MOON HANDBOOKS®

SOUTH KOREA
대한민국

© ROBERT J. NILSEN

Buseok-sa

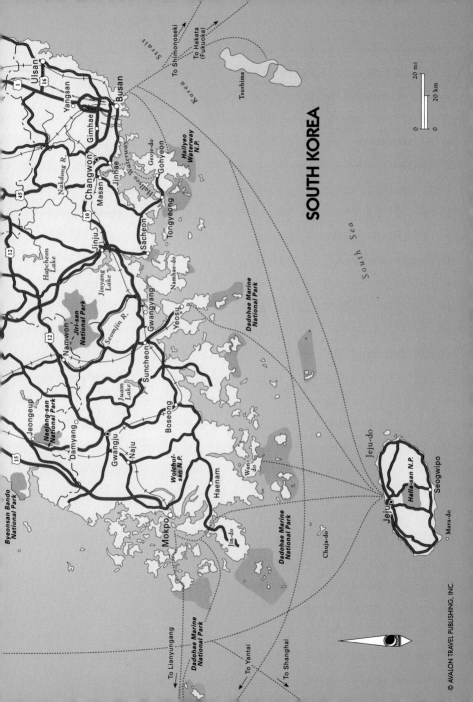

Suwon Fortress

MOON HANDBOOKS®

SOUTH KOREA

THIRD EDITION

ROBERT NILSEN

AVALON
TRAVEL

MAPS

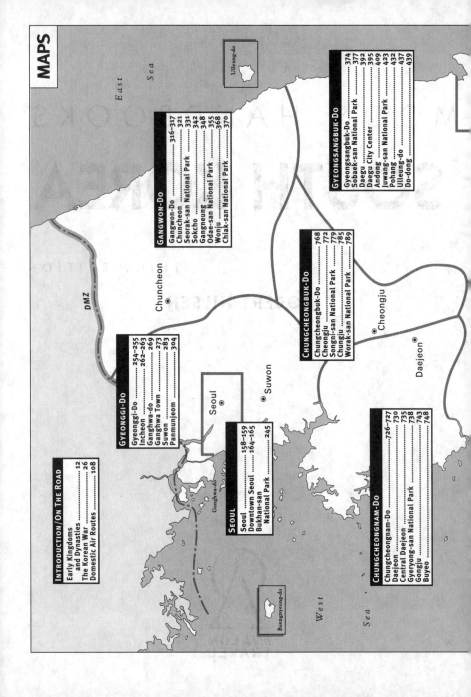

East
Sea

Ulleung-do

DMZ

Chuncheon

Cheongju

Seoul

Suwon

Daejeon

Ganghwa-do

Baengnyeong-do

West

Sea

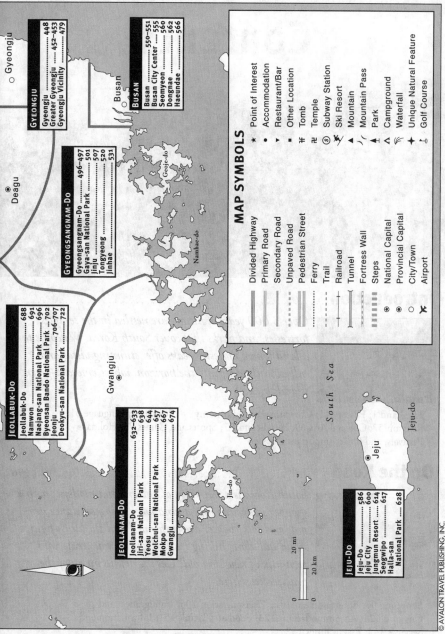

Contents

Introduction

Over 3,000 years of history are nestled in the temples, fortresses, and parks that cover South Korea. Welcome to a land where majestic peaks offer stunning vistas and hills undulate off into the horizon, where emerald-green islands beckon.

On the Road

South Korea is a marriage of ancient and modern: both a shopper's paradise and a land where masked-dance dramas and folk theater are performed and Buddhist figures stand tall along hiking trails. How do you create your own mix of new and old? Get the details on all of the practicalities here.

Seoul 157

A city of opportunity rushing enthusiastically into the modern age, Seoul offers quiet parks and secluded palaces, temples, and royal tombs amidst its skyscrapers and bustling streets. All South Koreans look to this city—no matter where in the country you are, you always go "up" to Seoul.

Gyeonggi-Do 253

This is a province of contrasts. Korean War memorials abound, while the ancient walled city of Suwon evokes a deeper history. Meanwhile, the beaches on Ganghwa-do island and the golf courses and river resorts of southern Gyeonggi-Do offer more upbeat pleasures.

Gangwon-Do 314

Home to the high granite peaks and serpentine valleys of Seorak-san, as well as the major temples of Odae-san and Naksan-sa, Gangwon-Do is what legends are made of. Drive along the rugged coastline, stroll through isolated fishing villages, and visit the "Lake City" of Chuncheon, the gateway to major mountain-recreation areas.

Gyeongsangbuk-Do 372

Daegu, South Korea's third-largest city, is the jumping-off point for visitors heading to the famous temple Haein-sa or the traditional Confucian stronghold of Andong. You can hike mountains studded with temples in and near stunning Juwang-san National Park. To the east, scenic Ulleung-do offers a remote island retreat.

Gyeongju 446

Capital of the once-great Silla Kingdom, Gyeongju is one of UNESCO's 10 most important ancient cultural cities. In this "museum without walls" you'll find hundreds of royal tombs, temples, palace sites (including famed Bulguk-sa), fortress ruins, pagodas, and rock sculptures. Don't miss the three-day Silla Cultural Festival in October.

Gyeongsangnam-Do 495

*Explore the two great temples, Haein-sa and
Tongdo-sa, and experience traditional local art and dance
at the cities of Tongyeong and Jinju, home of the weeklong
Gaecheon Arts Festival. Relax on beautiful beaches and
coastal islands, or visit the Bugok Hot Springs.*

Busan 548

*This is the San Francisco of South Korea: The cities
share roughly the same latitude, similar climates, a
coastal location, hilly topography, and a cosmopolitan
flavor. Take in all that this international port city has
to offer—parks and recreation areas, beaches, hot
springs, marketplaces, museums, and several dozen
temples, shrines, fortresses, and royal tomb mounds.*

Jeju-Do 584

"Emerald Isle," "Island of the Gods," "Island of Fantasy," "Korea's Hawaii" ... Jeju-Do offers beaches, forests, the majestic snow-capped Halla-san, and a slow, island-paced resort life not found on the peninsula.

Jeollanam-Do 631

Jeollanam-Do's 6,400-kilometer-long coastline is sculpted with contorted peninsulas and intruding bays, and nearly 2,000 islands lie just off the coast. Explore the province's rich cultural legacy by visiting numerous temples or take in its scenic delights, hiking along mountain trails and fishing bountiful waters.

Jeollabuk-Do 686

Visit Namwon, "City of Love," check out the fall colors in Naejang-san National Park, or see the fortress built by women in Gochang. Sample regional specialties like bibimbap *and* gongnamul gukbap *in Jeonju, South Korea's epicurean center. Or go rock climbing in Daedun-san Provincial Park.*

Chungcheongnam-Do 725

Once the heart of the Baekje Kingdom, this agricultural province takes pride in its deep cultural roots, complex historical past, and natural beauty, including many parks and fine beaches. The mountains of Gyeryong-san National Park are renowned as a site of supernatural power that still attracts believers today.

Chungcheongbuk-Do 766

Life in this land-locked province moves at a slower pace. Its eastern region features remote valleys and peaks, mountain fortresses and temples. In Songni-san National Park you'll find Beopju-sa, a temple featuring the 33-meter-high Mireuk Buddha—the tallest in Asia.

Resources 797

Abbreviations

H.S.—Historical Site
I.C.A.—Intangible Cultural Asset
KNTO— Korean National Tourism Organization
N.M.—National Monument
N.P.—National Park
N.T.—National Treasure
P.O.—post office

P.P.—Provincial Park
R.O.K.—Republic of Korea
T.—Treasure
Telecom—telecommunications office
W—before a number indicates the Korean monetary unit, *won.*
Y.H.—youth hostel

ABOUT THE AUTHOR
Robert Nilsen

Travel to South Korea was a big step for this young Scandinavian from Minnesota, but go he did with never a regret. Two years' experience in the Peace Corps were some of the best and worst of times, but always an education. Two more years of teaching privately in Korea were followed by a slow sojourn from Seoul to Bali, and from there across to the Khyber Pass, before returning to the United States. The author has returned to South Korea four times since, to total nearly seven years of living, working, and traveling in the country. In addition to writing *Moon Handbooks South Korea*, he has assisted in rewriting a travel guide to Indonesia, and revises the Hawaii series for Avalon Travel Publishing: *Moon Handbooks Hawaii, Moon Handbooks Kaua'i, Moon Handbooks O'ahu, Moon Handbooks Maui,* and *Moon Handbooks Big Island of Hawai'i.* Now that the third edition of this book is on the bookshelf, the author hopes to spend more time on other interests while the reader uses this book to explore one of Asia's least known yet wonderfully fascinating countries.

To my parents, for their faith and support

Introduction

The Land 육지와바다

South Korea comprises the lower half of the Korean Peninsula, a ruggedly mountainous land mass that dangles from East Asia, thrusting out of Manchuria toward southern Japan. The peninsula has roughly the shape of a rabbit held up by its ears and looking back at Asia. Its head is the northern tier of North Korea, with its mouth to the west, and ears running up the Manchurian border almost touching Vladivostok, Russia. The front and rear legs are the broad peninsulas that push out into the Yellow Sea. The curving east coast forms its slightly humped back, and the small projection of land between Pohang and Busan at the peninsula's southeast corner is its tail.

The Korean Peninsula is at about the same latitude as northern California, southern Spain, Syria, and Kashmir. It is approximately 1,000 kilometers long, and between 170 kilometers and 350 kilometers wide. The coastline measures approximately 8,700 kilometers. The entire peninsula covers 221,600 square kilometers, about the size of Great Britain or the state of Minnesota. About 45 percent of that, or 99,237 square kilometers, constitutes the Republic of Korea (South Korea), or R.O.K., nearly the size of Hungary or the state of Virginia; the remainder is the Democratic People's Republic of Korea (North Korea).

A natural border consisting of the mountain Baekdu-san and the Amnok (Yalu) and Tuman (Tumen) rivers divides the Korean Peninsula from China (and, for 16 kilometers, from Russia). South and North Korea are split by the 243-kilometer-long Demilitarized Zone (DMZ), which runs in a gentle S-curve from the Han River estuary to a point between Seorak-san and

© ROBERT NILSEN

view of Jeju-do's south coast as seen from Sanbanggul-sa

the Diamond Mountains. The West Sea (Yellow Sea) lies to the west of the peninsula, the East Sea (Sea of Japan) to the east. To its south is the South Sea, and, south of Jeju-do, the East China Sea. The 50-kilometer-wide Western Channel of the Korea Strait separates Busan and the nearest Japanese island; to the major Japanese island of Kyushu, it's roughly 190 kilometers. From Baengnyeong-do to the Shandong Peninsula of China is 180 kilometers.

Part of the same tectonic plate as East Asia, the bedrock of the Korean peninsular "block" was formed during the early Precambrian era. This foundation consists largely of granite, gneiss, and crystalline schist. For the most part, this bedrock is deep underground, but some pierces the surface—perhaps most dramatically in the mid-river peak Dodam-sambong, near Shin Danyang in Chungcheongbuk-Do. While nearly two-thirds of the Korean landmass is metamorphic rock, there are also large intrusions of limestone, sandstone, and additional sedimentary rock, with lesser amounts of basalt and other igneous rock. Limestone generally occurs in the Taebaek and Sobaek ranges, resulting in sizable areas of karst formations, including numerous caves.

The creation of the Korean mountains was followed by a long period of sedimentation and later by limited volcanic activity. Lying west of the Pacific "Ring of Fire," the Korean Peninsula experiences less volcanic and thermal activity than Japan, but relatively more so than Manchuria to the northwest. While there are no active volcanoes, Jeju-do (est. 1.2 million years old), Ulleung-do (est. 4.6 million years old), Baekdu-san (est. 28 million years old), and the upper Imjin River basin were formed from ancient eruptions. The most recent volcanic activity occurred on Jeju-do some 1,000 years ago. This ancient land experienced no glaciation, and today Korea remains surprisingly rugged and steep.

The Korean Peninsula is also not an earthquake-prone area. Earthquakes have averaged two per year throughout this century, but none have been severe. Only 48 of the 2,000 earthquakes that have been recorded since A.D. 2 have been destructive to any measurable degree.

KOREAN PENINSULA SHAPE

There has been some controversy about how Koreans have looked at the shape of their peninsula. Viewing its shape as being like a rabbit is attributed to the Japanese, Korea's long-time adversaries. Koreans previously, and more and more now, looked upon their peninsula as having the shape of a tiger with its back to Japan, its head and front paws up along the Chinese border, the bulk of the body down from there, both back paws as the projections into the West Sea, and a curled tail, its tip being the nub of land near Pohang. According to Eastern thought, the tiger has much more power and prestige than the rabbit and the Koreans would rather see their peninsula in this favorable light than as the more impotent version imposed by the Japanese. Disregarding any cultural context, it is perhaps easier to imagine the peninsula as the shape of a rabbit than as a tiger; however, viewing it in whatever shape one would like is certainly appropriate and acceptable.

Mountains

South Korea is roughly 70 percent mountainous. While the average elevation is quite low, ripples of hills undulate off to the horizon in every direction. The loftiest of the spiny mountain ridges rises to about 1,000 meters, and some peaks push to more than 1,500 meters. The highest elevation in South Korea is Halla-san (1,950 meters), on the island of Jeju-do; Jiri-san (1,915 meters) is the highest peak in peninsular South Korea. Baekdu-san (2,744 meters), on the North Korea/Manchuria border, is the highest peak on the peninsula.

South Korea has five mountain ranges. Running down the east coast are the Taebaek ("Great White") Mountains. The largest and most significant range, this is the "backbone" of Korea, the great watershed and peninsular divide. To the west of the range flow the country's major rivers; to the east run short, swift coastal streams. Diverging from this range, and curving through the center of

STRATEGIC KOREA

South Korea is strategically situated in East Asia. Historically, the Korean Peninsula has been a conduit of culture, language, religion, and the arts between China and Japan, yet filtered through Korean society. It has also been an important staging point for invasion by both China and Japan into the other's territory. In the modern age, increased economic strength and rising international standing have put South Korea in a pivotal geopolitical position, perhaps most evident when we consider its location in relation to the countries surrounding it. Seoul is approximately 190 kilometers from Pyeongyang in North Korea, 1,000 kilometers from Beijing, 900 kilometers from Shanghai, 1,500 kilometers from Taipei, 1,200 kilometers from Tokyo, and 950 kilometers from Vladivostok, Russia.

mond Mountains of North Korea are considered the peninsula's most picturesque. Their thrusting peaks, deep valleys, and thick forests made them a popular pilgrimage destination in the past, home to many Buddhist temples, and the subject of innumerable paintings, stories, and legends. A smaller version of them, the Seorak-san area just south of the border, is the most popular and dramatic in the lower half of the peninsula.

All but a handful of the country's highest peaks and most of the land-based national parks are in these ranges. The highest and most popular peaks, known for good hiking, pleasant scenery, or historical importance, are Jiri-san (1,915 meters), Seorak-san (1,708 meters), Deokyu-san (1,614 meters), Taebaek-san (1,566 meters), Odae-san (1,563 meters), Sobaek-san (1,440 meters), Gaya-san (1,430 meters), Chiaksan (1,288 meters), Worak-san (1,097 meters), Yongmun-san (1,064 meters), and Songni-san (1,058 meters). Other peaks not in the main ranges are Halla-san (1,950 meters), Gaji-san (1,240 meters), Palgong-san (1,192 meters), and Mudeung-san (1,058 meters). All except

the country, are the Sobaek ("Little White") Mountains. From these two north-south ranges run three smaller east-west ranges—the Gwangju, Charyeong, and Noryang mountains. The Dia-

© ROBERT NILSEN

Villages and fields find space where they can between the seemingly endless series of South Korean hills.

© ROBERT NILSEN

The contour of the land helps shape paddy fields in the lowlands.

Halla-san were created by geologic uplift. Formed by spewing lava, Halla-san *is* the island of Jeju-do. There's a crater lake at its summit, similar to Baekdu-san in North Korea. It also has several lava tubes; one (at over 13 km) is the longest known in Korea and one of the longest in the world.

Lowlands

The country's lowlands are generally coastal plains, by far the greatest in area, and flat river valleys. Forming the nation's rich alluvial farmland, the coastal plains are seldom uninterrupted flatlands. Bordered by mountains, they are dotted with low rounded hills and are not larger than 250 square kilometers. Most lie along the west coast. Smaller on the south coast, they become nothing more than narrow littoral strips on the east coast. River valleys are generally wide at rivermouths, quickly becoming narrower upstream. Upriver, wide areas have formed between mountains, often at the junctions of major tributaries, as near Daegu on the Geumho River, and at Yeoju and Chungju on the Han River.

Rivers and Lakes

Wide and shallow, South Korea's languid, liquid rivers contain little water for the majority of the year. Only a few are navigable—and then only by shallow-draft boats for short distances upriver. In days past, however, Korean rivers were important highways of commerce and travel. Sailboats that once plied these rivers have long since disappeared, and now only fishing boats, hand-propelled cross-river ferries, and a handful of excursion ferries can be seen.

The four major rivers in South Korea are the Nakdong (525 km), Han (514 km), Geum (401 km), and Seomjin (212 km). All have large tributaries. Eight smaller rivers of note in South Korea are the Imjin, Anseong, Sapgyo, Man'gyeong, Dongjin, Yeongsan, Taehwa, and Hyeongsan. Only the last two are on the east coast, and both are short in comparison to the others.

River flow varies greatly according to season, and only during the summer monsoon rains do the channels fill. Occasionally they flood from the rains, causing extensive damage. Rain causes other problems as well; sediment continually washed down from the mountains settles on the riverbottoms, raising water levels and reducing the amount of water the channel can carry. Along some stretches, the channel bottom is higher than the surrounding land, requiring levees to direct the course. During winter, only the swift rivers do not freeze.

The character of Korea's rivers is changing as more levees are raised and dams built to control floods, store irrigation water, and produce electricity. In all there are about two dozen major dams across the largest of the country's rivers and tributaries. Rivers that empty into the West Sea have the added problem of tidal backwash, which may travel upstream for many kilometers. Estuarine tidal dams—including those across the Yeongsan River at Mokpo, the Geum River at Gunsan, Sapgyo River, and Asan Bay—reduce this problem and, in effect, have created lakes on their inland sides.

Unlike the broad lowland rivers, east coast and island rivers are short, swift, and generally steep. Rushing down the mountainside, they cut narrow valleys and expose boulder beds. Slowing as they approach the coast, some widen and drop silt, creating sand beaches that block the rivers and form lagoons on the narrow coastal lowlands.

The country's only natural lakes are the crater lakes on Halla-san and Baekdu-san. All others are actually man-made reservoirs. Most have been constructed since the end of the Korean War, with a proliferation of them since the 1980s, yet a few have been around since the Three Kingdoms period. Small and medium-size reservoirs are sprinkled throughout the country, sparkling like scattered glitter from the air. Large dams have created more than a dozen huge lakes (the longest stretching over 70 km upstream) on all major rivers, and some necessitated the removal of entire villages, graves, and large cultural objects while flooding farmland and roads.

Hot Springs and Mineral Springs

Although there is no volcanic activity on the peninsula today, thermal activity does produce hot springs in the country, over 70 by one account. Generally enclosed and "developed," these have by and large been turned into gross commercial establishments that have only recently expanded sections to the open air and created more aesthetic surroundings. Most are around 50°C, two have water as hot as 60°C, and one has water at 78°C. While few are sulfurous, most are known for the minerals the water contains and their beneficial effects on the body and human health. While several dozen hot springs are scattered throughout the country—the majority in granitic areas, with a handful elsewhere—the following are the best known, warmest, or most historical: Bugok, Suanbo, Onyang, Dogo, Icheon, Deoksan, Yuseong, Osaek, Deokgu, Baekam, Dongnae, Haeundae, and Cheoksan.

Even more numerous than hot springs are the country's mineral springs. Popularly believed to prevent or cure specific ailments and disorders like indigestion, anemia, rheumatism, and eczema, they attract not only the health-conscious but also those who simply want an early-morning punch of mineral-rich ground water. Myeongam and Chojeong springs near Cheongju and Dalgi spring near Cheongsong are three of the best known.

The Coast, Islands, and Seas

Because of the movement of the earth's crust, the Korean landmass is tilting upward in the north and east. The relatively unindented east coast is characterized by rocky headlands that alternate with sand beaches. The rugged Taebaek Mountains parallel this coast. Their foothills roll down to the sea, only grudgingly allowing limited littoral plains. The one sizable coastal lowland area along this coast is north of Wonsan in North Korea. The east coast is marked by only two large bays, Yeongil Bay in South Korea and Wonsan Bay in North Korea, which protect Pohang and Wonsan, the peninsula's best natural harbors. Smaller harbors in the southern portion of the peninsula are at Ulsan, Donghae, and Sokcho; the much smaller coves and inlets up and down the coast suffice for small fleets of fishing boats. The only substantial island off this coast is Ulleung-do, created from the depths of the frigid East Sea by violent volcanic activity. The tiny double-island outcrop of Dok-do, 92 kilometers southeast of Ulleung-do, is South Korea's easternmost land mass.

The west coast, in contrast, is very indented. Shallow bays push deeply into the land and broad peninsulas thrust out into the sea. Languid rivers run across wide coastal plains between low, rounded hills, creating wide tidal estuaries. Because of the shallow nature of these bays, much land reclamation has been accomplished and more continues. Hundreds of islands dot this coast. Most are tiny, close to shore, and/or uninhabited—Ganghwa-do and Anmyeon-do being the major exceptions.

The south coast is the most sculpted and, with its many islands and good harbors, the country's most enchanting coastal region. Here the bays and peninsulas alternate in rapid succession, and the multitude of islands are sprinkled like emeralds on blue silk. While plains extend along its western end, mountains push toward the seashore for most of its length.

Korea has a surprising number of beaches. Although the "swimming season," roughly corresponding to summer business holidays, is from mid-July to late August, water is generally comfortable enough for swimming from June to mid-September. Still, even in summer, the sea is cool compared to the tropical countries of Southeast Asia. Generally, beaches run up to one kilometer long, with a few stretching to three kilometers, and are often bounded by rock outcrops at both ends. Those on the east coast drop off steeply, while those on the west and south coasts, and island beaches, are more gentle. East coast beaches are the least affected by tides, while the most protected are those on the south coast, as many of them lie in coves and bays.

Korea has over 3,000 islands, more than 400 of which are inhabited. The majority are located off the south and southwest coasts. Several hundred dot the West Sea, but only two lie off the east coast. Most are relatively close to the peninsula, although Ulleung-do, Jeju-do, and Hong-do lie 140 kilometers, 85 kilometers, and 95 kilometers offshore, respectively. Mara-do is the

southernmost landmass of South Korea, Dok-do the easternmost, and Baengnyeong-do the westernmost. Only Jeju-do (and the small islands surrounding it), Ulleung-do, and Dok-do were created by volcanic activity; all others were formed by drowned land. South Korea's largest islands are Jeju-do (1,810 square km), Geoje-do (383 square km), Jin-do and Ganghwa-do (320 square km), Namhae-do (298 square km), and Anmyeon-do, Ulleung-do, Dolsan-do, and Wan-do (each 60–90 square km).

The West Sea (Yellow Sea) is broad and shallow, with an average depth of less than 100 meters. Its light yellow-brown color is caused by sediment rinsed down the Yangtze and Huangho rivers of China and, to a lesser extent, the westward-flowing rivers of the Korean Peninsula. This sea has extreme tidal variation; the greatest (second only to Canada's Bay of Fundy) is nearly 10 meters, at Incheon. The movement of this vast amount of water causes swift tidal currents—up to seven knots—between the islands; hundreds of square kilometers of mud flats occur at low tide. Bottom-dwelling fish and sea creatures are the principal marine products.

Still on the continental shelf, the South Sea is only slightly deeper than the West Sea and has a tidal variation of two to five meters. Less affected by siltation, it has a soft, aquamarine color. Scattered islands lend it an intriguing character. Many were at one time peninsulas, and as the land continues to sink, today's peninsulas will become tomorrow's islands. Deep-sea and bottom fishing are practiced here, as are seaweed and oyster farming.

Beyond the very narrow coastal shelf, the East Sea (Sea of Japan) drops off quickly. Averaging 1,600 meters in depth, it's deep, cold, and a rich dark blue. The tidal variation along this coast is slight. In summer, the warm Kuroshio Current flows up from the Philippines, bringing warm summer monsoons. When summer turns to autumn, this current is pushed south by the cold Liman Current flowing out from the Sea of Okhotsk. This mixture of warm and cold waters creates great fishing conditions. Connecting the East and South seas between Busan and the Japanese island of Tsushima is the Korea Strait, a major shipping lane and, reputedly, a major route for American and Russian submarines. The currents in this bottleneck become very strong.

CLIMATE 기후

Korea has a temperate climate with four distinct seasons, similar to the mid-Atlantic states and Great Britain; only the subtropical valleys on the southern coast of Jeju-do and mountain areas above 1,700 meters differ. The weather is greatly affected by the Asian continent, with high pressure in autumn and strong winds and cold temperatures in winter. The surrounding seas also influence the peninsula's climate, particularly in the northward movement of humid monsoon air in summer. The north and central regions experience greater temperature variation throughout the year than the coastal areas. Winds come predominantly from the northwest in winter and from the south in summer. Generally, the east coast is slightly warmer than the west, as the high Taebaek Mountains block some of the cold winter air that sweeps down from Manchuria and Siberia.

Perhaps the best months to visit Korea are May and October. April, June, September, and November are also quite pleasant. Summer is bearable, but humid and intermittently wet. Winter is dull and harsh, with plenty of snow in the higher elevations.

Summer **temperatures** average 26°C and humidity runs 80–85 percent. August is the hottest month, but July the most humid. The hottest areas of the country are Jeju-do and the Daegu basin. Daegu has the dubious distinction of recording the highest temperature on the peninsula at 40°C in August 1942. The following August, Seoul recorded a temperature of over 38°C. The whole peninsula suffered during the summer of 1994, when there were abnormally hot temperatures for many days running, but one year earlier the summer was unusually cool. Winter temperatures average just below freezing for most of interior South Korea, just above freezing on the

coast, and 7°C on Jeju-do; humidity runs 30–50 percent. January is the coldest month, but February seems just as frigid. The lowest temperature ever recorded on the peninsula was -43.6°C at Junggangjin on the Amnok River in 1933! Snow falls on all but the south coast and southern islands, yet November–February see the least precipitation. Winter 2000–2001 was one of the coldest and snowiest in a century; it caused great hardship for the entire peninsula. Temperatures in spring are 10–12°C, in autumn 13–17°C; humidity during both is a comfortable 60–75 percent.

Precipitation over most of the peninsula averages 1,275 mm per year, with 1,200–1,400 mm along the south coast and Jeju-do, and 800–1,000 mm around Daegu. As little as 500 mm falls in the north-central region of North Korea. The greatest annual rainfall, 1,750 mm, soaks the south coast of Jeju-do near Seogwipo. Due to the concentration of rainfall in summer, every year sees some flood damage somewhere in the country. To mitigate this damage and better use the country's water resources, nearly two dozen multipurpose dams have been built on major rivers and dozens of small reservoirs have been constructed on smaller rivers and tributaries. Historically, once every eight years rainfall drops dramatically, in the past resulting in a poor rice harvest and famine. This happened in spring and early summer of 2001, creating the most severe drought conditions in a century. This condition of excessive rains or drought was a dire problem until the construction of reservoirs after the Korean War. Spring rains brought by winds out of China are essential for planting rice. Still, most rain comes during summer, primarily mid-July to early August, when up to two-thirds of the annual precipitation falls. Warm moisture-laden air blows up from the South China Sea in June, starting the monsoon season. These monsoons are much less severe than those in Southeast Asia. Generally, the monsoon rains are not continuous; usually a few days of rain are followed by a few days of clear skies. Most typhoons hit in late July or early September. While they usually play themselves out by the time they reach the peninsula, every few years a severe typhoon does strike, flooding the country and causing extensive and severe damage. Some snow falls between December and March; on high mountain peaks it comes in late October and stays through May.

The Four Seasons

Spring, a transition from dry to wet, lasts from mid-March through May. Early in the year, temperatures slowly start to rise and the wind picks up, bringing fine yellow dust from the Gobi

---

AUTUMN COLORS

Every autumn, the country's hardwood canopy turns a splendid mixture of colors, called *danpung*. Like a multi-color coat, the trees miss no shade from brown to gold to scarlet. Nowhere is this natural pageant more visible than in the mountain parks. While all mountain areas put on this display, some are particularly well known and loved—Seorak-san, Naejang-san, and Baemsagol at Jiri-san are three of the most revered. Although the change happens at slightly different times every year, varying according to temperature, humidity, and rainfall, as a natural phenomenon, it does follow a general pattern. Starting in the north in early October, the slow and steady march of color moves south at about 25 kilometers a day and down mountainsides at about 50 meters a day. In early October, the colors hit Bukhan-san and Seorak-san, the northern tier of the country. By mid-month Chiak-san and Odae-san are changing color also. The mid-peninsular mountains Gyeryong-san, Songnisan, and Deogyu-san are affected in late October, while Naejang-san, Jiri-san, Halla-san, and other southern areas usually turn last—in early November. There is no mistaking the change when it comes. When it starts the whole country is abuzz, newscasts are full of up-to-the-minute reports, buses to the most colorful and popular spots are packed, and highways are overcrowded. Everyone loves the fall colors, and no one likes to miss out. If you find yourself in Korea in the autumn, you owe it to yourself to have a look, and perhaps a hike, to appreciate this aspect of Korean beauty.

Desert of Mongolia. This is soon followed by moist air out of China and showers that farmers need to start the rice seedlings and flood the paddies in preparation for transplanting. Agricultural life begins anew. The winter barley comes up green, trees bud, flowers bloom, beehives are put out, and fields are covered with polyurethane greenhouses so farmers can get a head start on Mother Nature. While the rest of the peninsula is still in the grips of Old Man Winter, spring creeps in to the south coast of Jeju-do. The first budding trees herald the new season, and everyone knows it will not be long until the warm weather reaches them as well.

Summer comes quickly. The wind changes from the west to the south, pushing tropical air and warm water up from the Philippines. The air becomes thick and heavy, but coastal regions are blessed by sea breezes. Lush green of all shades is the dominant color. *Jangma* (heavy summer rains) start in late June or early July. Rain alternates with clear days through the majority of this period, but days of continuous rain predominate in late July. The hottest, muggiest part of midsummer (the dog days known as *sambok*) immediately follows these rains, and this is when most Koreans take their holidays.

Autumn, arriving around mid-September, is a transition from wet to dry. Winds switch from the south to the northwest, the heavy rains cease, temperatures drop, humidity wanes, and the skies clear, which helps the crops mature. This is the season of sunshine, crisp air, golden fields of ripening rice, and deep blue skies. Epitomizing this season is the favorite expression, *cheon'go mabi* ("high sky, fat horses"). Late in the fall is harvest, as busy a time as spring planting. It's also the time of many public holidays and the most important cultural festivals—many relating to the cycle of farming—the most significant being *Chuseok*, the harvest festival. In autumn, hillsides blaze with a patchwork blanket of yellow, orange, and crimson, while fruits and nuts ripen on the trees. Late in the season, when the warm days grudgingly give way to the icy fingers of winter, it's time for *gimjang* (*gimchi*-making).

In December, winter creeps over the land. Dull brown, characterless, and uninviting, this

SPRING CHERRY BLOSSOMS

When spring comes to Korea, the peninsula awakens from its wintry slumber and the natural cycle of life once again commences. Temperatures rise, the ground softens, early rains fall, birds return, grasses green, and flowers blossom. Perhaps the most colorful display heralding this new life is the delicate pink of cherry blossoms. While cherry trees are native to the slopes of Halla-san, they are well known and appreciated at countless other sites throughout the country. Jinhae, however, unquestionably offers the best show. This small port city grows over 150,000 cherry trees, all blossoming over a 10-day period in late March or early April. For the two or three days that the color peaks, hordes of people converge on this otherwise sleepy town to have a look, marveling at Mother Nature's finest. As quickly as it comes, the color is gone, and everyone reflects on this brief moment of beauty, then replaced by the ordinary task of growing other things.

FLORA 식물

Over 4,500 plant species, both coniferous and deciduous, grow on the Korean Peninsula, including 900 types of trees. Temperate plants abound; the few semitropical varieties are restricted to the south coastal areas and Jeju-do and other offshore islands. The high mountain peaks sport a few alpine species. Some 2,000 years ago, the land was covered by thick, mixed forest. Over the centuries, the trees were cut for construction, heating, and cooking. The problem of shrinking forests became increasingly worse until after the Korean War, when the country's forests were virtually gone. Only gnarled pines, scrub trees, and grasses were left or quickly grew back. Since the 1960s, a strong effort to reforest the land has been largely successful—quite unusual for a rapidly industrializing nation. Millions of trees have been planted over the past few decades, giving the countryside a new dimension and feel. The denuded hills often seen in Korean War photographs are now covered with a carpet of green. Still, few true virgin forests remain. They are small, legally protected, and usually in deep valleys or high on mountainsides.

Common trees are pine (many varieties), fir, spruce, larch, maple, oak, elm, ash, birch, alder, arborvitae, locust, sumac, willow, poplar, magnolia, sandalwood, and paulownia. Fruit trees include apple, peach, pear, plum, persimmon, tangerine, orange, citron, and quince. Some nut trees are the pine nut pines, chestnut, walnut, ginkgo, and jujube. Protected groves include the yew on Songni-san, nutmeg on Jeju-do, and juniper on Ulleung-do.

Flowers of many varieties also grow in Korea and bloom in the usual temperate climate patterns. Often seen are the rose of Sharon hibiscus (South Korea's national flower), rose, chrysanthemum, lotus, iris, Korean orchid, cosmos daisy, peony, and land cockscomb. In spring, the first to blossom are cherry trees, followed by azalea, forsythia, rhododendron, lilac, and magnolias. Flowers generally bloom later and carry on through the summer. The waist-high cosmos daisy lines many country roads and is the most predominant autumn flower. One of the few plants to give color

season becomes expressive only when snow falls, creating a vibrant contrast of stark white and black. Cold currents flow southward from the Sea of Okhotsk, and dry winter monsoons out of Siberia bring frigid air to the peninsula. Only occasionally do these monsoons drop snow. The south coast and islands receive only an occasional dusting; the interior mountain regions, northeast coast, Ulleung-do, and Halla-san receive the heaviest snowfall. Averaging over 1.5 meters, Ulleung-do gets the most snow. Icy winds blow strongly from the northwest and have the greatest effect on unsheltered Jeju-do. Thatched roofs on this island are tied down with rope to keep them in place. *Daehan,* the winter deep-freeze, comes in late January, but generally throughout this season temperatures follow a regular seven-day cycle known as *samhan saon* ("three cold, four warm"), in which three cold days are followed by four successive warmer ones. Although there is some variation to this rhythm, it's amazingly consistent.

INTRODUCTION

ROSE OF SHARON

The unofficial national flower of Korea is the *mugunghwa* (rose of Sharon), a hibiscus. *Mugung* means eternity or infinity and *hwa* means flower. This flower's tall yellow stamen is surrounded by five broad pink petals set against a background of dark green foliage. The flower blooms continually July through October, but each blossom lasts only a day, letting new buds open each morning. Koreans say that this flower has characteristics similar to their own. Not the most delicate or showy of flowers, it's modest, showing itself slowly, and yet it perseveres in a harsh climate and lasts a long time.

© ROBERT NILSEN

to the dull winter scene is the camellia tree. It blooms on the relatively warm south coast when all else has withered and died.

Bamboo grows throughout South Korea and into the southern portion of North Korea; the greatest concentration is in Damyang, Jeollanam-Do. There are several kinds of rush and sedge, some of which are used to weave mats, baskets, and art objects. Countless herbs and roots are cultivated; more grow wild. The best known is insam (ginseng), most of which ends up in Chinese medicine shops. Hemp is grown for its fiber, which is woven into lightweight summer clothing. Numerous varieties of wild and cultivated mushrooms are harvested, principally in mountain regions. Several kinds, including songi boseot, are edible and delicious. Dozens of wild greens and berries are also eaten.

FAUNA 동물

Generally, the peninsula supports temperate-zone animals, although a few subtropical and arctic species are present. Similarities exist with animals of eastern China, Manchuria, Siberia, and Japan. The musk deer and *Jindo-gae* dog are unique to Korea. Tigers, leopards, bear, and deer were once numerous, but because of over-hunting and shrinking forests most are now rare or gone. The 78 species of indigenous mammals include wild boar, wolf, red fox, roe deer, water deer, badger, weasel, marten, rabbit, black and brown ground squirrels, and chipmunk. Although they probably still live in deep mountain valleys of North Korea, Siberian tigers have not been seen in South Korea since the 1920s. Once nearly gone, the small black bear with a V-shaped white patch on its chest has made a slow comeback in deep mountain areas. Domesticated animals include cats, dogs, cows, oxen, horses, goats, sheep, pigs, and other farm animals. Since the 1990s, the popularity of pets (usually cats, dogs, and rabbits) has grown substantially. There are 25 species of reptiles, 14 types of amphibians, 130 species of freshwater fish, and innumerable kinds of butterflies and other insects.

Approximately 450 species of birds have been recorded on the peninsula; 50 are permanent residents and the remainder are migratory or vagrant. Korea is on the migratory route of many birds that summer in Manchuria and Siberia and winter in Japan, Southeast Asia, and Australia. Of the many "pit stops" throughout the country, perhaps the largest and most active is the Nakdong River estuary at Busan. Due to flight paths and favorable natural wetlands, other areas where bird-watching is rewarding are at and near the lagoon lakes along the east coast from

DINOSAURS IN KOREA

In 1973, the first dinosaur bone found in South Korea was discovered at Euiseong. Since then, numerous other bones, various eggshells, and literally thousands of footprints have been discovered in the country at nearly two dozen locations, the majority of which are in the southeast and southwest regions. One of the heaviest concentrations of prints is along the rocky seashore west of Goseong along the south coast; this is also one of the easiest to get to. A smaller set of varied footprints, also easy to reach, is located west of Haenam in the extreme southwest corner of the peninsula. While there is no conclusive evidence of the age of these remains, they are thought to be about 100 million years old.

ter also presents some fine bird-watching for those species that winter over in the peninsula, such as geese, ducks, Manchurian cranes, spoonbills, and swans. Bring high-power binoculars, telescopes on stands, and warm winter clothes. Common birds of the peninsula are the crow, magpie, dove, pigeon, jay, oriole, lark, sparrow, robin, tit, warblers, woodpecker, kingfisher, cuckoo, pheasant, quail, heron, ibis, crane, egret, peregrine falcon, sea hawk, cormorant, and seagull. Some of the migratory fowl are geese, bustards, ducks, swans, and teal. Species unique to Korea are the crested lark, Dagelet white-backed woodpecker, Quelpert white-backed woodpecker, and Tristram's woodpecker.

More than two dozen wildlife species are endangered, and a handful have recently disappeared. Eighteen localities have been set aside as breeding or wintering grounds and natural habitats. Twenty-four species of wildlife are protected as natural assets, including Tristram's woodpecker, Steller's sea eagle, Manchurian crane, white-naped crane, fairy pitta, Korean wood owl, musk deer, Amur goral, the long-horned beetle, the Jeju horse, and the *Jindo-gae*.

Gangneung north, Cheolwon along the DMZ, the island of Ganghwa-do west of Seoul, the Han river islets in Seoul, the Junam reservoir northwest of Busan, the Geum River estuary, Suncheon Bay, and the manmade lakes and tidal flats near Seosan and Haenam. Aside from the migratory times of spring and autumn, midwin-

History 역사

PREHISTORY

Evidence from a few scattered Paleolithic sites suggests that Neanderthals may have lived on this peninsula for half a million years or more, and that a Paleo-Asiatic people inhabited it from about 40,000 B.C. While little is actually known about these latter Stone Age humans, it's assumed from stone tools and weapons, bone artifacts, food remains, and fireplace sites that they were hunter-gatherers and fishers. Some lived on riverside flat land, yet most seem to have inhabited inland caves. It's likely that people moved from the Korean Peninsula to the Japanese islands about 20,000 years ago, when the Korean Strait was much narrower.

Artifacts from the peninsula's more numerous Neolithic sites indicate that Neolithic people

replaced the Paleo-Asiatics during several waves of migration from central and northeast Asia about 4000 B.C. (some suggest 8000 B.C.). The ancestors of modern Koreans, these people were of the Tungusic branch of the Altaic language group, which included the nomadic tribes of southeast Siberia, the Manchus, and the Mongols. Neolithic people lived along rivers and coasts. These hunter-gatherers and fishers used polished stone tools and weapons, and produced round-bottomed plain pottery.

A second wave of immigrants began around 3000 B.C. The plentiful archaeological sites from this period reveal a comb-pattern pottery similar to samples found in Manchuria, Mongolia, and southern Siberia. Small villages of pit dwellings were generally located close to water. Better tools and weapons were produced, and weaving began. With the inception of rudimentary cultivation

EARLY KINGDOMS AND DYNASTIES

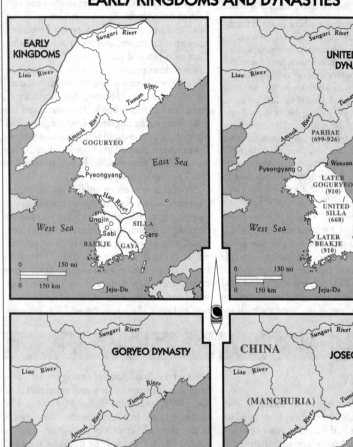

EARLY KINGDOMS

Sungari River
Liao River
Tuman River
Amnok River
GOGURYEO
East Sea
Pyeongyang
Han River
Ungjin
SILLA
Sabi
Saro
BAEKJE
GAYA
West Sea
0 — 150 mi
0 — 150 km
Jeju-Do

UNITED SILLA DYNASTY

Sungari River
Liao River
Tuman River
Amnok River
PARHAE (699-926)
East Sea
Pyeongyang
Wonsan Bay
LATER GOGURYEO (910)
UNITED SILLA (668)
West Sea
LATER BEAKJE (910)
Guemseong
0 — 150 mi
0 — 150 km
Jeju-Do

GORYEO DYNASTY

Sungari River
Liao River
Tuman River
Amnok River
East Sea
Seongdo
Han River
GORYEO (936)
West Sea
0 — 150 mi
0 — 150 km
Jeju-Do

CHINA

JOSEON DYNASTY

Sungari River
Liao River
(MANCHURIA)
Tuman River
Amnok River
East Sea
Hanyang
Han River
JOSEON (1392)
West Sea
JAPAN
0 — 150 mi
0 — 150 km
Jeju-Do

BOB RACE

Neolithic comb-pattern pot from Amsa-dong, Seoul

and the domestication of animals, people moved inland and became more sedentary. Along with a greater reliance on cultivation came an increase in population, with another probable migration to

Japan. During this time kinship relationships developed and blood clans exchanged goods and intermarried. Superior cultivation techniques, advances in tools and weapons, greater variety in the preparation of foods, storehouses, and objects of decoration and veneration indicate a growing sophistication.

A third wave of migrants arrived between roughly 1800 and 800 B.C. These people created new pottery shapes and designs, some painted. They developed a more advanced society that gave rise to specialized occupations, formalized social relationships, and some sort of order and rule of law. These clans grew in number and size, evolving into associated clan groups and tribes. Neolithic people were animists who believed that animate and inanimate objects have souls. As this belief became more important, the responsibility for the activities and interpretation of this religion was taken over by shamans who developed prestige and power within the community, and who may have become chiefs or respected elders.

FOUNDATION MYTH OF DAN'GUN

All nations have a historic past, and many also have foundation myths. Buried deep in the subconscious memory of the descendants of Asiatic tribes that moved into southern Manchuria and the Korean Peninsula lies the myth of Dan'gun. Hwanin, the heavenly king, had a son, Hwanung, who wished to live on earth among men. Accompanied by 3,000 followers, Hwanung descended from heaven and appeared under a sandalwood tree on Myohyang-san in North Korea. He ruled over the people that he found there, bringing them fire and teaching them agriculture, arts, and social behavior.

There were a bear and a tiger in his land who wished to become human. They prayed fervently to Hwanung to fulfill their wish, and he looked favorably upon them. Giving each 20 cloves of garlic and a bunch of mugwort, he told them to take only that for nourishment and to stay out of the sun for 100 days. They retired to a cave and took the food. Because of impatience and growing

hunger, the tiger left the cave. The bear, however, endured and was turned into a woman. Happy with the fulfillment of her wish, she prayed under the sandalwood tree to become a mother. Hwanung gladly obliged, and the bear-woman bore Dan'gun, the Sandalwood King. Dan'gun became the first human king of the people on the peninsula, establishing his capital at Wanggom (Pyeongyang) in 2333 B.C. and calling his kingdom Joseon, meaning "Morning Freshness" or "Morning Calm." He later moved his capital to Asadal, where he ruled until 1122 B.C. In that year, Dan'gun took on spiritual form, and a second legendary ruler, Kija, took his place.

Undoubtedly of shamanistic origin, this myth is similar to the bear myths and cults of the Ainu in Hokkaido and people of central Asia. While no one takes it as historical fact, the myth of Dan'gun is still told to foster Korean nationalism, and is the basis for the revitalized ancient religion *Daejong-gyo*.

About 700 B.C., bronze was introduced to the Korean Peninsula and peripheral regions of eastern Asia, most probably from central Manchuria and southern Siberia. Also, an influx of people at this time from eastern China brought advanced technology, metallurgy, more developed agricultural practices, including the cultivation of rice, animal husbandry, and the production of undecorated red pottery. While still depending in part on hunting, gathering, and fishing, people of the peninsula established permanent settlements in river basins and upland regions. They established a social hierarchy of commoner, privileged class, and leader. The society produced metal tools and effective weapons, and honored their leaders with dolmen tomb burials.

Tribal units developed into walled-town states where territory, not blood or relationship, was the dominant cohesive factor. Eventually, these began to form larger confederations, with one group among them becoming most influential. These states had a centralized government and were the foundation from which the first historical states evolved.

About 300 B.C., iron was introduced, allowing for improved agricultural implements (and greater food production), more numerous weapons, and the ability to use wood more effectively. From this time, houses began to be heated by the unique *ondol* system, in which hot air passed through flues beneath the floor—heating the floor and warming the air above it—and exited through a chimney on the far side. Because of the increase in population and the movements of people, warfare was common, causing shifting alliances and areas of control.

EARLY KOREAN STATES
Old Joseon
Sometime during the late Bronze Age, half a dozen loosely affiliated walled-town states grew powerful on the peninsula and in Manchuria, and kingships became institutionalized. Of these, the most significant were Buyeo [Puyŏ], in the middle Sungari River basin of central Manchuria; Old Joseon [Chosŏn], spread from the Liao River in southern Manchuria to the Daedong River in North Korea; and Jin [Chin], which occupied the peninsula's lower region. These states were the first to be mentioned in Chinese records. Old Joseon—closest to China—was the most advanced and the strongest. Its people were known to the Chinese as the "eastern barbarians" or "eastern bowmen." After repeated warfare with various Chinese kingdoms, Old Joseon was overcome in 190 B.C. by Wiman, an expatriate of one of those kingdoms. Wiman Joseon was easily overcome by Han China in 108 B.C., and the area between the Han River and the middle of Manchuria was made into four provincial commands, ruled by the Chinese as an outpost colony. In northern Manchuria, Buyeo continued to survive for some time, and Jin was basically left alone in the southern portion of the peninsula.

Lolang Commandery
Of the four Han Chinese provincial commands, Lolang was the most enduring and influential, the center for colonization in this peripheral region of their control. Although this commandery was operated primarily for military reasons, it was the means by which Chinese culture, writing, technology, and government had their first big influence on Koreans. The greatest effect was localized in the capital area near Pyeongyang, but it slowly seeped into the rest of the peninsula. However, with the emergence of the Goguryeo state, in the mid–Amnok River region, and the increased vigor of Jin, Lolang increasingly had trouble administering the colony and safeguarding its borders. In A.D. 313, Goguryeo drove the Chinese out of the Old Joseon territory, reestablishing Korean control.

THREE KINGDOMS PERIOD
During the Three Kingdoms period, the Goguryeo, Baekje, and Silla kingdoms and Gaya confederate states established hereditary monarchies and definite borders. Although their beginnings (late 1st century B.C.) are masked in a haze of uncertainty and myth (legend tells that the first rulers of Goguryeo, Silla, and the Bon Gaya state were mysteriously born of eggs), these nations

probably became recognizable entities by A.D. 200. After A.D. 200, direct Chinese influence on these emerging states diminished as China struggled with internal problems. A hereditary system of kingship and privileged aristocracy evolved, a state bureaucracy developed to deal with the increasingly complex domestic and foreign situation, explicit laws were promulgated, and military units were strengthened. Animistic and shamanistic beliefs and cultural rituals gained more significance. Buddhism became the state religion and Confucianism its ethical foundation; the first educational institutions were established during this period. Growing interest in literature and the arts spawned the writing of national histories, the development of a writing system that used Chinese characters to phonetically express spoken Korean, and the creation of religious structures. The potter's wheel was introduced, more and diverse metal objects were made, precious stones and glass began to be worked, and burial was done in wooden coffins and earthenware jars. Migration to Japan continued, affecting the formation of its early states by introducing such things as Buddhism and religious books, Confucianism and classic texts, Chinese and Korean political organizational structures, artisans and craftsmen, artistic and architectural designs, Chinese and Korean music and dance, styles of dress, astrology, and calendars.

Goguryeo

Rising from the old Yemaek territory of the central Amnok River basin, Goguryeo [Koguryŏ] was the nearest to China and most developed along Chinese lines. Located in the center of this highly contested area, Goguryeo was initially the strongest of the three kingdoms, but it was in constant warfare with China, Buyeo, and the nomadic tribes of northeast Asia. The strong military aristocracy eventually expanded the kingdom to include all lands between the Han River and the Liaotung Peninsula of China. After subjugating the eastern coastal people and absorbing Buyeo territory in A.D. 370, Goguryeo ruled until the 6th century. Responding to pressure

FORTRESSES

The Korean Peninsula is dotted with fortresses (seong) constructed over the last 2,000 years for protection from incursion by enemy forces. Because of their age and use during warfare, most have tumbled into ruin, yet a few remain as tribute to the skill and perseverance of the Korean people. From written records, it is known that early fortresses were made of mounded earth (toseong), sometimes fronted by palisades of wooden poles. Later, most were constructed or reconstructed with rough-hewn stone faces (seokseong), sometimes combined with brick. There are four general types of fortresses: mountain fortress (sanseong), city fortress (doseong), town fortress (eupseong), and long-wall fortress (jangseong). Most have long since been abandoned, but a few still contain communities. Most of the fortresses that survive today in good condition are from the late Joseon Dynasty. However, the Korean government has put much effort into reconditioning and rebuilding walls and battlements that are designated historical remains.

Mongchon Fortress in Olympic Park in Seoul and the Hangpaduri Fortress on Jeju-do are earthen-wall fortresses. A section of wooden palisade has been raised along a portion of the Mongchon Fortress wall to show what this feature must have looked like. Among the stone fortresses are the Suwon Fortress and Seongheung Fortress, south of Buyeo. Mountain fortresses are most numerous. Examples are Bukhan Sanseong north of Seoul and Sangdang Sanseong outside Cheongju. The best example of a city fortress is at Suwon. Fortress walls around small towns include those at Haemi and Nakan. The country's only long-wall fortress, similar in design and purpose to the Great Wall of China, was the Goryeo Dynasty 1,000 li wall, which stretched across the Korean Peninsula from the mouth of the Yalu River to Wonsan Bay. One of the smallest fortresses is Namdo Seokseong on Jin-do, only 360 meters around. The largest is Geumjeong Fortress, overlooking northern Busan. Its 17-kilometer-long wall encloses eight square kilometers.

from the north, Goguryeo moved its capital from the Amnok River to Pyeongyang, in turn putting pressure on Baekje to the south.

Baekje

Jin confederate states occupied the southern half of the peninsula. Because of wars with both the northern Chinese dynasties and Goguryeo, some Buyeo people fled as refugees to the southwest corner of the peninsula. These more advanced people overcame the indigenous population and evolved into the Baekje [Paekje] Kingdom. As a result of incursions into their territory by Goguryeo, their first capital on the Han River near present-day Seoul was moved to Ungjin (Gongju) and then, several decades later, farther south to Sabi (Buyeo). To counteract the strong Goguryeo state to the north and the growing menace of the Silla Kingdom to the east, Baekje allied itself with the Japanese and the Chinese of the lower Yangtze River. Thus, the Baekje Kingdom served as a conduit of culture from China to Japan. By sending an official envoy in A.D. 367, followed by diplomats, scholars, artists, and craftsmen, Baekje had significant influence on the Japanese Asuka culture.

Gaya

Byeonhan developed into a confederation of about half a dozen small states that, squeezed between larger and stronger Baekje and Silla, never was able to develop fully into one cohesive unit. The two most dominant Gaya [Kaya] states were Bon Gaya and Dae Gaya. Like Baekje, Gaya also had much contact and economic exchange with Japan. Although it is not known for sure, some scholars speculate that Japan had a foothold on the peninsula and some actual control over Gaya kings and the development of their territory. Most Korean scholars dispute this claim, and some suggest that the situation may have been the other way around, with Korean control and influence over some Japanese territory.

Silla

Silla grew out of the walled-town state of Saro (Gyeongju) in the southwestern corner of the peninsula. The last of the three great kingdoms to develop, it was less influenced by the Chinese, accepting Confucianism and Buddhism only in the early 500s. Although Silla was initially the least militaristic of the kingdoms, troubles with marauding Japanese and constant pressure from the Baekje and Goguryeo kingdoms led it to develop an effective army. One aspect of this rising military strength was the *hwarang,* elite soldiers with a chivalric code of leadership, unquestioned service to the country, and religious and ethical zeal—one of the primary forces in Silla's bid for control of the peninsula. The acceptance of Buddhism as the state religion gave new impetus to cultural development. By A.D. 562, Silla had absorbed the neighboring Gaya states and was gobbling up northern Baekje and eastern Goguryeo territory.

UNITED SILLA
A United Kingdom

The newly formed Chinese Tang Dynasty also had an eye on additional territory. Wanting to rule all of the Korean Peninsula, Tang allied with Silla, intending to walk right in after the defeat of the other two nations and take power from its ally. With combined armies, Silla and Tang easily overran Baekje in A.D. 660. The Silla/Tang forces then turned toward Goguryeo, which they defeated in A.D. 668. Tang then claimed the territories and set up military commands to maintain control. Silla too wanted control of the entire Korean territory, and by encouraging popular uprisings against this foreign domination, drove its former ally far to the north by A.D. 676. While Silla did not gain control of the entire Goguryeo territory, it did succeed in unifying the peninsula south of a line roughly from Pyeongyang to Wonsan Bay, thereby establishing the first united Korean kingdom. This unification was spearheaded by King Muyeol and completed under King Munmu, with the indispensable leadership of the great general Kim Yu-shin. Only in A.D. 735 did Tang formally acknowledge Silla's control over this territory. In the following centuries much contact and exchange took place between these two countries, Korea benefiting greatly from its more advanced patron. In fact, the United Silla Dynasty (A.D. 668–935) corresponds closely with the highly developed Tang Dynasty (A.D. 618–906).

Establishing Authority

With Silla in control, the country's administration was reorganized on the Chinese model, developing a complex bureaucratic system. The king's authority increased to a point where opposition was all but eliminated. The bureaucracy, run by members of the ruling class, was based on birth, not ability. Secondary capitals, numerous border garrisons, and a national army all helped solidify the king's control. In return for Korean autonomy, Silla kings sent periodic tribute to the Chinese emperor and recognized his authority in Asian affairs. Silla also received traders from China, Japan, and possibly as far away as the Middle East.

With unification, the cultural differences of Korea's various peoples blurred, leading to a more homogeneous culture throughout the land. Domestic tranquillity reigned in the 700s, and the Silla Dynasty reached its cultural apex: a highly developed artistry and high-quality craftsmanship in metal, stone, and pottery, some of which can still be seen in and around Gyeongju. Buddhism gained a strong hold on all classes and greatly influenced religious and governmental affairs. The spread of Confucianism, including the foundation of a Confucian university, gave rise to important rites. This was a time of great social and spiritual energy, when Silla grew as an international culture, reshaping what it received from China and funneling much of that to Japan.

Decline

By the mid-800s, however, Silla started to fall apart, due in part to corruption and factionalism. Increasingly weak and immoral rulers led to instability and the abuse of power by aristocrats. This situation gradually deteriorated into semi-anarchy in which private merchants controlled trade with China and Japan, and rebels and bandits took control of rural districts. In the 890s, peasant revolts led to the emergence of leaders who created rival states. One such leader, Gyeon

Hwon, established the Later Baekje Kingdom in the Jeolla-Do area; another was Gungye, who created the state of Later Goguryeo in the Gangwon-Do region. Both installed governments backed by strong armies that seriously challenged the Silla Dynasty, which shrank to a size not much larger than it was some 600 years earlier. In A.D. 918, Wang Geon ousted his superior, Gungye, and Later Goguryeo was renamed Goryeo. After establishing control over the middle of the peninsula, Goryeo took over Silla in A.D. 935 in an amicable transfer of power, and conquered Later Baekje in A.D. 936 after numerous hard-fought battles.

Barhae

When Tang conquered Goguryeo, many of its people fled to north Manchuria. There, along with the Malgal tribes of that region, they formed the state of Barhae [Parhae] (A.D. 698–926). After several decades, Barhae wrested control of much of the former Goguryeo territory from the Chinese, incorporating the area from Pyeongyang to central Manchuria. While maintaining an adversarial relation with Silla, it established friendly ties with Tang China, with the nomadic tribes of Mongolia and Manchuria, and with Japan. Development peaked during the 800s, shortly after Silla's golden age, but lost its vitality by A.D. 900. When it fell to Khitan tribes in A.D. 926, many of its people moved south to join the new Goryeo Kingdom.

GORYEO DYNASTY

With the unification of the country under Goryeo [Koryŏ] control, the capital was moved from Geumseong (Gyeongju) to Seongdo (Gaeseong). The Goryeo Dynasty (918–1392) took its name from Goguryeo, and from it comes the English name Korea. Government was completely restructured, agricultural reforms were made, a new educational system was initiated, and diplomatic relations were strengthened with China, ushering in a 200-year period of relative peace and prosperity. Power was centralized in the king, and the administration was carried out by bureaucrats and scholars who had achieved their position by examination, not birth. Unlike United Silla's government, where power was "tribal," the Goryeo system involved people from the whole peninsula and helped to create a unified national identity, and in this sense became the first true national government on the peninsula. Regional capitals were established, administered by appointed bureaucrats to check any possible emergence of a power base within the local gentry.

Rank and land became power and wealth, and this new bureaucratic social class eventually became hereditary. Increased interest in education led to the establishment of a national university and local schools. Although Confucianism continued to be important in politics, ethics, and daily affairs, Buddhism remained the primary spiritual inspiration and focus of religious fulfillment through the end of the dynasty. Land was given to Buddhist temples and monasteries, and certain Buddhist monks became involved in the mechanisms of power. At this time, the *seon* (Zen) sect of Buddhism became the predominant order. Much of Goryeo's art was religious in content; its most significant contribution, however, was the production of celadon, perhaps the best in the world. Other achievements of the dynasty were elegant wooden structures, literary histories, cast-metal movable type (created in 1234—200 years before Gutenberg!), and the production of gunpowder.

Early in the dynasty, additional territory had been added in the north, and Jeju-do was annexed in 1105. For a tighter defense, by 1044 a wall had been constructed across the peninsula —reminiscent of the Great Wall of China— from the mouth of the Amnok (Yalu) River to Hamheung. Civilian control ended in 1170, following a military coup that reduced the king to a figurehead. Power was concentrated in the Choe family, whose head became a virtual dictator. Private armies were established, including the *sambyeolcho*, an ultra-nationalistic elite force loyal to the Choes. This period saw harsh infighting and economic deterioration. It became obvious that the military was incapable of running the government properly, so civilian bureaucrats were soon reincorporated in large numbers.

In 1231, the Mongols invaded Goryeo territory, taking the capital. The royalty fled to the island of Ganghwa-do, where it set up a government in internal exile. Although unable to capture the island, the Mongols controlled the rest of the peninsula as a vassal state. The Goryeo king ordered the production of the *Koreana Tripitaka,* a collection of more than 80,000 hand-carved wooden printing blocks of the entire Buddhist canon, as a supplication to Buddha for aid in resisting the Mongols. (The Mongols remained for a century, but the printing blocks have survived and are kept at Haein-sa in Gyeongsangnam-Do.) Resistance to the invaders was led by the military, but when the Mongols laid waste the country, resulting in incredible hardship for the common people, opposition dissipated. Finally, the king sued for peace and returned to his rightful throne in 1270. The *sambyeolcho*, however, was not content with this settlement. This elite force struggled against a combined Goryeo/Mongol army, first setting up a small maritime kingdom on Jin-do, later being pushed south to Jeju-do, where it finally met defeat in 1273.

In 1280 the Mongols took the dynastic name Yuan, and for the next century they ruled China with a strict hand, greatly influencing Goryeo. Strong and independent before the Mongol invasions, Goryeo became a tribute state afterward. Korean kings had little say in domestic or foreign affairs, and forced intermarriage reduced the royal family to a branch of the Mongol royal family. One of the dramatic consequences of this partnership was Goryeo aid to the Mongol invasions of Japan in 1281, which led to untold human suffering and the destruction of the Goryeo/Mongol military force in a typhoon.

During the 1300s, Goryeo gained some independence while the Mongols were preoccupied with the rising power of Ming in south-central China. However, Japanese pirates were a constant nuisance to the peninsula's coastal regions, causing economic hardship. Extreme land reforms in the latter half of the century further ripped apart the fabric of this agricultural society, destroying the landed aristocratic class and Buddhist institutions, in turn worsening the situation for the common man. Neo-Confucianism, with its strict moral and ethical codes, stratified social hierarchy, and conservative doctrines of government and law gained strength, especially in the lower bureaucratic class, undercutting the influence of the nobility and power-abusing Buddhist monks. The once vibrant aristocracy and socially conscious Buddhist leadership began to sour.

In this setting of social and political turmoil and external badgering rose General Yi Seong-gye. After countering Japanese pirates along the southern coast, he was sent north to battle Mongol forces. Seeing this move as disastrous for the country, he returned to the capital, forced the abdication of the king, and put another on the throne. Still not satisfied with the state of affairs, he took the throne himself in 1392 and established the Joseon Dynasty.

JOSEON DYNASTY
Early Period

At 518 years (1392–1910), the Joseon [Chosŏn] Dynasty was the nation's longest-lived. Its founder, Yi Seong-gye, took the dynastic name Taejo ("Great Progenitor"), moved the capital to Hanyang (Seoul), and named the dynasty after the ancient Joseon Kingdom. This ended the Goryeo Dynasty Wang family's rule and supplanted it with the Jeonju branch of the Yi family. Referring to this family name, the Joseon Dynasty is often mistakenly called the Yi Dynasty.

Diplomatic relations were renewed with the Ming Chinese, and conflicts with northern nomadic tribes were resolved. During the reign of King Sejong (1418–50), the territory was extended to the Amnok and Tuman rivers, the present northern border of North Korea. At that time, the country was split into eight provinces, which have come down to this century basically unchanged. Regional capitals were set up in each province, and provincial armies and navies established. A system of beacon-fire communication sites and a series of postal relay stations were set up to transfer messages throughout the kingdom.

As Buddhism fell from favor, Confucianism arose as the dominant political and social force. The strict social hierarchy of Confucianism placed the king at the pinnacle with royalty directly below; under that was the aristocratic *yangban* class, which had expanded since the Goryeo Dynasty. Below that fell the commoners—tenant farmers and fishermen, many of whom had lost their rights and free status over the centuries as taxes and rents grew unbearable. At the bottom of the pile were outcasts, commoners who were employed in undesirable occupations, and slaves. Social classes became hereditary because intermingling was nearly impossible. This rigid system relaxed somewhat in the dynasty's latter years, when a merchant class arose (and some families were able to buy into or were granted the rank of *yangban*) and many traditional *yangban* families lost status and economic stability.

The system of government set up by King Taejo, and carried on by his successors, was one of counselors and department ministers. Final authority rested in the king, but suggestions were entertained at all levels. Government officials received land in relation to their rank. When land became scarce, salaries were paid. Although all land was officially owned by the king, *yangban* were allowed to collect rent on their allotted parcels and maintain slaves. Over the centuries, private holdings grew large, increasing the power and prestige of select *yangban* and reducing the leverage of the king.

To ensure a sizable pool of educated young men for government service, additional public and private schools were established, and civil service, military, and other exams were instituted. In the Confucian tradition, great importance was placed upon education, for through it one could achieve position and rank, and ultimately influence, power, and property. The strict Confucianist system seemed to work well through the first two centuries of the dynasty, and the integrity of public officials remained high. Moved by idealism, nationalism was strong, and the country's welfare primary. The emphasis placed on scholarship and the arts fostered output of national histories, scientific treatises, technology, medicine, increased use of printing to disseminate information, and interest in calligraphy, painting, and porcelain. One of Korea's proudest achievements, the indigenous *han'geul* script, was promulgated in 1446 by King Sejong.

Eventually, the *yangban* class became too influential for the king to tolerate. Between 1498 and 1545 there were four great literati purges. In response, many scholars went to the country to study and open *seowon* (private academies), while others returned to their ancestral homes to farm. The 1500s also saw a series of peasant uprisings and the emergence of bandits in response to excessive tax burdens, the land grabbing of *yangban,* and the deteriorating social condition of the lower classes.

Then, after some two centuries of Japanese raids on the Korean coast, a formal treaty was signed in 1443 that organized trade and opened three ports in the southeast corner of the peninsula. Korean trade was supervised by government agents; the Lord of Tsushima handled trade for Japan. Trade items from Korea were largely agricultural, handicraft, artistic, and religious; from Japan came raw materials and silver.

The Imjin War

The Imjin War (1592–98), also known as the Hideyoshi Invasions, was one of the most disastrous periods of Korean history. Shortly after consolidating control of Japan, the great general Toyotomi Hideyoshi decided to invade China in an attempt to become the ruler of all Asia. The easiest route to China cut through the Korean Peninsula. He asked the Korean king for help, or for unobstructed passage. As Korea had strong diplomatic relations with the Ming Dynasty, the king refused. To teach Korea a lesson, Japanese troops attacked Korea in April 1592 with their full military might. Although there had been voices in the Korean government calling for the strengthening of the military, the crown did not take note and Korea was virtually defenseless when Japan let loose its battle-hardened troops. Japanese troops pushed up to the capital in two weeks, forcing King Seonjo to flee. A few weeks later the Japanese were in Pyeongyang. Except in a few fortified southern towns, Korean opposition consisted largely of hastily organized guerrilla troops led by local *yangban.* Against Japanese rifles (copies of Portuguese models, never before seen by Koreans), they resisted bravely with arrows, cannons, and explosives, but still lost nearly every encounter. Finally, following the arrival of a large Ming force to assist the Koreans, the Japanese slowly retreated to the south coast. Peace negotiations were held between the Chinese and Japanese, with no agreement; skirmishes continued until 1596. In 1597 there was a second great invasion, which the combined Korean and Chinese armies confined to the two southern provinces. Still, there was great loss of Korean life and property.

Korea's saving grace was its navy. As in 1592, 1597–98 saw many great naval victories for the Koreans. The *geobukseon* was introduced and put to good use. It was a small, extremely maneuverable wooden warship roughly the shape of a turtle. Cannons were mounted on all sides, and spiked metal plates covered its humped top to discourage boarding. Moved by sail or oar, these ships could dart around and harass the larger and more ponderous Japanese boats. Led by Admiral Yi Sun-shin, the Korean navy crippled Japanese supply lines to the peninsula, sinking supply ships and troop carriers by the dozen. In 1598 Hideyoshi died and the Japanese decided to end the war and return home. During the last major sea battle in November 1598, Admiral Yi was killed.

Throughout this conflict, the Japanese had raped, pillaged, and plundered. Crops were razed, buildings burned, movable treasures taken, and other objects destroyed. Korea lost a great portion of its most valuable cultural properties. The government was drastically weakened, the economy was in shambles, and famine resulted. Ming China also suffered loss and economic decline, which contributed to its downfall. Unfortunately for Korea, its troops also looted the country after the war on their return to China. Japan, however, fared far better. Although it did not reach its goal of penetrating China, it boosted its economy and helped solidify the country under Hideyoshi's successor, Tokugawa Ieyasu. In retreat, the Japanese took many prisoners, including scholars, artisans, and craftsmen, and many religious and art objects and books. Because of what these reluctant émigrés were able to teach the Japanese, the religious, cultural, and artistic currents of Japan were greatly enhanced during the following centuries. From the early 1600s, trade and occasional diplomatic exchanges were resumed and continued until the 1800s.

Manchu Invasions
Within three decades of the ruinous Imjin War, Korea suffered another invasion. Under the leadership of Nurhachi, the Manchus overran northeast China and drove to control the entire nation and its neighboring countries. In 1636, the Manchus invaded Korea. Moving swiftly down the peninsula, they captured King Injo, who surrendered unconditionally and left the country open to Manchu domination. Tribute was paid, Korean princes were sent as hostages to the Manchu court, and Korea was obliged to aid the Manchus in their fight against the ailing Ming Dynasty. Within 12 years the Manchus took control of China. Establishing the Ching Dynasty in 1644, they ruled until 1912. From the mid-1600s through the close of the 19th century, there was close contact between the two countries.

Hermit Kingdom
In response to these drubbings, Korea closed its doors. Turning inward, Korea became a "hermit kingdom." It allowed virtually no outside contact, except for trade and periodic envoys to and from China and Japan, and built a series of fortresses throughout the country to better prepare for future invasion. Emphasis was on securing its borders, renewing state coffers, and putting the country back on a solid economic track, but the country never fully recovered from the Japanese and Manchu invasions. The upper class's authority and status weakened. Infighting and maneuvering for power became a constant concern for the ranks of bureaucrats, and greed and corruption were the standards of the day. Scholars turned their concerns from important questions to senseless bickering over philosophical trivia. During the 1700s, however, two enlightened rulers, Yeongjo (1724–76) and Jeongjo (1776–

a 17th-century sundial, one of the many scientific instruments employed by Joseon Dynasty scholars

BOB RACE

1800), brought to Korea a certain stability and peace, development and foresight. This period saw the expansion of mercantilism and the rise of a small middle class. Later, merchant control of products shifted to independent guilds of craftsmen and artisans who produced according to the demands of the market.

Like fresh air invading a stuffy room, a vibrant alternative to the narrow-minded traditionalism of scholars and bureaucrats arose. This was *Silhak* ("practical learning," or pragmatism), which proposed practical solutions to problems and acceptance of doctrines other than Confucianism. It was a challenge to the established order. New ideas included the equitable redistribution of land, loosening the rigid class system, government service by merit rather than class, aid for the poor, equal opportunity in education, and the introduction of *Seohak* ("Western learning") to help solve some of Korea's problems. Concurrently, new forms of literature were developed, and interest in Korean scholarship surged. Genre paintings of everyday scenes became numerous, and crafts were so widely produced that even the common man might have some. Scientific and technological instruments were created, and agriculture was improved. However, few substantive reforms were instituted in government, law, or social relationships.

Outside Contacts

Western ideas, in the guise of Catholicism, first influenced Korea in the late 1700s, when envoys to Beijing brought books back from the Middle Kingdom. Some scholars became interested in these new ideas, but the government, fearing challenges to the established ethical and philosophical order, discouraged contact with this "Western learning." A Chinese priest entered Korea in 1784 and a French priest followed in 1836 to "spread the word" and minister to the growing community of believers. Others came during the following decades, though frequent persecutions of Christians martyred thousands.

Korea's exposure to the West did not happen only through these religious contacts. There is evidence of foreign contact during the United Silla period, probably via overland trade routes from the Middle East. A Portuguese trader on his way from Lisbon to Japan reportedly landed on the coast of Korea in 1577 during a storm. A few years later, the Portuguese priest Gregory de Cespedes came to Korea with Japanese troops during the first winter of the Imjin War. In 1627, a lone Dutchman named Weltevree was shipwrecked on the southeast coast and taken into service by the Korean court because of his knowledge of warfare and the production of armaments. Twenty-six years later, 36 Dutch sailors washed ashore on Jeju-do. After being held captive for 13 years, survivors escaped to Japan. The ship's secretary, Hendrik Hamel, later wrote the first Western book about Korea. From 1832 merchant ships and warships occasionally entered Korean waters, probed for trade relations, or simply scouted the coast. But it wasn't until 1866 that there were any serious contacts with the West. Russia requested diplomatic relations, and an independent German entrepreneur asked for permission to trade with the country; both were denied. Later that year, an American gunboat sailed up the Daedong River to the doorstep of Pyeongyang to demand trade relations. Although this approach had succeeded in opening the door

to Japan a few years earlier, the ship ran aground on a sandbar in the middle of the river and the Koreans burned it, killing all on board. In response to the execution of French missionaries in a separate incident in 1866, the French navy invaded and held Ganghwa-do for a few weeks in 1869. Denied permission to address the king about their grievances, they left unsatisfied. Two years later the Americans showed up on Ganghwa-do, once again trying to force open the country for trade. After limited military skirmishes, they retreated. The Japanese came in 1875 to test the Koreans' defenses, and engaged in minor military encounters on Ganghwa-do. Returning the next year in force, they compelled Korea to sign the unequal Ganghwa Treaty, its first modern trade agreement with a foreign nation, opening the ports of Incheon, Busan, and Wonsan to the Japanese.

To counter Japanese influence, China convinced Korea to establish relations with Western countries. In 1882, Korea signed its first diplomatic treaty, with the United States. During the next four years, similar treaties were reached with Great Britain, Germany, France, Italy, and Russia, and economic relations were established with other Western nations. Korea's doors were opened, and during the following two decades diplomats, businessmen, and missionaries filtered into this previously unknown country.

Waning of the Dynasty

Aside from perceived threats from the West, Korea also faced serious internal problems during the last century of the Joseon Dynasty. The 1800s saw increasing corruption and inefficiency in government. The kings were weaklings and policies were made by powerful families or factions of high-ranking individuals at court. Cultural and artistic expression flourished, but the country was stunted politically and economically, poorly developed militarily, and naive in international relations. Voices of dissent were repressed and because of *yangban* oppression of the lower classes, dissatisfaction continued to ferment and sometimes boiled over. An effort, termed the Gabo Revolution, by upper-class pro-Japanese activists in 1884 to bring about drastic changes in gov-

MODERNIZATION

The following infrastructure was started during the late Joseon Dynasty (1880–1905) by Western nations and Japan:

1) First rail lines built connecting Busan to Seoul and Uiju; also Seoul to Incheon.
2) First telegraph lines laid connecting Busan to Incheon and Uiju.
3) King Gojong makes the country's first telephone call.
4) First electricity and public water service installed in Seoul.
5) First hospital constructed, later to become Severance Hospital.
6) First Western-style schools built by missionaries for males and females of all social classes.
7) First hotel built in Seoul: Chosun Hotel.

ernment and institute reforms (similar to those of the Meiji Restoration in Japan a few years earlier) also failed.

In the 1860s, the indigenous religion, *Donghak* ("Eastern learning"), had been formulated. Combining elements from Buddhism, Confucianism, shamanism, and other sources, it espoused the equality and dignity of all peoples, equal opportunity, national self-sufficiency, and independence from foreign influence. *Donghak* followers in 1894 protested against social conditions and the growing dominance of Japanese merchants in the Korean market. They engaged in violent clashes with the Korean army, prompting both China and Japan to send in troops to help suppress the demonstrations. As China and Japan were at this time vying for influence over the Korean Peninsula, the Donghak Rebellion brought relations between the two giants to a head and helped spark the Sino-Japanese War (1894–95). Partially fought on Korean soil, this was the first modern war engaged in by foreign powers on the peninsula. Japan won, dramatically ending Chinese influence in Korea. Japan subsequently demanded that Korea make sweeping changes in its policies to benefit Japanese interests. Because of

its loss in the war, China ceded Taiwan and the Liaotung Peninsula to Japan and was forced to recognize Korea as a fully independent nation, ending its centuries-long domination of the peninsula. After the murder of Queen Min in 1895, King Gojong and his heir fled to the Russian legation. Emerging about one year later, the king proclaimed himself emperor. The country's name was changed to Daehan Jeguk, or "Great Han Empire," symbolically equalizing the status of Korea, China, and Japan. It was an empty honor, however, as Gojong was nearly powerless in the face of foreign imposition; Korea found itself the pawn of foreign governments that had little concern for the people of the peninsula.

Japan, China, and Russia had vied for influence over Korea from the late 1800s. With China out of the way, and the policies of Korea largely in its favor, all Japan had to do was eliminate Russia. Russia had economic interests in Korea and Manchuria that it hoped to exploit. It also had influence at the Korean court in the last years of the 1890s. When Japan and the Western powers sent troops into China in 1900 to subdue the Boxer Rebellion, Russia moved troops into Manchuria. Early in the 1900s, Russia completed the Trans-Siberian railway, which enabled easy movement of men and supplies to the Far East. Japan saw all of this as too provocative and, using Korea as a conduit to Manchuria, attacked the Russians. Fought partially within Korean territory and partially on Japanese-occupied Chinese soil, the Russo-Japanese War (1904–1905) was the first major conflict between East and West. To the surprise of many in the West, Japan handily defeated the Russians and forced Western nations to look upon it as the dominant power in East Asia and a growing world power.

THE JAPANESE COLONIAL PERIOD

By 1905 Japan had thwarted Chinese and Russian bids for influence over the Korean Peninsula and felt comfortable in demanding of Korea a relationship to her benefit. The 1905 Taft-Katsura agreement in effect gave tacit U.S. approval to the Japanese colonization of the peninsula in exchange for Japanese recognition of U.S. influence over the Philippines. Without opposition in Korea, in November 1905 Japan concluded a treaty with King Gojong, making Korea a protectorate and giving itself control over Korea's foreign relations and external matters. The Japanese resident-general also slowly took over internal affairs. With the forced abdication of the king in 1907, his son Sukjong took the throne. Japan pressured him to abdicate three years later and formally annexed the country in April 1910. Both treaties were signed in secret; the king and his ministers were so weak by now that they feared the Japanese more than the retribution of their own people. It's no wonder that most Koreans felt as though they had been sold down the river! With an official stamp of approval, Japan acquired Korea without a shot. Calling the peninsula Chosen, Japan ruled Korea for the next 35 years (1910–45).

One of the first items of business was a survey (read: acquisition) of Korean land. Numerous Japanese came to Korea to farm and to fish its bountiful waters, while high taxes and fixed crop prices forced thousands of Korean farmers to move to Manchuria or relocate to Japan as laborers. Japanese big business and semi-governmental organizations established a near monopoly on commerce, industry, and mining. Progress in agriculture, energy, transportation and communications systems, monetary control, and commercial distribution was all for the benefit of the Japanese and to facilitate their conquest of Asia.

Broadly speaking, the first decade of colonial rule was one of stern military rule and suppression. Koreans were not permitted to participate politically and they were disenfranchised from nearly all aspects of economic, social, and political life. The '20s and '30s saw a move to civilian rule and a somewhat conciliatory mood. Social and political activity was relaxed and Koreans were allowed a role of consultation in some affairs. After 1939, the trend was to integrate Koreans into the mainstream of Japanese society, albeit only as an underclass.

After the Korean military was disbanded in 1907, an organization known as the "righteous army" was formed. For five years, this ragtag group of guerrilla fighters, although not broadly effective, was a thorn in the side of the Japanese. In 1919 during the public mourning for the late King Gojong, Korea experienced its largest popular uprising during the colonial period: the March First Movement. On that day, 33 religious leaders signed a declaration of independence in Seoul. When it was read to the public, people flooded the streets and rose up in popular support. This movement spread swiftly to the countryside, where tens of thousands participated in demonstrations and civil disobedience for several weeks. Taking the authorities by surprise, this outpouring of national sentiment was brutally repressed. In the end, the uprising brought about only minimal change. Ironically—or perhaps not so—this popular protest against repression won little support from Western governments then posturing as defenders of self-determination. However, it did stir Korean emotions, and enabled the formation of independence groups in the United States, Manchuria, and southern Russia.

In late March and April 1919, provisional governments were formed in Vladivostok, Shanghai, and Seoul, but they were ineffectual because of factional infighting. Most resistance to the Japanese took place on the peninsula in the form of mutual self-help groups and social clubs, in institutions and literature promoting Korean history, culture, and the arts, and in religious activities that pushed for freedom of thought. Vocal and violent outbreaks occurred in 1926 after the death of Korea's last king, and in a 1929 student demonstration in Gwangju.

With the Japanese push into China in the late '30s, Korea was used as a staging point for military activities. Crops were taken to feed troops and Korean boys were drafted. Others were taken to serve in fields and factories in other parts of the growing Japanese empire, and young women were forced into service as prostitutes ("comfort women"). At this time there was a concerted effort to extinguish the idea of "Korean-ness" and turn all Koreans into Japanese—though keeping them second-class citizens. Japanese became the official language; during the latter years of control, Korean was neither taught in schools nor allowed in public. In place of Korean history and culture, the Japanese equivalents were substituted. Koreans were forced to adopt Japanese names and accept Shinto as the state religion. The Japanese governor-general became the ultimate authority in Korea. Japanese held all top-level government positions, though Koreans were used as lower-level functionaries and local administrators. A Japanese-controlled police system was instituted and all dissent was stifled. Outspoken newspapers were shut down and all political activity was banned.

TRANSITION, CIVIL WAR, AND THE AFTERMATH

Military Government

At the Cairo Conference of 1943, the leaders of the United States, Great Britain, and China declared that "mindful of the enslavement of the people of Korea, (we) are determined that in due course Korea shall become free and independent." The Soviet Union agreed to it in 1945. Later that year at the Yalta Conference, it was decided to split the Korean Peninsula at the 38th parallel to effect the surrender of Japanese troops south of the parallel by the U.S. army and north of it by the Soviet army. Later, a joint trusteeship of Korea by the United States, Soviet Union, Great Britain, and China was proposed, on the premise that the Koreans lacked the mechanisms and political sophistication to govern themselves. Although the surrender of the Japanese army was carried out as planned, the trusteeship was never implemented.

Defeat in World War II ended Japan's 35-year occupation of Korea, but it did not, to the extreme regret of the Koreans, fulfill their hope of achieving immediate independence. U.S. and Soviet military governments were established in their respective sectors of the peninsula until countrywide elections could be held and a Korean government instituted. The artificial split of the country—never meant to be a political or permanent measure—and its control by foreign powers precluded Korean say in what happened to the peninsula immediately after the Japanese departure. The U.S. military government concerned itself primarily with immediate stability and basically carrying on the administration set up by the Japanese, while the Soviets were probably more farsighted in their goal of establishing a government in their own image. Split in two, the north was primarily industrial and the south agricultural. Neither sector was self-sufficient, so both were infused with economic aid. A joint U.S.–Soviet commission on Korea met in 1946 (Pyeongyang) and 1947 (Seoul) to discuss what was to become of this orphaned country. No agreement on unification could be reached, and talks were not resumed.

Independence

In 1946, the Provisional People's Committee for North Korea was established under Soviet auspices as an interim government; the following year it was renamed the People's Committee of North Korea. In 1947, the South Korean Interim Legislative Assembly was formed as a provisional government under the supervision of the United Nations. That same year, the U.N. General Assembly resolved to conduct supervised elections on the peninsula. The Soviets, however, would not permit election officials into their half of the country, so in May 1948 elections were held only in the south. The first National Assembly convened in May and the constitution was adopted in July, followed three days later by the election of Syngman Rhee as president. On August 15, 1948 the Republic of Korea (Daehan Minguk) was officially founded, recognized by the U.N. as the only legitimate government of all Korea. The following month, with the blessing of the Soviet Union, North Koreans formally set up their own government in Pyeongyang. Headed by Kim Il-sŏng (and under his control until his death in 1994) it was named the Democratic People's Republic of Korea. Both sides claimed to be the sole legitimate government of the Korean people, and each said it would fight to regain control of the whole country.

By mid-1949 U.S. troops were withdrawn from the southern half—Russian troops having already left the north—with only a small contingent left as military advisers to the fledgling South Korean army. North Korea, with aid from both Russia and China, was able to rebuild its industrial base and create an effective military organization more quickly than the south. Three important factors, then, led to the civil war the world knows as the Korean War: the North Korean military was much better equipped, there was strong sentiment to unite the land, and U.S. Secretary of State Dean Acheson publicly stated (mid-June 1950) that the Korean Peninsula was out of the U.S. perimeter of defense in Asia.

Korean War

Heavily armed and led by a phalanx of tanks, the Soviet-trained and -equipped North Korean army crossed the 38th parallel in the early morning of June 25, 1950 and invaded South Korea. War was on. Prior to the invasion, periodic conflict had occurred along the border; neither side seems blameless in its provocation of the other, and each added to the tension, distrust, and climate of uncertainty. As this border was an artificial creation of foreign powers, the North

THE KOREAN WAR

© AVALON TRAVEL PUBLISHING, INC.

Koreans denied it was an invasion, insisting their action was meant to reclaim what was rightfully theirs. South Korea naturally saw this differently, but its poorly armed military was no match for North Korean troops. Within days Seoul fell; preceded by fleeing citizens, South Korean troops made a strategic retreat. A special session of the United Nations approved U.N. intercession (the Soviet Union—which would have vetoed the action—was boycotting U.N. sessions for other reasons). Fifty-three U.N. member nations gave weapons, medical supplies, backup support, and money to South Korea; 16 countries provided troops. By far the largest supplier of troops and armaments was the United States, whose commanding officer was military commander of all U.N. operations.

North Korean troops continued to push south until September, when they were stopped by South Korean and U.N. troops at what became known as the Busan Perimeter, a line of defense that ran north from Masan, up and around Daegu, and over to a point south of Pohang. This southeastern corner of the country was the only area never overrun by North Korean troops. In September, General Douglas MacArthur gambled on an amphibious invasion at Incheon and a concurrent movement of troops up the east coast to break North Korean supply lines to the south. The now famous Incheon landing seemed a harebrained idea, so preposterous that most military leaders argued heavily against it, yet it went like clockwork and was a resounding success. Troops defending the Busan Perimeter were able to break out, capture thousands of North Koreans, and push into North Korea. By November nearly all of North Korean territory had been taken and some U.N. troops were at the Amnok (Yalu) River. Fearful that U.N. forces would cross into Chinese territory as Gen. MacArthur had urged, the newly established People's Republic of China sent troops to help the flagging North Korean army. With this horde of humanity crushing against them, the U.N. troops were forced back. Much of the heaviest fighting of the war took place that winter in the cold northern mountain regions; the U.N. troops suffered some of their most devastating defeats and highest casualty rates.

By spring 1951, this conflict came to a stalemate at roughly the 38th parallel. On June 23, the U.N. Security Council president, the Soviet delegate, proposed a cease-fire. Negotiations began on July 19 at Gaeseong, in territory held by North Koreans. After a brief renewal of hostilities, negotiations resumed at Panmunjeom. During these talks, both sides increased their strength, consolidated their positions, and dug in; several devastating battles also took place, including the infamous Heartbreak Ridge, Punch Bowl, and Porkchop Hill clashes. Cease-fire negotiations continued until July 27, 1953, when an armistice was agreed on.

Signed by the heads of the U.N., North Korean, and Chinese armies, the armistice was only a military agreement that formally ended the hostilities. President Syngman Rhee refused to sign, and South Korea has never been a signatory. The agreement provided for a cease-fire line (drawn roughly along the last point of contact between the opposing forces, representing the de facto border between the two countries) flanked by a four-kilometer-wide Demilitarized Zone (DMZ), and a bureaucratic structure to implement the armistice. It was not a peace agreement, and there has never been a political or diplomatic solution to this festering problem. However, such talks have taken place periodically since then. In 1954, negotiations were started in Geneva but quickly broke down. Secret negotiations were held in 1972, and public talks have been conducted several times during the 1980s and 1990s with few real results.

Neither faction won this fratricidal war. Destruction of the infrastructures of both countries was massive, and it's estimated that over a million Koreans died (some estimates say three million) and millions more were displaced. There were over 56,000 American casualties, as well as a lesser number from other participating countries. Figures for internal migration during the war estimate that two million people moved from north to south while a significantly lower number went in the opposite direction. The war left untold resentment on both sides, a twisted view of the sponsoring foreign nations, and deep psychological wounds. A siege mentality has permeated the South Korean government since the war, characterized by strident anti-communism, distrust of anything across the border, and an unbending military stance. Another reality of life in this formerly undivided nation is that the artificial border has proved to be even less porous than the Berlin Wall. Virtually no contact has taken place between the people of the south and north; propaganda is rampant and misconceptions are pervasive. A U.S.–South Korea Mutual Defense Pact was negotiated in 1953 and a treaty of friendship, commerce, and navigation was signed in 1956.

Forgettable 1950s

South Korea suffered serious economic stagnation after the war. As an agricultural country, it was able to start producing food again at a reasonable rate, but because most of the heavy industry and a great deal of natural resources were in the north, it had to build its industrial base virtually from scratch and rely upon foreign sources for raw materials. Despite large amounts of aid, development came slowly. Most businesses were still small-scale, and the few large industries were concentrated in the hands of a few wealthy families with the right connections in government.

President Rhee had been elected by the National Assembly in 1948, but in 1952, following a martial law proclamation in which many opposition leaders were jailed, the law was changed to permit presidential election by popular vote (to better ensure Rhee's reelection). In 1956, over muted opposition, a constitutional amendment was railroaded through the Assembly that allowed the president an unlimited number of terms. With little to show for his time in office and an increasingly authoritarian style, President Rhee's popularity dwindled. During the election of 1960, fraud was so rampant, party politics so corrupt, the economy so bad, and Rhee's rule so despotic that the majority of the people wanted him out. Students demonstrated in late February and early March. In mid-April, the discovery of the body of a student demonstrator in Masan Bay sparked renewed demonstrations that even brought university professors out into the street. On April 26, a bitter President Rhee resigned, and left for self-exile in Hawaii, where he died nine years later at the age of 89. His regime, downfall, and exile (courtesy of the U.S. government) are very similar to that of former President Ferdinand Marcos of the Philippines.

After four months of interim government led by Hŏ Chong, Yun Po-sun was elected the next president. Under the new parliamentary system, however, the real power resided in the prime minister, Chang Myŏn. More liberal than the previous government, Chang's eased political restrictions. While formulated with good intentions, this coalition of inexperienced leaders with weak personal power bases was not able to control the deteriorating economy, the fractured political situation, and continued student demonstrations. The parliamentary government ended nine months later in a bloodless military coup.

MILITARY GOVERNMENTS
The Park Chung Hee Era

On May 16, 1961, led by General Park Chung Hee, a group of mid- and upper-level officers forced the resignation of President Yun and established a military government in an effort to restore order to the political and social chaos and pull the country out of its economic malaise. Martial law was instituted, the National Assembly dissolved, political party politics stopped, and the first five-year economic plan created. All functions of government were taken over by the Supreme Council for National Reconstruction (chaired by General Park), which had many military and supportive civilian leaders in top posts.

Through 1963 dissatisfaction with military rule grew. The government had engineered no major breakthroughs and had seen many of its policies fail. An outcry of protest met Park's announcement that military rule would be extended for four additional years. In response to internal and external pressures, the extension was canceled and elections for civilian leaders took place in October 1963. Running as a civilian candidate, Park Chung Hee barely beat the recently de-

posed Yun Po-sun. He narrowly won—again over Yun—in 1967. Over vocal opposition from minority party members, a 1969 constitutional amendment allowed the president to run for a third four-year term, and in 1971 he squeaked by the new opposition leader, Kim Dae Jung. Realizing that he was losing control over the currents of Korean society, Park pushed for extensive revisions of the constitution. The Yushin Constitution was ratified in 1972 and Park Chung Hee was once again reelected. Among other powers, the revised constitution gave the president unlimited six-year terms of office, the ability to rule by executive order, and the right to appoint one-third of the membership of the National Assembly. The Yushin Constitution went into effect over loud cries of dissent. Martial law was declared and an executive decree made it illegal to criticize the president or his policies.

To its credit, the Park regime brought about considerable changes in Korean society, including rapid economic advancement. Big business became the bedfellow of government. (Small businesses grew at a much slower pace.) Broadening its economic base, Korea moved from agriculture into heavy industry and chemicals. The new export-oriented economy relied upon a constant flow of imported raw materials to produce exportable products. At first, most of the fruits of production were exported to gain needed revenue. By the late '70s, though, quality items began appearing on the Korean market, coinciding with a rise in the standard of living.

The military grew, and with the perceived increasing threat from North Korea, a homeland reserve force was instituted in 1968. Diplomatic efforts led to improved international relations and more involvement in Asian affairs. By the mid-1960s, Korea had about 50,000 troops in Vietnam—and they were some of the most feared of foreign troops—to fight with the southern half. In 1965, Korea renewed diplomatic relations with Japan, which had been cut since the end of World War II. Although protested by students, this was a healing of wounds and an opportunity to get much-needed financial aid to fuel the growing economy, the latter a key factor to the viability of the regime and its acceptance by the people.

The *Saemaul* ("New Village") program was instituted in 1971 as a self-help program for farmers. Although seen by some as a tool for government indoctrination, it did bring many benefits to the rural poor. The program later spread to fishing communities and then to urban areas. Due to various reforms, Korea became virtually self-sufficient in food production by the mid-1970s. Throughout the '60s and '70s, a reawakening of cultural activities was helped along by broadening mass communication and education.

With many of these advances, however, came the sacrifice of traditional values and a bit of the Korean "soul." With the emphasis on the country's overall improvement, the average citizen was often neglected. Human rights and civil liberties suffered, and dissent was squelched. Education and the media were heavily influenced and even censored by the government.

Even with the dissatisfaction in some sectors of society, if President Park had stepped down after his second term he would have been revered today as a farsighted national hero who helped bring economic vitality to the country, evolving its politics from chaos to the beginnings of democratic enlightenment. However, he did not step down but became increasingly autocratic. His last terms in office and the effects of the Yushin Constitution turned many Koreans against him, diminished his credibility drastically, and led to his untimely demise.

In 1968 and 1975, assassination attempts against Park by North Korean agents failed; in the latter his wife was killed. These incidents helped push President Park into seclusion. He ran again in 1978 and won. Students again took to the streets, while other segments of society were feeling fed up as well. There was growing sentiment that some drastic change had to occur before the glimmer of democratic process was snuffed. The country no longer had an unsophisticated populace, and voices grumbling for change became numerous. Change came unexpectedly. On October 26, 1979, President Park was shot and killed by his trusted associate Kim Chae-kyu, head of the Korean CIA.

Year of Turmoil and Transition

Following Park's assassination, Vice President Ch'oe Kyu-ha became acting president—and was later elected president. Great uncertainty marked the year of 1980. People from all sectors of society called for the institution of a real democracy. The economy, however, flagged because of the tumultuous political situation, and the military feared trouble from North Korea. In addition, the lack of dynamic leadership failed to redirect the country. Korea faltered. The economy spiraled down, demonstrations increased, and martial law was declared again. All political activity was banned, the National Assembly dissolved, universities were closed, labor strikes declared illegal, and major political leaders (Kim Chong-p'il, Kim Dae Jung, Kim Young-sam) arrested for corruption or sedition, or placed under house arrest.

In response to this crackdown, demonstrations mushroomed. The most serious took place during May 1980 in Gwangju, Kim Dae Jung's home district, where demonstrators overran the provincial office and held it for over a week. The army was sent in, hundreds were killed and thousands injured, and the generals took control. Military maneuvering during this period was directed by General Chun Doo Hwan, acting chief of the Korean CIA and head of the Defense Security Command. Troops used to quell the Gwangju riots were under the command of Gen. Rho Tae-woo, an army buddy and long-time friend of General Chun.

The Chun Doo Hwan Government

In August 1980, less than one year after he was elected, President Ch'oe resigned. Later that month, after resigning from the military, Chun Doo Hwan was elected president. For all practical purposes, this was just a formality as he had effectively held power since the Gwangju incident. After a new constitution was adopted in October 1980, Chun was reelected and sworn in for a seven-year term on March 3, 1981. Some of the new faces in government were military personnel, many from President Chun's class ('55) at the Korean Military Academy. Even though he had been elected according to law, because of his involvement in the Gwangju incident, many Koreans seriously questioned Chun's legitimacy. Yet his government was legitimized in the eyes of the U.S. government (and undoubtedly by many nations of the world) when he became the first foreign leader to pay an official visit to the newly elected U.S. president, Ronald Reagan. In 1984, following the Nakasone visit to Seoul the year before, Chun also became the first Korean president to make an official visit to Tokyo.

President Chun promised to usher in a "New Era, New Order." Martial law was rescinded in January 1981, and one year later the 2400–0400 curfew that had been in effect since 1961 was finally lifted. Political activity resumed, though watered down. Amnesty was granted to most imprisoned demonstrators, and the right of political involvement was reinstated to many who had previously been barred from political activity. After a period of strict censorship, newspapers and magazines were freed of many restrictions and agreed to self-censorship; radio and television, however, came under tighter government controls. The new era encouraged the expansion of cultural activities and sponsored the restoration and preservation of cultural sites. Although the presidency had a rocky start, it reached stability. Koreans began to believe in their country again, and the economy boomed. With more and better-quality goods available and with their wages higher, Koreans became more consumer-conscious. For the first time, Korea recorded a surplus in its balance of trade.

However, not everything was so rosy: political equity, social rights, civil liberties, and labor concerns took a back seat. Although a great disparity of wealth continued, the large and educated middle class that had been forming over the previous two decades began to voice its demands. Frequent student demonstrations and labor strikes brought about minor changes and much protest was countered by riot police—green versions of Darth Vader. Following the Gwangju incident, anti-Americanism rose dramatically among the student population. Despite the trappings of democracy, real power was still concentrated in the hands of the president.

President Chun promised to step down in 1988 after his one term in office to follow constitutional law and allow for modern Korea's first peaceful transfer of power. In the summer of 1987, majority party candidate Rho Tae-woo abruptly changed the party's stance and offered to rewrite the constitution and hold presidential elections by direct vote rather than by electoral college. Revision of the constitution was accomplished bilaterally and approved by national referendum in the fall of that year. Elections were held in November, the first direct vote for president in 16 years. Rho ran against Kim Young-sam, the main opposition party's candidate, and Kim Dae Jung, the major opposition figure. Unwilling to unite behind one candidate, Kim Young-sam and Kim Dae Jung split the opposition, and Rho won with 37 percent of the popular vote. While there was scattered violence and some accusations of fraud, the election seems to have been reasonably fair and valid. On February 25, 1988, Rho was sworn in as president while rioters once again filled the streets. His term limit under the rewritten constitution was five years.

The Rho Tae-woo Government

As major political parties began to work together to create changes in the constitution, the new administration started off on a positive note. The economy continued to grow, the country prospered, and social changes were instituted. Korea witnessed various substantive changes toward greater democracy in the political arena and detained politicians were granted amnesty and the reinstatement of their political rights. In 1988, for the first time, the major opposition political party, headed by Kim Dae Jung, won the largest number of delegates to the National Assembly. This ranked President Rho's party second, Kim Young-sam's party third, and Kim Chong-p'il's party fourth. The opposition-controlled assembly tested the democratic strength of the political process and the resolve of the president; the system held without falling into disarray. However, in 1990 the ruling party melded with the parties of Kim Young-sam and Kim Chong-p'il to form a new majority party that far outnumbered the party of Kim Dae Jung.

During this administration, much was done on the international scene to enhance the country politically and economically, including a concerted effort to approach former eastern-bloc countries. In 1989, South Korea established diplomatic relations with Hungary; since then, the list has grown to include nearly all the former Communist countries of Europe and Asia, including Russia in 1990 and China in 1992. The year 1991 also saw South Korea and North Korea sign a historic non-aggression treaty, and both entered as new members of the United Nations. Yet even with all the strides forward, there was a black cloud hanging over the administration because of Rho's complicity in the 1980 Gwangju Incident. Financial scandals plagued his administration, and student and labor demonstrations once again erupted.

CIVILIAN RULE

The Kim Young-sam Government

In 1993, Kim Young-sam was elected President of Korea, becoming the first head of state since 1961 who was not a former military general. Upon becoming president, Kim declared that one of his priorities was to rid the political/economic system of corruption and uncover public acts of misconduct. All responsible parties would be held accountable. Many public officials underwent investigation, and indictments were even leveled against former presidents Chun Doo Hwan and Rho Tae-woo for inappropriate use of military forces in the 1980 coup and for taking bribes from large corporations. In 1996, Chun was given a death sentence and fined $270 million for treason and embezzlement; Rho was sentenced to 22 years in prison and fined $350 million. In addition, 13 former military generals were given lesser sentences for their participation in the Gwangju Incident and 18 government official and business leaders were jailed for arranging bribes. While the former presidents were pardoned the following year, their sentences were a turning point in Korean democracy and the symbolism was pointed. From then on, even the highest officials in the land might be held accountable for their actions in a court of law. As in previous administrations, amnesty was given to numerous previously jailed political prisoners. Following the lead of the previous government, President Kim put much effort into opening social, cultural, educational, and scientific relations with other Asian countries and with former Communist countries. Trade with North Korea rose dramatically, yet diplomatic progress between the two countries saw no substantial improvement. The first local elections since 1961 were held in the country, with opposition party candidates winning the majority of positions available. With the slow opening of domestic markets, the manufacturing sector saw increased pressure from foreign competitors and the economy as a whole took a rather serious nosedive at the end of Kim Young-sam's presidency.

The Kim Dae Jung Government

How times change! After barely losing the presidential election in 1971, followed by long periods of house arrest, imprisonment, exile, and a death sentence—later commuted—former opposition leader Kim Dae Jung won the presidential election in December 1997 and was sworn into office on February 25, 1998. An important political and social step in the democratization of the country, it was the first time that an opposition party candidate had won election to the country's highest office. Even with the euphoria of such dramatic political change, however, Kim stepped into uncertain waters as the economy continued in a depressed state, due in large part to the Asian economic crisis. There was worsening social unrest due to the souring economic situation, and the relationship with North Korea continued to be adversarial. Over the next few years, the country pulled its economy out of a slump and managed to repay its International Monetary Fund (IMF) debt ahead of schedule. While internal corruption continued to plague this administration as it had done for all previous governments, Kim Dae Jung improved the relationship between South Korea and North Korea, and the leaders of the two countries held a historic first face-to-face meeting in Pyeongyang in June 2000. Following that event, additional ministerial meetings took place, more cultural and sporting exchanges have happened, family reunions have once again taken place, and greater economic cooperation has been instigated, including the development of rail and highway lines between the two halves of the peninsula. Kim's Sunshine Policy led to greater cooperation and lessening of tensions on the peninsula and in Northeast Asia as a whole. One result of this effort was that Kim Dae Jung was nominated for and awarded the Noble Peace Prize in 2000.

The Rho Moo-hyun Government

A member of the same political party as Kim Dae Jung, Rho Moo-hyun was elected president at the end of 2002. At that time, all indications were that he would carry on many of the same policies as his predecessor, including the Sunshine Policy of cooperative engagement with the North Korea leadership. While there had been

continued warming of the relationship between the two counties, events on the peninsula at that time became a major problem for the new president, even before he was sworn into office. At the beginning of 2003, North Korea took steps to restart an idled nuclear reactor (one that the United States and other nations feared could produce weapons-grade nuclear material for bombs) and withdrew from the Nuclear Nonproliferation Treaty. In addition, South Korea's workable approach to its northern neighbor began to diverge more prominently from that of the United States, which took a more hard-line approach in the face of the threat of world terrorism and the growing fear of the spread of nuclear weapons. What steps each nation will take will only be seen as events play out and as time goes by.

Government 정부

From its foundation as a modern state until the early 1990s, a crisis of authority troubled South Korea. The questionable nature by which several of the presidents had gained and held control had made legitimacy a key concern. Following two coups and several constitutional amendments that greatly expanded presidential powers, elections and referendums were held to put a democratic face on a skewed system. Power was concentrated in the hands of a select few, and politics was as much of personality and region of origin as it was of substantive issues and policies. All important political scenes were played out on center stage at the highest level or cloaked in secrecy behind closed doors. Government relied upon military backing to maintain control, with the occasional use of coercion and force. For years, government instituted policies that greatly benefited big business, and to a lessening extent still does today. In some instances, business pressed for changes, like a tail wagging the dog. The press was greatly suppressed, and censorship—voluntary and involuntary—was a key to control. Opposition parties were mostly weak and ineffective until the mid-1980s. The government operated under a siege mentality, con-

tinually harping on the possibility of invasion from North Korea. This authoritarianism was not only accepted but supported by foreign governments, who did little to protest its excesses.

From the 1980s and more so throughout the 1990s, the increasing political sophistication, education, knowledge of world affairs, and affluence of the populace made it imperative for the government to be more responsive to the people's wishes for a more equitable and socially and politically just society. Unprecedented bipartisan acceptance of constitutional changes instituted in 1987 and the first peaceful transfer of presidential power in 1988 pointed to a real evolution in Korean governmental democracy. With the election of Kim Young-sam as president in 1993 and the following election of former opposition leader Kim Dae Jung as president in 1997, the process of democratization took several great steps forward, and a multitude of reforms set forth by both governments eased the nation farther along the democratic path. The election of Rho Moo-hyun as president in late 2002 continued this peaceful transfer of civilian rule and also helped to cement the democratic reforms of the 1990s. While significant improvements

NATIONAL FLAG

Called *Taegeukgi*, the Korean national flag, first adopted in 1883, has represented the Republic of Korea since its founding in 1948. The white background symbolizes the land of Korea; the center circle, its people; and the bars, its balanced government and philosophical underpinning. The central *taegeuk* circle is an *eum/yang* (yin/yang) symbol representing the interrelatedness of opposing forces, the dualism of nature, and the harmony and balance of opposites. The red upper half is the positive (yang) half, representing light, day, fire, maleness, goodness, life, and heat; the blue lower half (yin) represents darkness, night, water, femininity, evil, death, and cold. Each is integral to the other and cannot be taken separately. Surrounding the central circle, set one in each corner, are trigrams taken from ancient Taoist and Confucian thought. These bars represent opposite yet harmonious aspects of nature. The three

solid bars represent heaven, east, spring, and generosity; the three broken bars are the earth, west, summer, and righteousness; two solid and one broken bar indicate the sun, south, autumn, and courtesy; and two broken and one solid bar represent the moon, north, winter, and wisdom.

have been made, crucial problems still hobble government policy, corruption remains a significant issue, and the question of reunification will greatly affect all coming administrations until South Korea and North Korea become one again.

CONSTITUTIONAL DEMOCRACY

Legislated by the constitution, South Korea has a democratic form of government. But democracy must be understood "in the Korean context," as officials are quick to point out: democracy with limitations. These limitations, however, are being reduced with each passing administration. Government is separated into executive, legislative, and judicial branches. Despite a system of checks and balances, the executive branch is by far the most dominant, yet the most recent constitutional changes have made the National Assembly a much more influential player than it ever used to be.

Ratified on July 17, 1948, the constitution has since had nine major amendments, the last in October 1987. Most constitutional changes have been imposed unilaterally by the majority party

in the legislature, with minority parties either excluded or abstaining. In 1987, however, amendments were worked out through a coordinated effort of the ruling and opposition parties, and ratified by a majority of Korean voters. Major limits were placed on the president's authority, the National Assembly was empowered with more investigative functions, and citizens regained rights in the areas of mass media, labor, search and seizure, arrest, and local autonomy.

Executive Branch

This branch is headed by the president, the dominant player in Korean government. The president is elected by popular vote to a single five-year term and must be at least 40 years old. His responsibilities are far-reaching: he is head of state, chief state administrator, domestic policy maker, head diplomat and foreign policy maker, chairman of the State Council (cabinet-level ministers), commander-in-chief of the armed forces, and leader of his political party. He appoints the prime minister and other high-ranking officials, pursues international relations, makes treaties, declares war and concludes peace, proposes legislation, and works toward reunification of the peninsula. He can grant amnesty and impose emergency measures and martial law. Numerous government agencies are under his direct control, including all state ministries, the Board of Audit and Inspection, and the National Intelligence Service. In addition, several commissions and councils are also directly responsible to the president; some of these include the National Security Council, Planning and Budget Commission, and the Advisory Council on Democratic and Peaceful Reunification.

The State Council includes the president, prime minister, and the heads of each ministry and selected government departments. This body has executive functions. Deliberating on public policy and governmental affairs, it advises the president. As the president's chief lieutenant, the prime minister directs the ministries, represents the president on certain occasions, and heads the Office of Government Policy Coordination and several other state boards.

High-ranking civil servants including ambassadors, ministry heads, and agency chiefs are appointed by the president upon recommendation of the appropriate minister or upper-level functionaries. The central government administration is run by about 500,000 national civil servants. Civil service was, by Confucian tradition, the only occupation, aside from scholarship, considered worthy of an educated man. It required scholastic training, freed one from manual labor, and necessitated influential relationships for advancement. While government service is still respected for its status and influence, interest in the profession has diminished recently due to questions of governmental policy, legitimacy, and a growing emphasis upon business and commerce. While semi-autonomous, provincial and local governments are considered an extension of the central government and these civil servants number some 350,000. In addition, teachers of the primary and secondary levels and all police officers nationwide are civil servants and their number runs over 250,000.

Legislative Branch

The lawmaking body of government is the 299-seat unicameral National Assembly. About four-fifths of the members are popularly elected by direct vote, one from each electoral district. The remaining seats are apportioned to parties receiving five or more seats in an election. Elected by direct ballot, members serve four-year terms, must be 25 years old, and are required to maintain a "high standard of integrity."

The National Assembly considers bills submitted either by its members or by the president. It must accept or reject the national budget presented to it by the president, approve constitutional amendments before they are set before the people in a national referendum, ratify treaties and other international agreements, approve the declaration of war, dispatch the armed forces, oversee government operations, and run investigations into affairs of state. It also has the power to pass a no-confidence vote against the prime minister or other cabinet members, and to initiate impeachment proceedings. The president may veto legislation, but the Assembly can override it. The National Assembly holds annual sessions of no more than 100 days and special sessions of up to 30 days upon request of either the president or at least one-fourth of the Assembly members. A speaker (usually from the majority party) and two vice-speakers (usually from the main opposition party) are chosen by the Assembly; there is no seniority system. Standing committees and special committees are maintained to consider proposed legislation and conduct inquiries.

Judicial Branch

The judiciary consists of the Supreme Court, five appellate courts, 12 district courts (with additional branch and municipal courts), one family court, one administrative court, one patent court, a courts-martial, and a Constitution Court, along with ancillary departments. All trials are held by judges; juries are not used.

Situated in Seoul, the Supreme Court hears appeals from lower courts, reviews the legality of governmental decrees and activities, and hears disputes concerning elections. Its decisions are final and it sets precedents for lower courts. Appointed by the president and approved by the National Assembly, the chief justice serves one six-year term, must retire at age 70, and may not be reappointed. Associate justices, of which there are 13, appointed by the president upon recommendation of the chief justice, also serve six-year terms but may be reappointed; all must retire at age 65. Lower-court judges are appointed by the chief justice and retire by age 63.

The five appellate courts are located in Seoul, Daegu, Daejeon, Busan, and Gwangju. They hear cases on appeal from district courts, family courts, and administrative courts. Appellate courts are presided over by one main judge and three associate judges. Located in major cities, district courts are the first step in civil and criminal litigation; branch courts and municipal courts in smaller cities are part of the district court system. These courts are nearly always presided over by only one judge. The one family court in Seoul hears matrimonial, domestic, and juvenile cases; the administrative court in Seoul hears administrative cases; the patent court deals with patent office decisions, and crimes of a military nature or those relating to national defense fall within the jurisdiction of the courts-martial. The Constitution Court hears cases involving the constitutionality of laws, impeachment, the dissolution of political parties, and issues involving constitutional rights.

Nine adjudicators sit on this court, and a majority decision must be reached by at least six. Public prosecutors are appointed by the minister of justice, and offices are located in all major cities.

Administrative Divisions

Korea's administrative divisions are broken down by area and population. Below the national level are nine provinces *(Do)*, the special city *(teukbyeolshi)* of Seoul, and the six metropolitan cities *(gwangyeokshi)* of Busan, Daegu, Incheon, Gwangju, Daejeon, and Ulsan. (Before 1995, these metropolitan cities were called *jikhalshi*.) The provinces range in population from 8.9 million (Gyeonggi-Do) to 513,000 (Jeju-Do). Of equal rank with the provinces are the metropolitan cities, which range in size from 3.6 million (Busan) to one million (Ulsan). Seoul, with one-fourth of the country's population, is set above the provincial level and dealt with separately as the nation's capital.

Below the provincial level are 93 counties *(gun)*. Within each county are provincial cities *(shi)* with populations over 50,000 (74 countrywide)—some have incorporated the county within their administrative boundaries—towns *(eup)* with 20,000–50,000 people (202 countrywide),

the National Assembly building

and townships *(myeon)*, with populations below 20,000 (1,214 countrywide). Within each *myeon* are villages *(ri)* and hamlets or small clusters of houses *(burak)*. Seoul and the metropolitan cities are broken down into districts *(gu)*. The next lower level, and the largest division for provincial cities, is the ward *(dong)*. Below that are the neighborhood *(tong)* and block units *(ban)*.

Local Government

Local government refers to provincial, county, and city governing officials and administrations. In true Confucian tradition, government administration is very centralized, with all policy moving from the top down. Except for a short, unsuccessful period of experimentation during 1960, there was no local autonomy until 1995; all heads of local and regional government units were appointed by higher officials and the local administration was simply the local extension of the central government administration. In 1995, the first popular election of provincial governors, city majors, and county heads was held, and from 1998, local elections are mandated to be held every four years. While local officials and administrative councils are popularly elected, local government still has limited autonomous authority to enact laws and legislation or to provide a tax and political base to support itself, and so is still in large part just a conduit for the administration of national policy and an extension of the executive branch of the national government.

Political Parties

Not having been developed until after its liberation from Japan in 1945, Korea has had a short, chaotic history of political organization. A multi-party political system is guaranteed by the constitution, and parties must allow for popular participation. Dominated by the ruling party of the president, the political scene has been strewn with numerous minor parties. These parties influence government policy and run candidates for national, regional, and local offices. Including independents, usually fewer than a half dozen parties manage seats in the National Assembly. Occasionally, during extreme situations such as martial law, political activities have been banned or parties disbanded outright. Communist and other left-wing parties are outlawed.

Generally, Korean political parties are organizations of politicians. There has been little grassroots activity or support—except that demanded of civil servants in decades past by the ruling government party. However, with the institution of local and regional elections in the 1990s, local political activity has grown in strength and influence. Parties generally orbit around personalities, and are not primarily policy-oriented. Policies are endorsed by the party membership after being formulated by party leaders. Few substantive differences can be seen among parties. All agree upon basic democratic principles, expansion of justice and civil liberties, the need for a strong national defense, continued economic development, expansion of international relations, and the reunification of the peninsula. Basic differences appear as to the methods and speed by which these policies will be carried out. Great inter-party strife is common, especially in opposition parties, due to the unbending resolve of individual leaders. Compromises within and among parties are often unattainable, leading to a less effective opposition and more fractured popular support, yet periodically parties do manage to coalesce behind an issue or candidate. Like most Korean organizations, political parties are greatly influenced by social relationships and friendships.

Political parties change names with frequency, according to the makeup of their political leaders, splits in factions, the occasional blending of two or more parties, or because of scandals and/or irregularities that might undermine the integrity of the party. During the '60s, '70s, and '80s, most political parties were full of former military men. Since the presidency of Kim Young-sam, however, more and more civilians have come into the political scene and the military has become a much less integral force. Major opposition leaders were Kim Dae Jung and Kim Young-sam, both politically active since the early '70s. Both had experienced house arrest, periodic denial of civil rights, imprisonment, and conviction on charges of sedition. Other important leaders are Kim Chong-p'il, prime minister under presidents Park Chung Hee and Kim Dae Jung; Lee Min-woo; and Lee Hoi-chang. While all minority party leaders have suffered under government repression, other politicized people have fared worse. Dissidents have been jailed, even tortured. While numbers are difficult to verify, reports indicate that several hundred political prisoners were in jail at any one time in the past and some are still in jail today.

Major pressure groups on the government are the military, business, students, intellectuals, media, the middle class, and foreign governments. The military is conservative; it stands for strict control, accepts slow, spoon-fed change, and stresses national security. The military, once the power behind the scenes and on occasion the power at the forefront, has taken a back seat since the mid-1990s and has generally left government administration and policy making to civilian leaders. Business leaders push for strong economic and business-oriented policies, and avoid upsetting the status quo. Intellectuals and certain members of the media generally have a liberal bent. They stand for more openness in and less corruption of government, and see their role as well-informed critics of current policy. Students are the idealists. Nationalistic in spirit, liberal in thought, they push for swift change, democratization, a strong unification policy, and less military influence and foreign meddling in government. The growing and increasingly sophisticated middle class pushes for greater equanimity, social justice, political participation, less corruption, and policies that continue the move toward a better life and standard of living. Foreign governments with the most influence in Korea are Japan, because of its huge economic ties, and the United States, because of economic interests and its military presence.

Elections

National elections are held for the president and National Assembly members. Local elections choose governors, mayors, and local council members. Elections are by direct and secret ballot; a simple majority wins. Voting age is 20 and elections usually have an 80–85 percent turnout.

Referendums on constitutional changes also come up for public vote.

Elections have historically been fraught with fraud and corruption. Perhaps the most blatant example of this was the 1960 presidential election, when the ruling party did everything in its power—from stuffing ballot boxes to arresting opposition leaders—to guarantee victory in the face of widespread dissent. Payoffs, influence peddling, and shrewdly timed concessions and benefits to the rural population were rampant through the 1960s and '70s. During the 1980s and '90s, elections become more legitimate due to increased political awareness by the citizenry, and major efforts by the government, opposition groups, mass media, and the church, as well as closer scrutiny by foreign governments and international organizations.

Until 1997, the ruling party had never lost a presidential election and, except for a short period during the beginning of Rho Tae Woo's presidency, had always maintained a majority in the National Assembly. Until 1988, when Korea experienced its first nonviolent orderly transfer of power, change in government had come only through popular uprisings (1960) and coups (1963 and 1980). Until the mid-1980s, opposition was relatively small, extremely fractured, and only moderately influential. In 1987, however, the opposition seemed to coalesce and capitalize on increasing public dissatisfaction and greater pluralism to make substantial gains in National Assembly seats, and the main opposition party actually captured more seats (although not a majority) than the ruling party of the president.

International Relations

While South Korea has had limited diplomatic relations with Western European and American countries since its founding in 1948, it started to cultivate formal international relations with democratic countries on all continents only in the 1960s. Through the last two decades there has been a push to establish diplomatic ties (currently at 184) with all nations regardless of political stance. In 1989, it established its first official diplomatic relations with a former communist state—Hungary. Since then, many have followed, including ties with both China and Russia. Although governments have changed, the foremost international policy of all South Korean administrations has been to maintain peace and stability on the Korean peninsula and throughout Northeast Asia.

On September 22, 1991, both South Korea and North Korea became members of the United Nations. Both belong to many of its organizations as well as numerous other non-governmental organizations and entities.

South Korea's relationship with North Korea has been rocky, adversarial, and often tense since the foundation of the two countries in 1948. The border between the two countries remains closed, and each maintains a strong and willing (if necessary) military to defend its territory. While there have been minor provocations across the border since the end of the Korean War, no major battles have ensued. Starting in 1972, when secret meetings were held between high government officials of both sides, there has been some diplomatic exchange and cooperation. In addition, cultural and artistic exchanges have taken place, economic food relief has been transferred, direct economic trade has been established, and there has been a continual softening of stance by both sides. In 2000, there was a major breakthrough when President Kim Dae Jung visited with North Korean leader Kim Jong Il in Pyeongyang, North Korea, and this too has furthered cooperation on many levels. Still far from reunification, the two Koreas are now on a friendlier and mutually cooperative footing and all hope that that will continue to lessen tension and eventually lead to the merging of the two countries.

Economy 경제

During centuries past, Korea's economy was based upon agriculture. Land and social rank determined wealth and power. Aside from the slow emergence of handicraft industries and small wholesale and commercial businesses in the 18th and 19th centuries, economic development didn't begin in earnest until the Japanese colonial period (1910–45). Under Japanese control, a few light industries, including textiles, were begun, mining was expanded, and power generation emphasized. As most mineral deposits, factories, and power plants were located in the north, this development benefited southern Korea little. While progress continued during the early years of Korean independence, the Korean War (1950–53) tore asunder the country's economic base and pushed it to disaster. Industry was destroyed, communication and transportation lines disrupted, the population displaced, and vast farm acreage lay fallow. Since then, relying upon an industrious and well-trained labor pool, government direction, and massive amounts of foreign aid and technical assistance, South Korea has pulled itself up from total collapse to create one of the world's most vigorous economies. A "newly industrialized country" (NIC), it is well on its way to joining the ranks of the industrialized nations.

The Five-Year Plans

Following the war, importation and production of consumable goods were paramount; almost nothing was exported. Growth was slow and undirected. This economic malaise changed quickly in the early 1960s, however, under Park Chung Hee. In 1962, the first five-year plan outlined development of basic industry and natural resources—a conscious effort to build an export-oriented economy and become a player in the big leagues. As Korea had few natural resources but a large pool of cheap labor, its first step was to pursue light, labor-intensive industry. Raw materials were imported and finished products exported. The income, plus great amounts of monetary and technical aid, fueled the growing economy.

The second five-year plan (1967–71) focused on developing heavy industries, chemicals, and electronics. Power production was greatly increased, port facilities and transportation lines expanded, and trade broadened to include European and Middle Eastern markets. Internal markets were also encouraged to produce needed goods to substitute for imports. The Land of the Morning Calm was experiencing a quiet revolution similar to Japan's economic revolution of some 20 years previous. The third five-year plan (1972–76) continued the same basic emphasis on heavy industry, but focused more on health and social-welfare programs, education, and living conditions. During that period, the *Saemaul* ("New Village") program was instituted to help country villagers raise their standard of living. Creating pride in the community and the spirit of cooperative effort, great strides were taken in that direction. Following success in agricultural areas, this movement spread to fishing communities and finally to urban areas. After weathering the 1973 oil crisis, Korea rebounded in 1976 with a 15 percent growth rate. A dramatic increase in overseas construction work (90 percent in the Middle East) boosted the economy. With the reduced vibrancy of the Middle Eastern economies after about 1980, Korean companies had to scramble for work elsewhere.

Extensive industrialization continued through the fourth (1977–81) and fifth (1982–86) five-year plans. Markets were expanded in South America and Africa, greater funding was allotted to research and development, and the climate for small businesses improved. With the headlong rush to expand, quality often took a back seat, though the quality of Korean goods rose somewhat in the 1980s. Following the assassination of former President Park (1979) and a year of economic and political chaos (1980 saw a minus 5 percent growth rate), Korea has moved to a somewhat freer economy, with less direct government control, liberalized trade regulations, and expansion of small industries. Still, the government wholly controls the postal and telecommunications systems, power production, railways, tobacco, and ginseng industries, while maintaining a majority interest in several public corporations including selected heavy industrial companies and half a dozen banks.

The sixth five-year plan (1987–91) continued the two-prong goal of economic and social development. It also set as goals balanced regional development, competition and the continued growth of small-scale businesses, and the growth of new markets to meet economic conditions and realities, both domestic and worldwide.

In recent years, Korea has begun cooperative overseas projects: mines in Australia, Canada, and the United States; electronics in the United States, Germany, and Portugal; oil in Indonesia and a dozen other countries; auto manufacturing and steel in the United States; and other types of manufacturing in Southeast Asia. To encourage foreign investment, the country has liberalized banking laws, reduced bureaucratic financial regulations, and relaxed other policies. In order to move into the ranks of the developed nations, Korea will need the scientific and technical edge it hopes to gain through greater research and development, and education in math, science, and electronics. To further that goal, it has made information and communications a major part of its economic thrust from the mid-1990s. By setting broad economic policies—but leaving much of the practicalities to private industry—future plans should create an atmosphere in which free-market forces can work to greater benefit.

Economic Issues

South Korea's economic success could not have taken place without strong leadership, massive foreign aid, and the education of young Koreans in foreign schools to create a pool of well-trained planners, managers, and technicians. Until the late 1980s, Korea was a debtor nation. In 1986, it balanced its payments and mostly met its payments until the Asian financial crisis of 1997. After borrowing some $57 billion from the IMF to overcome its problems, Korea fully repaid its obligation (ahead of schedule) by 2001 and once again has a strong financial base.

Exports have risen from nearly nothing in the early 1950s to $30 million annually in the early '60s to $170 billion today. They include textiles, footwear, electronic goods, computers and peripherals, ships, iron and steel products, machinery, vehicles, plastic, and wood products; heavy, chemical, electronic, and telecommunications industries lead the way. Earnings from these and other products contribute about 44 percent of the nation's GNP (agriculture claims 5 percent and services 50 percent). Crude oil, raw materials of various kinds, sophisticated electronics, machinery, and grains are the country's main imports. Through the mid-1990s, imports ran slightly more than exports; since 2000 exports have generally been greater than imports. Korea's major trading partners (together accounting for more than 50 percent) are Japan, the United States, and China. Western Europe and Southeast Asia follow, and new markets are being established in the rest of the world. The greatest increases in trade are being made with China and Southeast Asian nations. Since the early 1980s limited, unofficial contact between South Korean businesses and North Korea has led to secret (third-party) trade between the two countries. During the 1990s, some trade became official and was handled openly and directly, although volumes were relatively small. During the presidency of Kim Dae Jung, there was a normalization of shipping between the ports of Incheon in South Korea and Nampo in North Korea that has greatly increased the value and tonnage of trade. During the early 2000s, this inter-Korean trade amounted to about $400 million a year.

Except for a dip in 1980, Korea had an average annual growth rate of almost 9 percent—one of the world's highest—until the mid-1990s when it dropped to a still-respectable 5–6 percent. The Asian financial crisis of the late 1990s dealt the Korean economy a blow. It even contracted by some 6 percent in 1998, but by 2001 was again seeing growth rates in the 3–4 percent range, with anticipation of sustained upward growth. Its GNP stands at about $425 billion, making the per capita income in the vicinity of $9,000, a far cry from the 1962 figure of $87. With prosperity, a great disparity in wealth has arisen— the top 10 percent of the richest Koreans account for 25 percent of the nation's income. While the largest socioeconomic group by far is the working class, a white-collar middle class is swiftly growing. Because of the economy's rapid expansion, inflation averaged 16 percent during the 1970s and hit 29 percent in the chaotic year of 1980. It has now been reduced to a manageable 3 percent.

Korea's economy still has great problems: its huge conglomerate and monopolistic tendencies, coiled and ever-so-cozy relations between business and government, the concentration of businesses in small geographical areas, the snail's-pace growth of small business, an imbalance in wage distribution, protectionism from other countries, vulnerability to other "cheaper" developing countries, and excessive military spending. Associated concerns include poor environmental safety, ineffectual trade unions, and the deteriorating family unit due to employment relocation.

Agriculture

About one-fifth of South Korean land is under cultivation. Due to expansion of housing and commercial sites, however, this amount is slowly decreasing. Because the soil is highly productive, more than 50 percent is double-cropped. Before Korean independence, most land was owned by a small number of individuals and corporations that rented to farmers. Most farms are now run by families who own the land, although the number of corporate farms is again rising. Now accounting for only about 8 percent of the total population, the farming population slowly continues to shrink in proportion to the growing national population. More and more, young people are moving to the cities for better economic opportunities or for other reasons leaving the land and as a consequence a growing number of fields are being left fallow. In addition to their crops, a growing number of farming families rely on raising domesticated animals, making handicrafts, or children working in town for additional income. The average household farm is 1.4 hectares in size, nearly twice as large as in the 1960s.

For centuries, fields were generally hand-shaped to fit the lay of the land. Whether on a valley bottom or stepped up a gradual hillside, the free-flowing lines of their walls created tantalizing geometric designs of brown and green. Recently, however, the redistribution of land and redesign

© ROBERT NILSEN

Mechanized forms of machinery, like rice planters, tractors, and harvesters, play an ever-increasing role in the farm economy.

of these fields—in appropriately broad areas—has resulted in flat, squared-off sections. Where the ox and wood plow were once the only means of cultivation, the handheld, two-wheeled tiller or small farm tractor now predominates. More and more, mechanical rice transplanters, combine harvesters, binding reapers, and other farm machinery are also in use. Better irrigation and flood control (nearly three-quarters of rice fields rely on rivers for irrigation); high-yield, damage-resistant seed strains; increased use of chemical fertilizers; and efficient production techniques have multiplied crop yields. A dramatic profusion in the use of temporary vinyl hothouses has also been seen since the 1980s. Lengthening the growing season by weeks, they swathe fields in early spring, making the countryside shimmer in a sea of opaque plastic.

Primary crops are rice, barley, millet, wheat, cabbage, radishes, cucumbers, carrots, red peppers, garlic, onions, soybeans, sweet potatoes, sesame, ginseng, and tobacco. Others include corn, sorghum, apples, pears, peaches, grapes, oranges, persimmons, mushrooms, cotton, various nuts and seeds, tea, and mulberry leaves for silk production. Even with the impressive increases in food production over the past several decades, Korea is only about 60 percent food self-sufficient (95 percent for rice), meaning that the remainder must be imported.

Of the total cultivated land, approximately 1.9 million hectares, or 60 percent, are wet paddy fields, used almost exclusively for rice, which makes a vast majority of the principal grain harvest. Some terracing is done on low-gradient hillsides, but there is no extensive mountainside terracing as in the Philippines or Indonesia. Dryland fields are created on sloped land where paddies cannot be made. After the fall harvest, some paddies are planted with barley or wheat for a second crop.

In addition, Korea raises beef cattle, pigs, chickens, goats, and ducks, and produces a growing number of eggs and a variety of dairy products.

Fishing

Korea is one of the world's leading fishing nations, with an annual catch of two million tons. Korean fishermen supply both domestic and export markets. In the last 25 years, a great push to modernize the fleet (now some 95,000 boats strong) has resulted in at least a six-fold increase in catch. Deep-sea and coastal fishing bring in tuna, mackerel, pollock, cod, corvina, sole, anchovy, knife fish, squid, cuttlefish, shark, ray, and others. Inland fishing, mostly for trout and carp, has developed only recently. For centuries, sea farming has been practiced, especially seaweed and oysters. Other seafoods harvested are shrimp, clams, crabs, abalone, mussels, and sea cucumbers. From 1945 to 1986, Korea participated in commercial whaling on a small scale. It no longer does so; it now protects whales that swim in its territorial waters.

Industry

Employing about 25 percent of the workforce, manufacturing and industry produces about 30 percent of the country's GNP. Of this, heavy industry and electronics claim the lion's share. The 1970s saw the creation of industrial cities and an emphasis upon production of iron and steel products, ships, automobiles, refined oil, cement, chemicals, fertilizers, paints, farm and industrial machinery, and heavy equipment. Before the '70s, light industry was the predominant sector, producing textiles, footwear, food and beverages, cigarettes, furniture, plywood, paper, plastic and rubber goods, glass, pottery, porcelain, tile, electronic goods, appliances, sporting goods, and musical instruments. To facilitate exports, Korea has expanded its transportation lines, port facilities, and shipping fleet.

Although a majority of Korean businesses are small, the industrial scene is dominated by the *jaebol*, family-run, industrial conglomerates similar to Japanese *zaibatsu*. Wielding immense power, they have worked hand in hand with government to create the current economic conditions. The largest *jaebol* are Hyundai, Daewoo, Samsung, Lucky-Goldstar (LG), Sunkyong (SK), Ssangyong, Korea Explosives, Hyosong, and Hanjin. However, in an effort to stimulate growth in small businesses, a sizable percentage of all bank loans must now by law be made to small companies.

Workers are the muscle of the Korean economic strength. Of the 22-million-person workforce, only one-quarter work in companies that employ 10 or more. About 60 percent are male, 40 percent female. Although it varies up and down a little according to the strength or weakness of the economy, unemployment seems to average about 3–3.5 percent. It was, for example, 3.4 percent in the summer of 2001 when the country was recovering from the Asian financial crisis. When the crisis was at its worst, Korea hit 8.6 percent unemployment in February of 1999. The average workweek is 47 hours long—down from 55 hours in the 1970s. Since 2002, some businesses have gone to a five-day workweek and others are slated to do so as well. The average monthly wage for males is about ₩1,500,000, ₩1,100,000 for females. Women work mostly in labor-intensive, lower-paying industries. During the 1970s and '80s, wages did not increase proportionately to productivity or consumer prices, but from the 1990s they have been better in that regard. Labor relations have never been good. Past decades have brought repeated unrest and calls for better working conditions, higher wages, additional benefits, and independent unions. Strict new labor laws in 1980 reorganized (in some cases disbanded) and took the teeth out of unions. Independent unions are illegal. Only those sponsored by the government-controlled Federation of Korean Trade Unions are allowed, and then only in a single industry. This has led to relatively weak and ineffective leadership and great control by management and government. About 7 percent of the work force is unionized.

Mining

Small-scale mining has gouged the peninsula for centuries, and was expanded at the beginning of the 19th century. Unfortunately for South Korea, most minerals and other natural resources are in the north, out of reach since the Korean War. A large part of mining in South Korea is for coal, although its production has been cut drastically in the past two decades. The demand for anthracite coal as heating fuel, mostly for household use, increased through the 1960s and 1970s, but is now being offset by petroleum and electricity. Limestone has become the largest mined product, in terms of tonnage. Also mined, but in much smaller quantities, are gold, silver, copper, lead, zinc, molybdenum, tungsten, graphite, kaolin, clay, and talc. The vast majority is for domestic use. Additional minerals and quantities not met by domestic production must be imported.

Energy

To power the rapidly growing economy, several dozen thermal, hydro, and nuclear power plants have been constructed over the last four decades. Alternative solar and wind power is only in its infancy. Thermal power is produced by coal, liquefied natural gas (LNG), and oil at nearly four dozen facilities. As *all* oil must be imported, the country is working to cut dependence on it to prevent a recurrence of the hardships suffered during the oil crisis of the '70s. Currently, about 50 percent of energy is produced by oil. Over two dozen hydroelectric and 16 nuclear power plants produce the majority of the rest of the needed power. The first nuclear plant went on line in 1978; some in the power industry and government anticipate that number to be 30 by 2015.

Tourism

The newest contender for a slice of the expanding economic pie is tourism. From humble beginnings in the early 1960s (fewer than 50,000 visitors yearly), tourism has grown into a thriving industry. Over five million visitors (5,321,792 in 2000) now land each year in Korea, 44 percent from Japan alone. The next largest groups are from China (10 percent), the United States (9 percent), Hong Kong (4 percent), and Taiwan (3 percent). Returning Koreans make up 9 percent, ASEAN (Association of Southeast Asian Nations) member countries 10 percent, and Europeans 7 percent. Greater interest in the country, larger numbers of visitors, and a stronger economic ability to foster change has led to expanding and modernized tourist facilities at established sites, the opening of other cultural, historical, and natural sites, and the creation of a stronger and more broad-based infrastructure to support this ever more important sector.

Since the early 1980s, restrictions on foreign travel by Koreans have all but disappeared. In 2000, 5.5 million Koreans traveled abroad, mainly to Japan (1.4 million), China (1.3 million) the United States (748,000), and ASEAN countries.

People 국민

Koreans are one of the most homogeneous people in the world, part of the Mongoloid racial group, which comprises about 70 percent of the total human population. Culturally and linguistically related to the Tungusic people of Manchuria, Mongolia, and eastern Siberia, they are thought to have migrated in successive waves from central Asia some 3,000–6,000 years ago, absorbing minority groups in their path. While most remained on the peninsula, there were periodic movements beyond to the Japanese islands until the 8th century A.D. Despite strong animosity toward one another, Koreans and Japanese share deep cultural roots.

With roughly 47.8 million people (in 2002), South Korea is the world's 26th most populous country. At 475 persons per square kilometer, it has the third highest population density. Population growth is 0.89 percent annually, compared to 2.6 percent in the early 1960s; it's estimated to level out by 2030. The 2000 birth rate was 1.42 per female and is slowly declining —it was 1.59 in 1990. There are 100.7 males for every 100 females. However, the greater preference for boys over girls has created an unbalanced male/female split in the younger population and those of early childbearing ages up to age 25 where the ratio is about 110 males to 100 females. (Some men go outside the country, to Korean populations in China, for example, to find wives.) Greater medical technology has allowed women to know the sex of the child before birth, causing some women to abort female fetuses. Although abortion is still illegal, several tens of thousands are performed every year. Nuclear families now outnumber extended families, and the average household size is 3.1 people. Life expectancy is 72 years for males and 79.5 years for females. The median age is 32 years; 21 percent are under 14 and about 7 percent are

HANBOK

Traditional Korean dress has changed little over the centuries. Like much that is Korean, the *hanbok* seems to stem from Chinese or Mongolian counterparts, yet has evolved its own distinct style. Men's and women's dress is different in content and cut. Broadly speaking, royal and court dress, wedding costumes, and mourning clothing are all offshoots of and/or embellishments on ordinary dress themes.

For women, the basic outfit consists of a short bodice and long billowy skirt. The bodice *(jeogori)* has sleeves with slightly curved bottoms. It ties at the front with a half bow, the ends of which fall below the knees. The voluminous skirt *(chima)* wraps around the body under the armpits and is also fastened by a tie. Petticoats and bloomer-type trousers are worn underneath to puff out the skirt. During colder times of the year, a long formal coat, either half-length or full-length, is worn over the skirt and bodice, tying at the breast in a half-bow. This coat evolved out of the large hooded coats women wore during the Joseon Dynasty to hide their faces when they were away from home, keeping with the Confucian doctrine forbidding contact between unrelated males and females. Men wear trousers *(baji)* tied at the waist and ankles. A multi-pocket vest *(jokgi)* is worn over a square-bottom shirt, and a short waistcoat *(magoja)* is put on last. Men also wear an overcoat *(durumagi)* during cooler weather or on formal occasions. The women's bodice and coat, and men's shirts, vests, waistcoats, and overcoats, all have V-neck fronts.

Straight lines, gentle curves, and simple designs characterize the Korean *hanbok*. Variety and beauty come from the colors and patterns in the cloth. While everyday *hanbok* is not worn much anymore, fancier formalwear, often exquisite in material, texture, and color, is worn on ceremonious occasions, holidays, festivals, and other special events. Lightweight and lighter-colored clothing is worn in summer, while darker, thicker clothing is put on in winter. Silk, synthetics, cotton, ramie, and hemp are used for various types of clothes, some with embroidered designs or embossed or woven patterns in the cloth. Most designs are floral patterns, animal figures, and stylized Chinese characters. Fitted cotton socks *(beoseon)* are worn mostly by women and children, and shoes for women and children are made of rubber, felt, leather, or cloth. Men usually wear Western-style socks and leather shoes. Accessories for women include purses, knotted tassels *(norigae)*, fans, and hairpins; for men, amber buttons, fans, and hats.

---

65 and older. The most numerous age category is 35–39 years old. Because of the falling birth rate and longer life spans, the number of elder Koreans is also growing and this has the potential to put serious strain on social and welfare programs. Along with the increase in population and industrialization has come increasing urbanization: 6 percent of the population in 1930 lived in cities, compared to 86 percent today. This percentage only crept above the 50/50 level in the urban/rural split in the late 1970s. A full one-fifth of the South Korean population lives in the city of Seoul, and 46 percent lives in the northwestern corner of the country in Seoul, Incheon, and the surrounding province. Some 48 percent of Koreans live in the country's seven largest cities. Approximately 20 percent of the country's population changes residence every year—one-third of those move to another city or province, and about 10 percent go from country to city.

While the vast majority of ethnic Koreans live on the Korean Peninsula, an estimated five million (numbers vary according to source) have emigrated or were forcefully moved during the 20th century. Approximately 800,000 live in Japan, one million in the United States and Canada, one million in Russia (mostly eastern Siberia and Sakhalin Island) and Central Asia, and two million in China (the majority in Manchuria). A few tens of thousands live in Europe and South America. Movement to Japan, Manchuria, Russia, and Central Asia took place primarily during the Japanese colonization of Korea before World War II. While there was a short period of emigration to Hawaii at the turn of the 20th century, the big rush to the United States came in the late 1960s and '70s for political and economic reasons. Emigration continues today, and the greatest numbers of Koreans in the United States live in Los Angeles, the San Francisco Bay Area, and New York, where they have become successful in the greengrocery business. The largest contingent of Koreans in Europe is the roughly 10,000 in Germany.

Within Korea, the only significant minority group is the Chinese (approximately 20,000). Residents but not citizens, they fled from the mainland after the communist takeover in 1949. Approximately 150,000 other foreigners reside in Korea.

Names

Koreans have three-part (occasionally two-part) names. The family name comes first, followed by "generation" and given names. In total, there are about 300 family names in Korea; all but a handful are one syllable. The vast majority of Koreans have one of very few family names: Kim (Gim)—shared by an estimated 21 percent of all Koreans, Yi (Lee, Rhee)—15 percent, Pak (Park, Bak, Bahk)—8.5 percent, Ch'oe (Choe, Ch'oi)—5 percent, Chang (Jang), Chŏng (Jeong, Jŏng), Chŏn (Jeon, Chun), Cho (Jo), Han, Hong, An (Ahn), Hŏ (Huh), Kang (Gang), Kwon (Gwon), Ko (Go), Ku (Gu), Min, Im (Lim), Nam, Sŏ (Seo, Suh), Sŏng (Seong), Song, O (Oh), No

KOREANS IN JAPAN

Archaeological evidence makes it likely that people residing on the Korean Peninsula moved to the Japanese islands in successive waves of migration covering several thousand years prior to the establishment of the early Japanese states. During the Three Kingdoms period (4th through 7th centuries B.C.) Koreans principally from the Baekje and Goguryeo kingdoms traveled to Japan, introducing Buddhism, Confucianism, current Chinese thought, arts and crafts, dress, music, sciences, and governmental practices to the Japanese. Many of these people, and others escaping warfare between Korean states, stayed and assimilated themselves into Japanese society, creating families of significance and influence. The relationship between the Korean states and Japan at the time was, by and large, very positive and pursued by both sides for their mutual benefit. In the 6th century, Emperor Tenno is said to have boasted that his mother was Korean—an assertion that xenophobic Japanese would vehemently deny. By the 9th century, an estimated one-third of Japanese aristocracy possessed some Korean or Chinese blood.

For the next several centuries, most contact was by furtive pirate raids by both sides. In 1592, and again in 1597, Japan invaded Korea with full military forces, laying to waste the Korean nation. Thousands of Koreans, mostly artists and crafts-men, were taken to Japan as booty. Many of these Koreans made names for themselves by aiding the Japanese artistic community, and some became famous. Many of their descendants still live and thrive in Japan.

During Japanese colonization of the Korean Peninsula, Koreans escaped to China or Manchuria for political or economic reasons, or were once again forcibly removed to Japan to work for the Japanese war machine. At the end of the war about two million Koreans, 10 percent of the population, were in Japan. While many returned to Korea after the Japanese surrender, others chose to stay because of the rapidly deteriorating economic and social situation on the peninsula, and later because of the Korean War. Today, an estimated 800,000 Koreans reside in Japan, ninety percent of whom are second- or third-generation residents. Growing up totally within the Japanese milieu, they speak Japanese, attend Japanese schools, and function as productive members of the Japanese society. Nonetheless, because of their ethnicity, these people are considered "aliens." They are fingerprinted, required to carry alien registration cards, and face a multitude of discriminations. An estimated two million other Koreans live in Japan disguising their identity and their past, sometimes officially changing names and nationality in order to become fully accepted in Japanese society.

(Rho, Ro), Yu (Ryu), Yun, Shim, and Shin are among the most common. Two easily recognized two-part family names are Nam Gung and Sa Gong. The family name is passed from father to children. A married woman does not take her husband's family name, so a Miss Kim becomes Mrs. Kim after marriage, although she may be referred to as the wife of Mr. so-and-so. Generation names are usually shared among siblings in a family, indicating a specific stratum in the family genealogy. These rotate by generation between the second and third places. The third is the given name, unique to the individual. For example, two brothers may be named Kim Yeong-ho and Kim Yeong-hwan. In this case, "Kim" is the family name of their father, "Yeong" is the generation name, and "ho" and "hwan" are given names. The generation and given names are chosen by parents, grandparents, a respected elder, or a scholar whose job it is to divine auspicious names. Occasionally, a person will have only one name following his or her family name, as in the name Kim Ku. Male names often reflect characteristics that are honored by Koreans, like Ho (strength), Jong (justice), or Chul (brilliance), while female names connote beauty and virtue as in Sook (virtue), Mi (beauty), and Hye (benevolence). Some girls' names are sometimes dealt with more

RESURGENCE OF TRADITIONAL KOREAN CULTURE

Along with the modernization of Korean society, the Westernization of Korean culture, and the rising standard of living, there has been a resurgence of interest and preservation towards many aspects of traditional Korean culture. A few areas where interest has grown include Korean teas, the tea ceremony, and teahouses; Korean liquors; folk music, dance, and dramas; Confucian and Buddhist ceremonies; art and craft items of traditional design and material; sports and games; movies, television dramas, and books about historical figures and events; regional festivals; and the preservation of cultural sites and relics.

freely, typically poetically, as in the name Honghwa ("red flower"). Names are mostly derived from Chinese characters, but the use of indigenous Korean words (those without Chinese derivation) as names has become popular.

Personal names are seldom used except within the family or among close friends, as are nicknames. Titles or names of positions are more common for business or professional use. Married women are most often referred to as "so and so's mother." Artists and writers often use pen names rather than their given names. Signatures are seldom used in Korea, although it's seen more and more in translated documents and papers that have some foreign connection. Instead, a *dojang* (personal stamp) is pressed into indelible red ink and affixed to documents.

Life Stages

At birth, special significance arises if the child is male. He will carry on the bloodline, support the family, care for the parents in old age, and perform the ancestor memorial ceremonies. Although the preference for a male child—and the need for many children—is slowly changing, this deep-seated bias is tradition-bound. Children are considered one year old on the day of birth. At 100 days *(baekil)*, each is given a party, signifying a milestone of survival. (While modern medicine has greatly reduced infant mortality, in the past only children that lived this long had a good chance of surviving into adulthood.) The first birthday *(dol)* traditionally begins a male child's life's direction. Dressed in traditional clothes, he is set before a table laden with food. Numerous objects are also placed before him, and the one he selects indicates what will be in store for him. For example, a calligraphy brush points to a life as a writer or artist, a coin to riches. Although conducted in a playful manner today, the ceremony was taken seriously in the superstitious past.

A male was not considered a man and a female not a woman until marriage. Until the end of the Joseon Dynasty, couples were often married in their mid-teens. This led to odd situations, like a newly married boy of 15 being treated as a man while an unmarried male twice

TRADITIONAL WEDDINGS

Almost never seen today in their entirety, traditional Korean weddings and the preliminary ceremonies were solemn yet joyous events. Based on social status, family background, age, and astrological information, two families agreed upon the marriage potential of their children. This first stage, called *Oyihon*, was followed by *Napchae*, a formal exchange of documents binding the agreement. These documents included a letter sent by the bridegroom's family and prepared by a fortune teller giving exact information of his birth year, month, day, and hour. This constituted the formal proposal. In reply, a letter from the bride's family included an auspicious date chosen for the wedding according to the lunar calendar and agreed to by the bridegroom's family. On the day before, sometimes the day of, the wedding, the bridegroom's family sent a ceremonial box to the bride's family in the stage called *Nappye*. This gift box contained silk cloth and various items symbolic of fertility and longevity. Carried by a relative chosen because he was happily married and had already fathered a son, it was received by the bride's mother, who would evaluate the quality of its contents.

On the wedding day, the bridegroom, dressed in a formal blue gown and led on horseback by family members and other attendants, proceeded to the bride's house for the ceremony, formally receiving his bride in the stage known as *Chinyeong*. After greetings by the bride's family, the actual wedding ceremony began, often in the courtyard of the house in order to accommodate all the visitors. Facing each other across a high table, the bridegroom bowed to the bride, after which she, helped by two attendants, bowed low to the bridegroom. These *gyobae* bows were, in essence, the exchange of vows. After the bowing, the couple shared a cup of rice wine and the ceremony was over. No words were spoken except by the officiator, and no smile was supposed to cross the bride's lips. While individual items were often different, the high table was usually draped in cloth and covered with piles of the best food, candles, flower arrangements, and two wooden geese (or a hen and cock), indicating conjugal fidelity. Following the ceremony everyone was treated to a feast of noodles, after which the newlywed husband and wife were sent off to their bedroom. Sometime in the evening, family and friends would poke holes in the paper doors to see how the new couple was getting along! Following three days at the bride's house the newlyweds returned to the bridegroom's house, where they would live. Dressed in formal attire and carried in a fancy palanquin, the bride made her first visit to her new in-laws' house in a procession called *Urye*. At her future home, she bowed to her new parents-in-law and presented them with special foods brought from her parents' house.

Most Korean weddings today are Western-style affairs held in churches or wedding halls, the wife in a billowy white wedding dress and the husband in a new suit, but some people choose to hold traditional wedding ceremonies later at one of their parents' homes. Following a short honeymoon, newly married couples sometimes still live with the groom's parents for a time before getting a place of their own—though more and more couples are starting out with an apartment provided for, and furnished by, the bride and her family. You can see wedding ceremony reenactments at the Korea House in Seoul, the Korean Folk Village in Suwon, and at other folk villages around the country.

his age was still dealt with as a boy. Marriage brought great respect and responsibility to a male, who was then incorporated into the family's affairs and expected to carry out his duties. Marriages of the past were family matters, arrangements to ensure bloodline and social standing. Social status, and the time, day, month, and year of birth of the prospective couples were considered. Love had nothing to do with the arrangement; the bride and groom would often first meet on the wedding day! Matchmakers became common near the end of the Joseon Dynasty, and a few still ply their trade, yet only a small and shrinking number of marriages are arranged today. Marriage considerations now also include "character," education, and religion. More and more, people are being introduced by family or friends, or meeting at school or other social functions, and growing numbers of couples are marrying for love. Today, most females marry by the age of 25 and most males by 30. Great social stigma was, and still to some extent is, attached to the unmarried, especially to "old maids." However, this is greatly mitigated if the women reaches a position of respect and status within her profession. For women who have chosen the life of a Buddhist or Catholic nun, no stigma is attached, unless the decision to follow that path was not acceptable to the family.

The 60th birthday *(hwan'gap)* or *(hoegap)* is the next milestone. In the past, reaching 60 was a great feat. According to the Eastern zodiac, 60 years is the end of one "cycle" of life, the time for retirement and letting some responsibilities fall to others. A lavish celebration is given, piles of food are presented, and bows of respect made. Although reaching 60 is not so unusual today, *hwan'gap* is celebrated with enthusiasm, and it still marks a special step in life.

Finally come death and the funeral. According to Confucian custom, great care is given to funerals (like weddings); a proper send-off is necessary. Yearly ancestor memorials hold great importance. Even today, these gravesite ceremonies are some of the most significant traditional rituals that remain from the past.

Characteristics

Known as the "bow-wielding barbarians" by the ancient Chinese and pejoratively as "garlic eaters" by the modern Japanese, Koreans have more respectfully been called the "white-clad people," and Korea the "land of courtesy in the East" by the Chinese during the Joseon Dynasty. Koreans are spontaneous, earthy, talkative, and quick to laugh. They are expressive and unpretentious, and easily show their emotions among family and friends. Hospitable and gracious, they are a strong, proud people with great endurance. On the other hand, they can be aggressive, cutthroat, authoritarian, domineering, and obstinate. Through their joy of life runs a stoic streak that verges on fatalism that perhaps has been shaped by Korea's long, tragic, and often subservient past.

Loyalty to family and clan, filial piety, respect for elders, orderly relationships among men, deference to authority, proper education, and patriotism are some of the most important values. According to the Confucian model, all men fit into a stratified society where each has his place and duty; no movement was allowed among strata. Important relationships were king to subject, father to son, husband to wife, elder to junior, and friend to friend. While the social stratification is largely gone today, the relationship structure is fairly intact, except that king to subject has now become nation to citizen. Aside from friend-to-friend relationships, this structure is vertical and inherently non-egalitarian.

Although the extended family was the norm until recently, the nuclear family now predominates. Nonetheless, extended family ties remain strong, and family ceremonies are still honored. The oldest male of the principal bloodline is head of the family clan. He oversees the welfare of the entire clan and all familial responsibilities. Fathers are heads of the family, provide sustenance and security, and manage clan-related and external matters. The wife takes a secondary role in society, runs the household, and raises the children. Quite often they also control the family purse strings. Western ideas, including women's liberation, have by and large had minimal effect on Korean women. Today, however, women participate in many sectors of society, some even in supervisory positions and positions of authority, but the responsibilities of home life still rest on their shoulders.

Koreans love children. They dote upon and often spoil them until age seven, at which point their lives change dramatically: school starts, and strict obedience and discipline are expected. Traditionally, it was also at this age that they were segregated by gender to be raised separately. While no strict segregation of sexes exists today at home or in the elementary schools, by far most middle and senior high schools still operate as boys' or girls' schools, dress codes are still sometimes enforced, and discipline is mandatory. A carryover from the Confucian past, proper education is of utmost importance, and families make great sacrifices to that end. Primarily through education one can get ahead and reach a position of rank, power, and respect. However, the needs of the family take precedence over the desires of the individual. Relationships established at school are influential in business during adulthood. Relationships with one's teachers, business associates, church members, and neighbors are of lesser importance, yet they help provide the stability and cohesiveness of this tightly knit society.

The concepts of *jemyeon* (face) and *gibun* (mood or inner feeling) are key elements in relating to others. Especially in formal relationships, Koreans scrupulously avoid situations in which dignity or self-respect may be lost or embarrassment result. Likewise, it's important that the *gibun* be kept positive. It's necessary for Koreans to sense the mood of others by developing *nunchi* (the ability to "read" a situation), in order to maintain social harmony and personal dignity. Respect and propriety must be upheld.

Education

Education has been accorded great importance by Koreans. In the pre-modern era, education was the domain of upper-class boys only and entailed the learning of Chinese classics and Confucian doctrine. The first records of public education go back to the year 372, during the Goguryeo Kingdom. Both the Baekje and Silla kingdoms also established schools for the education of their aristocracy, and Baekje in particular sent many scholars to Japan. From the Goryeo era, lower level public schools as well as private schools were functioning throughout the country, and education incorporated Buddhist doctrine as Buddhism was the dominant religion at court. During this era, national civil service tests were instituted to select the country's best and brightest for public office. With the emergence of the strongly Confucian Joseon Dynasty, Buddhism was shunted aside and a proficiency in poetry and calligraphy was added to the classics and Confucian doctrine. Good education became a sign of social status and a means by which one achieved government rank, influence, power, and position. During the Joseon Dynasty, the top educational institution in the country was the Confucian academy Seonggyungwan; regional public academies were called *hyanggyo*. Private schools trained

ATTENDING SCHOOL IN KOREA

Aside from the Korean language programs that are offered by many universities and other organizations in the country, a number of universities offer summer session, semester, and year-long opportunities for foreign students to study various cultural topics. These programs range from easy to intensive, so be sure to check what's offered, what's expected, and what's required. The KNTO routinely puts out a brochure that lists some of the schools offering such programs, with short program descriptions and notes on costs. While not a definitive list, the following schools do have such programs.

Andong National University
Andong National University Language Center
388 Songcheon-dong
Andong, Gyeongsangbuk-Do 760-749
tel. 054/820-5774
http://korea.andong.ac.kr

Ajou University
Office of International Affairs, Ajou University
5 Woncheon-dong
Paldal-gu, Suwon 442-749
tel. 031/219-2922
www.ajou.ac.kr/~internat

Ewha Women's University (co-ed programs)
International Education Institute
Ewha Women's University
11-1 Daehyeon-dong
Seodaemun-gu, Seoul 120-750
tel. 02/3277-3161
http://home.ewha.ac.kr/~iei

Yonsei University
Division of International Education and Exchange, Yonsei University
134 Shincheon-dong
Seodaemun-gu, Seoul 120-749
tel. 02/2123-3486
www.yonsei.ac.kr/~ysid/

the scions of the landed elite class, the village schools being called *seodang,* and the higher-level institutions called *seowon.*

In the 1700s, about the same time as Western thought was beginning to filter into Korea via Chinese channels, there arose in Korea a mini-renaissance of thought called *Silhak. Silhak* (practical learning), often described as pragmatism, was a reaction against the staunchly unbending Confucian thought of the day and an attempt to address a wide range of concerns that would better the lives of the ordinary Korean. While innovative and practical, these scholars bucked the intransigent Confucian system, which eventually reduced their influence to naught.

With the opening of the country in the 1880s, Western education was instituted by missionaries who founded some of the country's most well-respected schools. Shortly thereafter, Koreans began to recognize the importance of Western education for the advancement of the country and also began to open schools. The educational system was expanded during the Japanese colonial period, but enrollment was limited and the focus was too "Japanese." After liberation, educational control once again reverted to the Koreans.

Although the content of the educational system has changed in the modern era, Koreans' fervor for the best education has not diminished and education is the privilege of all citizens. It is still considered virtually the only road to success. Because of the importance placed upon education, literacy is nearly universal (98 percent of adults by one report). As a measurement of this importance, education in Korea accounts for about 20 percent of the total governmental budget. The educational system is broken down into four basic units: preschool (one to two years), elementary education (six years), secondary education (three years middle school, three years high school), and higher education. Higher educational schools include four-year colleges and universities, graduate schools, two-year junior colleges, six-year medical and dental schools, teachers colleges, vocational colleges, correspondence colleges, and theological colleges. Aside from these are vocational schools, trade schools, company schools, and schools for the handicapped. The number of

schools throughout the country stands at about 20,000, and the number of students at about 11 million, roughly a quarter of the total Korean population. Students enter elementary school at age seven. Education is compulsory and free through middle school, and 99.5 percent go on to high school or its equivalent. Most students attend schools in their neighborhoods and towns; some country kids must travel to the nearest city for high school. Although elementary schools are not, most middle and high schools are segregated by sex. Although there has been some relaxation of these policies, most high school students wear some sort of uniform and have uniform hairstyles. A standardized national examination is administered to all high-school graduates who wish to attend college or university. The score on this exam, combined with high-school academic achievement records, and for some universities a test of their own, determines the qualification to enter particular schools. About 70 percent of high-school graduates go on to higher education.

The school year starts and ends in March. Students have a one-month vacation in summer (two months—July and August—at the university level), which roughly corresponds with the mid-July business vacation period, and a two-month vacation in winter, usually January and February. Through high school, students attend classes from about 0800–1700 on weekdays and 0900–1200 on Saturdays. Homework takes up many of their evening hours, and many students have tutors or attend special academies for additional study. Elementary-school class size averages 35 students, while middle- and high-school class size is about 38 students per class. These numbers are dramatically down from the 1970s when they were 50 percent higher. During the year, students may be required to study up to a dozen basic subjects; electives are extra. At the college and university level, students have a choice of dozens of major areas of study. For all levels, the main method of instruction is by lecture, with memorization and fact learning the most important learning tools. The importance of critical, analytical, and independent thinking is only slowly making an impact on this strict and authoritarian system.

Language 국어

Korean belongs to the Ural-Altaic language group, which occurs in a narrow band from Korea across Mongolia and central Asia to Turkey. Quite similar to Japanese in grammar and sentence structure, it's said to be distantly related to Hungarian and Finnish in basic form.

History

The ancestors of modern Koreans brought language from their native homes in central Asia down into the Korean Peninsula before the 4th century B.C. Distance, time, and the incorporation of local languages radically changed the form and content of their native tongue, which evolved in divergent ways in different parts of the peninsula. About 2,000 years ago, two dialects emerged, one spoken by the Goguryeo people in the north and the other by the Baekje and Silla peoples in the south. As the Silla people expanded their boundaries and unified the peninsula, their dialect blended with others, producing a homogenized language from which modern Korean stems. Efforts to standardize Korean have been made since the early 20th century with much success, yet some differences remain in vocabulary, word meaning, usage, and spelling, especially between South Korea and North Korea. Today, about 70 million people on the peninsula and several million more, principally in Japan, Manchuria, eastern Russia, and North America, speak Korean. With the continuing emigration of Koreans to all parts of the world, small groups of Korean-language speakers can be found in many countries, on all continents.

SPOKEN KOREAN

Characteristics

Korean is a non-tonal language, with agglutinative and polysynthetic elements; that is, phonemes, or sound elements, are combined to make whole syllables. Each whole syllable has a single and unified definite meaning or function, and elements of a phrase or sentence are joined to form one utterance but they do not exist independently.

Spoken Korean is a complex language with standardized rules for grammar, sentence structure, and sound combinations. There are few exceptions and even these follow regular patterns. The basic form of the sentence is subject-object-verb, the subject/object differentiation made by an additional particle of speech. Verbs consist of stems plus one or more endings, and these do not change with person or number. Dependent clauses precede independent clauses, modifiers precede the word modified, plurals and possessives are made by a suffix to the noun or pronoun, and gender is expressed by a character prefix. There are no articles. Statements, questions, commands, interjections, certainty or hesitation, and the "mood" of the sentence are all determined by the verb ending. Additional elements added to the verb, plus appropriate honorific words and/or a change in the pronoun, determine the level of speech. There are three basic levels, to be used appropriately with one's elders, equals, or subordinates. This highly developed system evolved to fit the social relationships of people in the complex structure of the Korean Confucian society. The Korean vocabulary is enormous, having a relatively large proportion of adjectives, adverbs, and words of emotion, feeling, and sentiment, and a relatively small proportion of words relating to abstract thinking.

Dialects

Today, standard Korean (pyojunmal) is taught throughout the country and used in nearly all mass media. It's basically a middle-class, Seoul-area dialect. Despite this standardization, dialects survive in provincial areas where pyojunmal is considered a "second" dialect used only with outsiders. Cadence and intonation of sentences, vocabulary, and grammatical endings make for the differences among the six distinct dialects associated with different geographical regions of the peninsula and Jeju-do.

Chinese Influence

It's estimated that 40 percent of the language is purely Korean in origin and about 60 percent is of Chinese derivation. Recent additions are from Japanese, English, and other Western languages. The debt to Chinese is profound. However, as Chinese is part of a completely different language group, this extensive extraction pertains only to vocabulary; grammar was not borrowed. Word meanings came with the imported Chinese characters, which were given Korean pronunciations to fit Korean sounds. Usually these Korean pronunciations are similar to the original Chinese pronunciations.

WRITTEN KOREAN

Development

Before a native script was developed, the Chinese writing system was used on the peninsula. Chinese characters (hanja) probably came to the peninsula with the movement of Chinese from Manchuria, about the 4th century B.C., but wasn't widely used until six centuries later. During the Three Kingdoms period (1st to 7th centuries A.D.), the Goguryeo, Baekje, and Silla societies became increasingly more complex, creating a need for accurate and sophisticated written communication. Chinese characters were adopted as there was official contact with the Chinese court, the dominant power in eastern Asia, and because it was the common script. Hanja was taught only to members of the upper class. Over time, three methods were developed to represent Korean words, syntax, and grammatical elements using the imported Chinese characters: Idu, Gukhyeol, and Hyangchal. They exploited the original sound value and meaning of Chinese characters for use with native Korean words, to fit appropriately within a Korean sentence. Even with their complexity, they were not thorough and represented Korean with much ambiguity.

New Script

The Joseon Dynasty's greatest king, Sejong, decided that all Korean people needed a simple script to accurately represent their spoken language so that everyone could benefit from learning to read and write. In 1440, he ordered a committee of linguistic scholars to look into this matter. After an exhaustive study of spoken Korean and Asian writing systems, their solution was the "invention" of the script we now call han'geul (hangeul), possibly based on a south Asian script of the period. Nonetheless, han'geul is perhaps the only methodically and scientifically formulated script in use in the world today, and it represents one of Korea's most noteworthy achievements. It's simple, yet captures all Korean sounds in a utilitarian manner. Han'geul was set forth in the document Hunminjeongeum in 1446. A national holiday, Han'geul Day, commemorates its adoption on October 9. Han'geul not only made all Korean sounds easily recordable but also facilitated learning the correct Korean pronunciation of Chinese characters. At its inception, the educated, "cultured" people resisted the use of this new script as beneath their dignity, and pejoratively called it eonmun, or "vernacular writing," connoting its benefit for only commoners and women. To them, nothing could surpass the beautiful and explicit script from China, the cultural heartland of the world. While han'geul eventually was widely learned

old-style Korean script

and used in some official documents, correspondence, and novels, *hanja* was preferred.

The use of *hanja* predominated until after World War II. Then, *han'geul* became the dominant script on the peninsula, and its relative simplicity worked wonders in making the Korean population literate. At over 95 percent, Korea now has one of the world's highest literacy rates. Yet there is still a certain degree of social status attached to being able to read and write *hanja* in addition to *han'geul*. The ability to use *hanja* proficiently indicates a strong and advanced education and is esteemed and aspired to by most students. In elementary school, *han'geul* is swiftly learned. *Hanja* is taught at the middle- and high-school levels, where 1,800 characters must be learned, enough to read basic textbooks, newspapers, and magazines. At university, students must learn additional characters to become experts in their fields of study. Yet some educators would completely do away with the use of Chinese characters and use Korean exclusively in all written communication. This has been instituted in North Korea, but in South Korea only cautious steps in that direction have been taken. Presently, *han'geul* and *hanja* are still seen together in most published works. Occasionally, Chinese characters are used in place of Korean words, but more often now they are put in parentheses behind the Korean word for clarification of meaning. Originally *han'geul* was written top to bottom and right to left in imitation of the Chinese system. Although it's still occasionally seen that way, now it's nearly always written left to right and top to bottom, an adaptation of the Western writing style.

The Structure of *Han'geul*

The Korean language has a syllabic writing system. Unlike English, where individual letters are strung together to make words, Korean vowel and consonant sounds are combined in *han'geul* to form syllables, which are then either used individually or joined together to make words. When created, there were originally 17 consonants and 11 vowels. Today, 10 lax consonants and 10 basic vowels are used in modern Korean. Nine aspirated and tense consonants are made

© ROBERT NILSEN

han'geul, Korean for "Korean script"

from the basic consonants, and 11 diphthongs are made from the basic vowels; counting these, there is a total of 40 letters. Of the possible vowel and consonant combinations, about 1,950 syllable combinations are used in spoken Korean.

Consonants are formed with angular or curved lines; vowels are formed with vertical or horizontal lines and short lines on either side of those, or combinations of lines. Although a bit angular or squarish in printed form, *han'geul* shows a pleasing geometric simplicity and beauty; amazing variations in writing styles can be seen, from bold block letters to fluid, cursive script. Originally, *han'geul* was based on a theory of construction much different from the Chinese use of one ideograph for one word. In *han'geul*, letters are grouped into syllables, each divided into three parts: initial, medial, and final positions. The initial position is filled by a consonant, or, if the word begins with a vowel sound, by a "o" symbol indicating no sound; the medial position is filled by a vowel or diphthong; the final position is filled by one or two consonants or simply left empty. Like *hanja*, however, Korean syllables are written in a "box" formation, each having the same relative size as its neighbor, no matter the complexity. This system is "scientifically" efficient, consistent in design, simple to read and write, and easy to learn.

Because of the volume of Korean words and the limited number of vowel/consonant combinations, most Korean characters have many and varied definitions. For example, the word *mal* may mean an 18-liter volume, language, word, speech, horse, the end, or a chess piece. Each is written and pronounced exactly the same way, the meaning to be understood by the context of the sentence. Only occasionally is the length of the vowel an indicator of meaning. For example, the word *nun,* when pronounced short, means "eye"; when the vowel is drawn out, it means "snow."

Certain Korean nouns appear throughout the text as suffixes to a place name or proper name. These are indicated by a hyphen (-) before the suffix as in Seorak-san (Seorak Mountain), Gwanghwa-mun (Gwanghwa Gate), Gyeong-gi-Do (Gyeonggi Province), and Bulguk-sa (Bulguk Temple). The meanings of these suffixes are usually self-explanatory, but all words and suffixes are listed in the glossary at the end of the book.

Translation

Translating Korean script into Roman letters has proved a difficulty. Early attempts at a systematic transliteration were made by the French and British in the years following Korea's opening to the world in the 1880s. Since then, there have been more than two dozen transcribing systems. These attempts were complicated by the fact that Korean pronunciation and written *han'geul* differ by region. While there is no internationally authoritative approach to transliteration, the McCune-Reischauer (M-R) system, set forth in 1939, has been the most widely used and accepted, and best represents Korean sounds in Roman script. Another, the Korean Ministry of Education (MOE) system, was more recent but its use was officially abolished in 1984. The MOE system misrepresents some sounds by its syllable-to-syllable transcription and does not account for some phonetic changes in sound according to the rules of spoken Korean. On occasion, the Yale-Martin (Y-M) system is seen, and it has proved most useful in linguistic study rather than everyday use.

In 2000, the Korean government—against a howl of criticism by a great number of Korean and international linguists and other scholars—instituted a new and official Romanization system that departs from the M-R translation system and is reminiscent of some aspects of the MOE system. Aside from costing an excessive amount,

it is seen by some to be a myopic nationalistic act that will undoubtedly cause more problems of communication both inside and outside the country. Time will tell. One thing that it does do well, however, is to make Romanized Korean easy to use on the Internet. Although many signs, textbooks, brochures, and other publications have been changed to reflect this new spelling system, not everything has been respelled by any means. The change will be a slow process, perhaps lasting until 2005, and some organizations vow not to make the switch at all. You will still find Korean transliterated both ways. With few exceptions, the Romanization system for this book has been changed for this edition from the M-R system to the new government system, not because it better represents certain Korean sounds—which the author believes is not necessarily the case—but because it will be easier for the visitor to match government-printed brochures and publications, and official signs and informational boards of all sorts. The major difference is that the new system does not include an apostrophe between an "n" and a "g" to indicate a break in syllable and to differentiate it from an "ng" sound. As the M-R system is still widespread and used in many sectors, the older M-R spellings for important place-names are still kept in the text and shown in brackets following the main entry of that name or where significant. Well-known Korean personal and place-names with "accepted" spellings have not been changed.

LEARNING KOREAN

When traveling in a foreign country, it's advisable to learn a few words and phrases of the language to facilitate your trip and make for easier communication. Time spent learning Korean will pay off in dividends, by opening doors, furthering understanding, and promoting acceptance. Language must be *learned;* it cannot be taught. The onus is on the learner; others can only augment the effort. Start with a few basic words and phrases, and *use* them. Don't be shy. Make your mistakes early and learn from them.

Written Korean is simple, and can be mastered in a few hours of intensive work. It's strongly recommended that you spend a little time learning to read and write *han'geul,* as nearly all street signs, notices, bus routes, transportation schedules, menus, and accommodation signboards are written only in Korean script. Spoken Korean is another matter. To speak Korean well takes years of practice. Yet learning a few basic words and phrases, correctly pronounced, comes nearly as quickly as learning the written script. You *will* need it at times. It is more difficult to learn to pronounce Korean correctly from Romanized Korean words than from Korean characters, so make it a point to learn to read and pronounce *han'geul.* If you speak even a little, Koreans will be pleasantly surprised, as very few foreigners even attempt the language. If you show an honest desire to learn, Koreans will reciprocate and become conscientious teachers. If you know more than a little Korean, they may think that you actually know a lot and speak in rapid-fire Korean, expecting you to understand all that's said. Don't be discouraged. Practice with people at the places you stay, with restaurant owners, shopkeepers, bus passengers, taxi drivers, and students. If you must communicate with a Korean in English, approach a high-school or university student, or a well-dressed young professional; they are more likely to understand and use English better than others. Japanese is spoken fluently by most Koreans older than about 70. Chinese is spoken by resident Chinese nationals.

Refer to the "Korean Vocabulary" appendix at the end of the book for pronunciation tips, basic vocabulary words, and standard phrases.

Intensive Korean Language Courses

For those who desire to learn Korean in a formal setting, only a handful of schools teach government-recognized language courses on a regular basis. The following is only a partial list of schools that offer language courses. See the tourist information center in the basement level of the Korean National Tourism Organization building in downtown Seoul for a more complete list. In order to receive a student visa and get sponsorship, you must attend a university program. Yon-

sei University's Korean Language Institute (tel. 02/361-3464, www.yonsei.ac.kr/~kli) has an intensive program in conversational Korean with students of many nationalities. Ehwa Women's University's Language Institute (tel. 02/312-0067, http://ile.ehwa.ac.kr), Sogang University's Korean Language School (tel. 02/705-8081, www.sogang.ac.kr/~sgedu), Seoul National University's Korean Language Program (tel. 02/880-5488, http://language.snu.ac.kr), GANADA Korean Language Institute at the Yonsei Institute (tel. 02/332-6003), and Korea University's Korean Language Research Institute (tel. 02/3290-1610, www.korea.edu), also offer language courses to foreigners. Most courses run 8–12 weeks in length and rates are generally in the ₩900,000–1,200,000 range.

Language Teaching Research Center (LTRC) (tel. 02/737-4641) has an ongoing program in intensive conversational Korean in Seoul. Other private organizations that teach Korean are the Korea Herald Institute (tel. 02/753-9155), Sisa Korean Language Institute (tel. 02/2278-0509), and the Korean Language Education Center (tel. 02/511-9314). The University of Maryland (tel. 723-4294) schedules Korean language classes on the Yongsan Garrison compound. Contact them at the Yongsan Education Center for information.

Texts and Dictionaries

Either for classroom instruction or self-study for serious students, the following books are recommended. For introductory grammatical and conversational Korean: *Speaking Korean,* vols. I, II, III, by Francis T. Park; and *An Introductory Course in Korean,* vols. I, II by Fred Lukoff. Several of the universities put out their own books, such as *Korean,* vols. 1–4 by Seoul National University; *Korean,* vols. 1–4 and *Korean Conversation,* vols. 1–6 by Koryo University; and *Pathfinder in Korean,* vols. I–III by Ehwa University. Specifically helpful for grammatical aspects of the language are the text and workbook *Korean Grammar for International Students,* by Yonsei University, *Easy Grammar for English Speakers,* by the Korean Cultural Society, and *Korean Grammar for International Learners,* by

Ihm Ho Bin. Perhaps more rudimentary are *Easy Korean for Foreigners,* vols. I, II and *Beginner's Korean,* both by the Sisa company. Sisa also puts out *Korean for Foreigners,* vols. I, II, which is accompanied by tapes. For a simple text and cassette tape of conversational Korean, try *Easy Way to Korean Conversation* or *Let's Learn Korean,* both published by Hollym Corp. The simpler pocket books *Let's Talk in Korean,* published by Hollym, *Korean in a Hurry,* by Charles E. Tuttle Co., and *Korean Phrasebook for Travelers,* by Hollym are easy to carry while traveling. The similarly small phrasebook and dictionary *Korean at a Glance* from Barron's is useful, as is Barron's *Talking Business in Korea,* which obviously puts a business emphasis on the language. For study involving the Korean use of Chinese characters, *A First Reader in Korean Writing in Mixed Script,* by Fred Lukoff, and *A Guide to Korean Characters,* by Bruce K. Grant, are indispensable.

For the traveler putting effort into learning *han'geul,* a dictionary will be indispensable. The *Elite Traveler's Dictionary* by Sisa fits into the pocket and is a very convenient two-way dictionary. Slightly larger but really too big to carry in the pocket are *Metro English-Korean, Korean-English Dictionary* and *Mate English-Korean, Korean-English Dictionary,* both by Dong-A, and *Handy English-Korean, Korean-English Dictionary* and *Pocket English-Korean, Korean-English Dictionary,* both by Minjung. Other larger dictionaries include *Essence: Korean-English Dictionary* and *Essence: English-Korean Dictionary,* both by Minjungseogwan Publishing Co., *Dong-A's*

Prime English-Korean Dictionary, Dong-A's Prime Korean-English Dictionary, Si-sa Elite English-Korean Dictionary, and *Si-sa Elite Korean-English Dictionary.* If a Romanized dictionary is what you need, the *Standard English-Korean Dictionary for Foreigners,* the *Standard Korean-English Dictionary for Foreigners,* and the *English-Korean Practical Conversation Dictionary,* all from Hollym, are good choices. Also available are the *Concise English-Korean Dictionary Romanized,* by Tuttle, and *Dong-A's Present-Day English-Korean Dictionary.* For decades it's been easy to find Korean-English, Korean-Japanese, and Korean-Chinese dictionaries, but for years there was little else available. Now, however, translation dictionaries are available in many languages including German, French, Spanish, Russian, Arabic, Indonesian, Thai, Vietnamese, Mongolian, Hindi, and more. For the serious student of Chinese characters as they are used in Korea, a Chinese character dictionary would be helpful. These list characters according to strokes and give definitions in Korean, sometimes with minimal added translations in Japanese and/or English. Various options are available, from the miniature pocket-size 10,000-character dictionary called *manja okpyeon* to full-size tomes.

All of the above-listed texts and dictionaries can be found at major bookstores in Seoul and some of the language texts can also be located at university bookshops. Dictionaries are stocked in virtually all bookshops around the country; however, the smaller the town and smaller the shop, the more limited the selection.

Religion 종교

The roots of Korea's religious traditions run deep. Brought by successive waves from Mongolia and Siberia millennia ago, shamanism is the most ancient. About 2,000 years ago, Taoism and Confucianism filtered into Korea, adding their unique concepts. Buddhism was firmly entrenched as the state religion of each of the peninsula's kingdoms from the early 500s until 1392, when it was supplanted by Neo-Confucianism, which remained dominant until 1910. Christianity was introduced in the late 1700s and became influential with non-traditional thinkers in the 1800s, but had widespread influence only after the opening of the country in the 1880s. The 20th century has seen a spurt of growth in a diversity of religions and sects. Korea has no state religion, so Koreans take freely from the old and the new, from East and West, to practice what best suits them. Although three-quarters of Koreans nominally subscribe to one religion or another, they are pragmatic in their approach and often "hedge their bets." For example, it's not uncommon for someone to go to church on Sunday, visit a Buddhist temple on Buddha's birthday, perform Confucian ancestor memorial ceremonies, and solicit the help of a shaman in order to rid the house of evil spirits. Broadly speaking, Buddhism (sometimes displaced by Christianity or other faiths) takes care of philosophical needs, is the wellspring of spiritual devotion, and is a refuge for solace; Confucianism provides an ethical foundation and social structure; and shamanism deals with the mysteries of life.

About 50 percent of Koreans are affiliated with one religious group or another. Even though Buddhism has not been the state religion for nearly six centuries and was severely repressed during the Joseon Dynasty (1392–1910), Buddhists make up about 23 percent of the population. Protestants make up about 20 percent, and Catholics 6 percent; smaller Christian and quasi-Christian sects account for another 5 percent. *Cheondo-gyo* (*gyo* means religion) and the Buddhist offshoot *Wonbul-gyo* both rank at about 2.5 percent apiece. Other indigenous religions have smaller percentages. While all religions draw from various sectors of society, each has its particular appeal. In general, Buddhist adherents are from the lower and middle classes, both rural and urban, and mostly women. Confucianism, the domain of males, runs across all socioeconomic boundaries. It is therefore possible that more than one religion be present in a single household. Christianity appeals mostly to the well-educated middle and upper classes. Shamanism is practiced primarily by rural and unsophisticated females. New religious sects generally attract those of the lower class.

SHAMANISM

Shamanism (*Museok Jonggyo*) is Korea's indigenous belief system. Not a religion in a strict sense, it functions as a spiritual foundation for the Korean culture and psyche. In numerous ways similar to shamanistic beliefs of central and eastern Asia, its pantheistic, animist doctrine attributes spirits to all natural phenomena, affecting every aspect of man and his environment. The veneration, placation, and influence of these spirits form the core of shamanism. Evil spirits must be appeased, and protection sought from the good. Only men and women with special powers are able to contact and communicate with these forces, usually in an induced state of psychological fervor, for the prosperity and well-being of the individual and community. The shaman, therefore, was the essential link between the spirit world and world of the here and now. The ancient shaman was a vital member of the clan and the males probably evolved into chiefs of the early Korean tribes. The Myth of Dan'gun, the foundation myth of the Korean nation, and the myths surrounding the births of the founders of the early Korean states all have heavy shamanistic, spiritual, mystical elements. Through much of Korean history, shamanism seems to have coexisted with religions introduced to the Koreans. Shamanism, however, suffered a decline through much of the Joseon Dynasty, with its predominant Confucian bent and distaste for things otherworldly, inexplicable, non-regimented, and emotional. During the last century, with the rise of the modern Korean state, shamanism remained, by and large, marginalized. It was suppressed by the Japanese, who wanted to stop its nationalistic elements, and even restrained by former President Park, who thought that it would slow the movement of the nation toward modernization and a modern outlook necessary to conduct affairs in an increasingly globalized world. Today, male shamans are nearly nonexistent, and female shamans are relegated to a lower-class, peripheral significance by society. However, it is interesting to note that in the last several decades, with the rise in consciousness of traditional Korean culture, shamanism has experienced a resurgence, once again becoming a more widely accepted practice, and the need for its preservation has been rendered significant.

Shamanism did not create an all-encompassing philosophical, religious, and ethical doctrine, or serve as the guiding light for a way of life. Rather, it was selective, and relative only to individual situations and events. Vestiges of the old shamanism remain, and shamans still perform ceremonies to intercede with the spirits—usually conducted in private homes or gidowon (prayer houses). Shaman shrines, spirit posts, and japsang rooftop figurines are still seen, while other elements have been incorporated into Buddhism. Crouched below gnarled oak trees, shaman shrines are still occasionally found in country villages. For special ceremonies, these shrines and trees are decorated with strings of prayer papers and human-shaped straw figures. Like shrines, the once-numerous and authentic spirit posts are now rare. These

JANGSEUNG

I n ages past, virtually every village had at least one set of spirit posts at its entrance. Today, authentic spirit posts are hard to find, although new copies have been erected at some folk villages to give modern Koreans and visitors a connection to this aspect of Korea's cultural past. Called *jangseung,* these totems are the guardians of the village, erected to protect it from harm and ensure peace and prosperity. Usually constructed of wood, those in the south-central coastal region of the peninsula were often made of stone—usually granite. Standing in pairs, they represent the male and female. The tops are carved in grotesque (some would say comical) faces: slanted bug eyes, huge stuck-out ears, and gaping mouths with prominent teeth. Down the front of the male run Chinese characters forming the words Cheonha Daejanggun ("Great General Under Heaven"), and down the front of the female, Jiha Daejanggun ("Great General Under the Earth"). In the past, these posts were venerated and well kept because of the protection they offered the village. While most are now gone and forgotten, they not only still grace villages in a few rural areas, but ceremonies are conducted to honor their spirits.

wooden poles capped with stylized male and female heads were set at entrances to country villages to ward off evil. Important government buildings of the Joseon Dynasty sport miniature human and animal figures set at the corners of roofs to protect the building from harm. Enshrined at temples are the spirits Sanshin, Chilseong, and Dokseong; temple doors are often painted with faces of fierce mythical creatures to scare away destructive influences.

Once the domain of both sexes, today's practicing shamans are nearly all female. Although the title varies according to location on the peninsula, female shamans are generally called *mudang,* and males are generally called *baksu.* These Korean words are similar to words for shamans in the languages of other East Asian peoples who also have a tradition of shamanism. Historically, shamans were of two types: hereditary and spiritual. Hereditary shamans follow in the steps of family members. As professionals who practice for economic gain, they are familiar with rituals and only perform ceremonies. The number of hereditary shamans is decreasing rapidly. Spiritual shamans receive a "call" from the spirits, usually through experiences that bring them much hardship and near-death. They have no choice in the matter, for to live is to accept the call. Not only do they perform rites and rituals, they also have been given the ability to communicate directly with the spirits in a trance state. Shamans of both types perform ceremonies called *gut.* The *gut* involves an offering of food or money at an altar, incantation, music and dance, special clothes and accoutrements, and often the involvement of spectators. At one point in the ceremony, the *mudang* lapses into a trance to be the receptacle of a spirit who then must be mollified. These ceremonies often last through the night and are a spectacle to behold. As one respected anthropologist said, shamans are "part priestess, part performer, part therapist."

Although individual parts of these rituals may vary, broadly speaking they fall into three sections: the evocation, or calling of the spirits; entertainment of the spirits and spectators; and sending off the spirits. Usually, four kinds of

SHAMANISTIC COMMA DESIGN

Excavations on the Korean Peninsula have revealed numerous artifacts in the shape of a comma or cashew nut. These artifacts are often made of jade, sometimes of flattened gold. Most have holes drilled through one end indicating that they were dangling ornaments. The fact that they are made of precious metal or jewel stone, and usually found in graves attributed to kings or royalty, leads historians to believe they were symbols of the ruling class. Similar-shaped ornaments have been found across eastern Asia. No one seems to know for sure the origin of this widespread symbol, but some have speculated that this design is shamanistic, perhaps representing a bear or tiger claw. Bear cults were a feature of the ancient peoples of east Asia and shaman rituals seem to have been used to protect these people from harm from Siberian tigers that were then much more numerous in this region. It is believed that male shamans of ancient tribes became tribal leaders and eventually kings, so the speculation that these shaman accoutrements became a symbol of early kings seems to hold credibility.

ceremonies are performed. Ceremonies for the dead are done to ease the deceased's transfer to the spirit world, and to ease the grief of and provide support for the survivors. Healing ceremonies are performed to end illness and sickness. Ceremonies for good fortune are held for individuals or communities, and involve such things as bringing peace to a household or village, casting off demonic spirits, appeasing household gods, helping ensure abundance for farmers and fishermen, and offering thanks to benevolent spirits. Initiation ceremonies formalize a new shaman's position. The first two types are performed only when deemed necessary. Ceremonies for good fortune are done on a regular basis, while initiations happen only when a spiritual shaman accepts the call and has undergone training.

TAOISM

While never an organized religion nor supported by the state, Taoism did contribute certain pantheistic and mystical elements to the spiritual makeup of Koreans. Known as *Do-gyo* ("The Way") and sometimes referred to as *Seondo-gyo* ("The Mysterious Way"), Taoism concerns itself with harmonizing man and nature and understanding nature's laws. Its pantheon of saints and sages was adored and used as a model toward which to strive. According to Taoism, perfection (or at least spiritual exultation) can be attained in this life. Other Taoist principles include harmony, simplicity, patience, contentment, purity, and a strong belief in longevity, strikingly symbolized by the oft-seen 10 signs of longevity. Medicinal and mythical herbs are prominent. Modern practices and symbols that hark back to Taoism are the use of celestial sages and mythical creatures in art, the use of symbols representing bliss and longevity, naming natural features after Taoist personages, and the pseudo-science of geomancy, prophecy, and divination; the trigrams on the Korean flag are taken from the *I-Ching*, an outgrowth of Taoist philosophy and divination. Hand in hand with an early form of Confucianism, Taoism filtered into Korea in the first few centuries A.D. and easily blended its belief and practices with Confucianism, Buddhism, and Shamanism.

BUDDHISM

Buddhism (*Bul-gyo*) came to Korea from China during the Three Kingdoms period. It was officially accepted as the state religion in 372 by Goguryeo, 384 by Baekje, and 528 by Silla. The first Buddhist university was founded in 682, and the religion flourished throughout the peninsula, maintaining a position of national religion during the United Silla period. Buddhism was a means by which the individual could strive for spirituality and the state could gain cohesiveness. At first, it focused on pragmatic, worldly elements that could be understood by an ill-educated and superstitious populace. Later, monks brought back from China and India new ideas and interpretations, texts, and paraphernalia. New sects were created and deeper understanding was reached. By the 8th century, Buddhism had shifted to a greater concern with meditation, ethics, morality, and attainment of Buddhahood through individual effort.

This religious code not only affected Koreans' spiritual development, but also played a great part in the arts and architecture, language, culture, and folklore. Monks sent to Japan as early as the mid-500s greatly influenced the formative years of Buddhism there, and records indicate that many Japanese monks came to Korea to study. During the Goryeo Dynasty (918–1392), Korea excelled in publishing, translating, and preserving Buddhist texts. Buddhism attained its greatest influence during this dynasty, when monks held positions of power in government, but toward the end it slowly became corrupt. Throughout the Joseon Dynasty, Buddhism was repressed by the strict Neo-Confucian administration, monks were treated with disrespect and disdain, Buddhist lands and property confiscated, and sects forcibly combined and reduced in number. Buddhist monks retreated to the mountains and Buddhism by and large became an underlying force in society, never disappearing but greatly reduced in influence. This wholesale suppression, plus the mass destruction carried out by the Japanese during the Imjin War of the 1590s, are the major reasons for the present scarcity of ancient Buddhist temple buildings and artifacts.

Sects and Temples

Mahayana Buddhism is the form practiced in Korea. After centuries of abuse and neglect, Buddhism is now experiencing a renewal. Buddhists number about 11 million, the largest religious segment of Korean society. With six major sects and over 50 minor ones, there are over 20,000 monks (*seunim*) and nuns (*bigunni*) at over 10,000 temples. The largest sect is Jogye-jong (*jong* means sect), with roughly half the country's temples and half its monks; Jogye-sa in Seoul is its head temple. Formed in the late 1100s, this sect was created to syncretize the then-dominant doctrinal and meditative branches of Buddhism.

After much change over the centuries, it was re-formed in 1941. Other major sects are Taego-jong, the married-priest sect headquartered at Bongwon-sa in Seoul; Hwaeom-jong (Hua-yen in Chinese), introduced to Korea in the late 600s, with its head temple at Hwaeom-sa in Jeollanam-Do; Cheontae-jong (Tien-t'ai in Chinese), brought to Korea in the late 1000s but recently revived at Guin-sa in Chungcheongbuk-Do; the Dyana sect, with Beomeo-sa of Busan as its head temple; and Daehan Beobhwa-jong, Jin'gak-jong, and Bomun-jong (a sect of nuns), all head-quartered in Seoul.

During Buddhism's early years, temples were built in urban and rural settings. During the Joseon Dynasty, many of the urban temples were destroyed and Buddhists retreated to the moun-tains. Although some are again being built in the city, most are still in distant, secluded valleys. Perhaps the country's most significant temples are Bulguk-sa, Beopju-sa, Beomeo-sa, Tongdo-sa, Haein-sa, and Songgwang-sa; many dozens of others are of regional or historical importance. There are three treasure temples: Tongdo-sa is the "Spirit of Buddha" temple and is said to pre-serve cremated remains of the Buddha's skull. Haein-sa, the "Spirit of Law" temple, houses over 80,000 hand-carved wood printing blocks that make up the entire Buddhist canon of liter-ature. As the "Spirit of the Monk" temple, Song-gwang-sa focuses on meditation and has special emphasis on the religious community.

Temples can be visited any day of the week during daylight hours. Go with a light heart, contemplative mood, and prayerful spirit. In general, well-known temples are crowded on weekends, holidays, and school vacations. They are quietest in the early morning and late after-noon hours—when the real serenity of temple life is most apparent. Large temples charge a nominal entrance fee which helps with maintenance; small temples are free. Always remove your shoes when entering a temple hall, and enter only through a side door. If you care to pray before the altar, kneel and follow the example of others who have come to do the same. The donation of a small amount of money (₩1,000–2,000 will do) is gratefully accepted but not necessary. Collection boxes are usually placed in front of the altar in the main hall; food can be brought to the temple kitchen. No smoking is allowed on temple grounds, and you should conduct yourself in a quiet and dignified manner. Dress respectfully and conservatively. If you are greeted by anyone who puts his or her hands together and bows to you, respond in kind. Taking pictures of temple grounds, monuments, and building exteriors is accepted, but always ask permission to photo-graph the insides of buildings, altar figures, and temple residents. Permission is not always grant-ed. Feel free to look around, but enter only build-ings that are open. Temple living quarters are off limits unless you are invited. It's usually not possible to stay overnight at temples unless you have had an invitation or participate in the Tem-plestay Program run by Jogye-jong (see the Spe-cial Topic "Experience Buddhist Temples from the Inside Out" for more information).

Although differing somewhat from sect to sect, the life of a monk (whether male or female) is relatively unencumbered, full of study and prayer. Monks rise around 0300 for the day's first chanting session, after which each attends to his or her own task—study, meditation, or chores. Breakfast is served about 0600. The morning hours are often devoted to teaching, as it is the time of day when minds are fresh. A sec-ond chanting session is held before lunch, which is usually the main meal of the day. After lunch and a short period of free time, each monk again returns to a personal task. About 1700, evening supper is served and an hour or so later a bell is rung to call all to evening prayers. Quiet study and meditation follow until bedtime. The year is divided into four segments devoted to two basic types of activities: summer and winter are de-voted to study, while spring and fall may be used to travel.

The most important Buddhist festival is Bud-dha's birthday, the eighth day of the fourth lunar month. On this day, paper lanterns are strung throughout temple grounds. In cylindrical, hexag-onal, or lotus-bud shape, each holds a candle il-luminating a ribbon attached to its bottom inscribed with names of those for whom a prayer is offered. Special ceremonies are held throughout the day, and, if the temple has one, a huge mural is unrolled in the courtyard—a once-a-year event. In cities, a parade is held in the evening in which participants carry paper lanterns and chant incantations as they trace a route through city streets to the temples. Anyone can hang a lantern at a temple or participate in the parade. Other important celebrations, all reckoned according to the lunar calendar, are the commemoration of Buddha leaving his home (eighth day of the second month), Buddha's enlightenment (eighth day of the twelfth month), Buddha's death (fifteenth day of the second month), and an All Saints Day (fifteenth day of the seventh month).

Buddhist Philosophy

Buddhism is an all-encompassing religion, providing a philosophical basis from which to view the universe and one's participation in it. It teaches morality and a universal ethical code. Buddhists believe in rebirth, wherein the afterlife attained is based upon conduct in this life. It postulates salvation through personal effort from the cycle of life in which all sentient beings are currently trapped. The object of Buddhism is to realize freedom from suffering. Each sect has its own method to best achieve that end, but the end is the same: Buddhahood, a fully awakened state, and a release from all attachment, Nirvana. The Buddha is the object of veneration, but only as an aspect of universal Buddhahood, showing the way to perfection for all beings. Pantheistic tendencies are exhibited in the number of bodhisattvas (those who have progressed along the path to enlightenment but who have stayed behind in the world to help all sentient beings escape the cycle of suffering and death) and the various gods absorbed from shamanism.

Buddhas, Bodhisattvas, and Guardian Figures

Four Buddhas are enshrined in Korean temples, each an aspect of the infinite Buddha. Seokgamoni (Sanskrit: Nirmana Kaya), the Historical Buddha or Buddha of the Present Age, sits on the altar of the *Daeung-jeon* ("Hall of Great Exultation"), flanked by Munsu (Manjusri), Bodhisattva of Transcendental Wisdom, and Bohyeon (Samanthabhadra), Bodhisattva of Universal Kindness. Seokgamoni is recognized by a protuberance on his head symbolizing supreme wisdom. He is the representation of Siddhartha Gautama, an Indian prince turned seeker and teacher, who was the founder of Buddhism in the 6th century B.C. Birojana or Vairocana (Dharma Kaya), godhead of the Buddhist trinity, is the Universal Buddha, the Buddha of Truth and Knowledge. Often enshrined alone, Birojana is easily recognized by his *mudra* (hand position)—one fist clasping the index finger of the other hand. Amita (Amithaba), the Buddha of Infinite Light, is seen in the *Geungnak-jeon* ("Hall of the Western Paradise"), flanked by the bodhisattva Gwanseeum Bosal (Avaloketesvara), also called Gwaneum, the Goddess of Mercy, and Daesaeji Bosal (Mahasthamaprapta), Bodhisattva of Saving Power. He is master of the Pure Land, where all reach enlightenment. The Pure Land sect of Buddhism, of which Amita is the most important Buddha, subscribes to the idea that salvation can be had simply by repeatedly chanting Amita Buddha's name. This has led to one of the most popular Buddhist incantations—often seen carved on rocks near temples—*Nammu Amitabul*, in Korean. The Goddess of Mercy often wears a crown, holds a bottle in her hand, and is sometimes depicted with 13 heads. If enshrined in a hall by herself, she is usually backed by a mural depicting her with 1,000 hands. The fourth Buddha is Yaksa Yeorae (Bhaisajya-guru Tathagata), the Healing Buddha. Master of the Eastern Paradise, he gives relief to those in poverty and pain, or afflicted by disease. Usually enshrined in a separate hall, he is seated and holds a bowl. Occasionally, he is flanked by Ilgwng and Wolgwang, the bodhisattvas of the Sun and Moon. One other Buddha, seldom enshrined in a temple hall, is seen in Korea. This is Mireuk (Maitreya), the Buddha of the Future. Depicted in small figurine form, he wears a crown and is seated in a meditative pose, often with one leg extended to the ground and chin in hand. If done as a large stone sculpture, he stands (occasionally sits) and wears a mortarboard hat.

The four Heavenly Kings (Lokapala), also called devas, are fearsome, armored guardians of the four cardinal directions of the Buddhist heaven. Jiguk reigns in the east and carries a lute, Gwangmok in the west clasps a dragon and thunderbolt (or jewel of life), Chungjang in the south wields a sword, Damun in the north holds a pagoda. Also protectors of the temple precinct, they chase away evildoers and trample demons beneath their feet. Whether a three-dimensional statue or a painting, they always stand at temple compound entrances.

Temple Design

No two temples are alike, and each has its distinct characteristics. However, certain common features are typical of all temples, large or small, rural or urban. After discovering what is alike, it is interesting to look for the differences.

Buddhist temple design is not only functional and blends well into the environment, it is also symbolic. Usually set on a hillside, the approach to a temple compound symbolizes an ascent from the mundane to the spiritual, a rise to a higher consciousness. The way is often bent, a reminder that the path to spirituality is not straight and easy. Often, this path crosses a stream, a symbolic purification from the taint of the ordinary world. In the center of the compound is the main hall.

The three major components of sizable temples are the approach gates, halls for religious activity, and living areas. These components may be combined or eliminated in smaller temples. The first gate is *Ilju-mun*, an open, wall-less gate whose heavy roof is held up by two or four stout posts. Here you "arrive" at the temple. The second gate is *Sacheonwang-mun*, which houses the four Heavenly Kings. Passing through it you reach the third gate (often missing), *Bulli-mun* ("Nonduality Gate"), the threshold to the inner sanctum. This gate is sometimes built to house the bodhisattvas Bohyeon (on the back of an elephant) and Munsu (riding a tiger). Each gate is separated by a short distance, giving all who approach time to drop the cares of ordinary life and prepare themselves for entry into the spiritual establishment.

The approach to the central courtyard leads underneath (sometimes around) a lecture hall—from the darkness into light. Usually an open

© ROBERT NILSEN

Located behind the larger halls at Buddhist temples, the Sanshin hall is dedicated to the Mountain Spirit.

post-and-beam structure, the lecture hall is sometimes enclosed to be used for study, houses a drum and bell, or is seemingly not used at all. At most temples, the bell pavilion also is placed toward the front of the compound. The bell pavilion contains the four large musical instruments found at temples: a bronze bell (to wake monks) suspended from a stout beam, a barrel-shaped skin drum (to wake creatures of the land), a flat bronze gong (to wake creatures of the air), and a wooden gong in the shape of a fish (to wake creatures of the sea). During prayers, a concave bronze gong and a wooden *moktak* (hollow wooden gong) are used.

On the far side of the courtyard (the main courtyard, if there is more than one) is *Daeung-jeon* or *Daeungbo-jeon*, the principal worship hall. Dedicated to Seokgamoni, his statue is centered on the altar, flanked usually by two but sometimes up to ten bodhisattvas. A mural of him with attendants backs the statue and a canopy is suspended overhead. Murals of religious scenes line its walls. At some temples, carved wooden animals dangle from the ceiling, dragon designs curl around the pillars to each side of the altar, fairy musicians grace the ceiling, and Buddhas are painted between the eave brackets to symbolically help hold up the roof. If the main worship hall carries the signboard *Geung-nak-jeon* ("Hall of the Western Paradise"), the Buddha enshrined is Amita. On occasion, Birojana, the Cosmic Buddha, is enshrined in the main worship hall, which will then usually be called *Daejeokgwang-jeon*. At large temples, individual halls are dedicated to various other Buddhas and bodhisattvas; the name of the hall indicates who is enshrined within: *Mireuk-jeon* for the Maitreya Buddha; *Wontong-jeon* for Avaloketesvara, the Goddess of Mercy; and *Yaksa-jeon* for the Buddha of Healing. Sometimes, portraits of former abbots of the temple or other important monks are housed in a small memorial hall, or if not there then inside the main worship hall. Larger temples have separate buildings set aside as museums.

ZEN MEDITATION FOR FOREIGNERS

There are few opportunities for foreigners to study Buddhism and Zen meditation in Korea, but it is not impossible. The major obstacle has always been a sufficient knowledge of the Korean language. While some serious seekers have managed to integrate themselves into the ordinary temple community, that path is virtually closed to non-Koreans. However, for others, and particularly for those who do not have either the language skills or a long-term commitment, there are still a few options.

Perhaps the easiest is through Lotus Lantern International Buddhist Center, 148-5, Sogyeok-dong, Jongno-gu, Seoul, 110-200, tel. 02/735-5347, fax 02/720-7849, www.lotuslantern.net, which is located just east of Gyeongbok-gung in downtown Seoul. This center (연등국제불교회관) offers discussion groups, study sessions, and Dharma meetings in English, as well as meditation sessions several times throughout the week, both during the day and in the evening. For those who have the desire to experience greater depth in meditation, this organization also offers periodic meditation retreats at the Lotus Lantern Meditation Center on Ganghwa-do. Contact them for all details.

In association with Hwagye-sa, a Buddhist temple on the eastern slope of Bukhan-san in Seoul, the Seoul International Zen Center (화계사국제선원), along with the Kye Ryong Sahn International Zen Center (계룡산국제선원무상사) at Mu Sang Sa near Daejeon, are the only two places in Korea that offer Zen study and meditation retreats for non-Koreans on a regular basis where participants live at the temple. Unlike at ordinary Korean temples, these retreats are open to ordained monks and laypersons, male and female alike. Study and meditation at these centers generally takes place during summer and winter sessions. At Hwagye-sa, there is a minimum of a one-week commitment and it's possible to stay for up to three months. Study at Mu Sang Sah (Musang-sa) is for the more serious person and the commitment there is for a three month Kyol Che retreat. A special application must be made in advance for participation in these sessions and a number of particular rules are enforced. For information and applications, contact the Seoul International Zen Center at Hwagye-sa, 487 Suyu 1-dong, Gangbuk-gu, Seoul, Korea 142-071, tel. 02/900-4326, fax 02/3297-5770, sizc@soback.kornet.net, http://soback.kornet.net/~sizc; or the Kye Ryong Sahn International Zen Center at Mu Sang Sah, Chungnam, Nonsanshi, Dumamyon, Hyanghanri, San 51-9, Korea 320-910, tel. 42/841-6084, fax 42/841-1202, krszc@soback.kornet.net.

Hwagye-sa is one of the major temples in Seoul and has a long and significant history. While Musang-sa is new and still in the process of being expanded, there is an interesting legend that relates to the mountain at its back. This temple sits below Guksa-bong (National Teacher Peak) and the legend states that at some time in the future, 700 Dharma teachers will live and study on this mountain. Perhaps the Mu Sang Sah Kye Ryong Sahn International Zen Center is the beginning of that community.

EXPERIENCE BUDDHIST TEMPLES
FROM THE INSIDE OUT

Tourists have long traveled winding mountain roads to reach Korea's temples. Most are content to stroll the grounds and peek into the Main Buddha Hall and shrines. But to commemorate Korea's co-hosting of the 2002 FIFA World Cup, 33 temples opened otherwise cloistered doors and invited foreigners to a monastic sleepover in "Buddha-Land." The official guidebook explained, "We are inviting you to this traditional space, which strives for perfect harmony between nature and Buddha's teaching of Dependent Origination, the concept that my neighbor, nature, and myself are not separate, but are all one."

The pre-dawn chanting, communal living, vegetarian meals, and *seon* (Zen) meditation tips proved so popular with foreign tourists and media that half the temples revived the program for the 2002 Busan Asian Games. To help cover the exorbitant costs of feeding, clothing, and housing thousands of guests, the organizing committee advised those near large cities to charge ₩50,000 per night.

Although temples are free to accept donations in place of a fee, some monks resent what they see as commercialization of the temples. Many, however, view the program as a chance to spread Buddha's teachings and learn from the visitors. While some temples may stop this program, others will likely continue hosting visitors indefinitely, albeit with some limitations to day or weekend stays. Those temples and their contact information are provided on the website below.

It's a great opportunity to get a close-up look at Korean Buddhism and architecture, and many temples include hiking and historical excursions as well as traditional art lessons on calligraphy, tea ceremonies, or making lotus lanterns.

Information is available at major Korean tourist information centers or from the TempleStay Committee, based near the Jogye Temple (Jogye-sa) in downtown Seoul: 46-22 Susong-Dong, Jongno-Gu, Seoul, Korea 110-140, tel. 02/732-9925-7, fax 02/720-7065, www.templestaykorea.net. Reservations: www.worldinn.com.

Program descriptions and directions to the temples are available in English and Japanese, but request directions in Korean as well in case you need to ask someone for help along the way.

©David Kendall

Nahan-jeon is dedicated to the disciples of Buddha. Inside, Seokgamoni Buddha is surrounded by 500 disciples (or some other representative number). Yeongsan-jeon is the hall of the Nahan (Arhat), where 1,000 disciples (or some other representative number) surround the central Buddha. Myeongbu-jeon is the judgment hall, where Jijang, with two assistants and 10 judges, passes judgment on all dead souls. Jijang Bosal (Ksitigarbha) is the bodhisattva of the afterworld, who intercedes with Yama, the King of the Underworld. Often murals on the outside of this hall depict in graphic detail some of the torments awaiting those who have not lived a righteous life.

Palsang-jeon contains murals depicting the eight famous scenes of Buddha's life. Where there is no separate hall, these paintings, or selections from them, are seen on the outside of other temple buildings. They are in order of appearance: Buddha's mother dreaming of a white elephant indicating the impending birth of a child; Buddha's birth; Buddha outside his castle seeing an ascetic, a sick man, and a dead man for the first time; Buddha escaping over the castle wall by horse with servant in tow in order to try to understand life; Buddha practicing asceticism alone in a forest under a tree; Buddha faced with the vanities in the guise of three beautiful women who try to tempt him from his path; Buddha preaching to disciples; and Buddha's death, where grieving disciples surround the coffin, from which his feet may protrude.

A second set of murals, the ox-herding pictures, are also often seen at temples. This series represents the training of the mind on the path to enlightenment. It starts out with the herder searching for the ox, then seeing its footprints, seeing the ox, catching the ox, taming the ox, riding the ox, the ox herder alone without the ox, and the empty circle. This classic series sometimes has the addition of a scene where the ox herder returns to the world. Other murals seen at temples depict scenes from Buddhist legends or famous Buddhist personages. Aside from altar figures and murals, the attractive features of temple buildings, like brightly painted woodwork and carved dragon heads, are above your head. Look up!

Up behind the main compound is a small building (sometimes two or three) dedicated to the three shaman spirits: Sanshin (Mountain Spirit) is always accompanied by a tiger and believed to help keep property safe; Dokseong (the Recluse or Lonely Arhat) is often portrayed as an old man with a servant or as a man with an enlarged forehead, and is seen as a person of exceptional intellect; Chilseong (the Seven-Star God) is prayed to by women who desire to become pregnant, usually with a son, and for his influence over human fortune and the length of human life.

Other objects at temples are stone lanterns, symbolically lighting the way to the spiritual sphere; stone pagodas; stone supports for banner poles; *sari budo,* stone water troughs; stone containers of calcified remains of holy men that are set outside the main temple compound; and various monuments which record incantations and such information as the history of the temple, a record of contributing donors, or biographical data about the person for whom a *sari budo* has been raised.

A spate of building frenzy seems to have taken over the Buddhist community during the past two decades. Temples large and small have built new or remodeled old structures. Perhaps the area least affected by this phenomenon, probably not for lack of want, is the southwestern corner of the country. In order to raise funds, some temples will, for a fee (around ₩10,000), write your name on a roof tile to be placed with all the rest when the building is roofed. This way devotees not only contribute to the construction but will have their name always in place as a prayer.

CONFUCIANISM

Confucianism *(Yu-gyo)* is an ethical and social system, not a religion per se. There is no worship of a higher being or striving to reach a higher level of existence. Still, as it attempts to improve human conduct and structure all human relationships, it's an all-pervading way of life. The strict doctrines of Confucianism are the basis for a well-ordered social system and fastidious ethical norm.

Confucianism divides human interaction into five important relationships: ruler-subject, father-son, husband-wife, elder-junior, and friend-friend. Proper conduct and social rank are all-important. Respect for one's elders and ancestors and maintenance of strong family ties are necessary elements of the proper attitude. Within this framework, loyalty, justice, knowledge, truth, virtue, piety, and decorum are ideals to be sought. Confucianism's fundamental desire is for peace and order in a controlled environment. Over time, these ideals became twisted and Confucianism turned rigid, overly ceremonial, moralistic, and oppressive. Neo-Confucianism, a "reformed" brand of this ancient system, was the norm throughout the Joseon

HYANGGYO

Of the numerous *hyanggyo* throughout the country, many have been renovated and restored during the past several decades. Several of historical or architectural interest are listed below, with founding dates in parentheses.

Naju Hyanggyo (1407)

Gyeongju Hyanggyo (1604)

Seongju Hyanggyo (1398)

Miryang Hyanggyo (1602)

Gwangyang Hyanggyo (1613)

Cheongdo Hyanggyo (1734)

Gangneung Hyanggyo (1413)

Daejeong Hyanggyo (1652)

Suwon Hyanggyo (1795)

Dynasty. With the advent of modernization, however, Confucianism lost much of its strength and continues to be eroded by the constant pressure of Westernization. Yet old traditions and practices die slowly, and Confucianism is still without doubt the primary ingredient of the Korean social structure.

Confucianism has no monastic order, organized churches, or worship rites. However, there are over 230 public Confucian academies *(hyang-gyo)* in the country, where periodic ceremonies honor Confucius and other Chinese and Korean sages and scholars. With some variation, these compounds contain a shrine, lecture hall, library, dormitories, and pavilion. While these academies no longer function as primary educational institutions, some have after-school classes in Confucian doctrine for the young. The shrines are simple and sparse. Unadorned outside, inside they contain only wooden tablets engraved with the names of honored sages and scholars set on table-like altars. They are opened only during yearly memorial ceremonies. *Seokjeon-je,* the most important Confucian ceremony, is held in September at Daeseong-jeon shrine on the Seonggyungwan University campus in Seoul. This shrine is the center of Korean Confucianism, and the ceremony involves traditional music and dance, ritual recitations, and food offerings seen nowhere else. Similar ceremonies held at other shrines throughout the country also mark the festivity. The yearly *Jong-myo Jerye* ceremony is held at Jong-myo in Seoul in honor of the Joseon Dynasty kings. Its pomp is a remarkable spectacle, a glimpse at the nearly lost traditional Confucian ceremonies. On a much simpler level, ancestor memorial ceremonies are held throughout the country by individual families to honor their forebears in a proper, decorous manner.

CHRISTIANITY

Christianity *(Gidok-gyo)* is the most dynamic religion in Korea today. After the Philippines, Korea is Asia's most Christianized country. If the rate of conversion continues as it has during the past several decades, Christians will soon outnumber Buddhists. Korea has several tens of thousands of churches (there are 5,000 in Seoul alone), often topped by red neon crosses on steeples (green crosses indicate hospitals). Protestants outnumber Catholics three to one, though the Catholic Church *(Cheongju-gyo)* is older, better organized, and much less fractured. The Protestants *(Shin-gyo)* are split into about 70 sects, some of which verge on quasi-Christianity. Current trends in Korean Christianity are fundamentalism, ecumenism, evangelism, revivalism, and mysticism.

Perhaps the most unusual fact about Christianity in Korea is that it was never imposed upon the people by foreigners. Introduced into Korea in 1784, Christian concepts were known through the Bible and other texts prior to that time by Confucian intellectuals and emissaries who had visited China in the 1700s. The interest in Christianity (read: Catholicism) parallels the rise of *Silhak* (pragmatism), a reaction to the increasingly rigid, ultra-conservative Neo-Confucianism of the day. *Silhak* scholars saw a need for flexibility in handling personal and communal affairs. Catholicism's early appeal was to intellectuals yearning for a revitalized spirituality, equity, and justice, and to people of the lower class as it offered them hope for this life and salvation in the next. This unorganized church grew by its own strength until foreign priests clandestinely entered the country in 1839 to minister to the large flock of believers. Even from the beginning this new faith was discouraged, with great persecutions dating back to 1801 and continuing through 1866; thousands of Koreans were tortured and beheaded. It largely remained underground until the opening of the country to Western nations in 1882.

Since 1882, Korea has been relatively open to missionaries of all sects. They brought things modern and Western, opened schools, established universities, built hospitals, and endorsed freedom, democracy, liberalism, nationalism, and the widespread use of *han'geul.* Protestants, especially Presbyterians and Methodists, had the greatest effect upon the country through the first three-quarters of the 1900s; the Catholics, on the other hand, had little organized strength until the 1970s. While there was a slow, steady increase in the numbers of Christian believers throughout the 20th century, only from the mid-1960s has there been a great burst of growth. In 1984, the Korean Catholic Church celebrated its 200th anniversary with a visit from Pope John Paul II and the canonization of 103 martyrs (93 Korean and 10 French). For Catholics, Korea has 90 holy sites, hundreds of martyrs, and is the country with the fourth largest number of canonized saints in the world. In 1985, the Protestants celebrated their 100th anniversary in the country, and its various sects have a number of shrines around the country.

The phenomenal growth of Christianity during the past few decades can be attributed to a variety of factors: the fall of monarchical government, dissolution of institutional Confucianism, imposition of a colonial power, and weakening of traditional values. Industrialization and Westernization required a different framework from the rigidly structured Confucian system, and Christianity fit the bill. After the disastrous Korean War, and through periods of political, military, and social unrest, Christianity has offered solace, security, and hope.

OTHERS

Other religions in Korea number more than 200, of which only a handful have any significant number of followers. The largest and most significant are mentioned below.

Cheondo-gyo

Founded in 1860 by Ch'oe Je-u and originally called *Donghak* ("Eastern learning"), this native monotheistic religion developed as a reaction to the plight of the rural poor and the influence of so-called decadent "Western learning" (*Seohak:* Catholicism). It was an attempt to restore dignity to the common people, raise their standard of living, and bring social and political stability through social action. Ch'oe was perceived as a threat to the government and beheaded in 1866, but his doctrine rapidly gained support. At first strictly religious, *Donghak* soon turned political and inspired popular rebellion and peasant revolt in the 1890s. After the turn of the 20th century,

the name *Donghak* was changed to *Cheondo-gyo* ("Doctrine of the Heavenly Way"), partly to shed its troublemaker image. Inspired by the *Cheondo-gyo* leader Son Pyŏng-hui, 33 *Cheondo-gyo,* Buddhist and Christian leaders signed and publicly promulgated a declaration of independence from Japan in 1919, provoking severe repression. *Cheondo-gyo* eventually ceased its political activity, but continues its religious and social work.

Cheondo-gyo doctrine is a unique amalgam of Confucianism's ethical foundations, Buddhism's self-cultivation and awakening to true nature, Taoism's cultivation of energy, and Christianity's personal God. It teaches equality among men and the unity of man and the universe. As all men are free and equal, it says, the political and social environment should be changed to reflect that reality. God is man and man God. With effort, heaven on Earth can be attained in this life. There is little concern for the future life, and there is no concept of original sin or need for atonement. With virtue and the infinite energy of the universe, the world can be changed in slow, constant evolution to benefit all mankind and secure peace for all people. The central headquarters of *Cheondo-gyo* is in Seoul, and a shrine dedicated to its founder is located near Gyeongju, at the village of his birth and place of his enlightenment.

Daejong-gyo

Daejong-gyo is a recent revival of the ancient myth of Dan'gun and the foundation of the Korean nation. Born of a heavenly father and an earthly mother transformed from a bear, Dan'gun represents a triune deity: heavenly creator, teacher and law-giver, and earthly ruler of the Korean nation. Legend says that Dan'gun was born in 2333 B.C. and ruled for 1200 years before ascending into heaven. Important doctrines of this nationalistic faith include service, love, and charity to others, cultivation of self, and truthfulness. Every October 3, National Foundation Day, white-robed believers make a pilgrimage to Mani-san on Ganghwa-do in celebration of the birth of Dan'gun and his dedicated service and instruction to the Korean people.

Wonbul-gyo

In 1924, the native Korean religion *Wonbul-gyo* was established to modernize and popularize Buddhism. It incorporates basic Buddhist beliefs with pragmatic social doctrines espoused by its founder, Pak Chung-bin, and its emphasis is on propagation of the faith, education, and charity. The object of faith is the attainment of Buddha-Mind for individuals and the relief of suffering for society on earth. No statuary is used or worshiped, but a circle symbol is used to represent the source of all beings and the enlightened mind of Buddha. *Wonbul-gyo* claims about one million members, 1,200 priests and nuns, and about 500 churches. While the majority of temples are within Korea, several have been established overseas.

Unification Church

Founded in 1954 by the messianic leader Reverend Sŏn-myŏng Moon, this quasi-Christian church (the Holy Spirit Association for the Unification of World Christianity) is extremely conservative and stridently anti-Communist. Believed to be the new-age son of God, Reverend Moon heads not only a religious organization but an associated business empire with a string of companies that deal in everything from food to weapons, chemicals, restaurants, newspapers, and banks. Because of questionable recruitment techniques and financial dealings, and unorthodox religious activities, the Unification Church has a tarnished image abroad.

Islam

Islam first came to Korea with Turkish soldiers during the Korean War, although expatriate Koreans living in Manchuria had been exposed to it around the turn of the 20th century. Since the mid-1950s, it has been helped along by close economic ties with Middle Eastern countries, where many Koreans have gone as construction workers. Domestic converts tend to be students. Korea has 10 mosques for the more than 20,000 faithful.

Cultural Arts 문화예술

Korean arts have long been overshadowed by the great and much better-known traditions of China and Japan. Indeed, Korea has acted as a conduit of culture from China to Japan. Yet it was not merely a channel. In the process, Korea altered what it received to develop its own artistic tradition, with as much individual character as others in Asia. In general, Korean art shows spontaneity, vitality, and naturalness. More emphasis is placed on the expression of emotion than on technique and precision. With some exceptions, Korean art is humble and unpretentious, not bold or grand like Chinese art, or sophisticated like the Japanese.

Early Korean art stems from the cultures of northeast Asia and the northern Chinese kingdoms. Pottery with repetitive patterns preceded those with plain and geometric designs; stone objects gave way to utilitarian and ornamental bronze items. The privileged class buried its dead in cists or under dolmen, which developed into mound tombs for the nobility of later ages. The earliest Korean paintings have been found in these mound tombs. During the Three Kingdoms period (1st century A.D. to 668) Goguryeo art was heavily influenced by the northern Chinese, being bold, simplistic, and "masculine," reflecting its hunter-warrior orientation in movement and animation. Baekje art, influenced by the southern Chinese, was more delicate and "feminine." Farthest from China, the early Silla Kingdom was the least affected by the Chinese artistic traditions.

New impetus to creatively use clay, metal, stone, wood, and paint came with the introduction of Buddhism in the 3rd century. The United Silla period (668–936) saw great influence from Tang China, particularly in religious subject matter. The 8th century was the golden age of Buddhist art. Gold continued to be crafted in consummate detail, and pottery began to be glazed, but this era's focus was on its stonework. During the Goryeo Dynasty, Buddhist themes continued to predominate. Wood plates began to be used for printing texts and illustrations, bronze items were inlaid with silver, and the casting of huge bells reached its apex. However, this dynasty is most noted for its unsurpassed skill in the production of celadon pottery.

During the strongly Confucian Joseon Dynasty, religious themes were suppressed. Bronze and stone were used less, wood and paper more. This dynasty is known for its painting and furniture making. Influenced by Western styles from the late 1800s, Korean art nearly died out during the Japanese occupation. Since the middle of the 20th century, however, there has been a vibrant resurgence of traditional art, and traditional themes and styles have been used in new ways.

NATIONAL MUSEUMS

The National Museum of Korea was established in Seoul in 1945 after the liberation of the country from Japanese colonial control at the end of World War II. This museum was an outgrowth and expansion of a Japanese colonial museum, the Yi Royal Household Museum, which was established in 1938, and the previous Imperial Household Museum, established in 1908 by the last king of the Joseon Dynasty. During the Japanese colonial period, branch museums were established in Gyeongju, Buyeo, and Gongju, as well as in Gaeseong and Pyeongyang, now both in North Korea. During much of the Korean War, pieces from the National Museum were moved to Busan for safe keeping. Following that war, these artifacts were returned to Seoul for display at Deoksu-gung Palace. In 1972, a new museum building was constructed within Gyeongbok-gung Palace to house the growing collection. In 1986, this collection moved into the renovated former Japanese colonial government building, known as the Capitol, and stayed there until its destruction in 1996, when the museum collection moved into an adjacent and much smaller building also within the palace grounds. Finally, in 2003, the collection of the National Museum moved into its new home on the south slope of Nam-san overlooking the Han River next to Yongsan Family Park. Aside from the central museum in Seoul, the National Museum has 11 branch museums around the country. These locations, dates of establishment, and main emphasis are listed below. For online information about the National Museum of Korea, see www.museum.go.kr.

Gyeongju: 1913: Silla Dynasty artifacts
Buyeo: 1929: Baekje Dynasty artifacts
Gongju: 1934: items from the tomb of King Muryeong and Baekje Dynasty artifacts
Gwangju: 1978: Sinan Sea shipwreck pottery and Jeolla-Do cultural artifacts
Jinju: 1984: artifacts from the 1592–98 Imjin War
Cheongju: 1987: artifacts from the central portion of the country
Jeonju: 1990: Buddhist art and artifacts from the Jeolla-Do area
Daegu: 1994: artifacts from the Gyeongsang-Do region
Gimhae: 1998: Gaya-era artifacts
Jeju: 2001: Jeju-Do historical and cultural artifacts
Chuncheon: 2003: artifacts from the mountainous north-eastern corner of the country

In addition to these museums, the **National Folklore Museum,** occupying the former national museum building within Gyeongbok-gung, is of great interest to visitors for its displays on aspects of Korean cultural life.

FINE ARTS
Painting and Calligraphy
The earliest known Korean paintings are in mound tombs in North Korea and Manchuria. Bold and bright, they convey a sense of the existing powerful warrior state. Scenes include horsemen hunting wild animals, wrestling matches, and brisk dancing. Mural paintings from Baekje Kingdom tombs reveal a refined sense of design, style, and execution. Depicted are floral and animal scenes in flowing lines and soft colors. Silla tombs have yielded little except for a flying horse painted on a birch-bark panel. Less skillful than the Baekje paintings, the horse shows Silla's connection with its nomadic ancestors and dependence on the horse for survival and warfare. The later Silla Dynasty produced religious paintings of great skill; the few remaining examples are now preserved in temples in Japan. The Goryeo Dynasty continued the emphasis on Buddhist themes in paintings, but landscapes were also introduced.

With the shift from Buddhism to Confucianism at the beginning of the Joseon Dynasty came a corresponding shift from religious to secular themes. Greatly influenced by Chinese styles, court painters were supported by royalty and followed formal styles dealing with limited subject matter. These official artists did mostly landscapes, court scenes, portraits, and plants. From the late 1700s, private painters developed a spirited, humorous, and casual genre portraying scenes of everyday life, still lifes, landscapes, and animals. As opposed to the formal, rigid, and stylized themes and methods of orthodox Confucian art, folk art was an expression of the informal humanist spirit. Official painters signed their work; most folk paintings were done anonymously. Court painters worked mostly in monochrome with very limited and subtle use of color; folk painters were much freer with color to give greater feeling and expression to the subject. *Dancheong,* the art of painting abstract geometric and floral designs on temple buildings, however, was the most colorful. Adjuncts to this were paintings of human and animal figures on inside and outside walls and on murals for hanging inside temple buildings.

Court, folk, and *dancheong* traditions continue today, although with greatly reduced emphasis. Throughout the Japanese occupation, artists were pressured to emulate Japanese styles and themes, and for the last 50 years there has been great interest in Western art—especially in the expressionist, abstract, and minimalist schools.

TREASURES AND CULTURAL ASSETS

National Treasures, or gukbo (indicated as "N.T." in the text), are rare, one-of-a-kind, or exceptionally crafted cultural artifacts of the highest order. Of the 400, the first is Namdaemun ("Great South Gate"), in Seoul; others include pagodas, gold crowns and statuary, celadon vases, stone statues, lanterns, stupas, memorial tablets, temple bells, and wood printing blocks. Treasures, or bomul ("T." in text), are second-ranking cultural properties of artistic or historical merit which number over 1,700. Intangible Cultural Assets, or jungyo muhyeong munhwaje ("I.C.A."), are skills, performances, games, and crafts—only sometimes producing a tangible result. The 124 designated Intangible Cultural Assets include the making of horsehair hats, the ganggangsullae circle dance, traditional tug-of-war, masked-dance dramas, the taekgyeon martial art, and traditional bowmaking. Practitioners, known as human cultural treasures, are honored and supported in their skill. Numbering over 425, Historical Sites, or sajeokji ("H.S."), are places of special historical significance (e.g. fortresses, royal tombs, or palaces). Natural Monuments ("N.M."), or Natural Assets, called cheonnyeon ginyeommul, are rare or significant physical features, plants, animals, and nature reserves. Some of the more than 330 are the Yongmun-sa ginkgo tree, virgin yew forest of Songni-san, Jindo dog, Seongnyu-gul limestone cave, and Hongdo nature reserve. In addition, there are over 950 nationally designated important folk cultural materials (jungyo minseok jaryo), some 1,775 other folk materials, and about 4,150 cultural assets, properties, and folk materials designated by provinces and cities. With periodic additions, these numbers slowly continue to rise.

Calligraphy has been admired since the adoption of Chinese characters in the 2nd or 3rd century A.D. Over half a dozen major styles, most taken from Chinese writers, have developed over the centuries, but some great Korean writers also evolved unique styles. Some are rigorous, studied, and formal, while others are cursive, playful, and bold. Not an art form like painting, calligraphy was seldom done as an end in itself. Good writing skills were considered an indication of scholarship and cultivation. The writing of *han'geul* has evolved into a calligraphic art form only since the early years of the 20th century.

Ceramics

Pottery has been produced on the Korean Peninsula since about 5000 B.C. A comb pattern was first to appear, similar to pottery found across Asia. Unglazed, probably hand-kneaded, gray or reddish in color, and fired at a low temperature, these earthenware pieces were usually medium to large and designed mostly for utilitarian use, but a few early pieces of statuary have also come to light. During the Three Kingdoms Period, pottery became, overall, more decorative and was fired at a higher temperature. Masterful floral and landscape roof tiles from the Baekje Kingdom have not been surpassed. Most pottery and earthenware figures of the Silla Dynasty are geometric, unglazed, and functional. Rather crude and simplistic in comparison to other pottery on the peninsula at that time, they are in some respects similar to early Japanese art. After the unification of the peninsula in the 660s, pottery styles changed. Influenced greatly by Tang Chinese artisans, there was a shift away from functional, geometric pieces to natural forms. Simplicity was still stressed, yet technique matured. About the 8th century, glazing was first used intentionally—before that, accidental ash glazing was the result of the firing process.

Korea's greatest contribution to ceramic art is Goryeo Dynasty celadon. First produced in Korea about 1050, it was based on Chinese Yuan pottery, which had a thin, full-cover, olive-colored glaze. Soon came the development of the unsurpassed, watery blue-green glaze called *bisaek*

("secret color"), for which Korean celadon is still famous and which has never been faithfully reproduced. Unlike Chinese pieces, Korean pottery was less perfect in execution. While elegant and graceful, it portrays a humble, relaxed naturalness. More spontaneous and independent, it was less confined by strict design, technique, and form. Although the blue-green glaze is best known, colors range from brown to nearly white. Until 1150, celadon was mostly plain, slightly incised, stamped, or molded. After that, inlay with white or black slip and underglazing with copper-rich glaze were also employed.

The decline of celadon production in the early 1300s coincided with the development of *buncheong* stoneware and white porcelain. *Buncheong* was pottery made for the common man, used mostly for food and drink storage. It was rougher than celadon, casual, and earthy. The largely natural or floral ornamentation was often done hastily, with little sophistication. Glazes are predominantly light gray, although they range from beige to dark brown. This unpretentious, carefree technique attracted the Japanese during their invasions of the country in the 1590s. Large numbers of Korean artisans transported to Japan greatly influenced pottery production there. Unlike *buncheong*, white porcelain was delicate and elegant. Its more formal style and technique were prized by the upper classes. Cobalt, discovered in the mid-1400s, was used for blue and white porcelain. Used sparingly at first, it later became overbearing and gaudy. Toward the end of the Joseon Dynasty, pottery production became much less innovative and of little note. Traditional pottery faded nearly to extinction during the Japanese colonial period, but with the increased interest of local artisans, government encouragement, and a more affluent and conducive environment, it has slowly revived since the end of World War II.

Most Silla kilns were in and around Gyeongju, Goryeo kilns were near Icheon and in the Jeolla provinces, and Joseon Dynasty kilns were near Gyeonggi-Do, Gwangju, Buan, and Gangjin. Today, many of the finest reproductions of these styles are still produced in those areas.

Stone

The peninsula's abundant granite was an obvious medium for early artists. Prehistoric petroglyphs of animal and geometric designs appear in several places, but not until the Three Kingdoms period were three-dimensional pieces made. Religious themes predominate throughout the entire history of stone art. Artisans of the early kingdoms followed styles in vogue in the northern Chinese regions; only during the Silla Dynasty did a unique Korean style emerge, although it too shows Chinese influence. Works from the Silla Dynasty represent the great age of stone art. More impressive than the grandeur of its structures is the subtle, graceful, and harmonious nature of its statuary. The Seokguram grotto cave —with the central Buddha statue, wall panels of the bodhisattvas and celestial spirits, and arched ceiling construction—is perhaps the finest stone work. Other items are pagodas, lanterns, and stone reliquaries; secular works included tortoise-base memorial slabs, zodiac figures, and grave figures. Stone sculpture continued through the Goryeo and Joseon dynasties, but its quality and importance declined. No one knows for sure when the *dolharubang* grandfather statues of Jejudo were carved, or why, but it's thought that they probably are several hundred years old and served a shamanistic and protective role. Modern sculpture, based largely on Western themes and styles, started during the middle of the 1900s but has not gained wide popularity.

Metal

Utilitarian and ceremonial bronze items appeared on the peninsula about 2000 B.C. About 1,500 years later, iron began to be used for more common objects. Shortly thereafter, gold- and silversmithing came to Korea from China. Gold was the specialty of the Silla Dynasty, used in everything from delicate filigree earrings to temple statuary. Casting bronze temple bells also began during the Silla period, but was perfected during the Goryeo Dynasty. Word of Korea's casting excellence spread as far as the Middle East. Slightly barrel-shaped, most bells have scalloped bottoms and are adorned with decorative floral bands and celestial figures in relief. Squat knobs punctuate the upper curvature; a sculpted dragon crouches around the sound tube on top. Like stone art, metal work reached its peak during the early dynasties. Following the Goryeo Dynasty, little of merit was produced and most metal sculpture today tends toward Western themes.

PERFORMING ARTS

The performing arts have developed at different periods with agricultural, religious, and secular emphasis. Little tangible evidence remains of the old forms. Ancient records show that the early Korean tribes performed ritual communal singing and dancing, either as religious or agricultural functions. Formal court music and dance developed during the Silla Dynasty and continued in altered form until the end of the Joseon Dynasty. The court was also once the scene of masked-dance dramas, but by the Joseon Dynasty these were excluded from court and taken up by the common people. Religious and secular music and dance, some from the Silla Dynasty, continued during the following dynasties and later were complemented by lyrical and epic songs. The court employed musicians and dancers for its own entertainment; roving theatrical groups kept alive stylized secular music and dance, while monks performed religious works. Preserving the most ancient traditions, farmers were themselves the source of the most inspired, hypnotic, and extemporaneous performing arts. Even with such deep roots, most of the traditional music and dance nearly died out during the Japanese occupation, when indigenous arts were strongly discouraged and even forcefully uprooted. Since 1945, however, there has been a resurgence of interest in preserving and performing known musical arts, and great attempts have been made at resurrecting forms fallen into disuse.

Instrumental Music

Korea's ancient folk musical tradition—esoteric shaman songs and vibrant farmers' music—stems from the nomadic tribes of Asia. Later, court music and instruments were brought from China and adapted to Korean tastes. Arising from Korean sources, some Japanese musical traditions—Bugaku, for example—are still kept alive there, though they have died out on the peninsula.

Korean music is based on a five-note (pentatonic) scale. This, combined with distinctive rhythms and melodies, may initially lead the Westerner to consider this music out of tune or dissonant. However, the more one listens, the more one understands and appreciates the complexity and its inner order. Korean music can be broken down into two broad groups: court and folk. Classical court music, *jeongak* (*ak* means music) is slow, ceremonial, and cerebral. One noted writer has said that it is the attempt to make audible the "hum of the cosmos." Formal and ritualistic, it comprises several different varieties: *tangak,* secular music from Tang China, which became ceremonial Goryeo court music in adaptation; *hyangak,* secular, native Korean music performed for entertainment at royal banquets; *aak,* ritual Confucian music performed at the Mun-myo shrine in Seoul for the royal ancestor memorial ceremonies; military; and chamber music. *Aak* is perhaps the best known, and the only one still performed in its original setting for its original purpose. Traditional court instruments are classified into eight basic types according to the material from which they are made. These materials, and representative instruments made from them, are metal (*jing:* gong), stone (*pyeon'gyeong:* chimes), silk (*gayageum:* 12-string zither), bamboo (*daegeum:* horizontal flute), gourd (*saeng:* panpipe), clay (*hun:* globular flute), leather (*nogo:* drums), and wood (*bak:* clapper).

Folk music (*sokak),* in contrast to court music, is lively, energetic, and emotional. Largely percussive, typical instruments are the *janggo* (hourglass drum), various handheld drums, cymbals, and the *taepyeongso* (conical wooden oboe). *Sokak* includes ritual shaman music to induce a trance state, Buddhist music performed in praise of Buddha, farmers' music played for pure entertainment or to accompany group field work, the *sanjo* improvisational solo, and accompaniment to lyrical or narrative songs. This was the everyday music of the common man.

A modern offshoot of *sokak* is what has come to be known as *samul nori.* Literally "the play of four instruments," this is *sokak* reorchestrated and set for the stage. *Samul nori* is a bewitching combination of percussion music that includes the hourglass drum, round drum, and large and small gongs. On occasion, the conical wooden oboe will be played to accompany the musicians when they get up to dance, twirl, and gyrate as they play.

Western music now also claims a piece of the Korean musical pie. Church music was introduced by missionaries in the 1880s; other forms have become widely popular and an important musical force from the mid-20th century. In recent years, Korea has seen the emergence of orchestras, chamber music groups, and solo artists in all sectors of Western music, and many outstanding musicians, including several internationally known musicians and conductors.

Vocal Music

Korea's long tradition of vocal music also breaks down roughly into court and folk categories. Vocal music is usually accompanied only by a drum, to keep the beat, or by a small ensemble. Court music includes the *gagok,* a long lyrical song with ensemble accompaniment that, in its entirety, lasts for hours; *gasa,* a slow narrative song; and *sijo,* a short lyrical song that is a musical rendition of a uniquely Korean type of poem. Among the types of folk songs are *minyo,* traditional folk songs of love, despair, and work from all locales on the peninsula. One, *Arirang,* has over 2,000 different lyrics and over 50 melodic variations. *Pansori* is a lengthy, dramatic, sung and spoken narrative accompanied by an hourglass drum. Like *gagok, pansori* runs through many episodes and lasts many hours, though it's now usually performed in short sections.

Koreans not only appreciate these traditional songs, but popular songs are also a great source of entertainment. Almost without fail, when a group gets together to party, songs are sung, hands clapped, and chopsticks beat on the table to keep time. Everyone takes a turn, and you'll be expected to participate. Talent is not a prerequisite—it's the convivial companionship that's important.

Dance

Like its music, the source of early Korean dance was the nomadic tribes of central Asia. From those groups that moved into the Korean Peninsula, ritual shaman and folk dances developed. Later, dances were brought from China and changed to fit the Korean character. They were more stylized and tended to be performed at court.

In any discussion about Korean dance, two terms are invariably used: *meot* and *heung*. *Meot* means something akin to grace or style, but it goes beyond merely graceful movement to encapsulate the inner expression of that movement. *Heung* refers to the joy, feeling, or inner "force" that is played out in the movement of dance. The dancer—his or her physical form—is of less importance than the dance itself. Greater emphasis is placed on expression than on the execution of correct steps. Korean dances do not tell stories; they create moods and attempt to express the inner spirit. If a story goes with a dance, it will be recited. The dancer, her movements, voice, and mask (if any), represent certain values, attitudes, and characteristics that the audience recognizes and can identify with.

Gestures are bold and definite, yet there is an economy of motion. Most movement takes place

FARMERS' MUSIC

Farmers' music is boisterous, seemingly free-flowing traditional percussive entertainment. This is the real thing, with a strong "country" flavor. Although it might be a bit overwhelming to the uninitiated, farmers' music can be mesmerizing. The constant and repetitive rhythm is produced by the clang of small cymbals, the throb of a gong, the sharp beat of skin drums, and the clack and muffled thump of the hourglass drum. Melodies repeat and continue for long periods, and the music is almost

musicians performing farmers' music

always accompanied by dance. Musicians circle as a group, or individually turn, twist, jump, leap, or bob to the beat, producing a kaleidoscopic color show. The more energetic dancers are nearly acrobatic. Their motion may be accented by a long ribbon that rotates from a swivel on top of their hats and is controlled by a jerk of the head. Others wear droopy, wide-brimmed hats splashed with rainbows of paper puffballs, and color sashes that vividly stand out against their baggy white clothes.

Country folk in any audience couldn't be happier than to be taken along by the music, and city folk get taken back to the country. At some performances, spectators get so caught up in the music that they get up and dance along with the performers—especially after they've had a few cups of strong rice wine. Long after a performance has ceased, the sounds of cymbals and drums will still reverberate in your head.

in the upper portion of the body, typified by the undulating movement of the shoulders, neck, and arms. Legs are covered and merely support the upper part. Dancers seem to glide rather than step, and most turns are executed on the heel.

There are three types of Korean dance: court, religious, and folk. Of Korean and Chinese origin, *jeongje* (court dances) were basically performed for entertainment. Although some stem from the Three Kingdoms period, they are, by and large, the newest dances. About 50 different dances or parts of dances have come down through the ages. Stylized and formal, they include the Dance of the Dragon of the Eastern Sea, Crane Dance, Sword Dance, Fan Dance, Nightingale Dance, Flower Crown Dance, and Queen's Unit Dance.

Shaman, Buddhist, and Confucian dances generally aim at a higher experience of spirituality. Of these dances, the shaman dances have the longest history. Religious yet humorous (with a bit of bold showmanship thrown in), the point of these dances is for the shaman to lapse into a trance so as to intercede with spirits. Many Buddhist dances, originally performed exclusively by priests and nuns, have become secularized and are now done by professionals. These include the Butterfly, Drum, and Cymbal dances, and the Priest's Dance, the most esoteric and spiritual. Confucian dances are newer, slower, and more formal. They are performed twice yearly (on the spring and autumn equinox) at Seonggyungwan University in Seoul, and on the first Sunday in May at Chong-myo royal ancestral shrine in Seoul. They take place in conjunction with royal court music.

While form and technique are all-important in court dance, and movement and mood are equally important in religious dance, the mood created and joy of performance are the most important aspects in folk dance. Stemming from ancient traditions, folk dances are improvisational, free in structure and interpretation, and sprightly. Performed with bright colors, great movement, loud music, and sometimes audience participation, farmers' dance is the liveliest in Korea. No degree of excellence is needed (although a great deal is shown); the dancers need only be performed with spirit. Other folk dances include masked-dance dramas, the Nine Drum dance, *ganggangsullae* circle dance, and *salpuri*. As with the Priest's Dance, *salpuri* unfolds the inner dance to its greatest extent.

Already weak at the end of the Joseon Dynasty, traditional dance forms largely fell into disuse during the Japanese occupation. Only since the mid-20th century have concerted efforts been taken to preserve existing dances, and to reconstruct some that have disappeared. Western ballet and modern dance are becoming increasingly popular, performed by large and small companies.

Drama

Dramatic forms seem to be the most narrowly developed of the performing arts. They include the masked-dance dramas, puppet plays, and *gugeuk* dramatic songs. Masked dances are combinations of dance and drama. Performed to music and song, the dancing tells the story. Dating from the Three Kingdoms period, masked dances developed into court plays during the Goryeo Dynasty. Later, they were banished from the court and taken up by the common people as a means of poking fun at the nobility, apostate monks, conjugal troubles, and the foibles of rural folk. Thirteen of these masked-dance dramas remain in the country today. Puppet plays are as old as masked-dance dramas, and some were adapted from them. All have been lost today except one, which has only a fractured plot. Modern theater was born at the beginning of the 20th century. Dealing mostly with social themes, it was tremendously popular, but interest in it has waned due to the advent of movies. While there are large companies—the National Theater was formed in 1949—small companies are now making a comeback with intellectual, thought-provoking, or humorous plays.

Handicrafts 공예품

Paper

About 2,000 years ago, China introduced papermaking to the Korean Peninsula. Seeing the beauty and usefulness of paper, Koreans excelled in its making. This art, combined with bookbinding skills, was exported to Japan around the 7th century. Through the Goryeo and Joseon dynasties, Korean paper products were appreciated by Chinese and Japanese for their high quality and durability. In the past, paper was made in all corners of the country, but today Jeonju is the undisputed papermaking center, accounting for about 90 percent of the country's production. Several handmade types include coarse wrapping paper; fine-quality paper for calligraphy and painting; paper with bamboo slivers, bark chips, colored thread, or other such materials for special artworks; tough paper for paper doors and windows, and thick oiled paper for covering the warm Korean *ondol* floors. Paper is also used on screens, incorporated into furniture, and made into fans and kites. Unlike chemically treated Western wood-pulp paper, which discolors and disintegrates within decades, natural Korean paper lasts for centuries—the National Museum in Seoul has an example from the early 700s.

Bamboo and Rush

Several varieties of bamboo grow on the Korean Peninsula, mostly in Jeollanam-Do, with Damyang as the center of bambooware production. Bamboo has been admired for centuries for its shape, strength, workability, and versatility. Some of the many uses include baskets, boxes, calligraphy brushes, mats and screens, furniture, bows, arrows, and quivers.

Like bamboo, a type of rush or sedge plant is fashioned into baskets and other containers, mats, curtains, and floor pillows. Naturally beige, dyed leaves are often woven into items to produce decorative designs. Traditional centers of rush production are the island of Ganghwa-do, west of Seoul; Hwasun, in Jeollanam-Do; and Inje, in Gangwon-Do.

Wood

Wooden home furnishings have been crafted throughout Korean history, but became widespread during the Joseon Dynasty. At that time, there was a great increase in production, variations of style, and construction techniques. Joseon Dynasty furniture is well known to antique dealers around the world, and wonderful reproductions are made. The Korean habit of living on the floor largely dictated the types of furnishings: most everything is built low. As Korean homes had few built-in storage spaces, many types of cabinets, trunks, wardrobes, chests, cupboards, and bookshelves were made. Other items include tables, trays, serving dishes, mirror and makeup boxes, and lanterns.

Because of their warm texture and grain, wood like paulownia, pear, and walnut was used to add an aesthetic touch to these utilitarian pieces, their richness brought out by dark stains and oils; carvings were included for decoration. Most furniture was left natural, but some was covered with lacquer and inlaid with mother-of-pearl, or decorated with painted oxhorn.

Brass

The production of brassware for common use started several hundred years ago in rural Anseong, south of Seoul, still the center for brassware. Small industries have now taken over most production. Some traditional items are bowls, utensils, pots, pipe bowls, urns, and ceremonial vessels, while small figurines, lamp shades, and beds are also made. Brass is also used for hinges, pulls, locks, and decorative plates on traditional furniture.

Cloth

Since the early dynasties, silk has been produced in Korea, but until recently this cloth was reserved for the wealthy. It was often embroidered for clothing, screens, and wall hangings—natural scenes and symbols of longevity were popular. Cotton was imported from China until the

1700s, when it began to be raised domestically. Hemp fiber is used in cloth worn during funerals and for cool summerwear, and ramie was woven for ordinary cloth. Today, Chuncheon and Ganghwa-do are known for silk, Andong for hemp, and Hansan for ramie.

Embroidery

The art of stitching colored thread onto cloth has a long tradition in Korea. References go back to the Silla Dynasty, when much embroidery was done for religious purposes. During the following centuries, religious and secular embroidery (for the court and common man) was crafted by the women of Korea and passed down from mother to daughter as a necessary skill. It is an art of patience and beauty, and is said to have rivaled painting for skill of creation and aesthetics during the latter part of the Joseon Dynasty. With the emergence of machine-stitched cloth in the 20th century, hand embroidery lost popularity and skilled artisans. However, with the recent resurgence of traditional Korean crafts, embroidery has once again gained popularity.

While natural dyes were once used exclusively, chemical dyes now make bright colors possible. It is said that there are over 50 techniques in stitching embroidery; flat and three-dimensional effects are possible. A whole host of motifs are commonly seen, including animals, birds, landscapes, and signs of longevity and good luck, and embroidery is commonly found on folding screens, traditional clothes, cushions, purses, pouches, carry containers, women's accessories, and scrolls.

Maedeup

Maedeup is the art of tying decorative knots and tassels of dyed silk. Having nearly died out in the early part of the 20th century, this craft has been revived. There are about three dozen traditional designs—butterfly, dragonfly, lotus bud, and chrysanthemum are several of the favorites—with many more modern creations. *Maedeup* are most often seen in *norigae*, a decorative ornament that hangs from a bow at the front of a woman's dress or coat, or incorporated into wall hangings, strung onto fan handles, or attached to metal furniture parts.

Sports and Games 운동경기와놀이

Koreans are athletic people. Whether participating or spectating, they are serious about their sports. Some Western team sports, such as soccer and baseball, have gained great popularity, but in recent years interest in traditional Korean sports has also grown. Many amateur athletic organizations have been established; government, schools, and businesses encourage exercise and fitness; and many athletic grounds and sports complexes have been built. Aside from school athletic grounds, private clubs, and municipal stadiums and sporting facilities, Korea's major sports facilities are the Seoul Jamshil Sports Complex and Olympic Park, constructed for the 1986 Asian Games and 1988 Summer Olympics, and the 10 stadiums constructed around the country for the 2002 World Cup competition. In addition, the Taeneung Athletic Village in Seoul is the major training facility for athletes competing in international sporting events. Founded in 1920 as the Korea Sports Council, the Korea Amateur Sports Association was reestablished in 1945 after being disbanded during the latter years of the colonial period. Currently nearly four dozen sports organizations are affiliated with this association with the goal of promoting their various sports for pleasure and enjoyment. Since it was formed in 1982, the Ministry of Sports (now a bureau of the Ministry of Culture and Tourism) has provided direction and funding for sports programs. Korean athletes have excelled in recent national, Asian, and world events, and during the last 25 years Korea has hosted numerous international competitions, perhaps the foremost being the 1986 and 2002 Asian Games, the 1999 Winter Asian Games, the 1997 Winter Universiade, the 1988 Summer Olympic Games, and the 2002 World Cup soccer games. However, the Korean experience with victory in international events is older. Korean long distance runners Son Ki-jŏng and Nam Sŭng-yong won a gold medal and a bronze respectively in the marathon in the Berlin Olympics of 1936 under the Japanese flag when Korea was under Japanese colonial control, and the 1947 and 1959 Boston Marathons were also won by Koreans. Since 1948, when Korea won 14 medals in boxing, many more have been won in subsequent years; in 1966, for example, the professional Korean boxer Kim Ki-su won the junior middleweight title of the World Boxing Association. While South Korea has participated in the Olympic Games since 1948 under its own flag, it wasn't until the 1984 Olympic Games in Los Angeles that Korean athletes really began to do well on a broad basis and since then the country has consistently placed in the top dozen list of medal winners.

Annual Korean sports events include the National Sports Festival, the National Winter Sports Festival, Children's National Sports Festival, and the National Sports Festival for the Handicapped. Traditional sports, like archery, taekwondo and *sireum,* are often held in conjunction with folk festivals or national competitions. Of the modern sports, soccer, baseball, volleyball, basketball, table tennis, and boxing are the most popular, and interest is growing rapidly in golf, skiing, tennis, cycling, ice skating, and swimming. Other sports seen mostly in competition are track-and-field events, badminton, field hockey, gymnastics, handball, rifle shooting, wrestling, and yachting. In addition, Koreans have always enjoyed hiking and fishing.

Advertisements for popular sporting events occasionally appear in the English-language newspapers. For additional information, check with tourist information offices.

TRADITIONAL SPORTS

Taekwondo

Practiced by both males and females, taekwondo [t'aekwondo] is a martial art of self-defense that also stresses sharpening of the mind and cultivating one's character. With its concentration on punching, kicking, and blocking, it is similar to karate and kung fu. This sport has roots going back about 1,500 years (mural paintings from Goguryeo Dynasty tombs depict these fighters), and developed out of an ancient martial art called *taekgyeon* (I.C.A. #76), which itself has gained popularity and has been reintroduced as a living martial art form. Practiced by a reputed four million Koreans at thousands of *dojang* (gyms) around the country, taekwondo is the nation's most popular amateur sport. Taekwondo has grown phenomenally in popularity abroad during the past 30 years, and is now taught in over 150 countries around the world. At the beginning, in the *beomsae* stage, one practices moves and steps with an imaginary opponent. In the *gyeorugi* stage, sparring is done with an opponent. *Gyeokpa* is an advanced stage where skills are mastered and demonstrated.

Taekwondo competitions are held in three rounds of three minutes apiece (two rounds to win), with one minute between rounds. Points are scored by striking the opponent's upper torso or face; protective gear is worn. There are eight weight classifications for both male and female participants.

Kukkiwon, in Seoul, is the World Taekwondo Federation headquarters. Periodic demonstrations and regularly scheduled national and international competitions are held here. Koreans always rank high in international competitions. A demonstration sport in the 1988 Olympics and 1992 Barcelona Olympics, taekwondo became a regular Olympic event beginning with the 2000 Olympics in Sydney, Australia.

Yudo

This martial art came from China during the Goryeo Dynasty and developed as systems called *subak* and *gwonbeop*. They were introduced to Japan from Korea around the time of the Hideyoshi Invasions (1592–97) and there developed into what is known today as judo. Having died out on the peninsula during the latter part of the Joseon Dynasty, it was reintroduced from Japan around 1910. *Yudo* stresses tossing, tumbling, and using an opponent's momentum to your advantage. *Yudo* is practiced by males and females of all ages. All policemen must maintain proficiency. A Yudo College has been built near Seoul. Periodic national competitions are held, and Korean *yudo*-ists always do well in international competitions. The less well-known martial arts of *hapkido* (aikido) and *shipbalgi* are also taught at gyms.

Ssireum

This Korean-style wrestling has some similarity to Japanese *sumo* and Mongolian wrestling. Like taekwondo, *ssireum* has a long history; depictions appear on tomb murals from the Three Kingdoms period (pre-660 A.D.). In a *ssireum* competition, two men face each other in a sand pit seven meters in diameter, both dressed only in a pair of shorts and a blue or red three-meter-long sash wrapped around the waist and the right leg. Shoulder to shoulder and leaning in toward one another, each man wraps one arm around the opponent's waist while one hand grabs the sash at the leg. The object is to toss the opponent to the ground; the first to let any part of his body other than his feet touch the sand loses. Some matches last only a few seconds, but most run longer. Rounds last three minutes and a match is three rounds; two are needed to win. If there is a draw after two rounds, the lighter man takes the match. Although outwardly quite simple, there are said to be over 100 moves for throwing an opponent. More than size or weight, speed, agility, and technique are important. *Ssireum* is played for fun by elementary school boys, and is part of middle- and high-school physical education programs. Since 1984, large companies have sponsored individual professionals and there are now professional teams. While competitions used to be open, three weight classifications have been instituted: Geumgang, up to 80 kg; Halla, up to 95 kg; and Baekdu, over 95 kg. Regular competitions are televised at least four times a year, and these are as popular as *sumo* is in Japan.

Gungdo

Japanese are known for swordsmanship, Chinese for their use of the lance, and Koreans for their mastery of the bow. Once a necessary element of hunting and warfare, this skill is now relegated to sport, practiced primarily by men.

gungdo archer

Gungdo (traditional archery) uses a short, double-curved bow made from water buffalo horn, bamboo, animal ligament, mulberry wood, and glue. Arrows are made from bamboo and partridge feathers; the string is silk. *Gungdo* is an amateur sport, and numerous schools, companies, and neighborhoods sponsor clubs. Periodic regional and national competitions are held, many in conjunction with folk festivals. Each contest consists of three rounds of five shots apiece. The bows are short but have great strength. Although the target is about two meters by two and a half meters, it stands 145 meters from the firing line!

In the last three decades, Western-style archery (*yanggung*) has gained popularity, and Korean women archers have done better than their male counterparts in international competitions.

MODERN SPORTS
Baseball

Baseball (*yagu*) was introduced to Korea in 1906. During the Japanese occupation, it caught on in Korea as it did in Japan. Until the 1980s, high-school baseball tournaments were the most popular team sporting events in the country. In 1982, a professional league was formed and all teams are sponsored by large corporations and located in different cities around the country. While high-school and college playoffs are still popular, the professional teams now generate the most enthusiasm. Korean games, though perhaps not up to the quality of U.S. or Japanese play, are still enjoyable to watch. In the early 2000s, the Korean pitcher, Park Chan-ho, played with the L.A. Dodgers and was followed avidly by Korean sports fans. While not the only Korean playing with an American (or Japanese) team, he was the best known.

Soccer

It's said that ancient Koreans enjoyed a ball game called *chukguk* played with the feet. Modern soccer *(chukgu)* was supposedly first taught to Koreans by British sailors in 1882. It is now Korea's number-one team sport, a professional league was established in 1983 and like baseball, these teams are sponsored by large corporations and based in different cities. Since 1971, the President's Cup Football Tournament, now called the Korea Cup International Football Tournament, has been held in Korea, with many foreign teams participating. Korea's national team usually does respectably in Asian competitions, and in 2002 pleasantly surprised even the South Koreans by placing fourth in the World Cup finals. It was an extremely proud moment for the country.

Table Tennis and Billiards

Introduced in the 1920s, table tennis *(takgu)* has become as popular here as in other Asian countries. Like soccer, children learn this sport from an early age and nearly everyone plays with some skill. Korean players perform well in international competitions in all categories. Table tennis parlors are ubiquitous—look for crossed paddles painted on windows.

Similarly, billiards *(danggu)* is popular, particularly with young men, and billiard halls are also found in every city and town (crossed cue sticks painted on windows). Tables can be rented for both by the hour.

Tennis

Until the mid-1970s, when its popularity mushroomed, tennis was played basically by college students and young executives. Once played primarily on a lawn, it's now mostly played on hard-surface courts. Tennis was a slow starter from the very early 1900s, but there are now numerous private courts in all cities; public courts are found at municipal parks and schools. Many large businesses and government offices have their own. Only recently have Korean tennis players been able to compete in international events with any success. Initially, women were more successful than men, but during the 1986 Asian Games, men won more medals.

South Korea's most promising young player, Lee Hyung-Taik, was ranked in the top 25 on the men's tour in early 2003.

Golf

Like tennis, golf is known by its Koreanized Western name. Korea's first golf course was set up in Wonsan (North Korea) in 1910. Before the 1970s, South Korea had only a handful, but with increased affluence, greater interest, and more leisure time, there are now more than 100 courses, usually called country clubs, the majority in the Seoul/Gyeonggi-Do area. Of these a handful are open for public play but the majority are membership-only courses. However, most of these membership courses have part of their course open to the public. Most are 18 hole affairs, with a few at 27 or 36 holes; some public courses are nine holes or less. Greens fees generally run about ₩100,000 during the week and a bit more on weekends. Tee time reservations are usually necessary, sometimes a few days in advance. For a list of the public courses, ask at the KNTO (Korea National Tourism Organization) office in Seoul. Many golf courses also have accommodations, a swimming pool, tennis courts, and other athletic facilities on site. The U.S. military also operates several courses—with more reasonable fees—for military personnel, their dependents, and civilian contractors. Here and there in suburban areas are huge green-net enclosures used as driving ranges. For a small fee, you can improve your swing without leaving the neighborhood. Golf clubs can be brought into Korea for personal use, but must be declared to customs officials. Korea is one leg of the annual Asian golf circuit. Once a sport of the well-to-do and the domain of very few, golf is becoming much more broadly popular, particularly with professionals and white-collar workers. One Korean who has made a name for herself in women's international play is Park Seri, perhaps the best known of Korean golfers inside and outside the country.

Skiing

While there was some skiing in the country before, Yongpyeong Ski Resort opened to the public in 1975 as the first modern commercial ski area. Quickly others followed. Until recently, skiing was pretty much an affair of the middle class and well-to-do, but now is getting more affordable for the average Korean. Young families and students seem to be the most avid skiers,

and now the young have taken to snowboarding in a big way. High-quality rental equipment, new facilities, snow-making machines, lights, good transportation connections, and moderate fees are all encouraging the sport's growth. The ski season is December–March.

South Korea's mountains, although not high, have great potential for ski slope development. The country's 13 ski resorts cater to everyone from rank beginner to advanced skier: Yongpyeong (Dragon Valley), Alps, Daemyung Vivaldi, Hyundai Sungwoo, Phoenix, and Korea Condo resorts are located in Gangwon-Do; Cheonma-san, Yangji Pine, Bear's Town, Seoul, and Jisan Forest resorts are in Gyeonggi-Do; Suanbo Blue Valley Ski Resort is located in Chungcheongbuk-Do; and Muju Ski Resort is the southernmost in Jeollabuk-Do. All have ski and snowboard rental and instruction, lifts and

NATIONAL PARKS

Korea boasts 20 national parks; 17 are land-based, and three are seashore and marine parks. The largest in area is Tadohae Marine National Park, covering over 2,300 square kilometers of sea and small islands off the southwest coast. The smallest, at 42 square kilometers, is Wolchul-san National Park, in the southwestern corner of the peninsula. Established in 1967, Jiri-san National Park was the first, and still is the largest, land-based national park. The last, Byeonsan Bando and Wolchul-sans, were dedicated in 1988. Entrance to national parks runs between ₩1,000 and ₩2,500. Of this, one-half goes for park maintenance and administration while the other half (if applicable) is set aside for the cultural properties and sites within the park. Entrance fees are payable each day, but if you enter two or more different park entrances in a single day, you need only pay the "cultural maintenance" portion of the fee on successive entrances following the first entrance of the day. Save your ticket! For additional information on South Korean national parks, see www.npa.or.kr.

1. **Jiri-san N.P.** (1967): Largest mountain massif in South Korea. Long hiking trails, many historic temples.
2. **Gyeryong-san N.P.** (1968): Petite, but rising precipitously. Historical and religious significance.
3. **Hallyeo Waterway N.P.** (1968): Numerous sections, occupying a historic and beautifully picturesque stretch of the south coast.
4. **Gyeongju N.P.** (1968): A "historical" park, in eight sections.
5. **Seorak-san N.P.** (1970): The most rugged and, by most accounts, the most beautiful mountain area in South Korea.
6. **Songni-san N.P.** (1970): Set in the middle of the peninsula, containing many trails and a deep religious significance.
7. **Halla-san N.P.** (1970): Occupies the top portion of South Korea's highest mountain. The

tows, a chalet, restaurants and coffee shops, and lodging; several also host winter snow festivals and national and international skiing competitions. Most resorts have less than a dozen slopes and half a dozen lifts, but Yongpyeong, Hyundai Sungwoo, and Muju have the greatest number of slopes at 18, 20, and 30, respectively, with an adequate number of lifts to match. All resorts offer special bus transportation arrangements from Seoul and/or neighboring provincial cities during the ski season, and some offer ski packages of transportation, accommodation, and reduced rates for lift tickets and rentals. Although each resort sets its own fees, lift tickets generally run about ₩40,000 a day, ski and snowboard rental about ₩25,000, and full-day individual ski lessons around ₩60,000 where they are offered. Most ski resorts also have sledding hills for the less adventurous and small children. Ski equipment and clothing is available for purchase in Seoul and at most ski resorts.

Hunting

Hunting is a big tourist draw for the Japanese. Although a handful of small birds can be hunted from September 1 to October 31, the big season is November 1 to February 28 for wild boar, roe deer, river deer, raccoon dog, badger, rabbit, squirrel, pheasant, quail, woodcock, certain ducks and geese, and other birds. Hunting is limited to restricted areas on Jeju-do, Geoje-do, and on a rotating basis in all eight peninsular provinces. The private Daeyu Hunting Club offers year-round hunting on its extensive grounds on the south slope of Halla-san, on Jeju-do. Licenses are mandatory. Hunting times and limits are strictly enforced. Hunting clubs rent equipment and can arrange guides. For more specifics, contact

only national park on Jeju-do.
8. **Naejang-san N.P.** (1971): Small, but renowned for its exceptional autumn colors.
9. **Gaya-san N.P.** (1972): Tall and rugged. Home of Haein-sa.
10. **Odae-san N.P.** (1975): High, rounded, and welcoming. Several temples, one deep twining valley.
11. **Deokyu-san N.P.** (1975): Tall ridge surrounding a long valley that historically has drawn domestic travelers to its scenic spots.
12. **Juwang-san N.P.** (1976): Little-frequented, low mountain park with unusual rock outcrops. Moderate hiking.
13. **Taean Coastal N.P.** (1978): Korea's only seashore park.
14. **Dadohae Marine N.P.** (1981): Largest national park, comprising eight sections and 1,700 islands.
15. **Bukhan-san N.P.** (1983): Partly within the Seoul city boundary. Known for its rugged peaks and historical connection to the Joseon Dynasty.
16. **Chiak-san N.P.** (1984): Little-visited park with broad vistas. Good hiking.
17. **Worak-san N.P.** (1984): Still largely undeveloped. Good surrounding scenery.
18. **Sobaek-san N.P.** (1987): Tall, broad, and rounded. Many trails, good hiking, several temples.
19. **Wolchul-san N.P.** (1988): Low but surprisingly craggy ridge.
20. **Byeonsan Bando N.P.** (1988): As part of a small peninsula, it incorporates water, lowlands, and hills.

In addition to its national parks, the country has 24 provincial parks and a growing number of country parks.

the Korean Hunting Association (tel. 02/972-6066). If you plan to bring your own gun and ammunition into the country you must complete a specific application procedure well before your arrival; documents include a gun license, photocopy of passport, a personal photograph, and application fee. For help with processing this information, contact the Korea Safety Engineering Association of Explosives and Guns (tel. 02/831-8157).

Hiking and Climbing

Although all mountains in South Korea are less than 2,000 meters in height, Koreans love to hike. It's become a national pastime. Summer months, autumn weekends, and national holidays are favorites, but any time will do. Hikers of all ages and both sexes attack the trails, and you'll hear the call "ya-ho" echo through the hills. Mountains close to Seoul are the most frequented, but the major national parks have the best hiking possibilities. All national parks have some hiking possibilities and aside from the established trails, larger parks also have short nature trails near their main entrances to teach visitors about the flora, fauna, and/or geology of the park.

Korean mountaineering has gone international, with climbers attacking the world's tallest mountains. The top of Mt. Everest was reached by Korean Ko Sang-don in 1977 and again by Chang Bong-won in 1988; Chang also conquered K-2 in 1986. Women's climbing groups have also done well in mountain ascents. Hikers in country are a lively crowd, usually found in groups, dressed to the hilt (often color-coordinated) in knee socks, knickers, vests, and feather hats, and having a grand time in the out-of-doors.

Dress for the weather and wear sturdy walking shoes. Pack in all you need, whether for a day hike or an overnight, and pack out all your trash. Bring plenty of food and water. Follow a good map or walk with someone who knows the area, and stick to designated trails. Don't hike trails closed during winter—could be a dress rehearsal for disaster. Korean outdoors shops sell medium- to high-quality camping, hiking, and climbing equipment, so whatever you forgot at home you can get here; butane is generally used for

stove fuel. Although rock climbing and ice climbing are done, they are not recommended for beginners. Favorite rock-climbing areas are Dobong-san and Bukhan-san (*san* means "mountain"), on the northern outskirts of Seoul; Ulsanbawi in Seorak-san; and Daedun-san. Popular ice-climbing spots are Towangseong and Daeseung waterfalls in Seorak-san, and Gugok Waterfall near Chuncheon. Hiking maps of Korea are available at most reputable bookstores and carried by outdoor sports shops. Unfortunately, they are printed only in Korean—good reading practice. National parks also print excellent maps, but you may have to ask for one when you purchase your park entrance ticket.

Others

Competition **swimming** (*suyeong*) has not traditionally been popular in Korea. However, after several Korean women won medals in Asian contests during the 1980s, there has been a push to develop this sport, including the construction of several world-class indoor pools. For the recreational swimmer, mid-July to mid-August is the "swimming season," when a majority of people take summer holidays. Beaches are full and sunbathers are everywhere. Although the weeks before and after this season are just as conducive, beaches are all but deserted.

During winter, ice forms on standing water and slow-moving rivers for a month or two in Korea's northern areas. Hunkered down on squares of wood with metal runners, children for decades have pushed themselves around the ice with short sticks skewered with a spike. Many now enjoy **skating**, speed skating being the most popular, and the number of indoor rinks is growing. Korea has produced a couple of international speed-skating competitors, including short-track medal-winners at recent winter Olympics.

Bowling has fast become popular, and lanes are popping up everywhere. Many lanes can be identified by a huge bowling pin set on the roof of the building it occupies or at the front entrance. Other ball games of more widespread appeal are **volleyball** (*baegu*) and **basketball** (*nonggu*), especially with high-school and college kids. In the past 20 years, male and female teams from both sports have done well in international competition. College rivalry between Yonsei and Korea universities has become legendary, almost to the point of becoming a national event. A professional basketball league was started in 1997.

Aside from taekwondo and *ssireum,* **boxing** (*gwontu*) and Western-style **wrestling** are the most popular contact sports. Particularly in the lighter-weight classes, Korean amateurs have won many medals in the Olympics and Asian Games, while pros hold several titles with international boxing associations. It wasn't until 1976, however, when a wrestler won Korea's first Olympic gold medal, that many turned their attention to this sport.

The Asian Games and the Olympics have also recently brought attention to gymnastics, weight lifting, badminton, handball, field hockey, track-and-field events, and shooting. Interest in bicycle racing, horse racing, leisure horse riding, sailing, long-distance running, windsurfing, water-skiing, scuba diving, motocross, car racing and other sports is still limited, but growing, and there is some interest in the more extreme sports of paragliding, white-water rafting, and bungee jumping.

GAMES

Like traditional sports, Korean games have developed over the centuries, some stemming from ancient practices of divination. Many have roots in China, one originated in Japan, and a few are indigenous to Korea.

Baduk

Baduk (Japanese "go") is an ancient board game of Chinese origin. The board has a grid pattern of 19 horizontal and vertical lines. Flat black and white stones are placed on any of the 361 intersections of these lines; there are no "sides." All stones have equal "value." Once placed, stones are not moved unless captured by the opponent. The object is to gain and maintain control of an area, and to surround and capture the opponent's stones. With such simple rules, strategy is paramount. *Baduk* is a battle of wits, and al-

most every Korean plays. It's a sophisticated games where quiet and concentration are necessary. Professionals play in periodic national and Asian competitions. Ranks are awarded according to skill level, as in chess. As some Western newspapers do with chess, Korean newspapers print and discuss *baduk* moves and strategies, and report on championship matches.

Omok is a child's game played on the *baduk* board. Here, two players alternate turns trying to get five stones of the same color in a straight line before his or her opponent can.

Janggi

This fast-paced, Korean-style chess game is played on a board etched with 10 horizontal and 9 vertical lines. Pieces are moved to intersections. Each player has 16 squat hexagonal pieces, each with a Chinese character written on it in red or green: one general, two palace guards, two chariots, two cannons, two horses, two elephants, and five foot soldiers. Capture of the general is the object, and play symbolically represents war between two Chinese kingdoms of the distant past. As in *baduk,* the first move is usually given to the younger or less experienced player. Unlike *baduk,* however, *janggi* is energetic, swift, and more a game of the commoner. It's accompanied by lots of noise and the participation of bystanders, and sometimes used as a medium for gambling. Often you'll see old men in parks bent over a *janggi* board like their Western counterparts intent on a game of chess.

Yut

Ostensibly brought by nomadic tribes from Mongolia, *yut* (also called *yut-nori*) was originally used for divination. Today, it's simply a game. Traditionally played on Lunar New Year, *yut* is accompanied by wild excitement, loud voices, and occasionally gambling. While sometimes played in the house, on the new year's day it's more often played on a straw mat in the courtyard. *Yut* uses four wooden sticks about 20 centimeters long, flat on one side and rounded on the other. These are "tossed" to determine a count which moves playing pieces around a board. The square board has 20 dots around its periphery, and nine dots make a cross through the center from each corner—old boards were round, with the lines through the center marking off four quadrants, or the four directions. Each team or player has four "horses," or playing pieces. The object is to move all horses around (or through the center shortcut) and off the board before the other players. Its background and manner of play make it similar to Parcheesi.

Golpae

Golpae, Korean dominoes, is played with 32 tiles incised with one to six dots; there are no blanks. Many different games are played, some in hands and others drawn from a pile.

Hwatu

Brought to Korea from Japan, *hwatu* ("flower cards") uses 48 small plastic cards—12 suits of four. Each suit represents a month, and each design of leaves, flowers, the moon, or rain is typical of the month that it represents. Many different games can be played, often accompanied by gambling.

Tuho

One of the oldest recorded games, *tuho* ("arrow toss") was once played primarily by aristocrats and royalty. Colored arrows or arrow-shaped sticks are thrown by hand into the narrow neck of a tall jar set about two meters away from the thrower. This game is played with several players, each having four arrows and tossing alternately. Several rounds are played, and scores awarded according to the number of arrows that make it into the jar. The player with the most arrows in the jar is the winner. Having lost much of its popularity during the 20th century, it's only now experiencing a slow resurgence of interest.

Neolddwigi

Neolddwigi, Korean seesaw, is played by two girls, usually wearing brightly colored *hanbok,* one standing on each end of a wide plank laid over a roll of straw or other fulcrum. A third girl squats on the fulcrum to steady the board. When the first girl jumps and lands on the end of the board, it sends the other girl into the air, and her landing in turn sends the first into the air. Good jumps go about two meters high. *Neolddwigi* is usually played on Lunar New Year's Day. It's sometimes explained that women of the noble class used *neolddwigi* to help them see over the wall that surrounded the house, as women at that time were rarely allowed out of the living compound except at night.

Geune

This long-rope swinging is nearly always done by women. Standing on a wide board suspended from a high branch (sometimes from a beam set over two tall poles), women swing as high as they can, sometimes alone, sometimes in doubles. During contests, the one who swings highest is the winner. Usually geune is done on *Dano* and other folk festival days, when the traditional *hanbok* is worn; the swingers look like flowers flying through the air.

Yeon

Korean kites *(yeon),* historically, were almost uniformly rectangular. Made of window paper glued over bamboo ribs, they averaged 50 centimeters by 75 centimeters—larger ones were used in areas of strong winds. Each had a round hole cut in the center, and various bold geometric or striped designs decorated the front. While Chinese and Japanese kites were (and still are) known for style and design, Korean kites were rather plain in shape but more maneuverable. While many are still rectangular, Korean kites these days are taking on a great variety of shapes (animal shapes predominate), colors, and sizes. No matter the size or shape, a spoked wooden reel is used to let out and pull in the silk or cotton string.

Kites are flown during the first half of the first lunar month, peaking on the full-moon day (15th). On that day, a special "kite of misfortune" is flown. When high in the sky, its string is cut, symbolically sending bad luck away.

For children and adults, annual kite-flying contests are held in large cities on the first full-moon day of the year. Competition is for the largest kite to stay up for more than 10 minutes, the highest-flying, and string cutting. String cutting is aerial dogfighting between two kites, where maneuverability is all-important. Abrasive material (glass or ceramic) is glued to the string with the object of rubbing string against string to cut the opponent's kite loose. Small boys love to scramble after downed kites. Many contestants enter these events, and greater numbers brave the cold weather to watch.

Although the venue and dates change yearly, an International Kite Flying Festival is held during the first month of the Lunar New Year. For current details, check with the KNTO office in Seoul.

Large-Group Games

Chajeon nori, a mock "tank" battle, is a large-group game where two teams propel an A-frame structure against the opponents trying to dislodge the tank "general." *Jul darigi,* tug-of-war, pits two teams against each other; the rope is made of straw wound to a diameter of about two feet, and down its long length are smaller branches of straw onto which the contestants grab to pull. Historically, the two teams of both these games represented two villages, and the winner was said to look forward to a good harvest in the coming year. Both games are most often performed now at cultural festivals for pure enjoyment and only symbolically represent the strength of one village over another.

Others

For the children, shuttlecock *(jegi chagi),* top spinning *(paengi chigi),* cat's cradle *(shil ddeugi),* pickup sticks *(sangaji),* and a kids' version of cockfighting *(dak ssaum)* are popular. The shuttlecock is a paper- or cloth-covered bundle of pebbles or clay (traditionally a heavy brass coin) with a feather top. It is kicked only with the feet and the object is to keep it from hitting the ground and losing one's turn to another. When played in a round, the shuttlecock is kicked from one person to another around a circle. In top spinning, which is almost always played by boys, wooden tops are kept spinning

SO SSAUM

So ssaum is bullfighting, but unlike the Spanish variety there is no matador in this traditional Korean sporting game. In the Korean contest, two beefy bulls are placed head to head in a ring and encouraged by their owners to push the other animal out, make the other animal turn and run, or in some other way concede. The owners are in the rings with the bulls but can only use verbal cues to spur their animals on. Although it's perhaps less so now, bullfights were once a popular means of gambling. These contests were a great diversion for a previously more agricultural Korean community when, in decades past, livestock was much more numerous. With increased mechanization in the countryside and a move toward modernization and away from the old ways, bullfighting ceased to be an event for most rural communities. Still, the tradition carried on in few places where the animals remained and the time and interest for old traditions allowed—Cheongdo being one of the most well-known. In recent years, bullfighting has gone through a revival and now a number of bullfight festivals are organized each year around the country and competitions are held.

by whipping the pointed bottom with a string attached to a short stick. Played by young girls, cat's cradle is similar to that played in the West, where various designs are made between the fingers by manipulating string. Almost identical to the Western version, pickup sticks are spread on a table and must be picked up one at a time without moving the others. "Cockfighting" is a balancing act in which one child tries to knock an opponent down while hopping around with one foot held up by the hands. Korean versions of tag and blindman's bluff are also played, but, unfortunately, interest in these and other traditional children's games is slowly being overtaken by television and arcade games.

Holidays, Festivals, and Other Important Days 축제일과문화재

Korea now uses the Western (solar) Gregorian calendar, but until the 20th century it utilized only the lunar calendar, which is still important for cultural events and agricultural cycles. Traditional holidays and festivals still follow the lunar calendar—dates vary each year. Most official holidays, many stemming from historical events, have fixed dates based on the Western calendar. The largest proportion of holidays and festivals occurs in October, with many also held in March, April, and May. Check with the tourist information offices, current brochures, or local residents for current schedules.

Seokjeon-je and *Jong-myo Jerye* are strict Confucian rituals. Most other festivals have events varying in emphasis depending upon the region and/or historical connection. Typically included are parades, performances of regional traditional music and dance, music and art contests, traditional sports competitions, and commemorative or shaman ceremonies. Most festivals last several days.

OFFICIAL HOLIDAYS

January 1–2: New Year's Holiday

This two-day period is a recent concession to Westernization, and the tradition of bringing in the new year with convivial celebration has been wholeheartedly adopted by many Koreans. Some folk celebrations and games are also scheduled at this time. At midnight on New Year's Eve, the Seoul city bell, in Boshin-gak on Jong-no, is rung 33 times to ring in the new year, and a fireworks display is presented from Nam-san.

January–February: Lunar New Year

Lunar New Year's Day, known as *Seol* or *Seollal,* is one of the most important traditional events of the year, more significant than January 1. The exact date changes by year, but it almost always occurs from late January to late February. Busi-

nesses are closed, and most people take several days off to visit their home towns to be with family. It's a time for families to renew ties, for youngsters to bow *(sebae)* in respect to their elders (in return, children receive good wishes and advice, and are given small amounts of money as gifts), for students to greet their teachers, and for all to wish their neighbors well. Many people dress up in their finest new colorful *hanbok.* The ancestral ceremony *jarye* is also observed on this day. A family feast is held, with specially prepared food such as *tteokguk* (rice-cake soup) and *sujeonggwa* (persimmon punch). Men play *yut* or fly kites, boys spin tops or play shuttlecock, and women jump on the Korean seesaw (*neolddwigi*). Traditionally, a new bamboo mesh dipper *(bokjori)* is hung outside the house to "scoop" in good luck for the coming year, and shoes which are generally placed at the entrance door are put in the bedroom because ghosts come around on New Year's Eve and take all shoes that are their size.

According to the Eastern zodiac, each year in a 12-year cycle has an animal representation and various distinguishing characteristics. Each Lunar New Year ushers in a new animal year, with all its influences. Often shortly after the Lunar New Year, people visit a fortune teller to determine what the year holds in store for them.

March 1: Independence Movement Day

Samil-jeol (March First Memorial) commemorates the Declaration of Independence—proclaimed on March 1, 1919 while under Japanese colonization—and the tenacious independence movement that followed. A reading of the declaration takes place in a special ceremony in Tapgol Park in Seoul, where the document was first read to the public. Additional ceremonies are held in provincial cities.

April 5: Arbor Day

This day *(Shingmogil)* reflects Korea's commitment to its reforestation program. Government workers, schoolchildren, and community groups head for the hills to plant trees, while others spruce up the cities with bushes and flowers. Largely because of this concerted effort, Korea is rapidly changing from a country of denuded hills to one covered by a thick carpet of greenery. In addition, the first week in November has been set aside as another tree-planting time.

May 5: Children's Day

In 1975, Children's Day *(Eorininal)* was created from Boy's Day (which showed the Korean preference for sons). Parents dress up the little ones and take them to children's parks, amusement parks, zoos, or the cinema for a full day of fun and games.

April–May: Buddha's Birthday

Established in 1975, this festival, *Seokga tanil,* is held on the eighth day of the fourth lunar month. Special ceremonies are held throughout the day at all temples in the country. These ceremonies include prayers in the main worship hall and chanting while circling a pagoda. Each temple courtyard is strung with paper lanterns, and in the evening these lanterns are lit, illuminating the compound with a dazzling display of light, and giving rise to the day's alternate appellation: Feast of the Lanterns. The biggest attraction in cities is the lantern procession, which threads its way through downtown streets to a temple. Symbolically, this procession illustrates the dharma of Buddha leading believers through the darkness of ignorance. Everyone is welcome to join the parade or have a lantern hung in a temple courtyard. In Seoul, the lantern parade makes its way through the downtown area to Jogye-sa. This festivity has broadened into the Lotus Lantern Festival, which includes, along with the parade, events like the construction of lanterns, exhibitions of calligraphy, paintings, sculpture and other art, and the performance of Buddhist music and dance.

June 6: Memorial Day

Memorial Day *(Hyeonchungil)* is set aside to honor soldiers and civilians who have given their lives for the country. The largest ceremony is held at the National Cemetery in Seoul, while others are held throughout the country.

July 17: Constitution Day

The Constitution of the Republic of Korea was promulgated on this day in 1948, and *Jeheonjeol* commemorates that event. Symbolically, it represents self-government after 35 years of colonial rule under the Japanese and three years of U.S. military rule.

August 15: Liberation Day

This holiday *(Gwangbok-jeol)* celebrates the freedom from Japanese colonial rule in 1945 and the establishment of the Republic of Korea as a self-governing, independent nation exactly three years later.

September–October: *Chuseok*

Celebrated on the 15th day of the 8th lunar month, *Chuseok [Ch'usŏk]* is the year's most important traditional holiday. Also called *Han'-gawi* ("Harvest Moon Festival") and *Jungchu-jeol* ("Mid-Autumn Festival"), *Chuseok* is Korea's equivalent of Thanksgiving Day. It's a celebration of the harvest—thanks for the bounty of the earth. Family members come from all corners of the country to visit their ancestral homes—causing great traffic congestion. In the early morning, an ancestor memorial ceremony called *jarye* is held in the home, at which a table laden with new grain, the best fruits and nuts, rice cakes, meat, fish, vegetables, and newly fermented white wine are symbolically offered to the family's forebears. Later in the day, and after some tidying up has taken place, another such ceremony called *seongmyo* is held at the ancestors' gravesites, affirming the importance of bloodline and kinship, and giving deference to the spirits of the ancestors who, according to traditional belief, still affect happenings in this world. These ceremonies are generally held for direct ancestors of the previous four generations and any others of significant personages for the family and/or country. Following this requisite ritual is the family feast. Special foods of the day include crescent-shaped white and green rice cakes (songpyeon) filled with a sweetened sesame-seed mixture or red bean paste and steamed with pine needles; a fluffy, bread-like rice cake covered with red bean paste, dates, or chestnuts; and dorantang (taro beef soup). Formerly, in rural communities, farmers' music and dance were performed in the afternoon, and in the evening people climbed a hill to watch the full moon rise, the largest and brightest of the year. Today, ssireum and tug-of-war contests and other folk activities are held. In some regions, other special events are performed including the ganggangsullae circle dance or geobuk nori, where villagers cover themselves in straw mats in imitation of turtles (symbols of long life) and, making a round of neighbors' houses, sing, dance, and good-heartedly beg for food.

October 3: National Foundation Day
This day, Gaecheon-jeol, also called Dan'gun Day, commemorates the mythical founding of the Korean nation in 2333 B.C. by the legendary god-king Dan'gun. A simple ceremony is held at an altar on the top of Mani-san, on Ganghwa-do. The altar is said to have been erected by Dan'gun to offer thanks to his father and grandfather, gods of heaven.

December 25: Christmas
As nearly one-quarter of the Korean population is Christian, Christmas (Seongtan-jeol) is becoming an important holiday. Although not yet as commercial as Christmas in the West, Christmas and/or New Year's cards are sent, and presents are exchanged by some.

NON-HOLIDAY COMMEMORATIVE DAYS
May 1: Labor Day
To honor all who work for family and nation, this day (Nodong-jeol) is set aside as a day of rest. Most businesses and government offices are closed.

May 8: Parent's Day
Set aside as a counterbalance to Children's Day, this day is one in which children pay respects to their parents and honor them for their love, guidance, and help.

May 15: Teacher's Day
In this society with its Confucian roots, education has always been pursued and teachers revered, and this day has been set aside to honor those who have chosen such an important profession.

May–June: Dano
Along with Seol, Chuseok, and Hanshik, Dano is one of the four most important Korean traditional festivals. Because it's an ancient agricultural festival, prayers for good crops, a bountiful harvest, and protection from disaster are offered. Celebrated on the fifth day of the fifth lunar month, Dano is a day of leisure, feasting, and play following the rigors of spring planting. Events include shaman ceremonies, masked-dance plays, ssireum and archery competitions, and the traditional long-rope swinging activity (geune) for women. Although adherence is somewhat lax today, traditionally everyone got up early, bathed, and put on new clothes. Following custom, women would ritually wash their hair in iris water to give it a dark sheen. As Dano occurred near the start of the hot summer season, friends exchanged fans and others were sent from each province to the king. Although festivities occur all over the country, the Gangneung Dano is the most famous.

October 1: Armed Forces Day
This day (Gukguneui-nal) gives tribute to all branches of the military for their defense of the nation. The largest parade, including a display of military hardware and an aerial show, takes place in Seoul.

October 9: Han'geul Day
Also called Korean Alphabet Day, this day (Han'geul-nal) celebrates the creation in 1446 of han'geul, the indigenous Korean script, one of the simplest and most scientific in the world. Perhaps the most honored of Korea's achieve-

ments, *han'geul* was designed after months of study by a group of scholars under King Sejong.

October 24: United Nations Day

Sixteen nations sent troops to aid South Korea during the Korean War, and this day has been set aside to honor all who gave their lives during this conflict. On this day, a commemorative ceremony is held at the U.N. Cemetery, in Busan.

TRADITIONALLY IMPORTANT DAYS

The lunar year was traditionally divided into 24 parts called *jeol*, sectioned by full-moon and new-moon days. These days were looked upon as turning points, and held significance not only for the agricultural community and what needed to be done in the planting/harvesting cycle, but also for festivals and special ceremonies. The summer and winter solstices and spring and autumn equinoxes were the most important reference points. Every three years, an extra month was inserted into the calendar in order to adjust it to the solar year. In addition, odd numbers were considered lucky, and double-odd-number days, such as the third day of the third month, were considered extra-special. With the modernization and urbanization of the country, many of these days and accompanying activities have been abandoned. Some of continued importance follow.

Seol (or *seollal*) is the first day of the first lunar month. Ancestral services are made at graves, a bowing greeting is done to living elder family members, traditional games are played, and traditional sweets are eaten. *Ipchun* ("Opening of Spring") signals the time to prepare for spring planting and a new cycle of life. *Daeboreum*, the first full moon of the new year, is a day when ceremonies are performed for village gods to ward off evil spirits for the coming year. Historically, on this day numerous games were played, including a lion's dance and the lighting of a bonfire on a nearby hilltop when the moon rose, and special foods were eaten. Today, most of these festivities are no longer observed but people still crack

and eat nuts with family members, eat *ogokbap* (five-grain rice), sip rice wine, and twirl cans with little fires inside on the ends of ropes. *Hanshik* is a traditional holiday celebrated on the 105th day after the winter solstice. A food offering is placed before ancestors' graves and a short memorial ceremony is held. In preparation for the ceremony, grass covering the tomb mound is cut and the surroundings are tidied up. In the past, cold food *(hanshik)* was eaten on this day, including foods made with mugwort, as a cooking fire was not permitted. On *Samwol Samil,* the third day of the third lunar month, special glutinous rice cakes are made with flower ingredients (typically azaleas) and fried in sesame oil, and a flower noodle or sweet noodle soup is also cooked. Boys hike in the hills and girls cleanse their hair. The fifth day of the fifth lunar month is *Dano,* a celebration of the completion of planting and a hope for good harvest. *Sambok* marks the three dog days of summer, the hottest period by the lunar calendar. To slack the heat and boost stamina, hot foods such as *samgyetang* or dog meat are traditionally eaten. The full moon of the eighth lunar month is *Chuseok,* the harvest celebration. On this day, newly harvested foods are offered to the ancestors at the home, a bowing ceremony is done at the gravesite, folk dances performed, and rice cakes with special stuffing eaten. Although not held on any specific day, *gimjang* (*gimchi*-making) is done after *Chuseok* in order to have plenty of food through the barren winter. The last festival of the year, *Dongji,* is the winter solstice, a time for reflection on the year past and anticipation of the year ahead. Traditionally, *patjuk,* a red bean porridge with rice balls, is eaten on this day.

For the agricultural community, several of the most notable turning points were *Ipchun,* the start of spring; *Junghwajeol,* the start of the farming season; *Gyeongjip,* end of hibernation for dormant animals; *Gogu,* when the rains begin to fall in earnest; *Ipha,* the beginning of summer; *Baengno,* the first dew; and *Sanggang,* the first frost.

MAJOR FESTIVALS

There are over four dozen well-established festivals and some 400 smaller local festivals held in

M

INTRODUCTION

the country throughout the year. The dates for many are designated according to the lunar calendar.

Seokjeon Daeje

This Confucian ritual is held at the Daeseongjeon shrine at Seoul's Seonggyungwan University. Performed twice a year, on the vernal and autumnal equinoxes, it's *the* major Confucian rite in Korea, honoring Confucius and Chinese and Korean sages. It's the best place to see traditional Confucian costumes and witness a performance of the classical court orchestra and dancers.

Jong-myo Jerye

An ancestral memorial ceremony for Joseon Dynasty kings is held at Jong-myo in Seoul on the first Sunday in May. This Confucian ancestral rite is performed by descendants of the royal family and is accompanied by royal court music and dance. Only during this festival are the buildings that contain the royal memorial tablets open for public viewing.

Jinhae Cherry Blossom Festival

Jinhae, a small port city on the south coast of the peninsula, is known for its cherry trees—some 70,000 of them. Every year when the cherry trees are in bloom (usually in the beginning of April), the city holds the Cherry Blossom Festival. In conjunction, the *Gunhang-je* Festival is held to honor the deeds of Admiral Yi Sun-shin, Korea's most renowned naval commander. Events include a parade, fireworks, commemorative ceremonies, a shaman ritual, music and dance performances, and a beauty contest.

Jin-do *Yeongdeung* Festival

The *Yeongdeung-je* is held on Jin-do, an island off the southwestern corner of the peninsula. It's a festival that's sprung up around a naturally occurring phenomenon called the "parting of the waters." For a day or two in April, the sea recedes when the tide drops nearly seven meters to reveal a mudflat that connects Jin-do and a nearby islet, allowing people to walk out across the mudflat. This yearly natural phenomenon

is becoming important to Christians, who see it as a reminder of the biblical story of Moses parting the sea. Aside from a walk across the mud, events include a ceremony to the god of the sea (or the dragon king), farmers' songs from the island, and a shaman exorcism ceremony.

Chunhyang Festival

Held in Namwon on the 8th day of the 4th lunar month, *Chunhyang-je* honors Chunhyang—Korea's Juliet—a symbol of feminine virtue and steadfast loyalty. This festival has grown out of the famous Korean tale of Chunhyang and her lover Yi Mong-ryong. During the festival, townspeople reenact the tale and host a parade; a *pansori* singing contest and *geune* long-rope swinging competition are also held, and a beauty contest picks a modern-day Chunhyang-for-a-day.

Gangneung *Dano* Festival

While *Dano* festivities are celebrated all over the country, the festival in Gangneung stands out as the most famous and, reputedly, the most authentic and traditional. Held for a week, over the fifth day of the fifth lunar month, *Dano* is a time for leisure after spring planting, and an opportunity to pray for a good harvest and invoke the help of the spirits for a successful year. Aside from athletic and musical activities, shaman ceremonies, a parade, and a masked-dance drama are held.

Jeonju *Pungnam* Festival

Held on *Dano* in the city of Jeonju, the *Pungnam-je* features music and literary contests, athletic games, and a local-products fair, but the highlight is a lantern parade. The *daesaseup nori*, a competition of 10 different folk arts, is held at the same time.

Halla Cultural Festival

The Halla Cultural Festival is the only large cultural festival on the island of Jeju-do. Held in October when the tangerines are ripe, it features distinctly provincial cultural activities, which include a ceremony to the mountain gods, horse races, a Jeju-do dialect contest, folk games, and a lantern parade.

Silla Cultural Festival

Held in Gyeongju every other October, this festival *(Silla Munhwa-je)* is the country's largest tribute to an ancient kingdom. Honoring its achievements, noting its famous men, and portraying its legends, events include a colorful parade, performances of classical music and dance, art exhibitions, Buddhist ceremonies, and athletic competitions.

Baekje Cultural Festival

Also held every October, this festival *(Baekje Munhwa-je)* alternates between Buyeo and Gongju, both former capitals of the Baekje Kingdom. Events include ceremonies commemorating the last king, loyal retainers who fought with him until the fall of the dynasty, and court women who threw themselves from a cliff rather than be debauched by invading troops. Music, dance, and athletic competitions are numerous, and a daytime parade and a nighttime lantern procession are held.

Gaecheon Arts Festival

Jinju has a strong artistic tradition. Held for a full week in late October or early November, the Gaecheon Arts Festival is the oldest and most renowned arts festival in the country. Literally hundreds of performances, exhibitions, and competitions are held in the areas of poetry, calligraphy, painting, photography, music, dance, and drama. The Jinju Sword Dance and a bullfight are special features. Athletic contests are also held, and the lantern ceremony and fireworks are popular.

OTHER FESTIVALS

January–February

Snow Festivals are held at several ski resorts on different dates during January and February. Aside from ski competitions and sledding, snow sculpture contests delight the crowds. A host of other cultural events are also incorporated. In addition, the **Daegwallyeong Snow Festival** is held near the Daegwallyeong Pass above Gangneung involving many outdoor winter activities, and the **Halla-san Snowflake Festival** of

Jeju-do incorporates mountain hiking, folk dances, and a ceremonial offering to the deity of the mountain.

Gwangju hosts the ***Gwangsan Gossaum Nori Festival*** on the first full moon of the new year. This event largely focuses on athletic competitions, traditionally held between villages, and farmers' music. The highlight of this event is the mock-fight *(ssaum)* between two *go,* huge constructions of looped-ropes and poles that are propelled by dozens of men, with the goal of pushing the opponent's *go* to the ground.

March

The ***Samil* Independence Movement Festival** takes place in Changnyeong on March 1, and commemorates the Independence Movement of 1919. In addition, the Battle of the Bull's Heads *(Yeongsan Soemori Daegi)* and the Yeongsan tug-of-war folk games provide entertainment.

The **Haengju Victory Festival** takes place at Haengju Fortress, just west of the Seoul city limits. This festival commemorates the victory of General Kwon Yul and his troops over the Japanese army in 1592. It was one of a handful of victories garnered by Koreans during the disastrous Hideyoshi Invasions.

A truly urban event, the **Myeong-dong Festival** takes place in the busy, crowded street of Seoul's historic entertainment and shopping district. Events include singing and beauty contests, an outdoor fashion show, and music and dance presentations.

The **Cheongdo Bullfight Festival** brings to modern crowds the traditional bull-to-bull power matches that once pleased a much more agricultural community. The festival takes place in the countryside of Cheongdo, south of Daegu.

April

The **King Danjong Festival,** held in Yeongwol, honors this young, deposed Joseon Dynasty king and his retainers. A stately ceremony is performed at the king's gravesite on the edge of town, while other festive events like music and poetry reading take place in town.

Celebrating traditional foods of the nation, the **Korean Traditional Drink and Cake Fes-**

tival is held in Gyeongju. Aside from watching the process of making these treats, the most fun is tasting them. Various traditional wines are also offered.

The **Wangin Cultural Festival** celebrates the illustrious Baekje Dynasty scholar and diplomat Wangin Baksa who traveled to Japan in the 3rd century and introduced literary documents and ideas of Confucianism and governance to the rulers of that country.

May

Among a number of natural fibers woven in the country, ramie is a well-known product of Hansan in Chungcheongnam-Do. To celebrate the enduring popularity and usefulness of this cloth, the **Ramie Cultural Festival** is held at the beginning of May. Events include weaving, dyeing, and clothes-making.

Yeosu hosts the **Jinnam Festival,** which honors Admiral Yi Sun-shin, who had his command center in this port city. Events include competitions in archery, literary composition, and deep-sea fishing.

A symbol of fidelity, the Silla Dynasty heroine, Arang, is honored at the *Miryang Arang-je.* Held along the riverbank in Miryang, this festival includes a Miss Arang contest, music and dance, and athletic contests. A bazaar is held throughout the affair.

For centuries, Daegu has been an important center for the production, processing, and marketing of medicinal herbs in Korea and the **Yangnyeongshi Festival** is held in May to celebrate all aspects of this traditional commerce and the beneficial effects of these plants.

As one of the centers of modern Korean green tea production and the place at which tea was introduced to the country, Hadong in Gyeongsangnam-Do holds the yearly **Mountain Dew Tea Festival** to honor this plant and the healthful benefits of its leaves.

June

A festival honoring an insect? The **Muju Firefly Festival** puts this bug at the center of an early summer festival, and it lights up the night.

July

The **Boryeong Mud Festival** is held at Daecheon Beach on the west coast to take advantage of the mineral-rich shore mud. The mineral content in the mud is prized for its skin cleaning and purifying properties so massages, wraps, and other such activities are offered.

Once one of the premier locations for the production of Goryeo celadon, Gangjin now hosts the **Gangjin Celadon Cultural Festival** to rekindle its connection with the past.

September

The *Yulgok-je* of Gangneung honors Yi Yulgok (Yi Yi), one of Korea's two most famous Confucian scholars. A ritual ceremony and traditional music are performed on October 26 in commemoration of his deeds, and a calligraphy contest is sponsored.

Every September or October, the **Geumsan Ginseng Festival** is held in the rural town of Geumsan to promote this region's most famous product. Events include traditional music and dance, athletic contests, fireworks, and a lantern parade.

Chungju welcomes participants and spectators from around the world to its annual **Chungju World Martial Arts Festival.** Chungju is center of the ancient indigenous martial art of *taekgyeon,* which many believe to be the precursor of the more famous and now widely practiced martial art of taekwondo.

Andong Hahoe has it famous masks and masked dance, but in late September or early October it invites masks and mask dancers from other countries to participate in the **Andong International Mask Dance Festival.**

October

Honoring one of the city's well-known crafts, Tongyeong holds the **Tongyeong Lacquerware Festival** in early October.

Andong Folk Festival is one of the largest such gatherings. Traditional folk events from the Andong area are performed, including the Hahoe Masked Dance, the *chajeon nori* "tank game," and the *notdari balki* "bridge-crossing game."

A combination of outdoor activities and folk events makes the **Mt. Seorak Festival** a major attraction in the Sokcho area when the weather and scenery are at their finest. A shaman ceremony, folk games, a mountain marathon, and climbing events are held.

The **Hansan Victory Festival** honors Admiral Yi Sun-shin and his crucial naval victory off Hansan-do during the Imjin War of the 1590s. Events take place on Hansan-do and in Tongyong, and include the Victory Drum Dance, an ancient military parade, and sporting competitions.

Jeongseon Arirang-je is held in the small mountain town of Jeongseon. This event centers around Korea's best-known traditional folk song. Throughout the country, *Arirang* has over 2,000 lyrics and 50 different melodies. The Jeongseon variations are the most famous.

The **King Sejong Cultural Festival** happens in Yeoju to honor this Joseon Dynasty king. Some athletic events, a lantern parade, and a *tapdori* (circling a pagoda in prayer) are held.

Held in Chungju, the **Ureuk Cultural Festival** commemorates the famous Gaya musician Ureuk. Ureuk popularized the *gayageum,* a 12-string zither that is still the most popular Korean traditional musical instrument. Music competitions are the focus, but other artistic events are also held.

The *Ganggangsullae* **Festival** takes place in the small town of Haenam and features the *ganggangsullae* circle dance, for which the town is known.

Icheon Ceramics Festival features the age-old tradition of pottery making in a town that has been producing pottery for centuries. Different styles are showcased and a kiln-firing contest is held.

The **Moyang Fortress Festival** of Gochang is held on the ninth day of the ninth lunar month, and is the first of the fortress festivals in the country. It celebrates the completion of the fortress in 1453, said to have been built solely by the labor of women. During this event, town women in traditional *hanbok* parade along the fortress wall. *Pansori* vocal music contests, archery and *ssireum* matches, and a parade are also held.

The second fortress festival is **Suwon Hwaseong Fortress Cultural Festival.** Erected as an act of filial piety of a son for his father, this festival not only honors the structure of the fortress but also the spirit from which it was conceived. Events include the pomp and ceremony of a royal procession.

The southwestern corner of the country is known for making some of the best *gimchi* and this edible identity of Korea is celebrated in Gwangju at the annual **Gwangju Kimchi Festival.**

In Busan, the city celebrates the bountiful resources of the sea during the **Busan Jagalchi Festival.** Most events take place around the Jagalchi fish market along the waterfront in town.

Hosted at the Suyeong Yachting Center is the **Busan International Film Festival,** where innovative films from around the globe are screened to appreciative crowds.

On the Road

Shopping 상업

If Korea is a "shopper's paradise," as tourist literature states, then Seoul is its Garden of Eden. There is plenty of merchandise in Korea, but not all is as cheap as some would like you to believe. Antiques, handicrafts, tailor-made clothes, athletic shoes, and furs are a few of the items sought after, and bargains can be found. With the increasing sophistication of the local economy, ties to international markets, and the demand for more and better products, the quality of Korean goods continues to improve.

Stores selling the same items tend to congregate together, and large cities have well-defined major **shopping districts** known for particular goods, such as the high-class boutiques and clothing shops of Myeong-dong and the antique shops and art supply stores of Insa-dong, in Seoul. These shopping areas are often coupled with entertainment districts. In smaller towns, the city center is the place to shop. **Multi-level markets,** like Dongdaemun Market in Seoul and the International Market in Busan, cover several city blocks. Each town has a **central market,** historically its commercial center, and numerous smaller neighborhood markets for the outlying areas. Here you can find virtually anything, from food to machinery, clothes to household goods. **Spe-**

remains of a gate from the Wibong-san mountain fortress

cialty wholesale markets, including Seoul's Yongsan Electronic Arcade, the Gyeongdong herb market, and Busan's Jagalchi Fish Market, are found only in large cities. At all these markets, cargo-delivery trucks, bicycle carriers, and men on foot shouldering wooden A-frames (called *jige*) are ready to transport bulky goods, for a price. While much more widespread only a few decades ago, five-day markets still grace small and medium-size towns and more rural areas. These markets operate once every five days, hence their name, when merchants congregate at a specified location to sell their goods. A few specialty markets worth browsing in the provinces are Yangnyeong Shijang in Daegu, which deals in roots, herbs, and Chinese medicinal items; the Damyang bamboo market; Geumsan ginseng market; Seongnam's Moran Market; the Sorae seafood market in Incheon; and the wild mountain vegetable market in Gurye.

Supermarkets have made their appearance on the Korean scene. Air-conditioned, sterile, canned, wrapped, and priced, these places are essentially the same as any other supermarkets in the world. Convenience stores such as 7-11 and Korean knock-offs like LG-25, often open around the clock, have also popped up seemingly everywhere, giving the corner mom-and-pop shops a run for their money. It was inevitable that big box discount stores would invade the shopping scene in Korea—but luckily (so far) only in the major cities. Never fear, you can find that cheap box of toilet paper, household item, or brand-name T-shirt at Wal-Mart or Kim's Club.

Like their counterparts in other countries, **department stores** have a wide selection of goods, fairly even quality, and moderate to high prices. Many have restaurant and food-product floors. Prices are usually fixed and marked. These stores, and others that carry name-brand items, hold storewide sales several times a year. Department stores are generally open 1030–1930, but each is closed one day a week. Most other stores and markets open earlier and stay open later. **Underground arcades** compete for the limited space in crowded downtown areas. Lying beneath major streets, these corridors of cubbyhole shops

© ROBERT NILSEN

ON THE ROAD

City markets often run for blocks and take up the whole street.

sell all imaginable goods. Prices tend to be high at hotel shops, above-ground arcades, and handicraft centers.

Look for **duty-free shops** at all international airports, the international ferry terminals in Busan and Incheon, and in Seoul, Busan, Gyeongju, and on Jeju-do. They sell the usual array of high-quality foreign goods and select Korean handicrafts not available domestically. The foreign goods are priced competitively, while the tourist handicrafts are expensive. These items can only be taken out of the country. For the busy person who doesn't have time to shop, online duty-free shopping, where you pick up your goods at your point of departure on exit, is now an option. For particulars, see www.dutyfreekorea.com.

Foreign currencies are accepted only in hotel arcades, some handicraft centers, duty-free shops, and specialty stores in such places like the Itaewon shopping district in Seoul. Most of these places, plus an ever-widening number of upscale and ordinary shops around the country, accept credit cards. Don't assume; ask before charging.

M

FIRST CUSTOMER OF THE DAY

While the superstition is slowly falling by the wayside, some shop owners believe that if the first customer of the day makes a purchase, business for the rest of the day will be good. If you intend just to browse, don't be the first into a store. If you are the first, it's nice (although not necessary) to purchase something, even if it's small and inexpensive.

American Express, Visa, MasterCard, and Diners Club are the most widely accepted. Some also accept traveler's checks.

While not everything is taxed, many items that are sold at tourist shops and department stores are. For incentive purposes, a number of **value-added tax refund** programs have been set up that return the equivalent of the sales tax paid on certain objects over ₩50,000 when those items are taken out of the country upon your exit, if it's within three months of the date of purchase. These programs operate only with participating stores and each store should display a sign indicating its participation. These tax refund programs are run under government regulation and so are legitimate, and sometimes the government itself will declare a specified period of time as tax-free for foreign visitors for certain types of goods. Either way, this presents a good opportunity to save on taxes for purchases that you might be planning to buy anyway.

All shopping complaints should be addressed to the KNTO's Tourist Complaint Center in Seoul (tel. 02/735-0101).

Bargaining

Bargaining is expected nearly everywhere except at department stores, duty-free shops, supermarkets, and select multi-level specialty shops in Seoul where prices are marked. If you don't bargain, you lose. Look around before you buy. Ask an impartial party what a fair price is, or check at stores with marked prices (these will usually be slightly more expensive). Generally, the asking price of unmarked goods is not wildly higher than the actual price. By and large, Korean merchants are out to make a good return on their investment, but not by ripping you off. There are exceptions, however, so be cautious. Don't be in a hurry; your impatience and lack of time work in the merchant's favor. Don't show your attachment to any one item; ask the prices of various goods. Make an offer that is substantially low and see how the merchant responds. The give and take starts here. Be willing to think about it, walk away, and look elsewhere if you can't agree. A shop selling the same item is undoubtedly just down the road. Often, if you start to walk away, a merchant will call you back and agree to your price if it's close enough to what he needs. If you buy several items at one time, you stand a better chance of getting a good discount. The sporting waltz of bargaining to an agreeable end satisfies everyone.

English is spoken by most clerks in hotel shops, handicraft centers, major arcades, and in most shops in Itaewon. Japanese is also widely spoken, especially in antique shops. Elsewhere, you must rely on your Korean, the shopkeeper's pidgin English, hand signals, body language, and a notepad and pencil.

Large shops in several of the major shopping areas in Seoul—Namdaemun Market, Dongdaemun Market, several large department stores near Dongdae-mun, the Yongsan Electronics Market, Techno-Mart, and in Itaewon—have, by law, instituted a **fixed-price** system for their goods. While contrary to the traditional bargaining system, the impetus seems to have been to create conditions where foreigners will not be overcharged at shops that they frequent. The smaller shops in these markets, however, do not operate under the same conditions.

Antiques

Korean antiques have been very popular for decades. While some are still available, they're quickly becoming more expensive and harder to find. Of most interest are Goryeo Dynasty celadon and Joseon Dynasty wooden chests. Other sought-after items are white porcelain, scrolls, paintings, calligraphy, woodblock prints, furniture, lacquerware, brassware, traditional craft items, folk-art objects, tools, and coins. Good-quality modern reproductions of antiques abound—a good, less expensive alternative if you aren't concerned with authenticity and don't care to deal with the paperwork required for export of genuine antiques. If you *are* looking for true antiques, however, shop at a licensed antique dealer (a certificate should be displayed) and know your stuff. For goods over 50 years old, you must get an appraisal and written permission to export. A bona fide dealer should help you through the appropriate paperwork. Beware those who will not. The majority of antique dealers in the country are in Seoul, particularly in Insa-dong, Janghanpyeong, and Itaewon. Others, in the country's major provincial cities, concentrate on regional items.

For certification of export for antiques, and for assessing an object for its status (valuable cultural properties may not be taken from the country), contact the KNTO information center for the nearest Art and Antique Assessment Office.

Furniture

Traditional-style Korean furniture (antiques and modern reproductions) has gained a following. Of interest are makeup boxes, document cases, blanket chests, multi-drawer medicine chests, bookcases, and huge wardrobes. Woods are carefully selected and cured before being cut. Heavy brass, nickel, or iron fittings are used for pulls, knobs, hinges, corner pieces, and ornamentation. Many pieces are left plain to show off their natural color and grain or are lightly stained. Lacquer with inlaid mother-of-pearl covers some furniture and other pieces are covered with painted ox-horn. During the past couple of decades, contemporary furniture has also been produced. Deviating from traditional lines, modern pieces tend to follow sleek Scandinavian, curvaceous European, or solid American designs.

Ceramics

Modern reproductions of antique celadon and porcelain have flooded the market. While some pieces are obviously mass-produced and of middling quality, fine examples—some by famous Korean craftsmen—are available at kiln shops and in select shops in Seoul. While the mysterious light-green celadon in traditional shapes and designs appeals to some, delicate white Joseon-style porcelain or the crudely beautiful Silla- and Baekje-style earthenware attracts others. Browse the shops in Insa-dong, Itaewon, the arcades, the Cultural Property Artisans Hall in the basement level KNTO Tourist Information Office, or the National Souvenir Center in Myeong-dong for an idea of what ceramics cost.

Silk

Korea produces high-quality silk, some of which ends up in famous Thai silks. From raising silkworms to spinning the thread and weaving the fiber, silk production is laborious. In the past a cottage industry, today the silk industry is dominated by large companies. Silk is produced in varying qualities and colors; bolts in plain, brocade, or embroidered patterns dazzle the eye. Shopkeepers are understandably proud of their wares and seem to take joy in showing you a variety of this wonderful fabric. You'll be pleased as well to have this cloth turned into something you can wear, but know that the real thing is expensive. The country's major silk center is the 2nd floor of Tongdaemun Market, in Seoul. Aisle after aisle of shops sell bolts of this fine material. If you're planning to have the cloth made into *hanbok*, the shopkeeper can recommend a good seamstress. Specialty silk shops, department stores, arcade shops, and tailors also handle silks.

Clothing

Traditional Korean clothing is called *hanbok*. Though simple in design, they are some of the most graceful garments in Asia. These and Western clothes of all designs can be bought ready-made or made to order. Tailors and dressmakers can produce slacks, shirts, suits, and dresses in a few days from pictures in fashion magazines. Clothes off the rack are plentiful, but unless you're of Asian size and proportion (smaller in the hips and buttocks, and shorter in sleeve length), an exact fit may be hard to find. The best place to shop for Western sizes is Itaewon, in Seoul, where dozens of shops handle everything from shoes and sportswear to dress slacks, knit sweaters, and winter coats. Natural and synthetic fabrics are available. Dress shoes can be made to order. Select from a mind-boggling array of athletic shoes (most are genuine, some are black-market imitations, others are seconds) for a portion of what they cost elsewhere. Shoes for a foot-size larger than 44 centimeters (men's size 10 U.S.) are uncommon, but they are available in Itaewon. Particularly in Itaewon, stores stock seconds and overruns, so check the quality and workmanship of each item before you buy. Name-brand labels are everywhere, but beware of false or misleading labels.

Korea has become one of the world's leading manufacturers of furs. With raw materials from Scandinavia, the United States, and other regions, skilled seamstresses sew these pelts into world-class furs that sell for far less than what they go for in most other countries. The largest producer is Jindo Furs, but others have also made a dent in this market.

Leather

Most leather is imported from abroad and fashioned into a wide variety of items including suede jackets, shoes, belts, and briefcases. Eelskin products—shoes, handbags, wallets, and more—are also popular. Be sure to check the stitching on these items, and scrutinize any metal parts, for quality. Skins from other animals—alligator and turtle for example—are also used on occasion, but they may not legally be imported into some countries.

Handicrafts and Native Products

Some of the most popular items for foreign shoppers are Korean handicrafts. Quality varies so shop around to get an idea of a well-made piece before you buy. Lacquerware boxes, bamboo and rush mats and baskets, brass bowls, dolls in Korean dress, masks, paper fans, paper and calligraphy sets, embroidered cloth and screens, *norigae* pendants, and carved wooden wedding ducks are common items.

In addition, *gimchi*, traditional Korean liquor and wines, dried laver, herbs, mushrooms, wild mountain vegetables, and other food products are widely available.

Brass

For several centuries, independent workshops produced brassware, and some old brass objects are still available in antique shops. Hefty, solid, and well-designed, these old pieces are of high quality. New brass tends to be thinner and less substantial, and the craftsmanship has generally gone down. While very fine pieces are still being made, most stores carry mass-produced, often gaudy examples, from tiny knickknacks to lamps and bed frames.

Ginseng

Ginseng (called *insam* in Korean) is a human-shaped root of medicinal and mystical qualities. Highly prized, *insam* is ingested for many reasons, including rejuvenation of strength; prevention of hypertension, diabetes, and illness; strengthening neurological and gastric functions; longevity; and sexual vigor. It's a common ingredient of folk and Chinese medicines. While often powdered and taken as tea, it also comes in capsule, tablet, and liquid-extract form and is

insam: ginseng

an ingredient in some candies and gums. For the aficionado, whole roots are put into glass beakers, covered with *soju* (or one's choice of fine liquor), and allowed to leech its powers before the liquid is drunk and the root consumed. Users wholeheartedly recommend this root. Requiring five to seven years to mature, *insam* is time-consuming to raise. White ginseng, called *baeksam*, is harvested after four or five years. Taken from the ground and washed, its skin and the small hairs on its main shoots are removed before it's dried. If it's not dried but used as is, it's called *susam*. *Hongsam*, or red, ginseng is not harvested for at least six years. Left unpeeled, it's steamed, resulting in its faint reddish color, and then dried. Wild *insam*, sometimes over 100 years old, is occasionally found, and this fetches a king's ransom. While ginseng is also grown in China, Russia, and the United States, Korea's is considered the world's finest. Even in Korea, however, quality varies. *Insam* from Ganghwa-do, a Gaeseong variety, is considered the finest. The red variety claims a higher price than white *insam*. Only specified amounts of red ginseng are allowed to be taken out of the country. Check with the KNTO office for particulars.

Semiprecious Stones and Jewelry

Of the gemstones, only smoky topaz, amethyst, and jadeite are mined in any quantity in Korea and sold at reasonable prices. As most precious stones are imported, Korea is definitely not the place to look for deals. Although loose stones are also sold, topaz and amethyst are usually cut and set into gold jewelry: rings, necklaces, bracelets, earrings, and pins. Ask for Korean amethyst, as stones from other countries are also sold in Korea. Be sure to always ask for a certificate of authentication. Reputable dealers will have them. Jadeite is also fashioned into jewelry, but more often large chunks are carved into decorative art objects. Ranging in shade from dark green to nearly white, it is less expensive than

its close cousin, Chinese jade. Gold is available in Korea, but it's comparatively expensive.

Electronic Goods

Every year Korea expands its catalog of electronic gadgetry and telecommunication equipment—and inches up its quality. Prices for audio, video, camera, telephone, and computer equipment, parts, and accessories have become quite competitive, and manufacturers are now catching up in design and quality to foreign goods. Imported products, including camera equipment, are all heavily taxed, so you'll find no bargains here. Korean, Japanese, American, and European film are all available, though not cheap. There are many electronics and camera shops in all cities, but the multi-building Yongsan Electronics Arcade and Techno-Mart in Seoul have the greatest variety, and perhaps the best bargains.

Sporting Goods

High-quality sporting goods of all sorts are available in the country and have been quite popular since the 1980s. Whether it's a tennis racket, baseball glove, soccer ball, running shoes, golf clubs, or camping equipment, it can all be found here at decent prices. With the increased interest in Korean sporting teams and individuals doing well on the international scene, the interest in better sports equipment has grown.

Shipping

If you've bought an article that's too big to mail, or you don't trust the postal system, ship it by air or sea freight. Air freight is much more expensive, but much quicker and probably safer. Rates for both vary considerably, so do some checking. For air freight, try one of the airlines that runs cargo flights to your country or try Federal Express (tel. 02/738-5331), DHL (tel. 02/716-0001), or UPS (tel. 02/3665-6016). For sea freight, try American President Lines (tel. 02/393-0707 in Seoul or 51/463-0156 in Busan) or Evergreen Marine (tel. 02/3702-1831 in Seoul or 51/463-8311 in Busan).

Entertainment 대접

Korea supports a diverse entertainment scene. Possibilities range from classical music concerts to disco dancing, melodramatic movies to Las Vegas–style floor shows, a drink with friends at a wine house to gambling at a casino. Large cities offer the widest choice, provincial towns have variety, but in rural areas you may have to make your own. Large cities generally have a concentrated "entertainment area"; Seoul and Busan have several. Koreans almost never go out on the town alone, instead going in couples or groups. If you are a single traveler, recruit someone to go with.

LIVE PERFORMANCES AND CINEMA

Theater

Large theaters such as the National Theater, Sejong Cultural Center, and the Seoul Arts Center in Seoul, and provincial cities' citizens' halls and cultural arts centers are the main venues for large-scale traditional and modern dramatic productions, music and dance performances, ballet, and opera, where both national professional groups and local amateur groups perform. Viewing a traditional performance is a good way to be introduced to Korean vocal music such as *pansori;* instrumental music played on traditional Korean instruments; various court, folk, and Buddhist dances; and the delightful masked-dance dramas. Occasionally, foreign groups or individuals are featured in modern performances. Shows start in early evening and generally draw large crowds. Ticket prices vary widely according to the performance, and are sold at the theater; Seoul and other large cities have selected ticket outlets at bookstores, music shops, department stores, and ticket vendors.

Small Theaters

Small theaters are becoming a viable institution in Korea. This seems especially true in Seoul, with such well-established and reputable theaters as the Munye, Cecil, and Nanta, but regional theater groups are enjoying growing support. Universities also sponsor theater programs. Generally, these small theaters present experimental, less well-known Korean works, and drama in translation.

Outdoor Theater

Traditional folk theater and music are also performed outside during fair weather. The Korean Folk Village, outside Suwon, and the Nori Madang, in Seoul, have regularly scheduled performances. National and regional cultural festivals also host productions as part of festival events.

Theater Restaurants

As in the West, theater restaurants offer dinner, a fixed number of drinks, and a floor show for a set price. Dinners are usually Western-style, and extra drinks are expensive. Floor shows are mostly Korean music and dance, with the addition of a Las Vegas–style performance or a foreign musician. Nearly all are in large cities at major hotels; a few are privately operated. Perhaps the best known and one of the most established in the country is Kayagum Hall at the Sheraton Walker Hill Hotel in Seoul.

Theater restaurants of a Korean nature are also available and these usually offer a traditional Korean meal followed by traditional Korean music and dance. Perhaps the foremost of these is Korea House in Seoul, although the most unusual may be Sanchon, also in Seoul, which offers vegetarian food and Buddhist dances. Although expensive, these are excellent introductions to fine Korean food and performance.

Both Korean and Western dinner shows are popular, so make reservations early.

Concerts

Indoor and outdoor folk and rock concerts are a relatively new and small phenomenon to the Korean music scene. As their counterparts do in the West, well-known Korean musicians, with the occasional Japanese or Western musician, play popular music to receptive university crowds. Look for posters and fliers for concerts around university campuses and along "Culture Streets." Busan sponsors an International Rock Concert on the beach each summer.

Cinemas

Many cinemas (geukjang) are huge halls that seat several thousand; however, multi-plexes and small cinemas with only a few hundred seats are popping up in larger cities. Movies are very popular with Koreans, and have lured some support and interest away from traditional performing arts. Historical and situational dramas, tear-jerker love stories, slapstick comedies, and anything to do with the South Korea–North Korea split are favored, although more serious themes are explored. The Korean film industry is becoming increasingly sophisticated, and a handful of films have done well in international festivals. Chinese kung fu films and American feature films are major imports. Large theaters seldom show European or other foreign films. Foreign films usually retain the original soundtracks and are subtitled in Korean; occasionally they are shortened or censored. Tickets generally run around ₩7,000 and seats are usually assigned; small theaters often charge nominally less. Shows start at 1100 and continue through late evening. Showtimes, available seating times, and admission prices are posted next to ticket windows. Go during the week or buy your ticket well before show time on weekend evenings to ensure a seat. In Seoul, movie listings appear in the English-language newspapers; in other cities, visit the theater for information. Most cinemas display huge painted murals over their front entrances depicting scenes from the film currently playing. New movies are often released during school holidays—December–January and July–August—but since Koreans have a reduced work week and greater leisure time, more releases are done year-round on weekends.

Video Rooms

If you would rather have more privacy, you can screen rental videos at video rooms. With seating for half a dozen or so, these rooms offer a great variety of choice, and snacks are available.

DRINKING
Nightclubs and Discos

Many hotels operate nightclubs or discos; others are privately run. Hours are 2000–0200 (some stay open all night); the cover charge varies. At some, an additional table fee or set minimum may be levied. The price of drinks is two to three times what you'd pay at other drinking establishments. You are expected to order anju (a snack), also expensive. At some nightclubs, a hostess may sit with you during the evening (your option); a tip is normal. Nightclubs have live music for dancing—occasionally with a foreign band. Discos spin records. Generally speaking, nightclubs cater to middle- and upper-income Koreans, businessmen with expense accounts, and foreigners. Less expensive discos draw younger crowds, mostly students.

Bars and Lounges

Many hotels have cocktail lounges in the lobbies. Their bars are like the Western variety, with subdued lighting and cushy seating, and are often strategically placed for the hotel's best view.

Independent bars and places called "salons" (sarong) are most often small, dark, and private affairs with muted music and secluded booths. Asked for or not, many provide their male guests the company of a "hostess," whose drinks must be bought and also compensated. Drinks are steep, name brands more so, and the same goes for the anju. Ask for a price list before you order. Pay as you leave.

Stand bars are generally large halls with dance floors like nightclubs'. Unlike nightclubs, however, they are divided into small bar stations. A hostess sits behind each bar and serves drinks only to the guests in her section. The hostess may drink or dance with a customer and the drink for the hostess can be twice as expensive as for the customers. Some stand bars have short musical variety shows or bands. For these, a small cover is charged.

A transplant from Japan, karaoke bar bands

provide the music and customers sing the songs — for a fee. Everyone wants their five minutes in the spotlight in front of the mike! Virtually anything can be requested, and if the band doesn't know the song they'll play an appropriate generic rhythm. Similar types of establishments are called *dallanjujeom* and *gayobanju; norae yeonseupbang* or *noraebang* are private rooms with video equipment that projects words to songs on a screen while playing their musical accompaniment. A microphone is hooked to the unit so everyone can have a chance to sing. Food and drinks can be ordered.

Beer Halls

Nearly always larger than bars and substantially less expensive than nightclubs, beer halls — also called Hof — are frequented by students and young professionals. Smoky and full of life, these halls often keep their music to low decibels; some halls now offer live entertainment. Beer is moderately priced, while *anju* is still on the expensive side. Most larger establishments serve both bottled and draft beer. Beer halls are found around the entertainment areas of cities and near universities. While most close in the early hours of the morning, some operate through the night for the die-hard drinkers.

Smaller and more congenial pubs can be found in neighborhood areas of the cities and in smaller towns. Crowded with low tables or high stools around a raised bar, these places usually seat only a few dozen. Along with the usual variety of *anju*, many serve deep-fried chicken. Find them by beer-company logos or pictures of frothy beer mugs or chickens on their opaque windows. Larger beer halls ask that you pay as you order; smaller places keep a tab and you pay as you leave. Open from late afternoon until around midnight.

Wine Houses

While the young are often drawn to fancier places for an evening's drink, the older crowd still frequents neighborhood wine houses. Called *suljip*, these places are the ordinary man's drinkery. Both the liquid refreshment and the *anju* are cheap — fit for the working-class pocketbook. *Makgeolli*

(fermented milky rice wine) and *soju* (clear potato liquor) are the usual drinks, although beer is sometimes sold. Crowded, lively, and noisy, *suljip* are full of down-to-earth charm. As the evening slides by, blue smoke fills the air and conversation becomes animated. Someone usually breaks into song and his buddies keep time by beating the edge of the table with chopsticks. Finally, the bill is paid — so the owner is happy, too — and everyone stumbles home satiated, not worrying about the work to be done in the morning. Singing almost always accompanies drinking. Learn a few songs so you, too, can join in.

Recently, rustic-style *suljip,* with period decor and music, waiters and waitresses in traditional garb, and liquor fermented by an age-old process, have been making a comeback. While these are more expensive than the ordinary wine house, and frequented by students and young businessmen, the atmosphere harks back to old Korea. These places are usually called *jujeom* or *minsok jujeom.*

Gisaeng Houses

For Korean food and entertainment in a traditional setting, the *gisaengjip* is the cream of the crop. *Gisaengjip* are exclusive restaurants, and *gisaeng* are women entertainer/hostesses, similar to Japanese geisha. While once a separate and privileged social class, today *gisaeng* are employees chosen for their beauty, grace, and talents. These places serve fine food and Korean or Western liquor. Hostesses help serve the meal, care for the needs of the customers, and perform music and dance in a private room. A visit to a *gisaengjip* is an unforgettable experience for the food, attention, and entertainment, but they are expensive. The bill can easily reach several hundred dollars — per person! It's the kind of place where if you are at all worried about the price — which should always be agreed upon in advance — you can't afford to go. The custom is for one person (or the company) to pay; if you're the lucky one, put it on the expense account. Most often used when business deals are in the making, by Japanese tourists on vacation, or on special days of celebration, *gisaengjip* are usually visited by small groups of men, and virtually never by couples or individuals.

Tearooms and Coffee Shops

Korea's numerous tearooms and coffee shops serve as gathering spots for friends, comfortable environments for business discussions, daytime meeting places for women, and lovers' rendezvous. Various coffee and coffee blends; green-leaf, root, and herbal teas; juices; soft drinks; and ice cream are served, though not necessarily all at each type of establishment. Regular coffee often tastes like dishwater; try a special blend or variety, if offered on the menu. If you want it black, say so—coffee often comes with cream or cream and sugar. Juice, soft drinks, and ice cream are also usually available. What seems to be universal, however, is that cups are never served full—a half-cup is standard. Classical, traditional Korean, Korean pop, soft rock, or Top 40 music is played to attract a certain clientele. Ordinary tearooms are often found in the basements or on the 2nd floors of office and commercial buildings. Usually low-lit places with fish tanks, they are the haunts of middle-aged and older Korean men. Classier places, and those with traditional decor, are more common in the shopping and entertainment districts of the city and near universities. Generally, these shops are brighter and frequented by younger Koreans, male and female. Outside, look for signs sporting coffee cups and the words *dabang* (다방) or *dashil* (다실) (tearoom), or *koepishop* (coffee shop) (커피숍); some sport signs in English. Traditional-style tearooms, generally called *dawon* (다원) or *chatjip* (찻집), often have carved wooden signs over their entrances, and are visited by the young, sophisticated, and avant-garde. Unlike other establishments, they often also have traditional Korean sweet punches, cakes, and cookies on the menu. Hotels have their own coffee shops. Open before noon, these places don't close until nearly midnight. When you order, you can stay as long as you want. Ordinary coffee shops and tearooms offer delivery service to nearby offices, commercial establishments, and *yeogwan* by smartly clad young women carrying cups and a thermos wrapped in an oversized cloth handkerchief. These young women work all day long and get two days off a month. A mobile group, they change job locations every month or two. Traditional tearooms and classier coffee shops usually hire college students, who work a more normal schedule.

GAMBLING

Limited and strictly controlled, gambling is allowed at 13 hotel-casinos in the country, eight of which are on Jeju-do. These **casinos** are at the Sheraton Walker Hill Hotel in Seoul (the largest in the country), the Olympos Hotel in Incheon, Sorak Park Hotel at the entrance to Seorak-san National Park, Kyongju Hilton Hotel in Gyeongju, Paradise Beach Hotel in Busan, and on Jeju-do at the Cheju Grand, Cheju Oriental, Cheju LaGonda, Cheju KAL, and Holiday Inn Crown Plaza hotels in Jeju City, at the Hyatt Regency and Cheju Shilla hotels in Jungmun, and at the Seogwipo KAL Hotel in Seogwipo. Try your luck at roulette, blackjack, baccarat, tai-sai, the big wheel, or the slot machines. Chips can be bought only with foreign currency. Instruction for games is available. Croupiers are tipped. These casinos are only open to foreigners, and a nominal entrance fee is usually charged. Some identification is usually required, and most have a minimum age limit of 20; casual dress is the norm although you certainly may dress up. In addition, most tourist hotels have a game room with slot machines and electronic games.

Until the late 1990s, all casinos were off-limits to Koreans, except for those that worked in them. Then the Gangwon Land Casino Resort was opened, the only casino in the country that permits entrance to Koreans. Others are anticipated. While gambling is legal for Koreans in this casino, the government has not made it easy. The Gangwon Land Casino is located high up in the mountains, away from just about everything except the small city of Taebaek. Like other casinos in the country, this one has all the typical casino games. Entrance is ₩5,000 and only open to those 18 years old or older.

Over the past two decades non-gambling game room arcades, called *orakshil,* have appeared. Frequented by young people, often to the dismay of their elders, these arcades can be distinguished by the universal beeps, bells, buzzes, and dings of electronic games.

Betting on **horse racing** is gaining in popularity. Races are held at the Seoul Equestrian Park and at the Jeju Race Track between 1100 and 1800 on weekends year-round. Win, place, and quinella bets are taken on each of the 10–12 daily races. Bets can be made in amounts from ₩100 to ₩1,000,000, and information in English is available. An admission fee of ₩900 is charged at the track.

Transportation 교통

AIR: INTERNATIONAL

South Korea is Asia's best-kept secret—but the word is getting out. In 1965 Korea had only 33,464 visitors; in 1976 that number swelled to 834,239; 1,659,972 visited in 1986; and the number grew to 3,753,197 in 1995. By the early 2000s, Korea was regularly getting 5 million visitors a year. By far the majority of visitors come by air. More than three-quarters of air arrivals land at Incheon International Airport, some 50 kilometers west of Seoul. Previous to the Incheon opening in March 2001, visitors arrived at Gimpo Airport, which is much closer to the Seoul city center and now used solely for domestic flights. Most other international flights arrive at Gimhae International Airport in Busan and Jeju International Airport on the island of Jeju-do. The smaller airports at Gwangju, Daegu, Cheongju, and Yangyang each receive only a handful of international flights per week. The opening of the newest domestic and international airport near Yangyang on the east coast in 2002 offers visitors easier access to the dramatic mountain and coastal areas in the northwestern corner of the country.

Korea receives several hundred international flights every week, and is connected to about 125 cities throughout the world. In the past several decades, flights to a multitude of Chinese and Central Asian cities have been added to the long-standing list of routes to Japan, North America, Southeast Asia, and Europe.

Airlines serving Incheon International Airport are listed in the Special Topic "Air Carriers Serving South Korea." Each has a check-in counter at the airport and an office in the city. Asiana Airlines, Korean Air, and 10 other airlines serve Gimhae International Airport; Asiana Airlines, Korean Air, and two Chinese airlines serve Cheongju and Yangyang international airports; while only Asiana Airlines and Korean Air service the Jeju and Daegu international airports and all the domestic airports. An airport use tax of ₩17,000 is levied on all foreign international passengers when they leave the country, except for those who leave on the same day as arrival and for children under two years of age. Korean nationals pay ₩25,000. For specific details on flight schedules, airline office telephone numbers, airport location and description, and local transportation to and from the airport, see the Transportation sections in the travel chapters.

Korean Air Carriers

Asiana Airlines entered the Korean domestic air market with three routes in 1988, the country's second airline. In 1989, it expanded its domestic routes and opened international flights to Japan, later inaugurating flights to the U.S. and Southeast Asian cities. Flights have since been added to China, Russia, Central Asia, Europe, and a few other destinations, in total servicing just over 50 cities in 17 countries. The vast majority of Asiana's flights leave from Incheon International Airport; however a few go to select Japanese and Chinese cities from Busan, Jeju, and Daegu.

Privatized in 1969, Korean Airlines has grown from a largely domestic carrier with one jet and seven prop planes to become one of Asia's largest airlines and one of the 20 largest in the world. In 1984, following the downing of a Korean Airlines jumbo jet over Russian waters the previous year, the company changed its name to **Korean Air** (also referred to as KAL) and adopted the *taeguk* symbol as its logo. Korean Air flies to 61 cities in

AIR CARRIERS SERVING SOUTH KOREA

The following airlines serve South Korea. (Numbers with a "02" prefix are in Seoul; numbers with a "032" prefix are at the Incheon International Airport.)

Aeroflot Russian Int'l Airlines (SU)
tel. 02/551-0321 or 032/744-8672

Air Canada (AC)
tel. 02/779-5654 or 032/744-0898

Air China (CA)
tel. 02/774-6886 or 032/744-3250

Air France (AF)
tel. 02/3788-0456 or 032/744-4900

Air Kazakhstan (9Y)
tel. 02/756-3700

Alitalia Airlines (AZ)
tel. 02/560-7001

All Nippon Airways (NH)
tel. 02/752-5500 or 032/744-3200

American Airlines (AA)
tel. 02/734-8820

Asiana Airlines (OZ)
tel. (toll free) 1588-8000 or 032/744-2626

Cathay Pacific Airways (CX)
tel. 02/311-2800 or 032/744-6777

China Eastern Airlines (MU)
tel. 02/518-0330 or 032/744-3780

China Hainan Airlines (HU)
tel. 02/779-0600

China Northern Airlines (CJ)
tel. 02/775-9070 or 032/744-3455

China Northwest Airlines (WH)
tel. 02/775-6699 or 032/744-6900

China Southern Airlines (CZ)
tel. 02/3455-1600 or 032/744-3270

China Southwest Airlines (SZ)
tel. 02/310-9988

China Yunnan Airlines (3Q)
tel. 02/777-7776

Delavia Far East Airways (HB)
tel. 02/777-2900

Delta Air Lines (DL)
tel. 02/754-1921

Garuda Indonesia Airways (GA)
tel. 02/773-2092 or 032/744-1990

Japan Air System (JD)

Japan Airlines (JL)
tel. 02/757-1711 or 032/744-3600

KLM Royal Dutch Airlines (KL)
tel. 02/733-7878 or 032/744-6700

Korean Air (KE)
tel. (toll free) 1588-2001 or 032/742-5175

Krasnoyarsk Airlines (7B)
tel. 02/777-6399

Lufthansa German Airlines (LH)
tel. 02/3420-0400 or 032/744-3411

Malaysia Airlines (MH)
tel. 02/777-7761 or 032/744-3500

Mongolian Airlines (OM)
tel. 02/756-9761 or 032/744-6800

Northwest Airlines (NW)
tel. 02/732-1700 or 032/744-6300

Philippines Airlines (PR)
tel. 02/774-3581 or 032/744-3720

Pulkovo Airlines (FV)
tel. 02/756-5050

Qantas Airways (QF)
tel. 02/777-6871/3, 032/744-3283

Sakalinsk Airlines (HZ)
tel. 02/753-7131

Siberia Airlines (S7)
tel. 02/501-6727

Singapore Airlines (SQ)
tel. 02/755-1226 or 032/744-6777

Thai Airways (TG)
tel. 02/3707-0011 or 032/744-3571

Turkish Airlines (TK)
tel. 02/777-7055 or 032/744-3737

United Airlines (UA)
tel. 02/757-1691 or 032/744-6666

Uzbekistan Airways (HY)
tel. 02/754-1041 or 032/744-3700

Vietnam Airlines (VN)
tel. 02/775-7666 or 032/744-6565

Vladavostok Airlines (XF)
tel. 02/733-2920

ON THE ROAD

27 countries and regions, including Japan, China, Mongolia, Russia, Southeast Asia, Oceania, North and South America, the Middle East, and Europe. Most flights leave from Incheon International Airport, a fair number fly from Busan to Japan, and a handful each use the airports at Jeju and Daegu.

AIR: DOMESTIC

Asiana Airlines and Korean Air both have extensive domestic networks, frequent departures, and reasonable fares. Fares are government-regulated, so both airlines charge the same rates. All standard fares are discounted about 6 percent for weekday travel, 10 percent for bona fide students, and 50 percent for children ages 2 to 13. With Seoul Gimpo Airport as the hub, direct flights go to 11 cities; from the southern city of Jeju, planes fly direct to 12 cities. In addition, there are direct flights between Busan and

Yangyang, and periodically flights will also be scheduled between other points like Busan and Wonju or Seoul and Yecheon. In order to facilitate better connections down-country for those flying in from abroad, a small number of domestic flights to Busan and Jeju City leave from Incheon International Airport.

For domestic flight information, reservations, and ticketing, contact the Asiana central reservations office (tel. 02/1588-8000) or the KAL central reservations office (tel. 02/1588-2001), either airlines' ticket offices throughout the country, or any domestic travel agent. Each airline has offices in the cities that it services, plus sales offices in other major cities. Both airlines issue monthly domestic and international timetables printed in both Korean and English that show routings and times of departure. Tickets are good for three months. All in-country flights are non-smoking, and because they are relatively short, serve only refreshments and snacks. Check-in starts about 60 minutes prior to scheduled departure. A travel card must be completed (available at the ticket counter). Your passport number must be recorded, and you may be asked to show your passport. An airport-use fee of ₩4,000 is levied on all domestic passengers, payable at the ticket counter when checking in if not included in the cost of your ticket. Upon boarding, you must show your ticket and completed travel card, and pass through at least one inspection point with X-ray for carry-on luggage and body search by metal detector. Except at the largest terminals, boarding entails a short walk from the terminal to the plane. There is a 15-kg free baggage limit; beyond that, an excess-baggage charge may be levied (₩330–1020 per kg, depending upon the destination). Limited carry-on luggage is permitted if it fits into the storage compartment above or under your seat. Keep your baggage-claim slip to retrieve your luggage. Both airlines have efficient service, and planes are fairly punctual.

All airports are connected by convenient airport- or city-bus routes to downtown areas. Taxis are also available, and some hotels offer free shuttle service for their guests, with prior arrangements.

DOMESTIC AIR ROUTES

Yangyang
Gimpo
Incheon
Han River
Wonju
Cheongju
Yecheon
Gunsan
Pohang
Daegu
Ulsan
Gwangju
Jinju
Busan
Mokpo
Yeosu
Jeju
Jeju-Do

0   50 mi
0   50 km

© AVALON TRAVEL PUBLISHING, INC.

DOMESTIC FLIGHTS

A lthough there are periodic changes to the schedules, the following gives a fairly good overview of domestic flights, incorporating both airlines' schedules.

The **Seoul-Busan** shuttle service (50 daily, 60 minutes) departs Seoul 0650–2020 and leaves from Busan 0700–2100.

Flights from Seoul

Destination	Frequency	Duration	Fare
Yangyang/Sokcho	5 daily	50 minutes	₩53,500
Daegu	19 daily	50 minutes	₩56,500
Pohang	12 daily	50 minutes	₩61,000
Ulsan	17 daily	60 minutes	₩64,400
Jinju/Sacheon	8 daily	60 minutes	₩68,400
Yeosu/Suncheon	11 daily	60 minutes	₩65,900
Mokpo	4 daily	60 minutes	₩62,000
Gwangju	13 daily	55 minutes	₩57,000
Jeju	55 daily	65 minutes	₩76,900

Flights from Jeju City

Destination	Frequency	Duration	Fare
Pohang	1 daily	60 minutes	₩68,900
Ulsan	1 daily	50 minutes	₩63,900
Daegu	8 daily	60 minutes	₩65,400
Yecheon/Andong	1 daily	65 minutes	₩66,400
Busan	18 daily	55 minutes	₩59,000
Jinju	1 daily	45 minutes	₩58,000
Yeosu	1 daily	40 minutes	₩53,000
Mokpo	1 daily	35 minutes	₩46,000
Gwangju	6 daily	45 minutes	₩52,000
Gunsan	2 daily	50 minutes	₩57,000
Cheongju	6 daily	60 minutes	₩67,400
Gimpo, Incheon	3 daily	65 minutes	₩76,900

Flights from Busan

Destination	Frequency	Duration	Fare
Jeju, Yangyang	2 daily	50 minutes	₩64,500
Wonju	when available	40 minutes	₩63,400
Gimpo, Incheon	2 daily	60 minutes	₩65,000

ON THE ROAD

FERRIES: INTERNATIONAL

Seaports for international ferry connections are Incheon, the closest seaport to Seoul; Busan, the country's second-largest city and principle port; Sokcho; Mokpo; and Gunsan. Occasionally, merchant marines, cruise-ship passengers, and steamship passengers land at these and other Korean ports.

From Incheon, ferries run to the Chinese port cities of Weihai, Yantai, and Qingdao on the Shandong Peninsula; to Tianjin, the port city for Beijing; to Shanghai in the south; and to Dalien and Dandong on the Liaodong Peninsula of Manchuria. Other connections may be forthcoming. These ferries leave from two separate terminals in Incheon but may eventually all depart from the new international ferry terminal on the outer harbor. **From Busan,** overnight ferries run to Shimonoseki and Hakata (Fukuoka), Japan, and to Yantai in China. Faster hydrofoil ferries to Hakata and Tsushima in Japan go and return in one day. All leave from the one international ferry terminal near the center of the city.

From Seoul and many other cities, it's possible to get to the Incheon international ferry terminals, purchase your ticket, and go through immigration and customs before departure time. From more distant cities, it would be best to travel to Incheon or Seoul the night before departure. It's also possible to travel to Busan from Seoul or most other major cities, make it to the pier, and purchase a ticket before boarding times for the overnight ferries. Start early! If you're leaving the country for Shimonoseki or Hakata and plan to reenter Korea with another tourist visa, it's possible on weekdays to return with the same overnight ferry. With multiple-entry visas, you can travel to Hakata or Tsushima and return the same day. For those traveling to Japan to apply for another tourist visa, the issuance of Korean tourist visas in Japan generally takes only a few hours; other types of visas usually require more than 24 hours to process, sometimes up to several weeks. While it is farther to travel and more expensive, Korean visas are also issued in Beijing, Qingdao, and Shanghai.

From other ports: Ferries to Zarubino near Vladivostok run from Sokcho. People often use the route from there, through Hunchun and Yanji, to get to the Chinese side of Baekdu-san, the Korean Peninsula's highest peak. From Mokpo, a ferry runs to Lianyungang, China, on the coast between Shanghai and Qingdao. The connection from Gunsan doesn't seem to be consistent yet, but there is a terminal and ferries may run to port cities serviced by the ferries that connect to Busan and Incheon.

Although tickets are available on the day of departure, it is best to make reservations and purchase tickets a few days in advance. Tickets are available at the ferry terminal ticket windows and through travel agents in large cities who handle international travel. Tickets will be issued only after you fill out the appropriate forms, present a valid passport and visa (if one is required of you), and pay your fare. Passengers should go through check-in at least 30 minutes prior to scheduled departure. A ₩1,100 harbor tax is levied on all departing ferry passengers. You must proceed through Immigration and Customs before boarding the ship, and you must already have a valid visa. Visas can be obtained from the Chinese, Japanese, and Russian embassies in Seoul, or from the Japanese, Chinese, or Russian consulates in Busan. For the Chinese visa, allow four working days to process the application, and several days for the Russian visa. If one is necessary, Japanese visas are usually available in the afternoon if the application is made in the morning. City-sponsored tourist information offices are located inside the international ferry terminal buildings, but they are usually open only when ferries arrive. Duty-free shops are located inside the bonded area of the terminal buildings. Foreign currency exchange counters are available for reconverting *won* to other denominations, or for buying *won* on entry into Korea. For additional information, see the Transportation sections of the travel chapters.

For those who suffer from seasickness, various over-the-counter brands of motion-sickness medicine are available. Usually little patches worn on the skin below and behind the ear, they are called *meolmiyak* in Korean.

FERRIES: DOMESTIC

A wide-ranging ferry network, stemming from 11 major ports and more than a dozen smaller ones, services Korea's hundreds of inhabited islands. Two inland ferries operate on Soyang Lake from Chuncheon to Inje, and on Chungju Lake from Chungju to Shin Danyang. By far the greatest number of ferries, however, are coastal. From Incheon, ferries go to the islands in the West Sea, in the northwest corner of the country. The ports of Daecheon and Gunsan serve the small islands directly to their west. Ferries from Mokpo run to all islands off Korea's southwestern corner, and to Jeju-do. From Wan-do, ferries ply the islands at the western end of the south coast and Jeju-do. From Yeosu and Tongyeong they serve the islands in the middle section of the south coast and Jeju-do. Masan has ferries to Geoje-do. From Busan they run to the islands off the eastern end of the south coast and to Jeju-do. Ferries from Pohang run only to Ulleung-do, as do those from Mukho and Sokcho, farther up the coast. The most popular and useful tourist routes for most travelers are the two lake ferries and those to Ulleung-do, Jeju-do, and Hong-do.

The three basic types of ferry are vehicular, passenger, and high-speed hydrofoil or catamaran. The largest, vehicular ferries, are capable of carrying vehicles, cargo, and several hundred passengers; they mainly serve the Jeju-do routes from Mokpo, Wan-do, Yeosu, and Busan. Passenger ferries vary greatly in size and speed, serve most of the inner islands, and are still mostly ordinary, round-bottomed ships. Of growing numbers are the hydrofoils, airfoils, and catamarans, and these now serve frequented routes to major tourist destinations like Baengnyeong-do, Hong-do, and Ulleung-do, plus the commuter route from Busan to the Geoje ports. Only sleek passenger ferries run on the inland lakes, and they are a good alternative to the bus, albeit a bit more expensive. Generally, small short-distance ferries have only one class and charge only by distance. A few have split pricing—lower fares for island residents and regular fares for visitors (Koreans or foreigners). Most long-distance ferries have third, second, and first classes—some also have second-class beds, first-class beds, or special rooms—and these charge by class *and* distance. Some of the fast catamarans assign seats, but the seat number is only important when the ship is full. Otherwise, you can sit anywhere you find a seat to your liking. In addition, although these large, enclosed ships are fast, passengers are not allowed outside for the sea breezes or photography. You have to be content to view the passing scene through water-splashed windows.

Fares vary greatly. For comparison, the fares from Busan to Jeju-do—one of the longest routes in the country—are: third-class ₩24,200, second-class ₩30,000, second-class bed ₩40,000, first-class bed ₩125,000–150,000, and special-class ₩180,000–220,000. On the other hand, the fare from Tongyeong to Jeseungdang is ₩3,500. More typical fares are ₩15,300 for the Busan to Okpo route, ₩49,000 from Pohang to Ulleung-do, and ₩28,100 from Mokpo to Hong-do. Generally, reservations are needed only on holidays. However, some of the heavily traveled routes can get very busy during the summer and autumn tourist seasons. When buying a ticket, you may need to fill out a travel card and present it (sometimes your passport is also requested) upon boarding.

© ROBERT NILSEN

ferry docked at Do-dong harbor on Ulleung-do

TRAINS

The most comfortable means of overland transportation in Korea is the train. In the late 1890s, concessions were given to the U.S. and France to build rail lines from Seoul to Incheon and Uiju (North Korea). In 1905, the Seoul-Busan line was opened, and just after the Russo-Japanese War of that year the Busan-Manchuria line was completed. From then until the Korean War, it was possible to train from Busan to Paris. Under Japanese colonization, rail lines were developed to major cities and mining areas. Much of this network was destroyed during the Korean War, but partially reconstructed during the 1950s and '60s. After the war, all lines that connected the northern and southern halves of the peninsula were severed and it was only after 2000 that effort was put into reconnecting two lines between the two countries: one, the line running north from Seoul to Pyeongyang and on to Shin Uiju, and two, the line up the eastern coast of the peninsula. With greater emphasis upon highway construction during the 1970s and early '80s, rail expansion slowed, but since the 1990s there has been another big push to upgrade and put in a high-speed line between Seoul and Busan. According to projections, the high-speed link between Seoul and Daejeon is due to open in 2003 with the entire line running in 2004. Today, the commercial rail network of some 3,100 kilometers (over 550 stations) connects all major cities on the peninsula. There is no train service on Jeju-do or any other island.

Three **classes** (ho) of train service this system. Although colors vary somewhat, they are generally as follows. The highest class is the *Saemaul-ho* ("New Village"). Blue or green and silver, with wide picture windows, these sleek air-conditioned luxury trains make limited stops on their routes. Each has a dining car, as well as two-person and family compartments. The orange *Mugunghwa-ho* ("Rose of Sharon") are air-conditioned limited-express trains. Most have dining and first-class cars, and some of the night trains have sleeping compartments. Both the *Saemaul-ho* and *Mugunghwa-ho* have individual reclining seats. *Tongil-ho* ("Unification") trains are the

green limited-express trains with fans. All seats can rotate so you may face to the front or rear; first-class cars have individual reclining seats. Some sleeper cars are available. For most purposes, the *Mugunghwa-ho* trains are the best for all-around travel. Reasonably priced and most frequent, they reach all major stations. For a luxury ride, at a higher price, use the *Saemaul-ho*. The longest train rides, from Seoul to Jinju and Seoul to Busan, via Yeongju, are just under 500 kilometers.

South Korea has 10 major rail lines and a handful of connecting and feeder lines. The busiest is the Gyeongbu line, which connects Seoul to Busan through the center of the country. On it, running the full length, run about five dozen trains a day. All other lines have less traffic. All three classes of train run on a majority of lines. Some of the shorter lines only run commuter-style *Tongil-ho* trains that stop at every station. The most numerous trains are the *Mugunghwa-ho*. Extra trains run on some lines on weekends and over major national holidays. Aside from the regular schedule of one-way routes, the railroad offers special package tours at certain times of the year—such as tours of mountain snow, autumn colors, and cultural highlights—and these may be purchased directly at a train station or through specified travel agents like Aju Tours (tel. 02/786-0028), www.ajutours.co.kr.

Fares are set according to class and distance. Sample fares for the three classes from Seoul to Daejeon are ₩10,900, ₩7,900, and ₩4,900; to Dong Daegu ₩21,400, ₩15,500, and ₩9,400; and to Busan ₩29,100, ₩21,000, and ₩12,800. Tickets are sold at each station, at Korean Travel Bureau offices, and at select travel agencies in major cities. Only reserved seats are sold for *Saemaul-ho* trains. Reserved seats are also sold for *Mugunghwa-ho* trains, but less expensive tickets for standing room, called *ipsok*, are also sold for this class. A seat in the first-class car on trains requires an extra charge depending on distance. These are, respectively, for each class: ₩4,000, ₩3,100, and ₩2,000 for up to 200 kilometers; ₩5,900, ₩4,700 and ₩3,500 for up to 400 kilometers; and ₩8,100, ₩5,900 and ₩4,600 for over 400 kilometers. Sleeper-car surcharges are ₩16,600 and ₩22,600 for the upper and lower beds, respectively, on the *Tongil-ho* trains; and ₩26,500 and ₩35,800 for the *Mugunghwa-ho*. Reservations are usually not necessary for most trains, but they are taken up to three days prior to departure. On the heavily traveled Seoul-Busan line, however, reservations are recommended; on national holidays, days preceding holidays, and weekends during the summer and autumn tourist season, they are absolutely necessary. Avoid traveling during those times if you can, although additional trains are put into service to handle the increased volume. Additional ticket windows are also set up at major stations around the country at these times. Round-trip reserved-seat tickets for weekdays are sold at a 10 percent discount; there is no discount on weekends. The origin and destination of travel; month, day, and time of departure; coach and seat numbers; class of train and seat; and fare all appear on each ticket. Usually, a few key words are printed in English for non-Korean readers. Tickets are punched upon departure and collected at your destination. Some travel agencies in major cities now also sell train tickets, but usually these do not advertise in non-Korean languages. Reservation and ticket purchase can also be done on the Internet.

Similar to rail passes in other countries and areas, Korea has a **Korail Pass** that is good for unlimited travel within a specified time frame. These passes are for use by foreigners only and available for purchase using foreign currency at designated ticket agents outside Korea in various countries. It is actually a voucher that must be exchanged in Korea at major train stations and other specified locations within 60 days of purchase and then used within 30 days of exchange. Normal, Youth, and Group passes are available, and for each category there are 3-day, 5-day, 7-day, and 10-day options. The normal pass is for either an adult or child ages 6–12; youth passes are for students ages 13–25 with a valid international student identification; group passes are for 2–5 adults traveling together. Pricing is as follows for adult, child, youth, and group, respectively: 3-day passes are US$47, US$24, US$38, US$43; 5-day are: US$70, US$35, US$56, US$63; 7-day are: US$89, US$45, US$71, US$80; 10-day are:

US$102, US$51, US$82, US$92. Persons with Korail Passes can also take advantage of associated discounts at participating hotels, tourist sites, and other transportation vendors. In addition, co-op passes to be used within Korea and Japan and within Korea and China are also available and could be pertinent for those traveling in two countries within a short length of time. For additional information and details, see www. korail.go.kr.

Most **stations** have numbered ticket windows with destinations (or rail lines, or class of train) written over them (also in English at larger stations). Major stations also have information and advance ticket sales windows, and a few have windows specifically for foreigners' use. Schedules and fares appear on large boards above the ticket windows at each station. Mostly labeled in Korean, some stops are also listed in English. At large stations, digital signboards are placed over each door, and, when lit, indicate the destination, class, time of departure, and platform number of the train then boarding. In smaller stations, these signboards are absent, but there are few enough trains that there should be no mistake as to which is boarding and on what platform. To be sure, ask. Many stations will announce departing trains in Korean and major stations will also make announcements in English. On board, upcoming station announcements are done in Korean on *Tongil-ho* trains and in Korean, English, Japanese, and Chinese on *Mugunghwa-ho* and *Saemaul-ho* trains.

All trains have several non-smoking cars which are usually placed at the front of the train. First-class and special cars are generally placed at the front or rear of each train. Each train has a snack cart that moves from one end of the train to the other. Typical items include hard-boiled eggs, milk, custard bread, fruit, candies, dried squid, soft drinks, and beer. Many trains also have someone selling coffee, boxed lunches, and magazines. Meals, beer, and finger food are available in the dining cars, on trains that have them. Noodle stands are located on the platforms at major stations. Trains stop for only a few minutes, so you must rush to the stand and gulp your noodles while paying attention so that the train doesn't pull out without you. Each station is marked by several large white signs on the platforms. These show the station name in *han'geul*, below which it is written in Chinese characters and in English. The next stations up and down the line are printed at the bottom.

SUBWAYS

Seoul, Busan, Daegu, and Incheon have operational subway systems; lines in Gwangju and Daejeon are under construction. Clean, efficient, punctual, and inexpensive, the subway is often preferable to city buses. At nearly 460 kilometers, the eight-line Seoul subway is one of the most extensive in the world. Running underground through the city's center, it rises aboveground in the suburbs and runs out to several surrounding cities. The shorter and newer three-line Busan subway system, which winds through that city's dense population districts, is almost completely underground. It and the Daegu and Incheon subways continue to expand beyond the presently operational number of lines.

These systems are fully automated. Tickets are dispensed from machines, although clerks also sell them at windows. Insert your ticket at the turnstile, then take it back as you walk through; you must insert it into another turnstile to exit at your destination. Subway cars are usually not crowded, except during rush-hour times when you may have to squeeze on and off and stand sardine-like with the rest of the crowd. Seats at the ends of each car are reserved for the elderly and handicapped. If they're not taken, anyone may use them. Subway lines are color-coded for easy recognition and transfers, and signs are written in Korean, English, and (usually) Chinese. Destinations are also written in Korean and English on the front and rear of each train, and on the side of all cars. Each subway station posts a map of the entire system with fares, the individual line, as well as maps of the station and neighborhood. Each car also displays maps of the subway line it serves and subways system-wide. Printed information about the subway system is available in each respective city, and for an online explanation of routes, fares, and other details on how the subway systems work, log onto www .seoulsubway.co.kr. Aside from the routes, details are similar for all the subway systems in the country. See the Transportation sections of the travel chapters for more specific details.

BUSES
Express Buses

Express *(gosok)* buses run to over 70 cities throughout the peninsula. More destinations will be added as new sections of the expressway system are completed. Half the bus routes run to and from Seoul, while the others connect provincial cities. For cities connected by rail and expressway, express bus fares are usually a bit more than *Tongil-ho* train fares and less than fares for the *Mugunghwa-ho* trains. Length of travel is nearly the same duration, but buses run more frequently. The shortest and cheapest route is from Seoul to Yongin (₩1,800; 50 minutes); the longest and most expensive is from Seoul to Nok-dong on the Goheung Peninsula (₩18,200; six hours). There are a dozen bus companies that service this system, but fares are regulated and all charge the same for the same routes. The most frequent run every 5–10 minutes from about 0600 into the mid-evening. The majority leave at least once an hour, and only a handful run at intervals of two hours or more. Slightly less frequent, but also interspersed throughout the day, are *udeung gosok* (superior-class) buses. Carrying fewer passengers in more comfortable seats, these buses charge roughly 50 percent more. Special *shimya* or *yagan* (superior-or-class night) buses also run between Seoul and most of the provincial destinations and between large provincial cities. Most destinations have only one a night, while others have up to 13. Buses leave from mid-evening to about midnight. No reservations are needed or taken, except on holidays, when they are absolutely necessary. Seats are assigned, but if there are empty seats you may switch. Destinations and fares are posted on or above express-bus terminal ticket windows; a departure schedule usually hangs over the booth. Destinations are also shown on buses, but these are mostly only printed in Korean. For specific details, see the individual travel chapters.

Express buses are direct, fast, comfortable, affordable, and punctual. These air-conditioned coaches have reclining assigned seats with space enough for all but the lankiest Westerners, reading lights, undercarriage storage compartments, and inside overhead storage racks. If your luggage can't fit on the overhead rack inside, you may have to ask for the undercarriage storage compartments to be opened. Every two to three hours, long-distance buses take a fifteen- to twenty-minute break at a rest stop. Remember the bus's license number so you get back on the right one! Each stop has restaurants, fast-food stands, a few shops, and bathrooms.

Intercity Buses

The highway system lies like a spider web over the country. The vast majority of these roads are paved, yet short stretches of the most rural may still be gravel. At some military checkpoints—particularly around Seoul and in the north near the border—buses are occasionally stopped and riders checked for identification; foreigners are almost never bothered. The MPs are looking for spies, military deserters, criminals, and contraband.

Intercity buses run between most cities and towns within a province, and to nearby towns in neighboring provinces. Some long-distance buses travel entirely through neighboring provinces. A few follow expressway routes, and others traverse back-country roads to rural mountain villages. All have comfortable padded seats, some that recline, and there is usually undercarriage storage. Ordinary intercity buses (known as *jikhaeng* buses) cover most of this system. Each has a scheduled departure, makes regularly scheduled stops, and is supposed to carry no more passengers than the number of seats on the bus. Some intercity buses, called *jiktong* or *mujongcha*, drive straight through to their destinations, or make only a few stops. *Gosok jikhaeng* intercity buses use the expressway for part or all of the route. Others, called *wanhaeng*, stop anywhere to let off or pick up passengers. None of these buses have assigned seats, and reservations are never taken.

Fares are based upon distance—generally about ₩60 per kilometer—route, and the length

of travel. *Wanhaeng* buses generally have lower fares, *jiktong* buses slightly higher. Although faster and more comfortable, *gosok jikhaeng* buses may be less expensive than ordinary intercity buses with the same destination because of route and number of stops. Some *wanhaeng* routes are slowly being taken over by expanding city-bus lines. In most cities and towns, the express- and intercity-bus terminals are separate, but close together. Sometimes they are combined, and may even service city buses. Routes from each station can be quite complex. While departure schedules and fares are posted, they are only in Korean. Few stations have English-speaking clerks.

City Buses

All cities and provincial towns have city bus systems with routes that often extend into the countryside. City buses are called *shinae beosu;* for those areas that have no cities, county buses, called *gunnae beosu,* serve the same purpose. The basic fare varies slightly throughout the country from ₩600–700 for any distance, increasing by increment beyond the city or town limits. All buses accept coins; some cities also use tokens (paper or metal), for which there is a slight discount in fare. Where they are used, tokens are sold at sidewalk kiosks and streetside shops near bus stops. Enter the bus by the front door and put the token or coins into the fare hopper next to the driver; exit via the back door. On routes into the country, the driver will collect the fare, determined by distance. City buses can be crowded, especially during rush hours. Expect to stand. If someone offers you a seat, take it and offer to hold that person's bags. Offer your seat to the elderly, the physically handicapped, and to women with babies. Especially in large cities, some bus drivers drive like wild men, switching lanes or hitting the brakes without a moment's notice. Hold on tight!

Express city buses, or *jwasok beosu,* are usually more civilized. They make limited stops on selected routes, and travel more swiftly through the city traffic; everyone is supposed to have a seat, and usually does, except during the peak of rush hour. Although these buses vary somewhat, they usually have only one front door for entrance and exit. The basic fare is ₩1,300 –1,200, depending upon the city—no tokens. Pay the driver as you enter. The largest cities also have commuter buses that connect the city center to surrounding satellite cities. These buses make few or no stops and fares are usually a bit more than for the express city buses. In addition, some cities with airports have special airport buses that run to and from the airport terminal and city center on established routes, making limited stops; fares are posted.

Bus routes can be mind-boggling. This is especially true in the largest cities. Periodically, these large cities will publish bus-route brochures that list all routes and their stops—unfortunately, no maps—and they are only written in Korean. Good practice!

RENTAL CARS

Self-drive and chauffeur-driven rental cars can be hired in major cities and tourist areas. Rates vary with the type of car, duration of rental, and season, and include vehicle hire, maintenance, insurance, and a 10 percent tax. There is no mileage limit. All companies charge roughly the same rates for same-size vehicles. There are several dozen rental-car companies in the country, but only a handful have agencies in several major cities. Car rental can be arranged at airports, at major hotels, or at company offices throughout the country. Consider renting a car from home before you arrive in Korea. Many of the worldwide rental agencies have agreements with major Korean firms that result in substantial savings. Several of the larger and more reputable companies are Kumho Rent A Car (Hertz) (tel. 02/ 797-8000 or 800/654-3011 worldwide), www .hertzkorea.co.kr, www.hertz.com; Sambo Rent-a-Car (National) (tel. 02/591-5711 or 800/227-7368 worldwide), www.nationalcar.com; VIP Rent A Car (Avis) (tel. 02/862-2847), www.avis .co.kr, www.avis.com; Seoul Rent-a-Car (tel. 02/ 472-0011), or Korea Express (tel. 02/715-0010).

Rates

Charges for a 24-hour day run roughly ₩60,000 –75,000 for compacts, ₩80,000–95,000 for medium-size vehicles, ₩127,000–150,000 for full-size sedans, ₩192,000–295,000 for luxury sedans, ₩92,000–128,000 for 4WD sport utility vehicles, and ₩90,000–142,000 for various size passenger vans. Six-, 10-, and 12-hour rates are also usually available, but they are proportionally more expensive per hour; rates go down substantially when you rent for multiple days and are discounted the most for rentals of a week or longer. Chauffeur-driven cars are substantially more expensive, and may be rented by the hour, day, or week. Sample charges are: ₩162,000 for 10 hours for a medium-size sedan and ₩325,000 for 10 hours for a luxury sedan. Payment is by credit card or advance deposit. The renter is also responsible for all parking fees, expressway tolls, gas, traffic tickets, and room and board for the chauffeur. With chauffeur-driven vehicles, there is a distance parameter beyond which an extra fee is levied for each extra kilometer. Gas tanks must be refilled when the car is returned. Fuel runs about ₩1,300 per liter.

Driving Tips

Any foreign driver must be at least 21 and have a valid passport and a valid local or international driver's license. Think before hiring a rental car. Although small-town and country traffic is not bad, driving in the cities can be a hair-raising experience. Big city traffic can be *very* congested; streets are often narrow and there is usually no sidewalk when you get off major thoroughfares. While expressways and highways are well-engineered, smaller roads are often narrow and with little or no shoulder. Korean drivers are not known for their skill, politeness, or timidity, and many Korean drivers drive too fast for the conditions or quickly change lanes without notice. Although it is not true of all drivers, you will see some cutting corners on curves, passing on curves going uphill, passing on the right, or passing on solid yellow lines. Although it's a generalization, it can be said that Korean drivers are aggressive and opportunistic—particularly bus and taxi drivers, others less so. A car that has its nose ahead goes first. Bigger vehicles usually take the right-of-way. Korean drivers are not particularly sophisticated and will play loose with driving rules and regulations. Watch out for speed bumps. Motorcycles have great leeway and seem to flaunt traffic rules, they dart in and out of traffic, drive on sidewalks, and even go the opposite direction of traffic flow. Keep your eyes open for them. Korea has the dubious distinction, supported by statistics, of having one of the world's worst traffic-accident records, and a high percentage of traffic fatalities. In fact, major cities have digital signboards set up on main boulevards that post daily death and injury figures as a deterrent (hopefully) to bad driving practices. Be forewarned, and be careful.

After a dramatic increase in the late 1970s, and continued growth into the 2000s, there are now about 13 million private passenger cars crowding the streets of Korea. The vast majority are Korean-made, but more and more imports are also taking to the road. While most are practical family sedans, there are a growing number of luxury vehicles, sports utility vehicles, and vans. As in the United States, unlike Japan, Koreans drive on the right side of the road. Unless otherwise marked, the **speed limit** is 100 kilometers per hour on expressways, 80 kilometers per hour on major highways, and 60 kilometers per hour on smaller roads. Highways and expressways are well signed so finding the way is generally not a problem. Major **traffic signs** indicating direction and distance are posted in Korean and English (and sometimes Chinese), and numbers are shown in Arabic numerals. Distance and speed are metric. Signs without writing are most often easily understandable and make common sense; they're designed to communicate. However, you'll probably have to put some time and effort into recognizing them so that it becomes second nature. Directional signs are rectangular. Speed limit signs are round with black numbers on a white background surrounded by a red outline. Most instructional signs are triangular. Where signs are not appropriate—usually in city centers—speed limits and other instructions are painted on the roadway. **Traffic lights** are of the red (stop), amber (caution), green (go) variety. If there is a fourth light, it is usually a left-turn arrow. Because of traffic conditions, most left turns are made only with this signal; without

the left-turn signal, make your turn when traffic allows. Be very cautious with traffic lights as there is usually little time given between the changing of lights and drivers are very eager to go. Be mindful of pedestrian crosswalk signals and yield to pedestrians when those crosswalk lights are green. Emergency telephones are placed every few kilometers along expressways for drivers in need of help. Locate these by the tall poles with photovoltaic cells on the top and a yellow box attached to the side with a telephone symbol and SOS letters printed on it.

Tolls are only charged on certain sections of the expressway. When you enter the expressway, you must take a ticket. This ticket must be given to the booth attendant as you exit at your destination. Your fare will be calculated electronically and shown on a digital display near the front of the car. Although they rise periodically, sample tolls for passenger cars from Seoul are: Busan ₩15,500, Gyeongju ₩13,200, Daejeon ₩6,300, Osan ₩1,900, and Suwon ₩1,300.

Parking is another concern. As Korean cities were not laid out for automobiles, inner city parking is at a premium. There are few parking spots along roads and fewer yet that are free. These parking spaces are indicated by a blue sign with the letter "P" on it. Otherwise, expect a pay parking lot or garage. Hotels usually offer free parking in a parking structure or underground garage. Most older *yeogwan* and other accommodations in city centers do not have any parking; newer accommodations often do. Once you get out and about you usually do find parking and most often it's free. Outside city centers and in the country, parking is less of a problem, but most tourist sites, parks, and other attractions also charge a fee to park.

Road System

Korea has over 90,000 kilometers of roads, about three-quarters of which are paved. Of these, the **expressway** *(gosok doro)* network (100 percent paved) is more than 2,000 kilometers long and extends to most corners of the country. The continued construction of expressways will open up new areas of the country to faster transportation. Mostly four lanes wide, some expressway sections have six lanes. In 1968, the Seoul-Incheon Expressway was completed as the first modern, high-volume motorway in the country. The completion of the Gyeongbu (Seoul-Busan) Expressway in 1970, however, was the first big stage in the nationwide expressway system. Major sections were completed in the 1970s. In the mid-1980s, the Jungbu Expressway was finished, and the mid-1990s saw another spate of construction, which continues unabated into the 2000s. Sections along the south coast are pretty, but the most spectacular is the Yeongdong Expressway, down the east side of the Taebaek Mountains from Daegwal-ryeong Pass to Gangneung. All

expressways and some national roads have rest stops at intervals along their routes. On the expressways, rest stops are identified by tall yellow signs with names in Korean and English. These rest stops have restaurants, snacks, and bathrooms, as well as gas stations and repair shops. Half a dozen level sections at various locations along this network have been widened and left without dividers. These are emergency airstrips, used during military exercises. Once or twice a year, traffic is detoured for a few hours to give the Korean Air Force time for training.

Aside from the expressways, there are **national highways** *(ilban gukdo)*, which are more ex-

ROLL ON KOREA: BIKE TRAVEL

If you're traveling with a bike in tow, Korea, surprisingly, has a lot to offer. In their race to develop, government planners originally looked down on bicycles as third-world transport, and the biggest vehicle has always had the right of way here. But with the drive to develop tourism and environmental awareness, bureaucrats have been heeding calls for a more bike-friendly course.

Bicycling in Seoul

The centerpiece is the 68-kilometer trail that loops Seoul's Han River. Cross-linked by some of the Han's many bridges, it is mostly flat and free of vehicles. Worn but sturdy, one-size-fits-all mountain bikes, tandems, and children's bikes can be rented at numerous parks along the river for ₩2,000–3,000 an hour with a picture ID. (Note: The sections running through parks are crowded, and pedestrians often step onto paths without looking. Give a shout or ring a bell if you see someone headed your way.)

Jeju (Cheju) Island

A scenic, well-maintained trail hugs Jeju's coastline. You can bring a bike over by ferry or rent one on the island. Bike rental companies will pick you up at the airport and get you fitted with a bike, maps, plastic bag and bungee cord to tie down your personal belongings within an hour of arrival.

Bomulseom (Treasure Island) Bike Rental (tel.

064/743-1407) has a variety of well-maintained 21-speed mountain bikes to choose from for ₩5,000–9,000 a day. The problem is they don't speak English; you need a Korean speaker to make reservations.

Give yourself at least four full days to circle the 41-kilometer by 73-kilometer oval island, with time to enjoy its beaches and lava tubes. You can't get lost, "just keep the ocean on your right." (Note: Locals sometimes spread crops out to dry on the trail's asphalt surface; kindly ride around the harvest. Remember, it was their taxes that built the trail, and they're the ones that will pick you up in a minute if you need help.)

Touring the Peninsula

PABLE, a non-profit group, is working with the government to lay out an extensive trail system, mostly along remote country roads that border rivers. Taking the train up into the mountains and heading back to Seoul offers some beautiful scenery far from the crowds, but don't expect to glide effortlessly downstream for three or four days. Before you can link up to the Han River trail system, you're going to have to fight at least one mean hill per day, some rough patches and a little traffic.

Still, despite having the reputation of being reckless, with the per-capita traffic deaths to back it up, Korean drivers, on country roads anyway, are just as courteous to bicyclists as those in the West.

tensive than the expressways and **provincial highways** (*jibang doro*), which in turn are more extensive than the national highways. Like the expressways, these too are virtually all paved. Running off these highways, connecting nearly every town and village in the country, is another network of paved and unpaved local roads. For weary drivers, rest stops also are located along these highways.

All expressways and national highways, as well as provincial and county highways, have been numbered for ease in finding one's way. Expressways are numbered as follows: Odd numbers run north-south and increase in size from west to east. All are two digit numbers that end in a "5" except for expressway no. 1, which runs diagonally from Seoul to Busan and was the first completed in the 1970s. Even numbers run east-west, increase in size from south to north, and end in a "0" or "2." Expressways with three digits are either circular routes around or feeder routes into major cities. For highways and other roads, the odd numbers run mostly north-south, while even numbers run east-west. Excellent street maps, usually printed only in Korean, are available at bookshops in atlas form. Tourist maps are good for general directions.

They seem to even give more leeway. If you need a lift up a steep hill or to the nearest town, stick out a thumb, and in a few minutes, a local "Bongo" driver will take pity on you.

You can carry a bike on board a train if it is in a bike bag, which bike shops usually offer for ₩25,000. Handlebars and wheels will likely have to come off (or be turned in), but built-in pockets hold them snugly. The bags fit easily behind the last seat in the car or in the space made when pairs of seats are turned to face each other. Intercity buses and domestic airlines also let passengers check bike bags as regular luggage.

PABLE has excellent maps that point out area attractions along the routes. Some are available in English, but it's good to carry Korean editions as well. Korean is Romanized in any number of ways, so even locals who speak English might not recognize the name of their own town. It's best to bring a guide to the national rail system so you can leapfrog from station to station if short on time or weak in the legs. PABLE can be contacted at tel. 2/2203-4225, fax 2/2203-4226, www.pable.or.kr. The staff in their office near the Olympic Park Station (Subway Line 5) speaks only a little English but is eager to hand out materials and advice.

Keep in mind that during the late-summer rainy season many of these roads and bridges are washed away, so check weather and road conditions before starting out.

The great thing about biking in Korea is that you don't need to carry a tent or food. Inexpensive *minbak, yeogwan,* and restaurants are always within riding distance if you don't mind eating with chopsticks and sleeping on a *yo.* (Note: Always set out with at least a liter of water. Refill empty bottles at restaurants. Temples are also ready sources for natural spring water.)

The Korea National Tourism Organization (KNTO) puts out a free English directory of low-cost, clean lodging with Western amenities, the *Budget Inns Guide.* Rooms run around ₩40,000 a night. Reservations are usually only needed on Saturday nights or holidays.

The budget inns guide, railroad guide, and bike rental information are all available at the KNTO's Tourist Information Center (TIC) in downtown Seoul, tel. 1330, fax 02/319-0086, www.knto.or.kr.

Hardcore Mountain Biking

Korea is 70 percent mountains, and expatriates and locals have been blazing hair-raising trails for some time. An Internet search under "Korea mountain biking" will bring up a load of information. These three provide some great free pictures, inspiration and safety advice for mountain biking and touring: www.geocities.com/mx44qj/korea06/; www.angelfire.com/ga/achamtb/; http://bora .dacom.co.kr/~boonstra/korea/cycle.htm.

©David Kendall

ON THE ROAD

TAXIS

There are two main types of taxis: ordinary and deluxe. All taxis are government-licensed and registered. Fares are the same, and are set by legislation. All taxis are metered. If a driver refuses to meter the ride, get another taxi. No tipping is necessary. Company taxi drivers must make a set amount each day for the company, and the rest is theirs. Individual owners make all their fares, but have to buy the vehicles and pay for gas, repairs, and insurance. It's no wonder that they hustle.

Ordinary taxis, or *ilban* taxis, are by far the most numerous. Mostly medium-size sedans, they are of various colors but all have taxi lights on their roofs. Generally, a blue light indicates a company car, a green light an owner-owned private vehicle. While it varies a little from city to city, the basic fare is ₩1,600 for the first two kilometers, and ₩100 for each additional 160 meters. In slow traffic, an additional ₩100 is charged for each 41 seconds. Fares increase by 20 percent between 2400 and 0400.

Deluxe taxis, or *mobeom* taxis, operate mostly in large cities. These are black with a gold strip down their sides and yellow taxi lights on top. In the gold strip is written "Deluxe Taxi." Larger, roomier, and more comfortable than the ordinary taxis, they are medium- or full-size cars. Fares start at ₩4,000 for the first 3 kilometers, and ₩200 for each 250 meters beyond that. A surcharge of ₩200 is also charged for each 50 seconds in slow traffic, but there is no increase in fare for nighttime rides. Deluxe taxis are equipped to give receipts and some also take credit cards. A call service is available. Some taxis in Seoul offer a free telephone translation service to help with communications and this is indicated by a sign on the vehicle's rear passenger door.

Taxi vans have begun to operate in some large cities. These vans can carry up to nine people and are used to best advantage with many people and/or lots of luggage. Rates and services are the same as for the deluxe taxis.

A third type, military (AAFES) taxis, are primarily for use by military personnel, though sometimes they will pick up other foreigners (pay in U.S. dollars only). These are black and operate under contract with the U.S. military for use in and around military bases.

Taxi stands have been set up in the downtown areas of large cities, but drivers will often pick up anywhere. Deluxe taxis sometimes have their own stands on major streets, as well as at hotels, bus terminals, and train stations. As a general rule, any taxi can be flagged down anywhere. A lit red sign in the front window indicates an available taxi.

While not as common as previously, *hapseung* (shared) taxi transport, in which drivers pick up additional passengers for an extra fare, is still practiced. In these cases, drivers slow down where people congregate to catch cabs and find someone going to roughly the same part of town as the first passenger. Each passenger will then pay part of the fare—less than the total, but more than half—so the driver ends up with a greater fare for the distance. Most riders don't mind—you can refuse if you want—but not all drivers will look for *hapseung* fares.

HITCHHIKING

By and large, hitchhiking is not worth it in Korea, except for the experience, since public transportation is relatively cheap, frequent, efficient, and far-reaching. Hitchhiking is possible, and there are no safety concerns to be especially conscious of—even for women—except to stand out of the lane of traffic. However, most Koreans still don't know exactly what hitchhiking is. Don't assume that they know what you're doing on the side of the road with your thumb out. Many will think that you are trying to get to a train or bus station, so don't be surprised if you're taken there. Hitching is best where you can stand along the highway on the outskirts of town, and out in the country on roads leading back into town.

Immigration and Customs 출입국

IMMIGRATION
Visas

All foreigners entering Korea must carry a valid passport or seaman's book issued in their names. Stateless persons, and those from countries that Korea does not recognize diplomatically, must obtain entry permits from a Korean embassy before coming to Korea or possess a *laissez-passer*, issued by the United Nations. Immigration laws were changed substantially in 1991 and to a lesser degree in 1995. As changes are made periodically, it's best to check with a Korean embassy or consulate to verify requirements for entry before departing for Korea. For additional information and current requirements, see www.moj.go.kr.

Most visitors with confirmed outbound tickets and sufficient funds may stay up to 30 days without visas. Exceptions are those from countries that have no diplomatic relations with South Korea, citizens of several former eastern-bloc countries, and citizens of countries that do not have such reciprocal arrangements. Entrance requirements are relaxed for citizens of specified countries if their visit is only to the island of Jeju-Do. All travelers who desire to stay more than 30 days must have visas issued by a Korean embassy or consulate before arrival in Korea, except for visitors from those countries with reciprocal visa exemptions, so long as they do not work; those countries follow. For citizens of Japan and the United States, visas are required for stays longer than 30 days. For all visitors planning to stay in Korea for longer than 90 days, a proper non-tourist visa must be obtained before entry into the country. To obtain a visa, you must present your passport, a completed application form, a recent passport-style photograph, the required fee (if applicable), and any other documentation that is required for the type of visa status that you are seeking.

Visa exemptions: 6 months—Canada; **3 months/90 days**—Antigua-Barbuda, Austria, Bahamas, Bangladesh, Barbados, Belgium, Bulgaria, Colombia, Costa Rica, Czech Republic, Denmark, Dominica, Dominican Republic, El Salvador, Finland, France, Germany, Greece, Grenada, Haiti, Hungary, Iceland, Ireland, Israel, Jamaica, Liberia, Liechtenstein, Luxembourg, Malaysia, Malta, Mexico, Morocco, Netherlands, New Zealand, Nicaragua, Norway, Pakistan, Peru, Poland, Romania, Singapore, Slovakia, Spain, St. Kitts-Nevis, St. Lucia, St. Vincent and the Grenadines, Surinam, Sweden, Switzerland, Thailand, Trinidad and Tobago, Turkey, and the United Kingdom; **60 days**—Italy, Lesotho, and Portugal.

Tourist visas are good for 90 days and may not be extended. It's illegal to work with this

SELECTED VISA STATUS

A-1: Diplomatic: valid as long as status is maintained.

A-2: Official duty of foreign government or international organization: valid as long as status is maintained.

A-3: Special agreements, including SOFA, not requiring residence registration: valid as long as status is maintained.

B-1: Visa waiver: according to diplomatic agreement.

B-2: Tourist/transit: according to diplomatic agreement.

C-1: Temporary correspondent: 90 days.

C-4: Short-term employment: 90 days.

D-2: Student: 2 years.

D-5: Resident correspondent: 2 years.

D-6: Religious worker: 2 years.

D-8: Business: 2 years.

E-1: University professor: 2 years.

E-2: Language teacher: 1 year.

E-3: Academic study and research: 2 years.

E-6: Professional artists, entertainers, and sportsmen: 6 months.

F-1: Korean national or foreigner living with family members or relatives: 2 years.

F-2: Married to Korean national: as long as status is maintained.

FOREIGN EMBASSIES AND CONSULATES

South Korea has full diplomatic relations with 184 countries, and maintains 143 oversees embassies and nearly four dozen consulates. There are 92 foreign embassies in Seoul, three consulate-generals in Busan, and one consulate-general in Jeju City. Some countries with diplomatic relations to Korea maintain an embassy in Tokyo or another Asian capital. Selected embassies are listed below. A list of addresses and telephone numbers for others can be found in KNTO literature or by asking at the KNTO tourist information center in Seoul.

Australia
11th Fl., Kyobo Bldg.
1-1, Jong-no 1-ga
Jongno-gu, Seoul
tel. 02/730-6490

Canada
10th Fl., Kolon Bldg.
45 Mugyo-dong
Jung-gu, Seoul
tel. 02/3455-6000

France
30, Hap-dong
Seodaemun-gu, Seoul
tel. 02/312-3272

Germany
308-5, Dongbinggo-dong
Yongsan-gu, Seoul
tel. 02/748-4114

Japan
18-11, Junghak-dong
Jongno-gu, Seoul
tel. 02/733-5626

Mongolia
33-5, Hannam-dong
Yongsan-gu, Seoul
tel. 02/794-1350

New Zealand
Rm. 1803, Kyobo Bldg.
1-1, Jongno 1-ga
Jongno-gu, Seoul
tel. 02/730-7794

People's Republic of China
83, Myeong-dong 2-ga
Jung-gu, Seoul
tel. 02/319-5101

Philippines
9th Fl., Diplomatic Center,
1376-1
Seocho 2-dong
Seocho, Seoul
tel. 02/577-6147

Russian Federation
1001-13, Daechi-dong
Gangnam-gu, Seoul
tel. 02/552-7096

Saudi Arabia
1-112, Shinmun-no 2-ga
Jongno-gu, Seoul
tel. 02/739-0631

Singapore
19th Fl., Samsung
Taepyeongno Bldg.
310, Taepyeongno 2-ga
Jung-gu, Seoul
tel. 02/774-2464

Thailand
653-7, Hannam-dong
Yongsan-gu, Seoul
tel. 02/795-3098

United Kingdom
4, Jeong-dong
Jung-gu, Seoul
tel. 02/735-7341

United States
82, Sejong-no
Jongno-gu, Seoul
tel. 02/397-4114

CONSULATE-GENERALS

Japan
1147-11, Choryang-dong
Dong-gu, Busan
tel. 051/465-5101

977-1, Nohyong-dong
Jeju City
tel. 064/42-9501

People's Republic of China
1418, U 2-dong
Haeundae-gu, Busan
tel. 051/743-7989

Russian Federation
8th Fl., Korea Exchange
Bank Bldg.
89-1 Jungang-dong 4-ga
Jung-gu, Busan
tel. 051/441-9904

visa status. **Entry visas** are necessary for periods longer than 90 days. There are several categories, with differing periods of validation. Most require a letter from the sponsoring institution (school, church, employer, etc.) including purpose of visit, length of stay, and proof of financial responsibility. Those with entry visas are required to apply for residence certificates at the nearest immigration office in Korea within 90 days of entry. Persons with entry visas who want to leave and return to Korea during their stays must apply for reentry permits at an immigration office. Their residence certificates must be surrendered upon exit from the country, but they can be picked up from the immigration office at the point of departure upon return. Visa extensions should be applied for at least one week before the expiration date. For visa extensions, changes of visa status, and additional information, contact the nearest immigration office.

The **Seoul Immigration Office** (tel. 02/650-6234) is located in the western part of the city at 319-2 Shinjeong 6-dong, Yangcheon-gu, and is open regular business hours. Conveniently, there is also an **in-town immigration office** (tel. 02/732-6215) on the 5th floor of the Jeokseon Building behind the Central Government Complex building near Gyeongbok-gung. The **Incheon International Airport immigration office** (tel. 032/740-7311) can also be approached for questions. For immigration questions in other areas of the country and for those residing outside the greater Seoul and southern Gyeonggi-Do area, the following offices may be of assistance:

Uijeongbu: tel. 031/876-5561, Seoyoung Building 7th Fl., 493-4 Uijeongbu 2-dong, near the Uijeongbu subway station.

Incheon: tel. 032/889-9904, 1-17 Hang-dong 7-ga, Jung-gu, near the port entrance.

Busan: tel. 061/461-3030, 17-26 Jungang-dong, Jung-gu, next to the International Passenger Ferry terminal.

Gimhae: tel. 051/972-1612, Gimhae International Airport.

Jeju: tel. 064/721-3494, 673-8 Geonip-dong, above the port to the west of Sara-bong.

Daegu: tel. 053/981-6854, 101-2 Geomsa-dong, in the eastern part of town near the Dongchon subway station.

Daejeon: tel. 042/254-8811, 16-8 Jungchon-dong, Jung-gu, northwest of downtown near the Sun Hospital.

Gwangju: tel. 062/381-0015, 366-1 Hwajeong 3-dong, Seo-gu, west of downtown.

Chuncheon: tel. 033/244-7351, 709-10 Hwanam Building 5th Fl. Hyoja 2-dong, near the Hyoja post office.

Jeonju: tel. 063/245-6161, San 27 Hoseong-dong 1-ga, Deokjin-gu, north of Jeongju Station.

Cheongju: tel. 043/262-0595, 77-2 Sugok 1-dong, Hongdeok-gu, near the Cheongju National University of Education.

Yeosu: tel. 061/665-2441, 332-3 Sujeong-dong, near Odong-do entrance.

Masan: tel. 055/222-9272, 2-6 Wolpo-dong, near the Dotseom ferry terminal.

Upon entry into South Korea, you must present your Arrival/Departure Card to immigration officials along with your passport. The immigration official will keep the Arrival Card. The Departure Card should be kept with your passport until you exit the country, when it will be collected by an immigration official.

Money and Shots

Up to US$10,000 may be brought into Korea without written declaration; greater amounts must be declared upon arrival. When exiting Korea, you may reconvert up to US$100 without a foreign-exchange receipt, and up to the amount exchanged with a receipt. You may take out as much foreign currency as you brought in. Remember to save ₩15,000 for the airport use tax —₩1,100 if leaving by ferry.

No vaccinations are required for entry into Korea, unless you have been in an area infected by cholera or yellow fever within 14 days of your trip.

CUSTOMS

Customs declaration forms are passed out on all arriving planes and ferries, or received from customs officials upon entry. A customs inspector will take the customs declaration card. To speed

SELECTED SOUTH KOREAN EMBASSIES AND CONSULATES

Australia
113 Empire Circuit
Yarralumla, Canberra
ACT 2600
tel. 612/6273-3044

Canada
150 Boteler Street
Ottawa, Ontario
K1N 5A6
613/244-5010

China
No. 3, 4th Ave.
East San Li Tun
Chaoyang District, Beijing
100600
tel. 10/6532-0290

France
125 Rue de Grenelle
75007 Paris
tel. 1/4753-0101

Germany
Schoeneberger Ufer 89-91
10785 Berlin
tel. 30/26065-0

Hungary
1062 Bp, Andrassy ut. 109

Budapest
tel. 1/351-1179

Italy
Via Barnada Oriani 30
00197 Roma
tel. 06/808-8769

Japan
1-2-5, Minami-Azabu
Minato-Ku, Tokyo
tel. 3/3452-7611

Mexico
Lope de Armandariz No. 110
Col. Lomas de Virreyes C.P.
11000
Mexico, D.F.
tel. 2/202-9866

Philippines
10th Floor, The Pacific Star
B/d, Makati Ave.
Makati City, Metro Manila
tel. 2/811-6139

Russia
14 Spiridonovka St.
Moscow
tel. 095/956-1474

Singapore
47 Scotts Rd. #08-00
Goldbell Towers
Singapore 228233
tel. 6256-1188

Thailand
23 Thiam-Ruammit Road
Ratchadapisek, Huay-Kwang
Bangkok 10310
tel. 2/247-5737

United Kingdom
60 Buckingham Gate
London SW1E 6AJ
tel. 20/7227-5500

United States
2450 Massachusetts Ave. N.W.
Washington, D.C. 20008
202/939-5600

SELECTED CONSULATES

Fukuoka
1-1-3, Jigyohama
Chuo-ku, Fukuoka
Japan

---

customs clearance, a physical inspection is not always done for all passengers. However, your bags may be inspected, if only in a cursory manner. An oral declaration of luggage is generally sufficient, though a written declaration is required with some luxury items, items over an allowable duty-free limit, agricultural products, and cash above $10,000 or its equivalent in monetary instruments. A reasonable amount of personal belongings may be brought in duty-free, including clothes, toilet articles, two ounces of perfume, personal medicine, a camera and inexpensive electronic goods, expensive articles that will be re-exported within six months, tools and equipment necessary for your work, one bottle of liquor (one liter), 200 cigarettes, 50 cigars, and 250 grams of other tobacco products. Some large luxury goods are subject to duty. Prohibited items include counterfeit money; articles of espionage; printed, audio, visual or other material considered pornographic, subversive, or detrimental to the welfare of the state, including material from or about North Korea; and illegal drugs. Some items can be put in bond—for a charge—and retrieved when you exit the country. Restricted articles must have prior authorized permission to be imported. These articles include but are not limited to hunting weapons, certain medicines, types of radio equipment, and items of commercial use. An additional customs check is done on arrival of unaccompanied baggage. You are allowed to take only a limited amount of ginseng from the coun-

tel. 92/771-0461

Hiroshima
5-12 Teppocho
Nakahu, Hiroshima
Japan
tel. 82/502-1151

Hong Kong
Consulate General
5-6 Floors, Far East Finance
Centre
16 Harcourt Road, Central
Hong Kong
tel. 5229-4141

Honolulu
2756 Pali Highway
Honolulu, Hawaii 96817
U.S.A.
tel. 808/595-6109

Los Angeles
3243 Wilshire Blvd.
Los Angeles, CA 90010, USA
213/382-9300

Nagoya
1-19-12, Meieki Minami
Nakamura-ku, Nagoya, Japan

tel. 52/586-9221

Niigata
1-13, Hakusanura
Niigata, Japan
tel. 25/230-3400

Osaka
2-3-4 Nishi-Shinsaibashi
Chuo-Ku, Osaka, Japan
tel. 6/6213-1401

Qingdao
#8 Qinling Road
Laoshan District, Qingdao
People's Republic of China
tel. 532/897-6001

San Francisco
3500 Clay Street
San Francisco, CA 94118
USA
415/921-2251

Sapporo
Kita 3-Cho Nishi 21-Chome
Chuo-ku, Sapporo, Japan
tel. 11/621-0288

Shanghai
4th Fl., Shanghai Int'l.

Trade Center
2200 Yan An Road (W) Shanghai
People's Republic of China
tel. 21/6219-6417

Shenyang
13/14 Fl., Mingzhe Bldg.
No. 51
14 Latitude Road
Heiping District
Shenyang
People's Republic of China
tel. 24/2385-7820

Taipei
Rm. 1506, 15th Fl., Int'l
Trade Bldg.
No. 333, Kee Hung Road
Section 1, Taipei
Republic of China
tel. 2/2758-8320

Vancouver
1600-1090 West Georgia St.
Vancouver, B.C. V6E 3V7
Canada
604/681-9581

try, and restrictions are placed on exporting antiques. Items of cultural value (including, but not limited to, designated treasures) may not be exported. For questions concerning items brought into or taken out of the country, contact the Customs Information office or the Art and Antique Assessment Office at any entry/exit port. For additional online information, see www.customs.go.kr.

Quarantine

All plants and plant products and animals and animal products must be declared and inspected upon arrival. A household pet must have a current health certificate showing a disease-free status; all animals are subject to a five- to 40-day quarantine. A one-day quarantine period is in effect for house pets from rabies-free countries and if a rabies vaccination has been administered with 30 days of arrival. Other animals and some plants are prohibited except by special permit from the Ministry of Agriculture and Fisheries. Prohibited products will be destroyed or sent back to the country of origin at the owner's expense. Check with a Korean embassy for details *before* transporting such items to Korea. In Korea, contact the National Animal Quarantine Service, Seoul branch (tel. 02/664-0241 or 031/467-1946) or the National Plant Quarantine Office, Seoul branch (tel. 02/664-3843 or 031/449-0524).

Accommodations 숙박

One thing is certain: no matter where you go in this country, you can always find a place to stay. Accommodations can roughly be broken down into five main categories: hotels, *yeogwan*, *minbak*, homestay, and youth hostels. Rates for hotel rooms fluctuate according to season, sometimes as much as 25–50 percent up or down. High season is spring to mid-summer and autumn; winter and the dog days of July and August constitute low season. Youth hostels have set charges. The rates for other types of accommodations do not fluctuate throughout the year, but may be negotiated down according to the season, time of arrival, and/or number of guests. Hotels accept cash, major credit cards, and traveler's checks; most all other accommodations take only cash, but traveler's checks can be used at some youth hostels. Accommodations listed in the following travel chapters can be recommended, with caveats where noted. General room rates are given in this introduction and hold true throughout the country. Only as exceptions are rates given in the travel chapters. Telephone numbers are included only when it's known or reasonably assumed that English (or Japanese) will be spoken at the other end. Addresses are left out for the most part as they are generally not used for finding locations in Korea—use maps and word descriptions for locations. Refer to individual travel chapters for particular accommodations in each area.

HOTELS

Large cities, tourist areas, and medium-size towns have hotels. All are registered with the government, must meet specified standards, and are ranked as super deluxe (SDL), deluxe (DLX), first-class (1), second-class (2), or third-class (3). A plaque near the front entrance of each hotel indicates the hotel's rank, showing five, four, three, or two flowers (similar to a star rating), respectively, for each of the above categories. The rose of Sharon, the national flower of Korea, is used.

Hotel names are virtually always displayed in Korean and English. The number of hotel rooms rose dramatically for the 1986 Asian Games and 1988 Olympics. With increased tourist growth since, the number of hotel rooms has continued to expand. In total, Korea has about 450 hotels, about half of which are located in the seven largest cities.

Hotels are Western-style, similar to those in any major city of the world. Depending upon its rank, a hotel's amenities might include various restaurants, bars, cocktail lounges, coffee shops, barber and beauty shops, tennis courts, a fitness center, swimming pool, sauna, nightclub, disco, theater restaurant, or banquet facilities. Many hotels have conference rooms, executive floors, and/or executive business centers which provide such services as secretarial help, computers, photocopy and fax machines, translation, appointment arrangements, courier service, and equipment rental. All have twin rooms and a small number of Korean-style rooms with *ondol* (heated) floors, and a Korean mattress (*yo*) and quilt. Most also have a few single rooms and suites. Rooms have private baths, heating and air conditioning, telephone, television, and music center, and many have stocked mini-refrigerators; some have telecommunication portals. In general, twin rooms in super-deluxe hotels run ₩330,000–380,000; ₩200,000–240,000 in deluxe hotels; ₩140,000–200,000 in first-class hotels; ₩80,000–100,000 in second-class hotels; and ₩50,000–80,000 in third-class hotels. Korean-style rooms are comparably priced, while singles are often but not always slightly cheaper. Suites often run double the price of a twin room, with some going for astronomical rates. Some hotels offer extended-stay and group rates. A 10 percent service charge is automatically added to the bill, and a 10 percent accommodation tax is also levied. Tipping is neither expected nor necessary. All hotels take reservations. Most top-class hotels outside of Seoul have reservation offices in Seoul, and some also have offices in other major provincial cities. Some hotels have reservation offices abroad, and many are connected to international reservation services. For contact information on hotels in the country, check the KNTO's free English-language *Travel Guide, Travel Planner's Guide,* or the *Meeting Planner's Guide.* Also check out the KNTO's website, www.knto.or.kr.

Recently, non-registered hotels have been popping up around the country. These hotels are virtually identical in quality to third-class registered hotels, but are usually smaller. They are also similar to top-notch *yeogwan,* many of which have "hotel," "motel," or "park" attached to their names. Most have a predominance of Korean-style rooms and limited or no amenities. They are clean, comfortable, and well-managed, and charge moderately less than a third-class hotel.

YEOGWAN 여관

The most numerous and most popular type of accommodation for Koreans and budget travelers is the *yeogwan* [*yŏgwan*], a Korean inn. They are everywhere; you'd be hard-pressed to find even the smallest town without one. *Yeogwan* range from basic to fancy, traditional to modern, mediocre to exceptionally clean and comfortable. Generally run as family businesses, they're more homey than hotels. Better *yeogwan* announce themselves in English, while the vast majority have signs only in Korean. The traditional *yeogwan* is a single-story Korean-style building surrounding a courtyard; newer ones are multistoried modern cement structures. While newer *yeogwan* have lost some of the feel of the traditional country inn, the rooms are still well-appointed.

Shoes are always taken off outside the room and stored in front of the door, inside the room on a shelf or mat, or in the entrance hallway. Most rooms have *ondol* floors covered with oilpaper (or more modern vinyl floor covering) on which you sit and sleep. Some now have Western-style beds, and a few have carpeting. The heated floors are great for drying damp clothes or towels, and for "pressing" pants if placed under the mattress. Each room has a *yo* (cotton-filled

mattress with removable cover), an *ibul* (cotton or synthetic-fiber quilt), and a *begea* (firm, cylindrical pillow filled with rice or wheat chaff) or Western-style pillow. The *ibul* come in summer and winter weights. Some *yeogwan* now use foam *yo* and pillows. Barley tea or filtered water and a facial towel are provided, and many have telephones, televisions, and wardrobes. *Yeogwan* do not have cooking facilities. In newer places, rooms have private baths connected to the sleeping rooms. When there is no attached bathroom, communal bathrooms and washrooms are located on each floor or perhaps outside in a separate building. Most *yeogwan* have now installed Western-style sit-down toilets, but some still have pit-style squat toilets. All but the cheaper places have hot tap water in the bathroom. While some places will serve breakfast at an extra charge if notified well in advance, most will not and guests must eat out.

Like hotels, *yeogwan* are ranked and priced accordingly. While it's not a definitive distinguishing factor, *yeogwan* with the word *jang* attached to the name, as in Samwonjang Yeogwan, are usually of higher quality. Some also add the words "hotel," "motel," or "park" to their names, seemingly to elevate their status and draw both Koreans and foreign travelers. Room rates for better places run ₩30,000–40,000, with a few above that. For regular *yeogwan,* average prices are in the ₩25,000–30,000 range, with a few older and rattier places down to 18,000–20,000. Accommodations are almost always rented by the room (single or double occupancy), but a minimal fee for a third person may be requested. Look for the posted rate schedule either in the room or at the front office. Ask to see the room first, and settle on the price before you agree to take it. Payment is expected in advance. If you don't know how many nights you will stay, pay each day. Most proprietors speak little or no English, and only the elders speak Japanese. If one *yeogwan* doesn't please you or is too much for your pocketbook, simply excuse yourself and look for another around the corner.

You can check in anytime of the day that there is a room available. Checkout is usually before noon but when a place is not busy there is some flexibility about that time. In the early evening you should have no problem finding a room, but it gets harder later. When business is slow, you can usually bargain the price down a little. If the bedding looks less than clean, ask to have it changed or find another place. During spring and fall, you may have to ask for a heavier (or lighter) *ibul,* or have the floor temperature adjusted. Modern *yeogwan* usually have doors that lock with keys. In older and traditional-style places, you may need your own lock. While it will not always be the case, you may be asked to sign the registration book on taking a room, and to provide your name, address, arrival and departure dates, sex, some identification number, and destination.

Aside from those *yeogwan* listed in this book, a whole list of others—mostly in the upper end of the economy range—are listed in the KNTO's publication *Budget Inns Guide.* To aid in locating and reserving economy rooms in major cities, the KNTO has created an online reservation system that is found at www.worldinn.com.

A new type of *yeogwan* has emerged in recent years. Whether located in the city or country, they are almost always new, a bit fancy, and discreet. Overnight room rates are usually similar to other *yeogwan* but the management will also charge for and accept guests by the hour. While much like ordinary *jang yeogwan,* they will most often have a rack of mildly pornographic videos near the front, a glass window with a sandblasted design between the bathroom and bedroom, and often a parking area half screened by a curtain or other such blind—ostensibly to give some anonymity to those using the place. Even though these places are a bit more expensive, they are not to be avoided and are generally as clean, comfortable, and safe as comparable *yeogwan* (unless you don't want to be exposed to that sort of environment).

Yeoinsuk 여인숙

From spartan to surprisingly homey, *yeoinsuk* [*yŏinsuk*] are virtually the same type of accommodation as *yeogwan,* only cheaper—and generally with lower standards of maintenance and cleanliness. Many are traditional-style houses

that have seen better days, although some are nondescript cement boxes. Surprisingly, there are still a few very clean, well-maintained, and homey *yeoinsuk* around, but their numbers seem to be diminishing rapidly as Koreans and foreigners alike demand more from a place to stay. Room rates run in the ₩15,000–20,000 range. Signs for *yeoinsuk* almost always appear only in Korean.

MINBAK 민박

These are private homes, almost always in rural and mountain areas, that rent rooms, by and large, on a seasonal basis to augment the family income. They may or may not have permanent signs advertising their location. Although they are located all over the country, Jeju-do seems to have a disproportionately large number of *minbak.* In mountain areas, most *minbak* operate during the fine-weather hiking season and often charge what the market will bear. In other rural areas, *minbak* are run like *yeogwan* and rates are comparable. Some bargaining is possible, but settle on the rate before you agree to stay. Payment is made in advance. Most will provide a standard breakfast or evening meal for a reasonable additional charge if arranged in advance. No cooking facilities are available in rooms.

HOMESTAY

An organized homestay program was created and run by the KNTO around the time of the 1988 Seoul Olympics. It has since been taken over by several private organizations including Labo Korea, Suite 317, Oyang Corporation Bldg., 76-3, 1-ga, Taepyeongno, Jung-gu, Seoul, tel. 02/736-0521, fax 02/736-0522; www.labo.or .kr. For other options see the websites www .homestaykorea.com and www.koreahome-stay.com. Homestays are the Korean equivalent of bed-and-breakfasts. These programs use homes that have been selected for location, cleanliness, comfort, affordability, and, in some cases, for the owners' ability to speak a foreign language. Generally, room charges are about ₩30,000 for a single person in a room, ₩50,000 for a couple,

₩40,000 for an adult and child, and ₩5,000 extra for each meal taken. Fees are paid to the owner in Korean *won* upon arrival. Arrival should be before 2100 and departure no later than 0900. Guests are requested not to remain at the home during business hours unless arrangements have been made to that effect with the owner. All reservations are handled by the individual home-stay organization. A reservation-request form must be filled out and sent in one month prior to your planned arrival—a later request is possible if done in-country. The arranging organization will return a confirmation to you. A reservation form can also be requested from the KNTO and is part of their brochure *Home-Stay in Korea*.

YOUTH HOSTELS 유스호스텔

Through the 1990s and early 2000s, Korea continued to add new youth hostels to its member list and the number now stands at over 55, all open year-round. While not necessarily conveniently located for the traveler without private transportation, these hostels are mostly located in provincial areas of scenic beauty near beaches, mountains, or ski resorts. All are large, modern buildings and many resemble small hotels. The smallest capacity is 120, the largest 1,370; most range between 200 and 600. For most of the year, getting a bed is no problem. However, during summer school holidays and on selected weekends throughout the year, especially in the autumn, blocks of rooms are reserved for busloads of schoolchildren. Call ahead to reserve a bed. See the individual travel chapters for specific hostels in each area.

All valid Y.H. cards from other countries are honored. Those without Y.H. cards are also welcome when there is room, but may be charged a higher tariff. IYHF (Hostelling International) cards can be issued in Korea for a fee of ₩20,000 for foreigners. Hostels generally have six- and eight-person bunk rooms (₩7,000–16,500 per person) and private family rooms (₩20,000–66,000 for the room). All bedding is provided. For those in bunk rooms, the toilet and showers are down the hall. Services include barley tea in the room, restaurant, coffee shop, souvenir shop,

money exchange, and, in the largest hostels, conference halls, gardens, and athletic grounds. For more information and a brochure listing all hostels and their contact information, contact the Korea Youth Hostels Association, Rm. 408, Jeokseon Hyundai Bldg., 80, Jeokseon-dong, Jongno-gu, Seoul 110-052, tel. 02/725-3031, fax 02/752-3113; www.kyha.or.kr.

The Korea Youth Hostels Association works in coordination with Youth Service Korea, a travel service catering mostly to Koreans going abroad. Domestic rail and airline tickets are also issued through this organization. The Youth Service Korea office is located in Rm. 409 of the Jeokseon Hyundai Bldg., next door to the Y.H. office.

CONDOMINIUMS

A rather new phenomenon in Korean accommodations is the emergence of condominiums. Located in tourist areas, and operating like their counterparts in the West, there are now many dozen around the peninsula. Units consist of bedrooms, bathrooms, kitchens, and living areas, and accompanying amenities run the gamut of athletic facilities, restaurants, and shops. Condos are membership organizations. Most heavily used during summer and fall (winter as well for those near ski resorts), they are open to non-members when demand is low. Arrangements can be made through a travel agent or directly through an individual condominium.

MOUNTAIN HUTS 산장

Called *sanjang*, mountain huts along trails in national parks are open nearly as long as the trails are open. Spartan affairs, they are usually faced with stone and have wood-floored sleeping areas. A space on the floor costs ₩3,000 per night. First come, first served. Capacity is usually limited to a couple dozen; some are smaller, but a few can hold well over one hundred. Because of limited space, it's easy to strike up friendships with fellow hikers. Each hut has a live-in caretaker. They are usually not heated, and only a limited supply of canned or packaged food, candles, and matches is available. Bring your own sleeping bag, pad, cookstove, food, and other supplies, although bedding is supplied at some. Outhouses are provided at each hut. In addition, there are camping areas at some huts for those who desire to pitch a tent. Periodically, these huts are closed for repair, so check with the park rangers to see about availability *before* you venture out on the trail.

BATHHOUSES 목욕탕

While all accommodations have some sort of bathing facilities, older and only the least expensive places will still sometimes not have a real bathtub or other bathing room. Indeed, you may have to go down the street for a bath, but these bathhouses are a real pleasure and a real cultural experience. You can use a *mogyoktang,* a public bath similar in style to the *sento* of Japan. *Mogyoktang,* now sometimes referred to as sauna (사우나) or *daejungtang* (대중탕), are virtually everywhere in the country, with some 2,000 or so in Seoul alone. Bathhouses were once quite easily spotted with their tall smokestacks, but most

are now lost amid tall city structures or incorporated into other buildings. In smaller towns and rural areas, they are more easily located. Look for a red and white sign that shows steam rising from a bowl. In addition, and to add to the confusion, most *yeogwan* and other similar accommodations also have this same symbol on their signs, which indicates that hot tap water is available in their bathrooms. At about ₩3,000, the entrance fee for the ordinary bathhouse is standard throughout the country; some fancy bathhouses may charge more. Small scrub cloths and bars of soap are available for a minimal fee. An additional fee, perhaps twice the entrance fee, is charged to have one of the attendants scrub you down. For men, a haircut and style can be had at most bathhouses for about ₩8,000, and coin-operated, handheld hair dryers are usually available. For a minimal charge, shoes can be shined. Most bathhouses provide two types of towels: a thin wash towel to be used while bathing, and a large thick towel to dry off with when you reenter the changing room. Some now

THE BATHING EXPERIENCE

Bathing is one of the joys of Korean life. Take off your shoes and step into the changing room, where you're given a small locker and a key. Shoe shelves or small cubicles matching the number on your locker should be used when available. Most keys have an elastic band to slip around your wrist or ankle while bathing. Showers are available and you can wash that way, but if you do, you'll miss the fun. Rather, with a rubber bowl, scoop water from the hot tub (or from a faucet) and wet yourself down. Sit on a low stool, lather up, and scrub away. Wash your hair, shave, and rinse well, then rinse off again. *Now* you're ready to get into the communal tub. Soak for as long as you want (or can), and then step out and do it all again. The heat has

bathhouse symbol, now also used to indicate a *yeogwan* that has rooms with attached baths

opened your pores so now is a good time to use that scrub cloth to remove any remaining dirt or dead skin. After the second soak, try a dip in the cold-water tub—some baths also have mineral water tubs and most also have dry heat, wood-lined saunas and steam rooms. Be sure to rinse off completely each time *before* you get into the big tub. Repeat as many times as you like, and stay as long as you want. Let the heat penetrate your skin and the warm water soothe your muscles. A soak in the tub is not recommended for heart patients, and is forbidden to those with contagious skin diseases. Plan to spend at least an hour or you won't get your money's worth. Step out, dry off, and relax before heading out clean and refreshed.

also have waiting rooms with lounge chairs, televisions, and soft-drink vending machines. Mirrors are abundant and there is always a scale to weigh yourself. Bathhouses open around 0600 and close at 2000. They are busiest in the early mornings before work and Saturday afternoon and evening. Each closes one day a week on a rotating schedule.

Food and Drink 음식, 음료

One of the least-known of Asian cuisines, Korean food is substantial, hearty, salty, and spicy. It's generally low in fat and high in carbohydrates. Rice is the principal grain. Various flavored or fermented vegetable side dishes and fish accompany the rice, and soups and stews are prominent. Only in the last 30–40 years has red meat become a regular part of the Korean diet in any quantity. Korean food is not as oily as Chinese food, and it's less aesthetic than Japanese. While not as sharply spiced as Thai food, for example, the spice is more pervasive. Soy sauce *(ganjang)*, soybean paste *(doenjang)*, crushed red pepper *(gochu garu)*, garlic *(maneul)*, ginger *(saenggang)*, sesame seed *(chamkkae)*, and salt *(sogeum)* are the principal seasonings in Korean cooking; red pepper, garlic, and salt are used liberally (the amount of salt may be of concern to someone with a salt-restricted diet). Aside from these, *gochujang*, a slightly salty, rice-and-red-pepper paste, is used as an ingredient in some foods, and soy sauce mixed with finely chopped scallions, sesame seeds, and crushed red pepper is used as both a broth and marinade. A mixture of salt and sesame oil, and the combination soy sauce and *gyeoja* (a yellowish mustard paste similar to Japanese horseradish wasabi) are used as dips for some meats. Whatever combination of spices used, the goal is to blend flavors harmoniously. For oils and liquids, Koreans mostly use vegetable oil, sesame oil, and various rice wines. Cooking methods include grilling, broiling, boiling, steaming, stir-frying, and pan-frying. Food is seldom deep-fried and Koreans traditionally do not bake food. Most preparation is done in the kitchen, but some meats and stews are cooked at the table.

A better and more nutritious diet, more food, greater variety, and more meat in recent years have resulted in taller Koreans and, for some, greater girth and weight. Unfortunately, there is an increasing number of overweight children and adults, by and large a phenomenon of the last 20–30 years.

THE KOREAN MEAL

Koreans love to eat, and eat together. When they sit down, they just eat; most conversation is saved until after the meal. Food is served all at once, instead of in courses. At home, all three meals are basically the same, with differing side dishes. Rice *is* the meal—all else is secondary. Although changing somewhat because of new prosperity and other alterations in the culture, this is obvious from the much-used greeting, *"Shiksa haeseumnikka?"* (literally, "Have you eaten rice yet?"). A bowl of rice is always accompanied by an individual serving of soup, and *banchan* (side dishes) which are put out for everyone at the table. *Banchan* include various types of *gimchi*, seasoned vegetables, fish, and meat. Vegetables vary according to the season, and are most numerous during summer. Refrigeration has increased the availability of foods somewhat, but some vegetables, fruits, nuts, and fish are still options only at certain times of the year.

Breakfast and dinner are the main meals; lunch is light. Breakfast often includes a fried egg, while dinner includes meat, stew, or extra fish. There are no desserts, but a meal may end with fruit. Sweets are also absent except on traditional holidays, when many kinds of sweet rice cakes and other goodies are available throughout the day. Other special foods are available on days of celebration and ceremony. *Boricha* (roasted barley tea) is always served with a meal—now sometimes replaced by filtered water; unboiled tap water is not. At home, *sungnyung* (scorched rice water) is sometimes on the table, and for a special treat for the kids *nurungji* (browned, crunchy rice from the bottom of the pot) is brought from the kitchen. Either filtered and (usually) chilled water or, to a lesser extent, *boricha* is also served at restaurants with ordinary meals, but beer, rice wine, or stronger alcoholic drinks are often had with fancy meat and fish dishes, and with some Chinese and Japanese meals. Eating vegetarian is not difficult at home, but much more of a problem at restaurants. Meat appears in many dishes.

Breakfast may be a problem for the budget traveler. Most public restaurants don't open until mid- to late morning, except for small eateries usually near train or bus stations that cater to early morning travelers. The few ordinary restaurants that open earlier generally serve food believed beneficial to upset stomachs and hangovers. In some cities, food carts are set up in the morning to serve quick Western-style fried foods or soups. It may be wise to arrange the night before for your breakfast to be prepared by the proprietor of your *yeogwan*, if that service is offered. Otherwise, buy milk, juice, fruit, hard-boiled eggs, or custard bread from the corner grocery, or stop for a quick bite at a bakery.

Utensils

Stainless steel tableware has mostly replaced brass and earthenware pottery. Plastic is sometimes used. Rice is put into a deep bowl, often covered when served; the soup bowl is lower and wider. Certain soups and stews are served in earthenware bowls at restaurants. Metal, bamboo, or plastic chopsticks are used in combination with a long-handled, shallow spoon. Knives are strictly for food preparation in the kitchen except for some Western dishes, so food is pre-cut into bite-size pieces or soft enough to be pulled apart with chopsticks. Plates are seldom used except for Western and some Chinese dishes and raw fish. *Banchan*, *gimchi*, sauces, seasonings, and condiments are all put in low ceramic bowls. Large metal pans or deep dishes are set in the center of the table for communal stews, along with a brazier or grill for meats. Except for leaves of lettuce or other greens and small wheat pancakes,

into which various ingredients are put before popping them into the mouth, food is not handled with the fingers. If you take a short break during the meal, put your chopsticks flat across the rice or soup bowl—this indicates that you are only resting and will continue. Don't stick them into the rice as this is done only at certain ceremonies, symbolically for the use of the dead. Never hold your chopsticks in your hand at the same time that you use your spoon. Bowls and plates are generally not picked up or held, except with some quick-noodle dishes. When finished, lay your spoon and chopsticks to the side of the rice bowl.

RESTAURANTS
Korean

These are, of course, most numerous. Many have the names of dishes written in Korean on the outside windows or on a placard next to the front door. Most restaurants post the menu and prices on the wall, often with specials written on individual papers. Fancier places, usually serving higher-priced meat dishes, have a picture-book menu in English. Restaurants that principally serve meat have gas burners on the tables or holes in the tables for charcoal pots. Some of these, as well as select Japanese, Chinese, and Western restaurants, display plastic models of dishes at the front door to show what's served within. These restaurants are usually a bit more expensive. Seat yourself; remove your shoes if you sit at a low table on an oil-paper floor. Many places now will bring a warm hand towel to the table to be used to clean your hands before eating. *Boricha* is brought when you order, and *banchan* comes automatically with the meal (though not served with some noodle dishes). Both are included in the price of the meal. A number of years ago, to the dismay of the general populace and many restaurants, the government tried to institute an a la carte ordering system for *banchan*. The idea was never widely accepted, but a few restaurants may still serve side dishes that way and add them to the bill. Some restaurants have a minimum charge (about ₩1,000) for an extra bowl of rice (*gonggibap*), while others will bring it for free.

The bowl of rice is never brought to the mouth. Leave the bowl on the table and use your spoon or chopsticks. It's all right to make noise while eating—like slurping soup, sucking in noodles, or sniffling—but blowing your nose at the table is a no-no. Toothpicks are usually provided; politely cover your mouth with one hand while you pick with the other. Toothpicks are also used to spear fruit if it follows the meal. Koreans never linger at a restaurant table. They adjourn to a coffee shop or drinking establishment for further socializing.

Restaurants in smaller towns are generally slightly cheaper than in large cities. Hotel, tourist, and specialty restaurants are more expensive. An average range for most ordinary soup, noodle, and rice dishes is ₩2,000–4,000; ₩1,500–2,500 for snacks and simple foods; ₩5,000–8,000 for the fancier rice and vegetable dishes; ₩4,000–7,000 for stews; and ₩7,000–12,000 for meat dishes. While most by far ask for payment at the end of a meal, a few (usually restaurants where there's a rapid turnover) will ask for payment in advance (*jeonbul*). They will let you know.

Chinese

These typically have their names written in Chinese characters above the doors. Most do not now have the formerly typical black wooden plaques with the restaurant's name on it draped by a red tassel hanging to the side of the door, although a few still retain this feature. Chinese restaurants range from ordinary neighborhood shops that serve basic food to ornate establishments that handle huge banquets. Food in ordinary restaurants tends to be a bit oily and greasy. The better places, run mostly by ethnic Chinese, offer a wider variety of foods and are of better quality. The predominant color at these better places is red. Many have Chinese characters pasted on the walls, fancy lanterns hanging from the ceilings, and pictures of former presidents of the Republic of China displayed. In the average Chinese restaurant, menus posted on the wall show only simple dishes, but in better ones the menu is brought to the table and may run to several pages. Most ordinary dishes are inexpensive (₩2,000–5,000), but communal dishes in authentic restaurants can be very costly (₩8,000–40,000). As prices for the same dish vary so little, look for a restaurant where the cook is ethnic Chinese. Most restaurants make their noodles by hand. Neighborhood restaurants deliver to nearby homes for no extra charge or tip.

Japanese

Less common than either Korean or Chinese, Japanese restaurants are often distinguished by the wood latticework on the front and the interior wood decor; often there is a sushi bar. Some have Japanese characters or cutouts of fish on the front windows. Although other food is served, they specialize in noodle and fish dishes. While simple noodle dishes are in the ₩2,000–4,000 range, most meat and fish dishes are on the expensive side.

Western

These restaurants specialize in various sorts of meat, rice, and vegetable dishes. Although the food is generally well-prepared—and excellent in some—Western establishments are expensive and not frequented by the average Korean. Often dinners will be in the ₩10,000–25,000 range. There is no standard decor. All hotels have Western restaurants or serve some Western food. Independent restaurants are located in large and medium-size cities. Both American and Continental cuisines, often a close approximation to the real thing, can be found in larger cities, but a rather generic Western food is more typical in smaller towns. Only in the larger cities—especially Seoul—can French, Italian, English, German, Thai, Indian, and Pakistani restaurants be found.

Relatively new to the food scene are the restaurants serving "fusion" foods. Typically, these combine the ingredients of the West with the flavors and spices of Korea and the Orient—although many variations are seen.

Cafés

These are a relatively new addition to Korea's food scene. Taking after European cafés, they serve coffee, tea, juice, cocktails, and a limited selection of quick foods. These places are popular with the young crowd, urban professionals, and the avant-garde.

Buffets

Also a relatively new concept for Korea and not yet very prolific are buffet restaurants. Similar to buffets around the globe, those in Korea offer a variety of meat and vegetable dishes, with fish and noodles, drinks and desserts. Like all buffets, you can go through the line as often as you like, but take only what you can eat so as not to waste. For the uninitiated, a Korean buffet might be a good place to get a first taste of some typical dishes—if you can find one. Generally, prices run from ₩5,000 to ₩10,000 or more for the better buffet.

Bakeries

A bakery is an option for a quick bite to eat. Found in both large cities and small towns, bakeries have grown in popularity in the last 30 years—the Koryodang Bakery in Seoul has been operating since 1945. Goods are displayed in glass cases, and all places provide seating. Check for freshness as not all items are put out daily or even baked on the premises. Items available are generally recognizable—these include various breads, rolls, pastries, and cakes. What is different, however, are fillings for some pastries (bean paste, for example), and ingredients for some frostings (lard is one). Generally, milk, juices, and ice cream are also available. All are priced individually, and are not cheap.

Fast Food

Slowly but surely, Western fast-food chains have entered Korea. At first it was the various doughnut sellers, then chicken, hamburgers, pizza, and ice cream came to fight for a share of the rapidly expanding fast-food market. Becoming relatively widespread, these places are popping up here and there throughout the country like chicks hatching from eggs. The greatest concentration of these fast-food restaurants is in the large cities and towns where foreigners and young Koreans congregate. Numerous Korean and Japanese knock-offs of these fast-food restaurants have also made their

FOOD HAWKERS

Fast-fading from the food scene in Korea are the evening sellers of *gimbap* (rice and vegetables rolled in seaweed laver) and *chapssal ddeok* (a doughy rice cake pastry with various fillings). Late in the evening, occasional peddlers still walk the alleys and byways of neighborhoods, shouldering their cases, and crying out *"gimbap, chapssal ddeok"* in rhythmic, melodious voices. While once more numerous and ordinary, these peddlers have largely gone the way of the *jigye* deliverymen, so if you are fortunate enough to hear their call, ask to try one of their snacks.

appearance. Whatever the derivation, they are not hard to spot, as the decor and signage are so incongruous with the surroundings that they almost jump out at you.

Movable Food Carts

Set up on sidewalks along major streets as well as back alleys, these carts offer mostly cheap, quick snacks, candy, and finger foods.

TYPICALLY AVAILABLE FOODS

Foods and dishes described below are representative of those found in Korea. This list is not all-inclusive, but broad in scope. Not all foods are available at all restaurants. While some are known for a certain type of food, such as meat dishes, and others are famous for and serve only one particular dish, most have a wide variety on their menu. Some dishes are only found in mountain areas and others along the sea. Have a good time discovering the foods of Korea, and be adventurous.

Key Food Words to Know

Since Korean food breaks down into several types, it would be beneficial to keep in mind certain food identifiers when choosing your meal. The main ones are *bap* (rice), *baekban* ("with side dishes"), *tang* (meat-base soup boiled for a relatively long time), *guk* (vegetable-base soup boiled a short time), *jjigae* (stew), *jeongol* (casserole stew), *juk* (porridge), *myeon* and *guksu* (noodles), *gogi* (meat), *gui* (broiled or grilled unmarinated meat), *jeon* (pan-fried), *bokgeum* (stir fry), *jjim* (steamed or stewed, usually in soy sauce), and *hoe* (raw fish).

Rice and Rice Dishes

Boiled, short-grain, polished white rice *(bap)* is the main staple of Korea, served in homes and restaurants. It is automatically served with all meals, except noodle dishes and Western foods. Mixed-rice dishes are few, although some restaurants serve rice mixed with barley *(boribap)* or millet *(jobap)*. On special occasions, bean sprouts *(kongnamulbap)*, red beans *(patbap)*, other beans *(kongbap)*, chestnuts *(bambap)*, or vegetables *(chaesobap)* are added for extra flavor and nutrition. Glutinous rice *(chalbap)* is cooked and beaten into rice cakes. The cities of Yeoju, Icheon, and Naju have the reputation for having the tastiest rice. At various stages, rice is known by different words: rice seedlings *(mo)*, unmilled rice *(pyeo)*, milled rice *(ssal)*, and boiled rice *(bap)*—the polite, formal form of which is *jinji*.

Typical rice dishes include:

Baekban (백반): A simple meal of boiled rice and *banchan*.

Sundubu baekban (순두부백반): Thick bean-paste soup with tofu, vegetables, and small clams, served with rice and vegetables.

Bibimbap (비빔밥): Boiled rice covered with an assortment of sliced vegetables, strips of beef, and an egg, to be mixed together at the table with a dollop of red pepper paste before eating. Favorite of Jeonju. Called *dolsot bibimbap*, and usually a bit more expensive, when it's served in a hot stone bowl.

Sanchae bibimbap (산채비빔밥): Bibimbap with covering of wild mountain vegetables. Usually found only in mountain areas.

Yeongyangbap (영양밥): Boiled rice and bean dish, with a mixture of meats, vegetables, nuts, herbs, and only nutritionally rich items.

Deobbap (덮밥): Bowl of rice covered with any number of vegetables or meats.

Japchaebap (잡채밥): Rice covered with a stir-fried mixture of clear noodles, meat, and vegetables.

Bokgeumbap (볶음밥): Stir-fried rice with various meat, vegetable, and seafood ingredients, and/or gimchi, often with some sesame oil added. Usually served in Chinese restaurants.

Ssambap (쌈밥): A variety of leafy greens (cabbage, lettuce, pumpkin, squash, sesame) into which rice, vegetables, condiment pastes, and sometimes meats are placed, before wrapping and eating as one small "package."

MOVABLE FEASTS

Where they all come from is a mystery, but when the sun goes down, *pojang macha* (movable food carts that sell finger foods and alcohol) seemingly appear from nowhere to dot the city's side streets and alleys and serve as sidewalk bars. Low wooden benches are placed in front of the carts for the customers, and an oil lamp is hung up for light. When the weather cools, a tarp is thrown over the top and wrapped around for protection from the chill and wind. These stalls primarily serve alcoholic drinks, but as an accompaniment they offer an assortment of *anju*, which may be anything from sliced vegetables to animal innards, or octopus tentacles to deep-fried sparrows. Each stall has its own special selection, as it probably has its own regular location. Those out for a late night on the town stumble onto (or into) the stalls for a last nightcap. On warm summer evenings, there are few pleasures like convivial companionship at one of these open-air stalls and they are very popular with working men and young professionals. On the other hand, few experiences can compare to downing your last swig of rotgut *soju*, followed by a slick and slimy sea creature, as the plastic tarp flaps in the breeze and you shuffle your feet for warmth late on a blustery winter's night! Try it, or at least go out and have a look at this slice of Korean social life.

Banchan

Every meal is accompanied by *banchan* (side dishes). The majority are vegetables—collectively known as *namul*—with some fish and meat, depending on the season and the region. Vegetables are from the field, mountains, or sea and are par-boiled, sautéed, or left uncooked. Dozens of these dishes are prepared in various ways, but some of the more common are: various *gimchi*, bean sprouts *(kongnamul)*, bellflower root *(doraji)*, fern brake *(gosari)*, watercress *(minari)*, spinach *(shigeumchi)*, Shepherd's purse *(naengi)*, black beans *(kong)*, tofu *(dubu)*, cucumber *(oi)*, eggplant *(gajinamul)*, anchovies *(myeolchi)*, dried laver seaweed *(gim)*, acorn jelly *(dotori muk)*, oysters *(gul)*, sesame leaves *(kkaetnip)*, and lotus root *(yeon'geun)*.

Gimchi

Perhaps the best-known Korean food is *gimchi* (*kimch'i*). It's served at every meal. Though it most often refers to a spicy cabbage mixture, *gimchi* is actually a generic term for any seasoned and fermented vegetable dish—with cabbage, turnip, radish, or cucumber as the usual main ingredient. Depending upon the recipe, crushed red pepper, garlic, salt, water, chopped scallions, pieces of carrots and cucumber, apples, pears, anchovies, clams, and other ingredients are added

for flavor. *Gimchi* is eaten fresh, ripe, or sour, and it varies from bland to spicy hot. It's generally spicier in the south, but the north traditionally has more varieties. About 200 types of *gimchi* have been documented from different parts of the peninsula. To attest to its popularity and importance in the Korean diet, and a growing awareness and acceptance around the world, a Kimch'i Museum has been created in Seoul.

Gimjang, or *gimchi*-making, takes place in November, when all the crops are in from the fields, and the temperature is cool. This is an important event as *gimchi* helps carry the family through the winter. Most people still make their own, but special kinds are bought. *Gimchi* is traditionally stored in huge earthenware jars buried with only their tops aboveground. This process allows the food to ferment while refrigerating. It's best in mid-winter, after having set for a month or two. *Gimchi* is not only rich in vitamins, but the process is a good means of preservation. With urbanization, *gimchi* pots are often set out behind the house on a cement slab, or on the roof of an outbuilding. Modern refrigeration has changed

© ROBERT NILSEN

gimchi pots

the traditional process somewhat, so *gimchi* is now made in small quantities at various times of the year when vegetables are available and when needed. In summer, it can ripen overnight.

Some of the *gimchi* most often seen at table are made from cabbage *(baechu gimchi)*, cubed turnips *(kkakdugi gimchi)*, small turnips and greens *(chonggak gimchi)*, stuffed cucumbers *(oi sobaegi gimchi)*, rolled cabbage and vegetables *(possam gimchi)*, leeks *(buchu gimchi)*, various vegetables in water *(mul gimchi)*, and radish sections in brine *(dongchimi gimchi)*.

Gourmet Foods

Certain Korean foods are generally served only at fine restaurants or formal gatherings.

Hanjeongshik (한정식), often shortened to *jeongshik*, is the Korean table d'hote, a traditional full-course meal of rice, soup, fish, and/or meat, and side dishes. The number of side dishes varies from half a dozen to several dozen. If you desire an authentic Korean meal, this is it.

Gujeolpan (구절판) ("Nine-sectioned board") is an appetizer tray in nine sections, eight of which are filled with different thinly sliced meats or vegetables, all surrounding a small stack of thin wheat pancakes in the middle. Small amounts of two or three of the foods are wrapped in a pancake before being popped into the mouth.

Shinseollo (신선로) ("Taoist Master Pot") is a highly seasoned stew of meat, fish, seafood, vegetables, tofu, herbs, eggs, and nuts in a beef broth simmered in a doughnut-shaped chafing dish over a charcoal fire. It is the first among *jeongol* stews, and was once a dish prepared for royalty.

Meat Dishes

In the last 30 years, principally due to increased prosperity and wealth, Koreans have dramatically increased their consumption of meat. Before that—and even today for some families—meat was a specialty food prepared only on traditional holidays and important occasions. Although Korea has always raised some beef cattle and pigs, many can now regularly afford higher-quality meat—mostly imported from Australia and New Zealand. Beef, pork, and chicken are virtually always thin-

ly sliced, and sometimes marinated. At times, meat strips and ribs are cut into bite-sized pieces with scissors when laid on the grill. Most meat dishes are cooked at your table and served with rice and *banchan*. Often, to help with digestion, pear slices are served after beef, and highly salted miniature shrimp follow pork. You generally find slabs of meat only in Western restaurants and those places that serve pseudo-Western and Japanified Western food. A few of the more common meat dishes include the following.

Bulgogi (불고기): Thin beef strips marinated in soy sauce, sesame oil, chopped scallions, red-pepper powder, garlic, and a pinch of sugar. Grilled on a convex pan surrounded by a trough for the broth.

Galbi gui (갈비구이): Grilled, marinated short ribs also called *bul galbi*.

Galbi jjim (갈비찜): Short beef ribs with a combination of potatoes, turnips, mushrooms, and/or nuts stewed in soy sauce–infused liquid over a low heat.

Deungshim gui (등심구이): Grilled sirloin.

Anshim gui (안심구이): Grilled tenderloin.

Sogeum gui (소금구이): Grilled salted beef.

Roseu gui (로스구이): Beef ribs simmered with garlic and onions.

Dwaejigogi gui (돼지고기구이): Grilled pork.

Dwaeji galbi (돼지갈비): Grilled pork ribs.

Samgyeopsal (삼겹살): Grilled, three-layered (meat, fat, meat), thinly sliced pork.

Yukhoe (육회): Shredded raw beef.

Sundae (순대): Sausage of pig intestine, with stuffing of pig's blood, rice, noodle, onion, and/or other ingredients and seasonings. Most often served with alcohol.

Dak galbi (닭갈비): Tangy chicken with vegetables, greens, and potatoes grilled on a flat pan. Famous in Chuncheon.

Yangnyeom Tongdak (양념통닭): Roasted chicken with a sweet herb covering.

Ori (오리): Duck.

Stews

Stews are prepared for each individual order, usually simmered at the table for a group of people. The flavor of this thick mixture is strong, and the seasonings permeate the entire dish.

Most are very spicy. There are two basic types: bean-paste base *(jjigae)* and water base *(jeongol)*. All are served with rice and *banchan*.

Doenjang jjigae (된장찌개): Vegetable and bean-paste base stew.

Gimchi jjigae (김치찌개): *Gimchi*, tofu, and pork stew.

Sundubu jjigae (순두부찌개): Spicy tofu and clam stew, sometimes with a bit of beef or pork.

Beoseot jjigae (버섯찌개): Mushroom stew.

Soegogi jjigae (쇠고기찌개): Beef stew.

Dwaejigogi jjigae (돼지고기찌개): Pork stew.

Saengseon jjigae (생선찌개): Fish stew.

Haemul ttukbaegi (해물뚝배기): Seafood stew in bean-paste base, usually served in an earthenware bowl.

Cheonggukjang (청국장): Similar to *doenjang jjigae,* but with whole beans and a distinctly stronger smell and flavor.

Sujung jeongol (수중전골): Seafood stew. A similar but spicier seafood dish is called *haemul jeongol.*

Gungjung jeongol (궁중전골): Meat, fish, and shellfish stew.

Soegogi jeongol (쇠고기전골): Beef stew.

Gopachang jeongol (곱창전골): Beef tripe and vegetable stew.

Nakji jeongol (낙지전골): Octopus stew.

Beoseot jeongol (버섯전골): Mushroom and beef stew.

Soups

Soups generally have a thin broth and a mixture of vegetables and seasonings that differs with each soup. They are prepared in large quantities, simmered in the kitchen, and served individually to the customer in metal or earthenware bowls. Those served in earthenware bowls usually come from the kitchen still boiling. While some, like seaweed *(mieokguk)* and certain fish soups, are usually served only in the home, others can be ordered at restaurants. These are served with rice and *banchan.*

Galbi tang (갈비탕): Short rib soup with clear noodles and scallions.

Seolleong tang (설렁탕): Beef and beef-bone stock soup. Comes bland. Season to taste with salt,

pepper, crushed red pepper, scallions, and hot-pepper paste.

Gom tang (곰탕): Beef stock and tripe soup with spices.

Gori gom tang (고리곰탕): Oxtail soup.

Yukgyejang (육개장): Heavily spiced beef, vegetable, and bean-thread noodle soup. Sweat-producing spice level.

Samgye tang (삼계탕): Ginseng chicken soup. Game hen–size chicken, stuffed with jujube (Asian date), garlic, persimmon, and glutinous rice and seasoned with salt, pepper, and scallion. Often eaten in the middle of summer to lessen the effects of the heat. When the chicken is larger and made for a group, this dish is called *baeksuk.*

Daegu tang (대구탕): Codfish soup.

Maeun tang (매운탕): Very spicy boiled-fish and vegetable soup.

Haemul tang (해물탕): Mixed seafood soup.

Saengseon maeun tang (생선매운탕): Spicy fish soup.

Tteok guk (떡국): Glutinous rice cake soup in beef stock. Always prepared for New Year's Day.

Mandu guk (만두국): Minced-meat and vegetable dumpling soup.

Tteokmandu guk (떡만두국): Rice cake and dumpling soup.

Ttaro guk (따로국): Spicy beef and vegetable soup, usually served with a bowl of rice. Specialty of Daegu.

Haejang guk (해장국): "Sunrise soup" of beef-bone broth, vegetables, and congealed cow blood. (Sounds yummy, no?) Good for a hangover! Settles the stomach.

Noodles

Korean noodles are made of wheat flour *(guksu* or *ramyeon)*, buckwheat and potato starch *(naengmyeon)*, or just potato starch *(dangmyeon)*. *Guksu* noodles are thin, flat, and whitish; *ramyeon* (ramen) are smaller, round, yellowish, and wavy. Both are usually served hot and in a broth, and dishes with these noodles are generally on the bland side. Usually served cold, most often in the summer, buckwheat/potato noodles are round, light gray, tough, and chewy, and are sometimes cut with a pair of scissors for easier eating. Potato starch noodles are coarse, semi-clear noodles most often mixed into rice, meat, or soup dishes. In addition, a thick, round, white wheat noodle—often hand-made at the restaurant—is often used in Chinese dishes, as is a small round vermicelli noodle.

Kal guksu (칼국수): Flat thin hand-rolled noodles in beef or chicken broth.

Kong guksu (콩국수): Cold noodles in soy milk broth.

Bibim guksu (비빔국수): Noodles and an assortment of vegetables, tofu, fish cakes, and red-pepper paste to be mixed up before being eaten—no broth.

Yubu guksu (유부국수): Noodles and fish cakes in broth.

Mak guksu (막국수): Thin potato or buckwheat noodles covered with sliced meat and vegetables, spices, egg, and red-pepper paste in chicken broth. Usually served cold.

Memil guksu (메밀국수): Cold buckwheat noodles served on a bamboo tray.

Mul naengmyeon (물냉면): Cold buckwheat noodles covered with meat strips, vegetables, spices, a hard-boiled egg, and red-pepper paste. Served in cold beef broth, often with ice cubes. Also called *Pyeongyang naengmyeon.*

Hamheung naengmyeon (함흥냉면): Cold potato noodles covered with spices, onion, garlic, and raw fish. Usually not served in water. Spicy.

Bibim naengmyeon (비빔냉면): Much like *Hamheung naengmyeon,* but not as spicy and with vegetables rather than fish. No broth. Mix in bowl before eating.

Ramyeon (라면): Cheap, instant noodles ("ramen" in Japanese and English), sometimes pronounced *namyeon.* With the addition of short pieces of rice cake, this dish is called *ddeong namyeon.*

Udong (우동): Thick wheat noodles ("udon" in Japanese).

Sujebi (수제비): Soup of misshapen and torn pieces of wheat dough boiled with onions and vegetables. Similar to *kal guksu* except for the shape.

Fish

Fish and seafood are prepared in a variety of ways. Fish is very seldom eaten as a meal in and of itself but rather as a complement to the meal, in soup, or as a side dish.

Saengseon gui (생선구이): Grilled fish.

Samchi gui (삼치구이): Broiled mackerel.

Gulbi gui (굴비구이): Broiled yellow corvina.

Songeo gui (송어구이): Broiled river trout.

Changeo gui (장어구이): Eel broiled in a sweet sauce.

Okdom (옥돔): Broiled sea bream.

Domi jjim (도미찜): Steamed red snapper.

Ke jjim (게찜): Steamed crab.

Saeu toekim (새우튀김): Deep-fried shrimp.

Nakji bokkeum (낙지볶음): Spicy sliced octopus, grilled.

Ojingeo bokkeum (오징어볶음): Spicy sliced cuttlefish, grilled.

Jeonbokjuk (전복죽): Abalone porridge.

Saengseon chobap (생선초밥): Sushi; vinegared white rice squares topped with slices of raw fish or seafood.

Hoe (회): Sliced raw fish and other sea creatures. Many varieties, including halibut *(gwangeo),* pollack *(bukeo),* skate *(hongeo),* snapper *(domi),* tuna *(chamchi),* eel *(gomjang),* shrimp *(saeu),* sea cucumber *(haesam),* and sea squirt *(mongge).*

Hoe deobbap (회덮밥): Rice covered with raw fish.

Porridges

Historically there have been dozens of kinds of porridge; during the latter part of the Joseon Dynasty, the king even started his day with a bowl. However, the popularity of this food has greatly waned in the last few decades. Still, several kinds are eaten on special occasions—*patjuk,* for example, on the shortest day of the year to ward off misfortune. Only one is now found with any regularity at specialized finer restaurants, and this is *jeonbokjuk.*

Jeonbokjuk (전복죽): Abalone porridge with a strong sesame oil flavor. Basically found only at seashore and island restaurants in the south.

Hobakjuk (호박죽): Pumpkin porridge.

Patjuk (팥죽): Red bean porridge.

Jatjuk (잣죽): Pine-nut porridge. Often served as one element of *jeongshik.*

M

Snacks

Many kinds of snacks *(bunshik)* are sold in snack shops, market stalls, hole-in-the-wall rice wine houses, and from food carts rolled out in the evening. A very few of the many are:

Odaeng (오댕): Boiled, pressed fish cake.

Pajeon (파전): Green onion pancakes.

Jeon (전): Slices of meat, fish, and vegetables pan-fried in an egg and wheat-flour batter. Many variations.

Bindaeddeok (빈대떡): Mung bean pancakes with vegetables and pork.

Gamja buchim (감자부침): Potato pancake.

Gimbap (김밥): Rice and vegetable strips rolled in seaweed laver. A type of sushi roll.

Twigim (튀김): Batter-fried vegetables or squid; "tempura" in Japanese.

Hoddeok (호떡): Oil-fried pancake filled with brown sugar.

Ddeokbokgi (떡볶이): Short cylindrical rice cakes heated in a red spicy sweet sauce.

Oksusu (옥수수): Corn on the cob.

Honghap (홍합): Steamed clams.

Ddangkong (땅꽁): Peanuts.

Bondaegi (번대기): Boiled silkworms.

Oddities

As with any country, Korea has a few foods that might not instantly appeal to the foreigner, or may even affront his or her sensitivity. None of these appear on regular menus, but they are generally served in shops that specialize in them. Due to international pressure before the 1988 Olympics, the government tried to do away with these foods, or at least move the restaurants to back alleys. This campaign met with limited success. Some of these dishes are snake soup, earthworm soup, dog meat, and dog soup.

Fruits and Nuts

Korea produces temperate-variety fruits and nuts, many of which have been introduced during the last century. Most are available fresh from late summer to early winter; dried fruits and nuts can be found all year. Follow the example of Koreans and peel all skinned fruits. Korea is rightly known for apples, and the best of the half-dozen types are huge and crisp. Pears are golden, crisp,

and shaped like apples. Aside from those listed, bananas, kiwi, and other "exotic" fruits not generally grown in Korea are imported and can be found most of the year.

Spring:

Eangdu (앵두): Bing cherry.

Ddalgi (딸기): Strawberry.

Boksunga (복숭아): Peach.

Cheondo boksunga (천도복숭아): Nectarine.

Chamoe (참외): Yellow sweet melon.

Subak (수박): Watermelon.

Podo (포도): Grape.

Autumn:

Sagwa (사과): Apple.

Bae (배): Pear.

Gam (감): Persimmon. There are hard and soft varieties. Dried persimmons are called *gotgam,* which are bright orange when ripe, brownish-orange and covered with white, natural sugar when dried.

Gyul (귤): Mandarin orange.

Gamgyul (감귤): Tangerine.

Jadu (자두): Plum.

Salgu (살구): Apricot.

Mogwa (모과): Quince.

Yuja (유자): Citron.

Seongyu (성류): Pomegranate.

Muhwagwa (무화과): Fig.

Daechu (대추): Jujube.

Bam (밤): Chestnut.

Jat (잣): Pine nut.

Hodu (호두): Walnut.

Eunhaeng (은행): Ginkgo nut.

Sweets

Aside from the various kinds of sweet rice-powder cakes served on holidays, only a few other sweets are made at home. Together, these are called *hangwa,* a traditional "cookie" made with fruit, nuts, powdered grains, and honey. More are sold at market stalls or at specialty shops in large cities, and some are now appearing at traditional-style tearooms as a complement to traditional teas. In Seoul, have a look at the shops behind the Nagwon Arcade near Insa-dong.

Songpyeon (송편): Crescent-shaped rice cake filled

with bean paste, sesame seeds, or ground chestnuts. Made only for *Chuseok.*

Chal ddeok (찰떡): Glutinous rice cake.

Akshik (약식): Cooked rice cake with chestnut and jujube.

Gyeongdan (경단): Ball-shaped rice cake.

Injeolmi (인절미): Rectangular steamed rice cakes coated with various bean powders.

Jeolpyeon (절편): Steamed rice cakes pressed by a wooden mold and coated with sesame oil.

Patshiruddeok (팥시루떡): Rice layered with pounded red beans and steamed in an earthenware pot.

Yakbap (약밥): Also known as *yakshik,* this is a steamed mixture of glutinous rice, sesame oil, sugar, and pieces of various dried fruits and nuts that's eaten cold.

Yakgwa (약과): Deep-fried wheat flour mixed with honey and nuts. Heavy and somewhat greasy.

Yugwa (유과): Deep-fried rice-flour and honey cake. Light and fluffy.

Maechakgwa (매착과): Twisted honey cake.

Songhwa (송화): Rice cake with dried and ground pine-tree sap.

Konggwa (콩과): Soybean cake.

Dashik (다식): Uncooked mixture of various flours; powdered seeds, nuts, and herbs; and honey, that's molded and dried in bite-size pieces.

Gangjeong (강정): Puffed rice cakes covered with sesame seeds, peanuts, and other ingredients.

Yeot (엿): Taffy of malt and molasses. Plain or covered with sesame or peanuts. Often sold from pushcarts in the evening, and perhaps the most common traditional sweet treat.

Japanese Foods

Sashimi: Raw fish. Called *hoe* in Korean.

Sushi: Strips of raw fish on top of vinegared rice squares. Called *chobap* in Korean.

Donburi: Various combinations of vegetables and meat placed over rice. Called *deobbap* in Korean.

Tempura: Deep-fried or batter-fried vegetables or fish. Called *twigim* in Korean.

Sukiyaki: Meat, fish, or noodles simmered in seasoned broth.

Shabu shabu: Similar to *sukiyaki* in that meat and vegetables are boiled in water and then eaten. Sometimes referred to as hot pot.

Teriyaki: Meat, chicken, fish, or seafood marinated and grilled in sweet soy sauce.

Tongaseu: Pork cutlet.

Udon: Noodle soup with various vegetable and fish ingredients.

Chinese Foods

Jajangmyeon (짜장면): Thick wheat noodles covered by black bean sauce, diced vegetables, and pork. *Jajangbap* is the same but over rice.

Jambbong (짬뽕): Thick wheat noodles in broth covered by vegetables, shellfish, and other sea creatures.

Bokkeumbap (볶음밥): Stir-fried rice.

Manduguk (만두국): Dumpling soup. Dumplings come with various ingredients, including a mixture of vermicelli noodles, vegetables, and meats.

Jinmandu (진만두): Steamed dumpling.

Yakimandu (약끼만두): Fried dumpling.

Japchae (잡채): Clear potato noodles, with vegetables, mushrooms, egg, and strips of beef. *Japchaebap* is the same, but served over, or to the side of, rice.

Tangsuyuk (탕수육): Sweet-and-sour pork.

Wantang (완탕): Wonton, dumpling soup.

Gyeran tang (계란탕): Egg drop soup.

DRINKS

As in most countries, beverages found in Korea run the gamut from water to fruit juice, soda, coffee, tea, and alcoholic drinks. Most can be found in markets, corner stores, and restaurants, but more and more, drinks are available from vending machines where the product and its price are clearly marked. Alcoholic drinks are not available from vending machines.

Cold Punch

Except for royalty and the wealthy, traditional drinks were not often made except during holidays and ceremonies, when both hot teas and cold punches *(hwachae)* were made. Most have largely been set aside in favor of other types of

ON THE ROAD

drink, but some traditional tearooms and other such establishments are now putting them on their menus.

Shikhye (식혜): A slightly sweet, fermented rice punch. Rice grains float on top.

Sujeonggwa (수정과): A sweet cinnamon, ginger, and dried-persimmon punch with pine nuts.

Omija hwachae (오미자화채): Red punch made of "five flavor" *omija* medicinal berry, often with azalea petals or steamed barley floating on top.

Fruit *hwachae:* Cold punch made with fruit pulp. Cherry, watermelon, peach, strawberry, plum, and grape are also used.

Tea

The Korean word for tea is *cha*. A variety of leaf, root, herb, fruit, and nut teas are served at ordinary tearooms called *dabang*. These plus more unusual teas, purees, and sweet traditional punches can be found at special tearooms called *dawon* or *chatjip*. Traditional teas usually run ₩5,000–7,500, while ordinary teas are perhaps half that. Not every tearoom has every tea. Certain teas have historically been ascribed healthful properties.

Hong cha (홍차): Red tea.

Nok cha (녹차): Green-leaf tea. Also called *Seollok cha*. Eases fatigue, headache, and indigestion.

Yulmu cha (율무차): Job's tears tea.

Deulkgae cha (들깨차): Sesame-seed tea.

Saenggang cha (생강차): Ginger tea. Sometimes taken to better digestion and blood circulation. Helps get rid of colds.

Gyepi cha (계피차): Cinnamon tea.

Yak cha (약차): Tea of various herbs.

Ma cha (마차): Wild medicinal herb tea.

Ssanghwa cha (쌍화차): Herbal tea with nuts and egg yolk. Often taken to help overcome a cold.

Yeongji cha (영지차): *Yeongji* mushroom tea.

Chik cha (칡차): Arrowroot tea. Helps control diarrhea.

Insam cha (인삼차): Ginseng tea. General tonic. Often taken to increase stamina and virility.

Gyulsam cha (귤삼차): Honey ginseng tea. Helps control blood pressure.

Gugija cha (구기자차): Boxthorn tea. Believed to protect liver and kidneys, and to help with muscle and skin tone.

Ssuk cha (쑥차): Mugwort tea.

Sol cha (솔차): Tea of early pine-needle shoots.

Yuja cha (유자차): Citron tea.

Mogwa cha (모과차): Quince tea.

Ogwahyang (오과향): Five-fruit tea (ginseng, jujube, chestnut, cinnamon, dried orange peel).

Omija cha (오미자차): "Five Tastes" Tea (sour, bitter, spicy, sweet, salty) from the *omija* fruit.

Gotgam cha (꽃감차): Dried persimmon tea.

Maeshil cha (매실차): Plum tea.

Gamip cha (감입차): Persimmon leaf tea.

Gukhwa cha (국화차): Chrysanthemum tea.

Gyulmaeshil cha (귤매실차): Honey plum tea.

Daechu cha (대추차): Jujube tea. Often taken to treat asthma, anemia or mental stress, or to delay aging.

Baesuk (배숙): Pear puree tea.

Jatjuk (잣죽): Pine-nut puree.

Traditional Alcoholic Drinks

Korea has a wide variety of traditional alcoholic drinks, the popularity of which has waxed or waned according to availability and economic conditions. Recently, interest in these drinks has grown, so traditional fermenting methods are being preserved. Three general types of traditional liquor were and still are produced: *takju*, an unrefined rice wine sometimes made from other grains; *cheongju*, a refined rice wine; and *soju*, a distilled liquor. In addition, there are wines made from fruits and medicinal wines. Some examples follow:

Makgeolli (막걸리): Sweetish, milky-white fermented wine made from rice or various grains. It's cheap, unfiltered, and sold by the pot or in bottles.

Dongdongju (동동주): Semi-clear, filtered rice wine where rice grains float on the top. Moderately cheap. Various kinds. Usually sold by the pot at festivals and on special occasions. Alternately known as *nongju*.

Cheongjong (청종): Purified rice wine ("sake" in Japanese), that is usually drunk warm. Expensive. Served mostly with fancy dinners.

Soju (소주): Clear potato liquor. Strong, cheap, and sold in glass bottles. Every region of the peninsula has its own brand.

Insamju (인삼주): Ginseng liquor.

Baemsul (뱀술): Hard liquor with a whole snake submerged in it. Often prescribed as a folk-medicine and sold in folk medicine shops.

The following are well-known, not widely distributed, expensive, and packaged in fancy bottles.

Gyeongju beopju (경주법주): High-quality rice wine made in Gyeongju.

Gyodong beopju (교동법주): Sweet, yellowish rice wine, also from Gyeongju.

Munbaeju (문배주): Sweet distilled liquor of wheat and millet with a crabapple flavor.

Dugyeonju (두견주): Liquor of rice and wheat, with azalea petals added for sweetness.

Igangju (이강주): Wine of pear and ginger.

Omaegiju (오매기주): Millet and dry-plum liquor made on Jeju-do.

Other Alcoholic Drinks

Maekju (맥주): Beer. The three Korean breweries are Oriental Brewery (OB), Crown, and Jinro. Most Korean beers are rather undistinguished light pilsner beers of about five percent alcohol content. A number of imported brands, including the perennial favorite Heineken are available at hotels, classier drinking establishments, and at some supermarkets.

Majuwang (마주왕): The best of Korea's grape wines. Semi-dry. Made from Riesling grapes.

Baegal (배갈): Chinese fire-water, made from sorghum. Over 75 percent alcohol content.

Goryangju (고량주): Chinese liquor much like *baegal* but slightly less potent.

Ogapi (오가피): Strong, dark medicinal Chinese liquor from the aralia root.

Various Korean-distilled Western-style hard liquors are available. Among them are whiskey, scotch, brandy, gin, and rum. Imported liquors can also be bought but are very expensive due to exorbitant tariffs.

Social Drinking

Drinking in Korea is not only well-accepted, it's encouraged and often necessary at certain social functions (such as family gatherings, weddings, and business dinners). Traditionally, only males could drink (at least in public), yet with the changing society young women now frequent some drinking establishments with friends. Koreans never drink alone—it's a social event. Hardly anyone drinks during the day, except for retired gentlemen who gather together for companionship, or those on holidays and outings. In all cases, when you finish a drink you pass the cup (or glass) to someone else and immediately fill the cup for them. That person, or another, will then pass you an empty cup and fill it. Never fill your own. On it goes until there is a mutual decision to stop. Receive an offered cup with both hands, particularly from someone older than you (or support the right with the left), and pour with two hands when filling someone else's cup. If you don't drink at all, there is no problem in refusing, but once you start it's beyond awkward to refuse another cup. Although it doesn't always happen, one drink usually becomes two. It's followed by another, and . . . you know. Sometimes, the first stop is followed by a second, and maybe a stop at a *pojang macha* on the way home. *Anju* (finger food) is always eaten when drinking. It's different for every kind of drink and varies among drinking establishments. There is little social disgrace in public drunkenness for males, yet overdrinking by females is condemned and ridiculed as a grave weakness. Problems do sometimes result from drunkenness, and these generally crop up in the home. Disgrace comes in situations where drink leads to confrontational behavior and stepping over accepted social bounds. As Koreans are hyper-aware of etiquette and manners, this rarely manifests itself.

ON THE ROAD

Information and Services 안내

TOURIST OFFICES AND INFORMATION

The **Korean National Tourism Organization (KNTO)** has its headquarters in downtown Seoul at 10, Da-dong, Jung-gu, Seoul 100-80, South Korea; www.knto.co.kr. With the most complete tourist information on the Internet, the KNTO website is available in Korean, English, Japanese, Chinese, German, French, Spanish, Russian, and Thai. The **KNTO information center** (tel. 02/757-0086) in the basement of this building is open 0900–2000 daily. It provides numerous helpful free brochures and maps, an information desk staffed with people who speak English, Japanese, Chinese, and Russian (some other languages may be spoken), a free Internet lounge, a reference library, audio-visual displays, an auditorium theater, a Korea Travel Bureau reservation desk for travel arrangements, and a shop that displays and sells traditional handicrafts made by noted artisans. The staff is very

OVERSEAS KNTO INFORMATION OFFICES

Bangkok
15th Fl., Silom Complex Bldg.
191 Silom Rd., Bangkok
10500
Thailand
tel. 2/231-3895
kntobkk@knto-th.org

Beijing
Rm., 408, B-Tower, COFCO
Plaza No. 8
Jianguomen Neidajie, Beijing
100005
People's Republic of China
tel. 10/6526-0837
bjknto@a-1.net.cn

Chicago
737 N. Michigan Ave.,
Suite 910
Chicago, IL 60611 USA
312/981-1717
kntocg@idt.net

Frankfurt
Baseler Str. 48
D-60329 Frankfurt am Main 1
Germany
tel. 69/233226
kntoff@euko.de

Fukuoka
6th Fl., Asahi Bldg.
2-1-1, Hakata-ekimae
Hakata-ku, Fukuoka
Japan 812
tel. 92/471-7174
fukuoka@knto.or.jp

Hong Kong
Suite 4203, Tower 1, Lippo
Centre, 89
Queensway, Admiralty
Hong Kong
tel. 2523-80650441
general@knto.com.hk

London
3rd Fl., New Zealand House
Haymarket, London SW1Y
4TE
United Kingdom
tel. 20/7321-2535
koreatb@dircon.co.uk

Los Angeles
4801 Wilshire Blvd., Suite 103
Los Angeles, CA 90010 USA
323/643-0025
kntola@mail.wcis.com

Moscow
4th Fl., Mosarlarko Plaza One
d. 16
ul Marksistskaya
109147 Moscow Russia
tel. 095/230-6240
kntomc@hotbox.ru

Nagoya
2nd Fl., Toyopet Nissei Bldg.
2-13-30, Higashi Sakura
Higashi-ku, Nagoya
Japan 461
tel. 52/933-6550
nagoya@knto.or.jp

New York area
One Executive Drive, Suite 100
Fort Lee, NJ 07024 USA
201/585-0909
kntony@ring3.net

Osaka
8th Fl., KAL Bldg.
3-1-9, Hon-machi,
Chuo-ku, Osaka
Japan 541
tel. 6/6266-0847
osaka@knto.or.jp

knowledgeable and can help with most any question. This is the best place in the country to gather travel-related information. KNTO also operates information desks at the Incheon, Gimpo, Gimhae, and Jeju-do international airports and at the international ferry terminals in Busan and Incheon. In addition, KNTO staffs an information center that is open daily in each of the metropolitan cities and provinces in the country. Some cities also staff an information office at a convenient location within the city. See the individual travel chapters for specific locations. To contact the nearest information center by phone during regular business hours from anywhere in the country, simply dial **1330**, and this connects you with the Korea Travel Phone Service in the city or province that you are calling from. For information about other areas, dial the area code for that city or province followed by 1330. These calls require the normal phone charges.

The Seoul city government maintains the **Seoul Tourist Information Center** (tel. 02/3707-9470) on the main floor of city hall in the center of the city. It's open Monday–Saturday 0900–1800 but closed Sunday and national holidays. Like the KNTO, it has a plethora of informational brochures and maps, a helpful staff to answer questions, and free Internet access. It also staffs a half dozen information booths at convenient locations around the city. For additional information, see www.visitseoul.net or www.metro.seoul.kr.

Tourist-information offices are distinguished by round brown signs with a white lower-case "i" in the middle.

Tourist Complaint Center

For complaints, compliments, questions, or suggestions, contact the Tourist Complaint Center (tel. 02/735-0101).

ON THE ROAD

Paris
Tour Maine Montparnasse
33, Avenue du Maine B.P. 169
75755 Paris Cedex 15
France
tel. 1/4538-7123
knto@club-internet.fr

Sendai
1st Fl., Nihonseimei Sendaik-
outoudai Minami Bldg.
1-5-15, Kamasugi
Aoba-ku, Sendai
Japan 980
tel. 22/711-5991
sendai@knto.or.jp

Singapore
#20-01, Clifford Centre
24 Raffles Place
Singapore 04862
tel. 533-0441
kntosp@pacific.net.sg

Sydney
17th Fl., Tower Bldg.
Australia Square, George St.
Sydney, N.S.W. 2000
Australia
tel. 2/9252-4147
visitkorea@knto.org.au

Taipei
Rm. 2005, Int'l. Trade Center
Bldg.
333 Keelung Rd., Sec.1
Taipei 10548
Taiwan
tel. 2/2720-8049
kntotp@ms5.hinet.net

Tokyo
Rm. 124, Sanshin Bldg.
1-4-1, Yuraku-cho
Chiyoda-ku, Tokyo
Japan 100
tel. 3/3580-3941
tokyo@knto.or.jp

Toronto
700 Bay Street, Suite 1903
Toronto, Ontario M5G 1Z6
Canada
416/348-9056
toronto@knto.ca

North America
toll-free information for USA
and Canada
800/868-7567

Goodwill Guide Service

For those who feel that they need extra help while in Korea or are in need of translation services on a short-term basis, KNTO offers the free Goodwill Guide service. Volunteers registered with KNTO—all can be identified by their official badges—can be enlisted for help in various locales around the country, and these guides speak a variety of languages including English, Japanese, and Chinese. No payment is necessary for this service, but you will be expected to pick up the cost of the guide's transportation, food, entrance fees, and other such items. Make application for a Goodwill Guide at least two weeks prior to your needing a guide. For information and application for this service, call 02/729-9446 in country or apply online at www.goodwillguide.com.

Electronic Information

Many sources of current tourist and general information about Korea are available over the Internet. Subjects include tourist sites, accommodations, transportation, entry requirements, weather, and activities. These are a few of the many websites available (and they have links to other sites): www.korea.net, www.koreainfogate.com, www.lifeinkorea.com, and www.1stopkorea.com.

For Military Personnel

The U.S.O. in Seoul near the west entrance to the Yongsan Garrison has a small tourist-information desk (tel. 02/795-3028, military 724-7003). Base Tour and Travel Centers offer travel tips, organized tours in-country, out-of-country travel arrangements, and discount airfares.

Books and Maps

Books about Korea are best found at the RAS (Royal Asiatic Society) office, several large bookstores in Seoul and major cities around the country, at hotel bookshops, and at some airport kiosks. See the travel chapters for details.

Get high-quality country, city, province, and special interest **maps** free from the KNTO, Seoul city, and local tourist information offices around the country. Other similar maps incorporating advertising are also widely available for free.

The most complete map store in the country is **Jungang Jido** (tel. 02/730-9191), also known as the Jungang Atlas Company. Located between Boshingak and Jogye-sa in Seoul, this store sells some tourist and road maps of the same caliber as the free maps from the tourist offices. It also has detailed maps of every section of the country (more detailed than travelers need), which might require a signature and passport number before purchase. For anyone looking for detail, this is the place to come.

Excellent **national parks maps** are published by the Korea National Parks Authority and are available at the entrance to each park for ₩500–1000. If you intend to hike, your best bet is to use the national park maps or, outside of the national parks, get detailed commercial topographical maps available at some large bookshops and many sporting goods stores. These commercial maps are published for the best mountain hiking areas in the country, cost about ₩2,000, and are printed on a non-ripping paper. Even though they are printed only in Korean, they are the best maps available as they show elevation, shading, trails, huts, springs, and streams, and give average walking times for each section of major trails.

Street maps and **road atlases** are sold at major bookshops throughout the country and at Jungang Atlas Company in Seoul. For the casual tourist, these maps and atlases are way too bulky and detailed. However, for someone renting a car and intending to drive in the country, they may be a necessity. The one huge drawback is that nearly all are printed only in Korean—good practice for those learning the language! A number of these maps and atlases are available and each has a sufficient but not overly thorough index. Whole country atlases are usually in the 1:100,000 to 1:150,000 scale; Seoul and other metropolitan city road maps are most often printed in a 1:10,000 scale. All show plenty of detail for good navigation. Depending upon the publisher, prices range from ₩12,000–20,000. For the driver, it's money well spent—if you can read Korean.

MONEY AND BANKING

Korean currency is called *won*—shown as a ₩ before monetary amounts. Denominations are ₩10, ₩50, ₩100, and ₩500 in coin; and ₩1,000, ₩5,000, and ₩10,000 in bills. The old ₩1 and ₩5 coins are no longer in circulation. Virtually all prices are in denominations of 10 or 100 and even banks will round up or down to the nearest 10 *won* when doing money exchange. The value of the *won* is closely tied to the U.S. dollar and fluctuates slowly. In 1964, the value of the *won* stood at ₩255 to the dollar; by July 1986 it had fallen to ₩899. Recouping some of its loss, it stayed in the US$1=₩780–800 range through much of the mid-1990s, but took a nosedive to about ₩1,800 as a result of the 1997 Asian financial crisis. Since then, the dollar/*won* ratio has rebounded to stay at roughly US$1=₩1,200. For the exchange rate of any foreign currency to *won*, see the Korean Exchange Bank website: http://ebank.keb.co.kr/exchange/fx_rate.htm. For currency converters, try www.x-rates.com, www.oanda.com, www.xe.com, and www.jeico.co.kr/currency1.html. It's illegal to exchange foreign currencies anywhere but at authorized banks, hotels, and money-exchange dealers, but there are plenty of them around. A currency black market operates in Seoul, Busan, and around U.S. military bases, but it's strictly illegal and cannot be recommended. A plaque next to the front door of a bank indicates exchange privileges; rates are posted inside. Each bank sets its own exchange rate, but there is little difference between the rates that banks offer, except for those at the airport, which are slightly less favorable. Hotels adjust rates more in their favor. Traveler's checks have a slightly better exchange rate than cash and these rates can and often do fluctuate several times during a single day. Nearly four dozen Asian/Pacific, European, Middle Eastern, and American currencies can be exchanged in Korea, the most widely accepted are the U.S. dollar and Japanese yen. Some currencies may not be accepted in provincial cities. If possible, exchange your money in large cities. It's perhaps best to exchange enough money for a week or two. If you exchange too much, your loss is greater if you lose your money or your money is stolen. In any event, a stack of Korean bills can get rather bulky. Traveler's checks are most easily exchanged at a branch of the bank of origin, but others will take them. Foreign currency exchange is usually handled at its own station along the bank counter and sometimes in a different section of the bank or at an upstairs office. The appropriate forms must be filled out, traveler's checks signed or bills counted, and your passport presented. The exchange procedure is quick, and in a few minutes you will be given the converted equivalent in *won* and a receipt—some banks ask you to step to a separate window to receive payment. Save your receipts if you wish to reconvert money when you leave the country. If you experience any problem in exchanging money, contact the nearest branch of the Korea Foreign Exchange Bank.

ATM cards may also be used to withdraw money from your accounts in Korean *won* from bank machines that have "global access" and from ATM machines located at Korean post offices. Credit cards may also be used for cash advances. Look for ATM machines that display logos for systems that your bank uses. Exchange rates will be calculated by the bank and are generally not as favorable as exchanging traveler's checks. Screen instructions on these ATM machines are usually written in English and Japanese. Be sure to use a numerical 4-digit PIN number only! If you access your account with other than a 4-digit PIN number and plan to use your ATM card while in Korea, change your PIN number *before* you leave your country.

Korean banks are located in all cities and towns. About five dozen foreign banks have branch or representative offices in Seoul. A dozen are also located in Busan, with a couple each in Incheon and Daegu. **Bank hours** are Monday–Friday 0930–1630 and Saturday 0930–1330 (some branches may open at 0900), closed Sunday and holidays.

Credit Cards

While credit cards are accepted at major hotels, department stores, duty-free shops, tourist restaurants, and some other establishments that cater mainly to foreign tourists, the best practice is to use them only in emergency situations. Most places will display a decal of cards they honor, but be sure to ask first before using them. The most widely accepted cards are VISA, American Express, MasterCard, Diners Club, and JCB. Some establishments ask for identification before accepting payment by credit card. Be sure to check your receipt carefully to make sure there are no additional charges.

Change Machines

While not numerous, change machines can be found in some hotel lobbies and department stores, at subway stations, at the entrances to some parks, and generally where there are automatic ticket machines. Only ₩1,000 bills are accepted.

THE POSTAL SYSTEM

The Korean postal system has been in continuous service since 1895. Today there are over 2,800 post offices in the country. Post office hours are Monday–Friday 0900–1800 (1700 Nov.–Feb.) and Saturday 0900–1300. There are special night hours at the Seoul Central Post Office and at the C.P.O. in each provincial capital for stamp sales only: Monday–Friday until 2200 and until 1800 on Saturday, Sunday, and public holidays. Service is friendly and delivery is efficient. Letters within the country take 1–2 days, 6–9 days outside the country; parcels

postal symbol

require 4–6 weeks. Every post office sells stamps and aerogrammes, and will post international parcels. The postal system reserves the right to inspect all outgoing mail, and printed matter must be sent tied but not sealed. Major post offices offer international money orders. The C.P.O.s in Seoul and Busan have poste restante service, and will keep mail for 30 days—longer if requested. Other post offices will keep mail upon request. With the increased use of email and to some ex-

tent cellular phones, the poste restante is seeing less use now than it did years ago. The Seoul C.P.O. also has a philatelic office, for commemorative and special-issue stamp sale, and a postal museum.

Postal Rates

In-country letters up to 50 grams cost ₩170, registered letters to 50 grams ₩1,050. These rates increase by ₩50 for each additional 50 grams. Within Korea, packages weighing up to two kg are ₩1,000, with an additional ₩500 for each extra kg; postcards are ₩150. Aerogrammes to anywhere in the world are ₩400, and postcards ₩350. The cost of airmail letters varies according to zone: ₩420 to Far East Asia; ₩450 to Southeast Asia; ₩480 to North America, Europe, the Middle East, and Oceania; and ₩500 to Africa and Latin America for the basic rate. Higher rates apply to certified and speed-post letters, printed matter, and packages over two kg. Air- and seamail packages up to 20 kg can be delivered to most countries of the world. The size and total dimension of packages accepted vary by country. Selected rates for a 10-kg air/sea-mail package are: ₩28,700/₩16,000 to Japan and East Asia, ₩41,800/₩16,500 to Southeast Asia, ₩81,000/₩20,000 to Europe, Middle East, and North America, and ₩120,000/₩22,500 to most of the rest of the world. Insurance is extra.

Package-Wrapping Service

Larger post offices provide a package-wrapping service. You get good work at reasonable rates, and using this service saves you running around to get box, paper, and tape to do the job yourself. Charges are levied by size of box, ranging from about ₩2,000 for a small parcel to ₩5,500 for a package about half a meter on a side. Odd-shaped objects and breakable items can also be wrapped but the charge is higher. Independent wrapping services, often found adjacent to post offices, charge about the same, and some hotels also offer the service to guests.

Private Providers

Several commercial providers also ship packets and parcels from Korea to nearly all points around the world, and they may do it more expediently than the postal system. FedEx (tel. 02/738-5331), DHL (tel. 02/1588-0001), and UPS (tel. 02/3665-3651) are three, while Mail Boxes Etc. (tel. 02/758-2157) can also make these arrangements through these and other providers. Although rates vary somewhat among providers and are adjusted periodically, all charge by the weight and zone. Depending upon the zone, document service runs approximately ₩16,000–32,000 for half a kilogram and ₩82,000–212,000 for up to five kilograms. Parcel service starts at about ₩55,000 for a half kilogram and runs up to ₩1,700,000 for 70 kilograms.

TELEPHONE

Domestic

Korean telephone numbers have 7 or 8 digits. Phone numbers for cellular phones have 10 digits. When calling within your area code no prefix is necessary. When making a call outside your area code, you must use a 2 or 3 digit area code prefix in front of the telephone number.

It seems that nearly everyone in Korea has a cellular phone (see the Cellular Phones section of this chapter for information on renting one), but for those who do not have a cellular phone, local telephone calls can be made from nearly any public phone. There are several types of public phones that accept coins and/or telephone cards. **Coin**-operated phones require ₩100 coins and calls last three minutes. Insert your coin to start the call, then add additional coins if necessary when the display runs down to zero or your three minutes are up. For long-distance calls, prefix the number by the area code and make sure that you have a pocket full of coins before you place a call—they are not cheap. Insert additional coins when you hear the beeps. Unused change is not refunded when you hang up. **Card** telephones can be used to make local and long-distance calls. Simply insert a telephone card in

TELEPHONE AREA CODES FOR SOUTH KOREA	
Seoul	.02
Busan	.051
Daegu	.053
Incheon	.032
Gwangju	.062
Daejeon	.042
Ulsan	.052
Gyeonggi-Do	.031
Gangwon-Do	.033
Chungcheongbuk-Do	.043
Chungcheongnam-Do	.041
Gyeongsangbuk-Do	.054
Gyeongsangnam-Do	.055
Jeollabuk-Do	.063
Jeollanam-Do	.061
Jeju-Do	.064

The South Korea **country code** is 82.

ON THE ROAD

the slot and dial away. A warning signal will sound when there are only 15 seconds left on the value of your card. A call can be continued by inserting a new card into the slot after pushing the "card change" button. Cards are issued in ₩3,000, ₩5,000, and ₩10,000 denominations, and are sold at most corner stores and street kiosks near phone booths. Operator-assisted long-distance calls can be made from any Telecom office and from some post offices. These calls are marginally more expensive and the rates are based on three-minute segments. Discounts of 30 percent are given for all calls made between 2000 and 0800 on weekdays, after 1600 on Saturday, and all day on Sunday and holidays. A business and commercial telephone directory is available in English, and directory assistance in English is available at 02/725-0114. Brochures are available at most tourist offices and Telecom offices detailing the steps for making any local, long-distance, or international call. Telecom offices are located in virtually all cities in the country.

International

Korea has telecommunications connections with the rest of the world by ordinary cable lines, fiber-optic links, and satellite. There is International Direct Dialing (IDD) to most countries of the world. The most convenient way to make an international phone call is by using a prepaid international phone card in a public telephone set up to accept these telephone cards. With IDD, dial 001 (or 002, or 008), then the country code, area code, and finally the telephone number. For discounted service, use a WorldPhone Card, available at Telecom offices, post offices, and some banks in ₩5,000, ₩10,000, and greater amounts. For these cards, you must dial an access number, the card number, then access code, country code, area code, and telephone number. Home Country Direct calling is also a possibility to certain countries from dedicated phones; charges will be billed to a number in the country that you are calling. Operator-assisted international calls can be made at a Telecom office or by dialing 00799. For international call information, dial 00794. Collect calls and calls charged on credit cards may also be placed with an operator. Calls can also be made from any Telecom office with rates set by country. Telecom offices have 24-hour service. Operator-assisted, station-to-station calls have the same rates as standard IDD calls, while person-to-person calls are 25 percent higher; operator-assisted calls are charged by an initial three-minute segment, followed by one-minute segments. International telegrams can be sent by dialing 00795, but to avoid errors, place the request in writing at any Telecom office in the country. Two services are available: ordinary and express.

Cellular Phones

Cellular or mobile phones can be rented while in country for domestic and international calls. This can be done by reserving a phone before arriving, by renting one at the airport when you arrive, or by renting at a city location. A number of companies offer this service. With this service, there is usually a rental fee (around ₩20,000), daily fee (perhaps ₩3,000–4,000),

and per minute charge (about ₩400). With some companies you can make a prepayment against total calling charges, but with others your bill will be tabulated when you return the phone. For additional information, contact Korea Travel Telecom (tel. 02/3472-1600 or 032/743-4300) or LG Telecom (tel. 032/743-4019) or stop by their booths at the Incheon International Airport.

Similarly, handheld PDA devices, which also double as cellular phones, can be rented at the Incheon International Airport and at the KNTO Tourist Information Center in Seoul. With a screen and keyboard, these have access to online tourist information, maps, money exchanges, email, simple translation, and much more. Daily rates run about ₩10,000 with additional per-minute charges for the phone connection. Try Mobiya (tel. 02/548-6627), SDK (tel. 02/776-8816), or Wink (tel. 02/318-6568).

Cellular phones will be of most use to business travelers and those looking for work in Korea; most tourists will not find one necessary.

HOSPITALS AND PHARMACIES

Korean doctors, dentists, nurses, optometrists, and other medical professionals are highly trained. Major hospitals dispense quality care on a level with developed countries. Most hospitals have some English-speaking staff. Some doctors and dentists speak other languages, but it's best to check with your embassy for names and telephone numbers of recommended medical providers. Except for Red Cross hospitals, hospitals are often topped by green crosses (red crosses cap church steeples). Medical facilities in Seoul accustomed to foreigners are Severance Hospital International Clinic (tel. 02/361-6540), open 1000–1200 and 1400–1700 weekdays and located next to Yonsei University; Asan Medical Center International Clinic (tel. 02/2224-5001), open 0900–1700 weekdays, located near Olympic Park; and Samsung Medical Center International Clinic (tel. 02/3410-0200), open 0900–1700 weekdays and 0900–1200 on Saturday, located in Gangnam-gu near Ilwon Station on subway line #3.

Pharmacies carry a mind-boggling array of drugs and health-care items, almost everything except narcotics. Labels are printed in Korean with some in English, but the names of many drugs are pronounced as in English, and most are reasonably priced. Most Korean pharmacists have not been trained as their Western counterparts have, but have learned their jobs from experience. While it's reasonable to rely upon their advice in alleviating minor discomfort, visit a doctor for major health problems. Hospital pharmacies, on the other hand, have qualified staff. Major hotels have house doctors and small pharmacies.

Alternatives include herbal medicine, folk remedies, and acupuncture. These treatments are generally prescribed for long-term prevention and not for quick cures. If you explore these health-care options, take along a Korean-speaking friend; few practitioners speak English.

MEDIA

Newspapers and Magazines

There are half a dozen major newspapers in Seoul, and several in each major city and province. Having suffered censorship and repression during the 1960s, '70s, and '80s, the news media is now relatively freer. The two English-language dailies in Korea are *The Korea Herald,* www.koreaherald.co.kr, and *The Korea Times,* www.koreatimes.co.kr. Published every day except Monday and national holidays, each costs ₩500 a copy. International news is sparse, and only "acceptable" items make the front page. Coverage of domestic political news, cultural events, and feature items is good, however. A third newspaper, the *Joongang Ilbo,* publishes an English-language insert that is put into the *International Herald Tribune.*

For English-language news published by other Korean dailies and news organizations, see http://english.chosun.com *(Chosun Ilbo),* http://english.donga.com *(Dong-A Ilbo),* http://english.joins.com *(Joongang Ilbo),* http://english.hankyung.com *(The Korea Economic Daily),* and www.yonhapnews.co.kr *(Yonhap News Agency).*

Hotel bookshops, large bookstores, and select sidewalk newsstands in large cities sell Korean newspapers, the English-language dailies, and a handful of foreign newspapers. Some of the foreign papers, which run ₩1,000–2,000 a copy, are the *Financial Times, Asian Wall Street Journal, International Herald Tribune,* and *USA Today.* The Pacific edition of the U.S. military newspaper, the *Stars and Stripes,* is available on U.S. military bases and at the U.S.O.

Korean-published English-language magazines and journals include the *Korea Journal, Korean Quarterly, Koreana: Korean Art and Culture, Korea News World, Business Korea,* and *Korea Economic Report;* the *Courier de la Coree* is published in French. A wide range of foreign magazines on multiple topics are also available in-country, including several that are translated into Korean for mass appeal. They are available at hotel kiosks and at large bookstores in Seoul. Some are: *Time, Newsweek, The Economist, U.S. News and World Report, Far Eastern Economic Review, Harvard Business Review, Foreign Affairs, Fortune, Money, Cosmopolitan, Rolling Stone, Architectural Digest, Sports Illustrated,* and *GQ,* and *Stern* and *Der Spiegel* in German and *L'Express International* in French.

Television and Radio

Television broadcasting in Korea started in 1956 with a private commercial station. In 1961, the government started the KBS (Korean Broadcasting Service) station, and in 1969 the private commercial MBC (Munhwa Broadcasting Corporation) station entered the market. SBS (Seoul Broadcasting Service) and EBS (Eastern Broadcasting Service) also now have broadcasting rights. Korean television went color in 1980. Since the 1990s, there have been cable and satellite stations. One cable channel which broadcasts in English is Arirang TV. In addition, the U.S. Armed Forces television station, AFKN (Army Forces Korea Network), broadcasts typical American programming in areas of U.S. military concentration.

There is more than one television set for every household in the country. As in the West, television viewing is taking up an increasingly larger percentage of free time for young and old alike. Typical programs are game shows, comedies, musical variety shows, serial dramas, sporting events, and dubbed foreign films. Perhaps the best shows for foreigners are the historical dramas and soap operas, which offer insight into historical and present-day Korea, its cultural values, traditions, and the inner workings of the Korean family and society. Even without speaking Korean, it's often possible to understand some of what's happening.

For those wanting domestic television news information in English without having to watch the tube, try online at www.arirang.co.kr/english (Arirang TV).

Numerous Korean **radio** stations, plus a U.S. military station, broadcast on both AM and FM bands. For the military AFKN station, turn to AM 1530 or FM 102.7.

Practicalities

WHAT TO TAKE

Korea has four distinct seasons. Dress appropriately. Lightweight, loose-fitting clothes should be worn during the hot, muggy summer. Not long ago shorts were worn only at the beach or when playing sports. Now they're acceptable as ordinary summer wear. Bring your swimsuit and towel for the beach, and a hat for the sun. Lightweight clothes are also good for spring and autumn days, though you'll need a jacket, sweater, or down vest for the evenings. Heavy clothes, down jackets, gloves, hats, long underwear, and wool socks will keep you warm during the winter. You'll need an umbrella (the collapsible type is most convenient) or a waterproof parka or shell (more protective) during the spring and midsummer rains. If you are in Korea on business, a business suit and dress shoes are necessary. Otherwise, casual clothes are the norm. High-quality, inexpensive clothes are available in Korea, but sizing may be a problem. Backless dresses, miniskirts, and "revealing," dirty, or torn clothing are unacceptable and should not be worn.

Slip-off shoes (Koreans step down on the backs of their shoes) or loosely tied shoes are the most convenient as you'll need to take them off whenever you enter a home, *yeogwan* room, some restaurants, temples, and various other places. Rubber thongs and sandals and shoes without socks are worn at home, in the neighborhood, and at the beach, but are generally not worn when going out or when traveling. If you plan to hike, sturdy walking shoes or boots are best, although jogging shoes are sufficient except on muddy and snowy trails.

Bring your own sleeping bag, water bottle, and cooking gear if you intend to spend more than a day in the mountains. Tents are not usually necessary as mountain huts are located along most trails. Camping spots are located in all national parks and most provincial parks.

Other items of importance: a small flashlight with extra batteries, small candle and lighter for power outages, travel alarm, Swiss army knife, sewing kit, thin nylon rope for a clothesline, several bandannas, combination or key lock for your travel bag or room without a locking door, folding paper fan (can be bought in Korea) for sultry summer days, toothbrush (one spare), toothpaste, soap, shampoo, razor, toiletries, suntan lotion, mosquito lotion, and plastic bags to compartmentalize and keep your goods dry. Take along extra eyeglasses or lens prescriptions, prescription medication (with a legible prescription) and generic names of drugs, and a compact first-aid kit. Prescription medication should be carried in original containers—it's easier getting through customs that way—and drugs containing narcotics should be accompanied by an explanatory letter from your physician detailing the necessity of the medication. Over-the-counter medicines are available at pharmacies in Korea, but it's not always easy to explain what you need. Antimalarial medication is not necessary. Be sure your insurance covers you for injury and illness while traveling abroad (also for theft or loss of personal affects), or obtain temporary travel insurance from another provider.

Carry your valuables and extra passport photos in a money belt or small bag hung around your neck under your clothes. Keep a photocopy of your passport, visa, traveler's checks, credit cards, driver's license, international driver's license, and other important documents and information in your luggage. Leave at home unnecessary credit cards, valuables, expensive jewelry, and anything that cannot be replaced. Bring a journal, notebook, and pens. Don't forget your camera and plenty of film for all the photo opportunities.

Travel light: a soft-sided travel bag (e.g. duffel bag, internal-frame backpack, or convertible backpack/suitcase) is easy to handle, comfortable to carry, and best for loading onto luggage racks. Label all pieces of luggage, and don't forget to put your name and address inside your luggage as well. A day- or fanny-pack is good for short excursions or a walk around town.

BUSINESS HOURS

Government office hours are Monday–Friday 0900–1800 (0900–1700 from November through February) and Saturday 0900–1300; closed Sunday and holidays. While most private businesses open at 0900 and close at 1800, some start at 0830 and operate until 1900. Banking hours are Monday–Friday 0930–1630 and Saturday 0930–1330 (some branches may open at 0900); closed Sunday and holidays. Hours for foreign diplomatic missions are generally Monday–Friday 0900–1700, closed weekends. Missions are also closed on Korean holidays and their own country's holidays. Some have limited hours for their consular sections, so inquire before visiting. Department stores are open 1030–1930; all are closed one day a week. Markets and commercial stores are open from mid-morning until late evening. Restaurants most often open in late morning and close at mid- to late evening. Tearooms also open at mid-morning but stay open until nearly midnight. Drinking establishments generally open in late afternoon and close after

midnight, while some stay open until dawn. Operational hours for palaces, museums, and royal gravesites vary by site but are usually 0900–1800; ticket sales usually stop one hour before closing. Palaces and museums are closed one day a week, usually Monday or Tuesday.

ENTRANCE FEES

Entrance fees listed in this book are given only for adults, except where children's fees are of particular importance, such as at children's parks. Usually, fees for young people ages 7–24 are reduced by about half. Small children and senior citizens are almost always exempt from entrance fees.

ADDRESSES AND PHONE NUMBERS

This book lists few addresses as they are almost never used for location, except by the postal system. Locations are described by indicating an area of the city or proximity to a large building or other landmark. In Seoul and other large cities, locations are sometimes given in reference to the *ga* (block) along certain major streets.

Telephone numbers are only listed where it is known or reasonably assumed that someone on the other end can speak English, Japanese, or another foreign language. Be aware that some telephone numbers change with amazing rapidity. For current numbers, ask at tourist-information offices or call directory assistance (English) at 02/725-0114.

LAUNDRY

Clothes can be hand-washed at *yeogwan* in your room's bathroom. For rooms with shared bathrooms, use the communal washroom. Some accommodations now have washing machines that can be used by guests for a minimal fee. Hang garments on a line outside or on the roof. During cool weather, underclothing can also be dried by laying them on a heated *ondol* floor, and outer clothes pressed by putting dry items under the *yo* mattress.

Laundries, called *setakso,* also wash, dry, and press clothing for reasonable fees. Ask for recommendations and directions from your *yeogwan* proprietor. Turnaround time is one or two days. Most hotels have laundry service, and while very convenient, it will certainly be more expensive than arranging this on your own.

TOILETS

There are relatively few public bathrooms in Korea, and these are not always clean. Most can be found in underground shopping arcades, subway or train stations, bus terminals, and at museums, parks, and recreation and sporting facilities. Much cleaner, and ones which you can expect to use without any problem, are bathrooms in hotel lobbies, department stores, cultural performance venues, and office buildings. Every restaurant also has a bathroom. From the late 1990s, there has been a concerted and government-subsidized effort in large cities to construct and maintain public toilets to better standards, to encourage private businesses to open their toilets to the public, to subsidize business for keeping their public toilets up to standards, and to install signs indicating where public toilets are located. Although not perfect, the situation is much improved over years ago, particularly in areas of big cities that see plenty of foreigners.

Hotels have Western-style toilets, similar to those found anywhere in the world. Most other accommodations have now installed Western-style toilets, but some still have pit-style squat toilets—face the end with the raised lip. Toilet paper is not always provided, so carry your own. When it's sold from a vending machine, it may be ₩200 for a small package. Often there will be a small wastebasket next to a Western-style toilet for soiled toilet paper—paper has a tendency to clog pipes. For pit toilets, toss the paper into the hole. Toilets are distinguished by male and female figures or by the Korean words *yeo* (여), for female, and *nam* (남), for male, on the door. If no picture or word appears, feel free to use either.

DRINKING WATER

Tap water in Korea is generally safe, but many people do not drink it because of the chemicals that are put in it to make it so. Bottled water (or boiled barley tea) will always be served at restaurants and tearooms, is supplied to most *yeogwan* and hotel rooms, and is sometimes available in public buildings and offices. Bottled spring and mineral water is sold at supermarkets, convenience stores, and corner shops. If you question the water at all, use bottled water to brush your teeth in place of tap water.

PEDESTRIAN TRAFFIC

Although automobiles drive on the right side of the street, as in most of the world, pedestrians walk and pass on the left and use the left side of stairways. Please, observe this habit unless the general flow of foot traffic is otherwise, the walkways are exceptionally wide, or arrows on the pavement or stairway indicate that you should do something else.

DRUGS

Illegal drugs are dealt with harshly in Korea. In 1975, marijuana was made illegal. While hemp is grown for its fiber (some grows wild), it's illegal to dry, distribute, or smoke the leaves. According to a government publication of some years ago, "Those who engage in the import, export, or manufacturing of drugs will be liable to a penalty of a minimum sentence of seven years in prison and a maximum sentence of capital punishment or life in prison. Those convicted of trafficking in drugs are subject to 10 years in prison." This applies to opium, narcotics, and other chemical drugs; marijuana laws are less stringent. Nonetheless, some drugs are available, and the methamphetamine Hiroppon and designer drugs are among the most popular. Some foreigners have been kicked out of the country for their use of drugs, and an unlucky few have experienced several years inside a Korean prison.

CIGARETTES

Many varieties of Korean cigarettes—unfiltered, mild, light, and menthol—are available, plus several American and European brands. Packs are sold over the counter and from vending machines. Like most East Asians, Koreans are voracious smokers, and they generally don't mind if you are too. Traditionally, only men, and women over about 60 years of age, smoked. Today, many young and middle-aged women have taken up the habit, but still may not do so in public except in the youth-oriented areas near universities, city center entertainment districts, and some restaurants and coffee shops. The government has instituted a multi-faceted campaign to reduce smoking, but the habit continues. This seems a bit contradictory because a government entity owns a monopoly on tobacco production, distribution, advertising, and marketing. Smoking is not allowed on buses and airplanes, and in some public buildings. More and more, No Smoking signs are in evidence but not always obeyed or enforced. Where there is a no smoking zone, such as at major airports, there may be a small contained and ventilated smoking booth for those who can't help themselves.

STORAGE LOCKERS

Storage lockers are located at most major transportation centers and at some subway stations. The largest lockers are big enough to take a medium-size soft suitcase or a couple of smaller bags. Although fees vary somewhat, the usual charge is ₩1,000 a day; slightly more for the largest lockers. There is a three-day limit (some have one-day limits), after which bags are cleared. Be aware that most bus and subway stations close at about 2400, so have your things out before then if you need them overnight.

PHOTO MACHINES

These are located at some subway stations, below-ground shopping arcades, and at many amusement parks. They give two (or four) small color shots for ₩4,000–5,000. Passport-size photos can be made at most small photo shops where the price will run about ₩10,000 for eight pictures.

FILM AND PHOTO DEVELOPING

Various brands of film, including Kodak, Fuji, and Agfa, are available in Korea in print and slide format. Prices are not uniform, so you must look around for the best price. As an example, Kodak 36-exposure ASA 100 print film runs about ₩3,600 per roll; slide film runs about ₩6,000. Most photo shops can develop print film in about one hour. Expect a fee of ₩1,500 to develop the roll and ₩200–250 per picture to print.

INTERNET SERVICE

While there are numerous Internet cafés and similar Internet access sites around the country that generally charge around ₩1,000–2,000 an hour, free Internet access is available at all major tourist information offices in Seoul and around the country. In addition, free Internet access is also available at most major post offices. Some budget travel accommodations also have free Internet access for their guests.

WEIGHTS AND MEASURES
Time

In international time designation, Korea is GMT + 9 hours. When it is 1200 in Greenwich, England, it is 2100 in Seoul, Korea. There is no daylight saving time in Korea. Sample time differences between Korea at 1200 and other parts of the world are: New York (-14; 2200 previous day), Los Angeles (-17; 1900 previous day), Honolulu (-19; 1700 previous day), Tokyo (same), Beijing (-1; 1100), Bangkok (-2; 1000), Riyadh (-6; 0600), and Frankfurt (-8; 0400).

Electricity

Korea is wired for 220-volt, 60-cycle electricity, but 110-volt outlets are also sometimes available. Major hotels in the country are wired for both. Check the voltage before plugging anything in. The 220-volt outlets accept two-prong round plugs while 110-volt outlets accept standard two-prong, flat and parallel plugs. Many 220 outlets are sunk into round cups. Adapters are available at electrical shops in Korea and should be found at full-service hardware stores and specialty shops in other countries.

Measurements

Korea primarily uses the metric system of measurement, followed by traditional Korean mea-

surements. A chart at the back of this book will help visitors accustomed to the Anglo-American system of measurement make the appropriate conversions. Provided here are a few Korean measurements.

1 *gan* = approximately 4 square meters, the area between four structural posts

1 *geun* = 600 grams, dry measure

1 *li* = 400 meters

1 *ma* = 91.4 centimeters, a measure for cloth

1 *mal* = 18 liters, wet measure

Seoul 서울

Seoul is a city of contrasts. In this rapidly evolving metropolis, the traditional co-exists with the modern in a state of harmony. For over 500 years the seat of Joseon Dynasty kings, Seoul is now the beating heart of modern Korea, the center to which all else in the country is drawn. It's the focus for government and politics, business and the economy, education, communication, transportation, culture, and the arts. All embassies, the main offices of all major Korean and foreign businesses and banks, the majority of the nation's most highly respected universities, and a multiplicity of research institutes, cultural foundations, and national sports facilities are located here. Seoul is also the principal international gateway to the country, one of the most significant cities of Asia, and one of the dozen most populous urban centers in the world.

Into the rich tapestry of its historical and cultural past have been woven threads of modernization. Rushing headlong into the modern age with dynamic enthusiasm, Seoul is in the process of continual evolution, a vibrant catharsis of change. Skyscrapers of glass and steel, broad industrial complexes, massive residential estates, modern shopping and entertainment facilities, convenient transportation systems, and swift communications all reflect long strides in development.

© ROBERT NILSEN

Traditional temple Bongeun-sa contrasts with modern skyscrapers.

SEOUL

GYEONGGI-DO

Hwajeong

Goyang

SEOO-NEUNG

JIN'GWAN-SA

Bukhan-san
National Park

SEUNGGA-SA

SEOBU BUS TERMINAL

SUBWAY LINE 3

OLYMPIA HOTEL

BUG
TUN

HAENGJU
SANSEONG

SAEGEOM-JEONG

BUG
SKYW
PAVILI

SUBWAY LINE 6

SWISS GRAND
HOTEL

JAHA-MUN

Bugak-san

CHEONGWADA
(BLUE HOUSE

SEOUL

Han River

Inwang-
san

GYEONGBOK-
GUN

SEODAEMUN
PRISON HISTORY
HALL

SEODAEMUN-GU

GEUMHWA
TUNNEL

DONGNIM-MUN
(INDEPENDENCE GATE)

WORLD CUP
STADIUM

BONGWON-SA
SINCHON STATION

YONSEI
UNIVERSITY

EHWA WOMEN'S
UNIVERSITY

SEVERANCE HOSPITAL

GREEK
ORTHODOX
CHURCH

SUBWAY LINE 5

SHINCHON BUS
TERMINAL

HOTEL PRINCE

MIRABEAU
HOTEL

GIMPO
AIRPORT

Ujang-san
Park

MAPO-GU

HONGIK
UNIVERSITY

SOGANG
UNIVERSITY

HOTEL
RAINBC

SEOUL
FOREIGNERS'
CEMETERY

SUKMYUNG
WOMEN'S
UNIVERSITY

YONGS
U.S. AF
GARRIS

JEOLDUSAN
MARTYRS' SHRINE

FERRY TERMINAL

Bamseom
Island

HOLIDAY
INN HOTEL

USO

WAR
MEMORIA
MUSEUM

Paris Park

NATIONAL
ASSEMBLY

YONGSAN
ELECTRONICS
MARKET

YONGSAN-GU

SEOUL INTERNATIONAL POST OFFICE

Yeouido Park

SEOUL
IMMIGRATION OFFICE

MOKDONG
STADIUM

GYEONGIN EXPRESSWAY

120

YANGCHEON-GU

LUCKY-
GOLDSTAR
BUILDING

FERRY TERMINAL

NATIONAL
MUSEUM OF
KOREA

THE SEOUL
IMMIGRATION OFFICE

DLI 63
BUILDING

SARYUKSHIN-MYO

Yongs
Fami
Park

Bucheon

GURO

YEONGDEUNGPO

NORYANGJIN
SUSAN MARKET

CHUNGANG
UNIVERSITY

NATIONAL
CEMETERY

SUBWAY LINE 7

SUBWAY LINE 1

SUBWAY LINE 2

Boramae
Park

SOONGSHIL
UNIVERSITY

CHUNGSHIN
UNIVERSITY

Gwangmyeong

0   1 mi

0   1 km

NAKSEONG-
DAE

SEOUL
NATIONAL
UNIVERSITY

GYEONGGI-DO

SEOUL

Anyang

Gwangk-san (629 m)

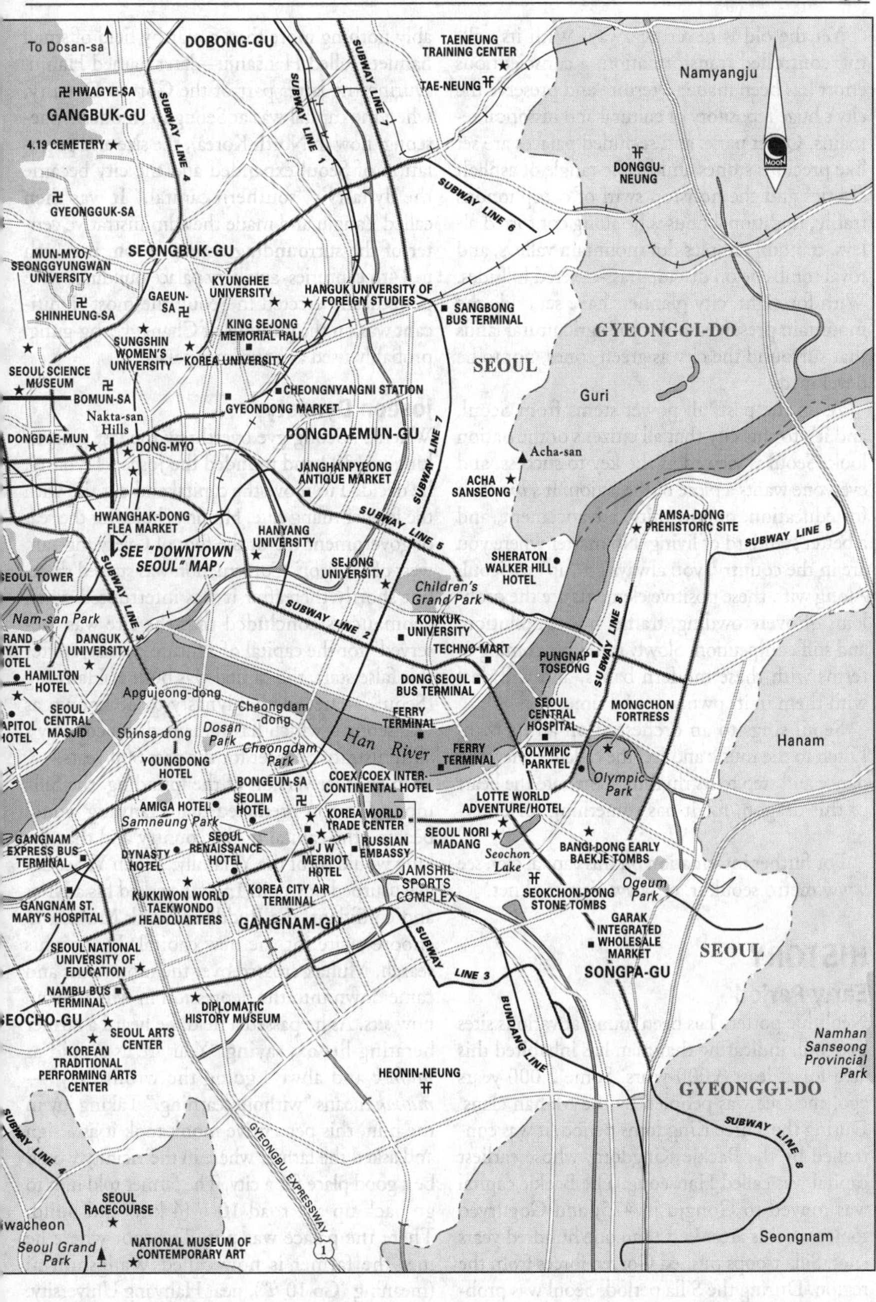
To Dosan-sa
DOBONG-GU
TAENEUNG TRAINING CENTER
TAE-NEUNG
Namyangju
HWAGYE-SA
GANGBUK-GU
SUBWAY LINE 4
SUBWAY LINE 1
SUBWAY LINE 7
4.19 CEMETERY
DONGGU-NEUNG
MOON
SUBWAY LINE 6
GYEONGGUK-SA
MUN-MYO/ SEONGGYUNGWAN UNIVERSITY
SEONGBUK-GU
KYUNGHEE UNIVERSITY
HANGUK UNIVERSITY OF FOREIGN STUDIES
GAEUN-SA
SHINHEUNG-SA
SANGBONG BUS TERMINAL
KING SEJONG MEMORIAL HALL
GYEONGGI-DO
SUNGSHIN WOMEN'S UNIVERSITY
KOREA UNIVERSITY
SEOUL
SEOUL SCIENCE MUSEUM
BOMUN-SA
CHEONGNYANGNI STATION
Guri
GYEONDONG MARKET
Nakta-san Hills
DONGDAE-MUN
DONG-MYO
DONGDAEMUN-GU
SUBWAY LINE 7
Acha-san
JANGHANPYEONG ANTIQUE MARKET
ACHA SANSEONG
HWANGHAK-DONG FLEA MARKET
SUBWAY LINE 5
AMSA-DONG PREHISTORIC SITE
HANYANG UNIVERSITY
SUBWAY LINE 5
SEE "DOWNTOWN SEOUL" MAP
SHERATON WALKER HILL HOTEL
SEJONG UNIVERSITY
SEOUL TOWER
Children's Grand Park
SUBWAY LINE 3
SUBWAY LINE 2
Nam-san Park
KONKUK UNIVERSITY
SUBWAY LINE 8
GRAND HYATT HOTEL
DANGUK UNIVERSITY
TECHNO-MART
PUNGNAP TOSEONG
HAMILTON HOTEL
Apgujeong-dong
DONG SEOUL BUS TERMINAL
SEOUL CENTRAL MASJID
Cheongdam-dong
SEOUL CENTRAL HOSPITAL
MONGCHON FORTRESS
CAPITOL HOTEL
Shinsa-dong
Dosan Park
FERRY TERMINAL
Cheongdam Park
Han River
Hanam
YOUNGDONG HOTEL
FERRY TERMINAL
OLYMPIC PARKTEL
Olympic Park
BONGEUN-SA
COEX/COEX INTER-CONTINENTAL HOTEL
SEOLIM HOTEL
AMIGA HOTEL
LOTTE WORLD ADVENTURE/HOTEL
Samneung Park
KOREA WORLD TRADE CENTER
SEOUL NORI MADANG
GANGNAM EXPRESS BUS TERMINAL
SEOUL RENAISSANCE HOTEL
J W MERRIOT HOTEL
RUSSIAN EMBASSY
BANGI-DONG EARLY BAEKJE TOMBS
DYNASTY HOTEL
Seochon Lake
JAMSHIL SPORTS COMPLEX
Ogeum Park
GANGNAM ST. MARY'S HOSPITAL
KUKKIWON WORLD TAEKWONDO HEADQUARTERS
KOREA CITY AIR TERMINAL
SEOKCHON-DONG STONE TOMBS
GANGNAM-GU
SUBWAY LINE 3
GARAK INTEGRATED WHOLESALE MARKET
SEOUL NATIONAL UNIVERSITY OF EDUCATION
SEOUL
SONGPA-GU
NAMBU BUS TERMINAL
SEOCHO-GU
DIPLOMATIC HISTORY MUSEUM
SEOUL ARTS CENTER
BUNDANG LINE
KOREAN TRADITIONAL PERFORMING ARTS CENTER
Namhan Sanseong Provincial Park
HEONIN-NEUNG
GYEONGGI-DO
SUBWAY LINE 4
GYEONGBU EXPRESSWAY
SUBWAY LINE 8
SEOUL RACECOURSE
Gwacheon
Seongnam
Seoul Grand Park
NATIONAL MUSEUM OF CONTEMPORARY ART
1

© AVALON TRAVEL PUBLISHING, INC.

SEOUL

Yet the old is never far away. With its willful, controlled transformation, a conscientious effort has been made to restore and preserve the city's huge repository of cultural and historical remains. Quiet parks and secluded palaces are set like precious stones amidst the tangle of asphalt arteries and the nonstop swirl of cacophonous traffic, traditional houses lie along contorted alleys, tranquil temples dot mountain valleys, and royal tombs lie on distant grass-covered hillsides. With foresight, city planners have set aside the mountain preserves and some agricultural lands that surround the city as green zones, not to be developed.

As in the past, all power stems from Seoul, and it's to this city that all citizens of the nation look. Seoul is viewed as the key to success, and everyone wants a piece of the action. It's *the* place for education, opportunity, advancement, and a better standard of living. No matter where you are in the country, you always go "up" to Seoul. Along with these positive elements are the problems of overcrowding, traffic, noise, pollution, and stiff competition. Slowly the city is coming to terms with these modern banes, and will deal with them in its own way and time.

Seoul sings to an orchestration all its own. Listen to the music and feel the cadence, view the dance and step to its rhythm. Penetrate the heart of this dragon, for it has something for everyone.

For further information on this capital city, see www.metro.seoul.kr. or www.visitseoul.net.

HISTORY

Early Period

Neolithic pottery has been found at various sites in Seoul, indicating that man has inhabited this area for at least 3,000 years. Some 2,000 years ago, the area was peopled by the Mahan clans. During the Three Kingdoms period, it was controlled by the Baekje Kingdom, whose earliest capital was called Hanseong. The Baekje capital was moved to Gongju in 475, and Goguryeo took over this area. Less than one hundred years later, Silla troops pushed Goryeo forces from the region. During the Silla period, Seoul was prob-

ably nothing more than a marshy field of small hamlets called Hansanju—later named Hanju. During the latter part of the Goryeo Dynasty, when the capital was at Seongdo (modern Gaeseong, now in North Korea), the size and population of Seoul expanded and the city became the dynasty's "southern capital." It was then called Yangju and made the administrative center of the surrounding county. From the 11th to 14th centuries, auxiliary palace buildings were periodically erected in Seoul; the most significant was on the grounds of Changgyeong-gung, probably used as a summer palace.

Joseon Dynasty

When Yi Seong-gye overthrew the last Goryeo king in 1392 and founded the Joseon Dynasty, he decided to move the capital and cut ties with the former ruling elite. His first choice for the seat of government was at the foot of Gyeryong-san, west of Daejeon. Construction was started there, but shortly thereafter it was interrupted when geomancers concluded that the site was "reserved" for the capital of a future dynasty. After this false start, the capital was built at Hanyang (Seoul)—later in the dynasty to be known as Hanseong—which has remained the country's administrative center for the past 600 years.

In another version of the founding, the Silla monk Doseon predicted that Hanyang would become the capital of the country and that the king would be of the Yi family. When Yi Seong-gye usurped power in 1392, he asked his adviser and confidant, the Buddhist monk Muhak, to choose a site for the new capital. During his search, Muhak crossed over the mountains and came down into the depression in which Seoul now sits. As he passed a field, he heard a farmer berating his ox, saying "You are as stupid as *muhak* and always going the wrong way"— *muhak* means "without learning." Taking joy in the pun, this perceptive monk took it as a sign and asked the farmer where in the vicinity would be a good place for a city. The farmer told him to go back up the road 10 *li* (4 km) and build. There the palace was put. The spot where he met the farmer is now called Wangshim-ni (meaning "Go 10 *li*"), near Hanyang University.

In 1394, construction of the capital palace and city walls commenced. The walled city was set up several kilometers north of the Han River at the foot of Bugak-san. Even though the city had a natural defensive location and a well-built perimeter wall, Seoul was overrun by better-trained Japanese troops in 1592 and by the Manchus in 1635.

Modern Era

In 1910, Japan annexed Korea, Seoul became the peninsula's colonial capital, and its name was changed to Keijo. During the occupation, Seoul started to lose its definition as a compact, walled city; it burst its seams and flowed into the adjoining plains. Long sections of the wall were taken down and the cityscape bubbled up in new forms and shapes. With the Japanese in control, commerce and industry began to blossom and the city started to take on a distinctly modern feel. With the fall of Japan at the end of World War II, Seoul became the seat of the U.S. military government (until the creation of the Republic of Korea, in 1948), and its name formally and officially became Seoul. During the Korean War, Seoul changed hands four times, and aside from a handful of buildings all was completely destroyed. An eyewitness account states that its destruction was worse than Berlin's after World War II. Out of this ash and rubble, and the grief and tragedy of its people, rose a thriving, modern metropolis, aptly called "the Phoenix City."

In 1963, after absorbing several adjoining provincial communities, Seoul was raised to "special city" status, equal to that of a province. Until 1991, the mayor was appointed by the president and responsible directly to the prime minister. In that year, the Seoul City Council was inaugurated. Its members and the mayor are now elected, and are responsible directly to the central government, although because of its size, population, and status as the capital of the country it does enjoy a certain amount of autonomy that other cities and provinces do not. The city is divided into 25 *gu* (districts)—14 north of the river and the rest to its south—522 *dong* (wards), and literally thousands of neighborhoods.

In 1994, Seoul celebrated its 600th anniversary. Among other commemorative events, a time capsule holding 600 items representing all aspects of modern city life was buried on the north slope of Nam-san.

The Name "Seoul"

During the Joseon Dynasty, Seoul was known as Hanyang; in the vernacular, it was simply called *Seoul*, meaning "the capital." Not derived from Chinese characters, the name can only be written in *han'geul*. Of uncertain origin, it's generally thought to be a shortened form of the name Seorabol, the ancient city-state that developed into the Silla Kingdom. A legend relates a second theory. After the monk Muhak had chosen the spot to found the city, he had to decide where to put the walls. One night, it snowed and laid a white circle of powdery fluff along the ridges surrounding the proposed city site. Along this line of snow, the city walls were built. From that time, the new capital, when not called by its proper name, Hanyang, was referred to by the name *Seoul*, a slightly altered combination of *seol* (the Korean pronunciation of the Chinese character for "snow") and *ul* (an indigenous Korean word meaning "fence").

Population

Seoul's population has increased dramatically since the end of the Joseon Dynasty. In 1900, the population was somewhere around 150,000. At the end of World War II it had risen to about 500,000. By 1950, it was close to one million. Today, with just under 10 million inhabitants—one-fifth of the country's total population!—Seoul is one of the world's most populous cities. With 17,200 people per square kilometer, the population density is nearly 40 times the national average; with 26,400 persons per square kilometer, Yangcheon-gu has the highest rate of density of any district in the city. Since the early 1970s there has been a concerted effort to locate people (and businesses, industries, and educational institutions) south of the Han River and to other areas of the country. This has largely been successful, for now approximately 60 percent of the city's population (as opposed to 30 percent in 1975) resides in this newer section of town. Until the early 1990s, Seoul grew despite government efforts to slow the tide of immigration from the provinces. Only since the mid-1990s has this trend been changed, resulting in a relative leveling off of population. This has been due in large part to the creation of several new cities, which in large part are bedroom communities in the provincial areas directly surrounding this metropolis.

About 40 percent of Seoul's land area is residential. While not long ago most people lived in single-family housing units, today the majority live in apartments. Many of the older apartment complexes are two- to three-story affairs, but it's obvious by looking over the city from any height that the five- to fifteen-story (or taller) variety now make up a fair chunk of the housing. Apartment construction started in 1962 but really mushroomed in the mid-'70s. Today, huge apartment estates are a common feature of the landscape.

In the 1980s, the city's squatter community was estimated to constitute about 10 percent of the total city population. This figure was down dramatically from the early '60s, however, when they were a full one-third of city residents. Today, these numbers are probably minuscule—much of this problem has been solved by massive subsidized-housing projects. While not a huge problem, the city's homeless are most noticeable in the late evening and early morning hours.

A City for Today

Seoul has enough diversity to keep the most energetic visitor busy for weeks. Primary tourist attractions are the palaces, shrines, monuments, museums, entertainment, and shopping areas. The city is a treasure house of historic and cultural remains with 124 designated National Treasures, 366 Treasures, and 64 Historical Sites. Countless other artifacts are kept in museums and private collections. For relaxation, Seoul has a wide variety of parks and green areas, art and cultural venues, as well as numerous mountains in the peripheral districts. The full spectrum of entertainment ranges from traditional concerts and masked-dance plays to casino gambling and

disco dancing. With competitive prices and a wide selection of markets and shops, Seoul has become to some a "shopper's paradise." One of Asia's fastest-growing and most outward-reaching cities, it's rapidly becoming a center for international conventions, conferences, athletic events, and transportation.

The event that created the greatest expectations was the 1988 Summer Olympics. Korea put its best foot forward and all energies were directed to make a successful and safe sporting event. For this event, as well as for the general development of the country, many changes were instituted. Important historical sites were renovated; major museums were moved to new quarters and upgraded; performance venues were expanded and performances professionalized; sporting facilities were created, expanded, or renewed; new parklands sprouted as fast as the spring flowers; the entire length of the Han River through the city was dredged and diked, while new levees were made for safety, and sporting fields were placed on the riverbanks; hundreds of additional hotel rooms were added; easily understandable traffic signs were hung; and it seemed everyone was attempting to learn some words and phrases of a foreign language. In like manner, the 2002 World Cup games were also a great incentive to spruce up again, construct new facilities, and bring the country into tip-top shape.

CITY LAYOUT

Seoul has one of the most striking settings of any large city in Asia. The mighty Han River bisects the city east-west, while pine-studded slopes counterpoise the broad white granite slabs that punctuate the cityscape in all directions. The walled city of Seoul was located in the bowl below the mountains Bugak-san (342 meters), Inwang-san (338 meters), and Nam-san (265 meters); on the fourth side are the Nakta-san hills, near Namdae-mun. As the population grew, the city spread, first beyond the walls into the surrounding bottomland toward the Han River and along the route that runs north toward China, then over the peripheral hills in all directions. Today it encompasses 605 square kilometers.

Surrounding the city in a protective embrace today are the mountains Bukhan-san (837 meters), Surak-san (639 meters), Namhan-san (480 meters), and Gwanak-san (632 meters). According to geomantic theory, the city needs a strong north and south anchor. Bugak-san and Nam-san met the criteria when the city was young, and today Bukhan-san and Gwanak-san provide these conditions. To the north, west, and south are the wide agricultural plains of Paju, Gimpo and Pyeongtaek; to the east are the undulating foothills of the great Taebaek Mountains, from which the Han River flows.

Although the central core is smaller, the greater downtown area is bounded on the west by the Seodae-mun intersection, on the east by Dongdae-mun, on the north by the Gyeongbok-gung and Changdeok-gung palaces, and on the south by the northern slope of Nam-san. While this downtown sector is still very much a commercial and financial heavyweight, in recent years there has been a movement to decentralize Seoul. Businesses, commercial establishments, banking institutions, and the like have been encouraged to move some of their operations to the city's newer areas or outside the city; universities have built satellite campuses in provincial cities, shifting student populations away from Seoul; and in 1975 the national legislature was moved from its offices next to Deoksu-gung to the domed National Assembly building on Yeouido. Later in the '70s, some national government offices and bureaus were relocated to Gwacheon, a newly developed city just south of Seoul city limits, and in the mid-'90s additional national offices were moved to Daejeon, a provincial capital some 170 kilometers to the south. To cut down on air and water pollution in the heart of Seoul, much industry has been relocated to the district of Guro, south of the Han River, to the many new peripheral cities in the surrounding province, and out of the city altogether to new and large industrial estates located throughout the country.

Wide boulevards crisscross the city, and streets in the newer sections south of the Han River are well-planned and gridlike. To help alleviate traffic through the heart of the city, a circular inner-city highway has been constructed. To divert through-traffic around its edges, another circular highway has also been constructed just outside the city limits; it connects with inner-city highways, provincial highways, and expressways. Most subsidiary roads are neither straight nor orderly, and in the center of the city they follow routes established decades ago when the city was growing without a plan. A complex network of twining alleys connects these roads and covers the inner-city hillsides. Old sections of the city have engaging personalities, while the new areas are squared and stark in comparison.

At the turn of the 20th century, no bridges crossed the Han River; several dozen free government ferries were provided for established transportation routes to the south. By the 1960s, there were four bridges and a rail line. Today, more than a dozen vehicular bridges and eight railroad and subway bridges span the Han River. Additional bridges are in the works and still more are planned. This rush to provide an adequate transportation network has not come without problems. In 1994, a span of one of the newer bridges collapsed, killing over 40 people and putting the government in an uncomfortable position of culpability for the bridge's shoddy construction.

To help the flow of traffic in the older sections of the city, over a dozen tunnels have been burrowed through its mountains, three under Nam-san alone.

Central City Orientation

One long block south of Gyeongbok-gung is the **Gwanghwa-mun intersection** [Kwanghwa-mun] one of the busiest in the city center. Although names of main boulevards change periodically along their lengths, this intersection marks one of the few spots in the city where all four roads radiating from it have different names. Dominating the intersection, sternly surveying the frenetic traffic below, is a bronze statue of Admiral Yi Sun-shin, Korea's most famous naval commander. A small replica of his invention, the metal-clad turtle ship, sits at the base of the pedestal with scenes of a naval encounter depicted on its sides.

DOWNTOWN SEOUL

NATIONAL FOLKLORE MUSEUM

THE NEST GUEST HOUSE

LOTUS LANTERN INTERNATIONAL BUDDHIST CENTER

GYEONGBOK-GUNG

THE CONSTITUTIONAL COURT

SEOUL SELECTION

Sajik Park

SAJIK ALTER

Gyeongbok-gung

GWANGHWA-MUN

Anguk

ANGUK-DONG ROTARY

UNHYEON GUNG

DONGNIM-MUN (INDEPENDENCE GATE)

SEOUL METROPOLITAN POLICE

JEOKSEON BUILDING

CENTRAL GOVERNMENT COMPLEX

JAPANESE EMBASSY

COMUNICATION MEMORIAL HALL

MINISTRY OF CULTURE AND INFORMATION

JOGYE-SA

JONGNO-GU

SUNG-DO YEOGWAN

Sejong-no Park

U.S. EMBASSY

SAM-O MOTEL

GWANGHWAJANG YEOGWAN

SEJONG CULTURAL CENTER

KOREA TELECOM

SAEMUNAN CHURCH

GYEONGHUI-GUNG

Gyeonghui-gung Park

SEOUL HISTORICAL MUSEUM

Gwanghwa-mun

INN-DAEWON

KYOBO BUILDING

KUK JE MOTEL

SEOUL HOTEL

SAE JONG JANG HOTEL

MILLENIUM TOWER BUILDING

PARADISE MOTEL

INSA-DONG

Jonggak

YMCA

JONG-NO

PAN KOREA BOOK COMANY

GWANGHWA-MUN INTERSECTION

GWANGHWA-MUN POST OFFICE

YOUNG POONG BOOKS

BOSHIN-GAK

Gwancheo dong

KANGBUK SAMSUNG HOSPITAL INTERNATIONAL CLINIC

CHEONGYEECHEON-NO

CHONGO BOOK CENTER

RED CROSS HOSPITAL

AGWAN

KOREANA HOTEL

NEW SEOUL HOTEL

KOREAN NATIONAL TOURISM ORGANIZATION

PRINTEMPS DEPARTMENT STORE

SEODAE-MUN INTERSECTION

Jeong-dong

BRITISH EMBASSY

CANADIAN EMBASSY

ULJI BOOK CENTER

AGRICULTURAL MUSEUM

CHONGDONG THEATER

ANGLICAN CHURCH

Uljiro 1-ga

Seodaemun

ROYAL MUSEUM

Seoul CITY HALL

METRO HOTEL

KOREA EXCHANGE BANK

JEONGDONG METHODIST CHURCH

DEOKSU-GUNG

City Hall

City Hall

SEOUL CITY PLAZA

LOTTE HOTEL

NATIONAL SOUVENIR CENTER

SEOU ROYAL HOTE

KOREAN AIR

RADISSON PLAZA HOTEL

WESTIN CHOSUN HOTEL

Myeong-dong

SAMSUNG BUILDING

MIDOPA DEPARTMENT STORE

COSMOS DEPARTMENT STORE

CHINESE EMBASSY

MYEONGDONG CATHEDRAL

FRENCH EMBASSY

HOAM ART HALL

DONGBANG PLAZA

DAEWOO MOTEL

BANK OF KOREA

SEOUL CENTRAL POST OFFICE

Seosomun Park

SHINSEGAE DEPARTMENT STORE

NAMDAE-MUN

NAMDAE-MUN MARKET

SUBWAY LINE 4

ASIANA AIRLINES

YAKHYEON CHURCH

Hoehyeon

PALACE HOTEL

0   300 yds
0   300 m

SEOUL STATION

DAEWOO CENTER

SEOUL HILTON HOTEL

Seoul Station

NAMSAN BOTANICAL GARDENS

CABLE CAR

GOETHE INSTITUTE

SUBWAY LINE 3

SUBWAY LINE 5

SUBWAY LINE 2

SUBWAY LINE 1

SEOSOMUN-NO

SHINMUN-NO

TAEPYEONG-NO

SEJONG-NO

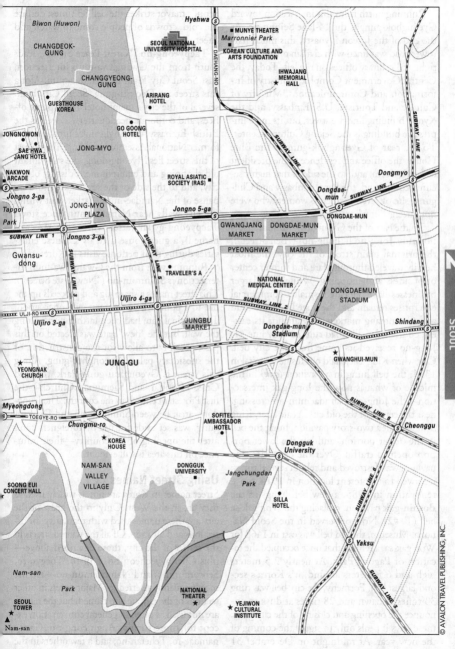

© AVALON TRAVEL PUBLISHING, INC.

SEOUL

Running north from this intersection toward Gyeongbok-gung is the 14-lane **Sejong-no.** At the end of the Joseon Dynasty, this much narrower road was lined with civilian offices on the right and military offices on the left. Today, the Central Government Complex, Ministry of Information and Communications, Ministry of Culture and Tourism, U.S. Embassy, and the Kyobo building line the street, but its most impressive building is the Sejong Cultural Center. To the rear of Gyeongbok-gung is the Blue House, the office and residence of the president of South Korea, and, to the side of that highly secured compound, the Papal Embassy and Chilgung, site of seven shrines to women who were not queens but whose sons became kings.

To the east of the Gwanghwa-mun intersection runs **Jong-no** [Chong-no] ("Bell Street"), the original main street of the city, the most heavily traveled thoroughfare and former center of business and shopping. While most larger businesses have relocated, smaller commercial enterprises remain and the huge Dongdae-mun and Gwangjang markets now anchor its eastern end. Under this road runs subway line #1. Jong-no received its name from the city bell. Cast when King Taejo laid out his new capital in 1394, the bell hung in a pavilion (*gak*) in the middle of what is now the Jong-gak intersection—the Jong-no/Namdaemun-no crossing, near the center of the old city. Years later, King Sejong built a two-story pavilion, hung the bell in the upper portion, and left the lower portion open to traffic. Over the centuries, the pavilion was destroyed and rebuilt several times; it moved to its present location in 1914. Since renovation in 1985, a new bell hangs in the **Boshin-gak** pavilion, replacing the Won'gak-sa bell (T. #2). Now preserved in the Seoul National Museum, the old bell was cast in 1468 for Won'gak-sa, a temple that once occupied the location of Pagoda Park. At nearly 2.5 meters high and 6.5 meters around, it's Korea's second-largest bell. Formerly, the city bell was rung 33 times at dawn and 28 times at dusk to announce the opening and closing of the city gates; these days it peals only to signal the coming of the new year. At midnight on December 31

Seoul's mayor strikes the bell 33 times; despite the cold, crowds of people come to watch and cheer.

Taepyeong-no ("Great Peace Street") leads south from the Gwanghwa-mun intersection, past Seoul City Plaza to Namdae-mun. Along this street are Deoksu-gung, Seoul City Hall, several of the city's major hotels, newspaper offices, and corporate headquarters, as well as the British Embassy, the Anglican Church, and the former National Assembly building. To the east of this street lies Myeong-dong, the still-vibrant old shopping and entertainment district of the city, and to the side of the south gate is the expanse of the Namdae-mun Market. Just within the city walls near Namdae-mun once stood Taepyeong-gwan (after which the street is named), a guesthouse used by Chinese emissaries during their periodic visits to Korea.

Running west from the Gwanghwa-mun intersection is **Shinmun-no** ("New Gate Street"). This street makes a sharp jog and proceeds up the hill to a point where the west gate once stood. The original gate had been farther north along the wall, but the "new" gate was erected on this pass, possibly to allow for the construction of the subsidiary palace Gyeonghui-gung. Along this street is Gyeonghui-gung Park, the Red Cross Hospital, and Saemunan Church—the first Protestant church in the country. The Jeongdong area, between Shinmun-no and Deoksu-gung, was set aside for use by foreigners soon after the opening of the country—their influence on this area is still evident.

Using Street Names

Street names in Korea are not as widely used as they are in the West. Only in the heart of the city are these names used with regularity for directions and location. Of all the named streets in the center of the city, those described above—plus Cheongyecheon-no, Ulji-ro, Toegye-ro, Seosomun-no, and Namdaemun-no—are the most frequently referred to. Major streets in other sections of the city are also named, but the names are not used as often in general conversation except for those such as Apgujeong-no, Gangnamdae-ro, Teheran-no, and a few others in the

Gangnam area south of the river. Much more common for location and directions is the use of *dong* (ward) names, or well-known buildings and landmarks. When going long distances in the city, especially by taxi, knowing the *gu* (district) name will also be helpful.

Negotiating the City Streets

Major streets have wide sidewalks. Smaller streets and alleys usually have none. On smaller streets, one must be very careful of cars, motorbikes, bicycles, and delivery trucks that approach from behind and always seem to be going faster than what is safe. Crosswalks are provided at most major intersections. Where crosswalks are not present, underpasses will usually be found, some in connection with shopping arcades or subway entrances. Overpasses are also a feature of major thoroughfares, usually found in the middle of the block. Unlike in the West, the general flow of pedestrian traffic is on the left side of the sidewalk and stairs, unless otherwise indicated by arrows painted on the pavement or steps.

Areas of the City

The Joseon Dynasty was a stratified society of upper and lower classes, each with its own neighborhoods. All the thatched-roof commoners' houses of the last century have long since gone, and most of the tile-roof upper class houses have also disappeared. However, certain areas still exist in a manner similar to decades ago. One such area is **Gahoe-dong,** an upper-class neighborhood during the Joseon Dynasty, set between Gyeongbok-gung and Changdeok-gung palaces. While not all the fine houses here are from the last century (some have been constructed, in the same style, since the war), this area has been set aside as a preservation zone for traditional-style houses. The intertwining alleys and byways of this neighborhood are chockablock with tile-roof homes set behind tall stone walls. Most houses are L-shaped, with traditional post-and-beam construction, sliding doors, *ondol* floors, wooden verandas, sunken kitchens, and landscaped gardens. They are restrained in ornamentation yet elegant and comfortable. This is the largest such concentration of old houses in

Seoul, and one of the few places where hints of the city of yesterday can be felt.

The section **between Nam-san and the river** has a high density of foreigners, with the Yongsan U.S. Army Garrison, military and business housing, and dozens of embassies. After the opening of Korea, it was occupied by the Japanese military during their occupation. Following the departure of the Japanese, the Americans moved in. Itaewon, one of the city's major shopping and entertainment districts, is located here, and in 2003, the National Museum moved into its new quarters within Yongsan Family Park. The remainder of Yongsan-gu, Seodaemun-gu, and Mapo-gu are relatively older and more established sections of town with plenty of historical connections. The 2002 World Cup soccer stadium in this area is one of the city's newest spots, however, and the Millennium Town is also slated to be built nearby, making this a district with great future potential.

To the east of downtown, the area between Dongdae-mun and Cheongnyangni Station and the surrounding districts are also older and well-established with plenty of small businesses, schools, and older-style residential and commercial areas. Beyond them, occupying the eastern fringe of the city and pushing up toward Uijeongbu are newer and fast-growing swaths of apartments for the expanding city population.

While universities are dotted here and there around town, the two major concentrations of these schools are several kilometers east and west of downtown. To the east, the best-known schools are Koryo and Kyunghee universities. In **Shinchon** to the west, they are Yonsei, Ehwa Women's, Sogang, and Hongik universities. Two out of every three persons living in the relatively small area of Shinchon are students. Because of this young crowd, it's also known for its restaurants, entertainment, and shopping. The most notable exception is Seoul National University, now located below Gwanak-san, but once occupying the hill directly east of Changgyeong-gung where the university hospital and School of Dentistry still stand.

Once just a big sandbar in the middle of the river and the site of the city's first airport, **Yeoui-**

do [Yŏuido] has gone through massive and intense development since the late 1960s. Between the National Assembly building, which anchors the west end of the island, and the graceful DLI 63 building pinning its eastern end are business and commercial concerns, banks and other financial institutions, the Korean stock exchange, the headquarters of the nation's major television and radio companies, as well as huge apartment complexes and shopping facilities—leading some people to call this island the "Manhattan of Seoul." Running through the center of Yeouido is Yeouido Park. In front of the Korean Broadcasting System headquarters is a place known as Reunion Plaza. Starting in 1983 and running for months on end, KBS broadcast names, pictures, and stories of Koreans separated by the Korean War. From all over the country, throngs came to stand here, hold pictures, and hope that surviving family members or relatives would come looking. Many found family whom they had not seen for decades and did not know whether they were alive or dead. The dream lives on and others still hope.

Yeongdeungpo [Yŏngdŭngp'o] is an established commercial, industrial, and residential area just to the south of Yeouido. With the exception of Yeongdeungpo, the whole area south of the Han River is the new city, having been built mostly since the early 1970s. Yeongdeungpo and Guro, which is farther southwest, have Seoul's major concentration of industries. (A secondary industrial district is Seongdong-gu, north of the Han River and east of Hanyang University.) Since 1971, when **Guro** was set aside as an export industrial zone, this area has grown to become the largest single industrial area of the city, with over 1,300 large plants. Major products of the city include metal fabrication, machine assembly, electronics, textiles, clothing, leather goods, and food items. **Gimpo Airport** bounds the city on the west, crowding farmland on the Gimpo Plain.

Although the most established fashion and nightlife district of the city is **Myeong-dong** [Myŏng-dong], located southeast of the City Hall Plaza, other areas have now established shopping and entertainment districts, particu-

larly **Itaewon** [It'aewon], on the southern slope of Nam-san, and the **Shinsa-dong** and **Apgujeong** districts of Gangnam-gu south of the river. Itaewon has been designated a Special Tourism Zone and this means lots of money and advertisement, particularly to attract foreign tourists and tourism revenue. **Gangnam-gu** has become the city's thriving new business center, with large and small business headquarters, international trade, telecommunications and electronics companies, the Korea World Trade Center, a convention and exhibition hall, and fine hotels and restaurants. The city express-bus terminal lies on its western edge, and to the east are modern and well-developed sports complexes. Throughout this area and the districts directly to the east and west one sees the further sprawl of houses and apartments.

the DLI 63 building, the tallest building in South Korea

© ROBERT NILSEN

Notable Architectural Structures

Until Korea was opened to the rest of the world, Seoul was a city of single-story houses and shops, with only a few palace halls and gates rising to any height. The remaining and rebuilt palace structures, shrines, and well-kept Joseon Dynasty homes are of greatest architectural interest from this period.

With the coming of the Westerner, buildings of other sorts began to be built, mostly churches, schools, and hospitals. Of particular note here are the Jeongdong Methodist Church, Myeongdong Cathedral (H.S. #258), the Anglican Church, and the first stone buildings of Ehwa and Yonsei universities. The missionaries were not the only ones who were busy, however, as the British Embassy building, the Russian Legation (H.S. #253)—known as Agwan and only part of which remains today—and the old Belgian Consulate are worthy examples of early construction. The first large Western-style building erected in Korea was Seokjo-jeon, at Deoksugung, used for a while by the royal family as its residence. During the Japanese occupation, new styles were tried; representative of this era are the Bank of Korea building and Seoul Station.

The Korean War destroyed much of what had stood in the city, and because the country was in such a poor economic strait, it built mostly utilitarian and rather unappealing buildings during its initial reconstruction phases. Once the country got on its feet and there was again money to work with, new directions were taken and bold designs tried. Fueled by the booming economy since the '60s, and guided by a desire to reshape the skyline, the city went through an architectural renaissance. From this period come the curvilinear Chosun Hotel, the French Embassy with its flowing lines, the contemporary Space Center building, needle-like Nam-san Tower, the Sejong Cultural Center with its mix of traditional and modern styles, the sprawling Seoul Arts Center, and more recently the bold Millennium Tower with its oval top floor suspended by three pillars above the rest of the structure. Before 1960, no structures exceeded 10 floors; by the early '70s, many buildings had 20. In 1971, Seoul saw its first real skyscraper, the 31-floor Samil building with smoked glass now occupied by the Korea Development Bank. Since then, office buildings and hotels have grown taller and, by and large, more architecturally pleasing—and the city is full of them. Today, Seoul's tallest building is the 63-story Daehan Life Insurance building (DLI 63). Others of note are the sleek Kyobo building, at the Gwanghwa-mun intersection; the dominating World Trade Center, in Gangnam-gu; and the twin tower Lucky-Goldstar building, on Yeouido.

Sights

PALACES

Palace Layout

Of all the tourist attractions in Seoul, its Joseon Dynasty palaces are the most tangible link between modern Korea and its not-too-distant monarchical past. Not merely inert relics, they are symbols of a deep history and rich culture. Although substantially reduced in number, the remaining palace buildings provide a glimpse at traditional architecture and the overall organization of palace grounds. Roughly square, these compounds were aligned north to south (with one exception) and surrounded by high, tile-capped walls, in each side of which were set large gates. The principal—often ceremonial—gate was in the south wall, the symbolic channel through which the king communicated with his people. The side gates were used for ordinary business, while the north gate was nearly always kept closed. (In Korean cosmology, north is the direction of winter, evil, and danger.) All authority stemmed from the palace. Appropriately placed at the center, the largest building was the throne hall. In the plaza to the front of the throne hall are rank markers on both sides of the central walkway. By these markers, civilian and military leaders stood according to their position for official and/or ceremonial occasions. Government offices, libraries, and auxiliary administration buildings were usually put close to the throne hall toward the front of the compound. The royal living quarters were sumptuous but modest, always set to the side or rear of the throne hall. Leisure areas, ponds, gardens, and pavilions were set back beyond the living quarters. Smaller in scope and architecturally distinct, Korean palaces are miniaturized equivalents of Chinese palaces. It is said that at its height, Gyeongbok-gung (*gung* means "palace") was the largest palace complex in Asia after the Forbidden City in Beijing.

Gyeongbok-gung, Changdeok-gung, and Deoksu-gung remain from the Joseon Dynasty. Changgyeong-gung dates from an earlier age, while the buildings of Gyeonghui-gung were mostly moved to other locations in the city. Most auxiliary palaces and private housing compounds for lower-ranking royal family members no longer exist. After 1910 and the beginning of the Japanese colonial period, Deoksu-gung and Changdeok-gung were used as private residences by royal family members until their deaths. Closed during the first part of the 20th century, Deoksu-gung was opened in the 1930s; Gyeongbok-gung and Changdeok-gung were finally opened to the public after Korea's liberation from Japan. A few buildings at Gyeonghui-gung were rebuilt in the 1990s. Conveniently located in the heart of this metropolis, Seoul's palaces preserve some of the city's largest green areas. Each deserves a look. Start with a tour of Gyeongbok-gung, and if time permits continue on to Changdeok-gung, Changgyeong-gung, Deoksu-gung, and Gyeonghui-gung.

Gyeongbok-gung 경복궁

General Yi Seong-gye (King Taejo) ordered the construction of Gyeongbok-gung [Kyŏngbokgung] ("Palace of Shining Happiness") in 1394, two years after founding the Joseon Dynasty. In its original form, it is said to have had about 500 buildings. For the next 200 years, Gyeongbokgung was the seat of government and the royal

THE FORMER CAPITOL

The broad and domineering, stone and cement former Capitol was constructed by the Japanese in 1926 as the administration office for the colonial governors-general. Significantly, it was placed within the boundaries of Gyeongbok-gung (the front wall of which had to be moved), directly in line between the throne—the traditional pinnacle of power in Korea—and Gwanghwa-mun, the figurative point of contact between the king and his people. This symbolically severed any vestige of royal authority, and replaced it with the supremacy of the Japanese governor. After World War II, the Capitol was used by the U.S. military government until a Korean government was formed in 1948. The building was burned in 1950, when North Korean troops were pushed out of the city. The gutted carcass was finally rebuilt in 1961, following the military coup that year. From then until 1986, when it became the new home of the National Museum, it was used for central government offices. As part of his campaign pledge, former president Kim Young-sam vowed to have this building torn down, removing one more symbolic vestige of the repressive Japanese colonial period. In 1995, the dome of this building was removed, perhaps symbolically "decapitating" the reminder of Japanese colonial rule on the peninsula; in 1996, the rest was destroyed. On one hand, it was sad to see such a historically significant building removed; on the other, the emotional component and desire for the building's removal were highly understandable and significant.

residence of Joseon Dynasty kings. During the Hideyoshi Invasions, Gyeongbok-gung was burned—not by the invading Japanese army, but by disgruntled palace slaves intent upon destroying the records of their servitude. The palace was left abandoned until 1865, when Daewongun, the former regent and father of Gojong (26th king: reigned 1864–1907), initiated its reconstruction soon after King Gojong ascended the throne at age 12. Building on the original foundation stones, Daewon-gun arranged for about 200 structures to be completed by 1872 in worthy representation of the palace's former splendor, but only by bleeding the already anemic Korean economy nearly to death. In that year, King Gojong moved in. Unfortunately, it was used for only 23 years. In 1895, Queen Min, King Gojong's wife, was murdered inside the palace grounds. In fear of losing his life, the king fled with the crown prince to the Russian Legation, Gyeongbok-gung then ceased to be the official seat of power, and a year later the king took up residence at Deoksu-gung.

The vast majority of structures at Gyeongbok-gung (H.S. #117) were taken down during the Japanese colonial period. Only about a dozen structures remained to attest to its former beauty and grandeur. Reconstruction of other major buildings has taken place since 1990, and in 2001, one main gate, portions of the inner walls, and several auxiliary buildings were finished. Additional renovation is planned until the late 2010s. This palace area also houses the National Museum (until its move in 2003) and the National Folklore Museum. Gyeongbok-gung is open daily except Tuesday 0900–1700 (until 1600 in winter); ₩700 entrance fee for adults, ₩300 for those ages 7 to 24. Entrance gates are on the east, west, and south walls. The palace is an easy walk from downtown; otherwise take subway line #3 to the Gyeongbok-gung Station, where one of the exits leads up inside the palace walls. Gwanghwa-mun Station on subway line #5 is close. By bus, use no. 6 or 8 to Sejong-no, or no. 205 and get off just west of the palace.

Palace Structures: Dominating the center of the palace grounds and surrounded by an inner wall is the throne hall, Geunjeong-jeon ("Hall of Government by Restraint"). The present structure dates from the 1860s reconstruction, although it went through a renovation in 2001. At 759 square meters, this enormous two-story building (N.T. #223) is the country's largest wooden structure, once the site of ceremonial functions and official audiences. Set on a double terrace, the throne hall has huge pillars upholding its heavy roof. Broad doors open to expose the cavernous interior. Backed by a screen showing

© ROBERT NILSEN

Geunjeong-jeon throne hall at Gyeongbok-gung

symbols of royalty, the modest throne rests on a raised dais below an intricately fashioned wooden canopy.

A stone balustrade circles the double terrace. The upper-terrace posts are topped by carved dragon, tiger, phoenix, and tortoise figures; the 12 Eastern zodiac figures are represented on the lower-level posts. The phoenix relief carved on an inclined stone slab between the steps of the main stairway symbolizes authority. Then used for the king, today it represents the presidency. A wide flagstone courtyard surrounds the throne hall, and running through it to the terrace steps is a walkway (its raised center was used exclusively by the king). Flanking the walk is a series of stone markers. Used by the appropriate official during formal audiences with the king and during other ceremonial functions, each slab denotes a specific rank in the hierarchy of government service—civilians on the right, military men on the left. Those who stood on the right side were more influential at court, and civilians always occupied the right-hand positions except during warfare. This civilian/military designation also held true for the palace gates; civilians used the right-hand door, the military used the left, and the central doorway was reserved for the king. In the collective Confucian mind of traditional Koreans, this ranking of civilian over military points to the supremacy of those who live and act by the pen over those who rely upon the sword. This division also held true for the other palace structures; living quarters were on the right-hand side of the palace compound, while government buildings were located on the left-hand side.

Behind the throne hall are several rebuilt structures. Sajeong-jeon ("Hall of Pondering Government") was used by the king for the daily affairs of state and is flanked by Manchun-jeon ("Hall of Ten Thousand Springs") and Cheonchu-jeon ("Hall of One Thousand Autumns"), offices used by government officials. Nearby is Sujeong-jeon ("Hall of Cultivating Government"), used for some official affairs of state. Directly behind these buildings was Gangnyeong-jeon, the living quarters of the king and queen and the king's personal office. This hall and its compound were rebuilt in 1994. The crown prince and his wife lived in a compound to the side, and two of its buildings, Jaseon-dang and Bihyeon-gak, and the surrounding walls were rebuilt in 1999. To the rear of Gangnyeong-jeon is Gyotae-joen, another hall, and beyond that is Amisan, a traditional Korean-style garden. Note the decorative clay and tile designs on a wall nearby to the east. Behind the wall is Jagyeong-jeon (T. #809), once used as a residence hall for other members of the royal family. Its six-sided brick and tile chimney (T. #810) has animal figures set into it, and its walls are perhaps the most pleasing in the palace.

A gateway to the side of Jagyeong-jeon leads to the rear of the palace compound. Hamhwa-dang, a private audience hall once used by the king, stands near a lotus pond and overlooks the beautifully proportioned pavilion, Hyangwon-jeong, on the island in the middle of this pond. A wooden bridge arches to the island, which seems to float on a carpet of lily pads—a favorite scene of photographers and painters. At times, entire classes of students try to render on canvas what man and nature have presented so perfectly. This pond is picturesque in any season, but perhaps most inspiring in spring, when deep pink buds bloom and plate-like lotus leaves spread out on the surface to pool silver droplets of rain. On the far side of the pond is the murder site of Queen Min, now noted by a stone marker.

To the west of the throne hall is Korea's largest pavilion (N.T. #224). Rising above the encircling pond, it sits on 48 huge stone pillars. Originally much smaller, Gyeonghoe-ru ("Pavilion of Felicitous Gathering") was enlarged in 1412 and set on an island in this lotus pond. While civil service examinations were once administered here, official receptions, banquets, and other festivities were more often held, and it has occasionally been put to such use in recent decades. The original building was destroyed in 1592, and the present structure dates from 1867. Suffering some damage during the Korean War, it has been reconditioned.

West of Gyeonghoe-ru is a wide grassy mall dotted with stone artifacts. Here and on adjoining lawns are over a dozen National Treasures and Treasures, fine stone lanterns, pagodas, *sari budo,* and commemorative monuments from the Silla and Goryeo dynasties. All of these objects were moved to the palace—principally during the Japanese occupation—for protection and preservation.

On the south wall of Gyeongbok-gung is the massive, three-arched Gwanghwa-mun ("Gate of Radiant Transformation") (광화문), the most impressive palace gate, constructed in 1395. Its central door was used by the king, while through the side doors went the fortunate few who were allowed to enter the palace via this front portal. Burned in 1592, it wasn't rebuilt until the late 1860s. During the Japanese occupation, it was moved to the east wall, north of the east gate, so as not to block the entrance to the newly constructed Capitol. During the Korean War, its wooden top was destroyed when the Capitol was burned. In 1968, it was moved back to its original site; the stone blocks of its base were moved one by one, while the double-tier roof was rebuilt in meticulous detail; only close scrutiny reveals that the upper portion was reconstructed wholly of cement rather than wood. To promote the government's emphasis on the Korean writing system, the Gwanghwa-mun signboard was written in *han'geul* by former president Park

Chung Hee—a unique departure from the normal Chinese characters. Flanking the gate are two stone *haetae,* mythical animals that protect against fire. Unfortunately, their power was not great enough to save the palace in 1592 or 1950.

Once the guard tower at the southeast corner of the palace wall, Dongshipja-gak now stands disconnected, an island around which modern traffic swirls. A guard tower at the southwest corner of the palace has long since disappeared. Original sections of the east, north, and west walls remain; the south wall is entirely new. Several inner walls and partitions have been added to the compound at various times. The south gate, Gwanghwa-mun; the east gate, Geonchun-mun ("Gate of Establishing Spring"); and the north gate, Shinmu-mun ("Gate of Divine Warriors"), have lasted throughout the years. Removed in 1926, the west gate, Yeongchu-mun ("Gate of Welcoming Autumn"), was reconstructed in the late 1970s.

Blue House 청와대

To the rear of Gyeongbok-gung, in a tightly secured compound below the cone-shaped Bugak-san peak, is Cheongwadae ("Blue Tile Mansion"). Known as the Blue House for the color of its tile roof, this stone structure, designed partially in traditional Korean style, holds the office of the president of Korea. Blue roofs were once reserved for the use of kings; this color denoted the seat of authority. While not a palace, the Blue House is the modern-day equivalent of the palaces of old. The presidential mansion is set to the side, an official guesthouse has been built next door for use by visiting heads of state and other dignitaries, and a press center, two secretariat office buildings, and a back garden also fill the compound grounds.

Since the presidency of Kim Young-sam, the road that runs in front of the Blue House has been open to foot traffic, so now you can walk under the shade trees along the high stone walls and consider what great state affairs are being discussed inside. This road passes the north gate of Gyeongbok-gung and a military compound for those entrusted with guarding the president and this vital area. A walk along this road is as close as most people get to the president. It's a highly sensitive area, so many of those you'll meet on this quiet street are either policemen or plainclothes members of the presidential bodyguard.

The Blue House is open to visitors on a limited basis. Shuttle buses leave from the east parking lot within Gyeongbok-gung on Friday and Saturday only during the months of April, May, September, and October for 45-minute tours at 1000 and 1320. Additional group tours for foreigners, with two weeks advance application, are run Tuesday–Saturday throughout the year. For a tour, reserve by phone (tel. 02/737-5800) or check with the tour booth at the parking lot for a first-come, first-served ticket. There is no cost, but you must show proper identification or a passport. For additional information, see www.cwd.go.kr.

Changdeok-gung 창덕궁

Donhwa-mun ("Gate of Mighty Transformation") leads from the hustle and bustle of city traffic into the tranquil Changdeok-gung [Ch'angdŏk-gung] compound. Smaller than Gyeongbok-gung, Changdeok-gung (H.S. #122) is the best-preserved city palace. In 1997, this palace was named a world cultural heritage site by UNESCO. Here, only traditional-style structures remain—no modern edifices spoil the landscape and distract the eye. Changdeok-gung ("Palace of Illustrious Virtue") was constructed from 1405 to 1412 as an annex to Gyeongbok-gung. Along with nearly all other palace structures in the city, these buildings were burned to the ground during the Hideyoshi Invasions; reconstruction finished in 1610. Originally not intended as such, Changdeok-gung served as the seat of government and the royal residence from then until 1872, when Gyeongbok-gung was rebuilt and the king moved back to the dynasty's original seat of power. Left in disrepair after the move, Changdeok-gung was renovated in 1907 and again used by Sunjong, Korea's last king. Although forced to abdicate in 1910, Sunjong continued to live here until his death, in 1926; Queen Yun, Sunjong's widow, made Changdeok-gung her home until her death in 1966.

M

SEOUL

The last crown prince of Korea died here in 1970, and the last royal family member lived here until her death in 1989.

Changdeok-gung is divided into four sections. The first contains the main palace buildings. Sandwiched between these structures and Changgyeong-gung is Nakseonjae. The third area is Biwon, located directly behind the main cluster of palace buildings. The last section is Seonwonjeon, stuck unobtrusively in the back corner of this enclosure. The buildings in the small Seonwon-jeon compound were moved here from the former Gyeonghui-gung palace. Seonwon-jeon (T. #817) is not open to the public, but the rest of the palace is.

Donhwa-mun (T. #383) is the oldest original palace gate in the city, dating from 1412, and is believed to have survived when Seoul was torched in 1592. A Yi Dynasty–style changing of the guards is performed here daily except Monday 1400–1530. Colorful and historic, it is not terribly exciting, but you get a feel for the pomp and ceremony, and the garb of Joseon Dynasty soldiers. Beyond this gate is Geumcheon-gyo ("Forbidden Stream Bridge")—such stone bridges are a feature of all Joseon Dynasty palaces. Smaller, yet as stately as the throne hall of Gyeongbok-gung, Injeong-jeon ("Hall of Benevolent Government") is the throne hall (N.T. #225). Its courtyard is paved with flagstones and is fronted by a well-figured gate (T. #813). Next door is Seonjeong-jeon, "Hall of Disseminating Government" (T. #814), used by the king for everyday government affairs and more informal audiences. An unusual feature—seen on no other Joseon Dynasty hall—is its blue tile roof. Only structures utilized by the king were allowed to have this feature.

Next to Seonjeong-jeon are Huijeong-dang (T. #815) and Taejo-jeon (T. #816), moved here from Gyeongbok-gung in 1920 to be used as the private living quarters of the king and queen. Taejo-jeon has an unusual feature: it has no central roof beam or dragon figures on the roof. (The dragon is a symbol of protection. As the king was the earthly personification of the dragon, it was not necessary to have a dragon protecting a dragon!) The interiors were remodeled partially in Western style when reconstructed in the 1920s. To the front of these quarters is the palace pharmacy, and across the wide path is a garage containing old cars, carriages, and palanquins used by the royal family.

Nakseonjae ("Retreat of Joy and Goodness"), a secluded private living quarters, was constructed in 1847 for one of King Heonjong's concubines. Although much less pretentious than the palace buildings themselves, it was used as the private home of the last descendants of the Korean royal family after the Japanese occupation. Princess Deokhye, a daughter of King Sunjong, and Princess Pangja, a Japanese princess and wife of Yi Un (Yeongjinwang)—crown prince and adopted heir to King Sunjong—last lived here. Yi Kyu, son of Yi Un, an MIT-trained architect and U.S. citizen, was said to have stayed here with his family when he visited Korea.

Biwon [Piwon] ("Secret Garden" or "Mystical Garden") is a 78-acre tranquil woodland originally constructed solely for the use of the royal family and palace women. This garden is also called Huwon, or "Rear Garden," as it used to be known decades ago, but everyone still refers to it as Biwon. This sylvan sanctuary of pavilions, ponds, hills, streams, and walking paths may be the epitome of Joseon Dynasty garden construction. After two years of renovation, it was reopened to the public in 1979. The first group of pavilions in the garden is clustered around the photogenic, stone-lined lotus pond Buyongji, built by King Jeongjo, builder of Suwon Fortress. On the pool's south side is Buyong-jeon, a multi-sided pavilion that extends out over the pond on pillars. The plain Sajeonggibi-gak shrine occupies the west side of the pond; on the east side is Yeonghwa-dang, an eminently simple pavilion once used to administer civil service examinations. Capping the knoll overlooking the pond is the two-story Juham-nu pavilion, said to have been the site of much bacchanalian debauchery by Yeonsangun, the 10th Joseon Dynasty king. He was one of two Joseon kings forced to abdicate the throne—and consequently not given posthumous honorary titles—for excessive self-indulgent and malicious behavior that scandalized

© ROBERT NILSEN

Buyong-jeon in Biwon

the state. Over the ridge is Aeryeongji, a second pond, fronted by two gates: Geumma-mun ("Gold Horse Gate") and a simple stone gate, Bullo-mun ("Gate of Eternal Youth"). Constructed on the opposite side of the pond in 1828 is a 99-*gan, yangban* manor known as Yeon'gyeong-dang. Periodically, kings would come to this house for a few days to pretend to live the life of a commoner. While not open to the public, over the next ridge to the north is a third, more natural lotus pond, roughly in the shape of the Korean peninsula. The pavilion Gwallam-jeong extends partly over the pond. Pathways connect a half dozen other ponds and two dozen more pavilions scattered throughout this northern section of the garden. A 1,000-year-old Chinese juniper tree (N.M.#194), a 400-year-old plum tree, and many other trees thought to be over 500 years old are preserved in this palace/garden complex. Over the wall to the east is Changgyeong-gung, to the south is Jong-myo shrine, and to the north is Seonggyungwan University.

Changdeok-gung and Biwon are open daily except Monday 0900–1700 and can only be en-

tered as part of a tour group; ₩2,200 entrance for adults, ₩1,100 for ages 7 to 24. Tours are offered in Korean, Japanese, and English. For English speakers, these tours are at 1130, 1330, and 1530; Japanese-language tours are scheduled at 1030, 1230, 1430, and 1630. More-frequent Korean-language tours are conducted throughout the day. Tickets for the 70- to 90-minute tour go on sale half an hour before the tour starts—no reservations are needed, and no tickets are sold in advance. Among others, city buses 6, 8, 20, and 205 stop down the road; the Anguk Station on subway line #3 is the closest.

Overlooking the road next to the main gate of Changdeok-gung is a statue of Min Yeong-hwan. A high-ranking military adviser to King Gojong and a relative of the murdered Queen Min, he committed suicide in response to the 1905 treaty making Korea a protectorate of Japan. Despite this unprecedented action—a dramatic and impassioned plea to the king and Korean people not to forsake their independence—Korea was annexed five years later. For Min Yeong-hwan's patriotic though futile gesture, this statue was erected in 1957.

Changgyeong-gung 창경궁

To the east of Changdeok-gung and Biwon is Changgyeong-gun [Ch'anggyŏng-gung] (H.S. #123), on a spot chosen by Goryeo Dynasty King Sukjong for a summer palace. It was constructed in 1104 as Sugang-gung; the name was changed to Changgyeong-gung ("Palace of Bright Rejoicing") in the 1390s, when the Joseon Dynasty's first king lived there while he waited for the completion of Gyeongbok-gung. The palace was destroyed in 1592 and rebuilt in 1616. A majority of the palace buildings were again reconstructed in the 1830s after a devastating fire. During the Japanese occupation a modern redbrick structure was erected on the grounds, a botanical garden was started in 1907, a zoo added in 1909, and the designation *gung* was changed to *won* (park). From 1983 to 1986, with the removal of the zoo to the Seoul Grand Park, extensive renovation, landscaping, and some new construction, this area was returned to a more palace-like setting—hence the name change back

SEOUL

WORLD CULTURAL HERITAGE SITES IN KOREA

In accordance with the Convention Concerning Protection of the World Cultural and Natural Heritage, UNESCO has designated certain sites around the world to be protected and preserved for their significance; see www.unesco.org/whc for more details. The following are those sites in South Korea that have been so designated—with their years of designation.

1995: **Seokguram** and **Bulguk-sa** in Gyeongju; the **Koreana Tripitaka wood printing blocks** and the **depository buildings** at Haein-sa; the **Jong-myo** ancestral shrine in Seoul

1997: **Changdeok-gung** palace complex in Seoul; the **Suwon Hwaseong Fortress** and its accompanying buildings in Suwon

2000: the **prehistoric dolmen sites** of Ganghwado, Hwasun, and Gochang; the **historical Gyeongju** sites of Daeneungwon, Cheomseongdae, Banwol-seong, and Hwangnyong-saji.

to *gung*. Changgyeong-gung is an emerald of green in a sea of city colors, well-known for cherry blossoms in spring.

Unlike the north-south orientation of other city palaces, Changgyeong-gung is aligned east to west, apparently a Goryeo Dynasty orientation. Entrance is through the huge Honghwa-mun ("Gate of Vast Transformation") in the east wall, across the street from the Seoul National University Hospital and School of Dentistry. This gate (T. #384) is in direct line with the throne hall. Between these two structures are Myeongjeong-mun (T. #385), the front gate of the throne hall courtyard, and Okcheon-gyo ("Jade Stream Bridge"), a twin-support stone bridge (T. #386) built in 1483 which may be the oldest in the city. Notice the carving on the bridge's supports, especially the faces of the beasts. Passing through the exquisite Myeongjeong-mun gate brings you to the courtyard before Myeongjeong-jeon ("Hall of Lustrous Government") (N.T. #226), the palace's principal audience hall. The present throne hall was constructed during the 1484 renovation; apparently having escaped the conflagrations of 1592 and 1830, it is the oldest throne hall in the country. Stone *haetae* stand guard at the bottom of the stairways that lead up the terrace to the throne hall, and a fine phoenix is carved between the steps. Flagstones pave the courtyard, and rank markers line the walk. Directly to the side of the throne hall, rebuilt in 1986, is Munjeong-jeon, a building used by the king to conduct daily business; to the rear of the throne hall is the open pavilion Haminjeong. Set farther back is a cluster of buildings, several recently remodeled, including Tongmyeong-jeon (T. #818), which was used as the principal residence of queens while they lived at Changgyeong-gung.

North of these palace buildings, walking paths surround Chundangji lotus pond and on its far side is the botanical conservatory with its great variety of orchids. On the western edge of the pond sits a seven-tier pagoda of Chinese origin (T. #1119). Unlike a typical Korean pagoda, this one has somewhat of a midriff bulge. Behind the throne hall is a five-tier Korean-style pagoda. Punggi-dae (T. #846), a stone support for a weather streamer, an astronomical device of the Joseon Dynasty, sits on the hill overlooking the main palace compound. Gwanchon-dae (T. #851), a second astronomical instrument, has been set up on the lawn south of the throne hall courtyard. The Changgyeong-gung palace grounds are open 0900–1700 April–October and 0900–1600 November–March, closed Tuesday; ₩700 entrance for adults and ₩300 for ages 7 to 24. Enter either through Honghwamun or from Jong-myo (described in the Shrines and Memorials section of this chapter). Entrance for either Changgyeong-gung or Jong-myo lets you into both; they are connected by footbridge over Yulgok-no. Among others, city bus nos. 6, 8, 20, 84, 205, and 710 stop in front of the palace's main gate.

Deoksu-gung 덕수궁

The smallest of Seoul's palaces is on the west side of the City Hall Plaza. Deoksu-gung [Tŏksugung] ("Palace of Virtuous Longevity") was originally constructed in the mid-1400s as the private residence for the grandson of King Sejo. Following the sacking of Seoul in 1592, this royal villa (H.S. #124), along with nearby *yangban* homes, was converted to a temporary palace in 1593 and given the name Gyeongun-gung. It was used by King Seonjo for the next 15 years as the official royal residence and seat of government. When King Gwanghae-gun ascended the throne in the first decade of the 1600s, he moved into the newly rebuilt Changdeok-gung, and in 1623 King Injo moved the throne there as well; Gyeongun-gung then reverted to a subsidiary palace. After Queen Min was murdered at Gyeongbok-gung in 1895, King Gojong and his son, the future King Sunjong, secretly fled to the Russian Legation, where they stayed for over a year while Gyeongun-gung was being renovated. It is said that a passageway from the tower at the legation building connected with this palace. In 1897, King Gojong moved into this new residence, and later that year he officially proclaimed Korea an empire and himself the emperor. He ruled from Gyeongun-gung until 1907, when the Japanese forced him to abdicate in favor of his more tractable son. King Sunjong renamed this palace Deoksu-gung. It was here that former King Gojong lived until his death in 1919. Left unused for over a decade, it was restored and opened to the public in 1933.

A great amount of building in the immediate area over the years, and a disastrous fire in 1904, greatly modified Deoksu-gung from its original shape and scope; consequently, it has the newest of the Korean palace buildings and a reduced size. Entrance into Deoksu-gung is through Daehan-mun ("Great Han Gate"). Once the principal gate in the south wall, Daehan-mun was later moved to the east wall, opening onto the City Hall Plaza. This single-story structure, the smallest palace's main gate in the city, once stood farther out in the plaza but was moved to its present location because of the traffic problems it created. Accompanied by martial music from a traditional military band, and wearing festive and authentic costumes, performers reenact the Joseon Dynasty changing of the guards ceremony from 1400 to 1530 (one hour later during July and August) at this gate every day the palace is open.

After passing through Daehan-mun, you cross over a stone bridge. To the right is a wide lawn at the far end of which is a statue of King Sejong. Farther down the path is Junghwa-mun. Through this inner-court gate you see the diminutive throne hall, Junghwa-jeon ("Hall of Central Harmony") (T. #819), set on a two-step terrace. Burned in 1904 along with most other buildings in the palace, it was rebuilt two years later and is the newest of the palace's throne halls. It was reconditioned in 2001. Behind the throne hall are Junmyeong-dang and Jukjo-dang, two traditional buildings connected by an enclosed walkway. A third, Seogeo-dang, is unusual in having a second story; it is the only remaining two-story royal residence hall from the Joseon Dynasty. With the Radisson Seoul Plaza Hotel rising in the background, a fine picture is created of contrasting traditional and modern architecture, harmonizing in this transfigured city. In a separate walled compound to the right of Seogeo-dang are additional buildings and a small flower garden. Look for the finely shaped arch gate in the wall! In Deokhong-jeon, the king conducted business. The L-shaped Hamnyeong-dang (T. #820) was the royal living quarters and is where King Gojong died in 1919. The building with Western-style metalwork to the rear is where the king took tea and held parties. Erected in 1900, it was the first Western-style building constructed within the walls of a Korean palace.

To the rear of the palace grounds is a European-style rose garden with a water fountain. It's a fine place to people-watch, especially during weekends and holidays. At the south end of this garden is Gwangmyeong-mun. Under the eaves of this gate a large bell cast in 1462 for the temple Heungcheon-sa and a water clock (N.T. #229) made in 1536 are preserved; a stone pagoda and several tomb statues stand nearby. At the opposite end of the garden is the neoclassical Seokjo-jeon ("Stone Hall"). Designed by an English architect, this imposing building was completed in 1909 as the first large Western hall in the country and was used for a time as the royal

SEOUL

residence. At the end of World War II, it was used for the inconclusive meetings of the U.S.-Soviet Joint Commission on Korean Trusteeship (see "Transition, Civil War, and the Aftermath" under "History" in the Introduction). From 1954 until 1972, it housed the National Museum; from then until 1986 it was home to the National Museum of Contemporary Art. After remodeling, Seokjo-jeon was reopened in early 1987 as the Research Institute for Cultural Development. Since 1992, it has housed the Royal Museum. In the second Western-style building to the side of the museum is a branch of the National Museum of Contemporary Art. Deoksu-gung is open daily except Monday 0900–1830 April–October and 0900–1730 November–March; ₩700 entrance, ₩300 for ages 6 to 24. Entrance to the palace includes entrance to both museums. On some Saturdays and Sundays throughout the year, pops concerts are performed in the fountain garden to the delight of visitors. City Hall Station on subway line #1 is directly to the front of the palace.

Gyeonghui-gung

There was a fifth palace, erected in 1616 near the old west gate of the city, called Gyeonghui-gung [Kyŏnghŭi-gung] ("Palace of Shining Bliss"). Gyeonghui-gung Park (경희궁공원) now occupies this site (H.S. #271). Around the turn of the 20th century the palace grounds were planted in mulberry trees, their leaves used in silk-making, and it became known to foreign residents of the city as the Mulberry Palace. Over the years, most of its buildings were moved to other sites in the city for safekeeping. In 1988, the main gate, Heunghwa-mun, was moved back and rebuilt on this site. In the early 1990s, numerous other buildings that had used this site (such as the 1910 Japanese-era Keijo High School —later known as Seoul High School) were torn down and replicas of several palace buildings erected. The Seoul Metropolitan Museum of Art and the Seoul Historical Museum now occupy portions of this site.

Unhyeon-gung 운현궁

Located between Changdeok-gung and Gyeong-bok-gung, just down from the Anguk subway station, is Unhyeon-gung [Unhyŏn-gung] (H.S. #257). Small, contained, and not as stately as the others in the city, this palace was not the residence of kings but the home of Heungseon Daewon-gun, father and regent for King Gojong. King Gojong was born and raised here and lived here until he ascended the throne at age twelve. During the king's regency, this palace was the center of Korean politics. Although reduced in size, this compound shows itself as a representative noble house of the late Joseon era. With men's and women's living quarters, a main house, adjunct buildings, and inner and outer courtyards, it has many of the pieces of such a typical Korean residence. During early afternoon hours on the last Saturday in April and October, the 1866 wedding ceremony of King Gojong and Queen Myeongseong is reenacted here, where it took place some 140 years ago. Open to the public, this ceremony is one of the best examples of Joseon Dynasty pomp that people can experience today. This small palace is open daily except Monday 0900–1800 (1700 in winter); ₩700 adults, ₩300 students, ₩1,000 for an optional audiotape guide.

CITY WALLS AND GATES

City Walls

When King Taejo moved his capital to Seoul, he immediately started construction of Gyeong-bok-gung, the Jong-myo ancestral shrine, and Sajik Altar. In order to protect these, and safeguard the city residents, a rough wall of earth and uncut stone was hurriedly built in 1396. Subsequent renovation added fitted stone blocks and topped the wall with battlements. Although only sections remain today, this 18-kilometer defensive perimeter (H.S. #10) encircled the old city. Suffering periodic damage and subsequent renovation over the centuries, remnants can still be seen on Bugak-san, Inwang-san, and Nam-san, and at various other sites throughout the city; the greatest portion has been removed for city expansion. From Inwang-san, a tangential, single-line wall connected the city wall north to the Bukhan Sanseong fortress wall.

Gates

Nine gates punctuated the Seoul city wall: a main gate was located in each of the four cardinal directions, while four secondary gates were placed amongst them; the last was a water gate which bridged Cheongyecheon Stream, which drained the city. All except the north gate were opened at daybreak and closed at nightfall on the signal of the city bell. The north gate was kept closed at all times, only to be used if the king needed to escape to the safety of Bukhan Sanseong or other fortifications. Five of the original gates have been renovated and set aside as cultural relics.

Namdae-mun (남대문), or the "Great South Gate" (N.T. #1), stands in the middle of the traffic circle halfway between the Seoul City Plaza and Seoul Station. It's a majestic structure, solid and sturdy, the old city's largest and principal gate. Once one of the city's tallest structures, Namdae-mun has been closed in by tall buildings which have sprouted around the rotary. Erected in 1396, it was rebuilt several decades later during the reign of King Sejong. It sustained damage during the Korean War and received its last major repair in 1962. The city walls connected to the gate were removed in the first decade of the 20th century to ease the flow of increased traffic. Although referred to by everyone as Namdae-mun, its official name is Sungnye-mun ("Gate of Exalted Decorum").

Gwanghui-mun (광희문) ("Gate of Bright Light") is in a market area near the Dongdae-mun Stadium, where the main streets Ulji-ro and Toegye-ro come together. All that remains of the original structure is its stone archway. This was renovated in 1975, when a new capping pavilion was built and a short section of wall re-erected. Smaller than the principal gates, this secondary gate is said to have been used primarily for transporting dead bodies for burial outside the city walls. Between Gwanghui-mun and Dongdae-mun is the site of the now-absent water gate called Ogangsu-mun. Removed in 1900, this five-arch stone structure once stepped across Cheonggyecheon Stream, the only outflow from the walled city, now covered by Cheonggye-cheon-no and the Cheongye Elevated Highway.

Dongdae-mun [Tongdae-mun] (동대문), or the "Great East Gate," officially named Honginji-mun ("Gate of Flourishing Benevolence"), stands in the traffic circle east of Dongdae-mun Market. Originally built in 1397, the present structure (T. #1) is from 1869 but was reconstructed after being damaged in the Korean War. An unusual feature is the semicircular defensive containment area that protrudes beyond the city wall, enclosing the actual gate entryway. Because there was only a small opening on the north side of this containment wall, people had to slow down and make two turns before actually going through the gate. In this way, anyone who entered could be inspected while in the courtyard, and in case of warfare, invaders would be open to easy attack. This design was probably inspired by the similar Suwon fortress gates.

Farther along the wall to the north, a short distance from the north end of Daehang-no, is the site of the Little East Gate. Called Hyehwa-mun ("Gate of Transformation by Benevolent Love"), it was taken down in 1939. Now only a marker indicates the spot, but a section of the city wall is still seen on the hillside above.

The north gate, **Sukcheong-mun** ("Gate of Solemn Purity"), can be seen below the Bugak Skyway pavilion. Erected in 1504, this gate replaced the original, which was farther west. Opened in 1968, the 19-kilometer Bugak Skyway runs from Donam-dong to Jaha-mun, roughly paralleling this north section of the wall. Partway along the skyway is Palgak-jeong, a restaurant and snack bar, from where you get a wonderful bird's-eye view of downtown Seoul to the south and the dramatic mountains to the north. On a clear day, the city seems like a map come alive. The mountain road's name changes to In-wangsangil at Jaha-mun, continuing to the south below Inwang-san and the western wall, exiting to the side of Sajik Park. There is no public transportation along this route.

In the northwest corner of the wall is **Jaha-mun** (자하문). Also called Changui-mun ("Gate of Revealed Righteousness"), this little gate is located near the western end of the Bugak Skyway, where portions of the old wall are visible in both directions from the gate. West of this gate, a secondary wall runs up into Bukhan-san

National Park. Along this wall in Saegeom-jeong is the gate **Hongji-mun,** and nearby are the pavilion Saegeom-jeong, which was used by noblemen for relaxation after its construction in 1704, and a Buddha statue carved into the broad face of a granite boulder and painted white. Before overthrowing the last Goryeo Dynasty king and founding the Joseon Dynasty, Yi Seong-gye prayed at this Buddha for guidance and inspiration.

Seodae-mun, or the "Great West Gate," was located behind Gyeonghui-gung Park. Officially called Donui-mun ("Gate of Abundant Righteousness"), it was moved south from its original site and thereafter called Shin-mun ("New Gate"). Due to increased traffic on Shinmunno, it was taken down in 1914. Located between the west and south gates, Soui-mun ("Gate of Bright Righteousness"), also referred to as Seosomun, or the "Little West Gate," was taken down one year later. Like Gwanghui-mun, it was used for taking the dead out of the city.

Independence Gate 독립문

Dongnim-mun [Tongnim-mun] ("Independence Gate") lies directly south of Inwang-san. Not a city gate, it was constructed on the site of an older gate used by Koreans who came out to greet Chinese officials sent to the city as emissaries. Modeled after the Arc de Triomphe in Paris, but of much smaller scale, Dongnim-mun (H.S. #32) was erected in 1896 to celebrate the formal "independence" of Korea from China, and the creation of the Great Han Empire. Over the arch, "Dongnim-mun" is written in *han'geul* on the side facing the city center, and in Chinese characters on the side facing China. Well outside the original city walls, it was moved some distance north of its original spot to make room for an elevated overpass and other road construction in 1979. Two stone pillars set next to Dongnim-mun are remnants from Yeongeun-mun (H.S. #33), the previous gate. Seodae-mun Independence Park and the Seodaemun Prison History Hall are located to the side. Dongnimmun Station on subway line #3 stops alongside, or use bus no. 146 or 158, or express-bus no. 158.

ANCIENT HISTORICAL REMAINS

Long before the Joseon Dynasty put its mark on Seoul, the greater Seoul area, particularly south of the Han River, had been used by preceding kingdoms and earlier peoples. Once circled by a moat, part of which has been redug, the remains of the Baekje Dynasty **Mongchon Fortress** (몽촌토성) take up a large part of the northern section of Olympic Park. This earthen fortress (H.S. #297) was probably built around the 3rd century (perhaps as early as the 1st century), and has a packed-earth oval perimeter just over two kilometers long. Although it has long since disappeared, the exterior was at one time protected by a log palisade. This fortress is assumed by some to be Wiryeseong, an early Baekje Dynasty capital; however, its exact history and significance are not known. Use Mongchontoseong Station on subway line #8.

Set along a tributary to the Han River, the Mongchon earthen fortress was undoubtedly an

© ROBERT NILSEN

Dongnim-mun, Independence Gate

important and integral early Baekje Dynasty site. It, however, is not the only such ancient historical site in the city. Set at riverside less than two kilometers north of the Mongchon Fortress are the remains of the Baekje-era earthen fortress **Pungnap Toseong** (풍납토성). Located next to the Han River near the Cheonho Bridge, only 2.7 kilometers of the original four kilometers of earth berm walls (H.S. #11) remain from this elongated fortress—the west wall was washed away during heavy flooding in 1925. Many prehistoric and Baekje-era pottery artifacts were discovered at this site when excavated in 1966. The 6- to 10-meter-tall remains are from the 1978 renovation, and its L-shaped wall wraps partly around the neighborhood. The Cheonho Station on subway lines #5 and #8 is close. Down the river near the Seongnae ("Inside the Fortress") subway station stood another earthen-walled fortress from the Baekje Dynasty, but nothing really remains from this site.

North across the river, crowning the top of the mountain behind the Walker Hill Hotel, is **Acha Sanseong** (아차산성) (H.S. #234). About one kilometer in circumference, this early Baekje Dynasty fortification apparently protected the northern flank of the capital from Goguryeo incursion when control of the area was in dispute. This site also saw battle in the late 500s, when Goguryeo and Silla forces vied for control over the peninsula. Part of the slope below this mountain has been turned into a recreational area, with hiking trails, archery ranges, and other athletic facilities.

Other evidence of Baekje occupation in the immediate area is its tombs. Southwest of Mongchon Fortress are the eight tombs of **Seokchon-dong** (석촌동백제고분군). Of these, several are tiered and have piles of flat stones around their periphery; two have been designated H.S. #243. One mound tomb is in this group, as are several pit tombs. One stepped tomb resembles a pre-Christian era Goguryeo tomb located in China, while another tomb with inner and outer stone rings has a fundamental design similar to early Japanese royal tomb construction. A quiet place, this open area is good for a stroll away from the frenetic activity of the Jamshil area to the north.

Closer to Mongchon Fortress, **Bangi-dong Early Baekje Tombs** (방이동백제고분군) (H.S. #270) is a group of 10 mound tombs. Authorities believe that this quiet, landscaped area may have been part of a larger burial site. Express city bus no. 41 from Gwanghwa-mun runs near both tomb groups.

About three kilometers east along the river from the Pungnap Fortress is the **Amsa-dong Prehistoric Site** (암사동선사주거지) (H.S. #267). Estimated to have been used around the 4th or 5th century B.C., this is the largest such prehistoric site in the southern half of the peninsula. Round and square, some with hearths, nine pit dwellings have been unearthed and several reconstructed to give visitors a view of what the site might have looked like when inhabited. A small exhibition hall on the site preserves comb-pattern pottery, stone tools, and other artifacts unearthed here. Open daily except Monday 0930–1800 (until 1700 in winter); ₩500 entrance. A 10-minute walk from Amsa Station on subway line #8 brings you to the site, and city bus no. 569 from Jamshil gets you close.

SHRINES AND MEMORIALS
Gojong Memorial
Set in front of the Kyobo Building, at the northeast corner of the Gwanghwa-mun intersection, is the memorial pavilion Bigak. Although it's widely accepted that this shrine was dedicated to King Gojong, some scholars believe that it was actually raised to honor his murdered wife, Queen Min, whom the Japanese wished degraded and forgotten. Erected in 1904 during the 40th anniversary of the king's reign, it was repaired in 1954 after suffering damage during the Korean War. Inside this open pavilion, a stone tablet rides on the back of a granite tortoise, and a small granite block used as "point zero" marks distances to various places in the country. The inscription Mansae-mun ("Ten Thousand Year Gate") on the arched stone lintel to the front was written by the king's then-six-year-old son.

Eclipsing this spot as the new center of the city is a location kitty-corner across the intersection and marked by an open geodesic white dome. Laid into the ground below this dome are directional arrows for compass points and brass plates indicating distance and direction to various cities in Korea and around the world. Here too stands the new zero milestone marker, called *wonpyo,* from which distance is calculated in the country.

The Altar of Heaven 원구단

When King Gojong proclaimed himself emperor in 1897, he, like the Chinese emperor, was of a rank to appeal directly to heaven. Between 1897 and 1910, the king made yearly sacrifices at Wongu-dan ("Round Hill Altar"), the Altar of Heaven, for this purpose. Located in a much reduced and confined spot, this altar (H.S. #157) is situated in the rear garden of the Chosun Hotel; enter via a small gateway to the side of the hotel's front entrance. Only one of the original shrine buildings is left standing today. Hwanggungu, an octagonal three-tier structure set on a raised stone foundation, stored memorial tablets for the spirits of Heaven and Earth. The Chinese architectural influence is obvious; it's similar in structure—although not round—and in function to the imposing and much larger Temple of Heaven in Beijing.

Sajik Altar 사직단

Located within Sajik Park, Sajik-dan, or Sajik Altar (H.S. #121), has a history as old as the city itself. After King Taejo located his new capital at Seoul, he set aside this area for ceremonial altars. Twice a year he performed sacrifices here to ensure successful planting and harvesting. (It's said that every spring the king himself would plow one furrow of ground within the city walls as a symbolic gesture of labor toward the enterprise upon which all Koreans depended for their sustenance.) These ceremonies continued at Sajik Altar until 1897, when the ritual was changed slightly and transferred to the Altar of Heaven. The altars, low flat mounds bounded by stone retaining walls, are just inside Pyo-mun (T. #177), the front gate of Sajik Park. The east altar was used in spring to sacrifice to the god of earth; the west altar was used in autumn for the god of harvest.

Jong-myo 종묘

Directly across Yulgok-no from Changgyeong-gung is Jong-myo [Chong-myo], the Joseon Dynasty Royal Ancestral Shrine, the most important shrine in the country. Constructed at the same time as Gyeongbok-gung, this shrine (H.S. #125) was originally built to house the tablets of four of King Taejo's ancestors. Tablets for the Joseon Dynasty kings and queens (and a few crown princes who did not rule) have subsequently been added. In 1972, Crown Prince Yi Un's tablet was ceremoniously added, undoubtedly the last. Jong-myo was burned in 1592, but reconstructed in 1608. It was first opened to the public in 1960.

Expansion of the original building followed periodically, and today two long buildings house these tablets. Fronted by flagstone courtyards and surrounded by high walls, each stands on a single terrace. Jeong-jeon (N.T. #227) is the longest wooden traditional building in the country. Tablets for 18 significant kings, their queens, and one crown prince are placed within. Tablets of the remaining seven kings, four crown princes, and other royal family members are housed in Yeongnyeong-jeon (T. #821), the hall with the raised central roof. Only two kings are not represented, Yeonsan-gun and Gwanghae-gun, the disreputable 10th and 15th kings of the dynasty. In this case, *gun* means "prince," a posthumous title indicating official demotion of rank. Across the courtyard to the front of Jeong-jeon is an auxiliary building which houses tablets of 83 meritorious subjects from throughout the dynasty. In addition, several other buildings dot this compound, all used in preparation for a yearly ritual ceremony.

Throughout the Joseon Dynasty, the king, as titular head of the Yi family, held ceremonies here five times a year. This memorial ritual (I.C.A. #56), discontinued by the Japanese in 1910, is now held once a year on the first Sunday in May 0900–1500. First seen by the public in 1960, this six-hour solemn rite officiated by members of the Yi family, called *Jongmyo Daeje,* keeps alive Confucian rituals of the past. Special food and wine are offered to each of the spirits of the departed kings; ceremonial recitations are spoken. The Royal Court Orchestra performs *Jongmyo Jeryeak,* traditional court music (I.C.A. #1) while dancers perform traditional court dances—everyone is in colorful court clothing. Don't miss it if you're in Seoul in spring! In 1995, UNESCO added Jong-myo and its ceremonies and music to the list of world heritage sites to be recognized and protected by the world community for its unique cultural value.

Although the grounds are open and the courtyards can be entered, the doors on the main shrines are kept closed except on the day of this ceremony and during other special events. A small exhibition hall is open daily. It displays traditional musical instruments, ritual food vessels, official seals, and a palanquin. Like the palaces, Jong-myo is a favorite spot for school outings—be prepared for crowds. Jong-myo is open daily except Tuesday 0600–1700 March–October and 0600–1630 November–February; ₩700 entrance, ₩300 for ages 19–24. Ticket sales stop one hour before closing. As Jong-myo and Changgyeong-gung are connected by a footbridge over Yulgok-no, entrance to one gives you entrance to the other. Jong-myo's main entrance is across the Jong-myo Plaza from Jong-no. Jongno 3-ga Station on subway lines #1, #3, and #5 is a few steps to the west.

Mun-myo 문묘

To the rear of Changgyeong-gung and Biwon is the Confucian Seonggyungwan University. Tucked into a secluded compound near its front gate is Mun-myo (H.S. #143), the central and most sacred shrine of Korean Confucianism. On individual table-like altars in Daeseong-jeon, the main hall, are memorial tablets for Confucius, his four principal disciples, and 16 Chinese and 18 Korean sages. Here as well are the Myeongnyun-dang lecture hall, east and west dormitories, library, auxiliary halls, and two tall ginkgo trees (N.M. #59), both about 500 years old. Mun-myo is used today strictly on ceremonial occasions—but Confucianism is still part of the curriculum at the university. While you can visit the compound at any time, you'll not get a look inside the buildings until they are opened for the *Seokjeon-je* ceremony. The

grounds are open daily 0930–1600, except Sunday and public holidays.

Founded in 1288, **Seonggyungwan** is the oldest continuously functioning institution of higher learning in Korea and was referred to in the past as the National Confucian Academy. *Seong* roughly translates as "accomplish," *gyun* as "uniform," and *gwan* as "academy." As one noted Korean scholar writes, the name Seonggyungwan means "to develop men from immaturity to maturity, make uniform the customs of those who differ." This fits nicely with the Confucian concept of what a learning institution should do and what effect society should have on its people.

In 1304, An Hyang, the foremost Korean Neo-Confucianist, enshrined portraits of the sages in Daeseong-jeon. Government examinations and official ceremonies were then held at the shrine while Confucian education was continued at the academy. In 1398, a new main hall and lecture hall were built, and the institute was given royal backing. Mun-myo was burned to the ground in 1592 but rebuilt a decade later. The present structures date from then. During the Joseon Dynasty, it was the only officially sanctioned institute of its kind. Seonggyungwan became a junior college during the Japanese colonial period but was elevated to university status immediately after liberation. In response to its continued growth and the confines of the city, several of the university's colleges have been transferred to the Suwon campus. Despite all the educational and social changes of the past century, it remains the undisputed center of Korean Confucianism, and heads 232 smaller Confucian academies throughout the country in an effort to disseminate Confucian principles and teachings. A museum here displays about 1,400 historical items relating to Korean Confucianism and Korean Confucian scholars.

Each spring and autumn, *Seokjeon-je* (I.C.A. #82) is held at Mun-myo to honor Confucius and his disciples; the whole affair is officiously ceremonial. It starts with a solemn procession; all participants are decked out in full traditional regalia, prayers are intoned, and special food and drink are offered. Music and dance are performed by students of the National Classical Music Institute; the shrill flute, thump of the drum, heavy ring of stone chimes, and clang of the bells counterpoise the slow, synchronized movements of the court dancers. Several hundred musicians and dancers participate. Usually held in late morning and lasting about two hours, *Seokjeonje* provides one of the few opportunities to witness a truly traditional, ancient ceremony. Don't miss it if you're in Seoul when it's being performed! Dates fluctuate yearly according to the lunar calendar; the ceremony is held to coincide with the spring and autumn equinoxes. Get there on city bus no. 6, 8, 84, 85, or 710; Hyehwa Station on subway line #4 is the closest.

Dong-myo 동묘

Less than one kilometer east of Dongdae-mun is Dong-myo [Tong-myo], a shrine dedicated to General Gwanu of the Chinese Han Dynasty (2nd century A.D.), who was, after his death, elevated to the position of the Chinese god of war. It was believed that Gwanu, through miraculous intervention, helped Koreans drive the Japanese off the peninsula during the Hideyoshi Invasions of the 1590s. (The real reason, however, was the death of Hideyoshi himself.) Nonetheless, this shrine, plus four others in the city, were erected in the early 1600s to pay tribute to the help rendered by Gwanu. Of the original five shrines, only Dong-myo (H.S. #142) remains. Wooden representations of Gwanu in two forms—a mortal figure, with a red face, and a spiritual figure, with a yellow face—preside in the main hall to the rear. Other statues are those of aides and retainers, moved here for preservation from other city shrines after their destruction. Although the roof is definitely of Korean style, the rest of the main shrine building has a Chinese "feel" because of its lattice wood front, tiled floor, and stone wainscoted sides. Until the 1980s, this shrine was not given much note and was left in a poor state of repair but since has been refurbished and the surrounding grounds made into a small park. No official ceremonies are now held here for Gwanu, nor have they been for decades; however, on occasion individuals will come to offer prayers or supplication. For the most part, it's now only a curiosity for the culture-conscious, a stop for Chinese tourists, and a place where locals come to while away the afternoon with friends. Of the dozens of similar shrines that once dotted the country, only four others remain—in Suwon, Namwon, Andong, and Jinju.

Backed up against Jong-no, the Dong-myo entrance is located one block off the main thoroughfare down a small side street. Take city bus no. 30, 38, or 131. The Dongmyo Station on subway line #6 is closest, but a 10-minute walk from either Dongdaemun or Shinseol-dong station on subway #1 also works.

King Sejong Memorial Hall
세종대왕기념관

The most highly respected and honored of the Joseon Dynasty kings, Sejong ruled over a land flush with social, literary, and scientific achievement. Many memorials, statues, and institutions throughout the country have been dedicated to him, and in 1973 this memorial was raised to exhibit samples of his achievements. He is best known for the promulgation in 1443 of the native Korean script, *han'geul,* and for the scientific and literary accomplishments of his time. In this hall is a pictorial history of events in his life. Replicas of sundials, rain gauges (including one set up in 1441—reputedly the world's first), and other scientific instruments, maps, and musical instruments used during his time are on display. *Han'geul* was perhaps the crowning achievement of Sejong's reign, and its creation is also represented by historical documents and examples of printing types and methods. Set on a wooded hill next to the diminutive Yeong-neung royal tomb, this memorial hall is open 0900–1800 (until 1700 in winter); ₩800 entrance fee. Use bus no. 134.

Ihwajang Memorial Hall 이화장기념관

This hall is dedicated to former president Syngman Rhee, an influential resistance fighter during the Japanese colonial period, a member of the provisional government in exile, and the country's first constitutional leader after independence. Occupying a simple and utilitarian home that Rhee used before his inauguration, and that his widow used until her death in 1992, this small, private museum/shrine explains Rhee's life and times and displays personal items used by him and his wife. Located in a residential district near the southern end of Daehang-no, the way is not well marked. Ihwajang is open daily 0900–1700, and is of most interest to the modern Korean history buff.

An Jung-geun Memorial Hall
안중근기념관

On the lower western flank of Nam-san is a large memorial hall dedicated to the patriot An Jung-geun. An was the man who assassinated Ito Hirobumi, the principal architect of the Treaty of 1905, which made Korea a protectorate of Japan. A portrait of An and his personal effects are on display in this hall, which was renovated in 2001. A huge statue of him stands outside. Open 0900–1700.

Jeoldusan Martyrs' Shrine
절두산순교기념관

On a bluff overlooking the Han River, across from Yeongdeungpo, is Jeoldusan [Chŏltusan] Martyrs' Shrine, at the Church of the Martyrs. *Jeol* means "decapitate," *du* means "head," and *san* means "mountain." Many of those who lost their lives during the numerous religious persecutions of the 1800s were beheaded on the sandy riverflats below. (Other spots, all outside the city walls, where Catholics were persecuted and martyred are the grounds of the Saenamteo Catholic Church, upriver near the railroad bridges; Jungnim-dong Catholic Church, behind Seoul Station; and Seosomun Park.) Built in 1967, Jeoldusan Martyrs' Shrine was raised to memorialize Korean and foreign Catholics who were killed for their faith. It has become well known since Pope John Paul II came here and canonized 103 Korean martyrs during an official visit to Korea in 1984.

The Koreans' first contact with Christianity came through envoys to the Chinese court in Beijing during the 1600s and 1700s. These men brought back books containing "Western" (i.e., Catholic) religious doctrine, and some who studied them were convinced that they contained

ideas of value. Gradually, scattered "conversion" took place with laymen heading small but slowly growing communities of believers. In 1794, the first priest, a Chinese father, surreptitiously entered Korea to minister to these people. In an effort to stamp out attachment to this religion, staunch Confucianists had him killed in 1801 during the first great Catholic persecution. The first foreign priest, the Frenchman Maubert, sneaked across the border in 1836 and was followed the next year by two others. These priests and many of their followers were beheaded during the persecution of 1839. Several other priests came during the next few decades, and large numbers of people continued to be converted despite pressure against the religion. Another persecution followed in 1846, and in 1866 nine French priests and thousands of Koreans were tortured and beheaded. After 1884, diplomatic and commercial treaties legally allowed foreigners into the country. Not only did the number of Catholic priests—and, consequently, converts—increase, but Protestants also entered to start their missionary work.

The modernistic Jeoldusan Martyrs' Shrine houses a chapel and a small museum containing memorabilia of the early Christian movement in Korea. A bronze statue of Kim Tae-geon, the first Korean Catholic priest, stands outside surveying the garden, and a bust statue of Pope John Paul II has been raised since the pope's visit. The museum hours are 0930–1830 (closed Monday); ₩1,000 entrance. This shrine can be reached after a short walk from the Hapjeong Station and along the east side of the tracks on subway line #2. City bus nos. 129 and 131 stop nearby.

Foreigners' Cemetery 외국인묘지공원
Capping a wooded knoll a few steps from Jeoldusan Martyrs' Shrine is the Seoul Foreigners' Cemetery. (This cemetery has been given the new and not entirely accurate name of Missionary Cemetery Park (선교사묘지공원), which appears on some street signs directing you to the site, yet the plaque at the actual entrance to the compound still carries the original name.) Nearly 500 are buried here: Americans, Canadians, Danes,

French, Germans, Italians, and Russians—government officials, missionaries, doctors, businessmen, scholars, journalists, and soldiers. Many of the tombstones are from the turn of the 20th century, but some are only a few years old. Well-known foreign names in early modern Korean history can be spotted here. The most oft-quoted epitaph from this cemetery is found on the headstone of Homer Hulbert (1863–1949), a missionary and scholar. "I would rather be buried in Korea than in Westminster Abbey," it says, and probably expresses the sentiment of most others lying at rest here as well. The Seoul Union Church is located within the grounds, and an exhibition room displays artifacts relating to foreign residents in Korea. A small monograph printed by the Yongsan military library and available through RAS discusses this and other foreigners' cemeteries in the country, and includes bibliographical notes on their occupants. Bounded by a major roadway and subway line, this cemetery is not as quiet as it used to be.

National Cemetery 국립묘지

The National Cemetery is located in an amphitheater-like valley on the south bank of the Han River. It was originally used as a military cemetery, but its scope was broadened in 1965. Gracefully landscaped, this sacred spot is reserved for select political and social leaders of the nation, some officials of the provisional government, policemen, military commanders, and Korean and Vietnam War dead. Former presidents Syngman Rhee and Park Chung Hee are interred here. Numerous buildings and monuments dot the grounds, and a memorial tablet has been raised for over 100,000 unknown soldiers from the Korean War. In addition, one display hall houses military paraphernalia. Commemorative ceremonies are held on this site during significant national anniversaries, including June 6, Memorial Day. Open daily 0800–1700. Use the Dongjak Station on subway line #4.

4.19 Cemetery

During the presidential elections of 1960, the authoritarian and intransigent President Syngman Rhee and his Freedom Party resorted to rigging the campaign process, buying votes, extorting funds, using force against opposition members, stuffing ballot boxes, and numerous other illegal tactics and acts of interference and repression. In response, students rose up in demonstrations in a number of provincial cities, and after the election a large demonstration erupted in Seoul. The students demanded that new elections be called and that the president resign. After perpetrating violent acts and causing destruction of some government property, the students were set upon by police and many were killed. The gravity of the situation resulted in martial law and the calling of military troops to restore calm. Following this ugly episode, large numbers of university instructors, then backed by the general populace, also put their voice to the call, forcing the reelected president to resign a week later and leave the country. Over 200 of the young people who perished in the Seoul conflict are buried at the 4.19 Cemetery and honored for their efforts to force true democratic processes onto governmental affairs. The name "4.19" refers to the date April 19, the day on which the bloody demonstrations started in Seoul. This cemetery is tucked into the eastern slope of Bukhan-san, in the northern section of the city. Use city bus no. 6-1, 8, or 23.

Saryukshin-myo 사육신묘

Set on a knoll in Yeongdeungpo overlooking the Han River is Saryukshin-myo, a shrine containing the graves of four loyal officials of King Danjong—three scholars and one military general. In 1455, the boy-king Danjong was pressured into abdicating the throne in favor of his uncle, Sejo. Seeing the orderly and prescribed system of succession crudely breached, these four men, with the help of two others, attempted to reinstate Danjong. Their attempt failed, and they, along with many other high-ranking court officials, were executed. Two years later, King Sejo had his nephew killed. Aside from the graves, Saryukshin-myo contains a memorial hall, memorial tablets, two ceremonial gates, manicured lawns, and walkways. This shrine is open 0900–1900. Use subway line #1 to the Noryangjin Station or take city bus no. 25, 26, or 85.

Nakseong-dae 낙성대

Dedicated to Gang Gam-chan, a Goryeo Dynasty general who repulsed a Khitan attack in 1018 and ended the strife along the country's northern border, the shrine Nakseong-dae lies at the foot of Gwanak-san, over the hill and east of Seoul National University at a site said to be his birthplace. A small memorial hall, stone pagoda, entrance gate, and a granite slab inscribed with the life story of General Gang are preserved in this well-landscaped, multi-level compound. Left to decay over the centuries, it was rededicated and refurbished during the years of the late president Park Chung Hee. Periodically throughout the year, traditional wedding ceremonies and other cultural performances are given free of charge within the park. This is one of the few places in the city where you can see what an old-style Korean wedding ceremony was like. The Nakseongdae Station on subway line #2, a 15-minute walk away, is closest.

TEMPLES

There are several hundred temples from all sects in and around Seoul (1,006 temples by one count). Aside from the few listed below, other well-known and frequented, but less conveniently located, temples are situated on the flanks of the mountains that surround the city.

Jogye-sa 조계사

The only major temple in the center of Seoul is Jogye-sa [Chogye-sa]. Neither ancient (founded in 1910) nor historic, it's the headquarters of the Jogye sect of Korean Buddhism, and the regional office of the World Fellowship of Buddhism. With over 1,500 temples, this sect is by far the largest in Korea and has the greatest number of monks. Jogye-sa is approached via a narrow alley from Ujeongguk-no. On the street nearby, shops sell Buddhist paraphernalia—candles, incense, bells, beads, alms bowls, robes, altars, statues, books, writing brushes—all the religious supplies necessary for a monk or a layman.

Squashed into a tightly packed downtown neighborhood, Jogye-sa has an atypical setting. Its main hall is one of the largest temple halls in Seoul. This colorful building has carved latticework designs on each of the front doors, and paintings of scenes of the Buddha's life and the ox-herding series paintings on its outer walls. Inside, the high ceiling creates a feeling of spaciousness, the long altar, a feeling of breadth. Set on a pedestal and seated on a cushion, a gilt image of the Seokgamoni Buddha is enclosed in a glass alcove. Done entirely in vivid red and gold, huge murals of the Buddha and his attendants have been painted to each side of this central figure. An ornate, somewhat angular canopy is suspended over the altar.

Behind it is the judgment hall, odd in that it is long front to back. Next to it stands the multistory administration building. A stone lantern of recent origin, seven-tier stone pagoda, and a bell pavilion stand in the courtyard along with a white pine tree (N.M. #9) that's over 500 years old, and a 400-year-old zelkova elm. It's said that relics of the historical Buddha were brought here in 1914 by a Sri Lankan monk and placed in the stone pagoda. In the alleys surrounding the temple are a number of Buddhist academies. At this always busy temple, prayers and ceremonies take place every day, and a special Sunday service is held. On Buddha's birthday, Jogye-sa is awash with activity and is the beginning and terminus of the popular lantern parade for the Lotus Lantern Festival.

Bongwon-sa 봉원사

Beyond the west end of the Geumhwa Tunnel is Bongwon-sa [Pongwon-sa]. Founded in 889 down the hill where Yonsei University is today, it was moved in 1749. Destroyed during the Korean War, it was rebuilt soon after. In 1970, it became the headquarters of the Taego sect of Korean Buddhism, the second largest in Korea. This sect allows priests to marry. The temple's main hall is a low structure with a cramped feel, but the unpainted 3,000 Buddhas Hall is one of the largest in the country. This large building, with its ornate altar canopy, has carved panels around its doors, which themselves are finely decorated. The main hall has many very fine murals inside and wall murals on its exterior. The judgment hall features larger-than-life figures of the judges of the underworld, and murals of the sufferings of those in hell. On the upper terrace is a shrine for Sanshin and Chilseong. A bell pavilion, study hall, and several other buildings make up the remainder of this compound.

While not the most exciting of temples, Bongwon-sa is known as the home of two designated Human Cultural Assets (#48 and #50): the head abbot is a master of *dancheong* painting, an art creating Buddhist murals and geometric and floral designs in bold natural tints, a type of decoration most often seen on wood surfaces in the upper reaches of temple buildings; the second priest's specialty is Buddhist ritual and chants. On Buddha's birthday, a huge mural is hung outside at this temple, special services are given, and ceremonial music and dance are performed. Ritual Buddhist music and dance performances called *Yeongsan-je* are held here yearly on the fifth day of May. To reach Bongwon-sa, use neighborhood bus no. 8 or 8-1 from in front of Yonsei University.

Hwagye-sa 화계사

Set on the eastern slope of Bukhan-san within Bukhan-san National Park, Hwagye-sa lies nestled in the forested hillside at the edge of the city. This temple was founded in 1522, repaired in 1619, and again in 1866. During the late 1800s, it was frequented by royalty who came to pray for the well-being of the nation. While rather undistinguished today, it is, however, a thriving and active institution. This temple's main hall sits on a high stone terrace. On its altar sit two urns, royal gifts from the 19th century; murals cover its exterior walls. To the right is the judgment hall. Its carved figures of the Buddha and judges of the underworld are attributed to the famous priest Naong. To the left is a hall with 500 stone bodhisattva statues on its altar. Just below the temple is a natural spring, and from there a trail leads farther up into Bukhan-san National Park. To reach Hwagye-sa, use bus no. 25 or 84 from Seoul Station or Myeong-dong.

In association with Hwagye-sa, the Seoul International Zen Center was established here by Master Seung Sahn. This center, along with the Kye Ryong Sahn International Zen Center at Mu Sang Sa near Daejeon, are the only organized entities in Korea that accept foreigners—ordained monks or laypersons, male or female—for live-in meditation study. Study and meditation take place at specified times throughout the year. For specifics about these centers and how to apply see the Special Topic "Zen Meditation for Foreigners" in the Introduction chapter. For those with a more casual interest, the Zen Center offers a worship service for sitting and questions nearly every Sunday 1330–1600; it's open to anyone.

Doseon-sa 도선사

Dedicated in 862, Doseon-sa [Tosŏn-sa] is the largest and best-known temple on Bukhan-san. This compact temple compound sits below the mountain's jagged eastern ridgeline. Although recently repaired, several of the halls are quite old, and the newer three-story cement prayer hall is one of the largest in the capital region. Gable roofs here display painted designs, and exterior walls are filled with murals. Buddha's birthday is the temple's most important event. At this time, the entire temple compound is strung with paper lanterns and awash with red and yellow colors. Up behind the main hall, to the rear of the compound, is an eight-meter-high bas-relief carving of the Goddess of Mercy, which, according to legend, appeared on the flat inner face of a boulder when it cracked in half. Another legend attributes its creation to the temple's founder, who is said to have done the work without chisel marks. The work, however, really seems to be of mid-Joseon Dynasty vintage. A bell pavilion, other stone work, a Mountain Spirit hall, and Myeongbu-jeon grace the temple, the last of which enshrines a portrait of former president Park Chung Hee and his wife, both supporters of this temple. Use bus no. 6 or 8 from Gwanghwa-mun. A 30-minute walk up a steep mountain road from the bus terminal brings you to Doseon-sa, or you can make this 2.5 kilometer distance faster and easier by riding the shuttle bus (₩600), which leaves from across the street.

Bomun-sa 보문사

A large temple for nuns and head temple of the

Bomun sect, Bomun-sa [Pomun-sa] is located north of Dongdae-mun. Established during the Goryeo Dynasty and reconstructed after the Korean War, this quiet yet slightly citified temple seems incongruous with its surroundings. The construction of a Buddha figure, placed in an artificial cave to the rear of the temple, looks like an attempt to replicate the Seokguram Buddha of Gyeongju. Tall and slender, a nine-tier stone pagoda stands to the side. Many halls crowd this confined compound, but they all seem to fit and create a harmonious whole. Use Bomun Station on subway line #6 or bus no. 23 or 32.

Bongeun-sa 봉은사

Formerly secluded on a hillside far from the bustle of the city, Bongeun-sa [Pongŭn-sa] now fronts a busy city boulevard opposite the COEX building and World Trade Center. Established in 794, this temple was one of the centers of Zen practice during the Joseon Dynasty. During the mid-1500s, Bongeun-sa was the home of the renowned priest Bou, who was instrumental in the revival of both the meditation and doctrinal branches of Korean Buddhism. Amidst great celebration, a meticulous translation of the entire *Koreana Tripitaka* into modern Korea was completed here in 2001 after 37 years of work. A pleasing place, this temple has for years been undergoing periodic reconstruction and construction of new and larger buildings and monuments. The main hall enshrines Seokgamoni Buddha and is finely adorned inside and out with brightly painted murals. Several other halls, study rooms, and dormitories, plus a large standing stone Mireuk Buddha statue, grace the compound. The old lecture hall is seated on pedestals of stone in front of the Mireuk Buddha and a new lecture hall was built in 1998 to the front of the main hall and central courtyard pagoda, which is said to contain a piece of the historical Buddha's *sarisa*. An archive holding 3,175 wood printing blocks of the *Avatamsaka Sutra*, with additional printing blocks for other sutras, stands next to the main hall. The front gate guards are perhaps the best examples of such figures in the Seoul area. Bongeun-sa is especially busy on weekends and holidays, when scores of people come to pray. Samseong Station on subway line #2 is the nearest, or use express bus no. 37.

Other Temples

North of Bomun-sa is **Shinheung-sa** (신흥사), established as the prayer temple for Jeong-neung, the tomb of Queen Gang, the first wife of King Taejo. Tomb and temple were originally built in what is now the Jeong-dong district behind Deoksu-gung, the old foreign settlement area which received its name from this tomb. Shortly after their construction, both tomb and temple were moved to their present location outside the city wall.

To the north of Shinheung-sa, set just within the boundary of Bukhan-san National Park, is the temple **Gyeongguk-sa** (경국사), one of the city's most finely landscaped and visually pleasing temple grounds. Its flowering bushes, trees, and terraces set off the comely buildings. Nearly a dozen other temples and hermitages are found nestled into the hillsides of this long valley. Several trails lead up to Bukhan Sanseong from farther up the valley. Bus no. 5-1 leads past entrance roads for both Shinheung-sa and Gyeongguk-sa.

On the western slope of Bukhan-san is **Jin'gwan-sa** (진관사). Erected in 1101, it was rebuilt in 1964 for Buddhist nuns. Neat and well-tended, this compound has many fine halls with numerous exterior murals. Bus no. 154 gets you closest.

To the rear of Goryeo University is **Gaeun-sa.** Founded in 1396 by Muhak, the teacher of King Taejo, the founder of the Joseon Dynasty, this temple serves as an institute of Buddhist education for the training of monks. To the rear of Gaeun-sa is the small hermitage Chilseong-am, and here is a large white image of the Goddess of Mercy, carved into the face of a boulder. Use Anam Station on subway line #6.

Lotus Lantern International Buddhist Center 연등국제불교회관

Founded in 1987 by Won Myeong Seunim, this center is associated with the Jogye order but is privately operated. Staffed by Korean and foreign monks, Lotus Lantern runs various meditation classes, workshops, and study groups on a regular schedule but does not offer a live-in option. You need not be an ordained monk or even a Buddhist to attend; a serious interest is all that's required. This center has a small library on Korean Buddhism and general Buddhist subjects, sells select books, translates Korean Buddhist works into English, and publishes other books and pamphlets on various aspects of Buddhist thought and practice. More broadly, Lotus Lantern seeks to make Korean Buddhism better known to the foreign community within Korea as well as to open up avenues of dialogue and understanding with proponents of Buddhism throughout the world. The creation of a medi-

tation center on Ganghwa-do expanded the center's options for retreats and additional meditation opportunities. Lotus Lantern is located up a tiny alley—a small sign in English hangs at the entrance—east of Gyeongbok-gung and north of the Anguk-dong intersection. For more information, call (tel. 02/735-5347), or write the Lotus Lantern International Buddhist Center, 148-5 Sogyeok-dong, Jongno-gu, Seoul, Korea 110-200.

CHURCHES

Aside from Buddhist temples, Seoul has a great

SELECTED HOUSES OF WORSHIP

For dates and times of church services in languages other than Korean, call the following churches directly, consult the Saturday edition of the *Korea Times* newspaper for others, or contact any tourist office.

Anglican Cathedral (English, Korean)
3, Jeong-dong, Jung-gu (tel. 02/730-6611)

International Lutheran Church (English)
726-39, Hannam-dong, Yongsan-gu (tel. 02/794-6274)

Jewish (English)
Yongsan Garrison South Post Chapel (tel. 02/793-3728)

Kwangnim Methodist Church (English, Japanese)
Shinsa-dong, Gangnam-gu (tel. 02/546-0151)

Lotus Lantern International Buddhist Center (English)
148-5, Sogyeok-dong, Jongno-gu (tel. 02/735-5347)

Myeong-dong Cathedral (English, Korean)
1, Myeong-dong 2-ga, Jung-gu (tel. 02/777-0281)
The midnight mass on Christmas Eve is well known.

St. Nicholas (Greek) Orthodox Church (English, Greek)
424-1, Ahyeon 1-dong, Mapo-gu (tel. 02/365-3744)

The Seoul Central Masjid (Arabic, Korean, English)
732-21. Hannam-dong, Yongsan-gu (tel. 02/794-7307)

Seoul International Baptist Church (English)
Located in Itaewon near Yongsan Garrison (tel. 02/793-6267)

number of churches and other religious meeting places—over 5,000 by one estimate. Western religions were first introduced to Korea in the early 1800s, but only since the end of the Korean War has there been a wellspring of support for these religions. Churches have sprouted all over Seoul to minister to the growing number of Korean Christians. From any vantage point in the city, steeples can be seen in all directions. Indigenous Korean religions have also sprung up over the past 150 years and play a significant social role in Korean society. The best known of these are Cheondo-gyo and Taejong-gyo, both of which only conduct services in Korean. Confucianists do not hold a regular worship service, only the yearly memorial ceremonies honoring the sages, and have no religious buildings other than their shrines.

Historical Notes on Various Churches

Although a few Catholics filtered into Korea during the early 1800s, it was not until 1882, when Korea began to establish diplomatic relations with other countries, that they and others were officially allowed into the country to practice and spread their religion. The building of churches started soon afterward.

The year 1887 saw the construction of the

Seoul International Zen Center (English)
At Hwagye-sa. 487, Suyu-dong, Gangbuk-gu (tel. 02/900-4326)

Seoul Union Church (Evangelical Protestant) (English)
144, Hapcheong-dong, Mapo-gu (tel. 02/333-7397)
Services adjacent to the Seoul Foreigners' Cemetery

Yeongnak Presbyterian Church (English, Japanese, Korean)
69, Cho-dong 2-ga, Chung-gu (tel. 02/273-6301)

Yeouido Full Gospel Church (Korean, Japanese, English)
11 Yeouido-dong, Yeongdeungpo-gu (tel. 02/780-5111)
With nearly a million members, this church has the largest congregation in the country.

Contact the following for information on indigenous Korean religions:

Central Mission of Cheondo-gyo
88, Gyeongun-dong, Jongno-gu
Services on Sunday

Taejong-gyo
13-78, Hongun 2-dong, Seodaemun-gu

Wonbul-gyo
1-3 Heukseok-dong, Dongjak-gu
Services on Sunday

Yudo-hoe (Confucian Society)
53, Myeongnyun-dong 3-ga, Jongno-gu

first Protestant church in Korea, the Saemunan Church, between the Gwanghwa-mun intersection and Gyeonghui-gung Palace site. **Yakhyeon Catholic Church** (H.S. #252), the oldest extant Catholic church in the country (1892), is located on a hill behind Seoul Station. This red-brick structure is done in semi-Gothic style, located just outside the old city walls. Many Korean Catholics were killed on this site during the persecutions of the mid-1800s. With its domed roof and Byzantine look, the **Greek Orthodox Church** stands out as it caps a small hill near Hyochang Park. Originally a Russian Orthodox Church located next to the former Russian Legation in Jeong-dong, it became a Greek Orthodox Church in 1956 with the aid of Greek and American soldiers. Historical religious items are displayed inside its entrance. Built in 1898 in the shape of a cross, **Myeong-dong Cathedral** is the premier Catholic church in the country, and the Korean archbishop often officiates here. The first large Western-style church in the country, it created a great fuss when built, because from its location it was possible to see into the king's palace. Musical concerts of all kinds are often performed at this stately structure. Around this spiritual sanctuary swirls the Myeong-dong commercial and entertainment area.

The **Yeongnak Presbyterian Church** across the road is known for its lofty gray granite facade. It is the principal Presbyterian church in the country, with a congregation of some 20,000. The red-brick and granite Romanesque **Anglican Church** sits next to the British Embassy and Deoksu-gung. Built in 1926, it's Korea's head Anglican church and home of the Anglican Bishop. A pioneer missionary to Korea, Bishop Trollope, is buried in this building—still the only person known to be buried within the old city walls. On the far side of Deoksu-gung stands **Cheong-dong Methodist Church.** The original Gothic-style stone church (H.S. #256) was built in 1910; in 1970 a modern red-brick structure was added.

Made of granite and brick in 1921, the **Cheondo-gyo Central Mission** building looks a bit like a colonial American structure. It houses a worship hall, and the adjacent Suun Hall is the church headquarters.

Since its introduction during the Korean War by Turkish troops, Islam has grown slowly in Korea. In 1972, the Arabesque **Yongsan Islamic Mosque** was built as the first mosque in the country. It sits high on a hill above the noise, glitter, and decadence of Itaewon.

PARKS AND RECREATIONAL AREAS

Public parks and green areas of all sorts have been developed in every corner of the city. Some, tucked into tight inner-city spaces, counterpoise crowded city streets; others lay over the many city hills; a handful have been created for amusement, recreation, and athletics. A few are relatively old, but most have been created within the last several decades, many of them in the areas south of the Han River.

Nam-san Park 남산공원

Rising like a stubby green thumb in the center of the city is 273-meter Nam-san ("South Mountain"), formerly Seoul's southern boundary. Today, as the city has swirled completely around it, Nam-san marks the hub of this metropolis. The old city wall, portions of which can still be seen at various spots on its thickly wooded hillside, ran up one ridge and down another. A fortress, part of the original defensive line, was constructed at the top. Placed in the saddle near the top of the mountain was the terminus of the nationwide **fire-beacon** communication network. Radiating from Seoul were five series of mountaintop beacons employed to relay daily messages from the farthest reaches of the country to the capital. When one beacon fire was lit, all was peaceful; two fires meant that something suspicious was happening; three, four, and five fires meant varying degrees of danger. Every night, these signals were relayed through the length of the peninsula to Nam-san so that the king and his court would know the state of affairs for each area of the country. This network was used until the late 1890s, when a telegraph system was implemented.

Today, the upper portion of this mountain is the three-square-kilometer Nam-san Park, the largest green area in the city's center. At the park's western end are the city library, a small botanical conservatory (open 0900–1800; ₩300), lawns, flower beds, walks, a children's playground, and a memorial to the patriot An Jung-geun. An octagonal pavilion, the renovated fire beacon towers, and the Seoul Tower cap the summit. On the eastern slope lie the National Theater and National Classical Music Institute. Here and there throughout the park are statues of civilian and military leaders, poets, scholars, saints, and martyrs. Nam-san's wild, tree-covered slopes are home to dozens of species of plants and animals, and from its sides issue several mineral springs. Running like a ribbon around the waist of the mountain is a scenic road; below, three tunnels have been burrowed through the solid granite.

Set on top of Nam-san and rising to a height of 236 meters is the most obvious landmark in the city, **Seoul Tower.** Completed in 1975 for television broadcasting, this needle-like structure was opened to the public in 1980. An elevator swiftly takes you to two observation floors and a revolving restaurant (plain but pricey) halfway up the tower. By far the best views of Seoul are had from this tower. From here you'll realize just how huge this city is. The views are best on a clear day, but the night scene is also spectacular and well worth a look. Pictures displayed along the glass outer wall of one of the observation floors indicate what can be seen in each direction, and distances to points inside and outside the country are indicated on a sign at each directional point. Here as well is a tiny exhibition area with several old photographs of Seoul and displays of Korean history. Coin-operated binoculars are available, as are stalls with the usual tourist trinkets. The Seoul Tower observation deck is open 0900–2430 daily; ₩3,000 entrance, ₩2,500 for students. In the basement of the tower are an animation theater, a small aquarium, and a folk museum. The **Global Village Folk Museum** exhibits mostly clothing, eating utensils, and ceremonial folk artifacts from some 150 countries around the world. There are separate entrance fees to the aquarium, Global Village Folk Museum, and animation theater; a combination ticket for all three plus the observatory

runs ₩9,000, ₩7,200 for students. Other gift shops and restaurants flank the base of the tower, and the plaza in front is a venue for occasional performances of folk music and dance.

For the energetic, a stairway leads up the steep western slope, and for the adventurous, a cable car (1000–2300; ₩3,800 one-way or ₩4,800 round-trip) leaves approximately every 20 minutes from the waist road on the north slope to just below the pavilion at the top. Operating since 1962, this system has recently been revamped with new cars and a new lower terminal. Nam-san Park can be approached easily from Seoul Station or Myeong-dong; city bus no. 83-1 from Gwanghwa-mun stops at the western entrance. Myeongdong and Hoehyeon stations on subway line #4 are a short walk from the cable car.

Nam-san Valley Village 남산한옥마을

At the bottom of the north slope of Nam-san is Nam-san Valley Hanok ("Traditional Korean House") Village. Several traditional Joseon Dynasty residences have been moved from other spots in the city to this site to represent examples of traditional upper-class residential architecture. Enter by way of the road to the side of Jungang University Hospital or through the Korea House grounds. Activities and musical performances are periodically held here, including a traditional wedding ceremony every Saturday at 1400. Some food is served at one of the houses, and a gift shop is open for souvenir hunters. Up behind this group of buildings is a still young and immature landscaped park and in an upper section a time capsule containing items from the modern age that was buried on the 600th anniversary of the founding of Seoul as the capital of the country. The hope is that this capsule will be opened in 2394, on the city's 1000th anniversary. Jungmuro Station on subway lines #3 and 4 is closest, or use bus no. 6.

Han-gang Riverside Park and Recreation Areas

An engaging feature of Seoul is its riverside development. From 1982 to 1986, the portion of the Han River that runs through Seoul was cleaned up and beautified; additional renova-

© ROBERT NILSEN

Yeouido as seen from Jeoldusan

SEOUL

tion and expansion has continued since. Over 35 kilometers have been dredged, the previously ragged river edge trimmed with levees, and athletic grounds, recreational facilities, extensive walking and biking paths, and performance stages have been built at nine park sites. Several of these sections have other attractions: riverboat piers are located at the Yanghwa, Yeouido, Ttukseom, and Jamshil parks; Banpo is a well-known fishing spot; water-skiing is done at Pungnap, Ttukseom, and Banpo; scullers take to the water at Mangwon, Ichon, and other areas; a replica of Adm. Yi Sun-shin's turtle ship, used as a ferry, is moored at Ichon; and there are flower gardens and nature study fields in various locations. In addition, the Olympic Expressway was constructed along the southern flank of the river, connecting the airport to the eastern edge of the city, and, more recently, part of the elevated circular city expressway has been erected along the northern bank. Attempts have been made to control the pollutants that flow into the river by purifying waste and moving factories away from the riverside. As a consequence, the fish population has increased markedly, and birds continue to feed along undeveloped sections. Bamseom Island, near Yeouido, has been set aside as a migratory bird sanctuary, and a bird observation station is open along the Yeouido riverbank during some of the winter months to view these wild pintails, mallards, pochards, and other winged creatures that make this a pit stop on their migratory routes. This river renovation has required great expense and effort, but it has had wonderful results.

In 1986, shallow-draft double-deck **riverboats** started operation on the river, giving riders a unique and special view of the city. One-way courses connect Yeouido to Ttukseom and Jamshil, about 15 kilometers in length, while circular courses run from each of the four piers. Schedules vary according to the season, but generally there are about 10 departures during the summer, running between 1000–2230. There are about half as many that run during the winter, and during spring and autumn that number falls somewhere in between. Trips last about 60 minutes. Daytime rides are popular with families, but the night rides see more businessmen, couples, students, and tourists. Each pier has a floating barge that doubles as a restaurant and coffee shop. The fare for any of these runs is ₩7,000 adult or ₩3,500 for children age 4–12. Reservations are usually not necessary. Evening musical shows are offered every day except Monday on the last two cruises. Dinner buffet cruises (₩30,000), with traditional music and dance accompaniment, can also be arranged for large groups. For information, contact the Semo Pleasure Boat Co., tel. 02/785-0393.

To reach the Yeouido pier, take subway line #5 to the Yeouinaru Station and walk five minutes. For the Yanghwa pier, bus no. 588 gets you close, otherwise it's a 20-minute walk from the Dansan Station on subway line #2. Shincheon Station on subway line #2 is the closest to the Jamshil pier. The Ttukseom Resort Station on subway line #7 brings you within a 5-minute walk of the Ttukseom pier.

Yongsan Family Park 용산가족공원

A large plot of land south of Nam-san near the Han River reverted from foreign control to use by the Korean public in 1992. In 1882 the Japanese military stationed troops in Korea and took control of this area. Following the Japanese departure from Korea at the end of World War II, it was set aside for use by the U.S. military as part of their headquarters garrison. For several decades, this plot had been used as a golf course and residential area. Once again in Korean hands, it is slowly being converted into a public green area of walking paths, park benches, shade trees, lawns, and ponds. The new National Museum of Korea is scheduled to open here in 2003. If and when the Yongsan Garrison closes and the U.S. military headquarters moves out of the city, a much larger area to the north has the potential to be the largest non-mountainous park area within the city limits. Yongsan Family Park is open 0500–1900 April–September and 0600–1800 October–March. Use bus no. 81-1 from Seoul Station, or walk from either the Ichon Station on subway line #4 or the Seobinggo Station on the suburban rail line that runs along the river.

Samcheong Park 삼청공원

North of Gyeongbok-gung, on the flank of Bugak-san below an old section of the city wall, is wooded Samcheong Park. The name roughly translates as "Three Purities Park" and is said to refer to a Taoist trinity once enshrined on this site. Royal housing also once occupied part of this area. Tucked away into a tranquil corner of this bustling city, Samcheong Park is seldom visited. It contains little more than walking paths that thread through the forest, a mineral spring, the restored north gate of the city wall, and a monument with poetry by Jeong Myeong-ju, a late Goryeo Dynasty Neo-Confucianist and contemporary of the founder of the Joseon Dynasty. What otherwise might ordinarily be a very pleasant environment is disappointing as all the walks are lined with tall steel-mesh fences because the park is adjacent to a tightly restricted military area. Samcheong Tunnel runs under the park to Seongbuk-dong on the far side of the ridge.

Olympic Park 올림픽공원

Built for the 1988 Olympics, Olympic Park contains several international-class sports facilities used for that competition and now used for national events. These facilities, plus both the Korean National College of Physical Education and the Seoul Physical Education High School, occupy the southern half of the park. The Korean Olympic Committee building and the Olympic Parktel Hotel/Youth Hostel next door are located on its northern edge. On the 3rd floor of the hotel is the Seoul **Olympic Museum.** Included in this exhibit are about 1,400 items relating mostly to the '88 Olympics: photos, equipment, commemorative memorabilia, the huge opening-ceremonies drum, and audio-visual materials. Included are a glimpse at previous Olympic games, a short history of Korean sports and games, video presentations, and cyber sports games. Entrance for adults is ₩5,000; open daily except Mondays and the first and second of January. Also within the park are an outdoor sculpture garden, with over 200 pieces from Korean and foreign artists; a water fountain coordinated with music and lights; broad lawns and picnic areas; a small lake; several kilometers of walking trails; the Peace Plaza; and the Olympic flame.

Occupying a good portion of this park is

Mongchon Fortress, an earthen-wall fortress from the early Baekje era. Within the fortress is the small **Mongchon Museum,** which displays Baekje Dynasty artifacts such as comb-pattern pottery, utensils, and jar coffins dug from this site during preparation for the Olympics and from other sites in the Seoul area. The Mongchon Fortress is open every day 0900–1800. Mongchontoseong Station on subway line #8 is at the main entrance, while Olympic Park Station on subway line #5 is at the rear entrance. Alternately, use the Jamshil Station on subway line #2 and take city bus no. 21-2 or 569 from there.

Pagoda Park 탑골공원

Designed in 1897 by an English employee of the Korean government, Pagoda Park, or Tapgol Park, as it's now more frequently called, was Seoul's first Western-style park. Built on the site of the Joseon Dynasty temple Won'gak-sa, this park was originally used by royalty for musical concerts but opened to the public in 1913. Rising from the center of the park is Won'gak-sa pagoda (N.T. #2). Erected in 1466, this 10-tier marble pagoda is the country's most elaborate and highly detailed, a masterpiece of Joseon Dynasty sculpture and construction. It rests on a three-tier granite base. Nearby is the Won'gak-sa memorial marker (T. #3). Set on the back of a stone tortoise, this slab has been inscribed with a short history of the temple.

Pagoda Park is an informal shrine to the Korean independence movement. It was from the octagonal pavilion here that the Declaration of Independence from Japan was read in 1919. A statue of Son Byeong-hui, the leader of this independence movement, and the entire Declaration of Independence, cast in bronze, are displayed here. Set into the park's curved outer wall are 10 bronze panels depicting scenes relating to this movement. Every March 1, a public ceremony is held to pay tribute to the scores of people who contributed to this nationalist movement.

Given a major facelift in 2001, this park is a favorite spot for elders to chat with their friends or play board games, and for young people to meet their dates. The park is open 0800–2200 Octo-

ber–March and 0800–2300 April–September; ₩500 entrance. Jonggak and Jongno 3-ga stations on subway line #3 are the closest.

Sajik Park 사직공원

West of Gyeongbok-gung, Sajik Park was the site of sacred altars used by the king during spring and autumn ceremonies in order to assure the country of bountiful crops and a good harvest. Aside from the altar remains, this wooded sanctuary has walks and benches, a swimming pool and children's playground, fresh-water spring, and statues of Confucian scholar Yi Yul-gok and his mother, Shim Saimdang, a scholar and artist of merit in her own right. A shrine to Dan'gun, the mythical founder of the Korean nation, occupies a spot on the wooded hillside.

Up the hill to the rear of the park is a **traditional archery range,** the only remaining range of five within the old city walls from the Joseon Dynasty. The building Hwanghak-jeong, which sits above the firing line, was moved to this spot in 1922 from its previous location as a palace building in Gyeonghui-gung. While once an important skill for warfare, archery is now only a sport in Korea. It's practiced year-round, and most enthusiasts shoot early in the morning or late in the afternoon. Archery contests are held here five times a year. The target at traditional ranges is set at 145 meters from the firing line (historically it was 250 meters distant). The target itself is about two meters high and 1.5 meters wide. When made in a traditional manner, arrows are slim bamboo rods with natural feathers; bows are a combination of bamboo, cow ligament, and animal glue. In order to shoot the distance, bows need to be very strong. Although short, they have great elasticity. When strung, they have an exaggerated curve with the back bent at the tip; when unstrung, they nearly curl forward onto themselves. Unlike modern versions made of wood, fiberglass, or carbon compounds, Korean bows are subject to weather conditions, so serious Korean archers may have several for various times of the year.

From the rear of the park, trails lead up to Inwang-san and Jaha-mun, running mostly along the old city wall. The road to the side of Sajik

Park also runs to Jaha-mun, and its extension is the Bugak Skyway. To reach Sajik Park use city bus no. 150 or 158, or express bus no. 158; Gyeongbok-gung Station on subway line #3 is the closest stop.

Seodae-mun Independence Park

West of Sajik Park is Seodae-mun Independence Park. Within this park stands Dongnim-mun, or Independence Gate, erected in 1896 after the king declared the country an empire and no longer under Chinese domination. To the side are refurbished buildings of the infamous Seodaemun Prison, where Koreans advocating their independence form Japanese colonial rule were held, tortured, and killed. Memorial markers, walkways, and landscaped gardens occupy the remainder of this site. Use the Dongnimmun Station on subway line #3.

Seosomun Park 서소문공원

Sandwiched between Seoul Station and an elevated road is the relatively tranquil Seosomun Park. Once the site of the city's secondary Little West Gate, or Seoso-mun, it was until the late 1970s a fish and seafood market. It was also, during the 1800s, the place at which more than three dozen early Korean Catholics died for their faith at the hands of an intransigent social system and a royal family bent on thwarting all "corrupting" Western influence. A statue of Goryeo Dynasty military General Yun Gwan surveys the park. He was partially instrumental in pushing the northern Goryeo border into Khitan territory. Landscaped with flower beds and bushes, the park creates a fine place for workers to come on fine weather days during their lunch hour to eat or chat with friends. This park was renovated in 1994.

Hyochang Park 효창공원

Behind Sookmyung Women's University, south of Seoul Station, is Hyochang Park (H.S. #330). This park has not only the usual walks and shade trees, but also an athletic stadium, tennis courts, and children's playground. It's here, in the tomb Hyochang-won, that Prince Munhyo, the eldest son of King Jeongjo, is buried. This park has

also become associated with the resistance movement against the Japanese. Kim Ku, Yi Bong-chan, Yun Bong-gil, Baek Jong-gi, and several officials of the Korean Provisional Government in exile are interred here as well. A statue of Wonhyo Daesa, one of Korea's most outstanding Buddhist monks, stands in the park; a road named in his honor passes nearby and extends over the Han River. Sookmyung Women's University Station on subway line #4 is the closest.

Jangchungdan Park 장충단공원

On the northeast slope of Nam-san is Jangchung-dan [Changch'ungdan] Park. This wooded public park of walks and recreational areas was originally set aside as a shrine for two loyal retainers who tried, unsuccessfully, to protect Queen Min from murder in 1895. The Jangchungdan ("Altar for the Commendation of Loyalty") shrine was erected here in their memory, but has since disappeared. Heunghwa-mun, the main gate of the Gyeonghui-gung, was moved to this site in 1910, later set up across the street as the main gate of the Silla Hotel, and more recently moved back to the palace site. Other palace buildings were also moved and renovated and now occupy a hillside site above this park on the campus of the Buddhist Dongguk University. Two ancient stone bridges are at the bottom end of the park. The most famous and one of the largest and architecturally most pleasing stone bridges in Korea is Supyo-gyo ("Water Gauge Bridge"). Built during the reign of King Sejong, this wide pedestrian bridge once traversed Cheonggyecheon Stream, but it was moved here in 1958 when the stream was covered with reinforced cement and made into a road. Marks on bridge supports were used to check the depth of water flowing through the stream and predict the possibility of flooding.

Prominent in the park is a statue of Yi Jun, a statesman who opposed the Treaty of 1905 making Korea a protectorate of Japan. In 1907, he and two others were sent to the Second Hague Peace Conference by the Korean king to seek international support for Korean independence. They were unsuccessful and, tragically, Yi Jun died before his return to the homeland. Here as

SEOUL

well is a statue of Sammyeon-daesa, one of the greatest of Korean Buddhist monks and head of a warrior monk force that opposed the Japanese invasions of the 1590s. In the upper portion of the park is a statue of Yu Gwan-sun, a 19-year-old student who helped organize anti-Japanese demonstrations in her home province of Chungcheongnam-Do during the 1919 independence movement. She was arrested, held at Seodae-mun Prison, tortured, and later killed for her activities. City bus no. 154 stops near the park; the Dongguk University Station on subway line #3 is at the corner of the park.

Marronnier Park 마로니에공원

Marronnier Park is a small city park set along Daehang-no, once part of the Seoul National University campus until its move south of the Han River. Surrounded by the Munye Theater, Fine Arts Center, and the Korean Culture and Arts Foundation, and set along a street filled with a plethora of shops, restaurants, coffee houses, and cafés, this park draws mostly the young and young-at-heart, who come to hang out under the tall chestnut and ginkgo trees or listen to amateur (and occasionally professional) musicians perform at the outdoor stage. At various times of the year, cultural events are held here and along Daehang-no. Daehang-no has become known as a "street of culture," and Marronnier Park fits easily into this setting. The Hyehwa Station on subway line #4 is closest, or use bus no. 25.

Small Inner-City Parks

New city parks are often created in the dense downtown area when older buildings are destroyed or removed to other locations. Set between the Sejong Cultural Center and the Central Government Complex is **Sejong-no Park** (세종로공원). Dotted with benches, water pools, and arbors, this small square is a fine spot for a midday rest. Once the site of the city police headquarters, the metropolitan police administration is now several blocks to the west. Across the wide boulevard, set next to the Ministry of Culture and Tourism, is Gwanghwamun Yeollin Madang Park (광화문열린마당), an open plaza with trees and park benches that also has a small

performance area. Similar in function is **Jong-myo Plaza** (종묘프라자). Set between Jong-no and the entrance to Jong-myo, this tiny green space of walkways, benches, and trees is a perfect spot to have a sit-down rest during the day. The plaza was created by clearing ramshackle buildings in order to spruce up the entrance to the country's most important ancestral shrine. When the road fronting the Blue House was opened to foot traffic in 1993 and some of the surrounding area and roads were reconfigured, the **Mugunghwa Garden Park** (무궁화동산공원) was constructed at its western end. Across the street, the modern Seoul City Sarangbang displays gifts that have been presented to the president and others by visiting dignitaries and pictorially presents, in brief, the history of Seoul.

Yeouido Park 여의도공원

Once an asphalt plaza, and the site of huge national rallies and parades, this strip is now landscaped and has broad lawns and ponds, trees and flower beds, many walking and biking paths, children's playgrounds, statues, outdoor theater stages, pavilions, snack shops, and an information center. There is also an underground connection from the plaza to the park at the edge of the Han River. A huge expanse nearly 1.5 kilometers long, it still has some broad open expanses that are used for roller skating, skateboarding, scooters and other such sports. Bike rental runs ₩2,000 and hour, ₩5,000 for a tandem. Use Yeouido Station on subway line #5.

Small Parks South of the River

By and large, the parks south of the Han River have grown with the great influx of population since the early 1970s. Of relatively good size, most occupy hilly, wooded areas. Within **Dosan Park** is a statue of An Chang-ho—promoter of Korean independence, education, and economic self-sufficiency during the Japanese colonial period—and the tombs of him and his wife. Also in Gangnam-gu are **Cheongdam Park** and **Hakdong Park**. In a similar manner, the neighborhood parks **Paris** and **Ujang-san** and others have been created in the southwestern section of the city and **Ogeum Park** in the southeastern.

Asian Park was built along with the athletic facilities at the Jamshil Sports Complex in preparation for the 1986 Asian Games. Nicely landscaped, it's an area of benches and walkways, pools and sculptures—good for a rest during the heat of the day.

Unlike the neighborhood parks, **Boramae Park** was created from the former Air Force Academy campus. Opened in 1986, this broad green area has ponds, walking paths, a small zoo, numerous sports facilities, and children's playgrounds.

Seoul Grand Park 서울대공원

No leisure amusement park in Seoul is of such grand scale as Seoul Grand Park, and none draws more visitors than the three million who come here every year. There is so much here that it's impossible to see it all thoroughly in one day. Wear comfortable shoes and come prepared for any weather. Opened in 1984 in the city of Gwacheon, just south of the Seoul city limits, this nine-square-kilometer recreation area is centered around a man-made reservoir. Within the park are a zoo and botanical garden in one compound, the Seoul Land Amusement Park, the National Museum of Contemporary Art, broad lawns and gardens, picnic spots, and rental boats for the lake. The subway station and city bus stop are located to the front of the entrance plaza, from where a broad walk takes you to an entrance pavilion with restaurants, shops, and a small natural history exhibit room. Walking around the right side of the reservoir brings you to the zoo and botanical garden, while the amusement park is most quickly reached by going around the left side of the reservoir; the art museum is above the amusement park. Connecting the front pavilion to each of these areas is an Elephant Train trolley (₩500 adult, ₩400 junior, ₩300 children 4–12). Board near the reservoir. For those who want a more scenic route to the far side, take the chairlift that whisks you across the lake from the right side of the front plaza to the zoo entrance. Fares for one-way and round-trip rides run ₩3,000/5,000 adult, ₩2,000/3,000 junior, and ₩1,500/2,000 children. Ticket sales start at 0900.

The **zoo** is the largest and best-equipped of any in the country. In an effort to create a more natural environment, this animal sanctuary has several dozen ditched and fenced open pens along with the usual enclosed buildings and cages. Moved in 1984 from its claustrophobic quarters at Changgyeong-gung in the center of the city, the zoo has 32 separate sections. The more than 3,000 animals of 360 species are from every continent of the world; over half are non-native to Korea. A touch-and-learn area has been set up for young children to pet and handle docile animals. Weather permitting, an inexpensive dolphin show is performed three or four times a day near the net-covered aviary in the center of the grounds. The **botanical garden** overlooks the central pens, and housed here are over 1,000 varieties of plants in eight sections. While many of the species are native, a great number have been imported from other climatic zones. For a panoramic, bird's-eye view of the zoo, a second chairlift runs from the zoo entrance to its upper section. The zoo is open 0900–1900 (1800 from October–March); entrance to the zoo and botanical garden is ₩1,500 adult, ₩1,200 junior, and ₩700 children.

Seoul Land is a Disney-esque amusement park split into five sections. Visitors can be entertained for hours by the three dozen state-of-the-art amusement rides, numerous arcade games, entertainment stages, and pavilions. Dotted throughout the grounds are restaurants and shops. At the front find a first-aid station, bank, lockers, and a stroller rental office. Daily street performances, holiday parades, and other seasonal festivals are also held. General admission is ₩7,000, ₩5,000 youth, ₩3,500 child. Admission plus five amusement rides is ₩18,000, ₩14,000, and ₩10,000, while the "Passport" admission, which includes all rides, is ₩22,000, ₩17,000, and ₩13,000. Tickets for amusement rides can also be purchased individually. Operating hours are weekdays 0930–1900 and weekends 0930–2100 April–October, with some extended hours through the summer, and daily 0930–1800 November–March. The easiest way to reach this multi-facility park is by subway line #4 to the Seoul Grand Park Station.

Seoul Equestrian Park 서울경마장

Located adjacent to Seoul Grand Park is the Seoul horse racecourse. The racetrack is open daily 0930–1700. Twelve races a day are held on Saturday and Sunday from February to October, and 11 races a day from November to January. General admission is ₩900. The track is a one-mile oval course and the horses are trained at the track's stables. Pari-mutuel betting is allowed. Win, place, and quinella bets from ₩100 to ₩100,000 are taken at the racetrack and at over a dozen offices throughout the city. (On a winning bet, the horse must place first; on a place bet, the horse must finish in the top three; and for a quinella bet, two horses must place first or second in the race.) Information booths are set up at the track to provide information to those who do not speak Korean, and restaurants are there for those with more than just betting on their minds. Free pony rides are offered on the weekends for children, and a playground is available for kids not interested in the races. The **Equine Museum** within the grounds is open daily 0900–1800 (1700 in winter). A one-of-a-kind in Korea, this museum displays horse equipment and accoutrements and items pertaining to Korean horse racing. The Seoul Racecourse Station on subway line #4 is at the track entrance gate. For information, see www.kra.co.kr.

Before Seoul Equestrian Park began operation, Ttukseom, the area below Hanyang University, had the city's only horse track. The Ttukseom racetrack still exists, but it's now used for other purposes. Situated at the wide, flat confluence of the Jungang-cheon Stream and Han River, it was through the Joseon Dynasty a place for the raising and training of horses for the palace and the military.

Lotte World Adventure
롯데월드어드밴쳐

Halfway between the Jamshil Sports Complex and Olympic Park is Lotte World Adventure. Connected to the Lotte Jamshil Hotel, department store, shopping mall, and sports and swimming clubs, this multi-story indoor/outdoor amusement park is the only one of its kind in Korea, and said to be the largest indoor theme park in the world. A multitude of rides, a monorail, arcade games, musical performance venues, a daily parade, an ice rink, shops, restaurants, and snack kiosks are here for the enjoyment of the hordes who visit every year. Connected by bridge from the indoor amusement area is Magic Island, an outdoor amusement area set on an island in the middle of Seokchon Lake. On the island are more rides, places to eat, and other attractions. Open daily 0900–2300; general entrance to Lotte World costs ₩15,000 adults, ₩12,000 youth, ₩10,000 children, with discounts after 1700; Big-5 and all-day passes are ₩22,000/25,000 adults, ₩18,000/20,000 youth, ₩14,000/16,000 children. Tickets for individual rides can be purchased inside.

In association with Lotte World is the **Lotte Folk Village Museum,** a combination historical and cultural museum. The many models, dioramas, and displays (some miniature) are exquisitely designed and constructed, showing important aspects of Korean cultural life through all major periods of Korean history. The most amazing and intricate are the scenes of Joseon Dynasty life, royal and common, through which you walk like Gulliver through Lilliput. The walk through this intriguing exhibit brings you to a small market selling traditional products and to several restaurants serving traditional foods. A ₩3,500 entrance fee is charged for the folk museum (free to those with Big-5 or all-day tickets). Lotte Folk Village Museum is open daily 0930–2200. The Jamshil Station on subway lines #2 and #8 is connected to the lower level of the adventure park. For information, contact tel. 02/411-2000 or check www.lotteworld.com.

Children's Grand Park 어린이대공원

Not far from the river on the eastern edge of Seoul is Eorini Daegongwon, or Children's Grand Park. Opened in 1973 on the site of Seoul's first golf course, this park has amusement rides, playgrounds, a swimming pool, roller rink, gardens, fountains, ponds, music stages, and pavilions. It not only has absorbing recreational facilities for children, but it's also set up for informal instruction. Young students can browse through the zoo, botanical gardens, and exhibition hall, or spend time at the Science and Cultural halls. One educational feature is a wonderful model park that displays several thousand miniature people and famous sites from around the world. It's a great place for a day of fun and frolic with the kids, or a leisurely picnic on the broad lawns. The park is open 0900–2000 in summer (until 2100 on weekends and holidays) and 0900–1800 November–March; ₩900 entrance, ₩500 for students, children and seniors free. There is a separate admission for most amusement rides and for some other activities. The Little Angels Performing Arts Center is next to the park's east entrance. Most convenient for the front gate is the Children's Grand Park Station on subway line #7; Achasan Station on subway line #5 is outside the rear (east) gate.

MUSEUMS

With several thousand years of history, deep cultural roots, artistic heritage, and a concerted effort in recent years to preserve artifacts, Korea has its fair share of museum pieces. The National Museum of Korea, with its main collection in Seoul, has branch museums in 11 provincial cities. Traditional objects of art and crafts, folklore artifacts, and special-subject items are also preserved in public and private folklore museums throughout the country. Provincial, municipal, university, and private museums also display historical and cultural material on a wide variety of themes. National museums and private collections have regular hours and charge nominal fees. University museums generally have free admission, but you must sometimes call for an appointment. Seoul and its immediate vicinity has the largest concentration of museums in the country. In addition, there is a growing number of art galleries in the city. Some are large public institutions, but most are smaller and private.

National Museum of Korea
국립중앙박물관
Established in 1945, the National Museum of Korea, in Seoul, was originally housed at Seokjojeon in Deoksu-gung. This collection was taken over from the Japanese, who had expanded the Yi

Royal Household Museum started in 1908. In 1972, the museum was moved to a newly built structure within Gyeongbok-gung, a building that is now the National Folk Museum. After extensive remodeling, following the exodus of certain government offices to the outskirts of the city, the vastly expanded collection of this museum was moved into the spacious former Capitol in 1986. Fulfilling a campaign promise to rid the country of a significant vestige of Japanese colonial imperialism, President Kim Young-sam had this building torn down in 1996. Consequently, an abbreviated collection of museum objects was moved to an adjacent building also located within Gyeongbok-gung. This temporary location will be the museum's home until a new National Museum building is completed in 2003 at Yongsan Family Park.

On display are about 5,000 of the 120,000 items of the collection that exemplify the essence of Korean artistic spirit and talent. Displays are attractively presented and well-lit; explanations are given in Korean and English, and some signs are also in Japanese and Chinese. This is undoubtedly the country's best collection of Korean artifacts; dubious sales and questionable expropriation in the past account for many priceless Korean art treasures being housed in public and private collections in Japan, the United States, and various European capitals. This museum contains over 150 National Treasures and Treasures. Represented here are artifacts from prehistoric Korea to the end of the Joseon Dynasty. You'll see Neolithic pottery shards and stone implements; roof tiles and pots from the Baekje and Goguryeo periods; clay pots and figures, metal containers and ornaments, bronze mirrors, and extremely intricate gold work on crowns and other kingly accoutrements from the Silla period. The Goryeo Dynasty is represented by what it's best known for—celadon pottery. White porcelain, blue and white ceramics, and calligraphy—plus a wide variety of portrait, animal, landscape, and fan paintings—come to us from the Joseon Dynasty. Metal sculpture, bells, and religious statues from all periods of history, and Buddhist paintings are well represented. The permanent collection also includes a limited number of works from Japan,

SEOUL

China, and central Asian countries. Special exhibitions on loan from other countries are also offered periodically.

A stroll through the museum is definitely worth a leisurely afternoon; it is in essence a walk through the history of Korean art. Each section has a chronological table and explanations of particular pieces, as well as of the artistic trends of the period. Audiotapes in four languages are available for rent (₩3,000) from the information desk inside, and free tours in English, Japanese, and Chinese are conducted once a day. The gift shop sells postcards, souvenirs, and a limited selection of books about Korean art, history, and culture. The museum is open every day except Monday 0900–1800 March–October (until 1900 on weekends), 0900–1700 November–February (closed January 1); ₩700 entrance for adults, ₩300 for ages 7 to 24. The Gyeongbokgung Station on subway line #3 is closest. For information on any of the country's national museums, visit www.museum.go.kr.

National Folk Museum of Korea
국립민속박물관

In 1993, the National Folk Museum moved to the old national museum building in Gyeongbok-gung from its former location at the rear of the palace compound. This museum exhibits about 4,300 traditional items typical of pre-20th century Korea, and offers a concise synopsis of important aspects of the culture. Exhibits are artistically displayed and explained in Korean, English, and Japanese; galleries show a comprehensive sample of objects dealing with life and work, handicrafts and technology, food and kitchen utensils, home furnishings, clothing, beliefs and rituals, musical instruments, masks and games, and aspects of education, communication, and medicine. Dioramas, miniatures, and full-size models are used to bring the displays to life. This collection is not to be missed for an introduction to traditional Korean culture. The museum's hours are 0900–1800 March–October (until 1900 on Saturdays and holidays), and 0900–1700 November–February; closed every Tuesday and January 1. The entrance fee for adults is ₩700, ₩300 for those 7 to 24. Audio guides are available for ₩3,000. The Gyeongbok-gung Station on subway line #3 is closest. For additional information, see www.nfm.go.kr.

Royal Museum 궁중유물박물관

It seems appropriate that the Royal Museum occupies a former Joseon Dynasty royal family building. Seokjo-jeon, once the site of the national museum, was the first large Western-style building erected on palace grounds. Opened in 1992, this museum displays not only court costumes, other clothes and accoutrements, furniture, food utensils, art objects, court paintings, and other pieces from the Joseon Dynasty royal family, but also items relating to science, education, and the indigenous Korean script, *han'geul.* Nearly 6,000 items are in the collection. Open daily except Monday 0900–1800 (1730 in winter); ₩700 entrance. Free docent service available if desired.

National Museum of Contemporary Art 국립현대미술관

In 1986, this museum moved from Deoksugung (where it now maintains an adjunct gallery) to its new contemporary building within Seoul Grand Park. Facilities include six galleries, an outdoor sculpture garden, seminar rooms, and hands-on classrooms. Paintings are the most predominant form, but wood, metal, stone, cloth, and paper sculpture, and a huge video display, are also presented. Each individual piece is of value, but most intriguing is the historical perspective: how the Korean approach to design, style, and color has changed, with influence from Western art, since the beginning of the 20th century. The exhibit of calligraphy is also worth a look, and many of the outdoor sculptures are quite engaging. By and large, this huge collection (3,400 works on display) has excellent pieces, a veritable snapshot of contemporary Korean art. Throughout the year, lectures, movies, and music and dance performances are sponsored, and special exhibitions, including some by foreign artists, are held on a regular schedule. In addition, the museum runs its own art school. Art books, postcards, reproduction prints, and other souvenirs are available at the gift shop. This museum is open daily except Monday 0900–1800 March–October (weekends and holidays until 1900), and 0900–1700 November–February; ₩700 entrance for ages 25–65, ₩300 for 19–24, free for those below age 19 and seniors. Take subway line #4 to the Seoul Grand Park Station, from where there is a low-cost shuttle bus to the museum entrance. For other information, check the museum website at www.moca.go.kr.

War Memorial Museum 전쟁기념관

Opened in 1994, this museum was appropriately constructed on the grounds of the former Korean military command headquarters in Yongsan, across the street from the Korean Ministry of National Defense. Done in Korea's inimitable monstrous style, it is nonetheless an attractive place. The outdoor grounds contain sculptures, a large-equipment display area, lawns, pool, and plaza. Inside, Korea's involvement with war is represented historically, with special displays for each branch of service, for military equipment, and for the Korean defense industry. The largest section, understandably, is that pertaining to the Korean War, still an unresolved issue for the nation. All seems well-displayed but it's unfortunate that there is so little foreign-language explanation. However, dioramas, paintings, models, replicas of historic relics, walk-through exhibits, and visual and audiovisual aids of all sorts help induce understanding. With this incredible display of some 8,500 items, plan at least several hours for this visit. Take your time and let it all soak in. Every Friday at 1000 on the plaza outside is a combination traditional and modern military guard demonstration. The museum is open 0930–1800 March–October and 0930–1700 November–February, closed Monday and the day after a holiday; ₩3,000 entrance fee for adults, ₩2,000 for youth, and ₩1,000 for children. Audiotape guides are available for ₩2,000. Use city bus no. 23 or 81; Samgakji Station on subway lines #4 and #6 is closest. See www.warmemo.co.kr.

Seodaemun Prison History Hall

Until recently, Dongnim-mun ("Independence Gate") was crowded in on all sides by buildings. With the removal of many of these buildings, the Seodae-mun Independence Park was created. A number of the buildings that were not removed were part of the old and notorious Seodaemun Prison, and these buildings with their displays are now the Seodaemun Prison History Hall. This prison represents the suffering of the Koreans under the Japanese and the fervent force for independence. So many anti-colonial citizens were imprisoned there and either suffered greatly or lost their lives. The main hall presents in graphic detail and diorama the detention, torture, and suffering of those imprisoned here. Throughout the grounds, and open for viewing, are several old red-brick prison buildings (H.S. #324), underground holding cells, a wooden execution building, and several memorials to those who suffered here. The prison is open 0930– 1800 (until 1700 in winter), closed Mondays and some holidays; ₩1,100 entrance and ₩550 for students. To reach Dongnim-mun and the Seodaemun Prison, take city bus no. 146, 150, 158, or express bus no. 72 or 158; Dongnimmun Station on subway line #3 is a few steps away.

Seoul Historical Museum
서울역사박물관

Located in a new contemporary building to the front of Gyeonghui-gung, this new museum (opened in 2002) lays out a historical sketch of the more than 600-year history of the city of Seoul as the capital of the country, the life of its citizens and their culture, education, and art, with some emphasis on the development of the city before the Joseon era. Open daily except Mondays and New Year's Day 0900–1800 (1900 on Saturdays and public holidays; 1700 in winter), the museum is set almost equidistant between Gwanghwa-mun Station and Seodaemun Station on subway line #5; alternatively, walk or use bus no. 146, 154, 302, or express bus no. 63, 130, or 720. Entrance is ₩700 for adults and ₩300 for children. For additional information, see www.museum.seoul.kr.

Postal Museum

An intriguing collection of Korean and foreign stamps, postal uniforms, post boxes, machines, and additional historical memorabilia illustrating the development of the Korean postal system since its inception in 1884, are displayed in the Postal Museum, on the 4th floor of the Central Post Office. Open 0900–1700 (until 1300 on Saturday).

Up the block from Jogye-sa is the country's first post-office building (H.S. #213), opened in 1895. Now called the **Communication Memorial Hall** (체신기념관), it was the site of the first national communications office, established in 1884. On display in this small traditional-style building are postage stamps from the late Joseon Dynasty, photographs, and other documentary materials relating to the development of communications systems in Korea. Open Monday through Friday 0900–1700 and until noon on Saturday.

Seoul Science Museum
국립서울과학관

When the new National Science Museum moved to its present quarters in Daejeon, the Seoul Science Museum took its place. Located just up the road from Changgyeong-gung and run by the Ministry of Science and Technology, it houses about 3,000 items in two buildings relating to natural science, technical science, technology, and scientific technique. A number of scientific instruments, models, and displays—some interactive—round out the offerings. Open daily except Monday and the day after a national holiday 0930–1730; ₩1,000 entrance fee.

Kimchi Field Museum 김치박물관

For the gastronome, the Kimchi Field Museum, in the underground COEX Mall of the World Trade Center, will be of interest; www.kimchimuseum.co.kr. Since 1986, this private museum, funded by the Pulmuone Food Co., has offered a complete exploration of Korea's most well-known food, a fermented, salted, and seasoned vegetable dish. Over the centuries and across the expanse of the country, more than 200 varieties of *gimchi* [kimch'i] have been de-

vised for various occasions. These recipes are not only wonderful creations of taste but also of food preservation. Sections on the history of *gimchi*, the *gimchi*-making process—called *gimjang*—the types of *gimchi* and all ingredients and utensils required for making *gimchi,* and the nutritional aspects of the food are exhibited. Research and educational activities are also offered; books and videos are available. Open Tuesday–Saturday 1000–1700 and Sunday 1300–1700, closed Mondays and some national holidays; ₩3,000 adults, ₩1,000 children. The Samseong Station of subway line #2 is most convenient, or use express city bus no. 37.

Suk Joo-sun Memorial Museum of Korean Folk Arts

This museum, established in 1981 at Danguk University, arose out of the private collection of some 3,400 pieces of Dr. Suk Joo-sun, a folklorist, scholar, and collector of traditional Korean costumes. This museum displays these items, plus several thousand more pieces of traditional Korean apparel, shoes, ornaments, and accessories from all social classes, many from the Joseon Dynasty period. Special exhibits are occasionally mounted. In addition, research is done, books published, and lectures and seminars held. Open daily 1000–1600, closed holidays and school vacations. For information, call 02/709-2188. Use city bus no. 83, or the Hannam Station on the riverside suburban rail line.

Museum of Korean Embroidery
자수박물관

Located south of the Han River near Dosan Park, this small museum was started in 1976 from the private collection of Mr. Huh Donghwa. The skill of fine embroidery was a treasured art among Korean women of old, largely forgotten because of mass-produced, machine-made, and cheaper imitations. There has been a revival of interest in both the art of thread embroidery and many of the traditional designs. More than 3,000 items are on display: screen cloth, wrapping cloth, cloth baskets, Buddhist scripture covers, clothing, decorations, and much more. Included are two designated Treasures. Open by appointment only during the week 1000–1600, tel. 02/515-5114, closed weekends and holidays. Use the Hakdong Station on subway line #7, or express city bus no. 37.

Forest Museum 국립수목원

The mountainous country of Korea has provided great opportunity for forests to flourish and diversify. Over the centuries, however, largely because of the need for fuel and building material, these forests have greatly diminished. Since the 1960s, Korea has made great strides in reforesting its bare hills, so the country is once again beginning to sport a thick green coat. One forest area in particular has been left fairly natural for about the last 600 years and is protected as the **National Arboretum.** This forest area is located just outside the city limits and up the road from the tomb of King Sejo at Gwang-neung. Opened to the public in 1987, this preserve has almost 3,000 species of trees and other plants, plus a couple hundred types of birds and animals—it's a designated woodpecker habitat. Paths run through a dozen gardens and several special forest sections—a perfect place for the person wanting a walk and an aromatic breath of fresh air.

The Forest Museum here has countless items and documents, displays on the history of Korean forests and the general life cycle of forests, types of wood in Korea, various wood products, and machines and instruments related to forestry. The museum and arboretum are open by reservation only weekdays 0900–1700, closed holidays; ₩700 adults, ₩500 students, ₩300 children. For information and reservations (preferably a week in advance), call 031/540-1114. Bus to Gwang-neung (₩1,600) from the Seoul Sangbong Bus Terminal, take city bus no. 7 from Cheongnyangni train station, or use Uijeongbu city bus no. 21 (₩900) from Uijeongbu to the forest/tomb.

Special-Interest Museums

The Seoul **Agricultural Museum** (농업박물관), just east of the Seodae-mun intersection, displays nearly 2,000 agricultural items covering the range from ancient times to the present. Open Mon.–Sat. 1000–1700, closed holidays; free entrance. Use the Seodaemun Station on subway line #5 or bus no. 152 or 154.

The **Cho Hung Bank Museum of Finance** (조흥금융박물관) is located on the 3rd and 4th floors of the Chohung Bank building near the Gwanghwa-mun intersection. It was opened in 1997 to commemorate the 100th anniversary of Korean banking and the opening of the Hanseong Bank, which later became the Chohung Bank. This is a specialized museum about the evolution of the bank, and the history of the country's finance in general. There is very little in the way of non-Korean explanation, but there are samples of Korean and foreign currency on display. The museum is open for free Monday–Saturday 1000–1800.

The 1st floor of the main Bank of Korea building houses the **Bank of Korea Museum** (한국은행박물관). Opened in 2001 on the fiftieth anniversary of the bank's founding, this museum displays bills and coins from Korea and around the world, as well as an overview of banking policy and practice to maintain fiscal stability and economic growth. Open for free 1000–1730 Tues.–Fri., until 1330 on Sat.

Relating the history of newspapers and newspaper printing in Korea is the **Presseum** (신문박물관), a museum located on the 3rd and 4th floors of the Dong-A Media Center building at Gwanghwa-mun. Samples of newspapers, presses, type, cameras, and other equipment fill this museum, which is open Tuesday–Sunday 1000–1800 (Thursday until 2000); entrance runs ₩3,000.

The **Korean Christian Museum** has a large collection of historical items relating to Christian missionary work and the development of Christianity in Korea. It's on the Soongshil University campus, over the hill from the National Cemetery. Hours are weekdays 0900–1700, Saturday 0900–1300. Use city bus no. 150, or the Soongshil University Station on subway line #7.

The **Jeoldusan Missionary Museum** exhibits items relating to the development of Catholicism in Korea and the persecution of early

SEOUL

Catholics, ritual items of historical interest, books and documents, and objects used by Pope John Paul II when he visited Korea. Open daily except Mon. 0930–1830; ₩1,000. Use the Hapjeong Station on subway line #2.

Located in the National Korean Traditional Music Institute at the Seoul Arts Center is the **Museum of Korean Traditional Music** (국악박물관). Old documents and compositions, old and new musical instruments, and famous Korean musicians are the focus of this unique museum. Perhaps of most interest to the general public is the room that displays over four dozen traditional Korean instruments, plus additional instruments from other Asian and African countries. Its audio-visual room and music library are used mostly by students and musicologists. Open daily except Mon. and Jan. 1 0900–1600 (1700 in winter); there is no admission fee.

The **Human Cultural Assets Gallery** has a permanent collection of traditional craft items made by individuals designated as Human Cultural Assets, and other professional craftsmen. Some items are for sale. Open 1100–1900, this gallery is located next to the New World Hotel at the northwest corner of Samneung Park, south of the river.

The small **Diplomatic History Museum** (외교박물관), located on the 2nd floor of the Institute for National Security, has a small but interesting collection of documents relating to Korea's diplomatic history and a number of old historical pictures. Open weekdays except holidays 1000–1600. Use the Yangjae Station on subway line #3 or express bus no. 46.

The Samseong Publishing Co. has established the **Samseong Museum of Publishing** at its building is Yeongdeungpo. Here the history of printing in Korea can be seen from the Goryeo Dynasty to the present. Open daily except Sun. and holidays 1000–1700; free. Dangsan Station on subway line #2 is close.

Art Galleries

Seoul has many dozen art galleries—the number grows every year. Most are in the heart of the city, but some are popping up in areas south of the Han River as well. While it varies by place, many are closed on Monday. Aside from the Museum of Contemporary Art, you can find fine displays at the Seoul Metropolitan Museum of Art at Gyeonghui-gung and at both the Art Gallery and Calligraphy Gallery at the Seoul Arts Center in southern Seoul. A few in the downtown area are the Sejong Cultural Center's various galleries, the Hoam Art Gallery at the Joongang Ilbo newspaper building near Seosomun Park, and the Rodin Gallery at the Samsung Life Insurance building a few steps up from Namdae-mun. Areas that have a concentration of galleries include the streets just to the east and west of Gyeongbok-gung. A number of these galleries have restaurants on the premises. Daehang-no near the Korean Culture and Arts Foundation, the long stretch of Insa-dong, and Cheongdam-dong near the Galleria Department Store also have many galleries. For specifics, check with the tourist information centers in town. Some shows are publicized in the English-language newspapers.

Culture

PERFORMANCE VENUES

Traditional Korean music, dance, and drama performances are of great interest to visitors. An introduction to any of these art forms provides a deeper understanding of Korean cultural roots. All the various traditional performing arts can be viewed in Seoul. Modern music, dance, and drama can also be seen, either in modernized versions of traditional Korean themes, or in purely modern forms. Many small, often experimental, theaters are located around town. The best-known venues for classical and traditional performances are listed in this section. For information on what is currently showing, refer to one of the following sources: Seoul City Tourist Information Center, KNTO Tourist Information Center, the English-language newspapers' entertainment pages, or the entertainment page in the free weekly tourist magazines. Tickets can be bought at the box office at each venue, and many are available more conveniently at large bookstores around town. While some are more expensive (up to ₩100,000) and others less (₩10,000), most tickets fall into the ₩20,000–40,000 range.

National Theater 국립극장
Dedicated in 1973, the National Theater (tel. 02/2274-1151, www.ntok.go.kr) sits on the lower slopes of Nam-san above Jangchungdan Park. It's the home of the National Orchestra, National Dance Company, and the National Drama Company. During the performing season, its two halls pulsate with sounds of music and voice. The largest hall has a capacity of 1,500; the lighting and sound systems are top-notch. Traditional dance and music are performed in the small hall every Wednesday evening at 1900 for ₩8,000–10,000. The center also has an indoor stage for experimental drama presentations and an outdoor amphitheater for less formal performances, particularly on summer Saturday eve-

nings. City bus no. 154 and Dongguk University Station on subway line #3 are the closest.

Sejong Cultural Center 세종문화회관
On Sejong-no near the Gwanghwa-mun intersection, the Sejong Cultural Center is one of the most impressive large buildings in the city, a combination of traditional and modern designs. As the city's principal venue for cultural performances, this center is busy nearly every night of the week. The 4,000-seat main hall is the largest performance hall in the city and is generally reserved for formal performances of orchestral concerts, operas, and large-scale productions (many by touring foreign companies), as well as major international conventions. Choir concerts and recitals are hosted in the small hall, and periodic free demonstrations are given in the patio outside. Constantly changing exhibitions of calligraphy, pottery, painting, and other arts are displayed in the downstairs galleries. A coffee shop and restaurant round out the facilities. For information, drop by the box office and pick up a program, call 02/399-1708, or visit www.sejongpac.or.kr.

The Sejong Cultural Center operates **Samcheonggak,** a secluded retreat in the wooded hills over the mountains from Gyeongbok-gung. This center offers half-day, full-day, and long-term programs in various cultural art forms, and a variety of public dance and music performances. There is shuttle service between the Sejong Cultural Center and Samcheonggak.

Chongdong Theater 정동극장
Located behind Deoksu Palace, the Chongdong Theater is Seoul's premier repertory theater. Aside from the variety of traditional and modern plays performed, this venue holds a continuing traditional music series on its Korean traditional stage, every day except Monday, April–September at 2000, October–March at 1600. The Chongdong Theater is the most convenient location in the center of the city for such a musical

performance and simply one of the best performances in town. Seats run ₩20,000– 30,000. Call 02/773-8960 for information and reservations, or visit www.chongdong.com.

Seoul Arts Center 예술의전당

The Seoul Arts Center is located at the foot of Umyeon-san, south of the Express Bus Terminal. A huge complex, this center includes the 2,600-seat Seoul Concert Hall, the nearly-as-large Seoul Opera House, Recital Hall, Hangaram Art Gallery, Seoul Calligraphy Hall, Seoul Art Library, and the Museum of Traditional Korean Music. National and international music performances make use of the large concert hall, while more intimate shows use the smaller recital hall. Opera, ballet, musicals, modern dance, and other theatrical productions use the opera hall, while the associated Dowol Theater stages smaller shows, and the Jayu Theater presents more experimental and small-scale theater productions. Art and calligraphy by prominent Korean artists and special exhibitions hang in the two galleries (open daily except Mon. 1000–1700); art classes, conferences, and seminars are also held. The art library is a tremendous resource for students and scholars alike. Information: tel. 02/580-1300; booking: tel. 02/780-6400; www.sac.or.kr.

Next door is the Korean Traditional Performing Arts Center and the National Classical Music Institute. The institute is set up for the purpose of preserving Korea's traditional classical music and instructing young people in those arts. Some classes are open to the public, so check the English-language newspapers for announcements. Students perform the music for the Confucian memorial ceremonies at Jong-myo and Mun-myo. Regular performances of Korean traditional music and dance are given in the small hall every Saturday 1700–1830 throughout the year; tickets are ₩8,000–10,000. Every Tuesday and Thursday at 1930 other traditional performances are presented in a larger hall. Performances feature different types of classical and traditional music and dance, and they are all crowd pleasers. These programs draw from court music, court dance, military music, *gayageum,*

gomungo, haegeum, and *piri* solo music, folk ensemble music, *pansori* lyrical recitation, *samulnori* percussion music, and folk-dance dramas. This center occasionally puts on performances by musicians who are designated Human Cultural Assets. They are a joy to hear as they perform their mastered arts. Some of these honored individuals instruct at the National Classical Music Institute. For information, call 02/580-3040; for booking call 02/1588-7890; or go online to www.ncktpa.go.kr.

To reach the Seoul Arts Center or the Korean Traditional Performing Arts Center, express city bus no. 42 or the Nambu Terminal Station on subway line #3 is most convenient. From the subway station, it's a 15-minute walk to the center.

Seoul Training Center for Important Intangible Cultural Properties

This educational institute, run by the Foundation for the Preservation of Cultural Properties, trains young people to carry on the important cultural arts of the country. Music and dance performances take place every Friday at 1900 at the performance hall in the foundation building near Seolleung Park south of the river. Call 02/566-5951 for information, or visit www.fpcp.or.kr.

Korea House 한국의집

A favorite of visitors to Seoul is a trip to Korea House, a restaurant and dinner theater operated by the Foundation for the Preservation of Cultural Properties (which also arranges the performances at Seoul Nori Madang, described later in this chapter). Established in 1957 to introduce aspects of Korean culture to foreigners, and renovated and enlarged in 1978–1981, Korea House is a showplace of performing arts and food. Monday–Saturday a traditional Korean buffet lunch (₩28,600) is served 1200–1400 and set menu *(hanjeongshik)* dinners (₩71,500) are offered at 1730 and 1920. Following each dinner, at 1900 and 2050, is a one-hour show (₩29,000 without dinner). This traditional entertainment includes dance, song, and instrumental music. On Sunday there is one dinner at 1830 and one show at 2000. Schedules may change according to the season. Although a bit expensive, the dinners and shows are well publicized and well attended, so make reservations (tel. 02/2266-9101, www.koreahouse.or.kr) several days in advance; open daily except holidays. On Saturday and Sunday a traditional wedding of court official and court lady is held in the courtyard, bringing this once-common but now rarely seen ceremony to life. Korea House is composed of four traditional-style buildings connected around a courtyard and three pavilions in the rear garden, each constructed and furnished in authentic style. In the main building, the exhibit of traditional musical instruments is worth a look, and there's a gift shop with books, postcards, prints, reproductions of cultural properties, and art created by designated masters. Korea House is located just south of Toegye-ro, near the Chungmuro subway station.

Seoul Nori Madang 서울노리마당

At the northwest corner of Seokcheon Lake in Jamshil is the open-air, semicircular, sand-floored amphitheater Seoul Nori Madang. Traditional folk music (instrumental and vocal), folk dance, masked-dance drama presentations, and an occasional ritual ceremony or martial arts demonstration are performed free of charge Saturday, Sunday, and holidays 1400–1700 April–October. These performances are given by non-professional but well-practiced groups from throughout the country. Performances at this informal setting are like those seen at provincial folk festivals outside the capital. The crowd often gets taken up with the music and onlookers participate with the performers. You can come and go as you wish. Use the Jamshil Station on subway line #2.

Private Halls

With 1,000 seats, the **Hoam Art Hall** is the largest and perhaps the most influential private performance venue in the city. Located on the 1st floor of the Joongang Ilbo newspaper building near Seosomun Park, it hosts Korean and foreign musical performances, conventions, and other large meetings throughout the year. On the basement level is the Ho-am Art Gallery. For information and tickets call 02/751-9997.

In a similar manner, the **LG Arts Hall** in Yeoksam-dong south of the river is a state-of-the-art concert hall that plays host to numerous large musical events throughout the year. For information call 02/2005-0114 or visit www.lgart .com.

Additional performances are also held at the **KBS Hall** of Yeouido; call 02/781-2242.

Smaller and more intimate than Hoam, the **Soong Eui Concert Hall** is often used for smaller musical performances and recitals. It is located on the campus of the Soong Eui Women's College, on the north slope of Namsan. Call 02/752-8924 for information on upcoming events.

CULTURAL ORGANIZATIONS

Korean Culture and Arts Foundation

This national organization was founded to help promote traditional and modern arts of all varieties in Korea and to provide information about these arts. On Daehang-no, the Munye Theater and Fine Arts Center are under its control. See www.kcaf.or.kr.

Korea Foundation

Korea Foundation (tel. 02/3463-5614, www.kf .or.kr) sponsors lectures, seminars, research, films, and cultural activities on Korea for visiting foreigners; promotes Korean studies overseas; offers fellowship grants to visiting foreign scholars; and publishes the weekly English-language quarterly journal *Koreana* among other publications. Located on the 10th floor of the Diplomatic Center Building in Seocho-gu.

Yejiwon Cultural Institute

Striving to preserve the values, ceremonies, customs, and crafts of and for Korean women, Yejiwon (tel. 02/2234-3325) offers cross-cultural educational programs for foreigner groups and Koreans alike. Courses are offered on the tea ceremony, flower arranging, calligraphy, wearing Korean clothes, Korean etiquette, Korean food preparation (including *gimchi*-making), Korean classical dance, and the Korean wedding ceremony. Courses are offered by arrangement only—it's not cheap, but it's quality instruction. Special classes for tour groups are given. Located behind the Tower Hotel on the eastern flank of Nam-san. Closed Sun.

Royal Asiatic Society (RAS), Korea Branch

Founded in 1900, RAS is a non-profit cultural organization dedicated to the dissemination of knowledge about Korea. Bimonthly free meetings feature authoritative speakers (in English) on a wide variety of Korean topics, and RAS organizes tours to a whole host of sites in Seoul and throughout the peninsula. These well-attended tours, open to all at reasonable rates, run on most weekends throughout the year. A quarterly newsletter is circulated to members. RAS publishes the annual scholarly journal *Transactions,* devoted to Korean topics, as well as publishing books on Korea and distributing numerous others. Few places in Seoul stock a wider selection. The RAS also maintains a reference library of books, magazines, journals, and other printed material about Korea and Asia. Annual membership dues for Korea residents are ₩40,000 for individuals, ₩60,000 for couples, and ₩20,000 for students; for overseas residents the fee is US$50 per person for two years. RAS is in the Korea Christian Building, Rm. 611, Jongno 5-ga (tel. 02/763-9483), and office hours are usually Monday–Friday 1000–1200 and 1400–1700. For correspondence, or to request a copy of their booklist, write C.P.O. Box 255, Seoul 100-602, Korea. For additional information, see www.raskorea.org.

Korean National Commission for UNESCO

Aside from sponsored activities, research, and publications, UNESCO has a library of books and magazines on Korean topics. Located in the heart of Myeong-dong along its main street.

EDUCATION

Little expense was spared for the education of the sons of the upper class during the Joseon Dynasty. While public and private academies were located throughout the land, it was to Seoul that students were sent for the very best training. Koreans still hold education in very high esteem, but now it also applies to women and all stratas of society. With such a huge population, this metropolis has an enormous number of schools, including a majority of the nation's most-respected universities.

Universities

Set below Gwanak-san, **Seoul National University** has one of the newest and most modern campuses in the city and is considered by most to be Korea's best university. **Ehwa Women's University,** with over 8,000 students, is the largest women's university in the country, and some say in the world. **Yonsei University,** established by Protestant missionaries around the turn of the 20th century, is one of Korea's oldest. **Koryo (Korea) University** is often ranked as Korea's best private school. Other universities worthy of mention are **Dongguk University,** the Buddhist university; **Hanguk University of Foreign Studies; Sogang University,** established and run by Jesuit priests; **Seonggyungwan University,** descendant of the National Confucian Academy and the center of Korean Confucianism; and **Hanyang University.**

To meet students, visit a campus. Many students are more than eager to practice their English (or Japanese, Chinese, German, or French), and it's a good place to practice your Korean. Near many major universities are student-oriented commercial and entertainment districts full of clothing stores, music shops, bookstores, restaurants, coffee houses, drinking establishments, theaters, galleries, arcades, and other entertainment facilities that are good places to contact students in a more relaxed setting than on campus.

Foreign Schools

Schools have also been set up to cater to foreign residents. Licensed by the government, they are independent of the Korean educational system and accredited by their respective countries. For detailed information, contact the individual school office.

Seoul Foreign School, 55 Yeonhui-dong, Seo-daemun-gu, tel. 02/335-5101, www.sfs-h.ac.kr.

Seoul International School, Songpa P.O. Box 47, tel. 02/2233-4551, www.sis-lhs.gyeonggi.kr.

Seoul Academy, 988-5 Daechi-dong, Gang-nam-gu, tel. 02/554-2475.

Korea International School, 155 Gaepo-dong, Gangnam-gu, tel. 02/561-0509, www.kis.or.kr.

Seoul American Elementary and High Schools, Yongsan Army Base, Yongsan-gu, tel. 02/7918-8822 or 7916-4378, www.korea.pac. odedodea.edu.

Seoul Japanese School, 84, Gaepo-dong, Gangnam-gu, tel. 02/574-0348.

Hanseong Chinese Primary, Middle and High Schools, 89-1 Yeonhui-dong, Seodaemun-gu, tel. 02/325-0664.

Lycée Francais de Séoul, 98-3 Banpo-dong, Seocho-gu, tel. 02/535-1158, www.lfseoul.org.

Deutsche Schule Seoul, 4-13 Hannam-dong, Yongsan-gu, tel. 02/792-0797, www.dsseoul.org.

International Christian School, 13-1, Yeoui-do-dong, Yeongdeungpo-gu, tel. 02/761-9972.

University of Maryland (tel. 723-4294) and several other American universities offer college-level courses, primarily for U.S. military person-nel stationed in Korea, on U.S. military installations; other resident foreigners are also accepted. Contact via the Yongsan Education Center (tel. 723-7194).

Accommodations

From 1914, when the city's first hotel opened for business, the number of hotels grew slowly until the Korean War, when all but one were de-stroyed. After the war, demand for accommo-dations began to rise, and by the '70s there were several dozen hotels. The mid-1980s saw a rapid rise in their numbers due to the strong economy, increased tourism, and the added impetus of the '86 Asian Games and especially the '88 Sum-mer Olympics. As a thriving international city, Seoul today has nearly 100 registered Western-style hotels. Of this total, 30 are rated as super-deluxe or deluxe class, comparable to major hotels in any cosmopolitan city of the world. While there are variations, broadly speaking, room rates for standard rooms are: super-deluxe class, ₩330,000–380,000; deluxe class, ₩200,000–240,000; first class, ₩140,000–200,000; sec-ond class, ₩80,000–100,000; and third class, ₩50,000–80,000. Korean-style rooms are usu-ally of comparable price, single rooms slightly cheaper (when available), and suites more ex-pensive—some exorbitantly so. All hotels have a variety of amenities, which might include restau-rants, coffee shops, cocktail bars, souvenir shops, barber shops, saunas, laundry, recreational facil-ities, and business centers, generally increasing in number and quality with the price of the hotel. A 10 percent service charge is automatically added to the bill, and 10 percent value-added tax is also levied. There is therefore no need for tip-ping. Generally small and scattered throughout the city, hotels without ratings are usually com-parable in value and quality to third-class hotels.

HOTELS

The following hotels are recommended. They are listed by area and their ratings are marked in parentheses as shown: (SDL)= Super Deluxe, (DLX)= Deluxe, (1)= First Class, (2)= Second Class, (3)= Third Class. For a complete list of hotels, contact the KNTO or one of its overseas branches for one of its brochures, or the Seoul city tourist information department.

Near Gwanghwa-mun

Koreana (DLX) (tel. 02/730-9911, www.kore-anahotel.com).

New Seoul (1) (tel. 02/735-9071) is popular with Japanese businessmen.

Seoul Hotel (2) (tel. 02/735-9001, www.seoul-hotel.net) is near Insa-dong.

Seoul Plaza and Myeong-dong Districts

Westin Chosun (SDL) (tel. 02/771-0500, www.westin.com) was founded in 1914 as Seoul's first hotel. Emphasis is placed on business travelers. Central to business, entertainment, and shopping.

Lotte (SDL) (tel. 02/771-1000, www.hotel.lotte.co.kr). With over 1,300 rooms, this is the largest hotel in the country; it's attached to a multistory department store.

Radisson Seoul Plaza (SDL) (tel. 02/771-2200, www.seoulplaza.co.kr) towers over the Seoul Plaza and Deoksu-gung.

Seoul Royal (DLX) (tel. 02/756-1112, www.seoulroyal.co.kr) is in the heart of Myeong-dong.

Metro (2) (tel. 02/752-1112) is also located in the heart of Myeong-dong, but it's more economical.

West Slope of Nam-san

Seoul Hilton (SDL) (tel. 02/753-7788, www.hilton.com) has a great location overlooking the city center and up at Nam-san.

East Slope of Nam-san

Shilla Hotel (SDL) (tel. 02/2233-3131, www.shilla.net/eng) is one of the city's finest; it hosts many foreign dignitaries and executives.

Sofitel Ambassador (DLX) (tel. 02/2275-1101, www.ambatel.com).

Itaewon

Grand Hyatt (SDL) (tel. 02/797-1234, www.seoul.hyatt.com) has a bold gold face and wonderful views over the Han River and southern Seoul.

Capitol (DLX) (tel. 02/792-1122, www.hotel.capital.co.kr).

Hamilton (1) (tel. 02/794-0171, www.hamilton.co.kr) is a remodeled old standby in the heart of the city's most prominent foreigner-focused district.

South of the River

Lotte World (SDL) (tel. 02/419-7000, www.hotel.lotte.co.kr) is connected to Lotte World amusement park and Lotte Department Store.

COEX Inter-continental (SDL) (tel. 02/3452-2500, www.seoul.interconti.com). Next to COEX and the World Trade Center, this opulent hotel caters to businessmen.

JW Marriott (SDL) (tel. 02/6282-6262, www.marriott.com) is at COEX and the World Trade Center.

Seoul Renaissance (SDL) (tel. 02/555-0501, www.renaissance.co.kr).

Oakwood Premier Coex Center (tel. 02/3466-7000, www.oakwood.com). Located next to the City Air Terminal, this is "hotel-style apartment" lodging for visitors on longer stays.

Human Touch Ville (tel. 02/552-3921, www.humantouch.co.kr). A cross between hotel accommodations and a condo apartment, the Human Touch Ville offers furnished extended stay facilities for those in Korea on business.

Coatel Chereville (tel. 02/6288-3400, www.coatel.co.kr). Another hotel/condo-like highrise accommodation with office space for long- and short-term visitors.

Amiga (SDL) (tel. 02/3440-8000, www.amiga.co.kr). Small European-style boutique hotel.

Youngdong (1) (tel. 02/542-0112, www.youngdonghotel.co.kr). Close to the Apgujeong-dong shopping area.

Dynasty (2) (tel. 02/540-3041). One of the most economical in this area.

Hotels in Other Areas

Mirabeau (2) (tel. 02/392-9511). Located in the Shinchon university area.

Holiday Inn (DLX) (tel. 02/717-9441, www.holiday-inn.co.kr). In Mapo-gu, across the river from Yeouido.

Swiss Grand (SDL) (tel. 02/3216-5656, www.swissgrand.co.kr). Peaceful setting north of the city center.

Olympia (DLX) (tel. 02/2287-6000, www.olympia.co.kr). Lies below Bukhan-san National Park in a quiet northern district.

Sheraton Walker Hill (SDL) (tel. 02/453-0121, www.walkerhill.com). On the eastern edge of the city. Has an art gallery, the Kayagum theater restaurant, and the city's only casino.

Non-Registered Hotels

Of the plethora of these hotels in the city, a few are listed here for their convenience, location, or reputation with foreigners. **Go Goong Hotel** (tel. 02/741-3831) and **Arirang Hotel** (tel. 02/745-4114) are across the intersection from each other near Changgyeong-gung. Slightly fancier, the Go Goong has rooms in the ₩45,000 –60,000 range, while rooms at the Arirang go for ₩30,000–45,000. Down the back alley from Jogye-sa temple is the **Sam-O Motel** (tel. 02/ 739-0604), where rooms run ₩40,000. On the north slope of Nam-san, very near the Namdaemun Market, the **Palace Hotel** (tel. 02/777-7731) has rooms for ₩45,000–60,000. Near Namyeong subway station, **Hotel Rainbow** (tel. 02/792-9993; military line 02/723-4350) has many military visitors and rooms for ₩55,000–60,000. In the Shinchon university district, **Hotel Prince** (tel. 02/313-5551) has rooms in the ₩35,000– 45,000 range. South of the river, the **Seolim Hotel** (tel. 02/546-2271) has rooms for ₩40,000.

YEOGWAN

Much more plentiful than hotels are *yeogwan*. Located in all sections of the city, they range in style from single-story traditional Korean tile-roof affairs to multi-story cement boxes, and in quality from mediocre to exceptionally clean and comfortable. By far, most rooms are Korean-style, but many now provide Western-style beds. Most rooms have baths attached, while some of the older and less expensive still share bathing and toilet facilities. Although not necessarily a distinguishing factor, the word "jang" attached to the *yeogwan* name usually means it is of higher quality. In addition, some better places attach the words "hotel," "motel," or "park" to their name. As in all cities, *yeogwan* can always be found in the vicinity of bus and train stations, close to universities, near tourist attractions, and in the center of the city. Select *yeogwan*, many used by foreign visitors, are listed below. For names, addresses, and telephone numbers of additional *yeogwan*, contact the KNTO city information desk, KNTO airport desks, or the city tourist office.

Just west of the Gwanghwa-mun intersection is **Gwanghwajang Yeogwan** (광화장여관), otherwise called the Kwang Hwa Hotel (tel. 02/738-0751). It has Korean-style *ondol* rooms and Western-style rooms with beds, some with fans and some with air-conditioning, and an attached public bathhouse. Room rates run ₩28,000-30,000 depending on the amenities. A short distance away, located on an alley across from the Seoul Police Headquarters, is the **Sungdo Yeogwan** (성도여관) (tel. 02/753-5507). Rooms there run about ₩30,000.

Set in the midst of the Bukchang-dong restaurant area behind the Seoul Plaza Hotel is the remodeled multi-story **Daewoo Motel** (대우모텔) (tel. 02/755-8067, www.daewoomotel.com). Clean, quiet, well-run, and safe, it has Korean- and Western-style rooms, some with baths attached. Room rates run ₩35,000, and amenities include television, air conditioning, laundry, and Internet access.

In the area between Gwanghwa-mun intersection and Jong-myo are several more places to stay. Down an alley up the street toward the Jongno Office is the **Kuk Je Motel** (국제장모텔) (tel. 02/732-0801), where rooms are ₩25,000. North of the Jonggak intersection is the older but serviceable **Sae Jong Jang Hotel** (세종장모텔) (tel. 02/732-7856). Turn into the first alley behind the Seoul Hotel. Korean- and Western-style rooms there run ₩25,000. Many other similar places are along this alley, including the **Shinjinjang Motel** (신진장여관) and **Dongwonjang Motel** (동원장여관). In the alley behind the YMCA is the rebuilt **Paradise Motel** (바라다이스모텔) (tel. 02/735-1558), where rooms are ₩30,000 –40,000. Nearer the entrance to Changdeok-gung, the **Sae Hwa Jang Hotel** (세화장여관) (tel. 02/765-2881) and **Jongnowon** (종로원) (tel. 02/763-4249) both have rooms for ₩25,000.

Several places are also available in Itaewon. Above the Seoul Arcade is the **Seouljang Motel** (서울장모텔), also known as the Seoul House Inn (tel. 02/795-2266). This small hotel has all air-conditioned rooms that go for ₩25,000 single and ₩35,000 double. Across the street and down the stairway from the Itaewon Arcade is the **Hangang Motel** (한강모텔) (tel. 02/795-5064);

rooms run ₩30,000. Down from the Hamilton Hotel is the **Geumseongjang Yeogwan** (금성장여관), where rooms are ₩25,000-₩30,000, and a bit farther along, the older **Obokjang Yeogwan** has rooms at the same price.

GUESTHOUSES AND OTHER ACCOMMODATIONS

Of the half-dozen places that were frequented by volunteers during the days of the Peace Corps in Korea, only the Korean-style **Daewon Yeogwan** (Inn-Daewon) (대원여관) remains. Converted from a Korean-style house, it advertises itself as "one of the cheapest"—and it is. Small, basic, clean enough, with shower rooms and telephones, it is frequented by low-budget travelers in town for a few days and by those who have found work, legally or otherwise, and are staying some time. Room rates run ₩10,000 for a dorm bed and ₩15,000 for a room. Located just a few steps from the Gwanghwa-mun intersection, to the northwest. Call 02/738-4308 to confirm that a room is available.

To the east side of Gyeongbok-gung, you'll find **The Nest Guest House,** (tel. 02/725-4418, fax 02/725-4416, www.outdoorkorea.com). More like a hostel than a typical Korean *yeogwan,* the Nest has dorm rooms for ₩15,000 and single rooms for ₩27,000. Clean and bright, with a living room, kitchen facilities, storage lockers, showers, and a washing machine, it is located in a quiet, secure section of town with friendly and helpful staff. A neighborhood bus runs up past the Nest from Sejong-no.

Down an alley to the front of Changdeok-gung is **Guesthouse Korea,** (tel. 02/3675-2205, www.guesthouseinkorea.com). A home away from home for many Japanese and European travelers, this is a somewhat funky place that's clean enough for a budget traveler and provides an atmosphere of community. Bunk beds run ₩15,000, a single room ₩25,000, and a double ₩35,000. There are basic laundry facilities, a television, and computer access. The closest subway stop is Jongno 3-ga Station on line #7.

Newer and well-kept is **Traveler's A** guesthouse (tel. 02/2285-5511, www.travelersa.com).

Located in a market area, this house is not the easiest to find, but Uljiro 4-ga Station on subway line #5 is closest. Dorm beds here are ₩12,000, ₩17,000 for a single, and ₩30,000 for a double room. Amenities include television and Internet, storage lockers, a kitchen, washing machine, and air conditioning.

A bit farther out, but offering the same basic service in a more family-oriented atmosphere is **Kim's Guesthouse** (tel. 02/337-9894, fax 02/3141-7203, www.kimsguesthouse.com). Dorms run ₩15,000, private rooms ₩25,000–35,000. Reservations preferred.

A 10-minute walk north of the Hyehwa Rotary intersection from Daehang-no brings you to **Friends House,** 33-15 Myeongnyum-dong 1-ga, Jongno-gu, (tel. 02/3673-1515, fax 02/3673-1513, www.friends-house.com). This Korean-style house with a front garden and five guest rooms offers comfortable accommodations on an *ondol* floor in the Korean manner, yet has a Western-style bathroom and a kitchen and laundry room with modern appliances that are for guest use. Air-conditioning offers more comfort in the heat of the summer, while the heated floor gives warmth in winter. The central living room holds a television and computer with Internet access. The room rate for one night per guest is ₩40,000, including a sit-down breakfast, but there is a 20 percent discount for groups of three or more. Subway line #4 is most convenient. Get off at the Hyehwa Station and walk north.

Other accommodations include the YMCA and Olympic Park Youth Hostel. A registered third-class hotel, the **YMCA** (tel. 02/734-6884) on Jong-no has rooms on its upper floors; the registration desk is on the 6th floor. All rooms have air-conditioning and color televisions. Credit cards are accepted and it offers foreign-currency exchange service. Singles are ₩40,000, doubles ₩50,000, twins ₩55,000, and triples ₩70,000; tax and gratuity are included. A restaurant in the building serves breakfast for ₩4,000–10,000, and lunch and dinner run ₩6,000–25,000. This is an older establishment and is rather worn around the edges, so you can find better value and a quieter environment for the same price elsewhere.

The only youth hostel in the city is the **Olympic Parktel** (tel. 02/421-2111) at Olympic Park in southeastern Seoul. It looks like a hotel but operates as both hotel and hostel. A bunk in the dorm room is ₩15,400 per person with a valid IYHF card; otherwise rooms are ₩60,500. For those in the dorms, the toilet and showers are down the hall. Several restaurants and lounges are in the building, as are a fitness center, indoor swimming pool, sauna, small shopping arcade, and the Olympic Museum. Foreign-currency exchange is provided, and major credit cards are accepted.

Food

RESTAURANTS

With an estimated 30,000 restaurants, Seoul has many more places to eat than to sleep. The most numerous are ordinary Korean restaurants, but expensive and more fashionable restaurants serving fine cuisine are growing in number every year. Located in every corner of the city, the ordinary restaurants serve meals at affordable prices. Chinese restaurants are numerous, but Japanese restaurants are fewer and farther between. Restaurants serving Western foods are becoming more numerous and varied in cuisine, and the ubiquitous fast-food restaurants have broken into the market and carved a substantial slice of the pie.

Deluxe hotels all have Korean, Japanese, Chinese, and/or Western restaurants which serve nothing but the best foods—prices are high. Other establishments are located throughout the city. The best of these have moderate to steep prices. Although reservations are not always necessary, they're recommended on weekends and holidays. A few recommended, non-hotel restaurants are listed below. For specific information on additional restaurants, locations, and telephone numbers, refer to the KNTO's *The Wonderful World of Korea Food* or similar brochures or contact either the KNTO or Seoul Tourist Information offices.

Korean

Yeongbin Garden and numerous others are in Insa-dong and the alleys near Jogye-sa. **Hanilgwan** is an old establishment, located kitty-corner across the intersection from Boshingak. **Jangan Samgyetang,** in Bukchang-dong behind the Seoul Plaza Hotel, is known for its ginseng chicken soup. **Jeonju Jungang Hoegwan** serves authentic Jeonju-style food, also in Bukchang-dong. **Nulbom** and **Samwon Garden** lie south of the Han River in Shinsa-dong. Both have indoor and outdoor dining areas. Near the Gangnam subway station is the newer restaurant **Our Story.**

In the same alley as the Sanchon vegetarian restaurant in Insa-dong is the **Arirang** restaurant, where a set Korean meal is served accompanied by traditional Korean music at 2000 for ₩15,000.

Japanese

Japanese restaurants with excellent reputations include **Songwon** behind the Radisson Seoul Plaza Hotel, **Hakata Udong** in Insa-dong, **Ariake** at the Silla Hotel, and the **Hakone** at the InterContinental Hotel at COEX.

Chinese

Several Chinese restaurants above the ordinary are **Ruran** and **Mallijangseong** in Shinsa-dong, **Lotus Garden,** in Yeoksam-dong, and **Paengnihyang** on the 57th floor of the DLI 63 building.

Thai

Thai Orchid is a few steps from the Itaewon subway station in Itaewon.

Sub-Continental

Moghul serves Pakistani dishes behind the Hamilton Hotel in Itaewon, **Ashoka** has Indian food on the 3rd floor of the Hamilton Hotel, and **Ganga** is in Apgujeong-dong.

Western

Wood and Brick offers gourmet Italian selections at their restaurants near Gwanghwa-mun and Hongik University, as well as breads, pastries, sandwiches, cheeses, and wines at a deli in Insa-dong.

Top Cloud grill and café is located on the top floor of the Millennium Tower building. The more formal and intimate grill offers a dinner menu and the more casual café is open for lunch and dinner. It's pricey, but people come here for the experience and the view.

Banjul in Gwancheol-dong is one of the city's most well-established French restaurants.

La Cantina offers Italian cuisine in a basement restaurant near city hall.

Scandinavian Club offers a smorgasbord-style feast; it's located on the grounds of the National Medical Center.

Chalet Swiss has—what else—Swiss food, in Itaewon.

L'abri, in the Kyobo Building, serves French dishes.

T.G.I. Friday's has standard American fare in Myeong-dong.

Tony Roma's serves ribs and other meat dishes near Dosan Park.

Vegetarian

Sanchon (산촌), in Insa-dong, is an excellent vegetarian restaurant run by a former Buddhist monk; open for dinner only. The cost is ₩29,000 for a set dinner with over a dozen dishes; the price includes a traditional music performance at 2030. Two streets down is Sanchon Sarangbang, an offshoot of the main restaurant which serves an à la carte menu for lunch and dinner for ₩5,000–12,000.

Also in this area are **Myeonginga** (명인가) and **Dagyeong** (다경), which provide similar, mostly vegetarian meals.

South of the river, **Shigol Saenghwal** (시골생활) is near the Shinsa subway station, while **Sanchae** (산채) is close to the Maebong subway station, both on subway line #3.

FINDING LESS EXPENSIVE FOOD

The streets and alleys in the neighborhoods of many of the *yeogwan* mentioned earlier in this chapter have eateries. Query the *yeogwan* owners and other travelers for the best places nearby.

The area behind the Kyobo Building is full of restaurants. In this maze of alleys, eateries are kept busy during lunch and dinner hours with businesspeople who seem to have left the cares of work at the office and are intent upon making short work of the food in front of them. The atmosphere is congenial and the food filling. This area is also known for restaurants that stay open very late to serve "hangover soup" to those who have partied too hard and drunk too much.

Running along the edge of this district, from the back side of the Kyobo building to Jongmyo, and paralleling this main drag with some interruption for modern office buildings, is an alley called **Bimat-gol.** Along this alley are numerous, mostly inexpensive and moderately priced eateries, with the addition of several higher-priced places like Hanilgwan. Off Bimat-gol in Insa-dong are additional alleys with plenty of drinking establishments frequented by university students. Historically, this alley was set just off the main street for the convenience of the commoner who was supposed to bow in respect as those of importance passed by on the main street. When such an entourage came down the street, people could duck into the back alley and go about their business while avoiding their otherwise mandatory social obligation.

In **Gwancheol-dong,** behind Boshingak, is a district full of all sorts of trendy restaurants and entertainment spots frequented largely by young people.

Along with its antique shops, art galleries, and gift shops, the back streets and alleys of **Insa-dong** are crowded with dozens of restaurants, many a cut above, and most serve some sort of traditional food.

An older area, visited principally by businessmen and office workers, the **Da-dong** district lies behind the KNTO building. In these cubbyhole restaurants, the food is often cooked at your table over a charcoal brazier. If done at the front, the exhaust smoke is blown out into the alley, where the pungent aroma serves as the restaurant's best advertisement. Either way, the food's savory smell saturates the air, drinks are passed, and voices fill the night.

The back alleys of **Myeong-dong** have innumerable restaurants, from cheap to expensive, all set up to serve the shoppers. You must search for one that looks inviting, or follow your nose to one that has that certain savory smell. It's a vibrant place in the evening, when the spirited are out for a good time.

Mostly in the mid- to upper price range, the restaurants of **Bukchang-dong,** behind the Seoul Plaza Hotel, offer a plethora of choices but mostly Japanese, Korean, and seafood. The area is frequented by businesspeople.

Near Marronnier Park, along both sides of the street along **Daehang-no,** you'll find a plethora of restaurants, coffee shops, clubs, theaters, beer halls, bars, nightclubs, and a long list of ethnic restaurants, mostly in the midrange, that caters to young students and professional people.

Areas near universities always have plenty of restaurants. While some cater to the well-heeled, most serve common food at affordable prices. Try the **Shinchon** district to the front of Ehwa and Yonsei universities, and a little farther west near Hongik University.

South of the river, the **Shinsa-dong/Apgujeong** area has developed into a high-class eating and entertainment area for the well-to-do young and young at heart. Here has flourished what some call the "café culture" of Seoul. Prices are higher than elsewhere, but good Korean and Western food can be found here.

For those interested, easily recognizable fast food restaurants are concentrated in areas of the city that are frequented by foreigners and young people, and/or are centers of nightlife. Such areas of Seoul include, but are not limited to, Myeong-dong, Gwangcheol-dong, Itaewon, and Apgujeong-dong.

Arcade Restaurants

For a less overwhelming introduction to Korean foods, head to the food court restaurants, where plastic models of various dishes are displayed and prices are marked. Most of these arcades are found on the basement level of large office buildings and the upper floors of major department stores. For a start, try the World Food Court in the Millennium Tower, the Daewoo Building, Dongbang Plaza basement, or the Lotte Department Store's 9th and 10th floors.

Markets and Stations

Major markets, like the Namdae-mun and Gwangjang markets, provide another place for basic Korean food—some of which you'll never have seen before and will, undoubtedly, have trouble identifying. Whether proper restaurants or stalls, all markets have great selections of eateries.

All railroad stations and bus terminals also have simple restaurants and snack shops, generally serving ordinary fare or fast food for people on the go.

Tearooms and Coffee Shops

According to one estimate, Seoul has approximately 10,000 tearooms. Those of the ordinary variety sell packaged teas and coffee. Rather pedestrian in decor, they are patronized mostly by middle-aged and older men who are catered to by young women hostesses. Another type of tearoom has emerged in growing numbers in the past several decades. This type serves leaf, root, herbal, and fruit teas, plus other traditional Korean drinks and snacks, usually in a setting of traditional decor with traditional Korean music. Insa-dong has many, and the areas near universities also have their fair share. To experience this slice of Korea and enjoy some wonderful drinks, start your search in Insa-dong at Jeontong Dawon (전통다원) or Yetchachip (옛찻집).

Coffee shops are just as numerous. Here, too, there are ordinary varieties serving ordinary coffee. Fancier places have been emerging over the years, so now it's possible to get any number of high-quality coffee drinks and blends from around the world, usually in a smarter and more modern setting. For these coffee shops, start your search in Myeong-dong, Shinsa-dong, Apgujeong, or near the universities.

Entertainment

Seoul supports a diverse entertainment scene from traditional music concerts to dance hall discos, melodramatic Korean movies to Las Vegas–style floor shows, a quiet evening at a neighborhood tearoom to a captivating casino. Entertainment spots are scattered throughout the city, but there are also several recognized entertainment districts.

ENTERTAINMENT AREAS

Myeong-dong 명동
Myeong-dong is Seoul's oldest and best-known entertainment/commercial district. East of Seoul Plaza, this concentrated area of narrow alleys and pedestrian streets is stuffed with department stores, clothing shops, restaurants, coffee houses, and a handful of theaters and clubs. It's a microcosmic hodgepodge of the Korean entertainment scene. Nightly, throngs of people crowd the streets and shop the brightly lit boutiques. Lovers find a dark corner in a tearoom, college buddies sing song after song in a smoky drinking house, and the show goes on at the nightclubs. It's a teeming, boisterous, active place, an area of bright lights, fetching sights, and cacophonous sounds. But change is afoot. This area in the heart of the city is losing its entertainment sector to newer districts, and in its place are coming more commercial establishments and financial businesses.

Gwancheol-dong 관철동
Not far from Myeong-dong, behind the Chongno Book Center, are the alleys of Gwancheol-dong. Although smaller and less sophisticated than Myeong-dong, this area, along with Gwansu-dong to the east, is full of nightclubs, discos, theaters, restaurants, beer halls, coffee shops, music rooms, and a number of clothing stores and silk shops. This area is frequented predominantly by college students and young businesspeople.

Insa-dong 인사동
Between the Anguk-dong rotary and Pagoda Park is an area generally known as Insa-dong, well-known for its traditional restaurants and teahouses, antique shops, upscale art galleries, and drinking houses that generally cater to Seoul's more affluent and growing middle class and foreigners. Quieter than many other evening places, it's still a destination for those out on the town.

Apgujeong-dong 압구정동
With the expanding population and push to decentralize the capital, huge tracts of land were developed south of the Han River. Wedged into a confined space in the heart of the city, Myeong-dong could not expand, so other entertainment districts arose. Shinsa-dong and the contiguous areas of Apgujeong-dong and Cheongdam-dong have become the new "Myeong-dong" on the south bank of the Han. Newer, broader, and moneyed, this thriving area is the city's rising star. Aside from the many and varied eateries, coffee houses, drinking establishments, fashion shops, galleries, and art stores, there are nightclubs, theaters, and cinemas.

Itaewon 이태원
While Itaewon was once geared almost exclusively to the foreign crowd, it now tries to garner the business of all. It's a bastardized district that's neither Korean nor Western, but a skewed yet intriguing combination of both. Itaewon is on the south side of Nam-san, to the east of Yongsan U.S. Army Garrison. Clothing, gifts, bright lights, brash sounds, swirling dance, pungent smells, thirst-quenching drinks, and the atmosphere of a place on the edge are just part of the essence of Itaewon. Great shopping bargains, bars, music halls, and Western food draw people to this area.

Dozens of clubs are basically G.I. hangouts, but other foreigners and a growing number of young Koreans also gravitate here. The rock-and-roll clubs perhaps draw the biggest and rowdiest crowds, while others play Top 40, mellow jazz, moody blues, and swinging country music. Stand-up bars, sit-down pubs, dance halls—there's a niche for everyone. Some have live bands and a dance floor. Others spin records, and every night is request night. One alley to the south of the main street holds vegetable and fruit stalls, and from tiny cubicle restaurants waft smoke and the smell of tangy grilled meat. Once a disreputable "den of iniquity," Itaewon has since developed some class, with new storefronts, lots of glass, aluminum and polish, higher-quality goods, and a wider variety of eating and entertainment establishments. It's humble pie grown to glitzy chrome, and it seems rather ironic that overlooking this very secular district is the country's central mosque.

The underbelly of this neon entertainment dragon is a red-light district. Bold and brash, painted ladies of the night circulate through the clubs like hawks in search of prey, or stand on street corners to proposition passersby. Some are as engaging as the girl next door, but most are strictly business-minded. Never go looking unprotected!

University Areas

Near most universities are places where students can hang out and enjoy themselves. Three in particular have an abundance of restaurants, coffee shops, bookstores, theaters, movie houses, art galleries, dance halls, bars, and other drinking establishments, along with boutiques and clothing shops of all sorts. They are **Daehang-no** (대학로); **Shinchon** (신촌), the area to the front of Yonsei University and the approach to Ehwa Women's University which is referred to as Edae Ipgu (이대입구); and the area called **Hongdae** near Hongik University.

OTHER POSSIBILITIES

Theater Restaurants

Aside from the prohibitively expensive *gisaeng-jip* (houses for professional entertainers/hostesses similar to the geisha in Japan), the highest class of social evening entertainment is the theater restaurant. Influenced by similar Western establishments, these places offer dinner and a floor show

for a fixed price. The dinner is usually Western fare and the entertainment often a sampling of Korean music and dance followed by a Las Vegas–style floor show, often with foreign entertainers. The floor shows at most independent theaters are a variety of traditional Korean music and dance, and the food is also usually Korean. Although prices vary, tickets are often in the ₩70,000–90,000 range. Call for additional information and reservations. The **Kayagum** (tel. 02/4555-0000) at the Sheraton Walker Hill Hotel offers the best Western-style entertainment in the city. Korean-style theater restaurants include **Korea House** (tel. 02/2266-9101), below Nam-san, which offers a set dinner menu and traditional entertainment twice nightly, and the **Arirang** Korean restaurant, in Insa-dong, which combines an authentic Korean meal and music once nightly. The **Sanchon** vegetarian restaurant, also in Insa-dong, puts on a short floor show nightly for dinner guests only. Seating at both the Arirang and Sanchon is on the floor, Korean-style.

Nightclubs

With house bands, colored lights, central dance floors, and expensive drinks, nightclubs and discos found in Korean hotels are virtually the same as their Western counterparts. Private establishments are most notably located in Gwancheol-dong, Myeong-dong, Apgujeong, Itaewon, Shinchon, and near Hongik University. By and large, hotel nightclubs are traditional, dressy, and expensive. In Myeong-dong and Apgujeong-dong, the clubs are modern, trendy, and also expensive. More casual and moderate in price are those found in Gwancheol-dong and Itaewon. Cover charges vary but may run up to ₩10,000.

Cinemas

Seoul has several dozen movie theaters. Of those, about a dozen show first-run Korean and Western films—most of these are multi-plexes located in the center of the city between Jong-no and Nam-san. Shows start at 1100 and continue until late evening. Listings of Western films and some Korean films appear in the English-language newspapers. In the center of the city are the

Danseongsa, Cinecube, Cine Core, Myeongbo, Seoul Cinema, Scala, Hollywood, Piccadilly, and Daehan cinemas. In Shinsa-dong are the Cine House, Broadway, and Oz; in Jamshil look for the Lotte World Cinema; and try the Megabox Cineplex in the COEX Mall. The DLI 63 building has an IMAX theater that shows a variety of nature-oriented films on its huge screen.

An alternative to the movie theater is Seoul Selection, a small shop near Gyeongbok-gung that previews subtitled Korean films on Wednesday, Saturday, and Sunday. Stop by or call 02/734-9564 for show times. Seoul Selection is located in the basement of the Korean Publishers Association Building, across from the southeast corner of the palace.

Gambling

Open only to non-Korean visitors, Seoul's only licensed casino is at the Sheraton Walker Hill Hotel (tel. 02/450-4825). Try your luck at roulette, poker, baccarat, Tai-sai, blackjack, or the slot machines. Most hotels have game rooms where you can play electronic games; some have slot machines.

The Seoul Equestrian Park allows betting on horse races held every Saturday and Sunday throughout most of the year. Win, place, and quinella bets ranging from ₩100–100,000 are taken at the track or at a number of offices in town.

Night Tours

For those who want their evenings scheduled, night tours offered by a variety of tour companies are an option. Often, dinner, entertainment, and a drive for a night view of the city lights are included. For more details, see the Tours section later in this chapter.

Fine night scenes can be viewed independently from Seoul Tower and the DLI 63 building, and a cruise on the Han River offers a unique city-lights perspective.

DLI 63 Building

Located at the eastern end of Yeouido, the golden, gracefully curved DLI 63 building has much to offer. The 60th-floor observation deck offers broad views of the city by day or night. Open 1000–2100; adult entrance is ₩5,500, ₩4,900 for students, and ₩4,400 for children. On the floors below are fine-dining Chinese, Japanese, and Western restaurants, and near the bottom is a Korean restaurant. Also in this building are the Seaworld Aquarium (adults ₩9,000, ₩8,000 students, children ₩7,200), and an IMAX theater (adults ₩6,000, ₩5,400 students, children ₩4,800). Changing every six months, movies are about 40 minutes long and run throughout the day 1000–2100. A ticket for all activities costs ₩17,500 for adults, ₩15,700 for students, and ₩14,000 for children. The DLI 63 building also has a shopping arcade, a food plaza, health club, bowling alley, bank, post office, and an information desk on the lobby level of the annex building. Use express bus no. 720 from Gwanghwa-mun, subway line #1 and bus no. 823 from Daebang Station, or bus no. 48 or 70 from Yeouinaru Station on subway line #5. Find out more at their website, www.63city.co.kr.

COEX Aquarium

Aside from Seaworld Aquarium, the COEX Aquarium presents marvels of the underwater world. Located in the basement of the COEX Mall, this aquarium is open daily 1000–2100; ₩14,500 adult, ₩12,000 student, ₩9,500 child. With half a dozen major pools, this aquarium presents fish and other sea creatures from all the seas, and includes an acrylic tunnel through one of the pools. See www.coexaqua.co.kr.

Shopping

The largest and most diverse markets in Seoul are the Tongdaemun Market and Namdaemun Market, adjacent to the east and south city gates, respectively. Smaller general markets, like those at Shinchon and Yeongdeungpo, and neighborhood markets (about 450 of them by one estimate) are located in every section of the city. Specialty and wholesale markets are fewer. Supermarkets, department stores, and arcades (in hotels, aboveground, and underground) are more recent phenomena in this transformed city.

Duty-free shops and specialty shops in Itaewon will accept both Korean *won* and U.S. dollars. Department stores, hotel arcades, and a growing number of established shops in the areas frequented by foreigners will take certain credit cards. Some also accept traveler's checks. But, by and large, the majority of markets and shops accept only Korean currency.

English is spoken by dealers in Itaewon and by clerks in most hotel shops, major arcades, and some department stores. Japanese is widely spoken as well in hotels, arcades, and department stores, and in the Insa-dong district. Outside of these areas, you must rely on your Korean, the shopkeeper's pidgin English, hand signals, body language, and a notepad and pencil.

SHOPPING DISTRICTS

Certain areas of the city have developed reputations as special shopping and commercial districts: Myeong-dong and Cheongdam-dong are the city's upscale fashion centers, shops near big universities also sell trendy fashions but usually at more modest prices, and Insa-dong is known for antiques, art and art supplies, and handicrafts. As the playground of American soldiers and other foreigners, Itaewon is full of shops that cater to their tastes. Other distinct areas in the city can be found for such diverse items as auto parts, used books, appliances, medicinal herbs, second-hand goods, and traditional Korean musical instruments. This concentration tends to create competition for the shopkeeper and easy price comparison for the buyer.

Myeong-dong

Myeong-dong is traditionally the busiest and most fashionable shopping district in Seoul. Its narrow streets and alleys contain hundreds of clothing and accessory boutiques, shoe stores, tailors and dressmakers, huge department stores, specialty shops, offices, banks, and hotels. The hustle and bustle of daily business activity is compounded at night with the savory scent of food and the throb of music. Like a magnet, Myeong-dong attracts great crowds, yet somehow this sea of humanity all seems to flow in relatively ordered motion.

Apgujeong-dong

Since the great push to move the population of Seoul south of the Han River, Apgujeong-dong, in Gangnam-gu, has established itself as the new and trendy fashion district, replete with department stores, clothing stores, shoe shops, and boutiques of all kinds that generally cater to affluent young people and young families. Here too are hotels, restaurants, cafés, coffee houses, nightclubs, cinemas, theaters, foreign auto dealerships, and numerous other commercial and entertainment spots. A place of money, it has wide streets and tall buildings, but lacks the warmth and homeyness of the older commercial and entertainment sections of town. Nearby in Cheongdam-dong, the street running southwest from the Galleria Department Store is referred to as Rodeo Street because of its trendy and high-priced shops; in the direction of Cheongdam Park are a series of several dozen art galleries. Apgujeong Station on subway line #3 and Cheongdam Station on the Bundang line are most convenient.

Insa-dong

Also known as Mary's Alley—named for some forgotten or fictitious "Mary"—this district is the most established antique center of Seoul. Interspersed among the curio shops are a slew of art galleries, art supply stores, furniture stores, many high-class restaurants, and teahouses. Most of the antique shops have been upgraded in the past few years; prices are not cheap, but the quality is high. It's intriguing to poke around just to see what's available, but if you plan to buy, know what you're looking for and what it's worth. Quality art and handicraft reproductions are plentiful here as well and may be a better deal than scarce and pricey originals. At the south entrance is a space for outdoor entertainment. Along the road are benches and shade trees, and at the north entrance is a tourist information booth and a small park with seats for relaxing. Jonggak and Jongno 3-ga stations on subway line #1 are clos-est to the south entrance; Anguk Station on subway line #3 is closest to the north end.

Itaewon

Not too long ago, this area catered almost exclusively to foreigners. Today, a growing number of young Koreans frequent Itaewon as well. This 1.5-kilometer strip has shops selling clothes and shoes (ready-made and tailored), fabrics, furniture, travel bags and luggage, leather and eelskin goods, brass, records and tapes, antiques and reproductions, handicrafts and trinkets. Tailored items can be made for reasonable prices—just describe what you want or bring in a picture. Western sizes and styles of clothes and shoes can easily be found. Some of what is sold here are export seconds. Most clerks speak English. Bargaining is necessary. Many Western fast-food restaurants have popped up here as well, so it's possible to go from one to the other without thinking about the delicious Korean food on the back streets. Use city bus no. 23, or Noksapyeong or Itaewon Station on subway line #6.

For related food, transportation, accommodation, attraction, and general tourist information online about the Itaewon Special Tourism Zone, see www.itaewon.go.kr.

SEOUL'S PRINCIPAL MARKETS

Its principal markets are outstanding features of Seoul. Covering huge areas, these multi-story hives of thousands of shops are stitched together by alleys and/or aboveground walkways. Nearly everything that you'd ever want to buy (and more) can be found in one or another of these markets. Shops generally open by 0800 and close about 2000; however, some shops are busiest in the wee hours of the morning when they cater to retailers and insomniacs. Every other Sunday is a holiday for most shopkeepers.

Dongdaemun Market 동대문시장

Adjacent to Dongdae-mun is Dongdaemun Market, the largest general market in the country. A four-level, several-square-block shopping complex, which includes the newer and taller Dongdaemun Chain Store section closest to the old

© ROBERT NILSEN

Full of art galleries, art shops, and antique stores, Insa-dong is one of the most well-known shopping districts in Seoul and is also a good place to eat and have traditional tea.

city gate, this complex has been operating since the early 1970s. It's enormous, a real rabbit's warren of shops, and most activity takes place inside and not on the street. Among other items, you'll find silks and other fabrics, clothing, leather goods, bags, bedding, carpets, towels, household goods, furniture, crafts, ceramic ware, china, and food. Bargaining is expected and necessary. The Dongdaemun Market is closed every first and third Sunday of the month. Almost an extension of the Dongdaemun Market is the Gwangjang Market, which runs farther west. It's older, having been established around 1910 as a market for barter between merchants of agricultural and other products from the country and those of the city. In this area are appliances and tools, camping equipment and army surplus items, a plethora of odds and ends, seafood, vegetables, grains, and dozens of ordinary restaurants.

Farther on, in the alleys of Yeji-dong, are shops selling jewelry, loose precious stones, watches, and cameras. Both foreign and domestic items can be found here. When buying precious stones, ask for a certificate of authentication. With watches and cameras, request the manufacturer's warranty. Some fakes and reproductions circulate through this market so be watchful. Almost across the street, the Jongmyo Jewelry Department Store has several dozen more shops. In the other direction from the city gate is a series of multi-story buildings that hold the Dongdaemun Shoe Market. Although these markets have sprung up in the 20th and 21st centuries, this has been an area for merchants since the mid-Joseon Dynasty, when Jong-no was *the* commercial street for the city.

New and used (mostly Korean) books are stuffed into shops lining the opposite side of Cheongyecheon-no from Dongdaemun Market. Above these and down the street are the clothing shops of the Pyeonghwa, Shin Pyeonghwa, Dong Pyeonghwa, and Cheong Pyeonghwa markets, which sell ready-made clothes (both brand-name and off-brand), shoes, and accessories. These markets, in association with other independent markets that stretch east down Cheongyecheon-no all the way to the Hwanghak-dong flea market, make the largest collection of clothing shops in the country. Behind these shops are numerous others, including sporting goods stores that are located mostly in the vicinity of Dongdaemun Stadium.

Namdaemun Market 남대문시장

To the east of Namdae-mun is the city's second-largest market, Namdaemun Market. Smaller than Dongdaemun Market, it's still as complex an array of separate and interconnecting buildings and alleys. Here, much of the activity takes place in the street. Wholesalers come in the wee hours of the morning (from 0200) to drop off goods ready to be sold when retailers and the general public begin to arrive about daybreak. Featured here are ready-made clothes, shoes, clothing accessories, eyeglasses, handbags, luggage, jewelry and watches, household furnishings, kitchenware, lacquerware, camping equipment, foodstuffs, seafood, flowers, stationery, wrapping paper, and imported goods. Outside the shops, vendors wheel huge carts into the already crowded alleys, stand up on them, and hawk the goods that lie at their feet. Numerous restaurants have stalls here and there. At the edge of this market, directly across the rotary from the city gate, is the Korean Handicraft Direct Sales Market, which sells only inspected craft items at reasonable rates.

Streetside moneychangers—usually middle-aged women hanging about with large purses clutched to their chests—also operate in the market. One of their favorite haunts is the alley next to a bank, across the street from the Bank of Korea! They exchange both ways, usually at close to the bank rate. These transactions are totally illegal. This clandestine money market is occasionally cleared out by the authorities, but it always resurfaces after the heat dies down.

DEPARTMENT STORES AND ARCADES
Department Stores

In the past, department stores have clustered in and near Myeong-dong. Recently, others have been built in newer sections of the city. They're little different from Western versions, except in a few of their goods and services—how often does

Sears line up salespeople at opening and closing hours to bow to customers as they enter or depart? Unlike their Western cousins, and in a manner similar to their Japanese counterparts, many Korean department stores have restaurants on one or more upper levels, and a supermarket selling food items on the basement level. Store hours are generally 1000–1930. Most are closed one day a week, but each on a different day.

Started in the 1930s and located opposite the Central Post Office, Shinsegae is the oldest department store in continuous operation and is still going strong. The Saerona, Metro Midopa, Lotte, and Printemps department stores are all within a few minutes' walk from Shinsegae. Others north of the river are the Samsung Plaza near Namdaemun, Hyundai Department Store in Shinchon, and Midopa and Lotte near Cheongnyangni Station. South of the river are many others including Shinsegae and Lotte in Yeongdeungpo; Yeouido on Yeouido; Hyundai, Galleria, and New Core in Seocho-gu and Gangnam-gu; Lotte in Jamshil; and Shinsegae in Cheonho-dong.

Duty-Free Shops

A handful of duty-free shops in Seoul handle imported luxury goods and select Korean items, many of which are heavily taxed on the Korean market, if available at all. Goods bought at the KNTO airport duty-free shop are taken directly out of the country. Articles bought in the city are delivered to your port of exit, to be picked up when you leave. Those shops in the city are Donghwa Duty-free at the Gwanghwa-mun intersection, Han Jin Duty-free at the KAL Building, Pungjun Duty-free south of Jong-myo, and duty-free shops in the Silla, Lotte, Lotte World, and Sheraton Walker Hill hotels.

Arcades

Arcades in Seoul come in several varieties: hotel arcades, office-building arcades, aboveground arcade complexes, and underground arcade corridors. Clothing, athletic goods, handicrafts, antique reproductions, electronic goods, ginseng, and jewelry are commonly sold. Most are open 1000–2200 daily. Major hotels have a small group of shops for use principally by hotel guests.

Several large office buildings, such as the Daewoo, Samsung, and Dongbang buildings have arcades. Independent arcades include the Shinsegae Arcade next to the Chosun Hotel; the four-block-long, multi-story arcade stretching from Jong-no to Toegye-ro; and the express-bus terminal arcade. Perhaps the most extensive are the underground arcades. Built under major thoroughfares in crowded downtown areas and at many subway stops, they are long corridors of tiny cubicle shops.

Similar to the underground arcades but on a much larger scale is the COEX Mall at the World Trade Center; www.coexmall.com. With its dozen sections and hundreds of shops, everything from fashion to food can be found here. The Kimchi Museum and COEX Aquarium are located here, and the COEX convention center, Korea World Trade Center, City Air Terminal, Hyundai department store, the Marriott and the COEX Intercontinental hotels are connected.

Handicraft Shops

While numerous shops and arcades around town offer Korean handicraft items, three in particular display and sell a wide variety of high-quality goods from excellent craftsmen and give you a quick overview of many traditional Korean products. In the center of the city is the Cultural Property Artisans Hall in the basement level KNTO Tourist Information Office. The National Souvenir Center (한국관광명품점) in Myeong-dong is next to the Seoul Royal Hotel. In Gangnam, look for the Important Intangible Cultural Properties Hall (인간문화재작품전시관) gallery, located next to Hotel New World, just around the corner from Seolleung Park. In addition, Mastercrafts, a shop that carries traditional items made only by nationally designated Korean artisans, is located in Itaewon, east of, but on the opposite side of the street from, the Itaewon Hotel. See www.mastercrafts.net.

SPECIALTY MARKETS

Antiques: With the crunch for space in Insadong, antique dealers had to shop for other space to sell their wares. Many relocated to (or established new businesses in) **Janghanpyeong** (장한평시장), which is located east of Dongdaemun and north of Hanyang University. About 150 shops in three main buildings here sell all sorts of antiques, but as opposed to fine art antiques that you might find in Insa-dong, here you find lots of furniture and household goods. Some people have come to regard this market as a "warehouse" area. Locate this complex by the many stone objects that crowd the sidewalk along the main drag. Open daily 1000–2000, except for the first and third Sunday of every month. These antique shops are surrounded by auto parts stores and repair shops. Use city bus no. 59 or express bus no. 959. The market is located between the Dapshimni Station and Janghanpyeong Station on subway line #5.

Herbs: Down the street to the west of Cheongnyangni Station is the **Gyeongdong Market** (경동시장), the city's principal market for herbs and herbal medicines, nuts, roots, and spices. Many herbal-medicine doctors have offices in the surrounding streets, and the alleys are full of herbal medicine pharmacies. Other shops turn bulk dry ingredients into liquid tonics for a small fee. The market is full of color and aroma, and the senses are tickled by a walk through it. This market was established in 1960, so unlike Yangnyeong Shijang in Daegu, it is not a traditional herbal market—yet a bountiful market nonetheless. To its side is an equally eye-pleasing fruit, vegetable, and ginseng market, open 0900–1900 daily except every third Sunday. Use the Jegidong Station on subway line #1, city bus no. 38, 134, or 302, or express bus no. 720.

Musical Instruments: A multi-story arcade on the edge of Insa-dong, the **Nakwon Arcade** has a multitude of shops selling all sorts of musical instruments. Traditional Korean instruments are also found in numerous shops along Jongno 3-ga.

Electronics: A group of nearly two dozen buildings behind the Yongsan Station, collectively called the **Yongsan Electronics Market** (용산전자상가), contains all sorts of consumer electronic goods, including computers and accessories, audio equipment, radios and televisions, home appliances, wires, parts, and tools. Open 0900–1900 except the first and third Sun-

day of each month. Yongsan Station on subway line #1 is closest. Rivaling the Yongsan Electronics Market, but inclusive in one large building, is **Techno-Mart** (테크노마트). Located across the road and subway line from the Dong Seoul Bus Terminal, this market offers a full selection of all the latest electronic, computer, and telecommunication equipment. The Gangbyeon Station on subway line #2 is out front.

Buddhist Paraphernalia: Shops along the street in front of Jogye-sa sell Buddhist images, clothing, music, and other such items. A number of shops along Jong-no also specialize in these items.

Flea Market: Seoul's flea market is the **Hwanghak-dong Market** (황학동시장). Second-hand goods, reconditioned appliances, antiques, cheap imports, giveaways, treasures, and junk can all be had here. A walk through this market provides insight into what older Korean items were like and what was used in days past. Open every day from mid-morning to mid-evening.

Agricultural Markets: A few steps from the flea market, the **Jungang Market** sells mostly agricultural products and was the city's major agricultural market before the creation of the Garak Integrated Wholesale Market. Use the Shindang Station on subway lines #2 and #6, or the Dongmyo Station on subway line #6 for both markets. Back into town a ways is the **Jungbu Market,** where dried fish, dried seafood, other dried sea products, and some agricultural products are sold. Use Uljiro 4-ga Station on subway line #2 or #5.

Moran Market: Although outside of Seoul, the Moran Market in Seongnam city is one of the largest open-air, "five-day" markets in the country, with an incredible amount of goods available. This market runs on days that end in the numbers 4 and 9. Use the Moran Station on subway line #3.

Wholesale Markets

Noryangjin Susan Market (노량진수산시장), a wholesale fish and seafood market, satisfies much of the city's needs. Merchants and housewives arrive in the early morning hours to get the freshest catch. Prices are lower than at neighborhood

SEOUL

markets. Fresh agricultural and seafood products are handled at the huge **Garak Integrated Wholesale Market** (가락동농수산물종합도매시장) in southeast Seoul. Here too the activity starts long before sunrise, when merchants and entrepreneurs from all over the city come to get the best that the earth and sea offer. Livestock is bought and sold at the **Dongmajang Market** (동마장시장), north of Hanyang University. Use the Noryangjin Station on subway line #1 for the Noryangjin seafood market, the Garak Market Station on subway line #8 for the integrated market, and the Majang Station on subway line #5 for the livestock market.

Supermarkets

Korean supermarkets are a relatively new phenomenon. Like their Western counterparts, they are the modern extension of the corner grocery store, well-stocked with canned and packaged goods, along with some fresh fruit, produce, fish, and meat. One of the first in the city was the Hannam Supermarket, east of Itaewon near Danguk University. Now they are found in all corners of the city. As with the grocery stores, Kim's Club, Wal-Mart, and other such wholesale and discount superstores can now be found around the city.

Information

M

SEOUL

TOURIST INFORMATION

Korean National Tourism Organization

Tourist information is available from the well-trained and knowledgeable staff at the KNTO Tourist Information Center in the basement level of the KNTO Building in Da-dong. Open 0900–2000, it provides tourist information for Seoul and the entire country, and an abundant variety of maps and brochures. If calling by phone, just dial 1330 within the city for a bilingual operator. The Korea Travel Bureau travel desk at the center can make in-country transportation reservations. Korean films are periodically screened in the auditorium and a computer room has been set up for the free use of guests. Detailed information about many of the country's major tourist sites is also available on computer in Korean and English, and you can request a printout of any information in the computer files. Check out the KNTO website at www.visitkorea.or.kr. The KNTO also staffs tourist-information counters at the City Air Terminal at Gimpo Airport and at Incheon International Airport.

While in Seoul, tourist-related complaints or compliments should be addressed to the KNTO Tourist Complaint Center (tel. 02/735-0101).

Seoul City Tourist Information Center

The Seoul City Tourist Information Center (tel. 02/3707-9470) is conveniently located on the 2nd floor of the Seoul City Hall building, just inside and up the steps from the front door. It's open Monday–Saturday 0900–1800; closed Sunday and national holidays. Helpful staff members answer questions, and if they don't have specific information on hand they'll make every effort to track it down for you. Useful maps, brochures, select newsletters and tourist magazines, and free Internet access are available. The city also runs tourist-information booths at the express-bus terminal, at both ends of Insa-dong, at Dongdaemun, at the entrance to Myeong-dong, in front of Deoksu-gung, and down from the Hamilton Hotel in Itaewon.

Tourist information about Seoul can now be accessed electronically, too. Visit Seoul's home page at www.metro.seoul.kr. See also www.visitseoul.net for additional tourist and cultural information.

Subway Information Center

The Seoul subway corporation runs an information center in the Gwanghwamun Station on line #5 for travel-related questions, particularly for those relating to subway travel, subway stations, and the areas around the subway stations.

BOOKS

Seoul's best selection of English-language books about Korea is at the **Royal Asiatic Society (RAS).** The RAS office (tel. 02/763-9483) is in room 611 of the Korea Christian Building, up from Jongno 5-ga. Its hours are Monday–Friday 1000–1200 and 1400–1700. If they don't carry a particular book on Korea, it's probably not available in-country. Many of these books are also found in the foreign-language book sections at large Korean bookshops in the city. Imported foreign-language magazines are also stocked. Store hours may vary, but most are open 1000–2100 daily except some holidays. The **Kyobo Book Center,** in the basement of the Kyobo Building at the Gwanghwa-mun intersection, has one of the largest selections. Other major book dealers that handle large numbers of foreign-language books are the **Chongno Book Center** (5th and 6th Floor), on Jong-no near the Jonggak intersection; the basement-level **Young Poong Books,** across from the KNTO building on Cheongyecheon-no; **Ulji Book Center,** located on the subway level at the Ulji-ro/ Namdaemun-no intersection; and **Pan Korea Book Company,** up Sinmun-no near the Salvation Army Center. South of the river, try **Bandi and Luni's** in the COEX Mall. Smaller bookshops generally have a tiny selection of English-language books and magazines, if they handle any at all; more often they carry a larger selection of Japanese- and Chinese-language books. Hotel bookshops also carry a select few foreign-language books and magazines.

Seoul Selection stocks books on Korea by foreign writers and translations of Korean works of literature and academic subjects. This store also carries DVDs and music CDs, serves coffee, hosts art shows, shows subtitled Korean movies three nights a week, has reservation numbers for nearby restaurants, ticket information for upcoming cultural events, and puts out a weekly newsletter with items of interest to foreign travelers. Seoul Selection (tel. 02/734-9564), www.seoulselection.com, is located across from the southeast corner of Gyeongbok-gung in the basement level of the Korean Publishers Association Building. The proprietor speaks English.

Major hotel kiosks and some newsstands in the center of the city carry the two English-language dailies, *The Korea Times* and *The Korea Herald,* plus a growing number of foreign newspapers and magazines.

MAPS

The best tourist maps of Seoul are printed by the KNTO and the Seoul Metropolitan Government. These maps are available for free at the KNTO and city information centers, airport information desks, and streetside information booths. Also available for free are the *Monthly Guide Map: Escort Seoul,* published by Unicom. Issued by various governmental agencies and private companies are maps with certain themes, such as shopping and nightlife or entertainment and cultural experiences, or with a concentration on a certain area of the city, like Myeong-dong, Insa-dong, or Itaewon. Major bookstores also carry tourist maps of the city and the country, but these you must buy. Bookstores also carry a variety of detailed street maps of the city and road map atlases of the entire country.

Services

Post Offices

Of the dozens of post offices in Seoul, perhaps the most useful to the traveler are the **Central Post Office (C.P.O.),** on the edge of Myeong-dong, the **Gwanghwamun Post Office,** at the southeast corner of the Gwanghwa-mun intersection, and the **Itaewon Post Office,** which is toward the western end of the main drag. Post office hours are Monday–Friday 0900–1800 (0900–1700 during winter) and Saturday 0900–1300. The C.P.O. has special night hours for stamp sales only: Monday–Friday until 2200, and Saturday, Sunday, and holidays until 1800. Major post offices in the city and around the country offer free Internet access for visitors.

Open regular postal hours only, the Seoul **Poste Restante** is on the 3rd floor of the C.P.O. This office keeps a written record of all letters and packages received, and their date of arrival; you must sign to pick up each piece of mail. The poste restante keeps mail for one month, but may extend that if you make a personal request. Much busier in the past, the poste restante seems to be getting less business since the advent of email. The engaging Postal Museum is on the 4th floor of this building, and the Philatelic Society is on the 5th floor.

Telecom Offices

To purchase an international telephone card, make an international phone call, or send a telegram or telex, visit the Telecommunications Authority building at Gwanghwa-mun.

Internet Access

Free Internet access is available at the KNTO tourist information center and the Seoul city tourist information office at city hall. Major post offices also have computers available for free Internet access. A number of accommodations that basically cater to budget travelers have computers set up for their use, most often at a nominal fee, and virtually all hotels offer Internet use, either in-room or at their business center. A growing number of Internet cafés charge a nominal fee, perhaps ₩1,500 for 30 minutes, but these fees vary.

Seoul Immigration Office

The Seoul Immigration Office (tel. 02/650-6234), located west of Yeouido in Yangcheon-gu, is open regular business hours. There is an in-town immigration office (tel. 02/732-6215) on the 5th floor of the Jeokseon Building behind the Central Government Complex building near Gyeongbok-gung. Additionally, the immigration office at the Incheon International Airport (tel. 032/740-7311) can be approached for questions.

Medical

About 60 percent of the country's hospitals are in Seoul. Major hospitals have English-speaking doctors. Hotels have house doctors, but for other travelers the following clinics can be recommended for medical emergencies: Severance Hospital International Clinic (tel. 02/361-6540), which is associated with Yonsei University; Kangbuk Samsung Hospital International Clinic (tel. 02/723-2911) near Gyeonghui-gung; Hannam-dong International Clinic (tel. 02/790-0857) in Itaewon; Gangnam St. Mary's Hospital (tel. 02/590-1114) at the Catholic Medical University near the Express Bus Terminal; and the Seoul Central Hospital (tel. 02/2224-3114) near Olympic Park.

Banks

Seoul has several dozen domestic and foreign banks. Most exchange foreign currency. A few are listed here; others can be located through the tourist information offices. Korean banks include Korea Foreign Exchange Bank, Korea First Bank, Chohung Bank, Hanvit Bank, and Seoul Bank. Foreign banks include American Express Bank, Chase Manhattan Bank, Citibank, Standard and Chartered Bank, Banque Nationale de Paris, Deutsche Bank A.G., Dai-Ichi Kangkyo Bank, the Hong Kong and Shanghai Banking Corporation, Development Bank of Singapore, Arab Bank, and the Indian Overseas Bank.

Transportation

Seoul is Korea's major transportation center. Gimpo Airport, on the western edge of the city, is its domestic airport. Until 2001, it was Korea's primary entry point and the largest of the country's international airports. In that year, the new and much larger Incheon International Airport opened for service and is now the country's major international port of entry for air traffic. Radiating from the city are two major and three minor rail lines. Three major expressways head down country, one rings the city, and others connect to them. Much more numerous are the highways that connect the capital to the entire country. Across the asphalt maze overlying this metropolis, more than 8,000 city buses race to their destinations, 50,000 taxis vie for riders, and over two million cars jockey for position. Partially burrowed underneath and partially aboveground, the extensive subway system runs eight lines through the city, with a ninth under construction.

BY AIR
Incheon International Airport
인천국제공항

Located some 50 kilometers west of Seoul on an island off the port city of Incheon is the country's new 24 hour international airport (www.airport.or.kr). Capable of handling the largest of planes, and a much larger volume of passengers than the Gimpo Airport, the Incheon International Airport not only boosts access to Korea for international travelers but also acts as a new "hub" for Northeast Asian air travel. Sleek and modern, the terminal is visually appealing, works well, and seems to have plenty of space to grow. The first level has baggage claim and customs, entry and immigration are above on the second level. The third level has ticket booths, departure lounges, and shops, while on the 4th floor mezzanine you'll locate Korean, Japanese, Chinese, and Western restaurants, and the Air Garden transit hotel. With 90 rooms, the hotel rates run ₩44,000–77,000 for six hours. The hotel also has several lounges, a business center, a game room, and meal and snack service. Outside of customs you'll find numerous money exchange counters, tourist information desks, telephones, bathrooms, snack and gift shops, a pharmacy, cellular phone rental booths, and counters to arrange transportation into Seoul or to other nearby cities. Inside the departure area are additional shops, including duty-free shops. Kiosks, restrooms, telephones, gift shops, money exchange booths, a lost and found office, post office, medical center, and information booths are located throughout the terminals building. Banks at the airport can exchange about 18 major world currencies, and those outside customs give a slightly better rate than those inside the customs area. The KNTO tourist information booth is open daily 0700–2200 and has general information, maps and brochures. The staff can arrange accommodations in Seoul and transportation to the city. For those leaving the country, the airport use fee, called a passenger service charge (P.S.C.), is ₩25,000 for Korean and ₩17,000 for foreigners. Pay this fee at any of numerous booths throughout the airport prior to entering the departure area. Be sure to save enough Korean *won* to pay for this fee so that you don't have to change any more money at the airport. Check-in for departure can also be done at the Korea City Air Terminal in Gangnam and at the old international terminal building at Gimpo Airport. There are good transportation connections from both locations to the Incheon Airport. Luggage storage at the airport is in the departure area; packing of items that cannot go into the plane as is can also be arranged at these shops. Storage rates per day run ₩5,000–8,000 for a backpack, ₩2,000 for a small bag, and ₩4,000 for a carry-on size bag. While there are only a few scheduled domestic flights out of this airport, more may be scheduled in the future to allow easy transfer to major domestic destinations. For those who need to transfer to flights that do not leave from the Incheon International Airport, both Asiana and KAL offer limousine bus service to the Gimpo Airport and express buses also transfer passengers for ₩4,000. Short-term and long-term parking lots are located to the front of the terminal building. Short-term parking runs ₩1,200 for 30 minutes and ₩600 for every 15 minutes after that.

Getting to and from the Incheon Airport: Until the rail connection between the Incheon International Airport and downtown Seoul is finished, bus transportation is the most convenient for the price. Buses generally require about one hour or a bit more during heavy traffic. Taxis are also available, but much pricier. Regular taxis charge ₩35,000–40,000 to get into the city or to the Gangnam area; deluxe taxis run ₩60,000–65,000. A multitude of very comfortable and convenient buses run into Seoul, to Incheon, and to other cities in the surrounding Gyeonggi-Do province. Get information and buy tickets for these buses at the transportation counters on the first floor of the terminal building. Buses leave from outside on this level. A few options are as follows. The KAL Airport buses (₩10,000) run four routes into the city that connect most major hotels; they operate approximately 0600–2100. Airport Limousine buses (₩10,000), operating 0530–2130, connect the airport with Seoul Station, the Gangnam Express Bus Terminal, and Itaewon. Express buses that run between the Incheon and Gimpo airports charge ₩4,000. Express city buses (₩5,000) also run on various routes between the city and the airport from 0430 until 2200 or later. Bus no. 600 runs to Gimpo Airport and various locations in the Gangnam and Jamshil areas; no. 601 passes city hall, Jong-no, and Dongdaemun; no. 602 goes to Gwanghwa-mun, Dongdaemun, and Cheong-nyangni Station; nos. 604, 606, and 609 run along various routes in Gangnam and Jamshil; no. 605 goes to Gwanghwa-mun and city hall.

City Air Terminals

Located at the Korea World Trade Center complex south of the Han River, the **Korea City Air Terminal** (KCAT) (도심공항터미날) opened in the early '90s to provide air passengers an in-town facility for domestic and international departure and baggage check-in formalities. Ticketing and baggage check are all taken care of at KCAT, as well as customs formalities for international passengers. From this facility, shuttle buses takes passengers to both the Gimpo and Incheon airports. For international passengers, there is a passport-control booth at the Incheon Airport especially reserved for KCAT shuttle passengers' use. Taking about one hour, this bus (₩10,000) departs from KCAT every 5–10 minutes 0600–2050. Not all airline have booths there, so call the KCAT information line (tel. 02/551-0077) or individual airline offices to make sure your carrier does. The city air terminal is most convenient for those staying in the southern and eastern sections of the city.

Built for the '88 Olympics, terminal #2 at the Gimpo Airport, otherwise called the **City Air Terminal,** is now also used for international flight and baggage check-in. Here you'll find check-in counters, a tourist information desk, a few snack shops, and departure for shuttle buses that run directly to the Incheon International Airport. This terminal is largely empty, but there are plans that call for this building to be put to a variety of other uses in the future, including restaurants, a shopping mall, and arts and entertainment venues.

The advantages of using these two locations include beating the crowds, having your baggage taken care of, use of a dedicated immigration control line, and a 50 percent discount on your airport use fee.

Gimpo Airport 김포공항

Located 18 kilometers west of downtown Seoul

is Gimpo Airport. With its upward sweeping roof, the domestic terminal was originally built as the country's first modern international terminal building. Remodeled and reopened as the new domestic terminal in late 2001, it has all the requisite amenities. The domestic terminal, the old domestic terminal building, and the City Air Terminal are connected by free shuttle buses that stop outside the lower levels.

Korea's extensive domestic air system is centered in Seoul, and it's serviced by both Asiana Airlines and Korean Air. Domestic flights connect Seoul to 13 provincial cities. Daily commuter flights to Busan leave about every 30 minutes 0640–2040. Spaced throughout the day 0700–2040, there are more than three dozen daily flights to Jeju. Roughly 18 times a day, flights go to Daegu and Ulsan. Gwangju, Yeosu, Pohang, and Jinju see about a dozen flights every day; while Sokcho, Gangneung, Mokpo, Yecheon, and Gunsan have less than half a dozen each.

The domestic airlines allow up to 15 kg free baggage, plus a small carry-on bag. Your passport is needed to purchase a ticket and tickets must be presented to board. With round-trip tickets, reconfirm your return at least 24 hours before departure time. For reservations, call Asiana Airlines (tel. 02/669-3114, 02/1588-8000) or Korean Air (tel. 02/751-7691, 02/1588-2001). Tickets can be purchased at airport ticket counters, any airline office in the country, or from travel agents. Pick up easy-to-decipher domestic air schedules—printed partially in English —at the airport, airline offices, or tourist-information offices in the city if you're planning an in-country flight.

Getting to and from Gimpo Airport: If you don't have someone picking you up or dropping you off at the airport, there are several ways to get between the airport and the city. Buses stop at the lower level of the domestic terminal. Generally, buses to Gimpo Airport from the heart of the city and the Gangnam area require 45–60 minutes. The KAL limousine bus service (₩5,000) operates on four separate routes about every 15 minutes 0600–2100 and these buses stop at the

Gimpo Airport on their routes to and from the Incheon International Airport and their various destinations in the city. Express city bus nos. 600, 601, and 603 (₩2,500) also run into town from the Gimpo Airport on their way to and from the international airport. Express city bus no. 63 runs to Gwanghwa-mun and city hall; no. 68 goes via Shinchon to Seoul Station and Myeong-dong; and no. 1002 runs via Yeouido to Gwanghwa-mun.

Perhaps the most convenient connection into the city is by subway. The Gimpo Airport Station on line #5 is located to the front of the air terminals and connects you with all parts of the city serviced by the subway system. Taxis also service the Gimpo Airport. Current fees to various destinations in the city for the two types of taxis are posted by the taxi stand. In general, a fare from the airport to the city center by regular taxi will be about ₩12,500 and to the Jamshil area about ₩20,000; by deluxe taxi, the fares are ₩17,500 and 29,000.

BY TRAIN
Stations
Seoul has two major train stations. Built in 1926, the Japanese colonial **Seoul Station** (서울역) (H.S. #284) is the major train station in the city and the busiest in the country. Although it was renovated and enlarged in 1989-1990, a new station is planned to open in 2003. You now enter on the right-hand side of the building and go up the stairs to the new lobby. Ticket windows, each designated by destination and class, are on your left. As this lobby is set over the tracks, the stairways to the platforms are to the side. Around the lobby are several restaurants, snack shops, coffee shops, and storage lockers, plus a travel information center. A bank and post office are located here as well. A number of the old waiting rooms have been turned into art galleries, and a small railroad museum is open in the old station building; ₩500 entrance.

About 120 trains a day run from Seoul Station to destinations to the south; only three a day run to the north. *Saemaul-ho, Mugunghwa-ho,* and *Tongil-ho* trains run south to Busan, Ulsan,

Pohang, Jinju, Masan, Dong Daegu, Suncheon, Yeosu, Gwangju, Mokpo, Janghang, and all points in between. To the north, two *Tongil-ho* trains (plus over a dozen more starting at the **Shinchon Station**) run to Munsan, and one a day (plus three more from the Shinchon Station) runs around the northern edge of the city to Uijeongbu. From **Uijeongbu Station,** over a dozen daily *Tongil-ho* trains run north to Shintan-ni. Uijeongbu Station can also be reached by subway from the center of the city on line #1.

Cheongnyangni Station (청량리역) is eight kilometers east of Seoul Station. From this, Seoul's second major train station, 20 *Mugunghwa-ho* and *Tongil-ho* trains run to Chuncheon. *Saemaul-ho, Mugunghwa-ho,* and *Tongil-ho* trains run 18 times a day south to Busan, Jecheon, Andong, and Gangneung. The staff at an information desk located in the station can provide assistance to foreign travelers.

Additional trains are put on line every weekend and several days before and after major national holidays in order to handle increased demand. Temporary ticket windows are erected on the front plazas outside the Seoul and Cheongnyangni stations before each major holiday to handle the increased volume.

Both the Seoul and Cheongnyangni train stations are stops on subway line #1. Seoul Station is also on subway line #4. The subway is the easiest way to get to these stations, but each is also serviced by a multitude of city buses. Among others, bus nos. 8, 20, 38, and 150, and express bus nos. 2 and 37 pass Seoul Station. For Cheongnyangni Station, use bus no. 38, 131, 134, or 302, or express bus no. 720.

Fares

Destinations (with fares) on the sleek *Saemaul-ho* include Busan (₩30,600), Gyeongju (₩27,800), Janghang (₩16,500), Gwangju (₩24,800), Mokpo (₩28,700), Yeosu (₩30,600), Andong (₩17,600), and Gangneung (₩24,700). Some *Mugunghwa-ho* routes are Chuncheon (₩4,700), Gangneung (₩17,000), Andong (₩12,100), Busan (₩21,000), Jinju (₩23,600), Dong Daegu (₩15,500), Gyeongju (₩18,300), Yeosu (₩21,000), Mokpo (₩19,800), and Janghang

(₩11,400). *Tongil-ho* fares are approximately two-thirds of the *Mugunghwa-ho* fares.

Tickets can be purchased at each station prior to boarding. There is usually no problem getting a ticket except on long weekends and holidays, when trains are packed and you must have a reservation to even think about riding. Tickets can also be purchased in advance at these stations. It's convenient to make train reservations and/or buy tickets at any of the city's many travel agents licensed to sell tickets. One of the most convenient is the KTB travel desk at the KNTO basement information center.

BY EXPRESS BUS

Frequent, comfortable, and affordable express buses connect Seoul to about 70 cities and towns throughout the country from three bus terminals. By far the majority run from the Gangnam Express Bus Terminal, with a dozen from the Dong Seoul Bus Terminal, and a half dozen from Seoul Sangbong Bus Terminal. As with the trains, no reservations are necessary except on long weekends and holidays, when it's best to buy ahead or you'll be left standing at the gate. The gigantic, pyramidal **Gangnam Express Bus Terminal** (강남고속버스터미날) has ticket windows on its 1st floor; buses depart from the sides. Although there is some overlap, buses leaving from the east side of the pyramid generally go to cities in southern Gyeonggi-Do, Chungcheong-buk-Do, Chungcheongnam-Do, Gyeongsang-buk-Do, and Gyeongsangnam-Do; buses from the newer terminal on the west side of the pyramid run to cities in eastern Gyeonggi-Do, Gangwon-Do, Jeollabuk-Do, and Jeollanam-Do. Buses from the Dong Seoul and Seoul Sangbong terminals go to the same destinations; those terminals are more convenient for the population in eastern and northeastern Seoul, and the ticket prices are virtually the same.

Departures at all stations are from ground level. Restaurants, coffee shops, snack bars, newsstands, and information booths are also located in the building. Commercial shops occupy the upper floors of the pyramid. Ticket windows post destinations, times of next departure, and fares; all seats are assigned. Buses also post their destinations and departure times in the window; nonetheless, make sure that you are on the correct bus because different bus companies run to the same routes. Most first departures are between 0600 and 0700; the last departure depends upon length of travel but most are before 2100. Buses run every 10–15 minutes for major destinations, every 20–60 minutes for the majority of destinations, and every one to two hours for others. Some only have a few buses a day. There are two types of buses, regular and first-class, and they are interspersed throughout the day. Both are fast and comfortable, but the first-class buses have fewer seats and more leg room. The cheapest fare from the Gangnam terminal is to Yongin (₩1,800), while the most expensive, with the longest run of 6.5 hours, is to Jindo (₩18,000). First-class bus tickets are about 40 percent more expensive.

Night buses to some 30 destinations also depart from the Gangnam terminal. Most depart 2200–2400. Half these destinations have only one bus, while the rest have multiple buses departing as late as 0200. These buses are of a slightly better class, and fares are about 10 percent more expensive than the first-class day fares.

To get to the Gangnam Express Bus Terminal, use the Express Bus Terminal Station on subway lines #3 and #7, or express city bus no. 37. Dong Seoul Bus Terminal sits next to the Gangbyeon Station on subway line #2. For Seoul Sangbong Bus Terminal, the Sangbong Station on subway line #7 is close; otherwise use city bus no. 302.

BY INTERCITY BUS

Intercity buses from four major and three small stations scattered throughout Seoul serve many more destinations than do express buses. While some routes overlap, buses from any one station generally service a specific section of the country. Running at regular intervals throughout the day, highway buses leave more frequently than express buses. Destination names, times of departure, and fares are all posted at each station, but mostly in Korean—it'll be good reading practice! These terminals generally do not have a

non-Korean information counter, but all have some sort of restaurant or snack shop.

Located near the Seoul Arts Center, the **Nambu Bus Terminal** (남부터미날) is the busiest. Buses from here run to southern Gyeonggi-Do, Chungcheongnam-do, southern Chungcheongbuk-Do, northern Jeollabuk-Do, and Gyeongsangnam-Do. Sample destinations and fares are Mallipo Beach (₩10,100), Onyang (₩4,200), Buyeo (₩9,400), Songni-san (₩10,300), and Jinju (₩20,500). To reach this station, use the Nambu Bus Terminal Station on subway line #3, or express city bus no. 42.

Dong Seoul Bus Terminal (동서울종합터미날) is nearly as busy as the Nambu Terminal. Buses to eastern Gyeonggi-Do, Gangwon-Do, northern Chungcheongbuk-Do, and Gyeongsangbuk-Do leave from here. Sample destinations and fares are Gangneung (₩10,000), Wonju (₩5,100), Yeoju (₩3,600), Cheongju (₩5,500), and Andong (₩16,700). This station is located near the Gangbyeon Station on subway line #2.

Sangbong Bus Terminal (상봉터미날) is located on the far eastern edge of the city. Buses from here service eastern Gyeonggi-Do and Gangwon-Do. Sample destinations are: Gangneung (₩13,900), Sokcho (₩14,200), Chuncheon (₩5,700), Wasu-ri (₩6,500), and Yongmunsa (₩4,800). Use express city bus no. 302, or the Sangbong Station on subway line #7.

Seobu Bus Terminal (서부터미날) is in the northwest corner of the city. Buses from here run north to Munsan and Uijeongbu. Selected destinations are Munsan (₩1,200), Bukhan Sanseong (₩600), and Uijeongbu (₩1,700). The Bulgwang Station on subway lines #3 and #6 is closest. Use city bus no. 154 or 156 or express bus no. 757.

One block south of the Shinchon rotary is the tiny **Shinchon Bus Terminal** (신촌정류장). Buses from here run only to the city of Gimpo, Ganghwa Island (₩3,700), and points on the island. The Shinchon Station on subway line #2 is closest.

The small **Yeokjeon Bus Terminal,** more like a bus stop, is located along the road just to the north of Seoul Station. Buses from here run to various spots in Incheon, including the Yeonan

M

SEOUL

passenger ferry terminal (₩3,300), and to the In-cheon International Airport (₩10,000). Use Seoul Station on subway line #1 or #4.

CITY BUSES

Seoul has an *extensive* city bus system, with over 350 routes. Buses crisscross this metropolis like ants on the march, handling over seven million riders every day. Unfortunately, the complexity of this network makes it difficult to master; persist, and it will become understandable.

There are three types of city buses: ordinary, express, and neighborhood. Most run from before 0500 to around midnight, and go most everywhere in the city. Some run out into the surrounding suburbs and countryside. There is no transfer option, so you pay for each individual ride. Bus colors are not standardized so you'll see many different combinations; however, the express buses just seem to look a little classier. The **ordinary city buses,** called *ilban* buses, come by every few minutes but don't stay long at each stop. During the day, ridership is down, but

rush-hour buses are as crowded as trays of fish at the market. You may have to run to the bus door and (occasionally) push to get on. Swiftly swerving from lane to lane and braking without warning, bus drivers race to their destinations. Hold on tight! Within the city limits, it's a flat fare of ₩600. Drop your coins into the collection box at the front of the bus as you get on. You can also use an electronic transportation card that is also good for the subway. Buy these at kiosks near bus stops and at subway ticket windows. Exit via the rear door. Drivers can make change for you if you don't have the exact fare.

Express city buses, called *jwaseok* buses, are more comfortable than ordinary city buses—everyone is supposed to have a seat. They run longer distances between stops and traverse the city more swiftly. The flat fare is ₩1,300. Deposit your fare in the collection box as you enter, or use your electronic transportation card. Most express buses have only one door, used both for entrance and exit, so wait until all riders get off before you get on. Deluxe express buses are much nicer. Many are commuter buses that connect

Seoul is crisscrossed by wide roads full of traffic.

the surrounding cities to the center of Seoul. At ₩1,500, fares are only marginally more expensive than express buses.

The **neighborhood buses** are called *maeul* buses. Mostly small shuttles, they run routes from neighborhood areas that are not serviced by the ordinary city buses to major thoroughfares or intersections. The fare is ₩350.

Some bus routes change periodically, particularly in the outlying areas of the city which are under development, so check with someone at the bus stop before boarding; most bus drivers do not speak English. To make matters worse, some buses vary one or more sections of their route. Unfortunately, there's no city bus map. However, the *Bus Route Booklet* (버스노선안내), available for ₩1,000 at streetside booths, lists all bus routes and most individual stops along each route for all city buses. Unfortunately again, it's printed only in Korean.

Convenient bus numbers have been included with the descriptions of most tourist sites in this book. What follows is a quick reference of buses that connect the Gwanghwa-mun, City Hall, and Seoul Station areas to selected city destinations. Although abbreviated, this list should prove helpful for getting around the city. (Express buses are shown in **bold**.)

Gimpo Airport: **63, 68, 130, 1002**

Incheon International Airport: **600, 601, 602, 604, 605, 606, 609**

Seoul Station: 8, 20, 38, 150, **2, 37**

Cheongnyangni Station: 38, 131, 134, 302, **720**

Gangnam Express Bus Terminal: **37**

Seobu Bus Terminal: 154, 156, **757**

Sangbong Bus Terminal: 302

Itaewon: 23

Yeouido: 53, **720**

Nam-san: 83-1

Daehang-no: 25

Gyeongbok-gung: 6, 8, 205

Changdeok-gung, Biwon: 6, 8, 20, 205

Changgyeong-gung: 6, 8, 20, 84, 205, 710

Dongnim-mun: 146, 150, 158, **72, 158**

Jong-myo: 5-1, 30, 38, 53, 131

Mun-myo: 6, 8, 84, 85, 710

Dong-myo: 30, 38, 131

Jeoldusan Martyrs' Shrine and Foreigner's Cemetery: 129, 131

Sajik Park: 150, 158, **158**

Nam-san Park: 83-1

Korea House and Man-san Hanok Village: 6

Jangchungdan Park and National Theater: 154

Yongsan Park: 81-1, **797**

Early Baekje tombs: **41**

War Memorial Museum: 23, 81

Seoul Art Center: **42**

Bomun-sa: 23, 32

Hwagye-sa: 25, 84

Bongeun-sa, COEX: **37**

Doseon-sa: 6, 8

Bukhan Sanseong National Park: 156 to the west entrance; 154, 155 to the Jin'gwan-sa entrance; 8, 135, to the south side Pyeongchang-dong entrances; 136-1 Gugi Tunnel area; 1, 3, 710 to the Jeong-neung entrance; 84 to the Hwagye-sa entrance; 6, 8, 23 to Uidong; and **2** to Dobong-san

Namhan Sanseong Provincial Park: **45**

Gwanak-san: 51 to the north side and Seoul National University; **797** to the east side and Gwacheon; and 103 from Shinchon to the south side and Anyang Yuwonji

Geumgok-neung, Donggu-neung: 165 from Cheongnyangni

Tae-neung: 45

Gwang-neung: 55-1 from Cheongnyangni

Heonin-neung: 36 from the Express Bus Terminal

Seoo-neung: 159

SUBWAY

Lines

City rail transportation started in 1899, when the first trolley line from Seodae-mun to Cheongnyangni was put into use; an electric trolley was started on Ulji-ro in 1912. Due to rapidly expanding bus service after the Korean War, however, trolleys were discontinued in 1968. Six years later, the first subway line started operation. Then 1983 saw the completion of the circular subway line #2, and lines #3 and #4 were put into service in 1985. The last of the current eight lines opened in 2001. The partially completed ninth line, the Bundang line, is to be finished by 2003.

Seoul was the third city in Asia to have an underground transportation system. With roughly 460 kilometers of track and over 350 stations, it's one of the world's longest systems. Through densely populated areas, tunnels have been burrowed through bedrock or tracks raised on elevated platforms. In outlying areas, lines shared with the national rail system run at ground level and extend as far as Incheon to the west, Suwon to the south, Ansan to the southeast, Uijeongbu to the north, Nowon-gu to the northwest, Seongnam city to the southeast, and Bundang, still farther south.

The subway network is color-coded for convenience. **Line #1** (dark blue) runs underground below Jong-no and Taepyeong-no between Seoul and Cheongnyangni train stations. It extends aboveground beyond both stations to Uijeongbu, Incheon, and Suwon. **Line #2** (green) is the 49-kilometer circular route that runs below Ulji-ro from city hall to Hanyang University, and circles around on the south side of the river before returning to city hall via Shinchon. Two short subsidiary lines connect Seongsu Station on this line with Shinseol-dong Station on line #1 and Shindorim Station with the Kkachisan Station on line #5. Cutting through the city from northwest to southeast, **line #3** (orange) tunnels through the mountains to reach downtown Seoul. There it plunges under the city center and ends its run at Suseo in the densely populated residential area south of the river. An extension of this line takes the subway along national rail lines to Daehwa in the northwest suburbs. **Line #4** (light blue) cuts across the city from the northeast to the southwest. Starting at the foot of Suraksan, it moves through the northeast periphery of Seoul. After cutting across the southern flank of the downtown area below Toegye-ro and skirting around Nam-san, it heads over the river to Namtaeryeong, where the national rail line picks up, passes Gwacheon, and continues through the provincial town of Ansan to Oido. In addition to these first four lines, an aboveground riverside **national rail line** starts at Yongsan Station and runs east along the Han River, joining

subway line #1 at Cheongnyangni Station. **Line #5** (purple) starts in the far west of the city and passes Gimpo Airport, Yeongdeungpo, and Yeouido before running up and through the center of the city. From there, it heads east and splits into two legs once it crosses the river at Gangdong. Staying completely north of the river, **line #6** (yellow ochre) makes a broad U-shaped circuit, running from the northwest, through Mapo and Itaewon, to the eastern residential areas. In a large reverse L-shape, **line #7** (olive), the longest at 87 kilometers, sweeps down the relatively new eastern residential sector of Seoul and shoots to the west after crossing the river, crossing the line to Suwon and meeting the line to Incheon at Onsu. **Line #8** (pink) operates in the southeastern corner of the city. It runs from Amsa-dong, down through Jamshil, and on to the city of Seongnam. When completed, the **Bundang line** (yellow) will run from Bundang, which is east of Suwon, up through Seongnam and central Gangnam, before crossing the Han River and meeting the national rail line near Wangshim-ni. In addition to these lines, Incheon subway line #1 crosses at Bupyeong Station and is connected there to the Seoul subway line that runs to downtown Incheon.

Each station is well marked by name (in Korean and English) and number. Schematic diagrams of the entire system are posted in each station and in each train car. Transfer points, indicated by three-color *taeguk* symbols, are at the intersections of lines. Exits are marked in yellow. Each station has maps that indicate station layout, including all subway exits, and area maps of the aboveground immediate vicinity are posted at each exit to help you orient yourself. Some of the newer lines were dug quite deep, so you'll have to go up or down several levels to exit or transfer.

On occasion, designated subway stations will play host to music and dance entertainment, performed during the afternoon on Friday, Saturday, and Sunday.

Particulars

Subway trains are swift, clean, and comfortable. Carrying up to three million passengers a day, cars are packed only during morning and evening rush hours. Although exact times differ with each line, the first trains generally leave their home station about 0530, the last cars about 2330 (2230 for the most distant stations). Trains run every four to six minutes through most of the system, and every three to four minutes during and rush hour. Those to Incheon, Suwon, and Uijeongbu, and from Yongsan to Seongbuk via the riverside rail line run every 3–12 minutes. A ride from Cheongnyangni Station to Seoul Station takes 15 minutes. From Seoul Station to Incheon, Suwon, Ansan, or Uijeongbu requires 50–60 minutes. To reach the opposite side of circular line #2 takes 45 minutes. A complete traverse of line #3, #4, #5, #6, or #7 runs 70–110 minutes. The shortest run, about 30 minutes, is on line #8.

Fares are based on zones and distances. The base fare is ₩600 within any zone or to connect with an adjacent zone. The fare rises to ₩700 to connect with a third zone, and increases from there by distance. Basically, to anywhere within the city limits will cost under ₩700. Fares from the farthest ends of the system into the city center run ₩1,000; the most expensive fares run ₩1,500 for rides from one distant terminus, through the city, to another distant terminus.

Purchase tickets at ticket windows in each station—state your destination clearly. Schematic maps of the subway system indicating destination names and fares are displayed at each stop above the ticket windows. Automatic machines also dispense tickets, and they too display a subway map with names and fares marked. One type of machine gives tickets for one and two zones only, the other type of machine dispenses tickets for all destinations. One-way and multiple-use tickets are available. Multiple-use tickets are available in ₩5,000, ₩10,000, and ₩20,000 values, and are perfect for riders who use the subway frequently. The ₩10,000 and ₩20,000 multiple-use tickets are discounted 10 percent for everyone, and 20 percent for students. Run your ticket through the turnstile machine and pull it out the far end. Hang onto it, as you'll need it to exit at your destination. One-way tickets are kept by the turnstile machine when you exit at your destination; multiple-use tickets will come out the other end.

When touched to an electronic pad, electronic tickets will have the fare electronically subtracted from your ticket's total value. If you get off at a point beyond which your ticket is valid, or use up the value of a multiple-use ticket, you must take it to an "Add Fare" machine. Insert your ticket, add the fare displayed by the machine, then retrieve and use the ticket to exit the station.

All stations are designed differently, often with artistic details that reflect the area in which it lies. Many stations have snack shops, photo booths, newspaper stands, paper money changing machines, benches, and an assortment of vending machines. Each station has several name signs written in Korean and English, giving the name of the station in bold letters and those in either direction in smaller letters (with arrows) below. Follow color-coded signs and arrows at transfer points. All important informational and directional signs are written in Korean and English. Each subway station is numbered, so this may be a help for those who do not read Korean. The first number indicates the line, while the following numbers indicate the exact station along that line. Some subway maps, but not all, list station numbers as well as names. At each station, announcements and digital displays indicate upcoming trains and destinations. A placard with the train's destination is displayed on the front and rear of each train. In-train announcements are given in Korean and English indicating the approaching station (some also have digital displays indicating the same), the following station, and which side of the car to exit. All train cars have line maps and system maps displayed over exit doors. The end seats in each car are reserved for the elderly and disabled; yield to them.

More information about the subway system can be found at www.seoulsubway.co.kr.

Stops

The extensive subway system makes it possible to reach many city sites and surrounding cities. Although the fare is the same as that of ordinary city buses, the subway is faster and cleaner. What follows are selected subway stations on each line, a few places of note near these stops, and transfer points.

Line #1

Uijeongbu: Uijeongbu City.

Dobong-san: Hiking trails and several temples of Dobong-san.

Cheongnyangni: Cheongnyangni (train) Station. Transfer to the riverside rail line.

Jegi-dong: Gyeongdong Market.

Dongdaemun: Dongdaemun Market. Transfer to line #4.

Jongno 3-ga: Jong-myo, Pagoda Park. Transfer to lines #3 and #5.

Jonggak: Pagoda Park, Insa-dong, Jogye-sa, KNTO

City Hall: City Hall Plaza, Seoul City tourist information office, Deoksu-gung, British Embassy, Myeong-dong, Gwanghwa-mun. Transfer to line #2.

Seoul Station: Seoul (train) Station, Nam-san. Transfer to line #4.

Namyeong: U.S.O.

Yongsan: Yongsan (train) Station, Yongsan Electronics Market. Transfer to riverside rail line.

Yeongdeungpo: Yeongdeungpo area.

Shindorim: Transfer to line #2.

Guro: Split for lines to Incheon and Suwon.

Incheon: West end of line #1. City and harbor.

Suwon: South end of line #1. City, Suwon Fortress.

Line #2

City Hall: Transfer to line #1.

Ehwa Women's University: Ehwa University and shopping district.

Shinchon: Yonsei University, Shinchon entertainment and shopping district. Shinchon Bus Terminal.

Hongdae Ipgu: Hongik University, entertainment, and shopping district.

Hapjeong: Jeoldusan Martyrs' Shrine, foreigners' cemetery.

Yeongdeungpo-gu Office: Transfer to line #5.

Shindorim: Transfer to line #1.

Daerim: Transfer to line #7.

Seoul National University: University, north entrance to Gwanak-san.

Sadang: Transfer to line #4.

Seoul National University of Education: Transfer to line #3.

Seolleung: Seolleung Park. Transfer to Bundang line.

Samseong: COEX, Korea World Trade Center, Bongeun-sa.

Sports Complex: Jamshil Sports Complex.

Jamshil: Lotte World Amusement Park, Seoul Nori Madang. Transfer to line #8.

Gangbyeon: Dong Seoul Bus Terminal, Techno-Mart.

Geonguk University: Transfer to line #7.

Wangshimni: Transfer to line #5 and the riverside rail line.

Shindang: Transfer to line #6.

Dongdaemun Stadium: Stadium, Dongdaemun Market. Transfer to lines #4 and #5.

Uljiro 3-ga: Transfer to line #3.

Uljiro 1-ga: Myeong-dong, KNTO.

Line #3

Bulgwang: Seobu Bus Terminal. Transfer to line #6.

Dongnimmun: Independence Gate and Park, Seodaemun Prison.

Gyeongbok-gung: Gyeongbok-gung, Sajik Park, Sejong Cultural Center.

Anguk: Insa-dong, Changdeok-gung and Biwon.

Jongno 3-ga: Transfer to lines #1 and #5.

Uljiro 3-ga: Transfer to line #2.

Chungmu-ro: Korea House, transfer to line #4.

Dongguk University: University, Changchung-dan Park, National Theater.

Yaksu: Transfer to line #6.

Oksu: Transfer to riverside rail line.

Apgujeong: Apgujeong shopping and entertainment area.

Express Bus Terminal: Express Bus Terminal. Transfer to line #3.

Seoul National University of Education: Transfer to line #2.

Nambu Bus Terminal: Nambu Bus Terminal, Seoul Arts Center.

Dogok: Transfer to the Bundang line.

Suseo: Transfer to the Bundang line.

Line #4

Danggogae and Sanggye: North end of line #4, Surak-san hiking trails.

Nowon: Transfer to line #7

Jangdong: Transfer to line #1.

Hyehwa: Daehang-no, Seonggyungwan University.

Dongdaemun: Dongdaemun Market. Transfer to line #1.

Dongdaemun Stadium: Transfer to line #2.

Chungmu-ro: Transfer to line #3.

Myeongdong: Myeong-dong entertainment and shopping district, Chinese Embassy, Central Post Office.

Hoehyeon: Namdae-mun Market, Nam-san.

Seoul Station: Seoul (train) Station. Transfer to line #1.

Samgakji: War Memorial Museum. Transfer to line #6.

Ichon: Yongsan Family Park, National Museum. Transfer to riverside rail line.

Isu: Transfer to line #7.

Sadang: Transfer to line #2.

Seoul Racecourse: Seoul Equestrian Park.

Seoul Grand Park: Seoul Grand Park.

Gwacheon: Gwanak-san hiking trails.

Government Complex-Gwacheon: National government offices.

Geumjeong: Transfer to line #1, south to Suwon and north into Seoul.

Ansan: Ansan City.

Line #5

Gimpo Airport: Gimpo Airport.

Omokgyo: Seoul Immigration Office.

Yeongdeungpo-gu Office: Transfer to line #2.

Shingal: Transfer to line #1.

Yeouido: Yeouido, National Assembly.

Yeouinaru: Yeouido Riverside Park, DLI 63.

Gongdeok: Transfer to line #5.

Chungjeongno: Transfer to line #2.

Gwanghwa-mun: Gwanghwa-mun, Sejong Cultural Center, American and Japanese Embassies.

Jongno 3-ga: Jong-myo. Transfer to lines #1 and #3.

Uljiro 4-ga: Transfer to line #2.

Dongdaemun Stadium: Transfer to lines #2 and #4.

Cheonggu: Transfer to line #6.

Wangshimni: Transfer to line #2 and the riverside rail line.

Janganpyeong: Antique market.

Gunja: Transfer to line #7.

Acha-san: Children's Grand Park back gate.

Cheonho: Transfer to line #8.

Olympic Park: Seoul Olympic Park back entrance.

Line #6

Bulgwang: Seobu Bus Terminal.

Hapjeong: Transfer to line #2.

Gongdeok: Transfer to line #5.

Samgakji: National War Museum. Transfer to line #4.

Itaewon: Itaewon entertainment and shopping district.

Yaksu: Transfer to line #3.

Cheongsu: Transfer to line #5.

Shindang: Transfer to line #2.

Dongmyo: Tong-myo.

Seokgye: Transfer to line #1.

Taeneung: Transfer to line #7.

Line #7

Dobong-san: Dobong-san hiking trails.

Surak-san: Surak-san hiking trails.

Nowon: Transfer to line #4.

Taeneung: Transfer to line #6.

Gunja: Transfer to line #5.

Children's Grand Park: Children's Grand Park front entrance.

Konkuk University: Konkuk University. Transfer to line #2.

Cheongdam: Cheongdam shopping and entertainment district, Cheongdam Park, Bongeun-sa.

Express Bus Terminal: Express Bus Terminal. Transfer to line #3.

Isu: Transfer to line #4.

Daerim: Transfer to line #2.

Garibong: Transfer to line #1 south to Suwon.

Onsu: Transfer to line #1 west to Incheon.

Line #8

Amsa: Amsa-dong prehistoric site.

Cheonho: Transfer to line #5.

Mongchontoseong: Olympic Park front entrance.

Jamshil: Lotte World Adventure. Transfer to line #2.

Garak Market: Garak Integrated Wholesale Market.

Bokjeong: Transfer to the Bundang line.

Sanseong: Catch bus here to Namhan Sanseong Fortress.

Namhan Sanseong: Catch bus here to Namhan Sanseong Fortress.

Shinheung and Sujin: Seongnam City.

Moran: Moran Market. Transfer to the Bundang line.

TAXIS

More than 50,000 taxis cruise the streets of Seoul and transport three million riders every day. Some designated taxi stands have been set up in the heart of the downtown area where you must queue for a ride. Still, most taxis pick up anywhere they're flagged down, as they do in the outlying areas of the city. Taxis seem most difficult to catch at rush hour, late in the evening, and during inclement weather. Make sure the ride is metered.

Regular taxis are mostly light-colored mid-size vehicles with lights on top. The basic fare is ₩1,600 for the first two kilometers. Deluxe taxis are black with a gold strip down the side and a yellow light on top. These charge ₩4,000 for the first 3 kilometers, and give receipts. No tipping is required. Taxi-vans are also in operation for up to nine passengers; these are perhaps best used when going to or from the airport with many people and/or lots of luggage. The rates for these vans are the same as for the deluxe taxis.

TOURS

Tour Companies

Many organized tours are available in English or Japanese (sometimes other languages) through city-sponsored or private tour companies for those who are short on time or leery about venturing into town on their own. These worry-free tours combine various sights of the city or focus on one particular site in the surrounding region. Numerous tours are available: morning, afternoon, evening, full-day, art and culture, entertainment, or other theme tours. Tours to locations outside the city are also given by these reputable companies. By and large, part-day tours run about ₩30,000, full-day tours ₩60,000–80,000, evening entertainment tours ₩70,000–100,000, and all others fall somewhere in between. For more information on these or other tours, contact the KNTO or Seoul city tourist information office, or the individual tour companies; some major hotels have tour desks. Several tour companies with long-standing reputations are the government-sponsored Korea Travel Bureau (KTB), tel. 02/778-0150, www.ktbonline.com; Global Tour, tel. 02/776-3153; Kim's Travel Service, tel. 02/572-9998; Star Travel, tel. 02/569-8114, www.startravel.co.kr; New Grace Tour, tel. 02/332-8946, www.newgrace.co.kr; and Hanhwa Tourmall, tel. 02/757-1232, www.goodmorningtours.com.

Seoul City Bus Tours

Daytime and evening bus tours on four somewhat distinct routes are offered 0900–2300 daily. These buses stop at a number of significant tourist attractions around the city, including Deoksu-gung, the War Museum, Itaewon, Namsan, Myeong-dong, Dongdaemun Market, Daehang-no, Changgyeong-gung, Changdeok-gung, and Gyeongbok-gung, as well as a number of deluxe hotels. Each route starts in front of Dongwha Duty-free shop near the Gwanghwa-mun intersection, and each stop is marked by a tall, narrow signpost. Tours start about every 30 minutes. Three of the routes require about two hours; the palace route is about an hour. You can get off and on at any stop that you want. The rate for daytime or evening rides is ₩8,000 per person, ₩15,000 for all-day use, or ₩25,000 for a two-day pass. Use of the bus from one stop to the next only runs ₩3,000. Guides accompany the bus and information about sights is broadcast in Korean, Japanese, and English. For information, stop by the starting point, call 02/777-6090, or visit www.seoulcitytourbus.com.

U.S.O.

The United States Service Organization (U.S.O.) (tel. 02/795-3028; 02/724-7003 military line), primarily set up to cater to the recreational and leisure activities of U.S. military personnel, also offers tours to the public. Their most popular tour is to Panmunjeom and they run various other tours to locations out of the city, but they also offer periodic evening shopping and entertainment tours throughout the month. For details on just what is scheduled when, stop by the U.S.O., across the street from the Yongsan U.S. Army Garrison's west gate, or see www.uso-center.org.

Royal Asiatic Society (RAS)

Except for short winter and summer breaks, RAS organizes daytime and some night tours to numerous sites in Seoul, and many down-country overnighters. For those in Korea for a short time, RAS tours are perhaps the best opportunity to learn about a specific topic of Korean culture or to visit a specific site. Although tours change periodically, tours offered within the city and the immediate surrounding area might include: a *bulgogi* dinner on the Han River; a *gut* (shaman ceremony); Buddha's birthday temple tour; markets of Seoul, Changdeok-gung, and Biwon; or a hike to Bukhan-sa National Park. These tours are conducted by experts, yet are casual and tend to be family-oriented. For more information, contact RAS (tel. 02/763-9483) or stop by their office on the 6th floor of the Christian Building, up from Jongno 5-ga.

Seoul Environs

ROYAL TOMBS

Burial practices and funerary rituals have long been an important cultural element for the Korean people. The preparation for interment, the ceremony itself, and the subsequent ancestor memorial ceremonies are serious affairs. The burials of kings and queens became significant events for the country as a whole as the selection of tomb sites, tomb construction, and the burial ceremonies developed into an art. No expense was spared for a proper funeral, and memorial services are still performed yearly.

Of 115 Joseon Dynasty royal tombs in existence, 105 of them are in South Korea. Nearly all are within 40 kilometers of the Seoul city center. While only one was constructed within the old city walls (now moved), several are encompassed within the current city boundaries. Most snuggle into the hills surrounding the city. The farthest from Seoul are the tombs of King Danjong, at Yeongwol in Gangwon-Do; King Sejong and King Hyojong, at Yeoju; King Jeongjo, south of Suwon; and King Jeongjong, near Gaeseong in North Korea.

There are three types of royal tombs: *neung*, *won*, and *myo*. Reserved for kings and queens, *neung* were the most elaborate. *Won* were for parents of kings and queens, and for crown princes and princesses. *Myo* were for the remaining royal family members. Principal tombs are open to the public daily, while a few are closed Monday. Although hours vary, most are open 0800–1800, with some open as early as 0600. Set on hills and surrounded by ancient trees, these tombs are places of historical and cultural importance that evoke feelings of respect, yet, curiously enough, they are often used as weekend picnic spots for family outings.

Tomb Sites

Royal tomb sites themselves were important for ensuring the good fortunes of the tomb's occupant in the afterlife, and they were carefully chosen by a geomancer well versed in the theories of geomantic selection known as *pung-su jiriseol*. In particular, all tombs were set on hillsides facing south, flanked by two ridges representing a blue dragon and white tiger, necessary signs for good fortune.

Although sites vary slightly, the following description provides a general understanding of Joseon Dynasty royal tombs. At the front are the tomb keeper's house and buildings used in preparation for gravesite ceremonies. Entrance to each tomb is by way of the *hongsal-mun* (red arrow

SEOUL

gate). Suspended between the two pillars of this open red gate is a spiked lintel, in the middle of which is set an *eum/yang* (yin/yang) medallion. To the right of this gate is a *banwi* (stone platform) once used by visitors to bow toward the grave before proceeding farther into the tomb area. From the *hongsal-mun* a stone pathway leads to a T-shaped building. Directly in front of the structure, the walk makes a right turn and an immediate left turn, ending on the right side of the building. This T-shaped pavilion is where the memorial ceremony takes place. To its right is a smaller building that houses a stone tablet inscribed with the name of and certain information about the tomb's occupant. To the rear of this is a water well and an incineration pit that's used to burn paper used in the memorial ceremony.

Set on a rise beyond is the tomb itself. About three meters high and nine meters across, the tomb mounds are faced with stone panels and ringed by a stone fence. A U-shaped retaining wall surrounds the mound on three sides, opening to the south. Around the mound, facing out, are stone figures of sheep and tigers. Positioned as protective devices, the tiger represents *yang* (strong, male force) and the sheep represents *eum* (weak, female force). To the front of the tomb is a low stone table set on four squat pedestals with grimacing demon faces carved on them. In front of this table stands an octagonal stone lantern, and flanking it are two *manjuseok* (stone poles) of unknown use, with squirrel-like animals carved into them. Guardians of the tomb, stone figures of civilian and military officials accompanied by their horses, stand to the front.

Geumgok-neung 금곡릉

Six kilometers east of the Seoul city limits is Geumgok-neung [Kŭmgok-nŭng] (H.S. #207). Here are the tombs of the last two Joseon Dynasty kings, Gojong (26th: reigned 1864–1907) and Sunjong (27th: reigned 1907–10). The most elaborate Joseon tomb, King Sunjong's, has some of the best examples of tomb stonework. The rows of stone guardians—greatly expanded, and patterned after the Imperial Ming Chinese tombs north of Beijing—are unique in Korea.

Flanking the walkway are two rows of nine figures. Closest to the tomb are civilian officials. Next come the military officials, followed by *haema* (mythical sea horse), elephants, lions, *haetae* (a mythical animal that eats fire), camels, and two pairs of horses. The figures at Gojong's tomb are a bit stilted, squarish and lifeless. In contrast, those in front of the tomb of King Sunjong are more skillfully rendered, life-like, evocative, and minutely carved in refined detail.

King Gojong was buried here in 1919, and his wife, the murdered Queen Min, was then moved here from her original grave at Hongneung, near Cheongnyangni. King Sunjong died in 1926. With him is buried his first wife, another Queen Min, and in 1966 his second wife, Queen Yun, was buried in the same mound. The last crown prince, Yeongjiwang, was buried in another compound nearby in 1970. To reach Geumgok-neung, take city bus no. 165 from Cheongnyangni Station.

Donggu-neung 동구릉

Donggu-neung [Tonggu-nŭng] ("East Nine Tombs"), H.S. #193, is a collection of nine tombs between Geumgok-neung and the city limits. This is the country's largest concentration of Joseon Dynasty royal tombs, representing various periods of the dynasty, including its first king, Taejo (reigned 1392–98), and King Heonjong, its 24th (reigned 1834–49). Others buried here are kings Munjong (fifth: reigned 1450–52), Seonjo (14th: reigned 1567–1608), Hyeonjong (18th: reigned 1659–74), and Yeongjo (21st: reigned 1724–76), and a prince and princess. Donggu-neung and Geumgok-neung are perhaps the best places to start an investigation of Joseon Dynasty tombs.

Between Geumgok-neung and Donggu-neung lies Sa-neung (H.S. #209), the tomb of Queen Jeongsun (wife of murdered King Danjong), and other royal family tombs.

Tae-neung 태릉

Just within Seoul city limits is Tae-neung [T'aenŭng] (H.S. #201). Here are the tombs of Queen Yun, the wife of King Jungjong (11th: reigned 1506–44), and her son, King Myeongjong (13th:

view over the tombs of King Heonjong and his two wives at Donggu-neung

reigned 1545–67). Although not open to the public, Gang-neung, the tomb of King Mun-jong's queen consort, is nearby. Take city bus no. 45 from Cheongnyangni or Seoul Station.

Gwang-neung 광능

The most picturesque tomb site is Gwang-neung [Kwang-nŭng] (H.S. #197). Graves of King Sejo (seventh: reigned 1455–68) and his wife, Queen Yun, lie in this national forest preserve north-east of the city, one of the few breeding grounds on the peninsula for the white-bellied Tristram's woodpecker (N.M. #11). Near Sejo's tomb is the temple Bongseon-sa. Its 2.5-meter-high bell was cast in 1469, and is said to be the third-largest bell in Korea. Many gardens and the Forestry Museum are within the National Arboretum here. To reach Gwang-neung, take bus no. 55-1 from Cheongnyangni Station, city bus no. 21 from Uijeongbu, or the intercity bus to Gwangneungnae from the Sangbong Bus Terminal.

Heonin-neung 헌인능

Near the southern boundary of the city is Heonin-neung [Hŏnin-nŭng] (H.S. #194). Set high on the hillside is Heon-neung, the graves of King Taejong (third: reigned 1400–18)—a son of the dynasty's founder and the father of King Sejong—and his wife. Nearby is In-neung, the tomb of King Sunjo (23rd: reigned 1800–34) and his wife. Originally placed north of Seoul near Paju, In-neung was relocated here in the mid-1800s, perhaps for better geomantic location. A visit here makes a fine stop between Seoul and Namhan Sanseong Provincial Park. Use city bus no. 36 from in front of the express bus terminal.

Seonjeong-neung 선정능

Within Samneung Park near COEX is Seon-jeong-neung [Sŏnjŏng-nŭng] (H.S. #199). Now engulfed by the great southern expansion of the city, the three tombs here were not long ago surrounded only by quiet countryside. Amongst the tree-covered knolls are the tombs of King Seongjong (ninth: reigned 1469–95); his son, King Jungjong (11th: reigned 1506–45); and King Seongjong's third wife, Queen Yun. Several ginkgo trees here are over 500 years old. Use Seolleung Station on subway line #2.

Seosam-neung and Seoo-neung

Northwest of the city are two groups of royal tombs. The farthest from the heart of the city is Seosam-neung [Sŏsam-nŭng] ("West Three Tombs," 서삼능), H.S. #200. Here lies King Injong (12th: reigned 1544–45), King Jeoljong (25th: reigned 1849–64), four queens, numerous concubines, several princes, and nearly two dozen graves of the children of Joseon Dynasty kings. Seoo-neung [Sŏo-nŭng] ("West Five Tombs," 서오능), H.S. #198, like Seosam-neung, actually contains more tombs than its name indicates, including the graves of the great fortress-builder King Sukjong (19th: reigned 1674–1720), King Yejong (eighth: reigned 1468–69), two queens separate from their husbands, and two princes. To reach Seoo-neung take city bus no. 159.

Other Tombs

On the southeastern slope of Bukhan-san is Jeong-neung [Chŏng-nŭng] (정능) (H.S. #208), the tomb of Queen Gang. She was the second wife of King Taejo, the founder of the Joseon Dynasty. Originally located near Deoksu-gung, the tomb was relocated here after foreigners were given land to build within the city walls near the palace in the 1880s. Queen Gang's tomb is the oldest Joseon Dynasty tomb. Use city bus no. 3 or 710. North of Seoul and west of the town of Geumsan is Jang-neung [Chang-nŭng] (장능) (H.S. #203), the grave of King Injo (16th: reigned 1623–49). Near the town of Gimpo is another Jang-neung [Chang-nŭng] (H.S. #202). Buried here are King Wonjong (a posthumous title), his wife, and the parents of King Injo. Use city bus no. 130.

Numerous other royal tombs are in the area surrounding Seoul. Generally small and plain, they contain mostly queens, princes, princesses, and lesser members of the royal family.

BUKHAN-SAN NATIONAL PARK
북한산국립공원

During the Imjin War (1590s), the invading Japanese army moved almost unopposed through the peninsula, pushing all the way through Seoul to Pyeongyang. The Korean king had to flee his capital for Uiju, on the Amnok River at the northern extremity of his kingdom. Four decades later, Seoul was overrun by the Manchu army. The need for a stronger defense of the capital was clear, but it wasn't until 1711 that the stone ramparts of Bukhan Sanseong [Pukhan Sansŏng] were constructed by order of King Sukjong—referred to as "the fortress builder." This fortress was to be used as a retreat for the king and royal retainers in case of enemy attack or internal rebellion. Luckily, it was never put to such use.

Bukhan Sanseong (H.S. #162), rings the rugged peaks of Bukhan-san, the principal guardian sentinel of the nation's capital. This eight-kilometer-long elliptical wall was a mighty affair that capped this natural defensive position. Encompassing the mountain's inner valley, the high fortress walls of Bukhan-san ran along the circular ridge and up its palisade of craggy peaks. In addition, a connecting wall ran down the mountain from the fortress to the Seoul city wall. Inside the mountain enclosure, palace structures, temples, military buildings, and storehouses were built. Several of those buildings remained until the 20th century, when they were destroyed by heavy fighting during the Korean War. The walls and gates that remain are from the late Joseon Dynasty. Although not as sophisticated as the Suwon Fortress, built a century later, Bukhan Sanseong has perhaps the most dramatic setting of any fortress in the country.

To the northeast of Bukhan-san is Dobong-san. In 1983, the Bukhan-san/Dobong-san range was designated Bukhan-san National Park. This 78-square-kilometer park is one of the country's smallest national parks. The ₩1,300 entrance fee is payable at any of the 30 trailheads. The park is open 0730–1800 (from 0700 on weekends and holidays), but trails are closed March–May and mid-November to mid-December. Approximately one-half of the park lies within the Seoul city limits,–the other half in Gyeonggi-Do. Although not exceptionally high, these mountains are steep and rugged; exposed ash-white granite peaks jut through the gnarled pine cover. The highest peak in the southern half is Baegun-dae

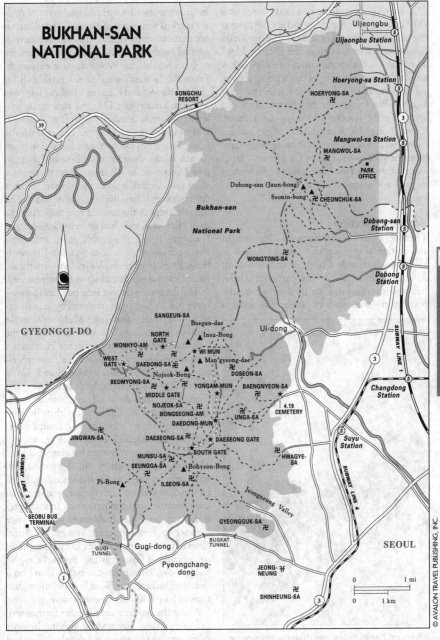

BUKHAN-SAN NATIONAL PARK

Uijeongbu

Uijeongbu Station

SONGCHU RESORT

Hoeryong-sa Station

HOERYONG-SA

Mangwol-sa Station

MANGWOL-SA

PARK OFFICE

Dobong-san (Jaun-bong)

Seonin-bong   CHEONCHUK-SA

Bukhan-san

National Park

Dobong-san Station

WONGTONG-SA

Dobong Station

SANGEUN-SA

Baegun-dae

Insu-Bong

Ui-dong

NORTH GATE

WONHYO-AM

WI MUN

Man'gyeong-dae

WEST GATE

DAEDONG-SA

Nojeok-Bong

DOSEON-SA

BEOMYONG-SA

YONGAM-MUN

BAENGNYEON-SA

MIDDLE GATE

NOJEOK-SA

BONGSEONG-AM

UNGA-SA

4.19 CEMETERY

GYEONGGI-DO

Changdong Station

DAEDONG-MUN

DAESEONG-SA   DAESEONG GATE

JINGWAN-SA

Suyu Station

MUNSU-SA

SOUTH GATE

HWAGYE-SA

SEUNGGA-SA   Bohyeon-Bong

Pi-Bong

ILSEON-SA

Jeongneung Valley

SEOBU BUS TERMINAL

GYEONGGUK-SA

GUGI TUNNEL

Gugi-dong

BUGKAT TUNNEL

SEOUL

Pyeongchang-dong

JEONG-NEUNG

SHINHEUNG-SA

0   1 mi

0   1 km

© AVALON TRAVEL PUBLISHING, INC.

SEOUL

SUBWAY LINE 1

SUBWAY LINE 3

SUBWAY LINE 4

(836 meters). It and the two peaks Insu-bong (810 meters) and Man'gyeong-dae (799 meters) rise close to one another and give the mountain its alternate name, Samgak-san ("Three Horn Mountain"). The park's interior valley below and to the west of these peaks is a popular place for picnics. The road up to the principal trailheads is lined with dozens of restaurants and shops. In the northern Dobong-san section, Chaun-bong (740 meters) is the tallest, and the valleys on its eastern slope also bring many summertime picnickers. Except for fortress's inner valley, nearly all of the broad swath of the western slope is a restricted zone, and no entry is permitted.

Southern Section

The inner valley of the fortress, and the southern and eastern slopes, contain literally dozens of trails, of which only a handful are often used. As in all national parks—and particularly here, because of its frequent use by the huge nearby population—some trails are occasionally closed to

hikers on Baegun-dae, overlooking Insu-bong

let nature rejuvenate itself. Although major trails are marked with signs in Korean, a good map is necessary to verify other trails. The best map is printed by the Korea National Parks Authority and is available for ₩500 at park entrances. From the fortress's west gate, a road leads up past restaurants and shops to a parking lot, from where you must walk. One trail runs up the valley to Wi-mun; another veers off to the south and heads to the south gate. The trail up the outer slope from the northeast is the closest approach to the summit; it leads from Ui-dong, past Doseon-sa, to Wi-mun. From that gate, a short trail continues up to the summit, another descends steeply into the inner valley, and a third runs the ridge to the south. From the south, the most often-used trails lead up from Gugi-dong to Seungga-sa and the south gate, and from Pyeongchang-dong to Ilseon-sa and Bohyeonbong. From Jeongneung Valley in the southeast, several alternate trails lead up to the fortress wall.

The flat granite faces of Insu-bong and Seoninbong (on Dobong-san) are used by experts for technical rock climbing. Many mountain climbers, including those who have braved the heights of Mt. Everest and other Himalayan mountains, have trained here. Don't attempt either unless you are fully equipped and *skilled!* About 200 meters high, both Insu-bong and Seonin-bong have about a dozen climbing routes apiece. Every year, climbers lose their lives on these faces due to accident or incompetence. Generally, hiking trails in this park are not rigorous, and can be traversed by average hikers. Through the inner valley and along the ridge, trails offer leisurely walks and inspiring sights. However, as you approach the bald granite peaks, trails become steep and strenuous. In some precipitous sections, metal cables and stairways have been set up. From the ridge, you get wonderful views of the metropolitan area and the provincial countryside of Gyeonggi-Do. From the top of Baegun-dae, Uijeongbu can be seen, and on a clear day, Incheon, the West Sea, and the mountains in North Korea come into view.

Along the Bukhan-san ridge are fortress wall and gate remains. Scattered throughout the inner valley are sites of long-gone palace buildings and temple structures. In this inner valley, as well as on the outer slopes of the mountain, are numerous newer temples and hermitages.

Inner Valley Trails

From Bukhan Sanseong's west gate, a road leads up into the fortress to a parking area. At this point, trails go in two directions. The trail to the left leads up along a sparkling mountain stream, first to Daedong-sa and then steeply up to Wimun, directly below Baegun-dae. Wi-mun sits in the deep gash of the high eastern ridge, and can be seen from the west gate as you enter the park. A short distance up a secondary trail before Daedong-sa, the small Silla Dynasty temple Sangeun-sa is tucked into the hillside below the north gate. At this temple is a white stone Buddha statue housed in a grotto. It's said to have been carved by a leper who was eventually cured of his disease by drinking the water that drips down from the inside of this cave. Because of this legend, it's now a pilgrimage site for others seeking a miraculous cure. Below Sangeun-sa is the hermitage Wonhyo-am, named after the famous monk Wonhyo, and dedicated to the Amita Buddha. This Silla Dynasty hermitage was rebuilt after being destroyed in the Korean War.

From the parking lot, the right-hand trail leads up past Beomyong-sa, through the Jungseongmun middle gate. From here, various trails go to the temples Nojeok-sa, Taego-sa, and Bongseongam, the sites of five former temples, former palace buildings, and defensive military structures. Founded during the Goryeo Dynasty by Bou Guksa, Taego-sa preserves this famous monk's *sari* pagoda (T. #749) and a commemorative monument (T. #611) for Wonjeung Guksa. Farther up the main valley trail is Daeseong-am, and beyond that the south gate. Nojeok-sa, a new temple built on the former Jin'guk-sa temple site, sits below the conical "sugarloaf" hill, Nojeokbong. According to legend, the famous Joseon Dynasty warrior-monk Sammyeong-daesa came to Bukhan-san when the Japanese pushed up the peninsula in the 1590s. He gathered his men in this valley to defend it from the invading troops. In order to outwit the more numerous Japanese, he had Nojeok-bong covered with straw bags to make it look like a huge pile of rice. Seeing it, the Japanese decided that there must certainly be too many Korean soldiers hidden in the valley for them to be successful in battle, and even if they were to lay siege, it would not be possible to starve them out. The trick worked, and the Japanese withdrew. So the story goes!

For many years, the trail past the middle gate was closed to civilians because of the threat of North Korean infiltration. In 1968, a group of North Koreans did slip across the border and camped in this valley prior to their attempted assassination of former President Park Chung Hee. You'll see that its deep valleys make good hiding places. All trails are now open to hikers.

Ridge Trail

Doseon-sa, the mountain's best known temple, occupies a spot on the eastern slope of the mountain above Ui-dong. From Doseon-sa, two trails head up to the ridge and peaks above. From the parking lot below the temple, the first trail leads two kilometers up the mountain, over the ridge, and into an adjoining valley before running up to Wi-mun. Because the trail is steep in sections, a steel cable has been strung along the most precipitous lengths to help hikers over slippery granite patches. From Wi-mun, a short trail to the north heads up to Baegun-dae.

A short distance down the inner valley trail, below Wi-mun, is a Y intersection. There, the ridge trail splits off the main trail and runs to the south around rock outcrops, past several small fortress gates, and partway along the top of the wall itself. The second trail from Doseon-sa, which runs up the valley behind the temple, meets the ridge trail at Yongam-mun. Farther south along the ridge trail is Daedong-mun. Here, trails go down the east slope to Baengnyeon-sa, Unga-sa, and the Academy House seminar center. Before reaching Buguk-mun, a trail drops from the ridge down to Hwagye-sa. At Buguk-mun, trails go into the inner valley as well as down the outer slope into Jeongneung Valley. Jeongneung Valley has many new temples, but the well-established Buddhist sanctuaries are Gyeongguk-sa and Shinheung-sa. Jeongneung Resort and the royal tomb of Queen Gang are also in this valley. From Daeseong Gate, a trail leads to the temple Ilseon-sa and on down to Jeongneung Valley, Pyeongchang-dong, and other trailheads. From the south gate, trails go down into the inner valley as well as out to the temples Munsu-sa and Seungga-sa. Founded in 1110, Munsu-sa's main hall incorporates a natural grotto. Below it is the older Seungga-sa, a temple of female monks, built in 756. A five-meter-high bas-relief Goryeo Dynasty seated Buddha figure (T. #215) has been carved into the flat rock behind the temple. A trail leads down from Seungga-sa to a point near the Gugi Tunnel. From a short distance east of the south gate, a rather treacherous trail leads out to the spire peaks of Bohyeon-bong. This is considered a power spot, and many people climb these pinnacles to spend the night chanting prayers or deep in meditation. From Bohyeon-bong, a path leads down to Ilseon-sa. The walk from Baegundae to the south gate requires about three hours. From the south gate, the ridge trail continues around to the west gate, passing three secondary gates and Munsu-bong; it is quite difficult in sections. From Munsu-bong, a ridge trail runs to the southwest to Pi-bong (560 meters). On the top of this peak stands a replica of the ancient marker Jinheungwang Sunsubi (N.T. #3). This monument was erected in 569 by Silla Dynasty King Jinheung on inspection of the northern border of his kingdom. From here, several trails lead down to the south. Directly north of Pi-bong is another of the mountain's cultural relics. The bas-relief carving of the Maitreya Buddha (T. #657) at Samcheon-sa was done during the late Silla Dynasty.

Northern Section

The northern section of this park, the Dobong-san region, has some of the best hiking in the Seoul area. A maze of trails leads up the mountain's eastern side; most trailheads are west of Dobong-san and Mangwol-sa stations on the subway line, but one each is reached from the Dobong and Hoeryong-sa stations. Trails also lead up from Ui-dong to the south, from Ui-jeongbu to the north, and from Songchu to the west. About half a dozen trails head up the hillside from Dobong Park, near Dobong-san Station. Perhaps the most well-used trail (an hour and a half) leads up to Cheonchuk-sa, founded in 673 by the famous monk Uisang. Above this temple, rock climbers try their skill at the bald rock face of Seonin-bong. Above that on the main ridge is Chaun-bong, Dobong-san's highest peak. Another well-used trail (about one hour) leads from the park's main office to Mangwol-sa, built in 639. From either here or Cheonchuk-sa, trails lead over the ridge and down to Songchu Resort on the western side (an additional two to three hours). Wontong-sa is reached in about two hours from the Dobong Station, or in a little over an hour from Ui-dong. It, like Doseon-sa, was built by the monk Doseon in the mid-800s. The fourth of the area's temples from the Silla Dynasty, founded in 681 by Uisang, is Hoeryong-sa, reached in about an hour from Hoeryong-sa Station. From there, trails lead to Mangwol-sa and up and over the ridge to Songchu Resort. Running south to north over the mountain spine, the trail from Ui-dong to Ui-jeongbu takes the better part of a day.

Mountain Huts

There are four shelters in the southern section of the park. Ui Daepiso is located just above the Doseon-sa parking lot, Insu Daepiso and Baegun Daepiso lie below Insu-bong, and Bukhan Sanjang is situated just below the fortress remains, high in the inner valley near Yongam-mun. In the northern section, Bomun Sanjang is above Wontong-sa, Dobong Sanjang is below Cheonchuk-sa and Seonin-bong, and the third is near Mangwol-sa. Each costs ₩3,000 a night for a space on the floor. Bring your own bedding, food, and cooking equipment. Camping also runs ₩3,000 for a small tent in either of the two designated camping spots.

Getting There

There are several possibilities for reaching Bukhan-san National Park. Seoul city bus no. 156 runs from Gwanghwa-mun and Seoul Station to the west entrance. A road from this bus stop leads up past the park's west office and through the west gate into the inner valley of the mountain fortress. No. 136-1 runs from Gwanghwa-mun to the trailheads near Gugi Tunnel, and no. 135 goes to Pyeongchang-dong and the trailheads near Bugak Tunnel. For the Jeongneung Valley trails, use bus no. 1, 3, or 710. Bus no. 84 runs to just below Hwagye-sa, and no. 127 stops below Baengnyeon-sa and the 4.19 Cemetery. City bus nos. 6, 8, and 23 from Gwanghwa-mun run to the Ui-dong bus terminus below Doseon-sa. From this bus terminus, either walk the 2.5 kilometers up the road or use the Doseon-sa shuttle bus, which starts across the street. Although city bus no. 12 from Dongdae-mun and no. 13 from Jong-no 5-ga run past stops that lead to Dobong-san trailheads, subway line #1 is perhaps more convenient. Stops along this line are at the Dobong, Dobong-san, Mangwol-sa, and Hoeryong-sa stations. Intercity buses from the Seoul Seobu Bus Terminal and from the Uijeongbu Bus Terminal, as well as trains from Seoul Station and Uijeongbu Station, stop at Songchu Resort for the trailhead up the northwest slope.

NAMHAN SANSEONG PROVINCIAL PARK
남한산성도립공원

Rising over Seongnam City, 25 kilometers southeast of downtown Seoul, is Namhan-san. Capping this mountain are the remains of Namhan Sanseong, used by the Joseon royal court in times of need. Namhan-san is a natural stronghold: its steep sides handicap approaching armies and its basin-like top is large enough to contain a large fighting force. Its strategic location and physical advantages became clear to Joseon Dynasty rulers when they saw the menacing Manchus looming across their northern border. In 1621, King Gwanghae-gun ordered the construction of a new fortress on the site of an old Baekje Dynasty fortress. This work was continued by King Injo, and by 1626 it was completed. In 1635 the Manchus invaded and conquered Korea, causing the king to flee to this mountaintop. The Manchus laid siege to Namhan Sanseong in the winter of that year. Royal advisers were split between surrender and fighting

to the death. After six weeks, King Injo surrendered and pledged his loyalty to the Manchu king. Defeat at Namhan Sanseong was undoubtedly one of the lowest points of the Joseon period, a disgrace still seen by some Koreans as a black spot on the tapestry of Korean history that can't be expunged.

In 1675, King Sukjong, the builder of Bukhan Sanseong, enlarged Namhan Sanseong; other additions and repairs were made during the following century. Wall and gate remains ring the mountaintop basin. Principal gates were erected at each of the four cardinal directions; in between these were 16 others, plus the basin stream's water gate. Palace buildings, military structures, temples, and ponds were built inside the fortress enclosure.

Provincial Park

In 1939, Namhan Sanseong was designated H.S. #57. In 1971, the fortress and 36 square kilometers of the thickly wooded mountainside were established as Namhan Sanseong Provincial Park, Gyeonggi-Do's only provincial park; ₩1,000 entrance. Portions of the nine-kilometer-long, eight-meter-high fortress wall and several of its gates have been reconstructed since the 1980s. Some of the old fortress structures have also been rebuilt, and are preserved within the walls; a halfdozen of these buildings have been designated provincial cultural properties. As the trees have grown big, it's not as easy to see the sites as it used to be, so have a look at one of the park signboards or procure a free map from the park office before you head up the roads and trails. Often used as an escape from the heat of city summer, Namhan-san is usually breezy and several degrees cooler than the streets of Seoul. From Iljeong-dae, on clear days you can get extraordinary views of the sprawling capital to the northwest. All too often, however, a smoggy haze lies low over Seoul, obscuring the view.

Remains

All the principal gates have been restored. The south gate is an excellent example of gate construction. Its solid rock wall, arched entryway, and topping pavilion offer a formidable defense while blending nicely into the lay of the land. Across the inner basin you can see the north gate. The road to Gwangju now runs to the side of the east gate, at a spot where a water gate once stood. Up a side trail from the east gate is Jang-gyeong-sa, the only surviving temple of the nine that once stood within the fortress wall—three others have been rebuilt since the end of the Japanese occupation of the peninsula in 1945. These temples housed the warrior-monks who served as the king's personal guards when he resided here. Not only were these monks part of the labor force that constructed the fortress, but many also lost their lives in defense of this stronghold. Farther into the compound, on the south side of the road, is Jisu-dang. Built in 1672, this pavilion, and the lotus ponds that front it, were said to be a favorite summer retreat for the royal family and court during much of the dynasty. Nearby are the park office and a new exhibition hall/museum with an explanation of events and artifacts from the fateful 1600s. Across the road and a bit up the hill sits Hyeonjeolsa, a shrine to five loyal counselors of King Injo. Four of them urged King Injo to resist the Manchus; for their loyalty, they were repaid with death by the enemy after the king's surrender. The fifth is Kim Sang-yong, King Injo's prime minister. He committed suicide by laying a match to a powderkeg in the south gate of Ganghwa town when the town was overrun by invading Manchu troops during their attack on the island. Along with himself, he blew the royal ancestral tablets to smithereens in order to keep those precious memorials safe from desecration. Near the center of the fortress, up behind the village shops, is Yeonmu-gwan, military headquarters for training soldiers stationed here. The present structure dates from 1674.

At the village are several stone monuments erected in memory of former governors of Gwangju. Behind them is Chimgwae-jeong, said to have been standing when the fortress wall was constructed in the 1620s. Legend relates that it was part of the personal house of King Onjo, the first Baekje king. Although obviously old, it could not have survived for 2,000 years! On the hill above Chimgwae-jeong is Sungnyeol-jeon, a shrine dedicated to the memory of King Onjo. Here as well is the site of a royal villa, a place used by the royal family when on an outing to this mountain retreat. At the beginning of the 20th century, these buildings were used by foreign missionaries during their summer retreats from the stifling city. Above this is Sueojang-dae, the two-story pavilion where King Injo stayed during his 45 days of resistance in 1636. To the rear of this pavilion is Cheonnyang-dang, a shrine to one of the two supervisors of the fortress construction. On Iljeong-dae (490 meters), the mountain's highest peak, the open pavilion Yeongchun-jeong has been erected. From here you can see Bukhan-san, on Seoul's northern edge. North along the wall is the west gate, and farther around, the fortress's north gate.

The mountaintop community is a growing cluster of shops, restaurants, a school, post office, accommodations, the park office, and the fortress history hall. Buses to and from Gwangju and Seoul stop here. Aside from being the Silla Dynasty's provincial capital, Gwangju was a principal Joseon Dynasty kiln site. It's still known today for artisans who reproduce that era's white porcelain. The other road from this village runs out through the south gate and steeply down the mountain to Seongnam.

It's possible to walk along the entire wall of Namhan Sanseong. Perhaps the easiest and most-frequented section is the stretch between the south and north gates, along the west wall. From the north gate, along the eastern and southern walls, the path is passable but overgrown; stay on top or just inside the wall itself. Bring along a bag lunch and canteen and make a day of it!

If you've come by bus, there's an alternate way to leave. From the park's western entrance, a short distance down the road from the south gate ticket booth, a path (two km) leads into a valley to the south to Seongnam. In this glen are several small temples and an exercise course. Several hundred meters beyond this exercise course is a peripheral residential district of Seongnam and a bus terminus for buses returning to Seoul.

The walking path to Namhan Sanseong from Seongnam can be reached by Seoul express city bus no. 45. Alternately, take bus no. 9 from

Sanseong Station on subway line #8. City bus no. 15-1 from Gwangju runs up into the park village from that city.

HAENGJU SANSEONG 행주산성

Haengju Sanseong (H.S. #56) is open 0900–1800; ₩1,000 entrance fee. Capping a low riverside knoll to the west of the city at an old ferry crossing point, this diminutive historical fortification is not as dramatic as either Bukhan Sanseong or Namhan Sanseong, yet the site offers pastoral scenes of the Han River and the agricultural lands west of Seoul, Goyang city, and Bukhan-san to the northwest. While resting in the pavilion, you can watch domestic planes take off and land at Gimpo Airport across the river to the south.

Older than either Bukhan Sanseong or Namhan Sanseong, Haengju Sanseong is the site of one of the few Korean successes during the Imjin War. In order to recapture the capital from the Japanese, General Kwon Yul, governor of the southwest corner of the country, moved troops up to the hills around Seoul. In 1593, he had Haengju Sanseong hastily built out of logs and earth, then manned by his limited troops. The Japanese came out from the city and surrounded the palisade. As the fight progressed, Korean archers ran out of arrows, and other supplies ran perilously low. During this battle, Korean women gathered rocks in their skirts for the men to use as projectiles. While not as effective as arrows, the rocks were enough to blunt the attack until support troops sailed up the river. These reinforcements turned the tide and gave the Koreans a victory.

This well-maintained area contains some recent constructions. A slender white monument commemorates this victory, and nearby a shrine with portrait has been dedicated to General Kwon. Set on a bluff above the ponderous river is a tranquil pavilion, a perfect place for an afternoon picnic. A small exhibition hall here displays historical items, and the building on top of the hill shows a short film about the history of the fortress. Sections of the original earthen wall have been reconstructed on the north side of the

hill. Every year in March the Haengju Victory Festival celebrates that event of four centuries ago. Aside from a ritual ceremony to honor General Kwon, an archery contest is held, and farmers' music and dances are performed. To reach Haengju Sanseong, ride neighborhood bus no. 15-1 from the Hwajeong subway station on subway line #3 to the fortress front gate. Otherwise, take city bus no. 82, 85-1, or 1008 from the Hwajeong station to the entrance road, from where there is a half-kilometer walk to the fortress.

GWANAK-SAN 관악산

The granite mountains near Seoul attract countless hikers, and Gwanak-san [Kwanak-san] (629 meters) draws its fair share. It and Samseong-san (481 meters), a secondary peak directly to its west, create a portion of Seoul's southern boundary. At their northern base is Seoul National University; to the southwest is the heavily industrialized city of Anyang and the Anyang Yuwonji recreation area; Seoul Grand Park and the Gwacheon national government office complex are to the southeast. Many trails run up its fluted north and south slopes, and one traverses its east-west axis. Pinnacles of ash-white granite thrust out here and there through the dark green pine cover. Clinging to the side of this thickly forested mountain are numerous temples and hermitages. The best known are Yeonju-am, a Buddhist sanctuary founded by the famous monk Uisang in the mid-600s, and its associated hermitage which clings precariously to the top of Yeonju-dae above. Entrance to the mountain is ₩300.

Three principal routes lead up this mountain, and the most often used starts to the west of Seoul National University. This trail runs through a broad area and up along the valley stream to a camping site, about 40 minutes away. While this valley trail continues up the valley to an intersection where trails lead up to either peak, a second trail splits off to the east at this campground and runs up the mountainside— one hour—to Yeonju-am [Yŏnju-am] (연주사). Yeonju-am has a hall that houses a statue of Gwaneum and what must be several thousand small

© ROBERT NILSEN

SEOUL

Yeonju-am

Buddha images. Smaller and older, the main hall is set to its side, and above that is a hall for the Mountain Spirit. Ten minutes above this hermitage, past a communications tower and perched precariously at the edge of the sheer cliff Yeonju-dae, is a tiny prayer hall; stones have been piled into the cracks of this vertically layered rock to support the buildings.

The second major route up Gwanak-san is from the mountain's east side. Starting from the Gwacheon Hyanggyo to the north of the national government complex and the Gwacheon city hall, this trail begins on the east side of the stream near the *hyanggyo* but crosses and recrosses it several times, leading past an emergency hut and several natural springs to Yeonju-am and the summit.

The third trail starts from Anyang Yuwonji, outside the city of Anyang, south of Seoul. From this recreation area, several paths lead up the mountain, but the most frequented heads first to Yeombul-am, and from there to Sammak-sa (삼막사) and the summit. In addition, a ridge trail runs northwest to the lower Janggun-bong peak, and from there several trails head down to the southern suburbs of the city, one past Hoamsa. Large plates of granite, some dislodged and precariously set and others forming shallow caves, are found at and near Janggun-bong. Any trail to either summit should take no more than two hours. From the summit, there are no better views of the southern half of Seoul. Anyang Yuwonji is a motley collection of small restaurants and arcade games, interspersed with several fine restaurants and a new hotel/hostel. It's best when there's water in the river; otherwise, there's not much to see nor is it very refreshing.

To get there, take city bus no. 51 from Gwanghwa-mun to Seoul National University. Seoul National University Station on subway line #2 is nearest the university; from there, take bus no. 413 to the mountain entrance. To get to the east side of the mountain, use express city bus no. 797 or Gwacheon Station on subway line #4. Bus no. 103 from Shinchon runs by the Anyang Yuwonji entrance.

Gyeonggi-Do
경기도

The province of Gyeonggi-Do [Kyŏnggi-Do] completely encircles Seoul. With nearly 10 million people, it has by far the largest provincial population, yet is only the fifth-largest in area of the nine provinces. Including the metropolitan cities of Seoul and Incheon, which both are administratively separate from the province, this rather small corner of the country has over 22 million people, or about 46 percent of South Korea's total population. Starting in the 1960s, gaining great intensity in the 1970s, and continuing thereafter, with a burst in the late 1990s, people have migrated from other areas of the country, dramatically swelling Gyeonggi-Do's population. By and large, they came for employment in the province's rapidly expanding industrial zones, and this great influx caused rapid urbanization and the accompanying problems of such swift growth. More than 80 percent of Gyeonggi-Do's population lives in cities or other urban clusters. The satellite cities directly surrounding Seoul have the highest growth rates in the country; the majority are new designations south of the Han River. Of the province's two dozen cities, Suwon, the provincial capital and largest of the cities, is also the most established and has the greatest historical and cultural remains.

the main hall at Jeondeung-sa

GYEONGGI-DO

North

Chuncheon

GANGWON-DO

DMZ

5

5

56

GYEONGCHUN RAIL LINE

NAMISEOM RESORT

Hwaak-san

47

Wasuri

Gimhwa

Shin Cheolwon

Sambuyeon Waterfall

Myeongseong-san

Senjeong Lake

CHEONGPYEONG RESORT

37

Gwangju Mountains

Gapyeong

45

SECOND INFILTRATION TUNNEL

GOSEOK-JEONG

Jiktang Waterfall

Sundam

43

Pocheon

47

Cheongpyeong

GANGBYEON RESORT

South Branch Han R.

Han R.

SETO RESORT

SEOUL RESORT

Dongsong

River

DOPIAN-SA

LABOR PARTY BUILDING

BEAR'S TOWN SKI RESORT

DAESEONG-NI RESORT

GWANGNEUNG

Namyangju

IRON TRIANGLE OBSERVATION POINT

Shintan-ni

Soyo-san

CHEONMASAN SKI RESORT

WHITE HORSE MEMORIAL

3

37

Hantan River

Yeoncheon

GYEONGWON RAIL LINE

Dongducheon

GWANGNEUNG NATIONAL ARBORETUM

Surak-san

NORTH KOREA

GYEONGGI-DO

Uijeongbu

Dobong-san

GYODE RAIL LINE

Bukhan-san National Park

SEOUL

HWASEOK-JEONG

YI YUL-GOK TOMB

Beobwon-ni

PAJU MIREUK BUDDHAS

39

SEOUL CIRCULAR EXPWY

Gori

38th Parallel

Imjin River

Munsan

1

100

SEOUL CIRCULAR EXPWY

Goyang

GYEONGUI RAIL LINE

ODU-SAN UNIFICATION OBSERVATORY

Geumcheon

DMZ

PANMUNJEOM

THIRD INFILTRATION TUNNEL

DORA OBSERVATION POST

IMJIN-GAK

Han R.

Gimpo

INCHEON AIRPORT EXPWY

48

Gaeseong

Keumcheon

Ganghwa

Mani-san

Ganghwa-do

Seongmo-do

Sido

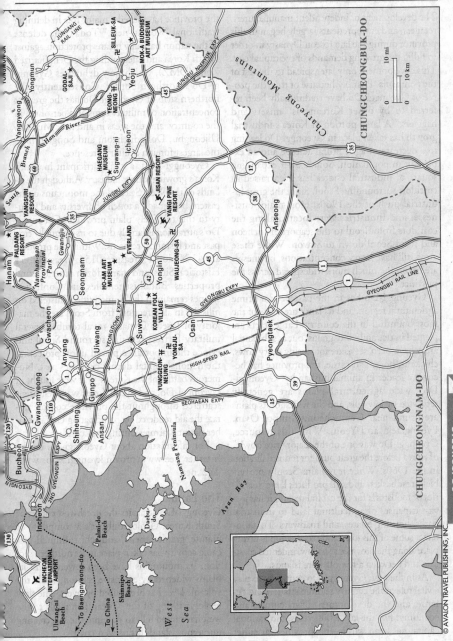

The development of independent manufacturers, retailers, and entrepreneurs largely began in this province during the late Joseon Dynasty in order to fulfill the growing demands of the capital city. This development only later spread to the rest of the peninsula. Possibly because of this, the people of Gyeonggi-Do have traditionally been referred to by other Koreans as "misers and hagglers." A large portion of Korea's industrial growth has taken place in Gyeonggi-Do leading to a decrease in agricultural acreage and an explosion in population. Square after expanding square of industrial estates has been raised in corridors surrounding Seoul. Since the great industrial push of the 1960s, most major businesses and industries were located along the corridors from Seoul to the seaport of Incheon and from Seoul down to Suwon. While these areas still have heavy concentrations, businesses are becoming much more widespread across the province.

Gyeonggi-Do has in the past been a prime agricultural region, and its lands are some of the most bountiful in the country. Large tracts are planted in rice and other grains, but as substantial areas have been set aside for raising dairy cows, chickens, hogs, and cattle, the province has become a leader in animal husbandry. Gyeonggi-Do's wide agricultural plains are generally separated by low hills, and the widest of its plains are found near Geumcheon, Gimpo, Osan, Pyeongtaek, and Yeoju. With this resource, Gyeonggi-Do was one of the major "rice bowls" of Korea before the great push for industrialization in the 1960s. While it remains Seoul's proverbial breadbasket, and still produces large quantities of foodstuffs for the capital region, it has lost vast expanses of agricultural land to industrial parks, housing estates, and roadways. To counteract some of this loss, land reclamation is taking place along the province's shallow, indented coastline and between a few offshore islands.

As in the past, Gyeonggi-Do continues to play a vital role in the country's administration and defense, and the development of its culture and economy. For the last 1,000 years, the national capital has been within this province, at either Seoul or Gaeseong (now in North Korea). Thus, the province has played a major role in defining traditional "Korean-ness." Today, the defense of the nation basically means protection against North Korea and safeguarding the Demilitarized Zone (DMZ), which now delineates Gyeonggi-Do's northern border. Consequently, the northern strip of Gyeonggi-Do has the greatest concentration of military arms and personnel in the country, and the areas in and near Munsan, Uijeongbu, Dongducheon, and Songtan have the largest foreign military presence.

Gyeonggi-Do is a vital participant in South Korea's growing tourist industry. Although the islands of the West Sea and the mountains on its eastern border add a touch of diversity and beauty to this relatively plain province, Gyeonggi-Do's attraction is largely due to its culturally rich past and historical remains. Within the province are 43 National Treasures, 154 Treasures, 54 Historical Sites, and many dozen other cultural properties. Buddhist temples and Confucian shrines remain in the countryside. Clustered on hillsides in all directions from Seoul are the majority of Joseon Dynasty royal tombs. Several military-fortress remains surround Seoul and evince the importance placed upon protecting the national capital during centuries past. Numerous battles of the Korean War were fought in Gyeonggi-Do, and over a dozen war memorials scattered throughout the province commemorate the aid rendered by participating U.N. member nations' armies during that conflict.

For information about Gyeonggi-Do on the Internet, see www.provin.kyonggi.kr or www.kg2.net.

The Land

Gyeonggi-Do occupies the northwest corner of South Korea. Geologically, it's a composite of granite, granite/gneiss, and schist; limited volcanic activity has taken place in its northern section. Its mountains have been lowered and its plains widened by extensive erosion, while the volcanic layer has been sliced by rivers. The slow geologic tilting of the Korean Peninsula to the west has caused hills to sink into the sea, creating numerous islands off its west coast.

Mountains and Rivers

This province has a low average elevation. Low hills and wide plains stretch across the province's south and west, while the hills rise in height and concentration in the north and east. Two mountain ranges run through Gyeonggi-Do. Coming southwest from Odae-san are the low Charyeong Mountains, forming its southern border. Yongmun-san (1,157 meters) stands as its highest peak. From a point between Anseong and Icheon, a spur of this range heads directly north toward Seoul in an ever-lowering line of hills. From the Diamond Mountains in North Korea come the Gwangju Mountains. They run across northern Gangwon-Do before plunging down through Gyeonggi-Do toward Seoul. Several of the well-known peaks in this range are Dobong-san, Surak-san, Soyo-san, and Hwaak-san (1,468 meters), the highest in the province. High or low, most mountains of Gyeonggi-Do have well-established trails, and are frequented by the mountaineering urbanites of Seoul, who leave the big city for fresh air, open vistas, and a day's exercise.

Both branches of the Han River run through Gyeonggi-Do. The northern branch starts in North Korea, runs through Gangwon-Do, and joins the south fork just above the Paldang Dam on the outskirts of Seoul. The south branch starts farther south in Gangwon-Do and cuts across Chungcheongbuk-Do before running up into Gyeonggi-Do. The only major dam on the Han River within Gyeonggi-Do is the Paldang Dam. The upper reaches of both branches of the Han drop rapidly as they slice through the mountains. When they reach the alluvial plains of Gyeonggi-Do, however, they slow down, widen, and become shallow. As they reach these plains, their sedimentary deposits create a sandy bottom and shifting sandbars, which tend to raise the level of the riverbottom; in some places the water rises above the level of the surrounding countryside, necessitating construction of levees and dikes. From the confluence of these two branches, the Han River runs through Seoul, splitting the city in two. Just a few kilometers before emptying into the West Sea, the Imjin River joins the Han from the north. The Imjin River, a slow-moving tidal river with a muddy bottom, is much shorter than the Han. Its drainage basin is entirely within the traditional Gyeonggi-Do provincial area, but its largest portion now lies within North Korea. The lower reaches of both these rivers are tidal—their levels rise and fall with the ebb and flow of the West Sea. No boats are allowed into the Han River estuary or the lower end of the Imjin River, as the actual border between South and North Korea runs right up the middle of them. In any case, for most of the year it's too shallow to be of use for commercial shipping and transportation, although it was used for such by shallow-draft sailboats in centuries past.

Coast and Islands

The most extensive intrusions of the sea along this heavily indented coastline are Asan Bay and the bays on both sides of the Namyang Peninsula. There is not one deep natural port in Gyeonggi-Do. The most extensive port facilities have been laboriously constructed at Incheon, and work continues on new harbor facilities west of Pyeongtaek. The tidal range along this coast—up to 10 meters—is the second greatest in the world, following only that of the Bay of Fundy in Nova Scotia. Hundreds of square kilometers of mudflats are exposed when the tide goes out. From these great expanses are gathered clams and other sea creatures.

Gyeonggi-Do's numerous islands are broadcast like seeds of grain in a paddy field. While most are tiny and uninhabited, the largest are in fact submerged mountaintops that are strung out like stepping stones from the Gimpo, Namyang, and Ongjin peninsulas. The largest of these islands is Ganghwa-do. Through land reclamation, the islands of Yongyu-do and Yeongjong-do have been combined and are now home to the Incheon International Airport, opened in March 2001. The far-flung island of Baengnyeong-do is the westernmost landmass of South Korea. Baengnyeong-do lies only a few kilometers from North Korean soil off the tip of the Ongjin Peninsula, some 120 kilometers west of Incheon.

While hampered by wide mud flats, Gyeonggi-Do does have some decent beaches—all located in the islands—but none that match the

BAENGNYEONG-DO
백령도

Lying some 120 kilometers west-northwest of Incheon, only 12 kilometers from the North Korean Ongjin Peninsula, is the island of Baengnyeong-do [Paengny'ŏng-do]. The island is closer to the North Korean capital of Pyeongyang than it is to either Incheon or Seoul. Opened only recently to tourism, after decades of restricted access to all except residents because of its military and strategic location, this island and the nearby islands of Daecheong-do and Socheong-do are now experiencing an influx of visitors interested in a look across the water into North Korea, coastal fishing, summer vacations, or just the novelty of visiting this very distant and once restricted island.

Baengnyeong-do is a rocky island with many offshore islets and coastal palisades. Many of these rock outcrops have been given names that represent their shape or have some legend attached to them. The western tip of the island has the greatest concentration of these rocks, but others are found at all points around the island. One rock island off the northeast coast is known as Seal Island because it is one of the few places in Korea where seals are found. Near the main port in Jinchon is the three-kilometer-long hard-pack-sand Sagot Beach, once used for landing aircraft. On the far side of the bay is the one-kilometer small-pebble Gongdol Beach.

country's best. Seopo-ri Beach is perhaps the best in the province and, at 1.5 kilometers long, the longest. Also popular are Ulwang-ni, Shimnipo, Palmi-do, and Shi-do beaches.

History

The history in Gyeonggi-Do sweeps from the very dawn of the Korean nation to the current geopolitical stalemate that plagues this peninsula. This province and the capitals that have been located here were in a real sense the vortex of change for the entire country, the point around which society revolved and, more often than not, the catalyst for its evolution.

Evidence of prehistoric society can be found on the island of Ganghwa-do in the form of Neolithic dolmen, and an altar attributed to Dan'gun, the mythical founder of the Korean nation. Dolmen stretch through Gyeonggi-Do from Ganghwa-do down past Suwon. These burial sites have been excavated, revealing pottery and metal objects. Perhaps the most outstanding of these huge stone tomb markers lies in a field on Ganghwa-do. That dolmen is speculated to have been raised over the grave of a leader or powerful member of the Neolithic people who inhabited this island.

Post-Neolithic inhabitants of Gyeonggi-Do are known as the Mahan. From them evolved the Baekje Kingdom, one of the three kingdoms that controlled the peninsula for the first 600 years of the Christian era. The first Baekje people seem to have been immigrants from the dissolving state of Buyeo, which had had its center near the Sungari River in upper Manchuria. These refugees moved down the peninsula, first establishing settlements in Incheon and Jiksan. They coalesced into an organized state with a capital near the city of Gwangju, southeast of Seoul. In 475 however, due to repeated incursions into its territory by Goguryeo, Baekje moved its capital to Gongju, in Chungcheongnam-Do.

When the Silla Kingdom united the peninsula in A.D. 668, the center of power and influence for the entire nation moved to Gyeongju. During this period Gyeonggi-Do was left with only a secondary capital at Gwangju. At the beginning of the Goryeo Dynasty, three centuries later, the capital was moved back to Gyeonggi-Do, this time to Songdo (modern-day Gaeseong), which is now just across the border in North Korea. With the establishment of the Joseon Dynasty, the capital of Korea stayed in Gyeonggi-Do, but was moved to Seoul. There was a plan in the late 1700s to relocate the capital from Seoul to Suwon; although the Suwon city walls and fortress were built, the actual move was never inaugurated. Seoul remained the capital of the Joseon Dynasty until its demise in 1910.

The Japanese occupation brought about many changes throughout the peninsula—and adverse reactions to its repressive colonialism. In March

1919, the Koreans declared independence, and demonstrations arose in Seoul, Suwon, Gaeseong, Gimpo, Yongin, and Gwangju, among other towns in the province. This common act of nationalism was cruelly repressed by the Japanese, and brought about only minimal reforms. During the Korean War, this province changed hands several times, and the armistice finally created the artificial boundary between South and North Korea, splitting this province in two. As a truce was never signed, the armistice commission still sits face-to-face across a table in Panmunjeom spouting accusations, looking for possibilities of rapprochement, and trying to defuse any conflict that could lead to armed aggression. Although confrontations still arise, these now occur by and large across a felt-covered table, rather than a battlefield.

Transportation

South Korea's major international airport is located on reclaimed land between two offshore islands just west of downtown Incheon. The Gimpo Airport, which was the international airport until 2001, is now the country's busiest domestic airport with flights to 13 other cities throughout the country.

Because of its population and density, many expressways run through Gyeonggi-Do. The Gyeongbu Expressway (no. 1) runs south, connecting Seoul to Busan. Paralleling it to the west is the Seohaean Expressway (no. 15), to the east is the Jungbu Expressway (no. 35), and farther to the east is the Jungbu Naeryuk Expressway (no. 45). The Gyeongin Expressway (no. 120) provides much-needed transportation between Seoul and the port city of Incheon, while the 2nd Gyeongin Expressway (no. 110) connects these two cities farther to the south. To facilitate traffic to the airport, the Incheon International Airport Expressway (no. 130) runs across northern Incheon from Seoul. Plans call for a rail link to Seoul as well by the year 2005 and a bridge/tunnel expressway is also planned to connect the airport to southern Incheon. Running around the periphery of Seoul is the Seoul Circular Expressway (no. 100). From Incheon, the Yeong-

dong Expressway (no. 50) heads east, toward the mountains of Gangwon-Do and farther on to the east coast. Three others will eventually run east to west, and while no expressways currently run north of Seoul, several are planned for the future, hopefully to be expanded north into a re-united peninsula. Southeast of Pyeongtaek, the Seohaean Expressway crosses the Asan Bay via the Seohae Grand Bridge. At seven kilometers in length, this bridge is the longest in Korea and has a one-kilometer-long cable-stay suspension section slung between two towers that permits ocean-going ships to pass beneath.

A plethora of trains run on a frequent schedule throughout the province. The Gyeongbu rail line starts in Seoul and runs south to Busan, through several of the province's cities. Also starting in Seoul and running to Busan, but through the center of the country, is the Jungang rail line. This line follows the wide Han River for a good ways once it leaves the city, and then cuts through Gyeonggi-Do's eastern agricultural lands on its way south. Running east from Seoul's Cheongnyangni Station to Chuncheon is the Gyeongchun line. The Gyeongui line runs north from Seoul Station to Munsan; the Gyeongwon line runs from Seoul Cheongnyangni through Uijeongbu and Dongducheon to Shintan-ni, the northernmost point on the South Korean rail system. From Uijeongbu, the Gyooe suburban rail line runs across to Neunggok on the Gyeongui line. Seoul subway lines, which run above ground much of the way, connect the city to the terminus points and provincial cities of Goyang, Incheon, Ansan, Suwon, Seongnam, and Uijeongbu.

The vast majority of ferries in Gyeonggi-Do leave from the Incheon Yeonan pier for the islands in the West Sea and to Jeju-do. Exceptions are the ferries from Wolmi-do to Yeongjong-do for access to the Incheon International Airport, those connecting Ganghwa-do to the small islands off its west coast, and the few that run from Daebu-do to both Deokjeok-do and Jawol-do. International ferries also run from Incheon to half a dozen ports in China.

Incheon 인천

With a population of 2.5 million, Incheon [Inch'ŏn] is South Korea's fourth-largest city. Being a "metropolitan city," with status equal to a province, it was administratively separated from Gyeonggi-Do in 1981 and since 1995 has incorporated Ganghwa-do and about 150 other smaller islands within its administrative jurisdiction.

Sprawling over seaside hills and plains southwest of Seoul, this rambling city has no distinct high-rise city center. Its older section lies below Jayu Park. A newer business/shopping district sprang up near the post office in the 1960s and has continued to push east and south since then. Expansive housing and industrial estates are situated both along the city's inland periphery and on reclaimed harborfront land. A new hub has been designated near the relocated city hall and another center rising in the Songdo area will concentrate on technology, communications, and advanced industries. Aside from its trade and industrial niche, Incheon has made a name for itself as a center of education, with one national university, two private universities, and half a dozen junior colleges.

Formerly called Jemulpo, Incheon was only a tiny port before its opening to foreign countries in 1883. Through this port early diplomats, businessmen, and missionaries entered Korea. Incheon was virtually unknown outside Korea until General MacArthur's famous amphibious landing here during the early weeks of the Korean War. Saturation bombing during September 1950 preceded this successful landing, after which U.N. troops moved quickly to recapture Seoul and cut off supply lines to the North Korean troops in the southern portion of the peninsula. This maneuver turned the tide of the war. Although undertaken against the advice of nearly all senior military officers, it was a brilliant success. MacArthur's brainchild, it was his greatest victory during the conflict. (For those who remember, "Green Beach" was the ocean side of Wolmido, "Red Beach" was the area around to the north, now occupied by the outer harbor, and

"Blue Beach" was near Song-do.) After the war, Incheon was slowly rebuilt. Through centralized planning, great expense, and hard work, the city has become a thriving metropolis, inextricably intertwined with the economy of the country as a whole. Incheon produces many items, some of which are fish and seafood products, processed, canned, and bottled food and drink, textiles, wood products and furniture, glass, machinery, automobiles, auto parts, fertilizers and chemicals.

Incheon has the country's second-largest harbor and is one of two major ports on the west coast. It's also Seoul's closest access to the sea. The city's international status has brought a variety of foreigners to the city, and it's now one of the few places in the country where a variety of foreign languages can frequently be heard. Extreme tidal variation, plus narrow channels, swift currents, and hundreds of square kilometers of mudflats have always plagued the harbor's development. Although the port facilities have periodically been revamped since its opening in 1883, the last 40 years have brought about phenomenal improvements in capacity and efficiency, making the harbor more attractive to domestic and international shipping companies. By connecting the islands of Wolmi-do and Sowolmi-do to the mainland, the harbor has been enclosed. The inner harbor is now entered through a sea lock, making it the largest lock gate harbor in Asia, with a capacity of nearly four dozen ships. Dredging the main channels to this lock gate has made it possible to enter the inner harbor at any time. Land reclamation in both directions from the inner harbor has added additional port and storage facilities, and while still affected by the tide, they are also accessible at all times. Incheon's current port facilities have just about reached their capacity and this has caused great growth in harbor facilities down the coast at Pyeongtaek and Gunsan.

In one of former president Chun's proposals for reunification of the peninsula, Incheon was recommended as an open port (along with one in

North Korea) for goods and passenger traffic between the two countries. Although nothing came from this intriguing idea, Incheon was once used for the transfer of relief supplies from the North after the disastrous flooding of Seoul in the summer of 1985, and it has been employed since then for other shipments from the South to the North. Its capacity and location makes it a natural link for such commerce.

For information about Incheon on the Internet, see www.incheon.go.kr or www.inpia.net.

SIGHTS

Aside from seamen or those catching an early ship to China, most travelers don't spend any time in Incheon but simply pass through on their way to Seoul. Although Incheon contains comparatively little of cultural importance, the city does draw domestic tourists. Many new city parks have been created for the enjoyment of the rapidly expanding and more leisure-conscious population, historical sites have been refurbished, temples and shrines given recognition as places of cultural and religious significance, and venues established for the city's new cultural awakening.

Jayu Park 자유공원

Capping a hill that overlooks the inner harbor is Jayu ("Freedom") Park. Opened in 1888, only five years after the first foreigners walked through the city, it is the country's oldest Western-style park. Its many shade trees and long walkways render it a peaceful enclave in the midst of a bustling city, a favorite of those who come for early-morning or evening exercise or to sit and play board games with their cronies, and it shows its best attire in spring when cherry trees in full bloom adorn the streets leading to the hill. Occupying a place of prominence is a statue of General MacArthur, erected in 1957. Resolute and confident, he gazes out over the much-changed harbor, near where he first approached this country. One of the best views over the inner harbor is from the pavilion near one of the entrances to the park; this vantage point yields a colorful panoply of city lights and the harbor at night. In another

section of the park is a much newer, modernistic monument, erected in 1982 to commemorate the centennial of Korean–U.S. diplomatic relations. In the center of this stone quadrangle is a sculpture of two intertwining, lumpy links of chain over which rise eight upward-thrusting triangular shafts that symbolize sails reaching toward the heavens.

Chinatown

An elaborately ornamented gate stands at the entrance to a street across from Incheon Station. This marks Incheon's Chinatown, and its main street runs up the hill, jogs, and heads up to Jayu Park. Mostly neglected for decades, this area is going through a reawakening. A number of well-decorated Chinese restaurants and a few other shops are in the side streets and alleys nearby. While this area is small, a few buildings still show some features typical of Chinese architecture. Perhaps the best of these are two blocks up from the gate and to the right, where several old two-story buildings sporting second-story verandas still line the street. In the late 1800s, the Chinese embassy was located in this neighborhood, and the site that it occupied is now home to the Overseas Chinese School. In the early 1900s, a simple Korean-Chinese dish called *jajangmyeon* was created here. This dish, which is wheat noodles covered with a black bean sauce, can now be found in nearly every Chinese restaurant in the country.

Old Town

The area of town below Jayu Park, just around the corner from Chinatown, was the center of the old city and one of the first places that foreigners settled in the country. Although most were destroyed, a few structures remain to speak of their influence. The Western-style Culture Hall on the slope below the park was built in 1901 and used by foreigners as a social club. The red-brick Dap-dong Catholic Church (H.S. #287), completed in 1897, was the first large Western-style church building constructed in the country, and the smaller stone Naedong Church is a reconstruction of the first Anglican Church in Korea (1891). Because of their long occupation of the country, the Japanese left the greatest influence.

INCHEON

Outer Harbor

FERRY

SEE
DETAIL

West

Wolmi-
do

Inner
Harbor

Sea

Sowolmi-do

Subong
Park

YEONAN FERRY
TERMINAL

FIRST INTERNATIONAL
PASSENGER FERRY
TERMINAL

FISH MARKET

★ NEW STAR
HOTEL

■ INHA
UNIVERSITY

DOHOBUCHEONGSA ★

INCHEON
HYANGGYO ★

MUNHAK
STADIUM ■

DETAIL

HWADOJIN
★

INCHEON
STATION ■

HWANGHAE
YEOGWAN ■

*Jayu
Park*

SWISS ■
MOTEL

INCHEON ■
DEPARTMENT
STORE

CENTRAL
MARKET ■

PARADISE
OLYMPOS
HOTEL ■

CULTURE ★
HALL

HONGYE GATE ★

DONG
INCHEON
STATION ■

■ POLICE

JAPAN FIRST ■
BANK BUILDING

58 BANK ■
BUILDING

NAEDONG CHURCH ★

● BAIK JAE HOTEL

*Shinpo-
dong*

DAP-DONG ★
CATHOLIC CHURCH

■ TELECOM

POST ■
OFFICE

KOREAN FOREIGN
EXCHANGE BANK ■

USEONG ●
MOTEL

E-MART ■

*Inner
Harbor*

SECOND
INTERNATIONAL
PASSENGER FERRY

NEUNGHEO-DAE ★

INCHEON MUNICIPAL
MUSEUM ★

INCHEON LANDING ★
MEMORIAL HALL

Munhak-san ▲

卍 HEUNGNYUN-SA

● HOTEL
SONGDO BEACH

SONGDO
AMUSEMENT
PARK

Songdo
New Town

INCHEON SUBWAY LINE

GYEONGGI-DO

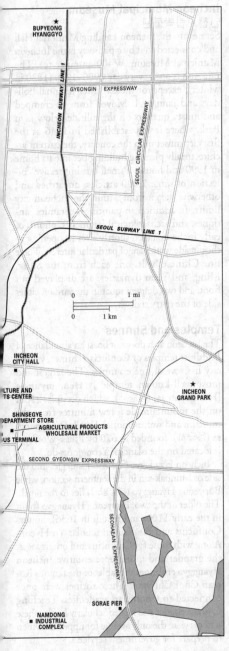

A few buildings from that time are the Japan First Bank building (1883), the Japan 58 Bank building (1892), the main post office (1923), Hongye Gate (1908) on the eastern end of Jayu Park, and the empty warehouses to the east of the post office that were used mostly to store goods for shipment out of the country.

Wolmi-do 월미도

An offshore island until the 1920s, Wolmi-do was connected to the mainland by a causeway and built up with salt-water baths, an amusement park, and other outdoor recreational facilities. Bombed to a pulpy mound during the Incheon landing in order to remove the North Korean soldiers ensconced there in fortified tunnels and gun emplacements, Wolmi-do has been remodeled and is now the scene of one of Incheon's most well-known seafood streets and the venue of a cultural festival in October. But Wolmi-do is more than this. Sometimes referred to as the "Street of Culture," its promenade features street musicians and other performers, caricature artists, occasional city-sponsored music, dance, and theater performances, art exhibitions and contests, one of the few places in the city where you can actually get down to the water, and on fine-weather days, one of the best sunset spots in the city. In addition, there are plenty of coffee shops and bars, amusement rides, and a handful of motels. Reminding you that this is a thriving international port, flags from around the world fly along the seafront walk, and the bridge to Yeongjong-do and the international airport is clearly outlined in lights to the north. From the Wolmi-do pier, commuter ferries run to Yeongjong-do and excursion ferries ply the outer harbor.

Songdo Amusement Park 송도유원지

About eight kilometers south of the city center is Songdo Amusement Park. Developed in the 1930s as a seaside resort for the city people, it was, until a few decades ago, at the end of the narrow gauge rail line that ran here from Suwon. Used by the military during the war, it went through its modern development in the 1960s. Hyped as a "beach resort," it's no longer at water's edge, due to land reclamation along the coast. Although the lagoon swimming area is free, the lap pool, amusement rides, golf course, arcade games, bungee-jumping platform, and boat rental all require separate admissions. Entrance is ₩3,000 adults, ₩2,000 students, and ₩1,500 children; with a Big 3 ticket at ₩8,500, ₩6,000, ₩4,000; and a Big 5 ticket at ₩12,500, ₩9,000, ₩6,000, respectively. Numerous restaurants, snack shops, and souvenir concessions—not all open throughout the year—dot the grounds. Once a leisurely getaway, this has become a mass frenetic experience on any given summer day. Families come with tents, mats, ice chests, bags of food, games, and air mattresses in hand to make a day of it on the sand. While not as pleasurable as it once was, it is still a perfect place to watch Koreans entertain themselves in a pseudo-beach park arena. To its credit, however, it does maintain a small but pretty flower garden, walkways of cherry trees that flood the area with a canopy of pink in the spring, and occasional open-air music concerts. As with Jayu Park and Wolmi-do, some come here on fair-weather days just to see the sunset. The best place for this, perhaps, is the tiny Aam-do islet, once reachable by picking your way across the mudflats at low tide on the backs of rocks but now connected by dry land.

Incheon Landing Memorial Hall
인천상륙작전기념관
Up the hill from Songdo Amusement Park is the Incheon Landing Memorial Hall. Against all bets, this amphibious operation turned the tide of the Korean War. While a heroic frieze graces the arch over the stairway leading up to the memorial, a tall spire of stone and a bronze statue of foreign soldiers crown the memorial sculpture. On the plaza below and to the side are military vehicles and war planes used during the war, and in the courtyard hang flags of participating nations. On display inside the exhibition hall are many emotionally moving pictures, numerous small weapons and military supplies, and other objects relating to the war. While you can visit the plaza at any time, the free exhibition hall is open 0900–1800 (1700 in winter); closed Mondays.

Incheon Municipal Museum
인천시립박물관
Set next to the Incheon Landing Memorial Hall and connected to it by a pathway is the Incheon Municipal Museum; ₩400 entrance fee. The museum is open every day 0900–1930 (1830 in winter), except for the day after national holidays and January 1. Moved from its cramped and musty quarters on the hillside below Jayu Park, where it was established in 1946 as the first city museum in the country, the current architecturally pleasing building became its home in 1990 and houses a small but impressive collection of some 2,000 articles, unearthed and otherwise, taken from within the Incheon city limits. In addition to paintings, ceramics, antiques, and archaeological fragments, photos of early Incheon, taken shortly after its opening to the outside world, are of particular interest. Three fine Chinese bells, one each from the Sung, Ming, and Yuan dynasties, are displayed out front, and two dolmen squat in the yard on either side of the entry stairway.

Temples and Shrines
The Incheon area does not boast an abundance of Buddhist temples or Confucian shrines, yet the city has several fine examples. The largest and most well-known temple is **Heungnyun-sa** [Hŭngnyun-sa] (흥륜사), which occupies a spot on the mountainside a few minutes from the museum and war memorial. Smaller **Yonggung-sa** (용궁사), founded in 670 by Priest Wonhyo, is located on the island of Yeongjong-do.

Incheon Hyanggyo (인천향교) snuggles into the side of Munhak-san in the southern section, while Bupyeong Hyanggyo (부평향교) lies to the north. The older of the two, **Bupyeong Hyanggyo** (built in the early 1100s and rebuilt in 1636), honors Confucius and the Korean scholar Yu Hyeon. Along with those for Confucius and others sages, the grander and more representative **Incheon Hyanggyo** enshrines the tablet of the famous Korean Choi Chi-won. These shrines were once connected to Confucian academies. Teaching Chinese classics and related scholarly books, these schools were the only avenue for upper-class men to prepare for government service.

Other Historical Sites

Inland from Songdo, the remains of a Baekje fortress features earthen walls; stone building fragments cap **Munhak-san**. This fortress was supposedly used by King Biryu when he moved his seat of government here in the early 300s. On the lower southern slope of this mountain, set next to the Incheon Hyanggyo, is the Joseon-era government office complex called **Incheon Dohobucheongsa** (인천도호부청사), that includes a magistrate's office and a visiting official's guesthouse. For most of the Joseon Dynasty, this and the area of Bupyeong were the seats of local government, and centers for commerce and population for the area west of Seoul. Remains of another ancient mountain fortress are to be found within the boundaries of Gyeyang Park to the north. **Hwadojin** (화도진), a Joseon Dynasty military command fortress from 1879, sits within a city park near Incheon Station. It was here in 1882 that Korean and American representatives signed a treaty establishing diplomatic and economic ties between the two countries. Buildings here have been rebuilt in the late Joseon-era style, and several hundred historical artifacts have been refurbished and put on display. Occasional cultural performances are held on these grounds, and a yearly cultural festival takes place here. Not far north of Songdo is the rebuilt **Neungheodae [Nŭnghŏ-dae] Pavilion** (능호대). As sea links between Korea and China have been reestablished after several decades of closure, it is appropriate that this pavilion be erected because it was from near here that Baekje envoys were said to have set sail for China over 1,500 years ago. Because of land reclamation, Neungheodae no longer sits at water's edge but it does still overlook the sea.

PRACTICALITIES

Hotels

As the most central of the city hotels, the deluxe-class **Paradise Olympos Hotel** (tel. 032/762-5181, www.olympos.co.kr) sits on a seaside knoll beyond Incheon Station, where it gets an unobstructed view of the busy inner harbor. Rates start at ₩160,000 for rooms and go on up to ₩450,000 for suites. The hotel has Korean, Japanese, and Western restaurants, banquet rooms, a coffee shop, souvenir shop, sauna, and a nightclub. For some, the hotel's strongest drawing card is its casino, oldest in the country and open to foreign guests only. The hotel offers guests free transportation to and from Incheon International Airport. The deluxe-class **Hotel Songdo Beach** (tel. 032/830-2200, www.songdobeach.co.kr) overlooks Songdo Amusement Park, yet has the most serene hotel environment in the city. Room rates start at ₩150,000 for Korean- or Western-style rooms and run ₩250,000–600,000 for suites; full amenities and services are provided, including a health club, sauna, theater restaurant, banquet rooms, and convention facilities. Smaller and less expensive is the first-class **New Star Hotel** (tel. 032/885-8111) which is conveniently located not far from the harbor.

Yeogwan

Perhaps the most convenient (if coming by subway) and inexpensive places to stay are the many *yeogwan* and *yeoinsuk* in the side streets below Jayu Park. On the street directly up from Incheon Station is Hwanghae Yeogwan (황해여관), a decent, clean, and relatively quiet low-budget establishment. Others here are Sumyeongjang Yeogwan (수명장여관), Buseongjang Yeogwan (부성장여관), and Deungdae Yeoinsuk (등대여인숙). A friendly and moderately priced place in a quieter neighborhood on the far side of Jayu Park is Swiss Motel (스위스모텔), with Korean- and Western-style rooms for ₩25,000–30,000. In the Shinpo-dong area, try the Baik Jae Hotel (백제호텔), where rooms run ₩35,000–40,000. Almost next door is the less expensive Incheon Yeogwan (인천여관) and across the street and down is the cheaper Silla Yeoinsuk (신라여인숙). Closer to the pier is the Useong Motel (우성모텔) with rooms for ₩25,000. You'll find many accommodations of various classes in other parts of the city—such as those across from the Yeonan Ferry Terminal, in front of Songdo Amusement Park, and on Wolmi-do. In front of the Yeonan

Ferry Terminal, check the Napoli Motel (나포리모텔) or the Uncheonjang Yeogwan (운천장여관). In Songdo, look at the Silk Road Motel (실크로드모텔) and the Alps Motel (알프스모텔), both up the street toward the Incheon Landing Memorial Hall. Among others, Samhaejang Motel (삼해장모텔) and New Star Motel (뉴스타모텔) are two average accommodations at Wolmi-do along its main street.

Food

Incheon's large fishing fleet brings in countless seafood delicacies for sampling. The area is famous for spicy clam soup and deep-fried prawns. Many well-known seafood eateries are along the pier on Wolmi-do. You'll find other such seafood eateries across from the Yeonan Ferry Terminal, while delicacies from the deep go to the table right from the ship at the Sorae Inlet pier in the south of the city. In the center of town, the Shinpo-dong market area is a place to find a variety of restaurants, including a number of Western restaurants and bars catering to foreigners. Other Western restaurants, plus well-heeled Korean, Japanese, and Chinese places to eat are found in the area surrounding the Songdo Beach Hotel. A handful of small but quality Chinese restaurants are located in Incheon's Chinatown.

Shopping

Incheon's major shopping district is **Shinpo-dong,** located not far from the main post office toward Dong Incheon Station. Like a miniature version of Seoul's Myeong-dong, this area has gained a reputation as a fashion center for all its fancy clothing, shoe, and accessory shops, but it also has a covered shopping mall with all sorts of goods, restaurants, accommodations, and cinemas. An underground arcade runs for several hundred meters under roads in three directions from the Dong Incheon Station, while other underground arcades are found in front of the Jemulpo and Bupyeong subway stations. Markets of all sizes appear all around the city, but three of note are the Central Market, located just north of Dong Incheon Station, the agricultural products wholesale market east of the bus terminal, and the wholesale fish market near the Yeonan

Ferry Terminal. The Central Market used to be the place for black market foreign goods before there was freer import into the country. Now it carries more pedestrian items and such things as silk, quilts, and clothing. At the east end of this market is the Baedari section where a number of shops make and sell traditional handicraft items and souvenirs. For department stores, perhaps the most convenient are Shinsegae near the bus terminal and Incheon Department Store at the Dong Incheon Station. The big E-Mart is not far from the main post office.

Tourist Information

Various tourist information centers are located throughout the city with plenty of good advice, maps, and brochures. You will find these in front of the Incheon Station, on the promenade at Wolmi-do, along the street in Shinpo-dong, at city hall, in the bus terminal, and at both international ferry terminals.

The city operates a tour bus service on several routes that stop at many of the most popular sights within the city. Fares generally run about ₩2,000 for a single ride or ₩5,000 for a day pass. Check with the tourist office for exact routes and times.

TRANSPORTATION
Subway

There is no national rail service to Incheon, however, there is a subway connection to Seoul. The Seoul subway line to Incheon stops at eight stations within the port city, making connection from the capital very convenient, and, in most cases, the easiest way to get to and from Seoul. As this train runs aboveground until it reaches the center of Seoul, it is in effect a suburban rail line. The ride from Incheon Station, in the heart of the old city, to Seoul Station takes about an hour. Within Seoul, all subway trains on this line (#1) continue on to the Seongbuk subway station, and many go out as far as Uijeongbu, an hour and forty-five minute ride. Running every 4–8 minutes throughout the day, the first train from Incheon leaves at 0500; the last heads into the heart of the capital at 2246. If you are heading south to Suwon or Ansan, change trains in Guro (and again in Geumjeong for Ansan). For Seoul subway line #2, transfer at Shindorim or at the Seoul City Hall Station. Both the Incheon and the Dong Incheon stations are equally convenient for hopping on the subway. You'll find Incheon Station at the end of the subway line; Dong Incheon Station, one station up, is larger and busier.

Incheon also has its own subway line—with a second and third line on the way. Line #1 runs north to south, crossing the Seoul subway line at Bupyeong. Although the subway is a great benefit to city residents, most travelers will not find this line particularly useful except to get to and from the bus terminal, city hall, and the Munhak World Cup Soccer stadium. Although roundabout, it's perhaps faster and less hassle to ride the subway from the bus terminal to the city center than to take the bus.

Ferries

From the **Wolmi-do pier,** vehicular ferries leave once every half hour 0530–2130 for the 15-minute ride to Yeongjong-do; ₩1,300 per passenger. Meeting each ferry at the Yeongjong-do pier are buses to the international airport and to island communities.

Coastal ferries from Incheon leave from the **Yeonan Ferry Terminal** (연안여객선터미날). Hourly ferries run to Jagyak-do Monday–Saturday and twice as often on Sunday and holidays; ₩7,000 round-trip. For the 120-kilometer ride to Baengnyeong-do, stopping at Daecheong-do and Socheong-do on the way, the airfoil ferry *Democracy 1* leaves Incheon at 0740 and makes the daily crossing in 4 hours. Two catamaran ferries also run this same route, leaving at 0810 and 1210. The fare to Baengnyeong-do is ₩43,200. For Yeonpyeong-do, halfway to Baengnyeong-do, a ferry goes Monday, Wednesday, and Saturday at 1000 and on Friday at 0800; ₩24,700. Occasional ferries also connect Incheon to other islands closer to the coast. During the summer, ferries bulge with swimmers, fishermen, vacationers, and local commuters. The islands with the best-known beaches are Deokjeok-do (Seopori Beach), Yeongheung-do (Shimnipo Beach),

Yongyu-do (Ulwang-ni Beach), and Shi-do (Shi-do Beach). Other islands have beaches and other leisure spots as well, but they are generally less developed.

Leaving at 1900 on Monday, Wednesday, and Friday for a 15-hour cruise, the overnight car ferry to Jeju-do runs ₩42,000–77,000. This ferry departs from the Incheon First International Ferry Terminal building next door to the coastal ferry building.

When boarding a ferry to any distant island, you may be asked to produce your identification and submit to a baggage check. This is especially true for the passengers going to Baengnyeong-do and Yeonpyeong-do, because these islands lie very close to North Korea.

Excursion Ferries

An excursion ferry leaves from the Yeonan pier park for a one-hour tour of the outer harbor and inner island sea off Incheon. These trips operate 1100–1730 and tickets run ₩7,000 for adults. Offering a similar program, the *Cosmos* and *Harmony* excursion cruisers depart from the Wolmi-do pier. Leaving once an hour from 1100 to 2000 (less often in winter), they run one-hour tours of the outer harbor and the sea between Wolmi-do and the international airport for ₩10,000 a person. On fine-weather days, this cruise is perhaps best near sundown. Twilight buffet dinners are also an option for an extra fee.

International Ferries

With ferry service from Korea to China resumed after more than four decades, Incheon has once again become an international ferry port. From the **Second International Passenger Ferry Terminal** (제 2 국제여객선터미날), located about a 15-minute walk from the main post office, the *New Golden Bridge* car ferry leaves for Weihai on Tuesday, Thursday, and Saturday at 1800 (14-hour crossing) and the *Hyang Soran* leaves for Qingdao on Wednesday and Saturday at 1300 (20-hour crossing). Weihai is located on the eastern tip of the Shandong Peninsula, Qingdao on its southern coast. Depending on class, fares range from ₩110,000 to ₩200,000, with discounts for children, students, and groups. For information and reservations in Incheon, call Weidong Marine Transportation (tel. 032/886-6171). In addition, the Jincheon Line connects Incheon to Tianjin, Beijing's main access to the sea. Leaving on Tuesday at 1300 and Friday at 1900, this ferry takes over one full day to cross; the return ferry from Tianjin leaves at 1300 on Monday and Friday. Fares run ₩115,000–250,000. For information, call Jincheon Marine Transportation (tel. 032/888-7911). Ticket counters, a city-sponsored tourist-information office, snack shops, and money exchange are located inside this terminal building, and a duty-free shop is located inside the bonded area.

The newer **First International Passenger Ferry Terminal** (제 1 국제여객선터미날) is located to the side of the Yeonan passenger ferry terminal building. Inside this modern structure are ticket counters, snack shops, duty-free shops, restaurants, money exchange booths, and a tourist information office. Out front are many restaurants and accommodations convenient for those waiting for a boat. From this terminal, ferries run to Yantai, Dandong, Dalien, and Shanghai, all in China. The *Da-In* to Dalien runs every Wednesday and Saturday at 1800, arriving the following day at 1200. Fares run ₩115,000–231,000, depending on class, with discounts for students, children, and groups. For information, contact the Daein Ferry Co. (tel. 032/891-7100 in Incheon or 02/3218-6500 in Seoul). The C&K Ferry Co. runs ferries to and from Yantai, leaving Incheon Tuesday at 1800 and Thursday at 1900. Fares for either of their two ferries run from ₩110,000 for a first-class room up to ₩336,000 for the VIP room. For information, contact the company (tel. 032/891-8880 in Incheon or tel. 02/360-6900 in Seoul). The *Eastern Silk* departs on Tuesday and Friday at 1800 for Dandong, and takes 16 hours. Fares are ₩115,000–210,000. Going the farthest, a Shanghai-bound

ferry requires 36 hours. It leaves Incheon at 1900 on Saturday, and fares are ₩135,000–438,750.

You must proceed through immigration and customs before boarding any of these ships, and you must already have a valid Chinese visa. Visas can be obtained from the Chinese Embassy in Seoul, located behind the Central Post Office; allow several days to process the application. Above and beyond the fare, there is a ₩1,100 use fee levied on all departing passengers.

Intercity Buses

The large and modern Incheon Bus Terminal (인천종합버스터미날) sits some distance from the center of the city, but near the expressway. It sits adjacent to a large multi-story shopping center, and lies near the new city hall complex and the Culture and Arts Center. From here, express buses run to Daegu (₩12,900), Busan (₩17,800), Gwangju (₩13,800), Daejeon (₩7,400), Jeonju (₩10,500), Mokpo (₩16,000), Sokcho (₩13,000), and Jinju (₩17,400). Intercity buses also leave from this station to various sites all over the peninsula including Seoul train station (₩2,600), Ganghwa (₩3,800), Munsan (₩4,800), and Suwon (₩3,000).

City Buses

Incheon has an extensive city bus system. Helpful for getting around town are the following:
Incheon Station: 2, 15, 23, 45
Dong Incheon Station: 2, 15, 12, 24, 28, 45
Wolmi-do: 2, 15, 23, 45, 101
Songdo Amusement Park, Municipal Museum: 6, 8, 9, 16, 99, 105, 107
Yeonan Ferry Terminal: 12, 24, 28, 33, 36
Incheon Culture and Arts Center: 3, 21, 41, 45
Incheon Hyanggyo: 27
Munhak Stadium: 6, 63
Sorae pier: 21, 38

Ganghwa-do 강화도

From either Seoul or Incheon, the trip to Ganghwa-do [Kanghwa-do] takes you across the fertile plains of the Gimpo Peninsula. Wide and flat, only low hills break the carpet of paddy fields that spread to the sea. Into this green cover intrudes the black tarmac of Gimpo Airport, and this neatly sectioned agricultural flatland was the first view of Korea that most arriving visitors saw before the opening of Incheon International Airport in 2001.

The 305-square-kilometer island of Ganghwa-do, South Korea's fifth-largest, was formed by the accumulation of Han River silt, and seems like an extension of the Gimpo Peninsula. Its hills, once separate islands, are now bonded together by alluvial plains, to which have been added limited tracts of reclaimed land. The island's ambience is distinctly rural, although the spate of development has made major inroads on this pastoral island, and some people from Seoul and Incheon maintain second homes or weekend retreats on the island. Ganghwa-do offers numerous prehistoric remains and historical attractions. Scattered throughout the island hills are several temples of great antiquity and cultural significance, a handful of the last dynasty's military forts and other fortifications, several kings' tombs, and prehistoric burial sites. In honor of Dan'gun, the mythical founder of the Korean nation, the Gangdo Cultural Festival is held every year in mid-October. Events include a parade and fireworks in the town of Ganghwa; a memorial ceremony for Dan'gun at

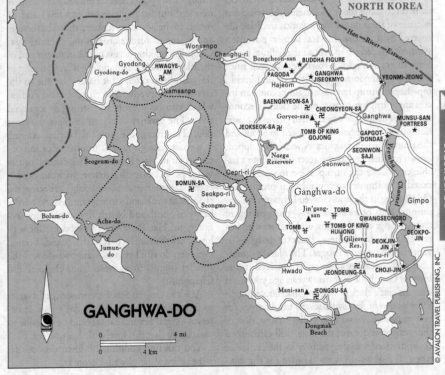

GANGHWA-DO

0   4 mi
0   4 km

© AVALON TRAVEL PUBLISHING, INC.

GYEONGGI-DO

LAND RECLAMATION

Although much land reclamation has taken place in the country, particularly along the west coast of the country, this phenomenon is not new. Since the Goguryeo Dynasty, Koreans have built dikes and levees and drained the enclosed water to create farm acreage in order to support a growing population. Much of this land reclamation seems to have taken place on small islands where it was relatively easy to enclose shallow bays and inlets, and Ganghwa-do shows some evidence of this work.

Chamseong-dan, an ancient stone altar at the top of Mani-san; a play relating to the Goryeo *sambyeolcho;* and farmers' music.

Along with the area surrounding Gaeseong (Songdo) in North Korea, this island grows some of the country's highest-quality *insam*. Here and there throughout the island, these fields stand out because of their raised frameworks, traditionally covered by straw thatch. Most farmers now use a synthetic shadecloth to protect the delicate plants from direct sunlight. Grown here as well since the Three Kingdoms period, the small, pinkish, top-shaped turnip has once again become an increasingly important part of the island's economy and of the people's diet. Often grown in plastic hothouses, this vegetable is trucked to Seoul and the nearby provincial cities. A wide, flat-topped, brown mushroom has also recently become a sizable crop. Like the turnip, these too are usually raised in hothouses to control their production. Originating in the mid-Goryeo Dynasty, the traditional craft of *hwamunseok*— the weaving of colored sedge mats, screens, and baskets with floral, animal, and Chinese character designs—is kept alive in country villages. The island's diminishing silk-weaving industry is centered in the town of Ganghwa. Not many years ago you could hear the clack-clack of weaving machines through the windows of the town's several small factories as you walked the town's back alleys. Now most of the weaving is done at the large, well-established computerized weaving factory in the center of town. Ganghwa-do is also known for the *bandashi,* a small wooden chest where the top half of the front opens for storage. The whole is decorated and hinged by decorative metalwork.

From the hilltops at the island's northern end and from the villages along its northern shore, you can see across the one-kilometer-wide Han River estuary into North Korea. From here you can also hear the blurred sounds of propaganda broadcast toward the south throughout the day. Because of its proximity to the north, Ganghwa-do has a large military presence and is virtually surrounded by a barbed wire–topped chain-link fence. Although the military keeps a low profile, defensive positions are seen all over the island, and the rumble of trucks or the whop-whop-whop of helicopters is not a chance occurrence. Although there is no longer a nighttime vehicular curfew, entrance to some villages along the north coast may be restricted to residents in the evening.

The old Ganghwa Bridge spans the Yeomha Channel at a point near an old ferry crossing. A new and sturdier highway bridge a few hundred meters to the north has replaced the old structure, and a second bridge crosses the channel near Choji-jin, making access to the southern end of the island much easier and quicker. Crossing to the island was often a bit hazardous due to the channel's unpredictable currents and eddies, which can be as swift and strong as a gorged river. The severity of action in these waters is due, of course, to the great tidal variation along this coast. Ganghwa-do's unusual location accounts for its place in history. This natural fortress was a perfect place for refuge; without experienced seamen, enemies could only glare across the channel at the island's inhabitants. As the border between South and North Korea splits this section of the Han River estuary, no boat traffic is allowed off the north coast of this island. Ferries, however, do run between Ganghwa-do and the smaller islands to its west, from Oepo-ri and Changhu-ri.

As it's so close to Seoul, the majority of tourists to this island come for only a day's visit. It deserves longer! Several days should be set aside to soak up all that this lovely isle has to offer.

You can find additional information on the website www.ganghwa.incheon.kr.

History

Ganghwa-do has played center stage during three dramatic periods over the last 800 years. In 1232, King Gojong fled the Mongol invasion and retreated to Ganghwa-do to set up his government in internal exile; throughout the entire Mongol occupation, this island was virtually the only piece of Korean real estate that was not overrun. Ganghwa-do was fortified, and a mini-capital created. The court stayed put until an understanding was reached with the Mongols, and only moved back to Songdo in 1270.

Ganghwa-do again became a royal refuge when the Manchu army began pouring through the country in 1636. King Injo moved his entire court here, but before the king himself could reach the island, he was cut off by Manchu troops. The Manchus overran Ganghwa-do, taking the royal family hostage, and King Injo eventually surrendered. As a result, Korea became a client state to the Manchus and was forced to fight alongside them against their former allies, the Ming Chinese.

In 1866, during a period of strong anti-Western sentiment, several French priests were killed after they refused an order to leave the country. In response, the French navy, led by Admiral Roze, invaded Ganghwa-do and captured two of its forts. The French held them for a few weeks, but were eventually forced to retreat.

In 1871, an American flotilla commanded by Rear Admiral Rodgers was ordered into Korean waters to try to repeat in Korea Admiral Perry's opening of trade relations with Japan. Rodgers encountered much resistance, and his ships drew cannon fire from several batteries along the Ganghwa-do coast. Like the French, the Americans landed on the island and overran several command posts and gun emplacements, but they suffered many casualties. Seeing that their mission could not be accomplished without great sacrifice, the Americans picked up and left.

Next came Japan's turn to demand trade relations, and they arrived in force in 1875. Able to present little effective opposition this time, Korea signed the Treaty of Ganghwa (otherwise acrimoniously known as the "Treaty of Amity") the following year. This pact opened the ports of Incheon, Busan, and Wonsan (in North Korea) to Japanese trade, granted the Japanese the right to live in these cities and establish businesses, and revised the diplomatic relations between the two countries. This foothold was the first step toward Japan's eventual annexation of the Korean Peninsula some 35 years later.

GANGHWA 강화읍

The island of Ganghwa-do and the smaller islands to the west, once a separate county area, have recently come under the administrative jurisdiction of Incheon city. The town of Ganghwa is Ganghwa-do's major population center. This laid-back seat of local government has a deep cultural foundation, numerous historical remains, and a small yet strong economic base. The effects of development are obvious here as the town pushes its perimeter out into the surrounding countryside. In the center of town, back-alley market stalls sell their wares in the shadow of a newer, multi-story central market building. Market day is every fifth day, falling on days ending in 2 or 7. Relocated next to the Telecom office, the agricultural market now sits on the site of the fortress's eastern water gate. **Insam Center** (강화인삼센타), located out beyond the Telecom office, was built to highlight the island's most famous product. Ginseng in all its forms—bulk, bottled, and packaged—as well as honey, mushrooms, and nuts is on display and for sale. A **Native Products Sales Center** (강화토산품판매장) is located just down the road from the south gate and built in a style reminiscent of a fortress gate. In its numerous shops you can find virtually anything that the island produces. Amongst the genuine articles, some generic manufactured souvenirs are also becoming available.

All sights within town are an easy walk from its center. Up the street to the north past the silk factory is the palace site, and farther up this road is the north gate of the old fortress. West of the market is the west gate. Occupying a spot in the middle of town is the police station; one block to the east is the town office, and beyond that the post office and Telecom office. To give it more room, the bus terminal has been constructed on the eastern outskirts of town, beyond the end of the agricultural market.

Fortress

The Ganghwa town fortress was constructed in the 1230s, when it became obvious that the Mongols were intent upon pushing into the peninsula to expand their control over East Asia. Before the onrush of barbarian invaders, the Korean royal house and court fled to this fortified town, making it the capital of the Goryeo Dynasty from 1232 to 1270. After the king returned to his rightful throne in Songdo, the earthen berm fortress fell into disrepair. It was rebuilt in the early 1600s, in expectation of a Manchu invasion. Walls and gates were constructed, this time of stone, and palace buildings and government offices erected. In 1636, the court once again fled, making Ganghwa-do their refuge. Early the next year, the Manchus captured the town and destroyed it. In 1677, this fortress was once again rebuilt, and went through a major restoration in the early 1700s by order of King Sukjong. The French burnt the fortress to the ground when they retreated from the island in 1866. The most recent restoration of select parts occurred from 1974 to 1977. These remains (H.S. #132) date mostly from the Sukjong period of the early 1700s.

Town Gates

Three of the fortress's original four main gates have been reconstructed. Partially covered with ivy, the gracefully arched south gate is connected to a short section of the old fortress wall. Other sections of this wall can be still be found in the hills above town. The gate's shuttered pavilion was the scene of a tragic yet honorable incident which occurred during the humiliating defeat by the Manchus. In 1636, with the royal court in exile here, this supposedly invulnerable island fell quickly to the Manchu troops. It's said that court ladies threw themselves into the sea rather than let the Chinese take them prisoner (or worse). The queen and royal family were captured and the fortress was ruined. A loyal retainer and former prime minister, Kim Sang-yong, saw an opportunity to save face. He

took the ruling family's ancestral memorial tablets to the pavilion over the south gate. With grandson and servants in attendance, he ignited a cache of gunpowder and blew the gate to smithereens, thus keeping these most precious items from the hands of the enemy. For his brave sacrifice, two memorial markers have been engraved and are now set up at the street corner near the town's largest silk factory. In addition, in 1658, the shrine Chungyeolsa was erected 2.5 kilometers south of town on the home property of the former prime minister in memory of him and two dozen other national martyrs.

The west gate resembles the south gate, with its arched opening, flat fitted stone, and painted pavilion. To each side is a short section of fortress wall, a portion of which was reconstructed in 1994. Like the south gate, the west gate was rebuilt in 1711 and has been renovated a number of times since. Across the road, a granite monument indicates the site of the former military drill pavilion, where the 1876 Treaty of Ganghwa was signed, opening the door to foreign influence in the country. Korea, until then cut off in self-imposed isolation from the rest of the world, was never the same again.

On the ridge of the hill north of the town center stands the reconstructed north gate. Looking to the north through the opening of this gate you see across the Han River estuary into North Korea, and you can easily hear the patriotic music and propaganda blaring from loudspeakers across the water. This gate has a flatter arched opening; through it runs a walking path to the fields and villages below. About 150 meters down the north side on a secondary path you'll find a natural freshwater spring. Stop and quench your thirst before heading back into town.

The east gate is gone, but the eastern water sluice, one of two original water gates, still stands. Built during the 1676 reconstruction of the fortress, this triple-arch stone structure was moved to Gapgot-dondae in 1900. In 1977, it was moved back and reconstructed on its original site, but returned to Gapot when the town's new agricultural market was constructed in the early 1990s. The western water sluice spanned the stream next to the west gate but is no more.

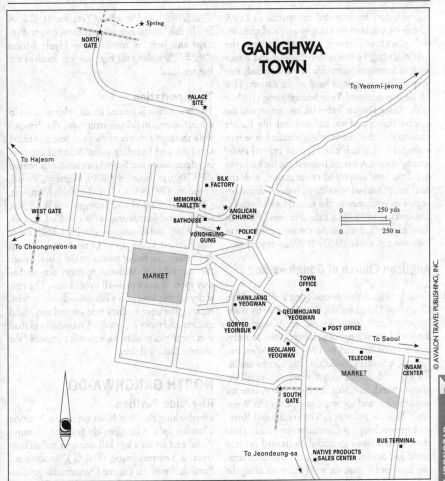

GANGHWA TOWN

To Yeonmi-jeong

★ Spring

NORTH GATE

PALACE SITE ★

To Hajeom

SILK FACTORY ★

MEMORIAL TABLETS ★

WEST GATE

BATHOUSE

ANGLICAN CHURCH ★

To Cheongnyeon-sa

YONGHEUNG-GUNG

POLICE

0   250 yds

0   250 m

MARKET

TOWN OFFICE

HANILJANG YEOGWAN

GEUMHOJANG YEOGWAN

GORYEO YEOINSUK

POST OFFICE

To Seoul

SEOLJANG YEOGWAN

TELECOM

MARKET

INSAM CENTER

SOUTH GATE

BUS TERMINAL

To Jeondeung-sa

NATIVE PRODUCTS SALES CENTER

© AVALON TRAVEL PUBLISHING, INC.

GYEONGGI-DO

Goryeo Palace Site 고려궁지
On the hillside above the town center is the site of a former Goryeo Dynasty palace (H.S. #133); open 0900–1800, ₩900 entrance. Only a few of the foundation stones remain. Constructed in 1232, two years after the court fled here to escape the Mongols, this was for 39 years the palace of internal exile for the Goryeo royalty. After an amicable conclusion of hostilities with these invaders, the court moved back to Songdo and this palace was left to decay. In 1636, this site was once again used as a temporary refuge for the royal family when they came here to escape the Manchus. The palace was occupied by the Manchus when the fortress fell into their hands in 1637. During the next several decades, government offices were built on this site; two of these buildings were reconstructed in 1977.

Royal Residence 용흥궁
In a tiny compound off a cul-de-sac down the alley from the police station is a rather unpretentious house that was the residence of King Che-

oljong before he ascended the throne in 1849. Cheoljong was born on Ganghwa-do and spent his early years here. Though a distant relative to the previous king, he was undereducated and somewhat of a country bumpkin; he was definitely unprepared for his role as head of the nation. This house was renamed **Yongheung-gung** ("Palace of the Rising Dragon") after his investiture, and the original thatch roof was replaced with tile. Rather small in size, the traditional-style main house is in a simple L shape; it employs the typical *ondol* heating system. A second house at the back also has the same basic shape and construction, with the addition of a raised wooden veranda. A shrine occupies an enclosure to the side. The site was reconstructed in 1974; a caretaker family lives in the compound. You may have to ask permission to look around. Open 0900– 1800; entrance free.

Anglican Church of Ganghwa-do
성공회강화성당

Directly behind Yongheung-gung is the Anglican Church of Ganghwa-do. Built in 1900 by Bishop John Corfe (some sources say Bishop Trollope) as the first Anglican church in the country, it was reconstructed in 1984. With Western, Korean, Christian, Buddhist, and Confucian influences, this is definitely the most unusual Anglican church in Korea. Its basic shape, interior construction, and rooftop cross speak of its Western Christian influence. The traditional Korean exterior design is Confucian-inspired, while the covered front gate and courtyard bo tree could just as easily be located at a Buddhist temple. Entrance is from the road that runs along the lower side of the silk factory.

Accommodations

While there are no upscale hotels in town, Ganghwa has many clean and friendly, less expensive accommodations. Primarily, these are clustered in the center of town, with a few newer, larger, and slightly more expensive ones popping up in the outlying areas. For about ₩20,000 you can get a simple room at the Goryeo Yeoinsuk (고려여인숙). For bigger, cleaner rooms—for ₩25,000–30,000—try the comfortable Geumhojang Yeogwan (금호장여관), Haniljang Yeogwan (한일장여관), and Seouljang Yeogwan (서울장여관). In this central area are numerous others. Perhaps the best in town is the Hyatt Motel (하얏트모텔), along the highway just south of the bus terminal.

Transportation

The bus station is located on the edge of town in a multi-story, multi-use structure. You have to walk through a cluster of shops to reach its ticket windows and boarding gates. Selected intercity bus destinations are: Seoul Shincheon Bus Station (₩3,700), Incheon (₩3,800), Hajeom (₩610), Oepo-ri (₩1,530), Hwado and Mani-san (₩1,300), Sagi-ri and Jeongsu-sa (₩1,990), Onsu-ri and Jeondeung-sa (₩1,040), Choji-jin (₩1,350), and Gwangseongbo (₩1,230). Buses also connect Choji-jin to Onsu-ri and Onsu-ri to Oepo-ri. To major points on the island, buses run every 15–30 minutes; to more out-of-the-way spots, buses run 4–10 times a day. The majority of the roads on Ganghwa-do are paved, making the once bouncy ride around the island quicker and more enjoyable. A round-island road is in the works to allow easier access to more of the island's historical sites.

NORTH GANGHWA-DO
Riverside Pavilion

Overlooking the Han River where the Yeomha Channel splits Ganghwa-do from the Gimpo Plain, and set on a low hill amongst tall zelkova trees, is **Yeonmi-jeong** (연미정), Swallowtail Pavilion. From the Goryeo Dynasty, this pavilion has an unusual design feature, perhaps of more interest than the structure's overall aesthetics. Rather than stocky wooden posts to uphold its simple but pleasing roof, head-high, tapered, octagonal stone pillars support short wooden posts, which in turn support the roof. Some say that during the last dynasty ships traveling to and from Seoul used to stop below this pavilion to wait for the change of tide before continuing on their way. Today, no water traffic is allowed in the estuary. From here you can easily see across the water into North Korea; however, a military observation post's presence limits access to the pavilion.

Ganghwa Jiseokmyo Dolmen
강화지석묘

The oldest of the island's historical remains, Ganghwa Jiseokmyo [Chisŏkmyo], also called Goindol (H.S. #137), is a granite dolmen from the Neolithic period. As it quiescently rests amidst farmer's fields, life blithely goes on around it as it has for untold centuries. More than two meters high, its one-meter-thick, five- by seven-meter, oblong capstone rests on two sturdy upright support stones. Open at each end, it's high enough to stoop and walk through. You'll find other whole and partial dolmen pieces just north of Goindol, in the fields on the north slope of Goryeo-san, and located above the Naega Reservoir.

Ganghwa Goindol is the largest of its kind in the country. Similar dolmen are found in the northern portion of the Korean Peninsula, Manchuria, Central Asia, and as far away as Europe. No one knows for certain what purpose these huge stone formations served, but the pottery and stone tools and a few metal implements and bones found at these sites have led most experts to think that dolmen were gravesites for powerful members of the ancient peoples who inhabited the region. An alternate theory holds that they were altars set up for ritual ceremonies. In either case, the manpower required to construct them indicates an organized community, and the fact that these objects are usually found in low-lying, richly agricultural areas leads one to think that the people were settled agrarians, not migratory hunter-gatherers.

To reach Goindol, take any bus from Ganghwa going toward Hajeom. You must ask to be let off at Goindol (about a 10-minute ride) as it lies one kilometer before Hajeom. Although there is only a small sign in English indicating the spot, there is a stone marker, souvenir shop, and a parking lot just off the highway. Walk up the path, now set with paving stones. On the landscaped lawn are a series of stones set up to illustrate how such a dolmen was created and nearby is a model of what a Neolithic house might have looked like. The dolmen is about 150 meters from the highway. On an ordinary day it's a pleasant trip, but a visit to this ancient relic might be more evocative on an autumn morning, when the crisp air tingles the nose and the fog is so thick that you must push through it, summoning visions of myth, mystery, and wonder. The story of these people remains as shrouded by time's passing as the dolmen is by the fog.

In lieu of their historical significance and because of the sheer concentration of their numbers, Goindol, along with the dolmen in Gochang, Jeollabuk-Do and Hwasun, Jeollanam-Do, were jointly designated a world cultural heritage site in 2000.

Hajeom 하점

A short distance beyond the dolmen is the tiny village of Hajeom. Here, individually designed religious, floral, and animistic designs, cut in various degrees of intricacy, grace the corrugated roofs of homes and lend each house a distinctive feature. Roof decorations on houses are found in few places other than on this island and Jeju-do; with the advent of cement houses and tile roofs, the number of houses with these roof decorations is dwindling, so find them while you can.

From the main intersection in the village, a hike of less than one hour to the north brings you to the top of Bongcheon-san (291 meters). Crowning this mountain, and visible from Hajeom and from Goindol, is the old beacon site, **Bongcheondae** (봉천대). This stone structure was originally constructed during the Goryeo Dynasty by a member of the Bong family. It served as an altar for their ancestor memorial services, but was converted during the Joseon Dynasty for use as a fire beacon. About five meters high, on its flat top fires were lit to relay communications of national security to Seoul. This was one of nearly 700 such mountaintop communication sites strung in several lines from the far reaches of the country to the capital at Seoul. On a clear day, this site makes a great vantage point from which to look over the Han River estuary into North Korea. A huge hillside billboard across the water displays a message in impolite Korean, that translates as "America, go home." At times, propaganda is broadcast from North Korea by huge speakers pointed south, rhapsodizing on the good life across the border.

Standing in a new-growth pine grove at the base of this mountain is a five-tier Goryeo Dynasty granite pagoda (고려오층석탑) (T. #10), which marks the site of a now absent temple. Around to the east is a Goryeo Dynasty standing Buddha figure (석조여래입상) (T. #615), carved in bas-relief on a thick granite slab. It's a bit of a caricature; the face is plump, the lips rounded and the eyes open.

To reach any of these three historical sites, get off the bus at the Hajeom post office and take the road running toward the mountain. This road splits about 100 meters from the highway, the left fork going to the pagoda and the right leading toward the stone carving. About .5 kilometer from the first split is the pagoda, where the mountain trail begins. About two kilometers down the right-hand road is a second fork; the left-hand road leads to the Buddha figure.

Tombs and Temples

West of Ganghwa is Goryeo-san. Snuggled into its slopes are a royal tomb and several temples. The tomb (고려고종홍릉) is that of King Gojong, the 23rd king of the Goryeo Dynasty. Forced to flee the advancing Mongol army in 1232, he never was reseated on his rightful throne in Songdo, and he died on Ganghwa-do, an exile in his own country. His tomb (H.S. #224) is a low, mounded affair, a small version of the Silla tumuli in Gyeongju. Girded by a stone fence, it sits on the top of the site's three terraces; the accompanying stone figures and a pavilion occupy the lower two. Farther south, below Jin'gang-san (443 meters) near the Giljeong Reservoir are three other royal tombs, each for a lesser Goryeo Dynasty king. The middle of these, called Seongneung (H.S. #369), is that of King Huijong.

Near King Gojong's tomb is a small Buddhist temple called Cheongyeon-sa [Ch'ŏngnyŏn-sa] (청년사). Farther down this highway to the west and up on the western slope of the mountain is a second temple, Jeokseok-sa [Chŏksŏk-sa]. Over the shoulder of Goryeo-san to the north is the slightly larger temple Baengnyeon-sa [Paengnyŏn-sa] (백년사), which houses a seated gilt-iron Amita Buddha statue (T. #994). A portion of the famous *Koreana Tripitaka* may have been carved at one or all of these three temples after being started at Seonwon-sa [Sŏnwon-sa], now only a temple site (H.S. #259) outside the village of Seonwon to the southeast, though most historians seem to think that the work was all done at Jeondeung-sa at the southern end of the island.

Changhu-ri 창후리

In the northwestern corner of the island is the tiny fishing port of Changhu-ri [Ch'anghu-ri] where vehicular ferries to Gyodong-do depart. Running throughout the day, these ferries charge ₩750 per adult with an extra fee for each car. You undoubtedly will have to fill out a travel slip with name, passport number, and reason for visit, as it's so close to the North Korean border. Notice all the barbed wire fencing along the water. Aside from residents of the island and the few who cross to have a look around, most people who stop in Changhu-ri do so for the fish restaurants and market where there is a variety of dried shrimp, shell fish, crab, and fish products for sale.

Lying off Changhu-ri and north of Seongmodo is the island of **Gyodong-do.** Wonsanpo is the port for ferries from Changhu-ri and Namsanpo is the major village and port for ferries from Oepo-ri. Inland are the remains of the Gyodong Fortress, Gyodong Confucian school, and small Buddhist hermitage Hwagye-am.

ISLAND FORTRESS

This island fortress had three lines of defense. Its most effective, after the treacherous channel, was the stone wall that ran the entire length of the eastern side of the island, combined with the cannon emplacements, armories, guard posts, and other such bulwarks placed at intervals around the island: five garrisons, seven fortresses, 53 other fortifications, and nine gun batteries in all. Overlooking the channel, several of the gun emplacements were restored in the 1970s; others are slowly being repaired. Here and there along the coastline lie ruins of several dozen other battlements and ramparts. Ganghwa-do is still a fortress island of sorts, with a large but relatively unobtrusive military presence. Along stretches of its coastline, where stone walls and battlements once stood, now stand sturdy chain-link fences and guardposts.

Gapgot Cannon Emplacement
갑곶돈대

At the west end of the Ganghwa Bridge is Gapgot-dondae [Kapgot-dondae] (H.S. #306); ₩1,300 entrance fee. As part of the external wall and the bastion that overlooked the primary ferry crossing to the island, this emplacement for eight cannons was of extreme importance, and part of a larger fortress. Erected in 1679, its walls were rebuilt in 1977; a 19th-century cannon is on display. Across the channel, on the slopes of Munsu-san, was another fortress, responsible for defending the land approach to the island. Its reconstructed gate can be seen to the north side of the road as you near the bridge when coming from Seoul.

Constructed in 1988, the **Ganghwa History Hall** is also located here. A large building with four exhibition rooms, it shows in brief the prehistoric life and major historical events that shaped this island community. Using descrip-

tion, diorama, and display of artifacts, this museum is a good introduction to the history of the island, and there are short and concise explanations for the foreign visitor. Also at Gapgot is the stone-arched water gate that once was part of the Ganghwa town fortress wall.

In a pavilion on the premises is a bronze bell (T. #11), cast in 1711. Originally located in the center of the city, it was struck at dawn and dusk to mark the opening and closing of the city gates. When the French were forced to retreat to their ships at the end of their abortive occupation of the town in 1866, they tried to haul off this two-ton bell. Finding it too difficult to move quickly, they abandoned it along the road at the edge of town. During the restoration of the palace in 1977, it was removed to that site but moved again to the Ganghwa History Hall in 2000.

Gwangseongbo Command Fortress
광성보

About nine kilometers down the coast, past the more recently rebuilt fortification Yongjin-jin, is Gwangseongbo [Kwangsŏngbo]; open 0900–

Gwangseongbo gun emplacement

1900, ₩1,100 entrance. This fortress (H.S. #227) was constructed in 1656, with additions in 1679 and 1745, and it commanded several smaller forts and gun batteries along this section of the wall. One of its gates and the artillery emplacement remain, restored in 1976. Topping the promontory above the gate is Sondolmokdon, a circular stone and brick armory. A long, curved walkway snakes down a spit of land in front of Gwangseongbo to Yongdu-don, Dragon's Head Battery. Thrusting out into the channel like a dragon on the prowl, its location made it one of the most important artillery positions along this shore. All three of these fortifications saw battle in 1866 against the French, and five years later against the American navy. To those 51 unnamed Korean soldiers who died fighting the Americans, a monument has been raised, and a group of seven graves has been constructed to represent them. For their slain commanders—two brothers—twin memorial stones have been placed in a small pavilion nearby. From Dragon's Head Battery, you can look down the coast and see Deokjin-jin Fortress, as well as the remains of Deokpo-jin Fortress and a modern military installation across the channel. From here, it's quite a sight to see the speed at which the tide moves in and out.

Deokjin-jin Fortress 덕진진

Two kilometers south of Gwangseongbo is Deokjin-jin [Tŏkjin-jin]; ₩700 entrance. Originally a naval camp, this fortress (H.S. #226) was later made an army command post. Of most interest here is the cannon battery. A crescent-shaped line of cannon openings with an unobstructed view out over the wide south end of Yeomha Channel, it was one of the most strategic of the nine artillery emplacements along the 20-kilometer-long wall that ran up the shore. Today, several cannons from the Joseon Dynasty again take their proper place in these openings. These cannons were employed during the French and American invasions of the island. During the latter encounter, this battery was the center of the heaviest exchange of fire.

Choji-jin Fortress 초지진

Another two kilometers farther down the coast, and near the new bridge to the island, is Choji-jin [Ch'oji-jin] Fortress (H.S. #225), constructed in 1656 and repaired in 1973; ₩700 entrance. It too saw heavy action in defense of the island against the French, the Americans, and the Japanese in the 1860s and '70s. One of the cannons displayed inside was used during these campaigns. The outer wall stands pitted with indentations and holes from cannonballs fired from a Japanese ship in 1875. Perhaps more than any other on the island, the community here is known for its seafood restaurants. Their specialty is raw fish, and you can literally choose your meal by picking your fish from the tank out front.

Getting Around

Gapgot-dondae is only about three kilometers from Ganghwa town. It can be reached by a long walk or a short bus ride from town. About once an hour, buses traverse the coastal road, part of the round-island route, connecting these fortifications on their way between Ganghwa and Onsu-ri. Between bus runs, you can take a leisurely walk between these points. A walk of 30 minutes is required between Gwangseongbo and Deokjin-jin, about 45 minutes between there and Choji-jin, and a little over an hour from there to Onsu-ri. There is a good possibility of hitching a ride here as well.

SOUTH GANGHWA-DO

Samnang-seong 삼랑성

Samnang-seong (H.S. #130) is one kilometer south of the village of Onsu-ri (온수리). Legend says that this ancient fortress was constructed in a day by the three sons of Dan'gun. Their sister helped by collecting the stones and bringing them to the site in the folds of her skirt. According to this story, Samnang-seong would be the oldest fortress in the country, as Dan'gun's traditional birth date is set at 2333 B.C. Samnang-seong is not large, but its 1.5-kilometer-long wall fits neatly into the fold of this low mountain, encircling pines, ginkgoes, and flowering cherry trees. Only legend remains of that ancient fortress; a newer one, called Jeongjok Sanseong, was constructed on its foundation. Here, in 1660, an archival storehouse for Joseon Dynasty official documents was set up, one of four such structures widely dispersed throughout the country to keep the kingdom's official records out of harm's way. Two centuries later, this fortress saw action when the French invaded the island. The Koreans triumphed that day, and a tablet has been set up inside the east gate commemorating that event. Its south gate has been completely restored with nicely fitting cut stone and is capped with a pavilion. This gate and other parts of the fortress wall were refurbished in 1976. Made of uncut stone and brick, the east gate is a bit overgrown but pleasantly welcoming. Down the hill from where the west gate once stood is the village of Seondupo, where Dr. Cornelius Osgood did his pioneering study of contemporary Korean culture and life in the late 1940s. His book, *The Koreans and Their Culture,* was published in 1951.

Restaurants and shops cluster in front of the south and east gates of the fortress. Several accommodations can be found in Onsu-ri, including the Koresco Family Hotel, where rooms are ₩40,000, and Ganghwajang Yeogwan (강화장여관).

Jeondeung-sa 전등사

Within this ancient fortress is Jeondeung-sa [Chŏndŭng-sa], the most famous and important temple on Ganghwa-do; ₩1,800 entrance fee. This temple compound is compact, and its structures are small. On windy days, chimes hanging from the eaves fill the compound with soft, melodious sound. Founded in A.D. 381 by the Goguryeo monk Ado, who traveled south to introduce Buddhism to the Baekje and Silla kingdoms, it's one of the oldest temples in the country. At its founding, it was known as Jinjong-sa. In 1299, Queen Jeonghwa, the wife of King Chungnyeol, gave this temple a jade lamp, and the temple's name was changed to Jeondeung-sa ("Temple of the Bequeathed Lamp"). That lamp is now gone, but Jeondeung-sa is the repository of three Treasures.

Here, in the 1230s and '40s, 81,258 wood printing blocks were made. Collectively known as the *Koreana Tripitaka,* these blocks were carved and stored here until they were moved to Haein-sa for safe keeping. About 120 of them, one complete sutra, are still kept in the main hall of this temple.

The temple's most interesting building, that fronted by a flagstone square, is the main hall (T. #178). Through its 1,600-year history, there have only been three main hall buildings. The first was constructed at the temple's founding; the present structure was built in 1615–21, after the second hall was burnt during the Imjin War. It's built rather high for having such a small floor area. This hall has a great deal of fancy woodwork; no nails were used. High over each corner post is a carved figure hunkered down on its heels, holding the weight of the heavy corner ridgebeam on its head. No wonder they make faces! It is difficult to determine if these figures are human or animal, yet one story has it that they were carved by a jilted lover, a carpenter of one of the temple's reconstructions, to represent his unfaithful wife in the hope that she too would find pain and remorse in her actions and suffer as these figures suffer under the weight of this heavy roof. Whatever the truth (they are often described as monkey figures, which they do resemble), these figures are a unique design feature for a Korean temple building. Although faded, the rather elaborate paint on the inside is said to date from the last construction. An incredibly intricate red and gold canopy hangs over the altar. Under the canopy hang tastefully carved and painted figures of a dragon, a phoenix, a bird of paradise, and lotus buds. Enshrined on the altar are three fleshy figures. In the middle is Seokgamoni, flanked by the bodhisattvas Munsu and Bohyeon. To each side of these altar figures is a mirror surrounded by a flame mandala and set on the back of a tiger. Bells are attached to the ceiling, and a metal line is strung from it to the altar. It's said that these bells ring every time someone dies and goes to the *Geungnak Segye* ("Western Paradise").

To the side of this building is Yaksa-jeon (T. #179), a hall dedicated to the Buddha of Medicine. In an open pavilion next to the temple's front steps is the temple bell (T. #393). Oddly, it is of Sung Chinese origin, from the year 1097. At the end of World War II, this bell was taken by the Japanese to be melted and used to make war machines. Luckily, before this took place, the war ended and the bell was returned to its rightful spot. Also in the temple compound are several other skillfully constructed and richly painted buildings, including a Mountain Spirit hall, as well as a 750-year-old bronze cistern and second temple bell. To the front is a teahouse.

Mani-san 마니산

Six kilometers west of Onsu-ri is the village of Hwado (화도). Above it rises the sacred mountain Mani-san, and at its top is the altar Chamseong-dan [Ch'amsŏng-dan] (H.S. #136). Mani-san lies exactly halfway between Baekdu-san, the highest mountain in North Korea, and Halla-san, the highest in South Korea. Both of the highest mountains, extinct volcanoes with crater lakes, have traditionally been considered sacred by the Koreans. From the top of Mani-san you get a panoramic view of Ganghwa-do, the island-sprinkled West Sea, Incheon, and the mountains surrounding Seoul and Gaeseong.

It's not the view, however, but the legends relating to this mountain that make it significant. According to the legend of Dan'gun, Chamseong-dan is over 4,000 years old. Many experts believe, however, that it's no more than several hundred. Nonetheless, its mystique still stirs the emotions of those who come here to worship, as Dan'gun is said to have done several millennia ago for the prosperity and well-being of his new nation. The altar is made of uncut stone, three meters high and five meters square, tapering up to its flat top. Attached to its front and connected by a stone stairway is a circular area rimmed by a low and broad stone wall, in the middle of which is a brazier where a fire is lit during worship ceremonies. In addition, a fire from this burner is relayed by runners to the designated stadium at the start of each national athletic event. Its circular portion signifies

"heaven," and the square altar "earth." When worshipers ("man") come here for a ceremony, there is a symbolic synthesis of these three essential aspects of nature. This is the most sacred spot for members of the *Daejong-gyo* religion. Every year on October 3, National Foundation Day, members make a pilgrimage to Mani-san. Donning white traditional clothes, they climb to the altar, bow to the west, chant hymns, and offer prayers to Dan'gun for peace and reunification of the peninsula.

About a half kilometer east of the Hwado bus station is the entrance to Mani-san, much of which has been declared a national tourism area, and the bottom end has been extensively developed. Among others, the accommodations Manisanjang (마니산장) and New Ganghwa Park (뉴강화파크) are found here. From the ticket booth (₩1,500 entrance fee) by the parking lot at the bottom, a wide cement path runs halfway up the mountain to a religious retreat. From there, Mani-san's major trail (stone steps most of the way) wends its way up the ridge to the altar at the peak. An alternate dirt trail just to the west also goes to the top. The climb to the top of this 468-meter-high mountain takes about one hour. A less frequented path leads down the next ridge to the east, exiting the mountain at Deokpo-ri. Another path follows the eastern ridge about two kilometers to Jeongsu-sa.

Jeongsu-sa 정수사

Jeongsu-sa [Chŏngsu-sa] is said to have been established in 639. Rebuilt in 1423, its main hall (T. #161) dates from that time but has been refurbished since. Especially nice are the finely carved floral designs on the front doors of its main hall. Above it, the temple's only other building, Sanshin-dang, is tucked up against a boulder. Quiet and remote, it is a nice contrast to the hubbub around Jeondeung-sa. To reach Jeongsu-sa, ride one of the infrequent buses to Sagi-ri and walk up the narrow valley trail from there. Steps of stone indicate the temple entrance. This route continues around the mostly undeveloped south end of the island and passes Dongmak Beach, the only beach of significance on the island.

Oepo-ri 외포리

A few kilometers north of Mani-san stands the village of Oepo-ri, a small fishing community with numerous fish restaurants and a ferry to Seongmo-do. Here as well are a handful of shops, *yeogwan*, and the Ganghwa Youth Hostel (tel. 032/933-8891), where a bunk runs ₩10,000 and a room ₩50,000. From Oepo-ri, buses run to Ganghwa, Hwado, Onsu-ri, and Seoul. From the newer ferry terminal, about 100 meters down the shore, and requiring about 15 minutes, a vehicular ferry crosses to Seokpo-ri once an hour from 0700 to 1900; ₩600 per passenger and a hefty charge for each vehicle. Meeting this ferry on Seongmo-do are buses that run to Bomun-sa; other buses run all the way from the town of Ganghwa to the temple. *Yeogwan* and restaurants are found at Seokpo-ri as well as in the village below Bomun-sa. Also in Seokpo-ri are a few rental shops that rent bicycles at ₩3,500 an hour for those who desire to spend the day leisurely biking around the island. From the old terminal, ferries leave for the several islands to the west. Aside from island residents, few people have cause to go.

Bomun-sa 보문사

Located on Seongmo-do, Bomun-sa [Pomun-sa] is the second most-significant temple on these islands. Founded in 635, it is dedicated to Gwanseeum Bosal, the Goddess of Mercy. One of three such temples in the country dedicated to this bodhisattva, it's given special significance by practicing Buddhists—the other two are Naksan-sa, below Seorak-san on the east coast, and the tiny hermitage Bori-am, on Namhae-do, off the peninsula's south coast. As it's believed that the Goddess of Mercy listens to supplication and takes pity on those in need, people come here to pray for something they ardently desire. Perched halfway up the mountainside, the temple looks to the west, out over the numerous islands scattered like sapphires on a molten gold sea.

Surrounded by pine trees, junipers, and gink-goes, the Bomun-sa compound is small and its buildings are plain, but it does have an unusual

natural stone grotto that enshrines 23 holy figures; ₩1,500 entrance. Legend says that a huge granite slab broke off the mountainside above and fell to this spot, creating this natural cave. One day while casting his net in the sea to the west, a fisherman caught 22 misshapen stones. He of course discarded them, wanting fish. That night, a monk appeared to him in a dream and told him that those rocks were Buddha figures. If he would retrieve them and enshrine them in this grotto chamber, all his wishes would come true. This he did, and the worn, ugly figures remain to this day. A plexiglass front, a flat stone floor, a finely carved stone altar, and one new image have been added to the cave. In the upper center group is the Seokgamoni Buddha, flanked by two bodhisattvas. To each side are celestial spirits and Nahan. The new image, one of Gwanseeum, is easily located in the upper right-hand corner of the left-hand group.

To reach Bomun-sa, ride the ferry from Oepo-ri to Seokpo-ri and take the bus from there for the 20-minute ride to the temple. Bus departures and arrivals at Seokpo-ri are timed to meet the ferry. You'll pass decorated island houses, rice fields, salt flats, and some reclaimed land on your way to the opposite side of the island. The last bus from the temple leaves in time to catch the last ferry back to Oepo-ri.

Eyebrow-Rock Buddha

High above the Bomun-sa compound is a dished, 10-meter-high rock sculpture carved in bas-relief below a granite overhang. It's from here that the stone slab that forms the grotto chamber below is said to have fallen. This seated figure of Gwanseeum Bosal is rather masculine in appearance, and its features are rather inexpressive. Its hands, thumbs touching, are folded together on its lap as a symbol of meditation; the palm of one hand cups a bottle. The folds of its garb flow gently over the lotus bud on which it sits, and a huge Buddhist swastika, an ancient symbol representing radiating divine power, is exposed on its chest. Sanskrit letters surround its crowned head like a halo. This interpretation of Gwanseeum is quite unusual. Only the crown, bottle, and lotus bud are features similar to other Goddess of Mercy figures. The monk who carved this figure about 80 years ago suspended himself from the overhang in order to do his work. You can still see a portion of the dangling metal hangers. The steep trail of over 400 steps up to this figure from the temple below starts at the left side of the grotto chamber.

Southern Gyeonggi-Do

South of Seoul and the north branch of the Han River are broad agricultural plains, split principally by low-elevation hills that run to the southeast from Seongnam. These plains provide much of the capital's food, yet here, too, because of the close proximity to Seoul and Incheon, you'll find a great concentration of industry and the accompanying growth of new cities. Perhaps the greatest concentration of industry in the country, this region spans the spectrum from textiles to heavy industry to ultra-modern electronics. The land's relative flatness and its close proximity to Seoul and the border have made it a favorite for air forces. The Republic of Korea (R.O.K.) Air Force has a major base in Suwon, while the U.S. Air Force has one in Songtan.

This area is not only one of industrial and military strength but also one of recreation and historical importance. The vast majority of the country's golf courses lie in the low hills of this region, and the country's rapid economic growth and greater leisure time have led many, particularly in the upper echelons of business and management, to seek a round of golf as a recreational and social outlet. Much more for the average citizen are the several river resorts that lie along the Han River east of Seoul, and the four ski resorts of the province offering easy-access, one-day ski trips for those in the metropolitan area. The well-known and respected Korean Folk Village outside Suwon gives Koreans and foreigners alike a glimpse of old Korea, while not far away, Everland amusement park provides a flipside opportunity to break loose and enjoy the thrill of modern amusement rides.

History has not passed by this southern section of the province either, evidenced by the several royal tombs, famous Buddhist temples, and fortifications located here. The Korean War raged through this province and many fierce battles were fought here. This is attested to by a number of monuments to troops who fought in those engagements. On the commercial side, Gwangju, Icheon, and Yeoju are centers of pottery production, and Anseong is known for brassware.

SUWON 수원

The walled city of Suwon, the provincial capital, lies one hour south of Seoul. The name Suwon means "water source," and the land depression that the city occupies was for centuries known for its clear-water wells. High above the city rises Paldal-san, a tall hill at its height of beauty in the spring, with its slopes awash with the color of pink cherry blossoms. In the late 1600s, the military established a garrison here as one of five principal fortifications set up to protect the approaches to Seoul. Intending to move the national capital from Seoul to Suwon, King Jeongjo, the 22nd Joseon Dynasty king, had the fortress wall constructed. Battlements and palace buildings were erected, but the king died before he could initiate the move. Although there were great plans for this city, they never had the opportunity to mature, as the decision was made to keep the capital at Seoul.

During the 1919 independence movement, many demonstrations were organized in Suwon. In one tragic incident, the Japanese herded a congregation of Christians into their church, then set it on fire. Those who tried to escape the inferno were shot. This incident is illustrated on a panel in Seoul's Pagoda Park. In 1949, Suwon was designated a city, and in 1967, the Gyeong-

DETAIL

DONGBUK
GONGSHIM-DON

BANGHWASURYUL-
JEONG

DONGJANG-
DAE

CHANGNYONG-
MUN

DONGPO-RU

BUKAM-
MUN

DONGAM-MUN

BONG-DON

MARKET

KOREA FOREIGN
EXCHANGE BANK

CHOHUNG
BANK

BROWN HOTEL

JANGAN-MUN

HWAHONG-
MUN

DONGBUKPO-RU

Gwanggyo
Stream

Jangan
Park

SEOBUK
GONGSHIM-DON

HWARYEONG-
JEON

HAENG-GUNG

POST
OFFICE

DAESEUNG-SA

PALDAL-
MUN

Paldal-san

SEONAM-MUN

SEONAMCHI

SEOPO-RU

HWASEO-MUN

SEOAM-MUN

CITY BELL

SEOJANG-DAE

SEOSAMCHI

PROVINCIAL
GOVERNMENT
OFFICE

SEONAM
GANGNU

SEOKSAN HOTEL

Wonchon
Reservoir

SAMSUNG
ELECTRONICS

GYEONGGI-DO
CULTURE AND ARTS
CENTER

Hyowon
Park

Art Park

SUWON

YEONGDONG EXPRESSWAY

50

Gwanggyo
Reservoir

GYEONGGI
UNIVERSITY

WORLD CUP
SOCCER STADIUM

AJU UNIVERSITY

HOTEL
CASTLE

CITY HALL

Olympic
Park

42

SPORTS
COMPLEX

TELECOM

**SEE
DETAIL**

Paldal-san

TELECOM

BUS TERMINAL

1

1

SUWAN
CONFUCIAN
ACADEMY

EXPRESS BUS
TERMINAL

INTERCITY
BUS TERMINAL

TRAIN
STATION

Seoho
Reservoir

SUNKYUNG
CHEMICAL

SEONGGYUNGWAN
UNIVERSITY

OFFICE OF RURAL
DEVELOPMENT

SEOUL NATIONAL
UNIVERSITY'S COLLEGE
OF AGRICULTURE

43

N

1 mi

1 km

© AVALON TRAVEL PUBLISHING, INC.

GYEONGGI-DO

gi-Do provincial administration was moved here from Seoul. Ever expanding, Suwon has 950,000 inhabitants and is the eighth largest city in the country.

Suwon depends upon the military, agriculture, light industry, education, and tourism for its livelihood. A Korean Air Force base is located on the outskirts of the city south of town, and a smaller U.S. Air Force contingent is located there as well. The national Office of Rural Development fronts Seoho Reservoir on the western edge of town, and south of there stands Seoul National University's College of Agriculture, one of the nation's foremost centers for agricultural education. Other institutions in or near the city are Aju University, Gyeonggi University, Suwon Women's University, and the Suwon branch campus of Seonggyungwan University. On the eastern side of town is the National Geographic Institute. Samsung Electronics and Sunkyung Chemical companies have large modern factories here.

Suwon is most famous for its lightly seasoned barbecued pork ribs. While some restaurants now use gas burners, traditionally ribs were grilled over a charcoal brazier. For ribs prepared the authentic way, ask for *sutbul galbi*. The Suwon Fortress is the main attraction of the city itself, but in the surrounding regions are Yeongju-sa, Yunggeon-neung royal tombs, the Korean Folk Village, and Yongin Everland. The Hwaseong Cultural Festival held yearly in October includes a procession through the city streets, a memorial ceremony at the graves of King Jeongjo and his father, art contests, photo exhibitions, and musical performances.

For information on the Internet, see www .suwon.ne.kr.

Hwaseong Fortress

King Jeongjo ordered the construction of Hwaseong, or Suwon Fortress, in 1794. Over five kilometers in length, the fortress wall averages nine meters high. Along its length are four principal gates and numerous parapets, pavilions, towers, sentry positions, command posts, gun batteries, and one fire beacon site. This was the last and most modern of the great Joseon Dynasty fortresses, constructed with the aid of the latest technological advances, and its bulwark of stone and brick is considered the masterpiece of Korean fortress construction. It was a magnificent endeavor, worthy of being a capital fortress and protecting the seat of national government. Through the 19th and 20th centuries, these walls slowly deteriorated and the whole complex fell into ruin. From 1974 to 1979, however, a concerted effort by the government restored portions of the wall and some of its numerous structures to their former splendor. Periodically since then, a portion of the wall or one of its structures has been rebuilt. The entire fortress with its remaining structures has been designated H.S. #3, and in 1997 it was designated a world cultural heritage site. It looks rather new today, and one gets a very clear understanding of its defensive capabilities. In years to come, when the stones settle, the wood weathers, and the ivy begins to crawl along the wall once again, these constructions will once again "mature" and resemble the fortress as it appeared at its height. Today you can walk along the entire wall—all except for short missing sections on either side of the south gate. Suwon's expansion has been so rapid that, like water pouring through an open floodgate, it has spread far beyond the narrow confines of this sturdy stone perimeter.

Tour of the Wall: Paldal-mun, the south gate (T. #402), is the best-preserved of the fortress gates. Built in 1794 as part of the original wall, it luckily was not destroyed during the Korean War. The gateway itself is made of a light-colored stone, over which sits a two-story wood pavilion; inside of this is preserved a bronze bell. The north gate pavilion also has two stories; the ones over the east and west gates are single-story structures. A semicircular walled enclosure of brick, with its own opening, extends out to the front of the south gate opening. This half-moon perimeter is topped with merlons and crenels, and a walkway for armed sentries. Similar security enclosures are found in front of the other three principal gates. Paldal-mun is in original form, and has had only minimal restoration and cleaning, like new roof re-

© ROBERT NILSEN

A world heritage site, the Suwon Fortress wall makes a great walk.

construction in 2001. The city wall ran from this gate directly up Paldal-san to the west, but now you must go one block to the west to catch it as it steps up the mountainside. Passing one pavilion and one lookout, you reach the tiny gate Seona-mam-mun, with its equally tiny pavilion, at the fortress's southwest corner. On the ridge out from Seonam-nu is the guard tower Seonam Gangnu. Going north is Seosamchi, a lookout site; Seopo-ru, a small firearms position; Seoam-mun, a secret gate; and a pavilion that houses a new city bell (1991). At the top of Paldal-san stands Seojang-dae, the west command post. Tall and stately, this two-story building is a regal cap to the mountain. The best views over the city and the surrounding countryside are had from here. Farther down the wall is another Seopo-ru, this one a sentry post. It's built over the outside of the wall, like Seosamchi, to allow for unobstructed views along the wall's exterior. Along this walk are a number of trails that head down the hillside back into town. In the northwest corner of the fortress is Hwaseo-mun, the west gate. Overlooking it is Seobuk Gong-shim-don, a lookout tower. These two (T. #403)

are both made of stone topped with brown brick. The tower is the only one of its kind in the country. The stones in this tower and those along the connecting northern wall have been fitted together without mortar in non-uniform yet harmonious order, somewhat akin to the magnificent stone masonry of the Inca Indians in South America. Passing several more pavilions and sentry posts, you reach the north gate. Jangan-mun stands in the middle of a traffic circle at the north end of the road running up from the south gate. Jangan-mun was damaged and its pavilion burned during the Korean War, but it has been restored to its original form.

Continuing on to the east you find Hwahong-mun, the water gate. This seven-arched sluice allows the water from the Gwanggyo stream to flow into the city. It's the most unusual of the fortress's many gates, and the only one of its kind in the country—its present open pavilion dates from 1931 but was refurbished in 1994. Above the water gate you'll find Banghwasuryu-jeong, an unusual, multi-sided pavilion with an inordinately complex roof structure. It overlooks a willow-fringed lotus pond outside the city wall. Banghwasuryu-jeong is a favorite spot for elderly Koreans to gather and chat or play a game of *baduk* during hot summer days. Along the walkway inside the wall is a memorial stela for National Priest Jin'gak (T. #14), tutor to the Goryeo Dynasty King Chungjong. This marker was constructed in 1386 in memory of the virtuous loyalty of this monk, and it was moved here for safekeeping during the fortress restoration. Just above this stone tablet, and looking very out of place, a modernistic monument honors citizens of Suwon and the province who participated in the Korean War. Farther along the wall past Bukam-mun, the north secret gate, Dongbukporu, and Dongam-mun, the east secret gate, you'll find Dongjang-dae, a military training ground and archery range, on which has been constructed a new range for those who still practice traditional-style Korean archery. At the corner is Dongbuk Gongshim-don, largest of the fortress's observation tower/battery sites, which crowns the very corner of this fortress. Directly to the south is Changnyong-mun, the east gate. Like the west gate, Changnyong-mun features a semi-circular protective outer wall opening to the side. This arrangement caused all who entered to slow down and change directions twice under the watchful eyes of armed soldiers before actually proceeding through the arch gate. South along this wall is Dongpo-ru, another sentry position, and beyond that is Bong-don, a fire beacon site made of brick. Between all the major structures on the wall are smller sentry posts and small arms positions. At its south end, the wall goes steeply down to food market stalls along the stream, and used to continue on through what is now part of the market area to join the south gate, making a complete circle.

Along the outside of the fortress wall between the west and north gates runs Changan Park, a landscaped city park of walkways and park benches that also houses the provincial tourist information center. Land outside much of the east wall has also been cleared and landscaped. Many of the gates and pavilions are lit at night creating a fine scene.

Other Sights

Inside the walls, at the foot of Paldal-san, you'll discover two structures of note. The first is **Haeng-gung** (행궁), once part of a 33-building palace site used by King Jeongjo when he came to Suwon to conduct memorial ceremonies at his father's gravesite. This palace was totally refurbished in 2001. The second building is the shrine **Hwaryeong-jeon** (화령전) (H.S. #115), constructed by King Sunjo—King Jeongjo's son—to house his father's portrait and to remind all following kings of his father's extreme filial piety. On the south slope of Paldal-san is the Suwon Hyanggyo. Farther afield is Seoho ("West Lake"), a reservoir constructed at the same time as the fortress to provide enough water for the city's residents.

Accommodations and Food

Most people who visit Suwon come down from Seoul in the morning and return in the evening. If you care to stay, many accommodations are clustered between the traffic circle in front of the train station and the bus terminal. Try the Onjang Yeogwan (온장여관), New Haeunjang Yeogwan (뉴해운장여관), and Grand Motel (그랜드모텔). For a quieter place in the heart of the city, you'll find accommodations to fit any budget in the lanes on both sides of the main street, between the post office and the south gate. For greater comfort and more amenities try any of the city's hotels. The second-class **Seoksan Hotel** (tel. 031/246-0011) and first-class **Brown Hotel** (tel. 031/246-4141, www.hpbrown.co.kr) are conveniently located just south of the south gate. Out toward the expressway is the deluxe-class **Hotel Castle** (tel. 031/211-6666, www.htcastle .co.kr), the best in town, with regular rooms for ₩225,000–275,000 and suites to ₩475,000.

As with accommodations, there are many restaurants scattered all over town. A concentration lies in the area southeast of Paldal-mun, toward the market, where many serve *sutbul galbi*. Directly across from the train station, in an alley that parallels the main street, you'll run across another part of town full of restaurants, coffee shops, and drinking establishments; it's one of the most popular night-scene streets in town.

Other Practicalities

The provincial tourist information center (tel. 031/228-2766), for brochures and maps and information in four languages, is located at Jangan Park on the lawn near the north gate of the city. Other information booths located along the wall are just west of Paldal-mun, near the top of the hill at Seojang-dae, near the archery grounds in the northeast corner of the fortress, and at the train station. The post office is located in the center of the old city. For money exchange, try either the Korea Foreign Exchange Bank or Chohung Bank, both located south of Paldal-mun; nearby are other banks and several large department stores. This area south of Paldal-mun is the city's main business and commercial center. Directly to the west, over the shoulder of the hill, is the Gyeonggi-Do provincial government building. With the expansion of the city, city hall has moved out to a more spacious location southeast of the city center, and two telephone offices have been built, one near city hall and the other north of Jangan-mun, near the sports complex.

Transportation

Suwon's new train station hosts about four dozen trains a day in both directions on the Gyeongbu rail line between Seoul and Busan. Additional trains run this line going to Gyeongju, Masan, Jinju, and Ulsan. Via the Honam and Jeolla lines, more than two dozen trains a day run to Mokpo, Gwangju, and Suncheon. Also through this city run 17 trains a day to Janghang. Selected destinations (with *Mugunghwa-ho* fares) are: Daejeon (₩5,900), Busan (₩19,100), Gyeongju (₩17,200), and Gwangju (₩15,100).

The subway (suburban rail) connects Suwon to Seoul, Ansan, Incheon, and as far as Uijeongbu. The subway station is attached to the Suwon train station. Trains to Seoul run every 6–10 minutes; the ride to Seoul Station takes about one hour. The first train leaves at 0513, and the last train of the day as far as Seoul Station goes at 2247.

Both the express and intercity bus stations are only a few hundred meters from the train sta-

NARROW-GAUGE RAIL LINE

Until 1994, the country's only narrow-gauge rail line, the 47-kilometer Suin line, ran between Suwon and Incheon's Songdo Station. Constructed in 1937 by the Japanese to aid their war effort, the Suin line originally ran from Incheon, through Suwon, to Yeoju. Sometime in the 1950s, the section from Suwon to Yeoju was taken up, and in 1994 the rest was dismantled. Running over alluvial coastal plains, through then pastoral and unfrequented rural Gyeonggi-Do this train bounced along from small village to small village, the train cars swaying from side to side as they rolled over uneven tracks. Here, in the rickety old miniature cars, you would jostle with local farmers in their baggy clothes, housewives with bundles twice as big as they, and an assortment of the proverbial cackling, crowing, and squealing animals. Even with its less than perfect comfort, there was seldom a dull moment on this miniaturized piece of antiquated rolling stock. Now no more, it lives only in the memories of the passengers who rode the line and as an attraction at the railroad museum in the city of Uiwang, a short distance north of Suwon.

tion, but because of their cramped quarters there are plans to move them to a location south of city hall. Express buses run to Jeollanam-Do Gwangju (₩12,200), Daejeon (₩5,600), and Jinju (₩16,000). Selected intercity bus destinations: Incheon (₩3,200), Dongducheon (₩6,400), Yongin (₩1,600), Yeoju (₩4,200), Songtan (₩1,700), Asan (₩4,900), and Wonju (₩6,000).

City bus no. 39 runs the main street of the city connecting the Suwon Station to both the north and south city gates. Others that run by Paldal-mun are nos. 8, 13, 36, 38. From the traffic circle in front of the station, bus nos. 37 and 600-1 go to the Korean Folk Village, and bus no. 600 runs to Everland. From just south of the station, bus nos. 24 and 46 go to Yongju-sa and Yunggeon-neung.

SUWON VICINITY

Yongju-sa 용주사

After one visit to his father's grave, King Jeongjo and his attendants spent the night at an abandoned temple site near the tomb. That night, the king dreamed of a dragon that held a round red jewel in its mouth. (This jewel, sometimes referred to as the "flaming jewel," is a Buddhist image typically seen in the mouth of a dragon or sometimes clasped in its claws.) Taking this dream as an auspicious sign, King Jeongjo had a new temple built on this site in 1790. He named it Yongju-sa, or Dragon Jewel Temple, and had it decorated with many dragon figures. Look for them above the doors and inside below the ceiling of the main hall. Yongju-sa was designated specifically for offering prayers to the spirit of King Jeongjo's father. Once a large establishment of several dozen buildings and hundreds of monks, Yongju-sa today contains fewer than a dozen original structures. In 1994, additional construction and renovation work was undertaken. It's finely landscaped with scrubs and trees —one of which, a boxwood tree (National Monument #10), was planted 200 years ago at the temple's dedication.

You approach Yongju-sa by a tree-lined walk; ₩1,000 entrance fee. The temple's lecture hall and dormitories form the front of the temple's central courtyard; proceed under the lecture hall to enter the inner compound. These front buildings are extensions of each other; their outer walls and rooflines meld together, similar to some palace structures. Architecturally, they are the most significant of the temple's structures. In the middle of the courtyard sits the main hall. The interior paint has faded, but you can still see the old designs on its wooden surfaces. On the altar are three rotund figures: Seokgamoni, Amita, and Yaksa Yorae. Hanging inside is an altar mural painted by Tanwon, a highly regarded artist of the early 1800s. On Buddha's birthday, a huge scroll mural is unrolled and hung outside during the temple festivities.

To the left of the main hall stands a small structure containing a Goryeo Dynasty bell (N.T. #120). Cast in 854 for Galyang-sa, the site's orig-inal temple, this 1,500-kg bell is one of only three bells in Korea from this dynastic period. (The other two, also National Treasures, are the Emille bell, at the Gyeongju National Museum, and the Sangwon-sa temple bell, in Odae-san National Park.) With a deep, resonating sound and pleasing design, the Galyang-sa bell is an exquisite example of metalcasting! On its top are the dragon-shaped hanger and sound tube. Figures seated on lotus blossoms and surrounded by a stylized cloud pattern grace its gently curved sides. Four sets of nine squat knobs are placed near the top, under which are round striking plates. Encircling its top and bottom are wide belts of floral designs. Below the bell is a shallow depression in the ground that causes the sound to reverberate and travel great distances.

Behind the bell pavilion is a small hall, on the side of which is painted a wonderful example of a "smoking tiger" mural. Tigers are often pictured with other animals in Korean folk art. This one sits peacefully under a tree smoking a long-stem bamboo pipe, attended by a rabbit, whose job is to see that the pipe stays full and lit. One look at the tiger's eyes and its quirky grin will make you wonder just what it is that he has in that pipe. This mural and the Three Spirits hall to the rear of the compound are examples of shamanistic influence in Korean Buddhism. On the outside of two other buildings are murals in bright colors depicting the eight scenes of the historical Buddha's life, and show scenes of what parents should do to deserve their children's devotion. Among the eave brackets of the hall with the Buddha murals are small portraits of saints and monks, a type of external decoration not often seen on temple buildings. The temple bell and two stone pagodas are all that have survived from the Silla period Galyang-sa. To get to Yongju-sa, take Suwon city bus no. 24 or 46 (₩600) from near the train station rotary.

Royal Tombs

A 20-minute walk to the west of Yongju-sa, down the road toward Suwon University, brings you to **Yunggeon-neung** [Yunggŏn-nŭng] (융건릉). Bus nos. 24 and 46 also run this road. Set on a low hillside are the tombs of King Jeongjo and his father, Prince Sado; ₩400 entrance, open daily except Monday. These two tombs (H.S. #206) are good examples of Joseon-era tombs of the latter period. King Jeongjo's grandfather, King Yeongjo, had a relatively progressive reign of 52 years—the longest of any Joseon Dynasty king. In his old age, however, he became senile and convinced that his son, Prince Sado, planned to usurp his power. The king had the prince sealed in a rice box until Sado died. Prince Sado's son, King Jeongjo, witnessed this ignominious event, and ever after honored and respected his unfortunate father as a proper, filial-minded Confucian son should. The prince, often referred to as the "rice box king," was posthumously elevated to the rank of king and given the name Jangjo by his son, King Jeongjo. Jeongjo moved his father's remains to their present location and had a tomb constructed befitting his new rank. He had Yongju-sa erected as its prayer temple, and some scholars suggest that the Suwon fortress and palace structures were built so that King Jeongjo could live closer to his father's grave. King Jeongjo requested that when he died, his tomb be placed here as well, so that he could be near his father even in death. This is a perfect example of filial piety and devotion, a quality still much respected by Koreans today.

Korean Folk Village 한국민속촌

A trip to the Korean Folk Village is not to be missed, especially if you have limited time to spend in Korea and want a diversified exposure to things traditionally Korean. Opened in 1974, expanded and renovated in 1977, and enlarged again in 1994–95, it now features approximately 250 traditional-style structures on as many acres. This open-air museum attempts to encapsulate traditional Joseon Dynasty life: housing, clothing, food, arts, crafts, customs, etc. It is representative of a way of life nearly gone now except in a few isolated communities around the country and with individuals who have intentionally preserved the old ways. Each change of season lets you observe what happened in the country at that time of year. Don't be fooled by all the hype and advertisement and dismiss it merely as a tourist trap! A living, working community, it's a quality reconstruction, and truly warrants a full day's visit. Being limited in size and scope, it is not, of course, totally comprehensive, but it's a worthy introduction to old Korea.

Beyond the village's broad front gate, and concentrated in a small plaza, you'll discover a Korean restaurant, a tea shop, post office, souvenir shop, and information signboard. Walk through the inner gate to the main folk village complex and several shaman totems will greet you. Traditional houses from every locale in the country have been constructed here; you can enter and examine nearly three dozen, including rural farmers' dwellings, island houses, middle-class city homes, and a *yangban* manor house. Buildings of wood, wattle, and mud, roofs of tile or golden straw thatch, and walls and fences

THE PROGRESSIVE REIGNS OF KINGS YEONGJO AND JEONGJO

The largely peaceful and progressive reigns of Kings Yeongjo and Jeongjo made great strides in the advancement of Korean society and culture. This period was the peak of the *Silhak* movement, during which utilitarian and practical concerns outweighed theoretical considerations in many branches of study. It was also the time of resurgent interest in Korean history and advances in science and technology. To the joy of many forward-looking scholars, Western documents started to filter into the country through China; to the regret of most other members of this staunchly Confucian society, Catholicism made its first inroads—the first religious repression promptly followed. Some major changes in the arts emerged: the development of genre paintings moved away from the rigid confines of prescribed subjects to portray scenes of ordinary life, and blue-and-white ceramics became highly developed. The 18th century saw a loosening of the tight hold that the *yangban* class had on this society. The influence of the literati/bureaucratic class grew in all aspects of Korean life, and the mercantile class started to emerge.

of stone and other organic materials abound. You will also find a Buddhist temple, Confucian school, Chinese medicine shop, and provincial governor's office here, set up in their entireties. The houses have been furnished as they would have been in the days of old: rooms filled with household items and art objects, kitchens full of utensils, farming implements and tools kept outside.

Dozens of people work in the village and you may feel out of place when you see them all dressed in traditional Korean clothing. Old gentlemen are dressed in flowing gowns and top hats, craftsmen in work clothes and straw shoes, women in puffy skirts. Unmarried youngsters of both sexes still wear their hair long and braided. Traditional arts and crafts are also practiced here. A potter's studio, blacksmith shop, water mill, and brewery are all producing industries. Skilled artists and craftsmen perform cloth, bamboo, and wicker weaving, the making of horsehair and bamboo hats, papermaking, fan construction, brassware manufacture, and woodworking. In the center of the village is a performance arena. Twice every day on a regular schedule, you can catch a performance of tightrope acrobatics or farmers' music and dance. The brash sounds and rhythmic cadence of folk tunes, with their dominant percussion beat, will assault your ears and make you move to the music; the colorful swirl of dancers' costumes and trailing ribbons will attract your eye. In another area of the village, a traditional wedding parade and ceremony is enacted, and on special holidays performances of folk dances, puppet plays, acrobatics, and/or traditional games are staged. Check with the information office at the entrance for performance times and locations.

Other items of interest include the traditional archery range and the women's swing and seesaw. A portion of the stream has been dammed for boating. At the far end of the village you'll come upon the open-air market. Admittedly commercialized, the market sells traditional wares made in this village at somewhat expensive prices. From the food stalls nearby you can sample regional variations of authentic food and drink. Don't leave without tasting some of the smooth rice wines, but don't let them keep you from seeing the rest of the village! They go down easily but pack a punch. Incongruously, an amusement area is located across the stream from the entrance plaza, but the Art Museum and Folk Museum (entrance ₩2,500) are worth a look, as is the Junghyeon Seowon next door.

The Korean Folk Village is located a short distance east of the Jungang Expressway, to the east of Suwon. It's open 0900–1800 (1730 in winter); ₩8,500 adults, ₩5,500 students, ₩4,000 children. City bus no. 37 (₩600) runs to the village from the traffic circle in front of Suwon Station. You can also get to and from the village by way of the folk-village shuttle bus. This bus leaves three times a day from the folk village sales office near the Suwon train station. If you buy your entrance ticket at the office on the plaza, you'll receive a free ride to the village and back. Also running to the folk village are Seoul city bus no. 1002 from Jamshil, Seongnam city bus no. 116-1, and bus no. 5500-1 from Gwanghwa-mun in the center of Seoul. Several tour companies in Seoul offer full- or part-day tours of (or including) the village for ₩45,000–70,000, transportation and entrance fee included.

Osan-Songtan

South of Suwon are the cities of Osan and Pyeongtaek. At Songtan (송탄), between these two cities, the U.S. Air Force maintains a large air base. The area outside the front gate of this base is a conglomeration of Korea and the West that is frequented by airmen, soldiers, and a variety of foreigners who mainly come down from Seoul. The main street of this area, called Shinjang Shopping, is closed to traffic, and along it and in the adjacent streets and alleys are a plethora of souvenir shops, clothing stores, accommodations, restaurants, and bars, many of which are staffed by young Filipino and Russian women. Especially active on the weekend, these bars offer rock, disco, R&B, and country music. Many of the restaurants cater to Western tastes, whether serving Western, Chinese, or Korean foods. This is one of the few remaining spots in the country where a mongrel mix of cultures can still be experienced. Take Suwon bus no. 300 or 301 to Osan and there transfer to Osan bus no. 2 to Songtan. Walk over the railroad tracks and this area is straight ahead. Alternately, take an inter-city bus toward Pyeongtaek, get off at Songtan, and walk from the bus terminal over the tracks to this area.

Yongin 용인

Twenty-five kilometers east of Suwon is the town of Yongin. The 3rd R.O.K. Army Headquarters and the National Police College are located here, as are the Cosmetics Museum and Waujeong-sa temple. This temple (와우정사) is the head temple of the small Yeolban sect, and the temple compound holds a number of unusual Buddha images, including a huge eight-meter-tall wooden head of the Buddha, a reclining wooden Buddha figure that is 12 meters long, and others that are made of white jade, stone, and bronze. But Yongin is best known for one other attraction—Everland.

For additional information, see www.yongin.kyonggi.kr on the Internet.

Everland 용인 에버랜드

Opened in 1975, Everland (formerly the Yongin Nature Farm) is a privately owned amusement park/zoo, water park, and auto racetrack; www.everland.com. It's the largest amusement park in Korea. The Festival World amusement park and Caribbean Bay water park are great places for kids, while the Everland Speedway racetrack slowly draws a crowd of enthusiastic adults. A small petting zoo, animal shows, and a bus tour through the open-air "Wild Safari" lion and tiger pens should keep young children entertained. Older children will enjoy the amusement rides at all thrill levels, musical performance areas, souvenir stands, and restaurants. You'll find medical stations and information booths scattered around the rest of the grounds. Near the west entrance are two wonderful rose and tulip gardens, with a water fountain set between. Every year rose and tulip festivals are held here, as are lily and chrysanthemum festivals. In addition, a hill to the south of the main grounds is used as a sled run in winter. The amusement park is open

0930–2100 (1800 in winter), with several admission options. The general admission ticket, which just lets you in the gate, is ₩15,000 adults, ₩10,000 for kids below age 13. The Day Pass admission, which includes a certain number of rides, runs ₩25,000 and ₩18,000, respectively. Many rides and other activities have separate admissions. Ticketing and information is available at each gate.

By separate entrance is the indoor/outdoor Caribbean Bay water park, which contains numerous swimming pools, water slides, tube rides, a water bobsled, wave pool, an artificial river, and a sand beach. With the basic entrance fee at ₩25,000 adult and ₩18,000 children, and with additional costs for rides, this is not a cheap adventure. The park is open 0930–1900 weekdays and until 2000 on weekends and holidays.

The first of its kind in Korea, Everland Speedway is set up for auto and motorcycle racing, a sport only slowly drawing the attention of Koreans. It's located outside the north gate of the amusement park. Nearby is the Samsung Transportation Museum, ₩2,500 entrance.

Overlooking a reservoir that's located above the amusement park is the renowned **Ho-Am Art Museum** (호암박물관); www.hoammuseum.org. Opened in 1982 with some 2,000 pieces from the personal collection of the late chairman of the Samsung Group, one of Korea's largest business conglomerates, the Ho-Am Art Museum is undoubtedly one of, if not *the,* finest private art collections in the country, and its largest private museum. The museum has some 15,000 objects from all periods of Korean history—mostly paintings, ceramics, metals, and sculpture, and among them over one hundred designated National Treasures. An outdoor sculpture garden occupies the lawn. For the art lover, this museum is not to be missed. Entrance is ₩3,000 (₩2,000 children); open Wednesday–Monday 1000– 1700, closed January and February. To the front of, and a perfect way to approach the museum, is the **Hoe Won Garden,** a traditional Korean-style garden. Finely landscaped in a very natural manner with lots of greenery, ponds, and stone sculptures from ages ago, this free garden is a quiet respite and contrasts greatly with the frenetic activity of Everland and Caribbean Bay below. Frequent free shuttle buses run from the amusement park entrance to both the Ho-Am Art Museum and the Samsung Transportation Museum.

Perhaps the easiest way to get to Everland and the Ho-Am Art Museum is to take the subway from Seoul to Suwon. From across the traffic rotary in front of the Suwon Station, city bus no. 66 (₩600), 600 (₩1,200), 600-1 (which also stops at the Korean Folk Village), or 6000 (₩1,400) brings you to the park's main entrance.

ICHEON 이천

Although today a center of light industry and the home of the OB brewery, Icheon [Ich'ŏn] has historically been associated with pottery-making. The yearly **Icheon Ceramics Festival** carries on this tradition, and international events, like the 2001 World Ceramic Expo held in Seolbong Park, help to bolster its reputation. Often held in association with the local Seolbong Cultural Festival in October, the ceramics festival showcases local wares, exhibits various styles and traditions of pottery, and encourages friendly competition with a kiln-firing contest and other folk events. During the Goryeo Dynasty, Icheon was one of the three major centers of celadon production in the country—the others were at Gangjin in Jeollanam-Do and Buan in Jeollabuk-Do. During the 20th century, there has been a remarkable revival of interest in and reproduction of this type of pottery. Much experimentation has been done with types of kilns—both the traditional incline Korean kiln and the stepped-incline Japanese kiln—firing techniques and fuel, and the composition of glazes and clay grog, and Icheon today still produces some of the country's finest celadon. Modern reproductions of old celadon ware are called *Goryeo Cheongja*. In town is the Icheon Pottery Village, a cooperative effort by more than a dozen artists to present the whole gamut of pottery production and their wares to the public. Each potter has a studio and an exhibition room here, and visitors can view work in progress.

One of the closest hot springs to Seoul is at Icheon. Even though its proximity to the capital makes it convenient, its relatively cool temperature and alkaline water create less of a reputation than other hot springs in the country. For a soak, try the deluxe-class mustard-yellow **Hotel Miranda** (tel. 031/633-2001), or the second-class **Seol Bong Hotel** next door (tel. 031/635-5701). Both are a five-minute walk from the bus terminal. You'll find numerous *yeogwan* and restaurants adjacent to the bus terminal.

You can easily get to Icheon by bus from Suwon (₩3,400), Yeoju (₩1,500), Gyeonggi-Do Gwangju (₩1,700), Wonju (₩3,500), Chungju (₩4,900), or Dong Seoul Station (₩3,000). Express buses connect Icheon only to Seoul (₩3,100).

Haegang Museum 해강도자미술관

Four kilometers north of Icheon (₩1,200 by city bus), in the village of Sugwang-ni (수광리), is Haegang Yo, one of the largest and most famous of the modern celadon pottery studios. Use city bus no. 114 (₩1,200). Located only a five-minute walk east of the highway from the police substation and traffic light, this kiln was started by the now-deceased Yu Geun-hyeong and is currently spearheaded by his eldest son Yu Gwang-yeol. The elder Yu was a master potter, and while alive he was honored as an outstanding practitioner of a designated cultural art form. From the 1930s, he almost single-handedly pressed for the revival of the art of making celadon pottery and experimented in all aspects to reproduce the best that the Goryeo celadon had to offer. Today, his eldest son runs the shop, which still produces these exquisite pottery pieces, and directs an institute for the study of celadon. He has also erected the Haegang Ceramics Museum, which displays work of Yu Geun-hyeong as well as Goryeo-period pieces, and gives a brief overview of pottery-making in general and the various types produced in Korea. There is almost no English explanation here, but the pieces on display are worth the visit. The museum shop sells work done at the studio. Entrance to the museum is ₩2,000; open every day except Monday and some holidays 1000–1700 (1600 in winter).

Other Kilns

Less than one-half kilometer up the highway to the north you'll find the **Goryeo Kiln** (고려요). Run by the well-known Chi Soon Taik until his death in the mid-1990s, this studio also produces Goryeo-style celadon and is open to the public. Stop by and see the process of turning out masterpieces and check the pieces in the showroom. Other studios and showrooms in the area are the **Hanguk Kiln** (한국도요), a large commercial place at the south edge of Sugwang-ni that caters to busloads of Japanese tourists, and **Haerim Kiln** (해림도요), a small unpretentious shop two kilometers before Sugwang-ni.

The area around Icheon is also famous for a white pottery known as *Ijo Baekja*. This type of porcelain production was at its height during the Joseon Dynasty, and many fine examples of this ware can be seen in the museums of the country today. Near Haegang Yo are several kilns that specialize in white pottery. Although Icheon is now known for white ceramic pottery as well as celadon pottery, Gyeonggi-Do Gwangju was the area most famous for its production during the Joseon Dynasty. Gwangju also produced a blue-and-white porcelain that proliferated during the later centuries of the Joseon Dynasty. While it still produces these delicate pieces today, Gwangju produces more of the country's utilitarian brown earthenware food-storage pots, called *dojagi* or *onggi*. From fist-size jars to those huge enough to climb into, you'll see these food-storage containers piled high in the kiln's front yard, at nearly every market, and of course at every house. Reputedly, several hundred pottery kilns operate in and around Icheon, Gwangju, Yeoju to the east, and between Yeoju and Yangpyeong to the northeast. Most of these produce

CELADON PRODUCTION

The production of one kilnful of celadon is a multi-stage process that takes about a month to complete; many artisans contribute to the various stages of producing each piece that enters the kiln. Ingredients for the base material are gathered from around the country. Clay, fine sand, and other materials preferred by the individual potter are mixed together. Water is added to this composite, which is then put through a sieve, rinsed, and dried. This base clay is made during the spring, summer, and fall for use the next year. When the mixture is to be used, it's kneaded by foot to give it adhesive qualities and work out the bubbles. It's then put on a turning wheel (either foot- or electric-powered) and shaped by hand. When partially dry, the surface is smoothed and either left plain, incised, or inlaid. Only four colored clays are used as inlays: black, white, oxidized copper, and gold. If inlaid, the additional clay must dry before the excess is scraped off and the surface once again smoothed.

At this point, the rough piece is baked at 800–900°C. When it cools, the glaze is applied. Each master potter has developed his own secret formula for this most mysterious of pottery glazes. While some glazes nearly match ancient celadon pieces, most experts agree that modern glazes are only approximations, and that the old glaze formulas have never been accurately reproduced. About once a month, glazed pots are fired. A ceremony is performed at the kiln beforehand to ensure success. Pots are then put into the multi-compartment hillside kilns. The side openings of the kiln are then blocked with brick, and a fire is started at the kiln's lower end. The firing continues for 24 hours at 1,200–1,300°C. Any over- or under-heating or accumulation of ash on the object may cause discoloration or defect.

Pots are left in the kiln for two days to cool before being removed. Each piece is examined minutely; those that don't fit the potter's expectations, even in the smallest degree, are discarded and broken. At near every pottery kiln you'll see this pile of shards, a junkheap of potential treasures. Successful pieces are displayed in the shop's showroom or packed and shipped to sales outlets. The result of each firing is necessarily different. Often, many objects are kept, but once in a while all but a handful are turned to useless, broken scrap. Although the base clay is made only three times a year, pots are thrown and fired year-round.

© ROBERT NILSEN

Step kilns have produced decorative and utilitarian pottery for centuries.

celadon or white pottery, but a few specialize in *Pungcheong* ware, an unpretentious and casual pottery, and some make utilitarian earthenware containers. In Gwangju, a Joseon Dynasty white porcelain kiln site has been designated H.S. #314. Near these kilns you can find numerous shops selling locally produced pottery at prices usually substantially reduced from those in Seoul shops. Although the prices are better, the selection may be limited to a particular type of pottery. South of Gwangju at Gonjiam was a second location for the 2001 World Ceramic Exposition.

YEOJU 여주

Yeoju [Yŏju] is well-known for its temples and tombs. The temple Shilleuk-sa and Godal-saji are both north of the Han River, while the tombs of King Sejong and Hyojong are west of town. Several influential *yangban* families of the Joseon Dynasty lived near here and claimed Yeoju as their ancestral home. Perhaps the family of most importance was the Min, which produced several queens for the Joseon Dynasty kings. The birthplace of one has been remodeled and opened to the public. A museum of Buddhist wood sculpture has opened outside of town, introducing many to this less-than-well-known art form. A rather unexciting community, Yeoju lies along the south branch of the Han River and is substantially smaller than Icheon. Just east of the town center, Yeongwol-lu pavilion caps a knoll where the highway crosses the river. Farther up the river on both sides are riverside recreational areas.

Several accommodations and restaurants cluster around the intersection near the market in the center of Yeoju, one block up from the county office, which is right along the river. Two of these are the mid-price Seouljang Yeogwan (서울장여관) and the more expensive Geumland Park Motel (금랜드파크모텔). The bus terminal for express and intercity buses is about one-half kilometer up the main street from the county office. A bit farther is the post office. Intercity bus destinations include: Dong Seoul Bus Terminal (₩3,600), Seoul Express Bus Terminal (₩3,600), Suwon (₩3,800), Icheon (₩1,500), Yangpyeong (₩2,300), and Wonju (₩1,800). Express buses run only to Seoul (₩3,700). From along the main streets, city buses run to the tombs, temples, and the museum.

See www.yeoju.gyeonggi.kr for more information about the city and surrounding area.

Ganghansa 강한사

West of the county administration office is a Joseon Dynasty government building and shrine, both remodeled in 1984. The shrine, Ganghansa, is dedicated to Song Shi-yeol, the most brilliant scholar and statesman of the 17th century, and a commemorative monument raised for him here is called Taenosabi. A voluminous writer and a staunch Neo-Confucianist, Song Shi-yeol has been referred to as the "Bismarck of Korea." His political and philosophical thought greatly affected the intellectuals of his day. Canonized in 1756, he is one of Korea's 18 most influential Confucian scholars. Song Shi-yeol was at Namhan Sanseong when King Injo surrendered to the invading Manchus. Because of this ignominious act, Song refused to take any government post as long as Injo ruled. When Injo's son, Hyojong, was made king, Song Shi-yeol became prime minister; he wielded great power and steered the country through a time of great internal disturbance. He seems always to have been embroiled in some scholastic controversy or political strife, and was twice banished from court, the second time to Jeju-do. In 1689, en route to Seoul to face public execution, he was ordered to drink a poison to kill himself. This he did with a steady hand and a steely eye.

Royal Tombs

Two kilometers west of Yeoju is **Yeong-neung** [Yŏng-nŭng] (영능), tomb of King Sejong, the Joseon Dynasty's greatest ruler. This tomb (H.S. #195) is open to the public 0900–1800 every day; ₩200 entrance. King Sejong died in 1450 at the age of 54. Buried with him is his first wife, Queen Shim. Originally located west of Heonneung in Seoul, the tomb was relocated here in 1469. This is considered a sacred spot and visited by many Koreans as a pilgrimage. Aside from the mound tomb and the usual stone lanterns, tablets, and attendant figures are the buildings for the memorial ceremony and the preparation and storage of ritual utensils and accoutrements. At the entrance of this well-tended, garden-like grave stands a statue of King Sejong and a small museum relating his achievements. Sejong's 32-year reign was a high-water mark in Joseon Dynasty culture, which saw the development of a unique Korean alphabet, for which Sejong is best remembered. A bronze plaque next to his statue shows these original Korean letters, and presents an explanation of them in Chinese characters. Lamps that light the area's walkways have these letters as part of their ornamental design. His reign is also known for other literary achievements, including the encyclopedic codification of medical knowledge, the foundation of a Confucian school in Seoul, the casting of metal type for the publication of worthy literature, musical notation, the creation of scientific and astronomical instruments, the creation of half a dozen fortresses, and the pacification of the Japanese island of Tsushima. In May, the Confucian ritual *Sungmo-je* is held at the grave site to honor the great king, and every October, as part of the King Sejong Cultural Festival, a memorial ceremony is also conducted here.

Adjacent is the tomb of King Hyojong, the 17th Joseon Dynasty king, who ruled for 10 years through the middle of the 1600s. As part of his father's agreement with the Manchus, Hyojong spent several years as a hostage in Beijing before ascending the Korean throne. Once king, he strengthened the defense of the country and created a climate of coexistence with the new Chinese dynasty. Hyojong admired King Sejong and desired to be buried near him. Although smaller than that of his predecessor, King Hyojong's tomb is a finer example of tomb construction, with separate mounds for the king and queen. Each is surrounded by a stone fence and carved animals, but only the king's has a retaining wall. In front of the tombs are the usual table, lantern, civilian and military attendants, and additional animal figures. At the bottom of the hill are a memorial stela, and buildings used in preparation for the yearly memorial ceremony. To reach these royal tombs, take one of the periodic city buses (₩600); it's even close enough for an inexpensive taxi ride.

M

GYEONGGI-DO

Shilleuk-sa 신륵사

Two kilometers east of Yeoju is the temple Shilleuk-sa [Shillŭk-sa]; ₩2,000 entrance. Established in 580 by the Silla Dynasty monk Wonhyo, this temple was enlarged, burned, and rededicated several times. It was home to Naong, the most famous monk from the end of the Goryeo Dynasty. During the reign of King Seongjong, Shilleuk-sa was made the prayer temple for the tomb of King Sejong. Set against a low hill on the north side of the Han River, this temple is especially nice during spring, when its many flowering trees are in bloom, and in autumn, when the leaves of its huge ginkgo trees turn from green to gold; there's a 500-year-old aromatic juniper tree at the temple as well. It's one of the most important temples in the province and is the repository of seven Treasures. The first is a six-tier brick pagoda (T. #226) overlooking the river, one of a handful of brick pagodas in the country. Below it on the riverbank are a smaller stone pagoda and an octagonal open pavilion, a perfect spot for a lazy summer picnic. Nearby is a Silla Dynasty memorial stone stela (T. #230), whose inscription concerns a library that once stood on the premises for the preservation of wood printing blocks of the sutras.

Circling the temple's central courtyard are the main hall, lecture pavilion, judgment hall, several additional halls, and the temple living quarters. The Amita Buddha is enshrined on the altar of Geungnakbo-jeon, Shilleuk-sa's main hall, which is rather lofty for such a small floor space. On the outside walls of this hall is painted an eight-section abbreviated version of the "ox-herding" series of murals that explain the process of reaching enlightenment. Between these two buildings stands a seven-tier marble pagoda (T. #225) from the early Joseon Dynasty. Pagodas made of such marble are almost nonexistent in Korea; sadly, much of this light-colored stone has turned blackish. The relief carvings of dragons, lotus, and "wave" patterns around its base are all done delicately, with consummate skill. To the side in an open-lattice building are a large Korean bell, a flat metal gong, two skin drums, and a wooden "fish" drum. One of the skin drums is played and the bell struck toward the end of the day to announce the start of evening ceremonies, and to help lay over the compound an aura of quietude, reverence, and piety.

To the side of the main hall is Chosa-dang (T. #180), a small, rather undistinguished building constructed with no ridge beam. This hall enshrines the portraits of three distinguished monks: Naong, the most famous monk of the late Goryeo Dynasty and, in his old age, a brief resident of this temple; Muhak, adviser to King Taejo; and Jigong, an Indian monk who came to Korea to preach. To the rear of these buildings and up the hill is an octagonal gray marble lantern (T. #231). It stands next to the bell-shaped *sari budo* (T. #228) of Naong. Next to it is a stela (T. #229) like the one near the brick pagoda overlooking the river. Two other *sari budo* occupy a spot farther to the side behind the judgment hall. The newest addition to the temple grounds is the brightly painted front gate. Set on two tall and sturdy tree trunks, this open structure symbolizes the boundary between the sacred and the profane.

While city buses run the route past the entrance to Shilleuk-sa, it takes only 30 minutes to walk from the town center. Follow any of the city streets east out of town to the Han River bridge. Cross the bridge and take the first road leading to the right on the north side of the river. At the temple entrance road is a large parking lot and a modern community of shops, accommodations, restaurants, and ceramics studios. The Ceramic Exhibition Center here was built for the 2001 World Ceramic Exposition. You must walk through this village to get to the peace of the temple grounds. Even with the noise from the river, greatest during summer weekends, this is still a fine spot and a good example of a temple with a full complement of halls.

Godal-saji 고달사지

Near a small village eight kilometers north of Yeoju is the site of one of the Goryeo Dynasty's most important Buddhist temples, Godal-saji [Kodal-saji]. While once a thriving religious community, this temple is now a memory. Only a few stone objects remain from its glory days, but they're some of the finest stone carvings that remain from the period. The foremost is a *sari budo* for priest Won'gam (N.T. #7). This squat, lantern-shaped reliquary has a low, rooflike capstone with sharply upturned ridgelines that end in teardrop-shaped decorations. In its bottom section are an exquisitely carved, dragon-shaped tortoise head and twining dragons playing below a stylized swirl of clouds. A similar *sari budo* (T. #7) was made for priest Wonjong. Nearby is a stone pedestal (T. #8) that once supported this temple's main altar statue. Double-petal lotus blossoms circle its base and top, while one huge lotus-bud outline is recessed into the flat side of its square spacer block. A tortoise-shaped stela base and its capstone (T. #6) also grace these grounds; the stone plaque that separated these two pieces is now housed at the National Museum in Seoul. Dragon figures in the capstone writhe in turbulent waters. Typical of carved tortoise heads from this period, this one resembles a grimacing dragon, with knitted brow and fierce eyes. Also taken to Seoul from this temple site was a roofless lantern (T. #282) with an unusual twin lion base.

Mok-A Buddhist Art Museum
목아불교박물관

About six kilometers east of Yeoju in the village of Gangcheon Iho-ri is the Mok-A Buddhist Art Museum. Get off the bus (there are only a handful a day) along the highway and walk the 100 meters up the country lane to the museum. Established in 1993 by Pak Chan-su, a master carver (I.C.A. #108), this museum is the reflection and dedication of one man's quest to give life and spirit to wood in the Buddhist religious tradition. A finely landscaped lawn dotted with stone and metal sculpture fronts the museum's ar-

chitecturally pleasing, yet somewhat out of place, three-story Western-style building. Inside, the galleries are filled with works in wood by all the important Buddhist personages, and many Buddhist stories are rendered in statuary and panel form. With each sculpture, the masterfully controlled detail is extraordinary; its essence emerges as easily as the color from the block of wood. Much that you would ordinarily see painted at a temple is chiseled here from a chunk of a tree. Aside from the strictly Buddhist images, mythical figures of Korea's cultural past and Taoist figures which have been incorporated into Korean Buddhist iconography also make their appearances. Exquisite examples of temple furniture, ceremonial objects, and other accoutrements are also displayed to show this more pragmatic aspect of Buddhist temple woodwork. In addition, a display of traditional woodworking tools has been set up to show what is needed to create these works of art. A collection of wooden religious objects from other Buddhist countries rounds out the museum's collection. All parts of the museum are presented in a simple yet evocative manner, and the quality of each piece speaks for itself—three have been designated National Treasures (N.T. #1144, #1145, #1146). While there is almost no explanation in English, a walk through the exhibit is well worth the effort if only to appreciate the consummate skill of the carvers and the beauty of these religious works.

A gift shop in the lobby sells small sculptures done at the studio, Buddhist paraphernalia, and ceramics from the surrounding area. A restaurant near the front gate provides traditional Korean food and drink. The museum is open every day except Tuesdays and holidays 0930– 1800 (1730 in winter); entrance fee is ₩3,000.

Eastern Gyeonggi-Do

Yongmun-sa 용문사

Yongmun-sa, or Dragon Gate Temple, was dedicated in 913 and expanded in 1395. Japanese soldiers burned it to the ground in 1592. Reconstructed, it was again burnt by the Japanese in 1907, because it had been used as a base for Korean guerrillas. In 1983–84, a new main hall was constructed, almost entirely by the use of hand tools and human-powered devices. The wood was split, sawed, shaped, notched, fitted, and carved by hand. It took a crew of a dozen about 15 months to complete the task. Rather lofty for its girth, the broadly overhanging, intricate bracket system supporting the roof is brightly painted, and vivid murals deck its exterior walls. A multi-story stone pagoda, several stone lanterns, and a standing stone Buddha figure were all added new at that time. About 300 meters up the hill behind the standing Buddha is a *sari budo* and memorial tablet for National Priest Jeongju (T. #531), erected here after his death in 1395. He traveled to China with the much more famous monk Muhak and studied under the well-respected Naong. Several other smaller and more recent *sari budo* for minor monks stand to the side of the main compound.

Still the most impressive object at this temple is the ginkgo tree (N.M. #30), which dominates this compound and is said to be the oldest and largest nut tree in the world. Over 60 meters high, and having a girth of 14 meters, it stands tall and stately, spreading its branches over the temple grounds. In the autumn, its delta-shaped leaves change from lush green to imperial yellow—once the exclusive color of Chinese emperors. Quite a sight in its bright yellow garb, this immense tree was supposedly planted over 1,000 years ago by Silla Prince Maeui. After the dissolution of the Silla Dynasty in 935, this prince decided to spend his remaining years as a monk in retreat. On his way to the Diamond Mountains, he stopped here and planted this tree, never knowing to what heights it would grow or what reputation it would amass. In fact,

because of its reputation and grand size, King Sejong bestowed on it an honorary courtly rank. Legend says that when the tree dies or when a principal branch falls off, some calamity will befall the country.

When the temple's main hall was reconstructed, the village below the temple was also rebuilt—a classic example of tourist development in Korea. Created from the ground up, a wide avenue was carved out of farming fields in this gently sloping valley. Along this road is a multitude of accommodations, restaurants, souvenir shops, other stores, a group camping area, and a bus stand. Made of cold cement, it has an extremely business-oriented atmosphere, typical of all such villages that sit below major temples in the country. It's a 20-minute walk from the village through the two-posted front gate, along a stream, and under a canopy of trees to the temple itself; ₩1,800 entrance. Buses to the temple village run from the town of Yongmun (₩600), Yangpyeong (₩1,400), and Seoul Sangbong Bus Terminal (₩4,800).

Yongmun-sa sits below Yongmun-san. At 1,157 meters, this mountain is not the tallest in Gyeonggi-Do, but some say it's the best-looking. Of its many hiking trails, the one that's perhaps most often used goes over the ridge to the west of Yongmun-sa and on to the hermitage Sangwon-am. This distance is approximately two kilometers and takes about an hour. From there, a path goes down the valley to the village of Yeonan Yeonsu-ri, from where buses return to the town of Yongmun.

Recreation

This region provides abundant all-season outdoor recreational opportunities for the citizens of the province and the city of Seoul. Along with Yongmun-san, other tall peaks in the area are used for hiking, usually weekend excursions from the city. Here too are several **river resorts** that draw large numbers in the summer. The north branch of the Han River is the most picturesque of the two branches. Along it are the older Paldang, Cheongpyeong, and Namiseom resorts and interspersed along the way are the newer Yangsuri, Gangbyeon, Seto, and Daeseong-ni recreation areas. The closest to Seoul is **Paldang Resort**, located below the Paldang Dam, constructed just below the confluence of the north and south branches of the Han River. Here, as at the other resorts, you'll find facilities for swimming, fishing, boating, water-skiing, and other water sports, as well as numerous restaurants that specialize in river fish. Most also have accommodations. **Cheongpyeong Resort** lies two kilometers outside of the town of Cheongpyeong, above the Cheongpyeong Dam. Its reservoir stretches nearly to **Namiseom Resort**, which is on the tiny island of Namiseom in the middle of the river just outside Gapyeong. From Cheongpyeong, the road and rail lines cut directly to Gapyeong, from which they again follow the river as far as Chuncheon. The section of the river from Gapyeong to Chuncheon is perhaps the prettiest. There is bus transportation to all these river areas from the Seoul Sangbong Bus Terminal, Cheongpyeong, Gapyeong, and Chuncheon. The Jungang rail line has a stop at Paldang, and stops for the others are on the Gyeongchun line to Chuncheon.

For winter recreation, the area offers five ski resorts. Smaller and lower than the more expansive resorts of Gangwon-Do, these ski areas provide plenty of fun and enjoyment at a reasonable rate, and they're all close to the big city for easy transportation. Flanking the highway just east of Seoul are **Cheonmasan Ski Resort** (tel. 02/2233-5311) and **Seoul Resort** (tel. 031/592-1220, www.seoulresort.co.kr). North of there is **Bear's Town Ski Resort** (tel. 031/532-2534, www.bearstown.com). To the south, Jisan Resort (tel. 031/638-8460, www.jisanresort.co.kr) and **Yangji Pine Resort** (tel. 031/338-2001, www.pineresort.com) offer skiing near Yongin. Of these, Bear's Town has the largest complex, Seoul Resort the smallest, Cheonmasan has gained a reputation for night skiing, and the other two are generally more family oriented. In addition, each offers accommodations and a variety of other activities, while Jisan, Yangji, and Bear's Town have summer recreational opportunities. All are within two hours of Seoul, and aside from public transportation there are regular winter shuttles. Generally cheaper than the resorts in Gangwon-Do, lift tickets here run at around ₩40,000 for a full day and rental fees are less.

Northern Gyeonggi-Do

North of Seoul is a region of contrast. From the Paju agricultural plain in the west to the rugged mountains of the east, this portion of the province encompasses everything from tranquil Buddhist monasteries to a heavily militarized border. As one might suspect, the key factor to this border region is its strategic defensive position, evidenced by the multitude of Korean and U.S. military bases, and the inordinate number of servicemen, military checkpoints, and defensive barriers. This militarized region is divided into two sections, the western and eastern corridors. The western corridor runs north from the northwest corner of Seoul, through the Paju Plain, to Munsan; crossing the Imjin River, it goes on to Panmunjeom. The eastern corridor runs along a fault valley north from the northeast corner of Seoul to Uijeongbu, Dongducheon, Shintan-ni, and the DMZ. Through these corridors run two of the country's most important military supply routes. They are also the most probable land routes North Korea would take if it should try again to invade.

An extensive defensive network has been created to impede the advance of any invading land troops. Not only has it been thrown up across the two corridors north of Seoul, it's in evidence across the entire border region of Gyeonggi-Do and Gangwon-Do. Aside from the permanent gun emplacements and mobile military units, there are other deterrents. In areas where tanks can run, a series of several-meter-high, bermedwall tank barriers have been erected with a perpendicular rock face on their north sides. Where these walls cross transportation routes and waterways, other impediments have been raised, like the huge cement blocks suspended over roadways and above rail lines, the supports of which can be exploded causing the top to drop and block the passage, and the series of concrete pillars that dot riverbeds and run across some fields. Continuous coils of barbed wire stretch across certain areas of these valleys, ready to be pulled across the roadway if need be. High storm fences topped with barbed wire run along both sides of the Imjin and other rivers, and it's rumored that land mines have been placed along sections of the riverbanks, and at other strategic points, to deter individual infiltrators. On very rare occasions, buses are stopped and searched, and occasionally passengers are asked for identification. This is usually done on buses bound for cities; almost never are foreigners questioned. The military police are looking for spies, military deserters, and subversive students, as well as arms, contraband, and other security threats.

PAJU 파주

Paju is the county farthest north in the western corridor. Geumchon is the county seat but Munsan (문산) is the last town of any size on the way to Panmunjeom. Its location sets it closer to Shin Uiju, on the North Korea/Chinese border, than to Busan on the south coast of the peninsula. Because of its location, this small agricultural community and its nearby towns are important to the Korean soldiers stationed in the vicinity. There are several U.S. military installations nearby as well. During the Korean War military armistice talks, the U.N. negotiators set up their headquarters near Munsan. Following the war, the rail line that once ran to Pyeongyang in North Korea, and from there on to China, Russia, and Europe was dismantled north of town. (In fact, it was possible at one time to ride from Busan to Paris, one of the longest train trips in the world.)

In accordance with an agreement between former South Korean president Kim Dae Jung and North Korean leader Kim Jong-il, this line has been rebuilt to the border to facilitate transportation between the countries, initially for commercial use, but hopefully for regular passenger traffic if relations between the countries continue to warm. A corresponding link is supposed to be reconstructed south from Gaeseong to the border. Until full passenger traffic is established, short train tours run twice a day at 1043 and 1443 on the new section of track between the Imjingang Station near Imjingak and Dorasan Station, 3.7 kilometers and five minutes away. Special permission must be obtained at the Imjingang Station as this trip runs through the military-controlled DMZ. Tickets are ₩1,100.

Munsan marks the northern terminus for regular passenger service on the Gyeongui rail line. A dozen and a half *Tongil-ho* trains run daily between Munsan and the Seoul Shinchon Station (₩1,600). Seoul city bus nos. 922 and 912 run from Seoul Station to Munsan for ₩1,300. Intercity bus destinations and fares from Munsan include Seoul Seobu Bus Terminal (₩1,200), Imjin-gak (₩600), Hwaseok-jeong (₩600), Beobwon-ni (₩900), and Geumchon (₩1,200).

For more information about Munsan and the surrounding area see http://city.paju.kyonggi.kr.

Unification Park 통일공원

One kilometer south of the center of town on the east side of the highway is Unification Park, or Tongil Gongwon. Seven war monuments stand within the park. Unveiled in 1977, the first erected was a 10-meter-high bronze monument dedicated to the 18 Korean War correspondents from five nations who were killed during that conflict. It is the only such memorial in the country dedicated to members of the press. In the shape of a "J"—for "journalist"—its form resembles an unrolled length of teletype paper or partial roll of film. On it a stylized hand grips a quill pen; into it has been set a skeleton globe. Written in glowing terms, the inscription lauds the efforts of these journalists. Set up some years later, a second monument is dedicated to pro-South, pro-democratic North Koreans who fought a guerrilla campaign against the North Korean army during the war. A third monument has been added to honor 10 South Korean soldiers who in 1949 made themselves into human bombs to blow up enemy positions near Gaeseong. The others have been added more recently.

Tomb of Yi Yul-gok 이율곡묘지

North of Beobwon-ni (법원리), some 13 kilometers east of Munsan, is the tomb of the Joseon Dynasty scholar Yi Yul-gok. He, and another Joseon Dynasty Neo-Confucianist, Yi Toe-gye, are recognized as Korea's foremost Confucian scholars. Yi Yul-gok, his mother, and other members of his family are buried here on this peacefully secluded hillside. Although he was born in Gangneung, Yi Yul-gok's forebears came from a village not far from here, hence his burial at this spot. An ancestor built the pavilion Hwaseokjeong, which overlooks the Imjin River some eight kilometers from the tomb; Yul-gok no doubt visited it periodically when he was growing up as he had his early education here. Next to the tomb compound is Jaun Seowon, a Confucian academy and shrine built in 1615 to commemorate this most influential thinker and two of his distinguished students. In 1868 this academy was destroyed by royal decree along with most others in the country, but it was rebuilt in 1970. An exhibition hall has also been constructed on the grounds, containing reproductions of works by Yul-gok and his mother, Shim Saimdang, but they are duplications of those displayed at Ojukheon in Gangneung. A scholarly research institute has been set up next to the shrine to study the works of Yi Yul-gok, how his philosophy and social ideas affected Korean thought and the society of his day, and how it has had a more widespread influence throughout Asia over the centuries. To reach this historic site, walk 100 meters to the west of the main intersection in Beobwon-ni. There, turn right onto a paved road that heads north, and follow it for about two kilometers. A taxi will cost about ₩3,000; there are no buses. Open 0800–1800 daily; ₩1,000 entrance.

Paju Mireuk Buddhas 파주미륵

On a hillside a few kilometers south of Gwangtan is the temple Yongam-sa, and its double Buddha statue, Paju Mireuk. Carved about 900 years ago, these tall granite statues (T. #93) represent the Mireuk Buddha (Buddha of the Future), and greatly resemble a similar single statue in Andong called Jebiwon. The Paju Mireuk statues are the only such twin figures in the country. The bodies have been cut in bas-relief into a flat rock face; their heads are made from separate stone blocks that have been positioned on top. The facial features are rather inexpressive and lifeless, but the gowns are flowing and the hands are held in natural positions. Like many Mireuk Buddha statues in the country, these have hats. One is round, like the face over which it rests—it's a male representation; the other is squarish, and complements the angular features of the female figure. In 1953, then-president Syngman Rhee had a tiny statue carved and placed near the right shoulder of the male figure—no one seems to know exactly why, or what significance it has. The temple below these statues was rededicated in 1953 on the site of an ancient temple, and its main hall was built in 1978. These figures can be reached by bus from the Seoul Seobu Bus Terminal (₩1,200) or Beobwon-ni (₩1,000).

Imjin-gak 임진각

North of Munsan, on the south bank of the Imjin River, is the small Imjin-gak Park. This spot is as far north up the western corridor as you can go without special military permission. In this park you'll find statues and monuments, a new bell pavilion, an old tank and military plane, fountains and flags, a restaurant, kiosk, an exhibition hall, and, incongruously, kiddie amusement rides. One 17-faceted, tower-shaped monument commemorates the 17 high-ranking government officials killed in Rangoon, Burma, in 1983 when North Korean agents tried unsuccessfully to assassinate then-president Chun Doo Hwan. A small exhibition hall here is dedicated to displaying life in North Korea by pictures and goods. Occasionally on *Chuseok* and Lunar New Year's Day, people who fled from North Korea during the war come to Imjin-gak to perform a prayer ceremony for the reunification of family and country. A three-car train here serves as a reminder that this rail line was cut during the Korean War.

Crossing the silty Imjin River is the Freedom Bridge. Across this trestle of metal over 13,000 war prisoners walked to freedom in the south after the armistice of 1953. A former railroad bridge converted to a roadway, this was the only access to Panmunjeom and the section of the province north of the Imjin River until a new vehicular bridge to the DMZ was constructed some distance to the east in 1998. A new railroad bridge has been built next to the old bridge as part of the new rail connection to North Korea. To the side of Freedom Bridge, cement support pillars of the bombed vehicular bridge that used to cross this river still stand in solitary witness to the war's destructiveness. Nets slung across this tidal river discourage underwater infiltration from the north, a possibility since the north borders the Imjin River several kilometers to the west, near its confluence with the Han River. Use bus no. 94 (₩600) from Munsan.

Third Tunnel Tour 제 3 땅굴

One kilometer southwest of Panmunjeom is an infiltration tunnel, the third found in the DMZ since 1974. Discovered in 1978, this tunnel was started in the northern half of the DMZ and dug into the southern half before its discovery. Lying 73 meters below ground, it is about two meters tall and two meters wide, and would have been large enough, according to some estimates, for carrying a full division of fully equipped North Korean troops per hour had it been completed and used to conduct enemy troops on a surprise invasion. An interceptor tunnel has been dug to meet this tunnel, and tours are conducted into it. The long descent into the ground gets cool and wet, and hard-hats are provided for tall visitors because of the rough, jagged rock walls. Once in the tunnel you can walk the half kilometer to a point just below the Military Demarcation Line, where the tunnel has been blocked and a military guardpost created. On a hill near the tunnel entrance, the **Dora Observation Post** has been set up where you have a good view into the north and can see Panmunjeom, Daeseong-dong, Gijeong-dong, Gaeseong, farming fields,

and the rusting remains of a steam engine left in place after the conclusion of the Korean War.

Shuttle tours of the tunnel and observation post leave daily except Monday and holidays from Imjin-gak Park at 1100, 1300 and 1500 for ₩7,700 per adult or ₩6,200 for those ages 7–19; passports are required. Arrange for this tour on the 1st floor of the Imjin-gak building. Other tours to the third tunnel, including transportation to and from Seoul, a briefing by Korean military escorts, tour of a small museum, and a meal, take about seven hours. Those offered by the U.S.O. run on Tuesday and Saturday 0730–1500 and cost $40 for civilians and $25 for active-duty military personnel. Chung-Ang Express Tour (tel. 02/2266-3350) and others run a similar tour on different days of the week for around ₩48,000 per person.

Odu-san Unification Observatory
우도산통일전망대

A good place to get a view into North Korea without the cost or the restrictions of a tour to Panmunjeom or the Dora Observation Post is the Odu-san Observatory. Set high on a hill overlooking the confluence of the Han and Imjin rivers, this spot once was the site of a Baekje Dynasty fortress (H.S. #351), and it's obvious why. Today, a modern, multi-story observation building crowns the hill. From this lookout, you can see the western suburbs of Seoul to the south, but you are closer to the North Korean city of Gaeseong, set beyond the hills directly to the north, than you are to the center of Seoul. Inside the glass-fronted observation room is a contour map of what you can see out the window, and on the decks outside you may rent 20x binoculars to get a closer look at what's going on across the river. Photography is permitted and you can use your own binoculars. Inside on another level are two exhibition halls, one displaying North Korean items of daily use with a brief explanation of contemporary North Korean society, and the other showing still pictures and videos of life in North Korea. Unfortunately for the non-Korean speaker, there are no spoken or written explanations in English or other foreign languages. Food and souvenirs are available in the basement, and several stalls sell a few select goods of North Korean origin. Admission to this lookout is ₩1,500 for adults and ₩1,000 for students. Hours are 0900–1800 (1700 in winter).

To get to the Odu-san Observatory, first go to Geumchon. Seoul city buses no. 158-2 and 912, and an intercity bus from Seoul Seobu Bus Terminal, run this route. A local train from Shinchon Station also stops at Geumchon (₩1,300). From Geumchon, take an hourly local bus (₩720) the 10 kilometers to the observatory parking area in Seongdong-ni. To catch the local bus, walk west from the train station to the first intersection. Turn right, go over the railroad tracks, and take the first road to the left about 100 meters to a small bus station. The walk takes about 10 minutes. Alternately, take a taxi from Geumchon to the observatory for around ₩10,000 one way. From the parking area, a free shuttle bus takes you up to the observatory itself. At the lower shuttle-bus stop are numerous restaurants and souvenir shops.

PANMUNJEOM 판문점
Demilitarized Zone

Stretching across the waist of the peninsula is the 241-kilometer-long Demilitarized Zone (DMZ), established at the end of the Korean War. Running from the Han River estuary, this strip makes an S-curve through the peninsula and reaches the east coast a short distance below the 39th parallel. Placed at regular intervals down the entire center line of this 4,000-meter-wide zone are 1,292 white markers holding signs that indicate the actual borderline, the Military Demarcation Line (MDL). This zone is, in fact, a no-man's land. A barbed-wire fence, with guardposts placed at regular intervals, borders this strip. While mobile units patrol the zone, there is no permanent military base within. As in the northern half, there is only one village within the southern half of the DMZ. Referred to by South Korea as "Freedom Village," Daeseongdong is a tiny farming community of about 250 inhabitants. While it's a productive community, it's maintained partially for its propaganda value. Villagers are exempt from taxes and conscrip-

tion, and as an added perk, in the past—when it was illegal in other parts of the country—they could ferment their own rice wine. Villagers here have received great help from the government. It's said that they each farm an average of 17 acres (as opposed to three acres in the rest of the country), and earn substantially more than their counterparts. Of course, there are some drawbacks. The village sits smack-dab in the middle of a likely invasion route from the north; should such an invasion come, the village would be pulverized in a matter of minutes. Farming can only be done in restricted areas, and movement is limited. Everyone must be in the village by dark. There is a 2200 curfew, when anyone caught outdoors is liable to be shot on sight as a possible North Korean spy. Because of the unusual circumstances and the resulting lack of human interference, there has been a profusion of wildlife within the zone. Spots within the DMZ have become feeding grounds on the migratory route of many winged creatures, including the rare Manchurian crane (N.M. #202).

The area just south of the DMZ is hyper-militarized, with numerous military bases, heavy artillery positions, mobile units, radar and communications stations, and other defensive positions. In the event of attack, the duty of troops stationed between this zone and the Imjin River is to slow down the invasion of enemy troops while support units move up from the south and in from nearby countries. For the more than four decades since the armistice, there has been no large transgression of the border, but numerous "incidents" have occurred within the zone involving the deaths of at least 500 South Koreans, 50 Americans, and an unknown number of North Koreans. In addition, six American soldiers and numerous South Koreans have absconded to the north, while some North Koreans have fled south. Four North Korean infiltration tunnels have been discovered within the DMZ since 1974. It's conjectured that the North Koreans continue to dig and there may be several dozen more in the works. The first was discovered by accident a few kilometers east of Panmunjeom, and since then the military has been looking hard for others. The following year, the

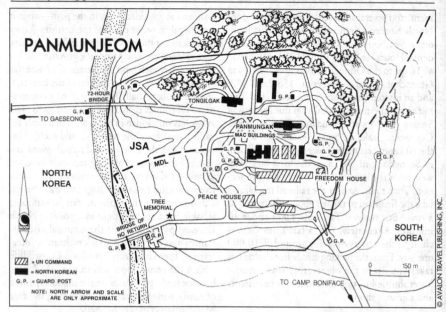

© AVALON TRAVEL PUBLISHING, INC.

second was discovered near Cheolwon, and in 1978 a larger tunnel was located only one kilometer southwest of Panmunjeom itself. A fourth was found in 1990 about 100 kilometers to the east, in Gangwon-Do. Panmunjeom is 56 kilometers by road from downtown Seoul. At its closest point, the DMZ is about 30 kilometers from the Seoul city limits. After crossing the border, fighter aircraft could reach the capital in a matter of minutes.

Joint Security Area

Straddling the actual border near the west end of the DMZ is the Joint Security Area (JSA), known as Panmunjeom [P'anmunjŏm]. An area of less than one square kilometer in size, it is the only place where mutually agreed-upon contact between U.N. and North Korean military representatives takes place, and it acts as the working area for members of the Neutral Nations Supervisory Commission. The JSA is the site of continuing meetings between members of the Military Armistice Commission (MAC), a place to defuse military tensions. Regularly scheduled administrative meetings provide continual dialogue, recurrent accusations, and, less frequently, constructive proposals relating to the truce agreement. While no longer a venue of warfare, Panmunjeom is still a battleground of minds and wills. Meetings of the International Red Cross, government representatives, and sports delegates are periodically held in the JSA. These specially convened political and cultural sessions are often viewed as lightning rods for political posturing by both South and North Korea.

Historical Sketch

On June 23, 1951, the Soviet delegate to the United Nations proposed a cease-fire. Less than one month later, on July 19, 1951, talks began at Gaeseong, the ancient capital of the Goryeo Dynasty, now 10 kilometers north of the DMZ in North Korea. After a breakdown, these meetings continued at the village of Panmunjeom, one kilometer north of the present JSA. Overnight, this tiny farming hamlet was hurled into the spotlight of world affairs. An armistice was signed on July 27, 1953, concluding more than 500 major meetings spread out over two years. Delegates from the U.N. joint military command and the North Korean and Chinese armies signed the document; South Korean representatives refused. This armistice was only a military document; no political agreement was ever offered, and no peace treaty was ever signed. Among other provisions, the armistice ended military hostilities, created the DMZ, repatriated prisoners, established the Military Armistice Commission to handle complaints of violations, and created the Neutral Nations Supervisory Commission, to see that the armistice agreements were kept. This commission consisted of four members, one each from Sweden, Switzerland, Poland, and Czechoslovakia, nations that did not participate in the Korean War. (In 1993, because of political developments in their own country, the Czech delegation withdrew from the Armistice Commission, leaving only the Polish delegation on the northern side.) Not only have subsequent truce talks been the longest in history, at well over 40 years—with still with no end in sight—but this is also the longest armed truce in history. Considering the imminent possibility of conflict, the immense amount of firepower, and huge number of soldiers (about one million) facing each other across the border, this truce has proved rather stable. By and large, sensibility has prevailed. Supporting national governments and world opinions have helped stabilize an admittedly volatile situation. Nonetheless, some experts believe Korea is the most likely spot in Asia for a large-scale outbreak of military activity including the use of nuclear weapons because tension between the two halves of the peninsula is still strong, nuclear weapons are still stored on the peninsula by the U.S. military, and both South and North Korea may soon possess the technology and capability (if they don't already) of producing their own nuclear arsenals.

The village of Panmunjeom no longer exists. Only the building that was hastily constructed for the signing of the agreement has been preserved, turned into a museum by the North Koreans. The actual site of the continuing talks (JSA) was moved one kilometer south, to a hilltop straddling the border. These temporary and spartan military structures soon turned into permanent buildings, accompanied by several guardposts for both sides within the confines of this small

© ROBERT NILSEN

view beyond Peace House into North Korea

acreage. The two-story buildings Freedom House (1965), built by the south, and Panmungak (1969), built by the north, were constructed to either side of the central row of conference buildings to better cater to visitors and provide office space for each country's Red Cross representatives. Set on a higher elevation and one meter wider than Freedom House, Panmungak got a 3rd floor in 1994. In the early '80s, the larger and much fancier edifices Peace House (1980), on the southern side, and Tongilgak ("Unification House"—1985), on the northern side, were erected for ministerial meetings and other such high-level contacts. The single-story Tongilgak found itself surpassed in height by the renovation in 1989 of three-story Peace House, and this perhaps caused the North Koreans to add a 3rd floor to Panmungak, which sits on the highest point in the JSA. Freedom House has since been enlarged and modernized. Some landscaping has also been done to "beautify" and soften the outer trappings of this no-nonsense conference spot.

Originally, the borderline was not drawn through the JSA, and the entire compound was open to free access by both sides. However, since an incident on August 18, 1976, a line has been drawn through the center of the JSA and no regular visitors or guards are allowed to cross to the other half of the compound. During a periodic tree-trimming detail from the south on that day, a truckful of North Korean troops crossed the Bridge of No Return and viciously attacked the civilian workers and their military guards with clubs, and axed to death two U.S. Army captains. This was the first act of armed conflict within this "neutral zone"; apologies were subsequently made by the north. In response, this bridge, which had been the north's only access to the JSA, was closed to their use, necessitating the construction of another bridge over the stream in their half of the area. This bridge is known as "the 72-hour Bridge," as that is how long it took to build. Prior to the axing incident, the most notable incident to take place at Panmunjeom was the release (in 1968) of the crew of the USS *Pueblo*. In November 1984, a 22-year-old Soviet tour leader dashed across the demarcation line and asked for political asylum in the

United States. A half-hour gun battle ensued, leaving three military guards dead. Not all crossings of the border have been from the north, however. In 1983, a U.S. Army private left his guardpost near the JSA and walked across the border into North Korea—apparently, North Korean propaganda does occasionally work.

Reunification talks started at Panmunjeom on July 4, 1974. By 1975 there was no progress and talks broke off; new rounds began in 1980 and once again in 1981. In 1985, these meetings once again resumed; this was the most significant attempt by both sides to come to some sort of understanding. While there was much discussion, many proposals, and a relatively positive atmosphere, few substantive agreements were reached. Yet these talks did result in reciprocal visits by International Red Cross workers, folk-art performers from both sides, and members of families split by the partitioning of the country. Since then, additional high-level discussions have been held, trips were conducted by upper-level ministers, and a summit between South Korean president Kim Dae Jung and North Korean leader Kim Jong-il was held in Pyeongyang, North Korea in June 2000.

Tour

The only way to visit Panmunjeom is to take an organized tour. The opening of the area is a goodwill gesture by the U.N. military command bearing responsibility for the security of this area. A trip to the DMZ presents an odd juxtaposition between the civilian and military spheres of this society. On the one hand, you as a tourist are on a "sightseeing tour" of rural Korea, with a helpful and friendly guide. On the other hand, that tour takes you squarely to the middle of one of the most militarized regions of the world. This is not a place of merriment and joy; it's rather bleak and stark. Panmunjeom is one of the few spots in the country where you can actually glimpse the forbidden north—one of the most tightly closed societies in the world—and it is the only place where you can walk up to the border itself. With the possibility of conflict never far away, you'll feel strong vibes of alertness, readiness, and tension. Everyone is on his or her best behavior here, where there's a studied practice of punctilious interaction. If you're at all versed in modern Korean history, you'll find a tour of Panmunjeom emotionally charged.

Your tour starts with a bus ride from Seoul. Just east of Imjin-gak, the bus crosses the Imjin River via a new bridge and drives on to Camp Boniface (formerly Camp Kitty Hawk), the advance camp for Panmunjeom, home of perhaps 300 U.S. soldiers. After a brief introduction to the zone, you will be given a guest badge and required to sign a release of liability to proceed further. This visitor's declaration begins: "The visit to the Joint Security Area at Panmunjeom will entail entry into a hostile area and possibility of injury or death as a direct result of enemy action." This is serious business, and the military is taking no chances. However, you needn't worry too much—there has never been an incident involving visitors to the area. From the briefing room, a military bus takes you to the JSA compound.

You'll be escorted to a two-story pavilion overlooking the light blue and silver buildings in the center of the compound, used for MAC meetings. Beyond that, on the far side of the MDL, is North Korea's most prominent building within Panmunjeom. Panmungak is a three-story affair with huge windows on the upper floor (the better to see you with!). Yet, for all its width and height, it's only six meters deep. While pictures are forbidden en route from Imjin-gak to Panmunjeom, feel free to bring along a camera to take pictures within this compound. You'll look through your camera lens at the North Korean guards, some of whom will be looking right back at you through binoculars and taking pictures of you! From the pavilion, you'll proceed into the MAC building. The MDL, the actual border, runs through the center of this building and its central table. This is the only place where you can freely step into North Korean territory, and just as freely step back.

While much serious discussion and debate takes place in this room, occasionally symbolic actions here have sunk to seemingly ludicrous depths. This is epitomized by the controversy over the representative flags. One day, a flag was brought in by one side that was larger than the flag of the other. At the next meeting, this smaller flag was replaced by a flag larger than that of the other side. On alternate meeting days, the respective sides brought in continually larger flags until the flags were too big to bring inside the building. The two sides finally agreed to limit their flags to their present size.

After leaving the MAC building, you'll stop at an observation post that affords the best vantage point for a view into North Korean territory. From that point you can see what is called "Propaganda Village" by the south, North Korea's only village inside the DMZ. While there are many new high-rise apartment buildings that appear to be able to house several thousand people, the South Koreans will tell you that the village has no permanent residents. To keep up the lived-in appearance, maintenance personnel and farmers are bused in on a daily basis from Gaeseong, only to be bused back in the evening, and children are brought in to play. In the center of this village is a flagpole that's 160 meters tall, with a proportionately huge North Korean flag draped from the top! Also visible from this vantage point is the building in which the armistice agreement was signed. You may hear music and propaganda broadcasts originating from North Korea. In fact, huge speakers are placed at regular intervals along the entire border. Since 1953, they periodically broadcast false information, defame South Korean leaders, fan anti-government sentiment, instigate anti-American feelings, try to make lonely South Korean soldiers homesick or cross the border, and praise the North Korean sociopolitical system. Propaganda leaflets have also been dropped from the air. Before returning to the advance camp, you'll drive past checkpoint no. 3, called "the loneliest guardpost in Korea." This checkpoint sits at the south end of the Bridge of No Return, across which the crew of the USS *Pueblo* walked from North Korea in 1968. Until after the axe murders in 1976, when another bridge was constructed for exclusive access to the JSA from the North Korean side, this was the only land link between the two nations. At the circle turning to the front of the guardpost was the stump of the tree that was being trimmed when the awful axing incident occurred. Subsequent to that incident, this tree was cropped about three meters high, leaving the stump of its two branches to form a mocking "V." In 1987, it was taken out completely and a plaque put in its place. All trees along this section of the road are now kept appropriately short.

Back at the advance camp, you'll have time for lunch before returning to Seoul. Next to the mess hall in Camp Boniface is the Officers' Club, dubbed "The Monastery: Home of the Merry Mad Monks of the DMZ." No females are stationed here, and until recently, none were stationed north of the Imjin River. At The Monastery, you can buy hats, T-shirts, postcards, and other souvenirs to prove that you've actually been to this highly sensitive border point.

Several companies arrange tours to Panmunjeom for foreigners. One is the Korea Travel Bureau. It runs tours daily except Sunday and holidays, leaving the Lotte Hotel in Seoul at 0730 and returning in mid-afternoon. The tour, including a full lunch, costs ₩65,000. Reservations (at least 48 hours in advance) can be made through the KTB desk at the KNTO Information Center (tel. 02/753-9870), the tour desk at the Lotte Hotel (tel. 02/778-0150), or at several other hotels in Seoul. The U.S.O. (tel. 02/795-3028; 02/724-7003 military line) also offers tours of Panmunjeom. Run on Tuesday and Saturday (0730–1230), these tours leave the U.S.O. office in Seoul, across the wide boulevard and down the street from the west gate of the Yongsan Garrison; a large U.S.O. sign marks the building. The charge for this tour is US$30 or $16 for active-duty military personnel (payable only in U.S. dollars); an optional lunch costs US$6. You'll often need at least a two-week advance registration, but if the list is not full you could get on the tour a couple of days before the departure date. Other companies that offer a similar service are Chung-Ang Express Tour (tel. 02/2266-3350), Global Tour (tel. 02/776-3153), Star Travel (tel. 02/569-8114), Panmunjom Travel Center (tel. 02/399-2180), New Grace Tour (tel. 02/332-8946), and Good Morning Tours (tel. 02/774-3226).

No tours are made on days when special meetings are held at Panmunjeom; in the event of an emergency meeting, the day's tour will be canceled without prior notification. You must carry your passport while on the tour. All active-duty military personnel must wear an "appropriate seasonal class-A military uniform." Civilians must be appropriately dressed and groomed. No shorts, jeans, sneakers, sandals, T-shirts, halter tops, "abbreviated items," clothing of the "sheer variety," unkempt hair, or the like will be permitted. Korean nationals and children under age 10 are not allowed on this tour. Separate tours for Korean nationals are operated by other tour companies. Tours of the JSA have been given for over 30 years, ushering about 150,000 visitors a year to this site. The north also runs tours from their side—but only about one for every eight or so from the south—with an unknown but much smaller number of visitors every year.

EASTERN CORRIDOR

Uijeongbu 의정부

The eastern corridor runs north from the Seong-buk area of Seoul. It is, like the western corridor, a heavily militarized region, but one with good hiking possibilities on nearby Bukhan-san, Dobong-san, Surak-san, and Soyo-san, and farther to the east on Hyeondeung-san, Myeongji-san, Hwaak-san, and Myeongseong-san.

Uijeongbu [Ŭijŏngbu] lies below the north slope of Dobong-san. Elevated to city status in 1963, it was the first of Seoul's satellite cities to be so designated. Uijeongbu expanded largely on account of its proximity to Seoul and the area's many military bases. A bustling city, but not one that will hold your attention for long, it has a multitude of accommodations and restaurants, many clustered around the train and bus stations. Like other areas of the country, Uijeongbu is home to many foreign workers, like field hands from Mongolia, Vietnam, and the Philippines, and traders and businessmen from Turkey. The road to Uijeongbu from Gupabal in the northwest corner of Seoul runs past several recreation areas, country restaurants, and the entrance to Bukhan-san National Park. A short distance north of Uijeongbu is the village of Yangju, home of the *Yangju Byeolsandae*, a traditional masked dance. Performed on some national holidays and during provincial cultural festivals, this satirical dance/play, like all other surviving masked dances, is an expression of cultural heritage from the peasant class. It satirizes apostate Buddhist monks, self-important *yangban,* court officials, broken-hearted lovers, and the foibles of the country bumpkin. Wearing masks of wood and papier-mâché and clothed in bright colors, dancers move to the rhythmic music of drums and cymbals.

East of the city, about half a kilometer north of the tomb of King Sejo, is **Gwangneung National Arboretum** (광릉국립수목원). As a national forestry center, this fine preserve has a whole host of trees in its forest land, as well as landscaped gardens, ponds, walks, and greenhouses. Of the trees with identification markers, most are signed in Korean with Latin names. Within the grounds is a botanical museum which offers a brief look at the life of a Korean forest, an encapsulation of the Korean forest industry, how Koreans have used wood in their cultural life, and Korean wood products. Entrance is ₩700 but reservations are necessary; call 031/540-1114. Use bus no. 21 (₩1,160) from Uijeongbu.

Uijeongbu is a transportation center. From it, two highways run north toward the border, while two others curve around the east and north sides of Seoul. The Gyeongwon rail line starts here and runs north to Shintan-ni (₩1,600) more than a dozen times a day. Uijeongbu is also the eastern terminus of the Seoul Gyooe rail line, which circles around the mountains north of Seoul to join the Gyeongeui rail line at Neunggok—these trains continue on to Seoul Shincheon Station (₩1,500). A more direct route back into the heart of Seoul is by subway. Bus destinations and fares from Uijeongbu include Seoul Sangbong Bus Terminal (₩2,200), Seoul Seobu Bus Terminal (₩1,800), Geumchon (₩3,100), Dongducheon (₩1,300), and Shin Cheolwon (₩3,800).

Dongducheon 동두천

North of Uijeongbu is Dongducheon [Tongduch'ŏn]. Designated a city in 1981, it, like Uijeongbu, also grew with the expansion of the military. While a sizable number of military personnel in Uijeongbu are Koreans, Americans make up a great number. The huge U.S. command center and divisional headquarters, Camp Casey, and other bases are located in and around the city. With the large number of soldiers, and all the activity, Dongducheon has become *the* entertainment spot for the military in the eastern corridor, with all sorts of bars, dance halls, clubs, coffee shops, restaurants, and the like. Look for the twining alleys, bright lights, and neon signs. The "ville" outside Camp Casey's main gate at the north end of town is a raucous community full of loud music, drink, and fast women. As a matter of course, this type of entertainment area spawns the ubiquitous streetwalkers, rowdies, pseudo-hip Koreans, and "slicky-boy" thieves. Its more wholesome side can provide hours of good entertainment, but if you're there for extracurricular activities, never go unprotected. There are many creepy-crawly things going around, including strains of social diseases not cured by a double-barrel shot of penicillin. Very much like "club districts" outside other military installations that were more ubiquitous years ago, this one generally is a funkier and less sophisticated version of the military entertainment area outside the air base in Songtan. The train from Uijeongbu to Dongducheon takes just 25 minutes. Select destinations and fares from Dongducheon are Seoul Sangbong Bus Terminal (₩2,800) and Uijeongbu (₩1,300).

Soyo-san 소요산

Soyo-san (559 meters high) is a natural formation of grace and beauty, with deep valleys, steep slopes, several waterfalls, and an old hermitage. In spring the azaleas bloom; in summer, the waterfalls provide refreshing coolness. Autumn brings a cloak of multicolored leaves that fall and give way to the stark white snowscapes of winter. As the walks here are not particularly difficult, it's one of the favorite weekend outings for city hikers. It's easily reached by bus from Dongducheon (₩600) or Uijeongbu (₩1,400). The Soyo-san train station is across the road from the entrance to the mountain's major valley. A walk of about 30 minutes up this valley (₩1,500 entrance), passing Wonhyo Waterfall on the way, brings you to the hermitage Jajae-am, established around 640 by the famous temple builder and monk Wonhyo during the reign of Silla queen Seondeok. The greatly revered Wonhyo is said to have studied and meditated here. Although he didn't travel widely as most learned monks of his time did, his writings and thoughts traveled far, influencing Buddhist thinkers in China and Japan. From Jajae-am, several trails loop up to the summit, one of which passes another waterfall and pool.

Sanjeong Lake 산장호

The eastern of the two major highways that run north from Uijeongbu goes through Pocheon and Uncheon to Shin Cheolwon and Geumhwa. North of Pocheon, the valley opens a little, its wide farming floor bounded by good-looking mountains. On this route, as well as on the route to Shintan-ni north of Dongducheon to the west, you'll cross the 38th parallel.

East of Uncheon is Sanjeong-ho [Sanjŏng-ho], a reservoir constructed in 1925 and a designated government tourist site; ₩1,500 entrance fee. This lake is being "developed" into a multi-use recreation area. Below the dam in the smaller development are several places to stay and eat. Along the lakeshore above the dam are boat rental shops, picnic areas, over six kilometers of lakeside walking paths, camping sites, swimming pools, amusement rides, and a road to the far side of the lake, which itself has additional amenities. Sanjeong-ho is tightly confined and recessed into a deep valley. Mountains rise steeply from the lake's edge, the highest of which is Myeongseong-san (993 meters). On its slope are hiking trails and the Buddhist temple Jain-sa. The hillsides are covered with thick forests of mature pines and huge swaths of granite that perhaps look their finest in autumn. The lake is rather small and its outlet makes a cascading waterfall, so the feel is perceptibly different than most other reservoir-lakes on the peninsula. Sanjeong-ho is as close as you will come in Korea to a diminutive alpine lake, but one wonders how long it will be so nice with the increase in tourism and expansion of water sports.

During the Korean War, North Korean strongman Kim Il-song had a retreat built along the southern perimeter of the lake. As a result of fighting in the area, this retreat was destroyed. Now occupying the spot is a small restaurant. Next to it is the waterfall over which excess reservoir water drains. To reach the lake, take an intercity bus from Seoul Sangbong Bus Terminal to Uncheon (₩5,000), and local bus no. 117 (₩600) from there to the lake, or bus no. 138 from Uijeongbu (₩1,200).

CHEOLWON AREA

The highway running north past the turnoff to Sanjeong Lake leads to Shin ("New") Cheolwon (신철원), a small community relocated to its present location after destruction of the original town site during the Korean War. Shin Cheolwon [Shin Chŏlwon], also known as Galmal, and the nearby communities of Dongsong [Tongsong] and Gimhwa [Kimhwa], are in Gangwon-Do, but access to this area is easiest from the south via the roads from Gyeonggi-Do, so discussion of this area is included here. Buses from the bus terminal in the center of town run to all nearby sights that are not restricted. Farther up the road is Gimhwa, from where occasional buses run over the mountains to the east to Hwacheon and Chuncheon.

Cheolwon Sights

Two kilometers to the east of Shin Cheolwon is **Sambuyeon Waterfall** (삼부연폭포). This "Three Cauldrons Falls" is a 20-meter-tall waterfall on three levels, where each pool is said to resemble a cooking pot. Legend relates that a dragon once ascended to heaven from one of these pools, giving rise to the nearby village name, Dragon Shining Village. Also close by is the small temple Buyeon-sa, and half a kilometer distant is a small cave.

This region of Korea has seen volcanic activity. Slowly but surely, rivers have gouged through this crust, creating a number of deep ravines and waterfalls. The Hantan River is one of these, and several scenic spots along its length draw visitors, especially in summer. About five kilometers northwest of Shin Cheolwon is **Sundam** (순담), one of these deep river gorges where sand-scoured smooth boulders line the river and high cliffs overhang clear pools and a few white-sand beaches. A fine spot to hang out for the scenery, this section of the river is also a favorite white-water rafting spot, closer to Seoul than those wilder rivers in Gangwon-Do.

A few kilometers up this twisting river is another spot that has drawn leisure seekers across the centuries. The octagonal pavilion **Goseok-jeong** [Kosŏk-jŏng] (고석전), originally built around the year 600, destroyed during the Korean War, but rebuilt in 1971, provides a great view over this, perhaps the most scenic section of the river; ₩1,500 entrance. It is here that a Joseon Dynasty Korean "Robin Hood" is said to have built a stronghold and plundered the wealthy until his eventual capture and beheading in 1562. The remains of his stone fort still lie on the hill across the river. During the mid-1500s, when increasing taxation forced many peasants into utter poverty and landlords with their large estates began to dominate the economy of the lower classes, Im Kkok-cheong, the son of a butcher, organized country folk to raid government warehouses and distribute grain to the needy. Im, and others like him who took measures against the establishment, was quickly neutralized but won the approval and admiration of the peasant class, who made him a folk hero. To the front of Goseok-jeong is a cluster of restaurants and souvenir shops and the Iron Triangle Memorial Hall. Inside this hall are displays and on the plaza to the front are military tanks and airplanes. Registration for tours into the DMZ is taken care of at this building. To the side of Goseok-jeong is the first-class **Chulwon Spa Tourist Hotel** (tel. 033/455-1234). Rooms here run around ₩80,000 but many people come for the baths. Other accommodations in this community, like the **Sun Park** (썬파크), offer comfortable clean rooms for around ₩35,000.

A short way farther on is **Jiktang Waterfall** (직탄폭포). Euphemistically referred to as the "Niagara Falls of Korea," water tumbles over its ragged, 80-meter-wide edge and cascades down steps of volcanic boulders to the broad pool three meters below. Unlike most waterfalls in Korea, this one is much wider than tall, and because of

IRON TRIANGLE

Some of the heaviest fighting during the Korean War took place in an area called the Iron Triangle. This was an area bounded by the old towns of Cheolwon and Gimhwa—both in South Korea's Cheolwon County—and Pyeonggang, just across the border in North Korea. To American Korean War veterans and those who followed the action of the war, the names Pork Chop Hill and Old Baldy bring back memories of bloody, heavy, and sustained fighting. Old Baldy was overrun and lost to Chinese ground forces about four months before the end of the war. Plans were made to retake the hilltop, but finally it was deemed not to be of strategic interest and the plans were dropped. Pork Chop Hill was attacked at the same time by other Chinese ground forces but did not give way. However, three weeks before the armistice agreement was signed, this hill was taken by Chinese forces, and due to great American casualties it also was deemed not worth the potential cost to retake. These peaks, and others that also played pivotal roles in the last month's jostling for boundary position, lie on the eastern periphery of the Iron Triangle. White Horse Hill, which was contested by Korean and Chinese forces, and other nearby battle sites occupy the western corner of this triangle. Much of this area that saw such heavy "static fighting" can now be viewed from the Iron Triangle Observatory on the southern boundary of the DMZ.

its rather unique nature it has been a favorite of photographers. While it's not overly impressive, you can see volcanic rock here.

The small Buddhist temple **Dopian-sa** [Top'ian-sa] (도피안사) was damaged during the Korean War. Originally constructed in 865 but rebuilt in 1957, this temple has little more than a main hall, bell pavilion, and the three spirits hall. The main hall houses an iron Vairocana Buddha statue (N.T. #63) and in the courtyard sits a three-tiered stone pagoda (T. #223). So close to the DMZ buffer zone, this small serene spot was closed to most visitors for years, but is now open once again.

© ROBERT NILSEN

gutted remains of the North Korean Labor Party building

Tour of DMZ

South of the southern border of the DMZ is a buffer zone that for decades was off limits to all but those who lived in the area. Since 1989, however, the government has slowly opened this area to tourists, so one can now see remains from the war, sites that have been repaired because of damage by the war, and the second infiltration tunnel. This has been one of the government's attempts to educate young people about the cruelty, damage, and lasting effects of that conflict. Tours to this restricted area are conducted by convoys that start at Goseok-jeong, so you must have your own vehicle, hitch a ride with someone going in, or be part of an organized bus tour from Seoul. Register at the Iron Triangle Memorial Hall near Goseok-jeong; you must carry your passport. Tours run at 1030, 1300, and 1430 daily except Tuesday and take 2.5–3.5 hours; the cost is W3,500. Within this buffer zone is one lone village. People who live there can come and go, but those who visit must be out by 2000. Partially as a result of this area's restricted condition and

partly due to its location, an unexpected bonus for this rich bottomland and natural flyway is that it has become a migratory-bird habitat and parts have been set aside for preservation.

Although tours vary somewhat, your first stop may be the **Second Infiltration Tunnel.** Discovered in 1975, this tunnel runs 50–100 meters below the ground, is two meters high and two meters wide, and 3.7 kilometers long. Access is allowed about half a kilometer into the tunnel to a point that is very nearly below the actual border. At the tunnel entrance is a small exhibition hall of North Korean gear and military clothing. On the way to the tunnel is the steel railroad bridge for the line that once ran from Seoul to the Diamond Mountains, and just beyond it are the remains of the Cheolwon First Methodist Church. Some distance to the west is **Woljeong Train Station**, where the rusting hulk of an engine and a few other cars bombed during the Korean War still lie to the side of the track. To the front of this station is the **Iron Triangle Observation Post,** from which you can look across the thickly vegetated border into North Korea and what was the Iron Triangle battle zone. Nearby is a wildlife refuge. Farther to the west is the **White Horse Memorial,** a knoll-top monument to the White Horse battle, where Korean and Chinese forces exchanged occupation of the White Horse hill some 24 times over the course of 10 days of fierce fighting. The hill is directly north of the monument, within the DMZ in South Korean territory. Heading out of the buffer zone, you pass the gutted and pockmarked shell of the cement building that held the offices of the North Korean Labor Party. This was very near where the old town of Cheolwon stood, and nearby are ruins of a cement ice storage house, an agricultural inspection building, and a few other old structures.

Route to Chuncheon

From Gimhwa (김화) and the small nearby community of Wasu-ri (와수리), buses run over the mountains to the east and down to Hwacheon and Chuncheon through an area that is full of military installations and road barriers and sees almost no foreign travelers. With higher peaks and deeper valleys, the eastern half is more picturesque than the western half of this route. If you're heading to the east from Wasu-ri, plan your trip early enough in the day so that you have daylight all the way. Buses from Wasu-ri run to Chuncheon (₩5,900), Hwacheon (change buses in Mahyeol-li), Shin Cheolwon (₩1,500), and Seoul Sangbong Bus Terminal (₩6,500).

Gangwon-Do
강원도

Gangwon-Do [Kangwon-Do] occupies the country's northeastern corner and, along with Gyeonggi-Do, creates the border with North Korea. The longest section of the Demilitarized Zone (DMZ) stretches across Gangwon-Do, and the heavily militarized mountain areas adjacent form a large part of South Korea's defensive perimeter against North Korea. Gangwon-Do was split in two after the Korean War, leaving valuable mineral resources and the beautifully rugged Diamond Mountains in North Korea. Named after the **Diamond Sutra**, a concise statement of Buddhist philosophy, this mountain area has historically been considered Korea's most awe-inspiring.

With 16,600 square kilometers, mountainous Gangwon-Do is the country's second-largest province; with only 1.5 million people, it has the lowest population density. Gangwon-Do has seven cities and 11 counties. With the highest average elevation, it also has the least arable land. Wetland farms are generally found in the river valleys and on its restricted plains, where the relatively small population is concentrated. Dryfield farms are on low-gradient hillsides. The people of Gangwon-Do rely more upon potatoes as a staple than those from other provinces, and for this reason, other Koreans refer to them as *gamja bawi*, roughly meaning "potato eaters," a slightly derogatory reference not only to their

Choenbul-dong Valley is the epitome of Seorak-san scenery.

© ROBERT NILSEN

diet but also to their relative poverty and backwardness. Many houses in this region were traditionally covered with wood shingles and held in place by stone due to the lack of rice straw for roofing material, and this architectural form also connotes poverty. Although infrequent today, wood-shingle roofs can still be seen in remote areas, and some have been preserved for their cultural significance. Another expression often used to describe these hardy and independent people is *amha nobul,* or "old Buddha beneath a rock," referring to their resolute, earnest, and serious character. These provincial people are, however, no less traditional than their neighbors, and every year they celebrate dozens of cultural and folk festivals.

The stuff of legends, a dreamland of ink-brush scenes, Gangwon-Do has traditionally been a region of uncharted mountains, high granite peaks, forested valleys, secluded temples, a rugged coastline, and isolated fishing villages. Though set apart, it's a wonderful vacation spot once reached. Its remote mountain valleys are favored by meditating Buddhist monks, and its outstanding scenery is inspiration for writers and painters. Because of its rugged topography, this province has always been hard to reach. However, with the ever-expanding rail and road networks, greater funds, and more emphasis upon development, tourism is now thriving. Every year, mountain parks and other tourist areas attract hundreds of thousands of hikers and campers, rock and ice climbers, skiers, skaters, and swimmers. Though good in every season, Gangwon-Do is the best region for winter sports as it receives more snow than any other province. Of the country's 13 ski resorts, this province boasts six. Gangwon-Do also has eight designated National Treasures (N.T.), 54 Treasures (T.), eight Historical Sites (H.S.), and numerous Nature Preserves, Natural Monuments, and local cultural properties.

For information on the Internet about the province, see www.provin.gangwon.kr.

Mountains and Rivers

From the west, Gangwon-Do rises slowly in a broad swath of foothills to the crest of the Tae-baek Mountains before it plunges steeply to the straight-line east coast. Running north to south, this range parallels the coast. Four major passes over the Taebaek Mountains connect the formerly isolated coastal region to the rest of the peninsula. Diverging from the Taebaek Mountains and running southwest across the bottom of the province are the Sobaek Mountains, with their limestone intrusions and numerous caves. The best-known cave is Gossi-donggul, near Yeongwol, but several others are located in or near Taebaek, Samcheok, and Donghae. North of the Sobaek Mountains lie the Charyeong Mountains. Starting at Odae-san, this lower-elevation range cuts through the peninsula to the southwest; Chiak-san is one of its major peaks. Farthest to the north are the still lower Gwangju Mountains. Originating at the Diamond Mountains in North Korea, they run southwest across the northern strip of Gangwon-Do, only stopping at Seoul's doorstep.

The Gwangju, Taebaek, and Sobaek mountains form the north, east, and south periphery of the upper Han River drainage basin—the vast majority of the province. The upper Imjin River basin, in the northwest corner, drains a much smaller area and is one of the few regions of the peninsula that have experienced relatively recent volcanic activity. Broad plains cover the fault valley in which Shin Cheolwon and Gimhwa lie, an integral component of the province's agricultural sphere. The Hantan River flows south into the Imjin River. Many other short and steep, boulder-strewn coastal rivers have grossly scored the eastern face of the Taebaek Mountains. Wave action and river-borne sediment have formed lagoons near where several of these coastal rivers empty into the sea.

The Coast and Beaches

Rocky headlands and jutting promontories intersperse long stretches of white-sand beach along the rugged coast. In the southern portion of the province, the Taebaek Mountains leave almost no room for a coastal plain. Farther north, on narrow littoral lowlands, the medium-sized cities of Sokcho and Gangneung have grown. Clustered fishing villages cling to the curves of tiny coves that march in a series down this shore. The families of these villages have long been isolated from Korea's main currents; they're hardy, independent people who have survived in a harsh and sometimes unpredictable environment. This side of the peninsula has minimal coastal shelf; both beach and headland drop off steeply into the deep, cold waters of the East Sea. The low tidal range and deep water would make for excellent anchorage, but this area boasts no large natural harbors. Along with landlocked Chungcheongbuk-Do, Gangwon-Do is the only province without a sizable island. Adjacent to North Korea, this entire coastline is defended against a sea invasion and the possible incursion of small groups of spies. Ample evidence includes camouflaged lookouts, gun emplacements, chain-link fences, and barbed wire; some beaches are raked to quickly reveal footprints leading up from the water. These precautions are not as silly or as far-fetched as they may seem because infiltration does occur. One major occurrence in September 1996 involved some 20 armed North Koreans who ran their submarine aground on the coast south of Gangneung and attempted to disappear into the hills. Military and police forces in the region hunted these infiltrators down.

The water is definitely colder here than elsewhere in Korea, but still swimmable in summer —by the hardy. Of about four dozen beaches in the province, perhaps the best-known are Hwajinpo, Sokcho, Naksan, Hajo-dae, Jumunjin, and Gyeongpo-dae. Numerous summer festivals are held on the province's beaches, including the Gyeongpo Beach Summer Festival, Sokcho Beach Rock Music Festival, Mangsang Beach Squid Festival, and the Naksan Sea Sports Festival.

History

A few Neolithic and Bronze Age artifacts have been uncovered near Chuncheon and Hwacheon, as well as along the coastal lowlands near Gangneung and Sokcho. The inland sites indicate a close connection with the more numerous Neolithic sites downriver near Seoul, yet the

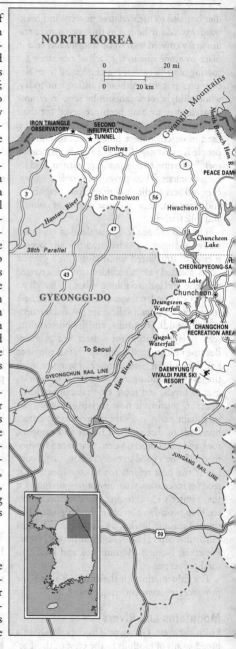

GANGWON-DO

Diamond Mountains

UNIFICATION TRIANGLE
OBSERVATORY

To Russia

Daejin

Hwajinpo Beach
Hwajinpo
Lagoon   Geojin

GANGSEONG
HYANGGYO

GEONBONG-SA   Ganseong

DMZ

GANGWON-DO

46

Songji-ho
Lagoon

Wanggok-ni   CHEONGHAK-JEONG

ULJI
OBSERVATORY
POST

Jinbu-
ryeong   ALPS SKI
RESORT   CHEONGGAN-JEONG

E a s t

FOURTH
INFILTRATION
TUNNEL

Sokcho

31   PUNCHBOWL

Sokcho Beach

S e a

Soyang
River

*Seorak-san
National Park*

SOKCHO
AIRPORT

NAKSAN-SA

Naksan Beach

Paro Lake

31

YANGGU
PREHISTORIC
MUSEUM

Yangyang

FERRY

Yanggu

Inje   44

Han'gye-
ryeong

Hajo-dae Beach

To Ulleung-do

46

*Naerincheon
River*

38th Parallel

YANGYANG
AIRPORT

HAJO-DAE

*Naksan
Provincial
Park*

Soyang
Lake

44

Jumunjin

7

Jumunjin Beach

56

*Gyeongpo
Provincial Park*

SUTA-SA

*Odae-san
National Park*

Gyeongpo-dae Beach

Gangneung

GANGNEUNG
AIRPORT

56

31

Daegwal-
lyeong

Jeongdongjin

Jinbu

DAEGWALLYEONG
MUSEUM

Hongcheon

Hoenggye

65

55

50

YEONGDONG EXPY

DRAGON
VALLEY SKI
RESORT

DONGHAE EXPY

Mangsang Beach

Mukho

FERRY

Charyeong Mountains

PHOENIX PARK
SKI RESORT

Gujeol-li

Taebaek

Donghae

To Ulleung-do

Hoengseong

HYUNDAI
SUNGWOO SKI
RESORT

31

42

35

MUREUNG
VALLEY

JUKSEO-RU

Samcheok

WONJU AIRPORT

Mtns.

Chiak-san

42

Pyeongchang

Jeongseon

HWAAM
CAVE

HWANSEON
CAVE

National

Dongang River

Park

Wonju

JANGNEUNG

Yeongwol

JEONGSEON
SOGEUMGANG

Gohan

19

CHEONGNYEONGPO

GOSSI-DONGGUL

GANGWON
LAND CASINO
RESORT

JEONGAM-SA

Taebaek

CHUNGCHEONGBUK-DO

TAEBAEK RAIL LINE

38

*Taebaek-san
Provincial Park*

S. Branch Han R.

Sobaek Mountains

GYEONGSANGBUK-DO

GANGWON-DO

small communities along the coast show that ancient man lived even in the very isolated regions of the peninsula. About 2,000 years ago, the Goguryeo Kingdom consolidated power in the mid-Yalu River area, near the present North Korea–Manchuria border. Slowly Goguryeo pushed south and incorporated the coastal and mountain peoples of this region. At the same time, burgeoning Silla was pushing northward. Around A.D. 500, Silla took control of the Gangwon-Do region, and it remained an integral, if isolated, part of that kingdom until its territory was lost to Goryeo, five centuries later.

Major currents of Korean history have swirled around this mountain stronghold, but seldom has it been at the center. This region was disturbed by the Mongol invasions of the 1200s, but suffered less than the southern provinces from the Hideyoshi Invasions of the 1590s. The 38th parallel became the de facto border between South and North Korea with the formal establishment of separate states in 1948. After North Korean troops transgressed this border in 1950, control of the province changed hands several times during the next year. The exhaustive battles of Pork Chop Hill and Old Baldy in the "Iron Triangle," and Heartbreak Ridge and Bloody Ridge in the "Punchbowl," took place within Gangwon-Do. These battle sites and others nearby that also saw aggressive fighting were roughly the line of last contact between the opposing armies; they consequently created a de facto border at the end of hostilities. As a provision of the armistice, this line was adjusted slightly northward on the east side of the peninsula for a counterbalancing readjustment on the Gyeonggi-Do end of the DMZ. Today, about one-third of the former Gangwon-Do provincial area remains north of this line, administered by North Korea.

Economy

Until recently, Gangwon-Do has been economically underdeveloped. Its limited industry is focused in Wonju and Chuncheon—cities with easy access to Seoul—and in Samcheok and Donghae, with their harbor facilities. Emphasis has been on mining, logging, and fishing—farming has taken a back seat. Potatoes, cool-weather

PEACE DAM

The Peace Dam was hurriedly built in the mid-1990s across the north branch of the Han River, northeast of Hwacheon and just south of the DMZ. It was built not to produce electricity but ostensibly to block an onrush of water from the north. It is said that such an onrush could destroy dams on the lower reaches of the Han River and flood out Chuncheon as well as Seoul and its suburban areas. Previously, North Korea had built the Geumgangsan Dam across the Han River on the north side of the DMZ for what they claim were peaceful purposes. Whatever the reason, if the dam was breached, either intentionally or by accident, releasing an onrush of water, catastrophic damage would result if the water was not contained, especially during the heavy rains of spring, when rivers are swollen and dams are ordinarily full.

vegetables, soybeans, corn, barley, and other dry-field grains are predominantly raised. Relatively little rice is grown outside the Hantan River basin and the western fringe of the province. Various mushrooms are cultivated, a multitude of vegetables are grown, and great demand exists for the wild, mountain vegetables collected here. Some honey is gathered, but the market for this expensive delicacy is still small.

Gangwon-Do's major fishing centers are Sokcho, Donghae, Samcheok, and Jumunjin, while smaller fishing towns are Daejin and Geojin. Squid may be the biggest catch, but sizable quantities of octopus, cuttlefish, tuna, salmon, red snapper, pollack, mullet, flounder, and shark are also netted. Fresh fish is sold daily at every village market, and several of the larger harbors now have refrigeration facilities for storage and export. A common sight up and down the coast is nets full of drying fish, some dried whole, others split and laid open to the sun. They make engaging geometric designs on their net backdrops.

Gangwon-Do produces about one-half of the country's mineral products, including anthracite coal, tungsten, lead, and limestone. Coal mining is much reduced from previous decades, but you'll still see some evidence of this dirty process in the Yeongwol, Jeongseon, and Taebaek area. Cement production is focused in Donghae and Samcheok. Of finer nature, the noble stone jade is also dug from the ground here and shaped into jewelry that's seen throughout the country.

With its tree-covered mountains, Gangwon-Do produces more timber than all other provinces. Its mountainous nature also provides great hydroelectric power-generation potential. Three large dams operate near Chuncheon, and one just outside of Hwacheon. A fifth, the "Peace Dam," has been built as a containment dam.

Transportation

The commercial airports at Yangyang and Gangneung link coastal Gangwon-Do to Seoul. The new Yangyang airport also allows international travelers easier access to the Seorak-san area, although there are still limited flights from abroad. Used minimally for domestic flights to Busan, the only airport in the interior of the province is located near Hoengseong, just north of Wonju.

The Jungang rail line slices across the southwestern corner of the province on its run between Seoul and Busan. South of Wonju, this line makes a spiral circle through a 3,650-foot tunnel. This is one of two such circle tunnels in the country and the second longest tunnel on this line. Two rail lines make their way over the Taebaek Mountains to the coast. The southernmost, the Yeongdong line, is the older and more scenic. It starts at Yeongju in Gyeongsangbuk-Do and runs via Cheolam to Gangneung. The Taebaek line branches off at Jecheon in Chungcheongbuk-Do and runs through Yeongwol, meeting the Yeongdong line at Baeksan. From Jeungsan, a short branch line heads north to the coal country of Jeongseon and Gujeol-li. The Taebaek line takes you through an extensive section of the province's mining district. The northernmost of the rail lines in the province starts at Seoul's Cheongnyangni Station and runs up the Han River valley to Chuncheon.

Traversing Daegwal-lyeong, the Yeongdong Expressway (no. 50) connects Seoul to Gangneung; the Donghae Expressway (no. 65) continues south from there along the coast to Donghae. When opened, an extension of the Donghae Expressway will continue up to Sokcho, while the route south will eventually continue past Donghae to connect with Pohang in Gyeongsangbuk-Do. The Jungang Expressway (no. 55) allows travel from Chuncheon to Wonju, and from there farther south to Andong and Daegu—speed and access the interior of this province never had before. Future plans call for three additional east-west expressways, one from Jecheon through Yeongwol to Samcheok, the second through Hongcheon to the coast, and the third north of there from the northern suburbs of Seoul passing north of Chuncheon to the coast north of Sokcho.

In 1978, the coastal highway was completed, creating an easy flow of traffic down the coast to Pohang—the 12-hour bus trip from Gangneung has been reduced by half. A full network of highways runs throughout the province, and an extensive highway bus system connects all provincial cities and towns.

Gangwon-Do's one inland ferry route connects Chuncheon to Inje (or to Yanggu when the water is low) via the beautifully twisting Soyang Lake. Catamaran ferries from both Sokcho and Mukho run to Ulleung-do, Korea's only island of size in the East Sea.

Chuncheon and Vicinity

CHUNCHEON 춘천

Lying below forested peaks in the western foothills of the Taebaek Mountains is the lovely city of Chuncheon [Ch'unch'ŏn]. It surrounds the riverside hill Bongeui-san at the confluence of the Han and Soyang rivers. Narrow and deep, these dammed river valleys have created a series of reservoirs, one of Korea's prime inland fishing and boating locales, referred to as Korea's "lake district." Chuncheon, the "Lake City," is also the principal gateway to Korea's northeastern corner, the country's major mountain-recreation area.

Chuncheon has been an important town and major population center since the Silla period, when it served as one of the provincial capitals. From the 17th century onward, Chuncheon was one of five fortress cities charged with the protection of Seoul. During the Korean War, this region sustained bitter fighting, and Chuncheon was almost totally flattened. Rebuilt after the war, this education and recreation center is now bursting with around 250,000 people and, since the end of the war, is once again the provincial capital. Although north of Seoul, Chuncheon is actually farther from the militarized border, and the region surrounding it has a high concentration of Korean military installations. The U.S. Army base Camp Page is located between the city center and the Chuncheon train station. Maintaining a low profile, the soldiers stationed here seem to have only minimal impact on the town. You'd hardly know that they were here except for the drone of their helicopters.

Like other major metropolitan areas in the country, Chuncheon has spread out considerably over the past few decades, pushing out into the surrounding farmland and up the low hillsides with housing estates and commercial and light industrial sectors. The older part of Chuncheon has stayed compact, however, though modernized and much fancier. The city's main street, Jungang-no, runs from the intercity bus terminal past the central market to the main traffic rotary, where it continues on to the provincial government building. Circling the central rotary is the business/entertainment district. In the evening, the back road from the market to the traffic rotary closes to vehicular traffic and becomes a pedestrian street. This area contains shops, restaurants, and drinking establishments. An underground shopping arcade runs for several hundred meters in each direction from the central rotary below Jungang-no, up toward the provincial government building, and below Nambu-ro. A secondary road, Soyang-no, heads northwest from the rotary past the Telecom office to the front gate of Camp Page, where it turns north and runs across the river. Nambu-no runs southeast from the central rotary, makes a jog, and continues out past Gangwon National University. Also within the city are Hallym University, Chuncheon National University of Education, and several technical colleges. On the city's southern rim you'll find various sports facilities, including the Chuncheon Sports Complex, an indoor gymnasium, ice rink, and velodrome. As the largest city between Seoul and the east coast, Chuncheon is the hub of transportation for the northern tier of the province.

Every year in autumn, the **Soyang Cultural Festival** is held in Chuncheon to celebrate the artistic culture of the region. Among others, events include a writing and recitation contest, photography contest and display, traditional music and song, a costume exhibition, an archery contest, and boating on Uiam Lake. In late summer, the **Chuncheon Puppet Festival** enthralls children and adults alike with its puppet shows and doll exhibits, and in early summer a **Mime Festival** captures the interest of everyone. Jade is mined in small quantities in Chuncheon and an exhibition center at a mine not far from the Soyang Dam is open to the public. When completed, the Chuncheon National Museum will display archaeological and historical remains of this inland region.

For more information, see www.chuncheon.go.kr.

Lakeside Sights

Uiam Dam, thrown up across the Han River about four kilometers south of the city, creates **Uiam Lake,** which fronts the west side of the city. At lakeside, beyond the railroad tracks, the Ethiopia Monument commemorates Ethiopian soldiers who were killed or injured in bitter campaigns for this region during some of the fiercest battles of the Korean War. Nearby along the lakeshore are boat docks where small rowboats and paddleboats can be rented. Several pontoon platforms farther along serve as floating beer halls on warm summer evenings, where you can sip a cold one, listen to music, and watch the sun go down beyond the distant hills. Along the lakefront runs a bicycle path and on the far side of this inlet is Citizens Park. Across the road opposite the Ethiopia Monument, a café and teahouse has been built over the Gongji Stream and a Sculpture Park created to its side. Within the sculpture park is a city tourist information booth.

The bank of Uiam Lake is a favorite fishing spot for locals, and the most convenient place

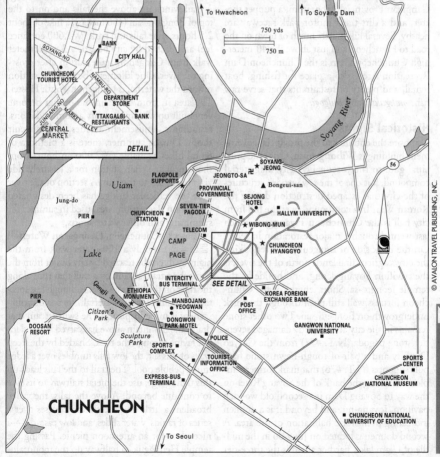

© AVALON TRAVEL PUBLISHING, INC.

GANGWON-DO

to put in your line. Not only can you fish from the bank closest to the city center but numerous rental pontoons are located along the opposite side of the lake. The islands **Jung-do** and **Wi-do,** in the middle of this lake, have been developed for water recreation (windsurfing, water-skiing, jet skiing, motor boating), camping, day hiking, and rental biking. Ferries to Jung-do run every 30 minutes for a 10-minute crossing from the pier near the Doosan Resort and the fare runs ₩2,700 one way. On the north bank of the lake shore is Yungnim Recreation Park, especially attractive to children because of the swimming pools and amusement rides. The Gangwon Provincial Arboretum, a puppet theater, and a dirt-track motor park raceway are nearby. Several kilometers north of town on the road to Hwacheon and just above the 40-meter-high Chuncheon Dam is the Chuncheon Dam Recreation Area, also a place for fishing, boat rental, and plenty of restaurants that serve raw fish, *makguksu,* and *bulgogi.*

Historical Sights

Opposite the entrance to the provincial government building is **Wibong-mun.** Once the principal gate to the Joseon Dynasty magisterial compound, it is one of the few wooden structures of the city that escaped destruction during the Korean War. In a compound over the hill from city hall is the **Chuncheon Hyanggyo,** which last went through a major restoration in 1960. On the back side of Bongeui-san, overlooking the city's agricultural lands north of the river, is the pavilion Soyang-jeong, and beside it, the temple Jeongto-sa. Short lengths of the Chuncheon fortress wall still push through the thick undergrowth on Bongeui-san. Two other stone remains in the city are a slightly damaged seven-tier stone pagoda (N.T. #77) from the Goryeo Dynasty and a pair of rough-hewn stone flag-pole supports (N.T. #76) that mark former temple sites. Along the bank of the Soyang River on the way to Soyang Dam is a second old wooden pavilion, Joyang-nu, and beyond it is a dolmen indicating prehistoric habitation of the area. A second dolmen is located on Jung-do in the middle of Uiam lake. Farther afield is the three-tier

pagoda at Seosang-ni. Located on the west side of the river above Uiam Lake, in the middle of a vegetable field, this 4.5-meter-tall stone structure marks the site of an unknown temple.

Waterfalls and Hiking Trails

A few short kilometers downriver from Chuncheon are the Gugok and Deungseon waterfalls. About 45 meters high, **Gugok Waterfall** (구곡폭포) tumbles down a craggy rock face in a quiet valley park. This lacy, bridal-veil curtain of water, whipped by the wind into an opaque screen in summer, freezes in winter, providing a more than adequate perpendicular face for ice climbing. A trail winds up above the falls and on to the top of Bonghwa-san (486 meters), a hike of about 2.5 hours. The falls and park (₩1,600 entrance fee) are reached by city bus, or a 3.5-kilometer walk from Gangchon train station after crossing the river. One kilometer beyond the station toward the waterfall is Gangchon Youth Hostel. The area in from the train station has become very built up with multi-story accommodations, restaurants, amusement arcades, and souvenir shops. During summer, there is a plethora of rental bikes available (₩2,000 an hour) from shops near the train station for a leisurely ride via a bike path to the falls. A section of the river near the vehicular bridge has been designated Gangchon Recreation Area, used in summer for swimming and other water sports.

Closer to Chuncheon, **Deungseon Waterfall** (등선폭포) is only a 100-meter walk from the highway. It can be reached by city bus or from the Gangchon train station by a trail that runs along the river on the highway side. Although less spectacular than Gugok Waterfall, its surrounding scenery is more inspiring. The swift stream that drains the mountain above has carved a very slender ravine through the rock. Shaded by the steep walls of this slit, the low falls tumbles over a ledge into a pebble pool. The trail to the falls leads up this tight gorge; use the metal stairway to its side to continue beyond. Above the falls, the valley broadens a little and the stream courses over a series of rapids, water slides, and low cascades—a nice place for an afternoon picnic. Passing the temple Heungguk-sa halfway up the mountainside, the trail continues to the top of Samak-san (654 meters), from where you have a view over the lake and city. This trail continues down the east side past the temple Sangwon-sa to Uiam Lake, exiting the hill a few hundred meters above Uiam Dam, from where you can catch a bus back into town. Both temples are said to have been founded during the Silla Dynasty but were rebuilt after destruction during the Korean War. Requiring about three hours, this six-kilometer-long trail makes an invigorating trip. Entrance fee is ₩1,600 from either end.

Accommodations

Of the three hotels in Chuncheon, the city's best is the first-class **Doosan Resort** (tel. 033/240-8000), overlooking the lake out beyond Gongji Stream. Western and Korean rooms, some with full kitchens, are ₩80,000 and up for up to four people. Amenities include several restaurants, a lounge, sauna, and nightclub, and the resort is affiliated with the Chuncheon Country Club golf course. On the hill above the provincial government office is the first-class **Chuncheon Sejong Hotel** (tel. 033/252-1191). It offers Korean- and Western-style rooms and restaurants, a coffee shop, cocktail lounge, and an outdoor swimming pool. Room rates start at ₩75,000. Smaller but with the same basic services and similar rates, the first-class **Chuncheon Tourist Hotel** (tel. 033/255-3300) is a few steps from the midtown rotary intersection.

There is a concentration of *yeogwan* near the intercity bus terminal. On the south side are Manbojang Yeogwan (만보장여관) and Dongwon Park Motel (동원파크모텔); to the front is the less expensive Worldjang Yeoinsuk (월드장여인숙). For a quieter place, and one nearer the center of town, try accommodations in the area just south of city hall.

Although often booked by groups, the **Gangchon Youth Hostel** (tel. 033/262-1201) has a bed in a bunk room at ₩10,000 for Y.H. members or ₩11,000 for non-members.

Food

Many mid-priced restaurants specializing in grilled chicken and *makguksu*, plus those that serve the whole range of other Korean foods, can be found in the area surrounding the central traffic rotary. If you want the city's tangy chicken specialty, *ttakgalbi*, head for the lively restaurants one alley in from the pedestrian walk. Marinated in seasoned juices, this meat is chopped into small pieces—most restaurants now serve it deboned—and cooked on a heavy flat griddle with a mixture of coarse-cut vegetables, potatoes, and pounded rice cakes. If you do find bones in the meat, just put them on the griddle to the side. A serving for two runs about ₩8,000 and should fill most hungry patrons; order rice and drinks on the side. Many restaurants that specialize in *makguksu* are found on the far side of the rotary, one block west of Jungang-no. Although each kitchen makes it in a slightly different manner, generally speaking it usually appears as a serving of darkish buckwheat vermicelli noodles topped with slivered cucumbers, a hard-boiled egg, hot red sauce, and perhaps a few other ingredients. Served cool, it is to be mixed together before being eaten.

As this is a university town, Chuncheon has many coffee shops and drinking establishments. Have your pick from the many along the pedestrian street or south of city hall.

For a good sampling of local Korean staples, visit the open-air market alley that runs in an arch to the east from a corner of the multi-story covered market. You'll find shops specializing in grains, spices, vegetables, prepared side dishes, fish, meats, and much more. Although not large, it's full of activity and color.

Information and Services

At the entrance to the Chuncheon Sports Complex is a modern, red-brick structure that houses a tourist information office and a local-products exhibition hall. Information booths are also located at the train station and at the sculpture park.

The Telecom office is located to the front of Camp Page, the post office on Nambu-no, and the police headquarters farther down that road near the sports complex. Exchange money at the Korea Foreign Exchange Bank or any of those around the main traffic rotary.

GANGWON-DO

Transportation

Chuncheon has no air service. The only train line out of town runs to Seoul. About once an hour 0520–2150, *Mugunghwa-ho* and *Tongil-ho* trains (₩2,500 and ₩1,600, respectively) ride down the Han River valley for Seoul's Cheongnyangni Station.

Express buses leave Chuncheon for Daegu (₩15,200) and Gwangju (₩16,000) from the express-bus terminal out past the sports complex. When the Jungang Expressway is finished and open for traffic, expect express bus service to Wonju, Andong, and other cities in the south and central parts of the peninsula as well.

The intercity bus terminal is close to the train tracks at the west end of Jungang-no. From here, buses run to all major cities in Gangwon-Do and to Seoul, Daejeon, Daegu, and Busan. Of those to the coast, most go directly to Sokcho via the Han'gye-ryeong Pass (the southern route), while a few go via the Jinbu-ryeong Pass (the northern route) and Ganseong. Those to Gangneung first go south to Hoengseong, and from there over the Daegwal-lyeong Pass to the sea. Buses also run north to Hwacheon and Yanggu, as well as over back mountain roads, past numerous army bases and tank traps, to Wasu-ri. The road to Wasu-ri is seldom traveled, yet lets you glimpse, as close as you're able, the fortified mountain region that lies along the DMZ. The route to Yanggu takes you over a twisting road through the mountainous hinterland. Selected intercity bus destinations and fares are: Seoul Sangbong Terminal (₩5,700), Tong Seoul Terminal (₩6,000), Wonju (₩5,300), Wasu-ri (₩5,900), Hwacheon (₩2,900), Yanggu (₩5,200), Inje (₩6,200), Sokcho (₩11,500), and Gangneung (₩12,000).

City buses ply the streets and run out to the surrounding communities. Bus no. 61 connects the train station and intercity-bus terminal to the central traffic rotary; no. 64-1 runs past the express-bus terminal; nos. 11, 12, and 13 go to the Soyang Dam through downtown; nos. 31, 32, 35, and 77 make runs to the Yungnim Recreation Area and Chuncheon Dam through downtown; nos. 50, 54, and 55 run from the main drag of town to the Gugok and Deungseon waterfalls and Gangchon Recreation Area; no. 82 runs on the west side of Uiam Lake; and nos. 65 and 74 to the Jung-do pier and Doosan Resort.

SOYANG LAKE 소양호

Thirteen kilometers from downtown Chuncheon is Soyang Dam (소양댐). Six years in the making, this pyramidal earthen dam was completed in 1973 to generate electric power, provide a regular source of irrigation water, and help control flood damage downstream toward Seoul. An impressive structure, it seems to leap right out of the Soyang River and climb up the valley walls. Rising to a height of 123 meters, it spans 612 meters and holds back the 64-kilometer-long Soyang Lake, the second-largest in the country.

Like a liquid dragon prowling through its green lair, the lake winds through a serpentine valley below lofty, pine-covered hills to Inje. Soyang Lake is stocked with carp raised at an experimental fish farm not far from the dam. Fried or in soup, the carp and lake salmon are served at the restaurant near the ferry pier and at many restaurants in Chuncheon. Fishing sites have been created along the bank of the lake, all reachable only by boat.

The 38th parallel, the former border between South and North Korea, cuts across the lake. The inundation of this valley necessitated removal of all rural communities, farms, and graves to new sites above the present waterline, all at government expense. A few farms at higher elevations were left where they were. Stuck along the bank or tucked away in inlets, they were isolated, depending solely on boat service for transportation, until new roads were built to them.

Every hour or so 0830–1800, high-speed ferries run between the Soyang Dam pier and the Yanggu and Inje piers. The fare is ₩10,000 to Inje (60 minutes) and ₩5,000 to Yanggu (30 minutes). When the water level is low, the ferry will only run as far as the Yanggu pier. City buses meet each ferry to take passengers into town—the bus fee is extra—where you can get an intercity bus on to your destination. Using the ferry is a scenic, although a bit more expensive, alternative to get farther into the mountains from Chun-

© ROBERT NILSEN

Soyang Lake pier

cheon. Another ferry (₩3,000 round-trip or ₩1,500 one way) runs every 30 minutes 0900–1800 from the Soyang Dam pier to the Cheongpyeong-sa pier. Tickets for all ferries are sold at booths on the quay.

An excursion ferry makes a 16-kilometer tour of the lower end of the lake for ₩6,000 when there are enough passengers. You can even hire a motorboat here to drive you around for a personalized tour—₩20,000–40,000 for 4–16 kilometers.

Cheongpyeong-sa 청평사

A 15-minute ferry ride from the Soyang Dam, followed by a 30-minute walk from the Cheongpyeong-sa pier, brings you to Cheongpyeong-sa [Ch'ŏngp'yŏng-sa]. Walk up through the village, cross the bridge, and continue up the stream to the temple; ₩2,000 entrance fee. This village caters to visitors; there is nothing here but restaurants, several *yeogwan* and *minbak*, and a group campground. There is no bus connection to this village, although a road does go over the hill to Oeum along the Chuncheon-Yanggu highway. Along the once-idyllic path to the tem-

ple, now dotted with food stalls and shops at the lower end, you pass **Guseong ("Nine Sounds") Waterfall**. It's said that when there's a great volume of water in the river, nine distinct sounds emanate from the falls. In these hills are wild boar and roe deer, occasionally seen with their young in the early morning and late evening by the riverbank or lakeshore.

Founded in 973 as a private study academy, Cheongpyeong-sa became a temple and was given its name in mid-1500s. The temple has been reconstructed several times, the last due to its demolition in the Korean War. Of the wooden structures, only the front gate, Hoejeon-mun (T. #164), escaped destruction during the war; a few of the original stone monuments and the fitted-stone terrace walls remain from the original construction. Plinth stones that supported structural pillars mark the site and size of each former temple building; together they indicate the extent of this grand complex when it was a major temple at the beginning of the Joseon Dynasty. One by one, new structures are being rebuilt, complementing the main hall, Geungnakbo-jeon, the Mountain Spirit shrine, and the bell pavilion.

GANGWON-DO

One has an unusual wooden balustrade that fronts the main hall. Several stone lanterns stand in the hills above the temple compound. Just below the main compound is a reconstructed pond, ostensibly from the time before this was a temple. This spring-fed pond is small in size but delicate in proportion and lovely in setting. Small carp swim its waters among reeds and boulders. Once a common feature at temples around the country, these ponds are rare today although some are being reconstructed. *Sari budo* line the trail approaching the temple .

From the temple, a trail leads up to Obong-san (779 meters), and continues down the opposite side to Baehu-ryeong Pass, on the road that connects Chuncheon to Yanggu. A walk from the temple over the mountain takes two to three hours. At the roadside trailhead, flag down a bus to either town.

HONGCHEON 홍천

South of Chuncheon is the mid-mountain town of Hongcheon [Hongch'ŏn]. Due to poor transportation connections, for decades this community and others in this hinterland have been outside the main swirl of events in Gangwon-Do and the country. However, it attracted those, especially Buddhist monks, who desired the remote tranquillity. Today several temples remain from centuries ago including Suta-sa. Not all in the area is of old vintage, however, as outdoor enthusiasts throng to several ski resorts in this intermountain region.

Suta-sa [Sut'a-sa] (수타사) lies within the twisting, boulder-strewn Suta Valley, through which runs the Hongcheon River. Built in 708 during the Silla Dynasty, rebuilt and relocated on the far side of the stream from its original spot in 1636, Suta-sa has gone through several metamorphoses. The largest building at the temple houses 1,000 Buddha statues and an altar statue that has several dozen heads and hands. Daejeokgwang-jeon, the main hall, is smaller. Two books written in the year 1485 have been discovered here, sealed inside one of the temple statues. In 2000, the front gate guardian devas were refurbished. Four times a day, a city bus

(₩920) runs the 10 kilometers from town to the end of the line. Beyond the few shops and restaurants, there's a five-minute walk past the collection of *sari budo* to the temple compound; ₩2,000 entrance. While the scenery here is not spectacular, it is pleasant, and there is a small waterfall and pool just down the hill from the temple.

Ski Resorts

Three of Gangwon-Do's ski resorts lie on the western slope of the Taebaek Mountains and all are within 2.5 hours of Seoul.

Opened in 1993, the **Daemyung Vivaldi Park Ski Resort** is located at the foot of Maebong-san, west of Hongcheon. Currently, there are 13 slopes—the longest at just over 1,600 meters—and 10 lifts, all with quad chairs and one gondola. Weekend lift tickets run ₩55,000 for adults; weekday, half-day, and night skiing are correspondingly less. Ski rental and lessons are available. Snow machines provide decent runs until late February or March. Rooms run ₩80,000 and up at the hotel and condominiums. On the less expensive side is the Daemyung Hongcheon Youth Hostel (tel. 033/434-8311) where rooms run ₩6,300 or ₩44,000 for a family room. Resort amenities include restaurants, a disco, a golf course, tennis courts, a bowling alley, indoor/outdoor swimming pool, and sauna. Year-round outdoor facilities are being developed. Bus by shuttle from Seoul via Daemyung Tour (tel. 02/422-6677), or take an intercity bus to Hongcheon and one of the resort shuttles from town to the slopes. For additional information and hotel reservations, contact the resort office (tel. 033/434-8311 or 02/222-7000 in Seoul). For information on the Internet, see www.daemyungcondo.com.

Southeast of Daemyung Ski Resort are two additional ski resorts. Outside Hoengseong is the **Hyundai Sungwoo Ski Resort** (tel. 033/340-3000 or 02/523-7111 in Seoul), with 21 slopes, eight lifts, and one gondola. Opened in 1995, this full-service resort has year-round activities and a small hotel and condo operation. Ski rental and lessons are available and lift tickets run ₩42,000 for adults on weekends, a bit more with gondola use. For a shuttle bus from Seoul to the resort, contact Lotte Travel (tel. 02/733-0201), Seoul Travel (tel. 02/564-1311), or Ojin Travel (tel. 02/739-1211). Additional information can be found on the website www .hdsungwooresort.co.kr.

East of there, in Pyeongchang, is the **Phoenix Park Ski Resort** (tel. 033/333-6000 or 02/508-3400 in Seoul). Also opened in 1995, this resort has 12 slopes, six lifts, and a gondola. Lift tickets for adults on weekends are ₩46,000 and ski rental is ₩27,000. Hotel and condo accommodations run ₩190,000 and up. Other facilities include golf course, swimming pool, bowling alley, nightclub, and mountain biking trails. Bus from either Seoul or Gangneung or use the resort shuttle from Seoul. Contact Dongyang Express (tel. 02/753-0011) or Smile Tour (tel. 022/730-5111). See the website www.phoenixpark.co.kr for more information.

CLOSER TO THE DMZ

Hwacheon 화천

About 40 kilometers north of Chuncheon lies the small provincial town of Hwacheon [Hwach'ŏn]. East of Hwacheon is Paro Lake, another favorite of anglers. This lake was created in 1942 after the Japanese had finished construction of the Hwacheon Dam, the first large-scale, modern, multi-use dam in the country.

Yanggu 양구

Yanggu is a quiet agricultural community which, because of its location close to the DMZ, has a strong military flavor. Situated on the east end of Lake Paro, it has gained a reputation for fine fishing. More recently, it has become a transfer point for travelers going between Chuncheon and the coast by way of Soyang Lake or for those visiting the Korean War "Punchbowl" battle zone.

The Yanggu ferry pier is several kilometers south of town. Buses from town meet each ferry when there is enough water in the lake for the ferry to make it to Yanggu. Other buses connect Yanggu to Chuncheon (₩5,200), Sokcho (8300), and Haean (₩2,800). Near the center of town are plenty of restaurants and the small Sejong

Hotel (세종호텔) and Seouljang Yeogwan (서울장여관).

At the north edge of town is the **Yanggu Prehistoric Museum** (양구선사박물관). Open 0900–1800 (1700 in winter) except Tuesdays and some holidays, there is a ₩770 entrance fee. This museum offers a look at the prehistoric remains of the inland region of Korea, mainly stone and pottery artifacts with some dioramas. In the yard behind are three examples of pit dwellings and several dolmen that have been moved from other locations nearby.

Punchbowl

North of Yanggu, in Haean, is the notorious "Punchbowl," the greatly eroded crater of an ancient volcano, where long and tedious struggles for territory were fought in August and September of 1951 during the Korean War. On the western edge of this natural basin are the peaks and well-known battle sites Heartbreak Ridge and Bloody Ridge. This was the heart of the Eastern Zone of battle, and other major confrontations here were Mt. Dosol, 949 High Ground Battle Zone, and Christmas Battle Zone. On the north edge of this crater, located within the DMZ, is the fourth North Korean infiltration tunnel. Although a quiet and seemingly prosperous farming community today, there is still a military presence as it's located so close to the border. In town the **War Memorial** (전쟁기념관) is open daily except Tuesdays 1000–1800 (1700 in winter). It is a small but heartfelt look at the horrors of war. Some military equipment is displayed. Next door at the office in the North Korea Exhibition Center, you can apply to visit both the infiltration tunnel and Ulji Observation Post (see following). As there is no bus traffic that runs to these points, both several kilometers up the hill on separate roads, you must either use a private vehicle or take an organized bus tour. A number of tour operators in Seoul include these two points in their tours. Entrance to both the tunnel and observation post, with a fee for a vehicle, is ₩4,000. Both are open daily until 1600 except on Tuesdays.

Discovered in 1990 but opened to the public

GANGWON-DO

in 1996, the **Fourth Infiltration Tunnel** (제 4 땅굴) runs about 1,000 meters into South Korean territory from the north side. Supposedly having taken over 10 years to drill—before discovery —it is nearly two meters high and contains a rail line, presumably for the easy movement of soldiers and equipment. A short section of South Korean–gauge track has replaced the original North Korean track to facilitate travel a short way into the tunnel by a sit-down rail car. On the ridge above is **Ulji Observation Post** (을지전 망대). At over 1,000 meters in elevation, this observation post has a bird's-eye view into North Korean territory and it's possible to see the Diamond Mountains off in the distance. Both the southern and northern boundaries of the DMZ are visible from this high point and it's easy to imagine the actual borderline. On both sides are propaganda signs and radio speakers that proclaim a better way.

Inje 인제

A farming community, Inje is little more than a transfer point for travelers between Chuncheon and the east coast, and the surrounding county has the lowest population density of any county or city in the country. Set along the Soyang River, the town is surrounded by thickly forested mountains, the vastly predominant feature in this region. Fueled by lots of water, **river rafting** is done through a stretch of the Naerincheon River southeast of town. One of the few places in the country where the water is right for this sport, the Naerincheon has good rapids with some tough sections, and is also used for kayaking. Even in this rural, mountainous region, Inje is changing from a dowdy backwater to one with modern shops, highway rest stops, and high-rise apartment buildings. From here, buses run west to Chuncheon (₩6,200), east to Daejin (₩5,600) and Sokcho (₩5,600), as well as to the Seoraksan National Park secondary entrances of Namgyo-ri (₩1,600) for Shibi Seonnyeotang, Yongdae-ri (₩2,500) for Baekdam-sa, Jangsudae (₩1,600), Han'gye-ryeong (₩2,300), and Osaek (₩2,900).

Mountain Passes

If busing to the coast from Chuncheon, Yanggu, or Inje, you have two possibilities: the southern route, over Han'gye-ryeong to Yangyang, or the northern route, via Jinbu-ryeong to Ganseong. The southern route features more spectacular scenery; from the pass itself, there's a splendid view of the boldly sculpted valley, at the far end of which lies the town of Yangyang, near the sea. This route takes you past Daeseung Waterfall, Osaek Mineral Spring, and several trailheads that lead into the remote back section of Seorak-san National Park. For the best visual snapshots along this route, sit on the right side when going toward the coast.

The northern route is wilder and more militarized, first paved in 1983. Along it are Namgyori and Yongdae-ri, two back entrances to Seoraksan National Park, as well as Jinbu-ri, the village below the Alps Ski Resort. While the mountain vistas are attractive from Jinbu-ryeong, there is no view of the sea. Buses running over Jinburyeong go either north, to Daejin, or south, to Sokcho. This northern route is faster and more direct for exploring the northernmost South Korean communities and the Unification Observatory north of Daejin before heading south to Sokcho or Seorak-san National Park.

For those with private vehicles, a third road has been opened over Mishi-ryeong Pass. This road skirts the northern boundary of the park, diving straight down to Sokcho, and like the road to Yangyang, it offers wide-open vistas of a deep and penetrating valley and distant views of the sea. There is a rest stop and restaurant on the pass, and while the view is pleasing, it can be windy.

Alps Ski Resort 알프스리조트

About 200 kilometers from Seoul, at the base of Masan-bong (1,052 meters) and along the spine of the Taebaek Mountains north of Seorak-san National Park, is the Alps Ski Resort (tel. 033/681-5030; 02/756-5481 in Seoul), the northernmost of Korea's ski areas. If you arrive by bus, get off at Jinbu-ri and either walk the two kilometers to the lodge, take a taxi, or catch the occasional bus that runs up from Ganseong. Shuttle

Ski resorts like Alps Ski Resort are growing in popularity and host thousands of skiers daily.

buses from Seoul also run daily during the ski season; ₩23,000 round-trip. Contact Ojin Tour (tel. 02/739-2111) or Lotte Travel (tel. 02/ 733-0201). For adults, ski rental runs ₩28,000 for a full day and lift tickets are ₩37,000, with half-day, afternoon, and night tickets available for less. This resort sports eight slopes of various difficulty—the longest is 2,200 meters—and has five lifts. Snow-making machines ensure adequate cover throughout the season, although the Alps gets perhaps the best and deepest natural snowpack of any resort in the country. Lights flood the hill for night skiing, and ski lessons are available.

There is a bit of European design in the ar-

chitecture of the hotels and condominiums at this resort. The community center has restaurants, a snack bar, coffee shop, game room, nightclub, and bowling. During summer, the resort is used by groups for golf, swimming, tennis, archery, camping, and other outdoor activities. Korea's only **Ski Museum** is located at the Alps Ski Resort. Displaying and preserving ski equipment and other snow gear from the past, the museum interprets the ski traditions and culture of Korea from its early use some 2,000 years ago to its modern incarnation—the first modern ski slope opened in 1974. Open daily 0900– 1800; admission is ₩1,000.

GANGWON-DO

Seorak-san National Park 설악산국립공원

Young, brash, and rugged, Seorak-san [Sŏrak-san] is the most strikingly dramatic of South Korea's mountain areas. This majestic region is a rampart of rocky peaks, many of which rise over 1,500 meters. Time and the elements have carved the sturdy gray granite into serrated ridgelines, battlements of crags, a bevy of spires, and lofty escarpments that rise above serpentine valleys. At the bottoms of these valleys lie emerald pools and sparkling streams of crystal-clear water. Fluid ribbons of silver tumble gingerly over rapids and cascades, or rush headlong over waterfalls to crash on the rocks below. Valley walls are shrouded with a thick mantle of pines and hardwood trees that soften the rough, raw nature of the mountain's base rock. Valleys to the east of the mountain's main ridgeline are deep, steep, and spectacular; those to the west are longer, broader, and softer. This awe-inspiring panorama of rock and tree is occasionally obscured by mist that dampens the valleys or clouds that blanket its peaks. On clear days, the view is truly engrossing—lofty heights rise precipitously from the wild, wave-crashed coast, leaving only the bare minimum of a narrow coastal plain. These rugged mountains tempt you to discover their secrets, their beauty, yet make you work diligently for the pleasure.

Seorak-san ("Snow Peak Mountain") refers not only to this well-known mountain region, but also to the northernmost of the country's national parks. Established in 1970 and encompassing 373 square kilometers, Seorak-san National Park is the second-largest land-based national park, and contains Daecheong-bong (1,708 meters), the country's third-highest peak. It is a national nature preserve (#171), and UNESCO designated this mountain area a world biosphere reserve in 1981; it is strictly protected for its unique botanical features and animal life. These thickly forested hillsides sustain over 800 varieties of plants, about 120 kinds of animals, and over 1,200 varieties of insects; nine of the animals and one of the plants are protected under

national law. The animals are mostly small mammals and birds, although there are some deer. A few bears inhabited the park until the 1980s. Despite unconfirmed reports of tigers deep in the park's trail-less valleys, their existence seems highly unlikely, as most experts agree they were driven from this area six or seven decades ago.

Every year in October, the **Seorak Festival** is held here to celebrate the wonder that nature has provided this region, and give local residents an opportunity to let loose in festive merrymaking. This festival draws great crowds to the mountain. One festival event is a mountain marathon. The long and strenuous courses take participants along hiking trails and over mountain passes. Various courses are used, and those who don't care to run can hike the distance.

Of the approximately five million yearly visitors to the park, most come during the middle to late summer and the few autumn weeks of peak foliage color. At these times, the parking lots are a sea of buses and the trails as crowded as busy city sidewalks! By far the majority of visitors stay in the Outer Seorak area, near the temple Shinheung-sa, and at the top end of the cable car. The more adventurous, however, hike into the Inner Seorak area to meet this unspoiled land face to face. A full network of trails covers these hills, providing for everyone from casual sightseer to serious hiker or rock climber. These trails open in late spring, after most of the snow melts, and close in late autumn, when the snow returns. Some winter hiking is allowed, though it's usually restricted to groups familiar with the trails. The easiest and most often used entrance to Seorak-san is from the east, at Seorak-dong. Less often used, but quicker for getting into the mountain hinterland, are the western entrances at Yongdae-ri, Namgyo-ri, and Jangsu-dae. Periodically, some trails close to hiking for extended periods due to overuse and the need for restoration. Be sure to check with one of the park offices for recent trail closures before you hike.

Major park trails are well-marked, but if you

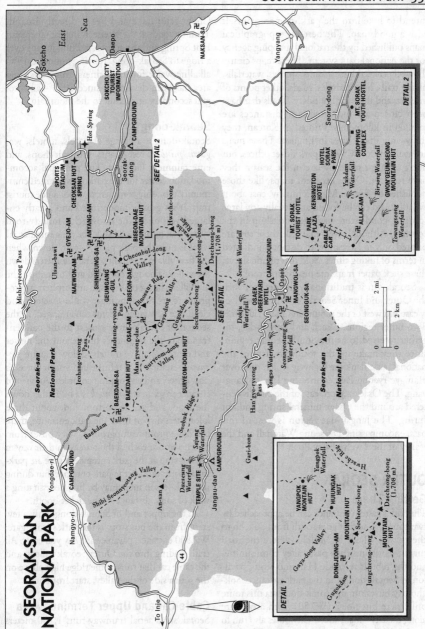

© AVALON TRAVEL PUBLISHING, INC.

SEORAK-SAN NATIONAL PARK

To Inje

GANGWON-DO

DETAIL 1

YANGPOK MOUNTAIN HUT
Yangpok Waterfall
HUJUNGAK MOUNTAIN HUT
Hwache Ridge
Gaya-dong Valley
BONGJEONG-AM
Socheong-bong
MOUNTAIN HUT
Gugokdam
Jungcheong-bong
Daecheong-bong (1,708 m)

DETAIL 2

Seorak-dong
MT. SORAK YOUTH HOSTEL
MT. SORAK TOURIST HOTEL
PARK PLAZA
Yukdam Waterfall
KENSINGTON HOTEL
HOTEL SORAK PARK
SHOPPING COMPLEX
Biryong Waterfall
CABLE CAR
ALLAK-AM
GWON'GEUM-SEONG MOUNTAIN HUT
Towangseong Waterfall

intend to hike into the park, prepare yourself with a good map. The best are topographical maps published by the national mapping agency for the national park system. These maps clearly show all peaks, ridges, streams, springs, waterfalls, hiking trails, huts, temples, roads, other points of interest, and the park boundary. Trails that have been closed are indicated, and distances are marked in kilometers. Printed in Korean, they show only major sites in English. These maps are available for ₩500 at park ticket offices, but don't be surprised if by late in the season they have run out. Other excellent maps, like those published by Sambu Map Company, cost about ₩1,000 and can be found at virtually any large sporting-goods store or large bookshop in the country. Although well-marked, these too are printed only in Korean, with distances indicated in terms of hiking times. Sold in a plastic sleeve, these slick paper maps are nearly rip-proof.

Seorak-san is traditionally divided between the Outer and Inner Seorak regions, respectively east and west of the mountain's main ridgeline. Two other regions, Osaek and Jangsu-dae, together referred to as the South Seorak region, since they make up the southern strip of the national park, flank the highway which runs over Han'gye-ryeong Pass connecting Inje to Yang-yang. The Osaek region, east of the pass, is centered around the Osaek mineral spring and hot spring. The Jangsu-dae region is west of this pass, encompassing Daeseung Waterfall and the Valley of the Twelve Fairy Pools.

OUTER SEORAK

Getting There

The park's eastern entrance can be approached by two routes. The first goes south from Sokcho to the coastal village of Mulchi, where the road turns inland and runs past valley communities and the rebuilt riverside Hangmu-jeong pavilion to Seorak-dong and the park entrance. Sokcho city buses run to Seorak-dong via this route only; take bus no. 7 (₩750) from anywhere along the city's main street. City buses also run to the Mulchi turnoff from Yangyang. The back route leaves Sokcho at the western end of

Cheongcho Lake and heads directly inland. Turning south at the intersection near Cheoksan Hot Spring and the sports stadium, it runs over a ridge to Seorak-dong. Relying upon the 45°C alkaline water for its business, this hot spring area has been developed since 1973—an integral secondary attraction to the mountain.

Seorak-dong

Seorak-dong is a village of hotels, motels, *yeo-gwan, minbak,* restaurants, souvenir shops, and entertainment facilities. The principal accommodation center for the park, this planned community is brashly commercial, a bona fide tourist trap. It's a grossly modernized and greatly enlarged version of the ramshackle muddy-road village that once stood inside the park entrance (at what is now the park plaza)—torn down when the new village was built several kilometers down the valley. Though crowded and unkempt, the old village had a truly rustic atmosphere appropriate to its surroundings; while spacious and clean, the new village seems too arranged. In the section of Seorak-dong closest to the park entrance are the high-class hotels and the newer and more expensive motels. Below that are *yeo-gwan,* restaurants, a refurbished youth hostel, a post office, and a shopping complex. An area of cheaper *yeogwan* and *minbak* is a bit farther down the road, and at the bottom end, about three kilometers distant from the park entrance, there is a large group campground. City buses from Sokcho stop at each of these areas on their way to the bus stop at the park entrance. There are parking lots just outside the park entrance, but during the peak season these may be full, necessitating a walk of some distance to the ticket booth.

At the upper end of Seorak-dong, only a few steps from the bus stop, is the park's front gate; ₩2,800 entrance, payable each day you enter. All trails leading into the Outer Seorak valleys, and the cable car that runs to the ridge high above on the south side of the valley, start from here.

Cable Car and Upper Terminus Area

Seorak-san's aerial tramway runs 1,100 meters from the valley floor to the ridge above. It operates daily 0630–1900 (later during summer evenings)

and costs ₩4,500—round-trip only. This five-minute ride offers a bird's-eye view of the Outer Seorak area. There may be long lines during summer school holidays or during the height of autumn colors. Just above the cable car's upper terminus is the Gwon'geum-seong mountain hut, used principally by rock climbers and hikers walking up the ridge trail via Hwache-bong to Daecheong-bong. This ridge trail is a moderate hike—six hours to the top—most used during spring to view the colorful azaleas that predominate here, but it is often closed. From this trail, you have a striking view down into Cheonbul-dong Valley and out toward the East Sea. Although of the typical spartan variety, the mountain hut has a surprise. While sitting on log stumps, gazing out at marvelous scenery, you can listen to classical music as you sip fine-quality blended coffee.

Very near the mountain hut are the deteriorated remains of Gwon'geum-seong fortress. The origin of this 2,000-meter-long stone wall is uncertain. One theory holds that it was built by Generals Kwon and Kim (Geum) during the Silla Dynasty after they were declared outlaws and forced to leave the service of the Silla king. Others claim it was constructed during the Goryeo Dynasty as a defense against the Mongols.

From the bare rock peak above and behind the hut is one of the best views of the mountain's main ridgeline, Ulsan-bawi across the valley to the north, Shinheung-sa in the valley far below, and Towangseong Waterfall as it tumbles over a high mountain cliff to the east. The view from here rivals that from the cable car. Be careful as you climb around this bald outcrop—there are no guardrails! If you look south and cock your head slightly to the side, you'll see the silhouette of a face looking skyward, formed by the contours of the distant mountain ridge.

About 100 meters below the upper cable car terminus is the tiny hermitage **Allak-am.** This religious aerie sits precariously on the edge of a precipice. On the sides of its main hall, colorful paintings depict scenes from Buddha's life and other familiar topics. Behind it a trail drops *steeply* down the mountainside, becoming a bit more manageable as it approaches the valley floor.

Meeting a second trail near the river, it continues over a footbridge to the park plaza. This trail is quite taxing, but an acceptable alternative for those in good physical condition who care to ride the cable car only one way.

Waterfalls

From the footbridge at the base of the Gwon'geum-seong trail, a second trail leads downriver and up a narrow side valley to three of the most easily accessible waterfalls in the park. The first is **Yukdam ("Six Pools") Waterfall**. The stream here is full of zest as it flows through a series of cascades, one of which makes an L-shaped water slide. The trail continues up the narrow ravine, crossing and recrossing the stream by suspension bridges. From the last few of these bridges, the uppermost falls comes into view high above as it roars over a distant cliff at the top of the valley. Within a few minutes you approach **Biryong ("Flying Dragon") Waterfall**, a 40-meter-long ribbon of water sliding down a scoured rock face into an emerald-green pool. An unfrequented trail leads from this pool around the left side of the falls and up to the end of this narrowing valley to **Towangseong ("Thriving Earthen Fortress") Waterfall**. Often sporting a rainbow, this falls cascades over a sheer rock face, pummeling the rocks below. It's one of the most enticing in the park, tackled in winter by expert ice climbers. From the bridge by the cable car terminus, it's a 40-minute walk to Biryong Waterfall, and another 20- to 30-minute climb beyond that to Towangseong. This is perhaps the nicest trail in the lower park area, but go early in the morning to beat the crowds.

Shinheung-sa 신흥사

A short, easy stroll from the park plaza brings you past a fenced-in group of *sari budo* and a huge new seated bronze Buddha statue to Shinheung-sa [Shinhŭng-sa] ("Divine Undertaking Temple"), the principal temple of Seorak-san. At the junction of two major valleys below high spired peaks, this small compound has one of the most spectacular settings of any temple in Korea. Established in 652 as Hyangseong-sa by the monk Jajang, the only remnant from that original temple is a three-tier (originally nine-tier) stone pagoda (T. #443), which for years stood in front of the Mt. Seorak Hotel but now has been repaired and moved to a point along the park approach road. Rebuilt in 1647 as Shinheung-sa after its destruction by the Japanese in the 1590s, its last major reconstruction was done in 1847, although repair work has been done periodically since the end of the Korean War. It is now the third district headquarters of the Jogye sect.

After passing through the temple's front gate, at the far end of the park plaza, you see the newest of the large additions to Shinheung-sa. This is a huge bronze Buddha that's seated on an equally large stone lotus bud, a bronze mandala placed behind its head. To the front stand two large bronze lanterns and an incense burner. On the far side of the stream and inside Shinheung-sa's enclosed front gate stand four of the best examples of deva guardians in the country, and those representative unfortunates downtrodden by them. These celestial kings not only guard the temple from evil influence, but are protectors of Buddhism in general; each reigns over one of the four Buddhist heavens. On the outside walls of this gate are several murals, including paintings of the first Zen patriarch and other familiar figures and tales. From under the lecture hall you approach the courtyard, on the far side of which is Geungnakbo-jeon, the temple's main hall. Look for the carvings on its stone stairway. Amita, enshrined in the central position on the altar, is flanked by the Goddess of Mercy and the Bodhisattva of Power. Its walls also sport intriguing murals, including a fine example of the ox-herding series. These 10 paintings, pictorially representing the spiritual path to enlightenment, end with the eternal circle, symbolizing full spiritual knowledge—with no subsequent paintings depicting the return to the world of man (as in some versions). Other buildings include the Three Saints Hall, Judgment Hall, new and old bell pavilions, and monks' quarters. The bell is said to be about 1,400 years old, while one of the Buddha statues is around 1,000 years old.

Gyejo-am 계조암

From Shinheung-sa, a one-hour hike leads up the right-hand valley, past Anyang-am and Naewon-am to the more well-known hermitage Gyejo-am [Kyejo-am] ("Succession of Founders Hermitage"). Set amidst huge boulders on the hillside, Gyejo-am is said to have been used by monks for study and meditation for the last 1,300 years. Established a year before Shinheung-sa, again by the monk Jajang, it was later used by the renowned monks Wonhyo and Uisang. These two great men followed the "founders" of Korean Buddhism as the country's most enlightened Buddhist priests of the age.

The diminutive hall contains statues of the Mountain Spirit, the Lonely Arhat, and the Seven Star God. A second hall incorporates a shallow grotto. Inside, a gilt seated image of the Buddha is illuminated by candles. Here, the resident monk intones daily prayers to the Enlightened One, while those who've come on pilgrimages bow in reverence and devotion. When this grotto is empty, the stillness and closeness create a holy, uplifting aura, enhanced when the muffled sounds of the clacking *moktak* and chanting voice of the monk softly penetrate from the other hall.

In front of this hall, the nearly round **Heundeul-bawi** ("Rocking Boulder"), twice the height of a man, balances on the edge of a broad, flat rock. It's situated so that even one person, with a hefty heave-ho, can rock it, but dozens of people cannot budge it from its perch. Give it a shove! Carved into flat rock surfaces here are the names of previous visitors to the hermitage, some possibly 400–500 years old!

Ulsan-bawi

From Gyejo-am, a trail leads straight up the hillside to the craggy rock outcrop Ulsan-bawi (873 meters). The 45- to 60-minute walk is tiring, the zigzag trail so steep that metal stairways, ladders, walkways, and bridges have been erected to make the climb possible without ropes. Over 800 metal steps lead up Ulsan-bawi. Its uppermost level, a flat observation area, is surrounded by metal railings, but be careful anyway as it's a long way straight down.

Rising precipitously skywards, Ulsan-bawi stands like an island in rolling green waves, offering a wonderful view of the mountain and an overview of Sokcho. It's one of the most dramatic of the huge rock outcrops in the park, and its sheer walls make commanding rock-climbing routes. Although it was pushed up by an ancient volcanic eruption, a mythical tale of its formation is more fetching. Legend relates that this rock outcrop (*bawi* means "large rock") was once located near the present city of Ulsan, in Gyeongsangnam-Do. When it heard the creator was putting together the Diamond Mountains, which were to be the loveliest on the Korean Peninsula, it wanted to become part of that formation. However, on its journey north this huge block of stone heard that the required 12,000 peaks had already been gathered and arranged—no more were necessary. In grief, it plunged to the earth and has remained where it fell.

Cheonbul-dong Valley

From Shinheung-sa, the left-hand trail leads into the most visually stimulating valley in the park. A 45-minute walk brings you to Biseon-dae ("Flying Fairy Rock"), a wide, flat rock surface where the river rapids drain into a clear pool. It is from here, legend says, that an angel ascended into heaven. Many pinnacles rise to great heights in the immediate area, perhaps imitating that angel's escape from the earth. One particular peak opposite Biseon-dae is called Mireuk-bong ("Buddha of the Future Peak"). Halfway up this immense spire is the shallow **Geumgang-gul** [Kŭmgang-gul] ("Diamond Cave"), said to have been used by the monk Wonhyo as a meditation site. From the top of the trail, steps and metal stairways reach this natural cubicle, which is dished out of the side of this vertical rock wall. Inside is an altar. The view from this height into the valley and up to the distant peaks is worth the climb. The trail beyond Geumgang-gul goes up to Madeung-ryeong Pass. It becomes substantially steeper as it approaches the top, then descends swiftly down the opposite side to the hermitage Osae-am and the Inner Seorak valleys. Views from this pass are unsurpassed. From here, you can look down into both Outer and Inner Seorak, and up the backbone of Dinosaur Ridge to Daecheong-bong.

The main trail from Biseon-dae continues into

© ROBERT NILSEN

Cheonbul-dong Valley

Cheonbul-dong ("One Thousand Buddhas") Valley, the most spectacular in the park. It is pure, unadulterated Seorak-san, the essence of this mystical mountain fairyland. Cheonbul-dong has hundreds of spires and pinnacles. Inspired religious minds of the past have looked at their shapes and seen images of the Buddha in each. Often clouds obscure these steeples of stone, playing hide-and-seek with those who walk amongst them. At the upper end of this valley are several waterfalls; perhaps the best is Yangpok, or "Yang" Waterfall, about two hours above Biseon-dae. The complementary Uempok, or "Yin" Waterfall, is only a few steps away. A short way below the falls is the Yangpok mountain hut, a place to replenish your supplies or stay the night. Sit on the balcony and watch the moon traverse the sky, or simply listen to the sounds of the night.

Daecheong-bong

From Yangpok hut, the last section of the trail rises steeply up the valley side to the small and spartan Huiungak hut, and from there continues in a roundabout way via Socheong ("Little Green") and Jungcheong ("Middle Green") peaks to the summit. Expect a climb of four hours from Yangpok hut to the top. Two other trails branch off from here. One runs north along Dinosaur Ridge to Madeung-ryeong, and the other goes down into Gaya-dong Valley. Neither is recommended for the casual hiker, and both are periodically closed to maintain their integrity. As you approach Daecheong-bong ("Great Green Peak"), vegetation becomes sparse. The stubborn bushes and trees that do grow at this height are twisted, stumpy specimens. At the top you're rewarded with an unprecedented view of the entire mountain area and the East Sea. Bring a sweater; the unpredictable weather at the summit is often windy and never very warm. At times, clouds come in within minutes and the temperature plunges, embracing the peak in stifling cold. While bright and sunny days are the norm during summer, snow covers the peak half the year. Two other mountain huts are located below Jungcheong and Socheong peaks, the latter being four times larger than the former.

Hiking

The Outer Seorak area has the best selection of half-day (or less) hikes in the park. If you're very energetic, several of these could be combined into a long day's excursion. Whichever you choose, start early to avoid the crowds. Options include: 1) Shinheung-sa to Gyejo-am and Ulsanbawi, return; 2) Shinheung-sa to Biseon-dae, Geumgang-gul, and Yangpok Waterfall, return; 3) the park plaza to Biryong and Towangseong Waterfalls, return; 4) by cable car to Gwon'geumseong ridge, the fortress, Allak-am, and a walk down the hill to the plaza. This walk down should not be attempted by those with weak knees (literally and figuratively). Many full-day and multiple-day hikes can also be made in the area. It's possible to walk from the valley floor up Cheonbul-dong Valley to the summit and return to Seorak-dong in one long day. For this strenuous round-trip, allow 10 hours or more—suitable only for those in strong physical condition. An alternate, although less traveled, route to Daecheong-bong is to take the cable car to the

top and walk the Hwache ridge. This round-trip should take at least nine hours, but the trail is often closed. For longer hikes, it's best to walk to the summit and stay the night at one of the mountain huts, continuing on the following day down to Baekdam-sa—the most common two-day hike in the park—or to Osaek. A hike along the Seobuk ridge from Daecheong-bong to Ansan (or Daeseung Waterfall) is the longest ridge trail in the park, even longer when combined with the walk up from the upper cable car terminus. Another long walk is from Shinheung-sa, over Madeung-ryeong to Baekdam-sa. This route requires eight to nine hours, often done in two days, staying one night at the Suryeom-dong mountain hut. A quick pace is energizing, but slow down to absorb your surroundings. Perceive what's visible, listen for what's audible, and sense what cannot be seen or heard.

INNER SEORAK

Inner Seorak, west of the main mountain ridgeline, is softer and more benevolent than Outer Seorak, generally less sculpted and more gradual, with longer and broader valleys. Wild, natural, and little touched by man, Inner Seorak is the mountain's hinterland, a locale of unspoiled openness. Because it's more distant from the park's main entrance and tourist sites, fewer people expend the time and energy to hike in and appreciate what Inner Seorak has to offer.

Baekdam Valley

The most often-used back entrance to Seorak-san National Park is the little village of Yongdae-ri, also referred to as Naegapyeong. Once just a muddy-street, wide spot in the road, Yongdae-ri gets wider and more developed all the time. Now it boasts numerous accommodations, restaurants, a highway rest stop, and your last chance for supplies when heading into the mountains from here. From the park office (₩2,600 entrance), a leisurely two-hour walk up the gravel road along the river in the long, serpentine Baekdam Valley brings you to the Baekdam hut. This is Inner Seorak's principal valley. With a 300-person capacity, the Baekdam hut is the largest in the park. For those who don't care to walk from Yongdae-ri to the hut, an occasional bus traverses four of the seven kilometers of this route. From August through October, it runs once an hour 0800–1800.

A few hundred meters before you reach the hut is **Baekdam-sa** [Paekdam-sa] (백담사), the major temple of Inner Seorak. It was founded as Bigeum-sa in 643 by Jajang, that busy monk, near the present-day town of Hwacheon. An incompatibility grew between the pacifist monks and the hunters in the nearby mountains, so about 650 years ago the temple was moved to a spot near the village of Han'gye-ri, just east of Inje. After a long series of mysterious fires, the location was judged inauspicious, and the temple moved to Yongdae-ri, then once again to its present location. Still, the fires did not cease. One night a monk dreamed that a venerable old monk tossed water from the top of the mountain into this valley near the temple. Taking this as a good omen, the temple's name was aptly changed to Baekdam ("100 Pools"), and in fact, there are innumerable pools in the river between this temple and the top of the mountain. Never again was this sanctuary bothered by fire, but it was destroyed during the Korean War. Although partially rebuilt, it has not regained its former grandeur. Within the main hall sits a white-robed wooden Amita Buddha figure (T. #1182) on the main altar.

The temple's most famous resident of the 20th century is the well-known poet/monk Han Yong-un. This talented, outspoken man worked toward the revitalization of Korean Buddhism when it was at an extremely low ebb during the beginning of the 20th century and helped instigate the Korean independence movement from Japan during the colonial period. He was one of the 33 signers of the Declaration of Independence, promulgated in 1919.

Bongjeong-am 봉정암

A short way beyond the Baekdam hut, the river turns sharply to the left, entering Suryeom-dong Valley, perhaps the essence of Inner Seorak as Cheonbul-dong Valley is the epitome of Outer Seorak. The meandering trail closely follows the boulder-strewn riverbed, and in its upper reaches the valley name changes again to Gugokdam. Crossing and recrossing the swift river, the trail makes its way up the narrow valley to the hermitage Bongjeong-am and on to Daecheong-bong.

At 1,223 meters, Bongjeong-am [Pongjŏng-am] ("Phoenix Summit Hermitage") is reputedly the loftiest in the country. Established in 643 by the monk Jajang, it backs up against a screen-like rock wall. It's said that when Jajang, one of the greatest Korean monks, returned from his journey to China, he brought back with him relic treasures of the historic Buddha. Several of these *sarisa* are supposedly kept in the five-tier pagoda to the side of the hermitage. A stone stairway leads to the pagoda, which looks out over Gaya-dong Valley. This pagoda is one of the country's five monuments that lay claim to containing a few sacred calcified Buddha remains. From here it's less than two hours to Daecheong-bong.

Osae-am 오세암

From the Suryeom-dong hut, a smaller trail leads into the mouth of adjoining Gaya-dong Valley. Its densely forested sides are steep and narrow, topped by a bald granite crest, and through its deep bottom runs a swift river, punctuated by falls and rapids. This valley is bounded by two craggy ridges with very telling names: Dinosaur Ridge and The great wall of Dragon's Molars Ridge! The only (well-worn) trail runs up the side of the valley from Suryeom-dong hut to Madeung-ryeong Pass. About 100 meters above the hut, the trail crosses the river and heads up the hill to Man'gyeong-dae lookout, an isolated, mid-valley peak with great views of the Gaya-dong Valley. This path continues a short way and meets a larger trail at a pass below the lookout. Going left here puts you back into Suryeom-dong Valley; right takes you to the hermitage Osae-am. When the clouds lower or the mist rises to obscure parts of the mountainside, this sculpted valley takes on the character for which Asian landscape paintings are famous.

Nestled into the mountainside some 20 minutes beyond Man'gyeong-dae lookout is Osae-am, occasionally referred to as Gwaneum-am. Founded by Jajang in the same year as Bong-jeong-am, this small, unpretentious hermitage has been the home of well-respected Buddhist monks. It's also said that the poet Kim Shi-seup, an unorthodox scholar well-known as one of the country's most talented poets and storytellers, an exemplary spirit and master craftsman of words, used it as a place of study. He's referred to as the "Rainhat Poet" because he refused to conform to the traditional models of strict Confucian society and wandered the country like a mendicant Buddhist monk, of which the broad rainhat was a symbol.

From Osae-am, the trail continues up the hill to Madeung-ryeong Pass, and descends steeply on the far side to the mouth of Cheonbul-dong Valley and farther on to Shinheung-sa. Also from this pass, a tortuous trail leads south over Dinosaur Ridge to Huiungak hut. This ridge is aptly named because its thrusting rock outcrops resemble the large, bony plates that protrude from a stegosaurus' back. Often closed, this trail is not recommended for those who have not been led through it at least once. Even then, it takes about five hours to traverse. Approach it with great caution.

Hiking

From Yongdae-ri, it's possible to make a day trip into the Inner Seorak area. A two-hour walk up this gentle river valley brings you to Baekdam-sa. It's another two hours to Suryeom-dong hut, from where you can easily return to Yongdae-ri in the afternoon. More often, however, hikers traverse this valley in order to get to Daecheong-bong or to go over the ridge to Seorak-dong. If you're going to the summit and you've lots of steam, it's possible to power up to the top in one long eight- or nine-hour day. Stay at one of the huts below Jungcheong or Socheong peak. From Daecheong-bong, most first-time hikers go down to Seorak-dong via the picturesque Cheonbul-dong Valley, while others take the trail down to Osaek. A shorter route from Yongdae-ri to Seorak-dong is by way of Madeung-ryeong. This trail is also possible to accomplish in one *long* day, about 10 hours. Rather than pushing over the mountain, it may be better to stay

the night at either the Baekdam or Suryeom-dong hut and negotiate the pass when you're fresh. Other possibilities are the trails from Baekdam hut over the Seobuk ridge to Daeseung Waterfall, about five hours, and the eight-hour trail over Jeohang-nyeong Pass to the park plaza, but both of these trails are periodically closed.

JANGSU-DAE 장수대

Situated in the western end of Seorak-san National Park, the Jangsu-dae region is the least-developed and least-visited section of the park. Its greatest attraction is Daeseung Waterfall, but the "sleeper" of the area, its beauty known only to the few who venture there, is the Shibi Seonnyeotang Valley. Entrance at the trailheads here is ₩1,300.

Set below An-san (1,430 meters) and Gari-bong (1,518 meters), Jangsu-dae [Changsu-dae] has a group campground located near the bus stop. Nearby the two three-tier stone pagodas (T. #1275, 1276) mark the site of the former temple Han'gye-sa. Erected in 1958, a memorial marker commemorates soldiers who lost their lives in this rugged mountain area during the Korean War. From here, a two-kilometer trail goes up past Sajung Waterfall to Daeseung Waterfall. At 88 meters, Daeseung Waterfall is the country's highest. While generally no more than a wispy stream, during the summer rains great quantities of water thunder over the cliff. Like Towangseong Waterfall in the Outer Seorak area, Daeseung is often used for ice climbing—one of the most difficult falls in the country.

Hiking

The walk to and from Daeseung Waterfall makes a pleasant part-day trip. Beyond the waterfall, it's a 1.5-hour walk up to Seobuk ridge. Going down the north side, you end up at the Baekdam hut. A seven-hour hike along the ridge trail to the right takes you to Daecheong-bong; the opposite direction leads to An-san. A secondary trail to the north drops down into **Shibi Seonnyeotang Valley** ("Valley of the Twelve Fairy Pools"). In the upper reaches is a quick series of cascades, falls, and pools. Tales of the region claim this valley was often visited in the misty past by fairies who bathed in its refreshing and attractive pools. The pools are enticing, but take care not to be overcome by magic if you happen to catch sight of a nubile naiad bathing in this isolated glen. If hiking this trail from the bottom end, get off the bus at Namgyo-ri and walk up the valley from there. Like the larger Yongdae-ri, Namgyo-ri has a few accommodations, restaurants, and shops for supplies.

OSAEK 오색

Directly south of Daecheong-bong is the Osaek Valley. Bounded by Han'gye-ryeong ("Cold Valley Pass") at its top end and the town of Yangyang at its mouth, this is the park's largest individual valley. Through it runs the major highway that connects Inje to the coast. Wide and open, dozens of side valleys lead into it. Through these hills run several trails, but the valley's major attraction is the developed area around the Osaek mineral spring and hot spring.

Osaek Springs

Legend relates that the Osaek ("Five Color") mineral spring is about 1,500 years old. During the Silla Dynasty, a temple apparently stood near this naturally gushing water, and behind the temple a flowering tree produced blooms of five different colors. Two small and rather unassuming temples, Mangwol-sa and Seongguk-sa, now stand nearby.

From the bus stop, a 10-minute walk brings you through a row of restaurants to a bridge. On the far side of this bridge, the mineral spring bubbles up from a fissure in the broad riverside rock. Containing iron and carbonic acid, it has a decidedly tangy flavor. Mangwol-sa is about 100 meters up the steps to the side of the bridge, and Seongguk-sa [Sŏngguk-sa], completely rebuilt in 1995, is about 1.5 kilometers up the path on the near side of the bridge, after passing the park entrance (₩1,300). About one kilometer beyond Seongguk-sa is Seonnyeotang Pool Waterfall, and another 1.5 kilometers above that is the higher Yongso Waterfall.

Discovered about 500 years ago, the Osaek Hot Springs now draws large crowds to its soothing waters. Containing sodium, fluorine, chlorine, magnesium, and calcium, among other trace elements, this water pushes forth from the ground at a relatively cool 29°C. At 650 meters, this is the highest known hot spring source in the country; it's piped from the source two kilometers to Osaek, where you can bathe in its warm waters at the hotel and *yeogwan*.

Because of the mineral spring, hot spring, and fine scenery, Osaek has recently become quite developed, a very miniature version of Seorak-dong. Here are the Osaek Greenyard Hotel, several upscale *yeogwan, minbak,* numerous eating establishments, shops selling dried, boxed, and bottled mountain vegetables and herbs, souvenir shops, and a city bus stop. City buses run from the stop near the parking lot down the valley to Yangyang (₩1,500). Intercity buses stop along the highway to let off and pick up passengers to and from Sokcho, Gangneung, Inje, and Chuncheon.

Hiking

The well-used trail from the Osaek mineral spring along the river to Yongso Waterfall makes a fine early-morning walk, about two hours roundtrip. While there are other, lesser-used trails of several hours apiece to waterfalls and peaks in the area south and west of Osaek, perhaps the most frequented is the shortest and most direct route to Daecheong-bong. Starting at Osaek Village, this trail goes up the north side of the valley to the summit, passing Seorak Waterfall on the way—plan for four hours going up. A lesser-used trail leads west into the next valley, past Dokju Waterfall to the Seobuk ridge. At 40 meters high, **Dokju Waterfall** is one of the three most spectacular in the park, and one of the tallest in the country. From Osaek, it's possible to go up to Daecheong-bong and down to Seorak-dong in one long day, but the route is very strenuous. It's better to stay the night at one of the mountain huts on the way.

PRACTICALITIES

Not surprisingly, a great number of accommodations are available in and near the national park. Whether it's the convenience and luxury of a hotel, the affordability of a *yeogwan* or *minbak,* or the location of the mountain huts, you can usually find what you want. Room rates are generally high, and their availability depends largely upon the season—summer school holiday and the autumn color period are the most heavily booked.

Hotels

The deluxe-class **Hotel Sorak Park** (tel. 033/636-7711, www.hotelsorakpark.com), with its wide, white, V-shaped front, is 1.5 kilometers below the park entrance. Nearly all of its well-appointed rooms have grand views of the distant peaks. Rooms run ₩169,000–181,000, with suites from ₩217,000. Here you'll find Korean, Japanese, and Western restaurants, a coffee shop, souvenir shop, game room, nightclub, bar, bowling alley, and the area's only casino. English and Japanese are spoken, and major credit cards are accepted. Much closer to the park entrance is the deluxe-class **Kensington Hotel** (tel. 033/635-4001), where rates for rooms run ₩129,000–199,000, with suites at ₩299,000. The third hotel, located within the park to the side of the plaza, is the third-class **Mt. Sorak Tourist Hotel** (tel. 033/636-7101, www.hotelsorak.com). This is the oldest of the park's hotels, and the least expensive, with rates starting at ₩90,000, suites from ₩130,000. The hotel's location and size give it a decidedly homier feel than either of its two newer cousins. In Oseak, try the **Osaek Greenyard Hotel** (tel. 033/672-8500), where rooms run ₩70,000–130,000.

Yeogwan

Near the Hotel Sorak Park are numerous *yeogwan,* also known variously as motels, villas, lodges, or *sanjang.* Most of these are fairly large and modern and some have their own restaurants. Western-style beds or Korean *ondol* rooms are available, generally for ₩40,000–50,000. Across the river and in the next community down is a greater predominance of more ordinary *yeogwan* where rooms run ₩30,000–40,000. Many of these places have numerous large rooms, good for sharing with several friends. Still farther down,

minbak rent for about ₩25,000 for a decent but usually spartan room. Additional *yeogwan* and *minbak* can be found at Osaek, Yongdae-ri, Namgyo-ri, and Jangsu-dae. Rates will be high during peak season, but can easily be bargained down during the off-season.

Youth Hostels

Conveniently situated near the shopping complex in lower Seorak Village is the **Mt. Sorak Youth Hostel** (tel. 033/636-7115). Relatively new with full facilities, this place is often booked by groups, but when not bunk beds run ₩11,300 for Y.H. members or ₩40,000 for non-members.

Mountain Huts

Located along the major park trails are eight huts, called *sanjang* or *daepiso* in Korean: Gwon'geum-seong, Biseon-dae, Yangpok, Huiungak, Socheong, Jungcheong, Suryeom-dong, and Baekdam. Ranging in size from 30 to 300 spaces, they charge ₩5,000 per night to use the sleeping area, which in most cases is no more than two tiers of bare board floors. You must have your own sleeping bag. Six huts operate only during fine-weather months when the trails are open to hikers; Gwon'geum-seong and Baekdam huts stay open nearly year-round. The huts stock a few canned foods and packaged goods—sold at inflated prices —so it's best to carry along and cook all the food that you'll need. Each hut has water. Generally, water is plentiful along the trails, although it should be boiled or treated before drinking. The only places where it's especially important to carry sufficient water are along the long Seobuk and Hwache ridge trails, where springs are few.

Camping

Aside from the designated camping areas at Seorak-dong, Osaek, Jangsu-dae, and Yongdae-ri, camping inside the park is prohibited. If possible, use the toilets at the huts, or bury your waste well away from any stream. Don't litter; pack out all your trash!

Food

Seorak-dong and Osaek boast many ordinary

restaurants; find finer food at the hotels. Yongdae-ri, Namgyo-ri, and Jangsu-dae also have growing numbers of restaurants, and more than just simple food. A limited variety of food is also available at the park plaza restaurants and snack shops, and at Biseon-dae. One special food of the area is *gamja buchim,* a potato pancake mixed with vegetables and fried in light oil. It's not usually a meal in itself, but is taken with some alcoholic drink. Another food you'll encounter here is *sanchae bibimbap,* a dish of wild mountain vegetables and spices that's mounded over rice and mixed together before being eaten—a full meal by itself. Individual wild vegetables, fresh or dried, pine mushrooms, and acorn jelly can also be found at shops at the various trailhead villages.

Getting There

Most visitors to Seorak-san National Park arrive at Seorak-dong. Buses that run to this entrance come from Sokcho (₩750) and Yangyang (₩1,500). City bus no. 7 from Sokcho stops at the Seorak-dong *yeogwan* and hotel areas before proceeding on to the park entrance. City buses from Yangyang also run to Osaek (₩1,500). Highway buses from Sokcho that traverse the Han'gye-ryeong Pass will stop at Osaek (₩2,800) and Jangsu-dae (₩3,800) on their way to Inje and beyond. Highway buses that run the northern route from Sokcho, via Ganseong and Jinburyeong, stop at Yongdae-ri (₩4,500) and Namgyo-ri (₩4,800), back entrances to the park. For those with private vehicles, an additional road from the newly developed community of condominiums and recreational facilities on the west side of Sokcho runs up and over the Mishiryeong Pass and is a quicker route to the western side of the park.

Sokcho and the North Coast

SOKCHO 속초

Sokcho [Sokch'o], an unassuming yet thriving harbor town of 90,000, is South Korea's northernmost city. It's a major fishing center, and the principal gateway to Seorak-san National Park. Situated in one of the province's wider coastal plains, it wraps itself around two lagoons (called lakes) and onto the surrounding hillsides. During the last several decades, with the expansion of the national park and subsequent development of surrounding recreational facilities, the entire area has become a center of year-round sports and leisure. To accommodate the increased population and growing number of visitors, apartments, condominiums, hotels, city parks, two golf courses, a water-theme amusement park and hot spring, and other facilities have been created—most of them directly west of the city in the foothills just north of the park boundary.

Along the city's main street are the Telecom office, central market, banks, post office, city hall, and police station. The nightlife, restaurant, and entertainment area is along the main street and adjacent alleys south of the central market to past the Telecom office. The channel of the southern lake is the old port. When Sokcho's many fishing boats are in harbor, they line the pier as tightly as sardines in a can. It's lively along the pier and good for pictures, especially in the morning when boats return and disgorge their catches or in the evening when the squid boats are brightly lit and ready to sail into the inky black night. There are other concentrations of fishing boats out near the lighthouse and at the small port of Daepo, south along the highway not far from the turnoff to the national park. As you might expect, a concentration of seafood restaurants front these harbor areas. Many are distinguished by tubs of water out front holding a variety of live fish and other sea creatures from which you can choose your meal. The selection varies according to the season, but common are flounder (sole), pollack, tuna, red snapper (sea bream), octopus, and eel. Most fish are served raw over a bed of shredded cabbage and usually dipped in red-pepper paste before they are eaten, but fried fish and fish soup are also served. The inner harbor restaurants have been eclipsed by the others, but there are many shops near this central

GANGWON-DO

location that sell all sorts of dried fish and seaweed.

Passenger ferries to Ulleung-do and Russia are located along the pier toward the north end of this central section of town. Just inland from there is the intercity bus terminal, while at the southeastern corner of Cheongcho Lake is the express-bus terminal. On the rocky spur of land that juts out and makes the northern curve of the harbor sit a lighthouse and pavilion. Set on a boulder at water's edge and now made of concrete to withstand the crash of waves, Yeonggeum-jeong pavilion is a good place to watch the lights of night fishing boats. On the hill above, the observation deck at the lighthouse gives an even better view of the sea and coast. At the narrowest point of the channel is a non-motorized pedestrian-only pontoon raft ferry. For the small fee of ₩300 you can cross to Sokcho Beach and the neighborhood on the spit of land that creates the lake, but you should help give the ferry a pull. The neighborhood on the lake side originally grew as a result of North Korean refugees settling in Sokcho after the split of the country. The 1999 Travel EXPO site, with its 74-meter-tall tower, has been created

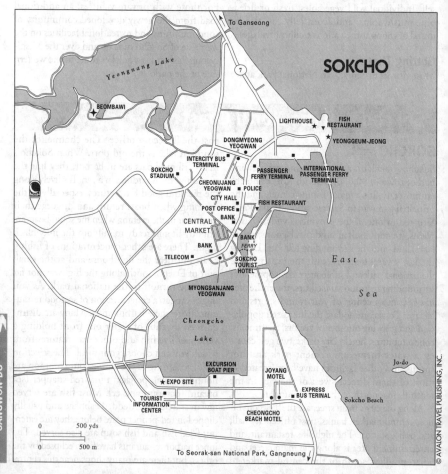

on the south shore of Cheongcho Lake. A tourist information center is located here. Excursion boats leave from the pier at the EXPO site for trips up and down the coast. Just off Sokcho Beach, across the spit of land to the east, is Jo-do, a small island frequented by a multitude of seabirds. Large sections of lakeshore park have been created around Yeongnang Lake, which a road and bicycle path circle. The huge boulder Beombawi sits on the south shore of the lake, and the lake itself is used for canoeing, kayaking, and windsailing.

Seorak Sunrise Park is located along the water at the Mulchi turnoff for the road up to the national park entrance. Relatively new, this park has yet to grow to maturity, but you can stop to have a look at the sculptures or ask for help at the tourist information center. Leaving from a pier at this park is a shuttle ferry that takes passengers to a tourist submarine. Rides are given along the coast up toward Sokcho a half dozen times a day or more and run ₩49,500 for adults, ₩39,600 for middle and high school students, and ₩29,700 for younger kids. Run by Tritone Marine, this sub carries up to 46 passengers, can dive to 75 meters in depth, has many large viewports, and delivers a narration in Korean. Dives last about 45 minutes; with the boat transfer, expect a time of two hours.

Every year in October the **Seorak Cultural Festival** is held in Sokcho and at Seorak-san National Park. While some rituals and climbing events are held at the mountain, music and dance, film previews, and fireworks occur in the city. In 1991, Sokcho proudly hosted the 17th Boy Scout World Jamboree at newly created facilities just west of the city.

Check the website www.sokcho.kangwon.kr for additional information.

Accommodations

While many visitors to the area stay at Seorak-dong, just below the park entrance, there are plenty of accommodations in Sokcho itself. Several dozen low-priced *yeogwan* and *yeoinsuk* are gathered around the intercity bus terminal. For a start, try the Cheonujang Yeogwan (천우장여관). Across the street and down an alley is the slightly cheaper Dongmyeong Yeogwan (동명여관). In town near the market is the mid-priced Myongsanjang Yeogwan (명산장여관). A few steps away is the second-class Sokcho Tourist Hotel, which has Korean and Western restaurants, a bar, and a coffee shop. Near the express-bus terminal are the Joyang Motel (조양모텔) and the Cheongcho Beach Motel (청초비치모텔), where rooms run ₩35,000–60,000.

Transportation

The Sokcho Airport (속초공항) is six kilometers south of the city, just beyond the Mulchi turnoff. It serviced daily flights to Seoul until 2002 when the Yangyang International Airport was opened and flights shifted there.

At the bottom of the street that runs by the intercity bus terminal is the passenger ferry terminal (속초항터미날) for boats to Ulleung-do. A high-speed catamaran ferry leaves Sokcho every Saturday and Sunday for South Korea's largest island in the East Sea. The crossing on this very comfortable cruiser takes about three hours, leaving Sokcho harbor at 0930 and 1730 from mid-July to mid-August and at 1100 during the remainder of the year. The fare one way is ₩34,000; no reservations are necessary except during peak holiday travel times. Before boarding, you must fill out a passenger travel card with name and passport number.

If the sea route is open for visitors to the Diamond Mountains, Sokcho (or Donghae) is used as the port of embarkation. There is a ferry connection to Russia, which many use to visit Baekdu-san on the North Korea-China border. This ferry leaves from the Sokcho International Passenger Ferry Terminal (속초국제여객터미날). For the convenience of travelers, this terminal has money exchange counters, ATMs, and a tourist information booth open during departure and arrivals. The ferry to Russia runs to the port of Zarubino, near Vladivostok. This ferry leaves Sokcho every Monday, Wednesday, and Friday at 1400 and the trip to Zarubino runs about 16 hours. One way fares vary from US$120 for a spot in an open cabin to US$240 for a VIP room; a ten percent discount is offered for round-trip fares. From Zarubino a one-hour bus trip gets you to Hunchun in China. From there, buses run to Yanji, where a change of bus will take you to Baekdu-san, another six hours or more. If required of you, you must get a Russian visa before you buy your ferry ticket, and you must have a Chinese visa before crossing into China.

Express buses run every hour to the Seoul Express Bus Terminal (₩12,800), every 2.5 hours to the Tong Seoul Bus Terminal (₩12,800), and nine times a day to Incheon (₩13,000). Selected intercity bus destinations and fares are Daejin (₩3,000), Inje (₩5,600), Chuncheon (₩11,500), Gangneung (₩4,900), and Pohang (₩22,200).

From in front of the bus station or along the main street, Sokcho city bus no. 7 runs to Seorak-dong and the national park entrance, bus no. 1 goes to Daejin and coastal pavilions and beaches to the north, and bus no. 9 runs to Daepo, Naksan-sa, and Yangyang.

NORTH OF SOKCHO

The white beaches along this littoral coast are set off like a string of pearls against a green dress. A few uninhabited rocky islets stand offshore, lending it a peaceful ruggedness. However pastoral it may appear, most of the shore is cordoned off by barbed wire; tank traps, army bases, and marine guard stations are placed at intervals along the entire coast. One prewar remnant is the raised bed for the rail line that ran up the coast from Pohang to Wonsan in North Korea. Perhaps this rail line will, at some point in the future, be reconnected and once again transfer goods and passengers between the currently divided halves of this country.

Lagoons

About six kilometers north of Sokcho lies the seaside Joseon-era pavilion **Cheonggan-jeong** [Ch'ŏnggan-jŏng] (청간정), and just north of there is a second pavilion, **Cheonghak-jeong** [Ch'ŏnghak-jŏng] (청학정). Both were obviously constructed with an eye on the sunrise. Known for fishing and its wildlife, particularly white swans, the lagoon **Songji-ho** is a short way on from the pavilions toward Ganseong. Bordered

by pine tress, Songji-ho Beach stretches for about four kilometers on the sea side of this lagoon.

Just inland from this lake is the folk village **Wanggok-ni** (왕곡리). Protected by surrounding mountain peaks, it was partially spared from the ravages of the Korean War. Some two dozen houses in this rural village were constructed during the last century in a style typical of this area. Hunkered close to the ground, most were constructed in an "L" shape, many with stables attached. Though having changed over the decades, these houses, taken as a whole and seen with some imagination, form a scene from old Korea.

Between Geojin and Daejin is **Hwajinpo** (화진포). At 16 kilometers around, it's the largest of the lagoon-lakes that appear at the mouths of rivers along this coast. Surrounded by pine forests, it attracts flocks of mostly migratory waterfowl to its fields of reeds. At the ocean here is the long, well-known Hwajinpo Beach. It's quiet here except in summer when the hordes flock to the beach. Set near the beach is the **Marine Museum** (해양박물관), a small museum dedicated to sea life and the seashore; ₩1,000 entrance. At the edge of the lake sits a renovated house once used by former South Korean president Syngman Rhee. On a wooded knoll overlooking the ocean is the rebuilt house used by North Korean president Kim Il-song, now an exhibition hall relating to the atrocities of the Korean War. Nearby is a home once owned by the first South Korean vice president, Yi Gi-bung. Each of these buildings displays items used by these men or items representative of the era and explains a bit about who they were and what influence they've had on the peninsula. There is a ₩1,500 entrance fee to these houses.

Geonbong-sa 건봉사

The only temple of note this far north is Geonbong-sa [Kŏnbong-sa]. Situated in the southern foothills of the Diamond Mountains, this small temple is said to have been built by the monk Ado in the year 521. Originally called Wongak-sa, its name was changed during the Goryeo Dynasty. A stone arch bridge transports you to the temple compound. Destroyed during the Korean War, its main hall has been renovated. Kept here is a container that supposedly preserves a tooth of the historical Buddha. Foundation stones mark other structure sites. Because it's so near the DMZ, it was closed to visitors until 1989. For those who want a look, take a bus from Ganseong to Haesang-ni and walk the remaining two kilometers. About eight kilometers north of Geonbong-sa is the smaller temple Sambul-sa, the northernmost in South Korea. Civilians are not yet allowed to enter this area which is set within the border buffer zone. It is said that from Sambul-sa it's possible to see Biro-bong in the Diamond Mountains across the border in North Korea. Closer to town, and with no entry restrictions, is Ganseong Hyanggyo. Set just off the highway, you can see this reconstructed Confucian school and shrine from the bus.

Geojin and Daejin

North of Ganseong are the fishing villages of Geojin [Kŏjin] (거진) and Daejin [Taejin] (대진). Daejin, the smaller, is a lazy harbor town, the country's northernmost fishing community. At both, buyers gather each day at the wharf to bid on the fish unloaded that morning. Each chalks a bid on a slate, then the fishing cooperative's representative notes the highest bidder and awards him the right to buy that particular pile of fish. Squid boats hang their catches out to dry like clothes on a line. Public bus transportation ends in Daejin, with intercity buses from Sokcho (₩2,400). Sokcho city bus no. 1 also runs this route. Daejin has a few simple *yeogwan, yeoinsuk,* and restaurants, while Geojin has more and larger of the same.

Unification Observation Area
간성통일전망대

To visit the Unification Observation Area, register your name and passport number at the ticket booth in front of the Unification Hall at Anbo Park, located a few hundred meters past the city bus station in Daejin. Inside, check out the short video program about Korea and the south's hope for reunification of the divided peninsula. Fortify yourself with a meal at the restaurant or one of the several snack shops, or pick up a souvenir of your trip. Beyond this point you must drive your own vehicle or hitch a ride with someone; there are no shuttle buses. Entrance is strictly regulated and the observation building is open daily 0900–1800 (1700 in winter); ₩2,000 entrance for the observatory, ₩2,000 extra for a vehicle. Ask to leave large backpacks with those at the ticket counter while you visit the observation post. The road north from here passes Myeongpa, the northernmost village in South Korea.

Twelve kilometers north of Daejin, the Unification Observation Area sits on a hilltop high above the coast, within a few thousand meters of the South Korea/North Korea border. The distant Diamond Mountains are visible from here on a clear day, as are the craggy granite coastal outcrops called the Diamond Mountains of the Sea. A small display and pictorial representation of North Korean life occupies the bottom floor, while the broad-windowed observation room is set above. A short presentation in Korean indicating points of interest on the border and within North Korean territory is given for each visiting group. For a small fee, you can rent powerful binoculars to get a closer look into the forbidden land; otherwise bring your own—and your camera. Hedging their bets, statues of both the Goddess of Mercy and the Virgin Mary have been erected here facing north in a bid to help with the unification process and hope that the border will someday disappear.

SOUTH OF SOKCHO
Naksan Provincial Park

Established in 1979 as Donghae Provincial Park, this park has since changed names. It stretches about 20 kilometers down the coast from north of Naksan-sa to south of Hajo-dae. Naksan-sa is the first and foremost of what are known as the "Eight Sites of Gwandong," Gwandong being an old cultural area that stretched along the east coast from northern Gyeongsangbuk-Do into what is now North Korea. Directly south of Naksan-sa is Naksan Beach, longest in the area and the most developed; on the north side is the smaller Seorak Beach. At intervals south of here are Susan, Osan, Dongho, and Hajo-dae beaches.

On the hill below Naksan-sa sit a youth hostel

and hotel. The first-class **Naksan Beach Hotel** (tel. 033/672-4000) has rooms for ₩110,000–165,000 with suites up to ₩350,000. Because of its location on the hill, some guest rooms have fine views out over the beach; amenities include restaurants, a lounge and bar, and a sauna. The **Naksan Youth Hostel** (tel. 033/672-3416) is tucked into the trees on the mountain side of the hill. A dorm bed with a valid Y.H. card is ₩10,000, while a Western-style or *ondol* room runs about ₩30,000. Below and back from the beach are many restaurants, shops, souvenir stands, arcade games, and a variety of *yeogwan* and *minbak*.

Naksan-sa 낙산사

Located twelve kilometers south of Sokcho, Naksan-sa is one of Korea's few Buddhist temples set at the edge of the ocean, rather than nestled into the folds of a mountain. Dedicated to Gwaneum, the Goddess of Mercy, Naksan-sa was founded in 671 by the traveling monk Uisang. After his return from China, Uisang came to this spot to try to meet Gwaneum face to face. In a seacliff cave, high above the crashing waves, he prayed and meditated for days, but she didn't show herself. In frustration, he threw himself into the ocean, whereupon Gwaneum immediately appeared and saved him from death. In response, Uisang established Naksan-sa on this bluff and dedicated it to her. The hermitage Hongyeon-am clings to the side of the cliff over the cave in which Uisang meditated. Renovated, enlarged, destroyed, and rebuilt a number of times over the centuries, the temple was completely reconstructed in 1953 due to damage sustained during the Korean War. Entrance is ₩2,500.

Enter Naksan-sa by way of the pleasing stone-arch gate, Honghye-mun. Topped with a tiny pavilion, this gate is made from cut-granite blocks and natural stones. This type of front gate is rare for a temple, but the ever-present enclosed wooden gate containing the four devas is here as well —farther into the compound. Preserved here are a seven-tier pagoda (T. #499) from the mid-1400s and a Joseon Dynasty bronze bell (T. #479), cast in 1469. Holes in the bell's side mark

weapon fire from the war. The main hall is pleasing but not extraordinary, yet it's surrounded by a mud, brick, and tile wall. Portions of the wall are said to be original, from the Joseon Dynasty, making this a tranquil and contained inner courtyard and another rather unusual feature of a Buddhist temple.

A modern addition to Naksan-sa is the 15-meter-tall statue of Gwaneum capping the bluff behind the main temple compound. Dedicated in 1977, this figure is one of the largest such granite statues in the country. Prayers and special ceremonies are held here, and some who live along this coast believe the statue keeps fishermen safe from harm. The newest addition to the temple, however, is Bota-jeon—an impressive structure in size and detail. Finished in 1993 and located below the old buildings, this hall is also dedicated to Gwaneum. Enshrined on the altar are seven different images of her, all skillfully carved with expressive detail. To the hall's front, and in contrast to the warm feel of wood, are fine examples of modern stone sculpture—lanterns, *sari budo,* and a stela tablet. To the front of all these is a newly dug lotus pond, presided over by an open pavilion.

At the edge of the cliff below, an old pine tree rising above its tile roof, is the hexagonal Uisang-dae Pavilion, touted as one of the country's best spots to view the sunrise. A short path from here runs to Hongyeon-am, clinging to the cliff's edge 100 meters away.

Yangyang 양양

South of Naksan-sa is Yangyang, a town known for pine mushrooms and as the entrance to southern Seorak-san. From here, the highway heads west past Osaek and over Han'gye-ryeong to Inje and on to Chuncheon and Seoul. From Yangyang, buses run to Osaek (₩1,500), Jangsu-dae (₩2,400), Naksan (₩700), Seorak-san National Park (₩750), and Sokcho (₩1,300).

South of Yangyang is **Hajo-dae** (하조대). Just outside the town of Hyeonbuk, this eight-sided pavilion is from the Joseon Dynasty, but the present structure was erected in concrete in 1998. Perched on a wooded promontory at seaside, it's no surprise that this spot was chosen for views of the sea and sunrise. Located as it is on this militarized coast, it's currently set behind barbed wire, but entrance is permitted until 2000 daily (1800 in winter).

A short distance south of Hajo-dae Pavilion is a highway rest stop located on the **38th parallel.** From the end of World War II until the border was adjusted at the signing of the Korean War Armistice in 1953, all the South Korean territory above this line was administered by North Korea. It was swapped for a nearly equal amount of land north of Seoul, below the 38th parallel, that now belongs to North Korea.

Yangyang International Airport
양양국제공항

Opened in 2002 just south of the town of Yangyang, this airport receives both domestic and international flights and has superseded the Sokcho Airport to become the predominant airport of the upper east coast area. Carved from seaside rolling hills, this airport handles larger aircraft and will hopefully be less affected by wind and fog than the old airport at Sokcho. Domestic flights from Yangyang go to Seoul Gimpo and Busan Gimhae airports. The airport is serviced by both Asiana Airlines (tel. 033/673-7700) and Korean Air (tel. 033/671-5858). International flights run from select cities in China but will probably open up to Japanese cities eventually. On the first level is check-in, information, and foreign currency exchange; boarding takes place on the upper level, domestic to the left, international to the right. Throughout the airport are all necessary and requisite amenities. As it's located outside of town, you must take a bus to get there unless you have a private vehicle. City buses run into town and then out to Osaek three times a day and up to Sokcho an additional seven times a day. Highway buses make a stop at the airport nine times a day, running north through Sokcho and going as far as the Unification Observation Area. The same number of buses heads south to Gangneung, Donghae, and Samcheok. Limousine buses also take passengers to various locations, including the Gangneung bus station (₩5,400) and the Gangneung train station (₩5,600).

Gangneung and the Coast

Gangneung [Kangnŭng] (강능), population 230,000, is the largest city on the east coast north of Pohang and historically its most vibrant city. During the Joseon Dynasty, Gangneung produced several famous intellectuals and influential families. Its many historical sites and nearby beaches, plus the nearby Odae-san National Park and Dragon Valley Ski Resort, now make Gangneung a tourist center. Gangneung is not only a cultural city but also an educational, commercial, and transportation center. Unlike other towns along this coast, it has no commercial port and is not an important fishing center. The post office, Telecom office, city hall, central market, and main entertainment area are all in the city's older section. Set between mountain and sea, the central market not only has the best produce from the fields, but also mountain vegetables and fish; next door, the dried-persimmon market is locally well-known, a perfect place to look for that delicious autumn fruit. The Dongbu market, a modern multistory affair, is found halfway between the city center and the train station in a newer part of town. The very helpful city tourist information center is located next to the bus terminals. Other tourist information booths can be found at the train station, at the entrance to Gyeongpo Beach, and at the Gangneung Airport.

See www.kangnung.kangwon.kr for information on the Internet.

SIGHTS
Old Buildings

Behind the post office is **Gaeksa-mun** (객사문). Erected in 936 as the front gate of a government rest house, this structure (N.T. #51) is one of

GANGWON-DO

GANGNEUNG

YONGJI-RO

FLAGPOLE SUPPORTS ★

DONGBU MARKET

TRAIN STATION

GANGNEUNG HYANGGYO ★

GYEONG-NO

OKGA-RO

HANSONG-NO

BANK ■

ASIANA AIRLINES ■

FLAGPOLE SUPPORTS ★

BANK ■

CENTRAL MARKET

Stream

HWABUSAN-NO

GAMNAMU-RO

TAESEONG-NO

JUNGANG-NO

GEUNSEONG-NO

IMYEONG-NO

HOTEL TONG-A ■

SEONGPO YEOGWAN ●

BANK ■

ROYAL HOTEL ●

0   300 yds
0   300 m

GAEKSA-MUN ★

POST OFFICE ■

BANK ■

CITY HALL ★

CHILSA-DANG ★

TELECOM ■

GANGNEUNG DANO GROUNDS

Namsan Park

Namdae-cheon

© AVALON TRAVEL PUBLISHING, INC.

SHINBOK-SAJI 卍

Inset map

East Sea

Gyeongpo-dae Beach

KYUNGPO BEACH HOTEL ●

HOTEL HYUNDAI GYEONGPODAE ★

Gangmun Beach

Gyeongpo

Songjeong Beach

Anmok Beach

Gyeongpo Lake

Provincial Park

Stream

GANGNEUNG AIRPORT ✈

To Donghae

7

To Sokcho

7

BANGHAE-JEONG ★

GYEONGPO-DAE PAVILION ★

HAEUNG-JEONG ★

SEON-GYO-JANG ★

OUK-HEON ★

Chodang-dong

CHOMSORI AUDIO MUSEUM ★

GANGNEUNG STADIUM ■

POLICE ■

KAL OFFICE ■

Namdae-cheon

Gangneung

MAP AREA

GANGNEUNG MUNICIPAL MUSEUM

GANGNEUNG NATIONAL UNIVERSITY

KANGNUNG TOURIST HOTEL ●

BUS TERMINALS ■

TOURIST INFORMATION CENTER ■

To Seoul and Daegwal-lyeong

DONGHAE EXPWY

YEONGDONG EXPWY

GWANGDONG UNIVERSITY ■

To Gulsan-saji

0   0.5 mi
0   0.5 km

the few such gates remaining in the country. Simple and unadorned, its slightly tapered persimmon-wood posts are capped with eave brackets and crossbeams which support the open rafters of the roof, which, unusually, has no upturn at the corners. The guesthouse that once occupied the grounds behind was used by officials visiting the province on government business. Once in

DANO FESTIVAL

Dano is the traditional spring agricultural festival, celebrated to insure a good farming year and bountiful harvest. Although celebrated throughout the country, the Gangneung *Dano* Festival (I.C.A. #13) is particularly well-known, and the country's largest traditional festival. Although most events take place during a five-day period both before and after the actual *Dano* holiday, which is the fifth day of the fifth lunar month (usually at the beginning of June), activity starts 45 days before that by making a "sacred drink," used later during the festival ceremonies. On the full-moon day of the fourth lunar month, a *gut* (shaman ceremony) is held at the Seonghwang-dang hall, high over the city about one kilometer up the mountain ridge from the Daegwal-lyeong. This ritual prayer, a carry-over from the strong agricultural and animist traditions of the past, honors Seonangshin, Beomil Guksa by name, the god who inhabits this pass and protects the people of the Yeongdong region. After the *gut,* Seonangshin is symbolically transported, in the guise of a maple branch, from Daegwal-lyeong to the city to preside over the festivities. *Dano* activities take place at various spots throughout the city and along the southern bank of Namdae-cheon, and include several ritual ceremonies for the peace and security of the local people and their homes, a parade, fireworks, the wordless *Gwanno* masked dance, Gangneung Nongak farmers' music and dance, the Haksan Odokttegi farmers' music, a *sijo* poetry contest, art exhibitions, and traditional sports and games like Korean wrestling and long rope swinging. Throughout the whole affair, entrepreneurs from all over the country gather along the river bank to sell their wares.

the 1400s, it was visited by King Gongmin, whose brush strokes of the gate's name were later carved into the name plaque.

A few steps from Gaeksa-mun and set under tall ginkgo trees is **Chilsa-dang** (칠사단), a fine example of a Joseon Dynasty city government office, appropriately standing within the Gangneung City Hall compound. Used during a great portion of the last dynasty, its intriguing design features a slightly raised rear portion of the main open porch floor, on which the most senior government official sat. Attached to the front of this building is a second-story enclosed veranda with removable windows. When not conducting business, the head official could relax here, or entertain friends while gazing out over the community. Chilsa-dang was refurbished in the early 1980s.

From the Goryeo Dynasty is the **Gangneung Hyanggyo** (강릉향교) and its shrine, Munmyo Daeseong-jeon (T. #214), which contains memorial tablets for Confucius and other sages. The shrine was erected in 1313, the *hyanggyo* added later. This school, one of the largest and best-kept in the country, was the training ground for many local Korean scholars, and Gangneung today continues this tradition of education. The school is arranged typically, with the shrine to the rear and lecture hall, library, and dormitories around the front courtyard. A stone-paved side courtyard is a unique feature. Having gone through several reconstructions over the centuries, this compound was last renovated in 1962. It is nearly identical to the Confucian shrine at Seonggyunwan University in Seoul, the center of Korean Confucianism, and, as there, the ritual ceremony *Seokjeon-je* is held here every spring and fall. North of the railroad tracks, this compound sits within the Myeongnyun school grounds.

Temple Sites and Stone Artifacts

South of the river and directly west of the Dong-hae Expressway is the former temple site **Shin-bok-saji** (신복사지). Two stone monuments remain at this once-grand Buddhist retreat: a well-proportioned three-tiered, double-base pagoda (T. #87) from the Goryeo Dynasty, and a skillfully carved seated figure (T. #84) from

N

GANGWON-DO

the same period. With right leg tucked underneath, and left leg forward and bent at the knee, the unusual seated position looks more offertory than meditative. The face bears an odd smirk, and its octagonal hat would be more appropriate topping a lantern. Except for the hat, it's almost identical in overall treatment to the seated stone bodhisattva figure facing the 13-tier pagoda at Woljeong-sa in Odae-san National Park, and its position in front of the pagoda is the same. While the overall designs of the pagodas themselves differ—this one being square and the Woljeong-sa pagoda octagonal—the base and roof sections of each have a distinct and similarly squat appearance.

Several kilometers farther down the road past Gwandong University, two other stone remains mark the site of **Gulsan-saji** (굴산사지). The granite *sari budo* (T. #85) here contains well-rendered fairy musicians carved on each of the granite block's eight sides, and numerous animal and floral representations. The somewhat misshapen flagpole supports (T. #86), said to be the largest in the country and marked with two sets of support holes, mark the front of the temple compound. One of the nine "Mountains" of Silla Zen Buddhism was founded here. At a stream nearby, "the virgin Moon is said to have drunk the water of the Sun and conceived Beomil Guksa." This relates to a legend in which a local virgin conceived and bore a son after drinking the water of the stream on which the sun had shown. Shocked and ashamed, her family forced her to abandon the child deep in the mountains. Unable to let go of the child, she returned the next day and found it still alive, nurtured by the animals. The child grew to become a respected monk, instructor of a king, and is said to have founded Gulsan-sa. After his death, his spirit inhabited Daegwal-lyeong Pass in protection of the people of Gangneung. Farther into the hills from here is the large two-story main hall of Beopwang-sa.

Near the mouth of the Namdae-cheon Stream close to the airport is a third temple site, at which the modern temple Hansong-sa has been built. Two seated marble Buddha statues from the United Silla period have been taken from this site and can be viewed at the Gangneung Municipal Museum. One is headless and missing its right arm (T. #81), the other, a better-preserved statue still with head intact (N.T. #124), has a depression in the forehead, presumably for a precious stone that's now missing.

Two pairs of Joseon Dynasty stone flagpole supports (T. #82, T. #83) stand rather unceremoniously in residential neighborhoods of the city. Although not much to look at in and of themselves, they are historically important for tracing the history of Korean Buddhist temples, and to have three pairs in such close proximity is a rarity since few still stand in the country. These supports are oblong carved stones set vertically into the ground and spaced to hold a tall metal pole between them, from which flags were flown or murals suspended. Fewer of the poles remain than the stones, as the metal probably was hauled off to be reused for other purposes. Not a common feature of temples today, they were an integral part of temples during the Silla and Goryeo dynasties.

Ojuk-heon 오죽헌

The most outstanding scholar/statesman from Gangneung is Yi Yul-gok (a.k.a. Yi Yi, 1536–84). He is considered one of Korea's two most important and influential Confucian scholars, the other being his contemporary and acquaintance, Yi Toe-gye. Precocious Yi Yul-gok could read and write Chinese characters at the age of three, and by seven could understand many of the writings of the great Confucian sages. At eight years old, he was taken to Paju, north of Seoul, to continue his study of the Confucian classics, as all male children of *yangban* families were expected to do. After studying and rejecting Buddhism, he met the elder Yi Toe-gye, who was to become his philosophical rival. Their different philosophies branched into the two major schools of Korean Neo-Confucian thought. After passing all government exams at the top rank, Yi Yul-gok held numerous high-level government posts, and was often squarely in the fray of political infighting. A man of foresight, Yi Yul-gok pressed unsuccessfully for the formation of a 10,000-man army for the defense of the country. Unfortunately, the Korean army was in a pitiful state of readiness when, only eight years after his death, the Japanese army ravaged the peninsula. Yi Yul-gok died at the age of 49, and is buried in Paju.

Three kilometers north of downtown Gangneung is **Ojuk-heon** [Ojuk-hŏn], Yi Yulgok's birthplace and his mother's family home. Shim Saimdang, the scholar's mother and early teacher, was a poet and intellectual in her own right, perhaps the most talented female artist of the entire Joseon Dynasty. Maintained by the family until 1975, Ojuk-heon (T. #165) was then taken over by the state and restored as a memorial to this pair. Two of the original household buildings have been rebuilt. One, Guga-ok, was used by the men of the family to entertain guests; the other, Mongnyong-shil ("Dragon Dream Room"), was the house in which Yi Yul-gok was born. It's so named for a dream Shim Saimdang had the night before she gave birth to Yi Yul-gok, in which a black dragon arose from the East Sea and entered the house with a child—dragons are considered auspicious by the Koreans, especially when appearing in dreams. Today, Mongnyong-shil enshrines a portrait of Shim Saimdang. Set on a higher terrace than Mongnyong-shil is Munseong-sa shrine. Built in 1789 as a memorial to Yi Yul-gok on orders from the king, it was rebuilt in 1976 and now houses a portrait of the scholar. To the rear of Mongnyong-shil is Eoje-gak, a small building set up in 1787 to house an inkstone used by Yi Yi and copies of his books, including one treatise on education (T. #602). Housing original paintings and written works of Yi Yulgok, Shim Saimdang, and other members of the family, the Yulgok Memorial exhibition hall stands below this small compound. Every year on October 26 the *Yulgok-je* commemorative ceremony is held at Ojuk-heon. It's a fine place to view this traditional ritual, listen to classical ceremonial music, attend a writing and speech contest, and see traditional clothing.

In separate but connected sections of Ojuk-heon are the **Gangneung Municipal Museum** and the **Folklore Pavilion**. The museum displays historical and archaeological objects from the city and surrounding Yeongdong region, while the focus of the folklore display is on articles of everyday life from the pre-modern era. Perhaps the most intriguing are the miniature dioramas of the Gangneung *Dano* Festival and a Gangneung farmers' dance troupe. It's worth a look. Open daily 0900–1800; there is a ₩1000 entrance fee.

Gyeongpo Provincial Park
경포도립공원

Across the highway and east of Ojuk-heon you'll find the nine-square-kilometer Gyeongpo [Kyŏngp'o] Provincial Park. Established in 1982, this park extends north from the mouth of the Namdae-cheon Stream nearly to Jumunjin, and pushes inland to encompass Gyeongpo Lake and the numerous old buildings that stand near it. The major attraction here is Gyeongpo-dae Beach, one of the country's longest. Basically, the entire seashore here is one long beach with several different names, according to the village that fronts its various sections. These beaches are full of swimmers during the heat of the summer, when there's also plenty of water sport equipment for rent, but nearly abandoned the rest of the year. Even in the off-season, the beach is fine for a stroll and reveals a wild and frothy character that's entirely different from its summer persona.

Four kilometers around—follow the bike path—**Gyeongpo Lake** is quite shallow; a small pavilion sits on the tiny island in its middle. Birds, migratory and permanent, are found mostly at the lake's quieter western end, part of which has been designated a migratory bird preserve. At the northern edge of the lake, near the beach, is a community of souvenir shops, restaurants, bike rental stands, a bus stop, and tourist information booth; around the corner are the post office and numerous accommodations. Stretching along the beach to the south is a long series of seafood restaurants, most of which nestle into the old pine grove that fronts the sea. Accommodations range from *minbak* to luxury hotels.

Along the road that leads away from the beach along the north side of the lake are several buildings of historical and cultural importance. **Banghae-jeong**, erected in 1859 by members of the Gangneung Yi family on the site of the former temple Inwol-sa, served as a gathering site for poets, calligraphers, and elders. A short distance away are a couple of traditional-style private houses with the small pavilions Geumnan-jeong, Sangnyeong-jeong, and Gyeongho-jeong between them.

On a knoll near the far end of Gyeongpo Lake is the pavilion **Gyeongpo-dae** (경포대); ₩600 entrance. Constructed in 1326 a short distance away at Inwol-sa temple site, it was moved to this scenic spot in 1508, rebuilt in 1873, and renovated in the 1970s. Many works of calligraphy, including one by Yi Yul-gok, hang in this finely designed structure. In the old days, *yangban* of the area (poets, calligraphers, and scholars) would gather here for good-humored banter and entertainment. They said that while sitting on the cool floor of this pavilion you can see five moons: the white orb in the sky, and its reflection in the sea, in the lake, off the wine in a wine cup, and in one's lover's eyes. Picturesque in all seasons, Gyeongpo-dae is perhaps best-dressed when the cherry trees push forth their blossoms and swath this hilltop in a robe of pink. Behind the pavilion stands a statue of Shim Saimdang, along with a memorial to Korean War dead.

Just past the Y intersection (both branches lead to the highway) is **Haeun-jeong** (해운정) (T. #183), a structure constructed in 1530 by Governor Shim Eon-gwang as his private quarters and study. In 1537, he received two Ming Chinese envoys here, one of whom wrote the calligraphy for the signboard that now graces this building. Haeun-jeong sits in a compact, walled compound, flanked by traditional-style houses, pine, maple, and persimmon trees, and stands of bamboo. Next door, the house of Shim Sang-jin is from 1530.

A few minutes farther west is **Seon'gyo-jang** [Sŏn'gyo-jang] (선교장); ₩1,000 entrance. This house of 99 *gan* was the maximum size allowed for any non-royal family. Seon'gyo-jang is one of a handful of *yangban* houses in the country still in such fine shape. It was built about 300 years ago by Yi Nae-in, a member of the Jeonju Yi family, from which the Joseon Dynasty kings came. Of traditional *yangban* style, it has separate compounds for the men and women of the household, and a long front of storage rooms and

servants' quarters split by the front gate. Most of the original house remains to this day; part of it is still occupied by the twelfth generation of its builder's family. About 6,000 family artifacts are stored in the house; the section open to visitors displays a fine collection of Joseon Dynasty furniture and kitchen equipment. Your best view of this country manor is from the low facing hill, above the scattered, thatch-roofed farmers' houses. To the front of Seon'gyo-jang is a square lotus pond, and partially extending out over the water is the pavilion Hwalle-jeong. Built in 1816, this little retreat must have been a perfect place to spend a hot summer afternoon. Today, you can still appreciate the beauty of the pond and try to imagine the life of nobility by treating yourself to a traditional meal and beverage in one of the restaurants on the far side of the pond. An exhibition hall stands to the front of Seon'gyo-jang, displaying period clothes and accessories from the last dynasty. Seon'gyo-jang and Haeun-jeong were once at the edge of Gyeongpo Lake, but over the past several centuries the lake has silted up and shrunk in size.

Other Sights

The village of **Chodang-dong** (초당동), close to the seashore, has traditionally produced an unusual form of *dubu* (tofu), made with fresh saltwater. This protein-rich food can be tasted here or at many restaurants near Gyeongpo Beach. Chodang-dong is also the home of Heo Gyun, the Joseon Dynasty author of the novel *Honggildong-jeon,* about a man who espoused an egalitarian social philosophy that ran counter to the strict social structure and Confucian values of the time. He wrote against the misuse of power and the exploitation of the lower classes by the nobility, and said that when needed the peasants could and should rise up against those in control of their lives. In essence, he campaigned for the dignity of the common man and equal opportunity among men. Every year in April, the *Gangmun Jinttobaegi* ritual is held near this village to protect it from harm. Central to this ritual are tall slender poles, on top of which are set three simplistically carved duck figures.

Another nearby sight, the **Chomsori Audio**

Museum (춤소리박물관), was opened in 1992 south of Chodang Village. An intriguing oddity, it's the only museum of its kind in Korea. It displays about 1,500 gramophones and phonographs, and preserves nearly 100,000 record albums and 2,000 music-related pieces of literature gathered from 17 countries around the world. Within the collection is an original 1899 Edison gramophone and a cylindrical music box from 1796. Aimed at presenting the development of this old-style audio equipment, it also seeks to protect old audio recordings and offers a brief early audio history. It's a delightful experience for the audiophile. Open 0900–1800 (0930 –1700 in winter); entrance is ₩3,500.

Located along the highway just below the pass west of the city is Gangneung's third museum, **Daegwallyeong Museum** (대관령박물관). Open 1000–1800, with a ₩2,500 entrance fee, this museum displays over 2,000 cultural artifacts from the region, including Buddhist religious art and prehistoric objects. Fitting nicely into the fold of the mountain, this building has a shape reminiscent of a stone-slab dolmen. Used as a rest stop for travelers, the restaurant serves hot meals.

A yearly **Daegwallyeong Snowflake Festival** takes place on the pass when snow blankets this area. Among the many events are snowmen-building contests, sledding, snow and ice sculpture, outdoor barbecue, and a snowflake queen pageant.

Coastal Sights

An unusual feature has popped up along the coast in the past several years, and this is the number of ships and structures that are built to look like ships that occupy spots along the waters edge. The real ships are displays, while the rest are either restaurants or accommodations. Some are set incongruously high on hills where a ship could never sail, others are closer to the water. Near Jeongdongjin, south of the city center and where the railroad tracks run right along the beach, are two of these "ships." A "Sunrise Park" and sculpture park occupy a spot next to them. A couple of kilometers north of there is a South Korean Navy vessel. Pulled up on shore next to it,

and also set up for display, is a captured North Korean infiltration submarine.

GANGNEUNG PRACTICALITIES
Accommodations

The best hotel in town is out at Gyeongpo-dae Beach. The deluxe-class **Hotel Hyundai Gyeongpodae** (tel. 033/651-2233, www.hyundaihotel.com) has rooms in the ₩180,000–220,000 range with suites from ₩280,000. Almost next door is the first-class **Kyungpo Beach Hotel** (tel. 033/644-2277, www.kyungpobeach.co.kr), where rooms run ₩112,000–300,000. Each has restaurants, a coffee shop, and a souvenir shop, while the Hyundai has a shopping arcade. Located east of the train station, the first-class **Kangnung Tourist Hotel** (tel. 033/641-3971) has rooms in the ₩110,000–120,000 range. In the center of town are the non-registered **Royal Hotel** (로얄장 호텔) and Hotel Tong-A (호텔동아), with rooms around ₩30,000–45,000.

Numerous less expensive *yeogwan* and *minbak* are also located along Gyeongpo Beach. Two of these are the **Meridian Motel** (메르디안모텔), at the north end around the corner from the post office, and the **Seoil Motel** (서일모텔), located behind the Hyundai Hotel. Expect room rates in the ₩30,000–40,000 range in summer, but reduced rates the rest of the year. In town, *yeogwan* can be found near the Royal and Tong-A hotels; try the **Seongpo Yeogwan** (성포여관) for starters. More accommodations are concentrated along the streets that run diagonally up toward the train station. While there are not many yet, more accommodations will eventually pop up near the new bus terminals on the west side of town.

Transportation

Gangneung is the major transportation hub on the east coast of Gangwon-Do. It's the eastern terminus of the Yeongdong rail line that runs over the Taebaek Mountains from the west and connects Seoul to the east coast. The Yeongdong Expressway traverses Daegwal-lyeong pass, highest in the range at 832 meters, from which it makes 99 turns on its twisting route down the mountainside to Gangneung; when going east by bus, sit on the right side for best views. The section of this expressway from Hoenggye, just west of the pass, to the city is being rerouted, so there will be fewer turns and more tunnels in the future. The Donghae Expressway continues south from Gangneung to Donghae, from where the coastal highway carries on down the coast to Pohang. Running north, this expressway goes to Jumunjin; an extension north to Sokcho is in the works.

Both Asiana and KAL have flights from Gangneung to Seoul; in addition, Asiana flies once a day between Gangneung and Busan. Get tickets and information at the airport, or from either airline office in the city: Asiana (tel. 033/643-9568), KAL (tel. 033/653-2004). Set along the seashore to the east of downtown, the small Gangneung airport can be reached in 20 minutes by city bus or in 15 minutes by taxi (₩5,000).

Seven daily trains run from Gangneung to Seoul Cheongnyangni Station. One *Saemaul-ho* (₩24,700) and five *Mugunghwa-ho* (₩17,000) trains make day trips via Yeongwol, and the one *Mugunghwa-ho* night train (₩19,500) runs via Yeongju. Aside from these, two daily *Mugunghwa-ho* trains run to Dong Daegu (₩16,700) and one to Busan (₩23,600). Intermediate stops and fares are Taebaek (₩5,200), Wonju (₩11,900), Andong (₩10,900), and Gyeongju (₩17,200).

The express and intercity bus terminals are located next to each other on the west side of the city. Express buses run every 15 minutes to the Seoul Express Bus Terminal (₩10,000), every 45 minutes to the Tong Seoul Bus Terminal (₩10,000), and about every hour to Wonju (₩5,400) and Daejeon (₩11,800). Intercity buses run up and down the east coast, and to all major cities in the province. Selected destinations and fares are: Sokcho (₩4,900), Chuncheon (₩12,000), Wonju (₩5,400), Jinbu (₩2,800), Donghae (₩2,400), Taebaek (₩7,400), and Pohang (₩17,300).

City buses of use are no. 7-7 to Sogeumgang; nos. 9, 10, and 19-7 to Ojuk-heon, Seon'gyojang, Haeun-jeong, Gyeongpo-dae, and Gyeongpo-dae Beach; no. 25 to city hall and the Daegwal-lyeong Museum; no. 28 to the airport; nos. 9, 21, and 48 to Chamsori Audio Museum; no. 31 to Jumunjin; nos. 11 and 12 to Jeongdongjin; no. 22 to Shinbok-saji; nos. 7-7, 9, 10, 11, 21, and 31 to the train station; and nos. 7-7, 15, 19-7, 21, 28, 35, and 48 between the bus station and city center.

During winter ski season, various tour companies run buses to the Dragon Valley Ski Resort, leaving early in the morning and returning in the early evening. These companies usually advertise and leave from near the bus terminals—make your reservation at least a day ahead. If you have a reservation at the Dragon Valley Hotel, you can take their free shuttle bus from the airport. No public transportation runs from Gangneung directly to the ski resort, but you can take an intercity bus to Hoenggye and from there get a taxi to the ski slope, or take one of the hourly shuttle buses for the 30-minute ride to the resort.

ODAE-SAN NATIONAL PARK
오대산국립공원

West of Gangneung, encompassing 298 square kilometers of the high Taebaek Range, is Odaesan National Park. At 185 square kilometers, the western and larger section is characterized by rounded peaks, waves of ridges, and fold after fold of hills and valleys. Rising less precipitously than Seorak-san, its hoary head thickly covered with pristine forests, Odae-san appears more aged. Broad and comely, this mountain is shapely but not overwhelmingly beautiful, and one of its streams turns into the south branch of the Han River. The highest peaks of Odae-san all rise to over 1,400 meters and together form a "U" shape; the highest, at 1,563 meters, is Birobong. Meaning "Five Terrace Mountain," Odaesan was once an isolated meditation retreat, and its old temples and many famous monks have been intimately linked with the propagation of Zen Buddhism in Korea. The Charyeong Range branches off from here and runs southwest to the coast of Chuncheongnam-Do.

In the park's central valley are two major temples, Woljeong-sa and Sangwon-sa, and five hermitages (perhaps a carryover of the "five terraces"

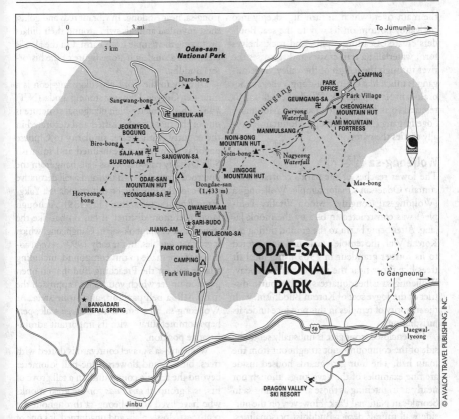

of ancient times). A road through this valley connects the two temples to the park entrance; from this road, short paths lead to the hermitages. Hiking trails run farther up into the hills, but fewer here than in most other mountain parks of Korea. Generally gentle and easy to follow, these trails lead through a blanket of fir, sugar pine, Mongolian oak, birch, and flowering rhododendron. One of the few such large stands of fir in the country, many of these trees are over 600 years old. Odae-san is especially known for wild boar and *sansam,* a wild variety of *insam* (ginseng) that's very rare, extremely difficult to find, and valuable; you may see villagers out on the hillsides searching for it. This elusive wonderroot can live to great age—some has been found to be over 100 years old. Special curative attributes are also associated with the clear, cold streams of Odae-san, and its water has drawn at least one Joseon Dynasty king for treatment. King Sukjong came to Bangadari mineral spring to be cured of a skin disease. Today, most people come only to drink its mineral-rich water.

East of the park's major valley, rising above the highway that splits the park in two and connects Jinbu to Jumunjin, is 1,338-meter Noinbong. This peak anchors the upper end of **Sogeumgang** [Sogŭmgang], the second and smaller section of the park. Sogeumgang is the antithesis of the western half of this park. It's deeply gouged and ruggedly sculpted, a tight gorge of craggy bluffs, precipitous cliffs, oddshaped pinnacles, and exposed rock outcrops. Streams rush down the steep side valleys into the main river, which in turn digs deeply into the valley bottom on its way to the sea. Boulders create cascading rapids, and rock shelves form waterfalls; a trail crosses and recrosses the river through the length of the valley. Sogeumgang is much like Cheonbul-dong Valley, in Seorak-san National Park. While Seorak-san is referred to as a miniature Diamond Mountain, Sogeumgang (Little Diamond Mountain) actually carries the name.

Woljeong-sa 월정사

The lower reaches of the park's central valley contain Odae-san's major temple. Woljeong-sa [Woljŏng-sa] (roughly, "Moon Vitality Temple") was constructed in 645 by the monk Jajang. After being burnt to the ground during the Korean War, the temple's main hall was restored to its former grandeur in 1969 using local fir trees like those near the park entrance. Today, Woljeong-sa is headquarters of the fourth district of the Jogye sect of Korean Buddhism, with the majority of temples in this province under its jurisdiction.

The enclosed front gate is unusually set to the side of the compound, not straight out from the main hall. The four gate guards housed inside are fine examples of the deva kings, though not nearly as frightening as those at Shinheung-sa in Seorak-san National Park. However, on the outside wall murals depict Buddhist personalities, including the first Patriarch of Buddhism, the bug-eyed Bodhidharma. He's shown walking on water, a symbolic portrayal of the transference of Buddhist doctrine from India to China. Also rendered on these walls are Hui-neung, the sixth Patriarch of Buddhism, and the two "crazies" of Buddhism, who wander through life laughing at the inanities and absurdities of worldly existence and reacting hilariously to the excessive importance that most humans give their earthly life.

Jeokkwang-jeon, Woljeong-sa's main hall, dominates the courtyard. This large hall is brightly painted inside and out; suspended high above the altar are carved wooden birds. To either side of the altar stand lavishly detailed "dragon pillars." Seldom seen, they are similar but newer versions of the much-faded pair in the main hall of Bong-

jeong-sa, near Andong. In vibrant reds and golds, these mythical animals swirl around their pillars protecting the temple from harm. On the altar is enshrined a single gilt stone figure of the historical Buddha.

Directly to the front of Jeokgwang-jeon is a nine-tier Goryeo Dynasty stone pagoda (N.T. #48). This 15-meter-high octagonal structure is one of the most finely crafted and decorated in the country, with greater similarity to Chinese pagodas than to the clean-lined and squarish Silla Dynasty pagodas. Brass bells hang from the upturned corners of each tier, and a tall decorative finial caps the top. Facing this pagoda is a Yakgwang Bodhisattva statue (T. #139). Although larger and more distinct, it has no hat like the stone statue of Shinbok-saji in Gangneung, which it greatly resembles. In the early 1990s, several additions were made to this compound, including a large hall for the Preaching Buddha, an open pavilion under which you walk to approach the main hall, a bell pavilion, and stone stela. At Woljeong-sa, all seems to be of large scale, perhaps commensurate with its important administrative position.

Woljeong-sa's gravel courtyard is dotted with trees, bushes, and flowers. One-half kilometer beyond the temple compound, in a tall grove of firs, is a group of *sari budo* for the great monks who have lived at Woljeong-sa throughout the centuries. Mostly plain and unadorned, it's one of the most comely collections of these stone monuments in the country.

Sangwon-sa 상원사

Seven kilometers up the valley from Woljeong-sa is Sangwon-sa. The bus stop here is the end of the line from Jinbu. Sangwon-sa, a Zen meditation temple, roughly translates as "Above the Ordinary," referring to its physical location and spiritual goals. Built about the same time as Woljeong-sa, again by Jajang, it astonishingly escaped destruction during the Korean War. The main hall is not typical in design. Built in an L shape, the short leg of which has a lower level, this building combines an austere altar room, dormitory, and other rooms under one roof. A gilt wood statue of Munsu Bosal, the Buddha of Essential

Wisdom, is enshrined on its altar. The second statue on the altar (N.T. #221), the smaller figure with black hair, represents the child aspect of Munsu Bosal. This hollow wood statue revealed over two dozen written scriptures and other records hidden inside when it was examined in 1984. These objects have been designated T. #793. Of greatest importance here is the temple bell (N.T. #36). Cast in 725, this bell is the oldest of only three remaining bells from the Silla Dynasty in the country; the others are displayed at the Gyeongju National Museum and the Gongju National Museum. Over the centuries, several others have been taken to Japan. Originally the city bell of Andong, this bell has been at Sangwon-sa since 1469. Nearly two meters high and one across, it weighs about 1,200 kg. Slightly potbellied, it has the same pleasing form as other bells from the Silla and Goryeo dynasties.

Hermitages and Shrine

Each of the five hermitages has been given a cardinal point: Mireuk-am (north), Jijang-am (south), Gwaneum-am (east), Sujeong-am (west), and Saja-am (center). Since these hermitages are used by monks practicing meditation, approach quietly and respectfully if you visit! The small temple Yeonggam-sa is up a short path on the west side of the road, halfway between Woljeong-sa and Sangwon-sa. Near here is a rebuilt two-story storehouse once used for Joseon Dynasty government records. One of five in the country, this one was first erected in 1606, destroyed during the Korean War, and rebuilt in 1989. While nothing is kept here now, this building represents the effort through which the old administration attempted to keep its history alive.

High above Saja-am is **Jeokmyeol Bogung** [Chŏkmyŏl Pogung], one of the country's five shrines said to be repositories of some calcified remains of the historical Buddha, brought back from China by Jajang. A mystique surrounds these relics akin to that which embraces the sacred tooth of Buddha enshrined at the Temple of the Tooth in Kandy, Sri Lanka, and the reverence of Westerners who claim to have a piece of the cross on which Christ was crucified. Jeokmyeol Bogung is only open for viewing when prayers are

conducted. Inside this well-kept structure sits an elaborate altar with an empty pillow, symbolizing the departed Buddha.

Hiking

Aside from the short and leisurely walks to Jijang-am and Gwaneum-am, the only well-used trail in the main valley leads up to and around its U-shaped ridge. From Sangwon-sa, a 40-minute walk brings you to Jeokmyeol Bogung, and another hour to Biro-bong. An alternate route to the summit runs via Sujeong-am, where you continue up to the main ridge, turn right, and follow the path to the top. From Biro-bong, it's possible to see a great portion of this park. The

SURVIVAL OF SANGWON-SA

During the Korean War, a tremendous number of structures in the country were destroyed, not only in the cities but also in the countryside and deep in the mountains. By luck or some odd turn of events, some, however, did survive. Sangwon-sa, in Odae-san National Park, was one of the lucky ones. One rendition of its survival is paraphrased as follows, and I'm grateful to Brian Zigmark for this information.

During the war, retreating South Korean troops destroyed as many buildings as possible to deny the advancing North Korean troops any place to stay and hide. The officer in charge of the operation in this valley ordered a lieutenant and his men to burn all the temple buildings here, which they did until they got to Sangwon-sa. There, the head abbot, sitting in meditation in the main hall, refused to leave the building in protest. Relating all this to his senior officer, the lieutenant was told to destroy the building, monk or not. Unable to follow the orders, the lieutenant removed and set fire to all the windows and doors of the temple instead, making it look to those in charge as if the whole compound were aflame. Some days later, the abbot died of old age while still sitting in meditation in the main hall, and the senior officer was killed in a helicopter crash while leaving the valley. The lieutenant survived the war.

GANGWON-DO

© ROBERT NILSEN

hikers on the trail in Sogeumgang

trail is fairly level from here to Sangwang-bong, but it dips down to the pass where the mountain road crosses into the outer valley, and then rises again to Duro-bong at the top of the valley. It runs through scrub bush and low trees much of its length, and in some sections is rather indistinct. Allow about 2.5 hours to reach Duro-bong from Biro-bong. Most hikers return down the ridge to the road, and from there to Mireuk-am before returning to Sangwon-sa or the Odae-san mountain hut. A lesser-used three-hour trail continues south along the ridge from Duro-bong to Dongdae-san, and from there down to the hut. For those intending to hike the entire ridge trail in one day, it's best to stay at the Odae-san mountain hut. No matter which trail you try, bring plenty of water as there is little along the way.

The park's second major trail takes you to Sogeumgang. The path from the Odae-san hut to Dongdae-san is in good condition, and the views from the top are expansive. From here, you can see the trail go down into the next valley, cross the road, and make its gradual climb up the opposite

side to Noin-bong, a three-hour hike. On the pass near the road is the Jingoge mountain hut. At Noin-bong, where there is yet another mountain hut, Sogeumgang is literally at your feet. From here, you can look out to sea, up the mountain range to Seorak-san, and down to Taebaek-san. From Noin-bong, one trail runs along the southern ridge of the Sogeumgang Valley to Mae-bong, where it turns south and continues on to Daegwal-lyeong, a hike of about seven hours. From this ridge trail, at least five others drop into the Sogeumgang Valley. However, the main and most-frequented route into the valley takes you a few hundred meters north of Noin-bong, and then *steeply* down to Nagyeong Waterfall. More often than not, the Sogeumgang Valley is hiked from the bottom up.

The Sogeumgang (소금강) trailhead is best reached by bus from Gangneung or Jumunjin. From the end of the bus line and park village, the valley trail runs up along the stream past the Cheonghak mountain hut and two T-shaped pools to **Geumgang-sa** (금강사), the valley's only temple. The main hall at this temple has been completely rebuilt and now sports a shiny copper-tile roof. Above Geumgang-sa are a flat rock slab that's fine for a picnic and a waterfall, and above those is **Guryong ("Nine Dragons") Waterfall**, a series of nine falls, that slithers down an abrupt side valley under a canopy of green foliage. High on the hill above and on the opposite side of the valley from Geumgang-sa lie the remains of the Ami mountain fortress, to which "the last crown prince of the Silla Kingdom is said to have retreated and mourned the fall of his country." The valley narrows to a deep gorge with many pools and scoured riverside rock flats. In this ravine are many rock outcrops; the most interesting is Manmulsang, a huge rock that from one angle resembles a human head. Through the remainder of the valley, the trail crosses and recrosses the river, passing at least three other waterfalls. The scenery in Sogeumgang is nearly as spectacular as that in the Cheonbul-dong Valley of Seorak-san; beautiful sights are hidden here and there throughout its length, and additional waterfalls, pools, and rock outcrops grace the side valleys. Its powerful river, piles of boulders, and blanket of pines and hardwoods make Sogeumgang an attractive hiking area, extremely different from the more open western half of this park.

Practicalities

The park entrance fee is ₩2,800 below Woljeong-sa and ₩1,300 at Sogeumgang. Small tourist villages at both park entrances have multiple *yeogwan,* restaurants, and shops for supplies. The large **Hotel Odaesan** (tel. 033/330-5000), about four kilometers below the Woljeong-sa park entrance, is by far the most luxurious in the area. The park's four spartan mountain huts have spaces for ₩3,000 per night per person—bring your own sleeping bag, stove, and food.

Numerous daily buses from Gangneung (₩2,800) and Wonju (₩4,400) run to Jinbu [Chinbu], from where you can take a city bus to Woljeong-sa (₩800) or all the way to Sangwon-sa (₩1,500). The buses to Woljeong-sa go about once every hour from Jinbu. A few in the morning and evening go all the way to Sangwon-sa, except on weekends and holidays, when they all seem to go that far. Every 30–60 minutes, Gangneung city bus no. 7-7 (₩2,000) runs to the Sogeumgang entrance. A few daily city buses run from Jumunjin over the Jingoge Pass to the Woljeong-sa park entrance and on to Jinbu, making a much shorter and quicker route between the halves of the park than going the roundabout way through Gangneung as you used to have to do.

DRAGON VALLEY SKI RESORT
용평리조트

South of Odae-san National Park and west of Daegwal-lyeong Pass is a high plateau. Near the town of Hoenggye (횡계) on this upland plain are several dairy farms, livestock ranches, and cool-weather vegetable farms. Six kilometers south of Hoenggye, at 750 meters, is Yongpyong Ski Resort, otherwise known as Dragon Valley Ski Resort (tel. 033/335-5757, 02/561-6255 in Seoul, www .yongpyong.co.kr), the first (1975), largest, and most developed in Korea. Lying below Balwang-san (1,458 meters), this resort has 14 lifts

and one gondola for its 24 slopes, the longest of which is 1,700 meters; more than 11 kilometers of cross country ski trails; and an indoor ice rink. The gondola offers a long ride of nearly four kilometers from the bottom of the hill to the peak, where you get an excellent view of the Seorak-san area and down to the sea. Ski equipment can be rented for ₩25,000 per day; adult, full-day lift tickets for weekdays are ₩55,000; they increase to ₩61,000 on the weekend. The ski season lasts from late November to late March. Snowmaking machines ensure adequate cover, but this region naturally receives a great deal of snow. An annual **Snow Festival** is held in January; a snow-sculpture contest is one of the highlights. An **International Ski Festival** takes place in February, with competition open to all resident foreigners in Korea. A year-round resort, Dragon Valley also has other activities available like bowling, racquetball, golf, tennis, archery, indoor swimming, an exercise gym, and sauna. To its credit, and showing to what caliber it has developed, Dragon Valley Ski Resort has held the International Alpine Ski Games every year since 1991, the World Cup Alpine Ski Games in 1998 and 2000, and the 4th Winter Asian Games in 1999.

At the bottom of the slopes, the deluxe-class **Dragon Valley Tourist Hotel** (tel. 033/335-5757) doubles as the chalet. Rooms start at ₩170,000 and go up to ₩330,000. It offers Korean, Western, and Chinese restaurants, a coffee shop, cocktail lounge, nightclub, sauna, health club, souvenir shop, and game room. Major credit cards are accepted, and foreign currency is exchanged. English and Japanese are spoken. Across the parking lot is the less expensive **Yongpyong Hostel** (tel. 033/335-5757), with *ondol* rooms for ₩45,000 and bunk space for ₩9,000 a person. Down the road are condominiums with units that run about the same as the hotel. The Valley Center has restaurants, shops, a game room, and a nightclub. The closest *yeogwan* and *yeoinsuk* are in Hoenggye.

To get to Dragon Valley Ski Resort, first take an intercity bus from Gangneung, Wonju, or Seoul to Hoenggye. From there, take a taxi or one of the numerous daily shuttle buses that operate during the ski season. Alternate methods during ski season include tour-company buses from Gangneung and Seoul. Round-trip buses from Seoul run ₩24,000. Contact Lotte Travel (tel. 02/733-0201) or Dae Won Express Tour (02/2201-7710).

DONGHAE 동해

Donghae [Tonghae] was created in 1980, combining the old port towns of Mukho and Bukpyeong with the surrounding residential and industrial areas. Hugging the coast, with mountains rising to the west, it stretches south to Samcheok, and, like that city, is a major domestic and international shipping center for all sorts of goods, particularly cement. Of the few sites in the city, perhaps the best known is **Cheon'gok Cave**. Discovered in 1991, and now with 700 meters open to public, it is the only cave in the country that's so close to a city center. Find it by walking 10 minutes up from the bus terminal and then turning toward the ocean from the sports stadium. Donghae is a city of high-rise apartments and burgeoning commercial sectors—not a very good-looking place. Showing its youthful strength, it has an eye on the future. It offers urban amenities, and is well-located on the Yeongdong rail line and the coastal highway, providing good transportation connections up and down the coast and into the interior. Express buses from Donghae run to the Seoul and Dong Seoul terminals (both ₩11,700). Selected intercity-bus destinations and fares are Gangneung (₩2,400), Samcheok (₩1,000), and Taebaek (₩5,000).

The old port of **Mukho** (묵호), at Donghae's northern end, is a busy fishing port and departure point for a catamaran passenger ferry to Ulleung-do. Requiring only 2.5 hours to cross, these ferries run every weekday at 1100. During the height of the summer holiday season, from mid-July to mid-August, they leave twice a day at 0930 and 1730. Adult tickets run ₩34,000. There is no city bus to the ferry terminal, which has moved to the south end of this harbor. From the train station or the main street, it's about one kilometer around the cement company's

port facility to the terminal. Buses let you off along the highway, where there is a shorter walk down the hill to the pier. City bus nos. 11, 12, and 22 run to Mukho from the bus terminal in Donghae.

For further information, see the website www.donghae.gangwon.kr.

Mureung Valley 무릉개곡

The major point of natural interest in the vicinity is the beautiful Mureung [Murŭng] Valley, located almost directly west of the city. While fetching and worth the effort to visit, you'd never know it from the ride up as the road passes a huge and ugly cement plant. City bus no. 11 or 81 (₩800) to Samhwa-dong brings you to this valley park; ₩1,000 entrance. Here you'll find a community of shops, simple accommodations, and a restaurant whose specialty is raw fish and a type of chicken soup. Less than one kilometer up from the park entrance, the river slips over a huge expanse of slab granite. In one section of this broad rock bed, large Chinese characters have been carved into the stone—characters of a poem from the 1570s. Just beyond this favorite picnic spot is **Samhwa-sa**, the valley's principal temple. This temple has had much reconstruction in recent years and now has several new buildings and a standing Buddha statue. Set high on an upper terrace, the main hall contains a seated iron Vairocana Buddha (T. #1292); in the courtyard to the front is a three-tier stone pagoda (T. #1277). Above Samhwa-sa, the main valley becomes more scenic, with waterfalls, pools, and numerous cascades; side valleys can also be explored. Three kilometers up the main valley is **Yongchu Waterfall**, perhaps the best in the area and the goal for most hikers. This short double falls tumbles through a deep cut in the granite and drops into a nice pool. Just below it is Ssang Waterfall, or Twin Waterfall, and just below that is Seonnyeotang Pool, a deep split in a huge rock. Above the valley to the south lie the stone remains of a two-kilometer-long fortress wall said to have been built about 1,000 years ago, rebuilt in 1414, and used by local residents for refuge in 1592, when the region was overrun by the Japanese during their invasion of the peninsula. These valleys and hills contain many hiking trails—all long and requiring the better part of a day.

SAMCHEOK 삼척

Samcheok [Samch'ŏk] is the southernmost of Gangwon-Do's coastal cities. It's a loosely cohesive community made up of fishing village, business center, and industrial/harbor districts. Coal mining in the area started in the 1930s, limestone and zinc extraction more recently. Although this was the site of one of the first *yeontan* factories in the country, these pressed-coal briquettes and coal in general are now a much smaller piece of the city's economic pie. One of the few cities in the province with an adequate harbor, its facilities are being surpassed by the growing port at Donghae just up the coast. While the harbor area is about two kilometers from the center of the city, the rest of Samcheok is easy to navigate on foot. The bus terminal is at the southern end of town. A short distance away, in the heart of the old center of the community, is the central market—most accommodations cluster nearby. Express buses run only to the Seoul and Tong Seoul terminals (both ₩12,300). Selected intercity-bus destinations and fares are: Donghae (₩1,000), Gangneung (₩3,400), Taebaek (₩4,000), and Uljin (₩5,100).

In the hills west of town is **Hwanseon Cave** [Hwasŏn] (N.M. #178); ₩4,500 entrance. At over 6 kilometers in length, it's supposedly the longest known limestone cave in the country. This cave has stalagmites, stalactites, and nearly a dozen pools, and the largest chamber is about 40 meters long. Inside it stays a constant 11°C year-round. The cave is encompassed by Daei-ri County park, and you can also see traditional-style wood shingle and wood-bark houses and a water mill here.

For additional information about the city, see www.samcheok.go.kr.

Jukseo-ru 죽서루

The most important historical site in town is Jukseo-ru [Chuksŏ-ru] ("Bamboo West Pavilion"); ₩550 entrance. Originally built in 1275, the present structure (T. #213) dates from 1403. This building has the most unusual construction. All 17 pillars supporting its floor are set on individual boulders at different heights. Twenty posts support the long roof—the three extra end posts sit directly on a huge boulder without supporting pillars. Jukseo-ru is perched at the edge of a bluff overlooking the Oship-cheon Stream. Facing west, you once had a wonderful view of the sun setting into the distant mountains, but now the opposite side of the river has a landscaped bank and buildings of the Cave EXPO site. A small folk museum within the pavilion compound contains a few hundred historical artifacts from the region, mostly pottery, paintings, writings, and tools of everyday life. Every year in February, the **Jukseo Festival** is held here to celebrate the area's unique cultural traditions.

GANGWON-DO

Southern Gangwon-Do

Like the rest of the province, southern Gangwon-Do is a rugged, mountainous region. It occupies large tracts of the Taebaek, Sobaek, and Charyeong mountain ranges. Wonju is situated in the far western corner, and Taebaek city occupies a relatively high-elevation, mid-mountain location. Smaller towns are dotted here and there throughout the mountains but are widely dispersed. Outside of Wonju and Yeongwol, little of national historical or cultural importance has taken place in this mountain region. Although picturesque in sections, much of the area was badly denuded from overcutting. To its credit, the national government has promoted a widespread program of reforestation since the 1960s, not only here but throughout the rest of the country, in an effort to re-green its mountains and provide wood products for the future. It shows, as the hills once again hold a mantle of trees. Sizable coal deposits in these mountains have spawned the country's largest concentration of mines. Anthracite coal is dug in huge quantities, and from the mine entrances grow ever-enlarging heaps of slag. Dusty trails lead from mine to town, where huge piles of coal stand at railside loading stations. Many towns and villages in the area are bathed in coal black; only the shiny rail line stands out against this bleak landscape. You'll see evidence of this activity when you travel through the area, particularly within the triangle bounded by Taebaek, Yeongwol, and Gujeol-li, but during the last several decades this activity has shrunk and the number of mines has grown smaller due to a greater dependence on other fossil fuels and nuclear energy.

TAEBAEK 태백

Like Donghae, Taebaek [T'aebaek] is a rather new designation—it combines the town of Hwangji with the surrounding communities, and extends as far as Taebaek-san. With just over 54,000 inhabitants, it has the smallest city populations in the country. Of these cities, Taebaek has the highest elevation, and Chujeon Station, one stop west of Taebaek Station, is the highest railway station in the country at 855 meters. Within the city limits are **Geomyongso Pond** (검룡소꽃), the source of the south branch of the Han River, and **Hwangji Pond** (황지연), headwaters of the Nakdong River. These are the two longest rivers in South Korea, the Han running 514 kilometers west across the waist of the peninsula, emptying into the West Sea, and the Nakdong heading south by a circuitous route, meeting the sea west of Busan after 525 kilometers. While Hwangji Pond lies smack-dab in the middle of town, Geomyongso is a few kilometers north of the city center; take bus no. 50. A coaling center, Taebaek is not an attractive city, yet it has all the necessary amenities and travel connections. In an effort to boost its image, attract winter visitors, and highlight the area's winter recreational potential, the city holds the annual **Mt. Taebaek Snow Festival** in February. Taking place at several locations around town and at the provincial park, events include a snow-sculpture contest, sledding contest, winter mountaineering activities, a Miss Snowflake pageant, and a national photo exhibition.

While the train and bus terminals are side-by-side at the north end of town, the post office, Telecom office, banks, accommodations, and restaurants are all located down the main drag of this long and narrow community. For starters, try the Meridian Hotel in the middle of town, where rooms are ₩40,000–60,000, or either the nearby Saeseouljang Yeogwan (세서울장여관) or Alpsjang (일프스장). Closer to the train station, look for the Seongnimjang Yeogwan (성림장여관) and Yonghae Yeoinsuk (용해여인숙). Other *yeogwan* and *minbak* can be found at the Taebaek-san Provincial Park village. From Donghae, a handful of daily trains run to the east down to Gangneung and west to Jecheon and Seoul Cheongnyangni. While there are no express buses from Taebaek, selected intercity-bus destinations and fares are: Gangneung (₩7,400),

Donghae (₩5,000), Jeongseon (₩4,700), Yeongwol (₩6,600), Wonju (₩12,400), and Yeongju (₩8,500).

See www.taebaek.go.kr for information on the Internet.

Taebaek-san Provincial Park
태백산도립공원

For most, Taebaek city's main function is as the gateway to Taebaek-san Provincial Park. Created in 1989, this park encompasses the Taebaek Mountains' highest peaks and their northern slopes; to the south it touches Gyeongsangbuk-Do. Within its borders are fine streams, broad mountain shoulders, 1,000-year-old trees, a mountaintop altar, four Buddhist temples, a shrine to Dan'gun, a cave, and a coal museum. It's considered one of the three sacred mountains in Korea; records indicate that since the Three Kingdoms period (pre-600s) religious ceremonies and offerings have been held in the autumn at Cheonje-dan altar, near the summit, to honor Dan'gun, the mythical founder of the Korean people. Commanding a high spot in this range, Taebaek-san has strength in its breadth, grandeur in its expansive embrace, and the dignity of age-old trees. From the top you can see the east coast, the Taebaek Mountain Range as it runs north and south paralleling the coast, and the Sobaek Mountain Range as it juts off to the west. Taebaek-san is famous for its winter scenes, and is most often visited then by avid hikers. A yearly **Mt. Taebaek Snow Festival** is held in February. Every June during the **Mt. Taebaek Azalea Festival**, more hikers and outdoor enthusiasts come to the mountain to enjoy it awash in shades of pink and red. In addition, the **Taebaek Festival** is held in October, not only to appreciate the autumn colors, but also to honor Dan'gun at the mountaintop shrine.

To get to the park's main entrance, take city bus no. 33 from the bus terminal in Taebaek to Danggol. Park facilities are in the early stages of development, so many accommodations, restaurants, souvenir shops, parking areas, and the like are yet to come. At the same time, trails are being improved and accessibility from other points increased. At the upper parking area, beyond the

ticket booth (₩2,000 entrance), are the Coal Museum (₩2,000 entrance), a cave, the temple Mandeok-sa, and Dan'gun Seongjeon, a memorial shrine dedicated to Dan'gun.

Hiking

The park's major trail starts at the main entrance. A hike of about one hour through this valley and then steeply up the right-hand hillside brings you to Banje ridge, where it meets another trail coming up from the north. As this trail crosses the river a couple of times on its way up the valley, it may be difficult to pass during periods of heavy rain, so take another trail. A 45-minute walk, mostly a slow upward gradient, takes you up the ridge, then across the side of the slope to **Man'gyeong-sa** (만경사). At this temple is **Yong-jeong Well**, considered by some to have the purest water in the country. From Man'gyeong-sa it's a short, .5-kilometer climb to the Cheon-je-dan altar on the summit of Taebaek-san (1,560 meters), passing a memorial monument to the Joseon Dynasty king Danjong on the way. A trail continues a short way directly north to the slightly higher summit of Janggun-bong (1,567 meters). At about 4.5 kilometers, this trail, from the park entrance to the summit, should take less than three hours.

Four other trails lead to the top. From the Baekdan-sa trailhead, walk up along the stream to a "Y." The right-hand path goes to the temple Baekdan-sa (백단사) and the left-hand trail to Banje, where it meets the main trail. Alternately, from the north you can start your hike at the Yuil-sa trailhead. This trail heads up the hillside, going in and out of several small valleys on the way. About halfway to the top, a short trail to the west runs down from the ridge into the next valley to Yuil-sa (유일사). From the ridge, a trail continues up to the peak. Either trail from the north should take about two hours. City bus nos. 30 and 34 run to both these trailheads.

The third and fourth trails are nearly twice as long. One starts at the park's main entrance and initially goes up the major valley. About one hour up, a trail branches off to the left and brings you up a secondary valley to the ridge, and then a short distance to the east, to Munsu-bong

(1,517 meters), in about an hour. The other starts at the park entrance but heads up the smaller valley to the east. This trail follows the stream, crossing and recrossing it a couple of times, eventually continuing up the slope to Munsu-bong. From Munsu-bong, it's more than an hour along the top ridge, past stands of ancient trees, to Cheonje-dan.

Lower-elevation valleys and hillsides are forested, but some spots appear to have been harvested and are in need of replanting. The top is alpine and full of grasses and scrub trees, giving it a very open feeling. As you approach the top, you pass patches of weatherworn trees, some buffeted by the winds and exposed to the rain for more than a millennium.

JEONGSEON 정선

Some 70 kilometers northwest of Taebaek and deeper into the mountains is the small town of Jeongseon [Chŏngsŏn]. Nestled into the bend of a river, this community is perhaps best-known for its version of the classical folk song Arirang. A lament for distant family members and loved ones, Arirang became very popular during the Korean War, when couples and families were split apart, many never to be reunited. Stemming from the early years of the Joseon Dynasty, over 2,000 lyric variations of the song exist, with about 50 melodic variations. Many of these can be appreciated for their beauty and passion during the singing contest of the **Jeongseon Arirang Festival**, held for three days every year in October.

Due to the shape of the mountains and twining rivers between Jeongseon and Yeongwol, whitewater rafting has become popular and this is one of few places in the country where it's feasible. The rapid-filled sections of the Donggang River, which in part is also called the Joyang River, is a premier site but not too difficult and sometimes touted as an experience for the family.

The surrounding mountains are full of coal, and many mining operations claw it from the earth. However, this mountainous area offers more than coal. Two kilometers from Gohan, a community along the highway back toward Taebaek, is the temple **Jeongam-sa** [Chŏngam-

sa] (정암사). Established in 638, the main hall of this temple has no Buddha figure on its altar and is in this way similar to Tongdo-sa, near Busan. Of veneration here are what are said to be sacred remains of the historic Buddha, protected in the Jeokmyeol Bogung hall, one of five shrines in the country that claim such relics. Also within this temple compound is a seven-tiered brick pagoda (N.T. #410), similar in many respects to one that stands in the city of Andong. To reach Jeongam-sa, take a city bus from Jeongseon or Taebaek.

Like Jeongam-sa, the relatively new **Gangwon Land Casino Resort** is closer to Taebaek than to Jeongseon. This casino is the only one in the country that's open to Koreans. All typical casino games are available here; entrance is ₩5,000 and only those over 18 years old are admitted. Attached to the casino is the deluxe-class Gangwon Land Hotel, where Korean- and Western-style rooms and suites run ₩120,000–320,000. Expansion plans for the resort include a 24-story hotel, a second casino, golf course, and ski resort.

Some distance north of Jeongam-sa, on the back road to Jeongseon, is the **Hwaam Tourist Area**. Designated as such in 1977, it encompasses a picturesque valley called **Jeongseon Sogeumgang** (정선소금강), sporting nicely shaped rock outcrops, palisades, and 12 waterfalls along its four-kilometer length. In another valley that opens onto Hwaam-ni is the well-known **Hwaam Mineral Spring** (₩1,500), and about a kilometer north of there is **Hwaam Cave** (₩4,000). At nearly three kilometers long, Hwaam Cave has one of the largest single cave chambers in the country and numerous limestone formations. This cave has been used for gold mining in the past, and some small seams of gold can still be seen in the cave walls. To reach this area, take a city bus from Jeongseon to Hwaam-ni.

Accommodations can be found in Jeongseon, Gohan, and Hwaam. Trains on the feeder Jeongseon rail line run north to Gujeol-li and south to Jeungsan. In Jeungsan, trains run to Seoul Cheongnyangni and Gangneung. Selected bus destinations and fares include Gangneung (₩6,500), Yeongwol (₩4,100), Gohan (₩2,800), and Taebaek (₩4,500).

YEONGWOL 영월

Lying along the south branch of the Han River, near the Chungcheongbuk-Do border, Yeongwol [Yŏngwŏl] is still known after 500 years as the place of the exile and assassination of the sixth Joseon Dynasty king. Danjong, grandson of the great King Sejong, was elevated to power at the tender age of 12, upon the death of his father, King Munjong. Because of his age, King Danjong was counseled by a group of advisers including his uncle, Sejo, who bitterly coveted the throne. After two years of constant intrigue and murder, Sejo forced King Danjong to abdicate in his favor. Several high-ranking ministers and generals loyal to King Danjong planned a coup against Sejo but were discovered and brutally put to death. Sayukshin-myo, a commemorative monument to the memory of six of these men, still stands at Noryangjin in Seoul, proclaiming their loyalty to King Danjong. King Sejo exiled Danjong to a location not far from Yeongwol. Two years later, on orders from King Sejo, the deposed king was murdered, ending one of the many tragic chapters of the strife-torn Joseon Dynasty.

Every year in April, Yeongwol hosts the **King Danjong Festival**. Events include a memorial ceremony commemorating the sad events and the injustice inflicted on Danjong, a parade, traditional dances, classical Korean music, and a poetry contest.

The Taebaek rail line runs through Yeongwol. Half a dozen trains in each direction run throughout the day from Yeongwol to Seoul Cheongnyangni and Gangneung. Selected bus destinations are Wonju (₩5,800), Jecheon (₩2,900), Gossi-donggul (₩750), Guin-sa (₩2,200), and Taebaek (₩5,900).

King's Tomb 장릉

Two kilometers north of town is **Jangneung**, King Danjong's grave (H.S. #196). After his death, the ex-king's body was irreverently thrown into the river, and King Sejo banned anyone from touching or burying it. Nonetheless, the local magistrate secretly retrieved and buried the body in an unadorned grave. A century and a half passed before this tomb was raised from commoner to royal status, and finished in a style befitting a king. Of all the Joseon Dynasty kings' tombs, this one is farthest from the capital. It is rather compact in size, set on a steep hillside, missing some of the usual attendant stone figures and railings, and it has a slightly different orientation and layout than other royal tombs. In addition to buildings used to conduct and store items for the yearly memorial ceremony, the lower portion of this compound also has one memorial tablet set up to honor Magistrate Eom, who buried King Danjong, and another to the loyal retainers who stayed with Danjong until his death. A short walk or city-bus ride brings you to the entrance of this serene compound; ₩1,000 entrance fee.

Up an alley on the city side of the tomb is Bodeok-sa, a small temple with bronze mirrors set on the altar. Closer to town, within the compound of Jangnang Seowon, is Jangjeolsa, a shrine erected to honor important persons loyal to Danjong despite his exile.

Historical Sites

Three kilometers west of Yeongwol is **Cheongnyeongpo** [Ch'ŏngnyŏngp'o] (청령포), site of King Danjong's residence in exile. Take a city bus to Gwangcheon and ferry across the river to have a look; ₩1,000 entrance. Located at an elbow in the Pyeongchang River, this tiny spit of land is covered with tall pines, backed by a rugged ridge of rock, and fronted by a sand riverflat. On this isolated riverbank, King Danjong lived out his two-year exile. A small monument on the cliff above the river marks this historic spot.

Located in town is what remains of a government compound used periodically to house King Danjong during floods. Within this compound was the hall Gwanpung-hyeon, site of the boy's murder, and the pavilion Jagyeong-nu, used by Danjong for study and relaxation. Gwanpung-hyeon, now known as Pogyeong-dan and converted for use as a Buddhist temple, sits in a walled compound on the main street of town; in a separate compound only a few steps away is Jagyeong-nu.

Grieving for their murdered king, exiled court

ladies threw themselves off the bluff upriver. Minchungsa, a memorial shrine dedicated to them, now stands on the bluff. Geumgang-jeong, a wooden pavilion built in 1428 for scholars and *yangban* of the region, is directly below Minchungsa and commands the best view of the river below. Nearby stand the village *hyanggyo* and a traditional archery range.

Gossi-donggul 고씨동굴

Gossi-donggul [Kossi], the most attractive limestone cave in the area, and one of the most intriguing in the country, lies nine kilometers south of Yeongwol. Bus from Yeongwol (₩750) to the small development of shops, restaurants, and accommodations now sitting along the road across the river from the entrance. Open 0900– 1700 (1600 in winter); entrance is ₩2,500. While not long ago you had to cross the river by ferry to reach the cave, now a pedestrian bridge has been constructed for easier access. This six-kilometer-long cave (N.M. #219) consists of narrow labyrinthine tunnels, nearly a dozen large open chambers, and four pools and water slides. There are fine examples of stalagmites, stalactites, fluted columns and curtains, and a large accumulation of other odd limestone shapes. The most interesting sections are farthest in. The cave maintains a cool 5–7°C throughout the year —a breeze blows out in the summer and in during the winter.

Stories from the past relate that in order to escape detection by the Japanese, members of the Go family (hence the cave's name) sought refuge in the front portion of this cave during the Hideyoshi Invasions of the 1590s. The full length of the cave was first explored in 1965, with one kilometer lit and opened to the public in 1974. Metal steps and bridges have been constructed in places to ease exploration. Only in one place is the clearance so low that you must get down on all fours and crawl. Wear clothes that you don't mind getting dirty, and bring gloves.

Tomb of the "Rainhat Poet" 김삿갓묘지

The tomb of Kim Sakgat is located on the north slope of the Sobaek Mountains, just outside the Sobaek National Park boundary, about five kilo-

© ROBERT NILSEN

shrine for the "Rainhat Poet," Kim Sakgat

meters up a side valley beyond Gossi-donggul. Nestled into the side of a gentle hill, this famous man's final resting place is accompanied by a memorial shrine that appropriately has an old-style bamboo rain hat on the altar. Rather a curiosity for most people, Koreans included, this tomb is way out of the way. You really have to have a liking for historical Korean figures to pay your respects here. Born near Seoul as Kim Shiseup (1807–1863) of the Andong Kim family, this poet extraordinaire was recognized as one of Korea's wittiest poets. About two kilometers farther up the valley is where Kim is said to have lived some of his life.

WONJU 원주

With a population of around 275,000, Wonju has surpassed Chuncheon as the most populous city in Gangwon-Do. Located near the Gyeonggi-Do border, it lies within the Charyeong Mountain Range. Over the centuries, Wonju maintained a close agricultural link with Seoul, and developed more significant lines of communication and transportation with the nation's capital than with the hinterland of its own province. During the United Silla period, this city was one of the five secondary capitals of the peninsula, and during the succeeding dynasty it was the seat of provincial power for the newly redistricted kingdom. Two structures in the city remain from the Goryeo Dynasty: Seonhwa-dang, a provincial administrative office building erected in 985, and Gamyeongmun-nu, its entrance pavilion, constructed around 1300. Both are preserved in the former compound of the Wonseong County office, now the new **Wonju Gamyeong Sajeok Park.** Bojeong-nu and Cheongun-dang, along with other structures and ponds will be rebuilt here as well before its completion, in a manner that re-creates, in part, the pre-modern provincial administration complex. The office of the provincial governor remained in Wonju from 1394 until after the Korean War, when it was moved to Chuncheon.

The city's old business/lodging/entertainment district is situated roughly between the train station and Wonju Gamyeong Sajeok Park. The covered Central Market, with its modern counterpart across the street, is in the center of the city; the Nambu Market is out toward the southern end of town. An underground arcade lies below the main intersection. Newer sections of town have been developed principally to the north and south of the city center. Wrapping around the south end are housing estates and the Wonju Sports Complex; to the north lie a mixture of residential areas, industrial factories, several colleges and universities, the headquarters of the 1st R.O.K. army, and a small U.S. Army compound. While the Wonju Hyanggyo is an academic hold-over from the last dynasty and the city museum preserves items of historic and cultural importance, Wonju is best known for its proximity to Chiak-san, the lofty highland at the city's eastern doorstep.

See www.wonju.kangwon.kr for information via the Internet.

Accommodations

Rising above the hubbub of the Central Market, the best place in town is the first-class **Wonju Tourist Hotel** (tel. 033/743-1241). Room rates run from ₩90,000 for either an *ondol* room or one with a Western bed, and facilities include Korean and Western restaurants, a lounge, nightclub, and sauna. Many *yeogwan* are clustered in the vicinity of the bus terminal, and some of these are the Yonggungjang Motel (용궁장모텔), Haniljang Yeogwan (한일장여관), Seouljang Yeogwan (서울장여관), and the less expensive Gil Yeoinsuk (길여인숙). Many places that may be quieter can also be found in the city center. One concentration of *yeogwan* lies between the train station and tourist hotel, while others cluster around the post office. Start your search by checking the Cheongujang Yeogwan (청우장여관) or the cheaper Gyeongnam Yeoinsuk (경남여인숙), the Yurimjang Yeogwan (유림장여관), or Tongiljang Yeogwan (통일장여관). For a nice place near the post office, head to the Yeongshinjang Yeogwan (영신장여관) or the nearby Daerim Park Motel (대림파크모텔). The Hwaseung Youth Hostel (tel. 033/732-1600) near the Guryong-sa entrance to the national park has bunks at ₩14,300 for Y.H. members and ₩18,590 for non-members.

WONJU

WONJU STATION

TONGILJANG
YEOGWAN

GYEONGNAM
YEOINSUK

GHEONGUJANG
YEOGWAN

YURIMJANG
YOGWAN

UNDERGROUND
ARCADE

CITY HALL

BANK

CHAYU
MARKET

WONJU
TOURIST
HOTEL

CENTRAL

MARKET

POST
OFFICE

YEONGSHINJANG
YEOGWAN

DAERIM PARK
MOTEL

Wonju
Gamyeong
Sajeok Park

BANK

0   100 yds

0   100 m

MAP AREA INSET

YEONGDONG
EXPRESSWAY

SANGJI
UNIVERSITY

EXPRESS BUS TERMINAL

INTERCITY BUS TERMINAL

YONGGUNGJANG MOTEL

TELECOM

MAP AREA

WONJU
POLICE
STATION

CITY
MUSEUM

NAMBU MARKET

WONJU SPORTS
COMPLEX

WONJU
HYANGGYO

CHIAK ART CENTER

JUNGANG EXPRESSWAY

0   0.5 mi

0   0.5 km

GANGWON-DO

Transportation

The nearest airport is located between Wonju and Hoengseong but much closer to Hoengseong, adjacent to an Air Force installation. Check-in is done at the terminal along the highway and then all passengers are transported the two kilometers by shuttle bus to the waiting plane. The terminal is small and has just the necessities. Running by the terminal, bus no. 62 connects both cities. As it's 15 kilometers from the center of Wonju, a taxi ride may cost ₩15,000. Flights from the Wonju airport don't seem to have a consistent schedule, so be sure to check with KAL (tel. 033/732-2001) to see if anything is currently flying. When flights do happen, they usually go to Busan.

Wonju is one of the major stops on the Jungang rail line, and nearly a dozen and a half trains of all classes run out of here in both directions every day. *Saemaul-ho* trains run to Seoul Cheongnyangni (₩7,600), Andong (₩10,200), and Gangneung (₩17,300). *Mugunghwa-ho* trains run to Seoul Cheongnyangni (₩5,100), Andong (₩7,000), Busan (₩18,600), and Gangneung (₩11,900). Of the trains to Gangneung, the day trains go via Yeongwol and the night train via Yeongju. The cheaper and slower *Tongil-ho* trains from Wonju run to Seoul Cheongnyangni (₩2,900) and Jecheon (₩2,900).

The Yeongdong Expressway cuts across the northern outskirts of the city, conveniently connecting it to both Seoul and Gangneung. Since the completion of the Jungang Expressway, Wonju is more directly and rapidly connected not only to the provincial capital in Chuncheon but also south to Yeongju, Andong, and Daegu, all places to which it was linked most readily by rail in the past. Express buses leave Wonju every 10 minutes for Seoul (₩5,200), and every hour or so for Dong Seoul (₩5,100), Gangneung (₩5,400), and Gwangju (₩13,600). Selected intercity bus destinations and fares are: Chuncheon (₩5,300), Yeoju (₩2,600), Jinbu (₩4,400), Gangneung (₩5,400), Yeongwol (₩5,400), and Chungju (₩4,200).

Frequent city buses run through downtown Wonju. Among those most useful, nos. 11, 34, 41, and 62 connect the bus terminals to the train station and city center; no. 62 goes to the airport and Hoengseong; no. 41 goes to Guryongsa and the north entrance to Chiak-san; no. 82 will take you to the Ipseok-sa trailhead; no. 81 runs to Haenggu-dong; and nos. 21 and 22 head to Geumdae-ri and Seongnam-ni on the south end of the mountain, from where there's a walk of about one hour to Sangwon-sa.

CHIAK-SAN NATIONAL PARK

치악산국립공원

Rising to 1,288 meters, Chiak-san [Ch'iak-san] is the most salient feature of the hilly area surrounding Wonju, one of the highest points along the Charyeong Mountain Range. Oriented north to south, Chiak-san has a slight crescent shape, its cusps pointing east, of which at least a dozen peaks rise above 1,000 meters. From the summit it's possible to see the Taebaek Mountains to the east and the Sobaek Mountains to the south.

Chiak-san is not nearly as spectacular as Seoraksan or Sogeumgang, but is as inviting as, though smaller than, Odae-san. Originally known as Jeogak-san ("Crimson Peak Mountain"), its present name means "Pheasant Peak Mountain." Large tracts of forest surrounding the peaks at the northern and southern ends of its main ridgeline, as well as one small grove on the southern slope, are set aside as nature preserves. Chiak-san played an important role in the defense of Wonju during centuries past, and the remains of three mountain forts can still be seen on its southern ridges. Once a stronghold of Buddhism, with as many as 76 temples, only seven remain today. Named a provincial park in 1973 with 182 square kilometers, this mountain was designated Chiaksan National Park in 1984.

To reach Guryong-sa, take Wonju city bus no. 41 or an intercity bus from Hoengseong, Seoul Sangbong or Dong Seoul terminals, past the Dream Land Amusement Park, and small lacquerware and *hanji* paper museums, to the small community of shops, restaurants, and *minbak* at the end of the line. The ₩2,600 park entrance fee also covers entrance to Guryong-sa; entrance at other trailheads is ₩1,300. City buses also run to other trailheads, where there are smaller villages with restaurants and accommodations.

Guryong-sa 구룡사

On the northern slope of Chiak-san is Guryong-sa [Kuryong-sa], the most important temple on the mountain. Founded by the monk Uisang, Guryong-sa was built in 668, the same year the peninsula was unified under Silla control. Legend says that long ago nine dragons lived in a lotus pond where this temple now stands. Because the area was deemed auspicious, the dragons were driven away and the temple erected. Eight of the dragons fled to the East Sea, while the ninth went to live in the pool below Guryong Waterfall. The original name meant "Nine Dragons Temple," but during the Joseon Dynasty the first character of this name was changed—even though the pronunciation is the same—to the character meaning "tortoise." Many well-known monks have resided here, and several of their *sari budo* can be seen in a small plot near the entrance path. The tiny main hall, built in the early years of the 20th century, has three altar figures flanked by several hundred small images. Across the courtyard is an open-fronted pavilion, where hundreds of Buddha figures sit on its two altars; the Three Spirits hall sits on the hillside above. A well-used skin drum, new bronze bell, metal plate gong, and wooden fish gong hang in the bell pavilion, and a huge new three-tier stone pagoda dominates the main courtyard. The older buildings were repaired in the late 1960s and early '70s. The newest building at the temple is Cheonwang-mun, a very pleasing and skillfully constructed double-roofed gate with its four guards. Portraying the heavenly kings who keep the temple safe from evil

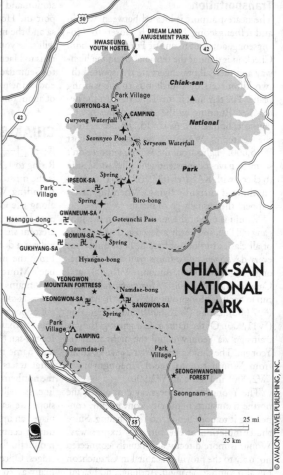

influence, each was carved from a single tree trunk and is particularly well done. You must pass through this gate to walk up the long, steep flight of steps and under the lecture hall to the main courtyard. Next to the entrance gate is a standing stone Buddha figure.

Hiking

Chiak-san's main trail runs up the valley from Guryong-sa to Biro-bong (1,288 meters), and from there along the ridge to Namdae-bong (1,182 meters) and down past either Sangwon-sa or Yeongwon-sa to park villages. It's possible to walk from end to end in about 13 hours, but many hikers descend one of the western trails for a shorter day. There are springs for drinking water below Biro-bong and Namdae-bong, and to the east side of Goteunchi Pass. There are no mountain huts in this park, but there are two campgrounds near Guryong-sa and one at Geumdae-ri. Chiak-san is not as well trodden as the other mountain areas in the country; on weekdays, the mountain may seem absolutely deserted. A few *yeogwan,* restaurants, and shops are at the Guryong-sa, Geumdae-ri, and Seongnam-ni trailheads. Carry all the food and water that you need, and get an early start.

From Guryong-sa, the trail leads up past Guryong Waterfall, Seonnyeo Pool, and Seryeom Waterfall before heading up three routes to the summit. From Biro-bong, the entire razorback ridge and the eastern inner section of the park are visible. Three towers of loose stone have been erected at the summit. Starting in 1962, it took one man from Wonju over 10 years to pile them up by hand. From the top, a 30-minute walk brings you to the turnoff for a very steep and swift trail that makes its way down a side valley, below huge rock outcrops, past the temple Ipseok-sa to the Hwanggol hamlet. A walk from Guryong-sa to Hwanggol should take about five hours. Farther south along the ridge trail, two

other trails run down into the western valleys, both ending at Haenggu-dong. The trail down from Goteunchi Pass leads past Gwaneum-sa, while the other goes past Bomun-sa and Gukhyang-sa. It requires about 90 minutes via either trail to reach this village from the ridge.

The ridge trail continues past Hyangno-bong to Namdae-bong. From a point about 10 minutes down the ridge trail directly south of Namdae-bong, a fourth trail leads steeply down into the southwestern valley to the temple Yeongwon-sa. High above the trail and this temple are the remains of Yeongwon Sanseong mountain fortress. From Yeongwon-sa, the trail continues down the valley to the bus stop at Geumdae-ri. The walk from Namdae-bong summit to Geumdae-ri should take less than three hours. Along this path are several apiaries, where honey and a honey liquor are bottled. A combination of honey, *soju,* and medicinal herbs left to sit for six months, this liquor is a potent drink.

Below Namdae-bong is **Sangwon-sa** (상원사). At about 1,000 meters, it's one of the country's loftiest temples. To its front are three cinnamon trees and a steep decline into the valley. A walk of less than two hours down from here brings you to the Seongnam-ni park entrance. Down this valley at Seongnam-ni is the Seonghwangnim Forest (N. M. #93), a tiny virgin grove of hardwood trees.

Gyeongsangbuk-Do

경상북도

Gyeongsangbuk-Do [Kyŏngsangbuk-Do] occupies the east-central region of the country, and at over 19,000 square kilometers (about 20 percent of the nation's landmass), is the largest of South Korea's provinces. With 2.7 million inhabitants, it ranks third in population. This province is the northern half of what was, until 1896, Gyeongsang Province; the southern half became Gyeongsangnam-Do. The old Gyeongsang domain embraced the whole southeastern corner of the country and is still referred to as the Yeongnam region.

Daegu (with an additional 2.5 million people) lies at the heart of Gyeongsangbuk- Do and has been its capital for four centuries. Ten other cities lie within the province, as do 13 counties. Despite its extensive coastline, Gyeongsangbuk-Do has historically been an inland-oriented, agricultural region. Only since the 1960s have the provincial cities started to grow rapidly, and only Pohang is situated on the coast. Koreans of this region are known as independent, self-respecting, and forthright in business. Colloquially, they are referred to as Gyeongsang-Do *mundungi* (lepers), due to a historically high incidence of leprosy in the region.

the second gate at Mun'gyeong Saejae

© ROBERT NILSEN

Gyeongsangbuk-Do embraces two national parks: Juwang-san, near Cheongsong, and the multi-section Gyeongju National Park, surrounding the city of Gyeongju; four others drape its borders: Sobaek-san, Worak-san, Songni-san, and Gaya-san. There are also four mountainous provincial parks within the province—Mun'-gyeong Saejae, Cheongnyang-san, Geumo-san, and Palgong-san—and a growing number of county parks.

For information online about the province, see www.provin.gyeongbuk.kr or www.gbtour.net.

The Land

The geology of Gyeongsangbuk-Do is characterized by deep layers of sandstone and conglomerate rock, with occasional surface patches of granite. The province is bounded on the north and west by the Sobaek Mountains, a largely granite formation with peaks averaging 1,000 meters. Some of the highest peaks along this range—Sobaek-san, Juheul-san, Songni-san, Hwanghak-san, and Daedeok-san—connect to form the provincial boundary. Down the east coast, within 25 kilometers of the sea, run the Taebaek Mountains. This range extends down from North Korea, through Gangwon-Do, and into Gyeongsangbuk-Do, ending near Pohang. Other notable peaks in the province are Palgongsan, Biseul-san, Juwang-san, Geumo-san, and Toham-san.

The relatively unindented east coast has one large impression, Yeongil Bay. On the inside edge of this bay sits Pohang, with the province's best harbor. Smaller ports, principally for local fishing fleets, are Jukpyeon, Uljin, Hupo, Ganggu, Guryeongpo, and Gampo. The coast alternates between long stretches of beach and craggy headlands of weathered rocks, with pockets of coastal lowlands, short steep rivers, and isolated fishing villages. Extolled by travelers as one of the most unexpectedly scenic areas of the peninsula, it's a patently picturesque coast, except for the barbed wire strung along the raked beaches and the marine guardhouses perched atop seaside promontories. Located some 140 kilometers east of Uljin in the frigid East Sea, Ulleung-do is the province's only sizable island.

At 525 kilometers South Korea's longest, the Nakdong River completely traverses Gyeongsangbuk-Do; virtually all of the province constitutes the upper half of the river's drainage basin. Its major tributaries are the Naeseong, Wi, Gamcheon, and Geumho rivers. All along the major rivers and their tributaries are dikes, levies, barrages, and weirs constructed to greatly mitigate the disastrous potential of flooding. One major dam, just above Andong, creates a 30-kilometer-long reservoir, and gives much-needed flood control. The newer and slightly smaller Imha Dam on a tributary nearby also helps to supply flood control—and electricity to distant Pohang and Daegu. Several other reservoirs, like Yeongcheon Lake north of Yeongcheon and Unmun Lake outside Cheongdo, have been constructed more recently for drinking water, flood control, and recreation.

History

Gyeongsangbuk-Do occupies much of the territory of the ancient Jinhan confederacy (A.D. 1st to 3rd centuries), when the walled-town state of Dalgubeol arose in what is now Daegu and the surrounding plain. Dalgubeol expanded and became an agrarian center, but was overcome by the more powerful state of Saro, to the east, which developed into the Silla Kingdom. By the 660s, Silla unified the entire peninsula. Gyeongju, its capital, became the heart and mind of the entire country, and by the 8th century it was one of the greatest cities of Asia, with an estimated population of one million. The Silla built palaces, temples, fortresses, public monuments, and efficient irrigation systems. They maintained an effective army and secured their distant borders. Education and arts grew prominent, and advanced agricultural methods created more fruitful fields. This society flourished and attained a level of cultural achievement that Korea would not surpass until the modern era.

When the first king of the Goryeo Dynasty took power in the 10th century, the capital was moved to Gaeseong (now in North Korea), transforming this southeastern region into a provincial backwater. In 1314, the new administrative region known as Gyeongsang-Do was established.

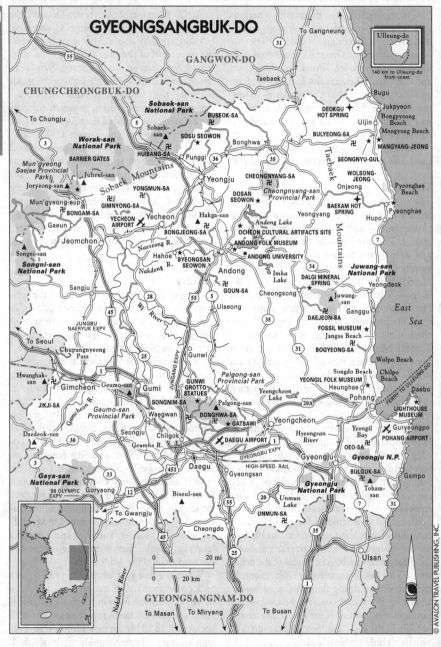

GYEONGSANGBUK-DO

GYEONGSANGBUK-DO

To Gangneung

GANGWON-DO

Ulleung-do

140 km to Ulleung-do
from coast

CHUNGCHEONGBUK-DO

Taebaek

Bugu
Jukpyeon

To Chungju

Sobaek-san
National Park

BUSEOK-SA

DEOKGU
HOT SPRING

Uljin

Bongpyeong
Beach
Mangyang Beach

Worak-san
National Park

Sobaek-
san

SOSU SEOWON

Bonghwa

BULYEONG-SA

MANGYANG-JEONG

BARRIER GATES

HUIBANG-SA

Punggi

SEONGNYU-GUL

Mun'gyeong
Saejae Provincial
Park

Juheul-san

YONGMUN-SA

Yeongju

CHEONGNYANG-SA

WOLSONG-
JEONG

Joryeong-san

GIMNYONG-SA

DOSAN
SEOWON

Cheongnyang-san
Provincial Park

Onjeong

Pyeonghae
Beach

Mun'gyeong-eup

BONGAM-SA

YECHEON
AIRPORT

Yecheon

Hakga-san

Yeongyang

BAEKAM HOT
SPRING

Pyeonghae

Gaeun

BONGJEONG-SA

OCHEON CULTURAL ARTIFACTS SITE

Hupo

Jeomchon

Naeseong R.

Andong Lake

ANDONG FOLK MUSEUM

Songni-san

Hahoe

BYEONGSAN
SEOWON

ANDONG UNIVERSITY

Songni-san
National Park

Nakdong R.

Andong

Imha
Lake

DALGI MINERAL
SPRING

Juwang-san
National Park

Sangju

GOUN-SA

Cheongsong

Yeongdeok

28

55

5

Uiseong

Juwang-
san

Ganggu

East
Sea

JUNGBU
NAERYUK EXPY

DAEJEON-SA

FOSSIL MUSEUM

To Seoul

Chupungnyeong
Pass

Gunwi

Jangsa Beach

BOGYEONG-SA

Wolpo Beach

Hwanghak-
san

Gimcheon

Geumo-san

GUNWI
GROTTO
STATUES

Palgong-san
Provincial Park

Songdo Beach

YEONGIL FOLK MUSEUM

Chilpo
Beach

JIKJI-SA

SONGNIM-SA

Palgong-san

Heunghae

Pohang

Daebo

Geumo-san
Provincial Park

Waegwan

DONGHWA-SA

Yeongcheon
Lake

20A

LIGHTHOUSE
MUSEUM

Daedeok-san

Seongju

Chilgok

GATBAWI

Yeongcheon

Yeongil
Bay

Guryeongpo

POHANG AIRPORT

Geumho R.

DAEGU AIRPORT

Hyeongsan
River

OEO-SA

30

GYEONGBU EXPY

Gyeongju N.P.

Gaya-san
National Park

Daegu

HIGH-SPEED RAIL

Gyeongju

BULGUK-SA

Gampo

'88 OLYMPIC
EXPY

Goryeong

Gyeongsan

Gyeongju
National Park

Toham-
san

Biseul-san

Unmun
Lake

UNMUN-SA

Cheongdo

Ulsan

0   20 mi
0   20 km

GYEONGSANGNAM-DO

Nakdong River

To Masan   To Miryang   To Busan

© AVALON TRAVEL PUBLISHING, INC.

During the Joseon Dynasty (1392–1910), its boundaries were slightly readjusted and the area popularly became known as Yeongnam. Because of its proximity to Japan, it suffered more than other provinces during the Imjin War of 1592–98. From 1905 to 1910, between the formation of the protectorate and the annexation of the peninsula by Japan, guerrilla forces known as the "righteous army" effectively harassed the Japanese troops stationed here.

When the country began to develop after the Korean War, Gyeongsangbuk-Do pragmatically took a lead. Daegu was one of South Korea's first three industrialized areas. Since the 1960s, the city's industrial sector has gone through great expansion, diversification, and modernization, concentrating on textiles, agriculture-related products, and light industry. Pohang produces iron and steel. Textiles, plastics, rubber, and electronics are made at Gumi, agricultural machinery at Gimcheon, and other light industrial goods at Yeongcheon. These inland industrial estates are conveniently located on expressways and rail lines, close to the ports of Pohang, Ulsan, Busan, and Masan.

Cultural Traits and Traces

Gyeongsangbuk-Do remains one of Korea's most traditional and conservative regions. Personal habits and relationships are maintained along traditional lines. Confucianism pervades society, remaining especially vital for the rural population. Confucian, Buddhist, and shaman ceremonies are often performed, and many people still maintain strong beliefs in fortune tellers, geomancers, and traditional medicine. Farmers' music, folk songs, and traditional art forms are actively kept alive, and cultural festivals are a mainstay of both rural and urban life. Slowly, though, even in this province, traditions and customs erode as modern influences creep in.

The Silla Dynasty, with its capital at Gyeongju, left thousands of ruins, and because of its legacy, UNESCO has selected it as one of the world's 10 most important ancient cultural cities. The Korean national government has designated Hahoe, in Andong County, as an important folk area because of its traditional lifestyle, houses, masked play, and prominent personages. Within this province you'll find the two oldest wooden structures in the country, both temple buildings. Gyeongsangbuk-Do has 52 National Treasures—the largest number outside of Seoul—258 Treasures, 94 Historical Sites, and dozens of other tangible and intangible cultural properties. The Gyeongju National Museum displays hundreds of artifacts, mostly from the Silla era, while the Daegu National Museum proudly portrays a broader cultural past. Dozens of famous temples pepper the misty mountainsides, homes to numerous influential Buddhist monks of the past, and many *yangban* families have left manor homes that are some of the best examples of Joseon-era upper-class houses in the country. Yi Toe-gye, a native son of the province, is regarded as the country's foremost Confucian scholar, and titular head of one of the two branches of Joseon Dynasty Neo-Confucianism. Dosan Seowon, a private academy dedicated to him and his work, sits on the bank of Andong Lake. Sosu Seowon, the first chartered Confucian Academy in the country also lies within this province, as do countless other lesser *seowon* and *hyanggyo*.

Agriculture and Fishing

Since the days of Dalgubeol, Gyeongsangbuk-Do has been an integral agricultural region of the country. It's favored by the extensive Nakdong River drainage basin, yet only one-fifth of its land is arable. The plains near Daegu, Gyeongju, Gimcheon, and Sangju are the widest flatlands in the province. Most of the farming must still be done on riverside flats, with some dryland farming on the gently sloped hillsides. Cultivation is intense; rice is the principal crop. Some fields are double cropped with barley or winter wheat. Soybeans, millet, white potatoes, green vegetables, peppers, legumes, apples (in Daegu), melons (Seongju), hemp (Andong), mulberry, tobacco, persimmons (Cheongdo), and *insam* (Punggi) are grown as well. Silk is produced in Sangju and Chilgok.

Tons of fresh fish and other sea animals, huge piles of dried fish, and slabs of frozen fish are seen at every fish market in the province. Screens full of fish in geometric symmetry dry in the sun at each port town. Ulleung-do is known for its tasty cuttlefish, and everyone knows of the long-legged red crabs of Yeongdeok. Pohang is the largest fishing port in the province; other coastal towns have smaller harbors and fishing-related industries like packing and refrigeration.

Transportation

Both KAL and Asiana Airlines serve the cities of Daegu, Pohang, and Yecheon. Daegu and Pohang are connected to both Seoul and Jeju, while flights from Yecheon go only to Seoul. Both the Gyeongbu and Jungang rail lines run through the province, while connecting lines run from Gimcheon to Yeongju and Daegu to Pohang. The Gyeongbu Expressway (no. 1) dashes across the southern part of the province, while southwest from Daegu runs the '88 Olympic Expressway (no. 12). South of Daegu runs the Jungbu Naeryuk Expressway (no. 45), which will have an extension north through Sangju and Mun'-gyeong. The Jungang Expressway (no. 55) slices through the middle of the province, connecting Daegu, Andong, and Yeongju north to Wonju and south through Cheongdo to Busan. Other expressways that are in the works will connect Sangju and Andong with the coast, link Pohang to Daegu and beyond to Seongju and Muju, will circle around Daegu, and shoot up the east coast to Gangwon-Do. Express buses travel to Sangju, Gimcheon, Gumi, Daegu, Yeongcheon, Gyeongju, Pohang, Andong and Yeongju; intercity buses travel to all corners of the province. The only ferry route here is from Pohang to Ulleung-do.

Northwest Gyeongsangbuk-Do

The northwestern corner of Gyeongsangbuk-Do lies on the southern slope of the Sobaek Mountains. Rugged and tall, these mountains have proven a barrier for communications and transportation over the centuries; they've also created a natural boundary with the neighboring provinces. Monks have found these forested hills a wonderful place for retreat, and numerous temples and other historical artifacts are still tucked away in their folds. Today, several national and provincial parks sprawl across the backbone of this sinuous range, preserving huge tracts for the enjoyment of hikers and other outdoor adventurists.

SOBAEK-SAN AND VICINITY

Sobaek-san National Park
소백산국립공원

The Sobaek ("Small White") Mountains sweep down through the middle of the country from the Taebaek ("Great White") Mountains, making a sickle-shaped arc to the south-central region of the peninsula. The first of the high peaks in this range is Sobaek-san, one of Korea's most famous; seven peaks in the immediate vicinity rise above 1,300 meters, the highest being Biro-bong, at 1,439 meters. Steep slopes predominate on the eastern side, while the west is a bit more gentle. With its long and graceful ridgeline, numerous spur ridges, and deep valleys, Sobaek-san is a smaller version of the great Jiri Massif at the southern end of this range. With no distinctive rugged features or unusual rock formations, Sobaek-san stands high and broad, yet gentle and unpretentious. Only a handful of trails, waterfalls, and temples lie in its folds. Even so, on good-weather weekends, nature lovers make their way over these long but easy trails. Sobaek-san is known for its wildflowers, especially edelweiss, which attracts hikers from all over the country when it blooms in the spring; azaleas also bring flower lovers in May and June. Below Biro-bong is a large virgin forest of yew trees (N.M. #244). From 200 to 500 years old, these evergreens average about seven meters in height. Elevations above 1,200 meters have been designated a nature conservation area. On Yeonhwa-bong (1,394 meters), to the southwest of Biro-bong, sits the mushroom-topped National Astronomical Observatory,

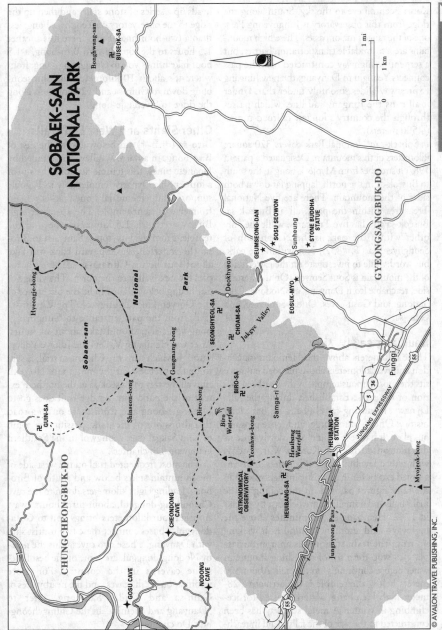

SOBAEK-SAN
NATIONAL PARK

CHUNGCHEONGBUK-DO

GYEONGSANGBUK-DO

Bonghwang-san

卍
BUSEOK-SA

Hyeonje-bong

Sobaek-san

National

Park

Shinseon-bong

Gungmang-bong

Biro-bong

GUIN-SA
卍

GEUMSEONG-DAN

SOSU SEOWON
★

Sunheung

STONE BUDDHA
STATUE
★

Deokhyeon

SEONGHYEOL-SA
卍

CHOAM-SA
卍

Jakgye Valley

EOSUK-MYO
★

BIRO-SA
卍

Biro
Waterfall

Samga-ri

Yeonhwa-bong

Heuibang
Waterfall

Punggi

55

36

5

ASTRONOMICAL
OBSERVATORY ■

HEUIBANG-SA
卍

HEUIBANG-SA
STATION ■

JUNGANG EXPRESSWAY

Myojeok-bong

CHEONDONG
CAVE

NODONG
CAVE

GOSU CAVE
★

Jungnyeong Pass

55

1 mi

1 km

0

0

© AVALON TRAVEL PUBLISHING, INC.

Korea's central eye to the sky. South along the ridge from this observatory is Jungnyeong Pass, one of the range's major passes. These high mountains are a formidable transportation barrier, but a serpentine highway constructed over the pass connects Yeongju to Danyang; the new Jungang Expressway glides smoothly under that. Under it all runs the Jungang rail line, which passes through the country's longest railroad tunnel (4,500 meters).

Sobaek-san National Park covers 320 square kilometers of this mountain. Designated a park in 1987, it stretches from Myojeok-bong in the south to Buseok-sa in the north, lapping far down both sides of the mountain. There are five National Treasures within the park, all at Buseok-sa. Buseok-sa also has five Treasures, while the only other within the park is the Nahan-jeon of Seonghyeol-sa (T. #832). Not within the park, but worthwhile to investigate on the eastern side of the mountain is Sosu Seowon. On the western side, reachable from Danyang, are Nodong, Cheondong, and Gosu caves, Ondal Sanseong, and Guin-sa.

Heuibang-sa 회방사

Three kilometers above the Heuibang-sa Station and two kilometers above the road entrance sits the most famous temple in the southern section of the park. Established during the Silla Dynasty, Heuibang-sa [Hūibang-sa] has a long history. Once a much larger and more prosperous place, it has been rebuilt only slowly since its destruction during the Korean War. Today, with only a few buildings, it is rather undistinguished except for shamanistic influences seen in the fairy figures painted on the ceiling of the main hall, and a small bronze bell cast by monks in 1742. Heuibang-sa, 45 minutes above the highway—add another 30 minutes if walking up from the train station—is an appropriate place to stop for a sip of refreshing mountain water before continuing up the trail. About 300 meters below the temple is the attractive 28-meter-high Heuibang Waterfall, used for ice-climbing in winter. A metal stairway has been constructed to the side of the falls to aid in reaching the temple. From the temple, the main trail heads up a series of stone stairs and then up the ridge to the observatory on Yeonhwa-bong, less than a two-hour hike. From there it is another 1.5 hours to the top. Beyond Biro-bong, a 1.5 hour hike brings you to Gungmang-bong; from where it's about 10 kilometers via Shinseon-bong down to Guin-sa and 12 kilometers along the ridge to Hyeongje-bong.

Other Sights and West End Trails

Biro-sa (비로사) sits below and to the east of Biro-bong, in a narrow valley. Surrounded by Japanese pines, this temple occupies the site of a former Silla Dynasty temple; only its flagpole supports and a memorial stone marker remain from that ancient temple. The 15-meter-high Biro Waterfall is 1.5 kilometers beyond the temple. From the bus stop at Samga-ri to Biro-sa, the waterfall, the top, and back will take about four hours. **Choam-sa** (조암사) occupies the next valley to the north. The village of Sunheung below claims to be the birthplace of the Goryeo king Chungyeol. The Choam-sa trail, from the park entrance to Gungmang-bong and back, should take about six hours. After the Heuibang Valley, the Jukgye Valley, through which runs the Choam-sa trail, is said to be the prettiest on the mountain. No path runs all the way to Buseok-sa at the northern extent of the park, but, a ridge trail does go to Hyeongje-bong and from there on to a road that drops out of the park, passing the tomb of Kim Sakgat (see Yeongwol in the Southern Gangwon-Do chapter).

The most frequented trail on the west side of the mountain starts below and south of Biro-bong, leading eight kilometers down to the cave **Cheondong-donggul**, about three hours away. Another four kilometers brings you to **Gosu-donggul**—buses connect these two tourist sites with Danyang. These two caves, plus the nearby Nodong-donggul, are some of the best limestone caverns in the country. For more information on the caves, and the nearby sites of Guin-sa and Ondal Sanseong, refer to "Danyang and Vicinity" in the Chungcheongbuk-Do chapter.

West End Practicalities

Admission to Heuibang-sa and the park costs ₩2,600; the charge at other trailheads is lower. If coming by train, get off at the Heuibang-sa Station, half a kilometer from the east end of the Jungnyeong railroad tunnel, and walk up the valley to the highway. City bus no. 25 from Punggi or Yeongju, or intercity buses between Danyang and Yeongju, let you off at the park entrance road along the highway. Walk the two kilometers to the temple by way of either the vehicular road or the much prettier valley trail. If going to Biro-sa or Choam-sa, city buses from Punggi run to Samga-ri and Deokhyeon. For Sosu Seowon, its nearby sites, and Buseok-sa, take a bus from Punggi or Yeongju.

While there are no mountain huts within the park, there are three camping areas: one lies below Heuibang-sa, a second below Biro-sa, while the third is on the west side of the mountain between Biro-bong and Cheondong-donggul.

Buseok-sa 부석사

On the wooded southern slope of Bonghwang-san, in the northeastern corner of the park, sits the famous temple Buseok-sa [Pusŏk-sa]. Established in 676 by the renowned monk Uisang, it's one of Korea's most venerated temples. Uisang studied Buddhism in China for 10 years, and on his return to Korea founded many temples. He used Buseok-sa as the base to introduce the Hwaeom doctrine of Buddhism to his countrymen. The temple's name means "floating rock," and is derived from a legend that tells of a huge rock that floated down from heaven and perched itself above the new temple's main hall to scare away demonic spirits and evil influence. This rock seems to have been successful, for the Hwaeom sect became dominant in Korean Buddhism. It remained so for five centuries, until its developmental creativity waned and the influence of other sects surpassed it. Today it still acts as the head temple of the Hwaeom sect under the more dominant Jogye sect of Korean Buddhism.

Five National Treasures and five Treasures, including the second-oldest wooden structure and some of the oldest mural paintings in the

the open pavilion on the upper level at Buseok-sa

© ROBERT NILSEN

country, are preserved at this temple. The temple compound sits on a terraced hillside, with many steep steps between each level. Its simple structures and natural colors present a stark contrast to the more common brightly painted temple buildings seen in the country, yet maple trees color the compound in multiple tints in autumn. Located at the end of a long road that traverses a peaceful valley, Buseok-sa is a bit out of the way, yet well worth the effort to get there.

The several daily buses from Yeongju (₩2,200), Punggi (₩1,510), and Bonghwa (₩1,850) stop at the small cluster of shops, restaurants, and accommodations below the temple. Luckily, this community doesn't yet have a long line of unsightly tourist shops to spoil the untainted beauty of the valley—but they are coming. Aside from the restaurants, a few *minbak* here also serve food to their guests upon request. Deep in the country, amidst fine scenery, this village makes a peaceful spot to spend the night. An alternate place, for a fancier and more comfortable room, is two kilometers back down the road at the village of Buseok, where the Koreana Hotel will set you up.

The Temple Compound: From the bus stop below Buseok-sa, the path leads up under a canopy of young ginkgo trees between apple orchards to the temple's unpretentious front gate; ₩1,200 entrance fee. Between there and Cheonwang-mun are multiple flights of steps and a pair of stone flagpole supports (T. #255), erected at the temple's founding. Inside Cheonwangmun stand four well-done, ferocious gate guards keeping the temple precinct free from evil influence. Dormitories, the administration building, twin pagodas from the Silla Dynasty, and Boho-gak occupy the lower terrace. Boho-gak was built in 1994 to house murals that were originally part of the Chosa-dang wooden structure. These polychromatic murals (N.T. #46) depict the four heavenly kings and two bodhisattvas. These are the oldest murals in Korea painted on wood, the best of Goryeo Dynasty temple paintings, and, aside from ancient tomb murals, some of the oldest paintings in the country. A second hall has been newly constructed next to and connected with, but on a higher terrace than, Boho-gak. This building houses and protects wood printing blocks (T. #735) of the Avatamsaka Sutra from the Goryeo Dynasty. They are said to comprise three versions of this sutra—in 40, 60, and 80 volumes, respectively. Not surprisingly, these have been kept here because the monk Uisang is said to have been "the progenitor of Avatamsaka philosophy in Korea." More recently, Jijang-jeon hall has been built behind.

Two pavilions set on huge pillars straddle the steps that lead up to the top terrace. Both are weatherworn and fine examples of open pavilion structures—the lower holds an equally old-looking skin drum. On the uppermost level is Muryangsu-jeon, the temple's main hall. This building (N.T. #18), the country's second-oldest wooden structure and the finest example of Goryeo Dynasty architecture, has looked out over the valley for more than 850 years. There is some disagreement among authorities as to the exact age of this building. While some still be-

lieve that it is the oldest wooden structure in the country, followed by Geungnak-jeon at Bongjeong-sa in Andong, most now agree that Bongjeong-sa's Geungnak-jeon is older by a few years. Whatever its actual age or number in the lineup of old wooden Korean buildings, the gentle upswing of the roof line, and the three-tier roof support system give the hall a simple, unpretentious dignity. The signboard over its front doors is carved from characters written by Joseon Dynasty king Sukjong (1674–1720). Inside, a statue of the Amita Buddha (N.T. #45) is seated in solitary repose, backed by an intricately carved gilt halo. Made of clay embedded with hemp cloth to give it strength and long life, and covered with gilt lacquer, this ancient figure is the only one of its kind in Korea, a masterpiece of Goryeo Dynasty statuary made during a period when talent was turned more toward creating exquisite celadon pottery than sculpture. Uncharacteristically, this statue sits along the short left wall of this tile-floored hall, rather than the long rear wall.

In the courtyard to the front of Muryangsu-jeon is a slender stone lantern (N.T. #17), ostensibly from the Joseon Dynasty. To the left rear of the main hall is the famed floating rock, and beyond that the Three Spirits hall. To the right is a sturdy three-tier stone pagoda (T. #249), and up the hill sits a rotund *sari budo*. From here a trail leads a couple hundred meters up the hill, the right fork going to Chosa-dang, the left going to Nahan-jeon. Built in 1372, Chosa-dang (N.T. #19) is the second of the temple's old wooden structures. Now a shrine to Uisang, its simple, unadorned construction is somewhat reminiscent of the main hall at Sudeok-sa. Nahan-jeon is a tiny hall containing two seated stone figures of the Vairocana Buddha (T. #220) from the 9th century. No matter how attractive the temple compound or how historic and culturally significant its treasures, one thing is for sure: the view from here along the spine of the mountain range to the west is superb.

Sosu Seowon 소수서원

Nine kilometers northeast of Punggi, on the way to Buseok-sa but just outside the park, is Sosu

Seowon (H.S. #55); ₩1,000 entrance fee. Many such *seowon* are seen in the country. Some are more tastefully restored, larger, or more scenic, but none matches the historical importance of this private Confucian academy. Founded in 1544, Sosu Seowon, then called Baegun-dong Seowon, was built to honor the brilliant Goryeo Dynasty scholar An Hyang (1243–1306), who introduced the Neo-Confucian philosophy of Chu Hsi to Korea, and to educate students in Confucian doctrine. Until the mid-Goryeo Dynasty, Confucianism was suppressed by the more influential Buddhists. Largely due to the efforts of An Hyang, this philosophy and its accompanying social and ethical beliefs began to flourish. In 1549, Korea's most famous Confucian scholar, Yi Toe-gye, then governor of this county, petitioned the king for an official charter for this *seowon*. The king granted the request, and this *seowon* became the first royally chartered private academy in the country, its name then changed to Sosu Seowon. Because of its very important historical and philosophical connection to the underpinning of the strictly Confucian Joseon Dynasty, Sosu Seowon escaped destruction during the nationwide closure of private academies in 1871.

Set in a grove of pines and 500-year-old ginkgo trees outside the village of Sunheung, with the Sobaek Mountains a short distance to the west, this academy houses one National Treasure and three Treasures. The walled compound holds a shrine to An Hyang, Confucius, and other scholars; a lecture hall; study hall; two dorms; two archives; and a handful of other buildings. In 1993, an extension was made to the rear of the compound; it houses an exhibition/education hall. While the old buildings are kept locked, opened only on ceremonial days, the two buildings housing portraits are open daily. In one hangs a well-preserved, 750-year-old portrait of An Hyang (N.T. #111), said to be the oldest portrait from the Goryeo Dynasty. Preserved in the second small building is a 300-year-old painting of Confucius and his followers (T. #485), and a portrait of Ju Se-bong (T. #717), the man who had the *seowon* originally constructed when he was governor of this county. The exhibition hall houses a number of historical items from this *seowon*, reproductions of other paintings, and a map that gives the distribution of all remaining famous *seowon* in the country. Unfortunately, there are no descriptions other than in Korean. The second half of this building functions as an educational hall for the teaching of Confucianism and the study of Confucian culture. Under the ginkgoes, near the entrance to this compound stands a pair of stone flagpole supports (T. #59) from the former temple Suksu-sa, which once occupied this site. It was from here that several small gilt-bronze figures were excavated in 1953; these are now housed in the Seoul National Museum. Across the stream, set right over the bank, is a much newer pavilion, a restful spot perfect for study or a lazy summer afternoon rest.

On a wooded knoll behind this village is one of the oldest *hyanggyo* in the country. Unlike private *seowon*, *hyanggyo* were government-supported village schools. Just north and across the road is Geumseong-dan, a small shrine set up for Prince Geumseong, who was banished to this village and later forced to commit suicide by his brother King Sejo, who had usurped the throne from Prince Geumseong's nephew, King Danjong, grandson of King Sejong. Set along the road back toward Punggi is Sunheung Eosuk-myo (H.S. #238), a Silla-era mound tomb with painted murals inside, now locked for preservation. Nearby stands the Seokgyo-ri stone Buddha image (T. #116).

Punggi 풍기

Six kilometers below Heuibang-sa Station, on the plains below Sobaek-san, is the town of Punggi [P'unggi]. Numerous shops and markets here sell *insam*, the local specialty and cash crop, and the October **Punggi Ginseng Festival** celebrates this root. Known the world over, this most prized medicinal plant was once sent to the emperor of China as a tribute. Today, most Koreans and many foreigners have used it in one form or another. This legendary root is praised as a cure-all, and often touted as an aphrodisiac. Needless to say, there is never a lack of customers! Wide fields surrounding Punggi are planted in *insam*, and in this area only white *insam* is produced.

INSAM FIELDS

While there are areas of Korea that are most well known for *insam*, it is grown throughout the country and the method of farming is fairly uniform. Gently sloping fields, requiring well-drained sandy soil, often face north. These delicate plants require painstaking care and protection from the weather, and they also must be properly pruned and safeguarded from bugs. A sloped support structure covered with thatch, shadecloth, and/or felt keeps the harsh sun off the plants in summer. In winter, the covering is lowered to the ground and straw placed over it to protect the delicate plants from snow and freezing winds. Every spring, small clusters of bright red berries bloom on tall stalks above the plant's mass of green leaves. Roots 2–3 centimeters in diameter and 20–30 centimeters in length take five to seven years to mature, often growing in a human-like shape similar to the mandrake root. Cultivation takes much time and effort, but profits are handsome. *Insam* fields should be left fallow for a number of years following a harvest in order to replenish their natural minerals. Because it's an expensive venture, *insam* fields are often bordered by fences or other barriers, letting people know to stay away.

After harvesting, the roots are peeled, bound so that the small bottom roots are partially bent, and dried. The *insam* grown here has never been considered as high in quality as that grown on Ganghwa-do, and it has much competition from *insam* grown in the Geumsan region of Chungcheongnam-Do. To help bolster the economy, apple production now creates a sizable slice of the economic income of the area.

Yeongju 영주

The gateway to Sobaek-san National Park from the Gyeongsangbuk-Do side is Yeongju [Yŏngju]. While this city has a few historical remains—there is a local *hyanggyo* and two Buddha triad stone carvings—and it is referred to as a place of scholars, it is perhaps better known today for apples and as an important rail transportation center. The Jungang rail line runs through the center of town, connecting Seoul to Busan via the mountainous interior. From here, the Yeongdong line heads across a more mountainous route to Gangneung on the east coast, and the Gyeongbuk line makes its way mostly through broad river valleys to Gimcheon. Highways fan out in four directions from Yeongju, and the new Jungang Expressway skirts the west side of town. The Yeongju Station is at the southern end of town; at the north end of the downtown area is the bus terminal. Among others, city bus nos. 1 and 5 run between the bus terminal and train station. Selected bus destinations from Yeongju are Huibang (₩1,800), Buseok-sa (₩2,200), Jeomchon (₩4,500), Andong (₩3,100), Uljin (₩10,200), and Danyang (₩3,800). For accommodations near the train station, try the Silla Gungjeon Hotel (신라궁전호텔), Cosmosjang Yeogwan (코스모스장여관), or the Royaljang Yeogwan Motel (로얄장여관). In the downtown center of the city are the Daewon Motel (대원모텔) and Samhwajang Yeogwan (삼화장여관), while a few steps from the bus terminal are the less expensive Haesanjang Yeogwan (해산장여관) and Yeongbin Yeoinsuk (영빈여인숙). Just north of town, on the way to the park, is the first-class Sobaeksan Tourist Hotel (tel. 054/634-7800), the best accommodation in the area.

For information online about Yeongju, Punggi, and the Sobaek-san mountain area, see www.yeongju.go.kr.

Bonghwa 봉화

Much smaller than Yeongju is the county seat of Bonghwa [Ponghwa], lying in an area known for *songi* (pine tree) mushrooms. It lies along the little-traveled but scenic highway that crosses over the Taebaek range to Uljin. The Yeongdong rail line runs through town, so from here you can hop a train to Gangneung, Yeongju, Seoul, or Andong. From Bonghwa, buses run the back route to Buseok-sa, south to the entrance of Cheongnyang-san Provincial Park, north to Taebaek, and over the Taebaek Mountains to the coast. The bus terminal is across the river to the west of the old part of town, and the train station about half a kilometer beyond that. Just around the corner from the bus terminal are the Nagwonjang Yeogwan (낙원장여관) and bathhouse and Ihwa Motel (이화모텔); near the main intersection in the center of town is the Sillajang Yeogwan (신라장여관).

MUN'GYEONG VICINITY

Mun'gyeong Saejae Provincial Park
문경새재도립공원

Five kilometers northwest of Mun'gyeong is the county's major tourist site, Mun'gyeong Saejae Provincial Park. Established in 1981, this park comprises several narrow valleys and high peaks of the Sobaek Range, the formidable natural barrier that has for centuries been the provincial boundary between the Gyeongsang and Chungcheong provinces. One of the five principal passes along the length of the Sobaek Mountains, this spot has played a strategic role in monitoring the flow of people along this route, deterred the influx of foreign troops from the south, has been the scene of several armed conflicts, and was for some reason often preferred by students from the Yeongnam region who were on their way to Seoul to take civil service examinations. During the reign of King Sukjong (1674–1720), a fortress wall (H.S. #147) and two of the three principal valley gates were constructed here.

Barrier-Gates

A city bus from Mun'gyeong deposits you half a kilometer below Juheul-gwan, the first barrier-gate; entrance to the park is ₩1,900. At the end of the bus line is a new development of shops, restaurants, accommodations, a museum, and park office. Get your last few supplies here if you are planning to hike up to the summit. Purchase acorn jelly, wild mountain vegetables, apples, and a local liquor called *hosanju* here also. The **Mun'gyeong Saejae Museum** is a small but likable display of the local culture and the importance of this fortified mountain pass.

Like the other two barrier-gates, the reconstructed **Juheul-gwan** gives a good idea of their daunting capability. The partially rebuilt fortress wall, a portion of which is connected to Juheul-gwan and contains a water gate, used to run up and around the ridge, creating a near-impreg-

nable fortification. In 2000, a very popular TV historical drama about the Goryeo King Taejo and events that led up to the founding of that dynasty was filmed here. The huge production set for this drama, which consisted of Baekje and Goryeo palace buildings, aristocratic homes, a village, market, and other structures, was created in the valley beyond and across the stream from the first gate of the park. This open-air set has been left for visitors to walk through and examine, and it has become quite an attraction in and of itself. Skirting this movie set village, a gravel road goes up the valley and over the pass, following a forest trail that has been used for centuries, a portion of which can be seen a short way above the second gate to the right side of the stream. The road through the birch trees between the first and second gates is possibly the prettiest part of the park. Dark gray squirrels with tufted ears and elongated bodies play here in this forest. They are quite distinct from the brown squirrels usually seen in the mountains of Korea. Villagers say that certain Chinese medicines made from parts of these gray squirrels are used particularly for nervous disorders. About 1.5 kilometers above the first gate are the reconstructed stone walls of a compound that once held lodgings for those whose job it was to man the gates and protect the pass. A short way above that is a *jumak* or winehouse. Stop and consider that such places once dotted all major travelers' routes to provide sustenance for weary wanderers along the road. Just above the *jumak* is Gyogwijeong, a reconstructed pavilion that overlooks a narrow and perhaps the most attractive section of the river called Yongchu.

Three kilometers beyond the first gate is the second, **Jogok-gwan**, at the opening of a side valley that ascends toward the mountaintop. Originally built in 1594 to repel Japanese invaders, it too is a sturdy sentinel. Stop for a sip of refreshing spring water once you pass through the gate. The third gate, **Joryeong-gwan**, is 3.5 kilometers farther along this narrowing valley, a short way past the tiny hamlet Donghwawon, which was used as a rest stop by government officers and others while making rounds to the provinces. Sitting on the Joryeong Pass, the gate marks the provincial boundary, and the pass itself delineates the drainage basins for the Nakdong River to the south and the Han River to the north. The view into either province from here is rewarding. A one-hour walk west down the road into Chungcheongbuk-Do brings you to the park's back entrance and highway, from where you can catch a bus either back to Mun'gyeong or the eight kilometers into Suanbo for a soak in one of its hot spring baths. Although not a vast area, this steep mountain region has an alluring beauty and historical significance, and once beyond the movie set, it's definitely not overcrowded by visitors.

Hiking

The first hiking route follows the wide road from the first gate to Joryeong Pass (two hours), and beyond to the highway on the far side of the mountain (one additional hour). The second route takes you to the summit of Juheul-san. From inside the first gate, follow the only track leading up to the right into the forest. Halfway up this steep and confined valley is **Hyeguk-sa**, a ramshackle temple attended by female monks, established over 1,100 years ago. Several of the present buildings are over 300 years old. They look their age as they lean precariously, seeming to need only a strong wind or heavy snow to topple them. In the past few years, new buildings have been erected here to make this temple a bit more serviceable and a periodic shuttle now reaches this temple from the village parking lot. A short way before you reach this temple is the 20-meter-high Yeogung Waterfall. Two kilometers beyond the temple is Juheul-san (1,106 meters). From the ridge at the summit, which connects its two peaks, a cliff drops off steeply to the south; Mun'gyeong can be seen in the distance. Looking back at the spine of the mountain—a perfect, natural fortress—it's easy to see how a barrier-wall and three small gates secured the area. The view from Juheul-san, south over the hills beyond Mun'gyeong and west into the interior of this park, is spectacular. About 100 meters below the peak is a crosspath that drops precipitously down and out of the park, leading back to Mun'gyeong. The trail heading back

into the park winds down from this intersection alongside a boulder-strewn stream to the barrier second gate. At one spot is a place where passers-by have piled rocks in neat stacks or conical towers called *seowon seongchwi-tap*—you'll find these along the main park road as well. Some people believe that when rocks are piled in this manner, and a fervent wish is made, one's desire will be attained. The lower half of this trail turns into a gravel track, which connects with the central valley road. Four hours should be allowed for this hike from the first gate to the summit and back down to the second gate.

Other hiking trails make their way through the park. One runs from Juheul-san, north along the ridge to Pu-bong, then farther along, passing two small ridgeline fortress gates to Mapae-bong, and from there either down to the valley road near Donghwawon or farther along the ridge to Joryeong-gwan. From Joryeong-gwan, one trail runs over the north ridge and down the mountainside to Mireuk-saji in Worak-san National Park. Another trail runs up along the ridge to the south to Joryeong-san, from where a trail drops down into the park to meet the valley road near the *jumak*.

Mun'gyeong-eup 문경읍

Mun'gyeong-eup [Mun'gyŏng-ŭp], a farming and former coal mining community, backs up against the towering twin peaks of Juheul-san. There's little of interest in the town itself, but it's the gateway to Mun'gyeong Saejae Provincial Park. The twisting mountain road over the pass west of town brings you to Suanbo and Worak-san National Park, both in Chungcheongbuk-Do. Mun'gyeong is so small that a few hundred meters in any direction puts you in the countryside, yet even here the town is beginning to spread a bit with the establishment of a hot spring spa at its south edge and the Mung'gyeong Ceramic Museum which opened in 2002. Mun'gyeong historically was a ceramic producing area, due in part to its abundant supply of high-quality clay. At the T intersection down the street from the bus terminal is the Chungangjang Yeogwan (중앙장여관) and bathhouse, and just south of the terminal is the newer and nicer Donghwajang Yeogwan (동화장여관). From Mun'-gyeong-eup, selected intercity-bus destinations and fares are Suanbo (₩2,100), Chungju (₩3,500), Jeomchon (₩1,800), and Andong (₩6,400). From the bus station, a city bus (₩1,050) runs about once an hour from 0700 to 1830 to and from the provincial park entrance.

Gaeun 가은

The area west of Mun'gyeong-eup is—or was—coal country. Although it produced great quantities of the black rock for decades, it never reached the output of the larger and more productive private mines in the Taebaek region of Gangwon-Do to the north. By the 1990s, the area's mines had all been abandoned and the rail line that once ran here and to Mun'gyeong-eup has been discontinued. In the tiny mountain town of Gaeun, the center of this coal region, is the **Mun'gyeong Coal Museum** (문경석탄 박물관); entrance ₩770. A 15-minute walk north of the bus terminal in town brings you to the entrance. Nearly 40 mines dotted these hills, about half of them large-scale government-sponsored operations. They drilled over 400 kilometers of tunnel, down to 700 meters below ground level, the deepest in the country. There is still plenty of coal left in these hills but for a variety of economic reasons, the last mine in this area shut down in 1994. About 150 meters of one mine can be viewed and it displays mostly the heavy equipment used in digging and in transporting men and coal; outside the mine are additional pieces of heavy equipment. Located to the front of this mine opening, the museum itself has a plethora of artifacts and smaller tools and equipment. There is a good but brief explanation of coal mining and related energy resource information, nearly all in Korean only. Great effort has been put into land reclamation here, reforesting the hillsides, greening former housing tracts, and cleaning up stream beds.

North of Gaeun is **Bongam-sa** (봉암사). Founded in 879 during the Silla Dynasty, then later transformed into a meditation school by Jeongjin Daesa, it became one of the "Nine Mountains" of Korean Zen, one of the principal schools of Zen practice. This sizable temple lies below the granite peaks of Hoeyang-san. A remote and distant place, Bongam-sa is known as the epitome of meditation temples in modern Korea. There are numerous temples throughout the country where meditation is practiced on a regular basis, but even among the monks, Bongam-sa is credited as the place for *serious* meditation. Basically, there is no distraction here, so meditation can happen without the usual comings and goings and happenings of ordinary life. Bongam-sa is closed to the public for all but one day a year. Only on the seventh day of the seventh lunar month will the temple open its gates for outsiders to visit. Among the usual collection of buildings, within the temple grounds are a stupa (T. #171) and stele (T.# 172) for Jeongjin Daesa; a stupa (T. #137) and stele (T. #138) for Jijeong Daesa, another meditation master; a less sophisticated stupa for Jigyeong Daesa; a three-tier stone pagoda (T. #169) that has an unusually well-preserved finial top; and the two-story, wooden pagoda-like, diminutive Geungnak-jeon, which is surrounded by an open veranda.

Mun'gyeong and Yecheon

Mun'gyeong (문경) was called Jeomchon [Chŏmch'on] (점촌) before the city and county merged administrations, and it is still often referred to as such. The much smaller community of Mun'gyeong-eup lies closer to the provincial park. The growing towns of Mun'gyeong and Yecheon [Yech'ŏn] (예천) don't have much that would be of interest to the casual visitor, save a Gaya-era mound tomb thought to be that of the founder of Goryeong Gaya (circa 40 A.D.) south of Jeomchon and a prehistoric northern-style dolmen east of Jeomchon. However, outside of each town lies a temple or two of some historical interest. North of Jeomchon is **Gimnyong-sa** (김용사). Founded in 588, it at one time had about four dozen buildings and several associated hermitages. Much smaller today, it still lays claim to Geumdang Hall, said to be the largest old-style Korean room heated with the traditional *ondol* system. Two of its structures are from 1661, and several others are from the early 1700s. A short distance to the east is **Daeseung-sa** (대승사). Founded one year earlier than Gimnyong-sa, this temple has a more open aspect. It preserves a broad and finely carved gilt wooden mural (T. #575) that stands behind the figures on the main altar, and a seated, gilt-bronze, Goryeo Dynasty statue of Gwaneum (T. #991) in another building. Outside Yecheon is the larger **Yongmun-sa** ("Dragon Gate Temple") (용문사). Established in 870, it preserves four Treasures. Daejang-jeon (T. #145), the main hall, contains a wooden bookstand (T. #684), royal decree plaque (T. #729), and a seated wooden Buddha image and wooden carving (T. #989).

This rural and traditional region has kept alive many of its old crafts. Mun'gyeong hangs on to a pottery tradition and today still produces mostly carefree and earthy *buncheong* pottery and the more sophisticated white porcelain, both styles that were popular during the Joseon period. Yecheon is particularly known for its traditional-style bows and arrows. Short, with a sharp recurve, the extremely flexible Korean bow is a powerful weapon. Layers of bamboo, dried animal ligaments, and mulberry wood are bound together with a type of fish glue. The arrows are made of thin bamboo rods. These hand-crafted items are sought after and command a high price from Korean archery aficionados. Properly cared for, they will last longer than their owners. In the past, Korean archers were feared throughout Asia because of their deadly accuracy.

Open to domestic flights only, one of the smallest airports in the country lies between Yecheon and Mun'gyeong, adjacent to a Korean Air Force base. It is serviced by both KAL and Asiana Airlines; there are two daily flights to Seoul. The airport is located six kilometers west of town, and buses and taxis make the trip to the terminal to meet each flight, but they don't hang around long, so don't waste your time inside the terminal building. Airport shuttle buses run to Jeomchon (₩1,500), Yecheon (₩1,000), and Andong (₩3,300).

Sangju 상주

In the broad agricultural plains between Mun'gyeong and Gimcheon, a short distance from the back entrance to Songni-san National Park, is Sangju, a quiet town known for rice, dried persimmons, and silk. During the Three King-

SILK

Of the areas of the country known for producing silk, Sangju is perhaps best known for its sericulture. Learned from the Chinese, Koreans perfected the art of silk production and weaving, and eventually passed the skill on to the Japanese. For hundreds of years, Sangju has been famous for its silk, and remains one of the country's principal silk-producing areas. Much is still produced in small quantities as a cottage industry, but a growing number of factories are generating large volumes of this soft, subtle, and strong material.

Silkworms feed on mulberry leaves cultivated in the area. Stripped from their branches, these leaves are placed on large mesh beds with young larvae; the larvae then gorge themselves. They'll mature in about six weeks; when round and plump, they begin to spin a cocoon. Through an opening on the lip, a continuous flow of sticky liquid turns into a thin filament when exposed to the air. As the cocoon grows, the silkworm shrinks. When finished, this soft white womb is about four centimeters in length. The worms are killed and fibers loosened when the cocoons are boiled or exposed to steam or hot air. Carefully unspun, the delicate strands are wound together with several others to produce a gossamer thread. From there, the thread is woven into fabric.

What you might not expect is that the boiled silkworms are saved, steam-heated, and sold as snacks called *beondegi* by pushcart vendors who ply the streets during summer and autumn evenings. Its earthy bitter taste is popular with young people out for an evening's entertainment, but it's definitely an acquired taste.

doms period, this region was an independent Gaya state known as Sabeol-guk. One of eight principal Silla garrisons was set up near Sangju. During the early 10th century, Silla's power began to atrophy. In its place rose the Later Baekje and Goryeo kingdoms. Several battles were fought near here between the forces of these three kingdoms, which resulted in the acquisition of land for the Later Baekje and Goryeo kings, and paved the way for the eventual dissolution of the

Silla Dynasty in 935. Sabeol, son of Silla king Gyeongmyeong, was sent to rule this region but was killed by Gyeon Hwon in about 930. A small mound tomb regarded to be that of King Sabeol is located some kilometers east of town. Interestingly, Later Baekje king Gyeon Hwon was born in Gaeun nearby. He ruled his short-lived kingdom from Jeonju in Jeollabuk-Do until its defeat by Goryeo forces in 936.

The intercity bus terminal is on the western edge of town. Selected destinations and fares are

Gimcheon (₩2,600), Mun'gyeong (₩3,500), Andong (₩5,900), and Daegu (₩6,400). City buses run to Hwabuk, from where a trail leads up the back route into Songni-san National Park, and to Songmyeon, the entrance to the Seonyu-dong section of the park. From the train station, south and east of the main intersection, daily trains pass through Sangju going to Jeomchon, Yeongju, Gimcheon, and Busan.

For additional information, see www.sangju.kyongbuk.kr.

Southwest Gyeongsangbuk-Do

Gimcheon 김천

Located in the southwest corner of the province, Gimcheon [Kimch'ŏn] (pop. 150,000) is close to the geographical center of the country, and Geumo Provincial Park and Songni-san, Gaya-san, and Deokyu-san national parks are all within a few hours' bus ride. Just outside the Busan Perimeter, it saw heavy and sustained fighting early in the Korean War, and was completely razed. After the war, the city was moved a short distance from its old location and rebuilt on higher land; it's now tucked into the hillside and surrounds the train station. The few remaining historical monuments of consequence are Bongh-wang-nu ("Phoenix Pavilion"), set in the middle of a lotus pond in the northern section of town; the Gimsan Hyanggyo, on the north side of the expressway; and Wongye Seowon, over the hill from the center of town. Although a city in size and population, and a bustling transportation center, Gimcheon is still very much an over-grown market town. The new industrial sector is located on the north side of the expressway.

West of the city is Chupungnyeong Pass, the major pass over the Sobaek Mountains, through which the country's central expressway and rail line run. Gimcheon is one terminus of the Gyeongbuk rail line, which runs north via Sangju and Jeomchon to Yeongju, and is one stop on the busy Gyeongbu rail line.

Hourly express buses service only Seoul (₩9,500); the terminal is next to the post office, 200 meters down the road to the right as you exit the train station. Intercity buses and city buses leave from their own terminal. Selected destinations and fares are Jikji-sa (₩600), Gumi (₩1,400), Daegu (₩3,900), Andong (₩8,500), and Daejeon (₩4,800). To get to the intercity bus terminal from the train station, take the pedestrian walk-way over the tracks or walk 200 meters up the road to the bridge over the rail line. There, go down the steps, turn left and follow the road 200 meters to the terminal. The frequent city bus nos. 11 or 111 running the 12 kilometers to Jikji-sa can be boarded at the bus terminal or along the main street in front of the train station.

As in any city, there are dozens of places to stay in Gimcheon. At the top end is the first-class **Kimchon Grand Hotel** (tel. 054/433-9001), where rooms start at about ₩80,000. At the other end of town is the third-class **Kimchon Tourist Hotel** (tel. 054/432-9911); rooms here are ₩40,000–70,000. Across the road and back in from the train station are the Yeongnam Yeogwan (영남여관), Aellimjang Yeogwan (엘림장여관), Heungnamjang Yeogwan (흥남장여관), Sujeong Yeogwan (수정여관), and others. Near the bus terminal, try the Yeonjeongjang Yeogwan (연정장여관) or the Oksan Yeoinsuk (옥산여인숙).

See www.gimcheon.go.kr online for more information.

JIKJI-SA 직지사

Along a gentle stream at the foot of Hwanghaksan is the temple Jikji-sa [Chikji-sa]. This 1,600-year-old temple was purportedly established by the famous Goguryeo monk Ado, who introduced Buddhism to the Silla Kingdom sometime in the early 5th century. Legend says that when Ado first saw this mountain, he pointed to it and said that a large temple should be constructed at its base. Thus, the temple was dedicated with the name Jikji ("Direct Indicator"); it's the oldest temple in the Yeongnam region. (Another take on the name indicates that the study and meditation of the Buddhist doctrine is the "direct path" to enlightenment.) During his reign, Taejo, Goryeo Dynasty's first king, expanded the temple to make it the largest in East Asia. Jikji-sa was the home of numerous well-known monks, including the military monk Sammyeong-daesa, who was ordained here. During the Imjin War, this national hero helped raise and command an army of warrior-monks. He built several fortresses, inspired the population to resist the invaders, courageously faced the Japanese forces, and caused them innumerable inconveniences. The Japanese army burned Jikji-sa in retaliation. After the war, Sammyeong-daesa was sent to Japan as a peace envoy, and there negotiated a treaty for better relations, receiving some recompense for the damage inflicted on the Korean peninsula; he also secured the release of thousands of prisoners of war.

Jikji-sa was carefully rebuilt in 1610, and throughout the 1980s went through extensive reconstruction and landscaping. In 1993, an International Buddhism Training Center was erected here for meetings, training, meditation, and ceremonies. Sitting below the original temple compound, its buildings are now the largest at the temple. Yet even with a variety of well-constructed buildings, their extensive and brightly colored paintings and realistically carved wooden figures, none is particularly outstanding. Five Treasures are kept on the premises. With its courtyards, tree-lined walks, and invigorating mountain atmosphere, the temple seems to welcome and embrace you with open arms. With its very pleasant compound, Jikji-sa is now one of the eight largest temples in Korea and has five associated hermitages in the hills beyond. Hwanghak-san is not the most alluring mountain (although it is known for its grand fall colors), but a 12-kilometer hike to the top rewards you with an expansive view.

Temple Buildings and Treasures

From the ticket booth (₩2,000 entrance) and informational signboard, a wide walkway takes you to the temple grounds. The first gate is the two-posted, open Ilju-mun. Its huge posts are made of arrowroot trunks and are over 1,000 years old. Nearby sits an excellent Goryeo Dynasty tortoise-shaped stela base and numerous stone monuments. The path threads its way through two small enclosed gates to reach the next and much larger gate in which stand huge brightly painted wooden figures of the four Heavenly Kings trampling demons into the ground; faded intertwining dragons are painted on the ceiling. Walk under the lecture hall to the main courtyard. On the far side sits the visually pleasing main temple hall. Behind the three seated images on the altar hang three scroll paintings (T. #670) from 1744. Out front stand twin United Silla period stone pagodas (T. #606)—elegantly tall and slender, in excellent shape, but topped with new finials. These two, and a third pagoda (T. #607) that stands in an adjoining courtyard in front of Biro-jeon, were moved here from other locations in the province and set up during the mid-1970s. A pavilion with drum, bell, and gongs stands to the left, and in front of another building stands yet another three-tier stone pagoda (T.# 1186).

To the side of the main hall is an arbor, with several stone objects not found at any other temple in Korea. At least one authority considers them related to procreation, similar to the *lingam* and *yoni* figures of Hinduism; some are obviously phallic, while others are deeply dished. One look will give you the idea! Behind this "fertility garden" is Gwaneum-jeon, inside of which is an ornate statue of the Goddess of Mercy, uncharacteristically seated with one leg folded onto her lap. Around an adjoining courtyard are the judgment hall, 500 Nahan Hall, Yaksa-jeon, and Biro-jeon. Biro-jeon enshrines on its very long altar an impressive collection of several hundred look-alike statues of the Buddha's disciples, all except one seated. Yaksa-jeon contains the temple's fifth Treasure. This seated stone figure (T. #319) from the United Silla period was unearthed during a previous building period. Unfortunately, its face and halo are badly disfigured, but judging from the bowl (bottle?) in its left hand, it seems most likely to be the Healing Buddha. Other buildings in the complex are Sammyeong-gak (a memorial shrine to Sammyeong-daesa), dormitories, a new teahouse, and a small museum (₩1,000 entrance fee) which displays other treasured temple items.

Practicalities

One kilometer below the temple is Jikji-sa village, a well-developed collection of souvenir shops, restaurants, *yeogwan*, post office, police station, and bus stop. City bus nos. 11 and 111 run all day, every 15 minutes or so, to and from Gimcheon. Remember that you won't be the only visitor. In good weather, especially on autumn weekends, busloads of camera-wielding housewives, old gentlemen in top hats and topcoats, and schoolchildren flock to see the colors, sing songs, and generally disturb the peace of this tranquil temple. Make a timely visit—go during the week!

GEUMO-SAN PROVINCIAL PARK 금오산도립공원

Geumo-san (976 meters) lies about five kilometers west of Gumi. This mountain area was designated Geumo-san Provincial Park in 1970; ₩400 entrance fee. During the Silla Dynasty a Buddhist monk came through the area in order to construct a temple in the mountains west of here. As he passed this mountain, he noticed a crow lit golden by the rays of the evening sun. Because of it, the monk called the mountain Geumo-san ("Golden Crow Mountain"), and decided to build a temple at its base. The temple is now gone, but the mountain's name has remained.

A short ride on city bus no. 12 or 12-1 brings

Geumo-san fortress walls and gate

© ROBERT NILSEN

you from town to the park entrance at the base of the mountain. Running every 10–15 minutes throughout the day, most go by both the train station and bus terminal. At the park entrance village are a group of restaurants, a few *yeogwan*, the recently remodeled Geumosan Tourist Hotel, and a small children's amusement park. Across the road is a reservoir, alongside of which sits Jaemi-jeong, the reconstructed study hall of Goryeo Dynasty Neo-Confucian scholar Gil Jae. Erected in 1768 and renovated in 1977, this shrine honors a Confucian scholar who served the last Goryeo Dynasty king and out of loyalty to that king refused to hold office under the first Joseon Dynasty king, a usurper of the title. A two-kilometer path from here leads up the narrowing valley through a reconstructed gate in a section of the old fortress wall to the 27-meter-high Myeonggeom Waterfall and the nearby temple Haeun-sa (해운사). From the late Silla Dynasty, this temple was destroyed in 1592, then rebuilt in 1925 and again in 1980. Set below a huge rock outcrop, this small compound has brightly painted buildings. The main hall enshrines a memorial portrait of former president Park Chung Hee. In the yard is a Buddha figure with mortarboard hat standing in front of panel carvings of disciples and guardians. Up a path to the side of the falls, and directly above Haeun-sa, is the shallow cave Doseon-gul; an iron railing helps you keep your balance as you make your way around the rock face to its opening. Said to have been originally used by a monk named Doseon, it was used by Gil Jae and later by refugees from the Japanese during the 1590s. A small altar sits against the rear wall today. Perhaps the most pleasant view down the valley is from here. For those not wanting to hike up the valley, a cable car runs to a point next to Haeunsa, pretty much following the hiking trail below. This cable car operates every 15 minutes from 0900 to 1930, and charges ₩2,400 one-way, ₩3,500 round-trip.

From below the waterfall, near the streamside mineral spring, a one-hour climb leads up the mountain to a standing rock-cut Buddha image (T. #490) and the hermitage Yaksa-am. Slightly misproportioned, the Buddha figure is rather bulky and static, yet some of the detailing shows a bit of skill. A local legend relates to tidy Yaksaam hermitage; it says that from a small hole in the rock here (from which water now flows), rice would fall, one grain at a time.

No access is allowed near the communications tower on the summit, but two trails lead down from the hermitage. The most popular trail cuts down the east side of the mountain past Beopseong-sa to the park entrance village. The other leads around the side of the peak to another section of the old fortress wall and down the back side of the mountain past two other temples to the trailhead, where buses can be caught for Gimcheon or Waegwan. The Geumosan fortress wall is of uncertain age, but it is known to have been repaired in both the Goryeo and Joseon dynasties, so it's at least 600 years old. Not high or difficult, a hike up and down this mountain offers a satisfying way to spend part of a day.

Gumi 구미

When Korea began to speed industrialization in the early 1960s, one of the first areas targeted for new development was Gumi [Kumi] (pop. 340,000). Halfway between Daegu and Gimcheon on Korea's main north-south transportation route, it seemed like a perfect spot. Still, it appears not to have been an arbitrary choice as this small rural town in the already relatively industrialized Yeongnam region was former president Park's home turf. Development funneled large amounts of money into this predominantly agricultural area for construction, housing, education, and other services. Gumi grew with light industry, and over 250 companies operate in the Gumi industrial estate. Many produce textiles and fibers, while others focus on rubber, plastic, metal products, and electronic goods.

Former president Park Chung Hee was born in Gumi. To visit his renovated birth home (고박정희대통령생가), take bus no. 15 to the end of the line and walk a few dozen meters to the house. While there is not too much to see except his humble home and many pictures, most of which were taken after he had grabbed power in 1961, it is still a shrine of sorts.

Daegu 대구

Daegu [Taegu] is the principal inland population center of the Yeongnam region, and has historically been the major market and service center for the central Nakdong River basin. The Geumho River flows along the northern and eastern edges of Daegu, and empties into the Nakdong River a short distance beyond the low hills west of the city. Daegu's surrounding plain forms a basin with mountains on the perimeter: Palgong-san (1,192 meters) on the north, Biseul-san (1,084 meters) on the south, and the foothills of Gaya-san (1,430 meters) on the west; the hills to the east divide this plain from the one on which Gyeongju lies. Like spokes on a wheel, valleys radiate from Daegu toward Andong, Waegwan, Goryeong, Cheongdo and Yeongcheon.

Having less than average precipitation throughout the year, Daegu is an area of temperature extremes. On average, it is the hottest area of the country in summer, a condition exacerbated as the surrounding mountains trap the hot sultry air in this basin. In 1940, it recorded the highest temperature ever recorded on the peninsula—40°C. With cold air lying in this valley in winter, it's nearly as cold as the interior mountain regions. While snow falls in the city, it usually doesn't stay long, but the winter winds keep the temperature low.

With more than 2.5 million inhabitants, this bustling metropolis is Korea's third-largest city; its population has more than doubled in the last 25 years. Daegu citizens have been characterized as modest, persistent, patient, and hardworking; the women in particular are said to be strong-willed—and the most beautiful in the country. Daegu is Gyeongsangbuk-Do's provincial capital. Now a metropolitan city, it's been administered independently of the province since 1981. Daegu not only has strong local political muscle, it is an important player in national politics as well; the city is the home of former president Rho Tae-woo.

Daegu is an educational center. Missionaries introduced modern schools and Western education in 1906; Keisung Boys Academy was the first Western school. Many other schools, founded by Korean educators, followed in rapid succession. Students from all over the province flocked here to study this new "Western learning." Today, Daegu and its sister city, Gyeongsan (located a dozen km to the east), boast over two dozen universities and colleges. Of these, Gyeongbuk National University, Keimyung University, Daegu University, Daegu National Teachers College, and Yeongnam University are the most well-known and -respected.

When the countryside was finally opened to Western missionaries in the 1880s, Daegu was one of the first places outside of Seoul to be targeted for proselytization. Although it was slow going at first, Daegu became a strong and vibrant Christian community. Daegu Jeil Church and Gyesan Cathedral stand testimony to this. Aside from the city's numerous churches, missionaries started hospitals, universities, and social organizations for Daegu citizens. While few Buddhist temples of significance are found within the city, many are situated in the surrounding mountains. In the heart of the city, however, stands the Daegu Hyanggyo (Confucian Academy). Here, yearly memorial ceremonies are conducted to honor Confucius, Korean Confucian sages, and local scholars who have had the most lasting influence on the ethics and culture of both contemporary Koreans and those of the preceding Joseon Dynasty.

A large and lively place, Daegu hosts the spirited **Dalgubeol Festival** every October. Named after the ancient city state that occupied this spot, the Dalgubeol Festival is one of merriment and good fun. It not only honors the city's cultural and historical past, it also celebrates the strengths of its present. Events include traditional music and dance, folk games, sporting events, a parade, athletic competitions, and art exhibitions. In addition, in October, the textile industry puts on a

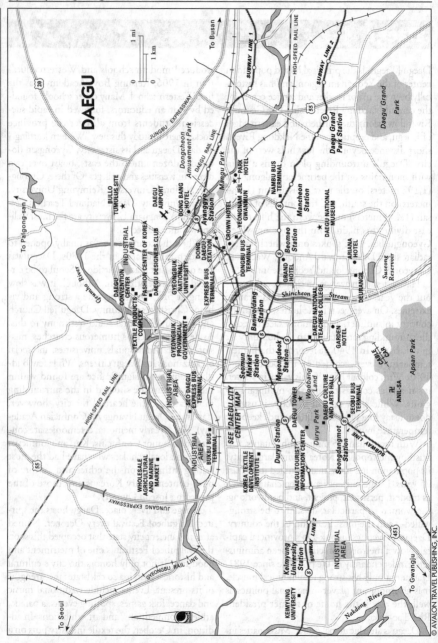

DAEGU

To Paigong-san

To Seoul

To Gwangju

To Busan

To Palgong-san

© AVALON TRAVEL PUBLISHING, INC.

Textile Festival and holds a Miss Textile pageant, while the Yangnyeongshi Festival celebrates the city's traditional herb market.

Once the hub of Korea's textile industry, Daegu now plays a less dominant yet still substantial role in the nation's textile market. Textiles make up nearly half of the economic base, with mills for spinning and dying thread, weaving cloth, and sewing clothes. Starting in the 1880s with silk production, the industry moved to other natural and then synthetic fibers when the country started its push to create an export economy in the 1960s. Today, fashion is also a focus, so design is an integral component. To help bolster this industry, the Korea Textile Development Institute promotes new types of textiles, the Fashion Center of Korea runs shows featuring fashions and promotes the city's textile industries, and the Textile Products Complex and Daegu Designers Club are huge retail shopping centers for fashions. In the recent decades, the city's economy has grown and diversified greatly. Medium heavy industries like machinery, chemicals, automobile parts, and light industries, particularly in electronics, communications, computer-related fields, and eyewear have most recently appeared. The city's industrial areas are mostly located along the river north of downtown and in the western periphery.

Apple production has historically been and continues to be another important driver of Daegu's economy. Whatever effect Daegu's bowl formation has on the human population, it's extremely good for the abundant apples. Although the indigenous crabapple grew in Korea for centuries, specifically in the Daegu region, a Western variety brought to Daegu in the early 1900s thrived; it was eventually planted throughout the country. Since then, other varieties have been introduced, and some crossbreeding has been successful. Today, there are over a dozen major varieties available. Over the decades, production increased markedly, making this and the surrounding provincial region the heart of the apple industry in Korea. The first apples are picked in late July; the season extends into early winter.

For several hundred years, Daegu has been the country's major retail center for medicinal herbs, and still commands that distinction. Throughout the Joseon Dynasty, Daegu's herb market operated every spring and autumn, with some trade even going to China and Japan. Its modern carryover, Yangnyeong Shijang, is still in operation and there is a revival of interest.

When the city outgrew its walls, a hodgepodge of winding alleys, houses, shops, and factories emerged. It haphazardly continued to expand, but in the last few decades, the city government has expended great effort to add color and personality to this once-drab city. It has erected more visually pleasing buildings; straightened, widened, and beautified its streets; pulled down many barrier walls and fences; expanded green areas; and created numerous recreational sites. Today, Daegu deserves an additional and appropriate appellation, the "City of Parks."

Daegu was one of the cities in Korea to host the 2002 World Cup Soccer tournaments. For this event, a new stadium was built in Daegu Grand Park, located to the southeast of downtown, toward the city of Gyeongsan.

See www.daegu.go.kr and http://tour.daegu.go.kr for more information about Daegu online.

History

Unlike other large population centers on the peninsula, Daegu's historical influence has been more local than national. During the early Three Kingdoms period, Daegu was the site of a fortified, earthen-walled town called Dalgubeol. The nearby clans slowly coalesced into a confederate state, which eventually lost its independence to the powerful and expanding Silla Kingdom to the east. The large group of some 200 graves at the Bullo Tumulus site (H.S. #262) northeast of the city center also evinces the existence of an organized society in this valley during the Three Kingdoms period. Smaller than the later Silla tombs of Gyeongju, they have yielded numerous items that show artistic skill and indicate an organized social system. Lying close to the vital Nakdong River water highway, the city became an important market for the surrounding prosperous agricultural regions, and a stop for government officials, merchants, military personnel, and other travelers. During the Goryeo Dynasty, the area was a stronghold of Korean Buddhism. The first set of wood printing blocks of the *Koreana Tripitaka* were stored at Buin-sa on Palgong-san, and the important cultural history of the Three Kingdoms period, called *Samguk Yusa,* was written at another of the mountain's temples. During the latter half of the Joseon Dynasty, Daegu served as the seat of regional government, and in the late 1700s a new city wall was built. Although it stood until the early 1900s, today nothing remains of the wall; a replica of the south gate, Yeongnam Jeil Gwanmun, however, has been constructed, overlooking the Geumho River on the eastern edge of town.

During the Korean War, North Korean troops were halted at the Nakdong River, a short distance west of the city. That point of contact became part of the Busan Perimeter. Luckily, the line held and Daegu was never invaded, though streams of refugees flooded the city. After the war, however, business boomed. Since then, its industrial sector has expanded rapidly, educational opportunities have greatly increased, and it has carved out a leading role for itself in the development of the nation. Since the Korean War, Daegu has remained an important military town, being the headquarters of the Second Korean Army. The U.S. military has also maintained a small and mostly low-key presence in Daegu with one Air Force base and two Army bases.

SIGHTS

For most travelers, Daegu has only attracted attention as the gateway to the famous temple Haein-sa to the southwest and the traditional Andong area to the north, or as a stop on the way to Gyeongju to the east. Stop a while and give the city a chance to grow on you. In Daegu's compact downtown, you'll find a concentration of banks, offices, accommodations and eating facilities, the central shopping and entertainment area, city parks, and the medicinal-herb

market. In the city's outlying areas are additional parks and markets, its many schools, and many of its historical and cultural remains.

Dongseong-no Shopping Street
동성로

Dongseong-no curves in a gentle arch down from Daegu Station to the east end of Yakjeon Golmok, making a Y split at its bottom end. A "pedestrian street," motor vehicles are barred along its length most of the day. This is the heart of the city, and along this street and its contiguous alleys are department stores, clothing retailers, tailors, sporting-goods shops, cinemas, music stores, bookstores, bakeries, tearooms, and dozens of restaurants and bars. At night, mobile carts cram the already crowded streets and alleys. Music blares from storefront speakers, lights dazzle the eyes, hawkers peddle their wares, and lovers walk arm in arm. There's as much activity here as along the midway of a large state fair. It's an eyeful, and there's never a dull moment; it's worth a look just for the people scene. A yearly street festival is held here in May to celebrate the vitality of this district.

The alleyways at the southern end of Dongseong-no, and those running to the east, form an area known as **Yashi Street,** a section chockablock with mostly small boutiques and shoe stores that largely attract a young female clientele.

Crossing the main boulevard south of Dongseong-no you find a street called **Bongsan Culture Street.** Along this road are a fair number of art galleries and art shops, and in October an art and culture festival is held here.

Yakjeon Golmok 약전골목
One kilometer south of Daegu Station, and following the curve of the old city wall, is a street where approximately 40 percent of all the medicinal herbs in the country are retailed. This is Yakjeon Golmok ("Pharmacopoeia Alley"), the only one of perhaps a dozen large traditional herb markets throughout the peninsula that is still functioning. Started about 1650, and held twice yearly near the old provincial government complex (the present Gyeongsang Gamyeong Park),

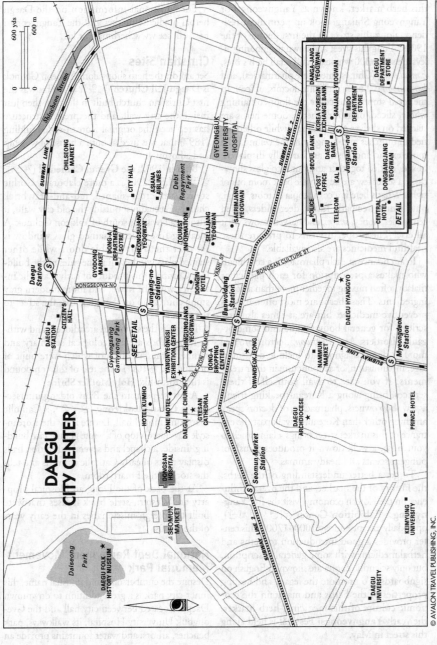

GYEONGSANGBUK-DO

DAEGU
CITY CENTER

Dalseong
Park

★ DAEGU FOLK
HISTORY MUSEUM

Shincheon Stream

600 yds
600 m

SUBWAY LINE 1

CHILSEONG
MARKET

CITY HALL

ASIANA
AIRLINES

Debt
Repayment
Park

GYEONGBUK
UNIVERSITY
HOSPITAL

SUBWAY LINE 2

Daegu
Station

GYODONG
MARKET

DONG-A
DEPARTMENT
SOTRE

CHEONGSUJANG
YEOGWAN

TOURIST
INFORMATION

SILLAJANG
YEOGWAN

SAERIMJANG
YEOGWAN

DONGSEONG-NO

Jungang-no
Station

YASIN ST

BONGSAN CULTURE ST

DONGIN
HOTEL

Banwoldang
Station

DAEGU HYANGGYO

DAEGU
STATION

CITIZEN'S
HALL

Gyeongsang
Gamyeong Park

SEE DETAIL

SHINGUNGJANG
YEOGWAN

DONG-A
SHOPPING
CENTER

YANGNYEONGSI
EXHIBITION CENTER

YAGJEON GOLMOK

SUBWAY LINE 1

Myeongdeok
Station

HOTEL KUMHO

ZONE MOTEL

DAEGU JEIL CHURCH

GYESAN
CATHEDRAL

DONGSAN HOSPITAL

GWANDEOKJEONG

NAMMUN
MARKET

DAEGU
ARCHDIOCESE
★

PRINCE HOTEL

SEOMUN
MARKET
▲

Seomun Market
Station

SUBWAY LINE 2

KEIMYUNG
UNIVERSITY

DAEGU
UNIVERSITY

N

DANGA-JANG
YEOGWAN

SEOUL BANK

KOREA FOREIGN
EXCHANGE BANK

SANJANG
YEOGWAN

DAEGU
DEPARTMENT
STORE

POST
OFFICE

KAL

DAEGU
BANK

MIDO
DEPARTMENT
STORE

TELECOM

POLICE

Jungang-no
Station

DONGBANGJANG
YEOGWAN

CENTRAL
HOTEL

DETAIL

© AVALON TRAVEL PUBLISHING, INC.

this herb market, known as Yangnyeongsi or Yangnyeong Shijang, took up permanent residence along this street in the first decade of the 1900s. Along this street and down neighboring alleys are some 300 wholesale and retail herb stores, *hanyakbang* (Chinese medicine pharmacies), and *haneuiwon* (Chinese medicine doctors' offices). In the retail stores, tubs cover the floor containing whole, sliced, or ground herbs. Some herbs are stacked on shelves in paper bags, while others are tied in bunches and hung from the ceiling. The more exotic and costly are carefully displayed, boxed, or tied together and put into glass showcases; a select few are kept in the back room out of sight. What's here is a cornucopia of roots, fungi, nuts, fruits, tree bark, leaves, deer antlers, dried centipedes, honey, *insam,* and heaven knows what all else! The proper utensils to prepare these healthful medicines are also available.

In attendance at each pharmacy is a consultant who makes a prescription for each particular malady, often mixing together more than a dozen ingredients. These herbs are most often used as preventive medicine, but are at times also prescribed for general body fatigue and some organic disorders. At *haneuiwon,* doctors provide more in-depth diagnoses to include diet, massage, moxibustion, or acupuncture in their treatments. If you care to avail yourself of these services, bring along a Korean-speaking friend as few shop owners, pharmacists, or doctors speak anything other than Korean. A walk past the entrance of this market street brings a faint smell to your nose; a walk down it produces a rush of pungent scents and heady aromas.

To get a better understanding of the herbs, the history of the market, and the overall influence on the Korean economy, visit the free **Yangnyeongsi Exhibition Center** (약령시전시관), open daily except Sunday 1000–1700. This center provides a good introduction to herbs and herbal medicine with some general description, but only scientific names are shown in English on signboards. To promote the legacy and healing properties of the herbs and maintain the economic culture of this medicinal-herb market, the yearly **Yangnyeongsi Festival** is held along this street in May.

For additional information on the Daegu herbal medicine market and the Yangnyeongsi Festival, see www.herbmart.or.kr.

Christian Sites

Set amidst the herb shops along Yakjeon Golmok is **Daegu Jeil Church** (제일교회). This was the first Christian church built in the city, then just inside the city wall, and the present structure has replaced the original Korean-style building (1897) that was used as both a house of worship and a hospital.

Built in 1902, the **Gyesan Cathedral** (계산동 성당) (H.S. #290) is a more elaborate, Gothic style, Latin cross–shaped, red-and-gray brick church. Erected just outside the old city walls, it sits just a few steps south of Yakjeon Golmok. A pleasing rose-shaped stained glass window is set over the front double doors while other stained glass windows line the sides of the building. Compair this product of early Catholic influence with the newer and more modern gray stone church up on the hill across the street to the west.

Daegu is the seat of an archdiocese and within its grounds are a theological seminary and nunnery, the buildings of which were built of brick in the 1910s. To the rear of this compound is the grotto-like **Holy Mother Shrine**.

A few steps from the Banwoldang intersection is **Gwangdeokjeong** (광덕정), a Catholic martyr memorial hall. Locate it by the Korean-style pavilion on top of a white granite face building. Inside, a chapel and several exhibition halls display relics of early Catholic converts and tells the story of their martyrdom.

At the back of the Dongsan Hospital property are Western-style brick houses that were built by foreign missionaries in the early years of the 1900s.

National Debt Repayment Movement Memorial Park

Despite the cumbersome and unusual name, this inner-city park is a great addition to downtown Daegu. Located between city hall and the Gyeongbuk University Hospital, its walkways, park benches, arbors, and water fountains provide an escape from the bustle of traffic. However, as the greenery is still young, it will take some years to mature. In the most prominent corner of the park is the huge Dalgubeol bell and pavilion, and at the back of the park the city's central library.

Gyeongsang Gamyeong Park
경상감영공원

Across the street from the mid-town post office is the old Jungang ("Central") Park, which, in recent years, has been expanded and renamed Gyeongsang Gamyeong Park. For being in the city center, this compact green acre is quiet. Created on the site of the former provincial government complex, it has finely sculpted gardens, many shade trees and park benches, a new octagonal city bell pavilion set partially over a fish pond, and two reconstructed Joseon-era buildings—Jingcheong-gak, a residence hall, and the pavilion Seonhwa-dang, an administration building. Both were erected in 1601, when the provincial government was moved here from Andong. They were used until 1965. During fine weather days, this is a favorite place for office workers to relax during their lunch hour and for elders to congregate, play board games, and gab with their cronies.

Dalseong Park 달성공원

A short walk west of Gyeongsang Gamyeong Park is Dalseong Park, open 0600–1900. Occupying the site of an ancient earthen-walled fortress (H.S. #62), the center of the city-state called Dalgubeol, it's one of if not the oldest of such fortifications in Korea, said to have been constructed during the Three Kingdoms period in the year 261. Daegu is traditionally considered the ancestral home of the Seo family; for centuries this fortress was its private land. In 1390, after the Mongol invasions, it was enlarged and strengthened, and rebuilt in stone. During the Joseon Dynasty, the land became state-owned and the fortress wall was rebuilt, but luckily its defensive capability was never tested. Now it's been transformed into a park that has become a favorite meeting spot for elderly Koreans and a place for young parents to bring small children. It has a central, well-tended lawn, many flower

beds, and a small zoo that lines its perimeter. A trail leads along the top of the 1.3-kilometer-long perimeter wall. Not the best of zoos, it is nonetheless a nice little collection of animals and birds. A bronze statue of the *Donghak* religion's founder and martyr, Ch'oe Je-u, has been erected in front of the green. Having lived and taught at Yeongdam, outside of Gyeongju, Ch'oe was brought to the provincial capital of Daegu and beheaded when the government considered his religious and social philosophies similar to Catholicism, then under a ban of punishment. The outgrowth of Ch'oe's thought is the relatively small religion now called Cheondo-gyo. On the north rim above the statue of Ch'oe Je-u stands the pavilion Gwanpung-nu. This pavilion originally topped the provincial government compound's main gate, until it was moved here in 1906. It was rebuilt in 1973. To the left of the park entrance is the small **Daegu Folk History Museum.** Open every day except Monday, it presents a brief history and life culture of the area for free.

Duryu Park 두류공원

To the southwest is the newer Duryu Park, a huge complex built on and around a series of hills. Basically, this park is one of recreational, amusement, music, and sports facilities, with the addition of the city's central tourist information center. Besides enjoying the wide grassy lawns, flower beds, long walkways, and the pond and water spout, you can swim in the outdoor swimming pool; watch baseball or soccer games; practice tennis or archery; or take in an exhibition or concert at the Culture and Arts Hall. A small Buddhist temple was constructed in 1984 on the hillside above the swimming pool.

Opened in 1995 and draping over the hill across the road to the north is **Woobang Land,** an amusement park which provides the whole spectrum of rides and games for the increasingly sophisticated and thrill-seeking citizenry, and musical and theatrical performances are offered on a regular schedule. Capping the hill within this amusement park is **Daegu Tower,** a slender spire similar to those in Seoul and Busan. The best views of the city are had from its observation deck. Also in the tower are a restaurant, tearoom, game arcade, and souvenir stalls. A ride to the top is ₩4,500 round-trip, and this includes general admission to the park. On the plaza at the bottom of the tower is the upper terminus of a gondola skyway (open 1000–2100; ₩2,500 one-way), the bottom terminus of which is located near the park's main entrances. Admission to Woobang Land with five major rides and a package admission including all rides are ₩12,000 and ₩18,000, respectively, for adults and proportionally less for the youngsters. The park is open daily until 2200.

Apsan Park 앞산공원

Directly south of the city center is the largest city park. Dedicated in 1965, and ten times larger than Duryu Park, this is Apsan Park. Blanketing the convoluted hillsides of the eight major valleys of this mountain, the beauty and natural surroundings of its oak and pine cover are impinged upon only by a small commercial venture at its main entrance. Also at the main entrance are a memorial marker dedicated to the Nakdong River battle, an important victory of the Korean War, and an anti-communism hall. In a dark and menacing room on the bottom floor of the hall are pictures and paintings of war atrocities, stories of horror, items of North Korean origin, and explanations of the evils of that totalitarian state. In contrast, the bright and airy upstairs gallery contains pictorial representations of the merits and achievements of the "better way" in the south. The overworked "message" of this dichotomy is obvious. Above this hall is a cluster of restaurants, and above that a small amusement park for children.

Several trails lead up to the three temples that nestle into this valley—Daeseong-sa below, and Daedeok-sa and Unjeok-sa above the amusement park. Another trail snakes its way up the valley to the pavilions on the ridge, high above the park's two flanking glens, for a very good view down onto the city and off toward Palgongsan to the north. The easy way up to the ridge, starting from the small amusement park, is by cable car (₩2,500 one-way, ₩4,000 round-trip), which operates from 0900 to 1930. From

the pavilions on the ridge, a wide gentle trail leads down and past the temple Anil-sa and, farther down the thickly wooded valley, past two other small temples, to a bus stop on the road that skirts the north side of the mountain. Additional temples (there are a dozen and a half on the mountain), trails, athletic grounds, and some 20 mineral springs lie in the valleys to the east and west, with some also on its south slope. Apsan Park becomes crowded on weekends; take to the trails during the week, when only nature and a distant temple bell are your companions. Maps of hiking routes with the locations of temples and springs should be available from the climbing offices at each of the major valley entrances. From the bottom, most trails are less than three kilometers to the peaks.

Suseong Josuji 수성조수지

Directly east of Apsan Park is Suseong Josuji, or Suseong Reservoir. Male students like to come here to row their girlfriends underneath the overhanging trees at the water's edge, or to sit under the multicolored umbrellas and drink soda. Pleasure boats ferry people around the lake for a small fee, or you can rent a sailboard to skim across the water. During summer months, people of all ages come here to escape the oppressive heat of the city. In winter, this reservoir is transformed into a skating pond where the few expert skaters make circles around the beginners, who cling to each other and spend more time on their bottoms than their feet. The area just to the north of the reservoir has become a restaurant district known as Deurangil, and its several hundred eateries offer the widest range of food options in the city.

Running north from Suseong Reservoir is Shincheon Stream. Much of its length has been landscaped and made into bicycle paths, athletic areas, and green space. Running north to Dong Daegu Station is Dongdaegu Boulevard, a wide tree-lined traffic artery which has become a new center for government and business offices.

Mangu Park 망우공원

East of the city center, atop a bluff overlooking the Geumho River, sits tiny Mangu Park. Its many trees and one pavilion give shade for the park benches, where you can sit and gaze at the bronze statue of General Gwak Jae-u, who sits astride his steed, facing south, looking determined to defend the homeland. Gwak was one of several well-respected and effective guerrilla leaders of the literati class who, during the Imjin War, raised forces to protect the Yeongnam region and tried unsuccessfully to drive the Japanese out of the country. Below Mangu Park along the river is Dongcheon Yuwonji amusement park. Here you can find a few rides and games, while on the river rowing teams sometimes practice their strokes.

Reached by a footbridge that crosses over the highway from the statue of General Gwak is **Yeongnam Jeil Gwanmun,** a reconstructed version (not the original, or the original site) of the former south gate of the walled city. The largest of the city gates, it was also the largest in the entire Yeongnam region. The original gate and the connecting walls were constructed after the Hideyoshi Invasions to protect the city from future Japanese incursions, which luckily never occurred. This gate was built in 1980. Across the road from the gate is a velodrome for the growing number of bicycle-racing enthusiasts.

Daegu National Museum
대구국립박물관

Opened in December 1994, the Daegu National Museum houses a collection of pieces previously stored in other public and private museums throughout the country, and serves to elucidate the history and culture of Daegu and the surrounding Gyeongsangbuk-Do provincial area. Three rooms display archaeological artifacts, art objects, and folklore material, with a fourth hall set up to display special exhibitions. Included in what the museum offers are earthenware and bronze objects, sculptures and paintings, swords and other military paraphernalia from the Japanese invasion of the 1590s, a standing gilt Buddha image (N.T. #184), and a *sari* container made of green glass and embellished gold (N.T. #325). To round out the displays are dioramas depicting houses of the region, Joseon-era scholastic life, ceremonies, games, and other aspects of the folk

culture of the region. Open daily except Monday and New Year's Day 0900–1700, 1600 in winter; there is a ₩400 entrance fee.

ACCOMMODATIONS
Hotels

Daegu has over two dozen Western-style hotels. While some are concentrated in the city center, others have cropped up on the periphery. With room rates generally in the ₩120,000–160,000 range and suites often double that, the three deluxe-class hotels are the **Grand Hotel** (tel. 053/742-0001, www.taegugrand.co.kr), near the regional court; **Park Hotel** (tel. 053/952-0088, www.ibtaegupark.co.kr), out along the river near Yeongnam Jeil Gwanmun; and the **Prince Hotel** (tel. 053/628-1001, www.princehotel.co.kr), near Keimyung and Daegu universities. First-class **Hotel Kumho** (tel. 053/252-6001, www.hotelkumho.co.kr), in the city center and the oldest of the city's fine hotels, has rooms for ₩110,000–150,000 and suites for ₩180,000–600,000. For others in the center of the city, try the first-class **Dongin Hotel** (tel. 053/426-5211) and the second-class **Central Hotel** (tel. 053/257-7111) where rooms run ₩53,000–71,000. Others of convenience are the first-class **Crown Hotel** (tel. 053/755-3001), near Dong Daegu Station; second-class **Dong Bang Hotel** (tel. 053/982-1551, www.dbhotel.co.kr), the closest to the airport with reasonable rates at ₩60,000–70,000; first-class **Ariana Hotel** (tel. 053/765-7776, www.ariana.co.kr), near the Suseong reservoir; and the first-class **Garden Hotel** (tel. 053/471-9911), where rooms go for ₩80,000–134,000. Farthest afield is the **Hillside Hotel** (tel. 053/982-0801, www.hillsidehotel.co.kr). Located at the tourist village below the Palgong-san cable car, it has rooms for ₩70,000–200,000.

Yeogwan

Near each train station and bus terminal are scores of new and clean *yeogwan* and cheaper *yeoinsuk*. Near Dong Daegu Station, try Dongyangjang Yeogwan (동양장여관), Dongdo Yeogwan (동도여관), Anamjang Yeogwan (아남장여관), or Royaljang Yeogwan (로얄장여관), all in the ₩25,000–35,000 range. Others are located in the heart of the city—check the following for starters. Down an alley at the city's main intersection is the small and inexpensive Sanjang Yeogwan (산장여관). East of there are the Cheongsujang Yeogwan (청수장여관) and DongAjang Yeogwan (동아장여관). Down separate alleys east of the Dongin Hotel, and on the periphery of the shopping district, you'll find the Sillajang Yeogwan (신라장여관) and Saerimjang Yeogwan (세림장여관). Nearer Yakjeon Golmok are the Shingungjang Yeogwan (신궁장여관), Dongnimjang Yeogwan (동림장여관), and Deokseongjang Yeogwan (덕성장여관). On a quiet street a few steps from Hotel Kumho is Zone Motel (죤여관) and farther up that same street is Dongbangjang Yeogwan (동방장여관). Most of these places are ₩20,000–30,000.

OTHER PRACTICALITIES

Food

Your best bet for a nourishing, ordinary meal in the town center is on the side alleys off the pedestrian street, where volume and competition keep the prices low and the food tasty. The department stores and some side-alley shops offer Korean "fast food," usually noodle soup, *gimbap*, or deep-fried finger food. Western fast food is making inroads here as well now, particularly in the central shopping/entertainment district. Movable stalls on Dongseong-no provide snacks in the evening. Near each bus terminal, and along most inner-city streets, are many average Korean and Chinese restaurants. Japanese and Western restaurants tend to be in or near the big hotels. You can find everything from Korean to Chinese and Japanese to Western at the 250-plus restaurants just north of Suseong Reservoir in an area called Deurangil. A new section of town with broad streets that's away from the center of town, this area has become popular with the rise of the automobile.

Daegu is well known for only one particular dish, *ttaro gukbap*, a soup of pork, beef, coarse-cut vegetables, and rice, usually served when the weather turns cold.

Entertainment

Daegu is still a "tea in the afternoon, cup of rice wine in the evening" town. Abundant tearooms and coffee shops are sprinkled throughout the city. Alternatives include beer or rice wine at a pub, loud music at a disco or nightclub, people-watching along Dongseong-no, or a movie at one of the cinemas near Daegu's main intersection. For the more urbane, a music concert or exhibition at the Citizens' Hall or Culture and Arts Hall, or a baseball game or soccer match at the stadium may be the ticket. Daegu, incidentally, is considered the home of Korean baseball. Before the advent of professional teams, the Daegu high school baseball team was nearly always the best in the country and had as many fervent followers as the professional Korean teams do today.

Markets

Aside from Yakjeon Golmok, huge markets for other agricultural and commercial products have evolved in the city where you can peruse a mind-boggling array of goods. Daegu's largest and oldest is the partially covered Seomun ("West Gate") Market, near where the city's west gate once stood. Within this several square block area, you find everything from gossamer silks to piles of cabbage. Mounds of delicious apples are prominently displayed from early August through winter. Nammun ("South Gate") Market is similar but smaller. Near the stream on the east edge of the downtown area is the smaller Chilseong Market, with an abundance of household items and furniture, everything from rice bowls to beautifully inlaid and lacquered clothes closets. The tiny Gyodong Market, embracing the narrow alleys east of Dongseong-no and south of Daegu Station, carries lots of clothes. A huge new wholesale market for agricultural and marine products has been constructed on the north side of the expressway just off the highway running north to Andong.

Department Stores and Arcades

Daegu's central shopping area has the Daegu, Dong-A, Mido, Migliore, Gangsan, and other department stores, plus the Dong-A shopping center. Along Shincheon Stream is the Debec

Plaza shopping center. Hundreds of underground arcades stretch for several blocks in both directions from the city's main intersection near Daegu Bank. This arcade has become a popular spot to do quick shopping, and is also a good place to beat the wind on a cold winter day. Underground arcades have also been constructed in front of Daegu Station and just north of the Seomun Market, and others will undoubtedly pop up as part of the subway system.

Tourist Information

The Daegu Tourist Information Center (tel. 053/627-8900) is located in Duryu Park. It is a complete center with brochures and maps, staff that speak Korean, English, Japanese, and Chinese, free Internet access for visitors, and a souvenir shop. Operating regular business hours, it has brochures of city and provincial sites, hotels, and rental-car companies, maps, and train and bus schedules. Information booths or counters are also located at the Dong Daegu Station, Daegu Station, at the National Debt Repayment Movement Memorial Park, in the lobby of the Daegu Airport, and at Donghwa-sa.

TRANSPORTATION

Daegu is a veritable transportation hub. Planes link this city directly to Seoul and Jeju-do. The Gyeongbu rail line, the main Seoul-Busan rail route, runs through this metropolis, as will the new high-speed rail line. Heading east, the Daegu rail line goes to Pohang, while it connects with the Donghae Nambu rail line that runs south through Gyeongju to Busan. Multiple expressways head in all directions from the city, and the Gyeongsangbuk-Do highway system radiates from Daegu like a spider's web, connecting all its cities and villages to this provincial capital.

By Plane

The **Daegu International Airport** (대구국제공항) is of modern construction and built on two levels: arrivals on the ground level, departures one level up. On the 1st floor are check-in counters, rental car booths, a tourist information desk, a foreign currency exchange counter, and snack shops. Upstairs you'll find additional snack shops, a restaurant, and gift shops. Domestic air service between Daegu and Seoul operates 17 times a day, and six daily flights go to Jeju-Do. While the bulk of flights in and out of this airport are domestic, several flights a week are to international destinations. Although routes may change as needs increase, there is connection to Osaka, Japan and Shanghai, China. For ticketing and reservations, call Asiana Airlines (tel. 053/427-8128) or KAL (tel. 053/606-2055), or visit their downtown offices. The airport can be reached by city bus nos. 104, 105, 131, and 718. There is limousine bus service only to Gumi. A taxi from mid-town Daegu takes less than 15 minutes and will costs around ₩5,000. The airport use tax for domestic flights is ₩3,000.

By Train

There are two train stations in Daegu: **Daegu Station** (대구역), the old station in the middle of the city, and the newer and larger **Dong Daegu Station** (동대구역), several kilometers to the east. Both are used for passenger trains, but the Dong Daegu Station handles the majority of train traffic. Direct trains to most major cities in the country can be boarded in Daegu; there are about 80 every day. While the majority run between Seoul and Busan, others go to Gyeongju, Jinju, Yeongju, Gangneung, Gwangju, and Jecheon. Sample fares from Dong Daegu Station on *Saemaul-ho* trains are Seoul (₩30,600), Daejeon (₩19,100), Busan (₩8,100), and Gyeongju (₩7,600). On *Mugunghwa-ho* trains, fares are Seoul (₩15,100), Daejeon (₩7,600), Busan (₩5,500), Jinju (₩8,000), Gyeongju (₩4,700), Andong (₩5,800), Seoul Cheongnyangni (₩17,900), Gangneung (₩16,700), and Gwangju (₩17,000).

By Express Bus

Daegu is connected to a dozen and a half large cities throughout the country, but rather than one, Daegu has three **express bus terminals** clustered within a few steps of each other just south of the Dong Daegu Station, and another one in the northwestern section of the city. For the three, while there is some overlap, each seems to have an area of coverage. If you don't find a bus going to your destination at one, try another. From the terminal closest to the train station, buses run mostly to points south like Busan (₩12,100), Ulsan (₩4,700), and Jinju (₩9,200). Across the street, buses go to Seoul and nearby destinations. Next door at the third terminal to the east they connect to Daejeon (₩6,300), Gyeongju (₩2,800), Jeonju (₩9,200), Jinju (₩6,100), and Busan. Across town at the **Seo Daegu Express Bus Terminal,** you can get buses for Daejeon, Masan (₩4,300), Gwangju (₩9,200), Jeonju, Cheongju (₩8,500), Suncheon (₩9,200), Chuncheon (₩15,200), and Eujeongbu (₩13,200). Frequency varies: every 10–20 minutes to Seoul; every one hour or less to Dong Seoul, Daejeon, Cheongju, Gyeongju, Ulsan, Busan, Masan, Jinju, and Gwangju; every two hours to Seongnam, Incheon, Suncheon, and Jeonju; and three or four times a day to Eujeongbu and Chuncheon. No reservations are required or taken except on major holidays.

By Intercity Bus

Intercity buses from Daegu go to all cities and towns in this province, and to major cities in the neighboring provinces. There are four widely dispersed bus terminals in Daegu. The **Dongbu Bus Terminal** (동부시외버스정류장) has buses going toward the east, and to towns along the coast, from Ulsan in the south to Gangneung in the north, with the addition of a night bus up the coast as far as Dean, north of Sokcho. From mid-July to mid-August, during the summer swim season, buses may also run to east coast beaches that do not usually have direct bus traffic from Daegu. Selected destinations are: Ulsan (₩7,300), Gyeongju (₩4,600), Pohang (₩5,100), Cheongsong (₩9,400), Uljin (₩13,900), and Gangneung (₩22,900). The **Nambu Bus Terminal** (남부시외버스정류장), the smallest of Daegu's stations, runs buses to the rural areas south and east of the city—Gyeongju (₩7,300), Unmun-sa (₩4,300), Miryang (₩4,800), and Pyochung-sa (₩6,600). The sizable **Seobu Bus Terminal** (서부시외버스정류장) has buses going to the south and west. Selected destinations:

Goryeong (₩2,200), Haein-sa (₩3,600), Tongyeong (₩9,600), Jinju (₩6,100), Yeosu (₩13,700), Namwon (₩7,800), Gwangju (₩11,300), and Jeonju (₩9,200). The **Bukbu Bus Terminal** (북부시외버스정류장) is the city's largest and busiest. It services the remaining area, basically to the west and north, from Deokyu-san National Park in the west to Taebaek in Gangwon-Do. Selected destinations and fares are Deokyu-san N.P. (₩9,800), Gimcheon (₩3,900), Andong (₩5,600), Mun'gyeong-eup (₩9,900), and Taebaek (₩15,400).

By City Bus

The Daegu city bus system is extensive; the base fare is ₩600 while the express buses cost ₩1,200. Routes change periodically; confirm your destination with the bus driver. Although not exhaustive, the following list of destinations and bus numbers will be of help for getting around Daegu.

Bukbu Bus Terminal: 303, 424, 427, 454, 717, 718, 903

Seobu Bus Terminal: 106, 306, 424, 454, 609, 906

Nambu Bus Terminal: 242, 309, 504, 609, 903

Dongbu Bus Terminal: 156, 301, 415, 514, 717, 903

Seobu Express Bus Terminal: 306, 424, 518, 613

Daegu Station: 104, 131, 401, 415

Dong Daegu Station, express-bus terminals: 106, 401, 415

Daegu Airport: 104, 105, 131, 718

City Center: 104, 105, 401, 424, 518, 609

Dalseong Park: 242, 301, 404, 514, 524, 808

Duryu Park: 424, 535, 601, 609, 906

Apsan Park: 616, 910

Suseong Reservoir: 104, 401

Mangu Park: 106, 156, 508, 518, 628, 808, 814

Donghwa-sa: 105, 131

Pagye-sa: 401

Gatbawi: 104, 131

Songnim-sa: 427

Daegu Confucian Academy: 301

Daegu National Museum: 204, 405, 424, 449, 704

Subway

Opened in 1997, Daegu's first subway line runs from the southwestern corner of the city, past the Seobu Bus Terminal, up Jungang-no, and through the center of the city, swinging behind Daegu Station and on to Dong Daegu Station, before finally going out past the airport. A second line running roughly west to east is scheduled to open in 2005, with two additional lines by 2010. Fares, operational procedures, schedule postings, and ticket windows and machines operate very much like those systems in Seoul and Busan. The basic fare is ₩600 for one zone and ₩700 for distances beyond the first zone. Schematic maps of the line are posted in each station and fares indicated. Tickets can be purchased from a clerk at a ticket window or from an automatic machine. For online information, see www.daegusubway.co.kr. Several of the stops that travelers will find useful are:

Line #1:
Seongdangmot Station: Seobu Bus Terminal
Myeongdeok Station: Daegu Confucian Academy
Banwoldang Station: Yakjeon Golmok, change to line # 2
Jungang-no Station: City Center

Daegu Station: Daegu Station, express bus terminals
Dong Daegu Station: Dong Daegu Station
Ayanggyo Station: closest to the Daegu Airport
Line #2:
Keimyung University Station: Keimyung University
Duryu Station: Duryu Park
Seomun Market Station: closest to Seomun Market
Banwoldang Station: Yakjeon Golmok, change to line # 1
Beomeo Station: Grand Hotel, district court
Mancheon Station: Nambu Bus Terminal
Daegu Grand Park Station: Daegu Grand Park, World Cup Stadium

Daegu City Tour Bus

If you only have a short time or wish to see major sights without transportation hassles, consider using the free Daegu City Tour Bus service. These buses run several different half-day and full-day courses daily. Admission to all sites is the responsibility of the rider. Get information and make reservations in advance at the Daegu Tourist Information Center.

Daegu Vicinity

PALGONG-SAN

Palgong-san, the region's tallest mountain area, lies just 20 kilometers north of Daegu. Its main ridgeline runs east to west. In the center is Birobong (1192 meters), to the east is Dong-bong (1155 meters), and to the west is Seo-bong (1041 meters). Farther afield are the slightly lower peaks Pagye-bong, In-bong, and Gwan-bong, which form the extremities of this slightly crescent-shaped ridgeline. In spring and summer, azaleas and magnolias make their appearance, and in the autumn the maples stand out as most predominant. Steep but not overwhelming, the mountain trails draw many hikers at all times of the year, but mostly during fine fall weather. In

1980, 122 square kilometers of this mountain were designated **Palgong-san Provincial Park,** the nation's largest provincial park.

On its slopes are half a dozen well-known temples and many smaller hermitages. A stone Buddha triad is enshrined in a grotto on the north side of the mountain, a seated Buddha passively surveys the hills from below Gwan-bong, and several other stone-cut Buddha figures are ensconced here and there on the mountainside. It is for these stone images and the numerous temples that the mountain is especially known. Dotting the undulations of its forest cover are unusual rock formations, crisscrossing its valleys and peaks are numerous hiking trails, and rising to a mid-slope peak (820 meters) is the **Skyline cable car,** from which you have the best view of the southern slope of the mountain. Running from mid-morning to about sundown, the fare for this 1,200-meter ride is ₩3,500 one-way or ₩5,500 round-trip. Below the lower cable car terminus is a tourist village, the principal entrance to the mountain, with large restaurants, souvenir shops, the Hillside Hotel, and a few expensive *yeogwan*. Running past Donghwa-sa to this village are city bus nos. 105 and 131. Smaller communities are also located below Pagye-sa, Gatbawi, Songnim-sa and Unhae-sa, and city bus transportation reaches each.

Hiking

A long trail runs along the entire ridgeline of this mountain, about a seven-hour hike. There is, however, a communications station on the highest peak where it's prohibited to enter, so the trail skirts it, connecting Seo-bong to Dong-bong. Connecting to this ridge trail are several from the south; one runs down the north side to the village of Daeyul, near Gunwi Samjeon Seokbul, and one heads east to Unhae-sa, each a bit over two hours long. Trails head up the mountainside from Donghwa-sa (perhaps the most often-used and about two hours in length); Pagye-sa (one hour); and Buin-sa (1.5 hours). A trail also runs from the upper cable car terminus to the ridge, and from the village to Gatbawi, which is also heavily used—both are about one hour apiece. Although there are no mountain huts along these trails, large group campgrounds have been established near the villages below Donghwa-sa and Pagye-sa.

Donghwa-sa 동화사

The most important temple on Palgong-san is Donghwa-sa [Tonghwa-sa] ("Paulownia Flower Temple"), founded in 493 by the priest Geukdal, and reconstructed in 771 by monk Shimji. Legend relates that during its reconstruction in 832, the compound's paulownia trees bloomed wildly, even through the dead of winter—thus its name. Today it headquarters the ninth district of Jogye order. Six Treasures are preserved here and at its six associated hermitages on the mountainside above.

This temple has had a tremendous amount

Yaksa Yeorae Buddha figure at Donghwa-sa

of new construction, reconstruction, and land-scaping during the last few decades; ₩2,500 entrance. By way of one entrance, a wide path leads past a gate, reservoir, and small hermitage to enter this temple compound from the side. To the right are the Tongil Buddha complex and the original entrance to the temple; to the left is the main temple courtyard. Next to the old entrance parking lot is a bas-relief carving of a seated Buddha figure (T. #243) said to have been done in the late 700s or early 800s during one of the temple's reconstructions under Shimji. This plump and smiling Buddha sits on a cushioned pedestal that floats on a sea of clouds, with hands in the "expelling evil" mudra, a halo around his head, flame nimbus around his body. The old path goes through the two-posted front gate, past a pair of stone flagpole supports (T. #254), over a stone bridge, and up a flight of stairs to the main temple area. Steps lead up under the Bongso-nu pavilion to the central courtyard. The bell and drum pavilion is on the right; a rare semicircular stairway steps up to the main hall, unusually small for a temple of such importance. Faded figures of the saints are still visible on both the outside and inside plaster walls. Note the carved dragons, phoenix, and other animals suspended above the altar, below the intricate wooden canopy! Above and to the left are separate small halls for the Mountain Spirit, the Seven Star God, and portraits of important abbots of the past. A great stand of bamboo grows like a shield behind these old buildings, as if helping to keep the fierce weather at bay. To the side of Donghwa-sa on a steep hillside is the temple's collection of *budo*. Of particular note is a well-preserved, octagonal stone *sari budo* (T. #601), which sits on a lotus base and is capped by a stylized cloud pattern finial top.

The newest addition to Donghwa-sa is the Tongil (Unification) Buddha complex. Cut into the hillside is a semicircular plaza paved with polished granite slabs, in the middle of which stands a huge (58 meters high) Yaksa Yeorae Buddha figure, dedicated to the peaceful unification of the peninsula. Finely sculpted, this Healing Buddha stands on a lotus pedestal around which are eight carved stone panels. Two huge flanking pagodas and two elaborate stone lanterns rise at its front and the surrounding elaborately carved wall contains many fine sculptures. The size, scope, and detail of this work is more than impressive. To the front of this plaza sits a three-story cement worship hall, one floor of which contains the temple museum.

Across the stream is the hermitage Geumdang-am.

Geumdang-am 금당암

Standing in front of Geungnak-jeon, Geumdang-am's pair of unadorned, three-tier stone pagodas (T. #248) are typical of those from the late Silla Dynasty. A *sarisa* container and 99 mini-pagodas were discovered inside the base structure of the western pagoda when it was repaired in 1959. At the hermitage **Biro-am** (비로암) nearby are preserved a seated Vairocana Buddha statue (T. #244) and a three-tier prayer pagoda (T. #247). With index finger of left hand grasped by the right hand, this statue, unusually, is painted white, with black hair and red lips; the lotus petals on the cushion base and the Buddha figures carved into the flame nimbus are also painted, as is the gold halo behind the Buddha's head. Almost identical to those at Geumdang-am, the pagoda here was discovered to contain a gilt bronze *sarisa* container and a small gilt wood pagoda.

Yeombul-am 염불암

Legend says that about 1,000 years ago a monk from the area heard the sound of a chanting Buddha emanating from a rock high on the mountainside. Such a strange occurrence indicated divine presence, so in 928 the hermitage Yeombul-am was constructed next to that huge boulder, and on two flat sides of the rock Buddha images were carved in bas-relief. Although flat of feature, each is done with substantial detail and indicates some sophistication. Munsu Bosal is on the south-facing side, Amita Buddha on the west.

Along the trail toward Yeombul-am is the small hermitage **Budo-am** (부도암), a meditation retreat for Buddhist nuns. Above Yeombul-am at the summit are two additional Buddha carvings. At Biro-bong, the seated Buddha of Medicine is much more refined and artistic. Larger, bolder, and cruder, that at Dong-bong is about the same age as Gatbawi.

Gatbawi 갓바위

At Gwan-bong (850 meters), on the eastern end of this mountain ridge, sits Gatbawi (T. #431), an imposing seated Buddha of Medicine sculpture from the 800s that gazes out over the southern foothills of Palgong-san. A wide flat rock sits on the figure's head like a *gat* on the head of a Korean gentleman. Very weatherworn but much revered by Buddhists, it is said that those who pray here on the first and fifteenth of each month will have their desires granted. In the hills below this figure are seven temples and hermitages. In the next valley to the west is the small temple **Bukjijang-sa** (북지장사). Established in 485, its tiny main hall has been designated T. #805. To the north and over the next major ridge from Bukjijang-sa, carved out of the hillside in terraces between 600 meters and 800 meters, is the new Palgong Country Club golf course. For Gatbawi, take bus nos. 104 or 377. Entrance to the park and its trails from here is ₩1,300.

Pagye-sa 파계사

West of Donghwa-sa is the temple Pagye-sa; ₩1,300 entrance. Dating from 804, also constructed by the industrious Shimji, Pagye-sa is neat and trim, and more modest than Donghwa-sa, and has an appropriately secluded location. Past the pond, a stairway leads under the pavilion lecture hall Jindong-nu to the flagstone courtyard. Wontong-jeon, the main worship hall, is from the 1695 reconstruction of the temple. However, the delicate paintings outside and in are quite new. On the altar sits an exquisitely detailed gilt wood Goddess of Mercy statue (T. #992). To the rear is a shrine with bold new murals of the Buddha, and to the side a new drum and gong pavilion. Also stored here are a set of royal clothes of King Yeongjo, an eight-fold screen brought back from Japan by the warrior monk Sammyeong, and two name plates carved from the script of Kings Yeongjo and Cheongjo. Take bus no. 401 from Daegu Station. The road

between Pagye-sa and Donghwa-sa greatly facilitates travel between the two and makes getting to Buin-sa, Samseong-am, and other trailheads more convenient.

Buin-sa 부인사

Founded sometime in the mid-600s, Buin-sa [Puin-sa] ("Temple of the Lady") is said to honor Silla queen Seondeok, then the ruler of this region. Four centuries later it had grown substantially, and was much larger and more significant than it is today, even though it is slowly growing in size again. The original set of wood printing blocks of the *Koreana Tripitaka,* the Buddhist canon of scripture, was stored here after they were completed in 1087. Originally done partially as supplication to the Buddha for defense from the Khitan northern invasion and partially as a codification of Buddhist doctrine, they were unfortunately destroyed two centuries later during the Mongol invasion of 1232. Buin-sa, which was burned to the ground, had been a base for military monks who were not only resisting foreign invasion but also resisting the usurpation of power by the Choe clan. A second set of blocks was subsequently carved during the 1230s and 1240s on Ganghwa-do, when the royal court was forced to flee the capital at Gaeseong. A true work of art, this second set is now stored at Haein-sa, southwest of Daegu. The temple's original site, scattered with remnants of stone, now lies some 300 meters away and is used as a vineyard. A short way above Buin-sa is the hermitage Samseong-am. There, a standing Buddha figure carved into a nearby boulder is covered with lichen. Less than an hour above this hermitage is another, and much better-done rock face Buddha carving. Seated on a lotus cushion and surrounded by a flame nimbus, the mudra of this Buddha of the Future is one of calling the world to witness.

Songnim-sa 성림사

On the west side of Palgong-san lies Songnim-sa ("Pine Forest Temple"). Established in the 9th century and destroyed in 1243, it was rebuilt in 1689. Its main hall enshrines what is said to be the largest wooden Buddha statue in the country. In this compound is a slender and well-balanced five-tier brick pagoda (T. #189) topped with a much newer ornamental metal finial. Although less hefty, it has a similar appearance to the Beopheung-tap brick pagoda in Andong. In 1961, two wooden Buddha images, a gold box, green glass *sarisa* bottle, and green glass cup, plus several other precious objects were discovered inside. Subsequently removed, these articles (T. #325) are now kept at the Seoul National Museum. Painted on the side of the judgment hall are graphic scenes of punishment administered to evildoers. It's worth a look! A tiny and cute Mt. Spirit hall stands next to the main hall. Take city bus no. 427 from the center of Daegu.

Above Songnim-sa but below Ka-san (902 meters) run the remains of **Gasan Fortress** (가산 산성). Erected in 1639 after the disastrous Japanese and Mongolian invasions of the 1590s and 1630s, this fortress was to help protect the Yeongnam region from future foreign incursions. Luckily, it was never needed. The fortress consisted of three rings of defensive fortifications, the innermost being about four kilometers in length; several of its gates and sections of its walls have been reconstructed.

East Side Temples

At the bottom of one of the mountain's eastern valleys sits **Unhae-sa** [Ŭnhae-sa] (은해사); ₩2,000 entrance. Bus no. 311 to Unhae-sa leaves from Yeongcheon. Established in 809, this large and important temple is the 10th district headquarters of the Jogye sect. Walk up past the small *budo* collection and cross the stream to enter the broad compound. After passing under the entrance pavilion, the main hall is straight ahead. It has old but elaborate woodwork inside and some fine old murals outside. A mural of the Amita Buddha (T. #1270) is kept here. On the mountain slopes behind it, you'll find at least seven hermitages. All, except Geojo-am, which is seven kilometers away, are within a two-kilometer walk of Unhae-sa. Enshrined at Unbu-am is a seated bronze Goddess of Mercy statue (T. #514). Baekheung-am preserves a

wooden altar (T. #486) from the Silla Dynasty and the Geungnak-jeon (T. #790) hall. Myobong-am has a 500-year-old main hall. On the ridge above is Gatbawi.

Culturally and architecturally, the small hermitage **Geojo-am** [Kŏjo-am] (거조암), which was founded in 738, is perhaps the most significant of this group. Built in 1375, Yeongsan-jeon (N.T. #14) is one of the country's oldest wooden buildings. Although it shows some evidence of renovation, this hall is a plain and simple structure with a double front door and latticed windows at the front and sides. It houses a statue of the Buddha and 526 small stone statues of the Nahan sit on narrow altars that wrap around the periphery of the building and take up much of the inner floor area. Each seated in a different posture, with distinct facial and hand positions, all are painted in a variety of pastel colors. This gathering of figures and altar arrangement are extremely unusual, and while the overall effect is one of fullness it is not too busy or overcrowded.

Gunwi Grotto Statues 군위삼존석불

On the far side of the mountain from Pagye-sa and Songnim-sa is Gunwi Samjeon Seokbul (N.T. #109), a natural grotto containing three sculpted figures. Set 20 meters above the stream, a stone stairway leads up the rock face to its round opening. Flanked by obeisant standing bodhisattvas, the 3-meter-tall Amita Buddha is seated in the center. These grotto figures are believed to have been constructed about the year A.D. 700, one century earlier (some sources say 250 years earlier) than the much more famous and inspiring Seokguram grotto of Gyeongju, of which it is undoubtedly the precursor. Although done with less skill, the Seokgamoni Buddha here resembles that in Gyeongju and the attendant figures are reminiscent of those on the surrounding wall panels in Gyeongju. It is understandable then that this cave is often referred to as the Second Seokguram Grotto. Attending this unusual work of art are several temple buildings, and an equally-unusual square and piled flat-rock pagoda. While the current temple buildings are from the 1980s, this temple was originally said to have been constructed by Ado Hwasang during the mid-400s (some say by Geukdal Hwasang in 493). Buses to the village of Daeyul (₩3,700), two kilometers below the grotto, leave from the Bukbu Bus Terminal in Daegu.

Andong and Vicinity

ANDONG 안동

Andong is a prosperous, medium-sized city (pop. 185,000), the largest in the northern half of the province, and it straddles the Nakdong River. Until the early 1970s, Andong fit snugly against the low hills on the river flat, but has since expanded across the river and spilled over the hills to the north and west. The surrounding region is one of concentrated low hills and narrow riverside plains, and its highest point is Hakga-san (882 meters). It has always been a market center for the flourishing agrarian region which surrounds it. More recently, however, it has become an educational center and tourist destination. Andong National University has grown out of the city teachers' college, and has developed strong departments in education and Korean folklore, a natural in such a culturally rich area, and even offers courses in culture and language to foreigners.

The Andong area has historically been (and still is) very conservative and traditional, a stronghold of Confucianism where traditional family organization remains strong. The people of the region are proud of their heritage, and they mean to keep alive the best of the region's customs and culture even while the area modernizes. The low hills of rural Andong contain numerous cultural remnants of old Korea. Buddhist temples snuggle into mountain vales, *yangban* manor houses stand proudly among thatched-roof peasant homes in country villages, and *seowon* sit amidst pine groves as a symbol of Korea's literary and educational past. Andong is the ancestral home of the Kwon and Jang families, and one branch of the Kim family. These and other *yangban* families not only greatly influenced the Andong area, but played a vital role in the historical, cultural, and academic development of the country as a whole, largely during the Goryeo and Joseon dynasties.

Traditional products of the region are red peppers, apples, medicinal herbs, hemp cloth called Andong *po*, a hard liquor called Andong *soju*, a sweet rice punch called *shikhye*, and mulberry paper which is used for decorative objects as well as door and window coverings. The government has targeted Andong as a secondary growth region for small-scale industry to help meet the planned decentralized and balanced build-up of the economy. Still, one large factory dries, processes, and packs tobacco.

On the west side of town, next to the tobacco factory, is the new police station; a few steps away and around the corner is the new central post office. A mid-town post office is located just around the corner from the pedestrian street and the city hall, train station, and bus terminal are only a few blocks away. Outgrowing its confined mid-town space, a newer and larger market has been built several blocks to the west. A tourist information center is located up from the train station, a counter in the train station has some material, and there is a booth at the entrance to Hahoe Village. Although Andong is not a transportation center, the Jungang rail line runs through it, connecting Seoul to Busan. The Jungang Expressway skirts the west side of town running north-south through the interior of the country, and a web of highways spreads out from here.

See www.andong.kyongbuk.kr for information on the Internet.

History

Some 2,000 years ago, Andong was populated by the Jinhan people. As the Silla Kingdom expanded its control over this corner of the penin-

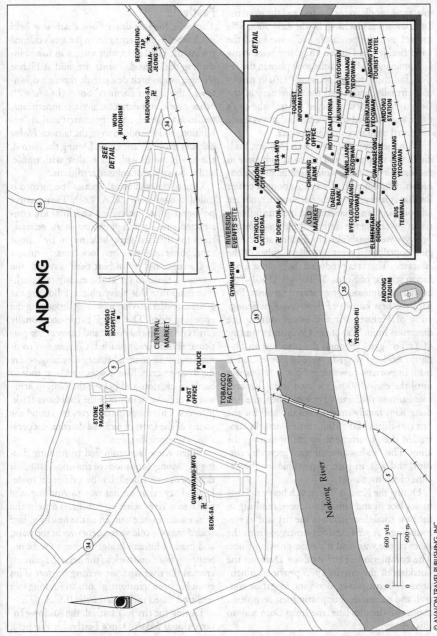

ANDONG

SEE
DETAIL

BEOPHEUNG-
TAP ★

GUNJA-
JEONG ★

HAEDONG-SA ♨

WON
BUDDHISM ★

RIVERSIDE
EVENTS SITE

GYMNASIUM

SEONGSO
HOSPITAL

CENTRAL
MARKET

POLICE ■

POST
OFFICE ■

TOBACCO
FACTORY

STONE
PAGODA ★

GWANWANG-MYO ♨
★

SEOK-SA ♨

YEONGHO-RU ★

ANDONG
STADIUM

Nakong River

0   600 yds
0   600 m

© AVALON TRAVEL PUBLISHING, INC.

DETAIL

TOURIST
INFORMATION ■

POST
OFFICE ■

HOTEL CALIFORNIA ■

ANDONG
CITY HALL ■

TAESA-MYO ★

CHOHUNG
BANK ■

DAEGU
BANK ■

CATHOLIC
CATHEDRAL ■

DOEWON-SA ♨

OLD
MARKET

ELEMENTARY
SCHOOL ■

BYEOLGUNGJANG
YEOGWAN ●

HANILJANG
YEOGWAN ●

BYEOLGUNGJANG
YEOGWAN ●

GWANGSEONG
YEONSUK ●

DAERIMJANG
YEOGWAN ●

MUNHWAJANG
YEOGWAN ●

DOWONJANG
YEOGWAN ●

ANDONG PARK
TOURIST HOTEL ■

ANDONG
STATION

CHEONGGUNGJANG
YEOGWAN ●

BUS
TERMINAL

sula, these people were absorbed and the town became known as Gochang. By the early 900s, Silla control over the peninsula had waned and the Later Baekje and Goryeo kingdoms were vying for dominance. Many battles took place in this region, but the battle of Gochang (930) in particular virtually guaranteed the supremacy of the Goryeo forces. With Goryeo control, the city's name was changed to Andong, and it was made a regional military command center.

With the coming of the Joseon Dynasty, Buddhism was suppressed and Confucianism came to the fore. Conservative Korea became more Confucian than China itself, and Andong a center for that conservatism. Scholar/bureaucrats were schooled in Confucianism and became influential in governing the country. Many *seowon* and *hyanggyo* were established in Andong and the region contributed greatly to the number of the educated. This area produced the greatest Confucian scholar of Korea, Yi Toe-gye (1501–70), as well as numerous government servants. Perhaps the best known of these was Ryu Seong-yong of Hahoe, prime minister during the disastrous Imjin War of the 1590s and a student of Yi Toe-gye. Through the mid-Joseon Dynasty, Andong *yangban* were largely excluded from important government posts. It was not until the early 1800s that men from this area rose again to positions of power. Then, the Andong Kim family married royalty and for the first two-thirds of the 19th century virtually controlled the government by manipulating the kings. This "in-law government" grew very corrupt, and was, in part, responsible for the decline of the monarchy.

During the Korean War, much heavy fighting took place in and around Andong, resulting in the near-total destruction of the city and its surroundings. A new Andong emerged from the ashes of the war, and it's been growing since. The completion of the Andong Dam on the outskirts of the city in 1976 provided much-needed electric power, flood and irrigation control, and recreational opportunities; completed about two decades later, the Imha Dam adds to this reserve.

Festivals

The week-long **Andong Folk Festival** is held in October to draw attention to the area's cultural traditions. Held at various venues in town, including the riverside events site, and at Hahoe Village, events include a parade through downtown, the Jajeon Farmers' Song (I.C.A. #2), other music and dance, athletic competitions, traditional games, a poetry contest and art exhibition, and a production of the famous *Hahoe talchum* masked-dance play. During the festival, the city is awash with color, alive with music, and a showplace of cultural traditions.

One of the traditional "games" performed is called *chajeon nori* (I.C.A. #24). Two massive pole-and-rope "tanks" (or chariots) are constructed, one for each of two teams. A "general" rides the uplifted tank, holding on by a stout rope. Some team members lock arms, forming a "V" wedge, and try to butt their way into the opposing ranks to get at the enemy tank; others manipulate this heavy object, following the general's orders, trying to win by dislodging the opposing rider. This rough battle occasionally carries on for several hours, and many of the participants come away bruised. *Chajeon nori* commemorates the ancient battle of Gochang, where the three generals, Kim, Kwon, and Jang, rode to battle in chariots and helped the Goryeo army win its decisive victory over the rival Later Baekje forces. This mock battle serves to remind the young of the spirit of national defense, cooperation, and esprit de corps.

When King Gongmin fled to Andong during the Mongol invasions of the mid-1300s, his daughter came as well, but by a different route. Legend says that on her way to Andong, she came to a river with no bridge. To help the princess across, the women of the nearby village waded into the cold water, bent over at the waist, and made a human bridge for her to walk on. Stepping from one back to the next, the princess crossed the river without wetting her feet. This event has been transformed into an Andong folk tradition called the *notdari balki* (I.C.A. #7).

During the city folk festival, the **Andong International Mask Dance Festival** is also held.

Not only is the Hahoe Mask Dance performed, but more than a dozen other Korean masked dances and several foreign masked dances are showcased. In addition, mask-making demonstrations are organized, traditional folk music performed, and foods of the area served. For additional information, see www.maskdance.com.

SIGHTS

Jebiwon Buddha 제비원

Five kilometers north of downtown Andong, on the road to Yeongju, you'll find a rock carving that has virtually become the city's unofficial symbol. Jebiwon (T. #115), now also called Icheon-dong Seokbulsang, is a Goryeo Dynasty Mireuk Buddha (alternate sources give the date of sculpture as 634, during the Silla Dynasty, and believe that it is a representation of the Amita Buddha). Cut into a 12-meter-high granite rock face are the graceful lines of the Buddha's robe and hands; one hand rests against its chest with thumb touching mid-finger, the other extends toward the ground. Carved in bas-relief, this form is difficult to distinguish from some angles, especially in low light. On top, carved from a separate and different type of rock, sits the two-meter-high head and hat. Below the partially destroyed hat brim are the Buddha's accentuated and dramatic facial features. Guarding the northern approach to Andong, Jebiwon tranquilly faces the setting sun and looks out over the distant valley hamlet. Over the Buddha's shoulder is a closely cropped pagoda, and below is the tiny temple Yeonmi-sa.

Koreans associate many legends with this spot, but one is of particular note. During the Imjin War, a Ming general came to Korea to aid the poorly prepared Korean army. As he neared Andong, his horse reared up and refused to go farther. Looking around to discover the cause of this problem, he saw the Jebiwon Buddha sculpture staring out at him from a grove of trees ahead. Thinking this was the reason his horse was frightened, he dismounted and beheaded it. Some time later, a monk had the head put back in its rightful position, and today you can still see

the cut at the neck and the symbolic traces of the blood (as streaks) running down the front of the Buddha's gown. City bus no. 54 lets you off below this martyred sculpture.

Taesa-myo 태사묘

In the center of the city is Taesa-myo, a small memorial shrine built in 1542 to honor Kim Seon-pyeong, Kwon Haeng, and Jang Gil, three local men who helped Goryeo king Taejo win the decisive battle of Gochang over Later Baekje troops. This victory led to the eventual unification of the peninsula under the Goryeo kings. For their meritorious service and contribution to the Goryeo state, each man was raised to the rank of general and given a family name, still the most prominent *yangban* families in this area. Taesa-myo, a symbol of loyalty, devotion, and patriotism, was completely rebuilt in 1958 after its destruction during the Korean War. This memorial houses 12 personal articles of the three men (together designated N. T. #451), including clothing, eating utensils, and seals.

Seoak-sa and Gwanwang-myo

Situated on the hill west of the tobacco factory are two old religious establishments. The first is tiny Seoak-sa (서악사). Founded during the early Silla Dynasty, it is the oldest temple in the city. After years of neglect, Seoak-sa has finally gotten a new main hall, with an intricate canopy over its altar and a finely carved mural on one wall. The main figure on the altar, a statue of Seokgamoni Buddha, is made of gilt clay, a rarity in Korea. The flanking bodhisattvas are painted *ssari* wood. Up to the side is a good example of a tiny Mountain Spirit hall.

Directly next to Seoak-sa is Gwanwang-myo (관왕묘), a shrine dedicated to Gwanu, the Chinese god of war. Gwanwang-myo is one of five such remaining shrines in Korea, remnants of a once-popular religious practice imported from China. Gwanu was a curd merchant who found himself in the ranks of the army. Even though a commoner, he rose to become a brilliant and feared general because of his unusual military skill and leadership talents. After his death, he was deified, and people began to call upon him for intercession in times of distress. It's said that during the Imjin War, an apparition of Gwanu appeared in Korea and helped stop the invading Japanese army. In gratitude for this help, his image was enshrined in memorial halls throughout the country and prayers were offered to him. Once widespread, this practice is now basically a curiosity. Set up in 1598 on the hill now topped by the Catholic cathedral, Gwanwang-myo was moved to its present location in 1831. Enshrined inside is the only such stone statue in Korea of this god of war. The red-faced figure's long black beard flows over the Chinese-style gown, and its "presence" is reminiscent of figures enshrined in Chinese temples.

Yeongho-ru 영호루

On the south side of the Nakdong River, perched safely on a bluff, sits Yeongho-ru, one of the older and more famous pavilions in Korea. The original structure was built in the mid-1300s on the north bank of the river, between the railroad and old vehicular bridges. Local *yangban,* scholars, and writers routinely frequented this pavilion, and inscriptions from some of them hang inside on the crossbeams. In 1361, Goryeo king Gongmin fled to Andong from his capital of Gaeseong due to repeated Mongol invasions of the country. While here, he often visited Yeongho-ru. Impressed by the pavilion and the loyalty of these people, he personally wrote the characters of the pavilion's name for a signboard to be hung below the roof. Three times since then, floods have washed away the pavilion. Each time the only retrievable article was the signboard. Following the last flood, when it seemed that *all* was lost, the signboard was miraculously found down the river near Sangju several days after the water receded, its brightly painted characters reflecting the light of the moon as if to signal its survival. In the early 1970s, this pavilion was rebuilt using cement following the original architectural style. To the side of Yeongho-ru is a Korean War memorial, and, a bit farther along, an archery range that stretches across a low draw.

While there are several *seowon* in the city and surrounding countryside, perhaps the easiest to access, and one that typifies others, is **Gosan Seowon** (고산서원). This traditional private school is situated several kilometers south of the city center at a bend in a tributary to the Nakdong River. It lies peacefully under tall pine trees; you can imagine what the daily life might have been for local boys who attended this academy. While somewhat dilapidated, the shrine, lecture hall, and dormitories give a sense of what this place was like when active. The riverside stretch to the front and above the irrigation barrage is now used for recreation—boating in the summer and skating in the winter. On the cliff across the stream is a stand of Chinese juniper trees (N.M. #252).

Brick Pagodas

Within spitting distance of the railroad tracks, on the way to the dam, is an impressive seven-tiered, 16.5-meter-high gray brick pagoda (N. T. #16) commonly known as **Beopheung-tap** (법흥탑) but now sometimes called Shinsae-dong Chilcheung Jeon-tap, which marks the site of a former Silla Dynasty temple. Set solidly on a granite base, it is said to be the oldest and largest complete brick pagoda in the country. On three sides of its base are relief panel carvings of the devas and other celestial beings. Somewhat worn, they were obviously done with skill and maturity. A chamber is recessed into the bottom story, and roof tiles cover several upper tiers. The original gilt bronze finial is gone. These physical characteristics make it similar to the brick pagoda at Songnim-sa, north of Daegu, and the Bunhwang-sa brick pagoda in Gyeongju.

Two other smaller brick pagodas are located south of the city in the countryside, one in Namhu-myeon and the other in Iljik-myeon (T. #57). In town, a smaller brick pagoda stands in the Andong railroad yard. This five-tiered construction (T. #56) originally had seven tiers, but was rebuilt in its present state after its destruction during the Korean War. Nearby is a set of flagpole supports which, along with the pagoda, remain from a temple that occupied this site. In a residential area of town is yet another pagoda. Although this six-meter-high United Silla stone structure (T. #114) is somewhat disfigured, it has graceful, upward-turning eaves and fine proportions.

Gunja-jeong 군자정

A few steps down from Beopheung-tap is Gunja-jeong, a 50-*gan*, mid-Joseon Dynasty house, and the study hall Imcheong-gak (jointly designated T. #182). Reconstructed in 1975, this compound backs against the steep hillside. The living quarters are a maze of rooms, verandas, passages, and courtyards on several levels. It is a unique structure, well worth a look. In its own walled section is **Imcheong-gak,** a T-shaped building constructed in 1515. A Confucian scholar's study hall, it has an intriguing floor design. One-half of the building, the top of the T, has an *ondol* floor; the other half has a wooden floor and removable doors. Thus, the occupant was able to stay comfortable in the heat of the summer as well as during the chill of winter. Occupied until the 1980s, this house and study hall was once used by Yi Sang-nyong, a one-time president of the Korean Provisional Government in exile. Next to Imcheong-gak stands a reconstructed memorial shrine.

Andong Dam and Folk Village

In 1976, after more than five years of construction, the pyramidal earth and stone Andong Dam was completed. The third largest in the country, this 83-meter-high, 612-meter-wide impressive structure creates a reservoir that twists like a contorted dragon for over 30 kilometers up its green hilly lair. The construction of this dam, like every other enormous dam in the country, necessitated the displacement of thousands of people to higher ground, the creation of new villages and fields, and the removal of numerous cultural properties to a safe haven. Created on the riverbank below the dam, one of these safe havens is Andong Folk Village (안동민속촌). Preserved here are 10 houses from the district, one *gaeksa*, and an ice-storage cellar. Taken from Yean township, the *gaeksa* (1712) is long and elegant. Its two tiny end rooms are separated by an open wood-floored porch. Set on sturdy vermilion pillars, the roof's central section has been elevated slightly above the adjoining end portions, giving animation to the building's long frontal plane. Next to it is *seokpinggo* (N.T. #305), an old-style ice house that resembles a mound tomb

from a distance. This cellar was originally erected in 1737 on the banks of the Nakdong River, some 30 kilometers north of its present site. Lined with stone, *seokpinggo* has an arched ceiling with three vents, and a floor drainage system. A stairway leads down into the chamber from a doorway on its long side. This cooler was packed with ice cut from the river in winter, and successfully stored river smelt caught during the summer; these fish were periodically sent to the king as gifts. The reconstructed houses at this village represent a variety of structure designs typical to the area. Several of these buildings are now used as restaurants that serve traditional-style Korean food and drink. Through the village and up a side valley are the remains of the TV drama set for a series about the Later Baekje king Wang Geon, aired in 2001.

Located nearby, the **Andong Folk Museum** houses smaller and more delicate artifacts of the region, and it has well-executed displays showing the stages of life in traditional Korean society, from birth to beyond death. Open every day except Monday and holidays, it has an entrance fee of ₩550. This museum is a wonderful introduction to the most socially meaningful of the traditional, personal events of a Korean's life, and is even educational for those who have more than a rudimentary understanding of Korean culture. This is a winner and a good place to expand your knowledge of traditional Korean ways and beliefs.

A little community of shops and restaurants that is the terminus for city bus no. 3 can be found 1.5 kilometers beyond the folk village and above the dam. At lakeside is a pier for occasional excursion ferries that may run as far as Dosan Seowon when there is enough water impounded in the reservoir.

Hyanggyo and *Yangban* House

East of town on the way to Imha Dam, and backed up into the hillside on the city side of Andong National University, is the **Andong Hyanggyo** (안동향교). This public school from the Joseon Dynasty once stood where the current city hall now stands, previously the campus of Andong Teachers College which became the university. As the university is the symbolic out-growth of the *hyanggyo,* it seems appropriate that they now sit side by side.

Farther along, at a point where the road to the dam splits from the highway, is the small village of Cheonjeon-ni. Here is a *yangban* house (T. #450) that belongs to the head clan of the Uiseong Kim family (의성김씨종택). Built around 1650, this traditional post-and-beam house is built in squares around two courtyards and has several additional buildings. It's still occupied, so be respectful and ask permission to look around. A family member from the 1600s was a ranking government official, and one of his diaries has been designated T. #484. This house gives a good idea of traditional *yangban* architecture from the Joseon Dynasty, as do other such family homes in the area.

Imha Dam

Completed in 1993 at 73 meters high and 515 meters long, the Imha Dam is slightly smaller than Andong Dam. Its reservoir stretches back several dozen kilometers along several arms, and the electricity produced is sent to the greater industrial areas of Daegu and Pohang. A small restaurant, shop, and observation hall have been built at the end of the bus line above the dam. While there is an excursion ferry pier near the shops, boats do not run regularly. As it occupied a spot in the inundation area behind the Andong Dam, the main shrine hall of **Hogye Seowon** needed to be moved and has been placed below the Imha Dam. Built in memory of Yi Toe-gye, it is in a better state of repair than Gosan Seowon, south of the city. Also in response to the inundation, other traditional buildings have been gathered together farther up the lake at **Jirye Art Village** (지례예술촌), where traditional arts and Confucianism are taught.

Since the creation of these dams, fog has been a problem at certain times of the year because of the vastly increased area of surface water in this part of the county. A third dam is under consideration for the rural area south of here at Gilan, and if that one is built, the problem of fog will be exacerbated. This has been a great concern to the farmers in the area, who have been vocal in their opposition to a new dam, because the current problematic fog condition has already adversely affected the production of their crops.

Practicalities

There are over 150 accommodations in Andong. The best in town is the first-class Andong Park **Tourist Hotel** (tel. 054/859-1500). Just down from the train station, it has Korean- and Western-style rooms from ₩60,000 and suites from ₩87,000, two restaurants, and a bar. The chic **Hotel California** (tel. 054/854-0622), in the center of town with rooms for ₩35,000–60,000, is much smaller, newer, and more of a boutique hotel. A great many *yeogwan* are clustered in the several-square-block area toward the city center from the train station and bus terminal. Start by looking at the Cheonggungjang Yeogwan (청궁장여관), Byeolgungjang Yeogwan (별궁장여관), Haniljang Yeogwan (한일장여관), or the more spartan Daerimjang Yeogwan (대림장여관) or Gwangseong Yeoinsuk (광성여인숙). A few steps farther away are the Munhwajang Yeogwan (문화장여관) and Dowonjang Yeogwan (도원장여관).

There are even more restaurants in the city than accommodations. Andong *hanu,* beef from Korean-grown cattle, is popular in town. Many restaurants are located between the pedestrian street and the road that runs up from the train station. The Asowon prepares a wide variety of Chinese dishes; for Western fare, try the Rose Garden at the Andong Park Hotel. Market alleys and street corners throughout town are crowded with movable food stalls on most fair-weather evenings.

The closest airport is west of Yecheon, some 40 kilometers to the west of Andong. Both Asiana and KAL fly between Seoul and Yecheon. Morning and afternoon flights make the 45-minute run, returning about a half-hour after they arrive. A direct shuttle bus (₩3,300) runs from Andong to the airport to connect with these flights and returns after picking up passengers. This bus leaves from in front of the elementary school down and across the street to the west from the bus terminal. For information and reservations on the shuttle bus, contact the airline offices in town: Asiana (tel. 054/854-4003) and KAL (tel. 054/852-4182).

More than two dozen daily trains of all classes run through Andong. These trains run directly to Seoul Cheongnyangni, Seoul Station, Yeongju, Gangneung, Ulsan, Daegu, and Busan.

With the completion of the Jungang Expressway, located a fair distance west of the city center, express buses connect Andong to the major cities along its route and to other large cities in the country. Intercity buses run to and from Andong from the bus terminal just down the street to the west from the train station. Selected bus destinations and fares are Daegu (₩5,600), Gimcheon (₩8,500), Mun'gyeong-eup (₩6,400), Yeongju (₩3,100), Yeongdeok (₩6,700), Juwang-san (₩5,500), Gyeongju (₩9,700), and Pohang (₩10,200).

While a few city buses make a circulation of the city streets, most start in the city and run to points in the surrounding countryside. From along the street between the bus terminal and the train station, bus no. 67 runs to Ocheon Cultural Artifacts Site, Dosan Seowon, and Onhye; no. 3 runs to Gunja-jeong, brick pagoda, and Andong Dam; and no. 11 to Andong National University and Imha Dam. Across the street, bus no. 46 goes to Hahoe, while no. 54 runs to Jebiwon. Bus no. 51 to Bongjeong-sa, no. 38 to Gosan Seowon and Goun-sa, and the airport bus start from in front of the elementary school to the west of the bus terminal.

HAHOE 하회
Traditional Village

Hahoe, 24 kilometers west of Andong, is one of the few officially designated "traditional villages" in the country. It occupies a knob of land that causes the mighty Nakdong River to form an "S" loop. Hahoe (pronounced ha-hway), with its markedly pastoral and rustic atmosphere, has produced many scholars and government officials, and is the wellspring of a folksy masked dance drama. It's one of the few remaining examples of a classical Joseon Dynasty Confucian village layout. The fewer than 500 inhabitants consider their community a living symbol of tradition, and not a showcase like the artificial (yet pleasing) Korean Folk Village near Suwon. Be-

cause of its cultural value, it has kept itself relatively free of the Saemaeul Movement's modernizing programs, and you get a feeling of stepping into old Korea when you arrive here. Yet modernization (in the guise of automobiles, television, power lines, and such) and the increased tourist trade (restaurants, *minbak,* and souvenir shops) have definitely made their marks on the village. Unfortunately, it is not nearly as pure and undefiled as it was even three decades ago, and it does not match the hype often used to describe it. Still, there is an obvious attraction. Mud-walled, thatched-roofed houses surround the tile-roofed *yangban* houses in the center of the village as they have done for centuries. High walls front the winding dirt lanes, and separate the individual housing compounds. A patchwork of fields surrounds the community as it has for hundreds of years. Tall ginkgo trees tower over the houses, complementing the prevailing earth colors. It's best experienced in fall, abuzz with activity and autumn smell in the air. Ruddy-cheeked men harvest the golden fields of rice and lay a new cover of thatch on their roofs. Red peppers are spread on mats to dry, and women keep busy making *gimchi* out of piles of cabbage and other vegetables. Even young children are active with household duties and field work. Stroll around and soak up the scene, look into the housing compounds and take pictures, but don't disrupt the daily activities of the inhabitants. A booth at the bus stop will collect ₩1,600 on your way into the village. For those who desire fuller understanding, an inexpensive guide service is available upon request. Bus no. 46 runs several times a day between Andong and Hahoe.

Ancestral Village

Hahoe is the ancestral home of the Pungsan Ryu family. The family planted its roots here about 600 years ago. In the late 1500s, this family produced two brothers of outstanding merit. Ryu Un-nyong was a noted Confucian scholar, and his younger brother, Ryu Seong-yong, was a statesman and prime minister during the disastrous Hideyoshi Invasions. The Ryu ancestral home, Yangjin-dang (T. #306), is a sturdy post-and-beam, tile-roofed *yangban* house about 400 years old. It sits in the center of the village, a stately old gentleman. Chunghyo-dang (T. #414), a second house of the family, is nearly as old as the first and located only a short stroll away. Ryu descendants still occupy parts of these homes. A small exhibition room next to Chunghyo-dang displays several designated treasures, numerous documents, historical artifacts, and personal effects of the Ryu family and village. One document, *Jingbirok* (N.T. #132), is an account of the Hideyoshi Invasions written by Ryu Seong-yong. Other writings are designated T. #160.

If you happen to be in the village during the tenth lunar month, you may be fortunate enough to witness the annual Ryu family *jesa* ceremony, which draws family members from all over the country to pay respect to their two famous ancestors. Old men with wispy gray beards, long topcoats, and specially woven horsehair hats, and young men in modern suits bow before the graves of these respected men, offer a table full of food, and recite a ritual eulogy. This is one of the authentic and traditional *jesa* ceremonies still religiously performed in the country today. Women, traditionally not part of this ceremony, provide food for everyone after the ceremony.

Hahoe Mask Dance

The *Hahoe Byeolshin Gut* shaman ceremony has, as a part, the Hahoe Mask Dance, or *Hahoe talchum*. Originating here during the mid-Joseon Dynasty, this dance was performed approximately every 10 years after a New Year's Day ceremony, and staged in the village square or in front of a sponsor's house. Stopped in 1928 by the Japanese authorities, who intended to repress Korean cultural activities, it resumed in 1958. While adjunct ceremonies and the opening act are done to placate the gods and drive evil spirits away, to pray for abundant harvests, and ensure the peace and tranquillity of the village, the remainder of the masked dance is performed with ribald humor in a much less serious manner: poking fun at lascivious monks; the stereotypical antics of the aloof *yangban,* government officials who exploit the farmers; and the buffoonery of the peasant. Originally performed to maintain goodwill between the social classes and as a ritual ceremony for the well-being of the community, it is now done simply for its entertainment and cultural value. One of the few masked dances in the country, this six-act play of satirical vignettes is performed for free at an outdoor the-

performance of the *Hahoe Byeolshin Gut* at Hahoe Village

ater-in-the-round near the entrance to Hahoe Village every Saturday and Sunday at 1500 from May to October and every Sunday at the same time during March, April, and November. Don't miss it if you're at Hahoe, or see it performed during the Andong Cultural Festival in town.

Hahoe Masks

Legend says that in the distant past this village was visited by ceaseless calamities. One night, a certain young man named Heo Do-ryeong had a dream. A spirit told him to carve 12 masks, keep them hidden until finished, then use them in a special shaman exorcism ceremony to stop the disasters. Hanging a special rope around his house to indicate to others that he was in seclusion, he set to work carefully carving each mask, devoting himself completely to this arduous project. However, a young village girl, who yearned after Heo, wondered what occupied her sequestered beloved. Finally, unable to control herself, she poked a hole in the window of his workshop to see what he was doing. Even though he had finished all but the last chin of the last mask, at that instant Heo Do-ryeong fell dead. Nonetheless, the ceremony and dance were held and the calamities ceased. The masks and the dance have been handed down from generation to generation. In 1980, this masked dance was designated I.C.A. #69, and has reached a place of prominence in the cultural traditions of the country.

Of the original twelve, only nine masks survive. They are the *yangban* (nobleman), *seonbi* (scholar), *halmi* (grandmother), *gaksi* (new bride), *bune* (an older married woman), *jung* (Buddhist monk), *baekjung* (butcher), *joraengi* (male servant), and *imae* (scholar's female servant). The extant originals (N.T. #121), kept in the Seoul National Museum, are the oldest wooden masks in the country. One special feature is the movable jaws, which allow the actors to portray a wide range of facial expressions with simple movements of their heads. Only one of the masks is missing its jaw.

Located before the entrance to the village, the private **Hahoe-dong Mask Museum** (하회동탈박물관) displays not only reproductions of the Hahoe masks, but some 250 other Korean masks and several hundred masks from other countries.

For more information on the masks and the dance, see www.tal.or.kr.

Buyeong-dae

Opposite Hahoe Village is a precipice called Buyeong-dae, or Lotus Bluff. Every year on the full moon of the seventh lunar month, a village tradition is staged with this wall as its background. Originating in the early years of the Joseon Dynasty, this event is called *chulbul nori,* or String of Lights. From a straw rope strung between Buyeong-dae and the pine grove on the village side of the river hang sacks of charcoal. In the evening, these sacks are lit and allowed to burn, illuminating the river, which reflects the fire's colored light. Men of the village row out on the water to drink, sing songs, and have a merry old time.

A wide sand flat at this curve in the river lies in front of the traditional-style house Ogyeong Jeongsa, set near the water's edge; beyond is the traditional village school, Hwacheon Seowon. Up the trail to the side of these buildings, you get an excellent view from the top. On the far side of the bluff is a second traditional house, Gyeomam Jeongsa. Built by Ryu Un-nyong as a place to study and teach, members of the family still reside here. Although all have been repaired, these buildings are about 350 years old. In years past, a flat-bottomed ferry, poled by an old man who was the ferryman for years, used to take you across the gentle river. The ferry no longer exists, so if you care to explore, you must either wade across or make the roundabout approach from the rear by car.

Byeongsan Seowon 병산서원

After Ryu Seong-yong left government office, he retired to Hahoe and devoted himself to writing and teaching. When he died, Bunggak Seodang was converted to a memorial shrine and academy in his honor and renamed Byeongsan Seowon [Pyŏngsan Sŏwon] (H.S. #260). Dormitories flank the courtyard, while the lecture hall and shrine are located up above. Several wood printing blocks of his works are stored here. At the front is a narrow pavilion, an excellent example of a clean-lined open structure, the most eye-catching building in this compound. Notice its unusual log stairway. Ask the caretaker in the house next door to unlock the compound if the gates are closed.

Byeongsan Seowon is about three kilometers from Hahoe. Walk east from the village through the fields. Just before you come to the river, a small trail leads up the hill past a grave site and along the riverside slope. Follow this path in and out of two gullies; it exits onto the sandy river beach at a point where the *seowon* is visible in the distance a few hundred meters away. The stream in front of the village by the *seowon* is used on hot summer weekends by families escaping the city. Return the way you came, or walk the 3-kilometer-long gravel road the other way around the hill back to an intersection one kilometer below Hahoe. Bus no. 46 to Hahoe runs to Byeongsan Seowon twice a day.

BONGJEONG-SA 봉정사

Andong's most historic temple is Bongjeong-sa [Pongjŏng-sa], or Phoenix Bower Temple; ₩1,300 entrance fee. It's set on a gentle hillside and surrounded by gnarled pines 16 kilometers northwest of Andong. Founded by Uisang in 672, part of this compound miraculously escaped destruction by the Japanese army during the Imjin War. During its last reconstruction in the early 1970s it was discovered that Geungnak-jeon (N.T. #15) was the oldest wooden structure in Korea, beating Buseok-sa's Muryangsu-jeon by about 30 years. Geungnak-jeon, however, is not as large or as aesthetically pleasing a structure as Muryangsu-jeon. Most of the woodwork in this building is original, but the wattle walls have been replaced. This diminutive 850-year-old building sits in the left courtyard of this compound.

Daeung-jeon, the main hall, Hwaeomgangdang, a study hall, and Gogeum-dang, a dormitory, have been designated T. #55, #448, and #449, respectively. The three altar figures of Dae-

ung-jeon are flanked by faded "dragon pillars." Not many such pillars, with writhing dragons circling them, exist in temples today. The paint on this building is said to date from the original construction. Daeung-jeon fronts the double-terraced central courtyard. Facing the main hall from the lower level is a weather-beaten pavilion that sits over the entrance to the temple compound, above a steep stairway of uncut stone. A building with character, its paint has totally faded, moss grows on the roof tiles, and the floorboards are uneven and irregular.

A few steps to the east is Yeongsan-am, a compact and somewhat dilapidated auxiliary hermitage. Its plain wood-and-plaster walls speak of spartan qualities, yet the verandas give it homeyness and warmth. Occupying a small hall, the altar figures here are larger than at Bongjeong-sa. Portraits of the temple's founder and famous monks who have lived here hang in a side hall. A 100-year-old stunted pine grows from a split in a courtyard boulder, giving this hermitage virtually its only bright color. This hermitage was used as a set for the Korean movie, *The Reason Why Dalma Went to the East*. Dalma refers to Bodhidharma, the first patriarch of Zen Buddhism.

Two hundred meters west of Bongjeong-sa sits another hermitage. Jijo-am is dedicated to Gwaneum, the Goddess of Mercy, and a Goryeo Dynasty statue of her, re-gilt in 1982, graces its altar. Behind this building is Samseong-dang, Hall of the Three Saints, estimated to be about 700 years old. The paintings on its altar date back several hundred years, and the pastel wall murals of heavenly beings look to be even older. It's used by monks for meditation, so approach it with reverence and quietude.

About a half-hour walk over the hill to the north brings you to Gaemok-sa, originally called Heungkuk-sa, a Silla Dynasty temple also built by the monk Uisang. Legend says that Uisang constructed one *gan* a day for 99 days, so this temple must have been a large complex at one time. Now all is gone except a gate and the hall Wontong-jeon (T. #242).

Andong city bus no. 51 runs to Bongjeong-sa (₩1,180). At the village about two kilometers down the road from the bus terminus is one of the

Andong Kim family's head houses and ancestral graves. Nearby are ancestral graves of both the Andong Kwon and Jang families, and in the town of Seohu-myeon is the reconstructed house (T. #112) of Kim Seong-il, a Joseon Dynasty scholar, and numerous items that belonged to him.

DOSAN SEOWON AND VICINITY

Dosan Seowon 도산서원

Possibly the greatest cultural asset in the Andong area is Dosan Seowon [Tosan Sŏwon] (H.S. #170), founded by Korea's foremost Confucian scholar, Yi Toe-gye (1501–1570). His portrait graces the front of the ₩1,000 bill, and a scene of Dosan Seowon is printed on the reverse. Yi Toe-gye (a.k.a. Yi Hwang) was respected for his philosophical understanding and writings, and was influential with scholars and politicians. His renown even reached China and Japan. He was a precocious youngster, and his family gave him the best education available. Yi Toe-gye easily passed the "lower" government exams, but didn't succeed in the "higher" examinations until he was 34! He subsequently held several high official posts, including governor of two neighboring counties and assistant deputy prime minister. Becoming disillusioned with the bureaucracy, he retired to his rural home to study, write, and teach classical Confucian doctrine. In 1561, Yi started his *seodang* (private school) to prepare students for the civil service exams, and in 1557 its first building was erected as his study and classroom. In 1574, four years after his death, this school was expanded, elevated to the status of a *seowon,* and a shrine was built in his honor.

Dosan Seowon is 28 kilometers north of Andong, tucked into a small fold in a hillside overlooking Andong Lake. Open 0900–1700; entrance is ₩1,100. A few small shops and one restaurant are located at the bus stop; use bus no. 67 from Andong. In 1970, all the *seowon* structures were rebuilt and the grounds landscaped. In spring, peonies and chrysanthemums color the courtyard, pines and bamboo provide a thick green backdrop in summer, and ginkgo and maple provide autumn color before the stark whiteness of winter arrives. The complex is an exemplary representation of classical Confucian architecture. Set on terraces, its many halls have a friendly, if somewhat pretentious, atmosphere; the renovation was too meticulous, the grounds are too clean, and the overall effect is too perfect for some visitors—it'll take some time to mature. A small and unpretentious building, the original *seodang,* is located on one of the lower terraces; the H-shaped first student dormitory is across the way. Each sits in its own walled enclosure. The main lecture hall (T. #210) occupies an upper level. The shrine to its rear (T. #211) contains Yi Hwang's memorial tablet. Every February and August a memorial ceremony is held here in his honor. On its gate doors are trifoliate swirling, circular symbols which represent the doctrine of harmony, balance, and the interdependence of heaven, earth, and man. In its own walled enclosure to the right of the lecture hall, a small archive contains hundreds of wood printing blocks, mostly works of Yi Hwang. On the left side of the grounds on a lower level is a tiny exhibition hall containing a few of Yi's personal belongings and samples of his writings. The museum office sells samples of some of his writings printed from wood printing blocks, and occasionally published papers about Yi and his work. Other buildings in the compound are study halls, two small libraries, dormitories, and caretaker's quarters. This is definitely one of Korea's most revered Confucian complexes, but when busloads of school children arrive, it can be anything but serene.

Out front, once at riverside but now in the middle of the lake on a manmade island, sits Shisa-dan, a marker commemorating official government examinations given here in honor of Yi's work and influence. Dosan Seowon was the only place outside of Seoul where these examinations were administered. In commemoration of Yi Toe-gye, and the government examinations that were once held here, a yearly writing competition has been started at Dosan Seowon. Scholars and others from throughout the country gather here for a day of essay and poetry writing, ritual ceremony, and other celebration. The winner of the writing contest is then paraded through the streets of Andong like those who passed civil service examinations of yesteryear.

In 2001, to celebrate the 500th anniversary of the birth of Yi Toe-gye, an International Confucian Cultural Festival was held here and at various venues in Andong. This event included an academic conference, writing contests, artistic performances, and various traditional ceremonies. Plans are to continue this event into the future. See www.confucianfestival.org for current information.

Other Yi Toe-gye Sites

Over the hill behind Dosan Seowon is the village where Yi Toe-gye was born and raised, the house in which he later lived, and his grave. On certain runs, Andong city bus no. 67 continues past Dosan Seowon and goes to the hamlet of Onhye. His birth house, **Toegye Daeshil** (퇴계대실), is in this village. From Onhye, a serpentine road runs east past **Toegye Jongtaek** (퇴계종택), his residence of later life, to the even smaller community of **Togye**, where his tomb is. His family home, a walled compound, is still occupied by the scholar's descendants. A new road now runs directly from Dosan Seowon to near this house. In Togye, a granite stairway leads up to a well-tended grave site. Pass the grave of Yi Toe-gye's wife and proceed to the top where Yi's grave is flanked by stone guardian figures and fronted by a stone altar. Several times a day, bus no. 67 continues on from Onhye to Togye; without a bus, it is less than a half-hour walk.

Ocheon Cultural Artifacts Site
오천문화재단지

Because of the inundation caused by Andong Dam, many cultural artifacts that lay in the valley behind it had to be moved. Some structures were gathered together below the dam as Andong Folk Village. A collection of other buildings, smaller artifacts, and two old written records (T. #1018, #1019) of the Gwangsan Kim family have been rebuilt for display at the Ocheon Cultural Artifacts Site, located about halfway between Andong and Dosan Seowon. This family had lived along the banks of the Nakdong River for some

600 years and these buildings are very good examples of Joseon-era *yangban* structures.

CHEONGNYANG-SAN PROVINCIAL PARK
청량산도립공원

Just over the county line north of Dosan Seowon is Cheongyang-san Provincial Park. Taken from the *Hwaeom Sutra* and referring to the Buddhist bliss of Nirvana, the name means "pure and refreshing." Designated a park in 1982, this 49-square-kilometer area is still rather undeveloped. Occupying a secluded section of Bonghwa County, it's a rugged mountain area of 26 peaks, the highest being 870 meters, which rise up in a U-formation and open onto the Nakdong River to the west. While there was once a temple below each peak, only one remains. At one point in his life, in order to concentrate on his studies, Yi Toe-gye withdrew to a retreat in these mountains. Cheongnyang Jeongsa, his study hall, can still be visited. A natural citadel, this area was used as a defensive fortress by King Gongmin during the mid-1300s, when he fled the capital of Gaeseong. Fortress wall remains can be still be seen on the northern slope of Chukyung-bong (845 meters). A huge *baduk* board carved on the flat rock top of this peak was used by the king and his courtiers in their leisure hours. The uppermost reaches of Andong Lake can be seen from here as well. It is said that someplace on the mountainside below this peak, lotus flowers blossom—an oddity, as they usually only bloom in a lowland lake or pond.

The road to the park entrance at Bukgok is paved all the way from both Andong and Bonghwa, but the park is best reached by the occasional bus from Bonghwa. Only a few simple *minbak* and restaurants are available at Bukgok and at the village along the park road.

Cheongnyang-sa 청량사
Set in the bosom of the best of the mountain's gray rock palisades, the temple Cheongnyang-sa has an outstanding location; it is perhaps best in the autumn, when the mountainside is robed

in all shades of red and yellow. Not only is the location very attractive, it is also said to have an outstanding position according to the laws of Korean geomancy. Founded in 663 by the monk Wonhyo, both he and his equally well-known friend Uisang stayed here. Now only a shadow of its former self, it still inspires. Approached by a walk lined with marigolds, the five-tier stone *sari* pagoda draws your interest first. It's set on the edge of the cliff to the front of the main hall. Although small and nothing special, the Yuri-pojeon main hall is friendly and intimate—it reputedly is the only temple hall in the country dedicated to the Healing Buddha that is not called Yaksa-jeon, the usual designation for a hall dedicated to this Buddha. In 1994, resident monks dedicated and installed a new altar mural and three altar figures. Unusually, Yaksa Bosal and Munsu Bosal are made of formed paper, while that of Jijang Bosal is of wood. This temple is also the repository of a huge old mural that is only unfurled on special ceremonial occasions. Here as well are a small three-tier pagoda and a hall dedicated to the Mountain God.

Set a few hundred meters below Cheongnyang-sa is Cheongnyang Jeongsa. Built around 1500 by an uncle of Yi Toe-gye, this simple and unpretentious retreat was used by the scholar as a place for solitude and study in his early years. Along a path above this study hall is Ungjin-jeon, a small hall associated with Cheongnyang-sa; it houses figures of the 16 Arhat. Above that is a shallow grotto cave called Kim Saeng Gul, in which the most famous Silla Dynasty calligrapher, Kim Saeng, is said to have studied and practiced his writing more than 1,000 years ago.

Trails

The park's several trailheads are located along the main valley's gravel road, the first section of which is now paved. Major trails are marked by signs, but a spider web of trails above the temple near the top of the north ridge are not. From the village of Bukgok on the highway, cross the bridge and walk up the park road past the ticket booth (₩800 entrance) to a small cluster of houses and a few spartan *minbak*.

Twenty minutes up from there brings you to another bridge near where a track rises steeply up the largest side valley to the left. Twenty minutes farther up the road is a second trailhead, called Ipseok. The trail from here heads around the side of the hill to the temple, and it is perhaps the most pleasant and gentle of the mountain's trails. About halfway along, the trail splits, the upper trail going to Ungjin-jeon and Kim Saeng Gul, the lower to the temple. Rounding a bend a short distance farther brings you to a point where you have the best view of Cheongnyang-sa nestled into the trees surrounded by huge outcrops of rock. From the rear of the temple, the trail continues on up to the ridge, from where you can reach several of the tallest peaks. From a spot along the road, a few hundred meters above Ipseok, the only major trail up the southern side runs up past remains of the mountain fortress to the *baduk* board at the top of Chukyung-bong. The main park road continues past a few shops and a small restaurant, and heads over the eastern pass to the village of Nam-myeon, from where there are occasionally buses to Bonghwa.

GOUN-SA 고운사

Between Andong and Uiseong, snuggled into a tight valley below lofty pines, is a temple with a glorious past. Goun-sa [Koun-sa], or Lone Cloud Temple, was constructed in 681 by busy Uisang and grew to become one of the district headquarters of the Jogye sect of Buddhism. It once had as many as 366 buildings and was then the main administrative temple of a 14-county area. Today, the temple maintains a low profile with a few more than two dozen buildings, which offer much for the curious to see. During the Japanese invasion of the 1590s, this temple was used as one of the headquarters of the warrior monks who fought against that aggression. As a result, the temple was burned, only to be rebuilt slowly in stages over the following centuries. Although the hills are not high and the valley not deep, the setting here is pleasant and the forest in the valley is protected.

A one-kilometer walk leads up from the bus stop to the temple's front gates. The first is a two-posted open-style gate; enclosed, the second contains four deva figures. Beyond the second gate, in a tiny shrine to the left side of the track, stand marred stone figures. Past this shrine you'll find a half-open weathered pavilion, the oldest structure in the compound. Set directly over the stream, which is partially covered, the pavilion's spindly foundation pillars seem too fragile to withstand the force of a raging spring flood. Yet it has stood through the years like the rock walls of the ravine itself, and will undoubtedly stand many more. Nearby sits a new bell pavilion. To its side, a stairway leads up to a small grassy court-yard. On the wall of the building above the stairs a tiger has been painted, the eyes of which follow you as you proceed up to the courtyard. Around this courtyard are the kitchen, administrative of-fice, and the Geungnak-jeon hall. On the altar of this hall sits the triad Amita, the Buddha of Infi-nite Light; Gwaneum, the Goddess of Mercy; and Daesaeji Bosal, the Bodhisattva of Power. This triad often occupies the altar when the Seokgamoni Buddha is not enshrined. Fine ex-amples of fairies are seen on the ceiling. One wonders if they are holdovers from shamanism, as is often stated, or Buddhist devotees intent upon opening the hearts and minds of diligent seekers of truth through a musical medium. Murals are painted on this hall's outside walls.

Beyond this small courtyard several other buildings include the judgment hall, with its large carved judge figures and door guards; a portrait hall for temple abbots and other wor-thies who have resided here; and a diminutive pavilion-like building with a wooden veranda which functions as the Mountain Spirit hall. Check out the spirit hall's artistic, though faded, floral designs, animal figures, and *eum-yang* (yin-yang) symbols on its ceiling and walls. Also here is a small new structure built to preserve the tem-ple's seated Seokgamoni Buddha figure (N.T. #246). This Silla Dynasty stone sculpture has excellent proportion and shape, and the light-colored stone seems to set off the contemplative facial features. A new and ornate main hall was built in 1990, and, unusually, occupies a place not immediately surrounded by the other temple buildings in this rather disjointed compound. This spacious hall is now the largest building at the temple and enshrines three good-sized figures on its altar under an intricate canopy. On the hill to the right side is a much-disfigured three-tier stone pagoda from the Silla Dynasty. The building to the front of which it sits functioned as the temple's main hall until it was removed to this spot and the new main hall built in its place. Along with the new construction and new paint, this entire compound has been freshened up.

Several times a day, city bus no. 38 runs be-tween Andong and Goun-sa. There is also a pe-riodic connection to Uiseong.

JUWANG-SAN NATIONAL PARK
주왕산국립공원

Juwang-san is southernmost of the great moun-tain areas in the Taebaek Range. Known as Seok-byeong-san ("Rock Screen Mountain") during the Silla Dynasty, it is one of the most scenic mountain regions in all of Gyeongsangbuk-Do. However, it's a bit of a surprise as the scenery is not so picturesque until you are right up in it. Es-tablished in 1976, Juwang-san [Chuwang-san] National Park is best known for its clear streams and waterfalls, a palisade of folding screen-like rock walls, and unusually shaped limestone pin-nacles. The 105 square kilometers of the park are divided into inner and outer regions, plus the appendage-like mineral spring area. The inner area is the park's central valley, open to the west and bounded by a ridge connecting Juwang-san (720 meters), Wanggo-am (910 me-ters), Myeongdong-jae (824 meters), and Geu-meun'gwangi (812 meters). It sees most of the park's visitors, has the majority of its trails, and contains the lion's share of superb beauty. Naked limestone peaks are found in various places in the park, but most prominently near the park's entrance at the lower end of the central valley. Gigantic, rounded spires seem to bubble out of the ground, forming sentinel peaks, sheer walls, cliffs, and waterfalls. The lower reaches of the valley resemble Asian landscape scenes drawn on an extended folding screen. The outer region bounds this central valley on three sides and boasts virgin forests, isolated vales, and only a few trails and hikers. Except for the leisurely valley path, all trails make moderate hikes.

In the spring, the lovely bleeding-heart flower blooms here in the valleys of Juwang-san, as if in respect for the spirit of King Ju. Although these forests are mostly pine, boxwood trees grow high on the mountain peaks, and moss covers the limestone boulders. Special foods of the mountain are the *songi beoseot* (a mushroom that grows only in pine forests), *sanchae* (wild mountain greens), *moruju* (wild grape wine), and a milky rice wine *(dongdongju)* with rice kernels still floating on the top.

Legend of King Ju

The whole mountain area—nearly every gorge, pinnacle, nook, and cranny—is somehow connected to stories of King Ju. A man of Chin China, he rose up in rebellion against the emperor of Tang China. Proclaiming himself the emperor of the Later Chu Dynasty (Ju in Korean), he was thereafter known as Juwang (*wang*

meaning "king"). After violating T'ang territory, Juwang lost a battle and was forced to flee for his life. He escaped secretly and made his way to this mountain in Korea, where his followers built a fortress wall. Here he retired to a life of solitude and meditation, seemingly far away from the perils and retribution of the T'ang emperor; but Juwang's whereabouts were discovered, and the emperor made an urgent request to the Goryeo king for assistance in capturing him. In the attempt, Juwang was killed in the gorge that now houses the hermitage dedicated to him. Since those days, this area has been known as Juwang-san, or Mountain of King Ju.

Park Village

The park entrance is 13 kilometers from Cheongsong. To the left side of the road as you approach the park, underneath huge oaks, crouches a *sadang* (shaman shrine). Old men sit out front and children play in the dirt, yet it seems a bit incongruous now as farmers drive by in tractors on their way to modern houses. The bus stops below the park office; one kilometer through the village is the park ticket booth (₩2,600 entrance fee). Becoming developed, this village has a small number of simple *yeogwan* and *minbak*, basic restaurants, and a string of souvenir shops. The Juwang-san Youth Hostel is here and charges ₩12,000 for a dorm or ₩50,000 for a family room. On the far side of the river is a large group-camping area.

Although known for its superb scenery, this park does not yet have the high volume of visitors typical of more easily accessible parks. Juwang-san is still a relatively tranquil, out-of-the-way mountain area, but the government emphasis on development and tourism may soon change all that, and the timeless rural peace will be broken. See the beauty of these eroded rocks and the sparkling streams before red vests and hiking packs block your view.

From the station at the park village, frequent city buses run to and from Cheongsong (₩1,300). Intercity buses run directly from here to Yeongcheon (₩8,600), Andong (₩5,500), Daegu (₩10,700), Busan (13,000), and Dong Seoul (22,200).

Temples

Juwang-san's largest temple, **Daejeon-sa**, lies just beyond the park entrance booth. It was named after Juwang's son. The date of this temple's founding is in question. Some scholars believe that it was constructed in 672 by the monk Uisang, while others say that it was started by Chinul in 919. Judging from the style of stone carvings on pieces of old pagodas that lie scattered in the yard, and other relics dug up from the ground, the earlier date seems more likely. Whatever the founding date, it was definitely used during the Japanese invasion of the peninsula in the 1590s to train Buddhist monk warriors. Today only three older buildings remain. Bog-wang-jeon, the main hall, is small and intimate. To its side sits a half-dilapidated judgment hall. Perhaps the most intriguing, however, is the diminutive and faded Mountain Spirit shrine. Located to the rear of the main hall, it sits up on posts off the ground. Towering over the temple grounds, standing as a sentinel to the valley, is the rock spire Giam-bong, resembling the Chinese character for mountain. Across the stream is **Baengnyeon-am**, a hermitage of nuns, dedicated to the eternal spiritual happiness of King Ju's daughter, Baengnyeon, said to have attained enlightenment while living here with her father. The trail to the side of Baengnyeon-am leads up to Gwangam-sa, above which rises the peak Jang-gun-bong.

Lower Valley

A path follows the stream past Daejeon-sa. A short distance beyond the first bridge are the remains of the Jaha fortress wall which collared this valley entrance. Near here, a side trail goes steeply up the hill to Yeonhwa-gul, a short tunnel through a huge slice of rock that has pulled away from the hillside. This trail continues to ascend beyond Yeonhwa-gul to Yeonhwa-bong, a peak that from Mangwol-dae appears like a lotus blossom in full bloom. Just beyond this point is an octagonal pavilion; here the path splits. The trail to the right goes over another bridge and up the hill, and branches in three directions. The right-hand branch goes off to Mujang-gul, a shallow cave where King Ju is said to have kept his ar-

© ROBERT NILSEN

The spires of Juwang-san tower over Daejeon-sa.

maments. The middle branch leads to the hermitage Juwang-am. At the rear of this tiny compound is a Mountain Spirit hall. One hundred meters farther into this box canyon is the grotto Juwang-gul, where the upstart emperor was struck down by arrow. Scooped out of the rock wall is a shallow opening containing an altar and a stone relief carving of the Mountain Spirit. High above this cul-de-sac thrust slender pinnacles of stone, many of them having religious names like Nahan ("Buddha's disciples"), Jijang ("King of the Underworld"), Gwaneum ("Goddess of Mercy"), etc. The left-hand path at the fork leads along the hillside past Mangwol-dae, a flat-topped pillar of stone where Juwang's children sat and learned the secrets of nature. Eroded pinnacles and rounded outcrops squeeze together along much of the northern side of this valley and, from the top of Mangwol-dae, give the impression of a long folding screen. The path continues under Geupsu-dae, a sheer limestone cliff, to a second octagonal pavilion. Between these two pavilions is a direct walkway that follows the watercourse. Beyond the second pavilion

is a short bridge. Directly above it rises the tall spire Hakso-dae, on which, it is said, a paired white crane and blue crane had built a nest. Some time later, a hunter shot one of these majestic birds, and since that time no cranes have been seen in the valley. Directly across the stream is Shiru-bong. Grossly eroded by wind and rain, from one angle it resembles a human face with a tuft of hair on its head, and from another it looks like an earthenware steamer.

From the bridge, the main trail continues up the valley via a raised walkway to the first and most picturesque of three waterfalls. Twisting and scouring its way through a bottleneck of boulders, it is as if it came straight off a scroll painting. It's no wonder that legends tell of supernatural Taoist hermits who came here to relax, and fairies who came to bathe. Farther along past the mountain hut, about 200 meters off the main path in an adjoining valley to the right, is the gracefully thin form of the second waterfall. Up the main valley, in a spot more open than the other two, is the two-step third waterfall, the largest of the three. This lower valley is the park's most frequented section. Beyond the second and third waterfalls are the park's upper valleys.

Hiking

Some of the best climbing in the park is up the steep slopes of the lower valley. Trails lead up along the rubble of the fortress wall, and go to the top of Giam-bong, Yeonhwa-bong, Mangwol-dae, Geupsu-dae, and Gwaneum-bong, among others. Trail or no trail, it's possible to blaze your way to the top of nearly any outcrop, but be extremely careful around all the loose rock.

For those who like to walk farther, several courses are recommended. The first follows the path past the second waterfall to Hurimaegi, a junction on the trail. Follow the right-hand trail along the stream, up the spur to the ridge, and right again to Juwang-san peak. Backtrack 100 meters and follow the trail down to Gwaneum-bong, or continue straight down the ridge to the park village. From Daejeon-sa, it takes about four hours round-trip.

The second trail requires about six hours. From Hurimaegi, follow the left trail into Sachang-gol, the loveliest glen in the park. This isolated trail runs for about a half hour up along the stream, then continues up the hillside past a grave to the ridge trail. Following the ridge trail, you come to Gamae-bong, the most outstanding peak along the horseshoe-shaped ridge. Farther along the ridge trail is the peak Wanggo-am. The south side of this escarpment drops off into the park's outer region, where the forest spreads like a broad green carpet below your feet. On a sparkling clear day, the East Sea is visible from here. A short distance along the ridge beyond Gamae-bong, trails drop down both sides. To the north, the trail exits this side valley about one kilometer above the village of Naewon-dong. Going down the south side, you end up at Jeolto, an old temple site. An additional six kilometers brings you to Ijeon, from where occasional buses run to Cheongsong. In an adjoining valley is Jusanji, an old reservoir constructed in 1720 and now popular as a fishing spot and a favorite site for photographers who come to take pictures of the huge willows that stand half submerged around the edge, pushing their skeletal branches toward the sky.

The third trail is one way from Daejeon-sa to Dalgi Mineral Spring. Just past the third waterfall, the trail crosses the river and continues up to Naewon-dong. Where it crosses, another trail branches off to the left and heads up the hill to the ridge, From the pass, it continues down the opposite valley to the small village of Neogu-dong. Dalgi Waterfall is about 30 minutes down the road, and five kilometers below the waterfall is Dalgi Mineral Spring.

Dalgi Mineral Spring 달기약수터

Three kilometers east of Cheongsong, at the far northern periphery of the park, is the Dalgi Mineral Spring. Considered the best mineral water in the country, this extremely carbonated fluid bubbles up through numerous streamside holes. It's said to be good for anemia and stomach disorders. More than 100 years ago, while constructing an irrigation system, a farmer uprooted a sapling and water gushed forth. Since this accidental discovery, the area has never been the same. Every year people flock to Cheongsong to drink this natural bubbly brew. Several simple restaurants and numerous *yeogwan* have been constructed in the village surrounding the spring, and the *samgyetang* chicken soup made with its water is said not only to have an attractive taste but also be extra-healthful. In recent years, two other such springs, both a short distance father up the road, have also been discovered and developed, and now the whole area is becoming very built up with shops, restaurants, and places to stay.

Cheongsong 청송

Cheongsong [Ch'ŏngsong], a relatively poor region, lies east of Andong in the lower reaches of the Taebaek Mountains. Economically behind most of the province, there is virtually no mining, industry, or manufacturing here, but you will see glimpses of old Korea and the slow process of transforming the nation's backcountry. Rural and traditional, it's still basically an agrarian area that depends heavily on the high production of tobacco—fields and mud-walled two-story drying sheds dot the countryside—and hot red peppers. The area's major tourist attraction is

Juwang-san National Park, and on the way to the park is the Cheongsong Folk Museum.

Most travelers who come this far continue straight on to the park, but there are several points of interest in town and in the surrounding county. Cheongsong is the original home of the Shim family, and as only one Shim family name exists in Korea, all members trace their ancestry back to this town. The Shim family produced a queen, wife of the Joseon Dynasty's greatest king, Sejong; her grave is across the river from the center of town. Near Cheongsong's central intersection, behind the town administration office, is the refurbished pavilion Chan'gyeong-nu. Built in 1429, it was used for *jesa* in years when the river was flooded and family members could not cross to hold the memorial ancestor ceremony at the grave site itself. A few steps away, below the county administration offices, is Cheongsong Hyanggyo, a refurbished Joseon Dynasty public school. A second *hyanggyo* can be found in Jinbo

to the north. Between Cheongsong and Jinbo are two *yangban* houses of note. One belongs to the Cheongsong Shim family and the other to the Pyeongsan Shin family.

The bus terminal in tiny Cheongsong is located at the northern edge of town. A few minutes' walk brings you to the main intersection. Near this intersection are the Dongseongjang Yeogwan (동성장여관) and Geumgangjang Yeogwan (금강장여관). On the way to Dalgi Mineral Spring is the third-class Juwang-san Tourist Hotel (tel. 054/874-7000), the best in the area, where rooms go for ₩55,000–110,000.

Every 15–20 minutes throughout the day, city buses run from town to the national park main entrance (₩1,300), while as many or more run to the Dalgi Mineral Spring entrance (₩650). Select intercity bus destinations are Andong (₩3,900), Jinbo (₩1,200), Yeongcheon (₩7,300), and Daegu (₩9,400).

East Coast

NORTH END

From the Gangwon-Do border, Gyeongsangbuk-Do's east coast stretches south in a fairly straight line until it hits Yeongil Bay at Pohang. Long beaches and rocky promontories dot the coast, and only a few scattered small harbors contain fishing fleets. Two remnants of old Korea, the pavilions Mangyang-jeong and Wolsong-jeong, look out to sea as they have for centuries, while the modern nuclear power plant north of Uljin takes its place along the seashore and produces electricity for the residents of this once-isolated coast—and the industrial areas of Pohang, Samcheok, and Donghae. Development of this region can also be seen at both Deokgu and Baekam hot springs, while the timeless beauty and natural setting of the limestone cave Seongnyu-gul remains constant. Up from the coast are ruggedly beautiful mountains and picturesque valleys, and in one of the most pleasing of these valleys lies the tranquil and hugely charming temple Bulyeong-sa.

There is suitable swimming along this section of the east coast, but it's not for the faint-hearted; the water is clean but *cold!* The most frequented and developed beaches are Bongpyeong, Mangyang, and Pyeonghae. Farther on toward Pohang are Jangsa, Wolpo, and Chilpo beaches.

Uljin 울진

Historically, Uljin has been a farming and fishing community, and aside from the Joseon Dynasty pavilion Mangyang-jeong, its major drawing card is Seongnyu-gul. Both Seongnyu-gul and Mangyang-jeong are located about six kilometers south of town, about 1.5 kilometers on either side of the coastal highway. The cave is located inland, along the river, and the pavilion on a bluff overlooking the rivermouth lagoon and the sea. City buses run to both.

Since the 1980s, however, the nuclear power industry has had a great impact on the economy of the area. The Uljin Atomic Energy Power Generation Plant (울진원자력발전소) is located 14 kilometers north of town in the village of

Bugu, at the turnoff for Deokgu Hot Spring. In 1988, reactor no. 1 was put on line and now four reactors are in use. Although it is not possible to visit the power generation facilities without special authorization, an information center has been set up at the entrance. While there are nicely done displays on how nuclear power is generated, how it is used, and a few personalities involved in its discovery and propagation, there is no serious discussion of the inherent problems or safety concerns associated with its production or the disposal of its byproducts. All explanations are in Korean only. There are, however, a few brochures in English. Korea is one of the dozen major countries of the world that satisfies a significant percentage of its electrical needs with nuclear power—about 40 percent in the case of South Korea. Currently there are 16 operating nuclear power plants at four sites in Korea. Up to 30 are anticipated to be in operation by 2015.

Uljin has a compact downtown area that has spread out, primarily along the one main street which passes through the center of the community. At the southern end of town is the bus terminal. Across the alley are the Daerimjang Yeogwan (대림장여관), Gwibinjang Yeogwan (귀빈장여관), and slightly pricier Alpsjang Hotel (알프스장여관). Next door is the police station. Just beyond the stream is the center of town, with shops, restaurants, and its central market.

City buses run along the main street of town before heading out into the countryside. Mangyang-jeong, Seongnyu-gul, Bugu, and Deokgu Hot Spring are all on city bus routes. Selected intercity bus destinations and fares are Gangneung (₩8,400), Bulyeong-sa (₩2,000), Yeongju (₩10,500), Daegu (₩14,500), Onjeong (₩4,000), Yeongdeok (₩5,300), and Pohang (₩8,800).

Seongnyu-gul 성류굴

Uljin's major tourist attraction is the limestone cave Seongnyu-gul [Sŏngnyu-gul]. Its hours are 0800–1800 April–October, until 1700 in winter; ₩2,200 entrance. At 472 meters, it's not the longest or most spectacular in the country, but as the first to be developed as a tourist site, it's per-

haps Korea's best-known cave. In 1963, the cave and the Chinese juniper-covered exterior rock cliff were designated National Monument #155. A riverside walkway of only a few hundred meters from either end and only a meter or so above water level runs to the cave entrance. It's merely a small opening in the rock, so you must stoop to enter this underground "Diamond Mountain." Inside it's a humid, constant 15°C; 31 life forms compete for existence in this stark environment. A walkway leads through narrow passages over pools and into each of the 12 chambers. Fluted columns, stalagmites, and stalactites appear around every corner of the passageway, jungle-thick in the open chambers. Colored lights accent these bizarre shapes, and give the whole scene an otherworldly feel. Each limestone form, pool, and cavern has, of course, been given a name to match its shape: "Treasure Island," "Three Buddhas," "Dragon Pool," "Maitreya Buddha," and "The Fairy's Secret Room" are a few. The highest chamber is 40 meters tall, the deepest of the three pools about 30 meters deep. Be aware that there are some narrow passageways and one place where you must duckwalk a few meters to get through. There is filtration through the rocks, so the depth of the pools inside rises and falls with the water level of the Wangpi River outside. Geologists have estimated its age to be about 250 million years.

Seongnyu-gul is close enough to walk to from town, but more convenient is the city bus to the north end of the riverside walkway. An intercity bus (₩700) can also drop you along the highway at Gunsan Il-li, from where there is about a one-kilometer walk to the south entrance walkway. At both ends of the riverside walkway are parking lots, and a string of restaurants and souvenir shops.

Bulyeong-sa 불영사

Although the coast road is full of fine scenery, the route from Uljin to Bonghwa, through the tightly twisting and picturesque Bulyeong Valley, up and over the Taebaek Mountain Range, and through small inter-mountain valleys is a real treat and delight. At the bottom end of the valley, starting about five kilometers outside Uljin and stretching for 15 kilometers, is the Bulyeong

Valley County Park, an area that has been named Scenic Site #6. Because the road winds its way along the hillside and there are few places to get down to the river, it is easiest just to appreciate its beauty from the road. If, however, you descend to the river, you are able to scramble over the boulder-strewn riverside from one great picnic spot and swimming hole to another. This valley is wonderful at any time of the year, but perhaps most beautiful at the height of fall color. Tucked into a side valley at the upper end of this park is Bulyeong-sa temple, and toward the upper end of the valley is the Tonggo-san nature area.

Established in 651 by Uisang, Bulyeong-sa was originally named Guryong-sa ("Nine Dragons Temple"), after nine of these creatures were driven from the pond at its front. Some time later, the temple's name was changed to Bulyeong-sa [Pulyŏng-sa] ("Buddha Shadow Temple"), because a rock outcrop on the hill to the west of the temple casts a Buddha-shaped shadow on the pond. As you pass the pond, turn and look to your left. On the ridge above is a slender rock with others to its front bent forward as if in supplication. Although some temples have lotus or fish ponds within their compounds, the pond here is unusually large and adds an attractive element to the temple grounds. This pond is fed by a spring at its western end, next to Geungnak-jeon; at its outlet is a 600-year-old ginkgo tree. Hidden in a side valley and unable to be seen from the larger Bulyeong Valley, this compound is perfect for the nuns who come here to meditate.

A half-hour bus ride from town brings you to the temple entrance road (₩2,000 entrance fee) and a small cluster of shops. A walk of about one kilometer from the highway brings you to the temple, which like most temples kept by nuns is as neat as a pin. Set around the courtyard are a lecture hall—still used for instruction—living quarters, a Silla Dynasty three-tier stone pagoda, and Daeung-jeon (T. #1201), the main hall. Daeung-jeon is a small but pleasantly square building. Weatherworn on the outside, with faded paint on the inside, it has gone through some recent repair. This building has one rather unusual feature. Two stone tortoises have been placed under the foundation stones flanking the front stair

way, and it is said that these are here to protect the temple from fire, as it was burnt to the ground in 1396. To the side of this central courtyard are the Myeongbu-jeon judgment hall, a hall for former temple abbots, the small and plain Ungjin-jeon (T. #730), and the Mountain Spirit hall. Around the far side of the pond is the Geungnak-jeon, Hall of the Western Paradise. Of more recent construction is a bell pavilion which sits at the edge of the pond. On your way out, stop at the *sari budo* of the monk Yangseongdang who rebuilt this temple in 1500. A portrait of him (T. #1272) is kept at the temple.

Deokgu Hot Spring 덕구온천

Gyeongsangbuk-Do has two of the east coast's three well-known hot springs (the third is Osaek Hot Springs, in Seorak-san National Park). Just south of the provincial border, 12 kilometers inland, is Deokgu [Tŏkgu] Oncheon. Discovered about 600 years ago by hunters out tracking wild pig, it had until a few decades ago the most appealing natural setting of any hot spring in the country. Set in a tight, twisting valley, water gushed out at 41°C and was channeled into a large concrete tub in the middle of the stream. Open to the sky, this bath was used all year round, and a soak here was exceptional when the air was crisp and the valley white with snow. Now, the tub has been filled and a silver streak of an eyesore runs three kilometers down this pristine valley, bringing hot water by insulated pipe to the Deoku Hot Spring, which currently has the only commercial bathhouse in this new development.

From the existing condo below the hotel, walk over the small dam and up the left side of the reservoir. This trail sticks close to the stream, and about halfway up passes the largest of the numerous waterfalls and cascades. A multi-step affair, it has clear pools scooped out of the rocks under each falls. Even though the pipe is visible nearly all the way up the valley, this trail makes a nice stroll. A four-kilometer, 1.5-hour walk brings you to the source of the hot water—and a new Mountain Spirit shrine. From here, the trail continues steeply up the hillside and then follows the ridge for another hour-and-a-half, bringing you to the top of Maebong-san (999 meters) for an encompassing view of mountains and sea. This valley is now Deokgu County Park.

City buses from Uljin to Deokgu Oncheon run 12 times a day (₩2,150). The bus terminus is in the parking lot at the front of the hotel. For a journey up the coast, change buses at Bugu. The largest and best place to stay, and the only place to bathe (₩5,000 per person), is the **Deoku Hot Spring Hotel** (tel. 054/782-0677), where rooms go for ₩100,000–200,000. On the approach road to the hotel is a string of less expensive *minbak*, motels, and restaurants.

Wolsong-jeong 월성전

Forty kilometers south of Uljin is the farming community of Pyeonghae. A few kilometers north of Pyeonghae is the Joseon Dynasty pavilion Wolsong-jeong, where you get spectacular views of the ocean and the mountains fading off into the setting sun. Uljin city buses run this route.

South of Pyeonghae is the small fishing port of Hupo. In the past, ferries have run to Ulleung-do from the Hupo pier. Although currently not in operation, there has been some discussion to restart this service. While not the most convenient harbor location, it is the shortest route to the island, matching that from Mukho in Gangwon-Do.

Baekam Hot Spring 백암온천

Some 12 kilometers west of Pyeonghae, in the "developed" village of Onjeong is Baekam [Paekam] Oncheon. Discovered during the Silla Dynasty by a monk named Baekam, it was used almost exclusively by monks and local inhabitants until it was turned into a public bath in 1953. At 45°C, the water is rich in sulfur, and contains the highest percentage of radium of any hot spring in the country. One of the best-known hot springs in the country, it's been designated Tourist Site #3. Be prepared for the throngs! In the center of the village is a palatial bathhouse/hotel, a monstrous, multi-storied, quasi-traditional building. Its sculpted pool is large enough to swim in, and is decorated with stone lanterns and shapely rocks—a rare ambience for a public bath. If you're in the area, stop in for a

dip, but if you're put off by the least bit of ostentation, you may be up the wrong valley.

Accommodations at Onjeong include the first-class **Paekam Tourist Hotel** (tel. 054/787-3500) and the second-class **Sungryu Park Hotel** (tel. 054/787-3711). Less expensive *yeogwan* and restaurants are found in the lower section of the village near the bus terminal. Frequent city buses run to and from Pyeonghae, where intercity buses going up or down the coast can be boarded. Direct buses from Onjeong run to Uljin (₩4,000), Yeongju (₩14,200), Daegu Dongbu (13.300), and Pohang (₩7,600).

Yeongdeok 영덕

Yeongdeok [Yŏngdŏk] is a sleepy town from where a highway goes west to Andong. This town is perhaps best known for the large tasty crab that are caught off the coast near here. These crab often grow to a size where the body is larger than a tea saucer and the legs stretch more than half a meter wide. Yeongdeok's fishing port of Ganggu lies six kilometers away at the rivermouth; use a city bus. Aside from crab, you'll see net-like drying racks filled with the day's catch along its beach. Small fish are dried whole, while others are butterflied and laid open to the sun. Dried fish are most often eaten as *anju*, or in soup or chowder.

Both the Cheonghwa Yeogwan (청화여관) and Murimjang Yeogwan (무림장여관) are located on the street directly to the side of the bus terminal. On the far side of the stream is the less expensive Gyeongdong Yeoinsuk (경동여인숙). Bus destinations and fares include: Gangneung (₩13,800), Uljin (₩5,300), Andong (₩6,700), Juwang-san National Park (₩6,600), and Pohang (₩3,500).

POHANG 포항

Pohang [P'ohang] (pop. 520,000), the province's second-largest city, lies on the western shore of Yeongil Bay at the mouth of the Hyeongsan River. Its climate is temperate, with a moderating effect from the sea. Until early in the 20th century, Pohang was just one of many tranquil fishing villages along this coast. The community slowly grew due to its protected location, bountiful fields, proximity to Gyeongju and Daegu, and convenient transportation connections. During the Korean War, the east end of the Busan Perimeter was just south of town; several bloody battles were fought in the city streets, with students also taking part. In 1962, Pohang was designated an international port and allowed to receive foreign vessels. In 1968, construction began for the Pohang Iron and Steel Company Ltd., now known simply as POSCO, and since then the city has been transformed into one of the province's three major industrial centers and the country's first and foremost steel city. Aside from POSCO, Pohang is known for the nearby temples of Bogyeong-sa and Oeo-sa, as a gateway to the lovely east coast, and as the principal port for ferries to Ulleung-do.

South of the sluggish Hyeongsan River are several square kilometers of POSCO workyards, along with factories of other heavy industries. During the day, workyards are hives of activity, and at night the whole area is brightly lit, like a modern art sculpture of light and steel. North of the river is the old port, used by fishing boats, ferries, and domestic cargo ships. This inner harbor is the narrow lagoon behind Songdo Beach. Between this inner harbor and the train station, surrounding the five-way and six-way rotary intersections, is central downtown Pohang. The city's main street, Jungang-no, leads past lively Jukdo Market, the city's largest, purveyor of food stuffs, clothing, and household goods. Many people come here for its fish market, one of the largest in the country. Once nestled into the side of this inner harbor, the passenger ferry terminal has been moved to a location near the outlet of the harbor, and new port facilities created. North of the breakwater is North Beach. A town with virtually no inner city park space, it does have Yongheung Park capping the low hills west of the train station, a place where you'll find pavilions, walkways lined with cherry trees, and a monument to the loyal student-soldiers of the Korean War. Pohang has modernized swiftly, evidenced by the wide streets, contemporary buildings, new recreational facilities, and housing estates at both the south and north ends of the city.

A tourist information booth is located next to the intercity bus terminal and a counter is at the Pohang Airport. The post office and Telecom office are situated between the six-way rotary and the train station in the heart of the city's shopping, entertainment, and restaurant district.

For additional information see www.pohang.kyongbuk.kr or www.pohangcity.net.

City Beaches

Songdo Beach (송도해수욕장) is the best-known in and around Pohang. It's a two-kilometer-long strand of sand, backed up against dozens of shops, restaurants, and the Pohang Beach Tourist Hotel. On summer days, especially on weekends, this beach is exceedingly popular and crowded! Backing the beach is a pine forest, planted at the turn of the 20th century as protection against strong sea winds. A far-sighted plan, this grove also provides a shaded picnic area and playground. On the far side of the harbor opening is the North Beach (북부해수욕장), an additional 1.5-kilometer-long swimming area. Once less popular than Songdo Beach, it too draws big crowds in summer.

Fronting the beaches of Pohang are dozens of seafood restaurants; those at Songdo Beach are generally older and most established, those at North Beach are more modern and seem to have a greater diversity. More expensive than the city's standard restaurants, they nearly always give good value. Look for those with tanks full of live fish at the entrance.

POSCO

POSCO is the city's largest company and employer. Since its opening in 1973, this enormous milling complex, one of the most advanced in the world, has played an integral part in Korea's rapidly expanding economic and modernization programs. With the addition of the newer steel plant at Gwangyang in Jeollanam-Do, also with several huge blast furnaces and mini-mills, POSCO as a company produces over 25 million metric tons of steel yearly for domestic and foreign consumption. Some of the iron ore and limestone needed in the steel making process comes from mines in the Taebaek Mountains

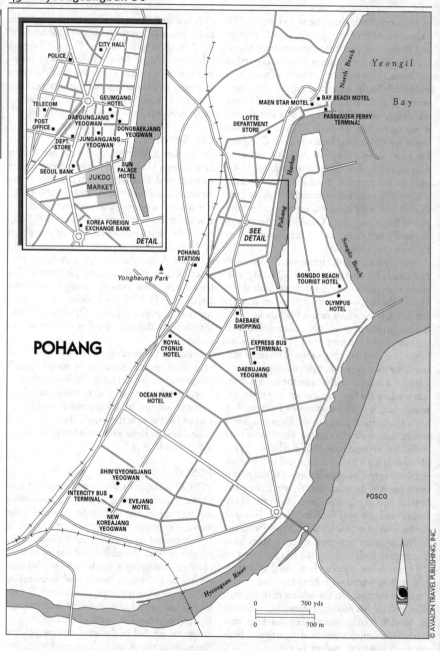

POHANG

Yeongil Bay

CITY HALL

POLICE

TELECOM

GEUMGANG HOTEL

POST OFFICE

DAEGUNGJANG YEOGWAN

DONGBAEKJANG YEOGWAN

DEPT. STORE

JUNGANGJANG YEOGWAN

SEOUL BANK

SUN PALACE HOTEL

JUKDO MARKET

KOREA FOREIGN EXCHANGE BANK

DETAIL

MAEN STAR MOTEL

BAY BEACH MOTEL

LOTTE DEPARTMENT STORE

PASSENGER FERRY TERMINAL

Pohang Harbor

SEE DETAIL

POHANG STATION

Yongheung Park

Songdo Beach

SONGDO BEACH TOURIST HOTEL

OLYMPUS HOTEL

DAEBAEK SHOPPING

ROYAL CYGNUS HOTEL

EXPRESS BUS TERMINAL

DAEBUJANG YEOGWAN

OCEAN PARK HOTEL

SHIN'GYEONGJANG YEOGWAN

INTERCITY BUS TERMINAL

EVEJANG MOTEL

NEW KOREAJANG YEOGWAN

POSCO

Hyeongsan River

0   700 yds
0   700 m

© AVALON TRAVEL PUBLISHING, INC.

in Gangwon-do, but most of the basic ingredients (ore, coking coal, and limestone) must be imported from abroad. POSCO produces pig iron, plate steel, bar steel, wire rods, rolled steel, electrical sheet steel, stainless products, and other specialty items. Korea has become one of the top 10 steel-producing nations of the world, and Koreans take great pride in POSCO.

For additional information on the company see www.posco.co.kr.

Accommodations

Once the only Western-style hotel in the city, the second-class **Songdo Beach Tourist Hotel** (tel. 054/241-1401) is still proud of the business it does and of its location on Songdo Beach. Well-run and clean, it has a coffee shop, bar, restaurant, and money-exchange facilities. With rooms for ₩60,000–120,000, it's heavily booked only during the height of summer. A few steps away up the approach road to the beach is the newer, second-class **Olympus Hotel** (tel. 054/241-6001), with rooms running ₩55,000–80,000. Of the many hotels in the city, others to try are the second-class **Sun Palace Hotel** (tel. 054/242-2800), where rooms run in the ₩50,000–70,000 range; and the first-class **Ocean Park Hotel** (tel. 054/277-5555), with rooms for ₩72,600–180,000. The finest place in town is the deluxe-class **Royal Cygnus Hotel** (tel. 054/275-2000), where rooms run ₩120,000–235,000.

Most of the once-abundant *yeogwan* that lined Songdo Beach have been turned into seafood restaurants and a handful of *minbak*, but along the main street running toward the beach, just before the hotel, are Neulbomjang Yeogwan (늘봄장여관) and Shinajang Yeogwan (신아장여관). If you intend to swim, these places are the most convenient. If you've come to Pohang to catch the ferry to Ulleung-do, try a place closer to the ferry terminal like the newer Maen Star Motel (맨스타모텔) or Bay Beach Motel (베이비치모텔). Close to the heart of town, between the six-way rotary intersection and the old ferry location, are the Daegungjang Yeogwan (대궁장여관), Dongbaekjang Yeogwan (동백장여관), and Jun-

gangjang Yeogwan (중앙장여관). Only slightly fancier and more expensive is the Geumgang Hotel (금강호텔). Around the periphery of the bus terminal, you can find many mid-range accommodations, including the Evejang Motel (이브장여관), New Koreajang Yeogwan (뉴코리아장여관), and the Shin'gyeongjang Yeogwan (신경장여관). The Daebujang Yeogwan (대부장여관) is located next to the express-bus terminal.

Transportation

The new **Pohang Airport** terminal opened in 2002. A dozen times a day, Asiana Airlines and KAL offer flights from Pohang to Seoul, and Asiana Airlines runs a once-daily flight from Pohang to Jeju-Do. The airport is east of the city, beyond POSCO and the turnoff for Ocheon. Depending upon your destination, a taxi into town might cost ₩5,000–8000. Express city bus nos. 200 and 200-1 run into town on the way from Guryongpo. For information and reservations, call Asiana Airlines (tel. 054/277-8884) or KAL (tel. 054/272-9229), or visit their respective offices in the city.

Ferries from Pohang run only to Ulleung-do. A large catamaran ferry makes one round-trip daily, requiring 3.5 hours one-way, leaving Pohang at 1000. The ordinary fare is ₩49,000, while a special first-class fare is ₩54,000. There may be a security check at the ferry terminal, where you and your bags could be searched and your ticket and passport examined.

The Daegu rail line, via Yeongcheon, ends in Pohang. Twice a day, *Saemaul-ho* trains connect Pohang to Seoul (₩29,600), with 10 *Tongil-ho* trains to Dong Daegu (₩3,200) and four to Gyeongju (₩2,900).

Express buses run every 20 minutes to Seoul (₩15,400), every two hours to Daejeon (₩9,800), every one-and-a-half hours to Masan (₩6,600), and every two-and-a-half hours to Gwangju (₩12,500). Intercity buses use their own terminal toward the southern end of the city, from where buses run up and down the east coast, to all cities in this province and major cities in neighboring provinces. The right-hand section of this building is used for some city bus routes.

Destinations and fares include: Busan (₩6,300), Ulsan (₩5,100), Bogyeong-sa (₩2,000), Gyeongju (₩2,000), Daegu (₩5,500), Andong (₩9,500), Uljin (₩8,800), and Gangneung (₩17,300).

Ordinary city buses charge ₩600 and express city buses ₩1,050. Some of the more useful numbers are as follows.

no. 101: North Beach, city hall, Jukdo Market, and express-bus terminal

no. 102: city hall, express-bus terminal, Ocheon (transfer to a country bus for Oeo-sa)

no. 103: Songdo Beach, intercity-bus terminal, train station, city center

no. 105: North Beach, train station, Jukdo Market, intercity-bus terminal, POSCO

no. 200: Ulleung-do ferry pier, city hall, intercity-bus terminal, POSCO, airport, Guryeongpo

no. 200-1: Ulleung-do ferry pier, city hall, express-bus terminal, POSCO, airport, Guryeongpo

no. 300: train station, express-bus terminal, intercity-bus terminal, Ocheon

nos. 107, 500: intercity-bus terminal, Yeongil Folk Museum

SIGHTS NEAR POHANG

Fossil Museum 경보화석박물관

North of Pohang along the coast is the Gyung-Bo Fossil Museum. While it seems an unlikely spot, there is actually plenty of traffic up and down the highway. This museum is open 0800–2000, 0900–1900 in winter; ₩1,000 entrance. You'll have to like fossils to appreciate this private museum, but if you do you'll find excellent examples of plants, animal parts, minerals, and wood. While many of the specimens are from Korea, there are fine examples from several dozen countries around the world.

Bogyeong-sa 보경사

The best-known and most oft-visited temple along this section of the east coast is Bogyeong-sa [Pogyŏng-sa], Treasure Mirror Temple. Established in 603, soon after Buddhism was introduced to the Silla Kingdom, its name refers to an eight-faceted mirror from China buried at the temple. Bogyeong-sa's 13 buildings create a harmonious whole, and trees, bushes, and flowers give the grounds an earthy touch. From the ticket booth (₩2,000 entrance) at the upper end of the village, a leafy corridor leads you past an 800-year-old *sophora japonica* tree to the temple's well-done front gate with its four finely carved wooden devas. Directly through the gate you see the slender five-tier stone pagoda standing in the temple's front courtyard. From 1023, its design is simple yet pleasing. To the left is a small hall with a skin drum set on a tortoise stand, wooden fish gong, flat metal gong, and a hefty bell—the four instruments always found at large temples. Behind the pagoda is Jeokgwang-jeon, under which the precious mirror is said to be buried. This structure is the oldest of the extant buildings in the compound, and on its altar is enshrined the Vairocana Buddha flanked by the bodhisattvas Munsu and Bohyeon. To the rear of Jeokgwang-jeon is the main hall, which contains several exquisite murals. New flagpoles and supports, an ancient feature of Korean temples, once again enjoying a resurgence, have been erected to its side. At the back of the compound are five smaller halls. Palsang-jeon contains murals depicting eight scenes from the Buddha's life. The Mountain Spirit hall was moved to its present location in 1914 from its former spot about 100 meters up the hillside. The 16 Nahan are enshrined in Yeonsan-jeon along with Munsu on his tiger and Bohyeon on an elephant. Wonjin-gak houses portraits of former abbots of the temple, including Wonjin Guksa, Bogyeong-sa's most respected abbot. His cremated remains are kept in the octagonal, five-meter-high *sari budo* (T. #430) on a rise behind the temple; his memorial tablet (T. #252), carved in 1224, stands on a Goryeo-style tortoise base, its fierce head resembling a dragon's. Set in front of the new judgment hall, presided over by Jijang Bosal, this beast must certainly put a scare into those approaching for evaluation and censure. Also preserved at this temple are a document written by the warrior-monk Sammyeong (1554–1610), and 12 wood printing blocks, exactly reproduced from the script of a poem written by Joseon Dynasty's King Sukjong (1674–1720) during a stay here.

Although not tucked away in a distant valley, there is a sense of peace and solitude at Bogyeong-sa, especially in the late afternoon, after all the tourists have gone. Take time to listen to the reverberation of the temple bell, the clack of the wooden fish gong, and the melodious clang of the metal gong as a monk calls for all other activity to stop and preparation for the evening ceremony to begin. Within a five-minute walk of the main temple are two hermitages, Dong-am to the east, and Seoun-am to the west; less than an hour's walk up the valley will bring you to Munsu-am, and, farther up, Bohyeon-am.

Waterfall Kingdom

Up the valley, through this lush, rocky river gorge, a trail leads to a series of 12 waterfalls, a veritable "waterfall kingdom," according to one ancient source. It's 1.5 kilometers to the first falls—a good-looking double cascade—and several more to the last. The valley narrows and deepens, and the stone-washed boulders and rock slabs take on more fantastic shapes as you make your way past each cascade. Number six is tall and slender and has a shallow cave scooped out of the wall behind the water curtain. A suspension bridge leads to the 30-meter-high seventh waterfall, **Yeonsan Waterfall**, which is the heart of the valley. Most visitors turn around here, but other fine sights can be seen along the trail that runs above this point. This valley is now administered as **Naeyeon-san City Park**.

From Bogyeong-sa, one trail leads up to Wonjin Guksa's *sari budo,* and from there up the ridge to Munsu-san—about one-and-a-half hours. Following this ridge for another five hours, the trail continues on to Naeyeon-san and from there up to the peak Hyangno-bong (930 meters). The valley trail passes each of the waterfalls, eventually leading up the hillside to the top, about four-and-a-half hours from the temple. A round-trip is possible, but it makes a long day.

Practicalities

There is a bright and modern group of multi-story souvenir shops, restaurants, *yeogwan,* and *minbak* below Bogyeong-sa that make up the tourist village. If you're staying, try Daedongjang Yeogwan (대동장여관) or others nearby. From this village, buses run many times a day to Pohang (₩2,200). For Yeongdeok and other points north, take any bus the four kilometers to the village of Songna (₩600), and there transfer to an intercity bus running up the coastal highway.

Yeongil Folk Museum 영일민속박물관

About 20 minutes north of Pohang, in the middle of the town of Heunghae (흥해), is the Yeongil Folk Museum. Of the 6,000 or so items in its collection, most have been donated by people of the area. They represent all classes of Korean people and all aspects of the farming and fishing life of the region. This folk museum is less pretentious than most others in the country, and there seems to be an authentic naturalness to the articles displayed here. While there are no non-Korean explanations, the items often speak for themselves. This museum is housed in Jaenamheon, a converted Joseon Dynasty county administration building, and a reconstructed farmhouse. At the entrance is a 200-year-old tree. A few years ago it was dying, so a mixture of *makgeolli* and water was fed to it and now it thrives with a full leaf cover! Open daily except Sunday and the day after holidays 0900–1800; there is a ₩330 entrance fee. Take Pohang city bus nos. 107 or 500 from the bus terminal.

Guryongpo

On the coast directly east of Pohang is the harbor town of Guryongpo [Kuryŏngp'o] (구룡포). This fishing port typifies all that makes for a thriving fishing industry. It is larger than Gupo down the coast closer to Gyeongju, but as in Gupo, many raw fish restaurants line the bay along the harbor. Near the bus terminal in town are the Geumgangjang Yeogwan (금강장여관) and Yeongbinjang Yeogwan (영빈장여관). Plenty of *minbak* can be found along the beach at the north end of town, where young people and families from town come during the summer for a holiday at the beach. Only a few buses a day run north along the coast to Daebo and the Lighthouse Museum.

Lighthouse Museum 호미곶등대박물관

In Daebo, at the point of land that forms the eastern tip of Yeongil Bay, stands Korea's tallest and oldest modern lighthouse. Janggigot lighthouse guides the heavy cargo traffic that not only enters this bay but also plies the increasingly important east coast ports. Here stands the country's only lighthouse museum; open daily except Monday and holidays 0900–1700. Use city bus no. 200 to Guryongpo and from there take the local bus running north to Daebo. The museum explains the origin and history of Korean lighthouses, displays items related to lighthouse operation and mechanics, and offers a brief look at the sea and Korea's link to it. Next to the lighthouse is the Homigot (Tiger Tail) Sunrise Plaza, used at various times of the year for public gatherings, particularly for a sunrise festival on the first day of the new year because this is the easternmost point of the peninsula and it receives daylight before any other sea level spot in the country. In geomantic theory and in the historical popular conception of the Korean people, this point of land was thought of as the tail of the tiger that is the form of the Korean Peninsula.

Oeo-sa 오어사

Twenty-four kilometers southeast of Pohang is Oeo-sa [Oŏ-sa], My Fish Temple. Originally called Hangsa-sa, it was founded by the monks Jajang and Uisang. One noted scholar tells the humorous story of the two eccentric monks Wonhyo and Hyegong as it relates to the naming of this temple. One day when these two monks were staying at the temple they decided to go fishing. As Buddhist priests do not eat fish, this was rather unusual behavior. As the day pro-

gressed they caught many fish and decided to eat what they had caught. After their meal both needed to defecate, which they did in the stream. Two fish immediately appeared from their feces, one swimming upstream against the current, the other floating lazily downstream with the current. Pointing to the stronger, Wonhyo exclaimed, "That's my fish," to which Hyegong retorted that it was, in fact, his. This amusing and peculiar incident caught the villagers' fancy and they thereafter called the temple My Fish Temple.

While the legend is more entertaining than the temple is interesting, it is still a convenient place to escape the city. Take city bus no. 102 or 300 to Ocheon and transfer there to a country bus that runs to the temple (₩700). From the terminus, follow the road up and around the reservoir and past a line of *sari budo* to the temple grounds. Oeo-sa is surrounded by bamboo. A small bell, wooden gong, and huge drum are kept behind the stern guards painted on the front gate doors. The gate opens onto a finely landscaped and well-tended courtyard full of flowering fruit trees. In its center sits the main hall, a building of grace and strength which years have given the look of a sage. Its shapely posts support a heavy roof, and inside curved roof beams have dragons' heads roughly carved at their ends, protecting the temple from evil influence and destruction. Carved cranes, suspended from the ceiling, contribute to the nobility of the hall. To the rear of this compound are halls enshrining the 16 Nahan and the Mountain Spirit. Across an arm of the reservoir, perched like an aerie on top of a bluff, sits the small hermitage Wonhyo-am; the second hermitage, Jajang-am, is 200 meters up the hill behind the main temple compound.

Ulleung-do 울릉도

One of Korea's best-kept destination secrets, the island of Ulleung-do [Ullŭng-do], lies unconcealed in the East Sea 137 kilometers directly east of Samcheok. Its 73 square kilometers are very rugged, shaped by the forceful elements of wind and water. With little historical, cultural, or religious significance, its main attractions are its tranquil remoteness and natural beauty. Few Koreans venture to this island, although a growing number are now making it a destination, and fewer foreign travelers even consider going. It's truly a place to get away from it all, and well worth the effort to get there. Recognizing the island's tourist potential, the government has put much energy into constructing port facilities, accommodations, increased commercial infrastructure, and a round-the-island road. For island residents, perhaps the most significant changes over the past several decades have been vehicles on the island, new apartment buildings, a decrease in population, and the increased number of visitors. Go before it becomes too well known.

Koreans say that Ulleung-do has five noteworthy characteristics, and lacks three. The five are strong winds, pure drinking water, handsome people, plentiful rocks, and juniper trees (the junipers are virtually extinct elsewhere in Korea). Thieves, beggars, and snakes are what

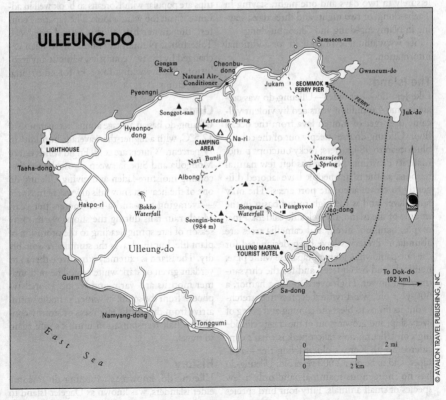

© AVALON TRAVEL PUBLISHING, INC.

the island doesn't have, although the latter have been introduced by man. The major festivity on the island is the yearly **Cuttlefish Festival** held in Do-dong in August.

Until 1976, there were no roads on the island; only trails connected the villages. In 2001, the completion of a road around the west end finally connected the older roads that run along the south and north coasts. Now only the east side road remains to be finished. Currently, to get from one section to the other on the east end, you must either use the remaining trail or take small vehicular ferries that run between Jeo-dong and Do-dong to Seommok. By using buses over the existing roads and walking the trails, it's possible to make a round-trip of the island easily in one day. However, without encountering too much traffic, a round-the-island walk can still be done leisurely in two days and one night, staying in Taeha-dong, or two nights and three days, staying in Namyang-dong and Cheonbu-dong.

See www.ullung.kyongbuk.kr for additional information.

The Island

Like Jeju-do—but older—Ulleung-do was created some 4.6 million years ago by violent volcanic upsurges of molten lava from the ocean floor. Ulleung-do rises steeply out of the cobalt-blue ocean to 984 meters; rocky outcrops punctuate its coastline. Nature has left few natural harbors, so the island people have labored diligently to create adequate port areas. The only fairly level land is the high round basin in the middle of the island, the volcanic caldera. Pine, maple, bamboo, birch, and camellia trees are abundant. Preserves have been designated for the rare paulownia, juniper, Japanese white pine, hemlock, and beech trees, and for the chrysanthemum flower. High over Do-dong harbor, a 600-year-old, wind-twisted cypress tree stretches out its limbs to bless the coming and going of every ship, and growing out of the craggy cliffside high on Ulleung-do's tallest peak is what's considered South Korea's oldest living tree—a juniper, said to be over 2,000 years old. Ulleung-do has no indigenous mammals and only a few species of small animals. Fifty-four bird species

have been sighted on the island. The waters of the East Sea provide massive amounts of fish, but the island is best-known for its cuttlefish.

Ninety-two kilometers southeast of Ulleung-do is the tiny island outcrop of **Dok-do** (.17 square km), the easternmost landmass of South Korea. Dok-do, the top of an extinct volcanic mountain that rose above the waves some 2.7 million years ago, is actually two islets, the westernmost rises to 174 meters and the eastern to 100 meters. These outcrops have been designated a protected breeding place for several varieties of seabirds (N.M. #336); seals also frequent this spot. Only police and naval personnel live on one—there is room for nothing else—and there is no habitation on the other. Once a month, the ferry from Pohang continues on to Dok-do for a look at this lonely outpost. These two-hour trips are popular with Koreans so book well in advance if you too want a look. The Japanese contest the ownership of this island they call Takeshima. Numerous "notes" have been exchanged by the two countries, without any resolution. See www.dokdo.go.kr for additional information.

Climate

Ulleung-do has an average annual temperature of 12.5°C, with a higher-than-average humidity of 77 percent. Winters are cold. Frigid winds out of Mongolia and Siberia sweep across the sea, becoming moisture-laden and giving Ulleung-do one of the heaviest snowfalls anywhere in Korea—averaging two-and-a-half meters per year. Much rain falls during the short, warm rainy season of late spring, leading to the profusion of plant life, but this leaves the summer reasonably dry. The island is extremely attractive either in its verdant green or stark white coat. The midsummer months are warm and see occasional typhoons from the south; in winter, periodic storms arrive from the north. High seas or stormy conditions halt transportation until it's safe again to travel.

History

Ulleung-do, known as Mureung-do to some elder islanders, was known as Dagelet Island to

Western cartographers until the early 20th century. Before A.D. 512, it was called Usan-guk, and was an independent area. In that year, the island was conquered by a Silla general, who later became its first governor. Ulleung-do was depopulated during the reign of King Sejong in the early 1400s. It was left uninhabited until 1882, when people came back to log timber which had grown thick and tall in the intervening years—and to gain a foothold on the island, as Japan was showing some interest in claiming sovereignty. Until 1906 it was part of Gangwon-Do, but today Ulleung-do is one of Gyeongsangbuk-Do's counties. The families of most islanders originate from other areas of this province, principally the Pohang and Daegu regions, yet some have come from Gangwon-Do and the Jeolla-Do provinces. With the smallest population of any county in the country, Ulleung-do is down to 10,000 inhabitants from a height of 30,000 some decades ago. Mostly, the young have left for school on the peninsula and have not returned, but older people have also left for better opportunities elsewhere. Life is not easy on the island. As a consequence, many farming fields and houses have been abandoned.

Farming and Fishing

A majority of the population lives along the coast, mostly at the island's southeastern corner. Villages run up the narrow valleys from the sea; farmland also ascends the mountainside. Rice, potatoes, corn, barley, watermelons, and pumpkins are grown; several varieties of wild mountain vegetables and medicinal herbs are gathered. Still, much needs to be imported from the peninsula, and you'll find prices a bit higher here.

Fishing, particularly for cuttlefish, is the major industry of the island, although gathering abalone, mussels, and seaweed is a growing occupation. Cuttlefish are caught year-round, but November and December are the best months. The dried product is considered the tastiest in the country. Fishermen fish all night and come in with their catches in the morning. Huge, brilliant lightbulbs are strung from bow to stern to attract cuttlefish into the nets. It's an impressive sight to see these bright vessels bobbing on the

waves against a black sky like a string of white Christmas lights on the horizon.

DO-DONG AND JEO-DONG

Do-dong [To-dong] (도동) is the administrative center of Ulleung-do, and has the island's only middle school. A friendly, quiet, overgrown fishing village, it's also the port where all ferries from the peninsula dock. In this postage stamp-sized harbor, fishing boats lie below craggy peaks that end the ridges that define this narrow valley. High on its eastern side is a protected grove of hardwoods (N.M. #51). Shore fishing is popular along the rocks at the edge of the harbor. From Do-dong, one road goes over the hill to Jeo-dong, another to the west along the south coast.

Although several doctors are scattered around the island, the only health center is in Do-dong. At the upper end of town is the Telecom office; the post office is located next to the Ullung

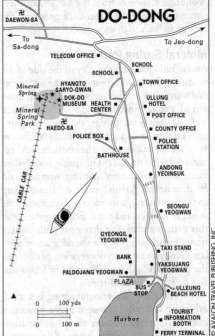

Hotel. Change money at the Agricultural Coop Bank, which is up the left alley. Use the police station or midtown police box for emergency assistance. A tourist information booth is located at the ferry terminal for all general questions, but may not be open when the tourist count is way down. Ticket sales for the ferries to the peninsula and for the round-the-island excursion ferry are handled at the office inside the ferry terminal. The bus stop is located at the town plaza just up from the water.

Seaside Path

One of your first activities on the island might be a stroll along the *sanchaengno*. This walking path along the water's edge runs in both directions from the harbor. To the west it skirts several well-used fishing spots, and to the east, starting from behind the harbor office, it passes a number of makeshift restaurants to a pebble beach. This path has been carved out of the volcanic rock and bridges small inlets. From the pebble beach about one kilometer from the harbor, an alternative but not very distinct path goes over the mountain back to town.

Mineral Spring Park 약수공원

About 300 meters up the alley to the side of the hospital is the island's most easily accessible mineral water spring. This carbonated punch flows out of a stone tortoise head stuck into a rock wall. Among other things, the water contains iron, calcium, and magnesium, said to be effective for anemia, indigestion, rheumatism, and eczema-like skin diseases. The spring is visited by many townspeople every morning, who take a sip for their health. A path leads from the spring up to the western ridge for spectacular views of the town, mountain, and coast. Eclipsing the use of this path is a cable car that now pulls visitors from the park to a point on the ridge where there is a short hike up to an observation pavilion on the peak. The cable car lift runs ₩3,000 one way or ₩4,500 round-trip.

To the side of the mineral spring is a small exhibition hall called **Hyangto Saryo-gwan** that exhibits a limited number of cultural artifacts from the island—mostly items of daily use—

and pictures of Ulleung-do and Dok-do. The **Dok-do Museum** (독도박물관), open 0700–1800, is a more recent construction that sets forth to explain the history of that lonely rock outcrop. Totally out of place on this island but nonetheless aesthetically pleasing, this modernistic structure offers a brief historical sketch of the possession of Dok-do from the late 1800s to the present via maps, photos, historical documents, and a video. The Koreans are making the point that this is their land, has been their land, and the Japanese have no claim to it, as past diplomatic communications have indicated. The ₩1,200 entrance fee to the park is good for the spring, exhibition hall, and museum; the cable car fees are separate.

Just below the park is Haedo-sa, a small temple with a small but relatively new main hall.

Daewon-sa

One of the five temples on the island is Daewon-sa, a small compound kept by nuns at the upper end of the Do-dong Valley. From the Telecom office, walk up the road along the channeled stream. Turn off and follow the footpath that runs under the bridge, continuing on about 150 meters to an intersection. Go left and you're shortly at the temple. The right-hand path leads up to the mountaintop.

Accommodations and Food

Several of Do-dong's comfortable *yeogwan* front the harbor. Try Paldojang Yeogwan (팔도장여관), Yaksujang Yeogwan (약수장여관), or Ulleung Beach Hotel (울릉비치호텔), where all rooms are ₩40,000. A short way up the left alley are Gyeongil Yeogwan (경일여관), Seongu Yeogwan (성우여관), and the cheaper Andong Yeoinsuk (안동여인숙). Up beyond the police station is the Ullung Hotel (울릉호텔), with rooms at ₩50,000–60,000. Here and there throughout town are numerous *minbak*. Proprietors will meet you at the pier upon arrival and vie for your business. *Minbak* ask around ₩20,000 a room, *yeogwan* about ₩25,000–30,000, and the hotels ₩40,000–60,000. These prices can usually be bargained down during the off-season—late fall to spring—when visitors are few. Two kilometers east of Do-dong, tucked up on the mountainside, is Ulleung-do's swankiest accommodation, the third-class Ullung Marina Tourist Hotel (울릉마리나관광호텔) (tel. 054/791-0020); room rates are ₩68,000, with suites higher. Amenities include a lounge, small nightclub, and tennis court.

The harbor restaurants' seafood is on the expensive side. Up in the middle of town are more reasonably priced restaurants. Dried cuttlefish can be bought in almost any market or shop on the island. Besides cuttlefish, the island has another specialty, called *hobangyeot,* a hard pumpkin taffy. It's tasty but tough—watch out for your teeth! While some is still made by hand, most is now turned by machine. The amber and light brown slabs of taffy and bags of individually-wrapped pieces range in price from ₩1,000. Look also for the jars of pumpkin jelly.

Jeo-dong 저동

A 10-minute bus ride from Do-dong brings you to Jeo-dong [Chŏ-dong], the island's commercial center. This town is larger and busier than Do-dong, and has had the most extensive port construction. Jeo-dong is also the island's principal fishing port, with about 200 fishing boats and a processing and refrigeration plant. During early morning hours, the long waterfront fish market is abuzz with activity. Throughout the day, nets are dried and repaired, and cuttlefish are hung out to dry. The local ferry to Seommok runs from here. Buy your ticket at the small office on the quay. It's located nearly across from the harbor entrance. Although there are many places to stay in Jeo-dong, it tends to be noisy. At the bus stop is the Cheongujang Yeogwan (청우장여관); around the corner and closer to the harbor is the Daehwajang Yeogwan (대화장여관). On the second street back, turn at the big old trees across from the police box to find the Jeiltang Yeogwan (제일탕여관). You'll find the Gyeongjujang Yeogwan (경주장여관) across from the post office.

Bongnae Waterfall 봉래폭포

Jeo-dong's main attraction is Bongnae Waterfall, the most well-known and accessible on the island. It's about three kilometers up the stream from the quay. Follow the cement road from the waterfront, or taxi for ₩5,000. From the entrance booth (₩1,200 entrance fee), a trail continues 750 meters up around a small water reservoir to the falls, passing Punghyeol, which is billed as a natural air conditioner. From April to September a small hole in the hillside exudes a constant stream of cool air. A refreshing breeze during a hot summer hike may be worth a stop on the way up to the waterfall. During the rest of the year air is pulled into the hole. A short distance farther up this narrowing valley is the three-step Bongnae Waterfall. Pretty at any time of the year, it's a refreshingly cool spot in summer. Water in this falls comes from mountain runoff and from an artesian well. During the early 1990s, this area was "improved," and now the air conditioner is enclosed in a glass-walled room, and a viewing tower has been constructed a short distance in front of the falls, allowing you a full-on look at the cascade but keeping you away from the pool! Along the path to the waterfall, a traditional island-style wood-shingle house has been built to give visitors a close-up look at the old housing style of the island without having to go up to Na-ri.

AROUND THE ISLAND

The interior of Ulleung-do is characterized by deep valleys, swift streams, thickly wooded hillsides, craggy ridges, and one flat agricultural area. The highest point, Seongin-bong (984 meters), rises majestically above the coastal towns. Look for old stands of Chinese juniper, found mostly on the south side of the island. To the north below the peak is the interior basin called Nari Bunji, the largest area of relatively flat land on the island and the caldera of the extinct volcano which created this island.

Hiking

One of the joys of the island is exploring its interior. From Do-dong, go up toward Daewon-sa, taking a right at the fork in the road just before the temple, and follow the steep road to the end. Don't be fooled by small paths leading off into fields; follow the most obvious trail up to the ridge. Continue up this trail, which then runs below and to the north side of the ridge. The entire trail is about four kilometers long; it rises nearly one kilometer in height and should take 2–2.5 hours. You are then in Seongin-bong Virgin Forest (N.M. #189). Sit down, rest, and appreciate how hard you've worked to get to the top! Running northeast from Seongin-bong is another ridge trail that takes you to two other peaks which are nearly as high. They now have a radar station between them. From there, the trail makes its way down the south side of the hill, exiting onto the trail a few hundred meters above the natural air conditioner below Bongnae Waterfall. Just below Seongin-bong, on its south side, is a trail leading around the side of the peak and along the ridge to the west. Follow it about 500 meters to a signboard where the trail leads steeply down through a hardwood forest, over several streams, and to the former community of Albong. Once a small cluster of island houses known for its community of chrysanthemums (N.M. #52), it now has only two island-style houses preserved by the county to show visitors what island homes looked like in decades past. The herb *yakcho* used to be grown in the fields here but this land is now fallow. A drivable road now reaches Albong from Cheonbu-dong. Na-ri (나리), where there is a camping area, is 1.5 kilometers below Albong. From Na-ri, one road goes down past the two Chusan hydroelectric plants—water for the power plants flows from an artesian spring that can be seen from along the road—and the other runs down to the village of Cheonbu-dong.

South Coast

Going west from Do-dong, the bus skirts the Japanese Wood Pigeon Habitat (N.M. #237) of **Sa-dong** (사동). A long breakwater and new harbor facilities are being constructed just west of this small village, and there are several *yeogwan* near the school. West past a gray cobble beach and around the point near the lighthouse brings you to **Tonggumi** (동구미). Near here are several stands of juniper trees which have been set aside as a nature preserve (N.M. #48). The old road and trail goes through the village and over the hill to **Namyang-dong** (남양동), a serene village with a pebble beach. Three tunnels have been cut

through the bluff at Tonggumi and a coastal road now reaches Namyang-dong. In Namyang-dong, there are several *yeogwan, minbak,* and a couple of simple restaurants. Right at the bus stop is the Namyangjang Yeogwan (남양장여관). A cup of herbal tea in one of the tearooms or rice wine in one of the pubs might be your only activity for the evening. On the other hand, *you* may be the main entertainment for the village people!

Taeha-dong 태하동

After passing through another two tunnels, continue along the coastal road to **Guam,** a tiny cluster of homes. The new road continues up the coast, spiraling to gain height, and punches through two new tunnels on its way to Hakpo-ri and Taeha-dong. From Guam, the old 5-kilometer-long road turns inland and rises very steeply as it makes its way up the valley, crossing the pass on a precipitous ridge road, and threading its way down the far side by way of an extremely narrow and winding path. Near the crest of this road is a preserve of pinion and beech trees (N.M. #50), and just before you reach the river near Taeha-dong, a road to the right heads up to Bokho Waterfall. Taeha-dong is the site of the first settlement on the island, and was the seat of local government until that was moved to Do-dong in 1903. The shrine Seongwon-dang is located in a grove of pine trees at the bus stop at the upper end of the village, a small Buddhist temple sits across the stream. A number of wind generators stand on the ridge above. Aside from a school and post office, there are a few *minbak,* restaurants, and tearooms in this laid-back village. There is not much to do here except observe the life of a small fishing community or watch the cuttlefish dry. A number of fields lie fallow in this valley as in other places on the island. On the promontory to the north of town sits a lighthouse, erected in 1958 for ships coming from the peninsula, and another stand of juniper trees (N.M. #49).

North Coast

About one kilometer back up past the post office in Taeha-dong is the road which zigzags over the ridge to the north to join the north coast road at **Hyeonpo-dong** (현포동), where

© ROBERT NILSEN

fishing boats in Taeha-dong harbor

there is a nice enclosed harbor. Along this spectacular north coast, the cliffs rise steeply out of the water as if trying to back away from the crashing waves. The most prominent peak is the steeply conical Songgot-san (430 meters), which rises up almost at water's edge, directly across from the islet Gongam. Follow the road past the lower hydroelectric plant to Cheonbu-dong (천부동), where there are several *minbak* and restaurants. Some people hold that Cheonbu-dong, not Taeha-dong, was the site of the first settlement on the island. At the west end of this community, an enclosed room has been built directly to the side of the road, which traps cold air emanating from the hillside—the island's second natural air-conditioner! One trail to the interior starts just to the east of the power plant, while another runs up through Cheonbu-dong. From this village, it's about three kilometers to Na-ri and seven kilometers to Seongin-bong.

From Cheonbu-dong, continue along the north coast road to the next village, Jukam (죽암). The bus continues around the north end and through another short tunnel to the ferry point at Seommok. If walking, take the trail at the east end of Jukam up the narrow ravine, over a bridge, and on up to a fairly level section on the east side of the island. From this trail you look out over Juk-do. The trail proceeds along the hillside, in and out of a deep valley, and back to the road that runs down to Jeo-dong, passing the Naesujeon mineral water spring and the newest of the island's power generation plants on the way.

Juk-do 죽도

Juk-do ("Bamboo Island") is the flat-topped citadel off the east coast where cattle are raised and vegetables grown. The island used to have more bamboo than it does today, but it can still be seen rimming its top. Young calves are taken to the tiny island by boat, and from the pier they must be carried to the top on the shoulders of a farmer. After the cattle are fully grown and ready to be sold at market, they are lowered over the edge in slings to boats waiting below. Three families still make Juk-do their home. More and more, tourists are visiting the island and ferries stop regularly on their routes to and from Jeo-dong, Do-dong, and Seommok. After paying your ₩1,200 entrance, trudge up the spiral stairway from the pier and have a look around the top.

TRANSPORTATION
Island Buses

Buses that service the island are of the mini-bus style and carry no more than a dozen passengers or so. Leaving from the Do-dong waterfront, buses run on two different routes on the south side of the island. Every 20–40 minutes from early morning until mid-evening, a bus goes over the hill to Jeo-dong (₩700). Most buses continue on to Naesujeon, while once an hour a bus runs up the valley to the Bongnae Waterfall entrance. Spaced evenly throughout the day until early evening are buses along the south coast to Namyang-dong (₩2,500). With the completion of the road around the west end, buses now are able to run to Taeha-dong and points on the north coast. In order to get over the hill to Sa-dong, this road spirals over itself twice to gain height in the steep valley behind Do-dong. At the saddle is a monument commemorating local Korean War dead, and the turnoff to the Ullung Marina Hotel.

On the north side of the island, half a dozen daily buses go all the way from the ferry pier at Seommok to Taeha-dong, with a few additional buses to Hyeonpo-dong and Cheonbu-dong. All buses are timed to pick up passengers with the arrival of each ferry. There are no buses to Na-ri, but taxis can make the trip.

The few taxis on the island are 4WD, jeep-style vehicles. A brief list of taxi fares from Do-dong harbor includes Jeo-dong (₩2,200), Bongnae Waterfall (₩5,000), Sa-dong (₩2,700), Namyang (₩7,500), and Guam (₩10,000).

Round-Island Excursion Ferry

One of the nicest ways to view the island is from the sea. Excursion ferries (₩13,000) leave Do-dong pier for an all-encompassing round-the-

island tour. Purchase tickets at the excursion ferry office, inside the ferry terminal building. Departure times change according to the season but, especially during the off-season, scheduled runs may not go if there is insufficient interest. From July 25 to August 15, excursions are scheduled nine times a day; the rest of the year, ferries go once at 0900 and once at 1600. This guided tour provides a running commentary in Korean, and takes more than two hours. The trip starts off fairly smoothly but soon turns choppy as you turn up the west coast, where several isolated villages can be seen. On the north coast, the boat passes an opening in Gongam Rock, a tiny islet that looks like an elephant's head—trunk and all—with a lone tree growing out of the rock where the eye would be. The northeast corner of Ulleung-do is the most dramatic, with its volcanic rock pinnacles and wild surf, stone grottoes and nesting seabirds. Off to the east, butte-like Juk-do is reminiscent of an immobile battleship. The ferry continues past Jeo-dong harbor and the lighthouse high atop the cliff at the island's southeast corner. Here, and at other similar places on the island, bats nest, only leaving their shallow caves in the sheer cliff at dusk to search for food.

Ferry Shuttle

Until the 1980s, private boats and a postal boat left Do-dong and Jeo-dong harbors every morning for the island's coastal villages. Today, however, because of the roadway and scheduled bus service, only two ferries operate on the island. One ferry (₩4,500) runs every two hours between Jeo-dong and Seommok: 0800 to 1800 from Jeo-dong, 0830 to 1830 from Seommok. The other runs from Do-dong to Seommok via Juk-do; ₩4,500 to/from Do-dong and Seommok and ₩3,500 from Do-dong to Juk-do or Seommok to Juk-do. From May 1 to the end of October there are five ferries a day, three the rest of the year.

Ferries to the Peninsula

Ferries to and from the peninsula run year-round. There are three ports of departure on the peninsula—Pohang, Mukho, and Sokcho—and one on Ulleung-do—Do-dong. Remember that weather conditions may interrupt these schedules. Check at the pier for times of departure on the day *before* you plan to cross.

A fast catamaran ferry makes this 3.5-hour run to Pohang (217 km) once a day throughout the year, leaving Pohang at 1000 and returning from Ulleung-do at 1600; during the busy summer season of mid-July to mid-August a second ship is also put into service at 1900. The fare is ₩49,000, or ₩54,000 for special first class.

A smaller catamaran ferry runs to Mukho (161 km) once daily during the week and the trip takes three hours. Requiring a slightly longer time, it leaves from Sokcho on the weekends. Departure from these two ports is at 1100, and it returns from Ulleung-do at 1530. The fare is ₩34,000.

In the past, ferries have also run from Hupo to Ulleung-do. While this connection is currently not in operation, there is a chance that it may be started again in the future.

Ferry to Dok-do: On the first Saturday of each month, with an additional run at times during the summer, the ferry from Pohang continues on to Dok-do for a look at those tiny islands. The added trip there and back takes about three hours and leaves from Dok-do harbor at 1400, shortly after arriving from Pohang. The additional cost, in excess of the fare from Pohang, is ₩37,000 and must be arranged when you buy your ticket from Pohang.

Gyeongju 경주

Gyeongju [Kyŏngju] is Korea's ancient cultural city, the capital of the once great Silla Kingdom. It is to Korea what Kyoto is to Japan. During its 1979 meeting in Thailand, UNESCO selected Gyeongju as one of the world's 10 most important ancient cultural cities, both for its position in the historical and cultural development of East Asia and for its role in the formation of the Korean nation. In 1995, Seokguram and Bulguk-sa were named by UNESCO as world heritage sites, to be recognized and protected by the world community for their cultural and historic value. In 2000, Daeneungwon, Cheomseongdae, Banwol-seong Fortress, and Hwangnyong-saji were added to that list.

Of the ancient kingdom, only the stone structures, a portion of its artwork, and its legends remain. Gyeongju and its environs contain hundreds of royal tombs, temples, palace sites, fortress ruins, pagodas, and rock sculptures. Finely crafted gold and silver ornaments, skillfully shaped clay figures and pottery, metal utensils and weapons, and an astonishing number of other objects discovered here are now displayed in the Gyeongju and Seoul national museums; scraps of Silla literature and legends are preserved in ancient books and annals. All these artifacts point to the wealth of the kingdom, the imagination and artistry of its people, and the cultural advancement of the civilization. This area luckily

Gameun-saji

evaded the wholesale plunder that usually beset culturally significant cities after their downfall. Every year, additional objects are excavated. Who knows what more lies yet to be uncovered by the shovels of future generations? Gyeongju offers the best of Silla Dynasty remains, as Kong and Buyeo do for the Baekje Dynasty, and Seoul does for the Joseon Dynasty. With 31 National Treasures, 76 Treasures, 73 Historical Sites, and over 110 other designated cultural properties, Gyeongju truly deserves its appellation, a "museum without walls."

On the modern side, new residential and light-industrial sectors have been raised, particularly on the northern side of town, for the increased local population. And additional accommodation, eating, entertainment, and shopping facilities have been constructed to handle the rising influx of visitors (over eight million annually). Gyeongju's most important places of cultural and historic interest have been renovated, and paved roads ease travel to these major sites. Yet countless other sites and artifacts lie off the beaten path and take some time and effort to reach. It's possible to see the more important sites and artifacts of Gyeongju in a few days, though weeks would be required to seek out all that the city, mountains, and surrounding countryside have to offer.

With a population of 160,000 and a slightly smaller number in the surrounding rural area, Gyeongju is an extensive population center that lies in the wide basin between Daegu and Pohang. A low rise to the south of the city separates it from the rift valley in which Ulsan lies. To the east, a coastal range that runs between Ulsan and Pohang separates this basin from the East Sea. The southern end of the Taebaek Mountains, bounded by the Hyeongsan River, stops just north of Gyeongju, while the Yeongnam Alps rise up south of the city and extend nearly to Busan. These mountains make a natural barrier around Gyeongju, on which military fortresses were erected to guard all valley corridors to the city. Gyeongju has the best of both worlds. It reaps the benefits of the sea, while the wide plain in which it lies, blessed with plentiful rainfall and good drainage, supports a healthy agricultural economy.

For more information, check out the website www.gyeongju.gyeongbuk.kr.

HISTORY

At the time when Julius Caesar was consolidating power in Rome, walled towns were forming on the Korean Peninsula. One of these, Saro (Seorabol) grew in size and influence, and took on a dominant role when the walled towns in this region formed a confederation. This state became known as Silla, and from its leading family clans (Bak, Seok, and Kim) sprang the entire line of Silla royalty. By the 3rd century, Saro became known as Geumseong ("City of Gold"), only later to be called Gyeongju. Although constantly strengthening its power, it was not totally free from the influence of the Goguryeo Kingdom, its stronger northern neighbor. During the latter part of the Three Kingdoms period (57 B.C.–A.D. 668), an alliance between the three Korean states of Silla, Baekje, and Goguryeo was ever-shifting, each state maintaining a shrewd diplomatic relationship with one or another of the Chinese dynasties. Silla developed a highly structured society dominated by its aristocracy. Originally the smallest and most isolated of the three, it received the least Chinese influence, and initially seems to have been the least militaristic. Yet, as its strength and confidence grew, Silla began to expand. By the mid-500s, the small and independent state of Gaya was absorbed. In 660, Baekje was conquered, and in 668, Goguryeo overrun.

Thus Silla became the first unifier of the peninsula, initiating 250 years of the relative peace and prosperity of the United Silla period, and ushering in a cultural renaissance. With broad advancement in government, education, military, science, technology, and the creative arts, Silla developed a highly complex and vibrant society. Silla exchanged much in trade and ideas with the more advanced Tang China, and also acted as a conduit to the Japanese islands, particularly for religion, philosophy, architecture, and arts. Confucianism (introduced in 503) and Bud-

GYEONGJU

DETAIL

SEONGNIMJANG
YEOGWAN
PYONGYANG CHIP ▼

THEATER
THEATER

CITY HALL

BUNHWANG-SA

HWANGNYONG-SAJI

PAGODA

GYEONGJU
NATIONAL MUSEUM

Tumulus Park

BEOPJANG-SA

SA RANG
CHAE
CHINESE
RESTAURANT

PONGHWANGDAE

SUBONGCHONG

GEUMGWANCHONG

MOKHWA
HOUSE

SAMHOJANG
YEOGWAN

GRAND
BUFFET

North Stream

GYEONGJU

ANAPJI

ICEHOUSE

Namcheon Stream

CHEOMSEONGDAE

BANWOL-SEONG

HYOBULHYO-GYO

Wolsang Park

GYERIM

HYANGGYO

SEONGDONG
MARKET

TELECOM

GYEONGJU
STATION

TOURIST
INFORMATION

HOSBUNG
YEOGWAN

SEGEOMJEONG
MOTEL

PALJEONG
ROTARY

GURO
SSAMBAP

SILLA
RESTAURANT

SUNHYE-JEON

TOMB OF KING MICHU

TOMB OF KING
NAEMAL

KYONGJU KALBI
RESTAURANT

SAMSO

KOREA FOREIGN
EXCHANGE BANK

POST
OFFICE

BOOKSTORE

SILLAJANG
YEOGWAN

YOURIM
TEAHOUSE

SELLOKWON

TOMB

TOMB

TOMB

HWANGNAM
DAECHONG

Tumulus Park

TOMB OF KING MICHU

STELA

GYEONGJU
FORTRESS

DEPARTMENT
STORE

POLICE

DEPARTMENT
STORE

CHORUNG BANK

DAEGU BANK

SEE
DETAIL

CHENMACHONG

SAMWON
GARDEN

JAEMAEJEONG

TOMB

HEUNGNYUN-SA

SAMNYANG-SAJI

CENTRAL
MARKET

HYUP SUNG
HOTEL

ANDONGTAEK

TOBIDAYAKI ▼

MADANG ▼

HANJINJANG
YEOGWAN

TAEYANGJANG
YEOGWAN

KYONGJU
PARK HOTEL

AG. COOP
SUPERMARKET

EXPRESS BUS
TERMINAL

INTERCITY
BUS TERMINAL

TOURIST
INFORMATION

Hyeongsan River

0   300 yds
0   300 m

© AVALON TRAVEL PUBLISHING, INC.

dhism (which became the state religion in the 530s) helped strengthen the social fabric and moral standards. The period from 600 to 800 was a time of high cultural attainment, relative affluence, learning, and artistic refinement, known as Silla's "Golden Age." As the vortex of the kingdom, with a population approaching one million, Gyeongju was as vibrant and creative as any city in Asia at the time, rivaling Changan (Xi'an), in China, and Nara, Japan.

Power and riches led to corruption, and the dynasty finally collapsed from a combination of inner turmoil and external forces. Near the end, the people's discontent with the royalty grew and the government's control of the country waned. By the early 900s, Silla had hit rock bottom, and by the 920s, Silla was a country in name only. Much of its land had been taken by the increasingly powerful Later Baekje and Goryeo states, themselves vying for dominance on the peninsula. Gyeongju was pillaged in 927, and eight years later King Gyeongsun unconditionally surrendered his title and country to Wang Geon, the Goryeo king, bringing to an ignominious close this 1,000-year-old dynasty.

Shortly after the surrender of Silla, King Wang Geon conquered the Later Baekje forces and once again united the peninsula under one monarch. A new national capital was established in Gaeseong; with its diminished status, Geumseong's name was changed to Gyeongju. For a short period during the Goryeo Dynasty, Gyeongju served as a regional capital, but its former significance was lost and this once proud city became a provincial backwater. In the mid-1300s, Gyeongju was ravaged in the Mongol invasions. Many wooden treasures were burned and stone monuments felled. In the 1590s it was invaded and razed by the Japanese army; countless treasures were put to the torch or carried off as spoils of war. Only the tombs seemed inviolable. Not until the early 20th century were the treasures of Gyeongju "rediscovered." Japanese and Korean experts first did the excavating; later, international organizations came to help. Digging continues, and every year new discoveries are made. However, the majority of tombs still lie unexcavated, and may never be touched.

Today, Gyeongju is a quiet town with a relaxed ambience. City streets have been beautified with ornamental trees and colorful flowers, and country roads are lined with poplars and willows. Agriculture, education, and limited, small-scale industry play a role in the economy, but Gyeongju's sustenance comes from tourism. This city has become one of the most fascinating places in Korea to visit, and a frequent tourist destination in East Asia.

Silla Cultural Festival

Every year in October—exact dates vary according to the lunar calendar—Gyeongju hosts the three-day Silla Cultural Festival, called *Silla Munhwaje*. Certainly one of the liveliest in the country, this festival, which has been held since 1962, helps revive the spirit of the Silla people, celebrates the dynasty's outstanding accomplishments, and honors the Silla Buddhist culture. Don't miss the entertainment if you're anywhere near! One of the highlights is the daytime parade. Floats carry the honorary king and queen, while others portray legendary personalities and stories. Musicians and dancers stream by in colorful costumes to the sound of staccato percussion music in what seems like a never-ending swirl of movement. An evening parade and fireworks are also staged. Folk games such as the *chajeon nori* (a "tank game"), the *gapae nori* circle dance, athletic contests (Korean wrestling, archery, and tug-of-war), farmers' music and dance, classical music and dance, art exhibitions of all sorts, and literary contests can be seen around town. A Buddhist religious service, the *tapdori* (circling the pagoda in prayer), is conducted in town, while the Yeongsan ceremony is held at Bulguk-sa temple. Large crowds come to Gyeongju for this event, as it's one of the finest Korean cultural festivals.

Numerous smaller festivals and events of lesser importance are held throughout the year, including the Korean Traditional Liquor and Cake Festival in March, the annual Cherry Blossom Marathon in April, and memorial ceremonies, held twice yearly in the spring and autumn, for the founders of the Silla Dynasty and Gen. Kim Yu-shin.

GYEONGJU

Gyeongju National Park

Established as a national park in 1968, this cultural arena maintains the artifacts, history, and legends of the Silla Dynasty. Gyeongju National Park comprises 138 square kilometers; unlike all of the other land-oriented national parks, it is split into seven distinct and separate sections, which cover more than one-third of the city area and large tracts of the surrounding mountains. These areas drape over Ongnyeo-bong, Seon-do-san, and Danseok-san to the west; Nam-san to the south; Sogeumgang-san to the north; Toham-san to the east; and land surrounding Gameun-saji and the underwater tomb of King Munmu on the East Coast.

Sights

CITY CENTER

While many important sites are scattered in the vicinity, Gyeongju, as the heart of the former Silla Kingdom, still has the largest concentration of such remains. No one site in the center of the city is too great a walking distance from another. To ease getting between a few of these sites, a pedestrian road now stretches through Wolseong Park, from the south end of Tumulus Park to Anapji with a branch that runs down to Gyerim, Banwol-seong, and the Confucian academy. These lanes run through open grassy fields, many of which are dotted with foundation stones of long-since-disappeared temples; a flower garden has been placed at one point along the way.

Short **carriage rides** leave from the beginning of this pedestrian road and take in Cheom-seongdae, Gyerim, and Banwol-seong; ₩3,000 adults, ₩2,000 children.

Tumulus Park 대능원

Containing 20 tombs from the Three Kingdoms era, Tumulus Park, also called Tumuli Park, Gobun Gongwon, or Daeneungwon [Taenūng-won], has the most varied concentration of Silla burial mounds. This walled compound lies at the southern edge of downtown, a few minutes' walk from the train and bus stations. Its hours are 0730–1900; ₩1,500 entrance. From 1973 to 1975, this disorderly section of the city was cleared of houses, several tombs were excavated, and a well-landscaped, park-like setting created. Tree-lined walks wind through the park, giving easy access to all tombs.

The first tomb beyond the entrance gate is that of King Michu (who reigned 262–284). This grassy knoll (H.S. #175), sometimes referred to as the "Bamboo Tomb," is surrounded by a low stone wall whose front gate is locked except during special ceremonies. Crown pendants of gold, jade, and glass, plus gold earrings and gray stone pottery were excavated here. A venerated man, Michu was the first of the Kim family to reign over the Silla nation; he repulsed Baekje invasions time and again, and even after his death his spirit was regarded as a defender of the nation, and this is illustrated by the following story. During the reign of the next Silla king, Yurye, the country was attacked by forces of the Iseo country. Even though they fought bravely, they were outnumbered and were losing the battle. From out of nowhere, a large number of unknown soldiers appeared to join the battle and the enemy was routed. Strangely, these soldiers had bamboo leaves growing from their ears. By the time of the Silla victory celebration, these same soldiers had disappeared and the only remnant of their presence was the bamboo leaves, which were strewn in front of King Michu's grave.

To the rear of the park is an immense double-humped tomb (H.S. #40), known as Hwang-nam Daechong. The largest in Gyeongju, it measures 23 meters in height, 123 meters in length, and 80 meters in breadth. Its depths have offered up earrings, bracelets, a belt, and pedestal cups, all of gold; silver bowls and cups; a necklace of glass beads; and an exquisite gold crown. Judging from these articles—most on display in the Gyeongju Museum—it is presumed to have entombed a royal couple. Some scholars suggest

TOMBS

Mounded tombs, the most obvious remnant of the city's past, dominate your view as you approach this historic city. Many of the early tombs were constructed near the Banwol-seong palace site—at one point the city center but now at the edge of downtown. Later, others were constructed outside the city boundary, in the midst of flat farming fields and at the foot of the low hills that rim this valley. Pre-unification tomb construction consisted of several layers. An inner wooden chamber, set directly on the ground or slightly recessed into it, contained the coffin and personal articles for the deceased to use in the afterlife. Over the wooden structure were piled round river rocks, and over these an earthen mound was made. Due to natural deterioration, the wood eventually collapsed, crushing the chamber contents. During the United Silla period, these wooden structures were largely replaced with stone slabs, possibly harking back to Neolithic dolmen construction techniques.

Early tombs were simple rounded mounds. Some were set on a raised earthen dais surrounded by natural stones, while others were rimmed with a retaining wall of cut stone slabs. Later these slabs were engraved with zodiac figures, the mounds surrounded by a stone fence, and civilian, military, and animal statuary set in front of the tomb as symbolic guardians. Most tombs are single mounds, but several are double-humped, presumably containing both a king and a queen. Tomb mounds range from a few meters in diameter and height to one that's 25 meters high. Gyeongju became in effect a royal Silla cemetery. Over 670 tombs dot the city and surrounding plains; dozens more are scattered throughout the former Silla territory. While many were erected for the 56 Silla kings and queens, some were made for members of the aristocracy, famous generals, or government officials. Of the royal tombs, only two have been accurately and indisputably identified. They are the tombs of King Munmu, west of the city, and King Heungdeok, just outside the town of An'gang to the north.

Over the centuries, these mounds have, by and large, been left unplundered—the task of surreptitiously removing all that dirt is an imposing impediment! Some informal excavation was done in the early 1900s, but the first government-sponsored excavations were authorized by the Japanese during the occupation. Many treasures were uncovered, and much of historical and cultural import was learned. Not until 1974 were the next official excavations done. Again, the earth yielded a treasure trove of artifacts—now primarily displayed in the Seoul and Gyeongju museums. Archaeologists have uncovered jewelry, utensils, belts, crowns, swords and other weapons, and accoutrements of decoration.

that it's the grave of King Soji and his queen, both buried around A.D. 500.

To its left is 13-meter-high Cheonmachong [Ch'ŏnmach'ong] ("Heavenly Horse Tomb"), the most well-known and treasure-yielding of this group. Presumed to be from the late 5th or early 6th century, it was excavated in 1973. Over 12,000 individual artifacts—including a gold crown, cap, belt, and many pieces of jewelry; earthenware funerary objects; and the first pre-Silla unification painting ever discovered on the peninsula—were unearthed here. This painting, after which the tomb was named, is of a galloping horse, a motif similar to mural paintings found in Goguryeo tombs of North Korea. The horse and skillful horsemanship were vital elements in the maintenance of a strong Silla military force. The reliance on this animal indicates a strong connection between the Silla people and the nomadic tribes of central and eastern Asia from which they sprang. Painted on layered birch bark stitched together with leather thread, and perhaps the most significant single artifact taken from the mound, this ceremonial saddle piece (N.T. #207) is thought to have been a mudguard. Considering its age, this long-buried piece is in excellent condition, its five colors still bright and vibrant after so many centuries. Cheonmachong has been reconstructed as a mini-museum, allowing you access inside to view a cross section of the tomb's square inner chamber and piled-rock dome construction. Reproductions

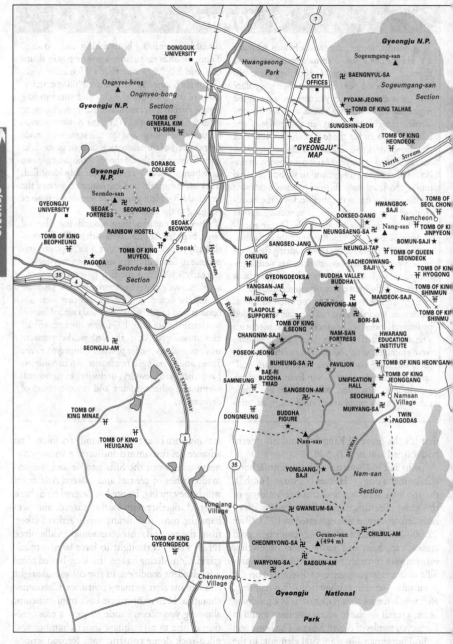

GYEONGJU

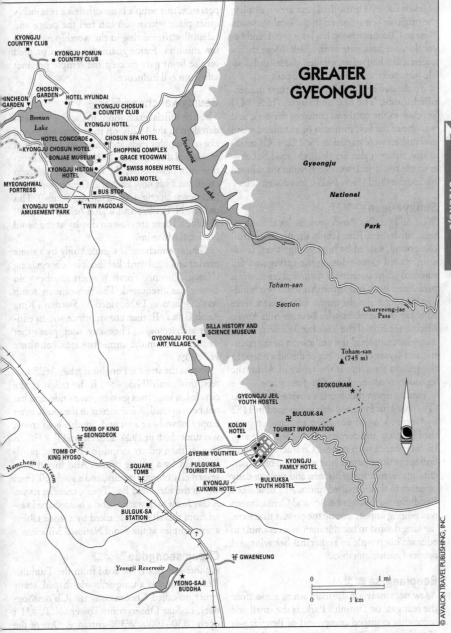

GYEONGJU

GREATER GYEONGJU

KYONGJU COUNTRY CLUB

KYONGJU POMUN COUNTRY CLUB

CHOSUN GARDEN

HINCHEON GARDEN

HOTEL HYUNDAI

KYONGJU CHOSUN COUNTRY CLUB

Bomun Lake

KYONGJU HOTEL

HOTEL CONCORDE

CHOSUN SPA HOTEL

KYONGJU CHOSUN HOTEL

SHOPPING COMPLEX

SONJAE MUSEUM

GRACE YEOGWAN

KYONGJU HILTON HOTEL

SWISS ROSEN HOTEL

GRAND MOTEL

MYEONGHWAL FORTRESS

BUS STOP

KYONGJU WORLD AMUSEMENT PARK

TWIN PAGODAS

Deokdong Lake

Gyeongju

National

Park

Toham-san

Section

Churyeong-jae Pass

SILLA HISTORY AND SCIENCE MUSEUM

GYEONGJU FOLK ART VILLAGE

Toham-san
▲ 745 m)

SEOKGURAM

GYEONGJU JEIL YOUTH HOSTEL

BULGUK-SA

KOLON HOTEL

TOURIST INFORMATION

TOMB OF KING SEONGDEOK

TOMB OF KING HYOSO

Namcheon Stream

SQUARE TOMB

GYERIM YOUTHTEL

PULGUKSA TOURIST HOTEL

KYONGJU FAMILY HOTEL

KYONGJU KUKMIN HOTEL

BULKUKSA YOUTH HOSTEL

BULGUK-SA STATION

7

GWAENEUNG

Yeongji Reservoir

YEONG-SAJI BUDDHA

0   1 mi

0   1 km

© AVALON TRAVEL PUBLISHING, INC.

of several objects unearthed here are on display, the originals being housed in the local museum. Next to Cheonmachong is a lotus pond, and beyond it, the back gate of the park. More than a dozen and a half other, smaller, single- and double-humped tombs lie within the park.

To the east of Tumulus Park lie three unidentified tombs. The first and largest (H.S. #41) lies close to the northeast corner of the park, and was one of the first tombs to be examined when excavations were started in the 1920s. Of smaller size, the next also lies along the road but closer to the rotary intersection. Beyond the railroad tracks, the third (H.S. #42) is less discernible.

Sunhye-jeon 순혜전

West of Tumulus Park's parking lot is Sunhye-jeon, an ancient Kim family shrine. This small compound, shaded by huge ginkgo trees, is seldom visited except during the spring and fall equinox, when an ancestor memorial ceremony is performed here. Inside the shrine are two buildings. One contains the memorial tablets for three Kim family members who became Silla kings: Michu, the first of the Kim family rulers; Munmu, who completed the unification of the country; and Gyeongsun, the last of the Silla rulers. In the second structure is the tablet of Alchi, the legendary founder of the Kim family line.

Farther down this lane is a covered stone stela (T. #68). This inscribed slab was erected in 1182 by Goryeo king Myeongjong to commemorate the filial piety and devotion of one Son Shi-yang. In compliance with correct Confucian custom, Son spent three years living at the site of his parents' grave, mourning his loss, and making daily offerings to their departed spirits. At a time when Buddhism was losing vibrancy and Confucianism was gaining import among the powers that were, the king desired to use this man as an example to educate his people in respectful behavior and proper Confucian ethics.

Beopjang-sa 법장사

A few steps away, on the main street, across from the rear gate of Tumulus Park, is the small and somewhat cramped compound of Beopjang-sa [Pŏpchang-sa]. Rather undistinguished in ap-

pearance, this temple is nonetheless a reasonably quiet place where you can feel the peace and solemnity after sitting in the worship hall for a few minutes. Fierce guards have been painted on the front gate to keep the temple precinct safe from evil influence.

Geumgwanchong 금관총

The first official excavations in the city were undertaken in the 1920s, on the tombs north and east of Tumulus Park, and only then as a result of accidental discovery. In 1921, during construction of a new house, the first gold crown was dug up at a site now known as Geumgwanchong [Kŭmgwanch'ong] ("Gold Crown Tomb"). This crown (N.T. #87) and a gold belt (N.T. #88) also found here are now on display at the Seoul National Museum.

Geumgwanchong is signaled only by a stone marker and signboard. Behind it is Subongchong ("Lucky Phoenix Tomb"), where another gold crown was discovered. This 5th-century tomb was dug into in 1926, aided by Sweden's King Adolf Gustav II, then crown prince and an eminent archaeologist. These two sites, plus other smaller tombs in the immediate area, constitute H.S. #39.

Across the street is Ponghwangdae. At 25 meters, this tomb (H.S. #38) is the tallest in the city. It has large trees growing on its side, and has not been opened. A few meters to the south, in an empty lot without a mound, another gold crown was unearthed, in 1924. This crown (T. #338), is smaller than others found in Gyeongju, possibly worn by a young prince. Also found were several clay objects, jewelry, and a gold bell, from which the site, Gold Bell Tomb, takes its name. A clay horseback warrior and a boat-shaped vessel from this site, also marked by a stone tablet, are on display at the Seoul National Museum.

Cheomseongdae 첨성대

A short way down the road from the Tumulus Park entrance is a unique bottle-shaped, stone structure called Cheomseongdae [Ch'ŏmsŏng-dae], or Star Observation Tower (N.T. #31); open 0830–1900, ₩300 entrance. One of the oldest structures in Korea, it's thought to be the oldest astronomical observatory in all of East Asia. Erected during the reign of Queen Seondeok (who ruled 632-647), it's speculated that the tower was employed to watch the movement of the stars, predict solar and lunar eclipses, aid farmers in determining the cycles of agriculture according to the moon, and even to predict the fortunes of government. At first, this nine-meter-high, gracefully curved structure looks simple and unsophisticated, but when studied, it reveals a systematic construction, fine workmanship, and some knowledge of mathematical principles on the part of its engineers. The square base is laid with 12 large stones, one for each month (or zodiac figure); each side represents one season. On top are piled hewn granite blocks, one for each day of the year. Including the base and two-tier square top, there are 30 levels, one for each day of the lunar month. On the south side is an opening; above and below it are 12 levels of stones. It's stated that the position and direction of the square top and stones projecting from its side have some relation to the position of certain stars. Although it now leans slightly to the north, Cheomseongdae is very well preserved. This observatory has come to symbolize the city of Gyeongju, and may be the single most recognized object of the area.

Gyerim 계림

Across the road from Cheomseongdae is a cool and quiet grove of gnarled old hardwood trees, mostly Chinese elm, called Gyerim [Kyerim] (H.S. #19); ₩300 entrance. A legend relates to the forest and the founding of the Kim family. One night in A.D. 65, King Talhae (the fourth Silla ruler) heard an imploring cock's crow from this grove, and he sent his prime minister to investigate. The official found a golden box hanging from a branch of a tree, with a white chicken sitting underneath. Brought to the palace and opened, the box revealed an infant boy. Pleased at this unexpected and unusual event, the king named the boy Alchi, or "young child" in the old Silla language, and gave him the family name Kim, the Chinese character for "gold." From that time, this grove has been known as Gyerim, or "Chicken Forest."

As King Talhae had no son, he adopted Alchi and made him the crown prince. When the old king died, the boy deferred the crown to a member of the Bak family, whom he considered to have a more natural claim to the throne—the first three Silla kings were of the Bak family. Head of the Gyeongju Kim family, Alchi never reigned as king, though many of his descendants did. His seventh-generation descendant was King Michu, the first Kim king; from the beginning of the reign of King Naemul (356), to the end of the reign of King Hyogang (912), Alchi's descendants ruled without break. In 1803, a memorial stone was set up in Gyerim by order of the king to commemorate the wondrous birth of Alchi.

Across the lane from Gyerim and below Banwol-seong, unearthed stones have once again been set in place where, centuries ago, they provided foundation for temple halls. Here and elsewhere in the area, excavation continues, giving a better idea of the extent to which this area had been built.

Yangban Village

Directly west of Gyerim is the tomb of King Naemul (H.S. #188), Silla's 17th king. Beyond it are several other low tombs with unknown occupants. Directly south and west of Gyerim is a neighborhood with many traditional-style *yangban* homes, and a *hyanggyo* built in the early 1600s. Last renovated in 1977, the *hyanggyo* is in very good shape. The lecture hall and dormitories of this Confucian academy can be visited, but the shrine remains closed except for ceremonies. Almost directly behind the *hyanggyo* is a house belonging to the Gyeongju Choe family, a fine example of old-style construction and layout. It is here that the high-quality Gyodong Beobju rice wine originated some 300 years ago. Other old-style homes are seen in this hamlet, including several that have been turned into exclusive restaurants.

At the eastern end of this village, just below the western edge of Banwol-seong, are the reconstructed foundation remains of a bridge that once spanned this stream. The following legend relates to this bridge, Hyobulhyo-gyo, the Bridge of Filial Piety and Impiety. Long ago, a widow with seven sons lived on one side of the South Stream. This woman worked hard to raise her boys properly and each grew to be a respectable young man. She, however, had a secret paramour who lived in the hamlet across the stream, and whenever she went to see him, she had to wade through the water. When the boys realized what was happening, they decided to build a bridge for her convenience. When the villagers came to know of it, they gave the bridge (gyo) its name, to symbolize the piety (hyo) of the sons toward their mother but also the impiety (bulhyo) toward the honor of their deceased father.

Heungnyun-saji 흥륜사지

West of the hyanggyo hamlet and across the first main street is a restored Joseon-era building called Samaso which was a place for local scholars to gather and a well called Jaemaejeong (H.S. #246), reputedly the site of the house owned and used by Kim Yu-shin, Silla's most famous general.

To the north of there and back behind a residential neighborhood are the remains of the temple Heungnyun-sa (Flourishing Dharma Wheel Temple). It is believed that this site (H.S. #15) is the spot on which the first Silla Buddhist temple was erected, sometime in the early 400s, during the reign of King Nulchi. Legend says that Buddhism was brought to Silla from Goguryeo by Priest Ado. At first, people were suspicious of these new beliefs and few were converted. At one point King Nulchi's daughter felt sick. None of the court physicians were able to cure the girl. Ado was called in to try, and after burning incense and saying prayers over the sick child she was cured. As a reward, the king built Heungnyun-sa for the priest. While Ado's powers impressed the king, few citizens turned to the new religion. After Ado died, the attraction to Buddhism seemed to die out until Yi Cha-don martyred himself for the belief some one hundred years later during the reign of King Beopheung, at which point Buddhism began to flourish amongst the people. Nothing of the first temple remains today, but a new temple has been erected on the site.

North of the bus terminal in town is the site of yet another very old temple. **Samnang-saji** (삼랑 사지) was said to have been built in 597, and its only remains are a pair of flagpole supports (T. #127). Set about a meter apart, they must have upheld a rather tall pole, perhaps indicating the size of the temple itself.

Banwol-seong 반월성

What is believed to be the principal palace and residence site of the Silla rulers lies beyond the tree-covered earthen wall a few steps from Gyerim—there is another entrance across the street and down from Anapji. Built sometime around A.D. 100, Banwol-seong [Panwol-sŏng] ("Crescent Moon Fortress") takes its name from its shape. The earthen wall that marks the boundary of this enclosure (H.S. #16) is topped with trees. Its interior once contained numerous halls, pavilions, gates, and other structures, but today only a few plinth stones dot the open field. A moat apparently once surrounded this fortress and part of that water-barrier has been reworked at the northeast corner. Just below and inside the northern wall of this enclosure is an ice house (T. #66), a man-made freezer of more recent age, moved here from some unknown location in 1741. Presumably there had been others here before this one, as historical records refer to such ice houses being built and used during the Silla period, some 1,000 years earlier.

Aside from Banwol-seong, other fortresses were set up in the vicinity to protect Gyeongju. The most important of these were Nam-san Fortress on Nam-san; Myeonghwal Fortress, draped over the hill above Bomun Lake; Seoak Fortress, high on Seondo-san west of the city; Busan Fortress, still farther west on Obong-san; Gwanmun-seong, south of the city; and Hyeong-san Fortress, north of Gyeongju toward An'gang.

Of much later date are the remains of the Gyeongju city fortress (H.S. #96), built in 1012 and repaired again during the Joseon Dynasty. A few sections can be seen in the center of town just north of the main drag, snaking through the neighborhood. Much is now overgrown.

Gyeongju National Museum
경주박물관

Across the road and southeast of Banwol-seong is the Gyeongju National Museum. Open 0900–1800 March to October and 0900–1700 November to February, it's closed every Monday and January 1; ₩400 entrance. After the Seoul National Museum, this museum has the best collection of Silla Dynasty artifacts. From 300 pieces in 1915, this collection has grown to about 100,000 today. Of this total, about 3,000 or so are shown at any one time, including 14 National Treasures and 20 Treasures. The eight display rooms in the main exhibition hall are spacious, well-lit, and attractive, though more copious notes and fully descriptive explanations would be helpful. Audio cassettes are available at the front for ₩2,000. One large annex building is devoted entirely to items unearthed from tombs and temples, and the other displays relics taken from Anapji pond. A new exhibition hall was constructed in 2001 to better display additional artifacts. In the outdoor exhibition area are numerous stone objects and statuary from the area, and reproductions of the two great pagodas of Bulguk-sa. From filigree gold crowns to earthenware pots and granite statuary, the sum total bespeaks the great craftsmanship of Silla artisans and is a graphic display of the tangible cultural heritage of the dynasty. This museum deserves a lengthy look. Its representative display of Korean artifacts is useful not only as a means of research and study, but also as a healthy glimpse at the treasures that this area has to offer for those with limited time to spend in Gyeongju.

Emille Bell: Hanging in the museum's yard is Korea's largest and most beloved bell. Popularly known as the "Emille Bell" (N.T. #29), it was cast in 771 to commemorate Silla's 33rd king, Seongdeok, and originally hung at Bongdeok-sa, a royal-sponsored temple. At 3.3 meters high, 2.3 meters wide, and reputedly weighing a phenomenal 23,000 kg, this skillfully wrought and gracefully embellished bell is one of the world's largest. It's suspended over a shallow echo chamber, which enriches its resonant sound when struck by a log on its side. Legend says that King Gyeongdeok commissioned the most renowned bell maker in the land to cast this bell. The king unfortunately died before it was completed, and it was King Hyegong who finally saw the bell cast. When the bell was first struck, it failed to ring. When recast and struck again, it cracked. After several unsuccessful attempts, a celestial spirit appeared in a dream to the head priest of the temple and indicated that the fire spirit dragon needed to be appeased in order for the bell to sound properly. In order to accomplish this, a young girl who was born in the year, month, day, and hour of the dragon needed to be found and thrown into the molten metal before it was poured. If this was done, the casting would succeed. This was done and when struck, the new bell did not crack. Yet, the sound of this unfractured bell resonated with the mournful cry of the child for its mother—*"emi"* or *"emille,"* in the language of ancient Silla.

Koreans have long been known for their bell-casting skills. Not only did the Japanese and Chinese give them high praise, but their reputation spread as far as the Middle East. The combination of casting skills and aesthetic tastes resulted in works of art. While most smaller bells ring with a melodious peal, the Emille Bell booms with the roar of a dragon (not the cry of a child), and can be heard 40 kilometers away on a crisp winter night.

Anapji 안압지

Across the road from Banwol-seong is the pond/pleasure garden Anapji. The grounds are open 0900–1900 every day except Monday and January 1; ₩1,000 entrance. Anapji (H.S. #18) was constructed in 674 by King Munmu to commemorate the unification of the peninsula by Silla forces during the preceding decade. In 679, the villa Dong-gung was built on the pond's west side. Most notable of the buildings within this auxiliary palace garden was Imhae-jeong, or Pavilion Fronting the Sea—a small-scale version was built overlooking the pond during recent renovation of the garden. This lotus pond, roughly the shape of the Korean Peninsula, let the king survey his "entire kingdom." Water was fed into this pond through stone channels from the South Stream on the far side of Banwol-seong. Three artificial islands were created in its middle, and 12 "mountains" placed around its periphery; flowering trees were planted at its edge, and rare animals were raised. Ironically, this site, built at the zenith of Silla strength, was also where King Gyeongsun, less than 300 years later, abdicated the throne and relinquished the kingdom to Goryeo king Wang Geon.

In 1975–76, this pleasure garden was restored. Over 30,000 items were taken from the pond's mud bottom, including a well-preserved royal barge, many items of bronze artwork, stone paving tiles, glazed roof-end tiles with demon faces, stoneware, lacquerware, and wood now on display at the Gyeongju National Museum. Three pavilions were rebuilt on the edge of the dredged and redefined pond; one contains a small-scale reproduction of what the whole area was thought to have looked like at its height. Foundation stones for several other long-lost buildings can be seen on the lawn, and stone conduits for the original water drainage system have once again been placed in proper alignment. On a sunny day, it's pleasant to sit in the cool of the pavilion and watch the ducks on the pond or the turtles sunning themselves on the rocks below, but it's also beautiful on a rainy day when raindrops ripple the smooth water surface and pool in huge silver beads on the wide, outstretched lotus leaves.

Hwangnyong-saji 황룡사지

Proceed north from Anapji, cross the railroad tracks, and follow paths through the fields to a six-meter-high, three-tier stone pagoda rising from the middle of a rice paddy. This 9th-century pagoda was re-erected in 1980, and marks the site of the former temple Mitan-sa.

Directly north of there is the site of Silla's largest and greatest of the *seon* meditation temples, Hwangnyong-saji, the Imperial Dragon Temple (H.S. #6). An artist's model stands in the national museum to provide everyone an idea of what the temple probably looked like at its height. Excavated from 1976 to 1983, over 40,000 items were dug up at this site. From a

mound in the middle of this compound, you can see that the individual buildings were numerous and the temple grounds extensive. Constructed in the mid-500s, its main hall is said to have had three huge gilt Buddha statues on the altar, and a bell four times the size of the Emille Bell. Paintings of pine trees on the side of this hall were supposedly so lifelike that birds tried to land on them. A nine-story wooden pagoda stood in the temple courtyard. Erected with the aid of the famous Baekje architect Abiji, it rose an estimated 70 meters! Records indicate that this wondrous wooden pagoda was destroyed five times during the ensuing six centuries. Finally, in 1238, with the Mongol invasion and sacking of the country, it was burnt to the ground, never to be rebuilt. Today, 64 massive foundation stones on the lawn indicate its monstrous size, while other foundation stones mark the sites of the many other temple buildings and corridors. A tall pair of flagpole supports stands a short distance away in the field to the north.

Bunhwang-sa 분황사

Across the lane and north from Hwangnyong-sa is Bunhwang-sa [Punhwang-sa] ("Famous Emperor Temple"); ₩1,000 entrance. Still an active place of worship, although very small today, it was one of the four most famous temples of the early Silla Dynasty. Its claim to fame is also a pagoda, but one much different from Hwangnyong-sa's. Erected in 634, during the reign of Queen Seondeok, the Bunhwang-sa pagoda (N.T. #30) is the oldest datable pagoda in the country, and, along with Cheomseongdae, one of the country's oldest stone structures. Originally nine stories high, only three remain today. If you look closely, the "bricks" are actually cut stones. This pagoda imitates the much-admired brick pagoda style popular in the South and North dynasties period of Chinese history, directly preceding this temple's construction. At its base level are chamber openings, with stone doors ajar, guarded by fierce figures. Stone lions squat at corners of the base. This partial pagoda is only one of five that are known to have been erected at this temple. During its renovations in 1915, a stone box found inside the structure contained jewelry, hairpins, needles, and other personal articles, now on display at the Gyeongju Museum. Aside from this pagoda, stone flagpole supports, a water well, and other miscellaneous stone objects from the same period are also found here. Within this formerly grand compound, only one worship hall now stands. A small weatherworn structure, it houses a disproportionately large Buddha figure that stands behind, unusually, a stone altar. Plans call for great future expansion of the temple grounds and several new buildings so that it more properly reflects the grandeur that it had during the Silla Dynasty.

This stone pagoda, the nine-story wooden Hwangnyong-sa pagoda, Cheomseongdae, and numerous other structures throughout the country were built during the reign of Queen Seondeok. She is credited with creating a climate where the building of religious objects was promoted, and the establishment of temples hastened. It was a time of great social and spiritual energy, a time of creativity. Although before the zenith of Silla society, and prior to the time when Buddhism was at its strongest, this period marked a surge in the advancement of the religion and seems to have been a heightened time for the consciousness of spirituality.

WEST GYEONGJU
Tomb of King Muyeol 무열왕릉

Two kilometers west of Gyeongju, along the highway to Daegu, is the tomb of King Muyeol (H.S. #20); ₩500 entrance. The 29th, he was one of the Silla Dynasty's greatest kings. Under his direction, the drive to unify the peninsula was carried out. Before he died, the Baekje Kingdom was firmly under Silla control; seven years after his death, King Munmu, Muyeol's son, defeated the Goguryeo state to finish unification. This is one of the few tombs in Gyeongju that can definitely be identified. An inscription on the tortoise monument (N.T. #25) at the tomb's entrance states his name. Unfortunately, the stela itself is missing, so the capstone is set directly on the back of this exquisitely shaped tortoise. This type of monument was a rather new feature to gravesite ornamentation of that time. Considering that

it's over 1,300 years old, it's in amazing condition! Set in a forest of pines, the king's tomb is large, and, unlike earlier tombs, natural boulders were used to reinforce the base of the mound—a few can be seen today sticking out around the tomb's perimeter. Four other tombs (H.S. #142), assumed to be for members of the king's family, stretch up the rise behind this one.

Directly across the street lie two smaller tombs, one of which is thought to contain the remains of Kim In-mun, King Munmu's younger brother and the second son of King Muyeol. The second tomb is said to be that of Kim Yang, a high-level Silla government official and direct descendant of King Muyeol. Set to the rear of these tombs is a second tortoise base (T. #70). Although done with much artistry, this piece doesn't quite match the excellence of its neighbor across the road, and it has no capstone.

Seoak Seowon and Other Sites

A few minutes' walk around the east side of this village brings you to Seoak Seowon [Sŏak Sŏwon] (서악서원). Reconstructed recently, this shrine holds the tablets of Kim Yu-shin, Silla's most famous general, and Choe Chi-won and Seol Chong, both brilliant Confucian scholars of the mid-Silla era.

Following the road less than half a kilometer up through the village will bring you past a humble yet traditional building that is used by the Hwang family for memorial ceremonies. Directly above this hall is a solitary, three-tiered stone pagoda (T. #65) of angular design that marks the site of the vanished temple Yonggyeong-sa. Across the dirt track, and at a spot that overlooks the much more impressive tombs of King Muyeol and family, are three small and rather ordinary royal tombs (H.S. #177, #178, #179), traditionally assigned to the four minor Silla kings Jinheung, Jinji, Munseong, and Heonan. Other Silla-era tomb mounds sit on an adjacent ridge.

From here, it's another 1.5 kilometers up a track to the small temple **Seongmo-sa** [Sŏngmo-sa] (성모사), near the top of Seoak-san. Here, a stocky Buddha statue (T. #62) has been carved into a rock wall, flanked by slender bodhisattva statues that, until recently, lay in pieces in the nearby brush. Around the top of Seondo-san and along several of its ridges lie the rubble remains of Seoak Sanseong, one of the five principal fortresses that guarded the ancient city of Gyeongju.

Tomb of General Kim Yu-shin
김유신묘

This most famous of the Silla generals was a man of great ability and ability, a strategist, patriot, and defender of the realm. Kim Yu-shin served as general under both kings Muyeol and Munmu, and was instrumental in unifying the peninsula. While in Gyeongju, you'll often read his name and hear a great many references to him. He accomplished extraordinary things, and when he died he was greatly revered.

His tomb (H.S. #21) is set at the base of Ongnyeo-bong, north of King Muyeol's tomb; ₩500 entrance. This tomb, while smaller, is more sophisticated than King Muyeol's, reflecting the influence Kim Yu-shin and his family had at court. On the base wall surrounding the tomb is a complete set of zodiac figures carved in bas-relief. All facing left, each animal is dressed in civilian attire but holds a weapon. These carvings

ZODIAC FIGURES

Eight tombs in the Gyeongju area have zodiac figures: six for kings and queens, one for Kim Yu-shin, and the square tomb near the Bulguk-sa Station, supposedly the tomb of Kim Dae-seong, the rebuilder of Bulguk-sa. The 12 zodiac figures were placed equidistant around the mounds, one at each compass point. Occasionally, three-dimensional figures were buried at each point around the grave, a practice imported from China around the mid-600s. The majority of these figures are relief carved in stone panels; the figures at King Seongdeok's tomb are the only extant three-dimensional statues. Nearly all are about one meter tall. The rat is always in the north position. From there, going clockwise around the tomb, are the ox, tiger, rabbit, dragon, snake, horse, sheep, monkey, chicken, dog, and pig.

are, by most accounts, the finest representations of zodiac figures in the region. There is no bus that runs from town to this site. Taxi or walk the two kilometers from the bus terminal.

Tomb of King Beopheung

Three other royal tombs are in the area—none easy to locate or get to. On the west side of Seondo-san is the tomb of King Beopheung (H.S. #176). Nearby is Hyohyeon-ni (T. #67), a plain three-tier stone pagoda typical of the United Silla era. This pagoda marks the site of the temple, Aegong-sa, to which King Beopheung is said to have retired and where he served as a monk until his death. Ancient records relate that King Beopheung wished to secure a time of peace and well-being for his subjects. He felt that Buddhism was the path, yet few turned to this new religion. A minor court official named Yi Chadon said that if the king would have Yi's head cut off, white blood would flow from the wound, and this would be a miracle that would cause people to accept Buddhism. His head was cut off in A.D. 527, and shortly afterwards temples were built and Buddhism spread rapidly throughout the kingdom. One of those temples was built on the site which Bulguk-sa now occupies.

South of Seondo-san and across the freeway are the tombs of King Minae (H.S. #190) and King Heuigang (H.S. #220).

Seongju-am 성주암

Over the hill to the north of King Minae's tomb is the tiny hermitage Seongju-am [Sŏngju-am] and its rock Buddha carving. To visit this spot, take a city bus toward Geoncheon and get off at the road running into Dudae-ri. Walk under the freeway, through the center of the village, and up a trail to the east side of this valley. After 20 minutes, you will reach the hermitage and its triad of rock carvings (T. #122). The central figure is that of the Amita Buddha; accompanying figures represent the Goddess of Mercy and Daesaeji Bosal, the Bodhisattva of Power. The figures are best seen in mid-afternoon, when oblique sun rays give them the appearance of greater depth.

NORTH GYEONGJU

Hwangseong Park 황성공원

Just north of the North Stream is Hwangseong [Hwangsŏng] Park. Dominating this forested glade is a small knoll majestically crowned by a bold statue of General Kim Yu-shin astride a horse. Even in the heat of the summer, cool picnic spots can be found along walking paths in the shade of the tall pines. To the rear of the park is an athletic stadium; a soccer field, archery range, tennis courts, and *ssireum* wrestling ring are also located here. Many events of the Silla Cultural Festival take place in this park.

Baengnyul-sa 백율사

Virtually the only historic temple in this northern section of the city, Baengnyul-sa [Paengnyul-sa] sits high on the hillside overlooking northern Gyeongju. It is dedicated to Yi Cha-don, the martyr whose inspiration helped Silla become a Buddhist nation. Although small, Baengnyul-sa was the repository of a standing, gilt-bronze, Healing Buddha statue (N.T. #28). Standing gilt figures this tall (about 2 meters) are rare indeed, and this one is skillfully done, representing a high-water mark in Silla's artistic metalcraft. It's now on display at the Gyeongju National Museum. Today, the temple's one small worship hall contains three smaller figures on the altar under an elaborate canopy. The terrace stonework is well done.

One day long ago, King Gyeongdeok paid a visit to Baengnyul-sa. As he approached the temple, he heard a rhythmic Buddhist chant emanating from the ground. He ordered the spot dug and found a carved square block of stone. To mark this wondrous encounter, the king had a temple constructed on the site, and named it Gulbul-sa [Kulbul-sa] ("Temple of the Excavated Buddhas"). Called Samyeon Seokbul, this carved block (T. #121) has representations of the Buddha and bodhisattvas on its four faces. The figure facing south is Seokgamoni Buddha; the Healing Buddha faces east; Amita, the Buddha of Infinite Light, looks west; and two undetermined figures face north. Foundation stones for a long-since-destroyed structure surround this carved block of stone. From here, a long flight of rough granite steps leads up to Baengnyul-sa.

Two Royal Tombs

From the bottom end of the path leading to Baengnyul-sa, a road leads south along the base of the hill to the **tomb of King Talhae** (탈해왕릉) (H.S. #174). The fourth king of Silla, Talhae was the first of eight kings from the Seok family, all of whom reigned in the early days of the dynasty. Next to this grave is **Sungshin-jeon,** a shrine containing King Talhae's memorial tablet, which has been moved from its original site, in Banwol-seong, where it was erected in 1898. Every year, members of the Seok family hold a memorial ceremony at this shrine. Sitting on a hill to the side of this tomb is the pavilion Pyoamjeong, an ancestral shrine of the Gyeongju Yi family, said to be the first of the six original clans of this region which eventually evolved into the Silla Kingdom.

The **tomb of King Heondeok** (헌덕왕릉) is located farther along. Surrounded by rice fields, this tomb (H.S. #29) is set like an oasis in the midst of encircling pines. From the tomb of King Talhae, follow the village lane and irrigation canal to the southeast, then walk the paddy dikes to reach this shaded circle. While this large tomb once sported all 12 zodiac figures, fewer than half remain.

Nawon-ni Five-Tier Pagoda

West of the highway and the rail line that run north toward An'gang and located in the village of Nawon-ni is a granite pagoda (나원리 5층석탑) which rises about nine meters tall. As one of the few five-tier pagodas in the region, it's an unusual artifact even though its basic form and construction technique are much like that of the common three-tier pagodas. This impressive and massive pagoda (T. #39) is in excellent condition except that the top finial is missing and the tips of the top two levels are broken. Unusually light in color, it is sometimes referred to as the White Pagoda. In 1996, several gilt objects were discovered inside when the pagoda was taken apart and repaired.

Tomb of Queen Jindeok

North of central Gyeongju and west of the Hyeongsan River, the tomb of this queen (진덕 왕릉) is surrounded by panels of zodiac figures in bas-relief, the smallest in the area. Following Queen Seondeok, Queen Jindeok furthered the spread of Buddhism throughout the Silla Kingdom. There is no bus service to this site (H.S. #24) so you must walk about two kilometers from the highway, passing a tiny grove of wisteria on the way. From the end of the country lane, head up through a series of newer graves then into the trees before reaching the queen's tomb. The new Gyeongju bypass highway passes to the side of this tomb.

Yongdam-jeong 영담정

The birthplace of Korea's first major indigenous religion is a few kilometers northwest of Gyeongju. Originally called *Donghak* ("Eastern learning"), the name of this religious group was changed to *Cheondo-gyo* ("Heavenly Way") in 1905. Yongdam-jeong is a memorial shrine to Ch'oe Je-u, its founder and inspirational leader. Son and grandson of poor Confucian scholars, young Ch'oe had a difficult early life. He saw that the neighboring peasants had an even tougher existence and resolved to help the lower classes. Using the best elements of Confucianism, Buddhism, and shamanism, in 1860 he formulated a humanistic philosophy and practical religion considered the antithesis of the "Western learning" (Catholicism) that was then slowly creeping into the country. He insisted that heaven could be achieved here on earth by the humanistic evolution of society, the equalization of all classes, and an improvement in the standard of living. Through the efforts of all people, he reasoned, governmental inequity and injustice could also be expelled. These new ideas proved anathema to the rulers, adding fire to an already unstable social situation. Members of this new religion were persecuted, and in 1864 Ch'oe was arrested and beheaded in Daegu. Nonetheless, his ideas flourished and were the impetus for the peasant uprisings in the latter part of the 1800s and a vital factor in the Independence Movement of 1919. While many of the activities of *Donghak's* early adherents were socially oriented, today they are by and large religious, with only undertones of social reform. Ch'oe's ideas have not been forgotten. Although claiming only a modest number of adherents, *Cheondo-gyo* functions today as a vital religious group.

Yongdam-jeong is a sacred spot for members of this religion. The shrine is set in a cool, thickly wooded vale next to a gently cascading stream. A one-kilometer walk from the country road brings you to its parking lot and entrance. A broad path leads up from the wide front gate into this secluded sacred spot. Near the front gate stands a statue of the venerable Ch'oe; a short way beyond are a prayer hall and office. Through the second gate, and on the far side of the footbridge, the reconstructed hall Yongdam-jeong enshrines a portrait of this religious leader. It is said that Ch'oe studied here and, in 1860, became enlightened about his philosophical purpose. Farther on, next to the pristine stream, is the hall Samgak-jeong, where copies of Ch'oe's writings are preserved. Only in 1974 was the shrine renovated properly, and due respect given this original thinker. On the ridge below Yongdam-jeong is Ch'oe Je-u's grave. Less than one kilometer up the road from the entrance drive to Yongdam-jeong is Gajeong-ni [Kajŏng-ri], the village of his birth. A memorial marker to the native son sits at the outskirts of the village.

NAM-SAN

The southern section of Gyeongju is dominated by Nam-san, and its highest peak (Geumo-san) rises to 494 meters. Although of low elevation, this mountain was held in the highest esteem by the Silla peoples. It was a spiritual spot, one of great religious reverence. In every one of the mountain's numerous valleys lie tombs, temple and pavilion sites, carvings and sculptures, pagodas and lanterns, and stone fragments of all sizes and kinds. Every valley has something to offer, every turn brings something new to view. By one authoritative account, there are over 450 points of historical and cultural interest on this mountain alone, including 127 temple sites, 87 Buddha figures, and 71 stone pagodas! It must have been magnificent at its zenith, about 1,200 years ago. Because of its cultural and historical significance, the entire mountain area has been designated H.S. #311. Though many trails crisscross this mountain like a spidery net, most are not well marked and some not often traveled. Recently, signs have been posted for the more important sites, so those should be easiest to find. Explore, but with caution! Major sites are listed below, starting on the mountain's west side, moving to the east, and then to those higher up on the mountain itself along trails.

Oneung 오능

Surrounded by ancient pines, south of the South Stream, is this group of five royal tombs [Onŭng] (H.S. #172); ₩300 entrance. It's believed that King Hyeokgeose, his wife Queen Aryeong, and Kings Namhae, Yuri, and Pasa are buried here, all from the Bak family. As they were four of the first five Silla kings, these tombs are of great importance to the cultural legacy of the region. Semi-annual memorial ceremonies are held here at Sungdeok-jeon. The buildings at the front of this park-like walled compound are used for the preparation of these ceremonies; no finer such structures are seen in all of Gyeongju.

Na-jeong 나정

In a copse of trees surrounded by rice fields is Na-jeong [Na-jŏng], birthplace of Bak Hyeokgeose, mythical founder of the Silla Dynasty. Inside this tiny walled enclosure (H.S. #245) is a water well, a memorial tablet (erected in 1805), and a stone marking the spot where he touched the earth after descending from heaven in an egg. At age 13 he was chosen to be the first Silla king. The year 57 B.C. is the traditional founding date of the Silla Dynasty. King Hyeokgeose ruled from then until A.D. 4. It's said that he and his queen—born from a dragon's rib—were benevolent rulers. Showing great concern for the well-being of their subjects, they traveled throughout the land teaching agriculture and sericulture, still important to this region's economy.

Other Nearby Sites

Up the lane that runs past Na-jeong is Yangsan-

jae (양산재), a shrine dedicated to the six ancestral chiefs of the pre-Silla period. They were posthumously given the proper family names of Yi, Choe, Son, Jeong, Bae, and Seol by King Yuri, and their descendants have carried those family names ever since. Every year in mid-autumn, a memorial ceremony is held at this shrine for these six men. Sticking up out of a rice field to the front of Yangsan-jae is a pair of flagpole supports (T. #909) from the former Namgan-sa. Unlike most others, this one has cross-shaped notches on the inside near the top for the supports that held the pole erect. A little farther up this lane is Gyeongdeoksa, a Bae family memorial shrine. Members of the Bae family were not only instrumental in helping found the Silla Dynasty, but also helped create the Goryeo and Joseon dynasties in later centuries. Beyond Namgan Village and its reservoir is the tomb of Ilseong (H.S. #173), seventh Silla king, and farther up the hill is a row of jumbled stones, remnants of the ancient Nam-san Fortress (H.S. #22), thought to have been constructed during the reign of King Jinpyeong around the year 590. Inside the wall, storehouse sites have been identified from which carbonized rice, presumably from a fire, has been taken.

Changnim-saji 창림 사지

Between Na-jeong and Poseok-jeong, but up above the fields in a grove of trees, is the site of the former temple Changnim-saji. This is said to have been the site of the first Silla palace, but in 858 the temple was built here. Many carved stone pieces lie scattered amongst the trees and the outline of terraces can be seen stepping up the hillside. One can imagine buildings rising from this site. Above the terraces is a tall, well-proportioned granite pagoda that has several sculpted panels. Recently re-erected, this pagoda is the largest on Nam-san.

Poseok-jeong 포석정

One of the most unique remains of the Silla period, and a frequent tourist stop, is Poseok-jeong [P'osŏk-jŏng]; ₩500 entrance. The name Poseok-jeong means "Abalone Stone Pavilion." Now located in a peaceful grove of trees on the west side of Nam-san, this site (H.S. #1) was once a large royal pleasure garden and banquet hall. Nothing remains now but a granite watercourse (roughly in the shape of an abalone), through which water was routed from the nearby stream. A favorite game was played here under the trees. One participant would start a poem, or propose a subject for a poem, and would then choose another of the group to finish it. A cup of wine was then floated down this winding channel. If the cup arrived at the chosen person after the poem was completed, all was fine. If not, he was required to drink the wine to the last drop. Undoubtedly for some guests, the poems came more haltingly (or perhaps more easily) with each emptied cup. Poseok-jeong was often the site of merriment and laughter, but one of the saddest tales of the dynasty was also played out here. In 927, while King Gyeongae was partying with friends, the rebel leader Gyeon Hwon invaded the city and set up his headquarters in the palace. He forced the king to fall upon his own sword, and appointed Gyeongsun, the king's tractable cousin, to rule instead. The queen and palace women were defiled, and soldiers plundered the city at will.

Bae-ri Buddha Triad 배리삼존석불

The eastern end of the Nam-san skyway, which winds up and over the mountain to Namsan Village, starts at the Poseok-jeong parking lot. From the far side of the parking lot, a path goes off between the fields and leads along the foot of the hill to the tomb of Jima (H.S. #221), the sixth king of Silla. The path continues on around the front of a reservoir, reaching the two small temples Sambul-sa and Mangwol-sa.

In a tiny walled enclosure above these temples, now capped by a roof, is a Buddha statue flanked by two bodhisattvas (T. #63). Presumed to be pre-unification figures, possibly dating from the sixth century, they are three of the oldest Buddha statues in the country. In 1923, all three were moved here from other locations on the mountainside. These images are best seen in the late afternoon, when the angle of the sun gives them "depth."

Samneung (삼능) and Other Tombs

The trail continues along the hillside to Samneung [Samnŭng] (H.S. #219), three tombs aligned like Oneung, one behind another, east to west. They're the tombs of Adalla, Shindeok, and Gyeongmyeong, the 8th, 53rd, and 54th kings of Silla, and like the occupants of Oneung all members of the Bak family. Set apart from these three is **Dongneung** (H.S. #222), grave of King Gyeongae, also of the Bak family and the last Silla king. Although a mere three kilometers separates Dongneung from the tombs of Oneung, nearly a millennium separates them in time.

Tomb of King Gyeongdeok

Located just west of Nam-san, the tomb of King Gyeongdeok (경덕왕능) is reached by crossing the stream, going under the expressway, and passing through the village to the pine trees on the hillside. Bus no. 501 runs past the entrance at the village, and from there, there is only a half-kilometer walk to the tomb. Gyeongdeok was an able ruler, and during his reign Bulguk-sa was constructed. Solemn and dignified, his tomb (H.S. #23) has a complete set of zodiac figures carved in panels around its perimeter retaining wall, and each figure is dressed in what appears to be military-style clothing. Stone posts encircle the mound grave, as if a railing were left unfinished.

Sangseo-jang 상서장

The eastern side of Nam-san has as many interesting sites as the western slope—or more. If walking, start your tour of the eastern slope at the bridge behind the museum. Walk through the village and along the west side of the South Stream. Immediately after emerging from under the highway bridge, go up the trail to Sangseo-jang [Sangsŏ-jang]. Just above the road is a memorial hall dedicated to Silla historian, scholar, poet, and sometime government official, Choe Chi-won. A steep stairway leads up to this shrine, which is usually kept locked except during official ceremonies. While still a young man, Choe Chi-won studied in Tang China, becoming imbued with Buddhist and Confucian thought. Although highly regarded at the Chinese court, he returned to Korea to try to effect changes in the deteriorating Silla administrative system, moving it away from its basis on birth and relationship and closer to the Chinese model, which is based on ability and merit. To the detriment of the dynasty, his suggestions fell on deaf ears. After some years of frustration at court, he retired to Gaya-san and spent his remaining days far from the capital.

Buddha Valley Buddha 감실석불좌상

About one kilometer from the highway is Buddha Valley; only a small stone marker set along the country lane near a grove of pine trees marks its entrance. A trail leads up this narrow gulch, eventually running up into Nam-san fortress near the remains of several storehouses. About 300 meters up this trail is a seated Buddha figure (T. #198) carved into a depression in a rock. Facing east, it catches the early morning sunlight. Sunk into a deep niche, this 1.5 meter-high image is robed, its head bowed slightly forward in composed meditation. The gown flows in folds over both shoulders and knees, leaving only one foot sticking out. Its long earlobes and *usnisa* set off the round but somewhat disfigured face, yet the peace and quietude of the whole is clearly felt. Still in good shape because of its protective cover, it is said to be the oldest rock carving on Nam-san.

Ongnyong-am Carvings 옥룡암

Less than half a kilometer east along the base of the mountain, and up a secondary road that leads into the thickly wooded Pagoda Valley, you'll find Ongnyong-am. On the road up, this road passes a deer farm, and a trail continues up from the temple into Nam-san fortress. This small but pleasing compound occupies the site of the former temple Shinin-sa. The real point of interest here is a large rock to the rear of the compound that contains the mountain's greatest concentration of bas-relief carvings—over two dozen images—and is the largest of the "four-sided" carvings from the Silla era (T. #201). Carvings cover all sides, although none are exceptional, so many in one place is extraordinary. They include a Buddha triad, other Buddha figures, disciples, a meditating monk, the bodhi

tree, and celestial devas. The most unusual carvings are those of seven- and nine-story pagodas, and those pictured here must represent a form built during the Silla Dynasty, possibly like the great wooden pagoda of Hwangnyong-sa. At one time, some of these images may have been covered by a roof and used as altar figures, as depressions have been chiseled into the rock that accept wooden beams.

Bori-sa 보리사

One kilometer farther around the hill, overlooking the South Stream, is Bori-sa [Pori-sa], a temple of nuns, and the largest functioning temple on the mountain. Unusually, the central figure, the Seokgamoni Buddha, is not a statue but actually the central figure of a gilt-wood panel carving on the wall behind the altar. A host of disciples appear in this panel surrounding the Buddha, and the entire carving is flanked by a pair of three-dimensional bodhisattvas. The combination is intriguing. In the yard is a three-tier pagoda, and to the left of

Buddha figure of Bori-sa

GYEONGJU

© ROBERT NILSEN

the main hall a new bell tower. Above it on the hill is a seated Mireuk Buddha statue (T. #136). An exquisite piece of stone sculpture, this 8th-century image not only exudes composure, but the work is well done. A flame mandala surrounds the body, and a second seated figure, the Buddha of Medicine, is carved in relief on the reverse side. Set to the side of this sculpture is the Three Spirits hall, visited in part by women who come to pray for sons. The roof of this temple's main hall can be seen from the road below, set in pine trees above a bamboo grove. Mushrooms are grown in the pine groves of this village. Look for the short lengths of pine logs leaning against one another in rows between the trees. The mushrooms grow on these teepees of logs.

Unification Hall 통일전

One kilometer farther down the road is Unification Hall, Tongil-jeon: ₩300 entrance. Opened in 1977, the compound was set up to commemorate Silla patriots who gave their lives for the unification of the peninsula, and to foster the same spirit of nationalism that could lead to the peaceful reunification of the peninsula—a goal as timely now as it was in the 660s. Three tortoise-base memorial markers, one for each of the enshrined men, are located on the middle level of this terraced compound north of Namsan Village. These three, King Munmu, King Muyeol, and General Kim Yu-shin, were most responsible for the unification of the peninsula in the 660s.

Minor Kings' Tombs

Between the Hwarang Educational Institute and Unification Hall, and set within the thickly wooded mountain slope, are the tombs of brother kings Heon'gang and Jeonggang (H.S. #187 and #186). They reigned as the 49th and 50th kings of Silla, during the peaceful but sad decline of the dynasty. The mound of King Heon'-

HWARANG

Originating in the mid-6th century, *hwarang* ("Flower Youth") was a military, social, and quasi-religious organization for young men, a type of youthful "knighthood." Predominantly the sons of the Silla elite, these youth were trained by the state and expected to serve the government in return. After marrying, they left the organization, but carried on its ideals and practices, by setting an example for the ordinary citizen, leading noble lives, and fighting for the country if necessary.

The young men were taught martial arts, warfare techniques, and strategy; instructed in social responsibility and grace, moral conduct and ethics; and given a literary education. Religious devotion and music and dance were stressed. They worshipped the Buddha of the Future, and there seems to have been some connection with *shinseon*, mythical Taoist beings of supernatural power. Their training, and consequently their lives, were based on five great precepts from Confucian, Buddhist, Taoist, and nationalist traditions; these were first enumerated by the Buddhist monk Won'gwang: loyalty to the king, filial piety, fidelity to and ami-

cability among friends, valor and non-retreat in battle, and the evil of needless and indiscriminate killing.

The *hwarang* not only served in the forefront of battle, they also acted as a cohesive force in society, fostering a spirit of national unity, a righteous social climate, and loyalty and obedience to the throne. Out of their ranks came numerous military and civilian leaders, highly respected men of the community. Many of the favorite stories and legends of that period have sprung from this organization.

Today there is a resurgence of interest in the *hwarang*. As one of the past glories of Korean civilization, principles still appropriate today are patriotism, loyalty to the country, harmony within society, pride in military ability and strength, and the spirit of national unity with a hope for unification. To that end, the Hwarang Educational Institute, located not far from the Unification Hall on the west slope of Nam-san, has been created as a training center combining some of the ancient ideals of the *hwarang* knighthood with the needs of the present society.

gang's tomb is ringed by four layers of stacked stones, while that of King Jeonggang is rimmed by only three layers. There are no signs pointing to these tombs but paths through the trees lead the way.

Seochulji 서출지

Just south the Unification Hall is Namsan Village, with Seochulji lotus pond, twin pagodas, and the small temple Muryang-sa. Seochulji [Sŏch'ulji] (H.S. #138) is wonderfully serene on an early summer morning when lotus flowers are in bloom and their color, heightened by the morning sun, contrasts with the unpainted pavilion, which partially protrudes over the water. Erected in 1664 but more recently renovated, the pavilion is called Arak-dang. The name Seochulji ("Letter-Issuing Pond") stems from a well-known legend. One day King Soji was out on a picnic with his courtiers near Nam-san. His queen had not come that day as she said that she had suddenly become sick. Buddhism was very new to the country at that time, and the Buddhist priest attached to the palace said that he would call a physician to look after the ailing queen. Later that day while eating lunch, the king was distracted by a noisy group of rats and crows. One of the rats came forward and after bowing to the king requested him to follow the black crow as it flew away. The king sent a soldier after the bird, but the soldier lost sight of the bird as he neared the mountain. Walking on a short way, he came to a pond where he was approached by an old man who gave him a sealed letter, on the outside of which was written the cryptic message, "One will die if left unopened, two will die if opened." When the king was given the envelope, he thought that it was better not to open the letter as only one life would be lost. The court astrologer, however, said that the one life lost referred to the king's and that he ought to open the letter. The king did so and found another message inside that directed him to go to his queen's bedchamber and fire an arrow through the clothes closet. The king returned to the palace and entered his wife's sleeping room. Caught unawares, the queen hurriedly gathered up the clothing that was strewn around the room.

Not responding to her protestations, the king shot an arrow through the door of the closet, which was immediately followed by a cry of pain. When the door was opened, the half-clad priest tumbled out. He and the queen had become lovers and were plotting the death of the king. Both were taken out and strangled as retribution for their adulterous and disloyal ways.

Muryang-sa 무량사

A few steps to the mountainside of Seochulji is the small but charming temple Muryang-sa. This tidy compound is unusual in a number of respects. Unlike many temples, the main hall here is not a large and brightly painted affair, but a plain and unadorned, U-shaped structure that has other rooms attached to both sides of the worship hall. Inside, the low ceiling is of normal room height and the long altar contains not only several statues of the Buddha and bodhisattvas but also murals of *Chilseong* and *Dokseong*. A granite statue of the Buddha is set in its own little courtyard to the side of the main hall, and it is done in imitation of the headless Buddha of Yongjang-saji high on the mountain above—but this one with a head. To the side of the temple's front gate stands a graceful bell pavilion, with a finely wrought bell and metal gong.

Twin Pagodas

Two hundred meters farther into the village are twin granite pagodas (T. #124); distinct features set them apart in time. An imitation of the brick pagoda design, the one closest to the road is simpler and older. Embellished with eight panel carvings of the devas around its base, the west pagoda is from the later United Silla period. Directly behind these pagodas sits the temple Bultap-sa, while a handful of smaller hermitages are scattered throughout the village. Other pairs of pagodas in the Gyeongju area are located at Bulguk-sa, Cheon'gul-li Village, Janghang-ni, Gameun-saji, Sungbok-saji, and Wonwon-sa. The trail up the mountain to Chilbul-am starts in front of the Namsan Village pagodas. Namsan skyway starts at the corner of the parking lot at Tongiljeon—where there is also a sketch map of the mountain, its relics, and trails—and passes to the rear of Seochulji before winding up the mountainside.

Nam-san Hiking Trails and Additional Mountain Sites

Although much has been carted off to the museum, countless stone artifacts remain on Nam-san. Operating temples and hermitages are few, but temple sites are plentiful. The following is a partial list of Nam-san hikes that will bring you to several of the remaining worthy sites. So many other possibilities remain that you could literally spend weeks taking different trails to seek out all that the mountain embraces in its many folds.

No. 1: West side hike. From Oneung, walk south to Na-jeong, Yangsan-jae, Poseok-jeong, the Buddha triad of Bae-ri, and Samneung. The Samneung Valley, from the tombs to Sangseon-am, is full of statuary and carvings (see No. 4 below).

No. 2: East side hike. From the museum, walk first to Sangseo-jang, and then on to Buddha Valley, Ongnyong-sa, Bori-sa, Tongil-jeon, Seochulji, the twin pagodas of Namsan Village, and, if you have time and the desire to climb for an hour, the hermitage Chilbul-am (see No. 7 below).

No. 3: The full-length walk of the skyway, with side trips to Buheung-sa, Sangseon-am, and Yongjang-saji, is a bit more strenuous, and provides not only a close look at the mountainside but a good view out over the valleys on both sides of Nam-san. Along this route are a few rock face carvings a short distance above Poseok-jeong, remains of the Nam-san Fortress wall, the skyway pavilion, and dozens of trailheads that lead into the mountain's many valleys.

No. 4: From Samneung, go up the valley following the stream—the trail starts between the three tombs and Dongneung. About half a kilometer up the trail is a headless, seated Mireuk Buddha, and a short way beyond that and about 10 meters above the trail is a standing figure carved into a rock face. Still farther up are six figures carved in outline on the side of a huge boulder. Two are Buddhas (look for the halos) and four are bodhisattvas. One hundred meters above this group is a lone, bas-relief Buddha image that's also cut into a rock face. You must keep your eyes open for all of these reliefs as you could easily walk by without ever noticing them. A short way up the trail, a relatively well-preserved seated Buddha figure on a pedestal (T. #666) has looked out over the valley for centuries, passively noting the changes. In the past it watched bullock carts raise dust on country lanes, but today it views transport trucks and buses cruising the expressway. From there the trail continues up to Sangseon-am [Sangsŏn-am] (상선암), a tiny hermitage high on the slope above the valley. The Mireuk Buddha above Sangseon-am is worth a look. With its body cut in relief on the rock face and the head in three dimensions above, the image must be about eight meters high. It catches the morning sun as it has done since the Silla Dynasty. From here, the trail continues up to the skyway. Two valleys to the south, Yaksu Valley holds the largest of the relief carved Buddha images in the Gyeongju area—nearly nine meters high. Much like the Sangseon-am Buddha image, this carving, however, is missing its head. It can be reached either by a trail that skirts the prison and runs up into the valley or by a short trail running down from the skyway near Geumo-san.

No. 5: A two-kilometer walk up from Yongjang Village brings you to the site of the former temple Yongjang-sa (용장사지), passing several Buddha figures and other temple sites on the way. Yongjang-sa was founded during the mid-700s by the monk Daehyeon, who, it is said, recited prayers while circling the temple's Mireuk Buddha. This seems to have been a common practice of later Silla Buddhists, and the current practice of *tapdori* (circling a pagoda in prayer) probably stems from this ancient ritual. The noted Joseon Dynasty scholar Kim Shi-seop wrote the novel *Geumo Shinhwa* while staying at the temple. It is considered to be Korea's first novel. Above the main temple site are its major stone remains. Set on a rock promontory is a six-meter-high, three-tier pagoda (T. #186). From here, you have a wonderful view out over the valley. A few meters below this pagoda, a headless Buddha (T. #187) sits on a unique, three-tier pedestal which looks like stacked doughnuts (the inspiration for the Buddha at

Muryang-sa). Behind it is a finely done seated Maitreya Buddha (T. #913), carved in relief on a flat rock face. A 15-minute walk up the hill on a seldom-used path will bring you to the skyway, from where this object can be seen.

No. 6: Farther south and an hour's walk above Cheonnyong Village is the site of the former Cheonnyong-sa [Ch'ŏnyong-sa] (천용사지), "Heavenly Dragon Temple." Follow the road through the village and up the hill to its end at Waryong-sa ("Sleeping Dragon Temple"). From there, the trail continues steadily up the hill for about one kilometer. As you approach this temple site, the ground levels out substantially, as if the mountainside formed a huge terrace. There is a small cluster of houses and the fields are farmed. A new temple has been established here. Lots of stones from the old temple lie strewn around, including a tortoise base for a stela, cistern for the temple, foundation stones, millstone, lantern, and a three-tier pagoda (T. #1188). From here, it's one kilometer over the hill to the north to Gwaneum-sa and the road down to Yongjang Village. To the east and over the ridge is a trail to the hermitage Baegun-am, and another kilometer farther brings you to Chilbul-am.

No. 7: A well-trodden trail (a drivable track the first half of the way) leads the three kilometers from Namsan Village to Chilbul-am [Ch'ilbul-am] (칠불암). This hermitage has a superb location; it looks out over the wide valley toward Bulguk-sa and catches the first rays of morning light. At the hermitage are seven figures (together designated T. #200). On the rock face is a seated Buddha flanked by two standing bodhisattvas. To their front is a large cubed rock with an image chiseled into each side that's much like the excavated rock at Gulbul-saji. All these figures are done with extreme artistic skill, and may be the best relief carvings in the Gyeongju area. Luckily, they have suffered little damage over the centuries. Don't miss them! Directly above these, you'll see a lone relief carving (T. #199), slightly recessed into a niche. From here it's about 200 meters up to the ridge. About three-quarters of the way up to Chilbul-am, in Cheondong Valley are the remains of two stone pillars, only one of which is now standing. Each of these pillars has about 100 small niches carved into its side and into each of these niches was put a Buddha statuette. Some have suggested that each of the 100 niches actually held 10 figurines apiece, giving rise to the name "1,000 Pillars."

Full-day hikes can easily be done by combining several of these shorter hikes. Three possibilities are listed below, with alternatives.

No. 1: From the west side, walk from Oneung to Samneung, and from there up the Samneung Valley to Sangseon-am and the skyway. From the skyway, take either direction down the road.

No. 2: Start by hiking up Samneung Valley to the skyway. At the skyway, go south until the road makes a sharp bend to the east. A narrow, little-used path leads several hundred meters down a ridgetop to the south, to the former temple site of Yongjang-sa. Alternately, come up the Yongjang Valley to this site. Backtrack to the skyway and continue to the east. About half a kilometer along the skyway, a second trail heads off into the trees to the south, along another ridge, and eventually down to a reservoir. Keep a sharp eye out here as this trail is not distinct. Follow it around the side of the pond and veer to the right. After about 200 meters, a side trail leads off to the east, up to the ridge, and down to Chilbul-am, from where you can make your way down to Namsan Village. From this reservoir, another trail goes to the south to the ridge, and then west to Cheonnyong-sa and down to the road that skirts Nam-san.

No. 3: Take the path along the east side of Nam-san from Sangseo-jang to Namsan Village. There walk over the mountain via the skyway to Poseok-jeong, or come down either Samneung Valley or Yongjang Valley.

EASTERN GYEONGJU

Bomun Lake Resort 보문단지

Opened in 1978, Bomun [Pomun] Lake Resort, called Bomun Danji, is about eight kilometers east of downtown Gyeongju. Most of the accommodations and attractions here line its northern shore, with the concentration at its eastern end. At the heart of this area is the convention center, which holds periodic seminars and has a useful tourist information desk. Here as well is a **shopping complex,** with numerous shops and restaurants, and an outdoor stage with a multi-story pagoda as backdrop. From April to November, music, dance, and other cultural performances are staged here free of charge at the **Bomun Outdoor Performance Theater.** During April and November they run 1430–1530; daily in April on fair-weather days except Wednesday and in November on Saturday, Sunday, and holidays only. From May to October, these shows are performed at 2030; on Saturday, Sunday, and holidays only in May and June, and daily except Wednesday for the remainder of the summer. From the nearby pier, rowboats (₩4,000 for 30 minutes) and paddleboats (₩9,000 per half-hour) can be rented, and a swan-shaped excursion boat (₩3,000) departs for a short tour of the lake. Bicycles can be rented from various vendors for ₩3,000 an hour. As this area is still being expanded, additional restaurants, entertainment facilities, accommodations, and tourist sites are either planned or in the works. Although one might not expect a museum at Bomun Lake, the **Sonjae Museum of Contemporary Art** is located on the grounds of the Kyongju Hilton Hotel. Open 1000–1800 (₩2,000 entrance) daily except Monday, this museum features works by contemporary Korean artists, with occasional exhibitions of works by foreign artists. An outdoor sculpture garden holds oversize pieces, which give you a preview of the style of the artwork displayed inside. Aside from the Kyongju Hilton, three other deluxe-class hotels line the lake; other accommodations are mostly located across the road to the east.

Three of Gyeongju's four golf courses—the 36-hole Kyongju Chosun Country Club, the 18-hole Pomun Country Club, and 9-hole Kyongju Country Club—are located to the west, also along the north side of the lake. At the western end of the lake, near the dam, is a new Korean-style restaurant complex, and along the south side of the river on the way back into downtown are more fine restaurants.

On the south side of the stream that feeds this reservoir is **Kyongju World Amusement Park**. Most enjoyable for young children and adolescents, this amusement area has rides, a swimming pool and other athletic activities, flower gardens (and periodic flower shows), snack shops, and restaurants. Entrance fees are ₩3,700 for adults, ₩2,700 for youth, and ₩1,700 for children. Entrance and the Big-5 rides is ₩13,000, ₩11,000, and ₩9,000, respectively; entrance and all activities is ₩19,000, ₩16,000, and ₩12,000 for the same groups. Across the road to the south is the Gyeongju World Culture Expo site.

Above Bomun Lake Resort is Deokdong Lake, a second reservoir, constructed at the same time as Bomun Lake. It's closely confined by the more wooded hillsides of the upper portion of this valley. One section of the Gyeongju National Park borders the eastern side of this lake. Following a country road north from Bomun Lake brings you to the temple site **Mujang-saji** (무장사지). Quite removed from most other sites in the area, this at one time was the repository of a huge temple hall built in memory of King Soseong. Now only a tall three-tiered stone pagoda (T. #126) and a double-headed tortoise base and stela cap (T. #125) remain. Unfortunately, both tortoise heads have been destroyed. The highway from Gyeongju to the East Coast skirts both these reservoirs on its way over the coastal mountains. A few kilometers along this road past the lake and into the major valley to the north are Pyochung-sa (표충사) and Hwangnyong-saji (황룡사지).

Fortress and Pagodas

To the south of Bomun Lake are the remains of **Myeonghwal Fortress** (H.S. #47). Today, only a ribbon of rubble winds its way around the top of this low mountain. If you look closely, you can see parts of the wall from the road and from the north side of the lake. One of the earliest fortifications surrounding the Gyeongju basin, it was probably built at the beginning of the 5th century.

Sprouting from rice fields in double symmetry below Myeonghwal Fortress are the **twin pagodas of Cheon'gul-li** (T. #168). Constructed in the 8th century and restored in 1939, these three-tier constructions mark the long-ago-destroyed Cheon'gun-sa (H.S. #82) temple site and are good examples of typical Silla-style pagodas.

Gyeongju Folk Art Village
경주민속공예촌

A road connects Bomun Lake Resort to Bulguk-sa Village. Near the Bulguk-sa end is the Gyeongju Folk Art Village. Created in 1986, this "planned" village of traditional and semi-traditional houses, showrooms, and a dozen and a half workshops produces ceramic, clay, wood, stone, metal, cloth, and precious stone items in various traditional styles. Walk through the village from shop to shop, watch the craftsmen at work, or peruse the cooperative showroom at the village entrance; open daily 0900–1700. There are excellent and high-quality examples of traditional Korean arts and crafts, but few items are cheap; many are marked in Japanese yen. Perhaps it is best to look here and buy elsewhere. Busy for most of the year, some shops close during the slow winter season. To the rear of the village is the **Silla History and Science Museum.** With an interpretive scale model of the Seokguram Buddha and grotto, it's set up to allow you a close-up view of this masterpiece of art and architecture; ₩2,000 entrance fee. Reproductions of Silla-era scientific works are also on display. After having a look through the shops, refresh yourself at the Korean restaurant and traditional wine shop set to the side and above the parking lot.

One of the ceramic shops at this village is the Silla-yo, set up along traditional lines and run by a man who has been making pottery since he started as an apprentice to his grandfather. Since the recent revival of interest in Korean crafts, he has focused on reproductions of Silla ware. A showroom/retail shop displays his work. While many items appear a bit crude and unsophisticated, others are quite graceful. To the side of the shop is a traditional-style hillside kiln, used every few months to fire the clay.

SOUTHEAST GYEONGJU

To the southeast of downtown Gyeongju is the low hill called Nang-san (H.S. #163), which is roughly 100 meters high. During the 8th century, with an estimated population of one million, Geumseong spread out on all sides of this hill. Today only fields surround Nang-san, and in these fields lie ruins of that ancient city. Running from Nang-san down past Bulguk-sa Station is "tomb alley," a series of royal tombs strung like beads along the neckline of these mid-valley hills. Aside from the tombs, there is a Silla Dynasty kiln site, a modern kiln, and the Gyeongju Beopju rice-wine factory. This winery produces one of Korea's tastiest commercial rice wines, a drink that slides smoothly down the throat but packs a punch.

Nang-san Temple Sites

Below Nang-san are three famous temple sites. Marked by an unadorned stone pagoda (N.T. #37) that sprouts from the edge of rice fields, the first is **Hwangbok-saji** (황복사지). From 692, this typical, United Silla–era pagoda's two-tier base supports three upper levels. Several small relics found inside during its most recent reconstruction include a standing gold Buddha statuette in a bronze reliquary box, glass beads, a bracelet, and gold threads (N.T. #79, 80). Now on display at the Seoul National Museum, the Buddha image is one of only a handful of Silla statues which can be accurately dated. Close by are some stone carvings and a stela tortoise base. At this temple, the famous Silla monk Uisang entered the Buddhist life.

The second site is **Sacheonwang-saji** (사천왕사지), the "Four Heavenly Kings Temple" (H.S. #8). Constructed on orders from King Munmu a year after Silla's unification of the peninsula, it was dedicated to those celestial beings, who protect temple compounds from evil influence. As the devas protect temples, this temple was built as protection for the country against Tang Chinese troops who, after helping Silla overpower both the Baekje and Goryeo kingdoms, targeted the whole peninsula for Chinese domination. Eventually, this problem between Korea and China was worked out diplomatically, without warfare. Flagpole supports and numerous foundation stones for the temple's large buildings dot this former temple site. Two stela tortoise bases hide in the tall grass—the head of one is now preserved at the Gyeongju Museum.

Cross the road onto paths that run along the edge of terraced rice paddies to the third temple site, **Mandeok-saji** (만덕사지), (H.S. #7). Set in a copse of trees, its granite flagpole supports (T. #69) complement those across the road at Sacheonwang-sa. Erected in 685, this set is among the earliest datable. Foundation stones for a wooden pagoda can be seen in the field to the side. These temples are considered three of the most important from the early Silla Dynasty.

East of Nang-san and about 300 meters southwest of the village of Namcheon is the minor temple site of **Bomun-saji** (보문사지). Here, stone rubble lies scattered in the rice fields. Several mounds indicate building sites, while stones from the terrace walls now hold up terraces for the fields. One pair of flagpole supports (T. #910) stands at this site, and of special note are the artistically carved lotus blossoms that appear on the outside of the upper ends. West of there by 200 meters is a second set of flagpole supports (T. #123), but it is not known if they were erected for the same temple. Nearby is a simple and unadorned stone tub (T. #64), from the original Bomun-sa, that was used as the temple's drinking-water cistern.

From Nang-san, walk the tractor trails and terrace walls to get to the Namcheon area. It is perhaps easiest in the autumn after harvest (or during winter), when the remains can be seen across the fields and it's easier to determine which path to follow.

Neungji-tap 능지탑

Just off the highway, at the base of Nang-san, is Neungji-tap [Nŭngji-t'ap], a square raised dais presumed to be the cremation site of King Munmu. Munmu ordered that when he died his body was to be burnt, and the ashes buried in the East Sea. He intended to transform himself into a dragon to protect the country from the Japanese pirates who were constantly pillaging Korean coastal villages during that period.

A few minutes to the north along the lane is the small and unpretentious temple Neungsaeng-sa. Carved into a rough rock face of a boulder to the side of the main hall and covered by a roof are three rather indistinct figures of the Maitreya Buddha and two bodhisattvas (T. #665).

Hilltop Tomb of Queen Seondeok 선덕왕릉

On the south knoll of Nang-san, between Neungji-tap and Sacheonwang-saji, is the tomb of Silla's most beloved queen, Seondeok (H.S. #182). Daughter of King Jinpyeong, the reign fell to her since he had no sons. Queen Seondeok grew to be a judicious ruler, one who understood the political and social makeup of her time. She was a skilled diplomat, maintained a peaceful relationship with the Chinese dragon to the west, and was well respected by her own people. During her reign, much of the best of Tang Chinese civilization and learning was adopted in Korea, and much was done to expand Buddhism on the peninsula. What she did for her people and the propagation of Buddhism in this country is still felt by some, as is evinced by bouquets of flowers that are still occasionally laid at her grave. Queen Seondeok was succeeded by Queen Jindeok, an able but less talented ruler. These were two of only three queens who ruled during the Silla Dynasty.

Tomb of King Jinpyeong 진덕왕릉

Set at the edge of Namcheon Village to the east, and also visible from Nang-san, is the tomb of King Jinpyeong (H.S. #180). Jinpyeong's 53-year reign (579–632) was one of relative peace, and a time when Buddhism was gaining influence among the people. Circled by trees, his grave is a plain round mound with a small altar at its south side.

Confucian Thinkers

On the far side of Namcheon Village is the mounded tomb of the Confucian scholar Seol Chong (설총묘). Son of the Buddhist priest Wonhyo, he was an eminent and original Confucian thinker during Confucianism's early development in Korea. Seol Chong is credited with creating the *Idu* script, a system of writing using Chinese characters to represent the sounds of native Korean words—before that, all written communication and literature was done strictly in classical Chinese. As at King Jinpyeong's tomb, a small altar stands in front of this rather undistinguished small mound.

On the northwest slope of Nang-san is Dok-seo-dang, a shrine to Choe Chi-won, the second of the two most important and influential early Confucian scholars. Surrounded by trees, this shrine occupies the spot that was used by Choe Chi-won as a study hall.

Because Buddhism had such a strong hold on persons of influence and power during much of the Silla Dynasty, the role of Confucianism in the intellectual sphere, and the influence of Confucian ethics in the social life of the Silla people, was relatively weak. Seol Chong and Choe Chi-won left only ripples in the history of their time. Yet those ripples grew in size and strength, and their greatest influence was felt centuries later, when Confucianism gathered momentum and became the socio-ethical doctrine upon which the Joseon Dynasty was founded. These two are the only scholars from the Silla Dynasty honored with a place among the 18 Korean scholars enshrined in Daeseong-jeon, at Seonggyungwan University—the highest seat of formal Confucianism in the country.

Tomb of King Shinmun 신문왕릉

The first tomb of importance south of Nang-san is that of King Shinmun, 31st king of Silla. This fenced, wooded compound (H.S. #181) is well-groomed and peaceful. Ringed by tall pines, it's stately yet simple, and, until some of the trees were felled, was one of the most pleasing tombs in Gyeongju. Bold but not over-ornamented, it seems to be an intermediate step in tomb development between the simple mounds and the more elaborate retaining-wall constructions.

The tomb of King Hyogong (H.S. #183) is located beyond the railroad tracks and across the fields to the northeast. It's a small, naturally mounded tomb set on the south side of a pine-covered knoll.

Four Other Tombs

Farther along this "alley," the tomb of King Shinmu (H.S. #185) is set peacefully in the trees to the side of a small village. From this tomb, you get a good view out over the valley toward the Hwarang Educational Institute and the east side of Nam-san.

KILNS

Near the tomb of King Shinmu is the site of an old ceramic kiln (H.S. #263). Discovered in 1979, this site was used during the Goryeo and Joseon dynasties to make roof tiles. The modern kiln Jinyong Togi is located in the nearby village. Another modern kiln, the Yeongji-yo, is located farther south and across the road from the Yeongji Reservoir. Items produced here are superbly done in both Silla and modern styles, and are shipped all over the country. With the growing awareness of traditional arts and the growing affluence of the Korean populace (and foreign visitors), a great number of kilns have been set up in the country to cater to the increasing numbers of people interested in buying traditional Korean pottery. Gyeongju has its share of these kilns, many of which reproduce Silla-era pottery while some produce modern pieces based on traditional designs and motifs. Aside from the Yeongji-yo, others include the Silla-yo, at the Gyeongju Folk Art Village, and those at Gameun-saji, Girim-sa, and at Cheon-gul-li, below Danseok-san.

Set close together, just across the tracks from the Naedong Elementary School, are the tombs of King Hyoso (H.S. #184) and King Seongdeok (H.S. #28), both sons of King Shinmun. Hyoso was the elder and first to rule. Although peaceful, his reign was rather unexciting and of little particular merit, and so is the tomb. Behind it is the much larger and more stately tomb of his brother, King Seongdeok. Between its stone wall and fence, three-dimensional zodiac figures circle the tomb. All are quite badly defaced except the monkey, which is now preserved at the Gyeongju Museum. Out front in the field is a large, somewhat worn tortoise base for a now-absent memorial stela, which was once probably part of a temple compound.

The last of these four tombs is most unusual. Referred to as the **Square Tomb** (H.S. #27), it's located at the Bulguk-sa Station traffic rotary. This low mounded tomb is a bit over seven meters on a side. The horizontal granite slabs of the tomb's retaining walls are spaced by panels of zodiac figures; a shallow chamber opening is located in the front wall. The stone slab inside was undoubtedly the base on which the coffin was laid. Some have suggested that it's the tomb of Kim Dae-seong, the filial son said to have rebuilt Bulguk-sa and constructed Seokguram in memory of his parents. In the middle of this rotary intersection stands a three-tiered stone pagoda that was moved from another location when the Japanese were doing historical excavations during their occupation of the peninsula. In the village below the Kolon Hotel near Bulguk-sa is another three-story pagoda of near identical style. Set in amongst houses, it occupies the Ungsu-sa (Honored Bear Temple), which legend says was constructed by Kim Dae-seong in response to a dream about a bear that he had killed that day while hunting on Toham-san.

Yeong-saji Buddha 영사지미륵불상

To the left side of the road that skirts Yeongji ("Reflecting Pond") Reservoir, is a large but badly defaced Buddha figure that marks the site of a former temple. Backed by a halo, this statue sits in solitary witness to the skill of a master craftsman of ages past. Legend tells that this figure was carved by a man named Asadal, who was commissioned to construct both pagodas at Bulguk-sa on the mountain above. He was a man from the conquered Baekje region of the peninsula who had left his new wife to work on the temple project. One night he dreamt that his wife was standing next to a pond waiting forlornly for him to complete his work and return to her. Unbeknownst to him, his wife had made the trip from their home but had been refused entry into the temple grounds while work was still in progress. She was told to go to the pond and there she would see the reflection of her husband and the one pagoda that he had finished. She went, but saw only the reflection of the pagoda. Afraid her husband was dead and that he would never again come to her, she called his name and threw herself into the pond. Hearing his wife call from afar, Asadal descended the mountain but was too late to find his wife alive. After some weeks of mourning near the pond, he thought that he caught a glimpse of her in the grove of trees on the far side of the water. Running there, all he found was a stone in the shape of a human form. As he stood there disappointed, the stone slowly changed its shape into that of a merciful Buddha. Asadal then put his stonecarving skills to work and refined the image, dedicating it to his loyal and loving wife. After completing this statue, he departed the pond and no one knows what became of him. A temple was then constructed at this site, but only the Mireuk Buddha figure remains today. Since that time, Dabo-tap of Bulguk-sa, that which was completed by Asadal, has been known as the "Reflected Pagoda" (or "Shadow Pagoda") while Seokga-tap has been called the "Non-reflected Pagoda" (or "Pagoda of No Shadow).

Gwaeneung 괘능

Past the Bulguk-sa Station and Gyeongju Beopju wine factory is Gwaeneung [Kwaenŭng], last tomb along the "alley." Located half a kilometer east of the highway, this tomb (H.S. #26) is set in a grove of pines at the foot of a low knoll; ₩300 entrance. Gwaeneung is said to be the tomb of King Wonseong (reigned 785–798), 38th king of Silla. The epitome of Silla tomb construction, it's well ornamented and contains all the requisites of a royal tomb. A stop here is recommended. All 12 zodiac figures are in their proper places, and represent some of the best in the city. To the front of the mound are placed a table for the *jesa* ceremony, stone pillars, and a lantern. On the level below the mound are parallel rows of sculpted military and civilian guards, and a pair of *haetae,* mythical animals who guard against evil and extinguish fire. Usually done with fearsome faces, these lion look-alikes have more friendly, "folksy" grins. The military guards portray foreign officials (possibly from Central Asia or the Middle East) who supposedly once served the Silla court; formal and stiff, the civilian statues are Asian in facial feature and dress. Gwaeneung means "suspended tomb." It is popularly held that at one time a small reflecting pool in front of the tomb made it appear as if it was floating, or suspended in the air over the water. Although it cannot be compared to the most grandiose Joseon Dynasty tombs around Seoul,

Gwaeneung

Gwaeneung is the most mature and evolved of the royal Silla tombs. City buses numbered in the 600s run by Gwaeneung and all the other royal tombs mentioned above.

Sungbok-saji 숭복사지

About 1.5 kilometers south of Gwaeneung and two kilometers up on the hillside to the east is the site of the former temple Sungbok-sa. The point of interest here is a pair of stone pagodas, one of only a few such pairs in the region. Somewhat disfigured and missing a few pieces, the deva relief carving around the base level shows skill and delicacy. An unbroken two-headed tortoise stela base, now located at the Gyeongju museum, was originally part of this temple.

BULGUK-SA 불국사

Rising directly east of Gyeongju is Toham-san (745 meters), the highest mountain in the vicinity, part of the coastal range. Today, two of Korea's greatest artistic testaments to Buddhism are found on the mountainside: Bulguk-sa, one of the most frequented and perhaps the best known

temple in Korea, and the Seokguram grotto hermitage. See www.bulguksa.or.kr.

History and Legend

About 1,450 years ago, King Beopheung, the first king of Silla to adopt Buddhism as a state religion, had a temple built on the side of Toham-san. Two hundred years later, in 751, its name was changed to Bulguk-sa [Pulguk-sa] ("Buddhist Country Temple"), and it was rebuilt by King Gyeongdeok's farsighted chief minister, Kim Dae-seong. During the disastrous Imjin War (1592–98), most of its buildings were burned down, and the Korean War wrought greater damage. In 1972, after three years of patient work, the last of nearly two dozen intervening restorations was completed. At its zenith, Bulguk-sa had 80 wooden buildings—10 times as many as today. It blends harmoniously into the surrounding hillside, and represents the pinnacle of Silla Dynasty architecture. After its renovation, Bulguk-sa and its environs were designated Historic and Scenic Site #1. On the premises are seven National Treasures (with one more at Seokguram) and one Treasure. A med-

M

itation center and monk's college have been established here.

Bulguk-sa sometimes generates a zoo-like atmosphere. During the fine-weather days of spring and autumn, hordes of people come to view this masterpiece and have their pictures taken in front. But don't miss it even during those times of the year! Go in the early morning, before the crowds congregate or in late afternoon, after they've left. The temple is open daily 0700–1800 April to September, and 0700–1700 October to March; ₩3,000 entrance. No photography is allowed inside the temple halls.

Temple Stairways

The temple compound has two entrances, both reached by walkways from either end of the parking lot. To the side of both ticket booths is a map of the temple grounds and surrounding mountainside. Inside the main entrance is a lotus pond. Two stairways lead to the temple's inner courtyards. On the right are Cheongun-gyo ("Blue Cloud Bridge") and Baegun-gyo ("White Cloud Bridge") (N.T. #23), the two sections of the stairway that lead up to Jaha-mun ("Mauve Mist Gate"). On the left are Yeonhwa-gyo ("Lotus Bridge") and Chilbo-gyo ("Seven Treasures Bridge"). This stairway (N.T. #22) rises to An'-gang-mun. Bold and symmetric, the flowing lines of these double-tiered stairways pull your eyes up to the front gates. Symbolically, these "bridges" lead the devotee up and out of the secular world and into the spiritual realm of Buddha. At the end of the temple's reconstruction in 1973, use of these stairways was prohibited to protect them from overuse. Today you must enter the compound via either of two side entrances.

Apart from a few recent additions, the stonework here is from the Silla period. All pieces have been put together without mortar; its endurance is a testament to the skill of the Silla craftsmen.

Temple Pagodas

In the temple's main courtyard sit its two famous pagodas, Dabo-tap [Tabo-t'ap] ("Pagoda of Many Treasures") and Seokga-tap [Sŏkka-t'ap] ("Pagoda of Seokgamoni"), considered the finest

from the United Silla period. Both constructed of granite, they represent opposites: physical/spiritual, active/passive, male/female, *eum/yang* (yin/yang). Dabo-tap (N.T. #20), the feminine aspect, is the more elaborate. Some say that the square pillars represent man in his coarse state, the flat midsection represents the four truths of Buddhism, the octagonal level represents the eightfold path to enlightenment, and the circular lotus top represents perfection. A short stairway leads up each side, and a small stone lion set on a stylized lotus base guards the pagoda from evil influence. Even with its mass, because of its open nature, it seems light; although complex, it never loses its unity of design. It has a grand overall appearance, and is one of the most unusually shaped pagodas in the country.

In complete antithesis to Dabo-tap is the three-tiered Seokga-tap (N.T. #21). Seokga-tap is the male counterpart—severe, austere, and stark in comparison. Its straight lines are well-balanced and proportioned, and this is complemented by the exquisitely carved, multi-level, circular finial top. This is typical of United Silla period pagodas found all over the peninsula as remains of that great building period. During its reconstruction, in 1966, a reliquary box was found inside containing many valuable items (jointly designated N.T. #126). A woodblock print of the Buddhist *Dharani Sutra* was also found here. Done on mulberry paper, this print, which must predate completion of the pagoda in 751, is claimed to be the oldest woodblock imprint of text in the world. It's displayed in the National Museum in Seoul, while the remaining items are in the Gyeongju National Museum.

Temple Buildings

At the front corners of Bulguk-sa's main courtyard are two pavilions. Cheong-nu contains a skin drum, while in Gyeong-nu hang a wooden fish gong and a flat bronze gong. Part of Cheong-nu sticks out over the front of the stone retaining wall and has a unique support pillar system. Daeung-jeon, the temple's main hall, is from the late 1770s. Dragons and boars inhabit the beams inside this hall, and the faded paint speaks its age. To its rear is Museol-jeon ("Hall of Silence"), largest at this temple. Up the steep steps to its rear, and located in a separate enclosure, is Gwaneum-jeon. On its altar stands a slender, gilt statue of the Goddess of Mercy, behind which is a painting of her with 1,000 hands stretched out to offer assistance to those who pray to her for aid. To the right of Gwaneum-jeon is a second enclosure, which houses Biro-jeon, with its statue of the Vairocana Buddha (N.T. #26). A *sari budo* (T. #61) stands to the side under overhanging trees. To the left of the main hall is Geungnak-jeon, in which sits the Amita Buddha (N.T. #27). The Vairocana and Amita Buddha statues, both cast during the United Silla period and recently regilt, are considered the best examples of ancient metal statuary. To the side of this compound is the bell pavilion and a small shop selling calligraphy, books, tapes, Buddhist paraphernalia, and other religious items.

SEOKGURAM 석굴암

High above Bulguk-sa, on the eastern slope of Toham-san, is the man-made grotto Seokguram [Sŏkkuram], or "Stone Cave Hermitage." Constructed at the same time as Bulguk-sa, Seokguram (N.T. #24) is an attempt to represent physically the highest spiritual aspirations. Set below the peak of the mountain, this grotto catches the first light of the morning sun as it rises out of the sea. Facing Japan, it is said to have been constructed as a symbolic protector of the realm, like Sacheonwang-sa and the underwater tomb of King Munmu. Seokguram is the crowning achievement of Silla religio-artistic work. Made to appear as part of the natural hillside, it was modeled after the cave temples of India and China. Built in a "keyhole" design—antechamber out front, a domed, circular inner chamber to the rear, and a short, narrower passageway between—Seokguram is impressive not for its size but for its subtle artistic quality and harmonious unity. It's a religious work of art unsurpassed by any other in Korea. This is all the more inspiring since, until a few years ago, the only way up to the grotto was via narrow and winding mountain paths. Its white granite was brought from a long distance.

Entrance to Seokguram is ₩3,000; the gate opens at 0630. A shuttle bus (₩2,000 one way, ₩4,000 round-trip) runs the eight kilometers approximately every hour 0840–1720 (1620 in winter) between the Bulguk-sa parking lot and the grotto parking lot. Board near the information booth. A three-kilometer trail also goes up to the grotto. This trail starts to the side of the ticket booth at the temple's front entrance and runs up to the bell pavilion at the upper parking lot; count on about one hour for this climb. A favorite activity of visitors is to climb the mountain to see the sun rise. If you have fair weather, you will undoubtedly not be the only one trudging up this trail in the dark early morning. Perhaps the best time of the year for sparkling clear mornings is in November.

Grotto Sculptures

The rectangular antechamber has 10 panels of carved figures. On the eight bas-relief side panels are the *palbujeong* (the Parivara, or guardian saints). Facing the front are two *inwang* (the Vajrapani, or guards), with clenched fists and grimaces on their faces. Fearsome and muscular, they are ready to stop any evil influence from entering. Facing each other in the passageway stand the four *sacheonwang*, each a king of one of the four directions of heaven, who keep the inner sanctum free of evil, safe from degenerate influence, and at peace.

Panels of finely carved relief figures circle the inner chamber. First are four bodhisattvas, two on each side. Unusually feminine and gracefully draped, they all carry some religious object in their hands. Next are the 10 Arhats, shaven-headed ascetics and disciples of the Historical Buddha. Each appears to have Aryan features, an almost certain indication of contact between Korea and the Indo-Persian area at that time. (Buddhism spread from southern Asia to China and then on to Korea, and along that path came the successive development of cave temples.) Last is the captivating figure of Gwanseeum Bosal, Goddess of Mercy, the favorite bodhisattva in Korea, the solid rock to which those awash in troubles can turn for aid and comfort. Uncharacteristically, her Asian face appears somewhat stern. Her position is directly behind the central statue, unseen from the grotto's entrance. In 10 arched niches high on the wall above these panel carvings are smaller carved figures, the exact identities of which are still unknown.

The focus of the grotto is the inner chamber's central figure. Sitting on a lotus pedestal, this 3.5 meter-high Buddha image is loosely draped. Its face is intent yet meditative, and its hands are in the mudra of "calling the earth to witness." It's a classical pose. The light-colored granite seems to radiate any light entering the grotto. Representing an elevated spiritual state, it is beyond doubt the finest stonecarving in Korea, and arguably one of the best in all of Asia.

This round room was constructed so that visitors would be able to circumambulate the central

figure. A similar practice is continued today (also in Tibet, Nepal, and Burma), as believers walk around pagodas praying or reciting chants. There is some question as to which Buddha is represented here. Some experts feel that it's the Seokgamoni Buddha, while others think that the figure is that of the Amita Buddha, the Buddha of the Western Paradise. Unfortunately, the front of the grotto has been closed off by a glass wall to protect the stone images from abuse and damage. While understandable, it still seems a pity that visitors are not able to enter the chamber to view at close hand these works of art, and to get a feel for their mastery and mystery. (Although not quite the same, a replica of Seokguram has been built at the Gyeongju Folk Art Village that can be examined up close.)

Gyeongju Vicinity

Like the city, the surrounding region provides ample evidence of the greatness of the Silla Kingdom. The area has also been the fertile ground from which communities and influential people from other dynasties have sprung.

WEST OF GYEONGJU
Geumcheok Mounds 금척고분군
A legend tells of a time when a man from this area possessed a golden rod that, when touched to a dead man, would bring him back to life. News of this miraculous wand spread far and wide and eventually the rod became overused. It was finally decided that nature would be allowed to take its course in determining the length of a man's life, so the rod was buried. However, to ensure the secret of its location, and to confuse those who might wish to unearth this magic stick, not one but dozens of mounds were raised. Although some have tried, the task proved too overwhelming and no one has discovered its whereabouts. These mounds (H.S. #43), known as Geumcheok [Kŭmch'ŏk] ("Gold Rod"), lie at the northern base of Danseok-san, not far from Geoncheon [Kŏnch'ŏn]. The highway from

Gyeongju to Daegu cuts through them, open fields surround them on the southern side of the highway, and an apple orchard has been planted around them on the northern side. About three dozen mounds remains.

Danseok-san 단석산
The highest point between Gyeongju and Daegu and the westernmost section of Gyeongju National Park is Danseok-san (827 meters), best known for the historic remains found in its thickly wooded valleys. Many temple sites, statues, and other stone objects have been found here (one as recently as 1984), but the mountain's historical association with the *hwarang* is of greater interest to the general populace. The youth of this group had military training on the top of Danseok-san; archery, swordsmanship, horse riding, military strategy, and war ethics were taught. This mountain fastness has remained quite undeveloped and inaccessible, and except for the trail up its west side, past Shinseon-sa to the top, few well-traveled paths exist.

Ujunggol Pottery Studio
From Gyeongju, take the bus to Ujunggol (우중골)

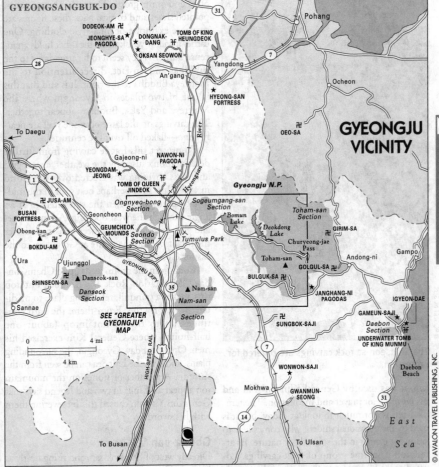

© AVALON TRAVEL PUBLISHING, INC.

(₩1,200); this bus carries on to Sannae. At the village directly below the bus stop is a small, family-run kiln, Haegyeom Toyae. For five generations, this family has been perfecting traditional Silla-style pottery. On the property is a rustic storeroom/showroom; next door is the workshop. The two kilns to the rear are fired two or three times a year with hardwood logs from the nearby mountainside. The smooth, sloped tunnel kiln is of Korean style, while the stepped kiln is Japanese-inspired. The proprietor speaks some English. The pottery is skill-fully thrown; much is done on commission, but some pieces are sold to those who make the journey to the workshop. At the lower end of the village is a handmade-paper factory, and below that a reservoir.

Shinseon-sa 신선사

From the upper end of Ujunggol, follow the drivable track about two kilometers up into the valley. A trail carries you the remainder of the way to the temple Shinseon-sa [Shinsŏn-sa]. Count on an hour's walk. Established about 1,300 years

The Shinseon-sa rock carvings are covered for protection.

ago, it was used by General Kim Yu-shin and his *hwarang* for prayer and meditation. The temple itself is not much to look at today, but it is used by the occasional student who comes here to study for exams in the solitude of nature. Its attraction is its fine group of rock carvings. Located some 50 meters to the right of the temple hall, these carvings (N.T. #199) line the inside walls of a split rock opening once used as a temple grotto. If it indeed was used during the time of Kim Yu-shin and his *hwarang*, at about the time of the unification of the peninsula (660s), it may be the oldest temple grotto in Korea. Three imposing Buddha figures are carved in bas-relief on three wall surfaces of this grotto, and a group of figures appears high on another inner wall, but the two most unusual figures are found low on the wall below the group, toward the open end of the grotto. Dressed in baggy pants, pointed shoes, and conical hats, these figures are two rare examples of Silla-style clothing. One carries a willow whisk while the other holds an incense burner. They seem to be attendants to the Buddhas and, in fact, direct attention to the Maitreya Buddha to the right. It is said that this is one of two places in Gyeongju where the Maitreya and Yaksa Buddhas appear together. The carvings on the large opposite wall are nearly gone—flaked off over the centuries.

To protect this fragile carving from further deterioration caused by the weather, a steel grid and glass covering was erected over the grotto in 1994. It is now perhaps best seen in the mid- to late afternoon, when the sun filters in at an angle through the west opening. A similar steel and glass covering has also been constructed over the rock face Buddha figure at Golgul-sa, to the east of Gyeongju.

A trail from the grotto leads up to Chamseon-dae ("Meditation Rock"), a flat rock outcrop that makes a tranquil, refreshing place to meditate, read, or write. From there, the path continues up to the mountaintop (about one half-hour), where General Kim exercised his men. On a clear day, Gyeongju, the surrounding plains, and even the East Sea can be seen from the summit. A number of stones on the mountain top appear as if split in two and legend says that Gen. Kim Yu-shin caused this by severing them with his sword.

Obong-san 오봉산

Directly west of Danseok-san, and rising nearly as high, is Obong-san ("Five Peak Mountain"). Obong-san was also used by the *hwarang*, as a training ground and a recreation area. Several temples cling to its wooded slopes. Twisting along the mountain's circular ridge are the serpentine remains of the wall of the old fortress (H.S. #25), called Busan Sanseong ("Wealthy Mountain Fortress"). The principal defense for the corridor running into Gyeongju from the west, it is said to have been constructed in 663. Fortress gates and storehouses can also be seen among the rubble. During the Silla Dynasty, its plateau was used for military exercises and farming; today it continues as a farming area for cold-weather vegetables.

Bokdu-am 복두암

About 2.5 kilometers up from Geoncheon is Songseon Village—₩1,000 by bus from Gyeongju. Follow the road on the left side of the stream past the far end of the village to the small temple Seongam-sa. To the side of this temple starts the trail, which zigzags steeply up the hillside. A 45-minute walk following the white arrows painted on trailside rocks leads to the hermitage Bokdu-am [Pokdu-am]. This trail passes a flat rock outcrop, a perfect place for a rest or a picnic. Enjoy fine views of the inner valley as well as a distant view of Gyeongju from here.

This hermitage has a feature found nowhere else in Korea. Nineteen niches have been scooped out of the rock wall beside where the tiny main hall stood; each holds a single stone figure. The central figure of the historical Buddha is flanked by the bodhisattvas Munsu and Bohyeon. On both sides are the 16 Arhat. While the carved figures themselves are not of great age, the niches look old and weathered. Directly above the three central figures are elongated, natural black streaks. Looking at the streaks, you can visualize figures—images of the Buddha and bodhisattvas—and imagine that Mother Nature herself has painted these indelible portraits. In 1989, the Bokdu-am worship hall was destroyed by fire. Now all that remains is an equally tiny Mountain Spirit hall. A few meters away stands a statue of Gwanseeum Bosal, mercifully looking toward the city of Gyeongju. Erected in 1980, she was lifted into place by helicopter. To the rear of this statue starts a trail that leads up along the ridge that circles this valley. At its start, this trail is well trodden; a short distance from the hermitage it passes one section of the old fortress wall. Soon, however, the trail peters out, when it reaches the high fields. Crossing the fields, you can continue down the rough road that circles around to the tiny community at the upper end of the valley below Jusa-am.

Jusa-am 주사암

On the far side of the old fortress is Jusa-am [Chusa-am], the mountain's oldest hermitage. Walk the trail from Bokdu-am or follow the valley road up into the mountain interior. Halfway up and 200 meters off the road is **Man'gyo-sa** (만교사), the valley's third hermitage. One trail to Jusa-am starts a few hundred meters up the road from the turnoff for Man'gyo-am. The main road continues up to a community at the relatively flat upper end of the valley. From the abandoned schoolhouse here, another trail leads up to the beautifully situated, 1,300-year-old Jusa-am, which sits above a section of the fortress wall amongst huge boulders. Founded by Uisang, this peaceful spot has been the home of several famous monks over the centuries. Small and compact, the main hall here is accompanied by the Three Spirits Hall.

Seventy-five meters west of Jusa-am is a flat-topped, sheer-faced cliff. It's said that General Kim Yu-shin brought his men here for banquets, parties, and other recreation. The circular depressions on this flat rock surface are said to be impressions of horses' hoofprints. Aside from the valley trails, one trail leads from Jusa-am to the west down the mountain and back to the highway. A second trail follows the ridge a short distance east, veers off to the north and heads straight down the mountain through Woman Valley to the highway.

Woman Valley

The best-known valley on the north side of Obong-san is so named because its shape resembles a female body reclining against the mountainside. A natural spring flows from the "crotch" and runs into the reservoir below. Pointing at Woman Valley from across the expressway is a spur ridge in the shape of the male form. As you can imagine, there are many tales about this spot. The most often told refers to the wisdom of Queen Seondeok. One day in winter, it was reported to her that white frogs had been heard croaking at the Jade Gate pond. In response, she told her trusted generals to go to Woman Valley and capture the enemy troops hiding there. They did as they were told, and to their astonishment, they found the troops at the spring; the enemy was easily captured and the planned invasion foiled. The queen explained: Croaking frogs on the winter solstice means an enemy disturbance. The color white refers to the direction west. Jade Gate is a poetic figure of speech for female genitalia. So, as there is a valley to the west with a woman's form, it can be assumed that there would be enemy troops hiding at the valley's crotch. Furthermore, the queen added with a gleam in her eye, everyone knows that no matter how strong and virile, after man enters the Jade Gate he will surely weaken and perish.

Ura Village

West of Obong-san, reachable by a long hike from there, or by a 20-kilometer road from the town of Sannae, is the village of Ura. Set at about 950 meters on the mountainside, Ura is a small Christian communitarian community founded in the early 1960s. Young to middle-aged, most of the nearly 100 inhabitants are women. They farm and garden, and do most chores together. They also eat together. This in itself is rather unusual, but the most unusual thing is that they eat only uncooked foods: grains, vegetables, roots, herbs, nuts, and the like. While not generally well-known, they are a strong and healthy group, and others have sought them out to cure certain diseases and bodily ailments. About half a dozen other such communities are scattered throughout the country. Although infrequent, bus nos. 304 and 351 run to Ura.

NORTH OF GYEONGJU

Yangdong 양동

Halfway between Gyeongju and Pohang is the traditional, Joseon Dynasty *yangban* village of Yangdong. Because it has no connection to the ancient Silla culture, visiting this village is like taking a step forward from the 8th to the 18th century. Since the 1400s, Yangdong has primarily been populated by members of the Son, Oh, Jang, and Yu families. Today, most of the villagers work the fields as farmers. Yangdong's strong Confucian tradition is evident in its architecture

and in the writings of its most famous native son, the Confucian scholar Yi On-jeok. Because of the wealth and importance of its material remains, this village, like Hahoe in Andong and Seongeup on Jeju-do, has been designated a Folklore Material Preservation Zone. It's so important, in fact, that over the past several decades the government has put several billion *won* into renovating its buildings, sprucing up the environment, and providing for better infrastructure. Through their bearing and speech, the inhabitants show strong kinship with their noble past and pride in the status and achievements of their ancestors.

Yangdong is one of the few traditional villages in Korea preserved well enough (at least in part) to be used as a historical movie set. If you're lucky enough to catch a film crew in action, you'll see actors in traditional dress and several buildings come alive with old-style interior decoration. This exciting experience evokes a slice of Korean history and prompts easier understanding of some Joseon Dynasty customs.

Village Buildings: A 30-minute bus ride from Gyeongju brings you to the entrance road leading into Yangdong, about two kilometers east of An'gang. Walk the kilometer up along the railroad line, under the tracks, and a bit farther to reach the village. On a signboard in the village is a pictorial representation of the village and the location of its important buildings. Set in the folds of a forested hill, Yangdong fronts on a meandering river and broad fields. In this lovely setting are roughly 150 buildings of historical importance and cultural value, some tiled and some thatched, including three buildings (the oldest about 450 years old) preserved as Treasures.

Occupying a prominent position on the hillside is **Gwangga-jeong** (T. #442), a wonderful example of a traditional square house. The combination of closed rooms, open porches, movable walls, storerooms, kitchen, and courtyard makes for a pleasing and utilitarian use of space. Stepping into its courtyard, you can imagine the daily activity of the house. Scurrying kitchen maids prepare food for the family, a muffled chatter and the thud of wood on cloth come from an inner room as women press clothes, and the smell of tobacco faintly filters from the study of the man of the house. Rice chests, clothes closets, calligraphy scrolls, embroidered cushions, books, ink brushes, stringed instruments, pottery, and foodstuffs recall the daily life of the landed gentry. A family shrine occupies a prominent position to the rear of this walled enclosure.

Around the hill to the east is the manor house, called **Hyang-dang** (T. #412), built by Yi On-jeok when he became governor of this province in the early 1500s. Large rooms in the front were for the head of the family, while smaller rooms were made in the back for others. The rooms are connected by covered walkways and porches—notice the angled design on the wooden railing. Over the hill from Hyang-dang sits the U-shaped Mucheom-dang (T. #411), an annex to the main house and the boyhood home of Yi On-jeok. Much smaller than the other two, it also has a pleasing combination of closed rooms and open porches. Next door is an example of a smaller home. This square house has men's, women's, and servant's quarters, with a shed making up the fourth side.

Across from Hyang-dang is **Shimsu-jeong**, the largest pavilion in the village. From 1560, this structure is of excellent design and craftsmanship. Having a good view over much of the lower village, it undoubtedly was prized as a perfect place to spend a lazy summer afternoon. To the rear of the village and up on the hillside is Sobaek-dang, the ancestral home of the Wolseong Son family.

Each small vale in this village has many intriguing houses to view. Whether a large tile-roof manor or a humble thatched home, all come together into an organic whole. Yet, modernization has not passed the village by. Power lines are strung along the lanes; television antennae protrude from rooftops; the steeple of a Christian church towers over the community; brightly colored, slate-roofed cement houses of the modern "box" style have been built here and there; trucks transport mechanized farming equipment and supplies, and passenger vehicles are used to get to and from market. Yangdong is a surprisingly large settlement and each little fold in the hills offers something new and exciting. Spend a good part of the day. Wander through the back lanes to see the other traditional-style houses, pavilions, shrines, and writing schools. While not wholly traditional, Yangdong is still worth a look. No matter what you might experience, typical country life still goes on here, and the importance of land, family, tradition, and ritual is still evident. Remember that while this is a cultural attraction for Korean and foreigner alike, it is *home* for the villagers. By all means, examine these elegant wooden structures, but respect the rights and privacy of the people who live here.

Oksan Seowon 옥산서원

Several kilometers west of An'gang is Oksan Seowon [Oksan Sŏwon], a private academy dedicated to the Confucian scholar and statesman Yi On-jeok. Built in 1572, it's one of the oldest, largest, and most important academies in the country. For hundreds of years, noble-class boys left their homes to come here and study. These buildings (H.S. #154) have been aesthetically reconstructed after long years of deterioration, war, and fire, but have not been changed beyond recognition. The three-door main gate—you must enter by a side gate—opens onto the front courtyard. Behind this are the lecture hall, dormitories, tablet house, a library storing wood printing blocks and over 4,000 books, the main shrine, and several other buildings and courtyards. Two written records of importance are kept here, a copy of the *History of the Three Kingdoms* (T. #525), one of the oldest early histories in the country, and a list of successful civil service examinees (T. #524). One piece of calligraphy (T. #526), attributed to the Silla Dynasty master Kim Saeng, is also preserved here. If, during the day, the inner courtyards are not open, ask the caretaker to unlock the gates.

While not totally an original thinker, Yi On-jeok was known for his bright mind and sharp analysis of traditional Confucian doctrine. Considered one of the wisest of pre-modern Korean scholars, his writing exerted tremendous influence on the learning of his time. Confucianism philosophically described the dualism of nature and reality: *I* is the form of existence, and *Gi* is the energizing element of that form. Yi argued the primacy of *I* over *Gi*, which led to a split in the intellectual circles of the time, causing the formation of the two major divisions of Korean Neo-Confucianism, later involving the two greatest Korean Confucian scholars, Yi Hwang (Yi Toe-gye) and Yi Yi (Yi Yul-gok).

After retiring from government office, Yi Onjeok (1491–1553) came back to Yangdong to write and teach. Rather than taking up residence in the family home in the village, he decided to live nearby in this tranquil valley. From the academy, walk across the log bridge and five minutes up through the fields or up along the road to the house Yi On-jeok built for himself in 1516. Set above the placid stream, **Dongnak-dang** (독락당) (T. #413) sits within a tightly walled compound, a maze of courtyards, gates, living quarters, and pavilions. A Chinese honey locust (N.M. #115) spreads its branches over the compound. As this compound is occupied by members of the Yi family, it may not be open to view.

City bus no. 203 runs from Gyeongju to Oksan Seowon and Dongnak-dang; check the return bus schedule when you arrive. At the cluster of houses near the *seowon* you can find a motel, *minbak*, and a small restaurant.

Jeonghye-sa Pagoda and Dodeok-am

Just off the road about 200 meters beyond Dongnak-dang is a pagoda (N.T. #40) that marks the site of the 9th century Silla Dynasty temple Jeonghye-sa. Differing dramatically from other Korean stone pagodas, this unique, 13-tier structure has shallow alcoves for Buddha images, one to a side, separated by four square pillars that make the base corners of this structure. Above this base lies a wide stone cap with gracefully upturned corners. Set on top are 12 thinner, equally spaced, and gradually tapering tiers. This bottom-heavy pagoda has an odd but pleasing shape; the base gives a feeling of strength, the narrowing upper section a feeling of elegance and purposeful flow toward the heavens.

From here, a one-hour walk will bring you to the hermitage Dodeok-am [Todŏk-am] (도덕암). About one kilometer above the pagoda, a track to the left heads into a side valley and up the hillside

to this tiny compound. Small in stature, Dodeok-am is big in scenery. A walk from Oksan Seowon to the hermitage and back makes for a pleasant journey.

Tomb of King Heungdeok 흥덕왕능

About four kilometers north of An'gang is the tomb of King Heungdeok (and his wife), one of the few that can be positively identified. Nestled into the hillside and surrounded by stately pines, this royal tomb (H.S. #30) is the farthest from Gyeongju, and one of six that have zodiac figures carved on panels that encircle the mound. This tomb is surrounded by posts and railings and fronted by an altar. Accompanied by four *haetae*, stone civilian and military guards protect the king from evil. Like at Gwaeneung, these military figures seem to have non-Asian features and may indicate that there was some contact with the "West"— perhaps Persia, India, or Central Asia. Out in front is a huge tortoise stela base. Unfortunately, most of the inscription and cap are missing. Constructed in the latter days of the Silla Dynasty, this is one of the few complete tombs, having all the elements of the advanced style of construction. While a worthy site, it is in less ideal condition than Gwaeneung and more difficult to reach. Use bus no. 200 to Yukdong-2-ri, then walk the 1.5 kilometers to the tomb site.

EAST OF GYEONGJU

Most of the Silla Dynasty construction was done on the Gyeongju plain, but several historical and religious sites, including an underwater tomb, are found along the coast. From the old Silla capital, a paved road runs past Bomun Lake Resort, over the lovely Churyeong-jae Pass, and down the serpentine valley below Toham-san, allowing easy access to this unfrequented coastal region. A trip here is worthwhile, but be aware that transportation between these individual sites is not necessarily convenient. If you don't have your own transportation, expect to spend time waiting for buses or hitching rides.

Girim-sa 기림사

Set below Hamwol-san in a quiet, secluded valley that turns colorful in autumn, Girim-sa [Kirim-sa] lies about five kilometers north of the village of Andong-ni, which is on the highway halfway between Churyeong-jae Pass and the coast. Originally called Imjeong-sa, this temple, according to legend, was founded by the Indian monk Gwangyu, who educated 500 other monks here. Renovated and enlarged in 643 during the flourishing reign of Queen Seondeok, its name was then changed to Girim-sa by the unorthodox Silla monk Wonhyo, and it became one of the largest and most important Silla temples. It played a vital role in the continuation of Buddhism in Korea, especially during the Confucian-dominated years of the Joseon Dynasty. During the Japanese invasion of the peninsula in the 1590s, Girim-sa was a command headquarters for warrior monks. Toward the end of the Joseon Dynasty, it had become one of the 31 major temples in the country. When Bulguk-sa was founded in 751, it was done as an outgrowth of and under the jurisdiction of the much larger and more influential Girim-sa; today Girim-sa is an adjunct temple of Bulguk-sa; ₩2,500 entrance.

A lone *sari budo* sits surrounded by bamboo below the temple to the side of the parking lot at the temple entrance. The main cluster of buildings are from the last quarter of the 1600–1700s, a medium-sized collection of relatively unadorned yet well-constructed structures built of weather-beaten brown wood and white plaster walls. A half dozen new buildings and a museum have been built during the last several decades, and this gives the space a grander feel. This expansion, unusually, has taken place to the side of and above the main buildings, putting the worship hall at a lower level. You approach the old courtyard by way of the new Cheonwang-mun and bell/gong pavilion, and the old Jinnam-nu lecture Hall. Daejeokgwang-jeon (T. #833), the main worship hall, sits directly across the courtyard. It is a broad structure, with pairs of lattice doors of different designs running across the front. A huge Vairocana Buddha (finger in fist), flanked by the Seokgamoni Buddha and the Bodhisattva Nosana, passively watches all

who enter the main worship hall. Imposing yet quiescent, this triad (T. #958) is made of gilt clay. Enshrined in the hall to the right is the Buddha of Medicine and to its front, under a towering Bodhi tree, are 16 foundation stones that mark the site of a former wooden pagoda. As wooden pagodas were generally constructed in the pre-Silla unification period (before the 660s), these foundation stones point to the temple's antiquity. In the autumn, the Bodhi tree drops hard, convoluted brown nuts that, when dried and peeled, are strung together to make prayer necklaces and rosaries. A somewhat-damaged three-tiered Silla Dynasty stone pagoda stands in front of Ungjin-jeon. On the long altar of this cramped hall are nearly 500 wooden Nahan figures, each distinct and individual.

In the new courtyard are several new halls and one that has been reconstructed. Unlike the old buildings, these are all meticulously and brightly painted. Gwaneum-jeon holds one of the most, if not *the* most, elaborate Goddess of Mercy statues in the country. This gilt figure has a multitude of heads and hands to see and help all those who ask for her aid and comfort. Check out the ox-herding murals on the exterior of this building. Also new are the Three Spirits Hall and the much larger Samcheonbul-jeon hall. On the huge altar in the latter sits the Seokgamoni Buddha, flanked by two bodhisattvas and what must be a thousand seated ceramic Buddha figures. On the exterior wall are murals depicting scenes from the life of the historical Buddha. The Myeongbu-jeon judgment hall has been relocated here and reconstructed.

With such a long history and major influence, Girim-sa has been the repository of numerous valuable cultural items. Until now, these items have been stored away out of sight of visitors for lack of proper display space. That changed with the construction of the temple's two exhibition halls—both worth a look. Don't miss them if you have time to visit the temple! Among the significant items here, and one of the most intriguing objects at the temple, is a one-meter-high gilt lacquer statue (T. #415) of the Goddess of Mercy. This unique figure is one of the few lacquer statues in the country. It differs from others in that it has a core of sculpted paper and silk, covered with several layers of lacquer over which gold leaf has been molded. Facial features and other marks are painted on. The face is South Asian, the nose aquiline. Legend relates that this figure was brought to Korea some 1,300 years ago by Indian monks, but during a recent cleaning the actual date of its construction (1501) was found written inside the statue. It's an inspiring, impressive piece of art. Of undetermined but obviously great age is a set of 54 sutras in 71 volumes (T. #959) found inside the large Vairocana Buddha of the main worship hall during its 1986 restoration. Some of these scriptures are hand-written (older) while others are printed from wood printing blocks (newer). Most have been written on white paper, while others employed blue or brown; black ink was used for most, while some were written with gold or silver. These sutras are from the Silla, Goryeo, and Joseon dynasties. While there is some overlap, as a general rule those from the Silla Dynasty are rolled, the folded ones are from the Goryeo era, and the Joseon Dynasty produced the bound volumes. In the second exhibition hall are wooden tablets relating special events of the past, and smaller wooden altarpieces and other objects of ceremonial use. Some metal objects are also kept here, including a *sari* container. Artistic renditions of the 10 kings who sit in judgment on those who enter the underworld are done on murals. Also displayed are a few stone articles and one huge roof end tile from a former temple building. The size of this end cap gives you an idea of the size of the original structure that stood underneath it and perhaps, by extension, the scope of the whole compound when at its peak.

A waterfall and several abandoned temple sites are located up the stream. Two annex hermitages, one across the stream to the temple's rear and the other on the hillside above the main compound, are only a short hike away. That to the side is Namjeok-am, and it is at the Hamwol Ceramic Studio here that the ceramic Buddha figures on the altar of Samcheonbul-jeon were made. Various other items, many with a Buddhist influence, are also produced here. A step kiln is on-site. At the bus stop are several shops,

restaurants, and a few *minbak*. Several times a day, city buses run to Girim-sa from Gyeongju, via Andong-ni, from where buses continue on to Gampo and Daebon.

Golgul-sa 골굴사

Between Girim-sa and the highway is the temple Golgul-sa [Kolgul-sa]. To reach Golgul-sa, walk one kilometer up the road toward Girim-sa to a point just beyond a factory. There, a cement approach road runs up into a narrow side valley to the west. From the parking lot, the temple's principal Buddha figure can be seen carved into a prominent rock outcrop. Recently, this hermitage was expanded and raised to temple status. New buildings were built and more religious figures enshrined. Unusually, the focus of this temple, instigated by its head monk, is the esoteric practice of *Seonmudo* (Zen martial arts). This practice apparently started during the Silla Dynasty, when the priests Won'gwang, Wonhyo, and others taught the discipline of mind and body to the aspiring *hwarang* elite corps of soldiers. Practiced by successive generations of monks, it was finally suppressed by the Japanese during their occupation of the country in the early decades of the 1900s. About 30 years ago, this martial art was revived by monk Yangik and taught to disciples at a hermitage of Beomeo-sa in Busan. Training for lay people started in the mid-'80s, and the

SEONMUDO

The fundamental aspect of *Seonmudo* stems from the very core of the Buddhist way, and this is to realize the harmony of body and spirit in order to attain enlightenment. This is accomplished by yoga postures, chakra breathing, body exercises, and mastery of dynamic martial art and weapon techniques. *Seonmudo* is not violent or fierce; its goal is not the development of offensive and defensive actions. Rather, it seeks to harmonize bodily composure and poise with a tranquil mind. For information about *Seonmudo*, contact the Geumgang Banyawon at Golgul-sa (tel. 054/744-1689) or the affiliate office in Seoul (tel. 02/763-2980).

Golgul-sa studio Geumgang Banyawon opened in 1990 for monk and layman alike. One program targets schoolchildren for the cultivation of physical education and spiritual refinement.

What has drawn people much longer to this site is its Silla Dynasty Buddha image (T. #581). On a prominent, light-colored rock face above the temple halls is a Buddha relief whose face, protected by a stubby overhang, has remained untouched by the ruinous elements of nature. Pieces of stone from its bulky body periodically flake off, as if dramatically and symbolically demonstrating the belief that the outward form and figure, the corporeal substance and body of a person, is temporal, and only the inner, spiritual essence of man is of supreme concern. The surrounding stylized flame mandala has also badly worn away. Similar to the rock face carving at Shinseon-sa on Danseok-san, this Buddha now has a steel and glass covering to protect it from the weather. Below this Buddha figure are various statues of Buddhas and bodhisattvas sized to fit the numerous niches in the pockmarked rock face. Below and to the left, in a shallow cave that has been made into the temple's main worship hall, a stone Goddess of Mercy occupies the altar, and smaller gilt Buddha statuettes have been placed in natural niches in the wall. To the left of the worship hall, a new Mountain Spirit shrine takes its place in a shallow grotto.

Janghang-ni Pagodas 장항리 5 층석탑

Along the back route to Seokguram and Bulguk-sa, standing on a terrace over a small river bed, are twin, five-tiered pagodas, presumed to be from the former Janghang temple (H.S. #45). These are two of only three pagodas in the region that have five stories. While the west pagoda (N.T. #236) is nearly complete, the eastern one is missing some pieces. Still, these two make a worthy pair. The eight images on each are carved with feeling. Other stone remains from this site are displayed at the Gyeongju National Museum.

Underwater Tomb of King Munmu 대왕암

Eight kilometers south of Gampo at Daebon, water flowing down from Toham-san reaches the sea. About 200 meters off the beach is a tiny islet called Daewangam (H.S. #158), which contains Korea's only underwater tomb, that of Silla king Munmu. Under one meter of water in the islet's concave center, a huge stone slab covers the gravesite itself. While frequented by Koreans, this unique spot is largely unknown to foreigners.

During the mid-Silla period, the coastal regions of Korea were often plundered by Japanese pirates, eventually driving the people away from the coastal lowlands and leaving the fields fallow. King Munmu was gravely concerned about this, and resolved to rectify it. When he died, his body was cremated and buried here. He willed to be turned into a dragon—then, even in death he could protect the kingdom and secure the land for his people. For the ancient Korean, the mythical dragon was a benevolent creature, one associated with water and kingly (or imperial) power.

On the far side of the river, on the bluff overlooking the sea, is **Igyeon-dae** [Igyŏn-dae] (이견대), or Dragon Viewing Terrace (H.S. #159). This pavilion, rebuilt in 1978, was built by King Shinmun, the son of King Munmu, to view the sea tomb of his beloved father. One legend relates that even after his death, Munmu sent his son, King Shinmun, a short length of bamboo by his messenger, the dragon. From that bamboo, Shinmun made a flute which he kept at a royal storehouse. This flute became the magical and legendary *Manpashikjeok*, which when blown in times of national crisis had the power to defeat invading enemies, stop disease, and counteract draught.

At Daebon Beach, you'll find a few spartan accommodations and several restaurants specializing in seafood. During fine weather, short motorboat rides are provided in the bay off Daebon (₩6,000 for adults and ₩3,000 for children).

Gameun-saji 감은사지

Approximately 500 meters inland from the mouth of the river are the remains of the temple Gameun-sa [Kamŭn-sa], started by King Munmu but finished in 682 by King Shinmun, who named it Gameun-sa ("Temple of Thankful Gratitude") in appreciation for his father's wish to safeguard the kingdom even after his death.

© ROBERT NILSEN

Gameun-saji

The most notable objects at this site (H.S. #31) are the twin 13-meter-high pagodas (N.T. #112). Although somewhat battered and cracked, and slightly defaced by graffiti, these stout sentinels are huge! An unusual feature of the site is the grid-pattern stone foundation work for the main temple hall. Sectioned block pilings and stone beams create an open space below the floor, above which the ordinary wood superstructure was built. This foundation construction technique is unique in the country. Pediment stone for other building foundations gives some clue to their size. On the level below the main hall is a pond, which was connected by a channel to the sea, dug to allow King Munmu, in the guise of a sea dragon, access to the temple to worship and to protect this sacred ground.

Legend relates that there was a bell at this temple, four times the size of the Emille Bell. This monstrous hunk of metal was supposedly hauled off as booty by the Japanese army during their invasion of 1592, but then sank in the waters off of Daewangam. Even though undersea expeditions have been mounted to recover the bell,

its location has eluded divers. Villagers say that its reverberating sound can still be heard when rough waters pound the dragon king's tomb.

Gampo 감포

The narrow coastal plain between Pohang and Ulsan is cut by swift and strong rivers that slice their way through the eastern foothills of the coastal mountain range. The rocky seashore and high promontories rise abruptly out of the water, and are parted by numerous white sand beaches. Abandoned most of the year, these beaches attract swimmers and sunbathers from Gyeongju and Pohang during the summer.

Directly east of Gyeongju is the compact port of Gampo [Kamp'o]. This secluded fishing village is tucked into the hills that surround this natural bay. If you've not yet seen a fishmarket in Korea, take a stroll through this one. In the early morning, fishing boats line the pier and disgorge their night's catch. Filling the dockside market are piles of fish and tubs of octopus, squid, crabs, mussels, sea cucumbers, and other sea creatures. The auctioneer moves from one catch to another as merchants chalk their bids on an erasable ledger. Off to the side, a group of women gut mounds of tuna. Over in the corner, away from watchful eyes, an octopus slings his tentacles over the side of a tub in a bid for freedom. There is activity everywhere, yet the market lasts only until late morning. A lighthouse across the bay gives the weathered fishermen direction to a safe harbor. To the north, the coast road runs to Guryongpo and, farther around the headland, to Pohang. Going south, the coastal highway passes numerous beaches and the Wolseong Nuclear Power Plant, and hugs the coast for many kilometers before it makes its twisted climb over the hills to Ulsan.

Several *yeogwan* are clustered around the Gampo bus station; others lie closer to the water. Near the breakwater, overlooking the line of fishing boats along the pier, are the Doseongjang Yeogwan (도성장여관) and Donggungjang Yeogwan (동궁장여관). Restaurants serving raw fish and savory fish soups are found along the harborfront road and along the main street. Intercity buses run every 20 minutes from Gyeongju to Gampo (₩2,410), and less frequently to Daebon Beach (₩2,350). From Gampo, frequent buses run the coast roads to Ulsan and Guryongpo.

SOUTH OF GYEONGJU

Gwanmun-seong Barrier Wall 관문성

Halfway between Gyeongju and Ulsan, just south of Mohwa, is a reconstructed section of the fortress wall (H.S. #48) known as Gwanmun-seong [Kwanmun-sŏng]. Constructed in the 720s, this 18-kilometer-long barrier ran from the sea to the mountains south of Gyeongju to protect the capital from southern invasion. High on the west side of this valley, sections of the original wall can be found, but along the road a short section has been rebuilt—right on the present boundary between Gyeongsangbuk-Do and Ulsan city.

Wonwon-saji 원원사지

In the mountains east of Mohwa are stone remains of the former temple Wonwon-sa (H.S. #46). Here, in what was the old courtyard, is a stone lantern flanked by imposing twin pagodas that stand facing each other as they have for centuries, adorned with unusually abundant carved panels. Of great artistic value, they alone make a trip here worthwhile. Although a few of the 12 are missing, zodiac figures grace the top sections of each base, while devas are carved into each side of the spacer blocks set between the base and the bottom tier. New temple buildings have been constructed below the original site. The stream in the valley bottom irrigates rice fields below, and hosts picnics during hot summer weekends. To reach the temple, walk under the railroad tracks at the north end of Mohwa Station and continue up the road for about four kilometers. Bus no. 600 runs from Gyeongju to Mohwa.

Practicalities

ACCOMMODATIONS

Hotels

Gyeongju has its share of fine hotels. The best are outside the city, at Bomun Lake and Bulguk-sa. The deluxe-class hotels Concorde, Hyundai, Chosun, and Hilton all front Bomun Lake, and offer Korean- and Western-style rooms, a variety of restaurants, and similar entertainment and recreational amenities. Rates at the Hotel Concorde (tel. 054/745-7000) are ₩169,400 for standard Western and ₩181,500 for standard Korean, and ₩193,600–338,800 for suites. Next door is the Kyongju Chosun Hotel (tel. 054/745-7701, www.chosunhotel.com), where standard rooms are ₩125,000–155,000, Korean-style rooms are ₩160,000, and suites run up to ₩222,000. Across the street and associated with the Chosun Hotel is the smaller Chosun Spa Hotel with rooms from ₩75,000–160,000. Displaying loads of artwork in the lobby is the Kyongju Hilton Hotel (tel. 054/745-7788, www.hilton.com). Opened in 1991, the Hilton's standard rooms start at ₩190,000, with suites from ₩450,000–3,200,000. This hotel has the area's only casino. Toward the middle of the lake is the Hotel Hyundai (tel. 054/748-2233). Room rates are fairly comparable, starting at ₩190,000, while suites range ₩350,000–3,000,000. The second-class Kyongju Hotel (tel. 054/745-7123) and Swiss Rosen Hotel (tel. 054/748-0094) are also located at Bomun Lake. Amenities are fewer but the rooms are much cheaper, starting around ₩60,000.

The second-class Pulguksa Tourist Hotel (tel. 054/746-1911), at the lower end of Bulguk-sa Village, has rooms from ₩75,000. Others in this complex, like the Kyongju Family Hotel (tel. 054/745-6050) and the Kyongju Kukmin Hotel (tel. 054/746-0601), offer pretty much the same facilities for similar prices. Just down the road is the deluxe-class Kolon Hotel (tel. 054/746-9001, www.kolonhotel.co.kr), another sub-

urb accommodation. In addition to its many restaurants, a bar, nightclub, and sporting facilities, the Kolon has its own eight-hole golf course. Korean and Western rooms run ₩132,000–247,000, suites ₩173,000–1,000,000.

Near the Gyeongju Intercity Bus Terminal are the eminently clean and comfortably third-class Hyup Sung Hotel (tel. 054/741-3335) and Kyongju Park Hotel (tel. 054/742-8804), both with rooms in the ₩40,000–60,000 range.

Yeogwan

There are numerous *yeogwan* at Bulguk-sa village, mostly large modern cement structures that cater to the hordes of visitors who come to view the temple. They are chockablock in the streets down past the row of shops and restaurants. Among them are the Han'gukkwan Yeogwan (한국관여관) and Ilseongjang Yeogwan (일성장여관), and at the lower end of the village, the Gyerim Youthtel (계림유스텔), where rooms run ₩30,000.

Several large *yeogwan* have also been built at Bomun Lake, mostly at the very eastern end. Clean, comfortable, and secure, they usually have both Korean- and Western-style rooms, and room charges are generally in the ₩25,000–40,000 range. Among others, there are the Bomun Sillajang Yeogwan (보문신라장여관) (tel. 054/745-1214), the Hwangnyongjang Yeogwan (황용장여관) (tel. 054/745-7771), Grace Yeogwan (그레이스여관) (tel. 054/745-0409), and Grand Motel (그랜드모텔) (tel. 054/745-7707).

In the city near the train station, try the Segeomjeong Motel (세검정모텔), Sillajang Yeogwan (신라장여관), Seongnimjang Yeogwan (성림장여관), or the Hosujang Yeoinsuk (호수장여인숙). Near the bus terminals, check the Mokhwa House (목화하우스), Samhojang Yeogwan (삼호장여관), or the Taeyangjang Yeogwan (태양장여관).

There are three budget *yeogwan* in Gyeongju that seem to attract the greatest number of foreign travelers. The oldest and most venerable is the Hanjinjang Yeogwan (한진장여관), also known as Hanjin Hostel (tel. 054/771-4097, fax 054/772-9679, kwon4097@hananet.net, http://hanjinkorea.wo.to). On a quiet alley only minutes from the bus stations, this place is conveniently located, and run by the friendly and vivacious proprietor, Mr. Kwon Yong Joung. He's an excellent source of up-to-date information about the city and surrounding region, including the less well-known points of interest, and will gladly speak to you in Korean, Japanese, or English. Aside from tourist information, he can direct you to the correct bus for your destination, suitable restaurants, banks, pharmacies, shops, and the like. As many foreign travelers stop here, it's a good place to gather information (about Korea and other Asian countries) or form a group for a day-trip. The Hanjin supplies hot water for beverages and the use of a small refrigerator and microwave for food. A small fee is charged for both the laundry facilities and a computer for checking email. In the summer, the roof is a favorite place for guests to gather, talk, drink, and catch the evening breezes. Some have complained of the rooms not being clean enough, others can't say enough about how comfortable they have been. It's all a judgment call—you decide. Rates for rooms with a common bathroom are ₩18,000 single, ₩22,000 double, ₩27,000 triple; with private baths ₩23,000 single, ₩26,000 double, ₩30,000 triple; and larger rooms with bath and a/c run ₩27,000 single, ₩30,000 double, ₩36,000 triple. Most rooms are Korean-style, while some have Western beds.

Centrally located up a short alley near the back entrance to Tumulus Park and close to the downtown area is Sa Rang Chae (사랑채) (tel. 054/773-4868, shilla7@chollian.net, www.kjstay.com). Since it is a traditional-style house with only five rooms for rent, the number of guests is limited. Twin, double, and Korean-style rooms are available and rates run ₩20,000 single, ₩25,000 for two in a room, or ₩30,000 for the Korean-style room; a simple breakfast is included. Guests share the showers and toilets. A kitchen and laundry facilities are available for guests' use. The wooden veranda outside the rooms and the courtyard provide a great place to meet other guests. The proprietors speak English and Japanese, are very helpful with information about town, and rent bicycles.

About two kilometers west of downtown and located in the Seoak-dong village beside King Muyeol's tomb is Rainbow Hostel (무지개집) (tel. 011/9741-8080). With only three rooms, this is the smallest in the Gyeongju area and the cheapest at ₩9,900. A single room and two dorms are available; the bathroom is shared. Guests can use the kitchen and a washer and dryer. The owner is a taxi driver so he can fetch you from the bus or train station. Very unusual for the time, the owner traveled the world off and on for 20 years when he was young and has many stories of his trips. Very knowledgeable about the area, he can point you in the right direction. As it is a place used almost exclusively by foreigners, you can garner information about other places from other guests.

Youth Hostel

There are two association youth hostels at Bulguk-sa village, both large hotel-like buildings. The Gyeongju Jeil Youth Hostel (tel. 054/746-0086) has dorm rooms at ₩12,000 for Y.H. members and ₩15,000 for non-members. The Bulkuksa Youth Hostel (tel. 054/746-0826) has similar rates. A non-association hostel is the Silla Youth Hostel (tel. 054/748-7333).

FOOD

The deluxe hotels have Korean, Japanese, Chinese, and Western restaurants. The lakeside restaurant Hobanjang, run by the Concorde Hotel, serves delicious Korean fare and, during the evenings, traditional music and dance performances are given free for the patrons. The Chosun Garden, Shincheon Garden, and other high-end restaurants at Bomun Resort also serve quality Korean meals. Close to the main entrance to Tumulus Park are the Silla Restaurant, Samwon Garden, and Kyongju Kalbi Restaurant, all serving fine Korean food. These are on the expensive side, so go as a treat to yourself. Nearby is Guro Ssambap, which serves less expensive *ssambap,* rice and vegetables that you

GYEONGJU

roll up in leafy greens before popping the little package into your mouth—a specialty of Gyeongju. Next to Beopjang-sa, across the street from the rear exit of Tumulus Park, is a restaurant serving better-than-average Chinese food.

Toward the center of town are numerous moderately priced Korean restaurants serving meat, fish, and soup. The P'yongyang Chip has a 50-year tradition of serving *naengmyeon,* a spicy, cold-noodle dish. Nearby are numerous Western fast-food imports. Several restaurants serving *haejangguk,* a soup made with bean sprouts that's often touted as a fix for a bad hangover, can be found along the street on the south side of the Palujeong rotary intersection, just south of the Gyeongju Station. Closer to the bus station, Andongtaek specializes in ginseng chicken soup, Tobidayaki is a Japanese restaurant, Madang serves up marinated grilled ribs, the 2nd-floor Grand Buffet offers an inexpensive Korean buffet, and the street-level Silla Byeolpanjeom almost next door serves basic Chinese dishes. Literally dozens of other eateries of all kinds and sizes are scattered throughout town, Bulguk-sa village, and Bomun Lake shopping arcade.

The markets are useful for quick noodle dishes or soups. Movable night stalls operate most of the year in front of the train station, along the principal shopping streets, in front of the theaters, and at select corners throughout the city. For fruit and packaged, canned, or bottled food items, a number of supermarkets now dot the city, including the Agricultural Cooperative at the Daegu Rotary just down from the bus terminals. Several bakeries in town specialize in *hwangnambbang,* a type of small round bread-like bun with sweet red bean paste filling. This specialty has been made in Gyeongju since 1939 and is well known around the country. To the uninitiated, the taste of the bean paste may take some getting used to.

To experience Korean teas, non-alcoholic drinks, and traditional cakes visit Yourim Teahouse or Seollokwon, with their quiet ambience, traditional music, and earthy decor. Of course, many coffee shops also can be found in Gyeongju. Often on the 2nd floor of downtown buildings, many have the words Coffee Shop written in English on their signs or windows.

To experience the alcoholic drinks special to the area, look for a bottle of Gyeongju Beopju, a rice wine made with herbs; Gyodong Beopju, rice wine with a different combination of ingredients; or Hwanggeumju, a rice wine infused with the flavor of chrysanthemums.

OTHER PRACTICALITIES
Entertainment

Once the sun sets, the city slows down considerably. But *you* need not! For drinking and dancing, head for any of the city's hotels. The Hilton Hotel has the only casino in Gyeongju (foreigners only), although slot machines can be found at other hotels. Several cinemas in the center of town show mostly Korean but occasional American or Chinese films, and a drive-in theater has been set up across the road from the shopping complex at Bomun Resort. Traditional music and dance are performed regularly at the performance area below the pagoda at Bomun Lake shopping complex. Kyongju World Amusement Park at Bomun Lake Resort is the city's only outdoor amusement center, with a variety of rides, a swimming pool, and various athletic grounds.

Shopping

At Bulguk-sa, the ubiquitous souvenir shops selling the typical tourist junk are monstrous! More of the same, but on a much smaller scale, are found in town near the entrance to Tumulus Park. Each hotel has its own. The arcade at Bomun Lake Resort is a pseudo-traditional shopping complex selling all sorts of expensive Korean arts, crafts, and other items. Numerous other independent shops dot the community at the east end of the lake; two duty-free shops are also located here. Traditional-style modern pottery can be purchased at the local pottery kilns mentioned above, while pottery and other traditional crafts are available at the Gyeongju Folk Art Village, where it's also possible to see them being made.

Shops of all sorts line the city center streets of town, and there are several reasonably large department stores. The Jeil Bookstore is perhaps the best in town. Use the more pedestrian Seongdong or Central Market for everyday items.

Services and Information

Near the back gate of Tumulus Park is the city hall; a second city administration office is located on the northern edge of the city on the way to Baengnyul-sa. The police station is north of the main drag. Both the post office and Telecom office are a few steps from the train station. The police, post office, and Telecom also have locations near the bus station at the south edge of Bomun Lake Resort. Exchange currency at the Korea Foreign Exchange Bank, Daegu Bank, Chohung Bank, or others in the city center—there are no banks at Bomun Resort. Major hotels also exchange money—at a less favorable rate, but they are open after banking hours. Haedong Pharmacy, Jungang Pharmacy, and others near the post office dispense over-the-counter medication and may have English-speaking clerks.

On the west side of the river north of downtown is the campus of the Gyeongju branch of Dongguk University, which has one of the few Chinese medicine departments in the country, and the university hospital. Beyond the tomb of General Kim Yu-shin, on the road to Geoncheon, are Sorabol College and, over the hill, Gyeongju University.

There are four **tourist information** booths in Gyeongju: one at the train station plaza, another between the bus terminals, a third at the Bulguk-sa parking lot, and the last on the 1st floor of the Bomun Lake Convention Center. All can provide useful suggestions, directions, and maps; it's best to ask specific questions. The train station also has an information desk inside that provides timetables and answers train transportation related inquiries. Hotel front desks can always be approached with questions, but perhaps the best sources of information about Gyeongju and the surrounding region for foreign travelers are the proprietors of the *yeogwan* that cater to these foreigners.

TRANSPORTATION

By Air

There's no air service to Gyeongju. The nearest airport is at Ulsan, but the Pohang and Daegu airports are not much farther. With prior notice, most city hotels offer paying guests free shuttle service from the Ulsan airport (and the Gyeongju train station) to the hotel. From the Ulsan airport, shuttle buses run four times a day to downtown Gyeongju and the Bomun Lake Resort hotels (₩4,500). Shuttles also run from the Gimhae International Airport to downtown Gyeongju and the hotels at Bomun Lake Resort (₩9,000), making this trip nearly a dozen times a day.

By Train

Two dozen trains a day leave the city, going to Busan, Ulsan, Pohang, Gangneung, Yeongju, Tong Daegu, Seoul Cheongnyangni, and Seoul. The fastest and most comfortable way to Seoul is the two daily *Saemaul-ho* trains (₩27,800); the *Saemaul-ho* also runs to Ulsan (₩7,600). The *Mugunghwa-ho* and *Tongil-ho* trains run to most other destinations. Sample fares are Pohang (₩1,400), Busan (₩5,400), Ulsan (₩4,700), Andong (₩6,300), Gangneung (₩17,200), Tong Daegu (₩4,700), and Seoul Cheongnyangni (₩18,300).

By Bus

Express buses run from Gyeongju to Seoul (₩14,600), Daejeon (₩9,000), Daegu (₩2,800), Busan (₩3,300), and Gwangju (₩11,700). Buses ply some two times a day to Gwangju, every two hours to Daejeon, and every 20–30 minutes to the other destinations. If you travel to or from Gyeongju for the Silla Festival or during major holidays (by either bus or train), be sure to buy your ticket well in advance. Everyone wants the same seat that you do!

Intercity buses run to all major cities in the province. Selected destinations are Busan (₩3,300), Daegu (₩2,800), Ulsan (₩3,100), Pohang (₩2,000), Andong (₩9,700), Gangneung (₩19,300), and Gampo (₩2,400).

Oft-used city buses are few in number. Most start from or pass along the street in front of the intercity bus terminal. The fare for ordinary city buses is ₩700; express city buses charge ₩1,050. The following buses will be of most use:

no. 10: Bomun Resort, Bulguk-sa, Gwaeneung, tomb alley, Seochulji, museum no. 11: museum, Seochulji, tomb alley, Bulguk-sa, Bomun Resort

no. 70: Gyeongju University

nos. 1, 100, 150: Bomun Resort, east coast

no. 200: An'gang, for tomb of King Heungdeok

nos. 201, 206: An'gang, Yangdong

no. 203: An'gang, Oksan Seowon

no. 230: Yongdam-jeong, tomb of Queen Jindeok

no. 232: Nawon-ni

nos. 300, 301, 304: Tomb of King Muyeol, Geoncheon

no. 350: Gyeongju University, Geoncheon, Danseok-san, Obong-san, Sannae

no. 600-608: tomb alley, Gwaeneung, Mohwa

no. 500-507: Oneung, west side of Nam-san

no. 501: tomb of King Gyeongdeok

Bicycles

This is the most rewarding means of getting around the city. Bicycles can be rented for ₩3,000 an hour or ₩5,000–10,000 a day; expect a rate of ₩12,000–15,000 for a tandem. Try the bicycle shops at the rear of Tumulus Park, across the street from the Kyongju Park Tourist Hotel, down the street from the train station, or at Bomun Resort. Bikes are also usually for rent at the beginning of the pedestrian lane near the south end of Tumulus Park, and a number of the inexpensive lodgings in town either rent bicycles or can point you toward the best bargains. Make sure the bicycle has a lock, and *use* it when you get off to look around or walk up into the hills. Flat paved roads run like ribbons to all major tourist sites in the area, and to within walking distance of most others; allow several days to see all the major attractions. Although not especially heavy, traffic on these wide roads is often quite swift. Be especially cautious on the twisting road to Seokguram, as cars generally drive recklessly on the curves.

Tours

Tours to the Gyeongju area are organized from all major cities in Korea through private tour companies as well as the Korean National Tourism Corporation. If you have limited time and resources, don't care to wait for city buses, or simply desire to "tour" independently, try the Cheonma Travel Co. (tel. 054/743-6001). Their Korean-language narrated tour stops at Bomun Lake Resort, Bulguk-sa, Silla History and Science Museum, Bunhwang-sa, Gyeongju National Museum, Anapji, Cheomseongdae, Tumulus Park, Poseok-jeong, and the tomb of General Kim Yu-shin. Board at the tour agency office, next to the express bus terminal. Departures are at 0830 and 1000 daily except Monday. Each tour lasts about seven hours and the cost is ₩10,000.

On a more low-key level, Kyongju Tour runs various moderate-priced tours to sites in the area and to evening entertainment. These tours leave from the Hanjin Hostel but can pick up at other locations.

Recommendations

If you only have one day to see the sites of Gyeongju, and desire an "orderly" visit, use the Cheonma tour bus. If you use the city buses or a bicycle, be sure to see Tumulus Park, Cheomseongdae, Anapji, the Gyeongju National Museum, the tombs of General Kim Yu-shin and King Muyeol, and Poseok-jeong. A second day might include Bulguk-sa, Seokguram, the Gyeongju Folk Art Village, and the Bomun Lake sites. For a third day, add Hwangnyong-sa, Bunhwang-sa, the Nang-san sites, Seochulji, and Gwaeneung. In addition, one or more days could be spent in each of the areas surrounding Gyeongju: Nam-san sites and hiking trails; Girim-sa and the sites toward the East Sea; Oksan Seowon, Yangdong, and the sites to the north of the city; Obong-san, Danseok-san, and the mountain areas to the west; Wonwon-saji and the sites to the south. After becoming acquainted with the area, you'll know what you want to see and when. There is much to see and you'll certainly not be at a loss for places to visit and things to do!

Gyeongsangnam-Do
경상남도

Gyeongsangnam-Do [Kyŏngsangnam-Do] occupies the southeastern corner of the peninsula. With an area of 10,515 square kilometers, this province is the country's fourth-largest; its 3.1 million inhabitants make it the second most populous. Farming and fishing are of course integral to the economy. The major domestic shipping and fishing ports are Tongyeong, Samcheonpo, Jangseungpo, Jinhae, Masan, and Jangsaengpo in Ulsan. Ulsan ranks as the country's third international shipping port, while the ports of Masan and neighboring

Changwon are growing in importance since the establishment of the Masan Free Trade Zone. Crabbing, and a great deal of oyster and seaweed farming, takes place among the numerous islands off the south coast. While riverflats are farmed throughout the province, the major farming areas are the plains near Gimhae, Miryang, Jinyeong, Hanam, Gaya, and Jinju. The mild climate, overall the warmest in the country after Jeju-do, and the length of the growing season allow extensive double-cropping.

roof lines at Haein-sa

© ROBERT NILSEN

Gyeongsangnam-Do has the country's highest coastal population, and is largely oriented toward the sea. The province's 10 cities are all located along the coast, except for Jinju, Miryang, and Yangsan—and even they are close to the sea. Another and larger city, Ulsan, was administratively separated from the province in 1994, and now is a designated metropolitan city like Busan. Aside from Busan and Ulsan, Gyeongsangnam-Do has developed a strong industrial base; the most important areas include Changwon, Masan, Okpo on Geoje-do, Jinju, Yangsan and Jinhae.

For additional information about the province, see www.provin.gyeongnam.kr.

Mountains

The southern section of the Sobaek Mountains, in conjunction with the Seomjin River, forms the western boundary of Gyeongsangnam-Do. Along this border are the range's two highest peaks, Jiri-san and Deokyu-san. Branching east from Deokyu-san is a short spur, of which the highest peak is Gaya-san. Running north-south, roughly between Busan and Gyeongju, are the Yeongnam Alps. Although not considered part of the Taebaek Mountains, they continue south in a straight line from the end of that range, petering out at the coast in Busan. Low coastal hills follow the entire southern coastline from Jiri-san nearly to Gimhae. The interior of the province is filled with rolling, round-topped mountains, limiting arable land but creating no formidable transportation barriers.

Rivers

South Korea's longest river, the Nakdong, cuts through the province and flows into the South Sea between Gimhae and Busan. Into this ponderous river empty the Nam, Hwang, and Miryang rivers. The Nam River is dammed west of Jinju and the Hwang River west of Hapcheon, creating the province's two major multi-purpose reservoirs. The only other sizable river is the Taehwa, which flows into the East Sea at Ulsan, where its mouth creates one of the few

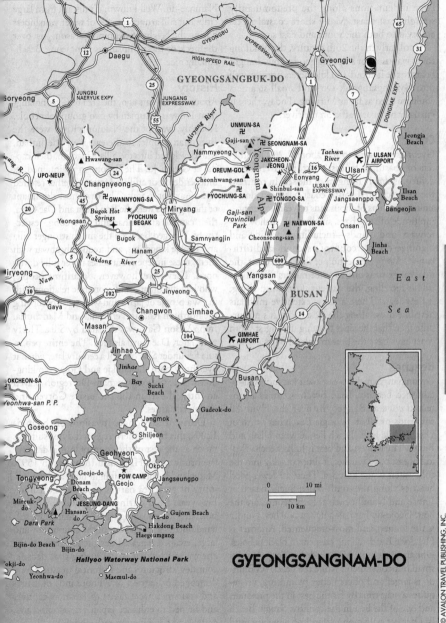

GYEONGSANGNAM-DO

large indentations along the predominantly straight east coast. Many short coastal rivers empty into both the South and East seas.

Until early in the 20th century, the Nakdong River was used for shipping goods. Low-draught boats made it about 250 kilometers upriver, well into Gyeongsangbuk-Do, and small steamers could be used as far as Miryang. Today, there is virtually no boat traffic on the river.

Coast

Gyeongsangnam-Do has about 2,200 kilometers of coastline. Its east coast, relatively unindented, is slowly rising from the sea. In contrast, the very sculpted south coast has been slowly sinking for tens of thousands of years, creating a multitude of large bays, small coves, shallow waterways, and islands—including Geoje-do and Namhae-do, the country's second- and fifth-largest. Along this section of the south coast, the tidal range runs one to three meters. When the tide is receding, the current flows west; rising, it flows east. There are few extensive mudflats here like those along the west coast. It's no surprise then that the cities fronting the largest south coast bays have the best mainland ports.

Beaches

Gyeongsangnam-Do's east coast has four well-established beaches. Ilsan Beach occupies a protected cove at Bangeojin, near the Hyundai shipyards of Ulsan. Jeongja Beach lies north of Ulsan, while Jinha Beach lies between Ulsan and Busan. The longest and best is Jinha Beach. Typical of east coast beaches, it drops quickly into the cold waters of the East Sea. There are fewer good beaches along the south coast; Suchi Beach at Jinhae and Namil Beach at Samcheonpo are the best. Geoje-do has half a dozen beaches; Gujora is the longest and most-frequented. Another is Hakdong Beach, a long crescent of black pebbles. Donam Beach on Mireuk-do in Tongyeong is small but convenient, while the beach on Bijindo is larger and offers better swimming, yet requires a boat trip. By far the best in the province, and one of the best in the country, Sangju Beach is a perfect half-moon strand of powdery sand tucked into a protected cove on the south side of

Namhae-do. Well-known, it's distant from large cities but still attracts hordes of water worshipers during the height of swimming season. Just over the neck of the peninsula is Songjeong Beach, equally nice.

History

About 2,000 years ago, the area of Gyeongsangnam-Do was occupied by two groups of people. Roughly, west of the Nakdong River were the Byeonhan people; to the east were the Jinhan, who developed into the Silla Kingdom, their capital at Gyeongju. The Byeonhan maintained six independent but affiliated states, together referred to as Gaya or Garak. The two most dominant of these groups were the Bon Gaya and Dae Gaya, their capitals at Gimhae and Goryeong, respectively. Wedged between the much stronger Silla and Baekje kingdoms, and frequently at war with them, these independent states never fully developed. They were, however, a maritime people, who had diplomatic and economic relations with the Wa people of Japan and with states occupying the northern Korean Peninsula and Manchuria. In 532, Bon Gaya was defeated by Silla. Thirty years later, Dae Gaya also fell. The entire peninsula fell under Silla control a century later when it overthrew both the Baekje and Goguryeo kingdoms. The Gyeongsangnam-Do region played an integral part in the successive Goryeo and Joseon dynasties.

During the Mongol invasions of the mid-1200s, this far-southern region did not suffer as much as the rest of the country, but it did take the brunt of the Hideyoshi Invasions in 1592. Many land battles were fought here, and the majority of great sea battles took place offshore. Five years later, during the second great invasion, this region, along with Jeollanam-Do, suffered once again. The rest of the country, by and large, escaped repeated destruction because the enemy was held at bay. During that decade, countless structures and historical treasures were destroyed or carried off. Thousands of artists and craftsmen were taken to Japan as captives and helped to enhance Japan's developing arts, crafts, and construction techniques.

The southeastern corner of the peninsula,

today comprising Gyeongsangnam-Do and Gyeongsangbuk-Do, was a single province and a distinct cultural unit known as Yeongnam during the Joseon Dynasty. At the turn of the 20th century, it was split into the present divisions. Jinju became the capital of the southern half and remained so until 1925, when the seat of government was moved to Busan. In 1963, Busan was designated a "special city," and administratively separated from the rest of the province. In 1983, Gyeongsangnam-Do's provincial capital was moved from Busan to its present location, Changwon.

Cultural Notes

Gyeongsangnam-Do's deep and strong cultural foundation includes a great number of festivals and numerous surviving dramas, dances, songs, and crafts designated as Intangible Cultural Assets. Four of the major festivals are the Jinhae Cherry Blossom Festival, the Miryang *Arang-je*, the Hansan Victory Festival in Tongyeong, and Jinju's *Gaecheon* Arts Festival.

Rush mats and baskets from Hapcheon, tea and bamboo products from Hadong, bamboo and porcelain from Sancheong, leather goods from Hamyang, paper umbrellas and persimmons from Jinju, citrus fruit from Namhae, lacquerware and kites from Tongyeong, carved gourds from Yangsan, ceramics from Gimhae, and amethyst from Eonyang are all traditional special products of the province. In addition, there are nine National Treasures, 93 Treasures, and 34 Historical Sites. Gaya-san, Deokyu-san, Jiri-san, and Hallyeo Waterway national parks are shared with the neighboring provinces, while Gaji-san and Yeonhwa-san provincial parks, and more than half a dozen county parks, are totally encompassed by the province. Gyeongsangnam-Do contains two of the five greatest temples in the country, Haein-sa and Tongdo-sa, and dozens of others dot the mountains.

Transportation

One of the international air entry points for Korea is at Gimhae, west of Busan. With flights to Incheon, Gimpo, Jeju, Gwangju, and Gangneung, it's also one of the country's busiest domestic airports. The two other provincial airports are located at Ulsan and at Sacheon, just south of Jinju.

Three major rail lines run from Busan through the province. The Gyeongbu line, the country's main line, runs north through Miryang on its way to Daegu and other points north. The Donghae Nambu line goes to Ulsan and Gyeongju, and from Yeongcheon takes the "back route," the Jungang line, to Seoul. The Gyeongjeon line heads west at Samnyangjin for Jinju, Hadong, and points in Jeollanam-Do. From Changwon, a short line runs south to Jinhae. A high-speed rail link between Busan and Seoul is scheduled to be completed by 2004. This line will skirt Ulsan on its way to Gyeongju, Daegu, and other points north.

Expressways reach all corners of the province. The Gyeongbu Expressway (no. 1) between Busan and Seoul is the major route; an artery, the Ulsan Expressway (no. 16), connects Eonyang to Ulsan. The Namhae Expressway (no. 10) conveniently joins Gyeongsangnam-Do and Jeollanam-do, while its branch line, the Namhae Branch Expressway (no. 104) skirts Gimhae and runs into south Busan. Running north to south, the Jungbu Naeryuk Expressway (no. 45) connects Masan to Daegu, the Jungbu Expressway (no. 35) connects Hamyang to Jinju and Tongyeong, and the '88 Olympic Expressway (no. 12) cuts across the northwest corner of the province, linking Daegu and Gwangju. When completed, others will ease transportation within the province. No. 600 will be a circular route around the cities of Busan and Gimhae, no. 102 will skirt the north side of Masan, the Jungang Expressway (no. 55) will drop down from Daegu to Busan and complete the connection through the center of the country, and the Donghae Expressway (no. 65) will run up the east coast through Pohang.

There is frequent ferry service from Jinhae and Masan to Geoje-do, and from three ports on Geoje-do to Busan, but the most extensive ferry service along this coast is from Tongyeong, and to a lesser extent from Samcheonpo, to the numerous outer islands south of there.

Gaya-san Vicinity

GAYA-SAN NATIONAL PARK
가야산국립공원

Branching southwest from Deokyu-san is a subsidiary ridge of the Sobaek mountain range ending at Gaya-san (1,430 meters). Named after the ancient Gaya Kingdom which, until 1,400 years ago, controlled this region, this massive mountain is basically one huge column of granite with a distinctive bald top. From the summit, a circular ridge connects half a dozen peaks over 1,000 meters in elevation, creating a cauldron-like inner valley. This thickly wooded bowl is drained by the Hongnyu River, running out through a narrow opening to the southeast. The road into the park passes through that gap and has some of the area's most attractive scenery. Its deep valleys create a refuge for a wide variety of plant and animal life. Gaya-san has long been known for its fine scenery, somewhat of a tourist attraction in centuries past for the few fortunate Koreans able to travel through the country.

In 1972, 57 square kilometers of the mountain were designated Gaya-san National Park, one of the smallest in the national park system. It has since grown to 80 square kilometers, and the entire mountain area, including the Haein-sa precinct, is designated Historic and Scenic Site no. 5. Its boundaries preserve three National Treasures, 15 Treasures, and over six dozen other cultural and historical properties. The cherry blossoms, azaleas, and rhododendrons in spring; the lush green of summer, and the colors of fall bring busloads of people to these hills, while others come as pilgrims to Haein-sa. Entrance to the park and temple is ₩2,800.

To handle these growing crowds, the park village has been enlarged and modernized. You'll find one tourist hotel, at least 30 *yeogwan* (₩20,000–30,000) and restaurants, a post office, police station, pharmacy, bus terminal, variety stores, souvenir shops, and a tourist center—all the amenities of a small village. The well-appointed, full-service Haeinsa Tourist Hotel (tel. 055/933-2000) offers rooms for ₩78,000–90,000, suites up to ₩242,000. There are a few camping areas (₩3,000) 15 minutes up the road past Yongmun Waterfall. From the park village, buses run frequently to Hapcheon (₩3,200), Goryeong (₩2,500), Jinju (₩7,200), and Daegu Seobu Bus Station (₩3,600), and less frequently to Busan Seobu Bus Station (₩10,400). Another hotel, additional *yeogwan,* and a second camping area are also located at Baegun-dong, the eastern entrance to the park.

Hongnyu Valley and Cheongnyang-sa

The road from the park entrance to the village leads through picturesque Hongnyu Valley. Azaleas in spring and the tints of fall colors inspired this valley's name—"Flow of Red Color." Anywhere along this river would make a fine place for a picnic. Several cascades, pools, huge riverside boulders, the rock parapets Nakhwa-dam and Chilseong-dae, and the strategically placed pavilion Nongsan-jeong, set on a tiny tree-studded island in the middle of the river, line the river's wooded route. Near Nakhwa-dam is the hermitage Gilsang-am. Set at riverside on the opposite side of, and easily seen from, the road are large new stone constructions including a tall Yaksa Buddha figure, a five-tier stone pagoda, and a semi-circular wall of carved stone panels containing bodhisattva figures surrounding a standing Mireuk Buddha image.

Lying in an adjacent valley south of the cauldron valley of Gaya-san, Cheongnyang-sa [Ch'ŏngnyang-sa] (청량사) is relatively isolated and seldom visited. It's a small, peaceful compound perched on a steep mountain slope. Preserved here is an impressive stone lantern (T. #253) set on a wide lotus base, as well as a three-tier stone pagoda (T. #266), and a seated stone statue of the Buddha (T. #265) that is the central altar figure of the main hall. Newly re-created, this main hall is highly decorated with fancy wood and stone work. In his last days, the great Silla Dy-

GAYA-SAN NATIONAL PARK

GYEONGSANGBUK-DO

Gaya-san
(1,430 m)

SHELTER

MOUNTAIN
FORTRESS
REMAINS

Gaya-san
National
Park

Yonggi Waterfall

BUDDHA
FIGURE

BAEGUN
TEMPLE SITE

HONJE-AM
YONGTAP
SEONWON

WONDANG-AM   HAEIN-SA
GEUMSEON-AM   JIJEOK-AM   HEUIRANG-DAE
SAMSEON-AM

CAMPING

BAENGNYEON-AM

BOHYEON-AM   GUGIL-AM
Yongmun
Waterfall   YAKSU-AM
Village

BUS TERMINAL
Nakhwa-dam

HAEINSA
TOURIST HOTEL   GILSANG-AM

NONGSAN-
JEONG

TICKET
BOOTH

BEOBSU
TEMPLE SITE

SAMWON
TEMPLE SITE

Baegun-dong

CAMPING

Hongnyu Valley

TICKET BOOTH

Chilseong-dae

GYEONGSANGNAM-DO

Nam-san
Jeil-bong

CHEONGNYANG-SA

Gaya-san
National Park

Gaya
To Hapcheon

0   1 mi
0   1 km

© AVALON TRAVEL PUBLISHING, INC.

GYEONGSANGNAM-DO

---

nasty scholar Choe Chi-won retired here, escaping the turbulent last years and disintegration of the dynasty. He later died here. While trails lead over the mountain from the park village and from Nongsan-jeong, a small 2.5-kilometer-long road to Cheongnyang-sa leads up from the park entrance road near an earthenware pottery factory.

Hermitages

The cauldron valley below Gaya-san holds more than a dozen hermitages and meditation retreats,

most set aside for *biguni* although several have resident male monks. One of the closest to Haein-sa is **Hongje-am**, where the famous monk and military leader Sammyeong died in retirement following his role as commander of Buddhist warrior-monks during the Hideyoshi Invasions. A monument has been erected in his honor, and in the hermitage hall his portrait hangs along with those of Seosan and Yeonggyu, two other inspirational leaders during that same conflict. Nearby is **Wondang-am**, the first hermitage built in the area, and, some say, the staging site for the construction of Haein-sa. A stone pagoda of 11 squat steps, and parts of a stone lantern (together designated T. #518) are preserved at Wondang-am.

Behind Haein-sa and beyond the hermitage Jijeok-am sits **Heuirang-dae**, said to be the meditation site for the Goryeo Dynasty monk Heuirang. The hermitage's tiny buildings are set precariously on the edge of a towering rock overhanging the narrow ravine below, making a fine photograph. Toward the upper end of this tight side valley is the hermitage Baengnyeon-am. The ridge behind it is beautifully sculpted—precipitous cliffs, rock boulders, and mature pine trees. Some say this is one of the prettiest spots in the park. Most of the other hermitages lie off the main walkway that leads up to Haein-sa.

Trails

The park offers a few short part-day walks. From Nongsan-jeong, a trail heads up the mountain to Nam-san Jeil-bong (1,010 meters). Halfway to the top, where the trail makes an abrupt right turn and goes straight up the ridge, a second trail descends the other side to Cheongnyang-sa, completing this two-kilometer walk. It is also possible to walk to Cheongnyang-sa by way of Nam-san Jeil-bong from the park village—a four-kilometer hike. A leisurely half-day hike takes in Haein-sa and the other hermitages in the immediate area. Starting at the tourist center, you can stop at Bohyeon-am, Samseon-am, Geumseon-am, Wondang-am, and Hongje-am, plus Yongtap Seonwon meditation hall on the way. From the side of Haein-sa, a path takes you up the hill past Jijeok-am and Heuirang-dae to Baengnyeon-am. Return down this ravine via Gugil-am and Yaksu-am.

If you plan to hike to the top of Gaya-san, count on spending all day. From the entrance to Haein-sa, follow the right side of the stream to an eight-meter-tall standing stone Buddha figure (T. #222), about an hour above the temple. The fleshy face and broad shoulders indicate that it's probably from the United Silla period. A 15-minute walk from there across the valley takes you to the junction with a second trail from below. Another hour's walk, past an emergency

shelter and a second standing stone figure, brings you to the top. On a clear day, Deokyu-san, Jiri-san, and Palgong-san can be seen from the summit. An alternate path down runs along the ridge to the south, past the remains of a mountain fortress. From the fortress, a four-kilometer-long valley trail takes you past the Samwon temple site to the Baegun-dong back entrance to the park. A second trail leads down another valley past the Baegun temple site and to the turnoff for the trail up to Yonggi Waterfall before ending at Baegun-dong, where there is a camping site. Three-tier stone pagodas mark both the Samwon temple site and the nearby Beobsu temple site.

HAEIN-SA 해인사
Treasure Temple

Haein-sa is one of Korea's three treasure temples, representing the doctrinal aspect of Buddhism. Founded in 802 by monks Suneung and Ijeong after their return from China, its original construction was made possible with the aid of Silla royalty, after the two monks cured the queen of a supposedly incurable disease. Burned by seven great fires over the centuries, only the stone pagoda and an iron flagpole and its supports remain from Silla times. Most of the present structures date from the end of the Joseon Dynasty. Today, Haein-sa is the Jogye sect's 12th district headquarters, with nearly one hundred sub-temples and hermitages under its jurisdiction. It is one of the half dozen largest temples in the country. Although you can wander around the complex on your own, periodic tours are offered in Korean and English.

Haein-sa is most often translated as "Reflection of the Sea Temple." A signboard at the temple states that this "suggests an analogy between an image reflected on calm water and the way Buddhist wisdom mirrors reality." This symbolism of a calm sea (and its antithesis) is stressed by the Hwaeom sect of Korean Buddhism, of which Haein-sa is an associate temple. The concept holds that the earthly existence of pain, suffering, and delusion can be compared to a sea in turmoil. A mirror-like, undisturbed sea, on the other

entrance walk to Haein-sa

hand, is an analogy for the "reality" of harmonious existence. Ordinary life in no way reflects "reality," which most sentient and unenlightened beings are not even aware of. The Wisdom of Buddha and the Truth, embodied by Buddhist doctrine is a reflection of that calm sea, and an understanding of "reality" and the nature of all things, comes only with spiritual enlightenment.

Temple Structures

Three rather unremarkable front gates lead up the entry path and past the Mountain Spirit hall to the first large courtyard at Haein-sa. Surrounding this open area are living quarters and a study hall. On the right a new tatami-floored hall has been raised, its altar atypically placed on the left side wall. A new bell/gong pavilion has been built to the left. Stairways lead around Gugwang-nu to the upper courtyard. Gugwang-nu is the temple museum, preserving over 200 arti-

facts including painted scrolls, documents, and a bronze incense burner in the shape of an elephant with a pagoda on its back; many are priceless, one-of-a-kind objects. Here as well sits a life-size, life-like wooden statue of the venerable third abbot of the temple, who developed extraordinary capacities for control over the body. Today, those who wish a cure for some disease or to conceive a child when it hasn't been possible before pray in front of this statue, hoping that some of the abbot's power will be transferred to them.

The upper courtyard has two levels. In the lower stands a three-tier stone pagoda and lantern; both have witnessed the changes at Haein-sa since its establishment. A broad stairway leads up to Daejeokgwang-jeon, the main hall, rebuilt in 1817, renovated extensively in 1971, and given a fresh coat of paint in 1994. Dedicated to the Vairocana Buddha, it is lavishly adorned inside and out, and seven figures occupy its huge altar. Also on this level are the Myeongbu-jeon, Ungjin-jeon, and the octagonal Dokseong-gak halls. To the side of the compound is a relatively new meditation hall.

The most important, valuable, and well-known items at the temple are located up a steep stairway behind the main hall. These are the famous wood printing blocks known as the **Koreana Tripitaka** (N.T. #32). Stored in two buildings called Janggyeong-gak (T. #52), the more than 80,000 carved wooden slabs represent the bulk of the Buddhist canon of literature and have been stored here since the mid-1200s. Additionally, 2,835 other wood printing blocks of Buddhist scriptures and related works, carved between 1100 and 1350 in the Goryeo Dynasty, are also kept here. Designated N.T. #206 and T. #734, they sit in smaller storage halls in the courtyard to the sides of Janggyeong-gak.

NEARBY TOWNS

Hapcheon 합천

South of Gaya-san National Park sits Hapcheon [Hapch'ŏn], a slow-paced provincial town tucked into the mountains along the banks of the Hwang

River, this stretch of which is sometimes referred to as the Ham River. Until recently, it seemed that time had largely passed Hapcheon by, but in the 1980s much new construction took place: a huge multi-purpose dam was built, roads were paved, and other improvements were brought to town. Former president Chun Doo Hwan hails from Hapcheon. For most, Hapcheon is just a stop on the bus route to Haein-sa.

The pavilion Hambyeong-nu lies below a small temple along the north bank of the river, a few minutes' walk from the center of town. Originally constructed in 1321, the present structure dates from 1871. An archery range lies within arrowshot of the pavilion. On warm summer days, young boys come here, strip, and take turns jumping into the cool water below the pavilion. To get to Hambyeong-nu, cross the main drag, walk up under the pedestrian overpass, and turn into the first street. Go past the elementary school, over a low rise, and around the hill. You'll see the archery range and river before you arrive at the pavilion, a fine place to spend part of a lazy afternoon out of the intense heat of the summer sun.

A good number of *yeogwan, yeoinsuk,* and restaurants are found across from or in toward the center of town from the bus terminal. Try the Yongmunjang Yeogwan (용문장여관), Bandojang Yeogwan (반도장여관), Saerimjang Yeogwan (세림장여관), or the Cheonil Yeoinsuk (천일여인숙) for a place to stay. From Hapcheon, buses run to Haein-sa (₩3,200), Goryeong (₩1,800), Daegu (₩3,800), Jinju (₩4,100), and Busan (₩7,900).

Additional information on Hapcheon and the surrounding county can be found online at www.hapcheon.kyongnam.kr.

KOREANA TRIPITAKA

In the early 11th century, the Khitan Tartar tribes of Manchuria launched several invasions into Goryeo territory. In an attempt to win favor and divine intervention from the Buddha, Goryeo King Hyeonjeong ordered a set of wood printing blocks to be carved, prompting a synthesis of the Buddhist canon then in use. This first set of printing blocks was stored at Buin-sa, near Daegu. Two centuries later, when the country was invaded by the Mongols, the printing blocks at Buin-sa were destroyed. In 1236, King Gojong ordered a second set engraved, again petitioning the higher powers to help expel the invading barbarians. Sixteen years later, the blocks were completed. Unfortunately, the Mongols remained in Korea for the next several centuries, greatly influencing domestic and foreign policy. Even with their failure to bring about the desired effect, the printing blocks stand as witness to the effort and intent of the Goryeo Dynasty royalty, remaining one of the greatest Asian religio-artistic works of all time.

These printing blocks are probably white poplar, birch, or silver magnolia. Although the process of production is under question, one procedure seems most likely. After the wood was selected and cut to rough dimension, it was submerged in sea water for three years, then in fresh water for an additional three years. The wood was then dried in an open-air, shaded environment for an additional three years—some even suggest it was buried underground for a three-year period before drying. Finally, the wood was sized and carved, and a natural lacquer finish applied for its preservation. In total, there are 81,258 blocks—6,791 volumes. Each measures 67 centimeters by 23 centimeters by 3 centimeters. All were hand-engraved on both sides, the characters necessarily being carved in reverse! An average block has twenty-three 14-character columns—as the writing is done top to bottom—for a total of about 320 characters per side. The block's position in the total sequence is designated on the end of each panel. The blocks are extremely well-preserved, it's said that to this day not even one has deteriorated by natural causes or been destroyed in any other way. Many complete sets of the entire canon have been printed and bound from these printing blocks throughout the centuries—some are still occasionally made today. Hand-printed and -bound copies of the complete canon are kept here at Haein-sa, at Tongdo-sa, and at Geumsan-sa.

According to authorities, this version represents

Goryeong 고령

East of Gaya-san National Park and west of Daegu is the small county seat of Goryeong [Koryŏng]. Goryeong is actually in Gyeongsangbuk-Do, but is discussed here since it has a cultural and historical affinity to Gyeongsangnam-Do because it was part of the Gaya region. Set to the side of an obviously productive agricultural valley and ringed by high mountains, this site was the center of the small Gaya kingdom called Dae Gaya. A pair of stone flagpole supports (T. #54) stands in good condition just down from the main intersection of town near the market, and outside of town there's a prehistoric flat rock carving (T. #605) of uncertain meaning. Between town and the river is a tomb (H. S. #165), now closed and locked for preservation, that displays (mostly disintegrated) painted wall murals and has a vaulted inner shape created by decorative brick that is similar to the Neungsan-ni painted tombs of Baekje outside Buyeo to the west. However the most well-known historical remains here are the numerous royal tombs that dot the hillside above town, the largest of which can be seen on the ridge to the west as a ripply silhouette backlit by the setting sun in early evening. (Other Gaya tombs can be seen at Changnyeong, Hapcheon, Gaya in Haman, Goseong, Gimhae, and Busan.) The Goryeong tombs (grouped together as H.S. #79) number over 200 and spread up the hillsides on both sides of the highway. The most prominent tombs are regarded as those of the Gaya kings, the smaller tombs of lesser royalty. Some have been excavated (early excavation was done during the Japanese occupation), and many of the unearthed items are on display at various museums in this country and in Japan. Later excavations were undertaken in 1977–78 and again in 1994. In the late

the most comprehensive and authentic version of the Mahayana Buddhist canon in existence, and it's of high technical execution. It is called the *Koreana Tripitaka*. *Tripitaka* means "Three Baskets," and refers to the three types of books: *gyeong*, the first, are the sutras and specific teachings of the historical Buddha and his disciples during the Buddha's lifetime. The second type, *yul*, contains the rules governing the lives of the Buddhist monks, and *non*, the third, holds commentaries on these religious/philosophical works by certain authorities of later centuries. This version was probably carved based on an edition of the canon printed in China and brought to Korea for study and distribution. Carved on Ganghwa-do while King Gojong was in exile there, they were moved to Haein-sa in 1399 during the reign of the Joseon Dynasty's first king, Taejo. One hundred and twenty-one matching plates are stored at Jeondeung-sa, on Ganghwa-do, where they were originally carved.

The original storehouse at Haein-sa was replaced in 1488 by the current, specially designed two-building library, Janggyeong-gak, which fills the uppermost level of the temple compound. These buildings miraculously escaped destruction during the Hideyoshi Invasions, as well as fires that have destroyed other parts of the compound. This unusually good luck accounts for the library buildings standing as the oldest original structures at the temple. They have been designed to keep out moisture, create an even flow of air, and moderate the temperature and humidity inside. Large lattice windows are placed in the bottom portion of the western walls, with smaller ones above. On the eastern walls, they are reversed. The printing blocks are stacked inside like books on a shelf, lined up on wooden runners and spaced for air circulation. Walkways run between the long stacks for easy access.

In 1995, the *Koreana Tripitaka* was added to the list of world heritage sites, designated by UNESCO for recognition and preserved by the world community for their cultural and historical significance.

While an extremely important cultural heritage, the *Koreana Tripitaka* has moved into the modern age. Not only has the entire work been placed digitally on a computer CD for easy study and research, the entire religious canon has been translated into modern Korean and portions have been translated into other languages of the world.

1990s, a domed **King's Tomb Exhibition Hall** was constructed along the highway where it passes through this line of tombs. Inside are displays of the structure of tomb no. 44 and reproductions of gold, bronze, iron, and earthenware tomb contents; ₩700 entrance. One gold crown (N.T. #138) is presumed to be that of King Geumnim. When finished, a new Dae Gaya History Exhibition Hall next door will expand this display and show some of the more than 6,000 items taken from these tombs. Periodic bus service from the center of town passes this exhibition hall. Gaya University lies a short distance past this site and is reachable by Daegu city bus no. 500.

A hike to the largest of these tombs is a 30–40-minute walk from the center of town; a leisurely round-trip makes a nice way to kill a couple of hours. From the bus terminal, walk into town past the police station and post office, turning left just past the fire department. Continue as the road curves around an athletic building; a driveway to the left brings you to Goryeong Hyanggyo

and several old stone relics standing on the lawn to its rear. You can also head up the street from the flagpole supports to this same spot. Continue straight on up a cement track. Soon it turns to gravel and runs into the woods, where it winds around the side of the hill to the top of a long line of tombs that descend like green gumballs down the ridge. From a point partway down this group, the craggy top of Gaya-san can be seen far to the northwest. On the hilltop above are the remains of a Gaya-era fortress (H.S. #61). Alternately, a shorter path leads up to the tombs from the side of the exhibition hall.

If you plan to stay in town, try either the Daegwang Yeogwan (대광여관) and bathhouse, or the Hanil Yeogwan (한일여관). Both accommodations, a second bathhouse, and a number of restaurants are clustered around the main intersection, only a few steps from the police station. The less expensive Unha Yeogwan (은하여관) is directly behind the bus terminal, from which intercity and city buses run.

Jinju and Vicinity

JINJU 진주

Straddling a bend in the Nam River, Jinju [Chinju] is the largest city (pop. 350,000) in western Gyeongsangnam-Do, and the principal marketplace and industrial, educational, transportation, and service center. It is one of the most pleasant cities in the country, with easygoing, hospitable people. Industrious but not frenetic, expanding but not bursting, creative, artistic and self-assured but not boastful, the city seems to rev up only during the yearly *Gaecheon* Art Festival. Expanding beyond its old core center, which lies between the Jinju Fortress and the riverside Dwibyeori palisade cliff, Jinju has pushed out its boundaries, particularly west toward the Jinju Dam and into a large broad plain to the southeast along the turn in the river, where the new city spreads out in broad streets, open areas, new residential and commercial sections, and the Sang-

pyeong Industrial Complex zone. Many mostly small factories are located here. The Namhae Expressway runs south of the city, while the newer Jungbu Expressway, connecting Tongyeong to Daejeon, is being cut between the city center and Jinyang Lake.

Close to the expressway entrance on the southern outskirts of the city is Gyeongsang National University. Near the express-bus terminal are the university medical school and hospital, and Jinju Industrial University. On the west edge of the city is the Jinju National University of Education. Half a dozen junior colleges are scattered throughout the city.

For cultural crafts, Jinju is known primarily for the production of ornamental silver knives. Today, these short knives are only decorative, but they were once worn by Korean women for protection against molestation or capture by invading armies. Jinju is also known for its pro-

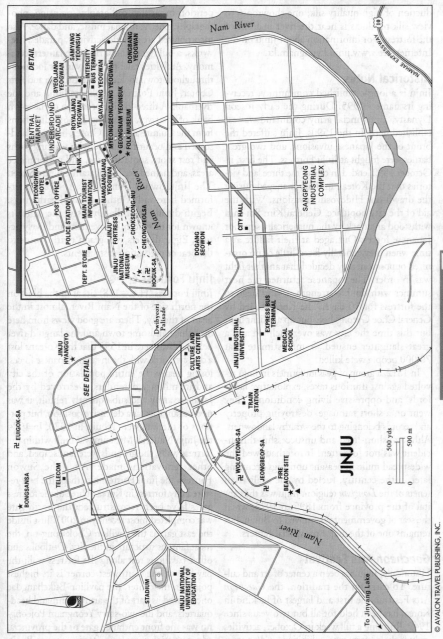

DETAIL

Nam River

CENTRAL
MARKET

UNDERGROUND
ARCADE

BYEOLJANG
YEOGWAN

SAMYANG
YEOINSUK

INTERCITY
BUS TERMINAL

DONGBANG
YEOGWAN

ROYALJANG
YEOGWAN

GAYAJANG
YEOGWAN

MYEONGSEONGJANG YEOGWAN

GEONGNAM YEOINSUK

FOLK MUSEUM

BANK

PYEONGHWA
HOTEL

POST OFFICE

POLICE STATION

MAIN TOURIST
INFORMATION

NAMGANGJANG
YEOGWAN

CHOKSEONG-NU

CHEONGYEOLSA

DEPT. STORE

JINJU
FORTRESS

JINJU
NATIONAL
MUSEUM

HOGUK-SA

Nam River

DOGANG
SEOWON

CITY HALL

SANGPYEONG
INDUSTRIAL
COMPLEX

Dwibyeori
Palisade

JINJU
HYANGGYO

JINJU
HYANGGYO

SEE DETAIL

CULTURE AND
ARTS CENTER

JINJU INDUSTRIAL
UNIVERSITY

EXPRESS BUS
TERMINAL

MEDICAL
SCHOOL

TRAIN
STATION

WOLGYEONG-SA

JEONGBEOP-SA

FIRE
BEACON SITE

JINJU

EUIGOK-SA

BONGSANSA

TELECOM

Nam River

STADIUM

JINJU NATIONAL
UNIVERSITY OF
EDUCATION

To Jinyang Lake

0   500 yds
0   500 m

GYEONGSANGNAM-DO

© AVALON TRAVEL PUBISHING, INC.

duction of high-quality silk; one showroom to view silk products is near the river in front of the fortress. For information about Jinju on the Internet, see www.jinju.kyongnam.kr.

Historical Notes

Jinju is a long-established community, receiving its name in 995. During the early Joseon Dynasty, a provincial army command was established here. In the 1590s, Jinju suffered the brunt of the Japanese invasions, and two great battles were fought at Jinju Fortress. The first, in October 1592, ended in one of the three land victories that the Korean military managed during the drawn-out Hideyoshi Invasions. With the aid of the city populace, General Kim Shi-min withstood an attack by the numerically superior Japanese forces. Outraged at their failure at a time when they generally faced little or no organized opposition, they decided that another fight was in order. The Japanese returned the next summer with double strength, laying siege to the fortress for 10 days. The Koreans, led by General Choe Gyeong-hoe, put up a valiant fight but this time the city was overwhelmed and a great slaughter ensued. Some estimate that 70,000 people were killed.

In 1812, a group of peasant farmers in Jinju revolted against usurious taxes, exploitative landlords, and oppressive living conditions. They went on a short rampage, destroying property and records belonging to the wealthy landowners. Although short-lived and unsuccessful, this incident was not forgotten. It foreshadowed the widespread militant peasant uprisings occurring later in the century, fueled by the egalitarian tenets of the *Donghak* religion. Jinju was the capital of the province from 1895 to 1925, when the seat of government was moved to Busan, but remains one of the major provincial centers.

Gaecheon Arts Festival

Historically, Jinju has been a center of art and culture. To carry on the tradition, the *Gaecheon* Arts Festival, the first and largest of its kind in Korea, has been held for all but two years since 1949. Running a full week in October, activities include the performance, exhibition, and/or competition in written calligraphy, painting, photography, poetry, drama, music, and dance. Also incorporated are athletic activities, parades, fireworks, a bullfight, and a riverside lantern ceremony. Activities take place at various locations throughout town including the Culture and Arts Center, Jinju Fortress, public stadium, and the riverbank. A three-kilometer stretch of the south bank of the river, spreading in both directions from the Culture and Arts Center, has been landscaped and beautified, filled with walking paths and rest spots, some artwork, and performance areas, and named the Namgaram Culture Street. The Jinju Sword Dance (I.C.A. #12) is performed here and at other cultural gatherings. Begun during the Silla Dynasty, the dance is known for its graceful movement and lively action. Eight dancers swing and twirl swords to the beat of percussion instruments.

Jinju Fortress 진주성

Jinju Fortress (H.S. #118) sits atop the bluff on the north side of the Nam River, almost in the heart of the city. There are good views from here over this handsome town and the languid river below. It was here in 1593 that the Koreans lost a decisive battle with the invading Japanese forces, losing nearly the entire population of the city and its military defenders. Destroyed by the Japanese army and subsequently rebuilt, it was never again used as a defensive position, but portions of the wall were rebuilt in 1970. In 1984 the Jinju National Museum was built within the fortress walls, the grounds were landscaped, and other renovations made. After the Suwon Fortress, the Jinju Fortress is perhaps the best-restored city fortress in Korea. Three of the fortress gates have been reconstructed; the north gate was completed most recently in 2001. Just inside the east gate is the pavilion Chokseong-nu, the most famous structure in the city. Outlooks and other pavilions rest along the fortress wall; the pavilion at the southwest corner is its highest point. In the center, the pavilion Bukchangdae once served as part of the army command headquarters, and the two-story Yeongnam Pojeong-nu was the front entrance gate of the provincial administration complex before its move to Busan in 1925. Nearby stand two shrines honoring residents of Jinju who fought foreign invaders and aided the economy of the region. Inside the west gate sits the small but friendly Hoguk-sa ("Protector of the Nation Temple"), home of the warrior-monks who fought with General Choe, protecting this garrison against the Japanese in 1593. To the side and up a steep flight of steps is the shrine Cheongyeolsa, holding memorial tablets for 39 patriots, including generals Kim and Choe, who both died during the Japanese attacks. This shrine was renovated in 2001. Entrance to the fortress is ₩1,000. At night, and making quite a sight, Chokseong-nu and the fortress gates are lit with floodlights, and to add dazzle to the river scene, the arches underneath the bridge crossing the river nearby are also strung with lights.

Jinju National Museum

The museum displays many earthenware and metal artifacts from the Gaya and Silla dynastie, but places special emphasis on items relating to the Hideyoshi Invasions, nearly all from this area. Not the best museum in the country, it is still worth a look. Set inside the Jinju Fortress, this museum is open 0900–1800 (1700 from November to February); ₩400 entrance fee.

Chokseong-nu

Chokseong-nu [Ch'oksŏng-nu], or "Luxuriant Vegetation Rock Pavilion" (T. #276), is one of the country's four noted ancient pavilions. Built in 1365, it was part of a military command center during the Joseon Dynasty, and preliminary civil service exams were given here for those aspiring to government office. Restored to its former grandeur and prominence in 1960 after being burnt to the ground during the Korean War, it's one of Korea's largest pavilions. Standing on sturdy posts, Chokseong-nu features a commanding view of the river from the bluff. It's attractive during the day, but the floodlit reflection off the evening river is inspiring.

To its side and through another gate in the wall stands Uigisa, a small shrine to Nongye, one of old Korea's best-known and most-respected heroines. She was one of several *gisaeng* selected to entertain Japanese generals following their victory over Korean forces in 1593. Nongye led one of the generals to the edge of the bluff called Uiam, clasped her arms around him and threw herself into the river below, drowning herself and the general. This shrine was erected in her honor in 1824. Every June 29 a ceremony here commemorates her bravery and loyalty. Down a stairway and through a gateway below the pavilion, you can walk to the rock ledge from where Nongye is said to have leaped.

Folk Museum 태종민속박물관

A few steps down the street from the east entrance to the Jinju Fortress is the **Jinju Local Folk Exhibition Hall: Taejeong Folk Museum**. This museum is open 0900–1800; ₩1,000 entrance fee. Once owned and operated at another location by Mr. Kim Chang-mun, a former shoemaker, this museum is now run by the city and displays a small collection of wooden chests and decorative brass ornaments and fittings for furniture. It's a fine display in itself, but what is shown is only a small portion of the approximately 200,000 individual traditional craft items—furniture, fittings, locks and keys, household wares, boxes, bags, gourds, food containers, wooden utensils, woodworking tools, and the like—that still are housed in the original one-room cramped showroom, reminiscent of an antique shop, that perhaps at some point in the future will again be shown to the public.

Jinju Hyanggyo 진주향교

It is said that the Jinju Hyanggyo, established in 987 during the Goryeo Dynasty, was Korea's first public academy. These local schools sprang up all over the country, educating children of the elite for public service by preparing them for the yearly national civil-service exams. Destroyed and repaired numerous times, it has appropriately been preserved in Jinju—the region's educational center. Standing on a hillside to the east of downtown, the buildings look newly remodeled, but the well-worn front gate shows signs of age. It's usually locked except during formal ceremonies; a pavilion, two dorms, lecture hall, and the main shrine stand inside.

Dogang Seowon, a private Confucian academy which once taught the classics to local nobility, has been reconstructed near the municipal library on the hillside above the city office.

Bongsansa 봉산사

On the slopes of Bibong-san behind the city is the shrine Bongsansa, erected to honor General Gang Il-shik, defender of Jinju during several battles around the year 600. His descendants, the Jinju Gang family, hold a yearly memorial ceremony on *hanshingnal* (150 days after the winter solstice) to honor him for protecting the region. Bongsansa is an impressive place as it steps up the hillside, but significant only for its historical connection. However, if you happen to be in the city on *hanshingnal,* visit the shrine and witness a very traditional ancestral ceremony. Those who visit will be rewarded by good views over the city and the back side of the fortress.

Temples

The road in front of Bongsansa leads around the lower slope of Bibong-san to the road heading to the temple **Euigok-sa** [Ŭigok-sa] (의곡사). Small and rather ordinary in appearance, except for the new main hall, it's the major temple in the city. Walk under the bell pavilion; bright deva murals line the corridor. The main temple hall has fine murals on its exterior wall.

Set behind tall apartment buildings on the south side of the river is the multi-story temple Wolgyeong-sa (월경사). Brightly painted, almost garish, this temple belongs to the Cheontae sect and is not unusual in ornamentation. In contrast, the smaller and more traditionally-decorated Jogye sect temple Jeongbeop-sa (정법사) sits up the hill. High above them both on the ridge above and at a spot with a good view of the river, city, and surrounding area is a reconstructed fire beacon site (망진산봉수대), which once served as part of a nationwide warning system for disaster and invasion.

Jinyang Lake 진양호

The Nam River, dammed in 1969 just west of the city, creates Jinyang Lake. This was one of the first modern multi-purpose dams in Korea, and the largest in the province. In the mid-1990s, a new, taller dam was constructed in front of the original, increasing the size of the lake and its potential uses. City buses run out to a small cluster of restaurants and accommodations, a kiddie amusement park, and a small zoo (₩1,000 entrance; hours 0900–1800) on the hill above the dam; ₩400 entrance to the area. Food and accommodations here are generally more expensive than in the city, but the location is pretty and tranquil. Near the bus stop is a pavilion which offers a good view over the lower portion of the lake. While no ferries operate on the lake, there are rowboats to rent in the summer and you may see scullers from a local rowing club practicing on the smooth surface.

Practicalities

The main tourist information office in the city is located just outside of the fortress's north gate. An information booth also is located next to its east gate. Along the river in front of Jinju Fortress you'll find a small silk center and the Taejeong Folk Museum. The police station and central post office are both in the city center; the Telecom office is several major streets toward the hills. City hall lies in the new section of the city. To exchange money, try the Korea Foreign Exchange Bank or other banks near the main rotary. An underground arcade runs under the street below the city's main traffic rotary intersection. Fancy shops, restaurants, and coffee houses are also located along the main street up from the river and in the adjacent alleys, principally near the post office, where several streets close to vehicular traffic at night and become the heart of the city's night scene. The city's central market lies east across the main road, while a vegetable and fruit market is located closer to the intercity bus terminal. Backed up against the levee in the old town area is the intercity bus station. The express-bus terminal is south of the river not far from the train station.

Accommodations and Food

In front of the train station you'll come across the

usual variety of accommodations. Decent mid-range *yeogwan* are located between the bridge and the intercity bus terminal, and below the eastern entrance to Jinju Fortress. The best in Jinju is the first-class Jinju Dongbang Tourist Hotel (tel. 055/743-0131). Set along the river, it offers a fine view over the city. Amenities include a restaurant, lounge, coffee shop, sauna, nightclub, and game room. Korean and Western rooms starts at ₩90,000, suites start at ₩150,000. Located next to the post office, the more pedestrian Pyeonghwa Hotel (평화호텔) offers rooms for ₩30,000–45,000. Among dozens near the bus terminal are the Gayajang Yeogwan (가야장여관), Royaljang Yeogwan (로얄장여관), Byeoljang Yeogwan (별장여관), and Samyang Yeoinsuk (삼양여인숙). Nearer the fortress you'll find the Myeongseongjang Yeogwan (명성장여관), Namgangjang Yeogwan (남강장여관), and Gyeongnam Yeoinsuk (경남여인숙). Others of course are located near the train station and express-bus terminals.

Many ordinary restaurants are located near the bus stations. A line of high-end eateries fronts the river outside the east fortress gate. Many other restaurants are located along the main streets up from the river and in the adjoining alleys, while the area surrounding the post office has more.

Transportation

Flights from **Sacheon Airport** (사천공항), 10 kilometers south of Jinju, connect 10 times a day to Seoul, and once daily to Jeju-do. Check with either Asiana Airlines (tel. 055/747-7015) or KAL (tel. 055/757-2295) for tickets and reservations either at their office in the city or at the airport. Inside the airport's tiny terminal are ticket counters, a small departure lounge, snack shops, souvenir shops, and a small tourist-information desk. A taxi to the airport costs about ₩15,000. Much cheaper and nearly as convenient is a city bus (₩1,100) that lets you off at the side of the terminal building along the highway. Airport limousine buses run from just outside the terminal building to Jinju (₩3,000), Tongyeong (₩6,300), and Geoje (₩7,800).

From Jinju Station, trains run five times a day to

Busan and Seoul, once a day to Suncheon, Masan, and Gwangju, and three times to Mokpo. Sample *Mugunghwa-ho* routes are Seoul (₩23,600), Busan (₩3,700), and Mokpo (₩6,200).

A few steps from the train station is the express bus terminal, with buses every 30 minutes to Seoul (₩16,600), every 20 minutes to Busan (₩4,900), every 40 minutes to Daegu (₩6,100), every two hours to Gwangju (₩6,900) and Daejeon (₩6,100), with four a day to Suwon (₩16,000) and Incheon (₩17,400). The intercity bus terminal sits along the river. Selected destinations include Tongyeong (₩4,800), Okcheon-sa (₩2,300), Samcheonpo (₩2,300), Namhae (₩3,800), Hadong (₩3,600), and Haein-sa (₩7,200).

City buses crisscross the city. Some of the most useful include no. 22, connecting the express-bus and intercity-bus terminals and the *hyanggyo*, nos. 15 and 25 to the Jinju Fortress, nos. 26, 70, 50, and 500 to Jinyang Lake, and no. 36, which runs up to Bongsansa.

HADONG AND JIRI-SAN SITES
Hadong 하동

South of the great Jiri Massif, the Seomjin River marks the boundary between Gyeongsangnam-Do and Jeollanam-Do. On the east bank lies Hadong, gateway to the Gyeongsangnam-Do section of Jiri-san National Park, the temples Ssanggye-sa and Chilbul-sa, and the traditional village of Cheonghak-dong. Some special products from the area include chestnuts, persimmons, pears, bamboo salt, dried laver, green tea, and mushrooms. Along with the low hills of Boseong, down the coast in Jeollanam-Do and the slope of Mudeung-san in Gwangju, the hillsides around Ssanggye-sa in Hadong are one of Korea's major tea-growing areas. Unlike the Boseong area, Hadong seems to have smaller acreage given to these trees and smaller companies producing the leaf. Fronting the Seomjin River, a 15-minute walk from the center of town, is a grove of stately pines called Songnim-sup. This shady stand borders a beach on the river, all now part of a town park. Fine for a stroll during the day, it's perhaps best in early morning or during the full moon. Tucked into the rear of this sylvan grove is an archery range. Indicative of development in the region, the glow to the southwest is not the red glow of the sunset but the lights of the Gwangyang steel factory and adjacent industries reflecting off the clouds.

Although you'll find a good number of restaurants in town, there's slim pickings in the way of accommodations. Look for one ordinary *yeogwan* just behind the bus terminal and the much better Hotel Silla (호텔신라) a short walk into town. The bus terminal is on the east end of town and the train station is half a kilometer farther. Selected bus destinations include Ssanggye-sa (₩1,800), Chilbul-sa (₩2,400), Cheonghak-dong (₩3,000), Jinju (₩3,600), Namhae (₩2,800), and Yeosu (₩5,400). More than half a dozen trains run through Hadong each day in both directions between Busan and Gwangju, with one traveling up to Seoul.

Ssanggye-sa 쌍계사

North of Hadong, tucked into a tight valley on the southern slopes of Jiri-san, sits Ssanggye-sa, one of the mountain's principal temples; ₩2,800 entrance fee. Four kilometers of the road that leads up to the temple entrance are lined with cherry trees, and the road passes small tea plantations. In May, the trees create a tunnel of blossoms, and thousands of people journey here to see this stretch of pink pour down the valley. Built in 722 as Okcheon-sa, its founding is related by the following legend: When the monks Daebi and Sambeop returned from China with the skull remains of the sixth patriarch of Zen Buddhism, they were instructed in a dream to find a valley on Jiri-san where arrowroot blossomed even through the snows of winter. They found such a place in this valley, founded Okcheon-sa here, and erected a memorial for their relic. In 840, the temple was enlarged and its name changed to Ssanggye-sa by Jin'gam Seonsa. Known as an exponent of chanting, Jin'gam is said to have planted tea seeds from China near the temple after finishing his study there. Tea is still grown on the mountain and the annual Mountain Dew Tea Festival is celebrated here. Today it's a district headquar-

ters of the Jogye sect, and the nearby Chilbul-sa and Guksa-am are under its jurisdiction. An hour above the temple is Bulil Waterfall, one of the tallest in the country at 60 meters, and above that Bulil-am hermitage. Over the mountain ridge is Cheonghak-dong.

Three entrance gates lead to the temple, the third housing four huge, well-sculpted wooden devas. Beyond the last gate is an unusually tall, nine-tier granite pagoda erected in 1990. Passing around the lecture hall and bell pavilion, you'll enter the main courtyard. It's said that in the lecture hall, Korea's first Buddhist music was created. A stone tablet (N.T. #47) with a detailed and stylized tortoise base stands in the courtyard, memorializing the temple's founder and meditation master, national priest Jin'gam. Unusually, Ssanggye-sa's tatami-floored main hall (T. #500) holds seven statues on its wide altar, and huge murals provide a backdrop. Other buildings at this good-sized compound include a Nahan hall, Three Spirits hall, a judgment hall with a well-painted ceiling, and a storage hall for wood printing blocks. Above this central compound, in a secondary courtyard, is Palsangjeon, where murals show the eight scenes of the Buddha's life (T. #925). Next door is Geumdang, which houses a stone pagoda said to contain a piece of the patriarch Heuineung's skull.

Guksa-am is half a kilometer up the hillside. Towering over its entrance gate is an old, four-trunk elm tree referred to as the Four Kings of Heaven Tree. The elm symbolically represents the four devas usually placed at the front gate of temple compounds to protect the grounds from evil influence. Quiet and neat, Guksa-am has an unusual feature—all of the altar figures and murals are in different rooms in the U-shaped hall. Near this hermitage is the *sari budo* raised for Jin'gam (T. #380). Farther along an adjacent trail is Bulil Waterfall, a narrow ribbon of silver that plunges down the craggy cliff face frothing into lace, constantly wetting the luxuriant vegetation.

Below Ssanggye-sa lies a small village with a few shops and a handful of accommodations and restaurants. Several private *minbak* also operate in the village. From the stop below this cluster of *yeogwan*, numerous buses run south to Hadong

(₩1,800) and Gurye (₩1,300), less frequently to Suncheon, Busan, and Gwangju. A number of buses run up the valley every day to Chilbul-sa.

Chilbul-sa 칠불사

Chilbul-sa ("Seven Buddhas Temple") is much smaller than Ssanggye-sa. Legend tells that seven *(chil)* monks (some stories say the seven sons of Gaya king Suro) meditated here, reached full enlightenment, and became Buddhas *(bul)*. Chilbul-sa was most famous several centuries ago as one of the country's leading and most renowned Zen temples. The temple still functions today as a meditation center, and at 800 meters in elevation it's appropriately high above the distractions of daily life. According to the theory of geomancy, Chilbul-sa has one of the most auspicious locations in the country.

About the same age as Ssanggye-sa, Chilbul-sa was largely destroyed during the Korean War, but underwent extensive renovation in 1984. From the parking lot, a long run of stairs leads up and through the new front gate to the main courtyard. The small main hall has more intricate woodcarving than most temples in the country. Parts of the altar, its back panel and statues, interior wall panels, and front doors are all delicately fashioned, and many fine murals decorate its exterior walls. However, this temple is best-known for the building Aja-bang, set to the left side of the compound. The interior floor space of this hall is split into two levels, a cross-shaped central walking space, and raised U-shaped platforms at each end for meditation. The meditation area, half a meter above the floor, is heated by an *ondol* system that takes about three days to heat—but warms for six weeks!

Bus from Hadong or Ssanggye-sa. From Chilbul-sa, a mountain trail leads to Tokki-bong, a peak in the middle of the Jiri-san ridgeline. For more details on Jiri-san, other temples, and trails, see the Jiri-san section of the Jeollanam-Do chapter.

Cheonghak-dong 청학동

About 10 kilometers over the ridge east of Ssanggye-sa, nestled high into one of Jiri-san's long valleys, is probably Korea's most traditional village. Cheonghak-dong [Ch'ŏnghak-dong], or "Blue Crane Village," is a tiny community caught halfway between old Korea and the 20th century. Repopulated in the early 1900s, it was a functioning religious community in past centuries, referred to as the Village of Taoist Masters. Today, over 200 people call Cheonghak-dong their home, and about 50 of these still practice a traditional way of life. Here, a thread of ancient Korean society still weaves its way through the present by means of old customs and traditions, and where a unique religious life is still practiced. A syncretic blend of Taoism and Confucianism, the villagers believe they can attain a "utopia" if they steadfastly follow their spiritual beliefs. Old-style baggy white garments and *gat* are still worn. As in centuries past, old men grow wispy beards and wear their hair in topknots; unmarried men's hair is grown long, braided, and allowed to hang down. Young women are married early. Some old-style farming methods are employed, many houses are still thatched with straw, and some verandas sport beehives topped with a conical thatched roof. Once the classical subjects were taught at the village school. Today, children are sent away to school to concentrate on their subjects and not be disturbed by visitors. Most days, there's not much to see at the village. The men are in the fields, the children are away at school, and the women are tending to chores at home. Although facing a tenuous situation, Cheonghak-dong survives as a cohesive, semi-traditional community, by law shielded from the onslaught of outside development. The future remains uncertain, and with the influx of weekend tourists, the village has in some ways become unrecognizably changed, a parody of its former historically traditional and spiritual self. Villagers insist, however, that change can be absorbed and a balance found between old and new. They insist that no matter what outward changes occur, their heritage and the focus of their spiritual life will remain the same.

Although Cheonghak-dong is Korea's gem of traditional village life, a microcosm of days gone by, outside influences are creeping in. Imports include electric lights, clocks, telephones, televisions, rolled flooring, and plastic of all sorts. A number of souvenir shops have opened to cater to visitors and driving a vehicle to and from town for supplies is not unheard of. Many buildings have been modernized, and modern farming implements are in use. No village in Korea exists today as it did a century ago, but Cheonghak-dong is still undoubtedly the most authentic relic of old-style Korea, changing as little and as slowly as possible in the nation's headlong rush through a cathartic evolution toward modernization.

While the outward lifestyle has changed irrevocably, most villagers still try to cultivate the spirit of their religious beliefs and carry on the ceremonies and rituals of their ancestors. An early-morning recitation is performed, and circle dancing periodically is conducted for a ceremony honoring their religious founder. The most obvious outward sign of the ceremonial religious life is the sacred area **Samseong-gung,** which is dedicated to Hanin, Haneung, and Dan'gun, the legendary progenitors of the Korean people. To get to Samseong-gung, walk back down the road about half a kilometer and turn onto the road running into the adjoining valley. From the end of this road, it's about 300 meters up a path to the grounds. Rock towers indicate the boundary, but a sturdy stone wall and a gate block your entry. Samseong-gung is not open to outsiders except when special public ceremonies are performed. Inside, rocks have been piled into pillars, ponds dug, altars erected, areas cleared for group ceremonies, and a few buildings built.

Five times a day from Hadong (₩3,000) buses run to Cheonghak-dong, which sits at about 800 meters in elevation. The bus follows a steep, twisting road up a rugged valley and past two reservoirs to what seems like nearly the top of the mountain. The road has improved over the years. Now paved all the way, it's not nearly the experience it used to be. Gaining in notoriety, the village now attracts tour buses, as well as more and more private vehicles. At the end of the bus line is a community of restaurants, drinking establishments, and accommodations that really plays host to all the visitors who come to look at their old-style brothers. Here too are souvenir shops and a Folk Hall, where village crafts and products are sold. From here it's a 10-minute walk to the core of the village, and after paying your park entrance fee, it's another eight kilometers west over the ridge to Bulil Waterfall, or 13 kilometers north to the Saeseok meadow on Jiri-san's long ridgeline.

NAMHAE-DO 남해도

South of Hadong, and lying between Yeosu and Samcheonpo, is the island of Namhae-do, the outline of which is reminiscent of the *janggu*, Korea's hourglass-shaped folk drum. Separated from the peninsula by the Noryangjin Strait, this 298-square-kilometer island—Korea's fifth-largest—is connected to the mainland by the Namhae suspension bridge. Fishing, and seaweed and oyster harvesting, are significant parts of its marine economy. Tall, rugged mountains create the two major bulges on this island, leaving narrow, agricultural plains clinging to its perimeter. With an increase in population, the island communities have slowly expanded. Every available flat parcel is intensely cultivated. Aside from a historical connection to the Hideyoshi Invasions, the suspension bridge, and Sangju Beach, Namhae-do is best known to Koreans for three varieties of trees. Together referred to as *samja*, individually they are *yuja* (Citrus janus: Chinese lemon), *bija* (Torreya nucifera: Japanese nutmeg), and *chija* (Gerdenia jasminoides: cape jasmine).

Travel to the island used to be there and back, but now it's possible to circle through and be on your way via the new bridge to Samcheonpo.

Noryangjin 노량진

Spanning the Noryangjin Strait is the Namhae suspension bridge. Slung from two tall towers, this graceful, 660-meter-long, 12-meter-wide arch of steel is often referred to as Korea's Golden Gate Bridge, which it resembles. Completed in 1973, it was the first of several suspension bridges in the country. Get off the bus and walk across—from this height, you can see distant islands in the waterway, squares of white oyster floats dotting the blue water, and some industrial areas to the west. At both ends of the bridge are rest areas, shops, and restaurants.

Set below the south end of the bridge, the tiny port of Noryangjin fronts the strait. Early in 1598, the last major naval battle of the Hideyoshi Invasions was played out near here. Victory came to the outnumbered Koreans, but the great Korean strategist Admiral Yi Sun-shin was killed—felled by an enemy bullet. Built in 1632, the unobtrusive shrine **Chungyeolsa** (H.S. #233) still stands on the knoll above the village at his original burial site; its front gate has been designated T. #293. Inside hangs a portrait of Admiral Yi and several murals relating to the battle. Outside but within the walls of the shrine are a memorial stela and a mound representing the admiral's original grave. An annual memorial ceremony is held here on the 15th day of the third lunar month. On the waterfront below this shrine is a turtle ship replica, ₩1,000 entrance, that is very much like the one at Yeosu. A look inside gives you a good idea of what kind of ship this was and what the living conditions were like on board.

A few kilometers into the island and located on a spit of land at the seashore is the shrine Yiraksa (이락사) (H.S. #232), supposedly just inland from the site where Adm. Yi fell in battle. Yiraksa houses a memorial tablet and out on the point is a pavilion where a signboard describes the fateful event. Where once the naval battle was fought below, you now look out on the POSCO steel factory in the distance.

Namhae 남해

A market town, Namhae is roughly in the middle of the island. There is little to see or do in this community, and most people bus right through on their way to the south end of the island. If you stay, you'll find the Hwajeon Motel (화전모텔), the town's best, a few steps down the main street from the central intersection not far from the post office. One street to the east are the Bangunjang Yeogwan (방운장여관) and Yeongnamjang Yeogwan (영남장여관). The bus terminal sits on the eastern edge of town along the bypass road. Bus destinations and fares include Jinju (₩3,800), Hadong (₩2,800), Suncheon (₩4,100), Noryangjin (₩1,000), Yongmun-sa (₩1,000), Sangju Beach (₩1,500), and Mijo (₩2,000).

B-24 CRASH SITE

On the night of August 7, 1945, one week before the end of World War II, an American B-24 on a bombing run to Yeosu (then a strategic Japanese military port) was shot down, crashing into the mountain that towers above the town of Namhae. In the morning, Japanese military authorities and Korean workers hiked to the crash site. Useful parts of the plane were salvaged, but the 13 bodies of the crew were left to rot. One Korean worker, Kim Dŏk-hyŏng, returned secretly that night and properly buried the men. He was found out and placed in jail, but, luckily, the war ended within a week and he was released. Furthering his commitment to honor the American airmen, he started collecting money for a monument. After the Korean War, Mr. Kim raised enough money to erect a four-meter-high granite marker at the rather inaccessible crash site, and in 1989 he established a small memorial hall in town, on the 2nd floor of a building just down from the main intersection in Namhae. His single-minded dedication made him an oddity in his own community, yet he has received coverage in U.S. newspapers, and official commendations from the U.S. Air Force, U.S. Department of the Army, and U.S. Forces in Korea. A memorial service has been held every year since the crash on October 26.

Yongmun-sa 용문사

Not far above the island's narrow waist, on the hillside overlooking the large south bay, is Namhae-do's principal temple, Yongmun-sa, or "Dragon's Gate Temple". Founded by Wonhyo on Geum-san nearby, it was later moved to its present location. Take a bus to the village of Yongso, and from there it's a 30-minute walk up the hill, under the viaduct, and into the forest. At Yongso, terraced fields step down the hillside in syncopated cadence to the edge of the bay.

Geum-san

Geum-san peak (681 meters) rises high over the eastern portion of this island, its summit scattered with huge boulders and rock outcrops. At the top stands a man-made structure of piled rocks, a centuries-old fire beacon site. From the summit, the southern half of Namhae-do comes into view, and you can see Samcheonpo in the distance. With the island-studded sea in the foreground, the sunrise from the summit is exceptional on clear mornings. A short distance below the peak, amidst huge boulders, sits the tiny hermitage **Bori-am** [Bori-am] (보리암), one of three religious retreats dedicated to Gwanseeum Bosal, the Goddess of Mercy. It's said that Yi Songgye, the Joseon Dynasty's first king, spent 100 days praying here before taking the reigns of power. At Bori-am you'll find a three-tier stone pagoda and a large temple bell. Ever wonder how a bell so large gets brought to a spot like this? A tall statue of Gwanseeum Bosal has also been erected at this hermitage and she looks out over the water to the south. At the Geum-san entrance to the south, a wide path from the highway leads about two kilometers through the forested hillside up to this hermitage and beyond to the summit. The trail starts about two kilometers up from Sangju Beach, at a point where several *yeogwan* and shops line the road. Alternately, a new road winds its way to the back of the mountain from near the waist of the island, passing a reservoir on the way. From the end of the road, a walk of less than one kilometer brings you to Bori-am. From either entrance there is a ₩1,300 entrance fee.

Sangju Beach 상주해수욕장

Sangju Beach, one of Korea's finest, lies below Geum-san. This two-kilometer-long crescent of silky sand nestles into a small cove protected by rocky promontories at each cusp and a diminutive island at its opening. Lined with pine trees, this beach slips into the calm, shallow waters of the bay, its placid surface disturbed only by infrequent punts and the ever-increasing tourist boats. Be aware, however, that although perfect most times of the year, this beach attracts hordes of campers (mostly students) during the summer school holidays. It can be crowded, noisy, and full of trash. Behind the pines that front the beach are many *yeogwan*, *minbak*, and camping space. Pricier during the swimming season, rates can be bargained down in the off-season. You'll find many other places to stay, as well as restaurants and shops in the village up from the beach, but many are closed during the off-season. Near the parking area facing the pine grove is the post office and the Gyeongsangnam-Do office of the Hallyeo Waterway National Park. The entrance fee for this beach area and to other portions of the park is ₩1,300. Between Mijo and Sangju lies Songjeong Beach, similar to, yet smaller and much less crowded than, Sangju Beach. It too is being developed.

Hallyeo Waterway National Park

한려수도국립공원

Like an emerald-studded blue cloth draped over the shoulders of a beautiful woman, this park embraces the south coast of Gyeongsangnam-Do. The many straits and channels of this waterway are its warp and woof, the patchwork of islands its precious stones. Like cloth, the length and breadth of this marine park must be seen, felt, and experienced at close quarters to be fully appreciated. View the park from the coastal hills or island mountaintops, skim across the surface by ferry, swim in its warm waters, or kayak near the shores, but by all means come and enjoy.

Established in 1968, 477 square kilometers of the southern coastal land (now increased to 510 square km), along with about a half million square kilometers of water, were designated Hallyeo [Hallyŏ] Waterway National Park. Of the 100 or so islands within the park's boundary, only 38 are inhabited. The six sections of the park are spread from the south coast of Geoje-do in the east to the island of Odong-do at Yeosu in the west, including the Noryangjin Strait, Geum-san/Sangju Beach area, Hak-do and the strait in front of Samcheonpo, and the large district comprising parts of Tongyeong, Mireuk-do, and Hansan-do. Numerous beaches, temples, small island scenery, and picturesque rock formations are encompassed within the park and the area is historically important for the sea battles directed by Adm. Yi Sun-shin and his famous turtle ships.

East Coast

The entire eastern coast of Namhae-do is marked by rocky promontories broken by half-moon bays, and one little fishing village after another. At the south end is the village of **Mijo** (미조), a small fishing port with a few *yeogwan* and restaurants, and buses to most points on the island and to Jinju. Although smaller, **Mulgeon** is another such village, with its gray pebble beach, protected harbor, and hardwood trees lining the water. North of Mulgeon is the Namhae youth hostel. Established principally for school groups, it occupies a rather uninspiring and isolated beach. At the north end is the community of **Jijeok**. Fish traps in the channel between the islands are perhaps like no others in the country. Constructed of stakes driven into the bottom, the 10- to 20-meter-wide round traps have 50-meter-long funnels attached. With the tide running in the direction of the round end, fish are directed into the funnels and through gates at the throats which close behind them. There is no escape. The fish are then easily harvested. What used to require a ferry ride now is done quickly by a bridge that crosses this channel to Changseon-do, from where a road continues on to the north end of the island and across the new bridge to Samcheonpo.

COASTAL SITES

Samcheonpo 삼천포

A fishing port of 80,000, Samcheonpo [Samch'ŏnp'o] lies across the channel from Changseon-do. Once a separate city but now administratively incorporated into the city of Sacheon, it's well-known in Korea for the variety of dried seafood processed and marketed here, including anchovies, octopus, shark, and stingray. A favorite of locals and guests, raw fish is served in the city's many seafood restaurants. A long stone's throw from the harbor, the tiny islet of Hak-do (N.M. #208) stands as a protected breeding and feeding habitat for white herons, egrets, and other migratory waterfowl. It and other small islands in the bay make up a small section of the Hallyeo Waterway National Park. During the Japanese invasions of the 1590s, Admiral Yi used the small and now partially restored port of **Daebangjin** as a naval harbor. This harbor lies just west of the present harbor. The most important historical

site in Samcheonpo is Gak-san Mountain Fortress, with its piled-stone fire beacon site overlooking the city to the west. A hike to the top takes less than one hour from Daebangjin. A closer vantage point for viewing the downtown area, as well as the harbor and offshore islands, is much lower No-san Park, situated directly east of the inner harbor. Namildae Beach, the best in the area, is farther east. It's a small secluded crescent that's only detraction is the red-and-white striped stacks of the electric power generation plant poking their heads up above the rise to the east.

While new facilities have been built a short way to the east, fishing boats and a few ferries and excursion boats crowd the old inner harbor. Ordinary ferries to Saryang-do depart from the pier directly in front of the Fishing Cooperative building. Until the completion of the bridge to Changseon-do, ferries to the island leave from a pier just to the west. These vehicular ferries cross every 30 minutes between 0710 and 1740 and run ₩400 for the 15-minute ride. On Changseon-do, buses meet each ferry and take passengers to Jijeok or Namhae. Among others, city bus nos. 30 and 71 run regularly between the harbor (one block up from the waterfront) and the bus station. Intercity buses go to Jinju (₩2,300), Goseong (₩2,800), and Busan (₩7,600). After the bridge to Changseon-do is completed, buses will run that direction to the town of Namhae.

The best accommodations in town are the second-class New Samhwa Hotel (tel. 055/832-9711), near the bus terminal up in town, and the Samcheonpo Beach Hotel (tel. 055/835-5212) out along the water west of the harbor. Near the pier, try the Samcheonjang Yeogwan (삼천장여관), or Geumgangjang Yeogwan (금강장여관).

Goseong 고성

In the lowlands between Jinju and Tongyeong sits the small town of Goseong [Kosŏng]. A provincial naval command center during the early Joseon Dynasty, today it's the seat of local government for this laid-back, coastal county. During the 1590s, several sea battles were fought against the Japanese invasionary forces off the

Sangjokam dinosaur prints

coast near here. The Danghangpo shrine has been raised to commemorate these events. Rice and vegetables are farmed, and oysters are harvested from the sea. The old oyster shells are strung on a cord and hung underwater beneath white flotation markers to attract live oysters. A two-kilometer walk from the center of town takes you past the girls' high school to the tiny port of Nampo. Restaurants here specialize in fresh shrimp and fish. While the fish is good at any time of year, the shrimp are best from the end of August to November, when they go directly from boat to pot.

One of the big events in town is the **Citizen's Day Festival**, an affair of music and dance, art exhibitions, sports contests, parades, and speeches. Sometime during the festivities, the *Goseong Ogwangdae* masked dance (I.C.A. #7) is performed. One of numerous such theatrical performances throughout the country, its religious significance

has now largely been overshadowed by its pure entertainment value. Incorporating dance, jesting, dialogue, and song, it purports to expel evil and bring good fortune, alternately poking fun at the corrupt but privileged *yangban* class, ridiculing lascivious apostate monks, and satirizing the triangular husband-wife-concubine relationship. Twenty-three troupe members perform the dance, each wearing a brightly colored wood or paper mask.

The bus terminal has been moved to the north end of town and there is a new post office at the large rotary just where the main street turns and runs through the town center. While there are no accommodations yet near the bus terminal, you can still find the Gyeongbokjang Yeogwan (경복장여관) directly behind the Gyeongnam Bank near the large rotary. A block or so farther along the main street are the Royaljang Motel (로얄장모텔) and several restaurants. Look for the tall smokestacks in town indicating bathhouses. Selected bus destinations include Busan (₩6,400), Tongyeong (₩1,500), Samcheonpo (₩2,800), Jinju (₩3,300), Gohyeon (₩3,200), Deongmyeong (₩2,800), and Gaecheon (₩2,200).

Sangjokam County Park
상족암군립공원

Located between Goseong and Samcheonpo is Sangjokam, seaside rock outcrops that have eroded in a stacked layer-like pattern indicating that they are sedimentary material. In 1981, **dinosaur footprints** were discovered at water's edge below these stacked cliffs—and they are prime examples! When the tide is right, water pools in these prints, making them stand out like plates of silver. Of various sizes, many of these three-toed imprints are about 30 centimeters in diameter and create a line. Numerous other prints are found along the coast nearby in both directions and at several other locations to the east, and a few have been uncovered on Namhae-do, in Jinju and Masan, and at other spots along the coast. Facilities will be added to this newly created county park. Located in Deongmyeong, buses run half a dozen times a day from Goseong to this isolated spot.

Yeonhwa-san Provincial Park
연화산도립공원

North of Goseong, on a back road to Jinju, lies the low-mountain area of Yeonhwa-san (552 meters). *Songi* mushrooms are raised on its slopes, some tea is grown, and wild berries are picked to make *bokbunja* liquor. In 1983, 29 square kilometers of Yeonhwa-san were designated a provincial park. The park has a few trails, but the principal temple, Okcheon-sa, and three hermitages—Cheongnyeon-am, Baengnyeon-am, and Yeondae-am—lie in its folds. Bus to Gaecheon (₩2,300) from either Goseong or Jinju. Buses run about once an hour throughout the day in both directions. From the eastern edge of the village, walk two kilometers up the narrow valley past a reservoir and the park entrance community to the temple grounds; ₩1,300 entrance.

Founded in 676 by Uisang, Okcheon-sa [Okch'ŏn-sa] (옥천사) functions as an educational center for the local Buddhist administrative district. Well-worn and well-used, it has seen only minimal reconstruction in recent years. A weathered pavilion near the creaky front gate is the first building to greet you as you come up the steps. Shuttered on the outside but open to the courtyard, it faces the temple's main hall. Originally erected in 676, the present structure dates from 1639. Squat wooden devas guard the doors of the diminutive main hall, only 20 years newer than the pavilion. Dragons circle the altar pillars, and one rises directly over it. Cranes fill the remainder of the ceiling squares. The three look-alike altar figures are attended by a well-used skin drum and bell. In the judgment hall, stocky and gruff carved wooden figures over one meter tall stand guard inside the finely detailed doors, protecting the well-cast incense burner and gong. Numerous other smaller halls crowd this compact compound, each level separated by granite retaining walls and steps. To the rear of the compound is a mineral spring, perhaps where the temple gets its name—Jade Spring Temple. While none of the buildings is exceptional in and of itself, taken together they make a fine whole. The newest construction of note is the temple museum which preserves old important objects and treasures. While all explanations are in Korean, the books, paintings, incense burners, a bronze gong (T. #495), and other objects displayed are typical of items kept and used by temples.

Tongyeong and Vicinity

TONGYEONG 통영

Tongyeong (pop. 140,000) is perhaps the country's prettiest medium-sized port. Located along the waterfront at the end of a peninsula, the city incorporates much of the surrounding countryside, the 39-square-kilometer Mireuk-do, and some 150 other islands within its boundary. Its protected outer harbor is framed by Mireuk-do, the fishing harbor is tightly encompassed, and a larger new commercial harbor now lies to the east. The center of the city fronts the harbor but newer sections have pushed back inland and across the bay to the northern edge of Mireuk-do. Once connected to the mainland by a muddy isthmus, Mireuk-do is now separated by a narrow, dredged channel. Jutting into this southern coastal waterway, yet protected by numerous offshore islands, Tongyeong has an unbeatable location. The unspoiled beauty and historical connections, particularly the naval command of Adm. Yi Sun-shin, make Tongyeong, Mireuk-do, neighboring Hansan-do, and the surrounding waters one of the largest and most significant sections of the Hallyeo Waterway National Park. The city is inextricably tied to the sea. It has the most extensive ferry network between Busan and Yeosu, and is home port for one of the largest concentrations of fishing boats on the south coast. Small cargo ships and wooden fishing boats are built and repaired here on a limited scale. Deep-sea and coastal fishing, oyster farming, and food processing are thriving industries. Appropriately, located here is the Fisheries Technical College.

While the post office remains in the heart of the old city, the Telecom office has been moved near the Ch'ungmu Bridge. City hall is now located out past the harbor, while the police headquarters is found near the bus terminal. A tourist-information booth is located at the Donam Resort Marina. The Korea Foreign Exchange Bank is located next to the Beach Hotel; others are near the post office. The central market sits across the road from the old harbor, and the newer Seoho Market fills the streets fronting the passenger ferry terminal.

See www.tongyong.kyongnam.kr for information on the Internet.

Hansan Victory Festival

Every year in the early fall, the Hansan Victory Festival is held in Tongyeong to commemorate one of the major Korean naval victories of the Hideyoshi Invasions and the accomplishments of Admiral Yi Sun-shin. A parade, farmers' music and dance, a masked dance, shaman's dance, the War Victory Dance, other cultural events, sports competitions, and a memorial ceremony for the

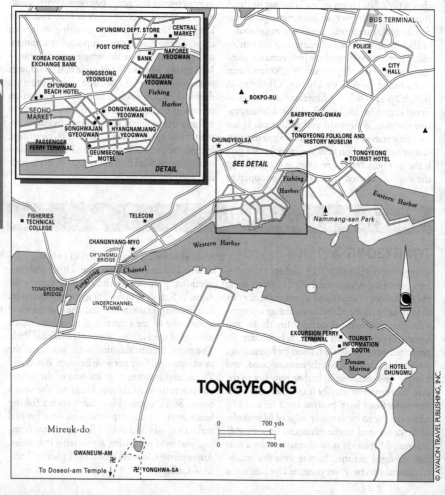

TONGYEONG

0 _____ 700 yds
0 _____ 700 m

© AVALON TRAVEL PUBLISHING, INC.

admiral at Jeseung-dang on Hansan-do are just a few of the events. In 1955 the city's name was changed from Tongyeong to Ch'ungmu in honor of Admiral Yi, who is often referred to by his formal title, Ch'ungmu-gong—*ch'ung* means "loyalty," *mu* means "military," and *gong* is an honorific title equivalent to "Lord." In 1995, the city's name was changed back to its historical appellation.

Cultural Assets

Tongyeong's several Intangible Cultural Assets include two local dances. The *Tongyeong Ogwang-dae* (I.C.A. #6) is a five-act, masked-dance drama performed by 31 dancers wearing colorful masks made mostly of gourds and paper. Like most others from the Joseon Dynasty, it stems from the common people. Witty and earthy in speech, most dances are improvised and accompanied by slow, languid music. The second, the Victory Dance *Seungjeonmu* (I.C.A. #21), commemorates the naval battle of Hansan-do. It's occasionally performed at cultural festivals throughout the province, at Jeseung-dang during the Hansan Victory Festival, and at memorial ceremonies at Chungyeolsa. Admiral Yi supposedly made his men perform the dance aboard ship and in camp to boost their morale. After the great victory of Hansan-do, it was danced in celebration. Today it's performed by a troupe of young women accompanied by a traditional orchestra. In addition, the *Namhaean Byeolshingut* shaman dance (I.C.A. #82) is particular to this south coastal area and is also performed at local festivals.

The remaining Intangible Cultural Assets are the skills of local craftsmen. *Tongyeong chit* (I.C.A. #4) is the production of the Korean *gat* (horsehair hat). As few gentlemen still wear these distinctive hats, only a few hat-makers are left to carry on the trade. Formed over a mold, *gat* are made from horsehair, silk thread, organic glue, stick ink, ash, and a natural varnish. Historically, the size and shape (and sometimes material) of each hat indicated social rank in the highly stratified Confucian society. Horsehair hats were most often worn by *yangban,* while commoners wore hats of bamboo. Basically, the wider the brim, the higher the social standing. An inner cap

under the *gat* covered the topknot of hair that every married man wore. *Gat* were worn both outside and inside, taken off only when another type of headwear was required, or while relaxing at home.

Najeon chilgi, the creation of mother-of-pearl lacquerware (I.C.A. #10), has been handed down from father to son for centuries. While there is evidence of its existence from the Silla period, it was only widely produced in the Goryeo Dynasty. During the Joseon Dynasty, even commoners might have owned a piece or two. Today, *najeon chilgi* is found in most households—everything from knickknacks to jewelry cases, tables, and clothes cabinets. Much is also exported. The abalone shells used are taken from the south coast near Tongyeong, said to have some of the world's best colors and iridescent qualities. Over the wood base a layer of natural lacquer varnish is applied. This lacquer is the processed sap-like exude of the lacquer tree. A pattern is then drawn on this varnished surface, to which the shaped mother-of-pearl must correspond. Each tiny piece is cut and set by hand—a painstaking and time-consuming task. Thin bronze or tin wire is sometimes used for certain design features. Geometric, floral, scenic, and Chinese character designs, or a combination, are most popular. Once the inlay is completed, additional layers of black (sometimes red) lacquer are applied, raising the surrounding surface to the level of the mother-of-pearl. Because drying is needed between each of the several dozen coats of lacquer, weeks are required to finish a project. To help celebrate this fine craft, a Lacquerware Festival is held every year in late September.

The skill of Korean furniture-making, *somok-jang* (I.C.A. #55), has also been handed down from father to son. Pieces often made today include chests, wardrobes, bedside cabinets, low tables, inkstone and bookcases, and mirror, stationery, and document boxes. Wood is selected for its particular grain and color. Often, four or more types are combined in one piece. After sufficient drying, the major flat surface pieces are "bookmatched" (split so that each piece mirrors and complements the other), their grain creating an overall harmonious feel. Depending on the piece, construction can take weeks or months, and while expensive, the work is exceptional.

Fine Korean furniture is decorated with brass, silver, tin, or alloy fittings including handles, pulls, hinges, locks, corner caps, and decorative plates. This craft is called *duseokjang* (I.C.A. #64). Designs are hand-drawn and made to order for each piece of furniture. Ranging from simple to complex, they are mostly animal figures, floral designs, and Chinese characters.

Nammang-san Park 남망산공원

Capping the low hill that forms the east side of Tongyeong's inner harbor is Nammang-san Park. A paved road winds around the forested hillside past the city's new Cultural Center to the summit, where a large bronze statue of Admiral Yi Sun-shin gazes out over Mireuk-do, Hansan-do, and the coastal waterway. Periodic music or theater performances and art exhibitions take place in the center's several halls, a small sculpture garden lies out front, and large *najeon chilgi* cabinets are displayed in the lobby. An archery range has been constructed on the south side of this hill, a pavilion has been placed for the best views, and circling the hilltop are wooded walking paths. Bordering the park at seaside are a number of shipbuilding concerns and fishery warehouses. On the inland side of this hill spreads most of the city. To the west of Nammang-san lies the tightly packed inner harbor, its line of fishing boats nosed against the quay. On this quay a broad open space called Tongyeong Culture Plaza has been constructed. It is used for outdoor performances and is a favorite place to stroll or sit on warm summer evenings. To the east side of the hill is the commercial Dongho Harbor.

Saebyeong-gwan 세병관

Built in 1603, Saebyeong-gwan [Saebyŏng-gwan] is one of the three largest old wooden structures in the country; ₩220 entrance. This open post-and-beam structure (T. #293) is all that remains of a much larger complex (H.S. #402), from 1597 the naval command headquarters of the country's southern province's division. This command center was used until 1896 when the last

admiral of the division died. It was subsequently abandoned. Memorial stele for him and his predecessors stand in an enclosed section. "Saebyeong" refers to soldiers washing their blood-stained clothing and cleaning weapons, and even today a traditional weapons-inspection ceremony is performed here as part of the yearly Hansan Victory Festival. Saebyeong-gwan was last renovated in 1973, but plans call for a major and long-term rebuilding of this former complex to show the site as it likely was some 400 years ago. At that time, the city was surrounded by a defensive wall. In 1993, Bokpo-ru, the north guard post of the fortification, was re-erected at the top of the hill to the back of the city and that pavilion is now a favorite place for short walks and good views over town.

Directly across the street from Saebyeong-gwan is the Tongyeong Folklore and History Museum (통영시향토역사관) and it has several rooms showing important historical and cultural aspects of the city. This is a good quick overview and signage is only in Korean, but the displays of handicraft items and the cultural arts legacy are well worth a look. Open 1000–1800 (1700 in winter) except Mondays and major holidays.

Guardian Totems

To the right side of the road leading to Saebyeong-gwan, standing unceremoniously in front of the *dong* (precinct) office, is a stone guardian totem referred to as a *beoksu*, or *seokjangseung*. Erected in 1906 to ward off disease and evil spirits from the village, its unnerving smile, bug eyes, and fangs must certainly have done the job! Smaller and more weathered examples can be found along the road at the entrance to the villages of Samdeok-ni and Dangpo on the western side of Mireuk-do. These guardian figures have been used for centuries in Korea. Totems in the southern regions are predominantly made of stone; elsewhere in Korea, they're generally wood.

Chungyeolsa 충렬사

Around the hill from Saebyeong-gwan sits Chungyeolsa [Ch'ungyŏlsa] (H.S. #236), a major shrine dedicated to Admiral Yi Sun-shin; ₩800 entrance. While the shrine was first erected in 1606, several buildings have been added in the intervening centuries. As opposed to the grandiose and imposing Chungyeolsa shrine to Admiral Yi erected in Onyang in the 1960s, this pleasant place is a fine representation of the old-style commemorative shrine, in scope, structure, and harmony with its surroundings. Built on several levels, the main hall is on the top terrace, while an exhibition hall is set below. The main hall houses the admiral's memorial tablet, and the exhibition hall preserves eight items (T. #440) presented to him by the Chinese emperor. These gifts include a stamp seal, battle flags and horns, and two gigantic swords. Admiral Yi's collected written works (N.T. #76), portions of which are still studied in schools, are stored here as well. Every year on *Chuseok,* a memorial service is held at Chungyeolsa to honor the admiral.

A separate memorial ceremony is held every April and November at **Changnyang-myo** (창량묘), near the peninsular end of the channel tunnel. Set on a low knoll, Changnyang-myo was the first of many such shrines erected throughout the centuries for Admiral Yi. It's usually kept locked.

Underchannel Tunnel 해조터널

Early in the 20th century, a single-span stone arch bridge crossed the narrow canal separating Mireuk-do from the peninsula. It was taken down in 1932, and the channel was widened and deepened to allow uninterrupted boat traffic. From 1927 to 1932, a tunnel—supposedly the first of its kind in Asia—was constructed under the channel with conscript Korean labor. Five meters wide, four meters high, and 461 meters long, it was originally for vehicular traffic, but now is only open to pedestrians. Even though it undergoes periodic maintenance, it is still obviously very solid and remarkably watertight after all these years. Have a walk through. It's cool on a hot summer day! The graceful Ch'ungmu Bridge, constructed in 1967, spans the Tongyeong Channel above this tunnel, and the newer Tongyeong Bridge also now crosses the channel farther to the west.

Mireuk-do

Above the small old reservoir on the north side of Mireuk-do [Mirŭk-do] is the temple **Yonghwa-sa** (용화사). Originally constructed in 632 and called Cheongsu-sa, its name was changed in 1628 after a devastating fire. The present buildings were all constructed in the 19th century. Set on the top terrace of the grassy courtyard, the main hall features a glass-enclosed altar enshrining the triad Amita, Daesaeji, and Gwaneum. On windy days, fish chimes tinkle under the eaves and incense wafts from the building's interior. Also of interest are the judgment hall and the eight-sided bell pavilion. The portrait of Hyogong, the temple's most recent well-known abbot, sits on the altar in Myeongbujeon. He died in the 1980s and his five-tier *sari budo* and statue sit to the side of the compound on the way up to other *sari budo.* Oddly, this pagoda and the entire temple compound are now guarded by replicas of four figures from Emperor Jing's tomb in X'ian China, not the usual deva gate guards. One former monk from the temple visited India in the '60s. When he returned, he had a replica of the Asoka Pillar built in stone, faithful in style except for the stone ball set on top.

From Yonghwa-sa, one trail continues to the top of the mountain, while another cuts across the side to the hermitage **Gwaneum-am.** A path from the bus stop below also leads to this hermitage, around the right side of the reservoir. A meditation center, this quiet retreat is dedicated to Gwaneum, the Goddess of Mercy. Its front gate is constructed of arched stone and capped with a small but elaborate roof—much like a city gate in miniature. Two stone *haetae* and deva guards painted on the doors guard the entrance. A green carpet of grass nicely sets off the stone lanterns, fish pond, and flowering bushes within the compound. In front of the small main hall sits a pagoda which, unusually, has an even number of roof tiers. To the rear of the compound is a painted, shallow relief carving of Gwaneum done on a stone stela block. Above Gwaneum-am is **Doseol-am,** the oldest hermitage on the mountain. Legend relates that long ago a dragon ascended to heaven from here.

Built below a pronounced rock outcrop, this hermitage stands in stark contrast to the beautified and trim Gwaneum-am precinct. From Doseol-am, you have a fine view of the island-studded waterway and distant Geoje-do. A trail from here leads to the mountain's summit. A round-trip hike from Yonghwa-sa to both hermitages and the top should take about two hours.

A road circles Mireuk-do offering great views of the coast and rural island life. On the south end of the island and perhaps the best place from which to get a sweeping view of other and smaller coastal islands is **Dala Park** (달아공원). Perched on a bluff, this rest stop offers exceptional coastal vistas. Bus no. 39 makes periodic rounds of the island. Farther along are ruins of a fortress from the 1300s and a couple of stone guardian figures at the north end of the village of Dangpo.

Donam Marina Resort 도남관광단지

A few kilometers east of Yonghwa-sa, past numerous small shipyards is Donam Bay. On the bay below Hotel Chungmu is Donam Marina Resort; the marina lies behind the breakwater. Excursion boats depart the terminal building; tickets are sold on the 2nd floor, souvenir shops and restaurants are located on the first. Out front is a tourist information booth. The round-trip to Jeseung-dang on Hansan-do costs ₩6,500 and requires 1.5 hours. Trips to Haegeumgang—for beautiful cliffs and rocky seashores—or Haegeumgang combined with stops at Maemul-do and Jeseung-dang cost ₩14,000–17,500. The combination trip, to Jeseung-dang and Maemul-do, is ₩13,000; the three-hour round-trip to Yeonhwa-do and Guk-do costs ₩17,500; and the shorter trip to the beach on Bijin-do runs ₩10,000. Departure times vary throughout the day and according to the season, but boats usually run 0900–1800 in summer and 1000–1600 in winter. Check times and cost before you make plans.

Accommodations and Food

The best accommodation in Tongyeong is first-class **Hotel Chungmu** (tel. 055/645-2091). Set on a bluff overlooking both the Donam Marina Resort and the tiny Donam Beach, this hotel has a near-perfect location. Standard rooms run ₩70,000, suites higher. In the lobby is a fine collection of approximately 20 *heungbae*, embroidered designs worn on the chest over formal wear to distinguish rank of royalty, and both civilian and military government positions of the past dynasty. The road south from the resort around the southern end of the island offers fine views of Donam Beach, Hansan-do, Bijin-do, Geoje-do, and the Geoje bridge. Closest to the passenger ferry terminal is the older and more dowdy **Ch'ungmu Beach Hotel**, where rooms start at ₩40,000. Set on a knoll near the new harbor you'll find the **Tongyeong Tourist Hotel** (tel. 055/646-7001).

Many *yeogwan* and *yeoinsuk* lie in the tightly packed area between the ferry terminal and fishing-boat pier. Try the Dongyangjang Yeogwan (동양장여관), Hangnamjang Yeogwan (항남장여관) and bathhouse, the Songhwajang Yeogwan (송화장여관), or the Geumseong Motel (금성모텔). For a more spartan, less expensive place, try the Dongseong Yeoinsuk (동성여인숙). Fronting the fishing harbor is the Haniljang Yeogwan (한일장여관) and on the far side is the Naporee Yeogwan (나포리여관). Many new and large accommodations are also available near the bus terminal, however, these are some distance from the center of town.

A variety of restaurants are found between the two harbors, mostly toward the main street, while a number of seafood restaurants line the street fronting the fishing harbor. Tongyeong is known for *gimbap* (a nutritious morsel of rice and sliced vegetables rolled in seaweed) sold at several small stalls near the fishing-boat pier. For ₩2,000–3000 you get enough *gimbap* to fill you, plus a little radish and sections of spicy octopus on the side.

Transportation

There is no train connection to Tongyeong. Leaving from the passenger ferry terminal, ferries connect Tongyeong with about four dozen ports on over a dozen islands. Excursion ferries leave from Donam Marina. Because of the beach, ferries to Bijin-do (₩11,500) are most often used by visitors during the summer months. The far flung islands of Maemul-do (₩14,100), Yokji-do (₩7,000), and Yeonhwa-do (₩8,000) attract visitors for the scenery, and boats to Hansan-do (₩3,500) go for the historical sites.

The bus terminal in Tongyeong is in the northern section of the city. Destinations include Jangseungpo (₩3,100), Haegeumgang (₩4,400), Goseong (₩1,500), Jinju (₩4,800), and Busan (₩7,800). From the terminal, nearly all city buses run through downtown. Selected bus routes are: nos. 10, 20, 21, 27, 35, 41, and 47 to downtown; nos. 20 and 21 to Yonghwa-sa; no. 41 to the under-channel tunnel; no. 51 to Hotel Chungmu; no. 39 for the Mireuk-do round-island route.

HANSAN-DO 한산도

Between Mireuk-do and Geoje-do, a half-hour ferry ride through placid waters from Tongyeong, you'll find Hansan-do. Although now a zone for fishing and oyster farming, this island witnessed a ferocious sea battle that ended in a Korean victory over Japanese forces in 1592. The following year, Admiral Yi Sun-shin moved the southern naval command headquarters here from Yeosu; it stayed four years until it was moved to Saebyeonggwan in Tongyeong. The compound sits on a tiny peninsula in a calm, diminutive bay on the north end of the island. The most prominent building, Jeseung-dang [Chesŭng-dang] (H.S. #113), is a re-creation of Adm. Yi's command headquarters. Completely renovated in 1976, this site was dedicated as a shrine to the admiral; ₩1,000 entrance. A memorial hall here houses Yi's portrait, and another building exhibits murals depicting scenes from the great Hansan-do battle. A pavilion overlooks the bay, and the archery range is unique because arrows must be shot at targets on the far side of a cove. Several defensive gates and other structures have been reconstructed, and a barracks site is in evidence. At the opening of this tiny bay is an unsightly cement lighthouse in the shape of a turtle boat.

Nearby Islands

Just south of Hansan-do you'll find bottle-shaped **Bijin-do** [Pijin-do], one of the nicest places to swim in the province. **Maemul-do, Yokji-do,** and **Yeonhwa-do** are known for surf fishing. Both Maemul-do and Yokji-do have lighthouses, while Yeonhwa-do [Yŏnhwa-do] has a small beach. As travel is time-consuming and accommodations are few, be sure there's a return ferry before you venture to these islands.

Geoje-do 거제도

In the azure coastal waterway just off the south shore of the peninsula is Geoje-do [Kŏje-do]. With an area of 399 square kilometers, it's Korea's second-largest island. While the whole of the island is administratively a city (pop. 170,000), the largest towns are still Gohyeon, Okpo, Jangseungpo, and Geoje. Known for its beautiful landscape, especially its rugged south coast, Geoje-do is mountainous, with a surprisingly large forested area. Its coastline is indented with a handful of sizable bays, and the numerous peninsular headlands create dozens of small coves and inlets. None of the half-dozen beaches is anything special, but Gujora draws sizable summer crowds and Hakdong is peculiar as a pebble beach. The island's more open northern and western sections contain a few broad agricultural valleys that run down to the sea. These valleys and the lower mountain slopes are heavily farmed, predominantly with rice and vegetables, but some pineapple and aloe are also grown. In contrast, the southern and eastern areas are characterized by limited coastal plains, narrow valleys, and hillsides sweeping down to the water's edge. Rocky seaside cliffs predominate in the south, culminating at Haegeumgang. This coast has been used as a movie location when a windswept, rugged coastline or dramatic, sheer bluff is called for. A great portion of this southern coast and the waters offshore are part of Hallyeo Waterway National Park.

Some areas of Geoje-do, such as the seaside grove of soapberry trees at Hannae and the forested slopes of Noja-san above Hak-dong, are set aside as nature preserves; the grove of camellia trees between Hak-dong and Haegeumgang is also protected (N.M. #233). Geoje-do is the wintering ground for several species of waterfowl, and Hak-dong is a breeding ground for the rainbow-colored fairy pitta bird (N.M. #204).

Farming and fishing have always been the keystones of the island's economy, but since the 1970s the industrial sector has expanded dramatically. Daewoo, one of South Korea's largest conglomerates, operates a huge shipyard in the Okpo Bay. Samsung, another mega-company, runs a smaller shipyard just outside Gohyeon. Development has brought increased tourism and the expansion of transportation, accommodation, and eating facilities, yet much of the island is little affected by these changes, remaining rural and relatively isolated.

Gohyeon is also the home of former president Kim Young-sam, the first popularly elected non-military leader of the country. Born in Oepo, on the east coast of the island, Kim's power base has traditionally been the Gyeongsangnam-Do area.

For several decades, Geoje-do has been connected to Tongyeong and the mainland by a bridge. During the mid-1990s, the highway from Okpo to Tongyeong was widened and straightened, and in an effort to alleviate traffic congestion across the channel, a second and larger bridge was constructed across the channel. With the completion by 2006 of a series of bridges to Busan from the northern tip of the island, Geoje-do will be opened to yet another transportation route. The area around Jangmok will be developed with modern tourist facilities, and older sites like the Jangmok Hyanggyo and former president Kim Young-sam's birthplace will be more accessible.

All highway buses to Geoje-do come through Tongyeong. Many run all the way to Jangseungpo, while a few stop in Gohyeon. Others bypass both those towns and run to Haegeumgang via the village of Geoje. City buses travel to all points on the island from Gohyeon and Jangse-

ungpo, including the picturesque south coast between Jangseungpo and Haegeumgang.

Geoje-do has lots of ferry traffic—the most pleasant way to reach the island. Geoje-do is most connected to Busan, with ferry traffic from Gohyeon, Okpo, and Jangseungpo. Ferries from Gohyeon also run to Masan, and there is a connection from Jinhae to the small port of Shiljeon near the northern tip of the island, from where you can catch a city bus to Gohyeon.

See www.geoje.go.kr for information online.

GOHYEON 고현

The county seat of Gohyeon [Kohyŏn] lies on the north coast of Geoje-do, at the head of a relatively broad valley. The establishment of the Samsung Shipyard on the outskirts of town brought a great influx of workers from other parts of the country, greatly expanding the population and creating many infrastructure demands. Much of the town, especially the harborfront, is going through a stage of massive expansion, and new residential areas are growing to the east. Generally, visitors to the island just pass through Gohyeon on the way to the south coast, but there is one site of interest in town for history buffs.

POW Camp

Built and maintained by the U.S. Army during the Korean War, a huge POW camp was located in the two valleys that the town of Gohyeon now occupies. It was one of the principal holding centers for captured North Korean and Chinese soldiers during the war. By November 1951, the prisoner population stood at about 170,000—nearly the same as the current population of the entire island! With such a large detained population—a combination of pro- and anti-Communist Korean prisoners and Chinese POWs—troubles were rife. Frequent and heated disturbances between these groups, and violence, were commonplace. At one point, a group of North Korean prisoners captured and held the camp commander, a U.S. Army brigadier general, for three days after he had entered the North Korean compound to negotiate the treatment of prisoners. Relieved of duty after his release, he was replaced

re-creation of Geoje POW camp

by a much tougher commander, who brought order and security to the camp. In an attempt to derail truce negotiations, former South Korean president Syngman Rhee released 27,000 pro-North Korean prisoners from this camp in 1953, using South Korean troops to overpower the U.S. guards and open several gates. After the armistice in July of 1953, this camp was closed and all prisoners were repatriated to their country of choice, North or South Korea for the Koreans, and Communist China or Taiwan for the Chinese.

Most of the camp was torn down after the armistice, but some two dozen structures remain, scattered around the periphery of the Gohyeon area. A couple are located at the lower end of town, east of the harbor; a few more stand on the hillside next to a school. Nearly all are vacant shells, their gaping window and door openings resembling the blank eye sockets and nose holes of huge skulls. The remains of this detention center (H.S. #24) have been set aside for preservation. A **POW Camp Site Exhibition Hall** (거제도 포로수용소유적관) sits next to those remains near the middle school, providing an explana-

tion of life at camp, displays of historical items from that time, and a scale model of the camp as it stood in 1951–53; ₩1,000 entrance fee. While very little English appears on signage at the exhibition hall, the pictures and displayed objects are graphic enough for you to get the picture. Next to this mini-museum is a re-creation of a section of the camp, complete with tents, guard towers, fences topped with barbed wire, and a tank and artillery pieces. This site is located up the street from the city government administration building, about a 15-minute walk from the center of town.

Practicalities

The best place to stay in Gohyeon is the **Geoje Tourist Hotel** (tel. 055/632-7002). In the center of town, only a minute from the bus terminal and ferry piers, it offers Korean and Western rooms for ₩55,000–78,000, suites for ₩180,000. Also on the premises you'll find a coffee shop, bar, nightclub, Korean restaurant, and a public bathhouse. Several *yeogwan* can also be found between the bus terminal and hotel.

There are two small ferry piers in Gohyeon. The one at the end of the town's main street departs ferries to Masan, while 100 meters west is the pier for ferries to Busan. Four times a day, a small ferry runs between Gohyeon and Masan (₩10,200), and four times a day a hydrofoil runs between Gohyeon and Busan (₩14,700). Once or twice a day, these ferries each stop at Jangmok on their way. For Jinhae, take a city bus to Shiljeon and catch the ferry there to cross the channel.

Intercity buses from Gohyeon run to Jangseungpo (₩1,400), Tongyeong (₩1,800), Jinju (₩6,500), and Busan (₩9,700) from a new bus terminal near the highway. City buses run to all points on the island, including Okpo and Jangseungpo, Haegeumgang, Geoje, Jangmok, and Shiljeon.

EASTERN GEOJE-DO

The old port of **Jangseungpo** [Changsŭngp'o] (장승포) was the principal population center for the eastern end of the island. A good example of a Korean port town, it maintains an active market, decent anchorage for a good-size fishing fleet, and frequent ferry connections, and it's the starting point for buses down the coast. Over the rise to the north sits **Okpo** [Okp'o] (옥포), which was smaller and a less important port. Since the 1970s, however, when Daewoo established its shipyard there, the community has grown rapidly, clawing its way up the hillsides, expanding around the bay, and incorporating the small port of Dumo in its grasp. It is more modern than Jangseungpo, now has a larger population, and is definitely a one-company town.

Most people going to Okpo either work at the shipyard or are related to the industry. There is little to draw visitors to town; however, the **Geoje Museum** would be a stop for those who do go. Located along the highway through town, this small museum focuses on the island's prehistoric and historic relics, offering a brief historical sketch of the island up to the Korean War.

Catering primarily to businesspeople and located up on the highway, the **Admiral Hotel**

(tel. 055/687-3761) is a homey, friendly place offering a multitude of restaurants and recreational opportunities. Less expensive *yeogwan* can be found down in the center of this community near the post office. Many other places to stay are located near the livelier port of Jangseungpo and restaurants line the roads fronting the water there. Perhaps the best of the accommodations is the **Jangseungpo Beach Hotel** (tel. 055/682-5151) where rooms run ₩80,000–180,000).

A great number of catamaran ferries ply the waters between both Jangseungpo and Okpo and Busan. Jangseungpo's spacious ferry terminal (장승포항여객선터미날) sits on the west side of the harbor, from where eight ferries a day go to Busan (₩15,300). Okpo has a smaller terminal and half a dozen ferries a day travel from there to Busan (₩15,300). Excursion ferries also leave Jangseungpo from a separate terminal located back in toward town from the ferry terminal. These boats run mostly to Haegeumgang, but depending on the season and demand, several other options are offered, including to Oe-do and Maemul-do.

Except for city buses running along the south coast, all intercity buses from Jangseungpo pass through Okpo and Gohyeon, and carry on to Tongyeong and other points on the peninsula. City buses run frequently between Jangseungpo and Gohyeon, but less often along the south coast to Dongbu or Haegeumgang. The intercity bus terminal sits to the east of the harbor on the way to Neungpo, where a city bus terminus is also located.

SOUTHERN GEOJE-DO

Much of the southern coast of Geoje-do is part of the Hallyeo Waterway National Park. It's rugged, and the few steep, narrow valleys allow only limited, intensely cultivated fields. The narrow plains are interspersed with headland promontories or forested hills that seem to push right up from the sea. Rocky outcrops abound, generally larger and more dramatic the farther west you move. Until 1984, the road along this coast was only a dirt track, but it has since been paved, alternately running along the seashore and high on the mountainside. One of the island's nicest sand beaches is at Gujora, and Hak-dong sports a pebble beach. Accommodations can be found at Gujora, Hak-dong, and other small communities along the coast. Summer excursion ferries to Oe-do and Haegeumgang depart from Wahyeon, Gujora, Hak-dong, Dojangpo, and the pier across from Haegeumgang.

Oe-do 외도

Oe-do is a tiny island in the bay between Gujora and Jangseungpo that has been converted into a botanical garden with various flowers, flowering plants, palms, cactus, and bamboo, many of them exotics to Korea. There is also a sculpture garden, numerous walkways and observation points, and seacliffs. Set within the national park boundaries, entrance is by excursion ferry from Jangseungpo or other points along the south coast of Geoje-do. Admittance to the island runs ₩4,500 and a couple of leisurely hours is enough for a good look. A trip to Oe-do is easy from anywhere on Geoje-do as well as from Tongyeong or Busan.

Haegeumgang 해금강

Like mountaintops protruding above a sea of clouds, the rocks of Haegeumgang [Haegŭmgang] poke their camellia-topped heads above the blue sea. Only half a kilometer offshore, Haegeumgang is the culmination of the rugged south coast. These steep and craggy isles are considered a miniaturized marine version of the Diamond Mountains, and this impression is heightened when the mist rolls across the sea in the early morning, partially obscuring the scenery and letting your imagination create the remainder of the mountain vista. As part of the Hallyeo Waterway National Park, a fee of ₩1,300 is changed for entrance to this area.

For a look down on this marine mountain, follow the path from the rear of the village's only *yeogwan* and proceed past the small hermitage Seoja-am to the high point on the cliff—about 20 minutes. You'll find many small trails here; all lead to the headland's highest point except the ones heading steeply down the hill to secluded fishing spots along the rocky shore. On the cliff,

you're about 100 meters above the rocky shore, looking straight down at the crashing waves below. Steady! This rocky promontory makes a nice place for an afternoon picnic. Watch boats come and go or view the full moon on a cloudless night. On a clear day, Halla-san, Jeju-do's majestic volcanic peak, can be seen on the horizon, four times as far as the highest point on the nearest Japanese island, Tsushima, to the southeast.

The somewhat seedy Haegeumgang Yeogwan offers Korean and Western rooms for ₩30,000; its restaurant and coffee shop are busy during the summer. Several *minbak* and seafood restaurants are also located in the village below. This is the end of the bus line, and buses from the village run to Gohyeon (₩3,500), Tongyeong (₩4,400), and Jangseungpo (₩2,800).

Seasonal summer ferries connect Haegeumgang to Tongyeong, Masan, and Busan, but their schedules seem not to be regular. When there is enough demand, local excursion ferries depart the Haegeumgang pier for a two-hour tour of Haegeumgang or Oe-do for ₩9,000. A second excursion ferry pier is located partway back up this peninsula at the Dojangpo fishing port. These excursion ferries are the best way to get a close look at the dramatic, rugged coastline and offshore islands.

Two roads reach Haegeumgang from the north, both running through Dongbu. The eastern road, by far the most picturesque, leads past the pretty Dongbu Reservoir, over the thickly forested pass to the pebble beach at Hak-dong, and out the long peninsula to its end. Passing through the village of Jeogu, the other road traverses the sparsely vegetated western slope of the southern peninsula before turning east to the Haegeumgang headland.

Geoje 거제

Overlooking the largest bay on the west coast of the island is the agricultural community of Geoje [Kŏje]. For most visitors, Geoje is merely a stop on the way to Haegeumgang. Yet it offers a lively market, and up from there a local *hyanggyo* and a reconstructed Joseon Dynasty government office building called Giseonggwan. The latter was used from the time of its construction in

1663 until 1914 when this community was the seat of local government. It is said to be one of the best examples of extant old important architecture in the province. On the hillside above town you can see the remains of Oksan Geumseong, one of the stone fortresses which protected this island during the Joseon Dynasty. Crowning the hill stands a new pavilion.

Cities on the Bay

One of the largest south coast bays is Jinhae Bay; taking advantage of its excellent position and adequate anchorage is the naval port city of the same name. Extending inland from Jinhae Bay is Masan Bay. The western half is incorporated into the industrial city of Masan, while the eastern portion lies within the city of Changwon. Most of the newly created heavily industrial sector of Changwon is some distance from the water, but a portion of its manufacturing enterprise zone has established itself bayside. Together, the population of Jinhae, Masan, and Changwon is just over one million, and along with Busan, Ulsan, and the smaller surrounding cities of Miryang and Yangsan, the southeastern corner of the peninsula has the second greatest population concentration in the country.

JINHAE 진해

Jinhae [Chinhae] is one of the prettiest communities along the south coast. A clean, compact, and neatly arranged port of 130,000, this burgeoning industrial city is slowly and inexorably pushing to the east along the water but is still dwarfed by its neighbors. Although Jinhae is only a small commercial port, it's the home base and headquarters of the Korean navy, and the location of Korea's Naval Academy. A small contingent of U.S. sailors is also stationed here. Unlike most other Korean cities, downtown Jinhae seems to have plenty of space and people seem to be unhurried. Jinhae is best-known for its cherry trees, originally planted when the Japanese occupied the city and established a naval base here at the beginning of the 20th century. Most trees were uprooted after liberation in 1945—Japan's national flower was seen as a symbol of oppression. The trees you see today have been planted since 1945

and are now legally protected. There are an estimated 160,000 in town—about 40,000 of them line the four-kilometer road from the city center to the hillside Jangbok Park. Depending on the weather, these trees bloom for a 10- to 15-day period at the end of March or the beginning of April. Aside from its cherry trees, the thickly-wooded **Jangbok Park** (장복공원) is a wonderful city asset, offering many walking trails, an archery range, several Buddhist temples, a restaurant, and great views of the city. A new amusement park and a Citizens' Hall have been built along the highway leading to the park.

Japanese influence is still obvious in the city's layout and architecture. Look for two-story structures with horizontal wood siding (fast disappearing), and notice the orderly array of broad streets with wide sidewalks radiating out from three major rotaries in the center of town. Dominating the city center is a forested knoll set aside in 1967 as **Jehwang-san Park** (제황산공원). Topping this hill is an observation tower offering fine views of virtually the entire city, the coastal range of mountains, and the few islands dotting Jinhae Bay. The 1st floor of this tower contains the free Jinhae City Museum which details the history of the city; open daily except the day after holidays. One step for each day of the year leads you from the street steeply up to the tower. Take your time and enjoy the cherry trees that line the stairway.

For additional information, see the website www.jinhae.go.kr.

Cherry Blossom Festival

Since 1952 the annual Gunhang-je (Naval Port) Festival has been held in Jinhae in the spring, when the cherry trees bloom. Activities relate mostly to Admiral Yi Sun-shin and his naval victories over the Japanese during the invasions of the

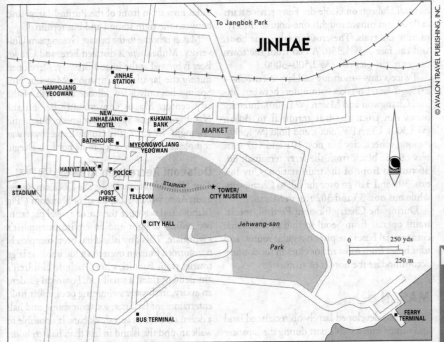

1590s. Over the years, a more broad-based cultural festival also began to be celebrated at this time. Today these festivals have been incorporated into a 12-day event often referred to as the Jinhae Cherry Blossom Festival. It's a festive time, when this sleepy town comes alive and hosts more than two million visitors from all over the country. Events include a parade, fireworks, an Air Force flyover, military band performance, an honor guard demonstration, a commemorative ceremony for Admiral Yi, sports contests and traditional folk games, a folk art competition, traditional and contemporary musical performances, a performance of the *ganggangsullae* dance, a shaman ritual, and a Miss Cherry Blossom beauty contest. Most of the festivities take place in the city streets, at the public stadium, and at Jangbok Park. However, special buses are arranged to take people inside the naval compound to view the cherry trees there and these leave from the traffic rotary outside the academy gate. Streets are filled with food vendors and arts and crafts

dealers. At night, colored lights strung from the trees cast a warm glow over the milling crowd and music wafts out of countless tearooms and drinking establishments. Everyone seems to be in the mood for a little levity. Still, the crowds do get a bit overwhelming, and transportation connections are somewhat disrupted.

Practicalities

Downtown Jinhae stretches several blocks, from the train station to the post office. In this area are numerous adequate accommodations, among them the Nampojang Yeogwan (남포장여관), New Jinhaejang Motel (뉴진해장모텔), and the Myeongwoljang Yeogwan (명월장여관). The closest tourist hotels are in Changwon and Masan. Like the accommodations, restaurants are numerous and abound in this area. Several seafood restaurants are near the ferry pier for those wanting to sample the local catch.

A vehicular ferry runs seven times a day (eight on Saturday, Sunday, and holidays) between Jinhae and Shiljeon on Geoje-do. Ferry service starts at 0700 and runs at roughly one-hour-and-forty-minute intervals. The crossing takes one hour, and the fare is ₩4,350. A taxi from the town center to the pier costs ₩2,500–3000.

Twice a day—morning and late afternoon—a *Tongil-ho* train takes commuters between Jinhae, Changwon and Masan (₩1,100). Intercity buses run from the bus terminal to Busan (₩3,300), Ulsan (₩7,900), and Jinju (₩4,900). Among others, city bus nos. 101 and 107 start service one block from the ferry terminal; no. 36 runs in front of the train station. City bus nos. 309 and 310 go over the hill to Changwon, while bus nos. 33 and 302 run to Masan.

During the Cherry Blossom Festival, special trains operate from Seoul to Jinhae, additional commercial buses are put on regular routes, and tour buses from most major cities in the country accommodate the hordes of visitors.

MASAN 마산

Masan was developed largely on reclaimed land and turned into a viable port during the Japanese occupation. During the 1970s, new life came into the city with the expansion of its port facilities and the creation of a Free Export Zone at the north end of the bay, used by foreign companies to manufacture goods that are directly exported. In exchange for preferential tax and tariff status, these foreign companies employ thousands of Korean citizens. This city of 450,000 will undoubtedly continue its economic growth as both domestic and foreign companies take advantage of the reasonable labor costs and high-quality workmanship.

The old city of Masan stretches along the west side of the bay, roughly from the passenger ferry terminal, past city hall, to the fish market. The newer sections push north past the train station. Masan claims several city parks, but its primary tourist attraction is Dotseom, an island amusement area in the bay. The major commercial/business area is located inland of the bayside markets, while a newer shopping/entertainment area has grown up north of there near the intercity bus terminal. Underground shopping arcades now sit in front of the Purim Market and between the train station and bus terminal.

Masan is home to the private Gyeongnam University. Muhak *soju* is distilled here, and Crown Beer is brewed at the Joseon Brewery. Developed during the Japanese occupation, Mageum Hot Springs lies only a few kilometers north of the city center. Masan conveniently lies on the Namhae Expressway which connects Busan and Gwangju. In 1977, the Guma Expressway was completed, offering a quick route north to Daegu.

Dotseom Recreation Area 돝섬유원지

Two kilometers from shore, the Dotseom Recreation Area, which occupies all of Dotseom ("Pig Island") and was once the site of a royal pig farm, is a child's delight and an environmentalist's nightmare. This tiny island has been completely transformed from an overgrown hill into one large tourist trap. Facilities here include children's amusement rides, a small zoo, botanical garden, an aviary, freshwater swimming pool, roller rink, entertainment facilities, souvenir shops, and half a dozen restaurants and snack bars. It's possible to walk around the island in less than half an hour, so you know there's hardly a square meter left untouched. The entrance fee, which includes the short round-trip boat ride from the ferry terminal, is ₩5,000 for adults and half that for children. Dotseom is open during daylight hours and ferry departures vary according to the season.

Practicalities

Masan's finest hotels are the **Crystal** (tel. 055/245-1112) and **Masan Royal** (tel. 055/244-1150), both with rooms in the ₩80,000 and up category. Next to Masan Station is the second-class **Masan Arirang Hotel** (tel. 055/294-2211), where rooms are about ₩60,000. Literally dozens of *yeogwan* surround the intercity bus terminals, fewer near the train station, and many in city center.

About a dozen trains a day in each direction run the Gyeongjeon rail line along the south coast between Busan and Mokpo, stopping at Masan. In addition, one morning and one afternoon train from each direction make the short trip through Changwon to Jinhae.

The Masan Ferry Terminal (마산항여객선터미날) is near the southern end of the city. Aside from the boat to Dotseom, four daily ferries run to Gohyeon (₩10,200) on Geoje-do, with one stopping at Jangmok (₩6,700).

A few hundred meters up the street from the train station is the major intercity bus terminal (마산시외버스터미날). Selected destinations from this terminal include Busan (₩2,900), Gyeongju (₩6,600), Miryang (₩3,500), Daegu (₩4,300), and Jinju (₩3,600). The city's Nambu bus terminal (마산남부시외버스터미날) is south of the ferry terminal and buses departing from it run mostly to the south of the city; the most useful may be Tongyeong (₩4,400), Jangseungpo (₩7,500), Haegeumgang (₩8,500), and Samcheonpo (₩5,600). Across the stream from the Free Export Zone is the express bus terminal (마산고속버스터미날), offering buses every 15 minutes to Seoul (₩15,200), every 30–60 minutes to Daejeon (₩9,600) and Daegu (₩4,300), with others to Pohang (₩6,600), Gwangju (₩9,000), and Seongnam (₩14,900).

City bus nos. 14, 28, 60, and 300 run between the intercity bus terminals, passing the train station and the city center. City bus nos. 53 and 40 take a similar route but pass the fish market; no. 12 runs by the express bus terminal, and nos. 22, 52, and 302 go past the ferry terminal. City bus nos. 33 and 302 connect the Masan city center and intercity bus terminal to Jinhae, while no. 10, among others, goes to Changwon.

CHANGWON 창원

Even though Busan was administratively separated from the province in 1963, the Gyeongsangnam-Do provincial government offices remained there for the next 20 years. When the decision to move the capital back into the province was finally made, several large cities were considered for the honor. As a surprise to many, Changwon [Ch'angwon] came away with the prize—selected over the seemingly more promising sites of Masan and Jinju. Today, this city of 500,000 boasts a sleek, officious-looking capitol building. The low coastal range makes a fine backdrop for this broad white structure. In many respects, Changwon is a planned community, a modern city designed for the future with little in the way of a strong cultural past.

With the rapid push for development and modernization, Changwon has developed as a heavy-industry, machinery, and manufacturing center. A grid of roads crisscrosses the city's huge industrial estates, largely in the southern half of the city. With the growing importance of modern industry and technology, it's appropriate that Changwon National University and other schools of technology are located here, national machinery exhibitions are held here, and the F-3 Grand Prix and other auto races are driven over its wrench-shaped track. Like the city of Ulsan, Changwon is visited mostly by businessmen and has little to offer the sightseer.

Information over the Internet can be found at www.changwon.kyongnam.kr.

Practicalities

The major strip in the center of Changwon runs south for about three kilometers from the university and provincial government offices, past city hall, the police station, post office, Telecom office, hotels, department stores, shopping arcades, and banks to the industrial area near the river. The best accommodations in the city are the deluxe **Changwon Hotel** (tel. 055/ 283-5551) and **International Hotel** (tel. 055/281-1101), the first-class **Canberra Hotel** (tel. 055/ 268-5000) and second-class **Olympic Hotel** (tel. 055/285-3331). *Yeogwan* and restaurants of all types are numerous and located in the city's central district, a few kilometers northwest near the bus terminal and beyond that near the Shin Changwon train station. Since the cities are located only one stop apart, Changwon's train schedule is virtually the same as that for Masan. Express buses run every 45 minutes only to Seoul (₩15,400), but intercity buses have numerous destinations including Busan (₩2,600), Daegu (₩5,700), Jinju (₩3,900), and Tongyeong (₩5,400). City bus nos. 309 and 310 connect Changwon to Jinhae, and bus no. 10 runs to Masan.

Central Gyeongsangnam-Do

CHANGNYEONG 창녕

Along the Guma Expressway, halfway between Daegu and Masan, is the provincial town of Changnyeong [Ch'angnyŏng], an old population center with a rich and lengthy history. Many stone structures from past dynasties remain in the area attesting to that fact. In a small park up at the top end of town you'll find a memorial tablet (N.T. #33) defining the national boundary after Silla king Jinheung defeated the Dae Gaya Kingdom in the mid-500s. Somewhat defaced and partially missing, this stone (진흥왕척경비) was probably erected in 561 and is important not for its appearance but for the message it bears. A similar stone record, now preserved at the Seoul National Museum, once stood high on the mountaintop over Seoul; two others are located in North Korea. These monuments bear four of the oldest datable inscriptions of any kind on the peninsula. Also within this park are a Silla Dynasty stone pagoda, a stone marker set up by order of the regent Daewongun commanding the Korean people to be vigilant against foreign influence at the time that Korea was opening to the outside world in the late 1800s, and a monument to U.N. forces who fought in the bloody battle of Changnyeong during the Korean War.

A few hundred meters to the north and lying close to the highway is a series of ancient mound tombs (교동고분군) (H.S. #80) from the Gaya era that are similar to those at Goryeong to the northwest. Across the road is the **Changnyeong Museum** (창녕박물관); ₩550 entrance. Displaying items mostly taken from the nearby tombs, this is a good example of a small-town museum. In the yard is a life-size re-creation of one of the tombs when opened. To reach the museum, walk from the bus station up to the main east/west street of town. Turn and head toward the hills, passing downtown, then veer left and follow the highway, which passes the muse-

um. For the Jinheung monument turn right at the intersection where the highway turns left.

Back in town near the market, marking the site of a long-forgotten temple, sits a well-preserved, clean-line, stone pagoda (N.T. #34) that very much resembles the famous Seokga-tap at Bulguk-sa. About one kilometer to the west stands its more blemished sister pagoda (T. #520). Nearby are two groups of dolmen and two carved Buddha figures (T. #75 and #227). Standing just off the main east-west street are the remains of a stone ice-storage house (T. #310) from 1742. A second similar but smaller icehouse (H.S. #169) is located some 12 kilometers to the south, in Yeongsan Village. Both are similar in design to the icehouses at Banwol-seong in Gyeongju and in Andong. Just off the highway in Yeongsan is a manmade pond with five small islands in the middle. A short way south of there stands a single-span, half-moon stone bridge (T. #564) that has graced this site since 1780. It lies at the entrance to Patriot Park, a public place set up to honor citizens of the area who fought against the Japanese invasions of the 1590s and those who rose up against Japanese colonization to start the Independence Movement in 1919.

The **Samil Folk Festival** is held in Changnyeong in late February or early March to commemorate the March 1, 1919 Korean Independence Movement. Activities include commemorative ceremonies, folk music and dance, archery, *sireum*, the Yeongsan Battle of the Bulls Heads (I.C.A. #25), and the Yeongsan Tug-of-War (I.C.A. #26). Other county activities include the Bugok Hot Springs Festival in September and the burning of the *eokse* reed on Hwawang-san in January.

The Changnyeongjang Yeogwan (창녕장여관) is located near the bus station; numerous others can be found on the way into and within the center of town. Buses from Changnyeong run to Yeongsan (₩700), Bugok (₩1,300), Daegu (₩3,300), Masan (₩2,900), and Miryang (₩2,900).

© ROBERT NILSEN

Changnyeong ice-storage house

Gwannyong-sa 관용사

In the mountains to the east of Changnyeong lies the diminutive temple Gwannyong-sa, founded in 583, only a few years after Silla took control of this region from Gaya. Set in a bamboo grove along a foot trail leading to the temple from the parking lot stands a pair of stone shaman posts, one set of some 100 or so said to still be in existence in the country. The stones of an entry gate greet you upon entering the temple compound. Around the courtyard are the main hall (T. #212), a Medicine Buddha Hall (T. #146) of early Joseon Dynasty style which has a seated stone Buddha (T. #519) on its altar, and several other buildings, each of which seems to be diminutive when compared to buildings of other temples. On a broad rock outcrop called Yongseon-dae, about one kilometer above is a larger seated Buddha statue (T. #295) from the United Silla period. Constructed at roughly the same time, the overall aspect of this figure is much like that of the Seokguram Buddha of Gyeongju. Resting on a stylized lotus bud, it sits in meditative silence, eternally gazing toward the

east over the valley below. Visibly pleasing, it is less well-executed than the Seokguram Buddha; with no cover, it's constantly battered by the weather. Elsewhere on the mountain is a second seated Buddha statue (T. #75). About five kilometers to the west, within Hwawang-san County Park, are the remains of the Hwawang Fortress (H.S. #64), built during the Gaya era and used successfully during the 1597 Hideyoshi Invasion of the peninsula by General Gwak Je-u to defend the Yeongnam region of the peninsula. A high-elevation meadow near the fort was probably used long ago for military exercises. Today, you can hike among azaleas in spring and *eoksae* reeds in the autumn. Every few years, the *eoksae* are burned in the evening on the first lunar moon as part of a local festival. Take the bus to Okcheon-ni for either the temple or fortress and walk from there.

Upo Marsh

Some distance west of Changnyeong is Uponeup (우포늪), or Upo Marsh, supposedly the largest natural wetland area in the country. Enhanced by a low levee (constructed in the 1970s to reduce the chances of flooding), this 19-square-kilometer marsh is the habitat of scores of water birds, including white egrets and white swans; butterflies, dragonflies; a host of wetland plants; and over 25 kinds of fish. Some of these are endangered species. This is an unusual feature in a country that has such little natural standing water except for that in rice paddies. From the end of the road—the closest bus stops in Hoeryong Village about two kilometers distant—walk the path down to the marsh and continue either way along the bank. This wetland is perhaps best in the early morning or late afternoon, and one could easily spend a leisurely couple of hours here watching the birds and appreciating the scenery. The northern arm of this marsh is referred to as Mokpo Marsh and not far to the east and west are the smaller Saijipo and Jokjibeol marshes.

Bugok Hot Springs 부곡온천

Southeast of Changnyeong, over low hills and through a series of fertile valleys lies Bugok ("Cauldron Valley") Hot Springs. At 78°C, Bugok boasts the country's hottest natural sulfur spring. Discovered in 1973, it's also the newest. This hot spring is said to be good for neuralgia, rheumatism, and skin diseases. As the largest hot springs resort complex in the country, Bugok incorporates public baths, indoor and outdoor swimming pools, a nightclub, souvenir shops, hotels, restaurants, and amusement rides, and because of all this has become a small town all its own. Most establishments are tapped into the spring; the largest is Bugok Hawaii. Because of its tropical theme, Bugok Hawaii exudes a crass commercialism like few other places in Korea. In fact, it draws Koreans by the thousands, playing host to over four million visitors every year. One kilometer down the road lie the remains of the old Bugok Village.

In this newly created community are the first-class Bugok Royal, Bugok Park, and Bugok Hawaii hotels, with rooms in the ₩45,000–75,000 range. The second-class Crown and Bugok Garden hotels rent rooms for ₩30,000–50,000. Several dozen motels and *yeogwan* charge ₩25,000–30,000. Many restaurants are on the pricey side, but economical places can also be found. From Bugok, intercity buses go to Miryang (₩1,600), Busan (₩5,300), Masan (₩2,800), Changnyeong (₩110), and Daegu (₩3,900).

MIRYANG 밀양

Miryang is situated in one of the wider agricultural areas of Gyeongsangnam-Do, straddling the Miryang River, a tributary of the Nakdong. Until its absorption into the Silla Kingdom at the end of the Three Kingdoms period, this district was under Gaya control. One branch of the Bak family claims Miryang as its ancestral home. Well-known in Korea for hosting the down-home *Arang-je,* it's less known for the utilitarian clay pots and finer porcelain made here. Perhaps due to its close proximity to Busan, Miryang (pop. 130,000) is growing rapidly, absorbing some of the surrounding farmland into residential and industrial zones. While city hall has moved out of the city center, and a university has been created on the western edge of town, downtown, with its shops, eateries, banks, and market, still occupies the area near the river between the downtown branch post office and Yeongnam-nu Pavilion.

East along the river, beyond the railroad bridge, is the Yongduyeon recreation area. Lying below the rocky bluff at the river turning is this relaxing place to fish, swim, or row a boat. Nearby is a riverside Sammun pine grove containing over 2,000 trees aged more than 100 years. About three kilometers outside of town on the way to Pyochung-sa you'll find the small pavilion, Wolyeonjeong next to the Giheo Pine Forest (N.M. #16). Both riverside tree groves make fine picnic spots and places to spend a relaxing afternoon. West toward Bugok Hot Springs is Pyochung Begak (표충비), a memorial stela and shrine set up to honor the Buddhist monk Sammyeong, who along with others helped lead the fight against aggressive Japanese invaders in the 1590s, and after the conclusion of the war went to Japan to arrange the release of several thousand Koreans who were captured and taken there as prisoners.

Yeongnam-nu Pavilion 영남루

On a riverside bluff in the center of town stands the stately pavilion Yeongnam-nu [Yŏngnam-nu] (T. #147), one of the country's four most-esteemed. Originally constructed in 1365, the present structure dates from 1844. This fine example of Joseon Dynasty construction is a gathering spot for town residents and is especially popular with older citizens. In summer they come here to escape the harsh sun and take advantage of the cool breezes that waft across the river below. Raised on sturdy posts, the main body is flanked by smaller side chambers set on lower levels in an appealing arrangement. Each post is supported by a natural stone that some say has the shape of an open flower. Directly behind Yeongnam-nu are two old wooden gates and the Cheonjin-gung shrine of a former government guesthouse. There's a ₩500 entrance fee to the pavilion and shrines; open 0900–1800 or until 1730 in winter.

To the side of Yeongnam-nu is a shrine to Arang, a local woman of beauty and talent who came with her maid one night to Yeongnam-nu; women of standing during the Joseon Dynasty were not supposed to be out during the day where they could be seen. That night at the pavilion, she was attacked by a man. Rather than be violated, disgracing herself and her family, she took her own life. Generation after generation, this story has been used as an example to urge young women to guard their virtue and marital fidelity in all cases. **Arang-gak** enshrines a portrait of this woman, and a stone set in the bamboo thicket to the side represents the spot where she is said to have ended her life. Farther on, perched on the side of this bluff, you'll find **Mubong-sa,** originally constructed in 773 but rebuilt after the Korean War. Small and unassuming, it's closely surrounded by a mantle of bamboo and hardwood trees. Unusually, a stone Buddha figure (T. #493) sits on its main altar. Above Yeongnam-nu and Mubong-sa is the city **museum** (₩500 entrance). Though not outstanding, this collection of over 450 artifacts from the area is representative of the utilitarian and decorative objects used by both the gentry and peasants in centuries past. The museum also contains some archaeological items and literary and artistic works by local scholars and artists. To the side of the museum stands a statue of the warrior monk Sammyeong, remains of the town fortress wall snake over the hill above in the cool shade of pine trees, and capping the hill is an octagonal pavilion offering views of the surrounding city and countryside.

Arang-je Cultural Festival

Since its start in 1957, the *Miryang Arang-je* has been held every May. Established primarily to honor the steadfastness, upright character, and propitious behavior of Arang, it also celebrates "the loyalty and righteousness of Sammyeong-daesa and wisdom and virtue of the Confucian scholar Kim Jong-jik, both figures from this area." This weekend-long celebration is sometimes raucous, sometimes sedate, featuring traditional music and dance performances, sports competitions, literary contests, memorial ceremonies, and crafts sales. More than 50 events are scheduled each year including a Miss Arang contest. Convivial crowds, abundant food, and liberal libation are the norm. Many activities take place on the sandy riverflat across from Yeongnam-nu, while others are held a bit farther south along the river in a pine grove, or at the nearby public stadium. Held during this festival and at other times of the year is the Miryang Baekjung Nori (I.C.A. #68), a farmer's festival dance and accompanying music particular to this area.

Practicalities

There is no cluster of accommodations in the center of town, and places to stay seem to be few and far between. Still, you can find a room at the Daeujang Yeogwan (대우장여관) or Unhajang Yeogwan (운하장여관) in the town center. A few others, such as the Shinhojang Yeogwan (신호장여관), are located closer to the bus terminal, which has been moved to the northern outskirts of the city, north of the Telecom office. The main post office has also been moved out of the confined city center to a new location near the train station at the south end of town. The central market remains in town, as do many restaurants and a majority of the shops. Select bus destinations from Miryang include Pyochung-sa (₩2,000), Oreum-gol (₩2,700), Seongnam-sa (₩3,800), Bugok (₩1,600), Busan (₩4,700), Changnyeong (₩2,900), and Daegu (₩4,800). The Miryang train station is three kilometers south of the town center. Miryang is on the country's main train line. Over four dozen daily trains of all classes stop at Miryang on their way south to Busan and north to Seoul. City bus nos. 1, 6, and 8 all run frequently between the bus terminal, city center, Yeongnam-nu, and the train station.

Yeongnam Alps 영남알프스

The Yeongnam [Yŏngnam] Alps are a short range of mountains running roughly between Gyeongju and Busan. Much of this region is within the Yangsan and Ulsan city limits, but not within the actual downtown areas; the remainder is in Miryang County. Eight peaks in this area rise to over 1,000 meters, while a half dozen others are nearly as high. The Gyeongbu Expressway splits the range into two distinct parts—a smaller eastern section and a broader, taller, western section. In the western half, the ridgeline swirls in a modified "S" shape connecting the peaks Unmunsan, Gaji-san, Neungdong-san, Cheonhwang-san, Chwiseo-san, Shinbul-san, and Ganwol-san, below which lie the temples Unmun-sa, Seongnam-sa, Pyochung-sa, and Tongdo-sa, the Oreum-gol Valley, and about a dozen waterfalls. A highway runs across the western section, from Eonyang, past Seongnam-sa and Oreum-gol, to Miryang. Although smaller and lower than its western half, the eastern section is perhaps the most expressive of the whole chain. Its highest peaks are Jeongjoksan, Cheonseong-san and Wonhyo-san, and below them are the temple Naewon-sa and several hermitages and waterfalls.

The five most important temples in these mountains are Unmun-sa, Seongnam-sa, Naewon-sa, Pyochung-sa, and Tongdo-sa. The first three are strictly for *biguni* (Buddhist nuns), and, along with Bomun-sa in Seoul, Donghak-sa in Gyeryong-san, and Wibong-sa outside Jeonju, are South Korea's largest and most significant temples for female monks.

Several trails through the Yeongnam Alps connect the temples and other well-known sites. Through the sprawling western section runs an interconnecting network of hiking paths. Across the expressway the eastern section is virtually a unit unto itself. This range is worthy of a few days' exploration, but short excursions to the temples and other sites are also worthwhile.

In 1979, 107 square kilometers of the Yeongnam Alps—in three separate sections around Naewon-sa, Tongdo-sa, and Seongnam-sa—were set aside as Gaji-san Provincial Park, which takes its name from the range's highest peak (1240 meters). Other sections of these mountains have been incorporated into Shinbul-san and Unmun-san country parks. Outside park boundaries, yet still within the Yeongnam Alps, are Pyochung-sa and Unmun-sa. Unmun-sa lies just across the border in Gyeongsangbuk-Do. The entire area is discussed here as a whole.

WESTERN SECTION

Pyochung-sa 표충사

With Cheonhwang-san towering overhead, Pyochung-sa [P'yoch'ung-sa] lies nestled in a remote, attractive valley, at the confluence of two streams. Situated on the western slope of the Yeongnam Alps, it's the least-visited of the major temples in this area. Founded in 654 by Wonhyo, its original name was Jungnim-sa ("Bamboo Forest Temple"). Even today, great stands of bamboo cover the hillsides above the temple. A legend claims that in 829 an Indian monk brought the real *sarisa* (calcified remains) of Buddha to this temple, and placed them in a three-tier stone pagoda (T. #467), which still graces the temple's courtyard. This same monk is said to have treated and cured a royal prince traveling the country in hopes of finding a remedy for his leprosy. During the Hideyoshi Invasions, 700 warrior monks from this temple served under the famous warrior monks Sammyeong, Seosan, and Giheo. For their bravery in defense of the nation, the temple was awarded its present name—translated as "Award for Loyalty Temple." A museum built in 1990 now contains over 300 personal items of Sammyeong, and other cultural artifacts. Perhaps the finest piece on display is a large silver-inlaid bronze incense burner (N.T. #75).

While the old part of the compound remains pretty much the same, there are several new buildings, and extensive reconstruction has taken place. The temple now contains more than 25 buildings, but is a miniature version of what it was centuries ago when the Goryeo Dynasty monk Ilyeon was in residence here, preaching to over 1,000 monks. A two-posted front gate greets visitors and the wide path leads up to the large front courtyard where you will find the temple museum. Through the Sacheonwang-mun opens the upper courtyard and the older buildings. Three large figures occupy the altar in the main hall. Notice the stone carvings on the steps up to this hall. Backing the altar figure in Gwaneum-jeon is an intriguing mural, predominantly in yellow, showing the Goddess of Mercy with 1,000 hands and eyes. Outside you'll see brightly painted ox-herding murals. Here as well are the judgment hall, and halls for the Nahan, Mountain Spirit, and Lonely Arhat. Across from the main hall rests a bell/gong pavilion. Five associated hermitages perch on the hills above.

Intercity buses run throughout the day from Miryang (₩2,000); buses from Cheongdo and Daegu run less often. A tourist community of *yeogwan*, restaurants, shops, and entertainment facilities has been developed about half a kilometer down the road. From the ticket booth (₩1,500 entrance) at the far end of the village, a wide, tree-lined path parallels the valley stream for the short distance to the temple.

Ice Valley

The entire northern slope of Cheonhwang-san is very steep. One particular side valley, Eoreum-gol [Ŏrŭm-gol] (N.M. #224), or Ice Valley, is unusually precipitous. Open to the north, it seldom gets sun; several ravines are so deep and narrow that streams and pools stay frozen until late in the summer. Several long rock slides cover the sides of this valley, and the trail can be tricky—about two hours up and one hour down. At the bottom are Cheonhwang-sa and a place to stay the night. Entrance to the valley is ₩1,000.

Seongnam-sa 성남사

Twelve kilometers above Eonyang is the temple Seongnam-sa [Sŏngnam-sa], situated along a cascading river in a verdant valley with Gaji-san at its head; ₩1,200 entrance fee. Numerous daily buses come here through Eonyang from Ulsan (₩1,000) and from Miryang (₩800). The temple was built in 824, and *biguni* have resided here since it was reconstructed following the Korean War. The stone *sari budo* (T. #369) was raised for the founding monk, Doeui; notice the fine carving. A tall Silla pagoda stands in the main courtyard. In the village below Seongnam-sa are several *yeogwan*, restaurants, and a bus stop.

Unmun-sa 운문사

Unmun-sa is by far the largest and most attractive of the three temples for nuns in the Yeongnam Alps. Set on a wide spot in the river valley, Unmun-sa is a combination temple and school. Much of the food eaten by the nuns is grown in the huge temple gardens. Behind the outer courtyard, separated by a wall and off-limits unless you're invited, are the nuns' living quarters and school—a multi-year course for females desiring to take Buddhist vows. At any one time, there may be as many as 200 nuns in residence. Entrance is ₩1,300.

Founded in the mid-500s by the monk Wone-ung, this temple has gone through the usual series of reconstructions and renovations. It may also have been where the monk Iryeon wrote the book *Samguk Yusa*, a history of the Three Kingdoms period. Unmun-sa ("Cloud Gate Temple") took its name at the beginning of the Goryeo Dynasty. A greatly weathered open pavilion sits to one side of this lovely front courtyard, and nearby stands a 400-year-old Japanese red pine

(N.M. #180) that spreads its wide branches over the lawn. (Some say that this tree is given several liters of liquor every year for health!) A stone lantern (T. #193), the memorial stone for Woneung (T. #316), a stone statue of the seated Buddha (T. #317), four stone panels engraved with deva figures (T. #318), a three-tier stone pagoda (T. #678), and a bronze vessel (T. #208) are also preserved here. Of the approximately 18 buildings, only the Biro-jeon (T. #835) has been declared a Treasure. Historically the most significant structure at this temple, it has fine woodwork, faded paint, and old murals behind the altar figures. In contrast, the new main hall is large and elaborate, but not overwhelming, and has seven figures on its altar. Despite the great activity and vibrant atmosphere, you'll feel peace and tranquillity as soon as you step through the front gate.

At the village below the temple you'll find inexpensive *yeogwan*, a few restaurants and shops, and the bus stop. From this village, buses run every hour to Cheongdo (₩3,500) with additional buses to the Daegu Nambu Bus Station (₩4,300).

Hiking

From the front of Pyochung-sa, one trail leads up the valley to the east. A 30-minute walk brings you to Hongyong Waterfall. Another 20 minutes brings you to Cheungcheung Waterfall, and an hour beyond that is the village of Gosa-ri. Beyond the village lies the Sajapyeong plateau. At about 800 meters, this slightly slanted, gently dished upper valley grows thick with grass, once used to graze sheep and other animals. A gravel road runs up the valley to Sajapyeong from the village below Pyochung-sa. Near Gosa-ri, a footpath leaves this road and leads east up the mountainside, crossing the next valley, and eventually taking you to Shinbul-san, Chwiseo-san, and Tongdo-sa.

A second trail starts behind the temple compound at the wall surrounding some *sari budo*. It runs along the mountainside to Gosa-ri. From there, the trail leads up to Jeyak-san, then across the saddle to Cheonhwang-san ("Heaven Emperor Mountain"), where there are fine views of the entire range.

A third trail starts to the left of the temple and heads north into the valley. A few hundred meters up is a Y intersection. One route crosses the saddle between Cheonhwang-san and Jeyak-san, while the other continues up the valley past Geumgang and Unryu waterfalls and Naewon-am, Han'gyeam, and Seosang-am, before running straight up the side ridge to Cheonhwang- san. From Pyochung-sa, it's about 3.5 hours to Cheonhwang-san and about 2.5 hours via Han'gye-am.

From Cheonhwang-san, this trail continues north and east along the ridge, where the path drops *steeply* into Oreum-gol—find this trailhead near a large distinctive outcrop along the ridge, about 25 minutes from the top. A second trail also heads down the north side of the slope to the village of Nammyeong. From Cheonhwang-san, you'll find the trail to Nammyeong *before* the trail into Oreum-gol. If you want to descend into Oreum-gol, but find yourself on a trail heading in an obviously westerly direction, you're on the wrong path.

From the bottom of Ice Valley, one path follows the major valley east, meets the highway, and crosses the pass to Seongnam-sa. The road over this pass connects Eonyang and Miryang. Down the valley, a path and road lead to the village of Nammyeong [Nammyŏng] (남명), where buses run every hour throughout the day to Miryang (₩2,300). From Nammyeong, it's equidistant to the three temples—Pyochung-sa, Seongnam-sa, and Unmun-sa. Going north, the trail crosses the river near the vehicular bridge. Heading through the village on the far side, take the left fork past an abandoned mine up to the pass—the border between Gyeongsangnam-Do and Gyeongsangbuk-Do—a two-hour hike. The easiest trail, straight down the opposite side, follows the stream through the forested valley, eventually meeting a dirt road that continues down the valley to Unmun-sa. More strenuous ridge trails lead up from the pass. One runs east to Gaji-san ("Buddha Wisdom Mountain"), three hours. There the trail splits. One branch heads south to meet the road near the point where the highway tunnel cuts through the mountain. The other goes to Ssal-bawi rock and from there follows an abandoned track and trail to a point about a hundred meters below the front gate of Seongnam-sa. Heading west, the trail heads to Unmun-san ("Cloud Gate Mountain"), two hours. From Unmun-san, the trail continues west along the ridge, dropping down into a valley on the mountain's north side, and eventually leads to Unmun-sa, a three hour walk. A second path heads southwest, via Sangun-am and Seokgol-sa, about 2.5 hours.

EONYANG 언양

Twenty-five kilometers due west of Ulsan is the small highway town of Eonyang [Ŏnyang], located at the interchange where the branch expressway leaves the Gyeongbu Expressway and heads toward the coast. Although most of the world's amethyst comes from others countries, Eonyang is well-known in Korea for this semi-precious stone. While mining has virtually stopped today, larger quantities of amethyst were taken from the ground in decades past. An amethyst mine museum has been created at one of the mines to elucidate the mining operation. Loose individual stones and jewelry are found in specialty shops in town, at the jewelry center in Iri, Jeollabuk-Do, and at specialty outlets in Seoul. Prices here are generally lower than in large cities, but the selection is not necessarily better.

Just south of town and standing along the river a short way up a valley toward Shinbul-san is the pavilion **Jakcheon-jeong** [Chakch'ŏn-jŏng] (작천정), said to have been built by local scholars for King Sejong. The lower reaches of this valley have plenty of places to eat and stay and are often used by local residents for hot summer getaways and picnic spots, a place to swim in the water and while away a long weekend afternoon. Left more natural, the upper end of the valley encompasses Shinbul-san County Park.

From Eonyang, buses run to Ulsan (₩1,000), Gyeongju (₩1,900), Shinpyeong (₩1,000), and Busan (₩2,600).

TONGDO-SA 통도사

Lying in a graceful valley below Chwiseo-san is the temple Tongdo-sa, founded in 646 to house holy relics of the historical Buddha (a bone from his skull, his robe, and his begging bowl), brought from China by the monk Jajang. The temple's oldest building escaped a conflagration in 1592, while the rest have been rebuilt more recently. In its heyday, about 600 years ago, the temple may have housed thousands of monks. Though smaller now, it is still one of the largest in Korea, with nearly three dozen buildings, and is the 15th district headquarters of the Jogye sect. Sprinkled on the hillsides above are 13 associated hermitages. Within its precinct are kept one designated National Treasure and 11 Treasures. The name Tongdo-sa roughly translates as "Transmission of The Way Temple," or, more loosely, "salvation of sentient beings by means of awakening the Buddha's teachings, Dharma." It means, in essence, "to master the whole truth and redeem the world, in the hope that the world would be saved through the perfection of Buddhism." It is one of Korea's three treasure temples (Haein-sa and Songgwang-sa are the other two). Tongdo-sa is the *bul* (Buddha) temple, focusing on the spirit of the Buddha. Haein-sa is the *beop* (law) temple, concerned with the spirit of the law, i.e. doctrine or Dharma. Songgwang-sa is the *seung* (monk) temple, focusing on the functioning community of monks and the individual practice of meditation.

Temple Structures

Tongdo-sa has three gates: the four-post Ilju-mun; Sacheonwang-mun, which houses the four imposing and well-rendered deva gate guards; and the simple, undecorated Buli-mun, entrance to the temple's inner courtyard and representing the division between the worldly and spiritual realms. Between Sacheonwang-mun and Buli-mun is the temple's outer courtyard, surrounded by several special halls. Yeongsan-jeon ("Holy Mountain Hall") is dedicated to the historical Buddha. It contains a statue of him, plus eight murals depicting poignant scenes in his life. Geungnakbo-jeon ("Treasure Hall of the Western Paradise") contains statues of Amita, Daesaeji Bosal, and Gwanseeum Bosal. Yaksa-jeon ("Healing Buddha Hall") is frequented by people praying for good health and welfare or a cure for

© ROBERT NILSEN

main temple hall, Tongdo-sa

disease. A shrine to the priest Jajang stands nearby containing a complete printed copy of the *Koreana Tripitaka*. Manse-ru, to the south side of the courtyard, has been set up as a shop for Buddhist paraphernalia—books, music, artwork. The large temple bell and flat metal gong are housed in the bell pavilion next to Buli-mun. On the 2nd floor of this weather-beaten structure is a *huge* skin drum, larger in diameter than the height of a man. Its deep voice reverberates through the valley, calling the resident monks to prayer. Kept here as well are two hollow logs said to have been used at one time as "rice bowls" by the monks of the temple! One can only imagine the crowds of devotees living here at that time.

The temple's most prominent building is the main hall, Geumgang Daeung-jeon ("Diamond Great Excellence Hall"). Set on a raised terrace, its stone retaining walls sport carved lotus blossoms. In the past, young men renounced their earthly ties here and formally entered the community of monks. This commanding structure has several peculiarities. Unlike most temples' main halls,

it does not face the front of the temple compound, but is turned to the side—to the south. It's deeper than it is wide, and is capped by an unusual T-shaped gable roof. Unlike in most other temples in the country, the three-tier altar holds no statuary. Directly behind this hall is the Geumgang Gyedan *sari budo,* holding the relics of the Buddha. Because the main hall is dedicated to Seokgamoni Buddha, and this *sari budo* contains his personal effects, the most revered of the temple's relics take the place of an altar statue. Geumgang Gyedan is a two-level square of stone. In the middle sits a stone-carved lotus bud supporting the squat, bell-shaped *sari budo,* the focal point of this temple. This is one of the five places in Korea where actual physical remains of the historical Buddha are believed to be kept. Together, Daeung-jeon and Geumgang Gyedan are designated N.T. #290.

To the side of Geumgang Daeung-jeon is Guryong Shinji ("Nine Dragons Sacred Pool"). A legend claims that when Jajang established Tongdo-sa, he found nine dragons inhabiting a pond on the site. In order to raise the temple buildings, he had to drive the dragons away. One dragon begged to stay, to guard the temple precincts, so this pool was dug for him. Nearby sit two halls—Yonghwa-jeon, which houses several large murals and is dedicated to the Maitreya Buddha, and Daegwangmyeong-jeon, dedicated to the Vairocana Buddha, the "source" from which all Buddhas emanate. Constructed during the end of the Goryeo Dynasty, it's believed to be the oldest wooden structure in the temple compound. In front of Yonghwa-jeon stands the unusual Bongbal-tap (T. #471), a covered, bowl-shaped cistern set high on a pedestal.

Over the centuries many important artifacts have been collected at Buddhist temples, and Tongdo-sa is no exception. This temple's treasures are now housed in a museum next to the approach path before you reach Buli-mun. Numerous metal statues, wooden carvings, paintings, printed scriptures (including an illustrated *Hwaeom Sutra* done in gold on blue paper—T. #757), and a three-series mural of Buddhas and bodhisattvas (T. #1042) are kept here. Another well-known item is a silver-inlaid bronze incense burner (T. #344). This museum has an amazing collection of some 30,000 items, and of these over 600 are Buddhist drawings and paintings, many of which are hung in the galleries. The museum is good for a quick look at historical temple items, and it also presents periodic traveling exhibitions. Hours are 0900–1800 (1700 in winter), closed Tuesday; ₩2,000 entrance. Nearby is the old museum, now an exhibition room, which displays other artifacts and items from the temple; ₩800 entrance. See www.tongdomuseum.or.kr.

Hiking

Several trails lead up the mountain from Tongdo-sa. One starts near the huge entrance gate at the top end of Shinpyeong Village, while another leads to the right from the group of *sari budo* and memorial tablets. Both start as drivable roads but soon turn into walking trails. About two kilometers up, they merge, and run a switchback course to the summit of Chwiseo-san. From the parking lot, a small road leads up a secondary

valley past eight hermitages. One of the first is Anyang-am, where you have a good view to the north over Tongdo-sa complex. A stop at several hermitages combined with other nearby trails makes a pleasant day hike. A fourth trail leads along the river, branching into two forks about a kilometer above Tongdo-sa. Along these tracks are Jajang-am, containing a rock-cut Buddha figure, and Geungnak-am, known for its lovely bridge spanning a small pond. Both routes lead to the ridge above; follow the ridge trail north to the summit. It continues to an intersection just below Shinbul-san; one trail leads east, ending at the village of Gacheon-ni, while the trail to the left crosses the valley and the far ridge, finally dropping into the second valley and on to Pyochung-sa. From Tongdo-sa to the summit of Chwiseo-san takes less than two hours; from Chwiseo-san to Gacheon is a two-and-a-half hour walk, while the hike as far as Pyochung-sa requires at least six hours. From the ridgetop intersection, the trail continues north to Shinbul-san ("Spirit of Buddha Mountain"), and along the spine to Ganwol-san. From a trough between these two peaks, a secondary trail leads into the valley to the east, past Ganwol Waterfall, and down to the pavilion Jakcheon-jeong. From Chwiseo-san to Jakcheon-jeong is a leisurely three hours.

Getting to Tongdo-sa

Take an intercity bus from Busan, Eonyang, or Ulsan to Shinpyeung [Shinp'yŏng] (신평), which offers several mid-range *yeogwan* and restaurants, plus several newer, pricier accommodations, most close to the temple entrance. Busan city bus no. 12 also runs the route between Busan and Eonyang. Incongruously, an amusement park is located a short way outside the temple's front gate. Just inside the temple entrance is a teahouse selling traditional Korean teas, music, books, and other related items. From the entrance (₩1,000), the road to the temple follows the stream up the valley for 1.5 kilometers under a canopy of trees. Along this road, ancient "graffiti" (actually the names of temple visitors from centuries past) have been engraved on flat rock surfaces. On several large stones, the meditative phrase *Nammu Amitabul* has been engraved.

Near the parking lot at the upper end is the Samseong Banwol-gyo, a gently arched, three-span stone bridge. Not from the distant past, this bridge was built in 1937. Across the stream from the parking lot, memorial tablets that once were set along the trail upstream have been gathered together as one of the country's largest collections of *sari budo*. Impressive for their size and variety, they just seem too neat and orderly in their new location. To see the temple at its best, come in the early morning, when the chill of night is still in the air, or return in the evening to watch the sun set behind the distant hills and the cloak of dusk settle over this peaceful community of spiritual aspirants.

EASTERN SECTION

Naewon-sa 내원사

Founded in 673, Naewon-sa was created for use by male monks. It was destroyed during the Korean War, but reconstruction began in 1958, spearheaded by the Buddhist nun Suok. Since that time it has been used solely by *biguni*. Set in a thickly wooded valley beneath prominent rock outcrops and the lofty peak Cheonseong-san ("1,000 Saints Mountain"), this tidy temple has the most attractive setting of any in the Yeongnam Alps, especially in autumn, even if the temple structures are not all that striking. Spring is also pretty, when rains turn the vegetation green on green and flowers fleck the hillsides in bright patches. With the rain also come the frogs. During the quiet evening they croak in melodious flirtation. Bright green on top and red on their undersides, these frogs are hard to miss.

Naewon-sa is a study and meditation center. By all means visit, but remember to stay quiet and respect the peace and harmony that reign there. Backed up against the bamboo on the hillside is the plain and rather unpretentious main hall, the only building most visitors are allowed to enter. To the side is the L-shaped meditation hall and kitchen. If the doors are open, you can see robes hung neatly in a row from pegs on the wall and food bowls wrapped in towels on the shelf above. Many of the remaining buildings are dormitories for the several dozen resident nuns, and a handful of hermitages are scattered throughout the hills above.

To get to Naewon-sa, take a local bus from the Busan Dongbu Bus Station or Busan city bus no. 12 to Yongyeon [Yongyŏn] (용연) (₩1,400); buses also run south from Eonyang. From the highway, walk over the freeway and two kilometers to the village below the temple, where there is a small cluster of *yeogwan,* restaurants, souvenir shops, and the temple's ticket booth (₩1,300 entrance). To the right is an attractive valley through which a paved road leads along the stream to Naewon-sa. The walk from the highway to the temple takes about an hour. Just below the temple is another small collection of shops and restaurants.

Mita-am

Of the half-dozen hermitages on Cheonseong-san, Mita-am has the most intriguing legend—and a lesson to boot. Long ago, an old man lived high on the mountainside in a cave near where the hermitage stands today. From a tiny hole in the cave ceiling, rice fell at a rate of one grain per second, sufficient for his needs. Wanting more, this man decided to enlarge the hole to increase the flow. After making the hole bigger, the rice stopped and water began to drip down instead. With his supply of rice gone, the old man starved to death. Still today, only water drips from the ceiling. Inside this cave is a standing statue of the Amita Buddha (T. #998). To the north of Mita-am, in a fold in the mountainside, is a second hermitage, and nearby is Hyeolsu Waterfall.

Trails

From Naewon-sa, a trail leads up a steep ridge to the summit, a little more than two kilometers. A short way above the temple, one branch splits off to the left and goes up the hillside. After about 40 minutes, this trail meets another coming from the left; that trail also starts at the village below, but it runs through the next valley to the north. From this juncture, the trail continues to the top. Each walk takes about three hours to the summit. On the far side, the shortest route heads straight down the mountain, passing Hyeolsu Waterfall before dropping to the reservoir and the village of Baekdong. An alternate course loops around the ridge to the south before going down to Mita-am. From there, one trail leads to the waterfall while another drops past a second reservoir, ending at the village to the south of Baekdong. From Baekdong, city buses run north to Ulsan and south to Busan.

Another trail over the range starts at the temple entrance village, but runs up a side valley to the north, first to Nojeon-am and then on to Anjeok-am in about two hours. From there it's a short distance to the pass, and another hour-and-a-half down the east side to the road. To the south, an hour-and-a-half walk from Daeseok brings you to the temple Hongnyong-sa and the nearby pavilion and waterfall.

ULSAN 울산

From Pohang to Busan, gradually diminishing hills front a coastline that's much less rugged and dramatic than the one farther north. Splitting this low coastal range is the Taehwa River, along which the city of Ulsan has grown. Along the river west of town, petroglyphs indicate that man was living in this region during the Neolithic Age. For a time during the early Joseon Dynasty, Ulsan (then known as Yeompo) was a provincial military command center, and one of three ports open to Japanese traders until the Hideyoshi Invasions. From that time until the 20th century, it remained an isolated farming and fishing community. Only since the 1970s has it become a significant industrial city, described by some as the Pittsburgh and Detroit of Korea. Today, most visitors to the city come for business. In 1994, its population reached one million and Ulsan was administratively separated from the province.

The Taehwa River empties into Ulsan Bay, the east coast's second-best anchorage. Ulsan's distance from the militarized northern border, its easily defensible position, its convenient transportation connections, and ample room for expansion have all contributed to the city's development as one of South Korea's primary industrial zones. The old section of town huddles along the north bank of the Taehwa River, while new residential areas have bloomed in the flatlands to the south and east. The concentrated districts of heavy industry are located away from the center of town, near the ocean, along both sides of the bay, and in pockets down the coast, particularly around Onsan. The area directly east toward Bangeojin is dominated by the Hyundai group, with huge factories producing automobiles, ships, ocean-use steel structures, pipes and fittings, electronics, wood products, paints and related commodities, and facilities for repairing ships. Chemical complexes, petro-chemical and fertilizer plants, power-generation facilities, fiber industries, other light industries, and harbor facilities dot the south side of the bay. Korea's first oil refinery was established here in 1964. Along with other cities in Korea, Ulsan hosted World Cup soccer games in 2002, creating a new stadium and accompanying facilities in the southwestern corner of the city on the edge of the Ulsan Grand Park.

The city's major shopping and entertainment district, a tight-knit cluster of streets and alleys, is located behind the Koreana Hotel in the center of the old town. You will also find restaurants in all price ranges. With broader streets and open spaces, the new city also has its department stores, eating and drinking establishments, and entertainment facilities. Additionally, shops, restaurants, and other facilities are located near the Hyundai shipyard.

The Ulsan city tourist information office is located in the heart of the new city at the city hall. While the main post office is up the street from city hall, the Telecom office is snuggled along a narrow, crowded street behind the Koreana Hotel in the heart of the old town. Foreign exchange banks are located throughout town, including the Korea Foreign Exchange Bank, across from city hall.

For additional information, see www.metro .ulsan.kr.

Sights

There are few historical remains in the old city of Ulsan aside from a rebuilt Joseon Dynasty local government building and village *hyanggyo*. Many more historical and cultural sites lie in the surrounding region, which now have been incorporated into the Ulsan city limits. Set near the river amidst pine and cherry trees is the site of a small Japanese fortress from the Hideyoshi Invasions called Woeseong (H.S. #9). Prior to that, the Buddhist temple Taehwa-sa occupied this site, evidenced by a one-meter-tall bell-shaped pagoda (T. #441), on which 12 zodiac figures have been wrought. This pagoda is thought to be one of the oldest in the country and the only one carved with zodiac figures. This spot is now known as **Hakseong Park** (학성공원), a knoll-top enclosure tightly surrounded by houses that's used mainly by locals to beat the summer heat. Topping the next hill to the north is Chungoisa, a shrine dedicated to the memory of Ulsan citizens who fought the Japanese in the 1590s. A bit farther out are the remains of an old stone fortress. While there are numerous dolmen, pagodas and other such stone remains from long-gone temples, perhaps the most intriguing ancient remains are two petroglyph sites. Bangudae Petroglyph (N. T. #285) and Cheonjeonni Petroglyph (N. T. #147) are near each other along the Taehwa River close to the expressway. While there is no easy access, the petroglyphs are carved and painted on the side of cliff walls and best seen in the late afternoon light. Mostly geometric shapes and figures, the significance of these flat-rock carvings is unknown.

At the tip of the peninsula protecting Ulsan Bay from the East Sea, is the fishing village of **Bangeojin** [Pangŏjin] (방어진). Site of a former coastal fortress, Bangeojin now sports a lighthouse on the bluff at the end of a short spit, now Ulgi Park. North of this promontory is Ilsan Beach, and south is the port, with its many raw fish restaurants. Hyundai employees fill the beach during summer and the restaurants all year.

Once a quiet whaling village on the south side of Ulsan Bay, **Jangsaengpo** [Changsaengp'o] (장생포) has been greatly affected by the intrusion of huge industrial factories. The coastal waters off Ulsan, part of the migratory route for gray whales, have been designated a protected zone (N.M.—#126). Although not a secret, many restaurants here still advertise whale meat on their menu.

Accommodations

There are numerous hotels in Ulsan. At the west end of town, on the south side of the river, the second-class **Taehwa Hotel** (tel. 052/273-3301) has rooms for ₩45,000–160,000. Across the river road in downtown Ulsan is the deluxe-class **Koreana Hotel** (tel. 052/244-9911); rates are ₩71,000–105,000 for standard rooms and ₩105,000–400,000 for suites. Closer to the new bus terminals is the deluxe **Ulsan Lotte Hotel** (tel. 052/960-1000) with all the amenities and luxury of any Lotte Hotel in the country. Opposite the Hyundai Shipyard main entrance is the deluxe-class **Hyundai Hotel** (tel. 052/250-6030); rooms start at ₩180,000 and rise to ₩500,000 for suites. Many of the Hyundai's occupants are foreign contract workers or businessmen. Near the bus terminals, behind the downtown hotels, are numerous medium- and low-priced *yeogwan*.

Transportation

Air service by Asiana Airlines and KAL runs 18 times a day between Ulsan and Seoul. The airport is north of town, along the road to Gyeongju. The terminal is small, with check-in counters, snack shops, rental car booths, a bank, and a tourist information booth downstairs; upstairs is the departure area, more shops, and a restaurant. For flight information and reservations, call Asiana Airlines (tel. 052/265-1406) or KAL (tel. 052/272-4597). City hotels offer free shuttle service if prior arrangements are made. City buses stop just outside the gate along the highway; use city bus no. 24 or 101. A taxi from the center of town is roughly ₩6,000. Airport shuttle buses run to Gyeongju four times a day (₩4,500).

Trains through Ulsan run 11 times a day to Busan. Going north, two or three trains a day go to Seoul, Seoul Cheongnyangni, Gyeongju, and Pohang, while trains run once a day to Dong Daegu, Yeongju, and Gangneung. Most of the shorter runs are *Tongil-ho* class, many of the longer ones are *Mugunghwa-ho* trains, while the two to Seoul are *Saemaeul-ho* trains. Sample fares: Seoul (₩30,600), Seoul Cheongnyangni

(₩20,200), Gangneung (₩19,100), Dong Daegu (₩500), Gyeongju (₩2,900), and Pohang (₩2,900).

Express buses run every 15 minutes to Seoul (₩16,200), every 20 minutes to Daegu (₩4,700), every hour to Daejeon (₩10,700), four times a day to Jeonju (₩13,400), and six times a day to Gwangju (₩13,400). Intercity-bus destinations include Busan (₩3,600), Haeundae (₩4,300), Tongdo-sa (₩2,000), Eonyang (₩1,000), Seongnam-sa (₩1,000), Gyeongju (₩3,100), and Pohang (₩5,100).

Busan 부산

Busan [Pusan], the country's principal port and second-largest city, lies at the southeastern corner of the peninsula. This hilly metropolis of four million fronts the Korea Strait and pushes west straddling the mouth of the Nakdong River—covering 760 square kilometers in all. A center for domestic and international trade and transportation, industry, commerce, and education, Busan became a "special city" in 1963, administratively separate from Gyeongsangnam-Do, and was renamed a metropolitan city in 1995.

The name Busan means "Cauldron Mountain," referring to the amphitheater-like valley and surrounding ridge of hills that front the south harbor. While there are narrow seaside plains, a central core of hills (the tallest rising to 804 meters) takes up much of the city. Additional hills rise up along the sea in the east, and the broadest agricultural land is located on the island in the river delta and adjacent lands to the west. The best natural port in the country, Busan's numerous bays lie deep and calm, well-protected by long fingers of hilly headlands that thrust out into the Korea Strait. The island of Yeong-do separates Busan's two principal bays and delineates its harbor areas. The relatively unindented east coast of the peninsula slides down in a gentle curve from the north. From Busan, however, it shoots off to the west, leaving an admirably indented coastline of large bays, countless coves, and dozens of islands.

Beomeo-sa

© ROBERT NILSEN

Busan harbor is split into two sections. The older, southern section is smaller, primarily used by the local fishing fleet and for small-scale ship repair and construction. North of Yeong-do lies the east harbor. Oryuk-do, a group of half a dozen rocky islets, thrusts out of the water at the bay's mouth like protecting sentinels, and a long breakwater helps to keep back the sea's agitation. Much larger and newer, and built on reclaimed land, the east harbor wraps itself north around the bay from the coastal and international ferry piers to the container pier at Shinseondae, while large ship construction takes place along the north shore of Yeong-do. Additional cargo capacity has been created at Gamcheon Bay, along the south shore of the city, and a huge new harbor project is taking place on Gadeok Island just west of the Nakdong River mouth. This island is slated to be connected to the peninsula by bridge, with a connection farther on to Geoje-do. Occasional cruise ships uses the east harbor or the newer docking facilities near Dadaepo. Through this harbor flows a great percentage of foreign imports, and over half of the country's exports. A majority of the country's container traffic enters and exits here.

After experiencing an adolescent burst of growth, Busan now is going through a period of adult midriff spread. From the narrow seaside plains, the city's developed sections have crawled up and over the low inner-city hills like creeping vines. In the outskirts, residential neighborhoods swirl around the taller hills like rivers around islands. Busan is an inconveniently long city, which creates an unusual phenomenon. The city has developed four major centers—the harborfront city center district, Seomyeon, Dongnae, and Haeundae. Aside from these, other large concentrations are located at Gwangalli, along the inner-harbor side of Yeong-do, and at Saha, Sasang, and Gupo along the Nakdong River. While still possessing distinct identities, all these areas are being run together by the indomitable, molasses-like ooze of urban development. In the harborfront **city center** you'll find business offices, the banking district, foreign consulates, primary markets, and shopping and entertainment areas. Here as well is a great concentration of accommodations in every price bracket, a plethora of restaurants, the central train station, and the international and coastal ferry terminals. **Seomyeon** also has many accommodations and restaurants, a number of markets, and city hall, but is almost devoid of tourist sites. It's the city's secondary business district, though its shopping and entertainment area grows increasingly fashionable and has begun to rival that of the harborfront area. **Dongnae** holds the express-bus terminal, Dongbu intercity bus terminal, a hot spring, a huge sports complex, and numerous historical and cultural attractions. **Haeundae,** with its famous beach, hotels, restaurants, shops, hot spring, and recreation facilities, is Busan's foremost "resort" area. Frequent bus and subway transportation connects these principal areas as well as the secondary concentrations.

Busan is the country's principal port for international commerce, and a vital link in the flow of domestic goods. Companies here produce everything from textiles and clothing to food products, rubber goods, ships, automobiles, steel machinery, toys, wood products, household items, and handicrafts; however, the city is working to establish a wide variety of modern factories to broaden its business base for the current century. Along with the recent, rapid population increase, Busan is expanding its manufacturing/industrial sector. Along with well-established areas, large complexes are being developed along the Nakdong River. To help propel the economic growth and care for the needs of the populace, the country's first nuclear power generator (Gori Atomic Power Plant) went online in 1978 on the northern outskirts of Busan; a second began operation in the early 1980s, and by 1985 plant no. 5 was producing electricity.

The development of a strong economic base and the growing population have led to the expansion of educational opportunities. The city now boasts over two dozen universities and colleges, with several hundred lower-level schools. The schools of most note are Busan National University (including its medical school), Busan National University of Education, Dong-A University, Korea Maritime University, Busan National Fisheries University, and Busan University of Foreign Studies. The hills of the city also abound with Buddhist temples, including the venerable Beomeo-sa, inspiring Seokbul-sa, grand Dongmyeong Bulwon, and Samgwang-sa. In all parts of the city, steeples rise over the many Catholic and Protestant churches, many of which have established and maintained hospitals and charitable organizations.

Busan is the San Francisco of Korea. Like its American counterpart, Busan is built along the sea at the site of an excellent harbor. The city stretches along the waterfront and steps its way up the hillsides. Houses and apartments carpet its lower knolls; industry fills the broader surrounding land, much of which has been reclaimed from the bay, and forested mountain peaks dot the entire area. As San Francisco is bounded on one side by the ocean and on the other by a bay, Busan also lies on a peninsula of sorts between the Korea Strait and the mouth of the Nakdong River. Although on opposite sides of the Pacific, these two cities are roughly at the same latitude and share a similar climate. Both are cosmopolitan, with a marked international flavor.

Busan is one of Korea's gateways. It is one of four cities in the country with international ferry connections and its international airport is located on an island in the river delta. From Busan you can easily travel along the island-studded south coast, or journey up the picturesque east coast via Gyeongju and Pohang to Seorak-san. The Yeongnam Alps stand close by, and Jeju-do is only a short ferry ride or flight away.

For information online, see www.metro.busan .kr and www.visit.busan.kr.

Climate

The mild climate here resembles that along the entire south coast of the peninsula—warmer overall than the rest of the country, except for Jeju-do. With comparatively less rain in summer and more in winter, Busan enjoys more even precipitation than most of the country. Temperatures hardly ever drop low enough for snow. Along the beach it's cooler and more refreshing; the city center can become humid and sticky

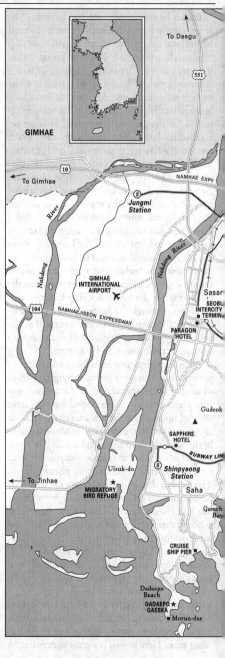

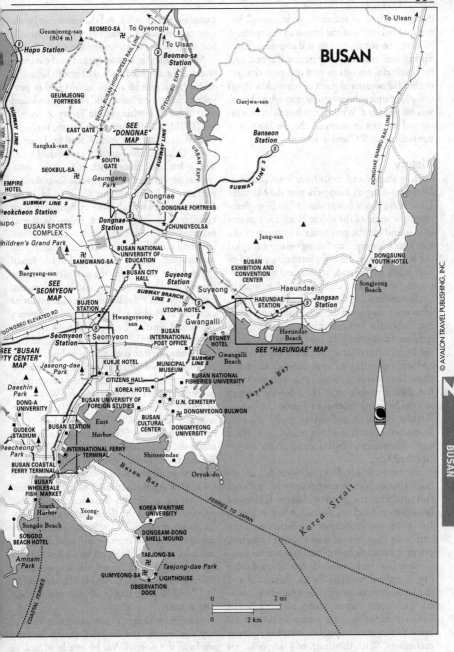

© AVALON TRAVEL PUBLISHING, INC.

BUSAN

during the heat of summer, yet its overall humidity level is one of the lowest in the country. Winter can sometimes turn damp and sharp. Spring and autumn are perhaps the best and most colorful seasons to visit this port city, yet during fall occasional gusts of wind blow in off the sea, at times almost strong enough to knock you off your feet. While it can be colder in winter and warmer in summer, the average winter temperature is 5°C and in summer 25°C.

History

Pottery shards and tools have been found at Dongsam-dong on Yeong-do, near the Maritime University; about 6,000 years old, these pieces represent some of the oldest Neolithic remains ever found on the peninsula. For most of the area's early history, tiny fishing villages occupied the land. During the early formative period of both states, regular trade and cultural relations between the Korean Peninsula and Japanese islands were handled through what is now Busan, what was then part of the Gaya Kingdom. However, when the two countries were not on such good terms, as during the late Goryeo Dynasty of the 14th century, Japanese pirates ruled the sea and often plundered the peninsula's southeast coast. In response, a fortress was built at Dongnae, then at water's edge. The following century saw trade flourish between Korea and Japan. Regulated and formalized by treaty in 1443, Busan was opened as a commercial port, and a tiny community of Japanese merchants was established here.

A century and a half later, however, friendly relations between the countries came to an abrupt halt. In 1592, the Japanese daimyo Hideyoshi launched an attack on Korea, landing at Busan. Jeong Bal, commander of the Busan garrison, and Song Sang-hyeon, magistrate of Dongnae, put up a valiant fight but found themselves overwhelmed by the numerically superior and more highly trained Japanese forces. Busan fell and the Japanese troops swiftly devastated the country. Subsequent naval battles off the coast of Busan, directed by the indomitable Korean admiral Yi Sun-shin, helped blunt further Japanese incursions. With the death of Hideyoshi, his

campaign was dropped, and the remaining Japanese troops returned home. Peace was negotiated, and small-scale private trade once again began.

Shortly after Japan was opened to the outside world, it forcibly tried to do the same to Korea. In 1875, Japan sent an armed naval vessel to provoke incidents near Busan and at Ganghwa Island west of Seoul, resulting in the Treaty of Ganghwa (1876), which opened up Busan, Incheon, and Wonsan (now in North Korea) for Japanese trade. Other nations quickly established trade and diplomatic relations with Korea—the country was never the same afterwards. Soon the importance of Busan became obvious. In 1876, Japan opened a branch bank in Busan, later establishing a coaling station on Yeong-do. Russia followed with a bid to gain trade access to this island and establish diplomatic influence. Communications inside Korea and with Japan improved in 1888 with the completion of the Busan-Seoul telegraph line, and its subsequent connection with the Busan-Nagasaki undersea cable. In 1904, due to increased tension between Japan and Russia, the Japanese took over the construction of the Busan-Seoul railroad line and connected it to the Seoul-Uiju line to facilitate much-needed transportation of Japanese troops across Korea to Manchuria, the eventual battleground of the Russo-Japanese War.

Busan was still relatively small when Japan annexed Korea in 1910. From 1911 to 1916, however, land was filled in along the shore to create the eastern harbor and new port facilities. Factories were built, commerce gained strength, and new residential areas sprang up. The Japanese made valuable contributions to the city (and nation), but along with assistance came colonial oppression. When the Koreans rose up in popular demonstration in 1919, the Japanese responded with cruel repression. By the end of the colonial period (1945), an estimated 50,000 Japanese dwelled in Busan, about one-sixth of the total city population. After the Japanese defeat in World War II, nearly all returned to their own country.

Along with Daegu, Busan was the only major city not overrun and occupied during the early weeks of the Korean War by swiftly advancing

North Korean troops; South Korean and U.N. troops held ground at what became known as the Busan Perimeter. Seoul, however, fell, and Busan for several months served as the temporary capital of the country. Refugees poured in, swelling the population to about four million (nearly equaling today's population!), creating an overextended city of ramshackle huts, dirt lanes, and a pitifully inadequate infrastructure. At the end of the war, most refugees returned to their homes, but great numbers stayed in the city permanently, particularly refugees from the north.

Cultural Notes

Unlike Seoul, Busan never served as a long-term center of national government, contains no palace or other royal remains, and enjoys no significant legacy or mystique. It has seen only sporadic incidents of major historical import, but does preserve four National Treasures, 14 Treasures, and four Historical Sites. Busan has its roots sunk in the past, experienced nurturing and growth in the 20th century, and looks forward to a robust future. Aside from its importance as an international port, the city is best-known for its tourist attractions: over two dozen parks and recreation areas, six beaches, two hot springs, major markets, museums, and several dozen temples, shrines, and fortresses. Haeundae is one of several sites in the country designated a tourism zone, which means that the government plans to pour money and energy into expanding the area's foreign and domestic tourism potential. During the 1988 Seoul Olympics, Busan had the honor of holding the yachting events; the city also hosted the 2002 Asian Games, and was one of the Korean cities to hold 2002 World Cup soccer games.

Held on October 5th, the annual **Busan Citizens' Day** festival features a boat parade in commemoration of Admiral Yi Sun-shin's military victory over the Japanese in a battle that took place here some 500 years ago. A street parade, games of all sorts, athletic competitions, cultural performances, artistic displays, and a beauty contest also make up part of the festivities. During the festival, the *Dongnae Yaryu* masked dance, Dongnae Crane Dance, Jwasuyeong Fishing Dance (all designated Intangible Cultural Assets — I.C.A.), and Suyeong Farmers' Dance are performed for the public, and music is provided by the city's orchestra and traditional music troupe. The *Dongnae Yaryu* dance is performed again at Haeundae Beach on the full moon of the first lunar month, during the **Moon Festival**. The **Jagalchi Festival**, with its numerous fishing related festivities and traditional ceremonies, is also held in October in adjacent Nampo-dong and Gwangbok-dong, in conjunction with the **Busan Citizens' Day festivities**. Getting good reviews, the Busan International Film Festival in October draws movies, actors, and directors from around the world and appreciative audiences from the city; www.piff.org. Films are shown at downtown theaters as well as the large outdoor screen at the Suyeong Yachting center. Gwangalli Beach hosts the **Busan International Rock Music Festival** for one week during late summer.

Citywide cultural and arts performances and exhibitions are often scheduled for the Busan Cultural Center, across the street from the municipal museum, or at the Citizens' Hall in Seomyeon. In addition, the Cultural Center stages weekly presentations of dance, song, and poetry on Saturday at 1500 in the small auditorium. Traditional folk performances are presented for free on the plaza at Yongdu-san park every Saturday, and on the second and fourth Sundays of the month additional folk dramas are shown at the Folk Art Hall in Geumgang Park.

Sights

SOUTHERN BUSAN

Busan Tower

Thrusting skyward from the top of Yongdu-san Park, high above the harbor, this 120-meter tower dominates the central business district. Completed in 1973 for television transmission and as an observation tower, it's Busan's most obvious and well-known landmark. An elevator glides to the octagonal top, with snack shops on the lower level and observation floor above. Through its huge plate-glass windows you have the best views of the entire southern section of this metropolis, its harbor, Yeong-do, and when conditions are right, the Japanese island of Tsushima. The nighttime view of the city lights is also quite spectacular! Open 0900–2200, a trip to the top for this view is well worth the ₩2,500 entrance fee. At the base of the tower is a small aquarium (₩1,500) and an adjunct art hall of the city museum. Entrance to both the tower and aquarium is ₩3,200.

Yongdu-san Park 용두산공원

Busan Tower crowns Yongdu-san Park. Formerly known as Songnim-san ("Pine Forest Hill"), this knoll was given its current name during the Japanese occupation, when a shrine was built on its top and named Yongdu Shrine. Yongdu-san means "Dragon's Head Mountain"; the peak to some resembles a dragon rising from the water. This wooded hilltop park is the quickest and easiest escape from the bustle of the city center. It has many walks and flower beds, flocks of pigeons, and a new city bell. To its front, a clock with a face of flowers and shrubs keeps time with sweeping hands two meters long. In the courtyard below the tower stands a statue of Admiral Yi Sun-shin, a detailed bronze sculpture of a dragon that appears to have just pranced off a scroll painting, and a monument to the March 19, 1960, student uprising that led to the downfall of former president Syngman Rhee. In a secluded section to the side of the main courtyard

is a monument to the Korean War dead—every city has at least one. Every day, all day, this oasis sees visitors, but it's busiest on weekends and holidays. It's a great place to people-watch! Schoolchildren come to the park in groups to ride up the tower, secretaries and clerks take their lunches here, and young people rendezvous here in the evening. The elderly come at all times of the day, dressed in brightly colored, voluminous *hanbok* to sit in the sun with their cronies, play *baduk,* or throw seeds to the pigeons. Stairways ascend to the park from the south and east, and a road leads up from the north. The stairway from Gwangbok-dong now also has a covered escalator that runs up the hill. From the late 1700s until well after the opening of Busan in 1880, a section of the city at the base of this hill was used almost exclusively as a residential enclave for Japanese traders. Although rapidly disappearing, this influence can still be seen in the architecture of some of the city's oldest buildings.

Fish Markets

The Busan Wholesale Fish Market, Korea's largest and most important wholesaler of marine products, and Jagalchi Market, Busan's most active fish-dealers' cooperative, both front the south harbor. Don't visit either without your camera! Early every morning, dozens of fishing boats unload their catches on the pier of the cavernous **Busan Wholesale Fish Market,** creating a pungent odor that wafts through the air. Stacked in boxes, heaped on the cement floor, live in seawater tubs, or hung from a cord to show the full length, an immense variety of fish, rays, eels, shellfish, shrimp, crabs, sea cucumbers, and other creatures go for sale daily—auctioned in bulk to wholesalers, dealers, independent shop owners, restaurateurs, and fish hawkers. The real action usually takes place well before 0600, so get there early.

Jagalchi Market [Chagalch'i Shijang] (자갈치 시장) means "Pebble Beach Market." The present market building and harborfront road have been

© AVALON TRAVEL PUBLISHING, INC.

DETAIL

- BYEOLJANG YEOGWAN
- GYEONGDONGJANG YEOGWAN
- TOWER HOTEL
- LOTTE UNDERGROUND ARCADE
- BUSAN TOWER ★
- Yongdu-san Park
- SEOUL BANK
- PUSAN TOURIST HOTEL
- KOREA FOREIGN EXCHANGE BANK
- BUSAN BANK
- BUSAN DEPARTMENT STORE
- ROYAL HOTEL
- DAESEONGJANG YEOGWAN
- PLUS PLUS
- ESCALATOR
- GWANGBOK-NO
- DONGHYEON YEOGWAN

BUSAN CITY CENTER

- JAPANESE CONSULATE
- STATUE OF GENERAL JEONG BAL ★
- CHORYANG GALBI ST
- CHORYANG MARKET
- HYOWONJANG MOTEL
- DONGBAEKJANG YEOGWAN
- DAEWON MOTEL
- GWANGJANG HOTEL
- TOURIST INFORMATION BOOTH
- BUSAN STATION
- Busan Station
- CHINESE MIDDLE SCHOOL
- ARIRANG HOTEL
- CHORYANG SHOPPING STREET FOR FOREIGNERS
- NAGWONJANG YEOGWAN
- GEUMHOJANG YEOGWAN
- SHANGHAI GATE
- MONACO YEOGWAN
- CHINATOWN
- PLAZA HOTEL
- KAL OFFICE
- MARINE CENTER
- COMMODORE HOTEL
- GEUMSU MOTEL
- TELECOM
- JUNG-GU POLICE STATION
- KOREA FOREIGN EXCHANGE BANK
- RUSSIAN CONSULATE
- CITIBANK
- SEOUL HOTEL
- KEUM KANG HOSTEL
- ASIANA AIRLINES
- GEUMHWA YEOGWAN
- BUSAN CUSTOMS OFFICE
- BUSAN IMMIGRATION OFFICE
- Jungang-dong Station
- INTERNATIONAL FERRY TERMINAL
- SORABOL HOTEL
- BUSAN POST OFFICE
- SERVICE CENTER FOR FOREIGNERS
- PIER 1
- Sumir Park
- TEZROC EXCURSION FERRY
- DAECHEONG-NO
- COASTAL FERRY TERMINAL
- GUKJE MARKET
- SEE DETAIL
- Yongdu-san Park
- GUKJE UNDERGROUND ARCADE
- DAEGAK-SA 卍
- LOTTE UNDERGROUND ARCADE
- Gwangbok-dong
- KOLON UNDERGROUND ARCADE
- GWANGBOK-NO
- EXCURSION FERRY PIER
- THEATER
- PHOENIX HOTEL
- LOTTE WORLD
- BOOKSTORE
- Nampo-dong Station
- BUSAN GRAND BRIDGE
- THEATER
- Nampo-dong
- DRY SEAFOOD MARKET
- HERB MARKET
- SAM HWA HOTEL
- JAGALCHI MARKET
- YONG-DO GRAND BRIDGE
- Jagalchi Market Station
- SHINDONG-A MARKET
- South Harbor

East Harbor

MOON

SUBWAY LINE 1

JUNGANG-NO

0   300 yds
0   300 m

BUSAN

constructed over the round, smooth stones that once lined this portion of the bay, a place that was for decades a streetside fish market. Aisle after aisle of stalls sell every imaginable type of fish—fresh, dried, or frozen, from tiny anchovies to hefty sharks and various seaweeds. Early morning and late afternoon are the most boisterous here, alive with bargaining housewives who come to buy fish for the day. Several seafood restaurants are set up inside the market, and here you can have virtually any kind of fish prepared until mid-evening. Ordinary grilled fish or fish soup is not particularly expensive; however, a meal of raw sliced fish or another delicacy can be pricey. On the street outside, pushcarts jockey for space with trucks and pedestrians as they maneuver around sidewalk vendors with tubs full of live sea creatures. Older women run a number of the informal sidewalk stalls. When the market started, during the Korean War, many of the women were war widows trying to eke out a living. Farther down the road toward the Yeong-do Bridge, numerous shops specialize in dried fish, processed fish products, seaweed, and other edibles from the sea. In amongst these shops are vendors of fruits, nuts, roots, medicinal herbs, and spices. In the other direction, the **Shindong-A Market** specializes in live fish and sliced raw fish, while vegetables are sold at the agricultural products market.

Gwangbok-dong 광복동

The area surrounding Jagalchi Market is known as Nampo-dong. In toward Yongdu-san Park from there, and stretching around as far as Daegak-sa, is Gwangbok-dong, the city's trendy shopping, entertainment, and eating area, a closely packed quarter of narrow alleys and side streets, bright lights, and a sea of movement. Although busy during the day, it really starts to hop when the sun goes down. Then, thousands of people of all ages jam these streets, further congested by food, clothing, and trinket carts. Gwangbok-no, the main street through this area, is lined with department stores, fancy boutiques, and other high-end shops, while the alleys contain smaller and more pedestrian stores. Toward the east end and behind the temple are many restaurants; you'll

find a concentration of movie theaters at the west end. Near these theaters is the PIFF (Pusan International Film Festival) Square, where many events of the October festival take place. Snack bars, coffee shops—mostly on 2nd floors—and drinking establishments appear here and there throughout the area. For many, it's the number-one night spot in the city and a great place to watch people. Beyond the Nampo-dong subway station, on the site of the old Busan city hall, is the new and huge Lotte World entertainment and shopping complex, a complement to Seoul Lotte World.

The farther you move from Gwangbok-dong toward **Gukje (International) Market**, the more ordinary the night scene becomes. Chock-a-block with small shops, this covered market carries everything from household items to clothes, jewelry, toys, and electronics. Here as well, pushcarts fill the already crowded, narrow alleys. Starting as a black market following the Korean War, Gukje Market has gained respectability and is now a vital part of the city's commercial scene. West of the Gukje Market is a long street of nearly 100 design and dress shops that specialize in fine traditional Korean fashions.

Foreigners Street

Directly across from Busan Station is an area formerly known as Texas Street (or Texas Town). Undoubtedly stemming from foreign contact during the Korean War (mostly American soldiers), it developed into a red-light and entertainment district, with restaurants and shops catering mostly to GIs. It was a hive of activity, a hybrid of Korea and the West. Once patronized almost exclusively by U.S. military personnel, it has become a rendezvous for Russian tourists and traders—so much so, in fact, that it would be more appropriate these days to call it Russian Road. Since the breakup of the Soviet Union and the opening of diplomatic ties between South Korea and Russia (as well as with other former Soviet republics), a steady stream of entrepreneurs has poured into Busan (and Incheon), and the Koreans are happily catering to them. These days, you see as many signs here in Cyrillic as Roman script and hear Russian spoken more than English. In fact, this area, and to a large degree the whole stretch between the International Ferry Terminal and this area, is plastered with Russian signs and has many shops and restaurants that now do almost exclusive business with these new visitors. The Russian Consulate is located near the port, and information booths with Russian-speaking staff are located at this shopping and entertainment area and at the City Information Service Center for Foreigners. Nonetheless, a handful of shops and clubs here still cater to English speakers, and this area remains a red-light district, hanging on to its reputation as a place to find Busan's seedier side of life.

In a ploy to bring respectability to the area and to help it become used more by all visitors to the city, Texas Street has now been dubbed Foreigners Street, or **Choryang Shopping Street for Foreigners** (초량외국인상가), and the small district just to its south has been re-created as a little Chinatown. An ornamental gate called Shanghai Gate stands at the entrance to one of Chinatown's streets, and several fancy Chinese restaurants and shops that sell Chinese goods have been opened here. For those familiar with the large and traditional Chinatowns in Western cities, Busan's Chinatown will be a disappointment. Nonetheless, it is an attempt to create a more cosmopolitan atmosphere, cater to the growing number of Chinese visitors to the city, play off the resident Chinese involvement in the area—Busan Chinese Association and Chinese Middle School—and tip the city's hat to Busan's sister city, Shanghai.

Daecheong Park 대청공원

Newer and taller than the Busan Tower, and resembling a skeletal church steeple, is a commemorative monument honoring local war veterans. Set high atop the ridge directly west of Busan Station, this monstrosity was constructed during the 1980s and dominates Daecheong Park.

Lying atop the ridge-end knoll below and to the front of this monument is **Democracy Park**. In this large area you'll find plenty of walkways and park benches, cherry trees, an open plaza, a sculpture garden, and a theater for performance events. The **Democratic Movement Memorial Hall**, which pictorially represents the struggle of Busan citizens against past dictatorial ruling regimes, and a public library are here as well. As it's at the top of the hill, there are some good views out over the city center, but for most nearby residents, it's just a great place to come to catch the breeze and hang out with cronies. City bus nos. 43 and 190 stop below the park.

Daeshin Park 대신공원

Neat and compact, the main campus of **Dong-A University**, the city's largest private educational institution, is tucked into the mountainside above Gudeok Stadium, the venue of many professional sporting events. To its rear is Daeshin Park. Once belonging to the school, this broad expanse of densely wooded mountainside is now managed by the city. A stream runs through it, and a mineral spring bubbles up from the ground. Opened to the public in 1970, it contains many walking and jogging trails.

Yeong-do

Yeong-do separates the two halves of Busan Harbor. The old bridge to this island, Yeong-do Grand Bridge, connects with the road that leads around the southern side of the island, along a pretty drive that ends at a cluster of raw fish restaurants. Paralleling this road for about three kilometers is an easy and well laid coastal walk. The newer of the island's double bridges is the gracefully arched single-span Busan Grand Bridge. This red structure helps offset the city's rather dowdy harborfront. A growing residential area pushes up the hill toward the center of the island; along the waterfront on the inner-harbor side lie the Hanjin Heavy Industry shipyards, drydocks, other small-scale industries, and the island's business district. The Korea Maritime University sits on a tiny islet in the harbor, connected by a causeway to Yeong-do. Near this causeway is **Dongsam-dong Shell Mound** (H.S. #266), one of the foremost stone age sites in the country.

At Yeong-do's southern tip, overlooking the Korea Strait, is **Taejong-dae Park** (태종대공원);

W600 entrance and open daily 0800–1800 (1700 in winter). This park is named after Silla King Muyeol, whose dynastic name was "Taejong"; "dae" in this case means "headland." King Taejong unified the Korean Peninsula under Silla control in the 660s, and it's said that he spent time here at a Buddhist hermitage after his warring labors. This park has a thick canopy of pines, and a rugged rocky coast on which stands a white lighthouse from the late 1800s. A stroll around the park's scenic circular road takes a leisurely two hours. An open-air tram also runs this route on a regular schedule, stopping at points of interest along the way; W1,500 for the entire route, along which you can get off and on at each point of interest, or W1,000 for the first section to the lighthouse. Hanging out over the sea from the top of the cliff at the park's southern end are a restaurant and an observation deck. The view here is gorgeous—on a very clear day you can even see the Japanese island of Tsushima on the horizon to the southeast. On the deck of the observation platform, a white stone statue of a mother holds two children in her arms. According to some accounts, this statue of motherly love was erected here to deter distraught people from jumping over the edge in suicide. From near the entrance to the park, down a stairway to the water, excursion boats make a 30-minute trip along the periphery of this peninsular for W5,000 per person. Shore fishermen throng to many of the rocky points here. Visit during the week to escape the weekend crowds. From Busan Station, take bus no. 88 or 101; from Nampo-dong try bus no. 8, 13, or 30.

Beaches

Busan's oldest "resort," and the beach closest to downtown, is **Songdo Beach** (송도해수욕장), famous for raw-fish restaurants and well known for swimming until the water became too dirty and better swimming beaches became developed. It lies at the opening of Busan's south harbor where you can see cargo ships parked out in the bay waiting to enter and unload their freight. Dozens of fish restaurants line the waterfront road. They're crowded most nights, and espe-

cially busy during the summer holidays. From the western end of the beach, a road makes its way around the small peninsula, at the end of which is Amnam Park and its many walking trails. To reach Songdo Beach, take bus no. 17, 30, or 134.

Farther west, on yet another peninsula, **Dadaepo Beach** (다대포해수욕장) stretches along the narrow waist of land that extends out to meet the wooded promontory Morun-dae at peninsula's end. Dadaepo is the widest beach of any in the city. Along its eastern side is a small harbor with fishing boats fronted by a tiny collection of seafood restaurants; beyond them are shipyards. Its western side, a wide expanse of sand, slips gently into the shallow, brown, sediment-laden water at the mouth of the Nakdong River. Even though the land here has been piled high with apartment buildings, it's easy to forget how close you are to the city center. After authorities caught a North Korean spy boat off this point in 1980, the wooded promontory was closed to civilians. While the very tip of the peninsula is still off-limits to casual visitors, the majority of the park is again open and makes a great place for a stroll and picnic, shore fishing, or simply a leisurely outing with a friend. Partway out is Dadaepo Gaeksa, a renovated structure that was once part of a government guesthouse. At low tide, clam diggers work the mudflats to the side of the promontory. Of course, the plovers are also there to get what they can scrounge. Take bus no. 2, 11, 96, or 98.

Ulsuk-do Migratory Bird Refuge

In the middle of the main Nakdong River channel, a short distance upriver from Dadaepo Beach, sits an alluvial island called Ulsuk-do. This designated wildlife preserve (N.M. #179) serves as the migratory nesting ground of well over one hundred species of birds on their way between Northeast Asia and Southeast Asia or Japan. Every year, tens of thousands of waterfowl make this estuary a pit stop. They're best viewed in late autumn, when huge flocks gather here on their way south for the winter. After the migrants disappear the few resident species can still be seen on the island. Rich in food and well-protected by broad reed beds along its sandy shore, this island is well-suited as a nature reserve. Largely uninhabited, the delta area does not completely freeze over, and is not disturbed by commercial riverboat traffic. However, the construction of a tidal dam across the mouth of the river between Ulsuk-do and the riverbank makes one wonder about its effect on this naturally formed reserve.

CENTRAL BUSAN

Seomyeon 서면

Located north of the east harbor, Seomyeon [Sŏmyŏn] has expanded into the city's second downtown area. In this upbeat enclave you'll find department stores, markets, business offices, banks, government offices, commercial establishments, and countless accommodations. Seomyeon has become a night spot to rival Gwangbok-dong—especially for college students and young working people. The many streets and narrow alleys south of the traffic rotary abound with clothing shops, variety stores, several cinemas, countless restaurants, tearooms, beer halls, and discos, as well as the ubiquitous pushcarts. While activity happens all around the Seomyeon traffic rotary, you'll find the bulk of activity southwest of the intersection. Drinking establishments and accommodations predominate on the periphery. Busy any night of the week, it's one of the best free shows in town. The Busan Citizens' Hall, Hialeah Compound (the city's only U.S. Army base), the Children's Grand Park, and Samgwang-sa also call Seomyeon home. Busan City Hall has been relocated to Seomyeon's northern edge from its old location at the harbor. Southeast of central Seomyeon is an odd district that's made up of tough industrial harbor facilities, half a dozen university campuses, and cultural spots like the city museum, city Cultural Center, U.N. Cemetery, and Dongmyeong Bulwon temple. Railroad and subway lines crisscross in Seomyeon, and the Dongseo Elevated Road runs through this area, connecting the Namhae Branch Expressway to the Urban Expressway.

Parks

At the southern end of Seomyeon is one of the city's historical sites. On the grounds of **Jaseongdae Park** [Chasŏng-dae] (자성대공원) stand the remains of **Busanjin Fortress**. Constructed as an auxiliary post to the larger Busan Fortress on the mountains to the west, this tiny knolltop fortification has at times also been occupied by invading Japanese and Chinese armies. Water once lapped at the fortress walls, but because of land reclamation and harbor expansion, the structure now lies a good ways in from the bay. Today, only the reconstructed east and west gates, a portion of the wall, and a pavilion remain.

The **Busan Children's Grand Park** (부산 어린이대공원) lies in a wooded fold of Baegyangsan, surrounding one of the city's reservoirs. This thickly wooded park features amusement rides and play areas, walkways and picnic spots, athletic fields, an observation tower, a science exhibition hall, and an "anti-communism hall." Use bus no. 28, 53, or 81.

Busan Metropolitan Museum
부산시립박물관

Although small, this museum has a decent collection of artifacts, most from the Gaya and Silla dynasties and collected from the Busan area. While some painting, calligraphy, and statuary are displayed, including a 7th-century gilt bronze standing Buddha figure (N.T. #200), pottery items predominate. Along with earthenware pots and tiles, there are fine examples of carved, inlaid, and crackle-glaze celadon, and white porcelain from the Silla and Goryeo dynasties. Look particularly for a light green celadon pitcher in the shape of a bamboo shoot! One of the revolving temporary exhibits focuses on folk paintings—don't miss it if it's there when you are. Opened in 1978, and totally remodeled during 2001–2002, the museum operates daily 0900–1800 (1700 in winter) except Monday and holidays; ₩200 entrance. Take bus no. 34, 51, 68, 134, 139, or 302 and get off at the Korean War monument. This white-spoke structure, surrounded by the flags of the 16 participating nations, stands in the middle of the rotary intersection in front of

the museum. For information online, see www
.museum.busan.kr.

U.N. Cemetery

Over the rise from the Busan Metropolitan Museum you'll find the United Nations Memorial
Cemetery in Korea, open daily 0900–1700 with
no admission charge. Within this well-tended
and landscaped memorial park lie the graves of
soldiers and medical personnel from 11 nations
who lost their lives during the Korean War. The
names and markers for each lie in neat rows on
the lawn. During the war, some 11,000 casualties

were buried here, and all but the remaining 2,300
have been returned to their respective home-
lands. This cemetery was brought under U.N. administration in 1959, and now stands as a
memorial to the united effort of these nations
in the defense of South Korean sovereignty. Near
the entrance gate, a non-denominational chapel
is open to visitors. Use bus no. 134 and get off at
the Busan Cultural Center, from where you must
cross the road for the cemetery. For additional information on the cemetery and related issues,
see www.unmck.or.kr.

U.N. Cemetery

Dongmyeong Bulwon 동명불원

This relatively new Buddhist temple and training center, is located adjacent to Dongmyeong University, which is a 15-minute walk up the road from the U.N. Cemetery and across the first major street. The main hall is by far the largest of the 17 buildings and one of the largest worship halls in the country. On its spacious altar sit huge statues of the Buddha and two bodhisattvas. Also of extraordinary size is the newly cast temple bell. Made largely from cement, the buildings still have graceful lines. Some suggest that the temple "is built in the S.E. Asian style." You decide.

NORTHERN BUSAN

Dongnae 동래

The area of Dongnae [Tongnae] in northern Busan is an old region experiencing new growth, spreading over the low rise toward Seomyeon, down the river toward Haeundae, and up the valley toward Beomeo-sa. Although smaller than either the harborfront downtown area or Seomyeon, Dongnae's business district forms a siz-

able center. Aside from the numerous shops and stores, there are many restaurants, theater restaurants, and drinking establishments. Dongnae hot spring is one of the oldest known in the country, having been referred to in the historical text *Samguk Yusa* with an accompanying date of A.D. 683. Modern development began in 1883. For a relaxing dip in the waters, try the **Heoshimcheong Spa** in the center of town.

Busan National University, Geumgang Park, the city zoo, and botanical gardens all snuggle into the hillside. To the south are the express-bus and Dongbu bus terminals and Busan Sports Complex. On the far side of the subway line, Chungyeolsa shrine sits at the base of a low hill above Dongnae Station, and over the shoulder of the mountain is the newer Bokcheon Museum. Above it are the remains of Dongnae Fortress and below it sits Dongnae Hyanggyo. The mountains above Dongnae are the highest in the city; Geumjeong-san, at 804 meters, is the loftiest. Ringing the top like a necklace are the wall and gate remains of the old Geumjeong Fortress. Strewn here and there on its slopes, like

DONGNAE

BUSAN NATIONAL UNIVERSITY

Busan National University Station

BOTANICAL GARDEN ★

Geumgang

Park

ZOO ★

FOLK ART HALL ★

CABLE CAR

MARINELIFE NATURAL HISTORY MUSEUM ★

MUNHWA HOT SPRINGS HOTEL

HEOSHIMCHEONG SPA

MANGMI-RU ★

DONGNAE HOTEL

Oncheonjang Station

HAEDONG YEOGWAN

HANVIT BANK

POST OFFICE

NEULBOM HOTEL

| 0 | 600 yds |
| 0 | 600 m |

DONGBU INTERCITY BUS TERMINAL

Myeongnyun-dong Station

SUBWAY LINE 1

LOTTE DEPARTMENT STORE

BOKCHEON MUSEUM ★

SUBWAY LINE 3

Express Bus Terminal Station

SUBWAY BRANCH LINE 3

EXPRESS BUS TERMINAL

BUSAN DEPARTMENT STORE

Dongnae Station

DONGNAE HYANGGYO ★

MOUND TOMBS ⌇

© AVALON TRAVEL PUBLISHING, INC.

precious stones on a green gown, are several temples and hermitages. Far below the north gate of the fortress, at the extreme northern end of the city, stands Beomeo-sa, Busan's largest and most significant temple. Not far away are two of the city's golf courses. Running from southern Seomyeon, where it joins the Dongseo Elevated Road, around the eastern edge of Dongnae is the Urban Expressway, which connects with the Gyeongbu Expressway at its northern end.

Chungyeolsa 충렬사

Chungyeolsa [Ch'ungyŏlsa] memorial shrine commemorates 91 individuals, including three officials, who gave their lives in defense of the Busan area during the Hideyoshi Invasion of 1592. The three officials are Song Sang-hyeon, magistrate of Dongnae; Jeong Bal, commander of the Dongnae Fortress; and Yun Hung-shin, commander of Dadaepo Fortress. A commemorative rite is performed here on the eighth day of the second lunar month to honor these men's courage and patriotism. Ironically—or perhaps not so—an inspirational and majestic statue of Jeong Bal stands resolutely in a small city square only a few steps from the Japanese Consulate.

Busan was the landing point for the first wave of Japanese troops during that invasion, and the Korean army garrisoned here, along with the Busan citizens, bore the brunt of this first onslaught.

Originally erected in 1605 inside Dongnae Fortress, Chungyeolsa (H.S. #192) was moved to its present site in 1652. During the Japanese occupation of early 20th century, the yearly memorial services were forbidden, and the buildings fell into disrepair. In 1976–77, this site was totally refurbished, and the grounds were formally set aside as a sanctified national shrine. The annual memorial service, which includes a ritual ceremony and classical music, has resumed, and you can witness it each May 25.

Memorial tablets for the three commanders and others are enshrined in two halls. Here as well are several other buildings and monuments, along with a small exhibition hall. Among other items, the hall displays period documents, several old scroll paintings (one a designated Treasure), modern murals depicting battle scenes, and a few 18th- and 19th-century gowns and other accoutrements worn by the commanders of the fortress.

Crowning the hill behind Chungyeolsa is a pavilion once part of Dongnae Fortress. Originally constructed in 1387, this walled fortification was destroyed and reconstructed several times over the centuries; some of the heaviest fighting of the 1592 invasion took place near here. In 1980, a portion of the old wall, the pavilion, and the north gate were rebuilt. Across the inner fortress area, now occupied by a residential neighborhood, is the north gate. Among others, city bus nos. 88, 305, and 307 stop in front of Chungyeolsa. Entrance is ₩200; free on Saturdays.

Bokcheon-dong Mound Tombs and Museum 복천박물분관

Over the hill north of Chungyeolsa, set amongst a hillside neighborhood, and occupying a portion of a ridge is a series of over 100 Gaya Kingdom mound tombs (H.S. 273) from before the 6th century A.D. This is one of several sites in the city from which archaeologists have unearthed artifacts from the ancient dynasties. Many relics have been uncovered here, particularly pottery, ornaments, metal weapons, and other accoutrements, some of which are displayed at the on-site museum. One of these tombs has been reconditioned and covered to show visitors what the excavations revealed and in what condition the remains were found. Although the mounds can be explored for free, admission to the museum runs ₩500; it's open 0900–1800 (1700 in winter) except Mondays and January 1. The road through the neighborhood to these tombs and museum is rather circuitous, but the neighborhood shuttle bus no.1 runs there from the Myeongnyun-dong subway station, passing the Dongnae Hyanggyo in the way, and shuttle bus no. 6 also goes from the Dongnae subway station.

Geumgang Park 금강공원

On the mountainside above Dongnae is the popular Geumgang [Kŭmgang] Park, a convenient place to escape the stifling city streets; open 0800–1800 daily, ₩600 entrance fee. Here it's green and forested, and especially pretty when the cherry trees bloom in spring. On the way to the park entrance stands Mangmi-ru, the front gate from the former magistrate's compound. Within the park are children's amusement rides, a folk art gallery stuffed full of traditional items, six small temples, a 13-tier pagoda, a lotus pond, and many walking paths. In 1994, a fine marine natural history museum (₩1,500) was added. Expanded in 2002, this museum displays several thousand ocean creatures and ocean plants, has displays on reptiles, birds, and dinosaurs, and also has a fish and marine life breeding program. From this lower section of the park, a cable car (₩2,500 one-way, ₩4,000 round-trip) runs the 1,300 meters up to a ridge, from which paths lead to the east and south gates of Geumjeong Fortress. Two hiking trails also start in the park and pass several of the temples on their way up the mountainside to the upper cable car terminus.

Just outside the park's back entrance lies the front entrance to the **Dongnae Zoo** (₩2,000); a few hundred meters farther along this road is the **Dongnae Botanical Garden** (₩700). Opened in 1969, this garden boasts over 2,000 varieties of plants. Set on a steep hillside, it is neatly tended and interspersed with lawns and pools. The road that passes the front of the garden continues up the hill to the east gate of Geumjeong Fortress.

To reach Geumgang Park from the main intersection in Dongnae, walk toward the mountain across the first intersection. From there, veer off to the left, cross another street, and proceed up the hill under Mangmi-ru. Beyond there you must cross a wider street to reach the park's front entrance.

Geumjeong Fortress

Constructed from 1703 to 1807, long after the Imjin War of the 1590s and the Mongol invasions of the mid-1600s—but at a time when their memory was still strong—this fortress (H.S. #215) was set up as protection against any future foreign invasion of the region. None came! Geumjeong [Kŭmjŏng] Fortress is the largest mountain fortress in Korea; the 17-kilometer-long wall (of which about four km remain) encloses eight square kilometers. In 1974, reconstruction of long sections of this wall, several pavilions, and the east, west, and south gates was completed. Many trails along its walls and through its vast interior make a fine part-day hiking course. Directly inside the east and south gates are small villages well-known for barbecued goat meat (grilled at your table over a charcoal flame) and homemade *makgeolli* (a milky rice wine), both of which live up to their well-deserved reputations. Most of the restaurants here have indoor rooms as well as open-air, canopy-covered seating areas. Note the goats grazing nearby! Don't fail to try these specialties before returning to the city.

To get here, ride the cable car from Geumgang Park and walk the trail from there, walk up the road from the botanical garden, or take bus no. 203 from in front of the garden. From the north, a trail leads up to the fortress wall from Beomeo-sa, and from the south, one goes up from Seokbul-sa.

Beomeo-sa 범어사

The name of Busan's greatest temple, Beomeo-sa [Pŏmŏ-sa], translates as "Fish of the Buddhist Scripture Temple." It's also called "The Temple Where Fish from Nirvana Play." Founded in 678 by Uisang, most of the present buildings date from reconstructions of the 17th and 18th centuries, representative of mid-Joseon Dynasty temple architecture. Two unique structures are the linear front gate and a three-section hall. Beomeo-sa now stands as one of the half dozen or so largest temples in the country. Two Treasures reside here, and an abundance of gaily painted ceilings decorate its halls. This multi-level complex sits peacefully on the gentle slope below the north gate of Geumjeong Fortress; from the left side of the front gate, a trail leads up through the pines to the fortress wall, high on the mountain above. A wisteria population near Beomeo-sa is a designated preserve (N.M. #176). Several dozen monks reside at Beomeo-sa's main compound; others live in the half dozen hermitages scattered in the hills above. With a great number of regular worshipers and a constant flow of tourist visitors, Beomeo-sa is well attended, enjoys a fine reputation, and is obviously well-to-do.

Temple Structures:

From the parking lot below the temple, follow the walk over a stone arch bridge to the first of the three temple gates; ₩1,000 entrance. On the way, you'll pass a series of stone stela, flagpole supports, and boulders carved with the names of temple visitors of ages past—old and permanent graffiti. This gate is of open style. Four squat posts (not the customary two), each set on top of a one-meter-high stone pedestal, uphold its widely cantilevered and intricately complex roof. A signboard at the gate claims that this single-row configuration symbolizes "a Buddhist doctrine that everything can be classified into one when . . . [a person] realizes all principles of the universe." The second gate is enclosed, with the four devas in attendance; the third displays paintings of nature scenes on its inside and outside surfaces.

The first building is the tatami-floored two-story lecture hall—walk around it to enter the wide courtyard. On one side is the bell pavilion/drum tower; within it stand a Silla Dynasty lantern and a three-tier pagoda (T. #250) from the temple's founding. Up a flight of steps is Daeung-jeon (T. #434), the temple's main hall; set at the bottom for protection are two *haetae*. Rebuilt in 1614, after the temple's destruction in 1592, this hall is not elegant but it's solid and serviceable. Unusually, each corner of this building is held up by a short wooden post set on top of a stout granite base half the height of the wall. Statues of the Seokgamoni Buddha and two bodhisattvas grace its altar below an ornate canopy. Dragons' heads are carved in the rafters, and fairy musicians play their way across the ceiling. An attractive painting of a tiger graces an outside wall panel. Granite retaining walls for the terrace, carved stone panels, and stone railings predominate around this courtyard.

An old and faded building that's split into three sections stands to the left of this main hall. The left section is the Palsang-jeon, where murals depict the eight major scenes of the Buddha's life. The middle section, Dokseong-jeon, is dedicated to the Lonely Arhat, and the remaining section, Nahan-jeon, houses statues of the Buddha's disciples. Its sectioned ceiling, too, is painted with fairy musicians and dancers. Not only is the structure of the building unusual, the arched middle lintel is something peculiar to this hall. On both sides of this opening are carved figures representing male and female. Half-hidden by a house-size boulder to its side is the Mountain Spirit hall. A few other structures also grace this compound, and a number of them have tatami floors.

To get to Beomeo-sa, take the subway to Beomeo-sa Station. From there, either walk the half hour up the winding road to the temple, or ride bus no. 90 to the temple entrance.

Seokbul-sa 석불사

South of Geumjeong Fortress, one kilometer above the west end of Mandeok tunnel, is perhaps the most intriguing small temple in Busan. Set below a rock crevasse, in amongst huge boulders, lies Seokbul-sa [Sŏkbul-sa] (Rock Buddha Temple), also known as Byeongpung-sa (Folding Screen Temple). Notice the unusual entrance— on the flat stone face of this crevasse opening,

artists have carved numerous Buddhist images. Expertly done in high relief, and with great attention to detail, they portray both a seated and a standing Buddha, Gwanseeum Bosal, the 16 Nahan, and the four celestial kings. From this temple, a trail runs two kilometers up the mountain to the south gate of the fortress, and farther on to the upper cable-car terminus. Take city bus no. 48, 110, or 111 from in front of the express-bus terminal and get off just after the tunnel. Walk toward the upper, older tunnel and you'll find the trailhead on the right.

EASTERN BUSAN

Haeundae 해운대

Because of its southern location, and the warming effects of the northward-flowing Kuroshio Current, the water in Busan remains swimmable until September. The city's most popular beach is Haeundae Beach, often exaggeratedly called "Korea's Waikiki." Possibly the most famous beach in the country, Haeundae's gently curved, soft brown sands slope gradually into the shallow Suyeong Bay. Over one kilometer long and 50 meters wide, the beach attracts several hundred thousand sunseekers each year. Frequented by young people, it's a popular honeymoon retreat. You may even see an intrepid windsurfer skimming the bay, one of the few places in the country where this sport is practiced. In fact, periodic domestic and international windsurfing competitions are held here. Haeundae also boasts a rare oceanside hot spring. Water exits the earth here at about 62°C and can be found only at a few select hotels up from the beach.

Not surprisingly, entrepreneurs are busily developing Haeundae and its peripheral areas as a major tourism zone. It hosted the yachting events of the '88 Olympics leading to the development of the Suyeong Yachting Center west of Dongbaek Park. In the year 2002, Busan held the Asian Games, which employed the yachting center and other local sporting facilities.

While the center of Haeundae is near the Riviera Hotel and Department Store and the train station is a few blocks farther back, major points of interest in Haeundae are along the water. A

HAEUNDAE

Art Museum Station

METROPOLITAN MUSEUM OF ART

HAEUNDAE STATION

POST OFFICE

Haeundae Station

RIVIERA HOTEL

RIVIERA DEPARTMENT STORE

GANGNAMJANG YEOGWAN

SUYEONG YACHTING CENTER

NEW BEACH HOTEL

PARADISE HOTEL AND CASINO

Dongbaek Station

BADA YEOGWAN

HOTEL MARRIOTT PUSAN

EXCURSION FERRY PIER

SYDNEY MOTEL

Haeudae Beach

TOURIST INFORMATION CENTER

WESTIN CHOSUN BEACH HOTEL

Suyeong Bay

Dongbaek Park

MOON

0   600 yds

0   600 m

© AVALON TRAVEL PUBLISHING, INC.

sidewalk promenade and park borders the beach; at night, food carts line this popular stretch. Near the center of the beach is the new aquarium, and at its western end, to the rear of the Westin Chosun Beach Hotel, is a wooded knoll called **Dongbaekseom** (동백섬), meaning "camellia island." Now connected to the mainland and more often called Dongbaek Park, this former island is famous for its flowering red camellia trees. The noted Silla Dynasty scholar Choe Chi-won supposedly came here during his travels and had the characters for *hae* (sea) and *un* (cloud) carved on a rock at Dongbaekseom; coincidentally, Haeun was his pen name. Since then, the name "Haeun" has stuck for this area. A statue of Choi has been raised near a pavilion at the top of this knoll. Perched on a rock at its tip is a well-rubbed statue of a mermaid, reminiscent of the Little Mermaid in Copenhagen harbor. A walk around the park's ring road takes a leisurely 30 minutes.

People flock to the many seafood restaurants here, yet, oddly enough, Haeundae is just as well-known for its barbecued beef ribs. Many coffee shops and tearooms, beer halls, and stand bars serve thirsty patrons in the byways in from the waterfront. Amusement arcades are busy and shops stay open late, as does Busan's only casino at the Paradise Hotel. Of course, the beach and bright stars bring couples out for a

stroll along the waterfront on fair evenings, and the sunrise over the East Sea provides a memorable sight for early risers.

Rent bicycles for about ₩1,500 per hour from several stalls along the promenade, or inner tubes to take out on the water. For windsurfing boards, try the sports shop on the basement level of the Paradise Hotel and Casino. A half dozen times a day from the pier at the eastern end of the beach, excursion boats offer one-hour round-trip sightseeing rides (₩8,000) around the bay and out to Oryuk-do. A regular commuter ferry (₩8,000 one way) also runs from this pier several times daily to the excursion ferry pier below Busan Bridge in the heart of the city. Among others, bus nos. 40, 140, 240, 302, and 307 run to Haeundae.

Busan Aquarium

Set within the beachside park is the mostly underground Busan Aquarium. An intimate look at living marine life, numerous pools here contain thousands of fish and other sea creatures from various locals around the world. Other attractions include a touch pool, an acrylic tunnel within one pool, an artificial coral reef, and displays on penguins, jellyfish, and deep-sea creatures. Opened in 2001, the aquarium is open Monday–Friday 1000–1900, weekends and holidays 0900–2100, and high summer season until 2300; entrance is ₩14,000 adults, ₩11,500 for students, and ₩9,000 for children; www.busanaquarium.com.

Metropolitan Museum of Art

Opened to the public in 1998, this museum exhibits mostly modern art by local artists, but also draws from the rest of the country and does periodic exhibits of international artists. Paintings and sculpture predominate inside, while large sculptures are placed outdoors. Open 1000–1800 (1700 in winter) except Mondays and several Korean holidays, ₩700 entrance. Located just up from the yachting center and across the road from the Busan Exhibition and Convention Center, it is conveniently easy to reach on the way to the beach. Use bus no. 36, 40, or 302.

Other Beaches

Like Haeundae, **Gwangalli** and **Songjeong** beaches are long and narrow. While these two are less well known than Haeundae, they each draw good crowds during the swim season and have plenty of facilities to cater to visitors—mostly

Koreans. Closer in toward the city center, Gwang-alli (광안리해수욕장) sports many seafood restaurants along its waterfront, with a concentration of them and a small amusement park at its northern end. Unfortunately, a new suspension bridge across the bay spoils the view from the beach when looking seaward. Beyond Haeundae, Songjeong Beach (송정해수욕장) has the city's only youth hostel. Although farther from the city center, **Ilgwang** and **Jinha** beaches (Jinha Beach is actually within Ulsan city limits) attract throngs of people from Busan and Ulsan during the hot summer months. An estimated 10 million people visit the beaches of Busan during the short swimming season!

Among others, bus nos. 39, 40, 109, 139, 140, 240, 302, 307, and 2002 pass Gwangalli Beach on their way to Haeundae Beach. Bus nos. 100, 140, 141, 302, and 2002 run as far as Songjeong, which is also one train stop past Haeundae on the Donghae Nambu rail line. Ilgwang Beach is also serviced by the same rail line and by city bus nos. 181 and 186. Intercity buses from the Dongbu Bus Terminal run to Ilgwang and Jinha beaches.

GAYA KINGDOM

Long ago, Gimhae ("Metal Sea") was an important source of iron and other metals for the tools and trade of Iron and Bronze Age peoples who inhabited this region. Eventually, these people coalesced into states jointly referred to as the Gaya (or Karak) Kingdom (A.D. 42–532), occupying an area south and west of the Nakdong River and east of the Sobaek Mountains. Though their sovereign lands were never extensive, the Gimhae Plain was under their influence until it fell to Silla control in the 6th century. Like a plant not given enough room to flourish, the Gaya Kingdom evolved slowly and died an early death. Squashed between the Baekje and Silla kingdoms, its larger and more powerful neighbors, the Gaya kings couldn't get it together to cooperatively challenge those nations, nor to combine into one vibrant social unit. Of the half-dozen Gaya states, the Bon Gaya and Dae Gaya were most influential. Bon Gaya centered around its capital, Gimhae;

Dae Gaya was located at Goryeong. According to traditional dates, the Bon Gaya kings reigned an incredibly long time—only 10 kings ruled during its 490-year existence. The first monarch, Suro, sat in power the longest, reportedly reigning for 157 years (A.D. 42–199)! Legends say that he was born from a golden egg and was "elevated" to the kingship by a group of nine chieftains of the Gaya clan. (Similar stories of miraculous births are told of Silla king Bak Hyeokgeose and Goguryeo king Dongmyeong.) King Suro's family name was Gim [Kim], and to this day the Gimhae branch of the Gim family claims Suro as its progenitor. It's said that King Suro married an Indian princess from the "Ayuta" state. Her family name was Heo, and she requested that the name of the king that her name be passed on to posterity after her death. The king's second son was then given the name, and it has come down through that line ever since.

GIMHAE 김해

Over the mountains west of Busan and across the Nakdong River lies the city of Gimhae [Kimhae]. Although a separate city, and located within the province of Gyeongsangnam-Do, it is discussed here due to its close proximity to and connectedness with Busan. Gimhae has one of the widest uninterrupted agricultural plains in Gyeongsangnam-Do, a rich delta land that grows most of Busan's food. Crisscrossing the bottomland below Gimhae, irrigation channels etch lines through this great agricultural heartland. Along this plain's northern edge runs Namhae Expressway; farther south, the Namhae Branch Expressway cuts through the middle of these expansive fields, eventually joining the other at Naengjeong.

Originally the center of one of the Gaya confederate states, the Gimhae region was absorbed into Silla territory. During the United Silla period, Gimhae was one of the five secondary capitals of the kingdom. After the disintegration of the Silla Dynasty, however, it lost all importance as a power center and regressed to a provincial agricultural community, eclipsed by the growing importance of the Busan area to the east. Today, it's again a thriving bustling city of some 320,000 people.

Gimhae's main street runs north from the bus terminal toward the hills. Along this street are major businesses, shops, banks, and restaurants. About one-half kilometer up and to the west is the tomb of King Suro; about two kilometers up is that of his queen. Over the hill to the west of the queen's tomb and sitting off the highway that runs north toward Miryang is the Gimhae National Museum. A visit to Gimhae is an easy half-day trip from Busan. Take Busan city bus no. 128 from Seomyeon, 130-1 from Dongnae, or 123 or 309 from the city center, and get off along Gimhae's main street.

See www.gimhae.go.kr for information on the Internet.

Royal Tombs

Occupying a spot in the middle of the city, the tomb of King Suro (수로왕능) (H.S. #73) is a graceful mound similar to, yet smaller than, those at Gyeongju. At its front is a stone table and a memorial stela inscribed with the words "Garak King Suro." Standing guard at its front are pairs of civilian and military stone figures, bear, sheep, and horses. The tomb's enclosure is tiny for such a legendary person, but it's peaceful and well tended. Every spring and autumn, a memorial ceremony for the king is performed here. In coordination with the spring event, the **Garak Cultural Festival** is held at various locations in Gimhae, and events include fireworks, folk music and dance, theatrical performances, and athletic and literary competitions. An extensive complex of associated buildings, lawns, ponds, shade trees, walkways, and park benches surrounds the tomb, and this whole park-like enclosure is a quiet enclave in the heart of the city. Although the accompanying buildings are relatively new and uninspiring, the exhibition hall warrants some attention; it displays reproductions of metal artifacts and pottery from the Gaya Dynasty. Other buildings house portraits of King Suro and his queen and memorial tablets for the second through the ninth Gaya kings. Entrance to the complex costs ₩700.

A 30-minute walk up the main street (or take bus no. 123 or 130-1) is the tomb of King Suro's wife (수로왕비능). Smaller than the king's, yet well tended, this mound tomb (H.S. #74) is surrounded by a low stone enclosure. Several buildings used for ceremonial purposes accompany this tomb. In an open pavilion to the front of the tomb stands a pile of stones stacked roughly in the shape of a pagoda, said to have been brought from India with the queen. The bottom course has a Buddha figure and Indian script faintly carved into it.

From here, a walkway leads across the road to the knoll Guji-bong. In amongst the trees at its top is a granite sculpture of six eggs surrounded by twining dragons and watchful tortoises. This represents the place and legend of King Suro's birth. From these eggs, King Suro was first born. Each of the remaining five hatched the head of one of the five Gaya states. To the side of this sculpture is a southern-style, low-slung and flat stone dolmen.

© ROBERT NILSEN

tomb of Gaya King Suro

Gimhae National Museum
국립김해박물관

This museum is one of the newest of the national museums, and its focus is on artifacts from the Gaya region, Gimhae, and elsewhere. While pottery predominates, there are many iron objects, most excavated from mound tombs. Interesting are examples of early iron military armor. Pottery ranges from early utilitarian bowls to later decorative pots and stands. One delicate object, an unglazed crescent-shaped vessel with wheels that's set on a stand (T. #637), may have been for ceremonial use. The Gimhae National Museum is open 0900–1800. It closes one hour later on weekends and holidays and one hour earlier in winter. Admission is ₩400; closed Mondays and the first day of the year. It's an easy walk west of Queen Heo's tomb, but Gimhae bus no. 4 runs past from the bus terminal.

Practicalities

ACCOMMODATIONS

Hotels

Busan boasts the largest number of Western-style hotels outside Seoul—about five dozen—mostly concentrated in its several city centers. Seven deluxe-class hotels operate in the city. You can't miss the **Commodore Hotel** (tel. 051/466-9101) high on the hillside overlooking the east harbor; its exterior lines and ornamentation mimic the style of traditional Korean structures. The interior also faithfully incorporates traditional designs and motifs. Also in the city center is the **Sorabol Hotel** (tel. 051/463-3511, www.sorabolhotel.co.kr). Like the Commodore, it is frequented largely by Japanese tourists. The **Hotel Lotte Busan** (tel. 051/810-1000, www.hotel.lotte.co.kr/pusan) is the newest and largest, with nearly 1,000 guest rooms, a profusion of restaurants and bars, a theater restaurant, multi-story department store, and duty-free shop, along with all the usual amenities. Rooms at the Lotte run ₩220,000–300,000 for Korean- or Western-style rooms or ₩370,000–3,000,000 for suites. All four of Haeundae's deluxe hotels have top-notch locations right on the beach, and unless you have business in the city center, it's much prettier on the water. With the quietest and perhaps most scenic site of any in the city, the **Westin Chosun Beach Hotel** (tel. 051/742-7411, www.chosunbeach.co.kr) anchors the west end of the beach. The oldest hotel in this area, it has periodically been remodeled and maintains a high standard. Rates run ₩160,000–260,000 and ₩420,000 for suites. Having undergone a thorough remodeling, the **Paradise Hotel and Casino Busan** (tel. 051/742-2121, www.paradisehotel.co.kr) lies at the far end. It has the city's only casino, an open-air hot spring bath, and duty-free shops. Room rates here start at ₩170,000. Focused more on business travelers, the newer and more contemporary **Hotel Marriott Pusan** (tel. 051/743-1234, www.marriott.com) sits next door. The Marriott has a full

complement of restaurants and recreation amenities. Its room rates run ₩170,000–250,000, with suites upwards from ₩350,000. The most unusual hotel in the city is the **Ferris Flotel** (tel. 051/749-0000), a converted Russian luxury cruise ship that's anchored next to Dongbaek Park. Aside from the restaurants, coffee shop, bars, saunas, and reception rooms, there are over 50 cabins that run ₩120,000–220,000 a night with suites up to ₩500,000. Numerous water sport activities are available. Even if you're not staying, it may be worth a look as it is an oddity.

In the central district, first-class hotels are the **Busan Tourist Hotel** (tel. 051/241-4301), and **Royal Hotel** (tel. 051/241-0151). Both on the slopes of Yongdu-san, they primarily receive Japanese guests. A short distance away on Gwangbok-no is the **Phoenix Hotel** (tel. 051/245-8061). These hotels have rooms in the ₩80,000–90,000 range. Nearby but less expensive are the third-class **Tower Hotel** (tel. 051/241-5151) and the **Sam Hwa Hotel** (tel. 051/246-4361). Conveniently located, the first-class **Arirang Hotel** (tel. 051/463-5001) sits to the south side of the Busan Station plaza and charges ₩60–70,000.

Of the dozen in Seomyeon, try the first-class **Kukje Hotel** (tel. 051/642-1330), a few steps from the Citizens' Hall; the third-class **Tae-A Hotel** (tel. 051/806-3010), at the Seomyeon intersection; or the **Ujeong Tourist Hotel**, south of the market. Dongnae has half a dozen hotels including the first-class **Dongnae Hotel** (tel. 051/555-1121), the second-class **Neulbom Hotel** (tel. 051/555-1800), and the third-class **Munhwa Hot Springs Hotel** (tel. 051/555-2858).

Others that may be of convenience throughout the rest of the city are the second-class **Utopia Hotel** (tel. 051/757-1100) in Suyeong, the third-class **Sydney Hotel** (tel. 051/752-0202) at Gwangalli, the third-class **Korea Hotel** (tel. 051/628-7001) up from the Busan Metropolitan Museum, and the second-class **Songdo Beach Hotel** (tel. 051/254-2000) across from the water at **Songdo Beach**. The deluxe-class **Paragon**

Hotel (tel. 051/328-2001) the first-class Sapphire Hotel (tel. 051/207-1300) and **Empire Hotel** (tel. 051/337-8811) are situated in newer, burgeoning sectors along the Nakdong River.

Yeogwan

Abundant *yeogwan* are found around each of the bus terminals and train stations. If arriving by ferry, you'll have to cross Busan's major thoroughfare or head toward the train station to find a place to stay. Overall, the *yeogwan* here are the same price as any in the country, with few bargains. The following are a sampling of *yeogwan* conveniently located near transportation connections and in the city's centers. Remember that aside from these mentioned, scores of others exist in the city, so if you don't like one for any reason, just walk down the street and find another.

At the edge of Gwangbok-dong, near the stairway up to Yongdu-san Park, try the Donghyeon Yeogwan (동현여관) or Daeseongjang Yeogwan (대성장여관). On the north side of the hill are Byeoljang Yeogwan (별장여관) and Gyeongdongjang Yeogwan (경동장여관).

On the far side of Daecheong-no and a closer walk from the International Ferry Terminal are the Seouljang Yeogwan (Seoul Hotel) (서울장여관), (tel. 051/469-7001), where rooms run ₩25,000; Geumhwa Yeogwan (금화여관), which has Korean-style rooms for ₩15,000 and Western-style rooms for ₩20,000; and at the top of the stairway is Geumgang Yeoinsuk (Keum Kang Hostel) (금강여인숙) (tel. 051/469-3600), the cheapest place in town at ₩11,000 with a couple of tiny rooms. Both the Keum Kang Hostel and Seoul Hotel have signs in English and the proprietors speak a little English. Look for the Geumhwa Yeogwan and Keum Kang Hostel on the street directly across from the Korean Foreign Exchange Bank, from where you can see the stairway. The Seouljang Yeogwan is just around the corner.

On the north side of the Busan Station plaza is the Gwangjang Hotel (광장호텔), and just beyond it is the Dongbaekjang Yeogwan (동백장여관) with rooms for ₩25,000. With similar rates, you'll find the homey Monaco Yeogwan

(모나코여관), and Geumhojang Yeogwan (금호장여관) on the south side of the plaza. Nearby is the Plaza Hotel (프라자호텔) with rooms for ₩40,000. A few blocks down, directly behind the KAL office, is the more upscale Geumsu Motel (금수모텔), where you can find a comfortable room for ₩30,000–35,000. Across Jungang-no, safe places to check are the Nagwonjang Yeogwan (남원장여관), and Hyowonjang Motel (효원장여관), where rates run ₩25,000–30,000. A little farther back is the Daewon Motel (Dae Won Youth Hostel) (tel. 051/467-5734), where a bunk in a dorm room runs ₩12,000 and a regular room is ₩25,000. Here too there is a sign in English and the proprietor speaks a little English. While close to the station, the sound of train noise seems muffled.

Seomyeon has its fair share of places. Near the Ujeong Hotel are many, including the Seouljang Motel (서울장여관), and directly behind the Lotte Hotel are others that include the Rose Parkjang Yeogwan (러즈파크장여관). In the streets north of Hotel Lotte and across the main boulevard is a cluster of *yeogwan* including the Oasisjang Yeogwan (오아시스여관). These generally run ₩25,000–30,000. As in Seomyeon, there are many places in Dongnae, including the Haedong Yeogwan (해동여관), which is down the street from the Dongnae Hotel. Across the road and up a bit from the Marriott Hotel in Haeundae is the Gangnamjang Yeogwan (강남장여관), down the road beyond the small New Beach Hotel is the Bada Yeogwan (파다여관), and beyond that the Sydney Motel (시드니모텔). Rates at the *yeogwan* run ₩25,000–30,000; it's ₩30,000–60,000 at the New Beach, and the motel falls between. Many others are located closer to the train station. If you care to stay at Songdo, try the Deokseonggwang Motel (덕성광모텔), Taewon Motel (태원모텔), Blue Beach (블루비치), or other similar places, all fronting the water across from this beach, with rooms ranging ₩35,000–45,000.

Youth Hostel

The only association youth hostel in Busan is the **Dongsung Youth Hostel** (동숭유스호스텔) (tel. 051/703-8466), located near Songjeong Beach way out beyond Haeundae. Not at all convenient to the city center, it's set in a quiet little community on a fine beach that sees great activity only during the summer swimming season. A 10-minute walk from the Songjeong Station, dorm rooms here run ₩10,000 or ₩30,000 for a family room. Use bus no. 139 or 2003.

FOOD

City Specialties

Busan has half a dozen special dishes. Already mentioned are the *so galbi* (highly seasoned charcoal-broiled beef ribs) of Haeundae and *yeomso gogi* (barbecued goat meat) and rice wine of Geumjeong-san. To the front of Busan Station is Choryang Galbi Street, known for pork ribs. Dongnae enjoys renown for *pajeon* (batter-fried onion pancakes), and waterfront areas specialize in *dodari hoe* (sliced raw flounder) and *paemjangeo* (river eel).

Restaurants

Busan has even more restaurants than it has *yeogwan*, and, like the accommodations, they are found in every corner of the city. All registered hotels serve a variety of Korean, Japanese, Chinese, and Western foods, but prices are dear. Characteristically fronted by wood lattice work with lots of wood trim inside, Japanese restaurants often serve noodle soups and sushi. For a wide variety of Chinese dishes, look for a restaurant crowded with decorative lanterns, scrolls, and paintings, Chinese-character decals, and a Taiwanese flag; you can bet that it's run, and the food cooked, by ethnic Chinese. Many ordinary Korean eateries are located in and around the area markets, while the side streets and alleys of Gwangbok-dong, Seomyeon, and Dongnae are chockablock with restaurants from austere to ritzy. Look also along the tree-lined boulevard near the post office and behind Daegak-sa near Gukje Market. In the evening, pushcarts set up in many areas to sell a variety of finger food and drink. Some of the large department stores also serve food; their restaurants are usually bunched together on the same level, often in the basement or on one of the top floors.

Fish is on many menus. The most popular places for seafood are the Jagalchi Market, the east end of Haeundae Beach near the excursion ferry pier, along Gwangalli Beach, and at Songdo Beach, with row after row of eateries.

ENTERTAINMENT

Long established as Busan's number-one entertainment district, Gwangbok-dong is frequented by everyone! This maze of alleys and lanes chockfull of buildings is as closely packed as the fish displayed in wooden crates a few steps away in Jagalchi Market. Seomyeon, on the other hand, has become an entertainment district more recently. Catering to a younger clientele, it's smaller and more casual, yet still full of life. In both areas you'll find bright lights, fancy shops, restaurants and bars, music halls and discos, food stalls, tearooms, curio shops, cinemas, and some of the best people-watching anywhere in the city. To best appreciate these areas, see them in the evening!

Most of the city's hotels have bars and lounges, and many have pricey nightclubs and discos. Dozens of other nightclubs, discos, and cabarets dot the city. Busan also has several dozen dinnertheater restaurants, of which the best known are probably the White House Nightclub in Seomyeon and Neulbeom in Dongnae. The Hotel Lotte has stage show presentations at the 3rd-floor Theater Restaurant Las Vegas. With two dinner shows nightly at 1800 and 2030, these presentations range from Las Vegas–style reviews to traditional Korean music and dance; tickets run ₩35,000 for the show only, ₩54,000 for the show and cocktail, and ₩70,000–125,000 for dinner and show. Call for reservations: 051/810-7000. The city's only legalized gambling establishment, the Paradise Casino, operates in the Paradise Hotel, offering blackjack, baccarat, roulette, daisai, big wheel games, and slot machines.

Beer halls, neighborhood rice-wine pubs, and other drinking places are found all over the city. Many congregate in the center of Gwangbokdong, Seomyeon, Dongnae, and Haeundae. With its loud music and numerous bars, one particular hot spot catering to foreigners is Foreigners Street. Across from Busan Station and one alley back, it's a favorite hangout for Western travelers, soldiers, seamen of all nations, and a growing number of Russian traders.

Both Gwangbok-dong and Seomyeon have theaters that show first-run Korean and imported American and Chinese movies. For a sedate evening's activity, try a stroll along the beach at Haeundae, or view the city from Busan Tower.

SHOPPING

Pusan has ample shopping. Each of the main centers of the city has its cluster of department stores, retail shops, boutiques, and markets. First and foremost, Gwangbok-dong is a tight quarter of chic clothing stores, specialty shops, and high-end department stores. The fashionable shopping district south of the Seomyeon rotary is adding to the city's shopping options by focusing on the younger generation. Both areas are lively all day, but really begin to buzz at night. Department stores generally open at 1030 and close at 1930. Although hours fluctuate slightly from shop to shop, other stores open about the same time in the morning but stay open a bit later in the evening. Generally, stores in the market raise their security doors to begin business about 0900 and stay open until 2000. Neighborhood stores and street markets on the whole tend to keep the longest hours. A few scattered neighborhood shops stay open all night, but these are rare.

When shopping in Busan you'll need to brush up on your Korean—and your sign language. As a general rule, English and Japanese are spoken only at hotel arcades, souvenir and handicraft shops, and duty-free shops. However, in the stores along Foreigners Street, English and Russian are used as much as Korean.

Department Stores, Markets, and Arcades

Busan has several multi-story department stores. Centrally located below Yongdu-san Park are the Busan, Let's Mihwadang, Plus Plus, and others. In Seomyeon you'll find the Taehwa, Lotte, and Hyundai department stores. In the same

building as the express-bus terminal in Dongnae is another Busan Department Store, while a second Lotte Department Store is located at the Dongbu bus terminal. Haeundae has the Riviera department store.

West of Yongdu-san Park is the Gukje Market, Busan's largest shopping complex. With over 1,400 shops, this covered market is one block wide and stretches along one of the city's major thoroughfares. Much like the East Gate Market in Seoul, block after block of two-story buildings is split by crossroads on the ground level but connected on the upper level by pedestrian overpasses. Here you can find anything from silks to sinks, tools to toothpaste, and farm machinery to fancy traditional crafts. A larger shopping district stretches out on all sides of this market. Near this area as well, you'll find the specialty Jagalchi fish market, Busan Wholesale Fish Market, a vegetable market, and herb shops. Busanjin Market stands at the southern end of Seomyeon near Jaseong-dae Park. Shops in this multi-story market deal predominantly in cloth and clothing. Between there and the Seomyeon traffic rotary, the Jayu, Pyeonghwa, and Seomyeon covered markets do business. These markets predominantly sell clothing, items for the home, and flowers. Just north of the Seomyeon rotary, with its huge selection of agricultural and marine products, along with daily necessities of life, is the Bujeon market.

An underground arcade fronts the Gukje Market on its west side; it's one of the city's oldest. Newer and much longer are the Kolon arcade, located between Gwangbok-dong and Nampo-dong, and the Lotte arcade, which stretches up the street near the Busan Department Store. Recently extended, the underground arcade in Seomyeon runs both north and south from the rotary, while the Lotte Arcade is underground in front of the Lotte Department Store. Others continue to be added here and there throughout the city in compact, high-density areas.

Antiques, Souvenirs, Duty-Free

Busan offers no concentrated district of antique shops like Insa-dong in Seoul. However, several such shops are located on the streets to the east of Yongdu-san, between Gwangbok-dong and Daecheong-no, catering largely to the ubiquitous Japanese tourists. You must look long and hard and be familiar with Korean antiques to strike a reasonable bargain here! Expect to see an overabundance of pottery and stone items, and a lesser variety of wood, paper, and other sorts of antiques.

Korean handicrafts and special products are found primarily in souvenir shops. These tourist items are generally well made, but also mass-produced and overpriced. Sometimes they pander to non-Korean tastes. Handicraft shops are located in most hotels, as well as at the airport, the International Ferry Terminal, and in Gwangbok-dong.

Duty-free shops carry foreign luxury items and select Korean-made goods at prices approximating those found in other duty-free shops throughout the country. These shops are located at the Gimhae International Airport and the International Ferry Terminal, the Nam Moon Duty-Free shop, in front of the Marriott Hotel in Haeundae, at the Paradise Beach Hotel in Haeundae, and at the Lotte Duty-Free Shop at Hotel Lotte Busan in Seomyeon.

Others

In business primarily for Western travelers and Russian traders, the Choryang Shopping Area for Foreigners opposite Busan Station is full of small shops selling souvenirs and other items like large-size shoes and clothes. Here as well you can browse through extravagantly embroidered jackets, exercise suits, leather goods, shoulder bags, soapstone chess sets, brassware, pirated tapes and records, trinkets, and a plethora of other goods seemingly common to stores with a predominantly foreign clientele. Be prepared for bright lights and colors, loud music, and fast talk. Some shops here also operate as (legal) foreign currency exchange vendors.

Foreign books (even pirated editions) are not readily available in Busan. Your best bet to find these is in the large bookshops in front of Busan National University and other large universities. Current foreign magazines, however, can usu-ally be found at most major bookshops, such as Nampo Mungyo in Nampo-dong and Dongbo Seojeok in Seomyeon.

INFORMATION AND SERVICES

Government Offices

From its former location at the harbor, the Busan City Hall has been relocated to new quarters between Seomyeon and Dongnae. Each area of the city has its police station while police boxes are located in most neighborhoods. Post offices are also located in each section of the city, but the central post office is at the corner of Jungang-no and Daecheong-no, between the International Ferry Terminal and Yongdu-san Park. Aside from stamp sales and domestic postal services, the central post office provides international service for ordinary flat mail and packages, poste restante, and free Internet access for visitors. The Busan International Post Office is out in Gwangalli and offers the same basic services, minus poste restante, but handles registered and certified foreign mail. While telephone cards are used mostly these days for long-distance and international calls, contact the Telecom office along Jungang-no between the post office and train station if you need assistance. Both the Busan Immigration office and Customs House are at the entrance to the International Ferry Terminal (pier #1). Immigration and customs also maintain offices at the Gimhae Airport's international terminal building.

Consulates

There are three consulates in Busan that issue visas for nearby countries. The **Japanese Consulate** (tel. 051/465-5101) handles visa applications at its side entrance Monday–Friday 1000–1200 and 1330–1530, except Korean and Japanese holidays. Expect a day for processing. Several hundred meters beyond Busan Station, this consulate sits near the statue of Gen. Jeong Bal. The **Russian Consulate** (tel. 051/441-9904) has an office on the 8th floor of the Korea Foreign Exchange Bank near the International Ferry Terminal. Hours for visa application are 0930–

1215 Monday, Tuesday, Thursday, and Friday only, except Russian and Korean holidays. Located out in Haeundae is the **Consulate of the People's Republic of China** (tel. 051/743-7989). Visa applications are accepted Monday –Friday 0930–1130, except Chinese and Korean holidays, and take about a week to process. Honorary consuls for about a dozen other countries also have offices scattered around the city.

Banks

The Korea Foreign Exchange Bank provides perhaps the most convenient place to exchange foreign currency in the downtown area. The exchange bank has several locations but the Busan Bank, Shinhan Bank, Hana Bank, and others also have branches in the city center. In Seomyeon, the Choheung, Busan, Hana, and Korea Foreign Exchange banks all operate near the traffic rotary. Korean banks have branches in all other areas of the city, while a dozen foreign banks also maintain branch offices in downtown Busan. Hotels also cash travelers checks, but at a slightly less favorable rate. Money may also be changed at the airport when the terminal branches are open, and at the International Ferry Terminal during arrival and departure of international ferries.

In addition, there are plenty of legal non-bank money exchangers, many of which you can find across from Busan Station. A surreptitious underground money market also exists in Busan. Operating much as it does in Seoul, mostly middle-aged and older women clutching oversized handbags stand on street corners or sit on chairs at curbside behind the Busan Department Store and ask in undertones if you care to change money. While some do choose this route, keep in mind that this practice is illegal and cannot be recommended.

Storage Lockers

One-day-limit storage lockers for about ₩1,000 are located at Gimhae International Airport, Busan Station, many subway stations, and the Coastal Ferry Terminal. None are available at the International Ferry Terminal. For short-term use, free lockers large enough for a backpack are located at the Busan Information Center of Foreigners.

Tourist Information

KNTO maintains two information counters in Busan, one at the Gimhae International Airport (tel. 051/973-2800) and one at the International Ferry Terminal (tel. 051/465-3471). The airport desk is open regular business hours and stocks a good supply of maps and pamphlets of Busan and the rest of the country. The ferry terminal information booth is manned only during the arrival of international ferries but a few brochures and maps may be available on the counter at other times. The city also operates information desks in the domestic terminal at the airport (tel. 051/973-4607), at the Busan train station (tel. 051/441-6565), directly across the street from Busan Station in the Choryang Shopping Area for Foreigners (tel. 051/441-3121), and along the beach in Haeundae. For things that go wrong while in the city, contact the city's tourist complaint center (tel. 051/888-3512).

Located one block up from the International Ferry Terminal, the Busan Information Service Center of Foreigners (tel. 051/462-2256) is a convenient place to garner tourist information in the city. Not only are brochures and maps available, but employees on staff speak Japanese, Chinese, Russian, and English, and can answer all your inquiries. From elsewhere in the city, call this office toll-free between 0900 and 1800 by dialing 051/460-1001. This service center also has an exchange bank, free storage lockers, free Internet access, public telephones, and a small souvenir shop. The Arum travel agency (tel. 051/ 463-0084) located here can help arrange accommodations, transportation, and other travel needs.

DOMESTIC TRANSPORTATION
By Air

Gimhae International Airport is located west of downtown Busan on an island in the Nakdong River estuary, www.gimhae.airport.co.kr. Both Asiana Airlines and KAL fly domestic and international routes out of this airport. (For international flights, see below.) This airport has separate domestic and international terminal buildings, and while it only takes a few minutes to walk between the two, they are connected by free shuttle buses that run about every 10 minutes. Both terminals offer the usual amenities along with the ticket counters, including storage lockers, money-exchange facilities, a post office, tourist information desks, duty-free shops, rental car companies, first aid stations, snack shops, and restaurants. The international terminal building also has immigration, customs, and quarantine offices.

Both Asiana and KAL fly many flights daily to Seoul Gimpo Airport, Incheon International Airport, and Jeju-do. Asiana Airlines also flies daily to Gwangju and Gangneung. Planes to Gimpo airport go about once every 30 minutes from 0700 to 2100, while those to the Incheon airport only fly once or twice a day. Asiana flies to Jeju-do half a dozen times throughout the day, but there is only one late morning flight to Gangneung. The airport use tax for domestic flights is ₩3,000.

While the subway does not run to the airport, connection from the airport to town is convenient. A KAL limousine bus (₩4,500) operates on two different routes into the city on a regular, frequent schedule throughout the day. Route #1 heads for the city center, depositing people across the street from the Sorabol Hotel, in front of the KAL Building, at Busan Station, and at Hotel Lotte in Seomyeon. Route #2 goes the northern route and lets people off at the Westin Chosun Beach Hotel, Marriott Hotel, Paradise Beach Hotel, and the train station in Haeundae. You can board the bus at any of the mentioned stops for a ride to the airport. Each route takes about 40 minutes to the end.

Express city buses (₩1,200) take about 50 minutes from the airport to the city. Bus no. 201 goes via Seomyeon to the International Ferry Terminal, no. 307 runs to the express-bus terminal and Haeundae; no. 310 runs past Dong-A University to Nampo-dong and the heart of the city. Regular city bus no. 66 (₩600) connects the airport to the Seobu bus terminal, directly across the river.

Taxi service from the airport is available but expensive. The fare from the airport to central downtown or the express-bus terminal is around ₩9,000, to Haeundae about ₩14,000. The deluxe taxis run about ₩15,000 and ₩23,000, respectively.

Other shuttle buses make runs to nearby cities, and each has a varied schedule throughout the day. These buses go to Changwon (₩4,500) and Masan (₩4,700), and to Ulsan (₩6,700), downtown Gyeongju and the hotels at Bomun Lake Resort (₩9,000), and Pohang (₩11,000). While both Ulsan and Pohang have airports, they do not accept international flights nor are there yet direct connections from the Incheon International Airport.

All buses and taxis pick up and drop off at both terminals.

By Train

Three major rail lines run out of Busan. Connecting Busan to Seoul, the Gyeongbu line is the central and most-frequented rail line in the country. The Jungang line also connects Busan to Seoul (the Cheongnyangni Station), but traverses the more mountainous region to the east of the Gyeongbu line. This line starts out as the Donghae Nambu line. Paralleling the south coast, the Gyeongjeon line runs from Busan to Mokpo. A fourth line, the high-speed rail link between Seoul and Busan, is scheduled for completion in 2004 and trains on this line will make stops in Gyeongju, Daegu, Daejeon, Cheonan, South Seoul, and Seoul, creating swift transportation between the country's two largest cities and a fast link to the capital for those coming from Japan.

The vast majority of trains leave from Busan Station. The Gyeongbu line boasts over 50 daily trains (*Saemaeul-ho* and *Mugunghwa-ho* classes) between Busan and Seoul, plus 10 trains a day as far as Daegu, three to Yeongju, and one that runs to Seoul from Haeundae. On the Jungang line, one daily *Tongil-ho*-class train runs from the Bujeon Station, while a nightly *Mugunghwa-ho* train leaves from the Busan Station for Seoul Cheongnyangni. Others run to Ulsan and Daegu, and via Gyeongju to Pohang and Gangneung. On the Gyeongjeon line, one daily train runs to Jinju, five a day to Masan, three to Mokpo and one to Gwangju.

Sample fares are: *Saemaul-ho* class to Seoul (₩30,600), Daejeon (₩19,100), Tong Daegu (₩8,100); and *Mugunghwa-ho* class to Seoul (₩21,000), Daejeon (₩13,200), Tong Daegu (₩5,500), Gyeongju (₩5,400), Gangneung (₩22,600), Jinju (₩7,100), and Mokpo (₩19,800).

The Busan Station has two floors. Ticket windows, boarding gates, and departure lounge for the *Saemaeul-ho* are located on the 1st floor; *Mugunghwa-ho* and *Tongil-ho* tickets are sold on the second level. Also in the station are shops, restaurants, a bank, automatic ticket machines, bathrooms, and storage lockers. A completely new station is planned for this same spot, to be opened by the fall of 2003. Above each departure door, a digital signboard displays the departure time, class, and platform number for departing trains. Arrivals exit the Busan Station from the 2nd floor, at the top of the ramp. Other Busan train stations are far smaller and easier to navigate.

By Express Bus

Four expressways lead out of Busan. Running through the middle of the country, connecting Busan to Seoul, is the Gyeongbu Expressway (no.1). Between Busan and Gwangju, the Namhae Expressway (no. 10) makes its way along the hilly and scenic south coast. Cutting across the Gimhae Plain from southern Busan, and running into the Namhae Expressway at the western end of this plain, is the Namhaejiseon (Namhae Branch) Expressway (no. 104). Starting in Sasang, crossing the Nakdong River and the Namhae Expressway, a branch expressway (no. 551) runs north and around the mountains to connect with the Gyeongbu Expressway at Yangsan. In the future this branch will connect with an extension of the Jungang Expressway running down from Daegu. In addition, future plans call for the creation of an expressway up the east coast which will branch off of the Gyeongbu Expressway in northern Busan. Within the city itself, the Urban Expressway runs south from the end of the Gyeongbu Expressway, skirting Dongnae and ending in southern Seomyeon. There it meets the Dongseo Elevated Road which cuts across Seomyeon to connect with the Namhae Expressway.

You'll find the **express-bus terminal** (고속 버스터미날) on the south end of Dongnae. Fares and destinations in Korean and English are written on each appropriate ticket window. When completed, subway line #3 will have a stop at this bus terminal. Until then, it's most convenient to go by bus. Among others, bus nos. 2, 10, 35, 105, 135, 157, 307, and 306 go past the terminal. Express buses run to Seoul (₩17,100), Tong Seoul (₩17,500), Uijeongbu (₩18,100), Incheon (₩17,800), Seongnam (₩16,800), Gyeongju (₩3,300), Daegu (₩5,700), Daejeon (₩11,600), Cheongju (₩13,100), Jinju (₩4,900), Jeonju (₩13,100), Gwangju (₩11,000), Yeosu (₩9,500), and Suncheon (₩8,200).

By Intercity Bus

An extensive highway bus system connects Busan to all major cities in Gyeongsangnam-Do and the neighboring provinces. The city has two intercity bus terminals. For buses headed west and northwest of Busan, use the **Seobu intercity bus terminal** (서부시외버스터미날), near the Sasang industrial area along the Nakdong River. Destinations include Jinhae (₩3,300), Jinju (₩4,900), Tongyeong (₩7,800), Hadong (₩8,800), Mokpo (₩19,900), Miryang (₩4,700), Daegu (₩7,800), Haein-sa (₩10,400) and Jeonju (₩16,100). To reach the Seobu terminal, take subway line #2 to the Sasang Station or use bus no. 66, 87, 110-1, 126, 128, 309, or 310.

Buses from the **Dongbu intercity bus terminal** (동부시외버스터미날) run mostly to the north of Busan, with a few also going to the west. Selected destinations are Shinpyeong (for Tongdo-sa) (₩2,000), Ulsan (₩3,600), Gyeongju (₩3,300), Pohang (₩6,300), Daegu (₩6,500), Andong (₩13,300), Gangneung (₩23,600), Jinhae (4300), and Yeosu (₩13,200). To reach this bus terminal, take subway line #1 to the Myeongnyun-dong Station or ride city bus no. 2, 10, 35, 135, 301, or 306. Though there are information windows at each of these terminals, they may be helpful only to Korean speakers.

By Ferry

Ferry traffic has been reduced greatly over the

past several decades. From Busan, ferries run to four ports on Geoje-do and to Jeju-do, leaving from the **Busan Coastal Ferry Terminal** (부산항여객선터미날) in the east harbor. Schedules and fares are clearly posted above the ticket windows, or ask at the information counter. One-day storage lockers rent for ₩1,000. You may need to fill out a travel card (name, ID #, and address) when you buy your ticket.

Hydrofoils and high-speed catamarans leave from Busan for several frequented ports on Geoje-do: seven times a day to Gohyeon, twice via Jangmok, four to Okpo, and eight to Jangseungpo. Fares are Jangseungpo (₩15,300), Okpo (₩15,300), Gohyeon (₩14,700), and Jangmok (₩12,150).

All running through the night, car/passenger ferries from Busan ply to Jeju City on Jeju-do. These large and comfortable ships take about 12 hours to cross. Either the *Cozy Island* or *Orient Star* leaves at 1930 every night except Sunday. Passage on these two ships varies slightly by class, but roughly it is ₩24,000 for third class, ₩30,000 for second class, ₩125,000–150,000 for a first-class bed, and 180,000-220,000 for the deluxe suite. Shipping rates for vehicles range according to size, starting at about ₩130,000.

Excursion Ferries

Excursion ferries offer rides under the Busan Bridge, around the harbor, out to Oryuk-do, and back. The downtown excursion ferry pier (유람선터미날) sits below the Busan Bridge, just down from the Coastal Ferry Terminal. Running half a dozen times a day or more, these one-hour rides cost ₩8,000. For the same price, a commuter ferry runs around Yeong-do and across the bay making a scenic connection to Haeundae. At Haeundae, the excursion ferry pier is located at the east end of the beach.

Departing from the pier in front of Sumir Park, which is little more than a widened and landscaped section of the pier just to the north of the coastal ferry terminal, the Tezroc excursion ferry offers 1.5-hour lunch and dinner cruises with meals and a drink (₩30,000), and a one-hour late afternoon cruise with a drink (₩15,000). The daylight trips run around Yeong-do, past Taejong-dae, and out as far as Morun-dae to Dadaepo before returning. To offer the best city-light views, the night cruises take a route past Oryuk-do to Gwangalli and Haeundae. Call 051/463-7680 for reservations.

By Subway

With the 1986 opening of Busan's first subway line from Beomeo-sa to Beomnaegol, this congested, strung-out metropolis took a giant step toward alleviating its transportation problems. Over the next couple of years, transit officials extended the line through the city center and out as far as Shinpyeong-dong on the lower Nakdong River, with a run time of about 60 minutes from end to end. This line runs through all of Busan's dense population centers except Haeundae. Most of the line lies underground, but short sections do rise above and follow the stream through Dongnae. A second line, opened halfway in 1999 but completed full length in 2002, runs from Haeundae, through Seomyeon, out to and north along the Nakdong River to Hopo. When completed, a third line will cut across the northern tier of the city from a point north of the airport, through Dongnae, and out to the Bansong neighborhood. A branch line will connect this third line to the second line by crossing the first line. For more information, see www.subway.busan.kr.

Operating from about 0530 to midnight, trains run every three minutes during rush hour and five to six minutes at other times. The basic fare runs ₩600 for one zone (up to 10 km) and ₩700 for crossing into a second zone (10 km or farther). It operates very much like the subway system in Seoul; tickets may be bought from a clerk at a ticket window or from a machine. Verify if your destination is within one zone or crosses into a second zone, insert your money (these machines will give change for bills), and wait for your ticket to drop into the box. Insert this ticket into the turnstile machine as you enter. Make sure to take the ticket from the far end of the machine as you'll need to insert this same ticket into another such turnstile machine as you exit at your destination—where it keeps the ticket. Value tickets are also available for those using the subway often. Maps of the subway lines, station neighborhood maps, and a fare schedule are displayed at all subway stations, and maps of the individual line and the entire system are also displayed in each subway car.

Important stops and nearby sites on **line #1** (orange) include Hadan Station (Ulsuk-do wildlife refuge), Seodaeshin-dong Station (Gudeok Stadium, Dong-A University), Jagalchi Market Station (Jagalchi Market, Gukje Market), Nampo-dong Station (Gwangbok-dong shopping area, Yongdu-san Park, the Coastal Ferry Terminal), Jungang-dong Station (the International Ferry Terminal, Asiana Airlines, central post office, Russian Consulate), Busan Station (Busan Train Station, KAL, Foreigners Shopping Street), Choryang-dong Station (Japanese Consulate), Seomyeon Station (Seomyeon business and entertainment district, transfer to line #2), Yeonje/City Hall (city hall), Yeonsan-dong Station (transfer to branch line #3), Dongnae Station (transfer to line #3), Myeongnyun-dong Station (Dongbu bus terminal), Oncheonjang Station (Dongnae, Geumgang Park, Geumjeong Fortress), Busan National University Station (Busan National University), and Beomeo-sa Station (Beomeo-sa). For **line #2** (lime green) stops include Deokcheon Station (transfer to line #3), Sasang Station (Seobu Bus Terminal), Seomyeon Station (Seomyeon shopping and business district, transfer to line #1), Munhyeon Station (Busan Citizens Hall), Daeyeon Station (Busan Metropolitan Museum, U.N. Cemetery), Geumnyeongsan Station (Gwangalli Beach), Suyeong Station (transfer to branch line #3), Art Museum Station (Busan Metropolitan Museum of Art, Busan Exhibition and Convention Center), Dongbaek Station (Dongbaekseom, Haeundae Beach), Haeundae Station (Haeundae downtown, Haeundae Beach). Some stops on **line #3** (brown) will include Deokcheon Station (transfer to line #2), Express Bus Terminal Station (express-bus terminal), Dongnae Station (transfer to line #1), and Allak Station (Chungyeolsa).

By City Bus

Even with the subway system in place, you must ride buses to many parts of the city. Bus stops are designated by signs that show which routes stop there. Buses run frequently along the city's major streets. Most come by every few minutes. Be quick to board and nimble on your feet. These drivers seem to do unimaginable and impossible things with buses—you'll see!

Most numerous are the ordinary buses (₩600). Ordinary buses that go beyond the city limits increase fares according to the distance. Conversely, express-city buses charge a flat ₩1,200 fare, regardless of distance. Deluxe city buses with numbers above 2000 stop at only a few stops between downtown and Haeundae. Buses should have the basic fare posted on the fare box inside next to the driver. Pay as you enter.

Although not complete, the list of bus numbers that follows will be helpful for getting around Busan. Keep in mind that a great many more buses than these listed run down Jungang-no and other major streets in the city. If you have any question as to which bus goes where you want to go, don't be afraid to ask someone. If possible, show them your destination written in *han'geul*.

Taejong-dae Park: 8, 13, 30, 88, 101

Songdo Beach: 17, 30, 134

Dadaepo: 2, 11, 96, 98

Yeong-do Bridge: 1, 18, 35, 39, 88, 109, 301, 302, 309, 310

Gwangbok-dong: 1, 18, 48, 103, 126, 201, 301, 302, 306, 309, 310

Daecheong-no and Gudeok Stadium: 126, 140, 309

Daecheong Park: 43, 190

Seomyeon: 2, 10, 18, 35, 48, 81, 88, 103, 140, 201, 301, 306

Metropolitan Museum and U.N. Cemetery: 34, 51, 68, 134, 139, 302

Haeundae and Gwangalli beaches: 39, 40, 109, 139, 140, 240, 302, 307, 2002

Songjeong Beach: 100, 139, 140, 141, 302, 2002

Ilgwang Beach: 181, 186

Children's Grand Park: 28, 53, 81

Express-bus and Dongbu bus terminals: 2, 10, 35, 135, 306

Seobu bus terminal: 66, 87, 110-1, 126, 128, 309, 310

Chungnyeol-sa: 88, 305, 307

Dongnae: 10, 18, 35, 100, 130, 301, 306, 307

Busan National University: 18, 19, 130-1

Beomeo-sa: 90 from the Beomeo-sa subway station

Gimhae International Airport: 66, 130-1, 201, 307, 310

Gimhae City: 123, 128, 130-1, 309

Busan City Bus Tours

Since 2002, Busan has offered city bus tours with information in Korean, English, Japanese, and Chinese. With stops at major sites along the way, two routes are offered; both start from the Busan Lotte Hotel in Seomyeon and pick up passengers at various hotels and other locations in the city. Some stops on the Haeundae Route include Chungyeolsa, Haeundae Beach, Busan Metropolitan Museum of Art, U.N. Cemetery, and Busan Museum. The Taejongdae Route makes stops at Taejongdae Park, Jagalchi Market, PIFF Square, Gukje Market, and Yongdusan Park. Departure times for each are 0900 and 1340 and both tours last about four hours. Fares run ₩10,000 for adults and ₩2,500 for children, and may be purchased from tour guides at the bus pick-up locations. For those with limited time or little desire to strike out on their own, this is a decent option for a quick view of the city. For additional information, call 02/851-0600.

Taxis and Rental Cars

Taxis are everywhere—but still seem less plentiful on rainy days! They pick up anywhere. When giving directions, first tell the driver the area of the city or the name of a hotel or a well-known landmark near where you intend to go, and point him in the right direction from there. Taxi drivers are generally amenable, but few speak English—it's a good time to practice your Korean! Fares for taxis run the same as anywhere in the country. Ordinary taxis charge ₩1,600 for the first two kilometers and ₩100 for each 280 meters after that. A surcharge of 20 percent is charged from midnight to 4 A.M. The black and yellow deluxe taxis charge ₩3,000 for the first three kilometers and ₩200 for each 250 meters after that—they also give written receipts.

For those with steel nerves, quick reactions, and excellent eyesight, self-drive rental cars are available from Hanguk Rent-a-Car (tel. 051/205-3240), Busan Rent-a-Car (tel. 051/469-1100), Yongnam Rent-a-Car (tel. 051/469-5000), Avis (tel. 051/973-4646), and Hertz (tel. 051/972-1515 or 051/810-5188). Generally, drivers must be 23 years old and have driven for one year. Cars are rented only after drivers produce a passport, valid international driver's license, and a current credit card.

INTERNATIONAL TRANSPORTATION

By Air

Asiana Airlines, KAL, and Japan Airlines have been and continue to be the major players in the international air market into and out of the Gimhae International Airport in Busan. However, China Eastern Airlines, China Northwest Airlines, Air China, Philippine Airlines, Sakhalinsk Airlines, Vladivostok Air, and a few others also have added flights out of **Gimhae International Airport** (김해공항), connecting Busan to Tokyo (Narita), Osaka, Nagoya, and Fukuoka, Japan; Vladivostok and Yuzhnosalkalinsk, Russia; Beijing, Qingdao, Shanghai, and Xian in China; and Bangkok and Manila in Southeast Asia. While the Japanese destinations have been fairly regular over the years, and the Beijing and Shanghai routes seem solid fixtures, the rest are relatively new and are apt to change over time. For information and reservations, contact the sales offices downtown: Asiana Airlines (tel. 051/464-8000), KAL (tel. 051/464-2000), Japan Airlines (tel. 051/469-1215), or visit their ticket counters in the international terminal building at the airport.

Asiana Airlines' downtown office is located beside the Korea Foreign Exchange Bank, near the international ferry pier. The KAL office is halfway up Jungang-no between there and the train station. For foreigners, the airport use tax for international flights from the Gimhae airport is ₩9,000.

By Ferry

International ferry routes connect Busan to Shimonoseki, Hakata (Fukuoka), and Tsushima, Japan, and to Yantai, China. Buy tickets or make reservations at the ticket windows on the 1st floor of the International Ferry Terminal. Tickets will be issued only after you fill out an embarkation slip, present a valid passport and visa (if required of you), and pay your fare. Tickets must be purchased by 1630 for the overnight ferries to Japan; boarding starts two hours before departure. Ticket sales for the ferry to China are on the morning of departure. Some of the ferry companies will sell advance tickets at their offices in the terminal building when their ticket window is closed. In addition to the ticket charge, a ferry terminal use fee of ₩1,100 is required from each passenger.

If you're coming from Seoul or most other major cities in the country, it's possible to travel to Busan by bus, train, or plane, make it to the pier, and purchase a ticket for the overnight ferries to Japan before boarding time. Start early! If you're leaving the country for Shimonoseki or Hakata and plan to reenter Korea with another single-entry tourist visa, it's possible on weekdays to return on the same ferry. The issuance of Korean tourist visas in Japan generally takes only a few hours; other types of visas usually require more than 24 hours to process, sometimes up to several days.

Used for arrivals, the ground floor of the terminal building also has a bank office, a snack shop, and a tourist information booth that is open when incoming passengers arrive. Departure is from the second level. There are no storage lockers in this terminal building. Spend your last Korean *won* here, as they aren't accepted or exchanged on the ferries, or good anywhere outside Korea. On departure, the bank office at the terminal building or any branch bank in the city will exchange *won* for the currency you entered the country with up to an amount equaling the receipt you have in your possession. The immi-

Sleek catamarans and larger cargo ferries make for a fast and convenient connection between South Korea and Japan.

gration and customs stations are located on the second level of the ferry terminal, and the departure lounge and a duty-free shop beyond that. Duty-free goods are sold on board each ferry, but prices generally run a bit higher.

Leaving at 1900 every day (1800 from November through February), the *Kampu* and *Hamayuu* ferries make an overnight crossing from Busan **to Shimonoseki.** Running from Busan **to Hakata,** the port of Fukuoka, the *Camellia* departs Busan at 1900 (1800 from November through February) on Tuesday, Thursday, and Sunday only, and departs from Hakata for a return to Busan on Monday, Wednesday, and Friday. These ferries are large car/passenger ferries. To either port, the crossing takes seven to eight hours. You arrive at the other end in the middle of the night, but must wait until 0830 to deboard. One-way fares for both of these routes are similar. The lowest fare for both is ₩75,000 (open cabin, second class) and a first class room is ₩105,000. The special room on the *Camellia* runs ₩150,000, while a deluxe cabin on the others is ₩214,000. Discounts are available for students traveling second class only with a valid student ID card, children, and infants, but you must inquire as to the current rate. Group rates are also available, and round-trip tickets are approximately 10 percent less than two full fares. Vehicles may also be shipped. Along with paying a steep charge of about ₩500,000, you must show the vehicle registration and an international or Korean driver's license. While there are restaurants, snack shops, and bars onboard ship, many people brown-bag it. To save money, take enough food and drink with you for your evening and morning meals.

A word of caution: These ferries may stop running for about a week over the New Year's holiday season for servicing. If you need to travel at that time, check the ferry schedule *prior* to your planned departure so that you're not left standing on the pier with no ship to board! For additional information, ticketing, and reservations, contact the Pukwan Ferry Company office in Busan (tel. 051/463-3165), Seoul (tel. 02/738-0055), or Shimonoseki (tel. 0832/24-3000) for the ferries to Shimonoseki; or the Korea Ferry

Company office in Busan (tel. 051/466-7799), Seoul (tel. 02/775-2323), or Hakata (tel. 092/262-2323) for the *Camellia* to Hakata.

The high-speed hydrofoil passenger ferries *Beetle 2* and *JB* depart every day at 1400 **for Hakata,** whisking you across the channel in comfort in about three hours. While the schedule is apt to change somewhat, these ferries generally run every day at 1215 and 1545, with the addition of four times a week at 0845 and 1400. The adult fare runs ₩85,000 one-way and ₩170,000 round-trip; the return portion may be used for up to six months. Discounts are offered for students, children, and infants. Get tickets and information at the International Ferry Terminal ticket window or call the Korea Marine Express company office in Busan (tel. 051/465-6111) or Hakata (tel. 092/281-2315).

Operating since 1999, the newest link between Korea and Japan is the route to **Tsushima** (Daemado in Korean), the closet of the large Japanese islands. Tsushima lies in the middle of the Korean Strait, halfway between the Korean Peninsula and the Japanese island of Kyushu, and is the closest point in Japan, cheapest fare, and fastest turnaround for foreigners who need to leave Korea for visa reasons and are able to re-enter on a multiple entry visa. The *Sea Flower* departs Busan at 1040 on Monday, Wednesday, Friday, Saturday, and Sunday for the port of Izuhara near the south end of the island, a two-hour crossing; and at 1200 on Tuesday and Thursday it goes to Hitakatsu on the north end, a one-hour crossing. The return run departs Izuhara at 1520 (1420 during winter months) and Hitakatsu at 1500. The same for both routes, the adult fare runs ₩57,000 one way or ₩114,000 round-trip; discounts are given to students, children, and groups. For information, contact the Dae-A Marine Express Company in Busan (tel. 051/465-1114).

Along with Incheon and Mokpo, Busan has a ferry connection **to China.** The *Ziyulan* cargo/passenger ferry runs from Busan to Yantai, which lies near the tip of the Shandong Peninsula. Running on a weekly schedule, ferries leave Busan at 1200 on Saturday and arrive in Yantai at 1500 on Sunday. From there it departs on Monday at 1700 for Incheon, arriving at 0900 on Tuesday, returning the same day from Incheon at 1800 and docking at Yantai at 0830 on Wednesday. This same ship leaves Yantai at 1700 on Wednesday and arrives in Busan at 1600 on Friday, after making a second stop in Incheon. One-way fares between Busan and Yantai range from ₩150,000 for a second-class four-person cabin to ₩450,000 for the best suite; round-trip fares are discounted by 25 percent. Discounts are also given to students, children, and infants. While it's not a luxury liner, amenities include a restaurant, sauna, game room, and lounge. For additional information, contact the Musung Shipping Company in Busan (tel. 051/441-8888), Seoul (tel. 02/752-8888), or Yantai (tel. 0535/623-8888).

Jeju-Do 제주도

"Emerald Isle," "Island of the Gods," "Island of Fantasy," and "Korea's Hawaii" have all been used to describe Jeju-do [Cheju-do], Korea's largest island and most "exotic" region. Until its incorporation into the Korean nation in the A.D. 900s, it was an independent region called Tamnaguk. Because of its distance from the mainland and the lack of knowledge about it, Koreans referred to Jeju-do simply as "that district over there." From the late 1600s, after its accidental "discovery" by shipwrecked Dutch sailors, until the early 1900s, Jeju-do was known to Westerners as Quelpert Island. More recently, the island has been called Samdado ("Island of Three Abundances"), referring to its ample supply of rocks, strong winds, and hardy women.

Jeju-do is one of Korea's premier tourist regions. In the mid-1960s, the government began to develop the island. In 1975, *Newsweek* named Jeju-do one of the world's top 10 undiscovered and unspoiled tourist destinations. Proximity, relatively low cost, and amenities draw Japanese men, the largest single group of tourists. Consequently, much of the tourist trade is geared toward them. They flock here for fun and games—to hunt, fish, golf, and pursue young women—making their brief vacations a liberating getaway.

For decades, Jeju-do has been a Korean honeymooners' retreat, a paradise where love can bloom in planned seclusion amidst the serenity of its easygoing ambience. Every season brings newlyweds to the island, but autumn is the busiest.

Biyang-do across the water from Hyeopjae Beach

© ROBERT NILSEN

Couples, she in traditional dress, he in a Western suit, are shepherded around by well-practiced taxi drivers. (One wonders where newlyweds of Jeju-do go to honeymoon, and it seems that most head to Seoul, Gyeongju, or Seorak-san National Park.)

In the past four decades, development has changed the face of the island. The airport and port facilities have been expanded, new roads made and existing roads paved, many new hotels constructed, historical and cultural spots renovated, and a huge tourist complex created above the island's finest beach. For island residents, new homes, expanded markets, better transportation, and greater economic opportunities reflect the rise in their standard of living. Much time and effort have been expended to draw visitors to its surf-splashed sand beaches, thick forests, and majestic, snow-capped mountain, Halla-san. Jeju-do offers sights and experiences not found on the peninsula, with enough to occupy anyone for days.

Because of its past isolation, the island's culture, language, and social system developed differently from those on the peninsula, but today its residents are very much in the mainstream of Korean society. The drastic modernization seems hardly to have affected them. Proud of their differences, yet happy with their inclusion in the broader Korean society, they're eager to welcome visitors to their slow-paced island home. Visit this most precious of Korea's island treasures.

To get information online, see www.jeju.go.kr.

THE LAND

Jeju-Do is the country's only island province. It encompasses the island of Jeju-do and 61 smaller islands, only eight of which are inhabited. About 100 kilometers south of the peninsula, the island of Jeju-do sits at the juncture of the Yellow and East China seas. It lies about 440 kilometers south of Seoul, an equal distance east of the nearest point in China, approximately 180 kilometers west of the closest Japanese island, and just over 250 kilometers from Busan. Seventy-one kilometers long and 41 kilometers across, the oval-shaped island of Jeju-do is noth-

ing but a shield volcano rising from the sea. At 1,845 square kilometers (of which 1,810 make up the island of Jeju-do), Jeju-Do is by far the smallest of the country's provinces, and has only about three times the area of the city of Seoul. Its population of 530,000 makes it the country's least populous province, with fewer citizens than each of the country's metropolitan cities as well as the larger provincial cities. Jeju-Do has two cities, Jeju City and Seogwipo, and is split into two counties. Jeju-do is roughly half forested, a quarter arable, and a quarter pasture and orchards.

At 1,950 meters, Halla-san is South Korea's highest peak. From the layering and formation of its rock, it reveals several dozen periods of volcanic activity (from as far back as 10 million years), which have left crusted lava beds, jagged outcrops, geometric basalt columns, lava plugs, and lava tubes. The major shape of Halla-san was formed perhaps 300,000 years ago, while the summit crater came into being some 25,000 years ago. Halla-san's last major eruption was in 1007, and while generally considered extinct, one wonders when the next "awakening" might be. Hot springs and other thermal spots on the vast slopes attest to the mountain's latent energy.

Halla-san's east, west, and north sides ascend gently. The steeper and more weathered south side stood through millennia as a bastion against the hot, humid, and sometimes violent summer weather. A crater atop the mountain holds Baengnokdam, South Korea's only natural lake, which swells during the summer rains but shrinks to nothing for the rest of the year. Halla-san's rocky top gives way to thickly forested slopes of evergreen and deciduous trees gouged by prominent valleys. Below this mixed forest spreads open grassland which carpets the vast rolling lower elevations. In general, coastal vegetation is found up to 50 meters, arable land up to 200 meters, grassland from 200 to 600 meters, the deciduous broadleaf forest to 1,100 meters, and evergreen coniferous forest to 1,500 meters, with alpine vegetation above that.

Throughout the island, but mostly on the east and west sides, are more than 350 secondary cones, or parasitic craters called *oreum* in the Jeju dialect, which dot the slopes like bubbles in a

JEJU-DO

JEJU-DO

South Sea

Yellow Sea

East China Sea

U-do

LIGHTHOUSE
Seongsan Ilchul-bong
Nan-do
beach
Seongsan
PIER
black sand beach
SEOP-JIKOJI
Shinyang Beach
Saehwa Beach
WINTER NESTING SPOT
Seongsando
Goseong
Shinyang
HONINJI
Gimnyeong Beach
BIJARIM
Saehwa
Pyoseon Beach
JEJU FOLK VILLAGE
MANJANG-GUL
CROWN COUNTRY CLUB
Hamdeok
Pyoseon
Gimnyeong
Hamdeok Beach
Seongeup
Pyoseon
DYNASTY COUNTRY CLUB
YEONBUK-JEONG
HANGIL MEMORIAL
SANGUMBURI
JEDONG RANCH
Namwon
SHINYOUNG CINEMA MUSEUM
PREHISTORIC VILLAGE SITE
Jocheon
WONDANG BULTAP-SA
Samhwa Beach
JEJU FOLKLORE MUSEUM
MOKSEOKWON
JEJU NATIONAL UNIVERSITY
SAMSASEOK
GWANEUM-SA
JEJU COUNTRY CLUB
SEONGPANAK REST AREA
Supseom
Jeju City
Halla-san National Park
Halla-san (1,950 m)
DONNEKO
Iho Beach
Shin Jeju
SANCHEONDAN
Orimok Vaolley
Seogwipo
HALLA BOTANICAL GARDEN
SHIN CHUN JEE ART PARK
Yeongshil Valley
KOREA BASEBALL HALL OF FAME
Shin Seogwipo
WORLD CUP STADIUM
Beomseom
Munseom
ORA COUNTRY CLUB
Goseong-ni
JEJU RACETRACK
Pass (1,100 m)
YAKCHEON-SA
Hagwi
HANGMONG YUJEOKJI
PINX GOLF CLUB
BEOPHWA-SA
JUNGMUN RESORT
Aewol
PARADISE GOLF CLUB
DAEYU LAND
Jungmun
JUNGMUN GOLF CLUB
Nabeup
Geumsan Park
ISIDORE RANCH
JEJU SCULPTURE PARK
Andeok Valley
Hwasun
Gwideok
Hallim
Hallim Park
Hwasun Beach
YONGMEORI
Songak-san
Jeoji
BONSAI GARDEN
Biyang-do
Gwakji Beach
CHUSA EXHIBITION HALL
SANBANGGUL-SA
Boseong
Sanbang-san
Mara-do
Kapa-do
JEOLBUAM
Hyeopjae Beach
Shinchang
Geumneung Beach
Moseulpo
Hamo Beach
Chagwi-do
Gosan-ni
Geumeung Beach

0 4 mi
0 4 km

© AVALON TRAVEL PUBLISHING, INC.

thick porridge. Below this pockmarked surface, the island's violent volcanic formation has left about 60 sizable winding caves. Known as lava tubes, they were formed by the outflow of molten lava from under a hardening surface crust. Several typical features of these tubes are striated walls, formed by the swift flow of hot lava through the tubes; pillars, where semi-stiff molten lava broke through the ceiling and oozed to the floor; thick rope-like formations; lava balls or chunks which dropped from the ceiling; "stalactites," formed by melted lava dripping from the ceiling or down the walls; and bridges made of hardened crusts within tubes by secondary flows. Near the coast, some show signs of limestone deposits from water filtering through layers of coral and seashells above. Found all over the island, the longest known individual tube is nearly 12 kilometers in length. Three of these lava tubes are open to the public, and exploring them is a wonderful experience. Aside from the cones and tubes, geometric basalt pillars, the ubiquitous volcanic rock rubble, raggedy pockmarked outcrops, and volcanic sand are also found throughout the island.

The island's volcanic soil has made the ground rich for farming, but its ubiquitous rocks cause problems. Taken from the fields, they're used to demarcate plots of land, construct houses, and build the fences that line the many lanes and alleys of the villages. The abundant rains, semi-tropical weather, and fertile soil create adequate citrus-growing conditions along the south coast. Even with the rains, however, the porosity of the soil leaves it too dry in many places for paddy fields, though well-irrigated rice fields are found around the periphery of the island. Dry land fields push inland, and the broad expanse of higher-elevation rangeland is perfect for raising horses and farm animals.

Jeju-do has none of the silted, ponderous rivers so common on the peninsula. Its streams are short and swift, and most are found on the southern and northern slopes of the mountain. Many are seasonal. Like watery knives, these streams have cut deep gorges into the basalt. A few waterfalls interrupt their flow on the mountainside and then again right along the south coast. Gentle cascades most of the year, they turn into gushing torrents during the spring rains. The island is rimmed by black volcanic rock, exposed to the elements by constantly crashing waves. Although some of the shoreline slides smoothly down into the navy blue water, there are long stretches of cliffs that thrust precipitously out of the sea. More than a dozen white-sand beaches punctuate this coastline, set like pearls around the neck of a beautiful woman. Farmland skirts the coast, and nearly every cove has its seaside hamlet. Jeju-do has only a few natural harbors, and these are poor. Its four major ports—Jeju City, Seogwipo, Moseulpo, and Seongsanpo, all dredged—have artificial breakwaters and port facilities to accommodate the growing fishing fleets and ferry traffic. In coastal villages, fishermen beach their boats on the same crescents of protected sand coves that their ancestors have used for generations.

Chuja-do 추자도

Lying about halfway between Jeju-do and the peninsula, the inhabited island of Chuja-do [Ch'uja-do] is the most far-flung of the province's many islands. Actually two smaller islands connected by a short bridge, Chuja-do is only seven square kilometers in area. Rising up in a number of low hills, it leaves little flat land. Peopled from Goryeo times, it now supports a population of some 3,500 in several villages. Although small, this island has all the requisite needs of an island community. Most people who come to Chuja-do come to visit relatives, or to try their luck fishing its rocky shores. Originally under jurisdiction of Jeollanam-Do, of which it has a close cultural identity, Chuja-do came under the administration of Jeju-Do in 1946.

Beaches

Korea's "tropical isle" has more than a dozen decent beaches. As on the peninsula's south and west coasts, the water here is warm. Generally, the island's beaches run smoothly into the sea, and many are set in coves or otherwise well protected; those on the southwest coast are the most exposed and drop off the quickest. North-coast beaches are peppered with numerous volcanic boulders; those along the southern shore have virtually no such rocks to interrupt the long white strands and aqua-blue water. All of the island's beaches consist of white sand except for the two below Ilchul-bong, which are volcanic gray. The vast majority of swimmers use the beaches only during the "swimming season," from mid-July to mid-August. Yet for several weeks before and after, the days are warm, the water pleasant, and the beaches nearly vacant. The most frequented beaches are Iho and Hamdeok, near Jeju City, and Jungmun, on the south coast. Two others of note are Hyeopjae (near Hallim, where pines trees front the gently sloping sand—good for kids) and Shinyang at the east end, a 1.5-kilometer crescent of sand, the bay of which is the spot of choice for windsurfers.

Those toward the ends of the island tend to be less crowded, used mostly by the local residents. Changing rooms are found at some of these swimming spots, and several have showers; *yeogwan* and *minbak* are located at nearly all.

Climate

Jeju-do is said to have a subtropical marine climate, but it definitely has four distinct seasons. While sometimes referred to as the Hawaii of Korea, Jeju-do only vaguely resembles those balmy isles, though it is warmer on average than the peninsula by 2–4°C. An important factor contributing to the higher temperatures is the warm Kuroshio Current and accompanying air, which pushes up in summer from the Philippines. Jeju-do has an annual average temperature of about 15°C (in summer the temperatures range 23–27°C, while winter gets cold—3–7°C) and the humidity, at 71–74 percent, is slightly higher than in the rest of the country. Because of its extremes in elevation, the island also has widely divergent climatic zones, from the semi-tropical south coast through the temperate mountain slopes to the alpine zone at the mountain summit. The peak's average temperature is 5°C, and for long periods in winter it drops well below freezing when winds sweep across the Yellow Sea from Manchuria picking up moisture, lay in a layer of cloud at about 700 meters, and drop great amounts of snow on the mountain.

The island also has a high degree of average precipitation. Most of its more than 1,400 mm comes during the summer rainy season (on average, about 500 mm in July alone), but some falls as winter snow on the mountain. Halla-san is capped from December through April, like a white-haired country gentleman, but may receive snow as early as October and as late as May. Although light rains occur in spring, the heavy monsoon rains start in the beginning of June and last well into August; Seogwipo and the south-central coast receive the greatest amount. Temperatures rise at their onset, but it is seldom muggy because of refreshing sea breezes. Few of Asia's seasonal typhoons make it as far north as Jeju-do, but often the associated weather does. Strong winds and heavy rains cause crop damage and high seas, and interrupt ferry traffic.

Weather at the mountaintop is extremely fickle. A bright clear morning may easily turn into a downpour by afternoon, or a misty morning chill may burn off by midday. Most days, the mountain plays peek-a-boo with eager hikers; it's exceptional when the mountain is clear from morning till evening. On the average, the summit can be seen only one day in ten.

Flora and Fauna

Jeju-do's vegetation is similar to that on the south coast of the peninsula and the coastal areas of southern Japan. Some 1,800 species of plants have been recorded; of those, 30 are endemic and eight have been designated as protected and important species. Of note are 15 native citrus fruits, 10 varieties of mushrooms, the *hallan* orchid, and the *nancho* amaryllis. Ferns, palms, and other semi-tropical plants grow in the gorges on the island's south side; camellia trees flower in winter. Inland from the coastal fields is the drier mountain skirt, with its hardy bushes and grasses; a few varieties of cactus live at this level. The mountainside above that is a mixture of evergreen and deciduous trees. Cherry trees grow wild in north-slope valleys and are especially pretty when they're abloom, in April. Meadows on the mountain's upper plateaus have a variety of alpine flowers, and are particularly noted for the azaleas and rhododendrons which bloom in spring. Toward the summit, only sturdy bushes, stunted trees, and frigid-zone plants survive.

Jeju-do's fauna is comparable to that of southern Manchuria and central China. In the past, wild boar and large deer were numerous, but they have long since been hunted to extinction. Today, the island supports roe deer, weasels, and 15 other small mammal species, a variety of game birds and over 200 other types of birds, numerous butterflies, eight species of reptiles, and about 1,600 species of insects. The small and stocky Jeju-do horse, called *jorangmal* (N.M. #347), is a breed that descends from the Mongolian ponies brought to the island during the Mongol occupation of the 1200s. While once used mainly as beasts of burden, they are now raised mostly for racing and as riding horses for tourists. With the introduction of gas-powered farm implements and vehicles in the 1960s and '70s, the horse population plummeted. However, since the mid-1980s their numbers have been increasing and now stand at about 3,000.

HISTORY

Pre-Goryeo Dynasty

That there was prehistoric habitation on Jejudo is confirmed by the presence of artifacts that have been found at various sites on the island. While less seems to be known about these people than those on the peninsula, bone and stone axes and other implements, and earthen burial jars and dolmens seem to indicate an organized community. It is supposed that the people of Jeju-do had some economic and cultural contact with both the Baekje and Silla kingdoms on the Korean peninsula, as well as with the western Japanese islands and eastern Chinese seaboard, as there was plentiful contact amongst those areas. While there is some reference in Silla literature to the island of Jeju-do, and some assume that toward the end of the Silla Dynasty Jeju-do had a tribute state status with the peninsular kingdom while maintaining control of its own internal affairs, it is not known for sure just what relationship actually existed.

Goryeo Period

Until the Goryeo Dynasty (918–1392), it is safe to say that isolated Jeju-do was largely unaffect-ed by events on the peninsula. In 1105, however, the island came under the direct control of the Goryeo court and was abruptly baptized into the world of political power and strained international relations. After Goryeo king Gojong bowed to the Mongols in the mid-1200s, loyalist rebels fled to Jeju-do to make a last stand. In 1273, they were soundly defeated.

The Mongols then set up a military commandery on Jeju-do, and for nearly one hundred years they controlled the island. With its favorable climate and plentiful pasturage, Jeju-do was turned into a huge livestock-raising operation to support the Mongols' insatiable need for horses and cattle, and it served as a staging and supply point during the Mongol invasions of Japan in 1274 and 1281. When the Mongols lost control of China in 1368, they were ousted from Jeju-do and it reverted to Goryeo control.

Joseon Period

A few decades later, the Joseon Dynasty's first king took control of the country from the Goryeo court. During the Joseon Dynasty (1392–1910), Jeju-do was pretty much left to its own devices and basically used as a place for political banishment. The two best-known exiles were King Gwanghaegun, who ruled 1608–23 and whose reign is considered the pinnacle of royal barbarity and duplicity; and the renowned statesman Song Shi-yeol (1607–89), prime minister under King Hyojong. Gwanghaegun was in exile for 18 years before his death on the island.

During a typhoon in 1653, a Dutch merchant ship, blown off course during its trip from Taiwan to Japan, was shipwrecked on the south shore of Jeju-do. The 36 survivors were the first large group of Westerners to see the Korean Peninsula and view Korean society firsthand. (In 1628, a lone Dutchman named Welteree was shipwrecked on the peninsula and spent the rest of his life in service to the Korean crown. He did have contact with this later group of Dutchmen, and was able to intercede for them several times during the first period of their forced internment in the country.) Korean policy kept shipwrecked sailors and never let them return to their homeland. The Dutch spent 13 years in captivity, both on Jeju-do and later on the peninsula, before eight of the crew were able to escape, sail a tiny boat to Japan, and be reunited with Dutch traders in Nagasaki. The leader of that group and former ship's secretary, Hendrik Hamel, later wrote a book about their experience. Translated and now known as *Hemel's Journal and a Description of the Kingdom of Korea, 1653–1666*, his writing was the first introduction of Korea to the Western world.

Contemporary Times

During the Joseon Dynasty, the administrative capital of Jeju-do was set up at Seongeup. Like most of the island's population centers of those days, Seongeup was set in the protected lowland hills. It was not until the 1900s that the majority of the villagers moved down to the coast. During their expansion into mainland Asia in the 1930s, the Japanese stationed troops on Jeju-do and used the island as a supply depot and mini-staging area. In 1946, Jeju-do was split from Jeollanam-Do and became an administratively independent province. Although not directly affected by the Korean War, this rugged island created a perfect stronghold for North Korean guerrillas who were only flushed out of the hills several years after the war ended.

ECONOMY

Like the coastal regions of the peninsula, Jeju-do's economy historically depended upon subsistence farming and fishing. Aside from the well-irrigated seaside paddy fields, the vast majority of the island's farmland consists of dry land plots. While some rice is cultivated, buckwheat, barley, soybeans, other legumes and pulses, rape and sesame seeds, millet, garlic, onions, and sweet potatoes are much more common. Persimmons and chestnuts are also harvested. On mid-elevation plots, under a canopy of leaning logs, shiitake mushrooms are also grown, making Jeju-do South Korea's highest producer of edible fungus. Honey from the mountain is also prized. The south coast is the only place in Korea where citrus fruits are grown commercially. Tangerine sales make up

the largest slice of the island's economy. Today, nearly 20 percent of Jeju-do farmers are involved in tangerine production, and this sweet and juicy fruit rivals any in Asia. More recently, the black berry *omija* has been made into a commercial tea, as has the *yuja* citrus fruit.

Sizable fishing fleets are based at Jeju City, Seogwipo, Moseulpo, and Seongsanpo, with other boats at many of the small seaside villages. Knife fish, snapper, sea bream, sea bass, mackerel, tuna, squid, octopus, shark, and other types of fish are caught. A whole variety of mussels, shells, and seaweed are also harvested. In a long-cherished custom on the island, *haenyeo* (women divers) search the coastal sea floor for shellfish and other sea creatures.

Large numbers of beef cattle, and to a lesser extent dairy cows, pigs, sheep, and chickens are raised on the island. There are approximately 120 private and cooperative ranches on the island raising these domesticated animals. The largest, at nearly 4,000 acres, is the Jedong Ranch, located on the eastern slope, near San'gumburi. Perhaps the island's most well-known meat product is pork from the black Jeju-do pig.

No large-scale industrial development exists on the island, but tourism brings in substantial revenue. Before 1960, only a trickle of visitors reached the island, nearly all of them Koreans. In the '70s, tourism began a push, and with *Newsweek*'s pronouncement it got a shove. The government has made great plans for its development, many of which are now being fulfilled. In the future, the island's economy will be as closely tied to its tourist industry as it is to livestock, farming, and fishing.

CULTURE, CUSTOMS, PECULIARITIES

Mongol Influence

The island people still show strong Mongol influence in elements of their language (although classed a dialect, the language of Jeju-do is almost unintelligible to the peninsular Korean) and their dress. Until recently, they wore leather and furs in a manner similar to that of the nomads of Mongolia and the steppes of eastern Asia, while cotton—stiff and shiny after being soaked in unripe persimmon juice until stained brown orange—was made into everyday work clothes. Now as a sort of fashion statement and throwback to the past, these dyed clothes, called *galot*, are made mostly into women's pants and blouses of a modern Korean style, some dresses, Korean-style men's wear, and various styles of hats. Unlike the custom on the peninsula, young children were not traditionally carried strapped to their mothers' backs. Rather, the child was put into a woven bamboo basket which was attached to cloth bands and strung over the shoulders, a practice said to have come from the Mongols. Narrow-necked pottery water barrels were also carried on the back, strapped onto a similar bamboo basket. Both these practices have almost totally died out today, seen only in old photographs, postcards, and re-creations of traditional island life.

Of course, the long period of Joseon control over the island (1392–1910) solidly enfolded Jeju-do into the structured Korean nation. Colonial and post-colonial influence resulted in great homogenization, and today only vestiges of the old culture can be observed by the astute student of Korean society.

Of Rocks and Residences

The farmers of Jeju-do have always had to deal with the island's loose volcanic rock; it's piled high into fences to separate village lane from courtyard, field from field, and to surround gravesites. Even though tall and thin, and built without mortar, these walls created strong shields against the island's forceful winds. The plentiful rocks were also used for houses, here mortared with mud. Straw and native grass thatch was the primary roofing material. To keep the roofs from blowing away, a latticework of straw rope (now sometimes replaced by strips of rubber) was laid over the thatch and kept taut by stones attached to the rope ends. Slowly, these traditional mushroom-top houses have been replaced by cement structures in the sweep of modernization. Topped with corrugated tin painted ocean blue, forest green, or tangerine orange, sheet metal cutouts

grace the roof ends. These new-style houses are easily spotted when you look down on a community from a height. Oddly, they are not as disruptive of the natural setting as the pseudo chalet-style cement boxes of the peninsula. Aside from fencing and construction material, volcanic rock is put to use for such things as street curbs, landscape items, and souvenir art objects. Anything that might be made of granite in another part of the country might be made of black volcanic stone here.

Until recently, Jeju-do had virtually no thieves or beggars, and consequently no solid front gates for the houses. A three-pole gate was used instead, and is still occasionally seen in the countryside. Traditionally, these poles were also used as a means of communication to visitors, indicating the presence or absence of the owner. If all three poles were up and placed in a crosswise position between the stone side uprights, it meant that the people of the house were gone. One or two poles down meant that they were out of the house but not far away. If all three were down and the walk was open, the owner was at home.

Traditional houses have another feature peculiar to the island, one greatly disapproved of by outsiders. The outhouse was put over a corner of the pigpen, from which the pigs would get a portion of their otherwise meager daily food supply. While not being the most hygienic, pigs raised in this manner are said to be some of the tastiest in the country! Still today in rural hamlets, this outhouse arrangement can be observed. If you happen to try these backyard privies, watch your bottom. The pesky little pigs have long tongues!

Dolharubang

Artistic uses for the volcanic stone were not overlooked. Large pieces were carved into what has become the de facto symbol of the island, the mysterious *dolharubang* (stone grandfather figure). Each of these male figures stands a little over one meter tall, with a wide prominent nose and round bug eyes. Arms bent at the elbow, the hands lie on the stomach, one higher than the other. A narrow brimmed round cap covers the head. Approximately 45 original figures survive today, most in Jeju City, Seongeup, and Dae-

© ROBERT NILSEN

The position of the poles on this gate indicates that the owners are not home but are not far away.

jeong (Moseulpo). Some scholars believe that these sculptures were erected at the entrances to the island's defensive fortifications as protective totems, similar to the wooden *jangseung* totems on the peninsula, or perhaps more similar to the stone totems found mostly in the southern fringe of the peninsula. Based upon their obvious phallic shape—and maybe also on their quirky smiles —others feel that they were fertility figures. Some people have tried to relate this statuary to similarly shaped figures of Okinawa, the central Pacific islands, and even to the monolithic figures of Easter Island. Replicas of these jovial rotund men, seen in all sizes at every souvenir shop on the island, have become one of the hottest items for vacation shoppers.

In a similar manner, piled stone towers like miniature mountains, with one round or horse-head-shaped stone on top, were used for the protection of a village from harm. Modern versions of these can be seen at Mokseokwon garden in Jeju City and at San'gumburi.

Haenyeo

From an early age, some Jeju-do females learn to dive to the sea bottom for edibles—not only in fine summer weather but also in the dead of winter when the sea provides its best. The divers seem oblivious to the conditions as they trudge to shore, change into swimwear, and plunge into the cool water. During decades past, these women averaged over 150 dives a year, staying in the water up to four hours during summer, when the water temperature is 27–28°C, and from 15 to 20 minutes in winter when it drops to 8–10°C. Now most dive only from fall to spring, and only when not employed at some other job. Still, however, for many their income is an important component for maintaining the family's standard of living. In the past, these divers wore only loose white cotton garments and used rope baskets for their catches and gourds as floats. It was unlawful for men to look at the women in these abbreviated clothes. You'll never see women dressed like that today, except for the young, scantily clad beauties painted on souvenir items and sold to romantic tourists.

Nowadays, the divers, who range in age from their thirties to well over 60, wear utilitarian, full-length wet suits. They look more like sea mammals than objects of romantic adoration, but are still a sight worth seeing. While their numbers are swiftly decreasing, about 5,000 divers are still active—that's down from nearly three times that number some thirty years ago. Constantly an object of tourist photography, they have become nearly as much a symbol of the island as the *dolharubang*. Photograph from a distance, or ask permission first if you want a close-up. Often the women will outright refuse or ask for a fee. While they dive at numerous spots all along the coast, and some now prefer to dive from boats offshore, good locales for viewing these modern-day mermaids are near Seogwipo and Seongsanpo, and on U-do.

Religion

Jeju-do has a long tradition of shamanism. Shaman ceremonies were important to community cohesion, and continue to have a strong influence in rural island life. Both male and female shamans are still active on the island, although recently the role of the male seems to have faded. The Mongols brought Buddhism to Jeju-do; whether it had been established before then is uncertain. Buddhism was not as well rooted here as on the peninsula before being supplanted by Confucianism at the beginning of the Joseon Dynasty. Unlike the rest of the country, there are only a few historical temples of note on Jeju-do, all long since disappeared, with only a few stones to mark their locations. With about 200 temples today, Buddhism is making a resurgence on the island. For the most part, these temples are small, unobtrusive, and not particularly attractive, however, in recent years several have been expanded and rebuilt in relatively large and ornate fashion. Christianity has fared better. While it had difficulty establishing itself and displacing the native shaman beliefs and rituals, the religion seems to have found fertile ground for its missionary work. Church steeples are now seen in nearly every village, and the number of adherents to the various Christian sects is growing steadily. During the Joseon Dynasty, Confucianism was the predominant shaper of society and the cultural framework. Annual Confucian ceremonies are still performed at the three Confucian shrines on the island.

Festivals

Jeju-do hosts nearly two dozen festivals and major events throughout the year. To help celebrate the uniqueness of this island and foster its folk arts, the **Halla Cultural Festival,** is held every year in October. Held at various places, this, the largest festival on the island, begins with a ceremony to the Mountain Spirit on top of Halla-san. Cultural activities of all types, literary contests, folk music, spoken dialect contests, and art exhibitions are presented, along with the usual parades, fireworks displays, and athletic events. Unlike other such festivals, however, the Halla Festival sports a horse race.

Smaller in size, the **Snow Festival** takes place on an appropriate spot of the mountain in mid-January to offer supplication to the mountain god and enjoy various snow sports. The **Cherry Blossom and Rape Flower festivals** happen in April, when the pink blossoms brighten up the mountainside and the oilseed flowers blanket island fields with a sea of yellow. In May, the **Royal Azalea Festival** is held when these bushes swathe the upper slopes of Halla-san in a robe of red, making it one of the prettiest times to climb the mountain. The **Tangerine Festival** is held every year in the autumn when this fruit ripens and dots the orchards with bright orange.

On the first day of the second lunar month of every year, the age-old **Chilmeori Shaman Ceremony** (I.C.A. #71) is conducted near Sarabong, in Jeju City, to pray for an abundant catch and the safety of the island's fishermen and *haenyeo*. Also known as *Yeongdeung-gut* because it addresses the Yeongdeung grandmother spirit who visits the island for 15 days during the second lunar month and helps assure a good harvest and catch, this shaman ceremony is performed at most coastal villages around the island, in numerous variations. This ceremony brings the diving community together in mutual cooperation, and highlights the traditional role of women in this community.

PRACTICALITIES

Accommodations

There are nearly three dozen registered hotels on Jeju-do, and scores of other mid-range accommodations, most located in Jeju City, Seogwipo, and at the Jungmun Resort complex. *Yeogwan* and *yeoinsuk* of all levels are found in all cities and towns and in many villages throughout the island. In addition, you can find several hundred registered *minbak,* most of which are located at beach villages and on the province's inhabited islands. *Minbak* are private homes, where the owners make their living at some other occupation and only rent rooms on the side. Room rates are comparable to those of inexpensive *yeogwan,* and food might be prepared upon request. While convenient for summer travelers, some of these may not accept guests during the off-season. Camping is approved anywhere on the island, beaches and select mountain trail spots being prime sites. Of the eight organized campgrounds on the island, only the Geumsansa campsite on the north flank of the mountain is within the national park.

Food

Standard Korean and Chinese food holds no surprises on Jeju-do. Western and Japanese cuisine are served at a few first-class hotels and select restaurants in Jeju City, Jungmun, and Seogwipo. Because of the surrounding bountiful waters, seafood appears on many menus—raw, fried, or in soups. Some popular specialties are *haemul ddukbaegi,* a savory seafood stew; *seonggyeguk,* sea urchin soup; *jeonbokjuk,* an abalone/rice porridge; *sora,* a conch shell mussel; *okdomgui,* grilled sea bream; *hoe* (sashimi), raw sliced fish; and various types of seaweed. Taking their fish right from the boat, harbor-front kitchens can always guarantee a fresh meal. Second best is any restaurant with water tanks of live fish out front. Traditionally, aside from the seafood, *ogokbab,* a boiled five-grain cereal, was often eaten instead of rice, and *bingddeok,* a chilled buckwheat pancake filled with vegetables and meat, was and continues to be a popular item on ceremonial days. Now often sold at fine restaurants,

omeagisul, a glutinous millet wine, was a staple island drink. As Jeju-do has been "ranched" for centuries, beef, pork, and chicken have been prominent here, but more recently, with the popularity of hunting, pheasant has begun to appear at some finer restaurants. It's usually served thinly sliced and simmered Japanese *shabu shabu* style, sliced and broiled teppanyaki-style at your table, or in soup. This distinctively strong game-bird flavor will be a special gastronomic memory of your trip to the island.

Tangerines are abundant in season, and somewhat cheaper than in other parts of the country. They make fine presents for friends living on the peninsula! Lemon, kumquat, pomelo, pineapple, banana, mango, kiwi, fig, and various melons are less numerous but also available. Although not all by any means, much of this fruit is now grown in huge hothouses on the south coast, where you will see plot after plot along the highways and small lanes. Growers are basically wholesalers, but some do sell at their orchards. The gentle slopes of Halla-san produce about 50 percent of the country's mushrooms, and most of these farms are located at about 700 meters in elevation. Bags of *pyogo peoseot* (shiitake mushroom) are sold in Jeju's central market, at the rest stops on the cross-island highways, and at tourist shops all over the island. More recently, honey from the mountain has been produced in greater quantity and is popular among island visitors.

For some, the night wouldn't be complete without a beer or other drink. As on the mainland, nightclubs, beer halls, stand bars, discos, cabarets, and the sky lounges of the taller hotels all offer drinks, music, and their own particular entertainment. More pedestrian are the back-alley pubs and canopied food carts that appear in the evening in almost every part of the city.

Sports and Recreation

Jeju-do, Korea's vacationland, is known for its varied sporting opportunities. Most organized team sports happen at the **sports complex** in Jeju City, which has two stadiums for both soccer and baseball, an indoor gymnasium, covered swimming pool, tennis courts, and other athletic grounds. The main venue of the **Halla Cultural Festival**, major sporting events are also conducted here, including the yearly provincial athletic competition in June. For the 2002 World Cup soccer tournament, a new stadium was built in Shin Seogwipo on the south shore.

With five major trails to the summit of Hallasan, one of the most obvious activities is **hiking.** (For details, see Halla-san below.)

Most non-residential, non-park public land on the island is open to **hunting.** Korea's largest designated hunting area is on the south side of Halla-san, from mid-elevation to the coast. In addition to public grounds, several private clubs stock game birds for their standing ranges. Some hunting of small birds is allowed in September and October, but the vast majority of hunting is for larger game birds—pheasant, quail, wild pigeon, and duck—only from November through February. Hunting equipment can be rented, and dogs and guides arranged. A three-day license runs about ₩100,000. Stringent hunting regulations are in effect in Korea, and detailed rules are in place for the importation of firearms. For current information on licenses, hunting areas, limits, and bringing in your own firearms, contact the Jeju-do office of the Korea Hunting Management Association (tel. 064/724-2682).

For the growing number of vacationing golfers, Jeju-do has seven **golf courses.** The best perhaps, with international standards, is the 36-hole Ora Country Club (tel. 064/747-5100), owned and operated by the Jeju Grand Hotel. Hotel patrons golf at a discount. Located at about 500 meters in elevation just off the cross-island highway is the 18-hole Jeju Country Club (tel. 064/702-0451). Also of international standards is the 18-hole Jungmun Golf Club (tel. 064/738-1202), at the Jungmun Resort on the south side of the island. Set along the coast for nice vistas, it is said to have the longest 18-hole course in the country at just over 6,800 meters. Other courses are the Pinx Golf Club (tel. 064/792-1886) and Paradise Golf Club (tel. 064/792-6688), both up the hill from Jungmun Resort; the Dynasty County Club (tel. 064/766-6200) in Namwon; and the Crown Country Club (tel. 064/784-4811) east of Jocheon. Although greens fees vary,

expect them to run about ₩130,000; club rental is ₩25,000, carts ₩40,000, or ₩5,000 for a pull cart when available.

Fishing is also a strong drawing card. Because of relatively mild temperatures, shore fishing and boat fishing are both possible year-round. Sea bass, sea bream, snapper, cod, and mackerel are the most common catches. The most promising waters are those around Biyang-do on the north coast, U-do and Seongsanpo on the east, Chagwi-do and Moseulpo to the west, around the islands of Chuja-do, and halfway between Jeju-do and the peninsula. Boat rental and guides can be arranged. For up-to-date information on rental arrangements, best fishing locations, and limits, contact the city or provincial tourism offices, hotel travel desks, or boat owners at any of the many piers around the island.

Scuba diving in the waters off the south coast of Jeju-do has become more common and more of an organized sport for Koreans and foreigners alike in the past dozen years. Although neither as prolific nor as spectacular as warmer regions to the south, the underwater south coast offers a variety of coral and rock formations as well as a multitude of fish species. If you aren't carrying your own scuba equipment, it is possible to rent all you need in Jeju City, Seogwipo, and Seongsanpo. All necessary equipment can be rented for about ₩120,000 a day. Contact the Dive Station (tel. 064/755-9934) or Pearl Scuba (tel. 064/751-1059) in Jeju City, Manta Dive Center (tel. 064/763-2264) or Poseidon Diving (tel. 064/733-1294) in Seogwipo, and Sea Life (tel. 064/782-1235) in Seongsanpo. Private instruction for certification can also be arranged. Jeju-do also offers the country's best snorkeling opportunities. North coast beaches are perhaps safer as they are generally more protected and shallower.

Windsurfing has caught on in Jeju-do in a small way. While several beaches offer equipment for rent, the best overall conditions are at Shinyang Beach near Seongsanpo on the far eastern end of the island. **Ocean rafting** is also becoming known, and a course has been set up from Jeju harbor to Samyang Beach. Contact the Jeju Events Club (tel. 064/722-7542) for details. **Paragliding** is also an option, but it too is not well known or well subscribed to by the general public.

For the less adventurous, **submarine** rides are available at Seogwipo and Seongsanpo for about ₩49,000 per adult.

A few **riding stables** have popped up recently, due to the growing attention paid to the Jeju-do ponies. Costing about ₩20,000 for 30 minutes, rides can be arranged at stables located mostly near Jungmun and San'gumburi. All rides are guided and gentle—don't expect any free-range gallop.

One of the most pleasurable ways to get around this island is by **bicycle.** All major roads are well paved and, except for the cross-island highways, relatively flat. Traveling on two wheels can be one of the most pleasurable ways to view the sights of the islands, but be aware that Korean roads were not made with the cyclist in mind—very few stretches have "safe" shoulders. Also, Korean drivers are not known for their caution, courtesy, or deference to pedestrians or bicycles, so be extra careful.

For those who prefer the nighttime recreation of **casinos,** there are eight on Jeju-do. Open to foreigners only, each has different hours of operation and requires a small admission fee. They are located at the Jeju KAL, Grand, Oriental, Lagonda, and Holiday Inn Crowne Plaza hotels in Jeju City, the Hyatt and Shilla hotels at Jungmun Resort, and Seogwipo KAL Hotel in Seogwipo. A few other hotels have rooms set aside for slot machines.

Information and Services

KNTO's information counter (tel. 064/742-0032) at the Jeju International Airport international terminal, and the province-sponsored information desk (tel. 064/742-8866) in the domestic area of the airport both have maps and brochures on the island and helpful staff. Similar counters at all three Jeju City ferry terminal buildings also offer information and brochures, but on a more limited scale. They may not be staffed for early arrivals, but brochures should be available. KNTO has a large new information center at Jungmun Resort on the south coast

(tel. 064/738-0326). The helpful staff there is able to provide additional brochures and plenty of information about the island and the country as a whole. All information desks are open 0900–1800 daily. For tourism-related complaints and suggestions, contact the provincial tourism department (tel. 064/746-0101).

For medical emergencies, try the Jeju Medical Center (tel. 064/750-1234) in Jeju City, or the Seogwipo Medical Center (tel. 064/730-3101) on the south shore.

TRANSPORTATION

By Air

Jeju-do is connected by air to 12 peninsular cities, four in Japan, and three in China. Capable of landing jumbo jets, **Jeju International Airport** sees increased traffic nearly every year. Domestic flights by Asiana Airlines and KAL to Seoul (₩75,000) run about every half hour from 0700 to 2100. Flights to Busan (₩54,000) are scheduled about every hour from 0800 to 2030. Six or seven flights a day connect Jeju-do to Daegu (₩63,500), Cheongju (₩65,500), and Gwangju (₩41,000), while one or two daily go to Gunsan (₩15,500), Mokpo (₩37,000), Yeosu (₩44,500), Ulsan (₩61,000), Pohang (₩65,500), Jinju (₩52,200), and Incheon (₩74,000). For information and flight reservations on Jeju-do, ask at the ticket sales counter at the airport or visit the airline offices in the city. The Asiana Airlines office (tel. 064/743-4000) is located at the main traffic rotary in Shin Jeju City, while the KAL office (tel. 064/752-2000) is across the street from the KAL Hotel in the old part of town. Each airline also maintains an office in Seogwipo. Major hotels and travel agents around the island can also provide information and make travel arrangements.

International flights from Jeju-do run to Tokyo (Narita), Osaka, Fukuoka, and Nagoya in Japan, and Beijing, Shanghai, and Hong Kong in China. Non-direct flights go via Busan.

The terminal has three levels. The third level is for departures, with its ticket sales and check-in counters, departure lounge, and shops. An art gallery and restaurants are located on the second level. The lower level is for arrivals, and here you'll find a tourist information booth, rental car agencies, telephones, foreign exchange banks, snack and souvenir shops, and free Internet connections. Transportation to Jeju City and Seogwipo leave from outside the first level doors, while the public parking lot is just beyond.

Taxis from the airport to the old city center charge about ₩3,500 for the 10-minute ride, ₩2,500 to Shin Jeju. City bus nos. 100, 200, 300, and 500 run from the airport into the city center, some going via Shin Jeju City on the way. Bus no. 600 runs across the island from the airport to Jungmun Resort and Seogwipo, stopping at the numerous hotels and condos on the south coast, and at the Seogwipo pier. The fare is ₩2,500 to Jungmun, ₩3,300 from the airport to Seogwipo, and the trip takes about an hour and a half. This bus runs from the airport on a 15-minute schedule throughout the day 0630–2200. Some major hotels provide free shuttle transportation to and from the airport for their guests.

By Ferry

Jeju-do is connected to six ports on the peninsula: Busan, Yeosu, Wan-do, Byeokpa (Jin-do), Mokpo, and Incheon, and to the island of Chuja-do. Jeju City is the only port on Jeju-do for ferries to the peninsula. Ferries also once left from Seogwipo but these are not in operation any longer. The increased ferry traffic over the years has led to a shortage of dock space, so the Jeju City harbor has been expanded with an extended breakwater and a third terminal building. Terminals 1 and 2 are set next to each other, while terminal 3 is about one kilometer down the shore along the same road. Terminal 1 has ferries to Mokpo, Busan, and Incheon. Terminal 2 runs ferries to Wan-do, Yeosu, and Byeokpa. Terminal 3, the International Ferry Terminal, has ferries to Wan-do, and Mokpo, and the occasional international cruise ship arrival. There is still no scheduled ferry service from Jeju-do to either China or Japan. Before departure, be sure to check which pier your ferry leaves from. When purchasing a ferry ticket, a travel card may need to be filled out giving your name, age, destination, and passport number. Each terminal building has ticket sales windows, a tourist information desk, and a handful of shops for gifts and basic food items. City bus nos. 100, 200, 300, and 500 all go through downtown Jeju City, out to the airport, and on to Shin Jeju.

From Jeju City, two ferries run to Busan Monday through Saturday. Leaving at 1930, they require 12 hours for the overnight crossing. Fares range from third-class (₩24,200) to a special-class room for ₩220,000.

Twice a day during the week and once a day on weekends, ferries leave Jeju City for Mokpo. The morning ferry leaves at 0700 and the afternoon ferry at 1730; each takes about five and a half hours to cross. Fares to Mokpo run ₩16,500) third-class to ₩45,200 for a first-class bed.

Car ferries also link Jeju City to Wan-do. Taking about three hours, these ferries leave at 0820 and 0900 every day except Saturday or Sunday. Fares run ₩14,000–23,000 depending on the boat. A third ferry also makes this run, passing Chuja-do on the way, two hours to Chuja-do and five to Wan-do; fares to Chuja-do vary ₩13,000–19,000. Chuja-do is also connected by ferry on the route to Byeokpa on Jin-do. Leaving every day except Sunday, this ferry requires a little over two hours to Chuja-do (₩13,000) and nearly five and a half hours to Byeokpa (₩17,000).

Leaving at 1800 daily except Sunday, the ferry to Yeosu pulls into port at 0830 and fares run ₩16,000–53,000.

The longest ferry route from Jeju-do is that to Incheon—16 hours. Leaving at 1900, fares run ₩42,000 third-class to ₩77,000 for a deluxe room.

While generally not necessary, reservations are taken on these ferries, particularly during high-volume travel periods, such as national holidays and school summer holidays, when you'd best make a reservation well in advance or you'll be on the island longer than you wish. Be aware that due to rough seas ferries may be canceled at any time without warning. If the weather looks threatening, confirm departure status beforehand with the staff at the terminal building.

Island Buses

Although there are no trains on the island, there is a reliable and convenient bus system. Six well-traveled highways and a web of interconnecting roads make for an abbreviated system that lends itself to easy travel. The flat round-the-island highway (182 km) is a pleasurable two-hour ride from Jeju City to Seogwipo, going either direction. From the main bus station in Jeju City, intercity buses run to Seogwipo every 15 or 20 minutes, from 0600 to 2100. *Jikhaeng* (express) buses are faster and stop only at major towns and tourist sites. The slower *wanhaeng* buses run virtually the same routes, but make more stops at the same fare rate. Fares for selected destinations are Jocheon (₩800), Manjang-gul (₩1,900), Seongsanpo (₩3,100), Pyoseon (₩4,300), Gwakji (₩1,500), Hallim (₩1,900), Moseulpo (₩2,900), and Seogwipo (₩6,000).

The East Cross-Island Highway is the safest way over the mountain, the fastest and cheapest route to Seogwipo (₩3,600), and the road to use if you intend to hike the east mountain trail from Seongpanak (₩1,600) to the peak. Buses run on this route every 12 minutes between 0600 and 2130. The West Cross-Island Highway rises to 1,100 meters (highest highway pass in the country) before plunging down the south slope to meet the round-the-island highway at Jungmun. From 0750 to 1550, buses run every hour over this pass to the south coast; fares are: Orimok (₩1,800), Yeongshil (₩2,600), and Jungmun (₩4,600). Every hour from 0630 to 2040, buses run the eastern mid-island highway (East Industrial Highway) to Pyoseon; selected fares are San'gumburi (₩1,100), Seongeup (₩1,900),

Pyoseon (₩2,800), and the Jeju Folk Village (₩2,900). Every 20 minutes, buses make a run down the western mid-island highway (West Industrial Highway) to Moseulpo. Selected fares are: Jeju horse race track (₩1,100), Poseong (₩2,600), and Moseulpo (₩2,900). Besides these, other less frequent buses from Jeju City run to Jedong Ranch and Namwon, from Hallim to the Jeoji Bonsai Art Garden, from Moseulpo to Sanbanggul-sa, and to Manjang-gul and Bijarim from Saehwa or Gimnyeong.

Rental Cars

Compact rental cars can be hired for about ₩70,000 for 24 hours or ₩55,000 for 12 hours. Mid-size cars are roughly half again as much, with luxury vehicles at least twice that rate. Vans and 4WD vehicles are also available from most rental agencies. Less expensive rates are available for multiple day, advertised specials, and off-season use, but when availability may be tight during the height of the summer season, you'll be lucky to find discounted rates. Rental cars with drivers run about double the rate for a self-drive car for a full day's sightseeing. While there are well over a dozen rental car agencies on the island, a few to contact are Jeju Rent-a-Car (tel. 064/742-3301), Halla Rent-a-Car (tel. 064/755-5000), Green Rent-a-Car (tel. 064/743-2000), Hanguk Rent-a-Car (tel. 064/748-5005), Avis (tel. 064/726-3322), and Hertz (tel. 064/755-8101). Most major hotels have a rental car company desk in the lobby. During the summer months, be sure to reserve a car well ahead of time as they are often booked in advance—especially from Jeju City.

Jeju City 제주시

Jeju [Cheju] City, capital and hub of the province, is the obvious place to start your tour. With a population of 275,000, it is home to a full half of the island residents. Set against the backdrop of majestic Halla-san, the city has one of the most inspiring locations of any in the country. Fronting the sea and pushing up against coastal farmlands, its mostly low buildings blend with the land. One structure, however, breaks this harmonious setting: the 21-story KAL Hotel rises over the downtown area like Devil's Tower over the Wyoming plateau. Though the city bustles, its pace is less frenetic than comparably sized cities on the peninsula. It's the most modern of the island's communities, and it has expanded rapidly in the past two dozen years. The harbor is a haven for one of Jeju-do's largest groups of fishing boats, and is its only ferry terminal. The island's only airport lies just west of the city. Some decades ago, Shin Jeju, or "New" Jeju, a modern appendage to the old town, was carved out of the farmland up the hill from the airport. This somewhat sterile area of government buildings, offices, hotels, shops, restaurants, and apartment complexes, along with new houses in other sections of the city, is pushing aside the old thatch-roof houses, which until the late 1970s, could been seen all over the city. Yet, Jeju City is the site of the island's oldest building, and, according to legend, the spot from which the island's progenitors sprang. In the city, the old mingles with the new in workable harmony. Not only the governmental and economic center of the island, Jeju City is the island's educational focal point and supports the Jeju National University, Jeju National University of Education, and half a dozen junior colleges.

For information online, see www.chejuro.net.

SIGHTS

Yongduam 용두암

One of the island's most touted tourist sites, almost the city's unofficial symbol, is the naturally sculpted volcanic rock Yongduam ("Dragon Head Rock"). Along the seashore west of the harbor, this animated black rock thrusts its raggedy head out of the ground as if trying to slip out between the land and the sea. Legend says that a cocky young dragon became dissatisfied with life in his watery world, and decided that he would go to live in heaven. Disregarding the dragon king's warning against this brash act, the young dragon set out on his merry way. No sooner had he thrust his head out of the dragon's world than his black body turned to stone. Planes to the island come in only a few hundred meters above the dragon that once wanted to fly away as the planes do today. In the evening, Yongduam is lit up with lights to dramatize its form. Some 100 meters in toward town from Yongduam is **Yongyeon**, a small, shallow, twisting gorge with steep basalt walls, said to have been shaped by wrestling dragons during a contest of strength. A walking path runs along the eastern side of this gorge; steps go down to the river on the west side. These two spots are perhaps most dramatic at sunrise and sunset. There is no admission fee to either.

Gwandeok-jeon 관덕전

Closer to the city center and just down the street from the post office is **Gwandeok-jeon** [Kwandŏk-jŏn], the island's oldest wooden structure. Built in 1448 during the reign of King Sejong and reconstructed in 1970, this building (T. #322) is representative of early Joseon Dynasty architecture, originally built for military training. Paintings on the interior ceiling beams have been noted for their design and technique and have been designated N.M. #322. Two *dolharubang* stand at its front. Down toward the sea from Gwandeok-jeon was a government complex (H.S. #380) called **Jejumok Gwanaji**, the seat of power for old Jeju-do from a time before the Mongols through much of the Joseon Dynasty. Since 1999, this former government center, with its half dozen structures, connecting corridors, and landscaped yard, has been reconstructed in a

JEJU-DO

JEJU CITY

To Seongsanpo

JEJU NATIONAL UNIVERSITY OF EDUCATION
JEJU NATIONAL MUSEUM

Esplanade
Sara-bong
MOCHUNGSA

TERMINAL 3

Jeju Harbor

Breakwater

TERMINAL 1
HANIL MINBAK
YANGSANDO YEOINSUK
TERMINAL 2
OHYEONDAN
JEJU FORTRESS WALL

Shinsan Park
FOLKLORE TOURIST COMPLEX
JEJU CULTURE AND ARTS CENTER

SEAWALL

SEE DETAIL

JEJU MEDICAL CENTER

JEJU-DO FOLKLORE AND NATURAL HISTORY MUSEUM
SAMSEONGHYEOL
CITY HALL
INSEONG YEOGWAN

To Seogwipo

CHEJU KAL HOTEL
TELECOM
YUSUJANG HOTEL
DAEGWANGJANG YEOGWAN

11

YONGDUAM
YONGYEON

JEJU HYANGGYO

SEOMUN MARKET

SURIM HOTEL
HOTEL YUSEONGJANG

BUS TERMINAL

TERMINAL YEOINSUK
ONCHEONJANG YEOGWAN
SPORTS COMPLEX

YUJEONG MOTEL

Shin Jeju

JEJU INTERNATIONAL AIRPORT

16

PROVINCIAL GOVERNMENT OFFICE
POLICE

HOLIDAY INN CROWN PLAZA
SHIN JEJU MARKET
HOTEL ROYAL LAGONDA HOTEL
SEJONG HOTEL
CHEJU GRAND HOTEL
GRACE HOTEL

12

To Hallim
To Moseulpo
To Jungmun

0   900 yds
0   900 m

DETAIL

SEAWALL

MYEONGSEONG YEOINSUK

CHEJU PALACE HOTEL
BAND SHELL
JEJU WATER PARK
SWISS HOTEL
GEUMSANJANG YEOGWAN

ORIENTAL HOTEL
SEASIDE HOTEL
TAPDONG YEOGWAN
NAMGYEONG HOTEL
TAEYANGJANG YEOGWAN
DONGMUN YEOGWAN
DONGMUN MARKET

JEJUMOK GWANAJI
GWANDEOK-JEON
POST OFFICE
HOTEL ROBERO
CENTRAL MARKET

© AVALON TRAVEL PUBLISHING, INC.

manner reflecting the original layout and design and seems a faithful representation of what this compound must have looked like in centuries past.

Other Old Structures

Along the city's main east-west thoroughfare out toward Yongduam is the old **Jeju Hyanggyo** (제주향교). Founded in 1392 and moved to its present location in 1827, this Confucian academy was, until the 20th century, one of the focal points of education on the island, and is still used today by Confucian scholars. Although smaller in size and not as visually pleasing as many such academies in the country, its age and importance suggest that the island was not always such a provincial backwater as is often portrayed. Having gone through numerous restorations over the centuries, its faded paint speaks of its antiquity. What in other regions of the country would be constructed of creamy granite, here is made with pockmarked, black volcanic stone. A statue of Confucius tops the rise at the back of the compound. As in ages past, every spring and autumn a ceremonial rite is celebrated here to honor Confucius and Korean scholars.

Up from the central rotary is **Ohyeondan** [Ohyŏndan] (오현단). Originally built in 1682 as the private academy Gyullim Seowon, Ohyeondan was refurbished in 1992 after its destruction in 1871. Now only an altar and a commemorative monument, it is dedicated to five scholars and military leaders. Two of these men, the Confucian scholars Song Shi-yeol and Kim Jang, were banished to Jeju-do during the Joseon Dynasty.

To the rear of this shrine is a reconstructed section of the old **Jeju Fortress wall.** Made of black volcanic blocks, this stone structure is perhaps 1,000 years old, although no one seems to know exactly when it was erected.

Samseonghyeol Shrine 삼성혈

Dolharubang also stand at the entrance to Samseonghyeol [Samsŏnghyŏl] (H.S. #134), the shrine to the island's three clan progenitors;

₩1,600 entrance. Legend tells that in the distant past three demigods emerged from the earth at a place called Moheunghyeol on the north slope of Halla-san. Samseonghyeol is assumed to be that place and in this attractive, garden-like enclosure are three depressions in the ground from which it is said the ancestors of the Ko, Pu, and Yang families sprang. They lived simply by hunting and gathering, and wearing animal skins. One day while out hunting they discovered a box along the eastern shore. From this box stepped three princesses who had been sent from Byeongnang, a distant island to the east, bringing five types of grains and six kinds of animals. The three demigods married the three princesses at Honinji pond in the southeast corner of the island and later returned to the northern part of the island, settled down, and started an agricultural community with domesticated animals. The island was then split into three regions, one for each of the couples. This partition took place by the three men shooting arrows to determine where their land would be. The stone marker **Samsaseok,** which is located a few kilometers east of Samseonghyeol near the Jeju Folklore Museum, marks the spot where the land division was conducted. The offspring of these couples peopled Jeju-do and ruled it as an independent kingdom called Tamna-guk until 937 when the Goryeo Kingdom took control.

Every year on the tenth day of the fourth and tenth lunar month, descendants of these three families gather here to pay tribute to their forebears and perform the traditional *chesa* ceremony (a rite in honor of one's ancestors). On the tenth day of the twelfth lunar month a public ceremony, the *Samseonghyeol-je,* is held at the site of the depressions to celebrate the history and mystery of these island forebears.

First dedicated in 1698, the shrine's altar, gate, and walls were constructed in 1926. Added later was a ceremonial hall which houses the ancestral tablets, and at that the twice yearly family ceremonies are conducted. Next to the hall, a fence surrounds the three depressions. Within this sanctuary are over 1,000 trees of about 50 varieties, with a whole range of flowers. The most prevalent of these flowers is the *myeongmuncho*, with spikes of lilac color and slender green leaves, which is said to be used in an herbal medicine for throat ailments.

Museums

A stone's throw east of Samseonghyeol is the **Jeju-Do Folklore and Natural History Museum** (제주도민속자연사박물관); ₩1,470 entrance. Open 0900–1800 (1700 in winter) every day except New Year's Day and a few other holidays, this small but decent exhibit is worth a visit. Constructed from blocks of basalt, the roofline of this museum resembles that of a tied-thatch roof. Several well-done life-size displays represent aspects of the culture peculiar to the island. Representative plants, animals, and minerals are also displayed. To the rear of this museum is **Shinsan Park**, the **Folklore Tourist Complex** where music and theater are performed throughout the year, and **Jeju Culture and Arts Center**, which offers additional performances and exhibitions. At the Folklore Tourist Complex, performances are held every evening at 2000 and 1900 during winter.

Just east of downtown Jeju City and set below Sara-bong is the new **Jeju National Museum** (제주국립박물관). Opened in 2001, this museum's focus is on artifacts pertaining to the culture of Jeju-do, from prehistoric times to the Joseon Dynasty. Open daily except Monday and January 1 from 0900 to 1800 (1700 in winter); the entrance fee is ₩400.

Five kilometers east of the city center is the private **Jeju Folklore Museum** (제주민속박물관), displaying a wide range of authentic items of everyday and ritual use, cultural objects, artifacts, and photographs that exemplify and explain the uniqueness of the island society. Cramped and rather hodgepodge, its casual displays give added dimension to the professional displays at the other two museums. This two-story modern building has a traditional-style house in its front yard along with a collection of stone spirit figures. Open every day 0900–1900; ₩1,000 entrance. Use bus no. 10 or 14 from the city center. Along the highway a few hundred meters back toward town from the entrance to the museum is Samsaseok.

Sara-bong

Rising above the harbor, with good views of the sea, city, and mountain, is the hill called Sarabong. A harbor lighthouse sits on the shore at the foot of the hill, and the small temple Sara-sa snuggles into the steep hillside. An exercise course drapes the top of the knoll below the cement octagonal pavilion, to the side of which is an reconstructed beacon site once used to report impending danger. On the inland side of the hill, Mochungsa shrine has been erected to commemorate those who fought against Japanese domination of Korea in the early years of the 20th century and also one woman who helped save many island residents during a period of famine centuries ago. While the view of the sunset from Sara-bong is one of the island's well-known sights, city residents will often come for an early morning walk around the waist of the hill along the "Esplanade."

Tap-dong Park

This plaza, entertainment, and amusement area stretches along the seawall from the end of the harbor breakwater to the west. It is the venue of outdoor theater and music at the band shell during the Halla Cultural Festival and Summer Band Concert series. Here too you'll find a few amusement rides, a bungee-jumping tower, and the small **Jeju Water Park** with its swimming pools and water slides. Open 1000–1800; entrance to the water park is ₩6,000 adult and ₩4,000 children. For those with nerve enough, the bungee-jumping option is open 1100–2200 for adults only at ₩25,000 a jump. On fine-weather evenings, people gather here for the cooling breezes, to stroll and chat with friends, to enjoy an outdoor meal at one of the fish restaurants, or listen to street musicians who entertain for free. From the seawall you can see the bright lights of the fishing boats bobbing on the water off the coast. It's also possible to walk out to the end of the breakwater from the plaza, and along the way you'll find sport fishermen, using illuminated bobbers at night, trying to catch supper for the family. Be extremely cautious, though; at times the wind is strong enough to push waves over the cement walkway.

Mokseokwon 목석원

Four kilometers up the hill is Mokseokwon [Moksŏkwon]; ₩2,000 entrance. This private collection of about 1,600 naturally sculpted rocks and dried tree roots imaginatively represents various animal and human forms and figures. Only wood and stone from Jeju-do have been used, taken from every part of the island over the last several decades. Some pieces stand alone as individual works of art, while others have been set in a series to illustrate the well-known story of Gapdori and his wife. A tale of honesty and truthfulness, it illustrates ideals and realities of married life. A lesson to all, it is perhaps most appropriate for the many newlyweds who visit here as part of their honeymoon. Another section, called the Garden of Underworld Rhapsody, displays perhaps the best of the root sculptures. Roots only of the rare *jorok* tree have been used. The hard, sap-infused roots of these mountain trees remain long after the trunks and branches die. Dug up and cleaned, the best of these have been arranged for their unique aesthetic forms. Along with the rocks and wood pieces are numerous *dolharubang*, front gateposts, grinding wheels, and island tools. While most of these objects are set amongst the trees, several open-air structures house some of the roots and a selection of photographs taken by the curator of the garden. Along with the root and rock sculptures, about 100 piled rock towers, each with a human-like stone head on top, have been set up representing the story of the 500 generals of Yeongshil. This garden makes a relaxing stop on the way to Sancheondan, the Seongpanak trailhead, or Seogwipo.

Sancheondan Altar 산천단

Sancheondan [Sanch'ŏndan] is an altar for the worship of the Mountain Spirit. In 1470, this small and rather unassuming altar was moved from the top of the mountain—where it had stood since Goryeo Dynasty days—because, it is said, too many people froze to death during the lengthy spring and autumn ceremonies conducted there. Today the mountain spirit rite is conducted in this grove of trees in relative comfort during the first lunar month. Five huge Japanese black pines (N.M. #160) standing around this altar are over 600 years old—supposedly the largest of their kind in Korea.

Gwaneum-sa 관음사

A short distance above Sancheondan is Gwaneum-sa [Kwanŭm-sa]. Small and unpretentious, it's one of the growing number of mostly small temples on the island. Reestablished in 1969, this temple was raised on the site of a former temple (from 1909), which had been destroyed by fire in 1948. Three kilometers off the East Cross-Island Highway—there is no bus service—Gwaneum-sa sits along the road that skirts the north side of the mountain. The temple is one kilometer before the national park's north entrance, from where a trail leads up the mountain's north side to its crater top. Beyond the front gate of the temple, the entrance walk is bounded by lava rock walls on which have been set dozens of Buddha statues. Past a small lotus pond is the main hall and beyond that is the Myeongbu-jeon. A third hall, Yeongsan-jeon, sits on the hillside behind while to the side are large carved statues of the bodhisattvas Bohyeon and Munsu and the temple bell pavilion. Spruced up over the past several decades, Gwaneum-sa is a tranquil enclave below the towering and powerful mountain.

Halla Botanical Garden

Less than one kilometer off the 1100 Highway, this botanical garden shows nearly 1,000 native and non-native plants on its 37 acres. Trees, flowers, flowering shrubs, herbs, and bamboo all have their own areas, and a conservatory houses more delicate specimens. Open 0900–1800; ₩1,000 entrance.

Temple Sites

Six kilometers east of the city center, on the north slope of a low seaside hill, is **Wondang Bultap-sa temple site.** Built around 1300, when the Mongols had control of the island, this temple was said to have been one of the centers of Buddhism on the island. Partially repaired in 1914 and again in 1962, today only foundation stones and a five-tier stone pagoda from 1374

(T. #1187), the island's only such Buddhist relic, remain from the original temple. Beyond the temple site is the town of Jocheon [Choch'ŏn], and in town stands **Yeonbuk-jeong.** Built in 1374, this pavilion was used by travelers to and from the island to perform ceremonies of respect to the king when Jocheon was used as the principal port for the island.

Ten kilometers west of Jeju City are foundation stones for a second old temple site, known as **Sujeong-saji.**

PRACTICALITIES

Accommodations

Jeju City has over two dozen registered hotels, located both in the old city and in Shin Jeju. Located near Samseonghyeol is the deluxe-class, 21-story **Cheju KAL Hotel** (tel. 064/724-2001, www.kalhotel.co.kr), the tallest building in the city. Standard rooms start at ₩145,000, with deluxe rooms from ₩257,000 and suites for more than ₩400,000. Amenities include a casino, health club, and indoor swimming pool. Also in the deluxe class is the **Cheju Grand Hotel** (tel. 064/747-4900, www.chejugrand.com), located at the top side of Shin Jeju. Newer than the KAL Hotel, standard rooms here start at ₩170,000, superior rooms are ₩200,000, deluxe at ₩240,000, and suites from ₩380,000 to ₩1,800,000. The Grand Casino at the hotel stays open all hours every day, and the 36-hole Ora Country Club golf course is associated with the hotel. Free transportation is provided to and from the airport and the golf course. Also in Shin Jeju are the deluxe-class **Holiday Inn Crowne Plaza Hotel** (tel. 064/741-8000), first-class hotel **Royal Lagonda Hotel** (tel. 064/743-2222), and the second-class **Grace Hotel** (tel. 064/742-0066). Conveniently located across from Gwandeok-jeon is the first-class **Hotel Robero** (tel. 064/757-7111, www.roberohotel.com), where standard rooms go for ₩75,000 and suites for ₩110,000–250,000. Among those along the waterfront near the seawall are the first-class **Cheju Palace Hotel** (tel. 064/753-8811), the deluxe-class **Oriental Hotel**, third-class **Seaside Hotel** (tel. 064/752-0092), and the first-class

Swiss Hotel (tel. 064/756-5359), where rates run ₩60,000 with breakfast and dinner or ₩40,000 without. Modern and sophisticated, the **Cheju Oriental Hotel** (tel. 064/752-8222, www.oriental.co.kr) has rooms from ₩145,000 and suites from ₩310,000, with a casino, restaurants and bar, bowling alley, and other amenities.

More pedestrian accommodation can be found all over the city. Nearest the pier are Yangsando Minbak (양산도민박) and Hanil Minbak (한일민박); both go for ₩15,000. At the first intersection up the road is the Geumsanjang Yeogwan and bathhouse (금산장여관). Across the stream near the Dongmun Rotary is the clean and comfy Dongmun Yeogwan (동문여관). This stream and its banks have been cleaned up recently and two new pedestrian foot bridges have been laid over it. From there toward the sea are plenty of places to stay. Directly behind the Palace Hotel is the Tapdong Yeogwan (탑동여관). Along the road running down to the sea is the Namgyeong Hotel (남경호텔), while one block closer to the sea and across the road is the Taeyangjang Yeogwan (태양장여관), and a few steps farther and less expensive is the Myeongseong Yeoinsuk. To the west of city hall in an area frequented by university students are the Inseong Yeogwan (인성여관) and Daegwangjang Yeogwan (대광장여관), both in the first alley back from the main street just up from the main intersection. Many convenient accommodations are located near the bus terminal. Try the Terminal Yeoinsuk (터미널여인숙), Oncheonjang Yeogwan (온천장여관), and Yu Jeong Motel (유정모텔), all one block back from the main street to the west of the bus terminal. To the east of the stream and in one block are the Yusujang Hotel (유수장호텔), the Surim Hotel (수림호텔), and Hotel Yuseonjang (호텔유성장). In Shin Jeju, inexpensive accommodatios are scarcer and harder to locate. Try the Sejong Hotel (세종호텔) near the Grand Hotel where rooms go for ₩30,000.

Food

Quick-food stalls are found in the market alleys, and restaurants are located in all areas of the city, but many eating establishments are located to the northeast and southwest of the central rotary in Jeju City. Here you can find a wide variety of foods in clean and congenial settings. Similarly, the area behind the city hall has many fine restaurants often frequented by government employees, office workers, and businesspeople, while across the main street to the west and in the small streets behind are scores of less expensive eateries that are largely frequented by university students and other young people. Waterfront restaurants serve all types of fish, raw, broiled, fried, and in soups. Small restaurants close to the entrance to the breakwater are perhaps a bit less expensive than those farther west, interspersed among the hotels. Western-style food is available in the larger, fancier, and more expensive restaurants in this area, as well as in the large hotels. Restaurants can also be found near the bus terminal and along the major streets in Shin Jeju.

Shopping

The traditional central market, Dongmun, and Seomun markets are all in the old town relatively close to one another, while the Shin Jeju Market offers the same type of shopping for those in the new city. Aside from the ever-present street-side shops, department stores, like the Lotte Champion and Royal Shopping, have popped up mostly in Shin Jeju, and an underground arcade has been constructed below the central rotary and under the city's main street downtown. Tourist shops near the waterfront sell the whole spectrum of souvenir items, as do the hotel shops.

Services

A post office and police box sit next to each other across the street from Gwandeok-jeon in cen-

tral Jeju City. The Telecom office is located up the hill near the KAL Hotel, and beyond that is city hall. The central post office, provincial police headquarters, and provincial government office all lie east of the main traffic rotary in Shin Jeju. For money exchange in Shin Jeju, use the Korea Foreign Exchange Bank or the Jeju Bank; in the center of town try the Korea Foreign Exchange Bank, Jeju Bank, or others near the central rotary, or Choheung Bank near the KAL Hotel.

Transportation

City buses run through the city and out to the surrounding rural communities on numerous routes. The regular bus fare is ₩650 while the express city bus fare is ₩700. Express buses run between the ferry terminal and Shin Jeju via downtown Jeju and the airport on a regular schedule from early morning until late evening. Selected city buses that will be of use are as follows:

nos. 10, 14: Jeju National Museum, Jeju Folklore Museum, Jocheon, Hamdeok Beach

nos. 30, 32, 36, 38: Iho Beach, Jeju National Museum

no. 38: Iho Beach, Yongdam, Mokseokwon, Sancheondan, Jeju National University

no. 52: pier, bus terminal, Shin Jeju

nos. 60, 61, 62, 63: Sancheondan

no. 100: ferry pier, Tap-dong Park, bus terminal, airport

nos. 200, 300: airport, Shin Jeju, bus terminal, downtown Jeju City

no. 500: airport, Shin Jeju, downtown Jeju City, Mokseokwon, Jeju National University

no. 600: airport to Jungmun Resort and Seogwipo

West Jeju-do

Iho Beach 이호해수욕장

Protected by a breakwater, this half-kilometer-long, 50-meter-wide gray sand beach is not the best on the island but is the closest to the city, is most easily accessible, and has some water equipment for rent. The beach has several *minbak* and restaurants, but unfortunately, as it's just past the runway, it also has noise from the airport.

Shin Chun Jee Art Park
신천지조각공원

Just outside the Jeju City boundary along the western highway is the Shin Chun Jee Art Park. Established in 1987, this open-air garden has a representative holding of modern Korean sculpture, mostly large and bold pieces of stone or metal, some imaginative and others less inspiring.

JEJU WOVEN HATS

Halfway between Hallim and Gwakji Beach is Gwideok Village, where handsome light brown, flat-brimmed hats are woven from roots of a bush that grows on the mountainside. This is a cottage industry. During slack winter months, when farmers are not busy in the fields, the roots are gathered, dried, stripped of their outer covering, and softened until pliable enough to bend into the desired shape. Finely woven and sturdy, these hats last for years, and may be just the thing for a trip to sunnier islands of Southeast Asia. Smaller numbers are being produced today than in past decades and this seems principally due to the fact that the older hat weavers are passing away and the younger generation does not want to learn this craft. Another factor is the greater production of *galot* cloth hats and their popularity with visitors to the island. These woven hats seem to be made principally for tourists as they are seldom worn by local residents. Depending on the size and quality, they go for ₩30,000–60,000 and are now sold only at a few tourist shops and at the five-day market in Shin Jeju.

The bulk of these pieces are angular geometric forms, free line objects, and nudes. Paintings, prints, and smaller sculptures are displayed in the indoor exhibition hall. Open every day 0900–1800; entrance is ₩3,000.

Jeju Racetrack 제주경마장

Beyond the art park is the Jeju Racetrack, established with the idea of increasing the number and value of, and interest in, the island's ponies, and increasing enjoyment of the sport of horse racing. This track holds races nearly every Saturday and Sunday of the year. Twelve races a day from 800 meters to 1800 meters are run from 1100 to 1730, with additional twilight races during July and August. Bets can be made for ₩100–100,000: win, place, and quinella. For inquiries or information on how to place a bet, contact the grandstand information desk. Entrance to the track is ₩800. From Jeju City, frequent buses (₩1,100) run every 15 minutes past the racecourse on their way to Moseulpo and Seogwipo.

Hangmong Yujeokji 항몽유적지

Down the hill from the racecourse is a reconstructed earthen-walled fortress and memorial site called Hangmong Yujeokji or Hangpaduri (H.S. #396). When the *Sambyeolcho* (rebellious, elite forces of the Goryeo army) fled from Jin-do to Jeju-do in 1271, it was here that they came to set up their last defensive position against the combined Goryeo and Mongol armies. While resisting valiantly, they were far outnumbered and were finally annihilated in 1273. The refurbished inner wall (1977) can be seen a short distance beyond a new commemorative hall and memorial marker. In the exhibition hall are a few earthenware artifacts from that time, patriotic paintings, and an explanation of the *Sambyeolcho* defensive forces. Part of the six-kilometer-long outer wall has also been rebuilt. Aside from the historical connection, there is little of interest to see. Take bus no. 808 (₩650) to Goseong-ni, and walk the one-half kilometer up the hill to the memorial; ₩1,000 entrance fee.

Nabeup Subtropical Forest Preserve
납읍금산공원

Tucked away on the rocky hillside up from Aewol and within Geumsan Park is the Nabeup forest preserve (N.M. #375). This small sanctuary of about 60 species of plants is thick with vegetation and almost seems enchanted as only shafts of sunlight poke their way through the dense canopy. Nothing is labeled and there are only rudimentary paths through the forest. This preserve has not been well developed or well publicized so is little visited. Infrequent bus transportation drops passengers at Nabeup [Nabŭp], which historically has been known as a village of noblemen. Walk about one-half kilometer toward the mountain through town to the forest entrance; no fee.

Gwakji Beach

A few kilometers east of Hallim is this attractive white-sand beach, with rugged volcanic rocks at each end and low sand dunes in back. Smaller than Hyeopjae Beach down the road, it attracts plenty of revelers during the heat of the summer when jet skis, boats, water-skiing, and other water recreation are available. During the summer swimming season, many private houses rent *minbak* rooms; several Korean restaurants open only for the summer. During the rest of the year, rental rooms are harder to find, but can be arranged, along with meals, if you stay a few days.

Hallim 한림

A sleepy yet thriving seaside community, Hallim is the largest town along the northwest coast. Fishing and farming are integral sectors of the local economy, and an electrical power generation plant lies inland from the center of town. Fields of onion, garlic, potato, and other vegetables surround the town, gradually giving way to pasturelands farther up the mountainside. Off in the distance, southeast of town, several parasitic craters are randomly spread over the wide and gentle mountain slope. Four kilometers west of Hallim in the village of Hyeopjae is the broad,

fishing boats in Hallim harbor

white-sand, but somewhat rocky **Hyeopjae Beach** (협재해수욕장). It boasts crystal-clear water and is a fine place to snorkel. Full during the short summer swim season, when all sorts of water toys are available for rent, it's virtually abandoned the rest of the year. A short distance farther is the smaller and less frequented **Geumneung Beach**. There are plenty of *minbak* at each. Between the beaches lies Hallim Park, and off the coast is the island of Biyang-do.

A fine place to stay in Hallim is the New World Motel (뉴월드모텔). Less expensive are the Yeongil Yeogwan (영일여관), and Jungang Yeogwan (중앙여관). All are located on the ocean side of the main street. A few restaurants are located on the main street, and other eateries can be found near the market. Buses to and from Jeju City stop at two spots along the main street of town, including directly in front of the Isidore clinic, across the street from the church. Periodic buses leave Hallim on routes that go by the Isidore Ranch and the Jeju Bonsai Garden. Daily ferries to Biyang-do leave from the pier at the south end of town.

HALLIM WOOL

One of the most successful missionary efforts in the country took place in Hallim. The mountain's mid-level elevation makes excellent pastureland for horses, cattle, and pigs, all of which have been raised on the island for centuries. In 1955, an Irish Catholic priest imported several hundred merino sheep from New Zealand in order to start a cooperative, generate employment, and improve the local economy. Those initial steps paid off bountifully and for years the Isidore Ranch raised several thousand sheep, pigs, and other domestic animals. This cooperative spread over nearly 3,000 acres above Hallim and was a great benefactor to the economy. In the late 1990s, the Isidore Ranch ceased most of its ranching operations and began putting its land to other uses.

In association with the ranch, Hallim Hand Weavers, a weaving and knitting cottage industry, was founded under the direction of Irish Columban Catholic nuns and based at the local church. These missionaries considered it important not only to serve the spiritual needs of the town residents, but also to help improve their economic base. Over the years, Hallim Hand Weavers expanded greatly, and established a reputation for quality goods. Irish fishermen's sweaters, gloves, mittens, caps, scarves, shawls, blankets, and bolts of tweed cloth were produced, most all were 100 percent wool from the ranch. At its height, the factory had 30 handmade hand looms producing cloth and blankets, and about 500 local women worked at home in their spare time knitting up to 4,500 sweaters a year. Initially, all steps in the process of producing yarn, including cleaning, carding, spinning, dyeing, and drying, were done at the factory—a lengthy and laborious process. Later, while the wool was still procured from the Isidore Ranch, it was sent away to Incheon to be processed into yarn. Later yet, some products were machine-made in Seoul, a few with the addition of man-made fibers. The last of the foreign nuns left Hallim in 1998, and due to changing economic conditions a decision was made to cease weaving and knitting operations all together. However, due in no small part to these pioneering efforts and the revenue that was funneled into the community, Hallim has a strong and diverse economic base and continues to be the principal community along the northwest coast of the island.

Hallim Park 한림공원

One hundred meters beyond Hyeopjae Beach, but on the inland side of the highway, is Hallim Park, a privately owned complex of two lava tubes, a subtropical botanical garden, bonsai garden, and a small folk village that's open daily 0800–1830; ₩4,000 entrance fee.

The Hyeopjae lava tube system (N.M. #236), composed of 19 separate caves including the 2,500-meter-long **Seocheon Cave**, is just over 17 kilometers long and supposedly one of the longest such complexes in the world. Of the numerous tubes, only two, **Hyeopjae Cave** and **Twin Dragon Cave**, are open to the public. The caves' discovery came accidentally in 1955, when a schoolboy fell into one of the openings and had to be dug out by his mates. A second, larger cave was discovered in 1969, the rest more recently. These flat-bottomed, arched-ceiling tubes were formed about 2.5 million years ago, when molten lava flowed out from under the already hardening upper crust of the disgorged volcanic vomit. Undoubtedly, long tubes still lie undiscovered below the surface. Although there is now a continuous exchange of air, these tubes maintain a constant and slightly humid 17°C year-round. Over the years, sand and finely ground shells have been blown up from the coast, covering the lava to a depth of about three meters. Slowly and steadily, "lime water" leaches through this "ionized" material and the rock below, creating stalactites and stalagmites inside the cave itself. The result is a bumpy patchwork of white, black, and gold color. These formations grow at a rate of about one centimeter per century. It is claimed that these caves are the only combination lava tube/active stalactite caves in the world and are a curiosity to scientists.

Started in 1971, the well-maintained botanical garden has grown to contain over 2,000 species of native and non-native subtropical trees, palms, bushes, grasses, and flowers, and the small bonsai garden and rock art garden were opened in 1997. Although small, the folk village has been tastefully created with buildings, implements, and furnishings typical of the island.

Biyang-do 비양도

Created by volcanic activity in 1002, Biyang-do [Piyang-do] is a nearly round island set about three kilometers off Hyeopjae Beach. Its two low cones are covered mostly by bushes and grass; a lighthouse caps the taller. Biyang-do now supports a small fishing community of about 300 people. From a pier at the south end of Hallim, a ferry (₩1,500, 20 minutes) crosses to this tiny island twice a day, at 0900 and 1500, returning immediately after dropping off passengers; an extra ferry leaves about noon at the height of summer season. It's possible to walk to the top of Biyang-do. The perimeter road takes about one and a half hours. On the north side of the island is a naturally sculpted rock in the shape of a standing pregnant woman (use your imagination). Biyang-do is often visited by fishermen who while away the hours along the rocky shore. A couple of *minbak* are located on the island, and they will prepare food upon request.

Bonsai Garden 분재예술원

Directly south of Hallim, in a fold of the undulating range land at Jeoji [Chŏji], is Korea's first garden dedicated solely to bonsai ("bunjae" in Korean). Bonsai Garden, also known as Bunjae Artpia was opened in 1992. Fine examples of these potted plants are displayed along paths that wind their way through green lawns amongst full-size native trees. Nearly 100 species are represented. Volcanic rocks are set here and there, symbolically anchoring these landscaped gardens to the land. A koi pond lies in front of the garden restaurant. While bonsai are familiar to most, the style of these miniature Korean trees may seem different as many are let to grow a little larger and not trained into such sculpted forms as the Japanese bonsai. Look at each plant from the bottom to the top. A healthy, good-looking root must underpin the whole plant. Above the root,

a stocky trunk must support the well-proportioned, though not necessarily symmetrical, branch system. Although shaped by the hand of man, the whole must not have an artificial look but appear as natural and harmonious as possible. However large or small, the plant must be imbued with a look of age. An intense interplay between man and nature, working with bonsai should increase the natural beauty of the tree through the grower's artistic skill. Occasionally visited by foreign dignitaries, this garden serenades guests with classical orchestral music and operatic arias and offers a fine restaurant for those who care to linger. Entrance to the garden is ₩5,000 and it is open 0830–2200 (0730 in winter). It's somewhat pricey, but the whole affair is artsy and modern. Catch the occasional bus (₩700) that runs between Hallim and Shinchang.

Jeolbuam 절부암

Just south of the village of Shinchang, set along the coast in an area of camellia and silver magnolia trees is the seaside rock Jeolbuam ("Faithful Wife Rock"), around which a tragic legend has grown. During the last century, a fisherman and his wife lived in a village nearby. The husband, tragically, was caught in a storm. Waiting day after day, the wife finally realized that her mate would not return and she would no longer be able to share her life with him. In her grief, she hanged herself from a tree next to the water's edge. The following day, as if in longing to be near his wife, the fisherman's body floated up to this rock. Every year on the 15th day of the third lunar month, a small ceremony is held here to honor the act of filial devotion and love shown by these two people for one another. Off the coast here is Chagwi-do, one of the island's preferred sport fishing spots. Near Jeolbuam is the Gosan-ni Prehistoric site, so far the oldest such Paleolithic site on the island.

MOSEULPO 모슬포

Most visitors to the island see Moseulpo [Mosŭlp'o], the largest town and most active fishing port on the southwest coast, only through the window of a bus, on the way to Sanbanggul-sa grotto or Jungmun. The port of Moseulpo is now also known as Daejeong [Taejŏng], an old name for this area which had its center up the hill in what is now Boseong [Posŏng]. There is little of interest in the town itself, except for small-scale construction and repair of wooden boats along the harborfront. Korean and Japanese tourists hire boats here to fish the clear waters off the west coast. The only permanent U.S. military presence on Jeju-do is the MacNab Compound Air Force radar station, which tops the hill to the back of town. Periodically, Korean and American soldiers come to the island for mountain-climbing training on Sanbang-san. The Americans have not been the only ones interested in this area, however. During the Japanese occupation, the Japanese military constructed an airfield here and camouflaged hangars for airplanes. These and some pillboxes can still be seen above town.

Up the hill from Moseulpo are the reconstructed remains of the **Daejeong Confucian Academy** (대정향교). Every spring and autumn a rite is performed here to honor past Confucian scholars. Built in 1416, it was moved to its present location in 1653. Farther up the hill, writings and other remains of the exiled scholar Kim Cheong-hwi (pen name: Chusa) are displayed at an exhibition hall (추사적거지) along with several *dolharubang* from the immediate area. Close by, portions of an old fortress wall have been re-created.

One kilometer south of town is Hamo Beach, frequented almost exclusively by locals. Three kilometers southeast of town is **Songak-san,** the island's southernmost tip. This seaside crater is the little brother of the more famous and visually dramatic Seongsan Ilchul-bong, which sprouted in a similar manner at the eastern end of the island. Measuring 180 meters high, 80 meters deep, and one-half kilometer around, Songak-san is smaller than Seongsan Ilchul-bong, but it, too, forms a short peninsula. On a clear day, the views past Sanbang-san to Halla-san and out to sea are spectacular. Pottery artifacts from the Bronze Age have been discovered on Songak-san. During the Japanese occupation, tunnels were dug into the outside wall of this crater as

storage facilities, as they were at Seongsan Ilchul-bong.

If you decide to stay in Moseulpo, try the Jeiljang Yeogwan (제일장여관) near the main intersection on the way down to the pier. The owner speaks English. Around the corner and down is the Hotel Daeheungjang (호텔대흥장) and a bit farther is the Dongwonjang Yeogwan (동원장여관). Korean restaurants line the road to the pier. Every 20 minutes, buses run in both directions from Moseulpo along the round-island highway, but only periodic buses run the coast road past Sanbang-san to Seogwipo and across the western-slope highway to Jeju City. Small inter-island ferries to Kapa-do and Mara-do leave daily from the Moseulpo pier. To Kapa-do (₩3,000), they run at 0800 and 1400 and take about 30 minutes; for Mara-do (₩4,800), the daily ferries leave at 1000 and 1400 and take about 45 minutes. A ₩1,500 use tax may be levied on arrivals at both Mara-do and Kapa-do, as they, the surrounding sea, and Songak-san make up the Mara Marine County Park. Excursion ferries also run to Mara-do from a pier below Songak-san. Leaving every hour 0930–1500, the round-trip costs ₩13,000 every day except when the water is too rough.

Gapa-do and Mara-do

Two of the province's inhabited islands lie directly south of Moseulpo. With fewer than 200 households, the closest and largest is Gapa-do [Kap'a-do] (가파도). Once used to run cattle, all available space on this flat and virtually treeless island is now cultivated in dry land crops. Strong winds whistle over the rock fences, wild surf crashes against the encircling pebble beach, and the surrounding water is clear to a great depth. Many islanders are prosperous fishermen, as they have been for the 150 years of the island's habitation. Yet even this traditional occupation is pursued by fewer people these days. Slowly, men are turning their hands to other trades, or leaving the island altogether. The effects of modernization have also swept ashore here. Thatch-roof houses are being replaced with cement boxes with gaily painted corrugated roofs; ubiquitous television antennas dot the island's two villages.

The south village has the island's only commercial pier and *minbak;* meals must be arranged with the owners. Between the time that the morning boat drops you off and the afternoon boat returns, take a leisurely stroll across the island or a walk around its perimeter. A prehistoric *dolmen* was recently unearthed here, indicating habitation from long ago.

Mara-do (마라도) is less than half the size of Gapa-do and twice the distance from Moseulpo. It is the southernmost Korean landmass, and a stone marker has been raised near its south end to note this fact. Unlike Gapa-do, Mara-do rises steeply out of the water to form pastureland on its slanted top. Precipitous cliffs, odd rock formations, and numerous cliff caves ring this isolated outpost. Once this island was densely forested; the trees were all cut down by the first residents in the 1870s to open the land for crops. About 80 residents make Mara-do their home, and the island has a school, a lighthouse, and a handful of *minbak*. If you don't care to walk, a bike can be rented for a spin around the island. Shore fishing has become popular among Koreans, who come here for an easy catch. A manned lighthouse sends a beacon from its spot on the island's east side to the vast ocean to the south. From both of these islands you have expansive views of southern Jeju-do, a sight seen by few travelers.

SANBANG-SAN

Sanbanggul-sa 산방굴사

Six kilometers east of Moseulpo, 395-meter-high Sanbang-san (N.M. #376) thrusts vertically out of the ground, a thick basalt plug, the core of an eroded volcanic peak standing in solitary contrast to the gentle gradient of the surrounding fields. Legend tells that in the misty past only a few people lived on the island, and gods inhabited the mountain slopes. One day a man took his bow and went up the mountain to hunt. Not being the best of archers, he accidentally shot a mountain spirit in the buttocks. Realizing that he had done something terribly foolish, the hunter raced down the slope toward his home. The spirit flew into a rage, ripped off the top of the mountain and threw it at the luckless hunter.

The piece he tossed became Sanbang-san, and the spot from which he tore it is Halla-san's dished summit crater. Its steep sides make for challenging rock climbing and rappelling.

Near the roadway sit the temple Sanbang-sa and a small collection of shops. Halfway up this peak's southern exposure is Sanbanggul-sa, a shallow natural grotto used as a place of worship since the Goryeo Dynasty; ₩2,200 entrance. A seated Buddha has been placed on an altar along its back wall, where services are held. Even though it's partially blocked by a tall pine tree, the view from this grotto—over the lowland fields, country villages, and offshore islands —is spectacular. The colors are especially mellow in late afternoon, when the sun meets its reflection as it sinks into the Yellow Sea. From the ceiling of this grotto comes the constant drip of pure, refreshing water—you'll want a sip after the climb up the hill.

A second legend relating to this peak says that once a very happy couple lived in this region, he a human, she a celestial spirit. The evil governor of the island came to know of her beauty and goodness, and wanted her. He had the husband falsely charged with a crime and permanently locked away, so as to take the wife for his own. The dutiful wife refused the governor's advances, and because of her grief turned into Sanbang-san. The water that drips from the grotto ceiling are her tears, still shed in longing for her unfortunate and maltreated husband.

Directly below Sanbang-san is **Yongmeori,** or Dragon Head, promontory. On this grassy headland, a plaque has been erected by a joint agreement between the Korean and Dutch governments to commemorate the first landing of foreigners on Korean soil, quite likely the shipwrecked Dutchmen's point of abrupt contact with Korea, although some believe that accidental landing was actually on Gapa-do. This seaside spot is a fine place to explore, have a picnic, or simply sit and contemplate the paradoxical beauty and peril of the sea. A reconstructed beacon site lies along the highway here while a windswept shoreline stretches to the south.

From Yongmeori, you can look down onto Hanguchi Beach. Beyond a low rise along the shore to the east is the longer and more frequented **Hwasun Beach,** and a little farther is a sea cliff palisade. In and of themselves these sights are pleasant, but as a whole they used to be more pleasing before the breakwater and electric power generator plant got added to the view. Both beaches are long stretches of tan sand that slide gently into the aquamarine sea. It's an excellent place to swim, and far from the crowds that flock to the island's better-known beaches. Accommodation and food are available at the village of Hwasun, just up from the beach.

Jeju Sculpture Park 제주조각공원

Opened in the late 1980s, this open-air garden displays over 150 sculptures by modern Korean artists. Mostly stone and metal, some abstract and some realistic, each depicts some aspect of human life. Stroll the paths or view the area from above, from the modernistic observation tower on the hill, which also gives you a great view of the entire southwestern corner of the island. Near the entrance are an indoor display room and a restaurant. Jeju Sculpture Park is on the north side of Sanbang-san. Open 0900–1830, the entrance fee is ₩3,000. Bus (₩700) from Moseulpo.

Andeok Valley 안덕계곡

Several kilometers past Hwasun is the lush Andeok [Andŏk] Valley. This short, tight, and winding valley (N.M. #182), more a good-size ravine, is thick with evergreen vegetation, representative of plants of the south coast of the island. It also holds some columnar basalt formations, and in the summer you're likely to see large, iridescent, green/blue winged butterflies and silvery-blue dragonflies. Legend says that long ago, when the earth quaked, the skies cried, and mists filled the land, this valley was formed in seven turbulent days. While not outstanding, it makes a pleasant side trip on a journey along the south coast. The entrance to the valley is just off the highway in the village of Andeok; use bus no. 130 from Seogwipo.

South Jeju-do

JUNGMUN 중문

This ordinary town [Chungmun], at the southern end of the West Cross-Island Highway, belies the attractiveness of the surrounding area, with its comfortable weather, deep ravines and lush green gorges, clear streams, waterfalls and pools, black volcanic rock, rich blue sea, white-sand beaches, grand views of the island's central behemoth Halla-san, and orchard after orchard of tangerines. Yet, in Korea's little corner of tropical paradise, "development" has become the watchword. This once laid-back farming community has been transformed into one of the country's premier resort complexes, its pristine environment nearly unrecognizable from what it was years ago.

Cheonjeyeon Waterfall 천제연폭포

At the west end of town is Cheonjeyeon [Ch'ŏnjeyŏn] Waterfall, a legendary bathing place of seven nymphs from heaven. It seems only proper that they should choose the most perfect of the falls and pools along this scarred coast. Before the steady arrival of tourists, it was possible to take a dip in these cool, clear pools without becoming the center of attention for a line of sightseers. Now, you can be one of dozens who only dip their toes into the refreshing water while soaking up the surrounding scenery.

Cheonjeyeon Waterfall lies in a gorge that contains a series of three falls and pools; ₩2,700 entrance. The first falls drops eight meters over a sheer basalt wall, almost directly underneath the highway bridge. A rock curtain of pentagonal pillars half encircles the blue waters of its round pool, and this wall evokes a feeling of strength and intimates the magical power of volcanic rock formations. During rainy weather, the stream crashes to the pool below, but in drier periods it only seeps down the cracks between these pillars. The second falls is slightly higher and wider, with a narrow lip overhang. Moisture-loving vegetation clings to the cliff, and thick foliage rising from the edge of this pool often erupts in a cacophony of calling birds. Farther down the boulder-strewn gorge, the stream rolls over the third falls on its way to the sea. This valley and its semi-tropical flora and fauna are part of sections along the south coast designated N.M. #182. There are about 100 species of subtropical plants in the valley, and a number of these trees have jointly been designated N.M. #378. It's more than pleasant at any time of year, but best in summer or fall.

With the development of the tourist complex west of the gorge, the footbridge Seonim-gyo spans the valley to facilitate safer passage to and from the waterfalls and offers a bird's-eye view of the valley. Each playing a musical instrument, seven winged nymphs in flowing robes glide across its arch. At the bridge's western end is the new Cheonje-ru pavilion.

Jungmun Resort 중문관광단지

Jeju-do's finest strand of white sand is a short walk below the Cheonjeyeon Waterfall. Jung-mun Beach, formerly known as Jinmosal Beach, is Jeju-do's most popular, attracting a circus of people in the summer. Aquamarine water laps at its powdery sand, and huge white dunes have been blown against the dark cliffs that isolate it from everything but the sea. A ramped cement walkway winds around the eastern end of the cliff, and a trail leads down the west end from the promontory. Following the top of the cliff is a trail that skirts the hotel properties, and at a high point along the cliff under some pine trees in front of the Shilla Hotel you'll find Swiri Hill, so called because the final scene of a very popular modern Korean film called *Swiri* was shot here. Beyond the west end of Jungmun Beach is a second, smaller, white-sand beach with a more impressive crescent-shaped basalt palisade backdrop. This once isolated area is being infringed upon by a massive resort complex, a place that has become *the* recreational area of the island and continues to expand yearly. This is Jungmun Tourist Resort. International-class hotels, condominiums, shopping arcades, restaurants, a convention center, botanical garden, golf course, an

Jungmun Beach

To Moseulpo

To Jungmun

JUNGMUN

GOLF

CLUB

Yeomiji
Botanical
Garden

Cheonjeyeon
Waterfall

CHEONJE-RU ★   SEONIM-GYO

JUNGMUN RESORT

SHOPS

TEDDY BEAR
MUSEUM

KNTO TOURIST
CENTER

CLUB HOUSE ■

HOTEL HANA

LOTTE HOTEL
CHEJU

HOTEL GREEN
VILLA

KOREA RESORT
CONDOMINIUM

JEJU KOREA
HOUSE

CHEJU SILLA
HOTEL

SWIRI HILL ★

To
Convention
Center

MARINA

PACIFIC LANDS

JUNGMUN
SEA-VILLAGE
RESORT HOTEL

FOLK
VILLAGE

Jungmun   Beach

HYATT HOTEL

Beach

JUSANGJEOLLI ★

0   300 yds
0   300 m

© AVALON TRAVEL PUBLISHING INC

JEJU-DO

aquarium, small marina, and folk fishing village have all been constructed here. Plans for the future include other accommodations, parks, and sports and amusement facilities, mostly on the east side of the stream, nearly doubling the area of the resort. Families mostly visit during the summer school vacation, and honeymooners flock here during the spring and fall. Anytime of the year is all right, but the winter months can be positively cool. Jungmun Resort is as close as Jeju-do comes to resembling Hawaii.

At the heart of this resort is a large and useful KNTO Tourist Center, which also houses a post office and bank. Information about Jungmun and the rest of Korea can be had here as well as help with accommodation and transportation arrangements.

Next to the tourist center is a shopping plaza, and across the way is the **Yeomiji Botanical Garden.** Anchoring the center of this garden is a 28-acre, round greenhouse with five separate gardens (flower, water lily, cactus, tropical rainforest, and tropical fruit). Rising through the center of this greenhouse is an observation tower from which all of Jungmun Resort, and the southern portion of Jeju-do—from Halla-san to Mara-do—can be seen. Surrounding this glass building are Korean, Japanese, French, Italian, sunken, and native-plant special theme gardens and broad lawns. Nearly 4,000 species of plants are represented here. Open daily, entrance is a steep ₩5,000, but well worth the cost for the true plant lover.

Next to the tourist information building is the much newer **Teddy Bear Museum.** With over 1,000 of these lovable stuffed animals, this museum is a one-of-a-kind for Korea. Teddys large and small not only sit on display but portray many important events and persons in history. The museum also has an outdoor garden, a restaurant, and a gift shop where you can purchase your favorite bear. Open 1000–1800 (2100 in summer), entrance is a stiff ₩6,000 adult and ₩4,000 for children.

Near the mouth of the stream is a newly expanded harbor for pleasure boats, a folk village, and a marine park. On the east side of the rivermouth is a **fishermen's folk village,** ₩1,400 entrance. With a dozen buildings, this small and neatly arranged folk village is a fine example of typical Jeju-do architecture. It was a real village of fishermen and *haenyeo* until the Sea Village Resort was built, at which time the people of the village moved elsewhere and the hotel preserved the buildings. Nearly 3,000 items relating to home furnishings, tools, and fishing equipment flesh out the display and give a feel for what village life was like along this isolated coast. Beyond this fishing village is a rugged coastline called Jisatgae or Jusangjeolli, a postpile of columnar basalt standing like a fortress wall against the sea. Activities at the **marina** include water-skiing (₩40,000), parasailing (₩40,000), jet skiing (₩30,000), and rubber rafting (₩50,000). Rent bikes from shops in town for ₩7,000 a day. On the west side of the harbor is **Pacific Land,** entrance ₩6,000. Although other activities are planned, a dolphin and sea lion show is currently held five times a day (four in winter), and an aquarium holds all sorts of sea life. On the cliff above the west end of Jungmun Beach is the public 18-hole Jungmun Golf Club, Korea's only seaside golf course. For those romantic spirits, old-fashioned horse-drawn carriage rides are available at night between the Lotte and Shilla hotels for ₩10,000.

Practicalities

The best accommodations at Jungmun are the deluxe-class **Hyatt Regency Cheju Hotel** (tel. 064/733-1234, www.hyatt.com), the **Shilla Cheju Hotel** (tel. 064/735-5514, http://cheju .shilla.net/eng/), and the **Lotte Hotel Cheju** (tel. 064/731-1000, www.hotel.lotte.co.kr). The octagonal pyramid-like Hyatt sits directly on the cliff overlooking the beach and, while finely designed, impinges on the beauty of the coastline.

The oldest hotel in the resort, it's been refurbished and maintains its high standard. Rooms, all of which have an ocean or mountain view and open onto the interior courtyard, start at ₩225,000, with suites from ₩600,000. Set back from the edge is the more classically-designed, lower and broader Cheju Shilla Hotel, where mountain-view rooms run ₩280,000–355,000, ocean-view rooms ₩310,000–450,000, and suites up to ₩4,800,000! Newest and largest is the imposing Lotte Hotel Cheju, where standard rooms run from ₩300,000, deluxe rooms are ₩380,000, and suites start at ₩1,000,000. All have the amenities commensurate with such international-class hotels, including a wide variety of restaurants, lounges, and fitness facilities, and each has a casino.

On the far side of the marina, above the folk fishing village, is the friendly and comfortable **Jungmun Sea-Village Resort Hotel** (tel. 064/738-5511, www.hotelseavillage.com), a cluster of low-slung bungalows (as you might find in Hawaii) and a restaurant; the 30 rooms here run ₩123,000–196,000 with suites at ₩492,000. Two other newer establishments within the resort complex, both located between the Shilla and Lotte hotels, are the visually pleasing boutique hotel **Green Villa Cheju** (tel. 064/738-3800, www.greenvilla.co.kr), and the boxier **Hotel Hana** (tel. 064/738-7001). Designed by an American firm and decorated by a French designer, the European-style Green Villa has the most distinctive style. An odd yet pleasing combination of mostly modern and contemporary styles, it has a predominance of pastel colors and wood, with a subtle island flavor. Rates at the Green Villa run ₩235,000–295,000, with suites at ₩450,000. At the Hotel Hana, rooms are less expensive at ₩145,000–195,000, with suites at ₩363,000.

A cluster of less expensive *minbak* are located near the entrance to the resort complex. Others are located up the hill in the town of Jungmun, particularly on its west side. Try **Eden Minbak** (tel. 064/738-0101), up the alley to the east of the post office, where a room in the house runs ₩20,000. The owner speaks English. Almost next door is another *minbak*.

Aside from the hotel restaurants, several pricey restaurants, including the **Jeju Korea House**, are found at the resort, while more ordinary eateries can be found at the resort entrance and in the town of Jungmun itself. Highway buses pass through Jungmun every 20 minutes, and frequent Seogwipo express city bus nos. 100 and 110 (₩700) run out as far as the resort hotels and botanical garden.

Hunting

The private **Daeyu Land** (tel. 064/738-0500), two kilometers west of Jungmun, offers skeet and trap shooting, pistol and rifle practice, and field hunting with a guide, as well as horse riding year-round on its huge reserve. The club also maintains a pheasant farm in order to stock its range, but in addition various pheasant recipes appear on the club's restaurant menu. Hunts are conducted twice a day at 0930 and 1500 every day year-round. A basic fee of ₩100,000 is charged for equipment rental and guide, with additional fees for practice and ammo. Reservations are required 1–2 days in advance. Daeyu Land can be reached by taxi from Jungmun for about ₩3,000.

Yakcheon-sa 약천사

Founded in 1930, Yakcheon-sa [Yakch'ŏn-sa] is of relatively new vintage. In the late 1980s and early 1990s much new construction was done, expanding the size of this temple dramatically and giving it one of if not the largest main halls and altar Buddha figures in the country. It's located a few kilometers east of Jungmun, one-half kilometer down a lane toward the sea. Yakcheon-sa is the 10th district headquarters for the Jogye sect. Its huge main hall has a three-tier roof. While its superstructure is made of concrete, there are many wood details like the finely carved door panels around the exterior and the large interior panels that stand behind the altar figures, which are impressive for their size and design. The whole building is highly decorated, but note especially the four dragons that entwine the pillars that front the altar. Unusual to such temple structures, this building is open on the inside for walkways that circle the hall on the second

and third levels, and there are interior partitions and walls. To the rear of the main hall, and set into the hillside, is a man-made grotto worship hall.

SEOGWIPO 서귀포

With a population of nearly 90,000, Seogwipo [Sŏgwip'o] is the island's second-largest city, and the southern terminus of the island-wide bus system. With the steep and etched slopes of Halla-san at its back and the cool blue waters and craggy-cliff coastline on its doorstep, Seogwipo is surrounded by awe-inspiring scenery. No wonder Seogwipo has become the favorite newlywed retreat! This quaint city is split by a lush gorge, and it has two of the island's most picturesque waterfalls. Just off the coast, three aesthetically placed islets, Munseom, Beomseon, and Supseom, where steep cliffs rise to thickly forested tops, accentuate its beauty. Munseom and Beomseon have jointly been designated N.M. #421. A fourth island, Saeseom, which lies just beyond the end of the harbor's western breakwater can be reached by wading across the short channel at low tide. On its south side is a fossil mollusk formation. Lying in the middle of the south coast, this city is the heart of the warmest region of Korea. With appropriate climate and rich soil, Seogwipo and this south-central coastal region have become the country's citrus-producing center.

It is written that about 250 B.C., Emperor Shi of the Qin Dynasty of China sent the envoy Seobul, accompanied by 500 young males and females, to Halla-san to gather the magical herb *bullocho*. Considered an elixir of eternal youth, *bullocho* was said to grow on Halla-san, one of the sacred mountains of the east. Unfortunately for the emperor, none of this plant was found and the envoy had to return empty-handed. His departure was made from Seogwipo, which means "Port of Western Return."

A few kilometers west of the city are the stone remains of **Beophwa-sa** temple. Built some time around 1300, it was said to have been the largest and one of the most important temples on the island until its destruction in 1410. Only founda-

SEOGWIPO

To Jeju City

To-Seongsanpo

SEOGWIPO KAL HOTEL

PARADISE HOTEL CHEJU

Waterfall

Jeongbang Waterfall

Seogwipo Harbor

Saeseom

TAMNAJANG YEOGWAN

DONGMYEONG DEPT. STORE

CENTRAL MARKET

DONGHWAJANG MOTEL

JEONGSHIL YEOINSUK

NAMYANGJANG MOTEL

FERRY TERMINAL

HANYANGGAK YEOGWAN

TELECOM

POST OFFICE

NAPOLI HOTEL

POKPOJANG YEOGWAN

SEOGWIPO PARK HOTEL

CENTRAL ROTARY

City Park

BUS TERMINAL

MANSUGAK YEOGWAN

STAR SONG MOTEL

SEOGWIPO LION'S HOTEL

EXCURSION FERRY TERMINAL

Cheonjiyeon Waterfall

JEJU PRINCE HOTEL

CAVES

Sammae-bong Park

To Jungmun

WOEDOLGOE

© AVALON TRAVEL PUBLISHING, INC.

500 yds

500 m

N

tion stones remain from that ancient temple, but a few types of roof tiles that were typical on royal structures have also been discovered near the temple site. New temple buildings were erected on this site in 1961 and the main hall raised in 1986.

The post office, an airline ticketing office, several banks, and most major businesses are located along the main east-west street through the city and on the street running up from the main intersection. The Telecom office is one block behind the post office, and the central market to its side. The five-day market is located in the northeast corner of town. Many restaurants and shops and much of the evening activity can be found east of the main intersection, both north and south of the main drag.

Following the example of Jeju City, Seogwipo has carved the new city of Shin Seogwipo out of land a few kilometers west of the old downtown area to meet growing governmental, commercial, and residential needs. The police office and city hall have been relocated there, and a soccer stadium was built for the 2002 World Cup games. The **Korea Baseball Hall of Fame**, entrance ₩1,000, is also there along the road that skirts the upper edge of town. How this city will develop is still unknown, but the old city is still the most vibrant center on the south coast.

A tourist information office (tel. 064/732-1330) is conveniently located at the entrance to Cheonjiyeon Waterfall. Open 0800–2100, it provides plenty of brochures, interpreters, and free Internet access.

For more information visit www.sogwipo .cheju.kr.

Orchards

Rich volcanic farmland spreads across the southern coast. Primarily planted in fruit trees, some vegetables and grains are also grown. During the Japanese occupation of the peninsula, the tangerine was introduced to Korea and has since thrived. Jeju-do has always grown a native variety of orange of inferior quality, but in 1965 imported varieties began to be grafted to native trees, yielding hardy, high-quality fruit. Some hybridization has been attempted. Orchards of

tangerine and other citrus fruit spread out in all directions from Seogwipo, but are concentrated near Jungmun, Seogwipo, and Namwon. Seogwipo itself produces about 60 percent of the tangerine crop. These trees need the warmth of the sun and protection from the wind, so groves are surrounded by high stone walls, windbreaks are created by rows of trees or cloth curtains, and now more and more fruit is grown inside huge plastic greenhouses. Ripening orange fruits fleck the green foliage, offsetting the black rock and complementing the deep blue sky of fall. A number of other native citrus fruits are grown and a variety of imported tropical fruits have been tried with limited success. Along these coastal roads, fields of pineapple lie open to the warm sun in summer and are covered by temporary plastic shelters when the weather cools. Mangos and orchids are also grown inside hothouses in this area.

Coastal Waterfalls

On the east side of Seogwipo, only a short walk from the city center, is Jeju-do's most famous waterfall. **Jeongbang** [Chŏngbang] (정방폭포) plunges 23 meters to the pebble beach at seaside. From the roadside entrance, a steep stairway brings you down to the rocky shore; ₩2,200 entrance. Most of the *haenyeo* (women divers) who used to dive here have moved on to other spots as the number of tourists has increased. Small rainbows are often formed here as the sun angles in on the mist created by the plunging water. A little farther east, below the Hotel Paradise, another, lower falls tumbles onto the rocky shore, this one next to the exit of a blocked lava tube. Along the edge of the cliff above, a short walk called the Paradise Promenade makes its way through the trees.

Almost directly below the center of town is the 22-meter **Cheonjiyeon** [Ch'ŏnjiyŏn] (천지연 폭포) and gorge, another spot said to have been used by heavenly nymphs for their nightly baths. From a parking lot near the harbor at the rivermouth, a walkway leads up into this ravine to a broad, idyllic pool below the falls; ₩2,200 entrance. A unique subtropical zone is found only along the south coast of Jeju-do. Protected as a nature conservation area, this valley is part of that zone and has been designated a unit of N.M. #182. Deciduous trees, broadleaf evergreens, and several varieties of bushes grow here, together designated N.M. #379. Because of its rarity and location, one of these trees has additionally been designated N.M. #163. *Anguilla marmorata* (N.M. #27), a type of nocturnal freshwater eel whose habitat is the coastal rivers and pools, lives in this river. Overlooking this valley, roughly from the Napoli Hotel to the Lion's Hotel, is a narrow landscaped city park that is flanked by a boardwalk.

Woedolgoe

Beyond Cheonjiyeon Waterfall is **Sammae-bong Park**. A pavilion sits atop the hill, while pine trees and grassy meadows run out to the cliff's edge. Local fishermen try their luck in the surf below, and townspeople come out for picnics. The view from this point in either direction along the coast is one of the best on the island! High volcanic cliffs give rugged definition to this sculpted coastline, and here you can see the dramatic effects of the island's violent creation in the tortured shape of its rock. Directly out from the cliff is a solitary pinnacle called Woedolgoe. Legend tells of a fisherman's wife who pined away after her husband was lost at sea. From this spot she gazed out across the water and waited for some sign of his fate. It never came. In grief she died, then became transformed into this lonely rock. Shortly after, as if in sympathy for her suffering, a boulder floated to the base of this pinnacle and attached itself. From a certain angle it looks like the body of a man.

At water's edge in the cliff east of Woedolgoe is a series of 12 natural caves. Beyond those, in the scrabble of jumbled rock at water's edge, are mollusk fossil remains (N.M. #195). The shoreline here, Woedolgoe, several small offshore islands, and Jeongbang Waterfall are all part of **Seogwipo City Marine Park**, ₩1,500 entrance.

Accommodations

On the east side of town are the deluxe-class **Seogwipo KAL Hotel** (tel. 064/733-2001, www.kalhotel.co.kr) and the newer **Paradise Hotel**

Cheju (tel. 064/763-2100). Refurbished, the older and more monolithic Seogwipo KAL Hotel has an unobstructed view of the sea, while the newer Mediterranean-style Paradise Hotel Cheju is tucked into the trees and has a much more homey and comfortable feel. Rooms at the KAL start at ₩200,000, while those at the Paradise run upwards of ₩250,000. The Paradise has rooms in six motifs—Korean, Mediterranean, Scandinavian, European, American, and African, and is architecturally the most unique on the island. On the grounds of the Paradise Hotel, the old Honeymoon Hotel, which was originally built as a getaway retreat for former President Syngman Rhee, has been turned into a fine restaurant. Both these deluxe hotels have a full complement of amenities. Closed for reconstruction after years of neglect, the **Jeju Prince Hotel** (tel. 064/732-9911) is once again open to guests. Set high on the cliff between town and Woedolgoe, it has the most dramatic location in the city.

In town, the third-class Seogwipo Park Hotel is closest to the harbor but has seen better days. Set high above Cheonjiyeon Waterfall and the gorge, the **Seogwipo Lion's Hotel** (tel. 064/762-4141) has the best location in town. Its rooms run ₩50,000–62,000. A number of other small hotels are also sprinkled throughout the city. Among these are the **Napoli Hotel**, down the road from the Lion's, with good views into the valley below and rooms for ₩40,000.

Yeogwan are found throughout town. Of these, try the **Pokpojang Yeogwan** (폭포장여관), the cheaper Jeongshil Yeoinsuk (정실여인숙), or the **Namyangjang Motel** (남양장모텔) near the harbor; the **Hanyanggak Yeogwan** (한양각여관), **Mansugak Yeogwan** (만수각여관), or larger **Star Song Motel** (스타송모텔) behind the bus terminal; or the **Tamnajang Yeogwan** (탐라장여관) or **Donghwajang Motel** (동화장모텔) near the shopping district.

Transportation

Approximately every 20 minutes, highway buses leave Seogwipo from the two small terminals near the central traffic rotary and run in both directions around the island, over both mountain highways, and via two mid-elevation highways to Jeju City. Selected destinations and fares: Jeju City via the round-island highway (₩6,000), Jeju City via the other highways (₩3,600), Jungmun (₩700), Namwon (₩1,200), Pyoseon (₩2,000), Seongsanpo (₩3,000), and Seongpanak (₩2,000).

City buses run throughout town and most have the central rotary on their route. Perhaps those of most use are the following. Bus no. 5 goes to the Donneko hiking trailhead, no. 7 runs close to Jeongbang Waterfall, no. 8 makes its way through the main street of town to the pier and Cheonjiyeon Waterfall, no. 12 goes out to Woedolgoe, and nos. 11 and 200 run to Shin Seogwipo; express city bus nos. 100 and 110 run all the way out to Jungmun Resort Complex, and no. 130 goes past Andeok Valley.

While ferries used to run between Seogwipo and Busan, via Seongsanpo, it seems that they have been discontinued. Check about tickets and departure information at the harbor terminal building if and when this route is reinstated.

Water Tours

Perhaps the most unusual experience in Seogwipo is an underwater tour on the yellow submarine *Maria*. During the tour, which lasts about an hour, the 48-passenger submersible dives off the south around Munseom island to give you a close-up view of the fish community, coral beds, stands of seaweed, and rock formations. With each meter of drop, light and colors change, slowly revealing the Jeju-do underwater world. Ex-

cept during storms, this sub makes seven or eight dives a day, once every hour and a half from 0720, but the dive schedule may change according to season and demand. Make inquiries and buy tickets at the submarine office on the west side of the Seogwipo harbor. Reservations are advised, particularly during summer; ₩49,500 adults, ₩39,600 students, ₩29,700 children.

Also from the Seogwipo harbor, several surface excursion boats make hour-long round-trips up and down the coast and around the nearby islands for ₩15,000–21,500 per person. For information and tickets, visit the tour company office next to the sub office at the excursion pier.

Shinyoung Cinema Museum
신영영화박물관

Located just west of Namwon, this museum gives a brief history of film, presents an overview of Korean movies, and displays technical equipment, posters, Korean movie star portraits, and other film memorabilia. While very little is in English, you can still garner something from the graphic presentation; ₩4,000 entrance. Outside on the lawn are a few sculptures and a refreshment stand. A few minutes down a path in either direction brings you to the rocky, boulder-strewn shoreline. Near here and at other points along this south coast are a number of small private condominiums, built to cater to the growing and increasingly sophisticated Korean tourists who are looking for something more than a stay at a city hotel or *yeogwan*.

East Jeju-do

Pyoseon 표선

Between attractive Jungmun Beach and Seongsanpo there is only one swimming area of note, and that's at Pyoseon [P'yosŏn], the southern end of the eastern mid-island highway. Protected from the sea by a low, sandy headland, a bay is scooped out of the rocky coastline here. Much of the shallow inner bay's bottom is exposed at low tide, but even at high tide the water is shallow, a good place for youngsters to swim. Accommodations, food, and services can be found a few blocks up into town. The mid-island highway connects Pyoseon to Seongeup, San'gumburi, and Jeju City, traversing the gradually ascending grassy mountain slope pockmarked with gumdrop craters, before meeting the East Cross-Island Highway. Buses run every 20 minutes on the round-island road and about every half hour on the road to Seongeup and San'gumburi.

Jeju Folk Village 제주민속촌

On the bay's sandy headland, the Jeju Folk Village was opened in 1987. Unlike the centuries-old village of Seongeup, and more along the lines of the Korean Folk Village in Suwon, this village has been put together to showcase Jeju-do architecture, furnishings, implements, and lifestyle, and its gardens are representative of the island's vegetation. However contrived in this way, most of the several dozen buildings here are authentic, many 100–300 years old, having been moved from their original locations on the island to enhance the learning experience of those who come to visit. Structures include commoners' homes, middle-class houses, a small shaman shrine, and a local government office complex, complete with prison. Periodic musical performances are scheduled and island craftsmen display and sell their wares. Well presented and well kept, worth the ₩5,000 entrance fee, and you can spend a couple of hours if you look at every housing compound. The Jeju Folk Village is open daily 0830–1830 (1730 in winter). Bus directly from Jeju City or walk the one-half kilometer through town toward the sea if you get off along the coastal highway. For additional information, check www.chejufolk.co.kr.

SEONGEUP 성읍

Eight kilometers inland from Pyoseon is Seongeup [Sŏngŭp], the only non-coastal town of significance on the island. From 1423 until just after the end of the Joseon Dynasty (1913), Seongeup was one of Jeju-do's three administrative centers. With its cluster of traditional houses, a Confucian shrine, reconstructed government building, fortress wall remnants, and numerous *dolharubang,* Seongeup is the island's best-preserved old community. Like Hahoe Village in Gyeongsangbuk-Do and Nagan-eup in Jeollanam-Do, Seongeup has been designated a "folklore preservation zone." Because of this status, it has remained free from many of the modernizing mechanisms brought about in other parts of the island by the *Saemaul* (New Village) movement and other government meddling. Here, you get a glimpse of rural island community life, complete with the traditional toilets perched over a corner of the pigpen. Try the back alleys for a look—they're a curiosity! But change has come to Seongeup too. Now you see more vehicles, paved back alleys, electrical wires, television antennae, yards full of modern conveniences, restaurants, and houses vacated only to be set up in a "traditional" manner, some selling trinkets and souvenirs. Still, the real thing exists in Seongeup. Among the 300 or so buildings in the community, several dozen traditional houses have been preserved pretty much the way they have come down through the generations, and these are marked by signboards with some explanation of their history and construction. Be aware that busloads of people come to look at this village, so, while tourists are expected, the obnoxious tourist is not appreciated. Be polite, and ask before entering housing compounds or taking pictures.

Ilgwan-heon, a replica of the former govern-

JEJU-DO

Dolharubang **still stand guard at Seongeup as they have for centuries.**

ment building, sits on the main street near where the highway buses stop. It was part of the local government complex that administered this section of the island from 1423 to 1914, an area known as Jeongeui. Jeongeui Hyanggyo is set back amongst the roped, thatch-roofed houses, which are the rule rather than the exception here. Built in 1416 and moved to its present location when Ilgwan-heon was moved to Seongeup in 1423, this Confucian academy is somewhat different from other Joseon Dynasty *hyanggyo* by facing east and having the main shrine hall and study rooms set side by side. Today, only the main hall, a secondary building, four small gates, and the walls remain. Special spring and fall ceremonies are carried on here as they have been for centuries. Three reconstructed town gates, plus parts of the perimeter wall, have also been reconstructed. Over the years, the village has spread beyond this perimeter enclosure.

Leave your bags at one of the restaurants on the main street while you stroll down these rock-fence-lined alleys, peer into the household compounds, and search for the old grandfather statues (several dozen are scattered throughout town). Plants grow in great profusion, and one 1,000-year-old zelkova elm tree (N.M. #161) stands proudly in the square near the center of town. Many other zelkova and nettle trees in the village are said to be several hundred years old, the remnants of a once much thicker forest. Try a cup of *gosokju*, a thirst-quenching, village-specialty rice wine. With it order *momiljeonggi ddeok*, a type of rolled wheat pancake, or charcoal-broiled pork. Buses pass through town going each direction about once every hour; ₩700 from Pyoseon or ₩2,200 from Jeju City.

San'gumburi 산굼부리

The mountain slope rises gently between Seong-up and the East Cross-Island Highway. Along with the numerous ranches and mushroom farms, a slew of parasitic craters are strewn over this rolling plain like chess pieces on a playing board. Although not the most prominent—it rises gently from pastureland and is not the top of a precipitous hill—San'gumburi is the second largest crater on the island and perhaps the most accessible. (*Gumburi* in the Jeju dialect refers to a major volcanic crater.) Bus from Jeju City, Pyoseon, or Seongeup. Over one-half kilometer across and 140 meters deep, this perfectly shaped crater (N.M. #263), with its thickly forested sides, is a natural botanical garden with over 400 varieties of plants. Set just off the roadway, it costs ₩2,000 to approach the rim; open 0900–1800. You're not permitted to enter the crater itself, but an observation deck on the west side offers a good view into its depth, down to the sea, and up the mountainside. Located in open rangeland, it can be quite windy here so bring a windbreaker. A handful of rock-wall graves dot the outer west slope.

While there are others around the island, several stables nearby and on the way to Seongeup offer group horse rides. Prices vary by time of the year and at each different stable, but expect to pay about ₩20,000 for a half-hour walk. No wild or free-range rides here!

EAST END

Honinji

While out hunting one day, the three progenitors of the Jeju-do people found a wooden box along the coast south of Shinyang. From the box emerged the three princesses from Byeongnang, whom they married. Their marriage took place at Honinji, a natural pond a short way in from the sea. After spending their wedding night at a nearby cave, they returned to the north to settle down, farm crops, and raise cattle.

Seongsan Crater 성산일출봉

Slightly smaller than San'gumburi is the Seongsan crater. Rising from the double-headed peninsula at the eastern end of Jeju-do, this fortress-like crater rises 182 meters straight up from the water. Also called Ilchul-bong ("Sunrise Peak"), this extraordinary upthrust of volcanic rock is considered the first of the 10 famous sights of Jeju-do. A 15-minute walk up the steep stone stairway brings you to the crater rim; ₩2,200 entrance—unless you beat the ticket takers in the morning! Fingers of lava rim the crater lip as if frozen in the action of exploding. Paths run around the rim and cross its basin, but you are not supposed to enter the crater itself now as you once were able to do. Horses often graze in this depression and on the grassy front slope. Have a look around, peer over the edge, but be careful—it's a long way down! Try climbing this crater to watch the sun rise. You'll need to start early—with a flashlight— but once on the top, you'll be treated to a splendid show if the weather permits. The bright morning sun silhouettes the far side of the crater rim, and the color of the sea slowly turns from red to gold to blue. Any month of the year can yield a good sunrise, but late autumn is perhaps best. The views of U-do, in the placid sea to the east, Shinyang Peninsula to the south, and the whole array of parasitic craters marching up the mountainside are also splendid. A second and much shorter pathway takes you from the parking lot to a point overlooking the black sand beach on the east side. Seongsan Crater, the island of U-do, and the seas between are all part of **Seongsan Ilchul-bong Seashore Provincial Park**.

Seongsanpo 성산포

Below Ilchul-bong is the village of Seongsanpo [Sŏngsanp'o], with the island's third-most active harbor and only black-sand beaches. One tiny crescent is tucked into a cove on the east side of the peninsula. The second is a narrow, ribbon-like beach stretching down the narrow isthmus toward Goseong [Kosŏng]. The Japanese dug several caves into the outer walls of the crater before World War II for storing supplies. Long since emptied, the front portions of these caves can still be entered. At the bottom of the horse pasture below the crater lies the small temple Dongam-sa. A tidal dam and highway across the inlet now allow buses to run to Seongsanpo without first having to go through Goseong.

The *munjuran nancho* flourishes along the coast just north of Seongsanpo. Nan-do in particular, some 50 meters off the coast and reachable at low tide, is covered in these flowers. In the amaryllis family, these flowers (N.M. #19) have showy multi-petal heads on tall stalks with long, narrow, dark green blade leaves. Blooming in July and August, they cover the island in a carpet of white. Nearby is an area of pond and reed beds that are used as a winter nesting spot for migratory storks, spoonbills, ducks, and herons.

Directly across the street and down an alley from the entrance to Ilchul-bong is the Sujijang Yeogwan (수지장여관). Around the corner and down near the main intersection in town are the Jaeseongjang Yeogwan (제성장여관) and Seongsanjang Yeogwan Hotel (성산장여관), and on the way to the pier is the fancier Hotel Ilchulbong (호텔일출봉), the best that the town has to offer. Besides these, there are several dozen *minbak* in town, and ordinary restaurants are located on the town's two main streets.

Frequent intercity buses stop in Seongsanpo. Additional intercity buses stop at Goseong on the round-island highway, from where you can transfer to a bus that runs out to this port town.

A small commuter ferry, which also can take a few vehicles, crosses to U-do from the Seongsanpo pier every hour from 0800 to 1800. Buy your ticket and board at the end of the pier beyond the cargo boats; ₩2,000 per person. The crossing takes about 20 minutes. Departure is one-half-hour earlier from U-do. At the other end of the enlarged Seongsanpo pier, tour operators run three excursion boats along the coast. One, a sightseeing tour to various spots nearby and around U-do, leaves hourly throughout the day for ₩15,000; the second is a fishing excursion trip for ₩20,000; and the third is a submarine ride at ₩49,500 for adults that runs several times a day 0730–1750. For each of these, an extra fee of ₩1,000 is tacked on for county park maintenance. The pier is a 15-minute walk from the center of Seongsanpo, but bus no. 701 runs from Goseong through town to the pier.

Shinyang Bay

Two kilometers south of Goseong is the village of Shinyang (신양). A long powdery crescent beach stretches along the head of the bay, and a second, more secluded, beach lies on the bay's east side a short walk from this village. Fossilized marine deposits have been found here. On the west side, a small breakwater has been built as anchorage for a few fishing boats. There are numerous *minbak* in town and an occasional bus stops here on its way from Pyoseon to Goseong. This bay is the place of choice for windsurfers on Jeju-do as the easterly winds swoop down across the mountain's eastern rangeland and across this sheltered inlet. Since 1988, **windsurfing** competitions have been held here. On the east side of the bay is the Korea Windsurfing Association shop where you can rent gear for ₩30,000 for four hours or ₩50,000 for the entire day. While windsurfing can be done throughout the year, it can get fairly cold from late fall to late spring. Scuba gear, raft boats, and water-skiing lessons can also be arranged here.

At the end of this peninsula, which is called Seopjikoji, is a *yeondae* (beacon site). During the Joseon Dynasty, 24 fire-signal towers on the mountain and 38 smoke-signal platforms along the coast were constructed to warn the islanders of enemy attack or other danger. Remains of others can still be seen at various points around the island. An unmanned light near the Seopjikoji *yeondae* now provides a beacon for seafarers. Several winding trails lead over the grassy sand hills of the peninsula to this stone platform, and

at the very tip of the peninsula are seaside rock outcrops and a small crater. From here, Halla-san rises up in the distance to the west, and Ilchulbong pokes out of the sea to the east, what seems like a stone's throw away.

Inland from Shinyang and Goseong are wide fields of rapeseed flower, a type of mustard plant. Known as *yuchaehwa*, these plants bloom a bright yellow in the late spring, and an island festival celebrates their beauty and contribution to the island economy. Pictures of these fields appear in nearly all tourist brochures about the island. Harvested in June, the seed is made into a cooking oil.

U-do 우도

Four kilometers across the narrow strait from Seongsanpo is the quiet farming/fishing island of U-do ("Cow Island"). The flat northern half of this island sweeps up to a cliff on its south end. Hundreds of Jeju-style graves dot the hillside below the lighthouse that tops this promontory. They are squat mounds enclosed by a low square wall of rough-hewn dark-gray volcanic stone. In the clear waters off this island, *haenyeo* dive for their day's catch. These women stay underwater an incredibly long time and explode with a shrill whistle when they break the surface for air. Often a group of 20 to 30 *haenyeo* dive in the cove below the lighthouse. Hardly ever visited by tourists, the women divers of U-do aren't as camera-shy as those on the big island. After their dive, these sturdy, ruddy-checked women change clothes, shoulder their catches, and head home to their household chores. At water's edge below the cliff is a large shallow cave called "Whale Cave." A short distance north of the U-do pier is the island's best beach. A short stretch of crushed white coral, it's a perfect place to watch the sun set behind Halla-san. In recent years, this island has undergone a partial transformation. A condo-style resort has been built on its northern tip and a new ferry pier created to service it.

Peopled in the mid-1800s, the island holds about 1,850 residents today. The main village is located in the center of the island. Where once they would have had only farm implements, many residents today have vehicles. Taking about

20 minutes, a vehicular ferry runs every hour 0800–1800 to and from Seongsanpo with periodic ferries from Chudalhang just up the coast from Seongsanpo. The fare is ₩2,000. Meeting each ferry is a bus that runs to the village in the center of the island. Ask and someone on the ferry should direct you to one of the half dozen *yeogwan* and *minbak* on the island. A few restaurants also are located here. Now part of a county park, an entrance fee of ₩1,000 is charged to all visitors to the island.

NORTH COAST ROAD

Bijarim Nutmeg Forest 비자림

Eight kilometers inland from Saehwa Village is Bijarim [Pijarim], a green botanical gem surrounded by dry land fields and pastureland. This forest of Gaya nutmeg trees (N.M. #374) is one of the few such concentrations in Asia. Over 2,500 trees range from 400 to 800 years old. To add to the delight, the forest harbors several varieties of orchid species. Aside from several walking paths, the forest is preserved in its natural state. The chatter of unseen birds, backlit gnarled branches, and shafts of sunlight streaming through the thick forest canopy creating dancing shadows in the dense ground cover lend a feeling of enchantment. You might expect to see Merlin resting under a tree as you round the corner of one of the trails. It's a pleasant place for a cool summer stroll. The trees' white flowers bloom in spring and the green nuts ripen and drop in autumn. Gathered, dried, and ground, the nuts are used in some herbal medicines and, it is said, were once used for lamp oil. The wood of fallen trees makes fine furniture and ornaments. Buses for Bijarim run between Saehwa and Gimnyeong [Kimnyŏng]. Get off at the Bijarim turnoff; you must walk the one kilometer into the preserve; open 0900–1900, ₩1,600 entrance. A group campground is located directly to the side of the nutmeg forest.

Lava Tubes

Six kilometers north of Pijarim as the crow flies is the most unusual of this island's unique natural phenomena—**Manjang-gul** (만장굴) (N.M. #98). This cave and others nearby are reputed to be one of the world's longest lava tube systems. Discovered in 1947 by a schoolteacher out collecting plants, this cave was not explored for several years because of the island people's strong belief that ghosts and supernatural beings inhabit places unknown to man. Eventually, scientific inquiry triumphed over superstition and a full-scale exploration was done. This lava tube ranges 3–20 meters in width and height and is big enough through most of its length to run a subway train through! Manjang-gul at 8,900 meters, Gimnyeong-gul at 700 meters, and three others nearby with a combined total of about 3,800 meters, make up a cave system that is over 13 kilometers long. The temperature inside fluctuates between a cool 10–13°C while the humidity runs 85–100 percent. Ferns inhabit the entrance, while bats and centipedes make the darker reaches their home. The well-lit first 1,000 meters can be entered. At a fee of ₩2,200, this cave is worth the entry price, especially for those who have never seen this type of formation. The Hyeopjae lava tubes at the opposite end of the island pale in comparison.

The cave's walls have been etched with countless parallel grooves, and these lines illustrate several distinct flowing and hardening periods, the last flow hardening into the relatively even floor. At certain points, sections of the ceiling have fallen, leaving rubble on the floor. One of these is called "couples rock." The reason is obvious—and appropriate for a honeymooners' island! Another fallen piece has been named "the tortoise"; set on a natural pedestal, it looks more like a relief map of Jeju-do than an animal. A broad-based pillar, formed as molten lava poured down from a hole in the ceiling, stands at the far end of this lit section. It must be one of the few "lava stalagmites" in the world—an odd yet intriguing sight.

Two kilometers below Manjang-gul, and one-half kilometer up from the highway, is **Gimnyeong-gul**, often referred to as Sa-gul ("Serpent Cave"). Much shorter than Manjang-gul, each of its four sections measures between 50 and 350 meters in length. This cave has been closed since the late 1980s for safety reasons. Legend says that in the distant past the cave was inhabited by a huge snake. Each year, a nubile virgin from a nearby village was sacrificed to this wrathful reptile to appease its anger and to protect the village from disaster. In the early 16th century, a new administrator came to the area. Deciding that this barbarous act must stop, he himself slew the serpent when it appeared at the cave entrance. The magistrate was praised for his heroic action, but soon afterwards he became physically and mentally enfeebled, and eventually died of an unexplained illness. This incident helps to verify the existence of an old snake cult that once existed on the island, of which the scanty details are imprecise and much speculation abounds. About a dozen buses a day run to the caves from Saehwa and Gimnyeong.

North Coast Beaches

Saehwa, Gimnyeong, and Samyang beaches are frequented mostly by locals. The swimming spot of choice along this coast is **Hamdeok Beach.** Gentle, shallow, and protected, this white beach is only a few minutes from the island's big city, from which large numbers of bathers arrive during the summer. Water toys are another attraction here and these include jet skis, water-skiing, raft rides, and motorboats. Several dozen *minbak* and motels are found in Hamdeok [Hamdŏk], and the Hotel Sunshine sits on a prominent spot just down the bay. The only one along this portion of the coast, the four-star **Hotel Sunshine** (tel. 064/784-2525) is a small but comfortable place with its own restaurant that has rooms for

₩120,000–200,000. Every year, a mini-Ironman marathon is held here; contestants swim 1.5 kilometers, run 10 kilometers, and bicycle 40 kilometers. For Hamdeok use bus no. 10 or 14. Closer in to Jeju City is the smaller **Samyang Beach**, used as much for baking under a pile of hot black sand as for swimming. One block from the highway on the way down to the beach is a **prehistoric village site** (삼양유적지) (H.S. #416) that is being developed with re-created village structures and an exhibition hall for artifacts taken from the ground.

Between Saehwa and Gimnyeong beaches, near the small Haengwon industrial area, are several wind-power electrical generators, an attempt to harness, if only in small part, the vast wind potential of the island. Another small group of wind turbines is located just west of Hyeopjae Beach on the west end of the island.

Hangil Memorial 항일기념관

Just west of the village of Jocheon, this memorial commemorates the effort made by Jeju citizens against the Japanese occupation in the early 1900s. A stone monument to the various movements stands on a knoll along the highway, and inside the exhibition hall are two rooms with photographs, paintings, dioramas, and movies that try to explain the struggle of Jeju residents against repression. Open daily except some holidays 0900–1800 (1700 in winter); the entrance fee is ₩2,000.

Halla-san

At 1,950 meters, Halla-san is the highest peak in South Korea. This mountain *is* the island of Jeju-do. Its low-elevation farm and rangeland rise to meet the dense mid-elevation forests, which in turn give way to mountain meadows, wildflowers, and scrub bush. A craggy-edged crater tops the mountain; the crater "lake," Baengnokdam ("White Deer Lake"), so called because legend says that mountain guardian spirits played here after descending from heaven on white deer, expands when the rains fall and disappears during drier autumn and winter months. Running along the south-central coast of the island is a semitropical climatic zone. The temperate zone blankets the rest of the mountain to about 1,750 meters. From there to the top, encompassing its steep volcanic cone, is a semi-frigid zone.

Heavy rains and swift runoff have cut deep, V-shaped valleys through the mountain's thick volcanic cover on the north, southwest, and south sides. The east slope is the most gentle, punctuated only by a few craters and leisurely streams. Pine, fir, holly, oak, elm, and maple mix together to form lush mountainside forests; stunted juniper, scrub grass, and a few hardy wildflowers cap the peak. Azaleas, rhododendrons, and chrysanthemums are the most common flowering plants in the high meadows. Mushrooms are grown in mid-mountain beds, and blueberries and strawberries grow wild along the streams. Of the more than 1,800 plant species, one of the prettiest is the speckled *hallan* orchid (N.M. #191). The "shaman" frog, several kinds of crane, the tiny rainbow-colored fairy pitta bird, a type of weasel, and many butterflies are indigenous to this mountain environment. Its upper elevation, virgin forest, and animal habitats have been designated Nature Preservation Area #182, and in 1970, 133 square kilometers of the mountaintop were set aside as Halla-san National Park, increased later to 149 square kilometers.

One of the three sacred mountains of Korea, Halla-san was considered the abode of gods. Its reputation even spread to China. The summit of Halla-san can be seen from almost everywhere on the island, and likewise the entire oval gem of Jeju-do, set in an indigo sea, can be seen from Halla-san's lofty peak. Unfortunately, the summit is free from clouds only about one day in ten. On other days, either the peak is entirely covered, or clouds continuously move in and out. The mountain's fascination changes with the year. During spring, colorful flowers bloom in the lowland fields and pink rhododendrons flush the highland meadows with color. All is green, lush, and robust in summer. Autumn colors of the hardwood-tree canopy add a touch of splendor to the hillside forests, and the bleached cream-colored *eoksae* reed indicates approaching cold. In winter, snow comes early and blankets this giant, giving the mountain a stark white purity.

HALLA-SAN NATIONAL PARK
한라산국립공원

Hiking

Halla-san National Park has four major entrances, each with a ranger station where you must register and pay your ₩1,300 entrance fee. Be sure to get a map of the mountain trails at the entrance if you haven't picked up one in Jeju City. From each entrance, one major trail rises to the summit; all are well marked, well maintained, and well used. A fifth entrance and trail starts at the rear of Seogwipo. For safety reasons, park rangers may request that you don't go to the top alone. If you are a single hiker, wait for others at the trailhead and join them for the climb. Almost without exception, Koreans gladly welcome others (especially foreigners) to join their hiking parties—an entertaining and pleasurable experience for all concerned. Be aware that on occasion some mountain trails or portions of them may be closed for the regeneration of the environment or because of inclement weather. Prior to climbing, be sure to verify with a ranger station

HALLA-SAN NATIONAL PARK

To Shin Jeju

To Jeju City

99

11

JEJU COUNTRY CLUB

GWANEUM-SA

CAMPING

CHEONWANG-SA

Ahanahop Valley

Oseungsaeng

CAVE GROTTO

HUT

HUT

Orimok Course

Gwaneum-sa Course

Halla-san National Park

HUT

SEONGPANAK REST AREA

Triangle Peak

HUT

Seongpanak Course

1,000 METER REST AREA

Spring

King's Crown Peak

HUT

Spring

HUT

Spring

Yeongshil Course

Halla-san (1,950 m)

Baengnokdam

PYEONGPUNG-BAWI

OBAEK NAHAN

Spring

Donneko Course

Donneko HUT

99

MOON

© AVALON TRAVEL PUBLISHING, INC.

DONNEKO

To Jungmun

0   1 mi

0   1 km

To Seogwipo

JEJU-DO

or through the tourist office that the trails you intend to use are open.

For those going to the top, rangers ask that you start your climb by 1000 on the longer trails and by 1200 on the shorter trails, and leave the summit by 1630 in summer and 1430 in winter to ensure that no one gets caught out along the trail after dark. If you plan to be on the mountain for more than the day, notify a ranger and stay either at the emergency huts (at least one on every trail), or in the camping spaces nearby. You should not camp inside the summit crater, so as to preserve its fragile ecological system. While on the mountain, use the toilets provided at each hut, or dig a small hole 20 centimeters deep and

completely bury your waste. The use of wood for cooking or bonfires is prohibited; take along a gas stove. A few basic foods can be bought at the Seongpanak, Orimok, and Yeongshil rest areas, and even at a few of the mountain huts during the busy summer months. Still, it's best to pack all you need from town. Carry water and other liquid refreshments with you; mountain springs are found along only three of the trails. The trails themselves don't follow the riverbeds, which in any case don't carry much water except during the early summer rainy season. Sneakers or walking shoes suffice, but take along a sweater or jacket, gloves, and a hat. Even in summer it's cool at the top. Although they are getting better,

Koreans are generally not very conscientious about maintaining a litter-free environment. You can set an example by packing out all that you packed in.

Trails are closed when there is an imminent threat of storm and during heavy snowfalls. Winter hiking is possible at other times, but it's recommended that you hike with someone familiar with the mountain. Weather on Halla-san is unquestionably fickle, so be prepared. Snow often starts in October and stays until April on the upper reaches of the mountain. The most severe conditions are from mid-January to mid-February. Through the winter, as much as four meters of snow can cover the north-slope valleys, two to three meters of snow on the high meadows. At these times, tall poles with bright red flags are put up along open meadow trails. During winter months, temperatures sometimes drop to -30°C, so if you hike the mountain then, be prepared—it's no picnic!

The following five trails ascend Halla-san.

No. 1: The **Yeongshil [Yŏngshil] course**, on the southwest side, is the shortest and fastest trail. From Jeju City or Seogwipo, catch a bus running the West Cross-Island Highway and get off at the Yeongshil entrance (영실입구). With no public transportation on the park road, you must walk the one-and-a-half hours (or hitch a ride) to the park office. From there, a walk to the top and back along this seven-kilometer trail can be done in a leisurely six hours or a more industrious five hours. Starting out gently, the trail quickly becomes steep as it goes up the side of the Yeongshil Valley, which is said to have been the remains of an early crater. Directly across the valley is a group of rock spires called Obaek Nahan ("500 Disciples"), said to represent the followers of Buddha. (Other stories refer to 500 generals or the 500 sons of the island woman Seolmundae.) A short way above these spires is a wide, columnar basalt wall called Pyeongpung-bawi ("Folding Screen Rock"). Once atop the ridge, the trail winds through groves of evergreens, past a spring, and eventually into open meadows. In spring, the meadows are covered with blazing pink rhododendrons. Beyond this

trail's emergency hut, a gradual walk heads through scrub bush and clumps of grass, climaxed by a short, steep climb (aided by metal steps and cables) to the summit.

No. 2: The seven-kilometer-long **Orimok [Ŏrimok] course** goes up the northwest slope, and should take about seven hours up and back. Bus via the West Cross-Island Highway to the Orimok entrance (어리목입구), and walk one kilometer to the park office. Near the office is a *sanjang,* where you can spend the night, and a short distance up the trail are two huts. The first third of this trail, through a dense forest of short pine and bamboo, is relatively steep and slippery. Between the spring, near the top edge of the forest, and the upper mountain hut, where this trail joins the Yeongshil trail, the path is more gradual and wends through grassy fields and around volcanic boulders.

No. 3: The **Gwaneum-sa course** leads up the north slope. Take a bus to the Jeju Country Club turnoff, and walk four kilometers to the park entrance from there, passing the temple Gwaneum-sa on the way. This nine-kilometer trail requires about five hours going up; its a continuously strenuous course, used by those out for a hard climb. It runs past a natural grotto and a mushroom farm before coming to two mountain huts. From here the trail leads up along Gaemimok Ridge, between the north slope's two deepest valleys. Continue on at an ant's steady pace, following the trail as it dips down into the valley. High above, flanking this valley, are two peaks. The one to the west is Triangle Peak, the one to the east King's Crown. Across the river is a third hut, from where it's a steep climb of over an hour to the crater rim. Of the five, this route generally has the most snow. It also offers the best spring and autumn colors, thanks to a profusion of cherry and maple trees along the way.

No. 4: The **Seongpanak [Sŏngp'anak] course** runs up the mountain's east slope. From either Jeju City or Seogwipo, take a bus over the East Cross-Island Highway and get off at the Seongpanak rest stop (성판악휴게소). Nearly 10 kilometers long, this is the most gradual of the five trails. It takes about five hours to hike from the rest stop to the summit. Starting out in thick woods over a rocky trail, the path opens up only in its upper reaches to grassy fields and meadows of azaleas, songbirds, and *shiromi*, whose nuts are used in some Chinese medicine preparations; closer to the top are fir and yew trees and various wildflowers. About six kilometers up is a freshwater spring with good drinking water. From the second mountain hut at the azalea meadow, about 1,400 meters elevation, it's at least an hour's walk before the final ascent to the peak. There are few distance views along this trail until you approach the top.

No. 5: The trail with the greatest rise in elevation, and by far the least often used, is the **Donneko [Tonnek'o] course,** on the mountain's south slope. Take Seogwipo city bus no. 5 to the trailhead. This 12-kilometer climb takes more than five hours going up, and the first third runs through private land. Three-quarters of the way to the top is an emergency hut, and farther

along, a secondary trail on the left comes in from below. The final ascent up the crater's sharp southern rim is very precipitous.

Aheunahop Valley

Below Oseungsaeng crater is the well-known Aheunahop Valley. Its jumbled contours, cascades, falls, and pools give great character to this unique section of the mountain, and make a fine getaway from the heat of the city. To reach this valley, take a highway bus along the West Cross-Island Highway and get off at the Cheonwang-sa entrance (천왕사입구). The trail leads one kilometer up to a Y, where the right-hand path leads to **Fairy Nymph Waterfall**. The waterfall is in a "wet" valley, where water stays in the stream year-round, and because of the thick forest cover it remains relatively cool even during the summer heat. The left trail goes up to the temple Cheonwang-sa [Ch'ŏnwang-sa] and farther on to a small cave grotto in this weirdly convoluted hillside.

Jeollanam-Do
전라남도

Jeollanam-Do [Chŏllanam-Do] occupies the southwestern corner of the peninsula. With 2.2 million inhabitants, it's the fourth most populous province; at 11,900 square kilometers, it's the third-largest in area. To the north is Jeollabuk-Do, the other half of the old Jeolla Province and the cultural region known as Honam. Gyeongsangnam-Do lies over the provincial boundary to the east, while the South and West seas wash its coast. A province of extremely varied physical features, broad, bountiful agricultural plains glide down its western side, while one of the peninsula's broadest mountain massifs rises along its eastern border. More than any other province, Jeollanam-Do's indented 6,400-kilometer-long coastline is sculpted with contorted peninsulas and intruding bays. Off the coast lie islands almost beyond count.

Jeollanam-Do has a rich cultural past. Historical and cultural remains are numerous, and traditional arts and crafts are still practiced. However, it is considered by many (particularly those who do not live there) a provincial backwater, out of the mainstream of Korean development—a situation that is only slowly being redressed. Although Jeollanam-Do has been less

©ROBERT NILSEN

Nagan Folk Village

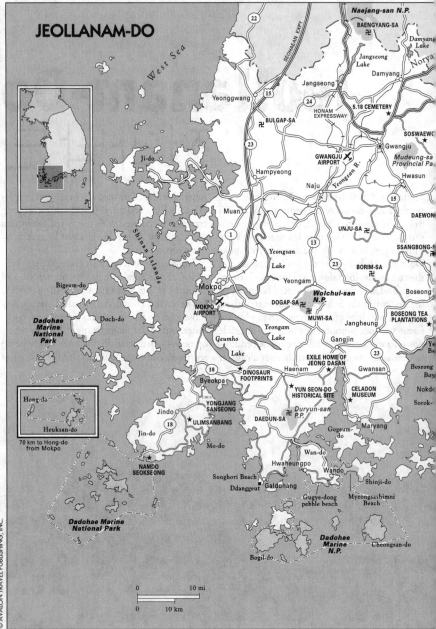

JEOLLANAM-DO

West Sea

Naejang-san N.P.

BAENGYANG-SA 卍

Damyang Lake

Jangseong Lake

Jangseong

Damyang

Norye

Yeonggwang

HONAM EXPRESSWAY

5.18 CEMETERY ★

SOSWAEWO

BULGAP-SA 卍

Ji-do

GWANGJU AIRPORT ✕

○ Gwangju

Soswae-sa

Hampyeong

Mudeung-sa Provincial Pa

Naju

Hwasun

Muan

DAEWON

UNJU-SA 卍

Yeongsan Lake

SSANGBONG-S

Shinan Islands

Yeongsan

BORIM-SA 卍

Yeongam

Boseong

Bigeum-do

Mokpo

Wolchul-san N.P.

DOGAP-SA 卍

Doch-do

MOKPO AIRPORT ✕

MUWI-SA 卍

BOSEONG TEA PLANTATIONS ★

Dadohae Marine National Park

Geumho Lake

Yeongam Lake

Jangheung

Gangjin

Ye Be

EXILE HOME OF JEONG DASAN ★

Boseong Bay

18

Byeokpa

DINOSAUR FOOTPRINTS

Haenam

Gwansan

Nokdo

Hong-do

Jindo

YONGJANG SANSEONG

YUN SEON-DO HISTORICAL SITE ★

CELADON MUSEUM

Sorok-

18

ULIMSANBANG

Duryun-san P.P.

Heuksan-do

Jin-do

DAEDUN-SA

Maryang

70 km to Hong-do from Mokpo

Mo-do

Gogeum-do

NAMDO SEOKSEONG ★

Hwaheungpo

Wan-do

Songhori Beach

Wando

Shinji-do

Ddanggeut

Galduhang

Gugye-dong pebble beach

Myeongsashimni Beach

Dadohae Marine National Park

Dadohae Marine N.P.

Cheongsan-do

Bogil-do

0   10 mi

0   10 km

JEOLLANAM-DO

economically developed than other regions of the country, it has not lagged in food production. Its wide agricultural plains produce some of the most plentiful harvests in the country. Above-average rainfall and mild temperatures add to the productivity of the rich soil.

Jeollanam-Do contains five cities. Yeosu, Suncheon, and Gwangyang are clustered in the southeastern corner of the province, and together make up the largest population concentration outside Gwangju. Gwangyang has arisen only during the last two decades, due to the establishment of industrial complexes. Like Yeosu and Suncheon, Mokpo and Naju are old communities that continue to expand in girth. In 1986, Gwangju was administratively split from the province. However, it still serves as the provincial capital until a new government complex is finished outside of Mokpo. Mokpo and Yeosu are the province's largest ports and most important coastal cities. The majority of Jeollanam-Do's established industry is concentrated in Gwangju, Yeosu, and Mokpo, while the new industrial area of Gwangyang specializes in steel and chemical production and related industries. Whether for business or to experience its rich cultural legacy, visit its numerous temples, climb its mountains, fish its seas, swim off its beaches, travel its islands, or explore its unfrequented places, Jeollanam-Do is worth a visit.

For additional information, see www.provin.jeonnam.kr on the Web.

The Land

The Sobaek Mountains slice through the middle of South Korea, ending in the Jiri Massif, the lofty stronghold in eastern Jeollanam-Do. Although its highest peaks lie in Gyeongsangnam-Do, Nogodan and Banya-bong are within Jeollanam-Do, the latter being the highest peak in the province. The Noryang Mountains strike off from the Sobaek range just north of Jiri-san, and run west to the sea. This relatively low range roughly corresponds with the province's northern border. Other mountains here, independent of these major ranges, are located in provincial parks. The most significant are Mudeung-san, Jogye-san, Wolchul-san, and Duryun-san.

Two major rivers flow through Jeollanam-Do. The longest, the Seomjin (212 meters), starts in Jeollabuk-Do, but its tributaries drain the west and south slopes of Jiri-san. Flowing through the rugged eastern region of the province and emptying into the sea at Gwangyang, this river creates a natural border with Gyeongsangnam-Do south of Jiri-san. The Yeongsan River (116 km) and its many tributaries, on the other hand, flow more gently through the wide agricultural plains of western Jeollanam-Do. Near the city of Mokpo, the Yeongsan River has been dammed by a tidal barrage creating Yeongsan Lake. Three reservoirs have also been constructed on Yeongsan River tributaries, creating Naju-ho Lake east of Naju, Jangseong-ho Lake south of Naejang-san Provincial Park, and Damyang-ho Lake north of the provincial town of Damyang. The largest reservoir in the province is Juam-ho Lake, west of Jogye-san Provincial Park, which captures the Seomjin River. Together these reservoirs help alleviate flooding, increase irrigation potential, create electricity, and provide for recreational opportunities. Numerous others have been more recently built and are sprinkled throughout the province.

Jeollanam-Do's southern coast is sculpted by huge bays and thrusting peninsulas. Its waters are deep and clear, unlike the silty waters of the shallow and less indented west coast. Although tidal fluctuation is great along both coastlines, it's most severe on the west coast. During low tide, huge mudflats are exposed, and the lower ends of rivers flow in reverse with the incoming tide. Jeollanam-Do's half-dozen peninsulas reach into the sea like twisted fingers on a chubby hand. The largest lie along the south coast on either side of Suncheon Bay. As the south coast has slowly been submerging over the millennia, islands have been created close to shore. Presumably, the remaining peninsulas will themselves become islands as water creeps across their narrow necks. The nature of this coastal area and inner-island periphery makes for slow transportation.

Jeollanam-Do has nearly 2,000 islands, about 275 of which are inhabited, with a total island population of just less than 200,000. (Due to land reclamation projects, the total number of islands, length of coastline, and island population have slowly been shrinking over the past several decades.) The largest island, Jin-do, is the third-largest in the country, while those of medium size include Dolsan-do, Gogeum-do, Wan-do, and Ji-do. Though hundreds are little more than specks of green and gray on a blue velvet sea, a great number of even the tiny ones are inhabited and cultivated. This punchbowl of islands is a fisherman's dream. Yellow corvina, sea bream, and rays are numerous. Eel, octopus, and abalone are harvested along the coast, while the sea between the coast and Jeju-do is known for its silvery knife fish. Most islanders are independent fishermen, but the ports of Mokpo, Yeosu, and Wan-do harbor the greatest number of fishing boats. Until the industry took a nosedive not so many years ago, Heuksan-do was one of the country's principal whaling ports (the other was Jangsaengpo at Ulsan).

As you might expect, there are a fair number of beaches in the province, yet due to the shallow, silted nature of the West Sea and the substantial tidal change, few are good. The largest and best beaches are along the south coast at Shinji-do, Yulpo, Sumun-ni, and Songho-ri. Smaller beaches are found close to Mokpo and on the Shinan Islands. Hong-do and Wan-do have pebble beaches. Manseong-ni beach in Yeosu is a black-sand beach. Naro-do, Banjukpo, and Mangdeok beaches all lie close to Yeosu.

History

When the early clans on the peninsula began to congeal into formative groups, the result in this region was the loosely related Mahan state. By the 4th century A.D., the Mahan people had evolved into the Baekje Kingdom, which had early contact and trade with the Chinese and Japanese. In 660, the Baekje Kingdom succumbed to Silla forces, and became an integral part of the united peninsula. During the Hideyoshi Invasions of 1592–97, Jeollanam-Do suffered great damage at the hands of the invading Japanese army. Land battles were fought, and most cities, fortresses, temples, and other important establishments were razed. Great naval battles took place amongst its islands; one in particular, between

Jin-do and the mainland, used an underwater cable to sink ships. During the Joseon Dynasty, Jeollanam-Do was often used to exile political and religious opponents, and dissenters of all stripes. Suffering with the rest of the country during the Mongol invasions of the 1600s and the Japanese occupation of the early 20th century, it has basically been out of history's limelight during the past several hundred years.

Arts and Culture

In the past, Jeollanam-Do was the site of officially sponsored ceramic kilns. The most well-known are the kilns of Gangjin. These kilns produced a great deal of famous Goryeo celadon, still prized for its lucid color and artistic skill. Today Goryeo celadon reproductions are fired at new pottery factories in this area. Remains of Joseon Dynasty kilns are located nearby in Gwansan. Other kiln sites are located near Suncheon, Boseong, Muan, Hampyeong, Yeonggwang, and Gwangju.

A branch of the national museum is located in Gwangju, the county's only maritime museum in Mokpo, and several other towns and temples offer small museums and exhibition halls. Jeollanam-Do claims 17 National Treasures (N.T.), over 100 Treasures (T.), 35 Historical Sites (H.S.), and 43 National Monuments (N.M.). Of the Intangible Cultural Assets (I.C.A.), the best-known are Gwansan *Gosaeum nori,* a "tank" game in which two teams propel massive wood and straw structures high on their shoulders, pushing them against the opponents' structure with the purpose of dislodging the opposing rider; and *ganggangsullae,* a gently swirling circle dance with accompanying song, traditionally performed on the full moon of the eighth lunar month. Nowadays, however, both are performed at cultural festivals nationwide.

Jeollanam-Do features more bamboo than all other provinces combined. Aside from its use in construction and furniture, baskets of all shapes and sizes, fans, mats, blinds, and artistic sculptures are made. Damyang is Korea's bamboo center. Roll-up rush mats and screens are made in and near Boseong. Of natural and dyed grasses, these household items have traditionally been presents

to newlyweds. Haenam is known for its skilled jade carvings. Although various designs are crafted, common pieces include vases, incense burners, votive objects, Buddhist statuary, and animal figurines. Small silver knives, traditionally used for self-protection by both men and women, have been produced in Gwangyang for centuries. Women also employed the knives to commit suicide when their virtue was violated and/or safety imminently threatened. The commercial centers of Gwangju and Naju have for centuries manufactured prized nacre lacquerware furniture. The fine craftsmanship is known throughout the country. Woven hemp cloth is made in Gokseong.

Jeollanam-Do is also known for its products of nature—one is man's best friend. A designated Natural Asset, the pure-bred Jin-do dog has been raised on the island of Jin-do since Neolithic times. Dried laver is a special product of Wan-do and Haenam, Yeonggwang is known for dried yellow corvina, small octopuses are taken in large quantities from Yeongsan Lake near Mokpo, and the fields surrounding Naju put forth tons of peaches and pears. In late summer, the hillsides of Mudeung-san, above Gwangju, sprout sweet watermelon. Along with the hills of Boseong, Mudeung-san also produces some of the country's best green-leaf tea.

Transportation

Gwangju, Yeosu, and Mokpo are connected to Seoul by daily air service. In addition, Gwangju is linked by daily flights across the peninsula to Busan and across the water to Jeju-do. With a scheduled opening in 2003, a new international airport is in the works at Muan, just north of Mokpo. Ground transportation to and from Jeollanam-Do is now quite convenient, though only since the late 1960s have major rail lines and expressways reached it and the highways been paved. The Honam rail line runs south from Daejeon to Jangseong, Songjeong-ni, and Naju before going on to Mokpo. The Jeolla line makes its way from Iksan via Namwon, Gokseong, and Suncheon to Yeosu. Starting in Mokpo, the Gyeongjeon line first runs north to Gwangju before turning east toward Suncheon and continuing on through Gyeongsangnam-Do to Busan. Four expressways thread their way through the province, two running through Gwangju. The Honam Expressway (no. 25) drops down from Daejeon and connects Gwangju to Suncheon. The Namhae Expressway (no. 10) starts in Suncheon and runs across the south coast to Busan, but an extension westward is being constructed. Crossing the Sobaek Mountains from Daegu to Gwangju is the '88 Olympic Expressway (no. 12), and this road is also getting an extension as far as Muan where it meets the Seohaean Expressway (no. 15) which runs up the western coastal region from Mokpo to Incheon. Future plans call for two additional expressways, one that circles the city of Gwangju, and another that runs from Jinju through Namwon to Suncheon, cutting across the eastern edge of the province. Major towns in every county are connected by the extensive highway system, and rural villages can be reached by bus from the county seats. Even with these extensive systems, the physical features of the province slow travel considerably. While Wan-do has long been connected to the peninsula by bridge, two graceful suspension bridges, both constructed in the early 1980s, connect Jin-do and Dolsan-do to the mainland. The highway across the new tidal dams near Mokpo allows for much faster connections to Gangjin, Haenam, and Jin-do.

Like thin threads drawn across an azure silk cloth, the extensive domestic ferry network spreads out from Mokpo to the numerous islands of this province and to Jeju-do, and there are international connections from Mokpo to Lian Yun Gang, China. The island port of Wan-do also has ferries to Jeju-do and the many small islands along the south coast. From Yeosu, the third major port in Jeollanam-Do, regular ferries connect to Jeju-do and the islands south of the Goheung Peninsula. Maryang and Nok-dong are secondary ports with mostly short-run local routes.

Jiri-san

Jiri-san [Chiri-san] is one of the sacred mountains of South Korea. At the tail end of the Sobaek Mountains, it rises in a broad massif not far from the south-central coast of the peninsula. Its highest peak, Cheonwang-bong (1,915 meters), is the highest elevation in peninsular South Korea. Cheonwang-bong is located in Gyeongsangnam-Do, at Jiri-san's eastern end. Nogodan (1,507 meters), on the other hand, lies in Jeollanam-Do, the western end of the central ridgeline. Between these two peaks, more than half a dozen others rise to over 1,500 meters in height. From this main ridgeline, long lean secondary ridges and six major valleys push out into the surrounding countryside. Within the valleys are 10 tall waterfalls. Primarily of granite, this mountain mass is characteristically rounded and gentle. Even though the valleys are deep and the peaks lofty, there's little dramatic rock formation like the spires and pinnacle towers of Seorak-san and Daedun-san. The more voluptuous, curvilinear lines of Jiri-san resemble those of Sobaek-san and Odae-san. Jiri-san stretches out its ridges like fingers of a hand, opening its palm in welcome, coaxing the hardy and adventuresome to come, explore, and be immersed in its charm. The whole of Jiri-san has been designated Historic and Scenic Site #7.

The sunrise from Cheonwang-bong and the sunset from Nogodan are without parallel. Often when the valleys are overcast, this chain of peaks sticks up like the scaly back of a contorted dragon floating on a sea of fleecy white clouds. Piagol Valley is best-known for its autumn tints, as splendid as anywhere in the country. Cool weather and the change of season paint the maple, oak, elm, and ash in flames of color. Baemsagol, Chilseon, upper Baengmu-dong, and the lower Guryong valleys have all long been appreciated for their rugged features, waterfalls, pools, rapids, boulder-strewn streams, and streamside scenery. An Azalea Festival takes place every year at Saeseok Meadow (1,600 meters) in late May or early June, when blossoms splash the field with tones of red and pink. If you're there, join the thousands of people who hike to the meadow to view this display of color.

Bold Jiri-san has a thick, virgin forest cover, with over 800 varieties of plants. Pines and other evergreens are the most prevalent trees, although in select valleys—Piagol being the prime example—hardwoods are in great number. Aside from the trees, about 200 kinds of edible plants, 175 medicinal herbs, 11 types of mushrooms, over 150 varieties of birds, and three dozen mammals find a home on these slopes. Once, when Jiri-san was a long hard trip from established communities, its slopes hosted larger populations of wildlife. Today, the tigers have vanished, and the bear, deer, and other large animals are few in number; badgers, sables, and other small animals and birds now rule the hills. Of these plants and animals, 11 are protected by law as endangered species. After years of strict maintenance, vegetation is returning to areas that were mostly barren or very degraded.

Only a few small farming communities have established themselves deep in the folds of this mountain, and until recently have largely been cut off from the rest of the country. The most notable example is the traditional village of Cheonghak-dong, high on the southeastern slope of the mountain above Hadong. Jiri-san proved to be a wonderful location for Buddhist monks seeking deep mountain retreats for their monastic way of life, and today seven major temples can be found around its base, and dozens of smaller temples and hermitages are strewn here and there throughout the hills.

During the early 1900s, missionaries built vacation homes high on the hillside below Nogodan. This community was used until World War II, after which it was largely abandoned and summer homes were newly established at Daecheon Beach, west of Daejeon. Gaping skeletal remains of these stone summer retreats can still be seen near the Nogodan mountain hut.

Jiri-san has also proved to be a (relatively) safe hiding place for military holdouts. During and after the Korean War, the deep valleys of Jiri-

san, like other rugged mountain areas in South Korea, were used as strongholds for bands of North Korean soldiers cut off during their army's northern retreat. It took several years to flush them from the hills.

JIRI-SAN NATIONAL PARK
지리산국립공원

Established in 1967, Jiri-san National Park was the country's first and, with 440 square kilometers, is still the largest land-based national park. Cloaking the mountain at an elevation of roughly 700 meters and above, the park spreads out over three provinces, each having a branch headquarters. The park entrance fee is W3,000, which includes entry to the major temples in each valley; ticket booths are located at principal trailheads and access points.

Hiking

Nine mountain huts conveniently located along the park's trails charge W5,000 per night for use of the wood-floored sleeping areas. All are open during the busy summer and fall seasons, but nearly all are closed through winter and spring. These huts now supply sleeping gear, so now all you need to bring with you is food to prepare in the community kitchen. Each hut also stocks a limited supply of basic food items, but never count on it; pack in all you'll require. Half a dozen large-group campsites have been cleared near several of the trailheads and a few small sites are located along the ridge trail.

Major trails are well marked and easy to follow. A long ridge trail connects Nogodan and Cheonwang-bong, and over a dozen major trails run up to meet it. The longest walk in the park (about 65 km), takes you from Hwaeom-sa to Daewon-sa. It takes three or more long days to walk from one end of the mountain to the other; most people simply enjoy a day-long or part-day hike up one of the valleys, returning by sundown.

For many, the first access to the mountain is by way of the trail that leads from Hwaeom-sa to Nogodan. This steep trail (four hours) takes you through the forest alongside a sparkling stream. One camping area is just below the temple and

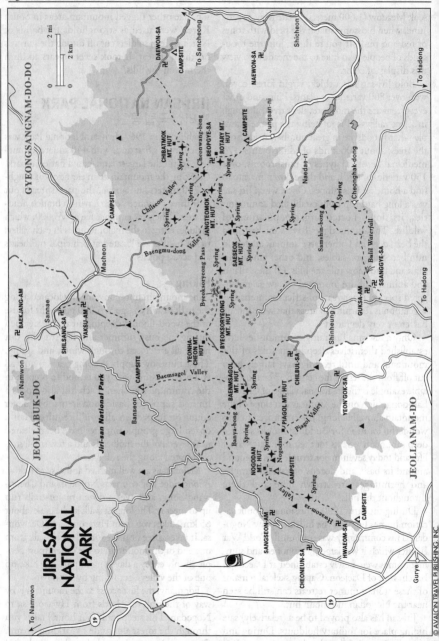

GYEONGSANGNAM-DO-DO

To Sancheong

DAEWON-SA
CAMPSITE

NAEWON-SA

To Hadong

Shicheon

Jungsan-ni

Cheonwang-bong
Spring
CHIBATMOK
MT. HUT
BEOPGYE-SA
ROTARY MT.
HUT
CAMPSITE
Naedae-ri

Chilseon Valley
Spring
CAMPSITE

Chilseon Valley
Spring
Spring
JANGTEOMOK
MT. HUT
Spring
Spring
Cheonghak-dong

Spring
Samshin-bong

Baengmu-dong Valley
Spring
SAESEOK
MT. HUT
Spring

Macheon

Byeoksoryeong Pass
Spring
Spring

BAEKJANG-AM
Sannae
SHILSANG-SA
YAKSU-AM
Byeoksoryeong
Spring
BYEOKSORYEONG
MT. HUT

GUKSA-AM
Buil Waterfall
SSANGGYE-SA

To Namwon
JEOLLABUK-DO

YEONHA-
CHEON MT.
HUT

Shinheung

To Hadong

Jiri-san National Park
Baemsagol Valley
CAMPSITE
Banseon
BAENMSAGOL
MT. HUT
Spring
CHILBUL-SA

JEOLLANAM-DO

Banya-bong
Spring
PIAGOL MT. HUT
Piagol Valley
YEON'GOK-SA

NOGODAN
MT. HUT
Spring
Nogodan
CAMPSITE
Spring

JIRI-SAN
NATIONAL
PARK

SANGSEON-AM

Hwaeom-sa Valley
Spring
CAMPSITE

HWAEOM-SA
CHEONEUN-SA

Gurye
19

To Namwon
19

© AVALON TRAVEL PUBLISHING, INC.

another is just beyond the mountain hut at the top of the trail. Below the Nogodan hut, a few brick chimneys poking out of the overgrowing vegetation mark the sites of the more than 50 houses once used by missionaries for summer holidays. Below the actual peak, which is off-limits, a piled-stone shrine has been erected to the goddess of the mountain.

Running mostly through low trees and bushes, the ridge trail leads from the Nogodan hut to Cheonwang-bong, with only a few short, steep sections on the way. Freshwater springs are located near each of the five huts along this trail. The Baemsagol hut is only 200 meters off this path, down the Baemsagol Valley trail to the north, and the Piagol hut is about 20 minutes down the Piagol Valley. The Piagol hut is managed by Mr. Ham, a mountain resident since the early 1970s. A personable, talkative fellow, he *knows* the mountain, and tries to inculcate in hikers a keen awareness of the environment and a spirit of oneness with nature. The Piagol Valley is one of the most spectacular in the mountain. Covered in virgin forest, with many trees several hundred years old, this valley has great autumn colors. A secondary trail leaves the ridge and runs up to Banya-bong (1,720 meters), where you'll see an inordinate number of dead trees standing in spindly disarray, a sign of one evolutionary step in the changing condition of the forest. From Banya-bong, one ridge trail and one valley trail lead down the north slope to the road below. From the Nogodan hut to the Baemsagol hut is about three hours, and from there on to the Yeonha-cheon hut another two hours or more. Another hour and a half brings you to the Byeoksoryeong hut which is located close to a track that runs over the mountain pass. Continuing on to the Saeseok hut requires about three hours, and from there to Cheonwang-bong, passing Jangteomok hut, is an additional three hours.

From Cheonwang-bong, one trail continues east, running down the ridge to the Chibatmok hut and on to the temple **Daewon-sa**—a five-hour walk. Established in 548 and now kept by nuns, Daewon-sa preserves a nine-story stone pagoda (T. #1112) from its earliest years. About a kilometer below the temple is a village and bus stop from where you can get a ride to Jinju (₩3,200) or Sancheong. Going south from the peak, a second trail leads steeply down the ridge to the tiny temple of **Beopgye-sa**. Dedicated to the Goddess of Mercy, its small halls cling to the side of the mountain. In its courtyard, seated solid on a well-placed boulder, is a three-tier pagoda (T. #473). Passing Rotary hut and a natural spring a few minutes below this temple, the trail continues down to the village of **Jungsan-ni** (중산리). The walk from Cheonwang-bong to Jungsan-ni requires about three hours, and from there buses run to Jinju (₩3,500). The Gyeongsangnam-Do branch park office is located farther down this road in the town of **Shincheon**. A third and much less frequented trail leads north from the top into the deep and twisting Chilseon Valley. Count on at least six hours to reach the village of **Macheon** (마천), from where buses run to Hamyang (₩2,000) or Sancheong (₩3,100).

From the Jangteomok and Saeseok huts, trails lead north into the Baengmu-dong Valley by three routes, each requiring at least three hours from the ridge. One trail from Jangteomok follows a ridge, but the other two run through narrow valleys flush with waterfalls. Buses from here run to Namwon, Sancheong, and Jinju. Also from the two ridge huts, trails lead down the southern slope of the mountain: from Jangteomok to Jungsan-ni and from Saeseok to Naedae-ri (each about a three-hour walk). Buses from Jungsan-ni and Naedae-ri run to Jinju. In addition, a long trail (nine hours) follows the ridge south of Saeseok hut to Samshin-bong, there turning west and continuing to follow the ridge. This trail finally drops down into the Ssanggye-sa valley, passing Bulil Waterfall. A shorter valley trail to the southwest drops down to the village of Shinheung (four hours). From Shinheung, buses pass Ssanggye-sa on the way to Hadong. Also from Shinheung, a little-used road runs up to the temple Chilbul-sa, and from there an infrequently used path goes steeply up to the ridge (about three hours). Yeon'gok-sa is the start of a four-hour trail through Piagol Valley to the ridge, most often visited in autumn, when the hillsides are awash with yellow and crimson, and the colors reflected in the many pools of the stream.

Perhaps the most picturesque of the mountain trails goes through Baemsagol Valley. This gradual five-hour walk takes you along a grandly beautiful, boulder-strewn river that races around rocks, tumbles over timbers, and falls from one pool to another via waterslides and rapids. Here you'll have fine water scapes, a palette full of colors in autumn, and plenty of places to picnic or simply cool your tender toes in the refreshing stream. At the bottom of this valley is the village of **Banseon** (반선), known for the honey that it makes, where there are buses to Namwon (₩3,200), a handful of *yeogwan* and restaurants, and the Jeollabuk-Do branch park office.

Hwaeom-sa 화엄사

Of the seven major temples of Jiri-san, the largest and most renowned is Hwaeom-sa [Hwaŏm-sa]. Founded in 544 by Yeon'gi Josa (said to have been an Indian monk), Hwaeom-sa was established during Buddhism's infant years in the country. Expanded and rebuilt by Uisang in the mid-600s and throughout the centuries periodically renovated, it was totally destroyed during the Imjin War of 1592, but rebuilt three decades later. Today, it's one of the most respected and largest temple compounds in the country. Preserved here are three National Treasures, four Treasures, one Natural Monument, and over a dozen other cultural properties. Around the year 850, tea was planted on the Korean peninsula on the mountainside above Hwaeom-sa, and some believe descendants of those tea bushes still live in the forest behind the temple.

About a kilometer up from the bus stop, past a long series of portly *sari budo*, you'll walk through the three front gates and around the lecture pavilion to the multi-level courtyard. The first two gates are rather small but the third holds large molded statues of the four heavenly devas. In the lower courtyard are two similar yet distinct five-tier pagodas (T. #132 and #133); the left-hand structure is highly embellished with relief carvings of the 12 zodiac figures. Directly ahead on the upper level is the main hall (T. #299).

Hwaeom-sa Gakhwang-jeon

This Joseon Dynasty structure has three large figures on its altar, the central one being the Vairocana Buddha. Gakhwang-jeon (N.T. #67) not only dwarfs the main hall but, with its two-tier roof, is also the largest of the older temple buildings in the country. What you see is the original structure. Constructed in 1703 and preserved by good fortune, it's open on the inside to the top roof—its cavernous interior is imposing. On the altar are seven figures. In the middle sits the Seokgamoni Buddha, usually enshrined in the main hall; the Amita and Dabo Buddhas sit to the sides. Flanking them are the bodhisattvas Gwaneum, Bohyeon, Munsu, and Jijeok.

Directly in front of this immense hall stands a five-meter-high stone lantern (N.T. #12), largest of its kind in the country. Next to it is a squat *sari budo* (T. #300), whose base stone consists of four lion figures. Behind and above Gakhwang-jeon is a unique five-meter-high granite pagoda (N.T. #35), with a three-tier top balanced on four lion-shaped pedestals. Each of the lions represents one of the four primary emotions—love, sorrow, anger, and joy—but their features are somewhat difficult to distinguish. Under the three-tier top stands a human figure with hands clasped together at its breast. Embellished with a lotus design, its base stone has been adorned with a dozen *aspara* figures. Other sculpted figures appear on different surfaces of this pagoda. To the front of the pagoda is an unusual lantern that has a squatting figure set under its upper portion in place of a thick pedestal. Some have suggested this figure represents the temple's founder offering obeisance to his mother, the standing figure of the pagoda.

Other buildings at this temple are the judgment hall, hall of disciples, hall of portraits (of its more famous priests), and a storehouse of wood printing blocks. Of a more fragile nature are a mural painting (T. # 301) and a stone-carved copy of part of the *Hwaeom Sutra* (T. #1040), after which the temple has been named. Here as well is an old higan cherry tree (N.M. #38). The trail to Nogodan starts to the right of the signboard at the temple's entrance, and passes the hermitage **Gucheon-am**, the main building of which has several pillars that are not rounded

in the usual manner but left in their attractive natural shape. A half dozen other hermitages lie on the surrounding hillside.

Just below Hwaeom-sa is **Namaksa.** Otherwise known as Haak-dan, this shrine is set up for the mountain spirits of Jiri-san, one of the five great mountains in Korea. Periodic ceremonies are done here in rites that stem from shamanistic origins. A typical Joseon-era structure, this shrine here functions very much like the similar Jungak-dan shrine on Gyeryong-san outside Daejeon.

The village below Hwaeom-sa is full of accommodations and restaurants. While numerous smaller hotels, *yeogwan,* and *minbak* are located here, the first-class **Jiri-san Plaza Hotel** (tel. 061/782-2171) is a short distance up the road toward the temple. Room rates run ₩121,000, with suites from ₩150,000–500,000. From the bus station at Hwaeom-sa village, buses run multiple times a day until late afternoon to Seongsam-jae and the track to Nogodan (₩2,950), and to Gwangju (₩5,500), Jinju (₩6,400), Namwon (₩2,600), Gurye (₩700), Busan (₩11,700), Yeosu (₩5,500), and Hadong (₩2,000).

Other Temples

Several valleys east of Hwaeom-sa is Piagol Valley, which hosts the temple **Yeon'gok-sa** [Yŏn'gok-sa] (연곡사). Built by the monk Yeon'gi in the same year that Hwaeom-sa was founded, it was destroyed in 1592 during the Japanese invasion, rebuilt in 1627, and once again destroyed during the Korean War. Partially rebuilt since then, it now has only a few buildings, but it's obvious from the size of the site and the number of terraced levels that this was a much larger place in the past. Several stone monuments from the early years have survived. The east and north *sari budo* (N.T. #53 and #54) are both highly decorated with relief carvings, while four other stone objects (T. #151-154) are plainer. While the new main hall is highly decorated and Myeongbu-jeon and Mountain Spirit hall are worthy of note, it's for the stone remains that most people come or when passing through for a hike in this beautiful valley during autumn. Use a city bus from Gurye (₩1,480).

In the valley to the west of Hwaeom-sa is the temple **Cheoneun-sa** [Ch'ŏnŭn-sa] (천은사)—a pleasant, meditative place. The original temple was constructed in 828; the present buildings date from the late 1700s. Along the path near the entrance to the temple, at the upper end of a small reservoir, a wooden pavilion sits atop a tightly arched bridge, over which the path leads to the temple's two-posted front gate. Steps around the old lecture hall bring you up to the main courtyard. To the front is the main hall, Geung-nakbo-jeon. While not old, this building sports much intricate woodwork and a fine series of ox-herding murals. Behind the figure on the main altar hangs a fine scroll painting (T. #924) from 1776 of the Seokgamoni Buddha surrounded by his principal followers. A full complement of

© ROBERT NILSEN

other newly refreshed buildings make up the remainder of the compound, and perhaps the most fetching is Gwaneum-jeon with its large seated gilt statue of the many-handed Goddess of Mercy set on the low altar. The living quarters here are comely and unpretentious with weathered wood posts and beams and plain white walls between.

Buses stop at the entrance to the parking lot, running either down the road to Hwaeom-sa and Gurye or up the road to Seongsam-jae and the track entrance to Nogodan.

The remaining temples are more easily reached from cities and towns other than Gurye—unless you walk over the mountain to them. Reach Ssanggye-sa and Chilbul-sa from Hadong, and Daewon-sa from Sancheong or Jinju; all are in Gyeongsangnam-Do. The best connection to Shilsang-sa is from Namwon in Jeollabuk-Do.

Gurye 구례

Set along the banks of the Seomjin River, the largely agricultural, rural town of Gurye [Kurye] is the southwestern gateway to the national park, and the closest town to the temples Hwaeom-sa, Cheoneun-sa, and Yeon'gok-sa. Every year in April, the **Jiri-san Mountain Festival** is held here. The five-day market in Gurye is well-known for the quantity of wild mountain vegetables and herbs. If coming by train, get off at Gurye Station and take any local bus the six kilometers into town. Buses from the in-town bus terminal run to Hwaeom-sa (₩700), Cheoneun-sa (₩1,200), Yeon'gok-sa (₩1,800), Hadong (₩2,400), Yeosu (₩5,100), Namwon (₩2,100), and Gwangju (₩5,100).

Aside from the temples on Jiri-san, two others nearby are also of historical interest. Closest to Gurye is **Taean-sa**. Built in 807, this temple is nestled in a deep mountain valley. It preserves two *sari budo*, a memorial tablet (T. #273, 274, 275), and a very large stone lantern. Closer to Gokseong is **Dorim-sa**, a diminutive temple of older vintage.

Southeast Jeollanam-Do

YEOSU 여수

Yeosu [Yŏsu] has one of the most picturesque locations of any city along the deeply indented coastline of Jeollanam-Do. It's no surprise that Yeosu ("Beautiful Waters") is the western end of Hallyeo Waterway National Park, which stretches east to Geoje-do and is one of the most scenic stretches of the coast.

About 400 years ago, Yeosu was the naval headquarters of Admiral Yi Sun-shin, Korea's most famous seaman. Held in early May, the annual **Jinnam Festival** celebrates the exploits of this naval hero and his victories over the Japanese navy during the wars of 1592–98. Then a small port, now a bustling city, Yeosu (pop. 325,000) is experiencing growing pains. New commercial port facilities have been constructed behind the train station, a new fishing port and related facilities, including a Fisheries College, have been built in the southern section of the city, residential sectors have popped up here and there throughout town, and the city administration and requisite infrastructure have been moved over the hill to the west. The rapidly expanding industrial sector north of the city houses a high concentration of chemical factories, oil refineries, and related industries dependent on international trade. Set along the southern periphery of Gwangyang Bay, it is a complement to the Gwangyang industrial area along the north side of the bay. Because of the rapid industrialization at Gwangyang Bay and in Yeosu itself, Yeosu's peripheral "beautiful water" is becoming somewhat polluted.

For more information, see the website www .yeosu.jeonnam.kr.

Odong-do 오동도

The westernmost point of the national park is the tiny island of Odong-do, or "Paulownia Tree Island." Set in the channel facing Yeosu's new harbor, this diminutive, tree-covered rock is connected to the mainland by a 750-meter-long breakwater; ₩1,300 entrance. It's open into the evening. For those who don't care to walk out along the breakwater, an excursion ferry (₩2,000) runs about every hour from the pier near the ticket booth at the breakwater's western end to the pier on the island, or you can ride the tram for ₩500. Unfortunately, the paulownia trees have long since been replaced by camellia trees and bamboo. Still, it's a great place to stroll, especially in early spring, when the camellias are aflame. The bamboo here is a special variety used for arrows by sharp-shooting Korean archers of days past. A lighthouse stands high on the south cliff, while a small temple hides amongst the trees in the middle of the island. Facilities on the island include several shops and seafood restaurants.

Three kilometers north is **Manseong-ni Beach.** Since the 1930s, Koreans have come to this beach to be covered by the warm dark sand that they believe helps alleviate the symptoms of neuralgia. Stretching along the curve of a short crescent bay on the fringe of national park, this gray sand and pebble beach faces Namhae-do across the channel. Many *yeogwan* and restaurants here cater to the crowds of summer bathers.

City Parks

Above the mainland end of the breakwater to Odong-do is **Jasan Park** (자산공원). A stairway leads up to the park from near the Odong-do ticket booth, while a road runs up the other side of the hill. A manicured hilltop park, its spacious gardens surround an impressive statue of Admiral Yi Sun-shin, standing resolutely in full battle armor, looking out over the bay that once sheltered his famous iron-clad turtle ships.

On the opposite side of the inner harbor are two newer and less developed city parks. At the western end of the Dolsan Bridge is **Namsan Park,** while the more developed **Dolsan Park** lies above the eastern end of the bridge. Below the Dolsan-do end of the bridge is a pier from which tour boats make trips into the island-studded

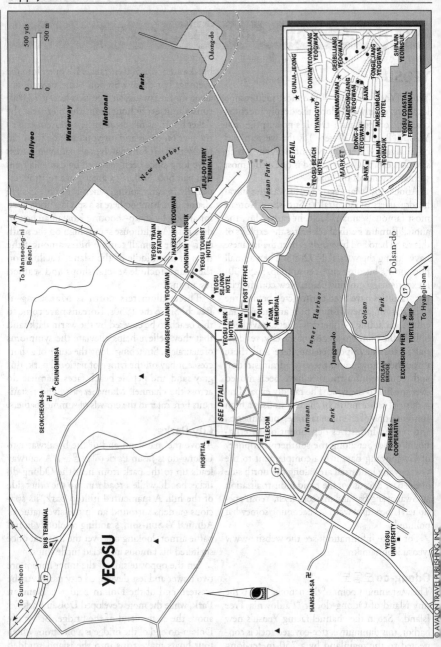

Hallyeo

Waterway

National

Park

Odong-do

New Harbor

Jeju-do Ferry Terminal

Jasan Park

DETAIL

GUNJA-JEONG

DONGMYEONGJANG YEOGWAN

GEOBUKANG YEOGWAN

JINNAMGWAN

HAEDONGJANG YEOGWAN

TONGILJANG YEOGWAN

SHINJIN YEOINSUK

HYANGGYO

MOBEOMGAK HOTEL

YEOSU COASTAL FERRY TERMINAL

YEOSU BEACH HOTEL

MARKET

DONG-A YEOGWAN

NAMJIN YEOINSUK

BANK

BANK

To Manseong-ni Beach

Yeosu Train Station

Hakseong Yeogwan

Dongnam Yeoinsuk

Yeosu Tourist Hotel

Yeosu Sejong Hotel

Post Office

Police

Gwangseongjang Yeogwan

Yeosu Park Hotel

Bank

Adm. Yi Memorial

Chungminsa

Seokcheon-sa

SEE DETAIL

Inner Harbor

Jangun-do

Namsan *Park*

Dolsan *Park*

Dolsan-do

Dolsan Bridge

To Hyangil-am

Excursion Pier

Turtle Ship

Telecom

Fisheries Cooperative

Bus Terminal

Hospital

YEOSU

To Suncheon

Yeosu University

Hansan-sa

0   500 yds

0   500 m

bay off Yeosu or to circumnavigate Dolsan-do: ₩7,000 for one-hour, ₩13,000 for two-hour, and ₩20,000 for three-hour tours. Anchored near the excursion ferry pier is a modern replica of an iron-clad *geobukseon* turtle ship; ₩1,200 entrance to board and have a look around. Dressed in period clothes, mannequins portray sailors at tasks typical of the day. Shown on the top level are sailors preparing for battle, while those below are attending to household chores. Smaller and more maneuverable than their Japanese counterparts, each of these ships had a crew of about 130 men. Across the channel is Yeosu's new fishing harbor. On Janggun-do in the middle of the city's harbor is a historical monument to an ancient general and the remains of a military fortress built to protect the city during the Japanese invasions of the 1590s.

Jinnam-gwan 진남관

By far the most historic, and perhaps the oldest, structure in the city (est. 1599) is Jinnam-gwan [Chinnam-gwan]; ₩440 entrance. Now surrounded by a hillside neighborhood and sitting on the site of an official government guesthouse burned down in 1597, this building (T. #324) occupies a portion of the site used as the naval headquarters by Yi Sun-shin during the Imjin War, before the command center was moved east to Tongyeong. Burned, rebuilt, and renovated several times, most recently in 2001, it's the largest and most impressive wooden pavilion in the country at seventy-five meters long and 14 meters high; 68 rotund pillars support its heavy tile roof. In the enclosed yard is a larger-than-life-size stone figure of a civilian official, one of seven said to have been carved and placed around the city during the Imjin War and used as some sort of decoy.

On the hill behind Jinnam-gwan is the local *hyanggyo,* and behind that the aging pavilion Gunja-jeong.

Chungminsa 충민사

On a hill north of Jinnam-gwan is Chungminsa, a recently renovated shrine dedicated to admirals Yi Sun-shin and Yi Ok-gi, and the statesman An Hong-guk. Originally built in 1601, this shrine

(H.S. #381) was one of the first of the many in the country dedicated to the deeds of Admiral Yi and other patriotic war heroes. From here, there are fine views over the eastern section of the city and the new commercial harbor. Nearby is the temple **Seokcheon-sa,** founded by a Buddhist monk who served under Admiral Yi during the Imjin War.

Closer to the city center and below Jasan Park, a small pavilion houses two memorial stone tablets (T. #571) dedicated to the honor of Admiral Yi and his victories during the war of the 1590s.

Hansan-sa 한산사

High on the hill west of the harbor is Hansan-sa, a temple that's undergoing a complete renovation. While the main temple hall has been rebuilt, the remaining structures will be erected when funds allow. The Hansan-sa temple bell is known for its sweet sound. A narrow concrete road winds steeply up the hillside up to this temple, from where you get fine views of the southern section of the city, the city's new fishing harbor, and the island of Dolsan-do.

Heungguk-sa 흥국사

About 10 kilometers north of the city center, on the edge of a huge industrial zone, is the temple Heungguk-sa [Hŭngguk-sa]; ₩1,000 entrance. This medium-size temple was founded in 1195 by Bojo Guksa before he took up residence at the more famous Songgwang-sa. Destroyed during the 1590s, it was rebuilt in the early 1600s. Of most cultural importance here are the main hall (T. #396), its altar mural (T. #578), and *honggyo* (T. #563)—a graceful stone arch bridge constructed in 1637 at the temple entrance and one of the most comely old arch bridges in the country.

Dolsan-do 돌산도

Dolsan-do helps form Yeosu's well-protected inner harbor. This island, the country's ninth-largest, was connected to the mainland in 1984 with the addition of a graceful half-kilometer-long suspension bridge. Banjukpo Beach is located midway along its eastern side, and west of the island is Musulmok, site of a naval battle fought between the turtle ships and the Japanese navy. Near the island's narrow waist is a large protected bay that is a wintering home of swans.

In the late 1990s, the **Jeonnam Fisheries Exhibition Hall** opened on Dolsan-do to afford a capsule glimpse at marine life in the seas surrounding the Korean peninsula. This hall unfortunately has virtually no explanation in non-Korean languages yet it does give scientific names for most live and stuffed fish on display. Here as well is a small but adequate display of ocean fishing techniques, a good introduction to this important aspect of the Korean economy. This hall is open daily 0900–1800 except Mondays and some holidays; ₩1,500 entrance fee.

The hermitage **Hyangil-am** (향일암), set amidst craggy boulders atop a cliff above the village of Impo near the southern tip of the island, appears to be set at the edge of the world. From Yeosu, take bus no. 101 or 111 to the end of the line, passing wide expanses of oyster beds in the numerous bays on the way. From the village, this hermitage is a 20-minute walk up the hill. The three predictably small buildings here cling to the cliff. A path from the main hall leads up through the rocks to another hall, set even more precipitously on the cliff's edge above. Constructed during the Silla Dynasty, this small hermitage is not known for its size or beauty but for its wonderful location. Perched a hundred meters above the roiling sea, it's a perfect place to watch the sunrise and view the small islands off the coast. Hyangil-am and the southern end of Dolsan-do are the eastern extremity of Dadohae Marine National Park.

Accommodations

The best place to stay in Yeosu is the first-class **Yeosu Beach Hotel** (tel. 061/663-2011). Located along the stream near the market, rates run from about ₩80,000 for either Korean- or Western-style rooms. The second-class **Yeosu Park Hotel** (tel. 061/663-2334) and **Yeosu Sejong Hotel** (tel. 061/662-6111) hotels have rooms from ₩60,000, while closer to the train station the **Yeosu Tourist Hotel** (tel. 061/662-3131) has rooms for ₩36,000–80,000. For less expensive accommodations, try the area below

Jinnam-gwan or near the ferry terminal. Below Jinnam-gwan, try the Haedongjang Yeogwan (해동장여관), Geobujang Yeogwan (거부장여관), Tongiljang Yeogwan (통일장여관), Dongmyeongjang Yeogwan (동명장여관), or the cheaper Shinjin Yeoinsuk (신진여인숙). Near the ferry terminal are the Mobeomgak Hotel (모범각호텔), Dong-A Yeogwan (동아여관), or the Namjin Yeoinsuk (남진여인숙). Near the train station are the Hakseong Yeogwan (학성여관), Gwangseongjang Yeogwan (광성장여관), and the Dongnam Yeoinsuk (동남여인숙).

Services and Information

The post office and central police station are located at the bend in the city's main street a short distance east of Jinnam-gwan. The Telecom office sits at the west end of this main street beyond the river. Between them is Yeosu's old city center: the bulk of businesses, shopping, markets, restaurants, lodgings, entertainment, shops, and the passenger ferry terminal. Numerous banks in the city center and near the post office can exchange foreign currency. There is a tourist information office at the entrance to Odong-do.

Transportation

Serviced by both Asiana and KAL, the small **Yeosu Airport** is located halfway between Yeosu and Suncheon. Planes fly 11 times a day to/from Seoul, split between the two airlines, while Korean Air also flies once a day from Yeosu to Jejudo. Due to its location, this airport is more often than others closed because of fog and/or rain. For alternate air transportation needs, try the **Sacheon Airport**, located just south of Jinju in Gyeongsangnam-Do. Yeosu city bus nos. 31 and 33 (₩700) and an airport shuttle bus (₩2,500) from the mid-town rotary run regularly to the airport. Taxis from either city will run about ₩15,000. For information and reservations, contact Asiana (tel. 061/666-4001) and Korean Air (tel. 061/641-2003).

Yeosu is the terminus of the Jeolla rail line. From here nine trains a day run to Seoul, and one a day each to Mokpo and Iksan.

Ferries from the **Yeosu Coastal Ferry Terminal** (여수항여객선터미날) run to Yeon-do,

Geomun-do, and other small islands in this coastal region. If you plan to travel by ferry on a weekend in summer, be sure to buy your ticket early. Destinations include Yeon-do (₩11,850) and Geomun-do by various routes (₩23,450). From Geomun-do, three-hour excursion ferries run to the more distant uninhabited Baek-do islands. Located between the train station and Odong-do is a ferry pier dedicated solely to ferries to Jeju-do (제주카훼리터미날). This car ferry runs daily except Sunday at 0830, arriving in Jeju-do at 1500; fares range ₩16,400 to 53,000.

Express buses from Yeosu run only to Seoul (₩17,400) and Busan (₩9,500). Select intercity buses run to Suncheon (₩2,600), Jinju (₩7,600), Songgwang-sa (₩5,500), Hwaeom-sa (₩5,500), Mokpo (₩12,400), and Gwangju (₩600). The majority of city buses make their way from the bus terminal through downtown Yeosu. Some useful numbers are as follows. To reach the entrance to Odong-do or to pass the train station, take bus no. 1, 2, 18, 85, 101, 103, or 105. Bus no. 6 runs out to Manseong-ni Beach. Passing Chungminsa shrine is bus no. 20, and no. 5 goes past the road entrance to Jasan Park. Going north from the station, bus no. 52 goes to Heungguk-sa. To reach Dolsan Bridge, take bus no. 100, 101, 102, 103, or 111; nos. 101 and 111 run all the way to Hyangil-am, passing the fisheries exhibition hall and Banjukpo Beach on the way.

SUNCHEON 순천

Suncheon [Sunch'ŏn] is nestled into the low hills at the upper end of the Yeosu Peninsula. This attractive city, a provincial naval command center during the early Joseon Dynasty, is today a transportation and educational center for the south-central portion of the peninsula, as well as an expanding industrial site. Suncheon is conveniently located near Jiri-san National Park, Jogye-san Provincial Park, and Yeosu.

In town, west of city hall, are the Suncheon Hyanggyo and Okcheon Seowon. East of city hall and across the river is **Jukdo-bong Park**, while near the public stadium south of the train station is Okgye Seowon. Capping the hill to

the east of Dongcheon Stream, the park has several pavilions, monuments, and walking paths. The view over the city from the park is perhaps the best and it's a relatively convenient place to have a stroll if you've got enough time while waiting for a train. Between the central market and intercity bus terminal is the city's central business district. Many accommodations are located here and in the area in front of the train station. The post office is down the road from the train station, while the police station is on the northern end of town, out past the express-bus terminal. At the northern end of town as well are the Suncheon National University and the city's most historic temple, Hyangnim-sa.

The city's two best hotels are the remodeled second-class **Suncheon Royal Tourist Hotel** (tel. 061/741-7000) in the heart of town and the **Geumgang Hotel** next to the market. Both have rooms in the ₩75,000 and up range. Down the street from the Royal are the Prince Motel (프린스 호텔) and Joseon Motel (조선모텔) and around the corner you'll find the Hilton Motel (힐튼 모텔) and the less expensive Cheonil Yeoinsuk (천일여인숙). To the side of the intercity bus terminal, have a look at the Sambojang Yeogwan (삼보장여관) or the Daeyeonggak Yeogwan (대영각 여관).

The **Yeosu Airport** is located halfway between Suncheon and Yeosu, with 11 flights a day to Seoul and one a day to Jeju-do. From Suncheon, take city bus no. 96 or 900 (₩1,100) from in front of the train station, the shuttle bus (₩2,500), or a taxi (₩15,000). The airport shuttle leaves from in front of the Suncheon Medical Center and stops at the train station rotary on the way. For information and reservations, both Asiana Airlines (tel. 061/742-4100) and KAL (tel. 061/744-5502) have offices in the city center.

From Suncheon, trains run 16 times a day to Yeosu; 15 daily trains go to Seoul, and one each to Mokpo, Iksan, and Jinju. Express buses run only to Seoul (₩15,900), Daegu (₩9,200), and Busan (₩8,200). Select intercity bus destinations and fares are Yeosu (₩2,600), Hadong (₩2,900), Jinju (₩5,000), Hwaeom-sa (₩2,900), Namwon (₩4,600), Songgwang-sa (₩2,950), and Gwangju (₩5,200). Most city buses with numbers 1–50 or so run between the train station and the express bus terminal, many of which also run by the intercity bus terminal. Some of the city buses that connect the train station and both bus terminals are nos. 1, 5, and 31. Bus nos. 1 and 100 run to Seonam-sa, no. 111 runs to Songgwang-sa, no. 8 goes by city hall, and no. 63 goes to Dolmen Park.

JOGYE-SAN PROVINCIAL PARK
조계산도립공원

Twenty kilometers west of Suncheon is Jogye-san Provincial Park. Created in 1979, the park encompasses 27 square kilometers of low rounded hills. Carpeted with pine trees and stands of hardwoods and bamboo, Jogye-san rises to 887 meters. At its base are the temples Songgwang-sa and Seonam-sa, both intimately associated with the introduction and expansion of Zen Buddhism in Korea. Above and around the hill from Songgwang-sa is the hermitage Cheonja-am.

From Songgwang-sa, one trail leads up the valley, over a ridge, and around the mountainside to Cheonja-am; another easily followed trail connects Songgwang-sa to Seonam-sa. From Songgwang-sa, follow the path up along the stream; at the fork, beyond the path that leads off to the right up to Cheonja-am, take the right-hand trail over the ridge and down to the wider valley on the far side. Pass several fields, cross another stream, then climb the far hillside, cross the ridge, and go down the long eastern slope to Seonam-sa. This hike takes about two-and-a-half hours. Another long east-west trail runs between Songgwang-sa and Seonam-sa over the tallest of the mountain peaks. Between these main trails are two connecting ridge and valley trails. Entrance to the park is ₩2,300.

Suncheon city bus no. 111 (₩2,500) runs to Songgwang-sa as do intercity buses from Suncheon (₩2,950), Gwangju (₩4,900), Beolgyo (₩2,000), and Yeosu (₩5,500). City bus nos. 1 and 100 run from Suncheon to Seonam-sa (₩2,500).

Songgwang-sa 송광사
On the western slope of Jogye-san stands Songg-

wang-sa ("Spacious Pine Temple"), originally constructed toward the end of the Silla Dynasty. In the late 1100s, when the famous monk Bojo Guksa was looking to establish a new temple, one of his followers found this nearly abandoned site, and rebuilt the temple as a center for the revitalization of Zen Buddhism in Korea. Bojo Guksa, otherwise known as Chinul, was one of the most influential Goryeo Dynasty Buddhist monks. At a time when Korean Buddhism was suffering from schisms and a lack of coherent identity, he worked diligently for its unification. This exceptional scholar and teacher founded a sect of Buddhism that blended the separate meditative and doctrinal ideologies into one syncretic system. While stressing the importance and necessity of both "ways," he gave predominance to meditative practice and its resultant "sudden enlightenment." While it was essential to study, to understand Buddhist thought, and to cultivate the Buddhist spirit (the doctrinal focus), it was ultimately more important to carry on from there, reach "enlightenment" by a sudden understanding of the mystery of true self, and thereafter live the life of an enlightened being (the meditative focus). Within a decade, the temple's name was changed to Suseonsa, or the "Society for the Cultivation of Seon (Zen)." At the same time the name of this mountain was changed from Songgwang-san to Jogyesan—the name of the mountain in China where Huineung, the sixth patriarch of Buddhism and godfather of Zen Buddhism, lived much of his life. Only toward the end of the Goryeo Dynasty was the temple's name changed to its present name of Songgwang-sa.

Songgwang-sa is considered one of the three treasure temples of Korea—the others being Tongdo-sa near Busan and Haein-sa in Gayasan National Park. It's the *seung* (monk) temple, emphasizing the community of monks and Zen meditative practice. In 1969, Songgwang-sa was reorganized as a monastic center for all sects of Mahayana Buddhism and an international meditation center was established so that non-Korean monks could train in traditional Korean meditation techniques. Again the center for the revitalization of Zen meditation, this was a fitting resurgence of the same spirit that led to the rededication of the temple seven centuries earlier. Over the centuries, this temple has produced 16 "national priests" (highest rank for a monk), and numerous other great monks and meditation masters. The last renowned meditation master of Songgwang-sa was Gusan Seunim. An instrumental force in the creation of the international meditation center, he was its guiding light until his death in 1983. Hwagye-sa in Seoul and Musang-sa near Gyeryeong-san have since taken over the bulk of Zen meditation training of foreign monks.

Temple Compound: As a living, growing institution, Songgwang-sa has experienced much renovation and rebuilding since the early 1980s. With nearly 50 buildings, Songgwang-sa is one of if not the largest temple complexes in the country. It also has several associated hermitages in the hills above. This temple preserves three National Treasures, 12 Treasures, and a handful of local cultural properties. Kept in the museum are a 14-centimeter-high, hinged votive tablet of carved wood (N.T. #42), 11 additional votive tablets (T. #175), an official document written by King Gojong (N.T. #43), a brass clapper (T. #176), and other small cultural objects. Guksajeon, or "National Priest Hall" (N.T. #56), contains the portraits of the 16 national priests this temple produced. Other buildings of note include Hasa-dang (T. #263), Yaksa-jeon, or "Hall of the Healing Buddha" (T. #302), and Yeongsan-jeon, a hall containing statues of the 16 Nahan (T. #303).

A small village sits below the compound, a typical collection of accommodations, restaurants, souvenir shops, and a bus station. From here a wide path leads up through the woods to the temple's double-posted front gate. Beyond it is an enclosed gate housing large statues of the devas, and farther yet is a tiny shop that sells books, tapes, prayer beads, statues, and other Buddhist paraphernalia. The hills above Songgwang-sa feed the stream that flows under the covered arch bridge leading to the temple's entrance. The entrance corridor leads under the bell pavilion, which also contains a skin drum, metal plate gong, and wooden fish drum, into the temple's spacious courtyard. To the right are Guksa-jeon and Yaksa-jeon, a lecture hall for the Buddhist seminary, and beyond that the kitchen and dormitories. Directly ahead is Daeung-jeon, the temple's main hall. Elaborately painted both inside and out, the Vairocana Buddha (index finger of left hand grasped by right hand) is enshrined on its altar with six other figures. Additional living quarters and the Gwaneum-jeon sit above the main hall, and beyond those the *sari budo* for Bojo Guksa. To the left and right, within separate walled compounds, are the meditation and living areas for monks studying here. During the day, you see little activity from those monks; most of the hustle and bustle is handled by novices. Only at certain hours, such as between meditation periods and theological classes, are the monks out and about. By all means visit this temple, but approach with a respectful heart, and be mindful enough of the lifestyle here not to disturb.

Cheonja-am 천자암

A one-hour walk above Songgwang-sa brings you to the tiny hermitage Cheonja-am [Ch'ŏnjaam], with its pair of 700-year-old Chinese juniper trees (N.M. #88). One legend says that shoots were brought from China and planted here. Another more fanciful story relates how the trees grew from the wooden staff of a monk who formerly called this retreat his home. These gnarled old junipers have extremely contoured trunks that, like a rope, curl around themselves as if someone twisted them from the top.

Seonam-sa 선암사

On the eastern slope of Jogye-san is Seonam-sa [Sŏnam-sa]. Founded in 529 by the monk Ado, this temple is one of the oldest in the southern section of the country. It has been destroyed, rebuilt, and renovated several times throughout its 1,500-year lifetime. While much restoration has happened here since 1992, most of the present structures date from the 1820s, and their unadorned weathered-wood exteriors definitely exude a feeling of age and grace. While regarded as the birthplace of both the meditative and doctrinal sects of Korean Buddhism, it has now been revived as a center of traditional Buddhist study. Smaller in size than Songgwang-sa, with fewer resident monks, it's no less important a place, and is, in fact, the head temple of the Daego sect of Korean Buddhism; this sect allows its monks to marry. Filled with flowers, bushes, and cherry trees, the temple courtyard comes to life in spring.

Approaching this temple from below, you cross the gracefully arched bridge Seungseon-gyo (T. #400), set below a pavilion that overlooks the stream. Dating from the mid-Joseon Dynasty, this bridge is made of granite, set on a natural rock foundation, and features a dragon's head in the center of the arch. It's a fine example of ancient bridge construction. Pass through the open gate and under the bell pavilion to the temple's front courtyard. Air vents in the shape of Chinese characters, trigrams from the *I-Ching*, and Buddhist swastikas have been cut into the walls of a building on the right. In front of the main hall, reconditioned in 2001, stands a pair of well-proportioned, three-tier stone pagodas (T. #395) of typical Joseon Dynasty design. Other cultural items preserved at the temple are a stone *sari budo* (T. #1117) at the Daegak-am hermitage and a portrait of the monk Daegak Guksa (T.#1044). Brass wind chimes that hang from the eaves of many of this temple's buildings play musical notes in the breeze, and create a friendly, homey environment. To display the temple's numerous artistic and religious treasures a small museum was opened here in 2001. Purposely oriented, Seonam-sa catches the first rays of morning sunlight.

BEOLGYO

Just south of Jogye-san Provincial Park is the town of Beolgyo [Pŏlgyo]. While the town itself is not of particular interest, one of the country's few remaining old stone bridges not near a temple is located on the edge of town. Beolgyo Honggyo (T. #304) is a graceful three-arch bridge, stout, sturdy, and well-made. It replaced a raft bridge, or *"beolgyo,"* at some date in the past and has been lengthened to bridge a widening river.

Nagan Folk Village 낙안읍성

The roads north lead to the provincial park and the one running to Seonun-sa passes Nagan Folk Village; ₩1,100 entrance. Like Goheung to the south, rural Beolgyo has remained relatively isolated over the years, leaving some communities more unaffected by modernization than others. One such community is Nagan, also referred to as Nagan Eupseong (Nagan Fortified Town), one of the few remaining walled villages in the country (H.S. #302). An oddity today, these flat-land walled towns were much more prevalent in centuries past, and this one was first constructed as an earthen-wall fortress during the late 1390s. While legend says that General Im Gyeong-eup took just one day to rebuild this fortress in stone in 1639, it took far longer when it was repaired in 1984. Along with the 1.5-kilometer-long wall which surrounds this community, several of its gates, gate pavilions and other historic structures, like the *gaeksa* and government office, were also refurbished. Outside the east gate, two stone guardian dogs help protect the village from harm. Neatly packed inside are geometric rice paddies, ponds, twining alleys, and one thatched-roof house after another, a handful of which are preserved for their historical importance. While not a village out of the last century, (witness television antennae, cars, and farm machinery), it still carries a flavor of traditional life. Have a walk through the village lanes or up along the top of the wall to get a sense of what a Joseon-era walled village was like, as this is the finest remaining and most authentically preserved small walled town in the country. To help bring alive the past, a folklore exhibition hall has also been built in the village to display artifacts of the old culture. During October every year, the village hosts the **Namdo Food Festival** in conjunction with the **Korean Folk Arts Festival** for memorable local foods, music and dance, dance competitions, and traditional ceremonies.

Dolmen Park, Sculpture Park, Memorial Hall

Nearly 12 dozen dolmen have been gathered together at Dolmen Park (고인돌공원), located north of Nagan village and east of Jogye-san Provincial Park; ₩500 entrance. These ancient burial stones have been removed from the submerged area created by Juam Lake, the largest man-made reservoir in the province. Mostly of the low southern style, a few dolmen are of the taller northern style. With so many examples, this group is a good representative glimpse at these burial structures. In addition, several replicas of prehistoric dwellings have been erected on the site and an exhibition hall displays items excavated from the original tombs before they were moved to this spot. Use Suncheon city bus no. 63.

Farther down the highway is **Seo Jae-pil Memorial Hall** (서재필기념관). Seo Jae-pil was one of the Independence Movement leaders from the late 1800s and early 1900s. A replica of the Independence Gate, which stands near Seo-dae-mun in Seoul, has been erected here and inside are historical relics of this man of foresight. Across the highway, on the banks of the lake, is a sculpture park. Just north of there, along the country lane that runs to Daewon-sa,

is the **Baekmin Art Museum** (백민미술관). In a seemingly unlikely spot for such a museum, it sits high on the hillside and holds a fine collection of mostly modern art pieces by a wide range of Korean painters.

Daewon-sa

The principal temple in Boseong County is Daewon-sa (대원사), reputedly built by the monk Ado in 503. All except for the main hall was burned during the Korean War but during the 1980s and 1990s was partially rebuilt. Daewon-sa is a small temple that, while like other temples in general, has a number of oddities. To start, a very graceful lotus pond lies before the front gate and numerous other smaller ponds dot various levels in the rest of the compound. The many terraces here are connected by a more than usual number of stone stairways. Before the main courtyard stands a stone house-like structure in which sit two Buddha figures set back to back in separate "rooms" under a slanted roof, very much like a similar structure at Unju-sa a short distance to the west. Rising over another diminutive

The entrance to Daewon-sa has a more mysterious feel than most other Korean temples.

pond is a bell pavilion in which hangs a gilt temple bell. The bell pavilion sits to the side of the compact main courtyard, which itself is well manicured with lawn, flowering bushes, and many small trees. Like other temples, the main hall has an old, venerable feel and behind it sit a small pagoda and statue.

The abbot of Daewon-sa has been interested in Tibetan Buddhism for decades and has had an opportunity to visit various Tibetan monasteries over the years. To preserve and display some artifacts brought back from his trips and to disseminate information about another branch of Buddhism, the **Tibetan Museum** has been built here. The only such museum in the country, one with a distinct architectural resemblance to a Tibetan temple, it opened to the public in the summer of 2001; ₩2,000 entrance. This three-story structure houses some 1,000 fine pieces of religious art, tanka paintings, and objects of ceremonial and everyday use.

South Coast

Dadohae Marine National Park

다도해해상국립공원

Established in 1981, Dadohae Marine National Park covers 2,345 square kilometers of coastal Jeollanam-Do, and is the largest of Korea's national parks. Split into eight separate units, this park encompasses about 1,700 small islands and parts of islands. Much larger than Hallyeo Waterway National Park in Gyeongsangnam-Do, the Dadohae Marine park stretches from the islands south of Yeosu in the east to Hong-do in the west. The eight sections of Dadohae Marine N.P. are: 1) the southern shore of Dolsan-do and the short string of islands to its south; 2) the southern tip of Goheung Peninsula and Naro-do; 3) the Geomun-do and Baek-do group of islands, south of the Goheung Peninsula; 4) the southern end of Wan-do, Shinji-do, and islands to their south; 5) the southern end of Jin-do and the islands to its south; 6) far-flung Manjae-do; 7) parts of Docho-do, Bigeum-do, and Euido, west of Mokpo; and 8) Heuksan-do and Hong-do, farther to the west. Ferry transport to sections 1, 2, and 3 is from Yeosu, to section 4 from Wan-do, and to sections 5, 7, and 8 from Mokpo.

The most easily accessible point of interest in the first section is the hermitage Hyangil-am, perched on a cliff at the southern end of Dolsan-do. Seen from here, the sun rises gently over the islands of the south coast. Within section two are Naebal Beach on the Goheung Peninsula and the beaches on Naro-do. The third section offers one of the largest lighthouses in Korea, shore fishing, *haenyeo* like the women divers of Jeju-do, and island life, but what brings most people to this area now are the bleached white rock pinnacles and spires that jut out of the sea at Baek-do. Excursion ferries from Geomun-do make a three-hour round-trip to these uninhabited rocky islets. Of historical interest on Geomun-do is the small British sailors' cemetery. This graveyard is what's left of a fortress erected on the island by the British navy in the late 1800s, when England was jockeying to influence affairs on the Korean peninsula. After a few years the navy left, leaving only their few dead. Perhaps the most well-known attraction of section four is Myeongsashim-ni Beach on Shinji-do, a short hop across the bay from Wan-do. Bogil-do features historical remains of cultural importance. It is here the exiled scholar Yun Seon-do lived for many years and wrote laudatory poems about the beauty of the island. The remaining sections, made up of scores of inhabited and uninhabited islands, are known mostly for the island-style life and great fishing.

GOHEUNG 고흥

The Goheung [Kohŭng] Peninsula dangles from Korea's south coast by a low and narrow isthmus. If the current movement of the Korean landmass continues, this isthmus will eventually sink and create an island off the peninsula. Goheung produces citrons, and the annual total of the fruit raised here is over half that grown in the country. Other notable products of Goheung are garlic, persimmon, seaweed, and laver. Rural Goheung County has no major towns, and because of its unique location and lack of major transportation connections is more isolated than most other non-island counties in the country. Located in the west-central portion of the peninsula, the town of Goheung is the principal population and administrative center. Gwayeok is a village through which buses run to Neungga-sa and Palyeong-san Provincial Park, and ferries to several islands south of Goheung leave from Nok-dong. Visited mostly by local residents, Daejeon, Pungnyo, and Naebal beaches are all reached by bus from the town of Goheung. The island beaches of Woenaro-do are now also easily accessible since a bridge spans the short channel between the peninsula and the island. A second bridge, one from Nok-dong across to Sorok-do and on to Geogeum-do, will make it more convenient to reach those islands in the future.

The town of Goheung stretches along a stream and nothing is very far from anything else. The bus terminal is at the south end of town and nearby are the **Goheunggak Yeogwan** (고흥장여관) and **Geumhojang Hotel** (금호장호텔). There is only bus transportation to and from Goheung. Selected destinations are Beolgyo (₩2,400), Suncheon (₩4,000), Gwangju (₩7,900), Narodo (₩2,400), Nok-dong (₩1,300), Gwayeok (₩850), and Geumtap-sa (₩1,000). The harbor in Nok-dong (녹동) is about 20 minutes by foot from the bus terminal at the north end of this small town. On the hill overlooking the harbor is a shrine that commemorates two naval commanders killed in battle with the Japanese in the 1590s. Lining the harbor are a series of *yeogwan* and seafood restaurants. Ferries from Nok-dong leave continuously throughout the day on a 10-minute crossing for Sorok-do (₩800). Other island destinations are Geumji-do, Shinpyeong-do, and Gogeum-do.

Sixteen kilometers south of town is the county's principal temple, **Geumtap-sa** [Kŭmt'apsa] (금탑사). Established in 637, the small compound is a refuge for *biguni*. Set far back into the mountains with only occasional bus traffic to the village below the temple, there is a steep hike up the hillside through a nutmeg forest (N.M. #239) to the temple compound.

Said to have been founded by the monk Ado in the early 400s, the temple **Neungga-sa** [Nŭngga-sa] (능가사) sits below the hill Palyeong-san to the east, a ₩700 bus ride from Gwayeok. Through Cheonwang-mun with its four wooden celestial devas is the broad and largely open courtyard. The main hall is directly ahead. From 1644, this building has some wooden wainscoting, and five figures sit on its altar in front of three huge murals. To the rear is the judgment hall, which unusually has some pierced wood carving above the front side doors. Here as well is preserved a one-meter-high bronze bell cast in 1698. Done with artistic flair, it has a dragon top, Sanskrit characters and arabesque floral patterns around its side and Buddha figures on facing sides. A stone memorial stele at the rear of the compound was also erected in the 1690s.

Palyeong-san Provincial Park drapes the mountain behind Neungga-sa. Not yet well developed, this area is relatively high—the highest peak rises to 608 meters—for being so close to the coast. From Neungga-sa, the major trail runs for about one hour up to the ridge. Traversing six peaks, along a line of spires and rock outcrops, the one-hour-long ridge trail heads east before dropping down another valley through pine forests and back to the temple.

Sorok-do

Across the narrow channel from Nok-dong, at the southwestern corner of the Goheung peninsula, is the tiny island of Sorok-do. Sorok-do has a long fine-sand beach on its east side, fringed with pine trees and washed by the aquamarine sea. It also has the country's only **National Leprosy Hospital**, established as a quarantined colony during the early years of the Japanese occupation. It's no longer forbidden for patients to leave or for others to enter the island. However, to keep this island community from the distraction of curiosity-seekers, entrance is still restricted to the beach and a small park behind the hospital. While many patients with Hansen's Disease (leprosy) and some others without the disease—usually relatives of patients—make their homes here, the vast majority of those with leprosy now live in other communities throughout the country. Due to better drugs and treatment programs, the resident population of the island has fallen to about 800 from a high of around 6,000. Almost all are elderly with the youngest about 40 years old. New patients in the country get treatment where they live and are not ostracized as they were in the past.

BOSEONG 보성

The hills south of Boseong [Posŏng] constitute Korea's major tea-producing area. South of Boseong is the **Daehan Dawon** (대한다원), Korea's oldest (est. 1959) and largest tea plantation. Employing hundreds of seasonal workers, this plantation harvests, dries, and packages a majority of Korea's green-leaf tea, much of which is exported. Various qualities are produced here, and packages of all kinds are sold at the gift shop.

Machine-processed packages generally run ₩15,000–40,000 for 100 grams while hand-processed tea runs ₩50,000–80,000. Farther south at a spot along the winding highway is an observation pavilion that overlooks a very curvaceous part of the tea plantation and the valley which drifts down to the reservoir below and to the sea beyond that. Along this road are several tea-tasting shops and other tea plantations like Dongyang Dawon.

South of Boseong, gracing the shore of Boseong Bay, are two of the few non-island beaches in the province: **Yulpo** and **Sumun-ni**. These long strands of powdery sand are filled with holiday-makers during the short swimming season. Both offer an ample number of *yeogwan, minbak,* and restaurants, and are connected by frequent bus service to Boseong and Jangheung. Here, you'll see not only fishing boats in the shallow waters of the bay, but also white floats indicating oyster beds, and the bamboo frames of seaweed farms.

Use a city bus from Boseong to Daehan Dawon (₩750). Other buses from Boseong run to Gwangju (₩4,500), Gangjin (₩2,700),

terraced fields of tea plants near Boseong

TEA

Long rows of well-manicured tea bushes spread across the terraced slopes of the Boseong coastal hills in a shade of green all their own. In autumn, these plants brighten with small, white, multi-petal flowers. In spring new leaves push forth, and it is these young leaves that are plucked and dried for tea. To the connoisseur, each of the three pickings has a different taste and character; each is given a different name and is sold at a different price. *Ujeon* is the first picking, *sejak* the second, and *jungjak* the third; *malcha* is a processed powdered leaf tea made from various pickings. Tea probably came to Korea from China about 1,000 years ago, during the late Silla period. It was first received in leaf form as a gift from the emperor; later seeds were sent. Used as an everyday drink for centuries, it slipped from popularity during much of the Joseon Dynasty. Only in recent years has there been a resurgence of interest in this drink and the ceremony surrounding its preparation and imbibing. As interest has grown, production has increased. Today, tea is also cultivated on the slopes of Jirisan and Mudeung-san, and in Hadong. While leaf tea from Taiwan is dark and curled, and Japanese tea lighter and rolled in on itself (sometimes powdered), Korean tea is lighter yet and has a crumpled look.

Yulpo Beach (₩1,000), and Suncheon (₩3,700). The bus terminal is on the west end of town, from where you'll have to walk into town for the train or for a place to stay. Trains along this line run to Gwangju, Mokpo, Suncheon, and Busan. Near the train station is the Donggwang Yeogwan (동광여관) and farther up the street is the Munhwa Yeoinsuk (문화여인숙).

Borim-sa 보림사

West of Boseong, but perhaps best reached by bus from Jangheung, is Borim-sa [Porim-sa] ("Precious Forest Temple"); ₩1,000 entrance. Founded in 759 during the Silla Dynasty, this temple was the headquarters of the Gaji sect of Korean Zen Buddhism during its early years. It was, in fact, an important center for Zen medi-

tation and, some say, where Korean Zen meditation started. This compound was a large complex until it was burnt during the Korean War, leaving only one of the front gates standing. The temple's stone monuments fared better. The twin three-tier pagodas and lantern (N.T. #44), east and west stupas (T. #155, 156), and priest Bojo Seonsa's *sari budo* (T. #157) and memorial stone tablet (T. #158) all survived and are in good condition today. In addition, Borim-sa preserves a seated, iron Vairocana Buddha figure (N.T. #117) cast in 858. Borim-sa has an unusual layout in that its front gates do not line up with the main hall. The small first gate has rather complex eave bracketing. From here the path leads to the Sacheonwang-mun gate, where the four carved-wood devas (T. #1245) fill the inside partitions. Straight ahead are the twin pagodas, which unusually have no missing pieces and therefore clearly show the overall design of early pagoda architecture. These pagodas stand in front of Daejeokgwang-jeon, a fully painted hall that houses the seated 1.5-meter-tall iron Vairocana Buddha altar statue. In the courtyard to the side is a two-tier bell pavilion and the main hall is a two-story affair with seven figures on its altar.

GANGJIN 강진

At the head of the long and narrow Gangjin Bay is the town of Gangjin [Kangjin], a farming and fishing center. To the north lies Wolchul-san National Park, and to the south Duryun-san Provincial Park. Established in 1998, **Cheon'gwan Provincial Park** lies to the east and drapes over a mountain area of rocky ridges that is similar to but a miniature version of Wolchul-san. Legend says that there were one hundred temples in this mountain at one time; today only three remain. On the north slope is **Cheon'gwan-sa** which preserves a three-tier stone pagoda (T. #759). Like the island of Jeju-do, and other areas in this region of the peninsula, Gangjin served as a place of banishment during the Joseon Dynasty for those in political or religious disfavor. The most famous exile to Gangjin was the scholar Jeong Yak-yong, whose nom de plume was Dasan.

Exile Home of Jeong Dasan
정다산유적지

The last of four boys, Jeong Yak-yong was born near Seoul in 1762. By the time of his death in 1836, he was considered one of the most influential intellectuals of his era. Growing up during a renaissance in Korean scholarship, this naturally inquisitive and intuitive man was steeped in Eastern thought. Yet, much attracted to the Western ideas slowly seeping into the country via Chinese channels, he and his family were some of the first Korean converts to Catholicism. Strong opposition to this new "Western learning" by dominant members of government led to periodic persecutions of Catholics over the following decades. As a result of the Persecution of 1801, Jeong Yak-yong was forced from government service, banished to Gangjin from 1808 to 1826, and suffered imposed retirement the last 10 years of his life.

Throughout his 18-year exile, he lived on the hillside above a tiny village south of Gangjin, his mother's ancestral home. There, he constructed a house just big enough for sleeping and writing. And write he did. He wrote voluminously, completing many of his approximately 500 books and briefs on a wide spectrum of subjects that include government administration, law, justice, philosophy, history, medicine, economics, agriculture, land reform, surveying, building, and astronomy. He is said to have been the foremost and most well-respected *Silhak* (pragmatism) scholar during an age when progressive Korean thinkers began to throw off some of the exceedingly restrictive Confucian thought and explore the possibilities of man. Dasan set forth his ideas of reform, criticized economic and social conditions of the period, argued for the breakdown of the strict hierarchical class system, called for more-equitable land distribution and ownership, and pushed for the acceptance of some Western learning to improve the lot of the common man. Many of his writings espoused both "democratic' and "socialistic" ideas, which were, of course, anathema to the entrenched order. He was a thorn in the side of Confucian scholars and government bureaucrats, but his ideas were much studied and appreciated by other pragmatic thinkers.

Jeong Dasan Yujeokji, Dasan's home in exile (H.S. #107), is located along the west side of Gangjin Bay. A bus ride and 20-minute walk from the road leads through the village of Mandeok, and gradually up the hill through a canopy of trees to Dasan's home. Because of the thick bamboo, pine, and fruit trees, this secluded compound appears to be cut off from the village below, perfect for study and scholarship. Although originally topped with thatch, the house, known as Jodang, got a tile roof in 1957. The small building to its side served as a dormitory for students. Set at the end of a short path that leads around the hillside, and overlooking the bay, is the pavilion Chonil-gak. Dasan would come here to discuss his ideas with others or turn his thoughts toward his unfortunate brothers. One brother was killed during the Catholic Persecution of 1801, and another was banished to the island of Heuksan-do where he wrote several scholarly works on fish. An exhibition hall has been built beyond the village and gives a simple overview of Jeong Dasan's life—but only in Korean. From this hall, a path leads over the shoulder of the hill to the upper end of the village, from where the trail leads up the hill to the Jodang.

Ceramic Kiln Sites

On the far side of Gangjin Bay in Daegu-myeon are remains of nearly 190 kilns (H.S. #68) from the Goryeo Dynasty; these produced some of the country's best celadon pottery, still admired and prized today for its color and artistry. This was one of the principal pottery-making centers of that day (800s to the 1300s); other Goryeo Dynasty kiln sites of importance were at Buan in Jeollabuk-Do and Icheon and Ganghwa-do in Gyeonggi-Do. While numerous of the best items from these kiln sites are now on display at the National Museum in Seoul, some artifacts are being preserved at the new **Gangjin Ceramic Museum** (강진청자자류박물관) at Misan, which also shows how celadon was made, displays many fragment pieces, and has re-created two kilns to illustrate what they were like. A workshop and new kiln behind the main building create new pieces based on traditional designs and techniques for sale to the public. The museum is open daily except Mondays 0900–1800; ₩1,000 entrance. Additionally, some reproductions and pieces of modern design are sold at several private art galleries across from the museum. To celebrate this artistic heritage, Gangjin celebrates a **Celadon Cultural Festival** every year in August. Across the peninsula to the east are sites of Joseon Dynasty kilns, which produced the white porcelain pottery typical of that period.

At the bottom end of this peninsula is the small port town of Maryang (마량), where ferries ply to Gogeum-do, Saengil-do, Geumil-do, and other small islands off the coast. When completed, a bridge will connect this peninsula to the two largest of these islands. Remains of a fortress wall can be seen on the hillside to the side of Maryang, which itself steps up the hill.

WOLCHUL-SAN NATIONAL PARK 월출산국립공원

Like an exhibition of granite spires and odd-shaped, bald-boulder peaks, Wolchul-san rises dramatically from the surrounding agricultural plains near Yeongam. It's a mountain of rugged rocks, deep narrow valleys, and moderate trails. Condensed in size yet bold in appearance, this multi-faced folding screen of stone provides good hiking and rock climbing. The mountain's highest peak, Cheonhwang-bong (809 meters), lies along its main ridgeline. A trail leads along this ridge, and a few run down the side valleys to the north and south. From the top Haenam Bay and Yeongsan Lake can be seen. In springtime, azalea blooms brighten the mountainside; it's lush green during summer. During autumn, the colored tops of maple trees partially camouflage the rocky slopes, and the *eoksae* reed is resplen-

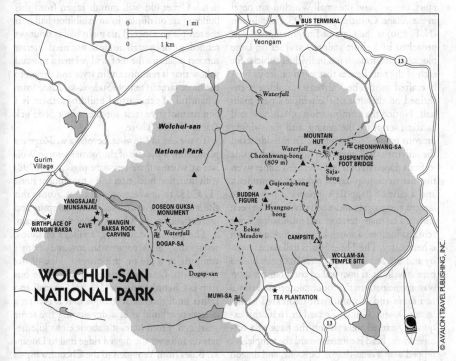

dent in the high meadows; its fleecy top radiates the mellow sunlight at dawn and dusk. Winter provides landscapes of stark white and black.

In 1973, 31 square kilometers of this mountain were set aside as Wolchul-san Provincial Park. In 1988, it was raised to national park status and expanded to 42 square kilometers, the smallest in the national park system. The mountain's two important temples are Dogap-sa and Muwi-sa, and several designated cultural properties are located within the park boundary. A suspension footbridge joins rock spires at the western end of the main ridgeline. The entrance fee is ₩2,500 at any of its entry points.

Dogap-sa 도갑사

Dogap-sa [Togap-sa] was founded by Doseon Guksa during the late Silla Dynasty. A path from the bus stop at the village below leads to the temple's front gate. You'll find a few shops, restaurants, *minbak,* and the small Wolchul-san hotel in the village. Constructed in 1493, Haetal-mun (N.T. #50) is the Gate of Enlightenment. Approached by a short stairway and set on large blocks of cut stone, it has individual cubicles for each of the four figures that stand under its finely crafted roof. The Vairocana Buddha is enshrined on the altar of the temple's new main hall. Notice the combination of Chinese and Sanskrit script on the ceiling, and the swirling dragons painted on its pillars. To the side stand the judgment hall, with two fierce guards inside its front doors. In the courtyard are a rather worn five-tier stone pagoda, an old stela monument, and a pair of flagpole supports; a new stone lantern and pagoda and a bell pavilion have been added. The many terraces and foundation stone remains indicate a much larger compound than is here today. The Three Spirits hall stands nearby and the Sumi Wangsa stela has been placed here as well. In its own walled compound a short way up the path to the mountaintop are various *sari budo* and a monument dedicated to the monk Doseon Guksa. Erected in 1636, this exquisitely carved stela sits on the back of a tortoise whose head is turned toward the temple. It's topped with a twin-dragon capstone, and dragon figures slither down its sides in high relief. Below

the walled enclosure is a small waterfall and above that is the hall Mireuk-jeon which contains a three-meter-tall seated statue of the Mireuk Buddha (T. #89), a fine stone image with a large *usnisa* and somewhat-worn flame mandala. Three city buses a day run to the temple village (₩850); otherwise, take a bus to the village of Gurim (₩700) and walk the three kilometers up to the temple.

Muwi-sa 무위사

On the south side of the mountain is Muwi-sa. Founded in 597 by Wonhyo Daesa, this early Joseon-era temple is known for its Geungnakpo-jeon (N.T. #13), or "Hall of the Western Paradise," and the famous mural of Gwanseeum Bosal painted on an inside wall behind the altar. Clad in white flowing gowns, the Goddess of Mercy appears with a small crown on her head, pendants around her neck, and an ewer in one hand. Other old wall murals taken from this building are on display in an exhibition hall near the temple entrance. This main hall is stout yet refined, small enough inside to not need interior support pillars for the roof, and painted a mustard yellow that is reminiscent in style and design to the more famous temple Sudeok-sa. Aside from a handful of other usual buildings, there is a commemorative stela for the monk Seon'gak Daesa (T. #507) here.

To the east of Muwi-sa, beyond a well-kept tea plantation, is the site of the former temple Wol-lam-sa, where a three-tier stone pagoda (T. #298) with imitation brick tiers and a monument stone (T. #313) sit in overgrown thickets. Above this site is a province-sponsored group campsite and one entrance to the hiking trails of the mountain.

The park headquarters, a village of shops, restaurants, and accommodations, and another camping area are on the eastern slope of the mountain. One-half kilometer above the bus stop is **Cheonhwang-sa** (천황사), a small and rather undistinguished temple that is getting a complete rebuild after a devastating fire some years ago. From here, it's about eight kilometers up and over the rugged ridge trail to Dogap-sa. Buses from Yeongam to the Cheonhwang-sa entrance run five times a day (₩630).

Hiking

There are only a few designated trails on the mountain, but the most-used is the main east-west ridge trail connecting Dogap-sa to Cheon-hwang-sa. Leaving Dogap-sa, the trail runs past the monument for Doseon Guksa and goes up the valley. Farther up, the trail traverses a meadow of *eoksae* on its way to the peaks Hyangno-bong and Gujeong-bong (738 meters). Fifteen minutes below Gujeong-bong on the north slope of the mountain is a massive rock-face carving of the Maitreya Buddha (N.T. #144). Sculpted during the Silla period by Baekje artists, this seven-meter-high Buddha is one of few such remaining sculptures from its time. Sitting in meditative repose, the hands of this Buddha image are in the *mudra* of "calling the earth to witness," and robes gently flow off one shoulder covering the crossed legs. Typically, an *usnisa* protrudes from the top of the head and the earlobes are extended. The whole figure is surrounded by a flame mandala. A similar figure adorns a flat rock face on Saja-bong, but that figure is rendered far less artistically.

About 45 minutes beyond Gujeong-bong is Cheonhwang-bong (809 meters), the mountain's highest peak. From here, one trail leads down past Saja-bong to a 52-meter-long suspension footbridge hung between two spires 150 meters above the slanting ravine floor, supposedly the highest in Korea. The other trail heads down into the valley to a mountain hut and waterfall. Both these trails continue on to Cheonhwang-sa and the park headquarters. A second popular trail leads down the south side of the mountain to the group camping site above the Wollam temple site, and a north slope trail descends from the top, past the Ucheon Waterfall to a point just outside Yeongam. The eastern-slope trails are steeper and more difficult than those on the west, north, and south slopes.

Gurim Village 구림마을

That this area was one of ancient habitation is evident by numerous historic and prehistoric remains. Just outside the national park below Dogap-sa is Gurim [Kurim] Village. Known as the birthplace of Wangin Baksa and Doseon

Guksa, it is also becoming known for its 4th- and 5th-century kiln sites (H.S. # 338), its new **Pottery Culture Center**, and artifacts excavated from the region that are displayed at the pottery center. A short distance northwest of Gurim village, at the edge of Eomgil-li Village, is a small collection of **southern-style dolmen** (엄길리지 석묘) from the 2nd century B.C., and about one kilometer to the west of that is a prehistoric settlement site from roughly the same era. Of much newer vintage, several Joseon-era pavilions and houses have been restored around Gurim and to better illustrate what various housing styles from the region have been like, a number of structures have been erected along the main highway running past the village.

The **birthplace of Wangin Baksa** (왕인박사 유적지) is believed to be the village of Seonggi-dong at the base of the mountain west of Dogap-sa. Wangin Baksa was a Baekje Dynasty scholar who is said to have taken the *Thousand Characters Book,* the *Analects* of Confucius, the *Book of Great Learning,* and other sacred books to Japan in 285 (some suppose it to have been between 375 and 405) at the behest of the Baekje king and became an adviser to the Japanese emperor. Though he's credited with introducing the Japanese to the Chinese-character writing system, Confucian thought, and some paper-making skills, it seems that at least the Chinese characters were already known in Japan. A memorial to this scholar, with portrait and monument, is located south of Gurim village; open 0900–1800, ₩800 entrance fee. This shrine is perhaps of most interest to ardent Korean scholars with a dedication to ancient Korean history. On the mountain not far away is a bas-relief carving said to be that of Wangin Baksa, a cave where he is supposed to have studied, and recreations of Yangsajae and Munsanjae, two buildings where his students studied and visited with friends. From the pavilion on the hill above the parking lot for the shrine (the stairway up to this pavilion has 1000 Chinese character impressed into its steps), you get a good overview of the productive surrounding countryside. It is said that Wangin Baksa left from the seaport of Sang-daepo only a few kilometers from here, now in the midst of rice fields due to the changing condition of the nearby bay and its shoreline. In April, the **Wangin Cultural Festival** is held at this shrine to honor this ancient Korean scholar and ambassador. The famous Silla Dynasty monk Doseon Guksa was also born at the foot of Wolchul-san not far north of Wangin Baksa birthplace.

Yeongam 영암

Yeongam [Yŏngam], a tightly packed town and county seat, is a thriving agricultural community that, along with rice, produces cucumbers, pears, persimmons, red and green peppers, and sesame oil. For about 300 years, fine- tooth bamboo combs have been made here, and the practice of this craft has been designated an Intangible Cultural Asset. Yeongam is the closest town to Wolchul-san National Park—for most visitors, the only reason for passing through.

If staying in Yeongam, try one of the *yeogwan* in the center of town. With the move of the bus terminal to the eastern edge of town, accommodations will eventually pop up there as well. Selected buses from Yeongam run to the Cheonhwang-sa park entrance (₩630), Dogap-sa (₩850), Gwangju (₩4,100), Mokpo (₩2,600), Gangjin (₩1,800), and Haenam (₩2,700).

HAENAM AND VICINITY

A navy command center during the early Joseon Dynasty, Haenam (해남) is currently both a sleepy farming community and the county seat for the southernmost of Korea's peninsular counties. Haenam is known for the large circle dance called *ganggangsullae* (I.C.A. #8), which is performed only by women at a festival in Haenam in October as well as on the first lunar full moon of the new year. It is said that this dance was first performed in celebration of naval victories over the Japanese during the Imjin War. One of the most notable battles, the Myeongnang sea battle, took place in 1597 in the strait between Haenam and Jin-do. The Jin-do bridge now crosses the strait there and a rest area overlooks the water. *Ganggangsullae* is also performed there periodically.

Between Haenam town and the bridge is a site where a number of **dinosaur footprints** have been discovered. Cast in the sedimentary rock along the bank of this deeply-indented bay, the prints from this site (우항리공룡화석지) are from various animals, some as large as one-half meter wide. It's only recently been made widely known; protective coverings over the prints will enhance the viewing ability of this rare find. From Haenam, bus to Hwangsan-myeon and walk the three kilometers to the site.

The most well-known craft of the area is the carving of locally mined jade, much of which is not the higher-quality, watery light green, but rather features shades of white to red and brown. In **Ok-dong** ("Jade Village"), in particular, a few kilometers southwest of Haenam, dozens of artisans produce everything from ashtrays to incense burners to Buddha figures from this workable stone.

The bus terminal is on the eastern edge of town. Near the traffic rotary here are the Gwibinjang Yeogwan (귀빈장여관) and Bandojang Yeogwan (반도장여관). Head in toward town from the bus station, passing a school, the post office, and the Telecom office, and the Hana Yeogwan (하나여관) is down an alley on the left. A little farther into town, before the bridge and on the left, is the Daeyangjang Yeogwan (태양장여관). The best in Haenam is the Haenam Tourist Hotel. Select buses from Haenam run to Jin-do (₩3,700), Daeheung-sa (₩700), Songho-ri (₩2,800), Wan-do (₩3,700), Yeongam (₩2,700), Mokpo (₩3,600), and Gwangju (₩6,800).

Yun Seon-do Historical Site
윤선도유적지

Like Gangjin, Haenam has housed its share of political exiles. The most famous was Yun Seon-do (1587–1671), an official in the Joseon civil service and a noted scholar, poet, and calligrapher. After criticizing government officials, he was unceremoniously kicked out of the National Confucian Academy and exiled to Bogil-so. The capricious political climate later led to Yun's pardon, a second fall from grace and exile, a second pardon, and subsequent exile until he finally decided to take up permanent residence in

Haenam, his ancestral home. His home in exile was four kilometers south of Haenam, in the village of Yeondong (연동). Backed up against a hillside of 300-year-old nutmeg trees (N.M. #241), the square compound, called Nogu-dang (H.S. #167), is typical of a *yangban* manor house of the Honam region. Apart from the 500-year-old living quarters, there are two shrines, several outbuildings, and an exhibition hall that displays several thousand items, including some of Yun's written works (T. #482), an old map (T. #481), an official government document (T. #483), a portrait of Yun Du-seo (T. #240), and other family treasures. A 500-year-old ginkgo stands guard at the front. Out of 31 generations, 21 have inhabited this house. The eldest son of the present generation and his family live here and farm the land. While the house is not open to the public, the museum is open 0900–1800; ₩800 entrance. Catch any bus going to Daeheung-sa, and walk the widened one-kilometer road from the highway to the compound.

Duryun-san Provincial Park
두륜산도립공원
Korea's southernmost peninsular mountain area is Duryun-san (703 meters), where thickly forested slopes run to a rocky top, from where the South Sea and the islands of Wan-do and Jin-do are visible. Daeheung-sa, southernmost of Korea's large temples and headquarters of the 22nd district of the Jogye Buddhist order, is nestled into its northern slope. Camellia and cherry blossoms color the temple in spring. Cooling temperatures swath the whole mountainside with autumnal colors. In 1979, 35 square kilometers of this mountain were set aside as the provincial park. Three kilometers below the temple is a sizable village of *yeogwan*, motels, restaurants, and typical tourist junk shops. From the park ticket booth, a free shuttle bus runs the first two kilometers for visitors who don't want to walk the distance. Entrance to the park and temple is ₩2,000.

Daeheung-sa 대흥사
Said to have been founded by the monk Ado Hwasang during the Baekje era, Daeheung-sa [Taehŭng-sa] (also known as Daedun-sa) is one of the oldest temples in the country—and still a thriving religious center of 30 buildings, with several associated hermitages in the hills above. As you walk up the path from the temple village you pass a small group of *jangseung*, wooden totem poles often referred to as spirit posts which are set up at temple or village entrances to keep evil away. Cherry trees (N.M. #173), thought to grow naturally only on Jeju-do, fill the approach to the temple. Passing through the double-posted front gate, you come upon a garden of stele and a wonderful collection of *sari budo*, erected for the 26 great monks and scholars associated with Daeheung-sa. All from the Joseon Dynasty, they show a remarkable diversity of design and dimension.

Crossing a stone arch bridge, the walkway passes through the lower level of the two-story bell pavilion to reach the temple's main courtyard. Directly ahead is the main hall. Murals depicting the Buddha's life, well-known monks, and other personages are painted on the walls, and tiny paintings of the Buddha have been added between the eave stacks to help support the roof. Three figures are enshrined on the altar between the "dragon beams," and carved-wood animals are suspended from the ceiling. To the right, a typical Silla Dynasty three-tier stone pagoda (T. #320) stands in front of a building that, unusually, is split into two sections. Three of the walls of this building feature a wainscot of stone, also unusual for a temple hall. Inside, judges of the underworld sit in passive silence waiting for all departed souls to come and be assessed. Dragons coil on the ceiling as if ready to pounce on those who fail. The mountain spirit and Lonely Arhat are enshrined in the other section. Between here and the main hall a bell with unusually bold and heavy fairy and floral designs hangs in an octagonal pavilion. Across the stream is Cheonbul-jeon; each of the 1,000 saffron-cloaked white statuettes sitting on the stepped altar has a slightly different body size, posture, and facial expression. They are believed to have been made over a period of six years from jade brought from Gyeongju after the building was repaired in 1813. Murals cover the outside walls. With no inner roof-support pillars, it's conveniently free of visual obstruction. The massive eave brackets, piled high on the structural pillars, support the roof which widely overhangs the building and makes it look larger than it actually is. To its rear is Yonghwa-dang, an unadorned meditation hall. Recent construction of new buildings here is slowly changing the face of this temple compound.

In a separate walled area to the side is **Pyochung-sa,** a venerable shrine with the feeling of age, erected in 1788 and dedicated to Seosan, Sammyeong, and Choyeong, generals of the warrior-monk troops who fought during the Imjin War against the invading Japanese army. A portrait of Seosan hangs in the main hall of the shrine and a statue of him stands to the side of the walk leading to its front gate. A museum nearby, closed Mondays, displays Seosan's personal artifacts, and also preserves the small Dapsan-sa bronze bell (T. #88) from the Goryeo Dynasty. Also associated with this temple is the monk Choeui Seonsa, who with Kim Cheong-heui helped revive the art of the Korean tea ceremony. In front of a small rock garden and pond, a small teahouse has been set up to taste locally grown tea and to sell paraphernalia for the tea ceremony.

Less than an hour's walk above Daeheung-sa is the hermitage **Bungmireuk-am,** with its great views of the valley and surrounding mountain walls. Here, a three-meter-tall Buddha figure (T. #48) chiseled into a flat rock face is protected by a wooden hall. Although done in high relief, this figure bears an unmistakable resemblance to the Seokguram Buddha of Gyeongju, and from it you get the same sense of serenity and tranquillity. A three-tier, moss-covered, stone pagoda (T. #301) stands close by, as does a second pagoda (this one missing its top tier). While many trails exist here, the most often used runs from Daeheung-sa to Bungmireuk-am and on to the top of the mountain. Others connect Daeheung-sa to its associated hermitages, and yet another makes a semicircle along the spiny ridge. When completed, a cable car will run from near the youth hostel at the top end of the village to near the tallest peak for easy access to this mountaintop. It will traverse the valley to the east of that in which Daeheung-sa sits.

Land's End 땅끝

South of Duryun-san Provincial Park is the southernmost point of peninsular Korea. Ddanggeut ("Land's End"), formerly known as T'omal, is located at exactly 34°17' 38" north latitude, according to a black marble tablet erected on the hill overlooking the sea. A pyramidal structure at water's edge marks the spot. A 20-minute walk around the headland from the port village of Galduhang gets you there. From the hill above, Jin-do, Wan-do, Bogil-do, and many other smaller islands off the coast can be seen; a road and trail from the village lead up to an observation pavilion. From the pier, ferries run to Bogil-do and other islands off the coast. This tiny village has turned into quite a community, with a small but decent complement of restaurants, accommodations, and shops. Buses from here go to Haenam, Gwangju, and Mokpo.

A few kilometers north is Songho-ri Beach, a long expanse of white sand at the fringe of a protected bay. Empty most of the year, this beach

Land's End

fills with vacationers during the warm summer months and *minbak*, condos, restaurants, and shops have been built to service them. Some evaporative salt beds can be seen on the way south and lashed bamboo frames poking up through the water in this area indicate seaweed farms. Seaweed is collected, rinsed, and sifted onto small squares of bamboo screens to make thin sheets of laver. These bamboo squares are then affixed to temporary walls of straw to dry—usually three hours in the sun is sufficient. The sheets of laver are then taken off the bamboo screens, folded, wrapped, and packed before being sent off to market. Much seaweed is now dried artificially in factories, but it doesn't have the same wholesome taste or texture of the naturally dried variety. Harvesting is done from fall to spring, but the greatest production is during January and February.

Wan-do 완도

Connected to the peninsula by bridge, Wan-do offers fine seascapes, a patchwork of vegetable fields, and lots of drying seaweed. This island hosted a Silla Dynasty fortress from which ships sailed to rid the coast of pirates and help protect trade with Tang China. Today, the town of Wando is one of the major ferry ports along the south coast—its only importance for most travelers. Several kilometers southwest is a long stretch of seashore called **Gugye-dong pebble beach,** which is strewn with large rounded black stones, pieces of shale that have been jostled together over the years by continual wave action. This 800-meter-long strand is bounded by rock outcrops and backed by a fine grove of trees, some over 500 years old, that shelter swimmers and picnickers during hot summer weather. On the island of Shinji-do, across the channel from Wan-do, is perhaps the best beach in Jeollanam-Do. Like the pebble beach at Gugye-dong, this four-kilometer stretch of white sand, called **Myeongsashimni Beach** (명사십리해수욕장), is part of Dadohae Marine National Park and is subject to a ₩1,300 entrance fee. Empty during the majority of the year, this beach comes alive once the swimming season rolls around, and ferries will continue to run frequently from

Wan-do bringing crowds of sunseekers until the vehicular bridge to the island is finished. Also off Wan-do, and connected by ferry, is the island of Gogeum-do, where Admiral Yi had a command post (H.S. #114) during the Imjin War. Some buildings here have been refurbished.

Every May or June, the **Jangbogo Festival** is held on Wan-do to commemorate the exploits of Silla Admiral Jangbogo, who used Wan-do's 9th-century Silla Dynasty fort **Jeonghaejin** to subdue pirates terrorizing the peninsula's south coast and to secure trade between Korea and China. Events include sea fishing, archery, windsurfing, and paragliding contests. The Jeonghaejin ruins (H.S. #308) lie on a tiny island a short distance off the coast, four kilometers north of the town of Wando.

Located at the north end of town is the **Sea World Hotel** (tel. 061/552-3005), the town's best, where you can get a room from ₩60,000. Convenient to the ferry terminal are the Hilltop Motel (힐탑모텔) and Naju Yeoinsuk (나주여인숙). A bit farther into town are the Mungak Hotel (문각호텔) and Gugiljang Yeogwan (국일장여관), while across from the bus station you'll find the Jeil Hotel (제일장여관). All manner of restaurants can be found in town, but seafood restaurants line the harborfront.

Ferries leave from the **Wan-do ferry terminal** (완도항여객선터미날) at the far south end of town. Two daily car ferries run to Jeju-do, leaving at 1500 and 1600 for the 3.5-hour crossing, and an additional ferry leaves at 0800. Every Saturday and Sunday, one of the afternoon ferries does not run. The second-class fare is ₩15,100 and a second-class bedroom is ₩19,350. Half a dozen ferries a day run to Shinji-do, while a few run farther, to Nok-dong and Cheongsan-do. On the west side of the island is the new port of Hwaheungpo from where additional ferries make runs throughout the day to Bogil-do.

The bus terminal is a 15-minute walk across town from the ferry terminal, and two blocks off the main drag; city buses connect the pier to the terminal. Buses run to all points on the island, as well as to Haenam (₩3,700), Yeongam (₩5,900), Mokpo (₩7,200), and Gwangju (₩9,800).

Bogil-do 보길도

An hour or so south of Wan-do is the smaller island of Bogil-do [Pogil-do]. Yun Seon-do lived here for some time after he left his official life in Seoul. Few artifacts remain from those days, except for parts of gardens and ponds he constructed. Not only a scholar, Yun is known as the best *sijo* poet of his day. On the south side of the island is Yeseong-ni Beach, connected by bus from the pier. You can reach Bogil-do from Galduhang and Hwaheungpo.

JIN-DO 진도

Off the southwestern corner of the peninsula is 320-square-kilometer Jin-do [Chin-do], fourth-largest island in Korea. About 250 other islands as well as Jin-do make up this island county. Since 1984, Jin-do has been connected to the mainland by a graceful, half-kilometer-long suspension bridge that resembles the bridge between Yeosu and Dolsan-do. In 1170, the 18th Goryeo Dynasty king was banished here. About a century later, elite troops of the Goryeo army (the *Sambyeolcho*), disgruntled by the deferential attitude of the royal court to the invading Mongol troops, occupied the island. Two fortresses—Yongjang mountain fortress (H.S. #126), in the north, and Namdo stone fortress (H.S. #127), at the south end—were constructed on Jin-do and battles fought. Eventually, rebel forces were driven from the island and defeated in battle on Jeju-do, where they had retreated to make their last stand. Near the end of the Imjin War, the Korean navy won a decisive encounter with the Japanese in the strait between Jin-do and the mainland. For the last 400 years, however, Jin-do has faded out of the historical limelight and slipped back to its normal preoccupations of farming, fishing, and seaweed harvesting.

This island has not only been a place of historical importance, but is also a rich cultural area with several natural treasures. Local artists here have long been known for their special natural-tint watercolor painting, called *suchaehwa*. Usually landscapes, the name of the recipient is often incorporated into the work. Both the *namdoteul norae* farmer songs (I.C.A. #51) and the *sshit-gim gut* shaman ceremony (I.C.A. #72) are cultural activities unique to the island. On Jin-do are found a wintering ground for a type of swan (N.M. #101), the Eushin-myeon evergreen forest (N.M. #107), and an indigenous dog called the *Jin-do gae* (N.M. #53). Some believe this dog has descended virtually unchanged from the Neolithic Age. Many of the dogs on Jin-do are still purebred, while the majority found on the mainland have been cross-bred. The *Jin-do gae* are muscular and short-haired, white to medium-brown, with pointed noses, close-set almond eyes, and short, up-curled tails.

The bus terminal is at the south end of the town of Jindo. Until accommodations get built nearby, walk the short distance into town and try the Daewonjang Yeogwan (대원장여관) at the first intersection or the Daedong Motel (대동모텔) a little farther on. The town is so small that all necessities are close by. Set on the hillside up behind the town is the Jindo Hyanggyo (진도향교). Enshrining memorial tablets for 25 Confucian scholars, this well-kept academy is a fine example of a Joseon Dynasty small-town private school.

From the town of Jindo, buses run to all points on the island; buses for peninsula destinations include Haenam (₩3,700), Mokpo (₩4,100), and Gwangju (₩10,500). The only ferries servicing Jin-do run between Mokpo and Jeju-do, and these stop at Byeokpa on the north coast of Jin-do. Before the bridge was built, Byeokpa was the principal entry point to the island. A bus meets the ferry for a ride into town. Above the harbor is another memorial marker for the able Admiral Yi Sun-shin.

Jin-do Strait

Between Jin-do and the mainland runs one of the swiftest tidal currents along Korea's coast. Reaching 13 knots, the current makes the water look like a river when at its swiftest. On one fateful day in 1597, a flotilla of Japanese ships chased a small number of Korean turtle ships into this narrow channel from the north, while the tide was rushing south. Just when the turtle ships reached Uldolmok, the strait's narrowest point at less than half a kilometer wide, they turned and headed for shore. Unable to turn so quickly, and swept along by the swift tide, the larger and more ponderous Japanese ships continued on through the channel. Unbeknownst to them, the brilliant tactician Admiral Yi Sun-shin had a steel cable strung just below the surface, so when the current pulled the Japanese ships into it, their hulls were split and the boats foundered and sank. This was known as the Myeongnang sea victory. Today, a large stone memorial monument and shrine (T. #503) to this event stands at Chungmusa on a hill just south of the bridge.

Fortresses

Walls of the two fortresses built by the *Sambyeolcho* (1270) remain on the island. Wanting to continue the fight against the Mongols, the soldiers established themselves here for a few short years, creating a tiny maritime state. After repeated battles, the rebels had to flee to Jeju-do, where they held out for a few years before their eventual defeat. **Yongjang Sanseong** (용장산성), the larger of the two fortresses, lies on the hillside between the new bridge and the town of Jindo. Part of its three-meter-high wall has been reconstructed and terraces for palace and military structures can still be discerned on the lower slopes. **Namdo Seokseong** (남도석성) stands at the southern tip of the island. Only 360 meters around, this fortress, with its three gate openings, now contains the village of Namdong. In 2001, some repairs were done to the wall, which can be walked, and two arched bridges again straddle the stream to the front.

Local Art

Located in front of the county office in the town of Jindo is the **Jin-do Folk Art Museum,** which contains craft items and artwork from the area. A few kilometers south of town is **Ullimsanbang** (운림산방), the residence and studio of Heo Yu, a famous painter of the Jin-do style of *suchaehwa*, sometimes referred to as the Southern School, a type of landscape painting that often depicts ethereal mountain scenes partially obscured by clouds and fog. Heo Yeong and Heo Geon, son and grandson, also became well-known painters, and a fifth-generation descendant is now also making a name for himself as a painter. Entrance to the landscaped garden, lotus pond, and exhibition hall is ₩500. Several kilometers away, in Sammak-ni, the private **Namjin Art Museum** shows mostly calligraphy and both Eastern and Western paintings, but also displays a few pieces of pottery; open 0900–1700 every day except Sunday.

Set next to Ullimsanbang is **Ssanggye-sa** (쌍계사), the most significant temple on the island. A temple of *biguni,* this sanctuary is not particularly fancy, but the exterior wall murals are enjoyable. Enter via the walkway under a new open pavilion that sits across from the main hall.

Parting of the Sea

Jin-do is the site of one of the most unusual natural phenomena in the country: the "parting of the sea." Affected by the pull of the moon, the tide draws water away from the shallow channel be-

JIN-DO SEA-PARTING LEGEND

Centuries ago, a man and his family were banished to Jeju-do. During the long journey, their ship was wrecked in a storm and the family washed ashore on Jin-do. They landed near an area known to have many tigers, and on occasion someone from the nearby village would disappear. For several generations, this man's descendants lived precariously in this village, leading a hard life. Eventually, the descendants decided to move to the small island of Mo-do for safety. In their rush, they left behind Grandmother Ppong. Grandmother Ppong was distraught and prayed to be united with her family. One night in March, the dragon king appeared to her in a dream and told her that she would be able to cross to the island on a rainbow that he would create for her. Going to the sea, she found that a rainbow-shaped opening had appeared between the two islands. Overjoyed, she began to cross, but as she was an old lady, she tired quickly and fell to the ground before reaching the far side. Her family came to meet her from the other side. Finally reunited, she passed away happily in their arms.

tween the village of Hoi-dong on Jin-do and Mo-do, a small offshore island, exposing a three-kilo-meter-long, 50-meter-wide muddy strip of land that can be walked across. Simply an odd occurrence for most, Korean Christians look upon it as a reminder of the biblical parting of the sea. Over the years it's received more and more publicity, and now attracts a great number of the serious and the curious. Many come to collect seaweed and edible sea creatures from the path. The sea parts several times during the year, and it's particularly evident in March and July when the water drops as much as eight meters. The **Yeongdeung-je Festival** is usually held to coincide with the spring occurrence of this phenomenon, and its main activities are a ceremony to the god of the sea for a bountiful catch, the *sshitgim gut* shaman ceremony to expel evil influences, folk dances, songs and drum music, and traditional games. This event has become a big deal. Easily seen from the observation pavilion on the hillside above, floats mark the route when the water is high.

Mokpo and the Islands

MOKPO 목포

Jeollanam-Do's major port city is Mokpo [Mokp'o] (pop. 250,000). Used for centuries by fishing boats and domestic cargo ships, it was opened as a "treaty port" for international commerce in 1897. Connected to Seoul by rail in 1913, Mokpo became a strategic harbor during the Japanese colonial period, evidenced today by some older architecture. In 1949, Mokpo was elevated to city status. Yudal-san (228 meters) thrusts its rocky head above Mokpo's harbor in the heart of the city; over this hill drapes Yudal-san Park. The city center is located to the front of the train station, and between there and the ferry terminal lies the old town, always a hive of activity. Besides the Pohae Brewery, limited small-scale industry is largely located on the eastern end of town, while larger industrial districts and harbor facilities are being created over the hill to the north of the city center, along the south side of the river near the airport, and on the back side of Goha-do island. A transportation and commercial center, Mokpo is also an educational center and the home of Mokpo National University, Mokpo University, Mokpo National Maritime University, and several colleges. In the late 1980s, a tidal dam was built across the Yeongsan River on the eastern edge of the city, creating Yeongsan Lake and providing flood control and new farmland along the riverbanks. Across inlet bays just to the south of Mokpo, two similar but smaller dams have also been built and future plans call for other similar dams to enclose shallow tidal waters between nearby islands and the peninsula just to the north. By 2007, a new provincial government complex and accompanying urban area will be built on the eastern edge of the city.

For more information, see www.mokpo.chon-nam.kr.

Yudal-san Park 유달산공원
Up from the harbor is a two-story brick building (H.S. #289), originally the Japanese consulate, later the city hall and municipal library, and now a cultural center dedicated to the literature of Park Wha-sung, the first of Korea's modern female novelists. To its left a stairway leads up to Yudal-san Park. A statue of Admiral Yi greets you as you walk up the steps; a huge new millennium bell hangs nearby. Adm. Yi looks back at Nojeok-bong hill across the street. A story relates that Nojeok-bong was covered with straw bags during the Imjin War to imitate a huge pile of rice in hopes of making it appear to the invading Japanese navy that more men were stationed here than really were. There is no indication whether this deception worked or not, but a similar story is told about Nojeok-bong in Bukhan Sanseong National Park in Seoul and how the trick worked

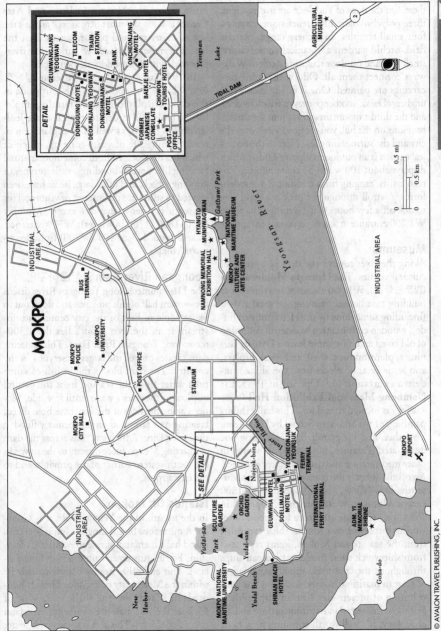

DETAIL

GEUMWANGJANG
YEOGWAN
TELECOM
TRAIN
STATION
DONGGUNG MOTEL
BANK
ONCHEONJANG
MOTEL
DEOKJINJANG YEOGWAN
DONGSHIMJANG
MOTEL
BAEKJE HOTEL
FORMER
JAPANESE
CONSULATE
CHOWON
TOURIST HOTEL
POST
OFFICE

Yeongsan
Lake

TIDAL DAM

AGRICULTURAL
MUSEUM

2

Yeongsan River

0.5 mi

0.5 km

Gatbawi Park

HYANGTO
MUNHWAGWAN

NAMNONG MEMORIAL
EXHIBITION HALL

NATIONAL
MARITIME MUSEUM

MOKPO
CULTURE AND
ARTS CENTER

INDUSTRIAL AREA

MOKPO

INDUSTRIAL
AREA

1

BUS
TERMINAL

MOKPO
UNIVERSITY

MOKPO
POLICE

POST OFFICE

STADIUM

MOKPO
CITY HALL

SEE DETAIL

Nojeok-bong

YEOCHEONJANG
YEONSUK

FERRY
TERMINAL

INDUSTRIAL AREA

Hatbori Harbor

MOKPO
AIRPORT

INTERNATIONAL
FERRY TERMINAL

ADM. YI
MEMORIAL
SHRINE

Goha-do

SCULPTURE
GARDEN

ORCHID
GARDEN

GEUMHWA MOTEL

SOELLIMJANG
MOTEL

Yudal-san
Park

Yudal-san

Yudal Beach

MOKPO NATIONAL
MARITIME UNIVERSITY

SHINAN BEACH
HOTEL

New
Harbor

Yudal Beach

there. On the slope of Yudal-san are five pavilions, three polychromatic high-relief stone carvings, four small temples, an archery range, exercise field, orchid garden, a botanical conservatory, small zoo, and outdoor sculpture garden. Walkways connect them all. Oddly, the stone-face carvings are painted. One is of the monk Heungbeop Daesa, another portrays a ferocious deva, and the third a mountain spirit. From the various pavilions on the hill, you get good views over the city and the surrounding sea. Next to the botanical garden is an outdoor sculpture garden which displays about 100 works by contemporary Korean artists, ranging from traditional to modern forms. A stroll through the park is a good way to tick off a few hours while waiting for a ferry; ₩1,200 entrance at any of its several entrances.

Museums

Along the river toward the dam is a group of cultural venues. The **Hyangto Munhwagwan** (향토문화관), ₩1,000 entrance, is a three-story building that houses paintings by local artists, (including some done by the Heo family of Jindo), wooden craft items, a wonderful collection of old coins and bills, some Joseon Dynasty furniture, plentiful rock, shell, and coral displays, and some ceramic pieces from the Shinan undersea excavation site. Opened in 1985, the **Namnong Memorial Exhibition Hall** (남농 기념관) is located next door. This hall exhibits paintings of the Southern School by Heo Geon, his father, and his grandfather, including some designated Treasure. Numerous art works in other mediums are also displayed; free entrance. Across the street is the **National Maritime Museum** (한국해양유물전시관); open 0900–1800 except Monday, ₩600 entrance. Opened in 1994, this riverside structure features a noteworthy display of two Korean ships excavated from the sea around Mokpo, items recovered from shipwreck sites, models of Korean ships throughout the centuries, and an explanation of Korean maritime history, including the contribution of present-day Korean shipbuilders. For those interested in maritime history and archaeology, it's well worth spending time here. For information on the Internet, see www.sea-muse.go.kr. The **Mokpo Culture and Arts Center** is along the shore here as well and it's the site of many cultural performances. Past the maritime museum is Gatbawi Park, a new riverside park with some oddly shaped rocks.

In 1993, an **Agricultural Museum** (영산호 농업박물관) was opened on the south side of the dam. Displayed here are farming implements, tools, and structures typical of the Jeollanam-Do region, as well as an explanation of rural farming life of years gone by, much of which has disappeared from contemporary rural farming life. Several buildings, various types of grinding wheels, and other large items have been erected to stimulate the interest of visitors. This museum is open every day except Monday 0900–1800 (1700 in winter); ₩770 entrance. Take bus no. 111 or 105 (₩700) from downtown Mokpo.

Yeongsan River Dam 영산호하구언

The 116-kilometer-long Yeongsan River drains the western half of this province and flows out to sea at Mokpo. East of the city center and upstream from the river mouth lies the 4,300-meter-long Yeongsan River Dam. This estuarine dam creates one of the largest reservoirs in the country. The dam blocks the inrush of saline tidal water from the sea and halts the natural outflow of the river's water until low tide. Sections along the sides of this lake have been diked, creating new farmland on the formerly flooded riverside plains. A highway runs across the dam connecting Mokpo more directly to the towns in the southwestern corner of the province and to the city airport.

Islands Off Mokpo

In the mouth of the Yeongsan River is Gohado. A munitions base during the Imjin War, this island has a memorial shrine to Admiral Yi Sunshin. Ferries run several times a day to the island. This and other nearby islands actually lie within the Mokpo city boundaries. Literally hundreds of islands dot the shallow sea west of Mokpo; the vast majority constitute the island county of Shinan. This area is strewn with oyster beds and seaweed farms. One unusual harvest from these waters has been the recovery of goods from a sunken 14th-century Chinese cargo ship, most of which are on display at the Gwangju National Museum, while some are now housed in the museums of Mokpo. Through these islands run the many tentacles of the ferry network that stems from Mokpo. The small islands off Jin-do, sections of Bigeum-do, Daecho-do, Daeya-do, and Eui-do, plus Hong-do and Heuksan-do are all sections of the Dadohae Marine National Park.

Accommodations

The city's best hotels are the first-class **Chowon Tourist Hotel** (tel. 061/243-0055), located just below Yudal-san Park, and the **Shinan Beach Hotel** (tel. 061/243-3399), out along the sea on the west side of Yudal-san. Korean and Western rooms at either are in the ₩90,000–140,000 range. The second-class **Baekje Hotel** (tel. 061/242-4411), in the heart of the old town, has less expensive rooms. One concentration of accommodations is directly in front of the Mokpo train station; another is up from the ferry terminal. Near the train station try the Deokjinjang Yeogwan (덕진장여관), Geumgwangjang Yeogwan (금광장여관), Donggung Motel (동궁모텔), Dongshimjang Motel (동심장여관), or the Oncheonjang Motel (온천장모텔). Up the street from the ferry, the Yeocheonjang Yeoinsuk (여천장여인숙), Soellimjang Motel (선림장모텔), and Geumhwa Motel (금화모텔), are a few to check out. Near the bus terminal, try New Hilton Motel (뉴힐튼모텔) or Gran Prix Motel (그랑프리모텔).

Transportation

Mokpo is an important transportation hub. **Mokpo Airport** (목포공항) is located on the south bank of the river, 18 kilometers from the city center. A small affair, but all necessary services are available. An airport shuttle bus (₩2,300) runs on a regular schedule down the main streets of the city, passing both the train station and bus terminal, arriving in time for outbound flights. Asiana Airlines and Korean Air together run five flights a day to Seoul. For reservations in the city, contact Asiana Airlines (tel. 061/284-

8000) or KAL (tel. 061/278-6072). In 2003, a new and larger international airport will open in Muan, just north of Mokpo, for greater access to this region.

Ferries run to most of the inhabited islands in the West Sea and to Jeju-do. Most ferries leave from the **Mokpo Passenger Ferry Terminal #1** (목포항여객선터미널). No reservations are necessary for any ferry except on holidays, when they're essential. The terminal has ticket and information windows, a domestic travel agency, shops, and storage lockers—and many movable food carts line the sidewalk outside the terminal gate. Of the approximately dozen-and-a-half routes, perhaps the most useful runs are to Hong-do, and Heuksan-do. Four ferries a day run to Heuksan-do and Hong-do, with one carrying on to Soheuksan-do. These catamarans require only about two-and-a-half hours to Hong-do; fares run ₩28,100 to Hong-do, ₩22,150 to Heuksan-do, and ₩39,800 to Soheuksan-so. Two leave in the morning and two go in the early afternoon. The smaller **Ferry Terminal #2** is located a few steps upriver to the east and has ferries to numerous small islands along the coast, including six a day to Goha-do for the shrine to Adm. Yi Sun-Shin. The newer **International Ferry Terminal** (목포국제여객선터미널) offers ferries to Lianyungang, China, which is south of Quingdao. Ferries to Jeju-do also leave from the international terminal. Ferries to Jeju-do leave daily at 0900 (except Saturday) and 1530 (except Sunday) for the five-and-a-half-hour crossing. Fares on the 0900 ferry run between ₩16,500 and ₩45,200, while the later ferry charges ₩39,000. The afternoon ferry stops at Byeokpa on Jin-do (₩12,600) and Chuja-do (₩33,000) on the way. When purchasing a ticket, passengers may have to fill out a boarding slip providing names and passport numbers.

Thirteen trains a day run from Mokpo to Seoul, with one a day to Daejeon and two to Busan. Express buses run only to Seoul (₩15,300) and Incheon (₩16,000). Select intercity bus destinations and fares are Gwangju (₩5,300), Yeongam (₩4,100), Haenam (₩3,600), Daeheung-sa (₩4,900), Jin-do (₩4,500), and Wan-do (₩7,200).

Frequently used city buses are nos. 1, 2, 3, 105, 200, and 300, which connect the bus station to the train station and ferry terminal; no. 7, which runs to the Maritime Museum; and nos. 105 or 111, which run out to the farming museum and the Yeongsan tidal dam.

HONG-DO 홍도

One of the most scenic sea journeys in Jeollanam-Do is to Heuksan-do and Hong-do. The first half of this route runs through the islands of Shinan County, passing under two tall bridges between islands on the way. Hundreds of thousands of years ago, the mountains of the Korean peninsula marched out into the West Sea. Due to the gradual sinking of this coastline, these mountains became islands. The channel water amongst these islands remains a light greenish color, but abruptly turns deep blue beyond Docho-do, reflecting the rich tone of the sky. The last half of this journey is through open water, first to Heuksan-do and then on to the red rocks of Hong-do. The sea is generally calm, but can produce waves up to several meters high during turbulent winter weather.

The Island

Located 120 kilometers west of Mokpo, this seven-square-kilometer island—about six kilometers north to south—is one of the province's most distant islands. It's surrounded by nearly two dozen uninhabited islets. Consisting mainly of quartzite and sandstone, Hong-do ("Red Island") has a definite reddish coloration in much of its exposed rock. There is no coastal plain. The island rises straight out of the exceedingly clear water to a height of 368 meters, and its steep, thickly wooded hillsides are sliced by short narrow valleys. Much of the island is bounded by sheer cliffs, slanted slabs of stone, series of spires, and wonderfully shaped masses of red rock. Sections give you the impression of an unapproachable fortress wall, while others resemble the scaly back of a huge sea dragon surging through the sea. Each unique formation has a name and a story, and all must be seen from the water as no trail runs along the water's edge. Seen most dis-

tinctly on clear days, the impression turns somewhat surreal—almost ghostly at times—when the island is enveloped by low clouds or fog.

As small as it is, Hong-do supports several hundred varieties of plants and animals, has been designated a nature preserve (N.M. #170), and is a breeding ground for the black-tailed gull (N.M. #335). White camellias are numerous on Hong-do, as is the native *bonchunhwa* flower, the dried stalks of which were used in the past to thatch roofs in the absence of sufficient rice straw. Up past the post office, next to the local administrative office, is a small building with a free display of various orchids that grow on the island.

Koreans often compare Hong-do with Ulleung-do in the East Sea. Some say that if you've seen one first, you'll not be impressed by the other. While both rise precipitously from the blue sea, Hong-do has the more fetching rock formations and vibrant colors and is more compact, therefore more quickly absorbed. Ulleung-do, on the other hand, is much larger, rises nearly three times as high, and has a greater diversity of attractions. You'll not be disappointed with either. Visit both!

Hong-do was first settled in 1679. Its population has varied over the years but now stands at 530. Hong-do has two villages. The larger, at the south end, has two ferry piers, numerous *yeogwan, minbak,* and restaurants, a school, post office, a Telecom office, and the island's only electric generator. Backlit by the morning sun, fishing boats bob in the cove below this village. *Haenyeo* can sometimes be seen diving for abalone, clams, and other sea creatures when the water is calm in the cove. A pebble beach and a second pier lie over the low hill beyond the school to the west. From the beach on a sunny afternoon or in the early evening, you can perhaps best experience "the crimson glow of the island." At the northern village are additional fishing boats, two short piers, and a lighthouse. There are no roads on the island and only a handful of motorcycle tricycle delivery carts. The island's only useful footpath connects these two villages—a one-hour hike. The path starts below the school and pretty much follows the ridgeline up the spine of the island. The traditional occupations on Hong-do are fishing, seaweed harvesting, and diving for abalone and other sea animals; however, money brought in by tourism (still mostly domestic) now makes up a healthy chunk of the island's income. Keep in mind that prices on the island are higher than on the peninsula; everything except fish has to be shipped in.

Round-the-Island Tour

The only way to fully enjoy the unique features of Hong-do is by boat. Many entrepreneurs offer two-hour rides around the island (₩12,000), leaving from the main pier at the south village. During summer these boats are full, but at both ends of the season they all compete for passengers. A running commentary in Korean describes each cliff, rock spire, arch, thrusting wall of stone, animal-shaped boulder, and cave to pay attention to, and briefly relates the history and legends of the island. If you've come this far to "see" the island, don't miss one of these rides.

Practicalities

Yeogwan and *minbak* are located in the south village. Among the many are the Gwangseongjang Yeogwan (광성장여관), Bangu Motel (방우모텔), Seoul Hotel (서울호텔), Beachjang Yeogwan (비치장여관), and Geumseongjang Yeogwan (금상장여관). As you would expect, restaurants in town serve mostly seafood dishes. *Jeonbokjuk* (abalone porridge) is one specialty to try. While a bit expensive at ₩12,000, it's just right for a cool morning. Raw fish, of course, is also a big favorite.

Tickets for Heuksan-do (₩7,550) and Mokpo (₩28,100) are sold from a booth on the quay. Crossing in about two hours, the sleek and modern enclosed catamarans give everyone a smooth and comfortable ride. During the summer months, additional ferries (₩34,000) also run to/from the port of Gyeokpa on the Byeonsan Peninsula in Jeollabuk-Do. Replacing a pier destroyed by a typhoon, the new pier on the east side of the south village is sturdier, encloses more of the harbor, and allows for passengers to disembark directly without the use of a shuttle boat as in the past. Over the hill on the west side of this village is a second pier. Generally, but de-

pending upon the weather, ferries land on the east side in winter and on the west side in summer. Because this is part of Dadohae Marine National Park, a ₩2,300 landing tax and park fee is collected from all arriving non-residents. Most tourists visit during July and August when they may outnumber residents, and there are additional ferries scheduled then. During the dead of winter fewer ferries make the crossing. Keep your eye on the weather as ships are subject to cancellation due to periodic rough seas. During storms, no boats run.

HEUKSAN-DO 흑산도

Heuksan-do [Hŭksan-do] is some 20 kilometers toward the mainland from Hong-do. The Heuksan-do group consists of 11 inhabited islands—of which Heuksan-do is by far the largest—and 89 uninhabited islets. Heuksan-do means "Black Mountain Island," and though not as dramatic as its neighbor to the west, it does have some fine dark rock formations along the coast. Stones are so numerous in the fields that they must be removed and piled to make fences or used in terrace walls. Some are attached to ropes and draped over roofs to hold down the straw thatch during high winds, similar to what is done on Jeju-do.

Heuksan-do (pop. 5,000) is larger, taller, and more populated than Hong-do; its coastal lowland supports farming. Heuksan-do has perhaps the best deep-water port of any island off Korea's southwest coast. It sports a sizable fishing fleet, and during severe storms is also used as a safe anchorage by fishing fleets from other Asian nations. Years ago, Ye-ri, the principal village and port-of-call, was a thriving whaling center, the counterpart to Jangsaengpo (Ulsan) on the east coast. Many of its seafood restaurants serve raw fish. These restaurants, as well as the town's many coffee shops and drinking halls, seem to employ an overabundance of young women, perhaps due to the small military base at the edge of town.

Round-the-Island Walk

Not long ago, Heuksan-do had no motor transportation beyond that between Ye-ri and Jil-li. If

Ye-ri Harbor at Heuksan-do

you needed to go anywhere, you walked or took a boat. The island's trails have been widened into roads but as there is no bus transportation you can still walk without too much concern for traffic. Taxis are used on the island, but these are four-wheel-drive vehicles and will continue to be used until the roads are paved.

Starting in Ye-ri, follow the road west around the large bay to Jil-li, where there is a short sand beach and a second pier. From the far side of this village, walk up past the reservoir and over the hill to Bi-ri, or follow the road to Eup-dong and up the hill past a three-tier stone pagoda and below the remains of a half-moon mountain fortress on the way to Ma-ri and Bi-ri. The road continues south around the side of the hill, high over the rough coastline, to the tiny hamlet of Gonchon. Make your way up the valley behind this settlement and over the hill to Shim-ni. A short walk over the rise to the east brings you to the larger village of Sa-ri and its white sand beach, from where you must follow the road around the hill to Sosa-ri. From Sosa-ri, the road parallels the shore as far as the next village, where it splits in two. In Cheonchon-ni, one road goes into the valley and over the ridge to Jil-li, while the other continues around the hill past the tiny Buddhist temple Shinwon-sa on the island's east coast and back to Ye-ri. This hike requires a full day. Start early to be back by sunset. For a tour of the island by taxi, expect a fee of around ₩60,000 for two hours.

Practicalities

New harbor facilities and a new ferry terminal have been built around the corner from the older section of the Ye-ri Harbor, around which you still find the post office, shops, and most restaurants and accommodations. Two accommodations to try that front the old harbor are Namdojang Yeogwan (남도장여관) and Gaechonjang Yeogwan (개천장여관); closer to the ferry terminal is the Sukso Town Yeogwan (숙소타운여관). The best on the island is the second-class Heuksan Beach Hotel. Located halfway between Ye-ri and Jil-li, it charges ₩60,000 a night.

Ferries from Heuksan-do run to Hong-do, Mokpo, and Soheuksan-do. Unscheduled private boats run periodically to the island's coastal villages and nearby inhabited islands; make arrangements at the pier with the captains of these boats. Following the arrival of a passenger ferry and when there is enough interest, excursion boats leave Ye-ri harbor for two-hour tours of Heuksan-do and nearby islands.

Gwangju 광주

Gwangju [Kwangju], capital of Jeollanam-Do (until the government center is moved to its new home outside Mokpo around 2007), is the political, economic, and art and cultural center of the province. It's been an established population center since the Three Kingdoms period (pre-660). Gwangju (pop. 1,400,000) is the fifth-largest city in South Korea, by far the largest metropolitan area in the southwestern corner of the province. In November 1986, it became the fifth city in the country to be administratively separated from its surrounding province and given the rank of a "special city," with status equal to that of a province. Its title was changed to a metropolitan city in 1995. In recent years, additional acreage has been incorporated into the city, mainly to the west in the section known as Gwangsan. This western section, along with the area north of the expressway, has the bulk of the city's large new industrial estates, while a few older establishments, like the Ilshin and Jeonnam textile companies, still occupy space closer in to the center of the city. The new Sangmu residential and commercial district has also sprung up between the city center and the airport in an attempt to ease the congestion of the city center. Although Gwangju is surrounded by great agricultural plains, the city itself backs up against Mudeung-san, the mountain mass towering above the city to the east.

The old section of town lies along the stream that flows through the city. Bounded at one end by the provincial capitol, this area stretches northwest encompassing the main business and entertainment area of the city. Jungjang-no, Geumnam-no, and adjacent streets and alleys, plus the area between the Grand Hotel and the provincial government building, are alive with the sights and sounds of after-hours Gwangju. Here you'll find dozens of clothing stores and other shops, theaters, restaurants, coffee houses, and drinking establishments; it's a good place to people-watch and pick up the "vibe" of the city. Closed to vehicular traffic, Jungjang-no is full of pedestrian activity. Geumnam-no is the principal traffic artery through downtown, along which major businesses have offices; beneath it for several blocks runs an underground arcade of shops. East of Geumnam-no, around the corner from Namdo Art Hall, and running for two blocks to Jungjang-no, lies an alley known as Art Street, or Avenue of the Arts. Many art-supply stores, galleries, studios, restaurants, and traditional tea houses are concentrated here. On Saturdays and Sundays only this street turns into the art and antique Gaemi Market. In the May 18 Democratic Square to the front of the provincial government office, a fountain erupts in a display of water and light, entertaining passersby on fine-weather evenings.

Special products of the city include handmade calligraphy brushes, nacre lacquerware furniture, globe-like watermelon, and tea grown on the slopes of Mudeung-san. Nationally designated master craftsmen of the Jindari writing brush, *gayageum* stringed musical instrument, Goryeo celadon pottery, and Korean wooden furniture live and work in the city, as do designated masters of *bansori* and *sijo* vocal music and the drumming technique that accompanies *bansori*. The Jeonnam National University, Gwangju National University of Education, Chosun University, Honam University, and nearly two dozen other institutions of higher learning are located in the city, and this seems appropriate as the region has produced numerous artists, writers, poets, and other literary figures in the past. Aside from its position as a political, cultural, and agricultural center, Gwangju serves as an important commercial hub, and its expanding industrial

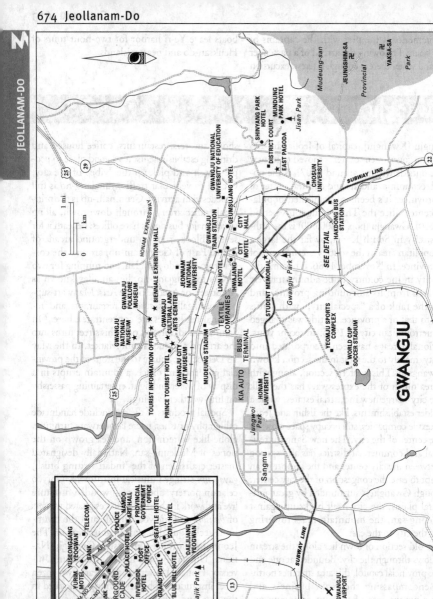

GWANGJU

Mudeung-san

JEUNGSHIM-SA

YAKSA-SA
Park

Provincial

HONAM EXPRESSWAY

SUBWAY LINE

SHINYANG PARK HOTEL
MUNDUNG PARK HOTEL
DISTRICT COURT
EAST PAGODA
Jisan Park
CHOSUN UNIVERSITY

GWANGJU NATIONAL UNIVERSITY OF EDUCATION

GEUMSUJANG HOTEL
GWANGJU TRAIN STATION
CITY HALL
CITY MOTEL HOTEL
LION HOTEL
IHWJANG MOTEL

HAKDONG BUS STATION

SEE DETAIL

Gwangju Park

GWANGJU FOLKLORE MUSEUM

BIENNALE EXHIBITION HALL

JEONAM NATIONAL UNIVERSITY

STUDENT MEMORIAL

YEOMJU SPORTS COMPLEX

GWANGJU CULTURAL AND ARTS CENTER

GWANGJU NATIONAL MUSEUM

TOURIST INFORMATION OFFICE

PRINCE TOURIST HOTEL

GWANGJU CITY ART MUSEUM

MUDEUNG STADIUM

TEXTILE COMPANIES

BUS TERMINAL

KIA AUTO

HONAM UNIVERSITY

Jungwoi Park

WORLD CUP SOCCER STADIUM

Sangmu

SUBWAY LINE

0   1 mi
0   1 km

© AVALON TRAVEL PUBLISHING, INC.

DETAIL

TELECOM
POLICE
NAMDO ART HALL
PROVINCIAL GOVERNMENT OFFICE

YUSEONGJANG YEOGWAN
YURIM MOTEL
BANK
ART ST.
SEATTLE HOTEL
SOFIA HOTEL

GEUM MUN-RO
CHUNGJANG-NO
BANK
PALACE HOTEL
UNDERGROUND ARCADE
POST OFFICE
DAEJIJANG YEOGWAN

RIVERSIDE HOTEL
GRAND HOTEL
BLUE HILL HOTEL

JUNGSAN-RO
Sajik Park

13

GWANGJU AIRPORT

SONGJEONG-NI TRAIN STATION

Gwangsan

22

25

29

22

1

sector includes textiles, electronics, heavy machinery, and automotive manufacturing. In contrast to the gray tile roofs found commonly throughout the rest of the country, many residential roofs here and in the province are red, with a distinctly sharper upturn at the ends. While common a few decades ago, these old-style red roofs are decreasing in number due to newer construction techniques and materials and the replacement of the old buildings with new.

Every year during the first lunar full moon, the Gwangsan *Gosaeum Nori* Festival is held in the city. *Gosaeum* is a traditional folk game that originated in this region as a lively and friendly exchange between villages during the slack time of year. In the game, two large structures of wood and straw rope (often referred to as "chariots" or "tanks"), propelled by dozens of youths and ridden by one "general," are pushed together and jostled until one of the structures is toppled and the rider felled. Aside from this "tank fight," other festival events include tug-of-war, Korean wrestling, other athletic contests, seesaw, and traditional music and dance. Residents and visitors also enjoy a Gimchi Festival that's held every October. Like Jinju, Gwangju has latched onto the appellation "City of Art." In August, the city hosts the **Gwangju Art Festival**, where nearly 1,000 pieces of art are displayed and eight categories judged. Local festivals are numerous, but in 2002, Gwangju was one of the 10 Korean cities to host the international World Cup soccer games, in the new stadium in the southwestern section of town. This facility, with the adjacent Yeomju Sports Complex, is the focal point for sporting events and competitions in the city. Other facilities include the Mudeung baseball and soccer stadiums.

Gwangju citizens are proud and independent, with a streak of opposition running through their veins. This opposition stance stems from the subjugation of the Baekje people by Silla at the end of the Three Kingdoms period, which continued into the Joseon Dynasty, when the province was regarded as little more than a backwater fit for political exiles. Even into the 20th century, less money and effort has gone into strengthening this region economically (and in other

ways) than into other regions of the country—in part because Seoul is considered the "center" of the country in all respects, and perhaps because four post-Korean War presidents have hailed from the Gyeongsang-Do region, the traditional nemesis of the Jeolla-Do region, and have directed money earlier to their own region. This changed somewhat after Kim Dae-jung was elected president, and more economic interest was given to Gwangju and the province as a whole as this is his home turf and power base.

Two events of the 20th century dramatically portray the pride and independence of the people of Gwangju. In 1929, during the Japanese occupation of the country, Gwangju students, like others throughout the country, demonstrated against discrimination by Japanese officials, and called for freedom from colonial rule. These protests turned into all-out bloody rioting, and scores were killed or injured in the city. In 1980, protesting the assumption of power by General Chun Doo Hwan and calling for less military participation in politics and greater democratization of government, the city once again erupted in several days of demonstrations and rioting, which resulted in a short takeover of the provincial government and culminated in the deaths of at least 200 and arrest of thousands. The military's participation in this event, often called the 1980 Gwangju Incident but now referred to by Koreans as the May 18 Gwangju Democratic Uprising, was directed by then-general Rho Tae-woo, later President Rho.

The provincial tourist information office, while full of brochures and staffed by helpful workers, is rather inconveniently located at the Gwangju Biennale site, next to the Folk Museum, in the northern part of town. Tourist information booths are also located at the train and bus stations and at the airport. For more information, check out www.metro.gwangju.kr on the Web.

SIGHTS

Sajik Park 사직공원

Sajik Park caps a low hill along Gwangju Stream. It was the first modern public park for the city, and from the multi-story pavilion at the top of the hill are good views of both downtown Gwangju and the western suburbs. Below the pavilion lie walking paths and gardens. Cherry trees turn the walks pink in spring, rosy acacia colors the hill in summer, and hardwood trees swath the hillside in hues of red, yellow, and orange in autumn. On the south side of the hill is the oldest Western-style house in the city, a large multi-story brick building constructed in the 1920s by an American missionary. Walk across the city's Central Bridge and up the hill, or take bus no. 8, 22, or 25 to the first bus stop west of the stream.

Gwangju Park 광주공원

Set on a second streamside hill only a short distance north of Sajik Park is Gwangju Park. A tight little area covered in zelkova trees, this park contains the Citizens' Hall, gymnasium, memorial to war dead, and memorial to An Jung-geun, who in 1909 assassinated Ito Hirobumi, principal architect of the Treaty of 1905 (which had led to Korea's protectorate status under Japanese control). Directly behind the modern gymnasium is the West five-tier pagoda (T. #109), a stone remnant from the past; the East five-tier pagoda (T. #110) stands amongst houses some 200 meters west of the District Court across town. Of typical Silla design, both are tall and slender, evoking uprightness and dignity. Below and to the south side of Gwangju Park is the **Gwangju Confucian Academy** (광주향교). Founded in 1398 but moved to this site in 1488, it's still used privately for the study of Confucian classics and doctrine, and religious ceremonies are performed here every spring and autumn.

Student Memorial

Starting with an incident in which several Japanese schoolboys insulted some Korean schoolgirls, fighting broke out, and eventually rioting erupted in Gwangju on November 3, 1929. The revolt was forcibly squelched by the Japanese constabulary, but not before much blood was shed and hundreds of people were arrested. Resistance movements spread throughout the country for several months afterwards. Dedicated to the participants in this incident, a tower-like monument stands in a well-manicured garden in the corner of Gwangju Jeil High School. Enter through the east wall gate of the school or via the newer exhibition hall that stands next to it, which attempts to put this event into perspective.

Recently, students have again precipitated in demonstrations when repression and inequity have become acute issues. Two notable examples are the student demonstrations that led to the downfall of President Syngman Rhee in 1960, and the Gwangju Incident of 1980. Throughout the 1970s and '80s, students have held periodic demonstrations against the rigid governmental system, lack of free choice in certain school matters, exceedingly slow movement toward democratization in the political sphere, and liberalization of civil rights for the populace in general. Generally more planned and focused than the 1929 incident, these incidents have also sometimes turned violent, eliciting a violent response from the riot police.

5.18 Cemetery

With great student involvement and wide general support, the May 18 Gwangju Democratic Uprising (Gwangju Incident of 1980) shaped the character of the city and the country like no other recent event. Starting as a non-violent demonstration that turned to massive repression resulting in many deaths, this social movement was a cry for democratization during a time of increasing authoritarianism and militarism within the country following the death of former President Park Chung Hee. Completed in 1997, the 5.18 Cemetery and accompanying shrines have been erected for those who died in that terrible incident while calling for political democracy and social justice. Officially, there were 259 dead, 3,549 injured, and 64 missing. Through the front gate is a huge plaza with several stone monuments, and beyond that on the low sloping hillside are the graves. Reinterred here from where the bodies were initially and hastily buried after the conflict (a public cemetery just up the road), these mounds make a formidable impression on visitors. One gallery to the side holds portraits of all those who perished, while a photo exhibition hall and outside photo displays on the far side of the plaza present pictures of the incident. For those not directly involved, the real effect of those days may not hit home until you see these photos. On the surrounding wall are relief carvings of other uprisings and peoples' struggles that have occurred throughout Korean history—in a sense, a pictorial representation of movements against repression. Use the infrequent city bus no. 25-2.

Amusement Parks

Situated at the northern base of Mudeung-san, **Jisan Park** (지산공원) is the city's first large-scale amusement area. It has, among other attractions, a reservoir with rowboats for hire, a few children's amusement rides, a swimming pool, a driving range, and a chairlift to the ridge above. The chairlift runs from the terminus next to the hotel to a point on the ridge above; ₩2,000 one-way, ₩3,500 round-trip. A footpath also leads steeply up to the ridge, starting next to the driving range at the upper end of the park. From the chairlift's top terminus, walk out to the pavilion at the end of the ridge or ride the excursion monorail (₩2,000 round-trip). A small snack shop occupies this pavilion. The view from here over the city and onto the western slope of the mountain is the best the city has to offer. From the pavilion, another trail (30-40 minutes) heads south along the ridge, eventually dropping down into the valley below Jeungshim-sa. A second trail runs up the "waist" trial that wraps around the middle elevation of Mudeung-san.

Located north of the Jeonnam University, about four kilometers beyond the expressway, is the city's largest amusement park, **Uchi Park** (우치공원). Like a smaller version of Seoul Land, this park has a plethora of amusement rides, a swimming area, roller rink and ice rink, water slides, a small zoo, and a botanical garden—all basically focused on children. In addition, various kid shows are performed on the weekends. The entrance fee to the park is ₩3,000. Tickets for the amusement rides are sold separately or as a package (₩2,000–15,000). The zoo, skating rinks, and swimming pools have additional entrance fees.

Jungwoi Park

Out beyond the large textile factories are the Mudeung soccer and baseball stadiums, and beyond them Jungwoi Park, in which are the Gwangju Biennale Exhibition Hall, Gwangju Folklore Museum, provincial tourist information office, gardens, walks, and monuments. Across the rainbow bridge is a small green area featuring walking paths, lawns, and a large pond, and over the hill the Gwangju Culture and Arts Center and the Gwangju City Museum. The biannual **Gwangju Biennale** is an exhibition and symposium of fine arts and culture that draws artists and scholars from around the world.

Perhaps the largest collection of folk items outside of Seoul is displayed at the **Gwangju Folk Museum** (광주민속박물관); open 0930–1750 except January 1 and the day after holidays; ₩440 entrance. Not just a static display of old objects, this museum has created engaging exhibits and dioramas of all aspects of Korean life, including occupations, crafts, clothing, food, games, rites, ceremonies, religion, folk beliefs, and important transitions of life, plus sections on music of the area and regional folk paintings. From the left side of this museum, an underpass leads to the road running in front of the national museum across the expressway. It's a 10-minute walk. Or you can walk across the expressway via the overpass bridge. On the ground floor of the building next to the folk museum is the **provincial tourism office,** where all manner of information and brochures can be obtained. Just down the hill is a children's amusement area with rides, a swimming pool, and athletic fields.

Back over the hill, set on the hillside, is the **Gwangju Culture and Arts Center** (광주문화 예술회관). Open 0930–1800, ₩500 entrance fee, the city art museum displays mostly paintings but also a limited collection of sculpture by Korean and Western artists—representative mainly of contemporary and modern styles. Additional sculptures stand on the lawn to the front. The large and small performance halls offer evening performances of traditional and contemporary music, dance, and song; other types of cultural events are held here as well.

JEOLLANAM-DO

Gwangju National Museum
광주국립박물관

On the far side of the expressway interchange you'll find the Gwangju National Museum, open 0900–1800 every day except Monday and New Year's day; ₩400 entrance. Well-displayed, the numerous examples of stone and metalwork, pottery, paintings, and religious art, including a twin lion base stone temple lantern (N.T. #103), cover all periods of Korean history, but its real attraction comes from the large collection of objects taken from a sunken 14th-century Chinese merchant ship discovered in 1976 in the waters off Mokpo. A local fisherman who happened to catch some pieces of pottery in his net spotted the ship. During the undersea excavation, celadon and white porcelain pottery, black and red earthenware pottery, clay statuary, lacquerware, bronze and ironware, coins, and silver and gold ingots were taken up from the murky bottom—possibly the largest excavation of Chinese pottery outside of China itself. These pieces of pottery can easily be compared to the delicate Korean artifacts on display in adjoining rooms. Larger stone pieces are set in the front lawn.

Mudeung-san

Mudeung-san [Mudŭng-san] ("Peerless Mountain") rises above and dominates the entire view southeast of the city. In 1972, 32 square kilometers of this mountain were designated Mudeung-san Provincial Park. At 1,187 meters, Cheonwang-bong ("King of Heaven Peak") is the highest in the province west of the Jiri Massif. Two other peaks on this mountain are Jiwang-bong ("King of Earth Peak") and Inwang-bong ("King of Men Peak"). Mudeung-san, a massive yet somewhat characterless mountain, has wide open valleys, grassy slopes, limited forests, broad scree slides, and only a few distinctively shaped gray granite outcrops near its top and down its back side. Wonhyo Valley, on the north slope, and Yeongchu Valley, on its south slope, are the prettiest. Below Inwangbong is Jeungsim-sa, the mountain's most important temple, as well as the smaller Yaksa-sa. The temple Wonhyo-sa is situated near the end

rock outcroppings on Mudeung-san

of the bus line on the north side, and the hermitages Gyubong-am and Seokbul-am are nestled into the rocks on the mountain's south side. At the northern base of the mountain is Jisan Park. While the stark black and white beauty of the mountain in winter is scenic, it is perhaps the most beautiful in spring when azaleas dot the hillside in shades of red.

Sweet watermelons, up to 50 centimeters across and weighing 20 kg, grow on the mountainside and have become famous. Tea grown on Mudeung-san is cultivated by monks near Jeungsim-sa, on a plantation that once belonged to an artist. The tea is called *chunseol cha* ("spring snow" tea), picked when new tender leaves are just budding, often while snow still covers the ground. This delicate drink can be tried at any of several tea houses near the temple, where a sizable community of restaurants has sprouted. From the bus stop there, bus nos. 15, 23, 27, 52, and 555 run into the city center.

Wonhyo-sa 원효사

The park headquarters and main mountain entrance are near Wonhyo-sa. Take bus no. 18 or

777. Wonhyo-sa is off to your right just before reaching the end of the bus line. Founded by Wonhyo Daesa during the Silla Dynasty, this small temple is the most significant temple on the northern flank of the mountain. Set on refurbished terrace steps, all the buildings have been rebuilt since the Korean War. One *sari budo* here is thought to be from the Goryeo Dynasty.

Jeungshim-sa 증심사

Located on the western slope of Mudeung-san is the ancient temple Jeungshim-sa [Chŭngshim-sa]. Founded during the late Silla Dynasty by meditation master Julgam Seonsa, this temple was destroyed during the Korean War and partially rebuilt since then. The temple's main hall is the largest building. To its rear is Obaek-jeon, reportedly the oldest structure on the mountain. Obaek-jeon houses not only the 500 Nahan statues—made of painted wood, with a wider variety of facial features, body figures, and clothing than those at Daeheung-sa, south of Haenam—but also the 10 judges of the underworld. A three-tier stone pagoda stands out front. Biro-jeon is a new and brightly painted building that enshrines a 540-year-old iron statue of the Vairocana Buddha (T. #131) that is set in front of a bright red, gold, and white altar mural. Also in the compound yard are several stone pagodas and a disfigured-yet-solemn standing Buddha statue wearing a large crown-like hat.

About one kilometer above Jeungshim-sa is the smaller temple **Yaksa-sa.** Said to be older than Jeungshim-sa, Yaksa-sa is the only city temple to have survived the Korean War intact. It houses a seated stone Buddha figure (T. #600) on the main altar and a slightly defaced stone pagoda in the yard, both probably from the United Silla period.

Round-the-Mountain Trail

From the end of the bus line that brings you to Wonhyo-sa, walk up the road past a small string of shops and restaurants to the park entrance. The trail initially runs steeply up the hillside, but soon levels off and stays relatively flat most of the way around the mountain. The majority runs through open, grassy slopes, while only a

short portion goes through forest—near the two hermitages on the south side. Near the hermitages, granite outcrops thrust skyward in stark geometric shapes through a carpet of green foliage. At Gyubong-am the trail splits, the lower path continues through the forest while the upper detours to Seokbul-am before meeting the lower trail again several hundred meters farther. Seokbul-am ("Stone Buddha Hermitage") preserves a rock sculpture of the Buddha. At Changbul-jae Pass, a one-kilometer-long trail heads up the mountain to Ipseokdae and Seoseokdae, two of the three large palisades of columnar rock outcrops on the mountain. Some of the top is off-limits to hikers, as communication towers occupy the highest peaks. From Changbul-jae Pass, the main trail goes west down the valley to the temple Jeungshim-sa, the longest and steepest section. At Jungmeori-jae Pass, part way down this valley, a secondary trail leads off to the right, runs past a mineral spring, and connects with the mountain road that leads back to the park headquarters. The walk (15 km) from the trailhead at Wonhyo-sa around the mountain to Jeungshim-sa should take five to six hours. It's not particularly taxing or overly spectacular, but it does offer fine vistas of the city and the surrounding hills that fade away in shades of green and gray as they roll out to meet the distant horizon. The trail around the north side of the mountain is much shorter in length and time. Starting at Wonhyo-sa, initially it climbs gradually, following a paved mountain road and then stays fairly level as it continues in gravel around the waist of the mountain to the mineral springs. Either way, it is preferable to start at Wonhyo-sa as this temple is at a higher elevation than Jeungshim-sa and the multiple trailheads from the Jeungshim-sa side can be a bit confusing.

Cultural Relics

In the wooded valleys east of Gwangju and on the slope of the mountain below Wonhyo-sa sit several shrines dedicated to residents of the area who were instrumental in defending the country against foreign aggression during centuries past, numerous refurbished pavilions of the last dynasty, and a nobleman's private garden. Aside from those on Mudeung-san, many of these lie along provincial highway no. 887 which runs past the manmade Gwangju Lake reservoir east of the city and north of the mountain. Unless you have a real keen interest in old buildings and the cultural legacy of this region and you have your own vehicle or rental car, these sites are very out of the way and spread out, and while bus no. 125 runs out along highway no. 887, transportation here is rather inconvenient. Along the road to Wonhyo-sa are the shrines Chungminsa and Chungjangsa honoring ancient Korean generals who fought for national sovereignty, a memorial to the rainhat poet Kim Satgat, and the pavilions Wasong-jeong and Bungam-jeong. Out near the expressway is Gyeongyeolsa shrine, dedicated to a late Goryeo Dynasty general. Along the highway running past the lake are Changpyeong Hyanggyo, Jungnim-jae, Hakgudang, Shikyeong-jeong, Chwiga-jeong, and Hwanbyeongdang pavilions, the Gasa Literature Center, Soswaewon garden, and Doksu-jeong pavilion. More than just a building, **Soswaewon** (H.S. 304) is a garden built during the mid-Joseon Dynasty. A quiet, peaceful spot in a small narrow valley, this very natural Korean-style garden has a pond and two aesthetic pavilions standing in a grove of bamboo, pine, zelkova, and maple. The pastoral drive along the reservoir has fine scenes, fishing spots, and numerous restaurants that cater to weekend visitors.

PRACTICALITIES

Accommodations and Food

The hundreds of places to stay in Gwangju range from high-class hotels to lowly fleabag joints. The best of the 12 registered hotels is the deluxe-class **Mudung Park Hotel** (tel. 062/226-0011), snuggled into the base of the mountain at Jisan Park. Room rates here run ₩121,000–133,000, with suites at ₩196,000–484,000. Nearby is the first-class **Shinyang Park Hotel** (tel. 062/228-8000), where rooms are ₩121,000–145,000. More conveniently located in the center of the city, but older and perhaps not as well cared for, are the first-class **Grand Hotel** (tel. 062/224-6111), with rooms from ₩78,000 and suites from

₩130,000; the first-class **Palace Hotel** (tel. 062/222-2525), where the charge is ₩82,000 for a standard room and ₩150,000 and up for suites; and the second-class **Riverside Hotel** (tel. 062/223-9111), where rooms are cheaper at ₩50,000. The **Geumsujang Hotel** across from city hall has less expensive rooms for ₩35,000–38,000, while out near the national museum, you can find a room at the **Prince Tourist Hotel** for ₩40,000–45,000.

Accommodations are located all over the city. Convenient are those near the train station. Set one after another down the road next to the station plaza are the Hongjin Yeoinsuk (홍진여인숙), Manmijang Yeogwan (만미장여관), and Byeol Yeogwan (별여관). Across the main street from the station is the better Lion Hotel (라이언호텔). Between the roads that angle out from the front of the station plaza you'll find City Motel (시티모텔), Yumijang Yeoinsuk (유미장여인숙), Ihwajang Motel (이화장여관), and Yeongdo Yeogwan (영도여관). A few steps from the north end of the Art Street in the center of the city are the Yuseongjang Yeogwan (유성장여관) and Yurim Motel (유림모텔). On the streets behind the Grand Hotel are the more upscale Blue Hill Hotel (블루힐호텔), Daejijang Yeogwan (대지장여관), Seattle Motel (시애틀모텔), and Sofia Hotel (소피아호텔).

While restaurants are also found all over the city, perhaps the greatest concentration is in the alleys near the post office. As the most active night spot in town, this area also has many pubs, tearooms, cinemas, and shops.

Transportation

The **Gwangju Airport** (광주공항)is located several kilometers west of the city center in the Gwangsan section of town not far from the Songjeong train station. Servicing domestic airlines only, there are 12 daily flights to Seoul, five to Jeju-do, and two to Busan. For information and reservations call Asiana Airlines (tel. 062/221-6300) or KAL (tel. 062/232-7770), both of which have offices in the city. City bus no. 999 runs to the terminal building (about 40 minutes), while bus nos. 555, 5, 6, 113 and 160 drop you off along the main highway from where there is a 15-minute walk to the new terminal building. A reg-

ular taxi from the center of the city will cost about
₩7,000–8000; call taxis cost half again as much.
A small but busy airport, its ticket counters and arrivals are downstairs, departures upstairs along
with a few shops and restaurants. Banks, rental
car agents, telephones, and all other services are
available. The tourist information desk at the airport provides useful brochures and maps.

There is a great flow of all classes of trains out
of the city every day. Seven daily trains run from
the **Gwangju Train Station** (광주역)to Seoul, six
to Mokpo, five to Suncheon, three to Busan,
and one each to Yeosu and Iksan. Trains can
also be boarded at the **Songjeong Train Station** (송정리역) on the western edge of town.

Gwangju is in the midst of a long-range subway construction project. When completed in
2003, the first line will run from below Mudeung-san, past the provincial government office,
under Geumnam-no, and under the main artery
that leads to the airport and Songjeong Train
Station. Two other lines are being planned.

Express buses and intercity buses leave from
the huge new semicircular **consolidated bus terminal** (광주종합버스터미널) in the western part
of the city. Express buses run to two dozen major
cities throughout the peninsula, the farthest being
Chuncheon (₩16,000) and the closest Jeonju
(₩4,500). Intercity buses run to all points in
this province and to major cities in the neighboring province. Some destinations are Damyang
(₩1,500), Baengyang-sa (₩3,000), Naejang-sa
(₩4,100), Jeonju (₩4,500), Namwon (₩4,000),
Gurye (₩5,100), Songgwang-sa (₩4,900), Yeosu
(₩7,600), Yeongam (₩4,100), Haenam
(₩6,900), Jin-do (₩10,700), Mokpo (₩5,300),

and Naju (₩2,000). A few much smaller bus
stations are still located around town for buses
going to the immediate surrounding area. Of
most use is the Hakdong station where bus no.
218 runs to Hwasun and Unju-sa.

Some **city buses** that run through the center
of town and may be of help to the traveler are as
follows:

nos. 16, 19, 26, 35, 55: Gwangju National Museum
nos. 1-1, 13: Gwangju Biennale Site
nos. 18, 771: city art center
no. 666: Uchi Park
nos. 22, 25: Sajik Park
nos. 2, 9, 17, 19, 117, 555, 777, 999: provincial
government office
nos. 3, 9, 19: East five-tier pagoda, District Court
nos. 1, 2, 9, 17, 18, 30, 50, 333, 999: train station to city center
nos. 7, 9, 13, 17, 21, 50, 113, 117, 555, 777,
999: bus terminal
nos. 22, 34: Yeomju Stadium, World Cup Stadium
nos. 19, 21, 109, 113, 777: Jisan Park
nos. 18, 777: Mudeung-san park entrance, Wonhyo-sa
nos. 15, 23, 27, 52, 555, 771: Jeungsim-sa
no. 225: cultural relic road
no. 25-2: 5.18 Cemetery
nos. 302, 303: Damyang
no. 21, 50, 555, 999: airport, Naju
no. 555: Naju
no. 218: Hwasun, Unju-sa (from the Hakdong
bus terminal)

Gwangju Vicinity

HWASUN 화순

Unju-sa 운주사

Hwasun is the county area just south of Gwangju. While Hwasun is known for its hot springs, and is becoming known for its collection of ancient dolmen (designated a world cultural heritage site in 2000), the most significant historical point of interest is the temple Unju-sa, which lies close to Naju Lake. Founded in 827 by Doseon Guksa, Unju-sa (H.S. #312) is a small and rather undistinguished temple today except for one feature—its one-of-a-kind collection of stone pagodas and Buddha figures. According to an ancient theory of geomancy, the Korean Peninsula was "unbalanced" because of the predominant mountains along the east coast. To counterbalance this phenomenon, thousands of pagodas and Buddha figures were constructed at various temples in the western half of the country. One of these was Unju-sa. Of the reputed 1,000 pagodas and 1,000 Buddhas said to have been built here, 18 pagodas and 70 images remain, scattered widely in the temple precinct, the largest such old collection in the country. While not the most skillfully done, they are impressive as a group for their number and variety. The remaining pagodas are of various shapes and sizes, and in different states of disrepair, but two—a nine-tier square pagoda (T. #796) and a six-tier round pagoda (T. #798)—are perhaps the finest examples. An imitation brick pagoda made of small stones is also of special interest. Peculiar to this temple is a stone house-like structure with sloping roof, inside of which sit two somewhat defaced Buddha figures, back to back in separate compartments. One of only two in the country, this structure (T. #797) is very unusual for a Korean temple although it may have been more common in the past. Most of the Buddha figures are defaced or partially broken; however, a pair of recumbent Buddha figures, the largest of which is 12 meters long, are still in fine shape. The only two such

lying figures in the country, they are located in a clearing on the hill above the temple. Plain in feature and stylistically uninspired, this pair pales in feeling when compared to the recumbent Buddha figures of South and Southeast Asia. Interestingly, up near these supine figures are unfinished round blanks for another pagoda still lying on the ground where they were being carved out of the surrounding rock. Use Gwangju city bus no. 218; ₩1,300 entrance.

Ssangbong-sa 쌍봉사

Southeast of Unju-sa and set in a small grove of trees along a well-paved back road is the isolated temple Ssangbong-sa. Founded in 868 by the meditation master Cheolgam Seonsa when he returned to Korea from study in China, it has a more illustrious past than present. Although Cheolgam's finely carved stone *sari budo* (N.T. #57) and memorial tablet (T. #170) are still preserved at the rear of the temple in a bamboo grove, and the secondary temple halls are of some interest, the temple's most unusual feature is its wooden pagoda, Ssangbong-sa's main hall. Tall and slender, this structure is of mid-Joseon Dynasty design. Although many such buildings exist in Japan and many graced the Korean countryside centuries ago (the large wooden pagodas of the Baekje era), the only similar structure in Korea today is the larger and taller Palsang-jeon at the more famous temple Beopju-sa. It's about three meters square at its base, with the bottom roof extending far out beyond that; sturdy pillars and complex eave brackets support its three roofs. Open on the inside to the ceiling, its predominant feeling is one of loftiness. In 1984, this building (then a designated Treasure) was disastrously burnt to the ground, but was rebuilt as an exact replica in 1986. To reach Ssangbong-sa, take bus no. 217 from Hwasun.

Below the temple, about one kilometer up from the highway, is a reasonably intact country village, set tightly against the hillside overlooking rice fields, with old-style houses, a shrine or two,

© ROBERT NILSEN

reconstructed Ssangbong-sa three-tier temple hall

and a streamside pavilion. Not "old traditional" by any means, this village still gives you the sense of what a rural community was like in the 1960s and 1970s, before the push to modernize.

NAJU 나주

Previously known as Geumseong, Naju is a small provincial city, the ancestral home of the Na family. Lying in one of the province's greatest agricultural plains, it produces bountiful crops. The best known is the pear, a golden orb shaped like an apple, large and firm yet sweet and juicy. There is a small museum in Naju dedicated to the pear. Naju is also known for *saetgolnai* (I.C.A. #3), the craft of handweaving cotton fabric and, like Gwangju, the production of nacre lacquerware furniture and decorative household items. In addition to the mother-of-pearl lacquerware, craftsmen in Naju also produce a type of low, plain lacquered table used for serving food and drink. The construction technique is particular to this town, but this type of table is a common item in all Korean households. Constructed largely of willow and ginkgo wood, the upper surface of these tables is rimmed with a low lip. The under-table skirt is bent, not cut and glued, and all joints are pegged with bamboo "nails." Connected with spacers for stability, legs on the multi-sided tables are usually slightly curved, while those on the square-edge tables are straight. Ornamentation and design features vary, as they do from region to region, and prices reflect the skill and reputation of the craftsman. Naju resident Kim Jun-shik, a master of this craft, has been designated Human Cultural Asset #1.

On the grounds of the county administration building are Geumseong-gwan—a Joseon Dynasty government rest house from the 1300s once used by visiting officials—and an aged three-tier stone pagoda (T. #50) from the Goryeo period. The pagoda once stood near the town's now-absent north gate and was moved to this site in 1915. At a spot once outside the east gate of the wall is an 11-meter-tall banner pole and its supports (T. #49). Usually banner poles front a temple and are used to suspend a huge religious mural; one can only guess what temple this one graced. As usual, the supports are tall blocks of granite. Unusually, the pole is also of granite rather than metal pipe. Topped with a diminutive roof-like stone finial, it's a fine piece of centuries-old stonework. In 1993, the south gate (H.S. #337) of the city fortress was re-erected.

Also in the city is the Naju Hyanggyo Confucian academy, a fine example and one of the largest in the Honam region. Daeseong-jeon (T. #394), its main hall, is large and in good shape. Once a seat of classical learning, Naju today boasts the small Dongshin University. Outside of town at Bogam-ni and Bannam are ancient tombs (H.S. #76, 77, 78, 404) believed to be from the Baekje Kingdom. Numerous objects, including a gold crown, burial jars, unglazed pottery, silver jewelry, and weapons, have been taken from these tombs, giving scholars insight into the kingdom that once controlled this corner of the peninsula before A.D. 660.

Between Naju and Unju-sa is the tiny temple Mireuk-sa. In the yard stands a somewhat pudgy stone Buddha figure with a flame mandala

(T. #462) and a smaller conical rock (T. #461) with six diminutive Buddha images (the seventh is missing)—four standing, two seated—that are carved around its sides.

YEONGGWANG 영광

Located in the northwest corner of the province, Yeonggwang [Yŏnggwang] is primarily an agricultural area. Of historical interest in this county is the Buddhist temple Bulgap-sa and the private Confucian shrine Naesan Seowon.

Gilyeong-ni, near the town of Baeksu west of Yeonggwang, is the birthplace of Pak Jung-bin, the founder of the indigenous Korean religion *Wonbul-gyo*. A sacred spot and place of pilgrimage for adherents to this religion, it is here that Pak reportedly gained enlightenment. An academy, memorial hall, and commemorative monument have been built on the site. By combining aspects of classical Buddhist theology with practical social theory, *Wonbul-gyo* seeks to rescue mankind from its destructive designs and direct it to a path of self-help and self-enlightenment.

Bulgap-sa 불갑사

The small temple Bulgap-sa [Pulgap-sa] nestles into the base of the mountain Bulgap-san, about 14 kilometers south of Yeonggwang. Founded in the early 600s by the meditation master Heangun Seonsa, it has been rebuilt several times. From the cluster of shops and *yeogwan* below the temple, a path leads to Cheonwang-mun, inside of which are four huge deva figures. Beyond this gate is the temple's courtyard. The diminutive main hall (T. #830), old and weary since it was constructed in the 1700s, yet obviously made with skill, has faded paint and fierce dragon heads projecting out over the main door posts, under the corner eaves, and on the points of the roof. It is notable in that its altar is set against the left side wall and not on the back wall, so as to face south. Other buildings here include a lecture hall, a bell and drum pavilion, and the judgment hall. A trail from the temple leads to the mountaintop through a virgin evergreen forest (N.M. #112), and from there around the ridge.

Four kilometers before Bulgap-sa, the bus passes **Naesan Seowon.** This 300-year-old private academy and shrine was erected in honor of the Joseon Dynasty scholar Gang Cho-toe, a man who was captured during the Imjin War in 1597, taken to Japan, and there taught Confucianism to the Japanese. After returning, he refused any government positions and retired to study and teach. Wood printing blocks and some of his writings are stored in a building on the premises.

DAMYANG 담양

Damyang [Tamyang], Korea's bamboo center, is 22 kilometers north of Gwangju. The majority of Korean bamboo grows in Jeollanam-Do, and Damyang has the greatest concentration of that —an estimated 70 percent. Bamboo craft has been practiced here for over 400 years, and the town is famous for the quantity and quality of its work. Although the production of bambooware has suffered because of the influx of mass-produced plastic items, interest in these bamboo products is once again growing because of the products' elegance and durability. Many excellent bamboo craftsmen reside in town, three of whom have gained national recognition for their skill and have been designated Human Cultural Assets. About 1,600 families in Damyang and the surrounding county make their livelihood by working this flexible material.

A few shops selling bamboo products dot the main street of this tiny town from the bus station to the river. Each has a wide variety of items. Check prices in several shops before you buy. You must bargain, but don't expect prices to drop dramatically, even if you buy in quantity. If you visit on market day (dates ending in the numeral 2 or 7), you'll have an even larger selection of goods to peruse. Starting about 0700 and running till mid-day, the **bamboo market** sets up on the Baekcheon riverflats at the north end of the town's main street. It's a bamboo bazaar, the largest market in Korea dealing strictly with products made from this grass. Bamboo products of all shapes and sizes are brought in from the country, stacked high on tarps and spread out on movable carts. Here you'll find literally dozens of products, from utilitarian baskets to ornamental souvenirs.

Craftsmen say that nearly 300 different types of items are produced out of this versatile plant. If you buy from the maker, prices should be marginally cheaper.

While in town, stop at the **Bamboo Museum** (죽물박물관), surrounded by rice fields one-half kilometer west of the bus station and several hundred meters off the highway. Open 0900–1800 every day except the day after holidays; there's a ₩500 entrance fee. Here you'll find a small display of old bambooware, modern bamboo products of daily use, bamboo examples from other countries, a brief description of the bamboo plant and its natural distribution, and several shops out front selling bamboo-ware items. According to museum information, bamboo of the world grows in seven families, 46 species, and 3,200 varieties. Found mostly in tropical regions of both hemispheres, several kinds also grow in temperate areas. Korea has four varieties, two of which are used for making bamboo crafts. One type grows as far north as 41 degrees north latitude on this peninsula, considered the northernmost distribution of bamboo in the world. Bamboo has, since ancient days, been admired in Korea for its strength, durability, workability, flexibility, light weight, straightness, and good looks. In a classical sense, bamboo's hardness represents virtue, its straightness man's righteousness and rise in social standing in society, its hollow core stands for truth, and its jointed connections for one's aims in life. The bamboo, pine, plum, and orchid, are the "Four Gentlemen" of Korean brush painting.

Today, Damyang is tied to bamboo, but one cultural artifact of note from the past is the stone flagpole and twin supports (T. #505) that stand just at the eastern entry to the city. While such supports are nearly always stone, and many remain throughout the country, few poles have survived and almost none are made of stone.

Intercity buses from the Gwangju bus terminal, and Gwangju city bus nos. 302, 303, 311, and 312 run on a regular schedule throughout the day to the Damyang bus terminal, located at the south end of the main street. Near the main intersection in Damyang are the post office, police station, a bank, and several accommodations; the Telecom office is east of the main intersection.

Jeollabuk-Do
전라북도

Jeollabuk-Do [Chŏllabuk-Do] constitutes the northern half (Jeollanam-Do being the southern half) of the Honam region, the cultural area encompassing the entire southwestern corner of the country. Slightly larger than 8,000 square kilometers, it's the third-smallest province; but with just over two million inhabitants, it's the fifth most populous. Jeollabuk-Do contains six cities (Jeonju, Iksan, Gimje, Gunsan, Jeongeup, Namwon), yet the majority of its citizens live in rural areas and engage in agriculture-related industries. Jeollabuk-Do borders five other provinces. Directly to the south (separated roughly by the Noryang Mountains) is Jeollanam-Do. To the east, across the Sobaek Mountains, is Gyeongsangnam-Do. At its northeast corner, Jeollabuk-Do touches both Gyeongsangbuk-Do and Chungcheongbuk-Do, while Chungcheongnam-Do bounds it on the north. This northern border starts at the mouth of the Geum River and shoots across hills and plains, following no obvious natural division, until it runs into the Sobaek Mountains. A handful of widely scattered islands push out into the West Sea on its fourth side.

For information on the Internet, see www.provin.jeonbuk.kr.

the small reservoir on the way to Jikso Waterfall

The Land

From the heights of the Sobaek Mountains, Jeollabuk-Do slides across the Jinan Plateau to the Honam Plain. Wider and flatter than any other area in Korea, studded only by an occasional low hill, the Honam Plain is the rice basket, the agricultural heartland of Korea. The importance of this area for agriculture is centuries old and is noted by the construction around the year 300 of the Byeokgolje irrigation dam and reservoir (H.S. #111) at a location south of present-day Gimje. Still this rich red earth, the plentiful rains, hot summer temperatures, and long growing season provide the country's most bountiful harvest of vegetables and grains. This region has also created a great variety of tasty Korean foods, and is rightly known as the epicurean center of the country.

None of the country's major rivers runs through Jeollabuk-Do, but two start here before running out into the neighboring provinces. The Geum River rises near Jangsu, flows north into Chungcheongbuk-Do, and swings around Daejeon before flowing out to sea at Gunsan. Starting northwest of Jiri-san, the Seomjin River skirts the Jiri Massif and slides by Hadong on its way to the South Sea. Two smaller rivers, with their many tributaries, drain the wide coastal plains near Jeonju and Jeongeup. The Seomjin Dam blocks the Seomjin River outside Imshil, creating Okcheong Lake, and the Yongdam Dam creates Jinan Lake. These are the two largest lakes in the province, while the Dae-A and Gyeongcheon dams, north of Jeonju, form much smaller reservoirs and recreation areas.

Three major bays and peninsulas line this deeply indented coast; wide stretches of farmland push to the interior. Hampered by a wide tidal range and shallow silted waters, Jeollabuk-Do has virtually no good natural anchorage. Only Gunsan has any large-scale harbor facilities and ferry connections. As the city's in-town old port is adversely affected both by sediment washed down by the Geum River and the in-rushing tide, a new outer harbor for domestic and international shipping has been created at the very mouth of the river through extensive land reclamation, dredging, and the creation of adequate port facilities. In addition, an ambitious land reclamation project is underway west and south of Gunsan. A combination of dikes, drainage, and landfill will encompass much of the area between the mouth of the Geum River, Shinshi-do, and a point near Byeonsan Beach on the Byeonsan Peninsula, and will yield not only additional farmland but also harbor space, a manufacturing and free-export zone, and recreational areas. A similar reclamation project is in the works west of Janghang near the north bank of the Geum River mouth.

Unlike its sister province to the south, Jeollabuk-Do has few islands, and fewer good beaches. Only Seonyu-do, Byeonsan, and Dongho-ri beaches are of interest and seem to have established any widespread reputation.

History

Jeollabuk-Do's history cannot be separated from Jeollanam-Do's; until the end of the 19th century these two provinces were one. Prior to 660, they constituted part of the Baekje Kingdom. Repeated incursions of Goguryeo forces from the north and Silla troops from the east stifled Baekje development, and their control over this corner of the peninsula ended in 660, when Silla troops defeated them in battle and absorbed these lands into the first unified Korean nation. For centuries Baekje had been an adversary of Silla, and this historical animosity still surfaces today in the simmering prejudice of the Jeolla-Do and Gyeongsang-Do peoples against each other. In the 890s, with Silla power and control over the peninsula rapidly eroding, the rebel guerrilla leader Gyeon Hwon attempted to revive the name of Baekje and establish control over the peninsula. With his capital at Jeonju, he ruled over limited areas of the Honam region until his defeat by the rapidly emerging Goryeo Kingdom in the 930s.

Dissidence again thrust up its hoary head in the 1890s, when the *Donghak* reform movement gained popularity and militancy. While dissatisfaction spread throughout the nation, cities in Jeollabuk-Do and Jeollanam-Do saw the lion's share of demonstration and armed conflict between the *Donghak* peasant army and military troops.

JEOLLABUK-DO

CHUNGCHEONGBUK-DO

GYEONGSANGNAM-DO

Daekyu-san National Park

BAENGYANG-SA

Jiri-san National Park

Muju

Sobaek Mountains

'88 OLYMPIC EXPY

JUNGSU EXPY

35

26

12

SHILSANG-SA

Sannae

Jinan Lake

30

19

Mai-san Provincial Park

TAP-SA

Jangsu

Namwon

Daedun-san Provincial Park

Dae-A Lake

WIBONG-SA

Jinan

SONGGWANG-SA

26

20

17

Mountains

Imshil

Gyeongchon Lake

17

Seomjin River

WANGGUNG PAGODA

Geumma

Jeonju

30

Okcheon

Noryang

Gangcheon-san County Park

Sunchang

MIREUK-SAJI

1

Lake

27

IKSAN TWIN TOMBS

23

Iksan

Moak-san Provincial Park

GEUMSAN-SA

25

29

12

HONAM EXPY

Gimje

Jeongeup

Naejang-san N.P.

NAEJANG-SA

Geum River

15

Gunsan

29

22

JEOLLANAM-DO

Janghang

Buan

SEOHAEAN EXPY

23

Gochang

MOYANG FORTRESS

1

GUNSAN AIRPORT

Byeonsan Bando N.P.

NAESO-SA

Seonun-san P.P.

Gyeokpo

SEONUN-SA

Mujang

15

JEOLLABUK-DO

22

West Sea

25 mi

25 km

0

© AVALON TRAVEL PUBLISHING, INC.

Jeollabuk-Do's economy has improved markedly since the 1960s, along with the nation's. Industry has developed primarily in the Jeonju-to-Gunsan corridor. Yet development here has occurred more slowly than in other areas of the peninsula, with less emphasis placed on large industrial estates and a continued stress on agriculture. Even though the province has a great many attractions, the growth of tourism has also been slow. Attention now is focusing on its more spectacular mountain areas, temples, and historical sites, as well as on Jeonju, a city of great cultural importance, heritage, and legacy.

Cultural Notes

Within the province are seven National Treasures (N.T.), 90 Treasures (T.), and more than 30 Historical Sites (H.S.). Folklore activities passed down generations include the *samgi* folk songs and *gisebi* farmers' dance of Iksan County, the Wi-do boating play, the women's *gawa* "bridge" performance, the *Donghak* festival ceremony, the Gochang Fortress ceremony, the Jeonju *Daesase-up nori* folk-art performances, and a traditional ceremony honoring the amorous devotion of Chun-hyang, Korea's Juliet. Craftsmen here have been creating special products for centuries. Continuing today on a small scale, they include the paper and bamboo fans of Jeonju, lathe-turned wood objects from Namwon, carved stoneware from Jangsu, and porcelain from Gochang. Much newer is the production of jewelry and man-made semi-precious stones at Iksan.

For its size and to its credit, Jeollabuk-Do has a great number of established parks, and a disproportionately large area of parkland. Straddling the province's borders are Deokyu-san, Naejang-san, and Jiri-san national parks, plus Daedun-san Provincial Park. Byeonsan Bando National Park, Mai-san, Moak-san, and Seo-nun-san provincial parks, as well as two county parks, lie completely within the province.

Transportation

With connections only to Seoul, the province's only commercial airport is at Gunsan. Several rail lines thread through the province. The Honam line runs south from Daejeon, connecting Iksan and Jeongeup to Mokpo. From Iksan, the short Gunsan line heads west to Gunsan, while the Jeolla line runs southeast to Jeonju, Imshil, and Namwon before going on to Suncheon and Yeosu. Frequent trains of all classes run the Honam and Jeolla lines, while only a commuter connects Gunsan to Iksan and Jeonju.

The Honam Expressway (no. 25) cuts through the heart of the province, the Seohaean Expressway (no. 15) skirts the coast, and the '88 Olympic Expressway (no. 12) slices its southeastern corner. When completed, the Jungbu Expressway (no. 35) will cut north to south just west of Deokyu-san National Park, and in the future, another will run from Gunsan, north of Jeonju, to Jangsu to meet with expressway no. 35. The highway system connects all major cities and towns and to those in the neighboring provinces; rural villages are connected to their county seats by local buses.

Due to the limited number of islands off this coast, only a few ferry routes operate. Ferries from Gunsan run to Seonyu-do and the small group of islands southwest of the city. Less frequent are the ferries to Gaeya-do and Ocheong-do, and those that connect Gyeokpo to Wi-do. The most frequent, however, are the commuter ferries that run between Gunsan and Janghang across the Geum River.

Namwon and Vicinity

NAMWON 남원

Namwon is a slow-paced, overgrown country town. Set along the Yocheon River, its compact center is only gradually spreading into the outlying area, principally to the east in a series of high-rise apartment complexes. In the center are the market, commercial and government offices, accommodations, and transportation terminals. Trees line the streets that run from the train station to the river.

For centuries the Namwon area has been known for its production of solid wooden tableware. Close-grain wood from trees that grow on the slopes of Jiri-san is cut into blanks and let dry under cover for two to three years. After being turned on a lathe to exact dimensions, these pieces are then left to dry for a few more days, after which they are sanded and finished with a half dozen or more coats of a natural lacquer that is harvested from trees that also grow on the mountainside. This lacquer turns these wooden pieces a reddish brown, and the finish doesn't fade but polishes to a richer sheen with use. Rice bowls, stacking bowl sets, ceremonial plates and stands, candle holders, and beverage containers are some of the variety of items produced. Having nearly disappeared over the last several decades because of the influx of cheaper and more readily available plastic, stainless steel, and aluminum items, the demand for traditional wooden tableware is on the rise today. Paegil-li Village, in the town of Sannae, near Shilsang-sa, is the center of this traditional craft.

A new tourism area has sprouted on the south side of the river. Among its many attractions are an impressive arts center, a small amusement park, open-air stage for musical performances, a National Traditional Music Institute, the movie set for a film about the city's most famous couple, accommodations, a variety of restaurants and souvenir shops, and a walk up the mountainside to two observation pavilions from where you get excellent views over town. A short way down the river is the older Gamam Park, with its walking paths and riverside pavilion, Geumsu-jeong.

Once one of the Silla Dynasty's secondary capitals, Namwon is today a growing tourism center because of its proximity to Jiri-san National Park. Yet Namwon is best known to Koreans as the setting for the love story of Seong Chun-hyang and Yi Mong-nyong, Korea's equivalent of *Romeo and Juliet,* and it's because of this and the cultural festival that revolves around this story that Namwon, referred to as the City of Love, draws big crowds.

For information via the Internet, check www.namwon.chonbuk.kr.

The Story of Spring Fragrance

During the 17th and 18th centuries, Korean literature went through great changes in style and form. Previously, classical Chinese was strictly employed for the written word, but at that time *han'geul* began to be used. Writers of the non-*yangban* class took up the pen, and many of the themes in their poems and stories touched on their discontent with the strict Confucian social and moral systems. Perhaps the best writing from this period is *Chunhyang-jeon,* a love story between the commoner Seong Chun-hyang ("Spring Fragrance"), daughter of a *gisaeng* (female entertainer), and a nobleman's son, Yi Mong-nyong. Despite their different backgrounds, these young people fell in love and were secretly married. A short time later, Yi Mong-nyong's father was transferred to Seoul to take a government position, and the young man had to accompany his family. At the same time, Namwon's licentious governor desired to have Chun-hyang as a concubine. Yet no matter how much she was cajoled, berated, and beaten, she would not yield to his advances. After some time, Yi Mong-nyong was appointed inspector of the Jeolla province. When he heard of what had happened to his love, he rightfully punished the wicked governor, publicly took Chun-hyang as his bride, and returned to Seoul. Well known

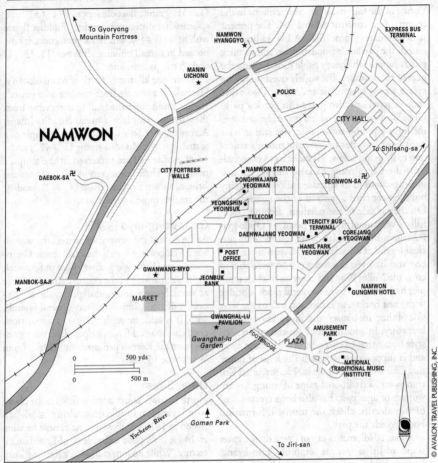

NAMWON

To Gyoryong
Mountain Fortress

EXPRESS BUS
TERMINAL

NAMWON
HYANGGYO ★

MANIN
UICHONG ★

■ POLICE

CITY HALL

To Shitsang-sa ↗

DAEBOK-SA 卍

CITY FORTRESS
WALLS

■ NAMWON STATION

DONGHWAJANG
YEOGWAN ■

SEONWON-SA 卍

YEONGSHIN
YEOINSUK ■

TELECOM ■

INTERCITY BUS
TERMINAL

DAEHWAJANG YEOGWAN ■

COREJANG
YEOGWAN ●

HANIL PARK
YEOGWAN ●

GWANWANG-MYO ★

■ POST
OFFICE

JEONBUK
BANK ■

NAMWON
GUNGMIN HOTEL ●

MANBOK-SAJI ★

MARKET

GWANGHAL-LU
PAVILION ★

AMUSEMENT
PARK ■

Gwanghal-lu
Garden

FOOTBRIDGE

PLAZA

NATIONAL
TRADITIONAL MUSIC
INSTITUTE ■

0 _____ 500 yds
0 _____ 500 m

Yocheon River

Goman Park ⬆

To Jiri-san ↘

© AVALON TRAVEL PUBLISHING, INC.

JEOLLABUK-DO

by all Koreans, this is a tale of passion, fidelity, and virtue, and a moral lesson that makes feelings of the heart, not social class, the most important factor in human relationships.

Every year starting on the 8th day of the 4th lunar month (April or May), and running for five days, the **Chunhyang Festival** is held in Namwon to praise Korea's most famous heroine, a symbol of female virtue. During this festival, the Chunhyang tale is reenacted, a "Miss Chunhyang" is selected, a *pansori* song contest and other music and dance performances are held, a lantern parade runs through the city streets,

young girls enjoy the long rope swing called *geune,* and archery competitions are held. One of the oldest cultural festivals in the country, it celebrated its 70th anniversary in 2000.

Gwanghal-lu Garden 광한루원
On the north bank of the Namwon stream is the finely landscaped Gwanghal-lu [Kwanghal-lu] Garden; open 0900–1800, ₩1,300 entrance. This garden park (H.S. #303) is the site of the annual Chunhyang Festival. Within is the pavilion Gwanghal-lu (T. #281), considered the trysting place of Chun-hyang and young master

Yi, one of the four most famous pavilions in the country, first constructed in 1434. The present structure dates from 1638. A low railing surrounds the pavilion's wooden floor, and its thick pillars support the heavy gable roof. During the heat of the summer, the widely overhung eaves create a cool spot to sit and relax. Two other smaller pavilions also grace this garden park. One, Wanwol-jeong, which protrudes out over the lotus pond on stout posts, was said to have been built in order to view the moon's reflection in the pond below. To the side of Gwanghal-lu is the Chunhyang Sadang shrine. Almost inconspicuous in its separate enclosure, this tiny building contains a portrait of the famous girl. On the far side of the pavilion, arching gracefully over one arm of the pond, is **Ojak-gyo** ("Magpie Bridge"). Its name relates to an ancient legend of celestial lovers, Gyeon-u the herd boy and Jik-nyeo the weaver, who were able to cross the Milky Way and meet only when magpies had flown up to heaven and made a bridge with their backs. An exhibition hall to the west side of the park houses paintings and relates this love story. In addition, look for the traditional-style house that has been built a few steps away and is supposed to represent the kind of house that Chun-hyang grew up in. Nearby, a tall Korean swing, a traditional game of young Korean women of ages past, has also been erected. For further details, check the tourist information booth inside the park.

About 10 kilometers east of town, on the lower slopes of Jiri-san, is the tomb of Chun-hyang. Because of the attention given to this story and the festival surrounding it, the gravesite has been tidied up in recent years.

Manbok-saji 만복사지

West of town beyond the stream is Manbok-saji, the site of a Goryeo Dynasty temple (H.S. #349) destroyed in 1597. Only stones remain to indicate the existence of this temple, but the arrangement of temple buildings can still be delineated by the foundation stones that poke up through the grass. Four designated temple treasures come down to us from the Goryeo period. They are a five-tier stone pagoda (T. #30), a pedestal for a Buddha image

(T. #31), granite flagpole supports (T. #32), and a somewhat disfigured standing Buddha figure with halo (T. #43), which, for protection, is now housed in a small building. Bus nos. 11, 13, 71, and 75 run past the site.

About one kilometer north of Manbok-saji is Daebok-sa, a temple from the late Silla period. Rather undistinguished, all that remains from the original temple is a metal Buddha image. Across town at Seonwon-sa, a fine example of a seated, gilt iron Buddha statue (T. #422) and a small bronze bell are preserved in the temple's main hall. Three kilometers out of town toward Jiri-san, a stone Buddha image (T. #42) stands at the small temple Yongdam-sa.

Gwanwang-myo 관왕묘

At the edge of the downtown area on the way toward Manbok-saji stands the small shrine Gwanwang-myo [Kwanwang-myo]. One of four such shrines remaining in the country (the others are at Seoul, Suwon, and Andong), this shrine honors the deified Chinese military general Gwanu, who, it is said, through the use of apparitions and other magical forces, helped drive the Japanese from the Korean peninsula during the Imjin War of the 1590s.

Other Sites

North of town across farming fields is the **Namwon Hyanggyo** Confucian academy (남원향교). Begun in 1410 but moved to its present location in 1443, it's a good example of old rural architecture. While no longer used as a learning institution, old gentlemen of the neighborhood still gather here to jabber, drink, and while away lazy summer afternoons. West of there is **Manin Uichong** (만인의총), open 0900–1800. Set on a low hillside, this shrine (H.S. #272) commemorates the valor of the 10,000 soldiers and citizens who fought valiantly, yet unsuccessfully, to defend Namwon Fortress during four days of siege by the invading Japanese army in 1597. A memorial service is held here every year on September 26. Take bus no. 71 to the turn and walk the 350 meters to the shrine's entrance. Bus no. 71 also runs past the express bus terminal, train station, post office, and Manbok-saji. Standing in the field across the river from the shrine are remains of the city fortress walls (H.S. #298). While not much is left of this fortification, you can get some sense of its defensive capacity.

On the mountain ridge to the northwest, some three kilometers from town, are remains of the Baekje-era **Gyoryong mountain fortress**. In the vicinity of the fortress wall is the Silla Dynasty temple **Seonguk-sa**. Its main hall dates from 1803. On the way up the mountain is a newly developing recreational area, which consists mainly of athletic fields.

Practicalities

For accommodations near the intercity bus terminal, try the Daehwajang Yeogwan (대화장여관) with its attached bathhouse, Hanil Park Yeogwan and bathhouse (한일파크여관), or the Corejang Yeogwan (코아장여관). In front of the train station are Donghwajang Yeogwan (동화장여관) and Yeongshin Yeoinsuk (영신여인숙). Within the tourism district on the south side of the river are plenty of better *yeogwan* and restaurants. Nearby and closer to the river is the **Namwon Gungmin Hotel** (tel. 063/33-3751) which has rooms of various sizes from ₩43,000–73,000, including 5-person youth hostel-type rooms for ₩49,000 a room.

Many fine restaurants and entertainment facilities are located outside the back gate of Gwanghal-lu Garden and in toward town from there. Between the park and the train station are the county government office, banks, Telecom office, post office, and medical center. A new city hall and the express bus terminal are located east of the city center. A short walk beyond the train station is the police station. The intercity bus terminal is closer to the river. Set in front of the post office, a piled boulder tomb has been re-created. Many such tombs were said to have been located within the old city wall before its destruction during the 1590s.

Trains run from Namwon to Seoul and Yeosu 15 times a day, with one each to Iksan and Jinju. Express buses from Namwon run only to Seoul (₩12,000). Select intercity bus destinations are Gwangju (₩4,000), Yeosu (₩7,200), Jeonju (₩4,100), Muju (₩6,700),

Daegu (₩7,800), Hwaeom-sa (₩2,600), Sannae—for Shilsang-sa —(₩2,500), Banseon—for Baemsa-gol Valley —(₩3,200), and Macheon (₩2,800).

SHILSANG-SA 실상사

The Jiri Massif thrusts up its broad shoulders in the southeastern corner of Jeollabuk-Do. Jiri-san National Park covers the upper elevations of this mountain mass like a blanket, and spreads into portions of Jeollanam-Do and Gyeongsangnam-Do. At 1,915 meters, Cheonwang-bong is the highest point in peninsular South Korea, and from there to Nogodan (1,507 meters) in the west is the longest high-mountain ridgeline of any park in the country. Dropping down from it are several deep valleys with a half dozen important temples and numerous cultural properties. A network of trails runs through the park, with mountain huts spaced here and there. (For more information see Jiri-san National Park in the Jeollanam-Do chapter.)

The most important temple in the Jeollabuk-Do section of the park, and the only major temple on the mountain's north slope, is Shilsang-sa ("Reality Temple"). Unlike the rest of the temples on Jiri-san, Shilsang-sa is not nestled into a deep valley, snug within the arms of lowering mountain ridges, nor clinging to a steep mountainside below a peak. This old establishment is set in a glade surrounded by broad agricultural fields at the foot of the mountain. One-half kilometer along the country highway toward Macheon from the town of Sannae, cross the stream that parallels the road, and follow the track through the rice fields to the temple compound; ₩1,500 entrance fee. On the far side of the bridge stands a duo of carved stone totems, set up originally to ward off evil spirits. Although similar in function and form to the wooden *jangseung* spirit posts throughout the country, and the stone spirit posts found in and around Tongyeong, the heads of these stone idols have a strong resemblance to the *dolharubang* grandfather figures of Jeju-do.

Built in 828 by the monk Junggak Daesa after returning from study in China, Shilsang-sa was the center for the then-nascent sect of Dhayana

Buddhism in Korea. At its height, this temple had several thousand resident monks and dozens of buildings, and may have contributed to the creation of the local solid wood tableware craft, as one of its traditional products is the wooden Buddhist rice bowl that every monk carries. Aside from the temple's present-day easy ambience, the real attraction is the age and craftsmanship of its stonework, pointing to the temple's more opulent and prestigious past. Set before the tiny and rather unadorned main hall are an exquisitely carved stone lantern (T. #35) and a pair of three-tier stone pagodas (T. #37). These typical United Silla-period pagodas are graceful and slender spires that stretch skyward from a sturdy two-tier base, showing an artistic sense of balance and proportion. Two *sari budo* (T. #33 and #36) and two memorial markers (T. #34 and #39) for former head monks also are preserved in the yard, but the best example of a *sari budo* is that raised for Junggak Daesa (T. #38), set in front of the Geungnak-jeon at the far side of the compound. In the small Yaksa-jeon to the right rear of the main compound is a seated statue of the Healing Buddha (T. #41), said to have been made in the 9th century from over two tons of iron! Shilsang-sa's weathered old compound has undergone a bit of a recent facelift with several new buildings set on old foundation stones and redug lotus ponds near the front entrance. About two kilometers up the hillside to the rear of Shilsang-sa is the hermitage **Yaksu-am,** which shelters an aged gilt carved-wood altar mural (T. #421). Five kilometers north of Shilsang-sa, in the yard of the associated hermitage **Baekjang-am,** stand a stone lantern (T. #40) (missing its cap) and a single three-tier pagoda (N.T. #10). Roughly from the same period as the twin pagodas of Shilsang-sa, this pagoda is more diminutive and decorated. Although weatherworn and partially defaced, each of the roof tiers has slightly upturned ends and a lotus-bud design on its underside. The solid spacer blocks between the individual roofs sport relief carvings of figures and geometric designs, the technical skill of which seems quite advanced for such an early date. Kept here as well is a bronze incense burner inlaid with silver script (T. #420).

Buses from Namwon run to Sannae on a regular schedule throughout the day.

Jeongeup and Vicinity

JEONGEUP 정읍

The gateway to Naejang-san National Park, Jeongeup [Chŏngŭp], formerly known as Chŏngju, is a small city with a small-town atmosphere. There is little to do or see in town except to take a quick look at the old *hyanggyo* or Chungyeolsa shrine, or to have a hike over the two-kilometer-long trail that runs through the hilltop **Chungmu Park**. This trail starts at Chungyeolsa shrine and runs along the ridge, returning to the road up and behind city hall. From the vantage point of the pavilion on the hill, you have good views of the city and distant Naejang-san. Visitors to Jeongeup are now greeted by the soaring steeple of a church that's sprouted in the dowdy neighborhood on the west side of the railroad tracks.

The tightly packed city center is squished roughly between the post office and the police station, about a 10-minute walk from the bus terminal. Transportation facilities are clustered at the west end of the town's main street, and nearby are many accommodations and restaurants. For a place to sleep, try the Rose Motel (로즈모텔) or Gyerim Park Hotel (계림파크), both only a few steps from the bus terminal, or the less expensive Dongnam Yeoinsuk (동남여인숙), which is a bit closer to the train station. Along the main street toward the center of town is the Daepyeongyang Motel (대평양모텔). In the center of town, check out the Geumo Hotel (금호호텔), where more expensive rooms start at about ₩50,000.

From Jeongeup, trains runs 27 times a day to Seoul, 14 times a day to Mokpo and Gwangju,

Jeongeup, one of South Korea's many small cities

twice to Daejeon, and once to Suncheon. The ticket counter for the bus terminal is back off the main street. Express buses run to Seoul (₩10,900) and Dong Seoul Station (₩11,400). Selected intercity bus destinations are Naejang-san N.P. (₩850), Namwon (₩5,700), Gwangju (₩3,200), Gochang (₩1,800), Naeso-sa (₩2,500), and Jeonju (₩2,600). City bus no. 71 runs to the Naejang-san N.P. entrance; most run through the length of downtown, starting along the road in front of the bus terminal.

NAEJANG-SAN NATIONAL PARK 내장산국립공원

South of Jeongeup past the Naejang Resrvoir, and draped over the Jeollabuk-Do/Jeollanam-Do provincial border, is Naejang-san National Park; ₩2,600 entrance. Established in 1971, it's one of the smallest national parks at 76 square kilometers. While relatively low in elevation—most peaks are 600-700 meters, the highest, Shinseon-bong, is 763 meters—it's a surprisingly rugged mountain area, famous for the country's grandest presentation of autumn colors

(there are 13 varieties of maple in the park) produced every year in excellence by Mother Nature. Embroidered into this canopy of leaves, like bright flecks on a bolt of cloth, are orange globes of ripe persimmon fruit. The northern of the park's three major sections is ringed by a horseshoe-shaped ridge, with the most dramatic rock outcrops in the area. In the valleys beneath this ridge lie the temple Naejang-sa, several hermitages, two waterfalls, a grotto cave, and a cable car to a lookout on the hillside. The temple Baengyang-sa, five hermitages, and a waterfall lie in the southern section. In the less visited and less dramatic western area are the remains of Ibam-san mountain fortress, of which the south and north gates remain and the wall is fairly well preserved.

Naejang-sa's placement is similar to Shinheung-sa's in Seorak-san National Park: it faces east and sits at the confluence of two secondary valleys beneath rugged peaks and steep slopes. Above both of these temples are viewpoints reached by cable cars. At Naejang-sa, the line (₩2,000 one-way, ₩3,000 round-trip; 0900–1800) is pulled from the valley floor to an oc-

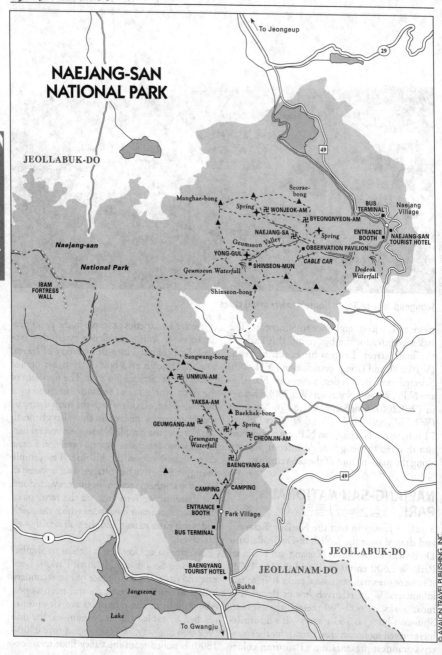

NAEJANG-SAN NATIONAL PARK

JEOLLABUK-DO

Naejang-san

National Park

IBAM FORTRESS WALL

To Jeongeup

Seorae-bong

Manghae-bong

Spring ┃ 卍 WONJEOK-AM

卍 BYEONGNYEON-AM

BUS TERMINAL

Naejang Village

NAEJANG-SA 卍

Spring

ENTRANCE BOOTH

NAEJANG-SAN TOURIST HOTEL

Geumseon Valley

OBSERVATION PAVILION

YONG-GUL

SHINSEON-MUN

CABLE CAR

Geumseon Waterfall

Dodeok Waterfall

Shinseon-bong

Sangwang-bong

卍 UNMUN-AM

YAKSA-AM

Baekhak-bong

GEUMGANG-AM 卍

Spring

卍 CHEONJIN-AM

Geumgang Waterfall

卍 BAENGYANG-SA

CAMPING

CAMPING

ENTRANCE BOOTH

Park Village

BUS TERMINAL

JEOLLABUK-DO

BAENGYANG TOURIST HOTEL

JEOLLANAM-DO

Bukha

Jangseong

Lake

To Gwangju

© AVALON TRAVEL PUBLISHING, INC.

tagonal pavilion, from where the entire valley lies at your feet. From the lookout, a trail leads back down the hill to Naejang-sa, and passes through a large stand of *gulgeori* trees (N.M. #91), seldom seen on the peninsula but found more frequently on the islands of Ulleung-do and Jeju-do.

On busy autumn weekends, when the colors are grand and the crowds are thick, a shuttle bus (₩770) runs between the park ticket office and the cable car terminus for those who don't care to walk the four-kilometer distance. Rental bikes are also available in the village for this long ride.

Naejang-sa 내장사

This temple ("Inner Sanctum Temple") was established in 636 by the monk Yeong'eun Josa. A casualty of the Korean war, it's been rebuilt since. The walkway from the park village to the temple grounds is flanked by tall maple trees that create a tunnel of flaming red color in fall; at the end of this tunnel is the first gate. This two-posted open structure has one peculiarity: its supporting tree-trunk pillars have not been artificially rounded, but have only had their bark stripped before being raised in place. A group of 16 egg-shaped *sari budo*, the second gate, a fish pond, a bell pavilion, and drum pavilion lie between here and the central courtyard. Directly across the courtyard is the main hall with its unusual stone pillars—these replaced wooden posts during some previous remodeling. It has many well-painted murals on its exterior walls. To the side of this hall is Gwaneum-jeon, containing a statue of the Goddess of Mercy with her many hands; it's unusually flanked by pictures of the Mountain Spirit and the Seven Star God. Here as well are the judgment hall and Geungnak-jeon ("Hall of the Western Paradise"). In 1997, a new stone lantern and large multi-storied stone pagoda were raised to grace this diminutive courtyard, and it's said that the pagoda enshrines the "real" *sarisa* of the Buddha.

Baengyang-sa 백양사

In 632, during the reign of Baekje king Mu, Baengyang-sa ("White Sheep Temple") was established. Originally called Baengma-sa, its name was changed in the late 1600s when a well-known monk preached so well here that even a white sheep came down from the mountain to listen. Last rebuilt in the 1920s, it's the 18th regional headquarters of the Jogye sect of Korean Buddhism. Unusually, this temple is entered through the Sacheonwang-mun at the side of the compound, not the front. Taking the predominant position, the main hall is a wide building with a complex eave bracket system. Inside, dragons and mythical animals dangle from the beams like model airplanes, and outside not a centimeter of exposed wood seems left without color. Directly behind the main hall is a pagoda of unusual design. Made of stone, its nine tiers are supported by four round pillar-like supports that in turn rest on a square base. To the front are two small stone lanterns. Probably from the 1500s, the oldest building is the Geungnak-jeon. Compact and quiet, this complex has a great location. Directly below is a wooden pavilion that overlooks a superbly dammed and visually pleasing section of the passing mountain stream. Nearby is a stand of nutmeg trees (N.M. #153).

Hiking

The valley and ridge trails of Naejang-san are generally not strenuous. Those leading up the side of the hill to the ridges, however, are quite steep. One of the major trails starts at Naejang-sa's first gate and leads north up the hill to the abandoned location of Naejang-sa and the temple Byeongnyeon-am. From there, it traverses the mountainside through nutmeg trees to Wonjeok-am, a tiny hermitage that dates from 1086, with an impressive gold-colored statue of the Goddess of Mercy. Have a drink at the fountain, then return to Naejang-sa via the valley below. Another easy trail heads up the Geumseon Valley behind Naejang-sa to the shallow grotto Yong-gul, Geumseon Waterfall, and the Shinseon-mun natural rock bridge. Either of these two trails should take two hours or less. Those with more time and greater stamina can continue from the resting place below Yong-gul up to the ridge and around to a point where the trail descends to the upper cable car terminus, where you can see all nine of the peaks of this U-shaped ridge, the hermitage Byeongnyeon-am on the hillside opposite, the park entrance road and meandering valley, and the road cut into the mountainside that runs south to Baengnyang-sa. There is no good view down onto Naejang-sa from the observation pavilion itself. If you have less time and want to stay closer to the park village, try the trail that runs south from the bridge near the park ticket office to Dodeok Waterfall.

More vigorous and time-consuming is the ridge trail. Close to 20 kilometers long, it requires one long day to complete. From the temple's front gate, head up the hill to the abandoned temple site. There a trail goes steeply up the hill to a spot below the cliff face of Seorae-bong. This path shadows the rock wall for a short distance but follows the ridge most of the way around this U-shaped valley. From the ridge, several trails run down into the valley—the trail up to and along the ridge and then back down via Wonjeok-am is the most popular hike in the park.

Several trails run up behind Baengyang-sa as well. One that heads up the valley past a waterfall and several hermitages eventually takes you to Ibam Fortress, but the most exciting is the trail *straight* up the hill to Baekhak-bong, the rock outcrop that towers over the temple. This trail passes a small hermitage and grotto on the way. From the top is a bird's-eye view of Baengyang-sa, the valley, and an expansive view of Changseong Lake and Mudeung-san off in the distance to the south.

Practicalities

The village below Naejang-sa has been turned into a full-scale commercial community. Buildings house the post office, souvenir shops, restaurants, and accommodations. Dominating this village is the first-class **Naejang-san Tourist Hotel** (tel. 063/535-4131), where rooms that start at ₩88,500 are at least three times as expensive as at the *yeogwan* and *minbak* below. Near the park entrance is Sarangbang Motel (사랑방모텔). Seouljang Minbak (서울장민박) and many others are lined up along this one-block-long street. Overall a bit cheaper are the accommodations of the newer section of the village set along the road up behind the bus terminal.

Newer and smaller is the community below Baengyang-sa, with *yeogwan* and *minbak,* two group campgrounds, and a handful of shops and restaurants. About three kilometers down the road, near the village of Bukha, is the **Baegyang Tourist Hotel**.

City bus no. 71, and intercity buses bound for Sunchang, run frequently between Jeongeup and Naejang-sa (₩850) until early evening. Other bus destinations from the park are Gwangju (₩4,100) and Jeonju (₩3,500). The bus terminal is at the lower end of the village, near the highway. Passing the north shore of Changseong Lake, buses run to Baengyang-sa from Gwangju. If coming from Jeongeup, change buses at Changseong Sageori for a bus to Baengyang-sa.

GANGCHEON-SAN COUNTY PARK 강천산군립공원

Jeollabuk-Do is not only full of national and provincial parks, it also has two county parks, one of which is Gangcheon-san County Park, located southeast of Naejang-san National Park, just outside Sunchang, an area known for its production of hot red pepper paste. Previously known to and visited mostly by residents of the area, it is slowly becoming more widely known. Small and petite, this mountain/valley area was the country's first (1981) to be designated a county park. Steep and narrow, this twisting valley cuts into the rugged mountains, beyond which is Damyang Lake. Through the valley runs a cool stream, the upper end of which has been dammed to form a small reservoir. Above the reservoir are the remains of a small mountain fortress called Geumseong Sanseong (H.S. 353). This valley is perhaps best in the summer, when the deep valley bottom and stream are still cool, or in autumn, when the leaves change the hillside to a colorful blanket. Buses from Sunchang (₩700) and Gwangju (₩3,500) run to the valley entrance and village; those from Jeongeup (₩3,200) stop along the highway a few kilometers below the village. At the village are several souvenir shops, restaurants, accommodations (including the small Gangcheongak Hotel) and the park entrance booth (₩1,000 entrance fee).

Many trails trace their way through the valley and hills, but the major trail runs up along the stream to the temple Gangcheon-sa, and farther up to a suspension bridge that drapes the valley. **Gangcheon-sa** is about two kilometers up the valley. Built in 887 by the monk Doseon Guksa, this temple at one time had over 1,000 resident monks and 12 associated hermitages. In the 1590s all was destroyed. Rebuilt shortly after, it was destroyed again during the Korean War. Since 1959, it has once again been slowly rebuilt. Small and rather unimpressive today, it does have a pleasant setting. About one-half kilometer above the temple, slung 50 meters off the ground from one side of the valley to the other, is a 75-meter-long suspension bridge that was erected in 1980. A trail leads across this bridge and steeply up the south hillside to a pavilion on the top of a ridge for the best views of the bridge, temple, and entire valley. Going under the bridge, the trail continues up the valley past a small waterfall to the reservoir. From the head of the reservoir, two trails head up the steep mountain to the fortress. The southern trail goes pretty much up the side of the mountain while the other runs up the ridge.

GOCHANG 고창

Southwest of Jeongeup is the small town of Gochang [Koch'ang]. On the hill overlooking this community is an ancient fortress (H.S. #145), supposedly constructed in 1453, solely by women, to protect the Honam region. The **Moyang Fortress** (₩770 entrance fee) is a 15-minute walk through town from the bus station. The road leading to the main gate of the fortress is directly across from the post office. Having undergone some reconstruction, it is in very good condition today. Three half-moon gates punctuate the four-meter-high, 1.5-kilometer-long walls. While many military and administrative buildings once crowded within its circumference, today it houses a handful of reconstructed structures, including a government office and the *gaeksa,* groves of trees and bamboo, and numerous paths. Every ninth day of the ninth lunar month (usually early October), the **Moyang Fortress Festival** is held here,

gaeksa inside Moyang Fortress

the only such fortress festival in the country. Girls, finely clad in traditional *hanbok,* line the top of the fortress wall in symbolic representation of the labor of their female ancestors. Take a walk along the wall, for legend says that if you go twice around (particularly in a leap year) your life may be prolonged by doing so—three times and you'll enter heaven after death!

Among other events held during these festivities are a lantern parade, an archery competition, *ssireum* wrestling matches, and a *pansori* song contest. The most renowned practitioner of this *pansori* vocal music was Shin Jae-hyo, a mid-18th century singer and composer who spent his life teaching others this uniquely Korean vocal tradition. It was due to the efforts of Mr. Shin that the six extant *pansori* compositions were taken from oral tradition, refined, and transcribed to notation. His restored thatched-roof house lies opposite the fortress's principal gate in a walled compound, and next door is the much newer **Gochang Pansori Museum** (고창판소리 박물관). Open 0900–1800 and free to the public, this private museum is a fine basic introduction to the history of this unique Korean singing style and its major virtuosos, but there is little in the way of non-Korean explanation. A few steps away and set next to the front gate of the fortress is a province-sponsored **Pansori Theater**, which not only teaches classes but holds periodic performances of *pansori* and *nongak.*

The bus terminal in Gochang is near the main intersection. Selected destinations from Gochang are Jeongeup (₩4,200), Seonun-sa (₩1,500), Buan (₩2,800), Jeonju (₩4,200), and Gwangju (₩3,000).

The area surrounding Gochang is known for its heavy concentration of dolmen, mostly of the southern style, which are usually flat rock slabs set low to the ground on top of several short upright stones. Nearly 2,000 of these artifacts have been identified in the area just west of town, and as a group, they were designated a world cultural heritage site in 2000.

Some kilometers west of Gochang in the village of Mujang is a second but smaller town fortress (H.S. #346). Originally constructed with two gates and a moat, this earthen fortress now has

one remaining pavilion-like gate along its wall while inside is a fine example of another *gaeksa.*

SEONUN-SAN PROVINCIAL PARK 선운산도립공원

Located in a low, seaside mountain area (its highest peak is 336 meters) to the west of Gochang is Seonun Provincial Park, one of the province's two parks near the ocean; ₩2,600 entrance fee. Established in 1979, this 44-square-kilometer park encompasses the temple Seonun-sa, several associated hermitages, a handful of cultural treasures, two natural grotto caves, one rock face sculpture, and some sensational scenery deep in the valley. From the temple, several quick and easy trails run up the valley to the hermitages and peaks. From the hilltop are fine views of the nearby coastal area, including the Byeonsan Peninsula across the bay to the north. In the greatly expanded village at the bottom end of the valley are a hotel, youth hostel, and a handful of *yeogwan,* restaurants, shops, and the bus stop. The first-class **Sansaedo Tourist Hotel** (tel. 063/ 561-0204) has rooms for ₩60,000–120,000. With mostly family rooms, the **Seonunsan Youth Hostel** (tel. 063/561-3333) charges ₩40,000 with some discount for youth hostel members. Frequent buses from the park go to Gochang (₩1,500); periodic buses connect to Gwangju (₩4,600).

Seonun-sa 선운사

Established over 1,300 years ago by the monk Gomdan Seonsa, Seonun-sa [Sŏnun-sa] is said to have grown to be the largest temple in the Honam region, with over 3,000 monks and seven dozen hermitages. Today just a ghost of its former self, it is still one of the district headquarters of the Jogye sect of Korean Buddhism. The streamside tree-lined entrance walk from the village to the temple compound is one of the prettiest in the country for a small temple. In the spring, camellia trees (N.M. #184) blossom wildly, and in autumn the path is lined with long-stemmed and leafless orange-topped *sangsacho* flowers, a type of amaryllis. Set like peas in a pod along one side of its long, narrow, grassy courtyard are the temple's most important buildings. The broad main hall (T. #290) is from the early Joseon Dynasty. Paintings of the saints are found up under the eaves and between the stacks of brackets. The inside ceiling is painted in a dragon motif, and on the altar below sit three large Buddha statues; murals of the Mountain Spirit and Lonely Arhat are unusually enshrined in this hall as well. In front stands a six-tier (originally nine-tier) stone pagoda from the Goryeo Dynasty.

In a newer building to the left side of the main hall is a one-meter-tall gilt bronze statue of Gwanseeum Bosal (T. #279) from the early Joseon Dynasty. As usual, she has a flowing gown and an intricate necklace but, unlike most representations, is seated and wears a relatively plain and simple crown-like headdress. This Goddess of Mercy sits unsmiling, lacking the usual expression of compassion. The building to the left contains a statue of the Buddha in the company of 18 disciples.

Dosol-am 도솔암

About two kilometers up the valley above Seonun-sa and along a side valley trail to the right is the hermitage Chamdang-am, whose stout main hall is a designated Treasure (T. #803). A short distance farther up the main valley is the grotto cave Jinheung-gul, and, beyond that, set in a grove of pine and bamboo, is the hermitage Dosol-am. Enshrined here is a Goryeo Dynasty gilt-bronze statue of Jijang Bosal (T. #280), lord of the underworld. One of only a few in the country to have Jijang Bosal as the principal image of its main altar, this hermitage and its accompanying prayer hall is, for many, more of a draw than Seonun-sa below as it is a special place to pray to Jijang for advantage in the afterlife or for special assistance with some more earthly need. On a rock face about 100 meters above this tiny hermitage is a large bas-relief carving of a Goryeo Dynasty Maitreya Buddha (T. #1200). Done with limited artistic skill, it's flat and stiff, but still impressive for its size. Holes in the rock face above this image once held beams for a cover, but now all is nearly gone. A steep set of stairs leads up and behind to a small prayer hall where devotees come for supplication. A second

trail and metal stairway runs to the rock outcrop across a side valley, while still another trail continues up to a second cave, Yongmun-gul, and farther on to the peak, which is well known for views of the sun setting across the West Sea. Trails continue around the U-shaped ridge and bypass the reservoir in an adjacent valley. A hike from Seonun-sa to the peak and back should take no more than four hours.

BYEONSAN BANDO NATIONAL PARK 변산반도국립공원

Across the bay from Seonun-san Provincial Park, occupying 157 square kilometers of the Byeonsan Peninsula, is Byeonsan Bando National Park. Established in 1971 as a provincial park and raised to national park status in 1988, this tightly knit coastal mountain park is slightly larger, higher (509 meters), and more diverse than its sister park to the south. These aesthetically contoured hills are surprisingly rugged for being so close to the sea and sprouting from the flat agricultural plains. Within the park's boundaries are narrow valleys, pine-studded hills, much exposed rock, several high waterfalls, good hiking trails, stands of silver magnolia and two types of holly trees (N.M. #122, #123, #124), one major temple, a handful of hermitages, a beach, and a seaside weathered rock formation. Not far beyond the park boundaries are broad areas of reclaimed land now used for farming, wide acres of salt flats for the production of naturally dried sea salt, and ponds for raising prawns.

Naeso-sa 내소사

Constructed in 633 during the Baekje Dynasty, and completely rebuilt exactly 1,000 years later, Naeso-sa is the largest and most important temple in the park (₩2,600 entrance). Through tall fir trees, a path leads from the village below past a group of *sari budo* and a grove of cherry trees to the temple precinct; within the temple compound is a 1,000-year-old zelkova tree. Walk under the front pavilion to enter the main courtyard; straight ahead is the main hall (T. #291), reputedly constructed without the use of any metal nails. Set on a terrace above the courtyard, its

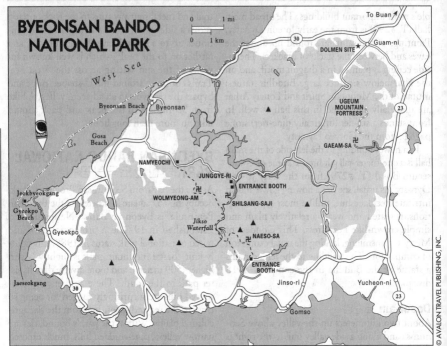

BYEONSAN BANDO NATIONAL PARK

West Sea

To Buan

DOLMEN SITE ★   Guam-ni

Byeonsan Beach   Byeonsan

UGEUM MOUNTAIN FORTRESS

GAEAM-SA 卍

NAMYEOCHI

Gosa Beach

JUNGGYE-RI

卍 ENTRANCE BOOTH

WOLMYEONG-AM

SHILSANG-SAJI

Jeokbyeokgang

Gyeokpo Beach

Gyeokpo

Jikso Waterfall

NAESO-SA

ENTRANCE BOOTH

Jaeseokgang

Jinso-ri

Yucheon-ni

Gomso

© AVALON TRAVEL PUBLISHING, INC.

JEOLLABUK-DO

fissured woodwork shows signs of age, but the carvings on its front doors are attractive. Below a ceiling of floral patterns and cranes are dragon beams; the head of one holds a *gusul* in its mouth and the other a fish. At the temple, and shown only periodically, is a huge painted mural of a white-robed, seated bodhisattva that is apparently the largest of its kind in the country. With its open lattice sides, the top-heavy bell pavilion sits on a raised stone platform to the left side of the courtyard. For such a small structure, its roof seems exceedingly massive; yet taken as a whole it's one of the most comely, diminutive bell pavilions in the country. Cast in 1222 for the former temple, Cheongnim-sa, which occupied a site on the north side of the mountain, the Goryeo Dynasty bell (T. #277) was moved here in 1850 and is a fine example of metal casting from that period. Displayed during a ceremony for longevity is a large mural (T. #1268) preserved at this temple. Two sacred sutras (jointly designated T. #278) from this temple are also now preserved at the Jeonju Museum. Written in gold ink on dark paper, they are the *Hwaeom (Hua-yen) Sutra* and the *Lotus Sutra*, the latter dated 1415.

Gaeam-sa 계암사

On the east side of the mountain is the smaller temple Gaeam-sa. First erected in 676, it, too, has gone through many reconstructions. In 1313, this temple was greatly expanded to include about 30 buildings, but is today much smaller. Of interest at this temple is its Joseon-era main hall (T. #292). Above this temple on the ridge are the remains of Ugeum mountain fortress, used by Baekje forces in the mid-600s during the time the Silla army was overpowering its neighbor state to form a unified country on the peninsula.

Trails

About 500 meters below the park ticket booth, walk to the far side of the village to a small group of graves. From there, follow the ridge trail over the pass and down to the stream. (Another trail starts about 50 meters below the *sari budo* at Naeso-sa and leads up to another ridge, where it winds around and connects with the trail from the village.) Follow the path downstream to the 23-meter-high narrow **Jikso Waterfall,** which falls into a rather large pool. Have a swim! During heavy rains, rivers of water course over the bare granite slabs here where no waterfalls ordinarily flow. Continuing on, the trail hugs the hillside as it skirts an old reservoir and cascades below, and farther down comes a Y in the trail. The right-hand path leads down the valley to the park ticket booth at Junggye-ri, from where buses run to Buan. The left-hand trail goes first to the hermitage Wolmyeong-am and then over the mountain to Sannae and the trailhead at Namyeochi. From the Silla Dynasty, **Wolmyeong-am** played a role in the "righteous army" uprising against Japanese meddling in Korean affairs in the late 1890s, and for its participation was destroyed. A half-century later, Korean War troops again rendered it unusable. The walk from Naeso-sa to Jikso Waterfall should take about an hour and a half, all the way to Junggye-ri about two and a half hours, and from the waterfall to Wolmyeong-am and over the mountain to Namyeochi a couple of hours. From the Junggye-ri entrance, an hour's walk brings you to the waterfall. On the way you pass Shilsang-saji. Some fifty years after having been destroyed, this temple is now being rebuilt.

Seaside Sites

On the oceanside of the park is **Byeonsan Beach** (변산해수욕장), a wide strand of fine sand sloping gently into the clear, shallow bay. Although relatively remote, it is one of the two best in the province. Dozens of accommodations and restaurants are set along the road through the town of Byeonsan, which fronts the beach. A few kilometers to the south is the less developed and more remote Gosa Beach.

Eight kilometers beyond Byeonsan Beach, at the very tip of the peninsula, is **Jaeseokgang** (채석강), an eroded seaside cliff and flatrock expanse. On the opposite point of this bay sits **Jeokbyeokgang,** a similar formation. Here the rock has settled in stratified layers like a huge pile of books. Winds and waves have constantly torn away at this formation, creating a jagged edge as the harder levels have remained more impermeable to erosion than the softer strata. Between these two points lies Gyeokpo Beach, site of the **Byeonsan Bando Sunset Festival,** which takes place on the last evening of the year. Aside from the cultural events, this festivity sees the launching of the ritual last boat of the year, set afire and sent off, symbolically removing bad luck from the year just past. Over the hill to the south is the tiny port of **Gyeokpo,** with accommodations, restaurants, and tearooms, from where ferries run three times a day to Wi-do and during the summer to Hong-do. Climb to the new pavilion on top of the hill overlooking the harbor if you have time before catching the ferry.

Gomso Saltflats

The stretch of land along the peninsula around Gomso has long been a producer of sea salt. Even though much salt is now produced in a commercial manner, many of the salt flats here produce salt in the time-honored, labor-intensive way that the ancestors did centuries ago. Broad flats at seaside are filled with sea water. This water is allowed to evaporate and the residue is scraped from the beds and sacked. After further drying, the salt is then packaged and sent to market. Once, workers here could be seen pumping water with an old-style water-wheel pump and carrying baskets of salt slung from bamboo poles carried over their shoulders; now electric pumps and trucks do the work. To expand the economic footing of the area, some of this seaside land has been turned into prawn farms, which you can recognize by wheels that stir up water in the enclosed ponds.

Buan

Gateway to Byeonsan Bando Provincial Park, Buan [Puan] is near an area of reclaimed land worthy of note. Due to the construction of two seawalls, approximately 4,000 hectares of productive farmland were created from what had been a broad tidal basin. These walls, together totaling 13 kilometers in length, connect the sides of this shallow bay with an island in its middle.

Started in 1962 during the country's first five-year economic plan, this massive civil engineering project was the first huge land reclamation program attempted by the Korean government. The land was readied by 1977, and mineral-rich rice has been harvested from this flat, square-sectioned land ever since. A much larger land reclamation project is currently underway. With dikes running from the Byeonsan Peninsula to Shinshi-do, and from there to the Gunsan Peninsula, much of this huge area will become agricultural land in the decades to come.

Aside from what is happening today, Buan is also known for relics of the past. Nearly a dozen prehistoric dolmen (H.S. #103), located in Guam-ni on the northern periphery of the park, indicate that this area was inhabited long before people began to record their history. Supported by eight upright stones, the largest has a top about six meters long by five meters wide.

Like Gangjin in Jeollanam-Do, the Buan area was the site of numerous Goryeo Dynasty kilns that produced fine celadon more than 600 years ago. Excavated kilns are found in concentration in Yucheon-ni (H.S. #69) and Jinso-ri (H.S. #70). Today, several pottery shops have been reestablished here to carry on this noble tradition.

Transportation

Frequent intercity buses from Buan run to Gunsan (₩1,800), Jeonju (₩3,000), Jeongeup (₩2,400), Gochang (₩2,800), Byeonsan (₩1,700), Gyeokpo (₩2,300), and Naeso-sa (₩1,900). From Gomso, buses also run to Gyeokpo and back to Buan. Three daily ferries depart Gyeokpo for Wi-do (₩6,100) and during the summer months also go to Hong-Do (₩34,000).

Wi-do 위도

The lonely island of Wi-do is located more than an hour's ferry ride off the Byeonsan Peninsula; ferries leave from the port of Gyeokpo. On this island of fishermen, residents have for centuries survived from the fruits of the sea. To ensure great bounty from the sea and reduce evil influences on the village, shaman ceremonies are conducted yearly. The greatest of these is called the *ttibae gut* of Dae-ri Village. Conducted on the third day of the first lunar month, during the depth of the cold winter, the *ttibae gut* follows and is combined with shaman ceremonies to appease various gods of the village, mountain, and household. For the *ttibae gut* itself, a straw boat is constructed and towed far out to sea, symbolically ridding the village of evil and enhancing the fishermen's good fortune for a successful year.

Jeonju 전주

Lying at the edge of the Honam Plain, Korea's greatest agricultural region, is Jeonju [Chŏnju], the provincial capital of Jeollabuk-Do, and the epicurean capital of the country. A traditional city with a long and strong culture, its history is intimately tied with the development of the nation as a whole, especially during the Joseon Dynasty (1392–1910). Jeonju is home of the Jeonju Yi family, from which the long line of Joseon Dynasty kings sprang. During the United Silla period, in 892, an upstart military leader, Gyeon Hwon, rebelled against the increasingly ineffectual Silla Dynasty and established the Later Baekje Kingdom. Before he was able to grasp control of the entire peninsula and make Jeonju the center of the nation, his troops were defeated in battle by the Goryeo army. After a lapse of over four centuries, Jeonju again became a provincial capital with the establishment of the Joseon Dynasty. Designated a city in 1949, it has a present population of over 620,000.

While the city and suburbs are rapidly expanding, sections of downtown have retained a venerable spirit and character. Jeonju is known for the preservation of its historical monuments and houses, including a remaining city fortress gate, a government rest house, the Yi family shrine, a *hyanggyo*, a noted riverside pavilion, and a district of traditional houses. Its industrial sector lies on the north fringe of the city; well over 50 factories, including the largest commercial papermaker in the country, make it the largest industrial center in the province. Not only is Jeonju a governmental and industrial center, it is also the major educational center of the province, with institutions like the Jeonbuk National University, Jeonju National University of Education, Jeonju University, Woosuk University, and several junior colleges.

Jeonju hosts the yearly **Pungnam Festival**. Starting on the fifth day of the fifth lunar month, it runs for a full week. The largest regional cultural festival, events include traditional folk music and dance, games, athletic contests, and a night parade through city streets. Held at the same time is the **Jeonju *Daesaseup nori* Festival**, which focuses on ten traditional performing art forms. Competitions are held in each, and the most enthusiastically appreciated seem to be *pansori* singing and *sijo* poetry. Other festivals include the Jeonju International Film Festival, Jeonju International Music Festival, and the Jeonju Paper Festival.

On the main street near Pungnam-mun is the **Jeonju Art Center** and near Deokjin Park is **Deokjin Hall**; both are venues for various cultural events. Other performance venues in the city include the **Provincial Institute of Traditional Korean Music** near Deokjin Park, which gives weekly reviews, and the **Sori Arts Center**, located near the zoo, which hosts major local, national, and international events at indoor and outdoor venues.

Art objects and handicrafts are tucked away in the many small arcades and shops between and surrounding Pungnam-mun and the *gaeksa*. A full selection can also be found at the Jeonju Specialty Products and Shopping Center across from Deokjin Park. For ordinary items, check the several city markets. Much shopping, however, takes place in the shopping district directly behind the *gaeksa*, where there is a concentration of department stores, small shops, boutiques, and restaurants, several square blocks of which are closed to vehicular traffic in the evening, and on

KOREAN FANS

There are said to be over 70 names for different types of traditional fans produced in Korea. Fans range in size from those that are held in the hand to those that must be mounted as decoration. Some can be folded out accordion-style while others are stationary in round or other shapes. The basic construction is of bamboo ribs that are covered with paper, silk, or other cloth. While some are left blank, the majority are decorated with calligraphy, paintings, or other kinds of artwork. Each fan has a purpose, whether to cool oneself during the hot summer heat, for use as a dance prop in a shaman ceremony, or to give as a gift to a friend. While specialty fans are still seen today, by far the most numerous are the ordinary handheld pivoting accordion fans, called *hapjukseon,* and stiff semi-round fans decorated with a three-part swirling red, blue, and yellow design, called *daegeukseon.*

its edge is a line of cinemas. This area and the district just west of the national university along University Street are the hot evening spots for young people. Saehana, Plus/Minus, F Sharp, E-Mart, and Ntepia are all located here, but the largest and most popular department store in the city is the Core Department store just a short distance away.

For more information online, check out www.chonju.chonbuk.kr or www.jeonju.go.kr.

Famous Crafts and Foods

Special products of the city are handmade sheet paper, writing brushes, and paper fans. This is one of the traditional papermaking centers of the country. This high-quality, handmade paper was not only used in-country, but was prized in China as long ago as the Three Kingdoms period (pre-668). Requiring great skill, the craft of making paper from mulberry bark has been passed down through generations. A quick look through any paper shop here shows many varieties and qualities. A good shop to peruse the types of paper (plus other items related to calligraphy and paint-

JEONJU

← To Gunsan

Jeonju Stream

KOREA SOUND CULTURE HALL

JEONJU ZOO

Jeonju Physical Fitness Park
★ JOGYEONGDAN

INSTITUTE OF TRADITIONAL KOREAN MUSIC

JEONBUK NATIONAL UNIVERSITY

HANSOL PAPER MUSEUM

JEONJU SPECIALTY PRODUCTS CENTER

Deokjin Park

Garyeon-san Park ▲

EXPRESS BUS TERMINAL

SYDNEY MOTEL

INTERCITY BUS TERMINAL

★ SUPJEONGI

CORE DEPARTMENT STORE

CENTRAL MARKET

JUNGANG CATHEDRAL

CORE HOTEL

Jeonju Stream

SEE DETAIL

Daga Park

Wansan Park

JEONJU NATIONAL MUSEUM

To Jeongup →

0   0.5 mi
0   0.5 km

DETAIL

NAGWONJANG YEOGWAN

HANSEONG YEOGWAN

GOWONJANG YEOGWAN

DAEDONG YEOGWAN

JEONJU DEPARTMENT STORE

GAEKSA ★

JEONJU TOURIST HOTEL

TELECOM

POST OFFICE

TRADITIONAL HOUSING PRESERVATION ZONE

HOLE-IN-ONE MOTEL

PROVINCIAL GOVERNMENT OFFICE

Jeonju Stream

POLICE

GYEONGGI-JEON ★

GAWONJANG YEOGWAN

JEONJU ART CENTER

PUNGNAM-MUN

JEONDONG CATHEDRAL ★

NAMBU MARKET

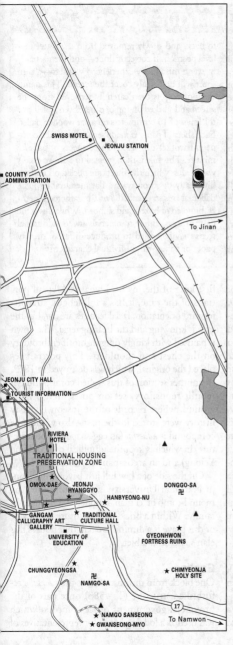

SWISS MOTEL

JEONJU STATION

COUNTY ADMINISTRATION

To Jinan

JEONJU CITY HALL

TOURIST INFORMATION

RIVIERA HOTEL

TRADITIONAL HOUSING PRESERVATION ZONE

OMOK-DAE

JEONJU HYANGGYO

HANBYEONG-NU

DONGGO-SA 卍

GANGAM CALLIGRAPHY ART GALLERY

TRADITIONAL CULTURE HALL

UNIVERSITY OF EDUCATION

GYEONHWON FORTRESS RUINS

CHUNGGYEONGSA

NAMGO-SA 卍

CHIMYEONJA HOLY SITE

NAMGO SANSEONG

GWANSEONG-MYO

17

To Namwon

JEOLLABUK-DO

ing) is Goryeodang Pildang, a small store down the street from Pungnam-mun. Some locally made paper is employed in fans. Like paper-making, this craft is having a resurgence after several decades of suffering from Western influences and these ubiquitous handicraft items are prominently displayed in many shops in the city.

As a city known for good food, Jeonju has a reputation to keep up. No matter where you eat, food here is well prepared and plentiful. Some of the best Korean recipes come from this epicurean center, but the city is especially known for two dishes: Jeonju *bibimbap* and *gongnamul gukbap*. Although ingredients vary by restaurant, *bibimbap* is a mixture of about half a dozen seasoned vegetables, strips of marinated beef, sesame seed, crushed laver, a fried egg, and a dollop of red-pepper paste laid over a full bowl of steamed rice. These ingredients, often coming from the kitchen in a heavy earthenware or fancy brass bowl, are to be mixed together in the bowl before being eaten. Two fine restaurants that serve this satisfying dish are the large and well-known **Hanil Gwan Restaurant**, in a back alley not far from the *gaeksa,* and **Jungang Hoegwan**, down an alley across from the post office. *Gongnamul gukbap* is cooked rice draped with bean sprouts and various vegetables (often with the addition of a hard-boiled egg) and covered with a thin broth. *Gongnamul gukbap* is considered more common than *bibimbap,* but it's still a nutritious, hearty meal and it's sometimes the food of choice if you have a headache after a night of heavy drinking. Another oft-served dish is *jeongshik,* a standard fare of rice, soup, and numerous side dishes of vegetables, fish, meat, and/or other delicacies. Although not special to Jeonju, this dish often comes with more and fancier side dishes here than in other cities in Korea. Unlike the rest of the country, most drinking establishments in the city serve complimentary finger foods with their drinks.

SIGHTS
Pungnam-mun 풍남문
The most well-known historical structure in the

HANDMADE PAPERMAKING PROCESS

While much less reduced in importance from decades ago, handmade papermaking is still a cottage industry in Jeonju with several small factories in back lanes of the city and villages outside of town. The entire operation, from stripping the wood to shipping the finished product, takes about seven days. To start, the *dak* (paper mulberry) tree is cut from the hillside, taken to the factory, and split open. After the bark is removed, its whitish pulpy inside is boiled until soft, then bleached. This matted pulp is put into another tub, where it's churned to break the fibrous strands into small pieces, remove excess bleaching dye, and loosen any foreign matter. This churned material is then strained and put into a tank of clear cold water. An extremely fine bamboo screen is dipped into this tank, deftly moved about side to side and front to back, and slowly removed from the water in a level position. If correctly done—and there's hardly ever a mistake by experienced workers—a thin sheet will uniformly cover the screen. This damp sheet of pulp is then carefully removed from the screen and stacked on top of other sheets, piled to a thickness of 10 centimeters on a flat wooden pallet. Each sheet of paper is made separately, and a competent worker can screen three sheets of paper a minute. This pile is then pressed to remove excess water, after which the sheets are peeled off and individually dried on warm, flat metal tables. The paper, at this stage called *hanji,* is gathered together, bundled or boxed, and shipped. While this is the basic process, different materials and/or additional steps may be added to produce different quality paper or paper with individual characteristics.

city is Pungnam-mun (T. #308), south gate of the city fortress. Originally constructed in 1389, the present structure, built in 1768 with the reconstruction of the city walls, was last renovated in 1979. When the city walls were torn down at the beginning of the 20th century to make room for expansion ("urban renewal" of those days!), only this gate, largest in the province, was left standing. The sturdy stone wall is punctuated by the wide graceful arch of the entryway, topped by a crenellated fence. The opening is fronted by a U-shaped protective area, similar in design and function to those of the Suwon fortress gates and Seoul city gates. Set over the entryway and surrounded by a low brick wall is a double-roofed pavilion. To each side is a small open structure; the one with staved sides contains the city bell, while in the other sits a cannon.

Gyeonggi-jeon 경기전

Across the main street and set in a walled compound of its own is Gyeonggi-jeon (H.S. #339), a shrine belonging to the Jeonju Yi family; open 0900–1800, entrance free. Within this compound is a small hall built in 1410 to preserve a portrait of Yi Seong-gye (T. #931), founder and first king of the Joseon Dynasty. Like all portraits of the time, it has a full-length, straightforward orientation; facial features are flat, but the gaze is knowing and the bearing regal. The gown is painted with kingly dragon-motif embroidery on the chest and shoulders. This portrait replaced the original, which was destroyed in 1872. In another section of this walled compound is a rebuilt repository, set on posts high off the ground, where records of the Joseon Dynasty history were stored in the past. Also within the compound is a *taeshil* (an egg-shaped stone structure, in which is kept the umbilical cord of King Yejong) and an accompanying tortoise stela.

On the side of a low hill just beyond the Jeonju National University is **Jogyeongdan,** the mound-tomb of Yi Han, founder of the Jeonju Yi family. Within a brick-wall enclosure to the side of this grave is a diminutive hall that houses this clan's ancestral tablet.

Gaeksa 객사

One block from the post office is the *gaeksa,* a refurbished structure (T. #583) once part of the provincial government office complex, which was used as a lodging house for representatives of the king who were in Jeonju on official business. The structure was built in two sections, the roof and veranda are offset and on different levels.

The present provincial government building is a few blocks south, the Jeonju city hall to the north, and the county administration building out near the train station. City hall is a one-of-a-kind structure, a U-shaped granite box with a facade that approximates the outline of a city gate and the arch of its entryway, and is obviously an attempt to gracefully combine traditional and modern architecture.

Other Joseon Dynasty Buildings

Along the river in the southeastern corner of town are the Jeonju Hyanggyo and Hanbyeong-nu pavilion. The **Jeonju Hyanggyo** (전주향교) (H.S. #379) was moved here from an earlier location and rebuilt in 1603. Enter through a gate around the west side. Its main hall enshrines memorial tablets for Confucius and 24 other Chinese and Korean sages. Huge ginkgo trees towering over the grassy lawn give this school a feeling of age and respectability. Until recently, students recited their lessons here during after-school classes.

To the front of this Confucian school, set along the riverside road, is a new **Traditional Culture Hall**, which has *pansori* as its main performance focus and also a craft exhibition hall. Down the way is **Gangam Calligraphy Art Gallery** (강암서예원), which exhibits over 1,000 hand-written works by some of Korea's well-known calligraphers. Free and open to the public, this is a unique collection and one of the only places in the country to get an encapsulated overview of this artform.

Hanbyeong-nu (한벽루) sits safely above the river on a sturdy rock tightly against the hillside at the far end of the road past the *hyanggyo*. This pavilion was constructed in 1404 by Choe Dam, who assisted King Taejo in founding the Joseon Dynasty. After serving in numerous high government positions in Seoul, he returned to his hometown and erected this structure. This was a refreshing place to hang out in the heat of the afternoon until a new highway was constructed

directly to its side. To its rear is an old railroad tunnel from an abandoned line constructed during the Japanese colonial period. The present rail line is now in use some distance to the east.

Above the *hyanggyo* and Hanbyeong-nu is **Omok-dae** (오목대), a pavilion set on the hilltop where a Goryeo Dynasty battle victory over Japanese forces was celebrated in 1380. From this knoll is the best vantage point from which to look down upon the sea of tile roofs topping several hundred traditional-style Korean houses, high compound walls, and the narrow alleyways and winding lanes concentrated in the eastern section of the city. This area, called **Hanok Maeul** (한옥마을), is one of the largest concentrations of such housing anywhere in the country, and because of its uniqueness has been declared a traditional housing preservation zone.

Mountain Remains

Capping the riverside hill opposite Hanbyeong-nu are the remains of the late Silla Dynasty **Namgo Sanseong** (남고산성) (H.S. #294). Erected in 901 by Gyeon Hwon, this fortress was used by the upstart general to protect the capital city of his newly proclaimed kingdom. All that remains are sections of its wall; the orderly piles of stone run through the trees along the mountain ridge that circles the amphitheater-like upper section of this valley. A short way up into this old fortress is **Gwanseong-myo,** a shrine dedicated to the mythified Chinese general Gwanu. Over the hill from the main section of the valley but still within the fortress walls is the temple **Namgo-sa** (남고사). Founded by Myeongdeok Hwasang, this now-small temple became an important site for Zen meditation practice after the Japanese invasions of the 1590s. From atop the boulders on the hill near the temple, you get an excellent view of the city to the north. In the village below is the shrine **Chunggyeongsa,** a newly constructed compound dedicated to Yi Jeong-nan, a general of the early Joseon Dynasty. On the mountaintop on the north side of the river below lie the jumbled remains of the smaller Gyeonhwon Fortress. It and the ruins of a palace site at the base of this mountain were also constructed by the Later Baekje ruler Gyeon Hwon who had established his capital here. Nearby is the temple **Donggo-sa,** founded in the Silla Dynasty by the well-known priest Doseon Guksa.

Christian Sites

Built in 1914, the **Jeondong Cathedral** (H.S. 288) lies just a few steps from Gyeonggi-jeon. Rising in brown brick on a site said to have been used for the execution of Catholics in the 1800s, it has a Romanesque style with touches of the Byzantine in its onion top–like steeple roofs. This is an attractive structure, larger and more formal than the Jungdong Cathedral farther into town. Supjeongi, which is located closer to Deokjin Park, is also said to have been a site of execution. Jeonju was as area of the country that saw early Christian converts and over the course of its history its share of martyrs. Located on the hilltop southeast of downtown Jeonju is the **Chimyeonja Holy Site,** a venerated shrine dedicated to a caste married couple who were martyred in the early Christian persecutions of 1802.

Parks and Zoo

On a hill west of Namgo Fortress is **Wansan Park** (완산공원). A winding road and numerous walking paths climb through a lovely grove of tall and stately Japanese cedars to an octagonal pavilion on the hilltop; Jeonghye-sa temple sits on the wooded hillside below. Looking north from the pavilion, the city spreads out before you; to the south is Moak-san. Before leaving the park, have a sip of natural spring water at the foot of the hill.

The much older and larger **Deokjin Park** [Tŏkjin] (덕진공원) is located adjacent to the national university campus north of downtown. Set in the middle and taking up a large portion of this park is a lotus pond, the remaining portion of a large moat constructed about 1,100 years ago to protect the city fortress. Lotus petals cover huge sections of the pond during the summer, willow and cherry trees line its bank. Good opportunities to people-watch abound as young and old come to stroll the many walking paths, picnic on the wide lawns, and row around the pond in rental boats. Suspension bridges lead from both

banks of this pond to a restaurant/pavilion set on an island in the middle.

Other newer parks, still in the process of establishing identities, are **Garyeon-san Park**, located on the hill across the main road from Deokjin Park; **Daga Park**, which caps the next hill north of Wansan Park; and the well-equipped **Jeonju Physical Fitness Park** near the zoo.

The **Jeonju Zoo** is an "open-air" type, where wide fenced areas house the larger animals, while smaller mammals, reptiles, and birds are still caged in close, claustrophobic quarters. Not the best zoo in Korea, it does provide city residents the chance to see a wide variety of animals not native to this country without going to a bigger city. Open daily; ₩1,000.

Jeonju National Museum
전주국립박물관

The Jeonju museum houses over 3,000 artifacts from this region of the country in three exhibition halls dedicated to archaeology, fine arts, and traditional culture. Not a large collection, there are, however, some fine items on display—including several national treasures—and well-constructed models depicting traditional and cultural events. Several highlights of this collection are a bronze incense burner (T. #420), which has silver inlay in floral patterns and Sanskrit characters; copies of the *Lotus* and *Hwaeom Sutra* (T. #278) hand-printed in gold on dark blue paper; and a gold box container for a green glass *sari* bottle (N.T. #123). A scale model of Mireuk-saji, as archaeologists believe it looked at its construction, will please those inclined toward architecture. Open 0900–1800 (1700 in winter), except Monday and January 1; there is a ₩400 entrance fee. Open since 1990, this museum is located on the southwestern edge of town.

Hansol Paper Museum
한솔종이박물관

Out in the western industrial section of town at the Pan Asia Paper Company factory is their brief but engaging paper museum. Displayed are a short history of paper, the Korean development of paper, paper uses, and paper production. There is a hands-on demonstration area where the traditional method of paper-making is done so you can take home a souvenir sheet of traditional Korean paper called *hanji*. Entrance is free; open daily 0900–1700 except Monday and holidays.

PRACTICALITIES

Information

Jeonju has several tourist information centers. There is one each at the train station and express bus terminal. At the entrance to Gyeonggi-jeon is a small booth that has plenty of information about the city. For additional information pertaining to city and provincial sights, check the province information center which is just down the street from city hall.

Accommodations

As usual, loads of cheap to medium-priced lodgings are near the bus terminals; more centrally located accommodations are available throughout the city center. Next to the Core Department Store is the deluxe-class **Hotel Core** (tel. 063/285-1100)—Jeonju's best. Rooms start at ₩136,000. This and the equally as nice **Riviera Hotel** (tel. 063/232-7000) have all the amenities that you'd expect from classy accommodations. Near the river and down a notch is the second-class **Jeonju Tourist Hotel** (tel. 063/280-7700) with rooms from ₩49,000. A few steps away is the slightly cheaper Hole-in-one Motel (홀인원모텔). In the city center, try the Hanseong Yeogwan (한성여관), behind the *gaeksa*. Nearby is the Daedong Yeogwan (대동여관), and in amongst the cinemas are the Nagwonjang Yeogwan (낙원장여관) and Gowonjang Yeogwan (고원장여관). Gawonjang Yeogwan (가원장여관) is located in a quieter part of town just near Pungnam-mun. Near the bus terminals, the Seongnimjang Motel (성림장여관), Anseong Yeogwan (안성여관), and Sydney Motel

(시드니모텔) are worth a look. Very close to the train station is the Swiss Motel (스위스모텔). Numerous other accommodations can be found in all these areas, with others near Deokjin Park and the national university.

Transportation

Jeonju lies on the rail line connecting Iksan to Yeosu. Jeonju Station is located in the northeast corner of the city. Trains from Jeonju run 15 times a day to Seoul and Yeosu, and once each to Jinju and Iksan.

Buses from the express bus terminal run to 11 distant destinations including Seoul (₩9,700), Dong Seoul Station (₩10,200), Daejeon (₩6,100), Daegu (₩9,200), Busan (₩13,100), and Gwangju (₩4,500). Selected intercity bus destinations are Gunsan (₩3,300), Gunsan Airport (₩4,100), Iksan (₩1,200), Jeongeup (₩2,600), Namwon (₩4,100), Jinan (₩2,700), Muju Gucheon-dong (₩8,300), Daedun-san (₩3,800), and Daejeon (₩3,800). Oddly enough, no city buses stop right in front of the bus terminals, so you must walk the short distance up to the main thoroughfare and catch a bus from there.

Jeonju's widespread city bus system not only services the city proper but also nearby country villages. The following numbers and destinations that pass through the city center will be of most help:

Bus terminals: 48, 79, 81, 45-1, 60, 69, 103, 112-1, 113

Jeonju Station: 21, 35-1, 44, 57, 60, 68, 77, 79-1, 81, 18

Deokjin Park and zoo: 21, 44, 79, 95, 97, 105, 83, 118

Jeonju Museum: 48, 50, 97, 118, 333

Hansol Museum: 77, 152, 166

Namgo Sanseong: 83

Songgwang-sa: 38, 106

Geumsan-sa: 79-1, 776

Wanggung Pagoda: 65

Jeonju Vicinity

MOAK-SAN PROVINCIAL PARK
모악산도립공원

Located some 15 kilometers south of Jeonju, occupying 42 square kilometers of the mountain Moak-san (793 meters), is Moak-san Provincial Park. Although not one of Korea's most picturesque, it does provide a decent backdrop for Geumsan-sa ("Gold Mountain Temple"), the province's most well-known and attractive temple. Three hermitages on the hillside above Geumsan-sa, and two temples on the east slope of the mountain, are also within the park. A trail over the mountain connects Geumsan-sa with these two temples, and continues down to the village of Gui, from where buses run back into Jeonju.

A handful of *yeogwan,* restaurants, and shops can be found in the village below Geumsan-sa. Here too is the **Moak-san Youth Hostel** (tel. 063/ 548-4401), where bunk beds start at ₩12,000 for members, ₩15,000 for non-members, and family rooms run ₩35,000–45,000. Jeonju city bus nos. 79-1 and 776 go to Geumsan-sa, and bus no. 75 runs to Gui. Geumsan-sa is also connected by bus to Gimje.

The trail from Geumsan-sa to Gui is approximately nine kilometers. Although it's not particularly strenuous, there are several steep sections, and it can get icy during the winter. Head up the valley behind Geumsan-sa. When you reach the cable freight lift, turn and follow the ridge trail up to the summit, where it passes below a broadcasting tower. Continuing down the east side of the mountain, the trail runs by the temples Suwang-sa and Daewon-sa before reaching Gui. This rural village has several houses roofed with flat slate tiles—an oddity. Several other trails run north over the mountain.

Geumsan-sa 금산사
Founded in 599, Geumsan-sa [Kŭmsan-sa] lies in a flat river valley on the western slope of Moak-san; ₩2,600 entrance. One National Treasure,

10 Treasures, and a complete printed edition of the *Koreana Tripitaka* (Buddhist canon of scripture) are preserved here. From the bus stop at the village, a long brookside path leads up to the temple's open-arch front gate and beyond, to the spacious courtyard ringed with buildings. In spring this complex is bathed in light-pink cherry blossoms, and during fall it's sprinkled with orange globes of persimmon.

The most distinctive structure here is **Mireuk-jeon** (N.T. #62), the only large temple hall in the country with a three-story roof. Bold and majestic, it dates from the 1626 reconstruction, and its maturity is evidenced by the faded paint and upturned roof ends now in need of structural support. Notice the small rectangular murals painted on its second- and third-tier wall panels! Open on the inside to the top roof, this building houses three huge wooden statues. The 12-meter-tall central figure is the country's largest non-stone, standing representation of the Mireuk (Future) Buddha. Flanking it are a pair of 9-meter-tall bodhisattvas, each wearing an elaborate crown. These golden figures fill so much of the interior that only a narrow strip of floor can be used by those who come to bow and pray!

Straight across the courtyard from the temple's entrance is **Daejeokgwang-jeon**. Tragically destroyed by fire in December 1986, it has since been rebuilt. Eleven figures sit on its incredibly long altar. Directly across the courtyard from Mireuk-jeon is **Daejang-jeon** (T. #827), whose front doors are said to be about 1,200 years old, supposedly the only objects to have survived the burning of the temple during the 1592 Hideyoshi Invasion. On the altar inside sits a statue of Seokgamoni Buddha backed by an intricately rendered halo. Its design harkens back to similar statuary from the Silla and Goryeo periods. Set around this courtyard are the bell pavilion, the judgment hall, and dormitories.

Geumsan-sa also preserves several stone structures. A square stone base (use unknown) called

Noju (T. #22), the round Seokgyeon-dae base stone (statue or lantern support) carved in lotus-bud motif (T. #23), a squashed-looking hexagonal 11-tier stone pagoda made of slate (T. #27), and a granite stone lantern (T. #828) are all found in the main courtyard. A pair of simple yet well-sculpted stone flagpole supports (T. #28) now stands below the lecture hall. In a separate enclosure to the rear is a Silla-style, five-tier stone pagoda from the Goryeo Dynasty (T. #25) and a bell-shaped *sari budo* (T. #26) said to contain relics of the Buddha set on an inordinately broad two-tier terraced foundation with finely carved stone panels. To the side of this pair of ancient stone monuments is Jeokmyeon Bugung hall which has no figure on its altar and a glass back wall that lets the pagoda and *sari budo* act as the objects of veneration.

In a walled enclosure a short distance up the valley is a group of stone tablets, the most prominent being the tortoise-base memorial tablet to Hyedeok (T. #24). A three-tier stone pagoda (T. #29) is located at Shimwon-am hermitage on the hillside above.

SITES TO THE EAST

In the mountains east of Jeonju are the temples Songgwang-sa and Wibong-sa, and the remains of the Wibong Mountain Fortress. Jeonju city bus nos. 38 and 106 run out to Songgwang-sa and the nearby village of Daeheung-ni. Daeheung-ni was a papermaking village, but unlike the thin sheets of writing paper made in and around Jeonju, the thick paper made here was used as floor covering. Like clothes hung out to dry in the afternoon sun, bleached white sheets could be seen hanging from the maze of lines that were much in evidence throughout this village. To reach Songgwang-sa (don't confuse this temple with the more famous temple of the same name near Suncheon), get off the bus at Daeheung-ni, cross the river, and walk up about 100 meters to the temple's front gate; ₩1,300 entrance. Bus no. 38 runs all the way to and past Wibong-sa, but you can get off about three kilometers past Daeheung-ni, in Oseong-ni, and

walk the four kilometers up and over the hill to the east as you used to have to do.

Songgwang-sa 송광사

A relatively small and quiet compound today, Songgwang-sa was undoubtedly a much larger institution when it was expanded in 1622. The placement and construction of its three front gates—the first was said to have been placed three kilometers down the valley—indicates a much larger complex than the few buildings that have survived to the present. Straight through the present front gate is the temple's main hall (T. #1243). The low-slung altar in this hall takes up a majority of its floor space, and on it sit three statues that dominate the room. Each over five meters tall, these Joseon-era seated figures (T. #1274) of Seokgamoni, Yaksa, and Amitabul are reputed to be the largest such figures in the country that are enshrined in a building. Behind these altar figures have been painted some exceptional interior murals. Done in brilliant red and gold, they represent a whole pantheon of religious characters. Animated figures of the more secular class have been painted on the hall's ceiling and walls. Look for the carvings of animals that hang from the ceiling and the carved panels on the altar.

To the rear of the main hall is the Nahan-jeon. Placed on shelves that line three walls of this hall are 500 statues of the Buddha's followers. On the floor to their left are two additional statues, one holding a snake and the other a tiger. These larger figures graphically show that all earthly attachment, even fear, can and should be overcome for those who seek truth and enlightenment. Perhaps the most visually fetching structure of this temple is the cross-shaped bell pavilion (T. #1244). This design creates the need for a more than usually complex eave bracket system to support its heavy roof. Unique for such a bell pavilion, its openness is refreshing. On your way out, have a look at the four celestial guardian figures (T. #1255) in the Cheonwang-mun gate. These statues are not carved from wood but created from molded plaster and painted, and represent some of the best of their kind in the country.

JEOLLABUK-DO

Wibong-sa 위봉사

Legend says that Wibong-sa ("Dignified Phoenix Temple") was placed on this site because three phoenixes were spotted in a nearby woods. Originally built in 604 during the Baekje Dynasty, Wibong-sa was at one time one of 31 major Korean temples. At its height, it had over two dozen buildings that occupied much of the gradually sloping hillside presently put to use as farming fields or overgrown with trees. Although unfrequented and partially dilapidated until a few short years ago, it has largely been rebuilt, creating a pleasant atmosphere, and is a place where you can feel the antiquity of Korean Buddhism. Neat and tidy, Wibong-sa exudes a feminine touch and in fact is now a study and meditation center for *biguni*. The main hall (T. #608), called Bogwangmyeong-jeon, has a crowded, almost cluttered interior, and on the back side of the wall behind the altar is an old mural of a bodhisattva. Painted with bold strokes, this three-meter-high figure is adorned with a headdress and a flowing white robe. While done in a simple style, there's a feeling of delicacy in its coloration,

the design of its jewelry, and the folding edges of the cloth. This mural is best seen when light can be let in through the door in the rear wall.

On the way up to the temple you pass one of the **Wibong Sanseong** gates. Only the stones of this mountain fortress gate still stand in place from the late 1600s. Like a river of rubble, the remaining disarray of rocks, once a strong defensive perimeter, can be seen running up and over the hills in both directions from the gate. While it's possible to walk for several hours along the top of the crumbling 18-kilometer-long wall, major sections are overgrown. Although it may not look like it from the temple, there is a very picturesque valley and waterfall just a short distance beyond the temple and below Wibong village. About four kilometers down this road is Dae-A Reservoir, an artificial lake built during the Japanese occupation by conscripted farmers from the area. The road used to dead-end at the reservoir, but this area will get plenty more traffic once the road is completed all the way past the reservoir, where it will connect with a highway running back to Jeonju.

remains of a gate from the Wibong Sanseong mountain fortress

© ROBERT NILSEN

STONE REMAINS NEAR GEUMMA

About 2,000 years ago, clans of people collectively known as the Mahan occupied the region of the peninsula in which Iksan County now lies. It's believed that the Mahan developed into confederate walled-town states with some sort of ruling elite, and that a fortified town once stood near the present community of Geumma. Every year in May, the **Mahan Festival** is held at various locations in Iksan County to celebrate its early culture and history. Events include music, dance, and activities related to Mahan legends.

Wanggung Seoktap 왕궁석탑

About two kilometers south of Geumma (금마) is a massive stone pagoda called Wanggung Seoktap, or "King's Palace Pagoda." Set on a raised mound with some evidence of surrounding dressed stone retaining walls, this well-proportioned, five-tier structure (N.T. #289) is one of the largest pagodas in the country. Evenly separated by spacer blocks, each of its broad roof tiers is slightly up-turned at the end, and smaller in ascending succession. It's tall, bold, and regal—definitely one of the most attractive unadorned pagodas in the country. In 1965, this pagoda was reconstructed. During the dismantling stage, valuable objects were discovered in an inside niche, including a tiny *sari* container, a dark green glass bottle with lotus-bud stopper and lotus-leaf base, sheets of gold engraved with Buddhist scriptures fastened into a folio, and a cover for that folio. These rare items (N.T. #123) are now displayed at the Jeonju National Museum. One legend says that Wanggung Seoktap was once within the fortress of a Mahan king. Some believe that it dates from a later period of Baekje control. It's likely, however, that the pagoda actually was constructed as part of a temple complex during the United Silla period, making it about 1,000 years old. Much archaeological work continues to be done at this site (H.S. #408). Sitting only 50 meters from the road, it can easily be seen from the highway when busing north from Jeonju to Geumma. Use bus no. 65 from Jeonju.

Standing Stone Figures
익산고도리석불입상

One-half kilometer northwest of Wanggung pagoda a pair of standing stone statues (T. #46) face each other across a distance of about 100 meters from separate square terraces in a paddy field. They are rather simplistic and squarish, with only faint carved details, and flat top hats shade their stark features. Their origin and significance remain a mystery, but their closest counterparts may be the much larger standing Mireuk Buddha statues of Gwanchok-sa and Daejo-sa, only a short distance to the north. Or they may be akin to wooden *jangseung* totems, stone village guardian figures seen predominantly along the south coast, or the grandfather figures that guard villages on Jeju-Do.

Mireuk-saji 미륵사지

The largest and most impressive of local stone remains is about three kilometers north of Geumma, at the long-since-abandoned temple Mireuk-saji [Mirŭk-saji] (H.S. #150). Constructed around 600 as Wangheung-sa, the temple, whose name was later changed to Mireuk-sa ("Buddha of the Future Temple"), was used until the 1700s. Excavation and initial renovation of this site were done in 1915, under auspices of the Japanese colonial government. Additional reconstruction was carried out in 1965 and again from 1980 into the 1990s. A ten-year study of this complex is currently underway to determine how best to preserve this piece of cultural history.

In the temple yard stands a pair of stone flagpole supports (T. #236), but the most impressive single object here is the huge stone pagoda Mireuk-tap (N.T. #11), one of the oldest in the country, and the last remaining of its type. Archaeologists believe that it was constructed along the lines of older wooden pagodas, and could have been the inspiration for the gigantic wooden pagodas erected in Gyeongju several centuries later, during the "Golden Age" of Silla culture. Looking more like a building than a typical pagoda, several square stone pillars, spaced with stone slabs, uphold crossbeams on which has been set the lowest of the four-step cantilevered tiers.

Above that, in alternating succession, rise vertical spacer blocks and the next smallest tier. An opening appears in each of the four walls on the lowest level, and from them a passageway leads in to the center. The number of extant stone pieces has prevented this pagoda from being more than partially reconstructed. Its six tiers rise to 14 meters, but it's almost certain that it originally had seven or nine tiers—due to the consistent practice of erecting pagodas with an odd number of roof levels. Mireuk-tap was halfheartedly reconstructed in 1915, and is reinforced by cement. This pagoda's twin was raised in 1993 in the eastern section of the old temple compound, not only as a counterbalance but also to show what the originals really looked like. The size, number, and position of the remaining foundation stones in this grassy area lets you imagine how expansive and grand this temple must have been. Many other stone pieces lie in the yard waiting to be put together in some way. This site is one of the most important Buddhist historical remains of the Baekje era. A model of how the entire temple once probably looked is on display at the exhibition hall here, a building that also displays several hundred of the 19,000 items excavated from this site. Mireuk-saji is open daily except Monday 0900–1800. Use Iksan city bus nos. 10 and 41.

To the northwest, on the mountainside, are a carved Buddha triad and a single seated Buddha figure. Also on the mountain are the remains of a mountain fortress and a functioning Buddhist hermitage.

While most are located at Gongju and Buyeo, a pair of royal tombs known as the **Iksan Twin Tombs** (익산쌍릉) (H.S. #87) are located a 10-minute walk off the highway between Geumma and Iksan. Similar to those found in Buyeo, these tombs are believed to hold King Mu and his queen, the monarchs reigning at the time Mireuk-sa was constructed. Excavated in 1917, several artifacts taken from the tomb are now on display at the Jeonju National Museum.

Iksan 익산

Halfway between Jeonju and Gunsan is the city of Iksan, the province's major rail hub. Formerly known as Iri, it's a growing industrial center,

well-known for its gem and jewelry industry, and, along with Jeonju and Gunsan, makes a thriving economic corridor in this corner of the province. Located on the eastern edge of town is a free trade zone where the Iri Gem and Jewelry Center is open daily except Tuesday for sales and the production of jewelry. On the more spiritual side, Wonbul-gyo, also called Won Buddhism, has its headquarters on the northern edge of town. Across the road is the well-respected Wongwang University, a private, non-sectarian school supported by the Won Buddhist church.

Iksan is not a city that has made a big name for itself, yet it did once make front-page news on account of a tragedy that happened there. The Iksan train station is a transfer point for large quantities of goods shipped by rail. One night in the mid-80s, a guard fell asleep in a boxcar full of explosives that was temporarily stored in the station yard. His cigarette apparently dropped from his hand and ignited the contents of the car, blowing himself to bits and creating a huge crater in the station yard. Worse, several hundred other people were killed, and about a third of the city was destroyed or damaged. From that disaster, much new has been built—including a train station. A monument has been raised in the city to remember this tragedy. Directly up from the train station is the city center. The market is two blocks back, and the bus terminal is toward the south end of town, down the road from the train station.

GUNSAN 군산

Just over 400 kilometers long, the Geum River is the third-longest in South Korea. It starts near Jangsu, on the western slope of the Sobaek Mountains, and flows north into Chungcheongbuk-Do. From there, this ancient waterway circles into Chungcheongnam-Do, passing both former Baekje capitals of Gongju and Buyeo, and creates the western extent of the border between Chungcheongnam-Do and Jeollabuk-Do before flowing into the West Sea at Gunsan. Opened in 1890 as an international port, Gunsan [Kunsan] has grown into a significant ferry terminal, and the third major shipping center on the west coast (along with Incheon and Mokpo). In order to combat the continuous problems of sedimentary silting caused by the river, plus the backwash and constant rise and fall of the tidal water, a new outer harbor has been developed partially on reclaimed land west of the city center, and an estuary dam has been constructed upriver from the inner harbor. A huge land development project is also under way, and this undertaking will dike the shallow mudflats from the mouth of the Geum River to Seonyu-do and from there on to the Byeonsan Peninsula. Much of the inner area will then be drained and put into cultivation. The new port and land development will promote increased international shipping and the construction of large industrial estates, and the dam-top road greatly facilitates traffic between Gunsan and Janghang across the river.

If you have a few hours to spare before catching a ferry or train, check out Wolmyeong Park. Stretching south for many kilometers in the western hills of town, it holds a temple, a water reservoir recreation area, many walking paths, and a small botanical garden.

Inexpensive accommodation can be found near the bus stations, ferry terminals, and behind the city hall. Try the Munhwajang Yeogwan (문화장여관) near the bus terminals; the Gongju Yeogwan (공주여관) or Oseongjang Yeogwan (오성장여관), to the side of the train station; or the Geumdongjang Yeogwan (금동장여관) and Dongbaekjang Yeogwan (동백장여관) near the Doseonjang ferry terminal. Larger and nicer is the Gunsan Tourist Hotel which is located at the major intersection near the bus terminals.

Transportation

Some 20 kilometers south of the city is Gunsan U.S. Air Force Base, one of the largest airfields in the country and home to advanced fighter aircraft. Adjacent to the air base is **Gunsan Airport** (군산공항); it's about a 40-minute ride on city bus no. 1, 4, or 9. The airport is small and basic, with only a few shops and other amenities; flights from here go twice a day and only to Seoul.

The Gunsan train station is located on the eastern edge of the rather claustrophobic and jumbled city center. The only trains to and from the city run seven times a day to Iksan, twice to Jeonju, and twice as far as Imshil. Beyond the railroad tracks and a bit farther to the east are the express and intercity bus terminals. Express buses run only to Seoul (₩10,300). Selected intercity bus destinations are Iksan (₩1,800), Jeonju (₩3,300), Daejeon (₩6,000), Jeongeup (₩5,500), and Buyeo (₩4,100). The city's two domestic ferry terminals are located along the river on the north edge of town. City bus no. 5 runs through town and connects these terminals to the train and bus stations. City bus nos. 20 and 67 also connect the bus terminals through the city center to the city hall.

From the **Doseonjang Ferry Terminal** (도선장), commuter ferries ply across the river to Janghang (₩1,000) every half hour, on the hour and half hour, from 0700 to 2200. About one-half kilometer up the river from the Doseonjang pier is the **Gunsan Coastal Ferry Terminal** (군산항여객선터미널). Ferries from here run to the islands off Gunsan, including Seonyu-do (₩11,700), Bian-do (₩14,400), Ocheong-do (₩21,800), and Gaeya-do (₩3,750). Seonyu-do is thirty kilometers southwest of Gunsan and located here is one of the two best beaches in the province. Ferries to Seonyu-do run every day, but during the summer swim season more are put on-line to handle the increased demand. Traveling up the coast from Ocheong-do, a daily ferry leaves at 0800 for Daecheon harbor in Chungcheongnam-Do. Located at newer port facilities is the **Gunsan International Ferry Terminal** (군산국제여객선터미널). While the facility exists, ferries between here and Yantai, China are not on an ongoing schedule so can't be counted upon. If you are interested in a water connection to China from here, check at the ferry company offices in Busan or Incheon about any current schedule.

M

Eastern Parks

DAEDUN-SAN PROVINCIAL PARK 대둔산도립공원

Nearly equidistant between Jeonju and Daejeon, straddling the Jeollabuk-Do/Chungcheongnam-Do border, is the 63-square-kilometer Daedun-san [Taedun-san] Provincial Park. Rising to 878 meters, this mountain area sits along a spur of the Sobaek Mountains. Varying shades of pink azaleas and rhododendrons assail the mountainside in spring. In winter, snow sharply contrasts with the stark black of the sheer cliffs and jutting rocks, like a scene from a classical Eastern landscape painting.

The park's southern section rises steeply and dramatically through curious rock formations. Dozens of stone spires, chimneys, and pinnacles thrust toward the sky, from which gnarled trees sprout. Deep crevasses between the pinnacles shelter thick foliage. Experienced Korean climbers consider this one of the foremost rock-climbing areas in the country. Be on the lookout for birds of prey which soar around these peaks. Strung between the tops of four prominent outcrops are a suspension footbridge and a metal stairway that provide bird's-eye views of this enchantingly sculpted hillside. A cable car now can whisk you partway up the mountains if you don't care to climb the whole way. The park's northern half is less dramatic and slopes gradually into the surrounding countryside. Here you'll find longer and wider valleys, little exposed rock, gurgling streams, a waterfall, and thick forests. In the folds of the mountain sit the temple Taego-sa and the remains of several mountain fortresses.

Hiking Trails

From the ticket booth (₩1,300 entrance) behind the hotel, walk up the narrow valley through its steepest section; alternately take the cable car (₩2,500 one way, ₩3,900 round-trip). At the upper cable car terminus is a freshwater spring. From here, one trail continues straight up to the mountaintop, while a metal staircase leads to the suspension bridge. A short way beyond the bridge, a steep rigid metal stairway transports you to another pinnacle, from where you join the main trail. Constructed in 1972, the suspension bridge is 50 meters long and 80 meters above the slanted chasm below. It's nearly identical to the suspension bridge at Wolchul-san in Jeollanam-Do. Because of its location, you can peer down from the 127-step stairway onto the suspension bridge. Continue up to the ridge, take a left, and walk to the highest peak. A modernistic silver marker has replaced the white cement monument that once stood on the top. From the bottom, it's about a two-kilometer, two-hour hike to the top. Backtrack to a point where the trail comes up to the ridge. There, go down the far side to a shelter and second spring. From the shelter there are three trails. The first heads back over the ridge into the deep Yong-mun-gol ravine, where a shallow grotto and another spring are found. Wind your way around the base of other pinnacles to the main trail just

suspension bridge at Daedun-san

below the upper cable-car terminus and back down to the village. The round-trip should take three to four hours. From near the top of the Yongmun ravine a branch trail continues along the ridge and eventually down the mountainside to Baetijae Pass, site of a bloody confrontation during the Imjin War. Outnumbered two to one, all 700 of the defending Korean soldiers lost their lives.

On the north side, one path leads down the mountain from the shelter to Taego-sa, a new temple on an old site. Periodic buses run from below Taego-sa to Geumsan. A second trail leads west down another valley, past Seokcheon-am, and out of the mountains to Surak Village—about five hours. An alternate route leads down the western ridge of the highest peak. Branching in the valley, the trail to the south goes to the temple Anshim-sa, and the trail to the north makes its way past a waterfall and on down to Surak. Be aware that all but the main trail are little frequented.

Practicalities

Daedun-san Provincial Park is usually a day-trip from the nearby cities, though accommodation is available at the base of the mountain. This little community includes a bus station, several restaurants, small shops, and a few basic and inexpensive *yeogwan* and *minbak*. At the upper end of the village is the Daedun-san Hot Springs Hotel.

Frequent buses run from Daedun-san to Jeonju (₩3,800), Gunsan (₩6,200), Geumsan (₩1,400), Daejeon Seobu bus terminal (₩2,100), and Daejeon Dongbu bus terminal (₩2,600). Less frequent buses run from Jeonju to Unju for Anshim-sa, Nonsan to Surak, and Geumsan to Taego-sa.

MAI-SAN PROVINCIAL PARK
마이산도립공원

Although bite-size, Mai-san ("Horse Ears Mountain") is certainly the most unusual mountain outcrop in the province, and perhaps in the entire country. With a V split between, its two steep peaks rise out of the surrounding flat agricultural plains, and from the town of Jinan, they do look like horse ears. The east peak (673 meters) is

MAI-SAN LEGEND

Long ago, a mountain spirit couple lived near Jinan with their two children. After living a comfortable life, it came time to ascend to heaven. This they decided to do during the middle of the night so as not to be noticed and prevented from reaching their goal. It was the wife's responsibility to wake the others, but due to fear of the night and fatigue from daily chores, she slept soundly and only awoke at daybreak. She wanted to postpone their journey but her husband persisted. That morning, a diligent housewife from a nearby village arose early and went to the well to draw water. When this woman looked off in the distance toward the home of the mountain spirits she was startled to see their buoyantly floating figures rising to the sky. When she screamed, the spirit husband became furious, took the children from his wife and put them on his back, hoping to make a mad dash for heaven. But it was too late. They had been discovered, and their ascension was halted where they were. In that position they hardened into the hills now called Mai-san. To this day, the husband and wife (male and female peaks) remain back to back, the man on the left with the children on his back, and the woman on the right, bent over in remorse for their failed attempt.

referred to as the male, the west peak (667 meters) as the female. Low hills stretch off to the west and then curve around to the south, while directly south of the horse ears is a lower yet distinctly similar tree-covered peak. Actually formed of sedimentary rock whose covering has eroded away, Mai-san appears to be a composite pebble mixture set in cement. Stories, in fact, tell of new settlers to the area asking how these hills were made and preserved so well, and what method was used to keep the little stones from falling off! Drainage from the mountain's north side eventually runs into the Geum River; water that flows to the south goes into the Seomjin River.

Called Mai-san today, it has had the names Soda-san, Yeongchul-san, and Seokgeum-san at various times in the past. Besides these, it's known by other names to the local population. In spring,

Mai-san is called Doddae-bong ("Mast Peak"), because the low-hanging clouds make the peak look like twin masts and sails of a ship floating through a misty sea. During the lush summer season, these hills are called Yonggak-bong ("Dragon Horns Peak"), the body of which is represented by the low hills that snake away in the distance. Mai-san appears most like horses' ears during the crisp days of autumn. The name Munpil-bong ("Literary Writing Peak") is given in winter because no matter how much snow falls in the area these peaks are always dark, like the black tip of a writing brush. Whatever this mountain is called, it's most dramatic and shapely from the north.

In 1979, 17 square kilometers were designated Mai-san Provincial Park. Not only are the peaks themselves of interest but here as well are several small temples, dozens of rock-pile pagodas, a hermitage cave, and a shrine.

From Jinan, a road runs up past a reservoir to the park's north entrance (₩1,400). From here a looooong flight of stairs goes up and into the V pass and down the opposite side. At the pass, a short trail to the left leads to a mineral spring in a narrow grotto in the east peak. A second trail goes off to the right, to the top of the female peak. Little piles of rocks have been left on top like signatures by those who have climbed up before. The male peak requires special climbing gear. The stairway continues steeply down to the small temple **Unsu-sa,** and farther on to Tap-sa. At the small and rather uninteresting Unsu-sa is an earthen platform used as an altar site for a ceremony during the local cultural festival. It is said that Yi Seong-gye came here to pray before establishing the Joseon Dynasty. There is bus service from about one and a half kilometers below Tap-sa back to Jinan.

Tap-sa 탑사

At Tap-sa ("Pagoda Temple"), about 80 neatly stacked rock pagodas were hand-piled by Yi Gap-yong, a hermit who made this valley his home. This group of stones, several of which rise to 15 meters or more, looks rather surrealistic in this confined valley. These pagodas are in reality a masterpiece of work, especially the aesthetic twins set directly behind the temple. Most of the rocks used were the rubble that had fallen from these peaks, but some stones were gathered from the various famous mountains throughout the country. Although fragile and unsteady-looking, none has ever been blown over by the wind that sometimes rushes through this gorge.

Yi Gap-yong was born not far away in Imshil around 1860. It's said that from an early age he showed signs of extreme filial piety. When his parents died, he spent three years in mourning at their gravesite, as correct (though rarely practiced) Confucian custom dictated. Afterwards he roamed restlessly from one well-known mountain to another, until he returned to his home at the age of 25. He came to Mai-san to pray and meditate, and received a revelation from a spirit saying that he could help succor the myriad masses then suffering in hell for their unrighteous earthly actions if he constructed stone pagodas as an unselfish act of grace. Until he died at the age of 98, he continued to live here and erect these pagodas. To honor his steadfastness and devotion, a statue of him has been placed amidst his fine handiwork. To the side of the tiny hermitage stands a modern granite statue of the Mireuk Buddha, the Buddha of Mercy, she to whom believers look for comfort and assistance.

One kilometer below Tap-sa is the temple **Geumdang-sa.** First erected in the Silla Dynasty, this temple preserves a nine-meter-high painting of the Goddess of Mercy. From the late 17th century, this mural is said to be one of the three most important Buddhist mural paintings in the country. The others are of the Goddess of Mercy at Tongdo-sa and the Maitreya Buddha at Muryang-sa. From near this temple a trail leads up into the hills to the grotto cave **Naong-am**, a secluded sanctuary once used for meditation by the great Silla monk Naong. Farther down the road is **Isan-myo,** a shrine dedicated to the spirits of Dan'gun, the Joseon Dynasty kings Taejo and Sejong, and select others.

Jinan 진안

This little town in the middle of the Jinan Plateau

is known for mushrooms and *insam* and as the gateway to Mai-san. The four-kilometer-long road to the mountain starts from the traffic circle at the west end of town. The major highways to Jinan come over the Sobaek Mountains from the east, and up over the serpentine Morae-jae Pass from Jeonju to the west. Every year in October the Mai Festival is held in town. North of town, on the northern flank of Unju-san, are the deep and picturesque Unilam and Banilam valleys, used by locals during the summer as a retreat from the heat.

If you decide to stay in Jinan, try the Munhwa Yeogwan (문화여관), near the bus terminal and post office, the Goryeo Yeogwan (고려여관), into town near the Telecom office, or the Jinan-jang Yeogwan (진안장여관), still a little farther into town. Buses from Jinan go to the Mai-san Provincial Park entrance (₩650), Tap-sa (₩1,200), Unilam (₩1,950), Jeonju (₩2,700), Daejeon (₩5,600), and Muju (₩3,000).

DEOKYU-SAN NATIONAL PARK
덕유산국립공원

Located in the northeast corner of Jeollabuk-Do, Muju County is the most mountainous in this agricultural province. The town of **Muju** is the gateway to the Gucheon-dong Valley, Deokyu-san [Tŏkyu-san] National Park, and Muju Resort. Nothing but a waystop for most travelers, this town preserves the pavilion **Hanpung-nu**. Last remodeled in 1783, this two-story structure is considered one of the three finest old pavilions in Jeollabuk-Do—the others being Hanbyeong-nu, in Jeonju, and Gwanghal-lu, in Namwon. In anticipation of the 2010 Winter Olympics being held at Muju Ski Resort, Muju is getting a facelift and sprucing up its infrastructure. Buses run from the terminal that's located along the south bank of the river near the pavilion. At the end of August each year, this town holds what is perhaps the county's strangest festival, the **Firefly Festival**. Encompassing numerous activities, the focus of this festival is that lowly bug that glows.

Muju Gucheon-dong, with its 33 scenic sights,

has for centuries been a tourist attraction for those fortunate Koreans able to explore their own land. In 1975, Deokyu-san National Park was created as an expansion of this famous valley, incorporating broad areas of the surrounding mountains; it now encompasses 219 square kilometers. Muju Gucheon-dong refers to the entire length of the valley, one of the prettiest valleys in the country.

Halfway between Jiri-san and Songni-san national parks, Deokyu-san National Park occupies a section of the Sobaek-san Mountains, and straddles the Jeollabuk-Do/Gyeongsangnam-Do border. Like other national parks along this mountain range, it's an expansive, high-elevation park with dramatic scenery and fine vistas from nearly any vantage point. Unlike the other parks, however, the several small temples here are not particularly significant; it's more appreciated for its natural beauty and hiking possibilities. At 1,614 meters, Deokyu-san is the fourth-highest peak in the country.

Many students come here during school holidays—August is the busiest month. Even during the sweltering summer, this valley and its clear streams stay cool and refreshing. Mid-to-late October is also popular because of the cooler weather and the patchwork of autumn colors. Spring brings bright red rhododendron blossoms, and winter a stark white snowscape.

Muju Gucheon-dong 무주구천동

The scenic sights of Muju Gucheon-dong start nine kilometers below the park village. The first is **Naje-tongmun**, a tunnel cut through solid rock that was for centuries the border "gate" delineating the Baekje and Silla kingdoms' territorial boundary. It's still used for vehicular traffic. From here, the next 31 scenic sights are sprinkled along this serpentine valley floor: waterfalls and cascades, pools, riverside rock cliffs and spires, and river turnings. Few people walk the length of the valley from Naje-tongmun to the park village. If you ride the bus, sit on the left side. The more spectacular sights are within the park beyond the entrance gate—the temple Baengnyeon-sa is the 33rd and last sight. Prepare for plenty of walking.

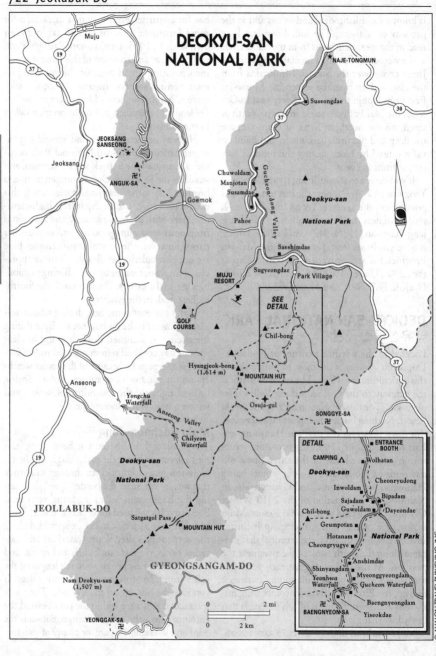

DEOKYU-SAN NATIONAL PARK

Muju

19

37

NAJE-TONGMUN

37

30

Suseongdae

JEOKSANG SANSEONG

Jeoksang

ANGUK-SA

Chuwoldam

Manjotan

Susamdae

Goemok

Pahoe

Gucheon-dong Valley

Deokyu-san

National Park

MOON

19

Saeshimdae

Sugyeongdae

Park Village

MUJU RESORT

SEE DETAIL

GOLF COURSE

Chil-bong

37

Hyangjeok-bong (1,614 m)

MOUNTAIN HUT

Anseong

Yongchu Waterfall

Osuja-gul

SONGGYE-SA

Anseong Valley

Chilyeon Waterfall

Deokyu-san

National Park

19

JEOLLABUK-DO

Satgatgol Pass

MOUNTAIN HUT

GYEONGSANGAM-DO

Nam Deokyu-san (1,507 m)

YEONGGAK-SA

0   2 mi

0   2 km

DETAIL

ENTRANCE BOOTH

CAMPING

Wolhatan

Deokyu-san

Cheonryudong

Inwoldam

Sajadam   Bipadam

Chil-bong   Guwoldam   Dayeondae

Geumpotan

National Park

Hotanam

Cheongryugye

Anshimdae

Shinyangdam

Myeonggyeongdam

Yeonhwa Waterfall

Gucheon Waterfall

Baengnyeongdam

BAENGNYEON-SA

Yiseokdae

© AVALON TRAVEL PUBLISHING, INC.

JEOLLABUK-DO

Baengnyeon-sa 백련사

Legend says that this temple, founded in 830, was given its name because a white lotus (*baengnyeon*) appeared here after the death of the monk Baengnyeon Seonsa, who had lived and meditated here in seclusion. In centuries past, there were many temples in this valley. Now only this one remains. Baengnyeon-sa [Paengnyŏn-sa] was expanded several centuries after its founding through the contributions of Ming Chinese princess Myeongwol in order to house 9,000 (*gucheon*) monks for strict meditation. This huge complex was partially destroyed in 1593 and burnt to the ground during the Korean War. Reconstruction began in 1964 and continues at a snail's pace today. At the temple entrance are several *sari budo;* one belongs to the scholar Kim Shi-seup, a high-ranking civil servant who would not switch loyalties and serve a usurping king. Somewhat of a nonconformist, this talented poet and storyteller left government work and spent many of the latter years of his life writing and wandering the countryside like a mendicant monk. Passing through the front gate, the path leads over a bridge and up 108 steps to the temple compound. Each of these steps represents one of the passions of man that Buddhism considers debilitating.

A kilometer or two above Baengnyeon-sa is **Osuja-gul**, a cave that's said to have been used for meditation by a monk called Osu. Ice in this cave, formed from water that drips through its roof, stays frozen virtually year-round.

Anguk-sa 안국사

The northwestern slope of Deokyu-san, seen from the road that connects Muju to Jangsu, is a spectacular palisade of cliff and spire. On top of the northern end of this formation lie the ruins of the 8-kilometer-long mountain fortress **Jeoksang Sanseong** (H.S. #146). Built around 1374, it had seen action in defense of the country. Three of its gates remain. Within the walls of this ancient mountain fortress, and incredibly near the top of the mountain, is a relatively new pumped-water reservoir and power generation plant. Rising from the north side of this lake is an observation tower from where you get a fine view

north toward Muju and south over the rest of the park where you can see the ski slopes distinctly on the hillside. The creation of this man-made lake necessitated the removal of the temple Anguk-sa to the site of the former temple Hoguk-sa, also within the fortress walls. Of the original four temples, only Anguk-sa remains. Constructed in 1277, Anguk-sa was used during the mid-Joseon Dynasty as one of several sites throughout the country for the storage of national archives as well as to station warrior-monks during times of national strife. At over 1,000 meters in elevation, this temple has a superb location overlooking the lowlands below and it's no wonder why this mountain was used as a fortification. Anguk-sa is rather unpretentious today, yet the hall Cheonbul-jeon has an unusual altar arrangement. On the front altar sit three figures as is usual, but there are also two tiered side altars that come all the way to the front of the building that hold a host of small seated Buddha images. Preserved at this temple is an old mural painting (T. #1267). A small museum here displays mostly Buddhist statuary, many pieces from other Asian countries. There is no bus service to the Anguk-sa.

Hiking

The most-frequented hiking trail in the valley takes you up the road from the park entrance to Baengnyeon-sa. This is the loveliest section of the valley; spend a leisurely half-day walking up and back. From the right side of the pavilion at Baengnyeon-sa, a trail of little more than one hour leads directly up the thickly forested hillside to the summit, Hyangjeok-bong. The main trail continues beyond Baengnyeon-sa into the upper reaches of the valley, eventually heading up the hillside past Osuja-gul to the top. Round-trip from the park entrance to Deokyu-san summit is close to 20 kilometers and requires about eight hours. For those who care to stay on the mountain overnight, a shelter is located just below the summit.

For those with sufficient stamina and enough food and water, a trail continues south from Hyangjeok-bong along the ridgeline to Nam Deokyu-san (1507 meters), and from there down past the temple Yeonggak-sa to the village of Sangnam, another tiring eight- to ten-hour day. There's not much water along this ridge, so be prepared. From the summit are three lengthy but shorter trails. One goes a short way up the main ridge to the north, turns down a side ridge to Chil-bong peak, and from there descends to the pavilion at Wolhatan. The second heads south along the main ridge and then turns to the west, dropping down into Anseong Valley, passing Chilyeon and Yongchu waterfalls on its way to the town of Anseong. The third goes along the ridge to the east and then down the south slope of the mountain to the temple Songgye-sa, from where buses run to Geochang. From the main park entrance, these hikes should take about eight hours.

The northern section of the park has a few shorter trails. One continues past Anguk-sa and heads down to the village of Goemok, from where periodic buses return to Muju. Another leads up from the west side of the reservoir to the west gate of the fortress wall and then steeply down the west side of the mountain to the village of Jeoksang, where there is also bus transportation.

Muju Ski Resort

Opened in 1990, Muju Ski Resort is the only ski area within a national park. It is also the most southern of Korea's ski resorts, but its elevation provides a long season. Good for skiers from beginning to advanced, Muju has 23 slopes including one that is over three kilometers long, the longest run in Korea. Lights have been installed for night skiing. Lift tickets are ₩38,000 a day for adults, ₩50,000 with night skiing, and ₩47,000 for the gondola to the top and all other lifts. Ski and snowboard rentals run ₩25,000–30,000, and ski lessons are available for about ₩30,000 a day. Packages are also available that reduce the cost. In addition, there are 48 kilometers of cross-country ski trails and two ski jumps. The resort also offers sled runs and ice-skating rinks and, for summer use, a golf course (at 950 meters, the highest in the country), water slide, swimming pool, and numerous other sporting facilities. Already having hosted several in-country competitions, and having been the site of the 1997 Winter Universiad, the resort has been chosen as the site for the 2010 Winter Olympics. Every February, the resort holds an international ski festival, featuring not only ski competitions but also a snow-sculpture competition, an exhibition of local craft items, and plenty of music and dance. During the winter season, a free shuttle bus runs between the park bus station and the ski resort several times a day between 1100 and 1700.

Practicalities

Entrance to Deokyu-san National Park is ₩2,600. A large tourist village at the end of the bus line includes numerous *minbak* and *yeogwan*, restaurants, tearooms, souvenir shops, a bus station, police station, and post office. Camping (₩3,000) is permitted within the park at the jamboree site. In the early 1980s, this jamboree site was created on the hillside near the park entrance, and this is still set aside for hikers, national and international scouting events, and as an outdoor training center for youth. There are two mountain huts on the mountain, one below the highest peak and another at Satgatgol Pass.

At the Muju Resort, rates at the **Tirol Hotel** (tel. 063/320-7200) run ₩266,000 and up, ₩192,000 and up at the **Family Hotel** (tel. 063/320-7000), and during ski season, ₩61,000–125,000 a room at the **Gungmin Hotel** (tel. 063/ 320-7000). In the town of Muju, try the Muju Tourist Hotel or the Muju Green Motel.

Buses from the park village run to Muju (₩2,500), Daejeon Dongbu bus terminal (₩6,900), Jeonju (₩8,300), and Namwon (₩9,200). During ski season, special shuttle buses run from Muju, Seoul, Busan, Daegu, Daejeon, and Gwangju directly to the resort.

Chungcheongnam-Do

충청남도

Situated in west-central Korea, Chungcheong-nam-Do [Ch'ungch'ŏngnam-Do] is bounded by Gyeonggi-Do, Chungcheongbuk-Do, and Jeollabuk-Do provinces, and the West Sea. Its Taean Peninsula is the westernmost tip of peninsular South Korea. In 1895, Chungcheongnam-Do was separated from its sister province Chungcheongbuk-Do.

Today, its population of 1.8 million and area of 8,323 square kilometers make it only slightly larger and more populous than its neighbor and previous "other half."

Once the heart of the Baekje Kingdom, the ancient capitals of Gongju and Buyeo have yielded countless historical and artistic prizes, many kept in their own national museums. Other objects of cultural value are found throughout the countryside. The repository of 30 National Treasures (N.T.), 85 Treasures (T.), 43 Historical Sites (H.S.), and numerous Intangible Cultural Assets (I.C.A.) and local cultural properties, Chungcheongnam-Do's wealth also extends to its natural beauty.

pavilion marking the site of the north gate of the Geumsan Fortress

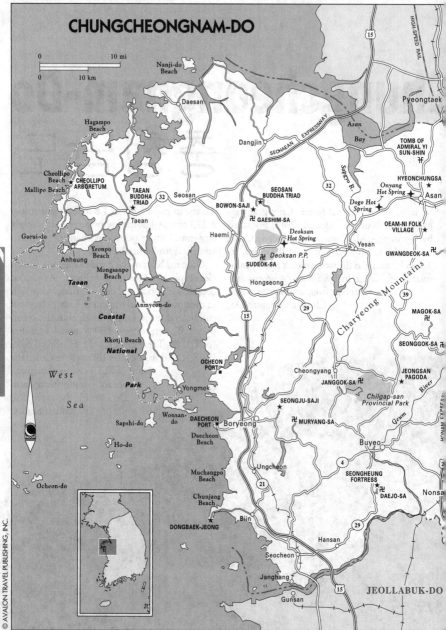

CHUNGCHEONGNAM-DO

0   10 mi
0   10 km

Nanji-do Beach

Daesan

Hagampo Beach

Dangjin

Asan Bay

Pyeongtaek

HIGH-SPEED RAIL

SECHAEAN EXPRESSWAY

TOMB OF ADMIRAL YI SUN-SHIN

Cheollipo Beach
Mallipo Beach
CHEOLLIPO ARBORETUM

TAEAN BUDDHA TRIAD

32

Seosan

SEOSAN BUDDHA TRIAD

32

Supyo R.

HYEONCHUNGSA

Onyang Hot Spring

Asan

Dogo Hot Spring

BOWON-SAJI

GAESHIM-SA

OEAM-NI FOLK VILLAGE

Taean

Haemi

Deoksan Hot Spring

Yesan

Gaeui-do

Yeonpo Beach

Anheung

Deoksan P.P.

SUDEOK-SA

GWANGDEOK-SA

Taean

Mongsanpo Beach

Hongseong

Charyeong Mountains

39

Coastal

Anmyeon-do

29

MAGOK-SA

Kkotji Beach

15

SEONGGOK-SA

National

West

Sea

Park

Yongmok

OCHEON PORT

Cheongyang

JANGGOK-SA

JEONGSAN PAGODA

Chilgap-san Provincial Park

River

HONAM EXPRESS.

Sapshi-do

Wonsan-do

DAECHEON PORT

Boryeong

SEONGJU-SAJI

MURYANG-SA

Ho-do

Daecheon Beach

Buyeo

Geum R.

Ocheon-do

Muchangpo Beach

Ungcheon

SEONGHEUNG FORTRESS

4

DAEJO-SA

21

Nonsan

Chunjang Beach

DONGBAEK-JEONG

Biin

29

Hansan

Seocheon

JEOLLABUK-DO

Janghang

15

Gunsan

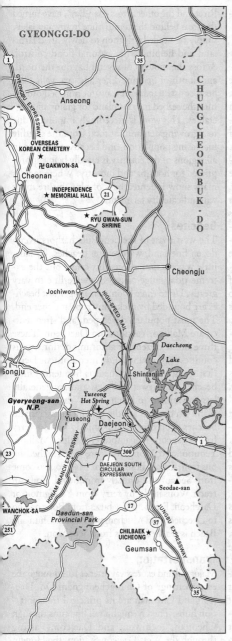

GYEONGGI-DO

1

35

Anseong

1

C
H
U
N
G
C
H
E
O
N
G
B
U
K
·
D
O

OVERSEAS
KOREAN CEMETERY

卍 GAKWON-SA

Cheonan

INDEPENDENCE
★ MEMORIAL HALL   21

RYU GWAN-SUN
★ SHRINE

Cheongju

Jochiwon

HIGH-SPEED RAIL

1

Daecheong
Lake

Shintanjin

ongju

Gyeryeong-san
N.P.

Yuseong
Hot Spring

1

Yuseong

Daejeon

23

300

1

DAEJEON SOUTH
CIRCULAR
EXPRESSWAY

HONAM BRANCH EXPRESSWAY

Seodae-san ▲

WANCHOK-SA

251

Daedun-san
Provincial Park

17

CHILBAEK ★
UICHEONG   37

Geumsan

JUNGBU EXPRESSWAY

35

Within its boundaries lie Gyeryong-san and Taean Coastal national parks, and Deok-san and Chilgap-san provincial parks; the northern half of Daedun-san Provincial Park also spreads into the province. Special products of the region include red and white *insam* from Buyeo and Geumsan, ramie cloth from Hansan, stone carvings from Ungcheon, walnuts from Cheonan, melons from Seonghwan, and apples from Yesan. Of the numerous festivals held in the province during the year, perhaps the most well-known are the Baekje Cultural Festival, held in October in either Gongju or Buyeo, the September Geumsan Insam Festival, May's Ramie Festival, held in Hansan, and the summer Boryeong Mud Festival.

While the area takes pride in its deep cultural roots, complex historical past, and natural beauty, it's also known historically for its loyal and patriotic citizenry. Yi Sun-shin, a native son and the country's most admired admiral, led the Korean navy to decisive victories over the Japanese navy during the Hideyoshi Invasions of 1592–98; 700 volunteer soldiers also died then, near Geumsan, in a rally to protect the motherland. Similarly, to voice their displeasure at Japan's maneuver to make Korea a protectorate in 1905, 900 citizens lost their lives in a conflict at Hongseong. During the occupation of the peninsula, individuals like Yun Pong-gil, who assassinated several top Japanese officers and civilian administrators in Shanghai, and Ryu Gwan-sun, a 17-year-old girl who led a contingent of citizens against the occupation force during the 1919 independence movement, sprang from this soil.

The people of Chungcheongnam-Do are rural folk, intensely tied to the soil. This province is first and foremost an agricultural province, and, with its broad coastal and riverine plains, one of the greatest food-producing regions of Korea. A growing industrial sector is concentrated in Daejeon, the provincial capital, and Cheonan, with a newer establishment at Daesan. Some smelting and refining of precious metals takes place in Janghang. Aside from Cheonan, the province's other cities are Asan, Seosan, Boryeong, Nonsan, and Gongju.

M
CHUNGCHEONGNAM-DO

For more information about the province online, check out http://chungnam.net.

The Land

With three-fifths of its land area below 100 meters in elevation, Chungcheongnam-Do has the country's lowest average elevation. Its wide fields, summer temperatures averaging 24°C, and an average annual rainfall of about 140 centimeters give this province optimal conditions for farming. Still, only a bit over 30 percent is arable.

Cutting diagonally across the province, petering out at the coast south of Boryeong, is the western extent of the Charyeong Mountains. Basically low rounded hills, few peaks stand over 500 meters. A spur of the Sobaek Mountains runs up into the southeastern corner of the province. Between these two ranges runs the 400-kilometer-long Geum River, third-longest in the country; half its length runs through this province. Traversing the wide coastal plain north of the Charyeong Mountains is the short Sapgyo River. Other short rivers trace their routes through the littoral plains of the Taean Peninsula and the coastal regions south of there. The province's widest agricultural areas are the Yaedang plain at Dangjin and the river plains around Buyeo. Four of the country's major hot springs are located in Chungcheongnam-Do: Yuseong, Deoksan, Onyang, and Dogo.

Although only 120 kilometers in a straight line from north to south, Chungcheongnam-Do's deeply indented coastline stretches over 1,200 kilometers. Huge bays cut into the land and several dozen mostly tiny islands hug its shore. By far the biggest and the only island of appreciable size in the province is Anmyeon-do, the country's sixth-largest. The West Sea has great tidal variation and strong currents; it creates huge mudflats at low ebb. These characteristics, and the absence of good anchorage, eliminate fishing as a major component of the economy. However, local residents endeavor in some small-scale sea farming. In addition, there is a great push for land reclamation to make use of some of the wide shallow bays for profitable crop production. Two long dikes constructed northwest of Cheonan (one across the mouth of the Sapgyo

River and the other across Asan Bay), have turned the areas behind them into huge freshwater lakes, supplying needed irrigation to newly dried farmland and helping with seasonal flood control. Across the mouths of several bays to the north and south of Seosan, dikes and sea walls have been constructed, and seawater pumped out, to turn the seabed into farmland for grains and vegetables. This work is exceedingly important due to a growing demand for food from the steadily increasing population, and because farmland in all regions of the country is rapidly being appropriated for housing and industry. Where today's maps show indented bays of blue, future maps will indicate dry farmland.

Beaches

The west coast of the peninsula harbors over a dozen fine-sand, warm-water beaches. Usually, little wave action affects this coast, but the extreme tidal range causes the waterline to vary greatly. Up to three kilometers long, most beaches are bounded by rocky outcrops at either end. The most-popular, -developed, and -frequented are Mallipo, Yeonpo, and Daecheon. These three boast dozens of accommodations, plus countless restaurants and entertainment facilities; transportation to them is frequent. Other beaches offer fewer facilities, and are generally less convenient to reach. The Wonsan-do and Nanji-do beaches are the province's two island beaches. You can reach Nanji-do best by ferry from Incheon. Hagampo, Cheollipo, Mallipo, Yeonpo, and Mongsanpo are best reached by bus from Taean, but buses for Mallipo also come from Seosan and directly from Seoul. You can reach Wonsan-do by ferry from Yeongmok or Daecheon. Frequent city buses from Boryeong go to Daecheon and Muchangpo beaches. Chunjang Beach is reached by bus from Seocheon.

Transportation

Major rail and expressway arteries run through the eastern fringe of Chungcheongnam-Do. Daejeon and Cheonan are its principal transportation hubs. The Gyeongbu rail line runs through Cheonan, Jochiwon, and Daejeon. Passing through the West Daejeon Station, the Honam line splits off the Gyeongbu line and makes its way to the Jeolla provinces. From Cheonan, the Janghang line runs via Asan, Hongseong, and Boryeong to the port of Janghang. Jochiwon is the western terminus of the Chungbuk line, which darts across Chungcheongbuk-Do to Jecheon.

Crossing and recrossing the Chungcheongnam-Do/Chungcheongbuk-Do border, the Gyeongbu Expressway (no. 1) passes through Cheonan and Daejeon before heading southeast toward Daegu. The rerouted Honam Expressway (no. 25) runs from Cheonan through Gongju and Nonsan, and then heads south to Jeonju and Gwangju. Cutting across the northern fringe of Daejeon and meeting the Honam Expressway is the Honam Branch Expressway (no. 251) which shoots across the corner of the province. Splitting from the Daejeon South Circular Expressway (no. 300), the Jungbu Expressway (no.

35) heads almost straight south into Jeollabuk-Do. The Seohaean Expressway (no. 15) ties the coastal fringe of the province to Incheon in the north and Mokpo in the south. Future plans call for additional expressways from northern Daejeon through Gongju to Dangjin, and from Gongju to Seocheon. In Chungcheongnam-Do, because of its low elevation, mountains cause virtually no transportation problems.

Dozens of islands dot the coast; Anmyeon-do connects to the Taean Peninsula by bridge. With only a handful of the rest inhabited, the ferry system is not extensive. The province's most active port is Daecheon, which has ferries to Wonsan-do, Yeongmok on Anmyeon-do, Sapshi-do, Ho-do, and Ocheon-do. One ferry from Ocheon plies to Yeongmok and Chojeon on Wonsan-do. From Anheung, ferries run to Gaeui-do.

Daejeon 대전

With 1.4 million people, Daejeon [Taejŏn], capital of Chungcheongnam-Do, is the country's sixth-largest city. In 1989, it was administratively separated from the province and given "special city" status. Like all other "special cities," Daejeon was redesignated a "metropolitan city" in 1995 and additional lands have been incorporated into the city boundary. Expanding rapidly since replacing Gongju as the provincial capital in 1932, it enjoys the province's largest concentration of industry, operates as its commercial and educational center, and is one of the primary transportation hubs of the nation. Occupying a wide plain between mountain peaks, Daejeon has incorporated the former towns of **Yuseong** (유성) and **Shintanjin** (신탄진) into its boundary; part of Daecheong Lake also lies within the city limits. Completed in 1980, the Daecheong Dam blocks the Geum River and produces electricity and drinking water for the city, and provides irrigation and flood control for agriculture. Because the lake is often used for fishing, no ferries operate as on Chungju or Soyang lakes, but you can bus from Shintanjin to have a look at the dam.

Since the 1970s, the national government has decentralized some of its offices. After Daejeon was given special-city status, a large area called **Dunsan New Town** was developed between downtown Daejeon and the 1993 Expo site. This area is one of huge apartment complexes, commercial blocks, city parks, schools, and new government offices. The new Daejeon City Hall was moved here and several national government offices have been relocated here as well. While this area has perhaps the greatest concentration of multi-story apartment buildings, other apartment clusters have also begun to ring the city, giving Daejeon a modern high-rise look.

Most industry is concentrated directly north of the city center, in the Daejeon Industrial Complex, and farther north, in Shintanjin. With more than one hundred companies, these areas produce, among other things, small machinery and engines, tires, textiles, clothing and footwear, bottled goods, food stuffs, chemicals, and pharmaceuticals. Also in Shintanjin is one of the nation's largest cigarette factories. Modern industrial goods and science and technology are not the

DAEJEON

Daecheong Lake

Secheon Park

Shikjang-san

GYEJOK SANSEONG
Gyejok-san

ONGNYU-GAK

GYEONGBU

DONGCHUN-DANG

Uam Historical Park

DAEJEON UNIVERSITY

GOSAN-SA 卍

GYEONGBU RAIL LINE

HIGH-SPEED RAIL

EXPRESSWAY

SUBWAY LINE

SEE "CENTRAL DAEJEON" MAP

DONGBU INTERCITY BUS TERMINAL

CHATEAU GRACE HOTEL

CHAMONIX HOTEL

EXPRESS BUS TERMINAL

HANBAT EDUCATION MUSEUM

HANBAT STADIUM

Bomun Park

Bomun-san

Sajeong Park

CHUNCHU FOLK MUSEUM

YUHOE-DANG

Gapcheon Stream

DAEJEON INDUSTRIAL COMPLEX

EXPO SCIENCE PARK

KKUMDORI AMUSEMENT PARK

DAEDEOK LOTTE HOTEL

Dunsan

DUNSAN PREHISTORIC SETTLEMENT SITE

CITY HALL

DOSAN SEOWON

MOKWON UNIVERSITY

WEST DAEJEON STATION

SEOBU INTERCITY BUS TERMINAL

Daedeok Science Town

CURRENCY MUSEUM

NATIONAL SCIENCE MUSEUM

KOREAN ADVANCED INSTITUTE OF SCIENCE AND TECHNOLOGY

PAICHAI UNIVERSITY

HONAM

RAIL LINE

CHUNGNAM NATIONAL UNIVERSITY

YUSEONG EXPRESS BUS TERMINAL

YUSEONG TOURIST HOTEL

RIVIERA HOTEL

Yuseong

DAEJEON SOUTH CIRCULAR EXPRESSWAY

Gubong-san

WORLD CUP SOCCER STADIUM

SUBWAY LINE

YUSEONG INTERCITY BUS TERMINAL

DAEJEON UNIVERSITY OF TECHNOLOGY

HONAM EXPRESSWAY

DAEJEON NATIONAL CEMETERY

Gyeryong-san National Park

1 mi

1 km

0

0

only important factors in the area's economy. Also important, but on a different level, are grapes, strawberries, pears, and ornamental flowers, and the crafts of small lacquered mother-of-pearl furniture, porcelain ware, leather goods, and traditional drums.

To the northwest of the city center, beyond the Daejeon Expo site, is **Daedeok Science Town**, an area of more than five dozen private, government, and academic institutes dedicated to research, development, and education. Within this area are such organizations as the Korean Advanced Institute of Science and Technology, Korea Research Institute of Standards and Science, Korean Atomic Energy Research Institute, Korean Research Institute of Chemical Technology, Korea Electronic and Telecommunications Institute, and the Korea Aerospace Research Institute. Here as well stand the National Science Museum, Currency Museum, and Chungnam National University, one of Daejeon's 14 universities and colleges. Other schools of note in the city include the Daejeon University of Technology, Paichai University, Daejeon Baptist Theological College and Seminary, Mokwon University, Hannam University, and Daejeon University. The combination of well-established scientific and technical research institutes, a broad educational foundation, and a growing industrial base has made Daejeon an important player in Korea's leap into the 21st century and in the country's rise to the level of a fully industrialized nation.

With the advancement in industry, science, and education, Daejeon has also created additional parks and recreation areas for its citizens, and has gone to some lengths to preserve its historical remains and cultural legacy. Three large-scale festivals are held yearly in Daejeon. With a parade through downtown, cultural arts performances of all kinds, folk games and contests, scientific and technical exhibitions, and a beauty contest, the **Hanbat Festival** is the city's largest cultural event. It takes place in the beautiful month of October. Also held in October is the **Yuseong Hot Spring Festival**, a celebration of local cultural heritage. The **Shintanjin Spring Flower Festival** occurs in April when the cherry trees push forth in shades of delicate pink. Events include traditional music and dance performances.

Directly below Bomun-san is the **Hanbat Stadium**. Consisting of a soccer field, baseball stadium, indoor swimming pool, gymnasium, tennis courts, and archery fields, this complex hosts all sorts of public athletic events throughout the year. Often on fine-weather evenings, you can look down on a brightly lit stadium from the observation area on Bomun-san and see a game in progress. A new stadium was built in Yuseong for the 2002 World Cup soccer tournament.

One of the many attractions that Daejeon is most proud of is the **Yuseong hot spring**. Gushing from the ground at about 50°C, this hot spring has been known since Baekje times and was said to have been used by ancient royalty. In the modern era, it once again became popular after the first public bathhouse was constructed here in 1915. Now about a dozen hotels and bathhouses use this water, offering a soothing, mineral rich bath to those looking for relaxation or for relief from some ailment. Containing some 60 minerals, this water is believed to benefit those who suffer from skin diseases, arthritis, and diabetes. **Yuseong** [Yusŏng] also boasts a well-maintained golf course. Across the road from the golf course you'll find the Daejeon National Cemetery. A broad expanse of lawn punctuated by several monuments and memorial halls, those who are buried here are war dead, as well as patriots and martyrs who died for the causes of freedom and democracy on the peninsula. Along with other areas of the country, Yuseong has been designated a "special tourism zone," ensuring that additional money and energy will be poured into the area in the coming years to enhance its tourism potential and attract more visitors.

For information online about the city of Daejeon, check out www.metro.daejeon.kr.

PARKS AND RECREATIONAL AREAS
Mokcheok Park

As there was no spare space in downtown Daejeon, the city's most central park has been built over a portion of the stream that runs through its center. A perfect place for a noontime lunch with workmates or as a place to relax on a sultry summer evening, this park is a tight mix of walkways and fountains, covered arbors and park benches, and sculptures and street lamps, all dotted here and there with potted trees and flowers. It's a much-needed addition to the city's previously austere center.

Bomun-san Park 보문산공원

Located directly south of the city center, Daejeon's premier green area is Bomun-san [Pomunsan] Park, a large forested area that drapes over the mountain. At the entrance to the park stands an area of restaurants, accommodations, and game arcades; the Chunchu Folk Museum is located here as well. Running until 1800, a cable car climbs part way up the mountain (₩1,300 one-way or ₩1,700 round-trip). Unexpectedly, from the cable car you have a good view of well-tended Korean graves on the hillside below. On this mountain you'll find several walking trails, the remains of an ancient fortress wall, a small kiddie amusement park and swimming pool, an outdoor concert hall, numerous small Buddhist temples, several commemorative war monuments, and an army of pigeons. By far the best bird's-eye view of Daejeon, and the most accessible, is from the **Boundae Observation Area** above the kiddie park. You also have a fine view over the city from a pavilion on the mountain peak within the fortress wall, a half-hour walk above the observation area. A pedestrian roadway runs up into the park, and just above the upper end of the cable car terminus, it splits. The left-hand fork takes you to the observation area; going straight ahead will bring you past a natural spring to the fortress. Turning to the right leads to the western slope of the mountain and to the Sajeong outdoor athletic and physical fitness area, a botanical park, and zoo.

Ppuri Park

At the bend of the Yudeung Stream west of Bomun-san Park is Ppuri Park. An area of flower beds, walking paths, trees, and hiking trails, this park also has stone tablets carved with Korean family names and their origins, thereby elucidating the roots (*ppuri*) of the Korean people.

Expo Science Park 액스포과학공원

In 1993, Daejeon hosted an International Exposition on this site, with the theme "The Challenge of a New Road to Development." This was the first time that a developing country ever hosted the International Exposition; over 110 countries each presented a display at an international pavilion, and over two dozen domestic and foreign organizations also constructed their own pavilions. While the exposition is long since over, a dozen-and-a-half pavilions stand as permanent structures in the now renamed Expo Science Park, which has as its theme science and technology. Aside from a handful of permanent displays, several offer techno-visual showings at regular intervals during the day. Other facilities are used as teaching tools in order to open the minds of and promote interest in science and technology among Korean schoolchildren who visit the park. Open every day of the year from 0930 to 2200 (1000–2000 in winter); general admission is ₩3,000, with entrance to three pavilions at ₩7,000 and five pavilions at ₩9,000. Rates for children are cheaper. Allow a good portion of the day to see everything here. Aside from school trips and during summer holidays, this park is very nearly deserted. Eating facilities, information booths, and other amenities are conveniently located in the park.

Adjacent to the Expo Science Park is **Kkumdori Amusement Park.** Typical of such parks, rides include a Ferris wheel, roller coaster, carousel, bumper cars, and a flume ride. Here also you'll find arcade games, entertainment stages, information booths, shops, restaurants, swimming pool, roller rink, a first-aid station, and lost and found. This could be a perfect place for high-spirited kids on a long summer day. Entrance to the park costs ₩2,500. Entrance with three rides is ₩10,000, with unlimited rides it's ₩18,000; children's entrance fees with rides are ₩2,000, ₩8,000, and ₩14,000, respectively. Entrance times are the same as the Expo Science Park.

Mountain Recreation Areas

Recognizing the need for city residents to get out into the surrounding countryside, the city has developed two mountain recreation areas that, because of the size of the city, still fall within city limits. Designed for fun and education, they contain athletic areas, playgrounds, and open fields, along with pathways through the forested hillsides and along the streams in which they lie. These two are **Manin-san Recreational Forest** and **Jangtae-san Recreational Forest,** both in the southernmost sections of the city. Manin-san is free; the entrance fee to Jangtae-san is ₩1,000.

Although not developed, **Gubong-san,** southeast of the city center and closer in than Jangtae-san, is also often hiked by city dwellers. Set along a turn in the river, its craggy nine-peak ridgeline offers good views of the surrounding countryside.

HISTORICAL POINTS OF INTEREST

The number of prehistoric remains in the city is small, yet a group of low-slung dolmen occupy a site some 500 meters west of the government complex, and the construction of Dunsan New Town has unearthed stone tools and pottery pieces from the Paleolithic and Neolithic age. Although it has a few dolmen and reconstructed pit-style dwellings, the **Dunsan Prehistoric Settlement Site** (둔산선사유적지), is not much to see, but is of important historical note to help trace the ancient habitation of this region.

Over the centuries, many important people have either lived or spent time in Daejeon and the surrounding area. Perhaps the most renowned of these is Song Shi-yeol, king's tutor and political adviser from the mid-1600s. On the eastern edge of the city, just north on Daejon University, is **Uam Historical Park** (우암사적공원), a park created to honor this scholar. Just inside and to the left of the front gate is **Namganjeongsa,** a 300-year-old tile-roofed building used by Song Shi-yeol as a study. Within a separate compound of its own, this building straddles a small rivulet flowing from a spring behind the house to a fish

pond in front. His desk and inkstone, along with wood printing blocks of his written works, and his portrait are preserved in an exhibition hall just up the hill. In the upper part of the compound, and built in a style thought to have been in use at the time, are re-creations of a lecture hall, dormitories, eating and resting places of a private Confucian school, and a memorial shrine dedicated to Song. This park is open 0500–2100 with free admittance. Bus no. 310 stops close to the entrance; bus no. 190 is more frequent but stops along the main street, a 15-minute walk down the road.

North of there, and close to each other, are **Dongchun-dang** (T. #209), **Ssangcheong-dang,** and **Songae-dang.** All three of these traditional-style buildings have tiled gable-over-hip roofs. All have an enclosed section heated by *ondol,* while the remaining two-thirds is a wood-floored room with walls of paper-clad lattice doors that can be opened or removed. This construction lets the occupant stay warm inside during the cold winter months and cool in the open-air section during the hot summer. Typically, these buildings were constructed for scholars and noblemen, who used them as a study halls or places to entertain, and were set apart from the living quarters of a house. On a hillside nearby you'll come across the well-preserved *yangban* house of Song Yong-eok, and, on the far side of the expressway from there, **Ongnyu-gak,** a partially open pavilion set on sloped ground on pillars of different heights. Just north of there, on the west side of the expressway, is **Jewol-dang,** another study hall, and Ogoje, an attached building. On the south side of Bomun-san, tucked up into a narrow valley, is the study hall **Yuhoe-dang.** All of these buildings, except Dongchun-dang, have been designated cultural properties for their age and structural characteristics.

Another local cultural property also of historic interest is **Dosan Seowon Confucian Academy,** not to be confused with the more well-known *seowon* of the same name north of Andong. Erected in a rural setting, but now surrounded by houses, this shrine is an example of a private school of the last century. Dosan Seowon honors Gwon Tteukgi and Gwon Shi, members of the Andong Gwon family, who taught Confucian philosophy and ethics here in the late 1600s. This compound contains several restored buildings, including a shrine and study halls once used by students. A ritual memorial ceremony is conducted here every spring and fall. The tombs of these two scholars lie below the tall pine trees on the hill to the west. An obscure site for foreign visitors, it is open 1000–1700 weekdays and until 1400 on Saturdays.

Northeast of the city is the mountain fortress **Gyejok Sanseong** (계족산성)(H.S. #355). Once the site of battle between Baekje and Silla armed forces, only a number of fortress walls remain to speak of the past. A modern observation pavilion now stands within the fortress walls where, presumably, an ancient observation post once stood.

Southeast of the city center is Shikjang-san, said to have been along the border between the Silla and Baekje kingdoms before their merger. On its slopes are a well-preserved forest area and several Buddhist temples, including **Gosan-sa** (고산사), one of the oldest and most well-known temples near the city. Although it has been reconstructed, the main temple hall here is a designated local cultural asset. Tucked into the hills on the northern edge of the mountain, surrounding a small reservoir, is **Secheon Park.** More a broad area of forested hills, open fields, and pathways, it's perhaps prettiest in spring, when the ornamental trees push forth their white and pink blossoms.

MUSEUMS

National Science Museum
국립중앙과학관

Moved from Seoul in 1990 to its new location, appropriately in the Daedeok Science Town section of Daejeon, the National Science Museum is not only a museum but an educational institution. The first section of its permanent collection explains the evolution of the universe and the geological and natural history of the Korean Peninsula. Other sections show the process by which nature works and how man has succeeded in manipulating and utilizing nature for his own ends. Of special interest for those studying Korea's past is the section on

the history of Korean science and technology. Included here are numerous Korean inventions, including a concave brass sundial, a rain gauge, mechanical devices, weapons, and displays discussing the making of pottery and the *ondol* Korean underfloor heating system. A few Western items are also included, including models of the Wright brothers' biplane and the space shuttle. Interactive displays and videos enhance the learning experience. Unfortunately, there is little in the way of explanation in English or other non-Korean languages for foreign visitors. The attached planetarium runs periodic programs about the universe, while the theater presents nature-related movies four to five times a day. The museum is open 0930–1730 (1630 in winter) except Monday and some national holidays, and the ₩1,000 entrance fee is good for the exhibitions and movie. For information online, see www.science .go.kr.

Currency Museum 화폐박물관

Located behind and to the west of the Science Museum is the Currency Museum, which traces the history of Korean money. Aside from Korean coins and bills from the last thousand years, here you'll find a good sampling of foreign currency, some Korean stamps, past Olympic commemorative coins from other nations, and a money printing machine. This is a fine historical representation and a good quick survey. Open Tuesday–Saturday 1000–1600 except the day after national holidays; admission is free. To go by taxi is most convenient, but if you walk here from the Science Museum, proceed around the back, then cross and walk along the stream for about 20 minutes until you see the Currency Museum inside a fenced compound.

Chunchu Folk Museum
춘추민속박물관

Located at the entrance of Bomun-san Park, the Chunchu Folk Museum stands stuffed full of everyday items from previous decades and the last century. These folk material pieces help illuminate how Koreans of the past dealt with the task of daily living. The building is somewhat close and claustrophobic and there is nothing formal about the presentation, making the displays seem all the more natural.

Hanbat Education Museum
한밭교육박물관

A few city blocks north of the train station is the Hanbat Education Museum. With some 6,000 items, the displays and dioramas here take you through the history of the educational process in Korea. Open 0930–1800 except Monday; free.

ACCOMMODATIONS

Hotels

Of a dozen-and-a-half hotels in Daejeon, the three best are the deluxe-class **Riviera Hotel** (tel. 042/823-2111) and **Yuseong Tourist Hotel** (tel. 042/822-0811), both in Yuseong, and the deluxe-class **Daedeok Lotte Hotel** (tel. 042/865-7012) for clientele visiting Daedeok Science Town. With full amenities, room rates run in the ₩100,000 and greater range. You'll find a

full host of other accommodations also located in central Yuseong. In central Daejeon, try the smaller and much less expensive second-class **Life Tourist Hotel** (tel. 042/253-5337) near the train station, or either the second-class **Daerim Tourist Hotel** (tel. 042/253-2161) or **Family Tourist Hotel** (tel. 042/255-4083) near the provincial government building, where rooms run in the ₩40,000–70,000 range. Slightly less expensive is the **Prince Hotel** (tel. 042/253-5853). Near the express bus terminal is the first-class **Chamonix Hotel** (tel. 042/621-8400) and the **Chateau Grace Hotel** (tel. 042/634-5600), with rooms a bit more expensive.

Yeogwan

Clustered around the express and Dongbu intercity bus terminals are many new *yeogwan* and *yeoinsuk*. Generally clean and comfortable, they mostly serve late-evening travelers. Among the multitude in this area, check out the Daejeon Park (대전파크) or High Motel (하이모텔), or for a less expensive place the Cheonghojang Yeogwan (청호장여관). The area around the Seobu

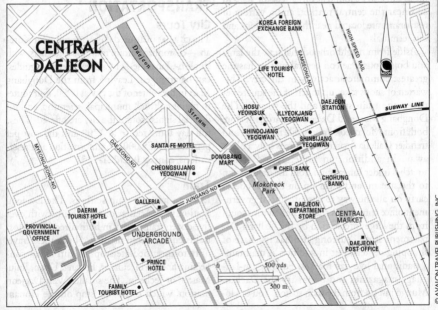

CENTRAL DAEJEON

KOREA FOREIGN EXCHANGE BANK
LIFE TOURIST HOTEL
HOSU YEOINSUK
ILLYEOKJANG YEOGWAN
DAEJEON STATION
SUBWAY LINE
SHINDOJANG YEOGWAN
SHINBIJANG YEOGWAN
SANTA FE MOTEL
DONGBANG MART
CHEIL BANK
CHEONGSUJANG YEOGWAN
Mokcheok Park
CHOHUNG BANK
GALLERIA
DAEJEON DEPARTMENT STORE
DAERIM TOURIST HOTEL
CENTRAL MARKET
PROVINCIAL GOVERNMENT OFFICE
UNDERGROUND ARCADE
DAEJEON POST OFFICE
PRINCE HOTEL
FAMILY TOURIST HOTEL

HIGH-SPEED RAIL
SAMSEONG-NO
DAEJEONG-NO
MYEONG-JEONG-NO
JUNGANG-NO

0   500 yds
0   500 m

CHUNGCHEONGNAM-DO

intercity bus terminal is less developed and has fewer accommodations, but if you need a place here try the Sanseong Yeogwan (산성여관), near the terminal's back gate. A dense concentration of lodgings is located mostly on the north side of the main street running up from the train station. For a place close to the station, try the Shinbijang Yeogwan (신비장여관), Illyeokjang Yeogwan (일역장여관), or the Shindojang Yeogwan (신도장여관). Less expensive and more basic is the Hosu Yeoinsuk (호수여인숙). On the far side of the stream, in another concentration of accommodations, check out the Cheongsujang Yeogwan (청수장여관) or the Santa Fe Motel (산타페여관).

Practicalities

The area just to the south of Jungang-no, between the stream and Daejeong-no, is full of restaurants, tearooms, coffee shops, drinking establishments, cinemas, and fancy shops and boutiques. This is the city's major restaurant/nightlife/entertainment area. Crossing this area are several pedestrian streets that are closed to traffic in the evening. Quick and inexpensive meals can also be found at tiny streetside stalls in and near the central market, and a variety of restaurants are located near the train stations and bus terminals.

Aside from neighborhood markets, the large and boisterous Daejeon central market has the greatest commercial activity in the city. This warren of shops takes up much of the square between the train station and the stream. The Dongbang Mart and Daejeon department store both front Mokcheok Park, while the newer and trendier Galleria department store is only a block away. In addition, an underground arcade stretches under Jungang-no from the train station to the stream, and picks up on the far side to carry on all the way to the provincial government office complex. A shorter section runs south from the large intersection by the Galleria Department store. Yuseong also has its share of shopping centers, but in addition it maintains a traditional five-day market. For English-language magazines and books try the Daehun Mungo just up from the train station. You can lo-

cate many herbal shops and doctors practicing traditional medicine in the back streets of the quarter on the far side of Jungang-no from the central market.

The central post office is conveniently located down from the train station, and the Telecom office down from the provincial government offices. For changing foreign currency, the Korea Foreign Exchange Bank, Cheil, and Chohung banks, among others, are conveniently located in the city center.

The city-run tourist booth in front of the express-bus terminal is helpful; the province mans a similar tourist information booth at the Daejeon Station plaza. Both maintain a stock of brochures and maps of the city and entire province. The city general tourist information center (tel. 042/861-1330) is located inside the Expo Science Park. Open daily 0900–1800, with Korean-, English-, Japanese-, and Chinese-speaking staff, this center also provides brochures and maps, a souvenir shop, computer Internet access, and occasional film screenings.

TRANSPORTATION

City Tours

The city has instituted daily bus tours for Koreans—customized group tours for foreigners, with English-, Japanese-, or Chinese-speaking guides, can be arranged. Leaving from the Dongbang Mart in the center of the city at 0930, four routes to major cultural, municipal, scientific, and industrial sights around the city are offered. These full-day tours return at 1700 and the cost per person runs ₩5,000. For information and reservations, contact 042/221-5451.

Train

Daejeon has two train stations. The Daejeon Station in the center of town hums with over five dozen trains a day in both directions. Most trains end in Seoul or Busan, but others travel only to intermediate stops or run along connecting lines to Haeundae, Pohang, Ulsan, Jinju, Masan, or Jecheon. The smaller West Daejeon Station, which is the first stop on the Honam rail line, serves nearly four dozen daily trains north to Seoul and south to Mokpo, Gwangju, Suncheon, Jinju, and Yeosu.

Like most metropolitan cities in the country, Daejeon is moving toward an underground transportation system. Scheduled for completion in 2003, line #1 will run under main thoroughfares connecting the express bus terminal, Daejeon Station, the city center, the provincial government building, city hall, Dunsan New Town, and Yuseong.

Express Bus

The express bus terminal is on the east side of town, and service connects Daejeon with 13 major provincial cities and three terminals in Seoul. Destinations include Seoul (₩6,500), Tong Seoul Station (₩7,100), Seoul Sangbong Station (₩7,000), Incheon (₩7,400), Suwon (₩5,600), Jeonju (₩3,800), Gwangju (₩7,600), Daegu (₩6,300), Gyeongju (₩9,000), and Busan (₩11,600). In addition, there is a direct express bus connection between Yuseong and Seoul (₩6,600).

Intercity Bus

The **Dongbu intercity bus terminal** (동부시외 버스터미날) is located to the side and up from the express bus terminal. Buses from here fan out to numerous destinations in this and adjoining provinces. Destinations include Asan (₩4,300), Cheonan (₩3,100), Songni-san (₩4,700), Cheongju (₩2,600), Jeonju (₩3,800), and Muju Gucheondong (₩6,900). Across town is the **Seobu intercity bus terminal** (서부시외버스터미날). Destinations from this terminal include Daedunsan (₩2,100), Gongju (₩2,600), Buyeo (₩4,200), Boryeong (₩7,100), and Taean (₩11,500). Yuseong also has an intercity bus terminal for those going directly there.

City Bus

Daejeon has an extensive city bus system. Although only a partial list, the following destinations with bus numbers should prove helpful. Most run through downtown Daejeon and by Daejeon Station. As in all major cities, there are regular city buses and express buses. Fares for express buses, which make fewer stops, are twice that of regular buses and should be posted on the collection box.

Express bus terminal: 102, 202, 703, 841

West Train Station: 223, 851

Seobu Bus Terminal: 703, 841

Bomun-san Park: 310, 711, 724

Sajeong Park: 888

Ppuri Park: 310

Gubong-san: 202, 220

Jangtae-san Recreational Forest: 230

Gyejok-san: 703

Donghak-sa and Gyeryong-san National Park: 102, 103

Dongchun-dang: 851

Ongnyu-gak: 104

Yuhoe-dang: 888

Dosan Seowon: 140-1, 180

Daecheong Dam: 702, 724

Daejeon Station: 841

Uam Historical Park: 310, 190

Dunsan Historic Site: 103, 513, 801

Expo Park, Science Museum, Currency Museum: 105, 105-1, 113, 180

Gosan-sa: 510

CHUNGCHEONGNAM-DO

Daejeon Vicinity

GYERYONG-SAN NATIONAL PARK 계룡산국립공원

Gyeryong-san [Kyeryong-san] is one of the few rugged mountain areas close to a major metropolitan city. Within 20 kilometers of downtown Daejeon, this solitary highland stands as a granite sentinel on a jutting spur of the Sobaek Mountains. Gyeryong-san means "Chicken Dragon Mountain"; its numerous peaks stand in a row like a cock's comb, and the mountain's twisting spine resembles the back of a dragon. Of its two dozen temples and hermitages the three largest dominate principal valleys: Donghak-sa, a cloister of female monks, in the east; Gap-sa, the mountain's oldest sanctuary, in the western valley; and Shinwon-sa, in the southwest. The abandoned temple site Guryong-saji once anchored a northern valley, where stone flagpole supports and *sari budo* alone remain to mark the site. Two accessible waterfalls grace the valleys: one above Gap-sa, the other above Donghak-sa. In 1968, 61 square kilometers of the mountain were set up as Gyeryong-san National Park, and since the park's opening much has been done to preserve and protect the natural environment, create adequate trails, and improve the religious precincts.

After a barren winter, spring brings bright flowers to the mountainside. Pine, elm, oak, and maple cover the steep valleys during summer with a carpet of dappled green. In autumn, the deciduous trees turn riotous colors, like a painter gone

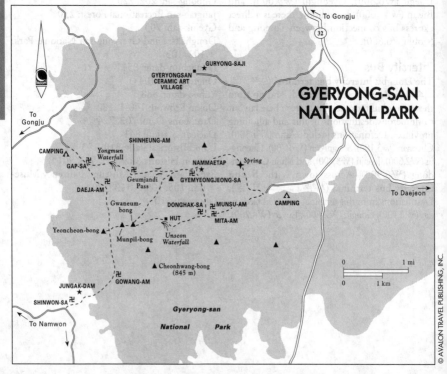

© AVALON TRAVEL PUBLISHING, INC.

crazy with his palette. A variety of common birds, squirrels, and other small animals are frequently seen, and you may be lucky enough to spot one of the furtive raccoons, fox, or deer.

The remote village of Seokgye-ri on the southern flank of the mountain was the original site chosen by King Taejo for the new capital of the Joseon Dynasty. Construction was stopped shortly after it began when geomancers informed the king that this was an inauspicious location. Seoul was then selected as a more propitious spot. Today, only a few foundation stones mark the proposed townsite, but the Korean military command headquarters, Gyeryongdae, is now located nearby. For years, however, several kilns remained which produced pottery during the early Joseon Dynasty. Many intact pieces, mainly *buncheong* ware, have been unearthed here. These kilns have been closely associated with the Buddhist temples of the mountain, and the manufacture of pottery by resident monks helped garner income for the temples. Today, the **Gyeryongsan Ceramic Art Village** produces pottery on the north flank of the mountain, carrying on this centuries-old tradition.

Gyeryong-san has been known for centuries for its myths and legends based on divination, its alleged supernatural powers, and its mystery. These qualities have especially drawn religious cults to the mountain, many of which amalgamate the tenets of shamanism, animism, Buddhism, and even Christianity. Although less pervasive today, this locale is still a mini-hotbed of cults that believe in the mysticism of the mountain, and even a number of established religions have churches here.

Donghak-sa 동학사

Donghak-sa [Tonghak-sa] was founded in 724 by priest Sangwon Josa. Originally built for monks, it is now one of Korea's few temples that function as study centers and teaching institutions for Buddhist nuns. Women come here to sharpen their minds and tread the religious path toward enlightenment. Along with the usual daily activities, you may see *biguni* out under the trees chanting sonorous hymns, while others meditate in back rooms or secluded hermitages. Be

© ROBERT NILSEN

stairway to Munsu-am

sensitive to the needs of those living here, and try to keep the noise level down. The grounds and buildings are well-kept. The halls are typical, except for a perceptible elegance and refined grace. Have a close look at the main hall, with its brightly painted front doors, intricately carved with crane, bamboo, cherry-blossom, and other floral designs. You'll rarely see such elaborate doors! Of less elegance is the Three Spirits hall. The lecture hall of the Buddhist college is the large building above and behind the main hall.

Directly to the right side of the temple is the memorial shrine Sungmo-jeon, originally constructed in 1456 by Joseon Dynasty scholar and official Kim Shi-seup for the deposed boy-king Danjong, whose throne was stolen by his uncle, King Sejo. Kim Shi-seup and several other officials refused to shift loyalty to the usurper and were banished and eventually killed for their "insubordination." Destroyed and rebuilt many times, the present structure is of recent vintage. Just below Donghak-sa stand the hermitages Mita-am, with an attractive stone stairway leading to its front gate, and Munsu-am. Across the stream near here is a small collection of *sari budo*.

Gap-sa 갑사

On the west side of the mountain lies Gap-sa [Kap-sa]. One of the oldest temples in the country, it's said to have been founded in 410 by Ado, the proselytizing Goguryeo monk credited with introducing Buddhism to the Silla kingdom. Gap-sa was repaired several times during the Silla Dynasty, and again rebuilt in 1604 after its razing during the Hideyoshi Invasions. The oldest of the present buildings dates from the renovation of 1604, the newest from 1994. Faded paint and weathered wood show the temple's age, and several of the buildings lean slightly, as if tired from long years of vigilance.

Set up on a stone terrace, the main hall marks the center of the compound. Erected in 1604, this hall hosts seven figures on its wide altar, three seated Buddhas and four flanking standing bodhisattvas. Above and to the left of this hall stands the newly painted Three Spirits hall. Among the other buildings at the temple is Pyochungwon, which houses a portrait of Yeonggyu Daesa, the warrior-monk leader of the 1590s, and the lecture hall, which sits directly to the front of the main hall. Near the front gate stands the temple's bronze bell (T. #478). Cast in 1584, this one-meter-tall bell is a bit stouter than the average Korean bell, but of excellent detail in shape and design. Locked away in one of the halls are over 100 wood printing blocks (T. #582) in both han'geul and hanja, representing two Buddhist writings. At a spot outside the compound is an inscribed stone monument, dating from 1659, which relates the history of the temple. About 100 meters to the side of the temple, a standing figure of the Buddha of Medicine occupies a small trailside grotto. Below the main compound was the original temple complex. There stands Daejeok-jeon and in a clearing in front of that hall is an elaborately carved *sari budo* (T. #257), radically different in design and execution from the much more common unadorned bell-shaped *sari budo*, like those found to the front of this temple compound and often found throughout the country at other temples. Set on a base of swirling dragons and lotus buds, the main block is decorated with figures of the heavenly kings, while the whole is capped with a simulated tile roof. In an open field below this reliquary stands a very rare temple banner pole (T. #256) from the United Silla Dynasty. Made from 24 iron cylinders (originally 28), each about 50 centimeters in diameter, it was once regularly draped with banners, flags, paintings, and cloth pennants. Gap-sa preserves a very large and old mural (N.T. #298), the likes of which were regularly hung on banner poles at temples throughout the country. It's unfurled on special occasions and is about 10 meters by 13 meters in size. Only one other such ancient pole still stands where it was erected centuries ago, and that is in cramped quarters in central Cheongju. During the past several decades, a few similar flagpoles have been reworked or created anew and raised at various temples around the country as they had been in centuries past.

Shinwon-sa 신원사

Newer than Gap-sa, older than Donghak-sa, Shinwon-sa was constructed in 651, when Baekje controlled this territory. Rebuilt several times over the centuries, it underwent some repair in 1982. Small, neat, and simple, Shinwon-sa has perhaps less historical significance than the mountain's two other, more famous temples. Dedicated to the Amita Buddha, the main hall is diminutive, yet elaborately adorned. Standing in the grass courtyard to its front are two stone lanterns and a five-tier stone pagoda. Here as well are several other buildings, including an international Zen study center. While foreign monks study, worship, and meditate at Hwagyesa in Seoul for most of the year, they and their teachers come to Shinwon-sa during the winter for a strict silent-meditation retreat. If you visit during these months, please respect their time of seclusion and do not disturb.

In a separate compound to the right of Shinwon-sa stands **Jungak-dan** ("Middle Mountain Altar"), an altar used for performing a yearly ritual to the Gyeryong-san mountain spirit, a ceremony supposedly enacted by King Taejo, the first Joseon Dynasty king and the famous Joseon Dynasty monk Muhak. This ritual is believed to be of shamanistic origins and probably predates all established religions on the peninsula.

Originally called Gyeryong-dan, the name of this building was changed at the end of the Joseon Dynasty when two other altars were built: Sangak-dan ("Upper Mountain Altar"), on Myohyang-san in North Korea, and Haak-dan ("Lower Mountain Altar"), on Jiri-san. In outward aspect, the building housing this altar is similar to a Buddhist temple structure; despite its faded paint, it's a fine example of late Joseon Dynasty construction.

Hiking

Trails connect the mountain's three major temples; the most-frequented runs from Donghak-sa to Gap-sa. Starting at the stone stairway to the front of Donghak-sa, follow the path straight up the hill for about one hour to **Nammaetap**, a "brother-sister" pagoda pair that once graced the yard of a now absent temple. A small and relatively new temple, Gyemyeongjeong-sa, has been built nearby. Alternately, a three-kilometer-long trail starts at the park entrance and runs past a natural spring to the pagodas. It is said that during the Silla Dynasty the monk Sangwon meditated here. One day he saved the life of a tiger who had a bone caught in its throat. Some time later, this same tiger brought a half-conscious girl to the monk to be looked after and Sangwon nursed her back to health. When recovered, the girl expressed a desire to remain with the monk and become his wife. This he refused because of his religious vows, but instead proposed that they live here like brother and sister, and cultivate the Buddhist path. This they did, and when the father of the girl found out what had happened he was moved by the kindness and purity of the monk and raised these pagodas as a testimony to the two. From these pagodas, continue up the trail less than a kilometer to Geumjandi Pass, where there are fine views down both sides of the mountain. Heading down the west side, you pass the hermitage Shinheung-am and Yongmun Waterfall before arriving at Gap-sa.

From Donghak-sa, a second trail heads straight up the long valley to Unseon Waterfall, where celestial spirits descended from heaven to bathe in the pool. For those who plan to stay on the mountain, a hut has been constructed here. From the waterfall, the trail rises steeply to Gwaneum-bong and the best views of the mountain. Hikers are not permitted to climb to Cheonhwang-bong, the mountain's highest peak, as there are telecommunications towers capping it. From the saddle between Munpil-bong and Yeoncheon-bong, the trail to the north descends to Gap-sa via Daeja-am, and the trail to the south proceeds first to Gowang-am and then on to Shinwon-sa. The trails between any of these temples should take three to four hours.

Practicalities

Entrance to the park and each of the three major temples runs ₩2,600. You can easily make a day trip to Gyeryong-san, though lodging is available at the villages below Donghak-sa, Gap-sa, and Shinwon-sa. In addition to the usual *yeogwan,* you'll find the Gyeryong-san Youth Hostel (tel. 041/856-4667) at the Gap-sa entrance, where bunks run ₩10,500 for members and ₩11,600 for non-members, or ₩27,500 for a family room. Each of these villages also has a number of restaurants and souvenir shops, and a bus station. Group campgrounds are located near the Donghak-sa and Gap-sa entrances, while a mountain hut rests at Unseon Waterfall.

Daejeon express city bus no. 102 or 103, from the express bus terminal or Daejeon Station, runs frequently to the park entrance below Donghak-sa. These buses go through Yuseong before reaching the park itself. It's perhaps easiest to reach Gap-sa by city bus no. 2 from Gongju or Yuseong, but buses also run to Nonsan. Buses to Shinwon-sa start in Nonsan and Gongju; from Gongju, use city bus no. 10.

GEUMSAN 금산

Set in the hills directly south of Daejeon is the rural town of Geumsan [Kŭmsan]. Outside of town is one of the country's telecommunication satellite stations, which directly links Korea to all but a few of the countries of the world via satellites above the Pacific and Indian Oceans. Farther to the northeast is Seodae-san (904 meters), the province's highest peak. Known for outstanding scenery, a number of trails thread

insam fields put to bed for the winter

through the mountain and there is a suspension bridge strung between two high peaks near the top. Just three kilometers north of town is **Chilbaek Uicheong** [Ch'ilpaek Ŭich'ong] (칠백의총) (H.S. #105), a monument to 700 soldiers and monk-warriors who lost their lives battling invading Japanese forces in 1592. Led by Jo Heon and the Buddhist priest Yeonggyu Daesa, this confrontation took place at Paetijae Pass below Daedun-san a few kilometers to the west. The Koreans were lost to a man, and the single tomb at the rear of this compound represents the group. An exhibition hall here displays personal affects of Jo Heon and other relics relating to this struggle. This commemorative monument was destroyed by the Japanese during their occupation of the peninsula as an attempt to get rid of all vestiges of anti-Japanese sentiment, and it was only rebuilt in the 1950s after the Japanese were forced from the country at the end of World War II. Entrance to the shrine is ₩200; take a city bus from Geumsan.

What Geumsan is perhaps best known for, however, is the *insam* grown in the surrounding county. For centuries, farmers have cultivated the finest-quality ginseng here. To bolster this product and its marketing potential, a ginseng market has been created and the Geumsan Ginseng Festival is held every September. The ginseng market is held on dates ending in 2 or 7, and buyers come from all over the country to select the finest. A reputed 80 percent of ginseng traded in the country is traded here. While *insam* is processed in many different ways, that which is sold here is almost all strictly unprocessed, whole dried roots, referred to as "white" ginseng. Although of varying size and quality, 300 grams of 4-year-old white ginseng root generally go for about ₩30,000. In addition, market vendors sell many varieties of herbal medicines, honey, mushrooms, nuts, and a multitude of other herbs, but most are only available fresh during certain times of the year. Other merchants in town, as well as a shopping arcade at the Geumsan Hotel, also carry this root, but many of these shops also have *insam* in all its other forms. Accommodations and restaurants abound in town. Bus destinations and

fares from Geumsan include Daejeon (₩2,500), Daedun-san (₩1,400), Muju (₩1,900), Jinan (₩3,100), and Jeonju (₩5,100).

Gongju 공주

The presence of Paleolithic man's presence near Gongju some 20,000–30,000 years ago is evidenced by the excavation of a cave site, the first prehistoric discovery in Korea, in the vicinity. The tools, weapons, and other artifacts unearthed resemble objects found in Manchuria and the Lake Baikal region of Russia. No one knows for sure if those people are related to modern-day Koreans, but by 4000 B.C., other migrants (Koreans' ancestors) moved onto the peninsula from the same regions of Asia. Around the time of Christ, the Mahan people, living in the peninsula's southwest corner, organized themselves into clan groups and developed walled-town states. Later, overcome by refugees from a more advanced kingdom to the north, the area be-

came Baekje territory. These Baekje people credit the founding of their nation to King Onjo in 18 B.C.; however, this region seems to have become a cohesive unit only by the early A.D. 200s. By the 4th century, Baekje was expanding north into Goguryeo territory, and had relatively peaceful relations with the nascent Silla Kingdom to the east. It also maintained diplomatic relations with some Chinese states, and traded with the Wa people of Japan. By the mid-400s, pressure from Goguryeo was mounting, and in 475, the capital was moved from Hanseong (near Seoul) to Ungjin, as Gongju was then known. Baekje continued to lose control over portions of its territory, and after 63 years the capital was moved farther south, to Sabi, as Buyeo was then known.

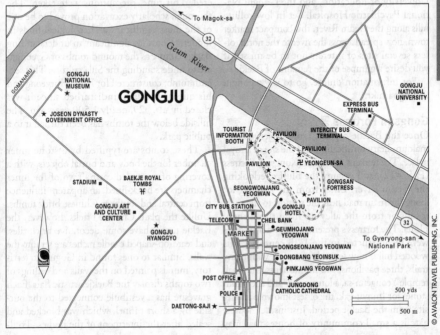

CHUNGCHEONGNAM-DO

Baekje culture was greatly inspired by the Chinese, and it eventually passed on aspects of ceramics, architectural design, and handicrafts to Silla and Japan. In 384, Buddhism was officially adopted by Baekje, and by the 500s, this too had spread east. By the mid-600s, both Goguryeo and the increasingly strong Silla Kingdom were at Baekje's throat; after years of skirmishes, Baekje fell to Silla troops in 660, bringing to a close an integral chapter of ancient Korean history. Although it's been centuries since Baekje influenced the peninsula, you can still feel its presence in Gongju and Buyeo, as you can for the Silla Dynasty in Gyeongju and the Joseon Dynasty in Seoul.

Throughout the Joseon Dynasty, Gongju was the capital of the combined Chungcheong Province until it was split into two units in 1896. In 1931, the seat of provincial government moved to Daejeon. While once a thriving and strategic city, Gongju [Kongju] (pop. 140,000) today seems small and slow-paced, yet is home to Gongju National University, Gongju National University of Education, and the Gongju National Psychiatric Hospital. Set in low rolling hills along the Geum River, this compact market town, now spread across the river to the north, offers several sites of interest not to be missed if you desire a glimpse of the remains of Baekje.

For information online, go to www.gongju .chungnam.kr.

Gongsan Fortress 공산성

Once the Baekje capital, Gongju served as a major military fortification and the site of a royal palace. The remains, Gongsan [Kongsan] Fortress (H.S. #12), still occupy the bluff overlooking the Geum River. Enter from the parking lot along the main road near the turnoff to the royal tombs or from the alley up from the Gongju Hotel. The fortress's present walls and four gates were reconstructed in the 17th century. This wooded hill is now set aside as a park, with many trails, three pavilions, two monuments, the small temple Yeongeun-sa, a lotus pond, and the plinth stones for Imnyu-gak, the oldest known building site from the Baekje period. Just inside the west gate is a small community of houses that may

have been the location of the palace buildings, and at other spots inside this fortress are foundation stones for what may have been government and military buildings. You can walk along the top of the 2.6-kilometer outer wall; the steepest section is near the lotus pond and temple. In the hills surrounding Gongju are the remains of more than half a dozen other ancient fortresses that once helped to defend this region from foreign incursion.

Songsan-ni Gobungun 성산리고분군

A 20-minute walk or short bus ride from Gongsan Fortress brings you to Gongju's principal point of interest. Known as Songsan-ni Gobungun, these Baekje-period hillside tombs (H.S. #13) are open 0900 to 2000; ₩800 entrance. Four tombs were discovered in 1927 and robbed of their treasures. Five years later the fifth and sixth tombs were uncovered; before any investigation could be undertaken, these tombs too were looted. During a restoration project in 1971, a seventh tomb was accidentally discovered. This time, precautions were taken. The thorough scholarly excavation proved to be one of the most significant archaeological finds in modern Korea, as significant to understanding Baekje culture as the mound tombs of Gyeongju are to understanding the Silla culture. This seventh tomb, constructed for King Muryeong and his queen, had lain undisturbed since it was closed in A.D. 529, nearly 1,500 years ago. The hillside below the tombs has been turned into a public park.

These tombs are typified by a stone inner chamber for the body and burial objects, with a covering of mounded earth. Two of the inner chambers are brick-lined, an apparent influence from central and southern Chinese brick tombs. Unlike the plain Chinese bricks, however, the Baekje tombs have some decorative brick tiles, and teardrop-shaped candle niches are set into the walls. Similar to ones found in Goguryeo territory, murals painted on the walls and ceilings of two tombs display the Baekje artistic flair. Each gravesite has a vestibule connected to the outside by a short tunnel, which was blocked and sealed after the interment of the bodies. To illustrate the construction technique, a cutaway model of King Muryeong's tomb has been built at this site, and an exhibition hall raised to display models of artifacts taken from the tombs.

Until 1998, three tombs of this group could be entered as far as the vestibule, from where you could view the inner chamber. They have now been resealed for preservation. Tomb no. 5 is constructed of stone and has an arched ceiling. The other two are lined with tile bricks and have vaulted ceilings and wall niches. Tomb no. 6 contains a rare example of a Baekje tomb mural. Although the paint has faded, a blue dragon, white tiger, red phoenix, and tortoise, images of the four cardinal directions, cavort on the walls. The third tomb is King Muryeong's, with alternating rows of horizontal and vertical tiles, some of lotus design. Over 2,900 items taken from this tomb include a gold crown, silver accessories, lacquered wooden pillows, and a stone guardian animal. The artifacts, 12 of which are designated treasures, are displayed in the Gongju and Seoul national museums. Generally they show subdued ornamentation, refinement, and great artistic skill.

Gongju National Museum
공주국립박물관

Moved to its new location beyond the royal tombs in 2002, the Gongju National Museum now occupies a new structure with expanded exhibition capacity. Open 0900–1800 (1700 during winter months) every day except Monday and January 1; the entrance fee is ₩400. This museum houses the best collection of Baekje artifacts in the country, including gold, silver, bronze, stone, and wooden items (N.T. #154–165) taken from the tomb of King Muryeong. Dozens of other-period objects from this region—bronze spear tips, earthenware pottery, silver ornaments, and an exquisite jade flute—are also well-displayed. Among these objects are a late Baekje period standing gilt bronze Goddess of Mercy statue (N.T. #247) and a stone block inscribed with a Buddha triad and 1,000 seated bodhisattva images (N.T. #108). Large stone remains include statues, pagoda parts, and two huge water basins (T. #148, #149) carved from

single blocks of granite, a pair of stone flagpole supports (T. #150), and a seated Buddha figure from the United Silla period (T. #979).

Other museums and exhibition halls in Gongju are the **Forestry Museum,** located close to the Geum River in the direction of Daejeon; the **Gongju Folk Drama Museum,** displaying masks, dolls, instruments, and other items used in the production of indigenous plays, dances, and dramas; and the **Seokjangni Paleolithic Settlement Site** exhibition hall, where you can see some of the first Paleolithic objects discovered in Korea.

Other Sights

Beyond the royal tombs are the Gongju Art and Culture Center and Gongju public stadium, two venues for the local cultural festival. Down toward the Gomanaru recreation area along the river, along the entrance road to the museum, are **Seonhwadang** and **Donghyeon,** restored Joseon-era government office buildings, removed to this site from elsewhere in the city and renovated. Moved from its previous location in 1623, the **Gongju Hyanggyo** enshrines tablets of Chinese and Korean Confucian scholars and sages. Spring and autumn memorial services are performed at this shrine. Dominating one of the highest hills in town and set across from the old national museum is the **Jungdong Catholic Cathedral.** Semi-Gothic in style, this church and the education hall next door are done in red and black brick. Founded in 1897 but completed in 1936, they are the oldest extant historical buildings in town and some of the most historic Western religious buildings in the country. Along the stream in town near the police station you'll find a pair of stone flagpole supports that belonged to the temple Daetong-sa, which, according to records, was one of the largest Baekje temples. In 2001, this site was cleaned up.

Practicalities

For information about Gongju and the area, check the tourist information booths at the parking lot below Gongsan Fortress and at the entrance to Songsan-ni Gobungun.

Gongju offers many decent places to stay. The

best in town is the small, second-class Gongju Hotel, set along the back street that runs up to the south gate of Gongsan Fortress. It has rooms in the ₩35,000–60,000 range. Moderately priced are the Geumhojang Yeogwan (금호장여관), Seongwonjang Yeogwan (성원장여관), Dongseonjang Yeogwan (동성장여관), and Pinkjang Yeogwan (핑크여관). The Dongbang Yeoinsuk (동방여인숙) is cheaper yet.

The express and intercity bus terminals are located on the north side of the river. Express buses run only to Seoul (₩5,600). Selected intercity bus destinations are Buyeo (₩2,600), Nonsan (₩2,400), Gap-sa (₩1,300), Daejeon (₩2,600), Boryeong (₩4,500, and Cheonan (₩3,200).

A city bus station is crowded into the center of town. City bus nos. 22 and 25 run by the royal tombs, while no. 25 continues on to the sports stadium, old government buildings, and national museum. No. 2 goes to Gap-sa, no. 10 to Shinwon-sa, no. 12 to Jochiwon Station, no. 5 to Yuseong, and nos. 1, 22, and 25 run between the center of town and the bus terminals. Bus no. 7 connects Gongju to Magok-sa from the bus terminal.

MAGOK-SA 마곡사

Set in gentle mountain folds 24 kilometers north of Gongju is the temple Magok-sa, headquarters of the sixth district of the Jogye sect of Korean Buddhism; ₩1,500 entrance. Founded in 640 by the famous Silla monk Jajang Yulsa, this compound is divided by a stream, and connected by an arched stone footbridge. In the first half of the compound stand the two front gates and two halls. The first gate contains the four devas, the other shows Munsu Bosal riding a blue tiger while Bohyeon Bosal straddles his white elephant. In Myeongbu-jeon sit the judges of the underworld, while in Yeongsan-jeon (T. #800) seven statues occupy the altar in front of 1,000 disciples of Buddha. In the courtyard on the far side of the bridge stand a cross-shaped bell and drum pavilion and a slender stone pagoda (T. #799) from the Goryeo Dynasty crowned by a squat bronze finial. The finishing touches of

this five-tier structure differ drastically from the basic Silla-style pagodas; the chorten-shaped top resembles stupas of Tibetan origin seen in Nepal. Behind it is Daegwangbo-jeon (T. #802), a wide hall similar to Muryangsu-jeon of Buseok-sa, near Yeongju; its altar is on the short west wall facing east, not on the back wall as in most temple halls. It's dedicated to Vairocana, the Buddha of Infinite Light and is highly painted, although faded, inside and out. Have a look at the back of the wall behind the altar for a very large wall mural of the Vairocana Buddha. Behind this is the temple's double-roofed main hall, Daeungbo-jeon (T. #801). Rebuilt like Yeongsan-jeon in 1651, this sturdy structure has a spacious interior, open to the top roof, and houses the Seokgamoni Buddha, Amita Buddha, and Healing Buddha, set in front of a three-part hanging mural (T. #1260). Several hermitages lie in the hills behind the main temple compound. The early '90s saw much reconstruction here, and plans for the future include a huge bronze Buddha seated on the hill overlooking the temple.

Magok-sa's pleasant atmosphere makes an easy day trip from Gongju. Gongju city bus no. 7 runs every half hour to the temple. In the newly expanded community below are shops, restaurants, a post office, several simple accommodations, and the bus stop.

Seonggok-sa 성곡사

Closer to Gongju and much newer is the temple Seonggok-sa. While not known for its buildings, it does however have a huge collection of Buddha and bodhisattva statues of various sizes and shapes. The construction of these images was started in 1984 as a 30-year project of the temple's head monk. On the ridge to the side of the main compound is a 12-meter-tall seated bronze Buddha figure with an intricate mandala. At 78 tons, this figure is set on a lotus base and backed by a tiered semicircle of 1,000 standing life-size bodhisattva statues with 333,333 hand-size Buddha statues to their rear that can be backlit at night. Near the entrance road is a 33-meter-tall standing Maitreya Buddha and at its feet is a 37-meter-long lying Buddha that's made of copper plates and is more angular. Down the hill a few steps is an even taller standing copper Buddha statue, and around the hill is a 27-meter-tall statue of Jijang Bosal that's surrounded by dozens of attendant figures. While the size and number of images are impressive, the aesthetic element seems less than perfect and, overall, one gets the feeling of excess. Perhaps when the compound is landscaped and the metal has had a chance to age, it will look more congruous. From Gongju, bus to Oseong-myeon and walk the four kilometers up the valley to the temple.

Buyeo 부여

Because of repeated incursions into Baekje territory by the powerful Goguryeo Kingdom, the Baekje capital moved south in 538 from Ungjin (Gongju) to Sabi (Buyeo). During the 123 years that Sabi served as center of the kingdom, Baekje society, art, and culture flowered. Buyeo [Puyŏ] is proud of its rich heritage and remains a traditional community, a repository of Baekje artifacts from its golden age, and a preserver of the Baekje legacy. As an obvious link with its distant past, some of the town sidewalks are laid with paving tiles that replicate those taken from local excavation sites.

Set along a broad bend of the Baengma River (a stretch of the Geum River by a different name), this clean and quiet town (pop. 95,000) is embraced by fertile agricultural lands. Although many grains and vegetables are grown, the region is especially known for red *insam,* which is grown, treated, packaged, and exported in great quantities.

Because of the town's cultural and historical importance, the central government has declared this region the Baekje Cultural Zone, and is actively seeking to improve the area's tourist potential and infrastructure. For additional information, see the website www.buyeo.chungnam .kr.

Baekje Cultural Festival

Alternating between Buyeo and Gongju, the Baekje Cultural Festival is held for four days every October to celebrate the greatness of the Baekje society, and to give descendants an opportunity to honor the spirits of their ancestors. One of the three largest of Korea's cultural festivals, it helps bring Baekje culture into focus and

preserve traditions relating to that long-lost dynasty. Though a daytime parade of brightly clad participants in traditional costumes, groups of musicians, and historical floats is a highlight, the nighttime Buddhist lantern procession and fireworks display also draws great crowds. Other events include theatrical, musical, and dance performances, poetry readings, art exhibitions, and various athletic competitions including Korean wrestling, archery, and kite flying. Memorial services are held for the Baekje kings, three royal retainers who stood by the last Baekje king as his kingdom crumbled around him, and the 3,000 court ladies who committed suicide rather than fall into enemy hands.

Inspired by a similar spirit the three-day *Unsan Byeolshin gut* is held every third year in February (or March) in the rural village of Unsan, several kilometers north of Buyeo. This ritual pays tribute to the soldiers who died defending the Baekje Kingdom from Silla incursion during the 660s. Part Confucian ceremony to worthy ancestors, part quasi-religious shamanistic performance, and part military tribute, this ritual honors the greatness of the Baekje defenders.

Buso-san

The Baengma ("White Horse") River runs past Buyeo. The combined Silla/Tang forces crossed here in order to storm the fortress and crush the last resistance to the Silla bid for the takeover of Baekje territory. Legend says that the advancing Tang general was afraid to cross the river because it was inhabited by a dragon who protected the Baekje people. So, he went fishing! Using the head of a white horse as bait, he caught and killed this pesky reptile. With the dragon gone—

CHUNGCHEONGNAM-DO

BUYEO

To Gongju

BAEKJE KILN

BAEKJE ROYAL TOMBS

To Nonsan

Geumjeong-san

WANGHEUNG-SAJI

FERRY PIER

GORAN-SA 卍

SAJA-RU

GUNGNYEOSA

Buso-san

MILITARY STOREHOUSE

YEONGIL-LU

SAMCHUNGSA

NAKHWA-AM

SEOBUK-SAJI

BANWOL-LU

TOURIST INFORMATION BOOTH

GUDEURAE PIER

Gudeurae Park

SAMJUNG BUYEO YOUTH HOSTEL 卍

BUYEO GAEKSA

CHEONWANG-SAJI

KILN SITE

BUYEO HYANGGYO

KILN SITE

BUYEO NATIONAL MUSEUM

GUNGNAMJI

SEE DETAIL

COUNTY OFFICE

GUNSURI-SAJI

DONGNAMNI-SAJI

POLICE

SUBUK-JEONG

Baengma River

To Gongju

DETAIL

BANK

MARKET

BUS TERMINAL

POST OFFICE

SILLAJANG YEOGWAN

TELECOM

JEONGNIM-SAJI

BANDOJANG YEOGWAN

SEOULJANG YEOGWAN

MOTEL SKY

0   0.5 mi

0   0.5 km

© AVALON TRAVEL PUBLISHING, INC.

and no protection for the city residents—the general then crossed the river, defeated the defending Baekje troops, and overran the fortress. This battle, in 660, caused the downfall of the Baekje Dynasty.

Flanking the Baengma River and dominating the town is the hill Buso-san [Puso-san] (H.S. #5), upon which the central Baekje fortification and royal palace stood. Once a compound of many fine buildings and stout walls, today only a handful of pavilions and shrines, one temple, scattered foundations stones, and sections of an earthen wall dot the hill. ₩2,000 entrance fee at either of the two entrances; open from 0700 (0800 in winter). Thrusting out of the water at this gentle river bend is Nakhwa-am ("Falling Flowers Rock"). Rather than be taken prisoner by the invading armies and chance being "deflowered," 3,000 Baekje court ladies chose to commit suicide by flinging themselves off this cliff onto the rocks below, air puffing their billowy skirts as they fell to their deaths. A small hexagonal pavilion atop this rock commemorates these fallen flowers of Baekje society.

Below Nakhwa-am is the small temple Goransa [Koran-sa]. Its name stems from gorancho, a type of medicinal herb that grows on this cliffside. Behind the temple is a mineral-water well that springs from the rock. Legend relates that one Baekje king would only drink water from this well; he ordered that a sprig of the gorancho be put into each water container to verify its purity. The temple's tiny hall is brightly painted, with one unusual glassed-in end. Three murals on the rear wall depict incidents from the temple's history; one portrays several Japanese nuns who came to study Buddhism after its introduction to Japan by Baekje priests. From a pier below the temple, summer excursion boats ply to the pier at Gudeurae Sculpture Park and to Subuk-jeong, a pavilion topping the knoll at the west end of the highway bridge. Fares are ₩2,200 to Gudeurae and ₩4,000 to Subuk-jeong. Additional tour boats run from the pier at the sculpture park.

A military storehouse once stood at the highest point on Buso-san. Carbonized grains of rice, presumably burnt when the fortress fell, have been discovered here. At the east end of the hill's circular pathway is Yeongil-lu, a pavilion from which the Baekje kings watched the sun rise over their kingdom. On the west end of the hill is Saja-ru. Together with Yeongil-lu, this pavilion symbolized eum and yang (yin and yang); royalty watched the moon and stars here. Between these two stands a third pavilion, Banwol-lu, which offers a fine view over town. Next to it lie excavations of two pit dwellings, the upper portions of which have been re-created as they must have looked when used during the Baekje era. Nearby is Gungnyeosa, a shrine dedicated to the 3,000 "fallen flowers"; inside, a painting of three women represents the 3,000. On the hillside below this shrine is Samchungsa, dedicated to, and enshrining portraits of, three loyal retainers who stood by the last Baekje king. Every year during the Baekje Cultural Festival, commemorative services are held at these shrines.

Below Buso-san, set between two of the entrance gates and next to the old museum building, are the Buyeo Gaeksa and Buyeo Donghyeon, a Joseon-era government rest house and office building. Another structure from this latter dynasty is the Buyeo Hyanggyo, which is located to the rear of Jeongnim-saji.

Jeongnim-saji 정림 사지

In the center of Buyeo is Jeongnim-saji [Chŏngnim-saji] (H.S. #301), a Baekje Dynasty temple site; ₩1,000 entrance fee. While nothing but two stone objects and a lotus pond remain, it was at one time an important Buddhist center. The five-tier granite pagoda (N.T. #9) sits at one end of this open courtyard. One of two remaining pagodas from the Three Kingdoms period (pre-A.D. 660), it's a prototype of Korean stone pagodas, undoubtedly modeled after the more common wooden pagodas of the age. While solidly anchored on a broad base, its roof tiers are slender and graceful. Facing it is an extremely weatherworn Buddha image (T. #108); only its flat facial features are at all discernible. Approximately the same age as the pagoda, it's certainly not the carving itself but the age that makes this piece significant. To preserve this figure from more damage, a building has now been constructed around it, and to create a more park-like space, the entire area has been spruced up.

In its heyday there were many temples in and around Buyeo. Other temple sites include Seobuk-saji on Buso-san, Cheonwang-saji near the main traffic rotary in town, Wangheung-saji north across the river, and Dongnamni-saji and Gunsuri-saji (H.S. #44) west of Gungnamji lotus pond, the last of which has yielded two Treasures.

Buyeo National Museum
부여국립박물관

The Buyeo National Museum is open 0900–1800 (1700 in winter) every day except Monday and January 1; ₩400 entrance. Like the Gongju museum, it contains mostly Baekje artifacts. The courtyard holds a number of stone objects, but the real treasures are well displayed inside. Prehistoric pottery, bronze weapons, musical instruments, religious images, roof tiles, and gold, silver, and brass artifacts all line the display cases. Worth the entrance fee alone are the square tiles of dragon, phoenix, cloud, lotus, and landscape designs. Selected roof tiles of the various dynasties complete the collection of artistic tileware. Among the many treasures are an exquisite gilt bronze seated Buddha (N.T. #83), stone seated Buddha figure (T. #329), a standing bodhisattva image (T. #195), a standing Gwaneum statue (T. #293), and an earthenware tile impressed with a mountain, tree, and cloud motif (T. #343). A granite slab inscribed with 56 characters, considered invaluable to linguists as the only example of writing from the Baekje era, is also preserved here. A number of objects have been taken from a nearby 7th century B.C. village site, described as the largest Bronze Age village site in Korea. The most recent important find displayed at the museum is a tall and masterfully carved gilt bronze incense burner (N.T. #287), supported by the rising figure of a slender but powerful dragon and topped with a phoenix, that was unearthed at a temple site near the royal Baekje tombs in 1993.

Gungnamji 궁남지

At the south end of town is Gungnamji [Kung-namji], a circular lotus pond (H.S. #135) ringed by willow trees, constructed in 634 as a pleasure garden for the royal family, and perhaps part of a detached palace. Reached by an arch bridge, a small pavilion occupies the tiny island in the center. Supposedly, the Baekje Kingdom produced excellent gardeners. Some historians suggest that designs, techniques, and gardeners were sent to Japan, helping it develop its own exquisite command of gardening. A short walk from the noise of town, this lotus pond is a pleasant place for a picnic or a stroll with a friend.

Neungsan-ni Gobungun 능산리고분군

Three kilometers southeast of town is a closely packed group of seven Baekje tombs (H.S. #14) known as Neungsan-ni Gobungun [Nŭngsan-ni Kobungun]; ₩1,000 entrance fee. Similar in appearance to the Gongju tombs, these grassy burial mounds contain inner burial chambers. Some are made of stone and others of brick; several feature flat ceilings, while a few have arched tops. Each is different from the next and all are different still from the tombs of Gongju. On the ceiling of one of these tombs is a rare example of tomb mural paintings from the Baekje period. As all have been resealed after the latest excavations, an exhibition hall on this well-tended site explains the various tomb-construction techniques.

Just to the west of these tombs stands a section of an eight-kilometer-long earthen wall that once swept down in an arc from Buso-san and its hilltop fortress. Now mostly destroyed, small portions of it remain here and there in the hills. Remains of other small mountain fortresses, a defensive perimeter for the capital, dot the hills to the west and east.

Baekje Kiln 백제요

Four kilometers outside Buyeo on the road to Gongju is the Baekje Kiln. Opened in 1992, this showroom and working studio not only sells Baekje-style pottery but also teaches art students. All pottery is done with as much authenticity as possible, based on archaeological evidence and research by the owner. Although some are covered with a clear glaze finish, most pieces are a dark natural gray, fired without glaze. Vases of various shapes predominate, but bowls and stands are also in evidence. While many items here are unadorned, some show understated design details that, while similar, clearly set them apart from contemporary Silla pottery. Behind the studio is a hillside kiln, and every two or three months it's filled and fired to about 1300°C.

Two Baekje Dynasty kiln sites have been identified in town, one just below Buso-san and the other a short distance east of there.

Practicalities

Located between Jeongnim-sa and the bus terminals are the central market, business center, post office, and Telecom office. A tourist information booth is located at the parking lot below the south entrance to Buso-san.

There are no registered hotels in Buyeo, but a number of better accommodations (some using the name "hotel" or "motel") operate in town. Try the Bandojang Yeogwan (반도장여관), Seouljang Yeogwan (서울장여관), or Motel Sky (스카이모텔) behind the Telecom office, or the Sillajang Yeogwan (시라장여관) closer to the central market. In addition to the above, the **Samjung Buyeo Youth Hostel** (삼중유스호스텔) (tel. 041/835-3101) has rooms. For members, bunk beds in a dorm room are ₩10,600, for non-members ₩14,500; private rooms are also available for much more.

The intercity bus terminal is on the main street; one block back is the express bus terminal. Intercity bus destinations and fares include Imcheon (₩1,000), Nonsan (₩1,500), Daejeon (₩4,200), Gongju (₩2,600), Boryeong (₩3,100), and Jeonju (₩4,600). You can board city buses on either the main north-south or east-west streets; there are no bus numbers. Buses run to the Baekje tomb site, Buyeo Kiln, Subuk-jeong, Muryang-sa, and Imcheon.

BUYEO VICINITY

Gwanchok-sa 관촉사

Backed into a low hillside four kilometers south of Nonsan (논산) is an ordinary temple with an extraordinary statue. Gwanchok-sa [Kwanch'ok-sa] has in its compound the Unjin Mireuk Buddha (T. #218), the country's largest free-standing stone Buddha image; ₩1,500 entrance. After

Unjin Mireuk Buddha of Gwanchok-sa

passing the four heavenly kings, approach the temple compound by a steep stairway and enter either under a simple stone lintel, a unique diminutive gate, or through the underpassage of a new temple hall. The Unjin Mireuk dominates the temple grounds and looks out passively over the productive countryside. This Buddha of the Future from the Goryeo Dynasty, a bit over 18 meters high, supposedly took 38 years to complete. Carved from granite, the body and head are one piece; its double-level mortarboard hat is cut from separate stones. Although this huge sculpture is well-carved, its head is noticeably out of proportion. The face has a peaceful stare, and its earlobes are longer than a man is tall. Its oversize hands are carved with feeling; toes peek out from beneath the lengthy robe. The mortarboard hat has a lotus carved on its underside, and brass wind chimes dangle from the hat's corners. While it looks as if the face is periodically washed, the monks say that no one cleans it; the body is partially covered with a dark lichen.

In front of the Unjin Mireuk is a lantern (T. #232) from the same period. Like the statue, it's massive, yet delicately carved; the roof ends up-turn sharply at the corners. A four-tier pagoda stands in front of the lantern, and a stone slab, with its intricately carved lotus design, lies in front of that.

The hall set directly in front of the Buddha has a back wall of windows and no image on its low altar. The Unjin Mireuk, seen from inside the building, serves in place of an altar figure. Fairy musicians are painted on the central beams of this hall. Look also for murals painted on one of the other temple buildings. Note particularly the Goddess of Mercy, riding a dragon across the water, and the bug-eyed Bodhidharma being offered the severed arm of the second Zen Patri-arch as a lesson in enlightenment. In the mid-1990s, a new main hall was constructed here and the other buildings repainted. Plans still call for a huge stone pagoda to be raised a short dis-tance around the hill.

Frequent city buses run to Gwanchok-sa from the Nonsan bus terminal. Other city buses run to Donghak-sa, Shinwon-sa, and the village of Surak, back door to Daedun-san Provincial Park. Select intercity bus destinations and fares from Nonsan are Geumma (₩2,000), Jeonju (₩3,700), Daejeon (₩2,700), Gongju (₩2,400), and Buyeo (₩1,500).

Imcheon Daejo-sa 임천대조사

Twelve kilometers south of Buyeo, on the moun-tainside above the village of Imcheon [Imch'ŏn], is the temple Daejo-sa [Taejo-sa]. In this com-pound is a standing Buddha statue (T. #217) re-markably like the Unjin Mireuk—only the details differ. A mortarboard-like hat is set on the figure's head, which is more in proportion to its body. Its facial features do not signal the typical compas-sionate or contemplative mood of the Buddha, but show a more human quality. Again, the face is clean while the body grows with lichen. Al-though the figure is more finely garbed than the Unjin Mireuk, its hands are not as lively; no feet are visible. A heavy stone slab in front of this 10-meter-tall image serves as an altar; a worship hall is set slightly down the hill. Constructed like that at Gwanchok-sa, this hall has a glass rear wall and no figure on its interior altar. In front of the newly painted main hall stands a stone pagoda. Discovered in pieces during the temple's recent re-construction, the pagoda was rebuilt with new pieces taking the place of missing ones.

City buses from Buyeo and Ganggyeong take you to Imcheon. To get to Daejo-sa, follow the paved road from the village school about one kilometer up the mountainside. At the Y, the right-hand track continues on a few hundred meters to Daejo-sa. The left-hand path goes up to the wall remains of the **Seongheung Mountain Fortress** (H.S. #4). Originally constructed in 501, this fortress was the principal defensive for-tification protecting the southern flank of the Baekje capital. This fortification was built by a Baekje nobleman who later killed the king in an attempt to usurp the throne. He himself was killed by the king's son, King Muryeong, who put an end to the rebellion. The fortress walls have been partially rebuilt, and within stand a shrine and pavilion. Given the commanding view of the surrounding farmland and Geum River from this fortress, it's easy to understand why military strategists chose this spot.

Muryang-sa 무량사

Twenty kilometers northwest of Buyeo, in an open valley rimmed by low hills, is the temple Muryang-sa, repository of four designated Trea-sures; ₩1,500 entrance fee. In front is a two-posted, open-style front gate. Notice that the sturdy tree-trunk posts have not been turned to make them symmetrical. A second gate encloses the four finely painted devas. To its side is a pair of flagpole supports. An octagonal stone lantern (T. #233) set in front of a five-tier stone pagoda (T. #185) occupies the central courtyard. Some-what squat and heavy, yet with thin eaves, the pagoda is rather ponderous in comparison to the older one of Jeongnim-sa in Buyeo. During its last renovation in 1971, a gilt Buddha figure and *sari* container were discovered inside. At the far end of the courtyard, dominating the compound, is Geungnak-jeon (T. #356), the two-story main hall, one of the largest in the country. Built dur-ing the 18th century, it's typical of mid-Joseon

Dynasty architectural style. The elaborate and multi-layered roof-support system rests on a sturdy post-and-lintel frame, lending the whole structure a majestic elegance. It's rather plain on the outside, but the meticulous interior is spacious and open to the top roof. Windows between the roofs help illuminate the five-meter-tall Buddha triad that sits on its altar. On special occasions, an old mural from 1627 of the Mireuk Buddha (T. #1265) is unfurled in the building. A bell pavilion, Mountain Spirit hall, judgment hall, and 1,000 Buddhas Hall, also with largely unadorned exteriors, complete the compound, and three hermitages nestle into the hillside behind on the flank of Mansu-san. Set to the side is another small building that houses a portrait of the early Joseon Dynasty scholar Kim Shi-seup. This painting is apparently an original that has not been retouched over the years and therefore an excellent example of such early portraiture.

Located at the village below the temple are a few spartan accommodations, restaurants, and a bus stop. More accommodations await two kilometers down the road in Oesan Village. Buses from here run to Buyeo, Cheongyang, and Boryeong.

Seongju-saji 성주사지

About 10 kilometers west of Muryang-sa, accessible by city bus from Boryeong, is Seongju-saji [Sŏngju-saji]. Built in the mid-800s on the site of a Baekje temple, Seongju-sa was one of nine great Silla Dynasty temples. Only stone objects survived its destruction by invading Japanese in 1592. The three sizable five- and three-tier pagodas (T. #19, 29, 47)—it's unusual to find so many at any one temple—as well as lanterns, steps, and building foundation stones indicate just how large this complex was. A huge, inscribed memorial stela (N. T. #8) for the temple's founder has been placed under a roof for preservation.

Chilgap-san Provincial Park
칠갑산도립공원

Established in 1973, 32-square-kilometer Chilgap-sa Provincial Park lies between the towns of Buyeo and Cheongyang. Rising to 561 meters, it's the highest point in the lower reaches of the Charyeong Mountains. From its summit you'll

enjoy fine views of hills that undulate toward the West Sea. Chilgap-san is known for its cherry trees and azaleas, which add color to the brown hillside in spring. Boxthorn trees grow wild in these mountains. In autumn, they produce a crimson nut that is picked, dried, and used in Chinese medicine and *gugija* tea. About 85 percent of the country's *gugija* nut harvest comes from this mountain. Edible berries and hazelnuts also grow along the mountain paths.

Snuggled into a valley on the west side of the mountain's main ridge is the temple **Janggok-sa** [Changgok-sa] (장곡사). Founded in 850, this unusual temple has two main halls. The upper hall (T. #162) enshrines two cast-iron statues, one a seated figure of the Vairocana Buddha (T. #174), and the other a standing Buddha of Medicine (N.T. #58), both presumably from the United Silla period. The small white healing Buddha has a halo painted on the flame mandala rising at its back. It's set on a stepped stone dais adorned with bas-relief lotus-blossom designs. A third and newer figure is also enshrined here, and each of these figures is set on an individual altar, an unusual configuration. Preserved in the lower hall (T. #181) is a gilt bronze statue of the healing Buddha (T. #337). In addition, a large mural of the Maitreya Buddha (N.T. #300) is unfurled on certain Buddhist holidays. Janggok-sa is a quiet place with lots of trees. It is a bit out of the way, but many people come to view the statuary. To reach Janggok-sa, bus from Cheongyang or Buyeo.

Trails through Chilgap-san are short and easy. From the village of Jicheon, it's about two kilometers to Janggok-sa, where a trail leads up the ridge to the mountain's highest peak. Stay on the main ridgeline as many side paths lead back down into the adjoining valleys. Bring water—there are no springs along the trails. From the summit, a second trail runs north along another ridge to the highway—you'll walk over the Daechi Tunnel on the way. The route from the temple to the highway should take about three hours.

Jeongsan Pagoda

Some kilometers east of Chilgap-san is **Seojeong-ni nine-tier stone pagoda** (서정리 9 층석탑).

This early Goryeo-era pagoda (T. #18) sits in slender symmetry in the middle of a rice field near the highway intersection in the town of Jeongsan. While now the sole remnant, it undoubtedly marks the site of a long-disappeared unnamed temple.

West Coast

Janghang 장항

This port lies on the north bank of the Geum River, opposite the much larger and more important city of Gunsan. Ferries traditionally have been a strategic transportation link between these two communities and for traffic up and down the west coast. Although commuters still use this method of transportation, the ferries have recently been superseded by a new highway across the Geum River tidal dam and expressway bridges across the river a short distance inland. Janghang [Changhang] is the southern terminus of the Janghang rail line, which runs north through Boryeong, Hongseong, and Asan to Cheonan, linking the rural, coastal regions of this province to major rail and highway arteries. Since 1936, a metal smelting plant in town has refined gold, silver, copper, and other precious or scarce metals. On the drawing board is a huge industrial complex that will entail land reclamation along the north side of the river mouth, encompassing several small islands currently off the coast.

Ferries (₩1,000) across the Geum River between Janghang and Gunsan run every 30 minutes from 0645 to 2115. Although the bus terminal is only a short distance up from the pier, many buses conveniently pick up passengers in front of the ferry terminal building. Selected bus destinations and fares are Hansan (₩1,400), Dongbaek-jeong (₩2,340), Boryeong (₩3,600), Buyeo (₩3,500), Gunsan (₩1,100), and Daejeon (₩7,700). The Janghang Station is a 20-minute walk into town from the ferry pier. Trains of all classes run 18 times a day to Seoul; two additional daily trains go only as far as Cheonan. Accommodations and restaurants can be located between the ferry terminal and train station. If you stay, try the Daehojang Yeogwan.

Jutting out into the Yellow Sea, just west of the small town of Biin, is a narrow peninsula known for a forest of flowering camellia trees (N.M. #169) that turns the tip of this headland into a carpet of blazing red in spring. On its promontory sits the pavilion **Dongbaek-jeong** (동백정). A few kilometers up the coast is the newly developed **Chunjang Beach**. With its powdery white sand and gradual grade, it's typical of the beaches along this coast. In Biin is a slender five-tier stone pagoda (T. #224), a skinnier version of the robust five-tier pagoda in Buyeo.

Hansan 한산

Twenty kilometers up the Geum River is the rural community of Hansan, known throughout Korea for its production of the highest-quality hand-woven ramie cloth and its ramie cloth market. The weaving of this linen-like material is a time-consuming traditional craft that's been designated a cultural asset, and the **Ramie Cultural Festival** is held in town every May to celebrate this unique product. Fine of texture and natural in color, ramie has historically been pre-

RAMIE MAKING

Producing ramie is a simple yet lengthy process. The stem of the ramie plant, a member of the nettle family, is stripped of its bark and then split open to reveal a coarse, fibrous interior. These short fibers are rubbed together between the palms of the hands to make long threads. Somewhat brittle, the thread must be woven in humid conditions to keep it from breaking. Once woven, the cloth is steamed and later boiled with ash to turn it a delicate cream color. It's sometimes dyed today, in defiance of tradition. Wrapped in mulberry paper, it is then set aside in a dry place for up to two years to give it its smooth sheen and delicate feel.

ferred as the cloth of choice for cool summer clothing. With the introduction of mass-produced cloth, hand-woven ramie slipped in popularity during the middle of the 20th century but is making a comeback. Ramie cloth, called *moshi* in Korean, is most often woven in long, narrow bolts, about 30 centimeters wide and 22 meters long. Hansan has numerous shops, a **Ramie Museum**, and an information center for those who wish to buy or simply learn about the production of this fine cloth.

Though much less known for this than for its textiles, Hansan played a part in the final days of the Baekje Kingdom. This town was once a military fortress, one of the last strongholds to fall to the combined Silla/Tang Chinese forces when they made their move to take over Baekje territory. After Baekje forces were defeated in Buyeo and the king surrendered, diehard Baekje loyalists led by members of Baekje royal families gathered at the Hansan Fortress and put together an army to oppose the takeover of their land. Undaunted by the defeat of the regular army, these irregulars intended to push back the invaders. Initially, there was some success, but soon they too were defeated. The loss of the Hansan Fortress signaled the death knell for their bid to reestablish sovereignty and rid their country of aggressors.

BORYEONG 보령

Along an alluvial stream a short distance inland from this extremely indented coastline lies the small town of Boryeong, formerly known as Daecheon [Taech'ŏn]. A large market sprawls across its center. This county seat is surrounded by wide agricultural fields; salt beds line the road to the sea. The salt is still made by the natural, time-honored, and time-consuming method of seawater evaporation. However, these salt factories, and others up and down the coast, are slowly disappearing with the increase in chemically manufactured salt. The Charyeong Mountains end near Boryeong in low rolling hills. Slag heaps seen in the hills surrounding town are remnants of coal mining operations, once a big industry here, and to elucidate this vanished sector

of the economy a **Coal Museum** has been constructed on the hillside overlooking town. It's perhaps appropriate that a large power plant has been built just outside of town, and an electricity-generating dam has been built inland from here. The rural region south of Boryeong is known for obsidian stone, and for the skill of its carvers. Stonework of all kinds is done here, from tiny, intricate inkstones to huge, swarthy statues. Many stone yards are in evidence at Ungcheon.

Boryeong is conveniently located on the Janghang rail line. Over a dozen daily trains run through town going south to Janghang and north to Cheonan and Seoul. The bus terminal is located in the center of town across from the train station. Select intercity bus destinations and fares are Buyeo (₩3,100), Daejeon (₩7,100), Cheongyang (₩1,800), and Hongseong (₩2,500). City buses run to Daecheon Beach and Daecheon harbor, just a kilometer or so north of the beach. From the harbor, three vehicular ferries a day (with additional ferries during the height of summer season) ply to Yeongmok at the southern tip of Anmyeon-do, a half dozen run to Wonsando, and fewer go to the inhabited islands to their south. The most direct ferry to Yeongmok crosses in an hour and a half (₩7,000). Other more circuitous routes through the islands require two and a half hours (₩13,200). A ferry from here also runs to Ocheong-do (₩22,700), where another ferry continues on to Gunsan (₩21,800).

Daecheon Beach 대천해수욕장

For the fun-seeker, the major attraction to this area is Daecheon Beach. Located 12 kilometers west of town, it's the most developed beach resort on the west coast. Arguably the best swimming spot along the entire west coast, it's gained a grand and uncompromising reputation. This fine, three-kilometer-long white strand can accommodate thousands of sunbathers, and does! The water's comfortable temperature makes this beach a perfect swimming spot and water playland. It's crowded from mid-July to mid-August, and perhaps most crowded at the beginning of this period during the **Boryeong Mud Festival**, which celebrates the rejuvenating astringent qualities of the tidal mud to benefit the skin.

Before and after that, while the temperatures are still warm, you'll have the run of the sand. Islands off the coast are visible from here on clear days. Many long-term foreign residents of Korea maintain summer homes near the south end of the beach. This well-kept and quiet enclave contrasts with the hodgepodge of accommodations, restaurants, bars, nightclubs, and amusement establishments that line the beachfront road to the north, nearly blocking the view of the water until it's lapping your toes. As development has taken place, the extension toward the south end has been better planned and is a more homogeneous mix of fancy shops, seafood restaurants, tearooms, drinking establishments, and finer accommodations, and even the north end is getting spiffed up a bit and developed more thoughtfully. For most of the year, this community is sedate and relaxed, but when summer rolls around it starts to hop. The empty streets turn into rivers of bodies, and the sound of water lapping on the beach is replaced by human voices and the din of music. People come to the beach to relax, and work very hard at it. The beach does, however, have visitors at other times of the year, those who come to walk the sand, enjoy the wind and waves, and absorb the atmosphere of the beach in another temperament. Daecheon Beach and its mini city-like community is in many respects an equal counterpart to the very similar Gyeongpo Beach area just north of Gangneung on the east coast. An alternative to this ever increasingly crowded beach is Wonsan-do Beach on the island of Wonsan-do. Regular city buses run between the center of town and the beach, with fewer going all the way to the pier.

Muchangpo Beach

Some kilometers south of and reachable by bus from Boryeong is the little-visited Muchangpo Beach. Of particular note here is a natural phenomenon where the departing tide exposes a portion of the bay floor for a short period twice a month, in a manner similar to the much more famous "parting of the sea" on Jin-do. On the first and 15th days of the lunar month, water recedes to open a 20-meter-wide, 1.5-kilometer-long crescent strip of rock and mud that, for an hour

and a half, connects the mainland to the island of Seokdae-do. When this strip is exposed, locals walk out and gather bottom-dwelling sea creatures.

TAEAN PENINSULA AREA
Taean Coastal National Park
태안해안국립공원

Stretching from the southern end of Anmyeon-do to the northern tip of the Taean Peninsula you'll find Taean Coastal National Park. Established in 1978, this park covers 325 square kilometers; it's the smallest of Korea's three marine national parks, and the only one in one section. A majority of this heavily indented coastline and about 150 offshore islands fall within the park boundaries. Most are tiny uninhabited specks; only Anmyeon-do is of any size. The park's twisting coastline resembles the back of a contorted dragon. It's a long series of bays and crescent coves, interspersed with rocky capes and promontories. The white-sand beaches contrast with the black rock, and both complement the green vegetation. Sixty plant families and over twice that number of animals have been recorded. Vacationers come to swim, fish, and watch the sunset from several of the longest and finest beaches on this unspoiled coast: Mallipo, Cheollipo, Yeonpo, and Mongsanpo. (Mallipo Beach is the beach of "ten thousand *li*." A *li* is a distance of about 400 meters. Cheollipo is the "one thousand *li* beach." North of there in succession are beaches called Baeknipo, or "one hundred *li* beach," Shimnipo Beach, "ten *li* beach," and Illipo Beach, or "one *li* beach.") Because of the shallowness of the West Sea, these beaches have a gradual drop-off, and are usually very calm during the summer months; the great change in tide, however, causes extreme variation in the water level. For the swimming season, extra buses handle the influx of holidaymakers. Most visitors only see the shoreline of this marine park. To ride through the park or reach the outlying islands, you must take a boat from Anheung or Yeonpo. Recreational fishing is possible in these waters; commercial fishing is done farther out. Among the most common fish are perch, red snapper, blowfish, and flounder.

Lobster and crab are also taken. Steamed king shrimp is a specialty of the area; they're expensive and most are exported. Spicy crab soup and seafood relishes are also local favorites. Particularly well-known and sought after is a concoction of pickled oysters and hot peppers.

Anmyeon-do 안면도

Connected to the mainland by a bridge, this rural and not overly crowded island extends south from the Taean Peninsula. At its southern tip is the tiny port of Yeongmok, from which ferries run to Daecheon. Along its west coast are four beaches. In 2002, a floriculture exhibition was held at Kkotji Beach and a new hotel/condominium complex with water park and golf course was constructed there. In the middle of the island is the town of Anmyeon, and above it a large area of low rounded hills covered with tall pines. This rare cover of trees must be one of the largest lowland forests in the country. Near Anmyeon as well is a stand of Chinese soupberry trees, also called bladdernut trees (N.M. #138). A rarity in Korea, the trees produce a yellow flower in summer and a hard nut in autumn used to make Buddhist rosaries.

Taean 태안

Taean holds little interest for most travelers, yet high on the rocky hillside above town, carved onto the flat face of a large boulder, you'll find the **Taean Buddha Triad** (태안마애삼존불) (T. #432) made during the Baekje Dynasty. Located at Daeyul-am hermitage, this triad is similar to the better preserved and more animated Buddha triad of Seosan, but the figures here are more weatherworn with less distinct features, and there are two Buddhas flanking one bodhisatvar. Protected by a roofed enclosure to keep the elements at bay, this sculpture is considered to be one of the two oldest Buddhist rock carvings in the country. Above the hermitage are the remains of a mountain fortress and a fire beacon site. There is no bus service up this steep mountain road, so a walk of over four kilometers one way is required from town.

Taean is basically a small town on the way to the coast, roads to all parts of the Taean Peninsula

and Anmyeon-do fan out from here. Along many of these roads are wide, leveled areas used for producing sea salt. These cement beds are filled five centimeters deep with seawater. Over a period of 5 to 10 days, depending upon the intensity of the sun, the water evaporates, leaving only the salt as residue. Shoveled and raked until thoroughly dried, it's then packed into sacks and sent off to market. This labor-intensive process is increasingly threatened by the chemical production of salt in factories, as well as land reclamation, which is turning acres of prime seaside land into grain-producing areas.

Bus destinations from Taean include Hagampo (₩1,600), Cheollipo (₩1,220), Mallipo (₩1,200), Anheung (₩1,300), Yeonpo (₩950), Yeongmok (₩3,500), Seosan (₩1,200), Cheonan (₩7,600), and Daejeon (₩11,600).

Mallipo Beach 만리포

At the western end of this dragon-like peninsula is Mallipo Beach. Knolls rise up at each end of this popular bay, beautifully framing the crescent of sand. Unfortunately, ugly rows of closely packed shops, accommodations, and raw fish restaurants incongruously push right up to the sand. Accommodations are usually full to capacity during the swimming season, but for the majority of the year, you might think you're visiting a ghost town. A 30-minute walk beyond the far end of this beach brings you to **Cheollipo Beach** [Ch'ŏllip'o], a smaller dowdy cousin with a handful of places to eat and a few basic *minbak* and a working fishing harbor.

Cheollipo Arboretum 천리포수목원

Draped over the hill separating these two beaches, with additional acreage in half a dozen plots some distance to the north, is the privately owned and operated Cheollipo Arboretum. Started in 1966 by Ferris Miller, an American expatriate who became a naturalized Korean citizen, it's now managed by his son. A wonderful collection of about 7,000 trees and shrubs has been put together here, and among them are magnolia, holly, camellia, oak, maple, azalea, daphnia, and various conifers. Everything on the property, except the tall pines, has been planted here.

While the majority of these plants are Asian temperate varieties, some have been brought from the Southern Hemisphere, and a few exotics have come from Europe and America. This project not only grows plants for their beauty and/or scientific and educational use, but the intention is also to work in harmony with nature by employing environmentally sound, chemical-free methods of arboriculture. Some experimentation is done and hybrids have been created. Yet, with all the care that goes into this work, there's a deliberate attempt to let nature take its course, and refrain from "artificial" means of growing and caring for plants. Although it's not a public showplace, plant lovers may be allowed to walk through. If you have the opportunity to view this private arboretum, take care where you walk and don't even think of picking a flower! Open to group tours, but closed Wednesday and some holidays; reservations are necessary. Contact the office at tel. 041/672-9310, fax 041/672-9727.

Anheung 안흥

At the tip of this peninsula, past Yeonpo Beach, lies the tiny port town of Anheung. In the mid-1600s, a fortress was built here to help protect the country against potential invasion. Never used, today only the front-gate stones remain. Within the ruined walls you'll find a few houses and the small temple Daeguk-sa. Three times a day throughout summer and once a day during the winter, ferries make the one-hour crossing to Gaeui-do (₩2,800).

SEOSAN 서산

Seosan [Sŏsan] lies at the throat of the Taean Peninsula. With its splayed fingers, this deeply indented peninsula rushes out into the West Sea like flames from a dragon's mouth. While radically sculpted today, the coastline seems to change even before your eyes. Seawalls are being constructed across some of the shallow bays both north and south of Seosan. When the water behind these dikes is drained and the land dried, these wide plains will become farms. Fishing has always played an important part in the lives of the local residents here, and a ritual fishing play is

performed to help favor a good catch. Special products of the area include seaweed, salted oysters, garlic, and ginger.

Bus destinations and fares from Seosan include Mallipo (₩2,400), Taean (₩1,200), Haemi (₩730), Gyoran-sa (₩730), Hongseong (₩2,800), and Cheonan (₩6,400).

Seosan Buddha Triad and Other Stone Remains

In the hills east of Seosan is a Baekje Dynasty rock sculpture (N.T. #84)—a smiling Buddha triad (서산마애삼존불상). The central figure stands nearly three meters high, while the attendants are almost two meters. Finely carved in bas-relief, their smiles are set off by elaborately etched teardrop halos. The central figure and left attendant are standing; the right attendant is seated, with one leg pulled up onto his lap. This triad is considered by art experts to be the finest extant Baekje-era stone carving. From Seosan, take a bus to Yonghyeon and the tiny temple Gyoran-sa and walk 10 minutes up to the shelter that houses this sculpture.

Just one kilometer up the road is **Bowon-saji** (보원사지). Although long since abandoned, this former temple site is still marked by one five-tier pagoda (T. #104), *sari budo* and a memorial stela to Buddhist priest Beobin (T. #105, 106), a huge stone cistern (T. #102), and flagpole supports (T. #103). One can assume from the location of the remains and the skill of their carving that this was a large and important temple, presumably from the Baekje era, and the valley surely would have supported a sizable resident population.

The northern section of Deok-san Provincial Park is over the mountain to the south from Bowon-saji. The temples Gaeshim-sa and Illak-sa are in valleys to the southwest; bus from Seosan. The square main hall of **Gaeshim-sa** (T. #143) is from 1484; inside is a fine mural painting of the Western Paradise and in the courtyard stands a five-tier stone pagoda. The temple environs are especially known for cherry blossoms, which brighten the valley in spring.

Haemi 해미

In the town of Haemi, 12 kilometers southeast of

Seosan, lie the reconstructed remains of the **Haemi Fortress** (H.S. #116). Like other small town fortresses, this fort, built in 1491, lies on flat land to surround and protect the community. Two kilometers around, it has three gates, two pavilions, and several reconstructed buildings inside. Used as a military training center, the famous Admiral Yi Sun-shin even spent time here with troops before the Japanese invasions of the 1590s. In 1866, about 1,000 Catholics were executed outside the west gate for their belief in the then relatively new foreign religion. Additional believers were killed at other times and a monument to these martyrs has been raised near the west gate.

Hongseong 홍성

Halfway between Boryeong and Seosan is Hongseong [Hongsŏng], known for its fortress, which is older than the nearby and similar Haemi Fortress. This stone barrier circles the low rise in the center of town. With the increase in population, the wall, which once surrounded the town, is now surrounded by the town. Originally built during the Baekje Dynasty with packed earth, it was later reconstructed and faced with stone. Partially destroyed by an earthquake in 1978, it was rebuilt in 1982. Long sections remain and beg to be walked on. Go for a hike! During one reconstruction (1870), the new Joyang-mun east gate was raised, which now sits in the middle of the business district, creating a traffic rotary. Within the old walled fortress is the county administration office. Located there is a restored magistrate's office from the Joseon Dynasty, the front gate to its compound, and a pavilion at the edge of a lotus pond. Along with the fortress wall, Joyang-mun and the other old structures have jointly been designated H.S. #231.

In 934 a great battle was fought in Hongseong between the Goryeo and the Later Baekje armies, both vying for control over the peninsula during the last years of the tottering Silla Dynasty. This battle was a turning point for the Goryeo army; a year later, Goryeo accepted the surrender of the Silla king and gained control over the whole peninsula. Hongseong is also the site of a more recent rebellion of Korean freedom fighters. Following Min Jong-shik, citizens gathered in town in 1905 to protest the pact making Korea a protectorate of Japan. In the resulting melee, about 900 people lost their lives. Just outside the center of town, a shrine has been erected to honor and commemorate the nationalistic spirit of these people.

To the side of Joyang-mun is the Telecom office, and behind that, the post office; two banks are only a few steps away. Reasonably priced accommodations and restaurants are found in the vicinity. If staying, look for a room at the Joyangjang Yeogwan (조양장여관), Dorimjang Yeogwan (도림장여관), or the less expensive Gwangshin Yeoinsuk (광신여인숙).

The train station and bus terminal are located next to each other on the east edge of town. Over a dozen times a day, trains go through Hongseong to Janghang, Seoul, and Cheonan. Bus destinations include Asan (₩3,200), Seosan (₩2,800), Sudeok-sa (₩1,560), Gongju (₩4,400), and Daejeon (₩7,900).

DEOKSAN PROVINCIAL PARK 덕산도립공원

A short distance north of Hongseong, Deoksan Provincial Park lies in two sections surrounding Gaya-bong peak in the north and the boulder-strewn Deoksung-san peak to the south. At 21 square kilometers, it's one of the country's smallest provincial parks. The park boundaries encompass the famous temple Sudeok-sa, but just outside are Deoksan Hot Spring and the Yun Pong-gil memorial shrine.

Two kilometers from the town of Deoksan is **Deoksan Hot Spring**. Mention of its existence appears in the writings of Yi Yul-gok (1536–84), one of Korea's most eminent Confucian scholars. The list goes on and on, but two ailments the 46°C water supposedly ameliorates are rheumatism and neuralgia.

Less than a kilometer down the road toward Sudeok-sa is the shrine **Chungeuisa** (충의사) (H.S. #229), dedicated to the young loyalist Yun Pong-gil. Across the road, a small exhibition hall houses some of his personal belongings (T. #568), while the restored home of his birth is also preserved here; ₩500 entrance fee. This man killed for the sake of his suffering people. In 1932, while in Shanghai, he threw a bomb into a group of high-ranking civilian and military leaders of the Japanese colonial government. Many were killed and more were seriously injured. Yun was arrested and, after a short trial, executed. He was 24 years old. Every year on April 29 (the anniversary of his deed), a ceremony held here memorializes the action he took against the oppressive colonial Japanese.

Sudeok-sa 수덕사

Nestled into the base of the granite mountain Deoksung-san, north of Hongseong and five kilometers west of Deoksan, stands Sudeok-sa [Sudŏk-sa]; ₩2,000 entrance. Founded in the late Baekje period, this 1,300-year-old temple is one of the oldest in the country and the most significant in the region. Monks who lived here in the late 1800s and early 1900s helped to revive the practice of *seon* (Zen) meditation amongst Korean Buddhists. Sudeok-sa's principal point of interest is its main hall (N.T. #49). The original structure was built about A.D. 600, and through its long history has been renovated or completely rebuilt six times. During its last reconstruction (1936–40), workers found the date 1308 carved into a ridge beam, proving that this hall is one of the few spared by the all-consuming conflagration of the Hideyoshi Invasions, and one of the oldest wooden structures in the country. A mural painted on an inside wall by a famous Goguryeo artist was also discovered during this last renovation and, along with similar murals at Buseok-sa in Gyeongsangbuk-Do, it is one of the oldest such paintings in the country. Unlike the bulky and more elaborate structures of the mid-Joseon Dynasty, this building has a refined elegance and grace. The post-and-beam frame is simple and linear, and the rafter system is akin

to Japanese architecture. Note especially the framing design from the side of the building, and the open rafter system and ceiling beams on the inside. The outside wall is painted in a mustard color. Unusually, this structure has only a single front door. Five figures sit on the altar of its spacious interior. If you enter, remove your shoes and go in through one of the side doors. In the judgment hall to the right, notice the finely carved wooden murals set around the elaborately carved altar. Two slender stone pagodas sit in the courtyard in front of the main hall, and a large bell hangs in a pavilion to the side. A small museum (₩1,000 entrance fee) has been built to show valuable temple artifacts and elucidate its history. Also worthy of note are the dragon-figure drum stand and finely wrought flat gong in a second open structure, and the granite posts upholding the front gate roof. Much new stonework, including the tall central stairway and lotus pond, has been done recently to spruce up the yard.

Reached by a long stone step trail, a meditation center and monastic college sit on the hillside above the main hall, and three hermitages for nuns are snuggled into the trees to the west. Less than one-half kilometer up the steep trail behind the temple is a tall Mireuk Buddha sculpture, carved into the flat rock face of a huge mountainside boulder. Although elegantly garbed, its facial features are flat; on its head sits a two-tier hat. Nearby stands a pagoda, and between there and the mountain summit is the temple Jeonghye-sa.

The village below Sudeok-sa has numerous shops, restaurants, and simple accommodations. This area is known for *sanchae deobbap*, a mixture of cooked fresh mountain vegetables set over rice. From the bus stop at the lower end of the village, buses run directly to Hongseong (₩1,560), Yesan (₩1,450), and Hongseong (₩1,560).

Asan-Cheonan

The wide plains of northeast Chungcheongnam-Do lie on the south side of Asan Bay, one of the largest bodies of water that thrust deeply into the west coast, helping to create a portion of this heavily indented lowland. The Sapgyo River, a shallow silty estuary, empties into Asan Bay from the south. Across its mouth and across the neck of Asan Bay are two of the country's longest tidal breakwaters, 3,360 meters and 2,564 meters, respectively. Here, excess river water is let out through dam openings, and inrushing saline water is blocked. The dikes create freshwater lakes, minimize flooding, and provide irrigation for newly created farmland. A highway has been laid across each breakwater to help expedite the flow of traffic through this coastal region, and the longest and tallest expressway bridge in the country now spans the mouth of the bay west of these two breakwaters.

ASAN 아산

The new city of Asan incorporates the town of Onyang, as it is generally known and has been called for decades, with the surrounding countryside. Aside from the fame of its hot spring, Asan is a rather undistinguished city. It is perhaps best known as the birthplace, and final resting spot, of Korea's most famous military man, Admiral Yi Sun-shin. Lesser known are the gravesite of Kim Ok-gyun, a political progressive and leader of the failed 1884 coup attempt, and the birthplace and gravesite of former president Yun Po-sun. While not a cultural stronghold by any means, Asan has the best private folk museum in the country, offering a splendid introduction to Korean folk culture. A living example of how these cultural roots have carried over into modern times can be seen at Oeam-ni Folk Village. On a small scale, white jade is mined in the area.

Of related interest is the **Onyang Cultural Festival**. Held in late April, this event commemorates Admiral Yi Sun-shin. Folk events

of all sorts are held in town, including a Joseon Dynasty royal parade.

Although well-known for several hundred years, the **Onyang Hot Spring** wasn't popular until the completion of the Janghang rail line in the 1930s. Gushing from the ground at 57°C, this water is now piped to the indoor baths of several of the town's large hotels. As at all hot springs in the country, while the bath itself is soothing, these indoor artificial tubs tend to lack the uplifting natural element of baths open to the sky. In response, several hotels have now made outdoor bathing tubs with pleasing natural surroundings.

Fourteen kilometers west of Asan, near the Sapgyo River, is **Dogo Hot Spring**. At 40°C, it's cooler than the Onyang Hot Spring. Not cramped by the confines of a city, Dogo Hot Spring has developed into a recreational resort with health club, tennis courts, and 18-hole golf course.

Onyang Folk Museum 온양민속박물관

One kilometer north of Onyang Station is the Onyang Folk Museum, open 0830–1730 (0900–1730 in winter); ₩3,000 entrance. Use city bus nos. 41 and 90. Established in 1978, this museum displays more than 14,000 artifacts of the Korean people, an excellent collection of Korean folk materials. Although not absolutely complete, it is an excellent overall introduction to traditional Korean customs, beliefs, and practices of everyday life. In its four exhibition rooms you'll discover displays relating to agriculture, fishing, life rituals, marriage, death, housing, clothing, crafts, games, customs, music, masks and masked dances, printing, calligraphy, inkstones and seals, astrology, medicine, woodworking, and chests. The curators have paid great attention to detail and accuracy, with life-like mannequins and informative explanations. All articles are well-displayed, and the soft background music creates an appropriate atmosphere. A Folk Art annex is also located on

CHUNGCHEONGNAM-DO

the grounds, displaying and explaining the peculiarities of Korean folk art. In the finely landscaped yard are several hundred stone objects, mostly items found at gravesites, but some also of religious nature. In addition, a pavilion, a wood-shingle house from the mountains of Gangwon-Do, totem poles, and several types of mills have been re-created here to add further dimension to this fine museum. Don't miss the place if you desire more than a peripheral understanding of the Koreans—and the traditions, customs, and culture of this complex and fascinating land.

Hyeonchungsa 현충사

Four kilometers north of Asan is Hyeonchungsa [Hyŏnch'ungsa], considered by some the country's most important shrine. Hyeonchungsa (H.S. #155) is dedicated to Admiral Yi Sun-shin, an esteemed patriot and perhaps the most brilliant Korean naval commander. Yi was credited with inventing the famous ironclad "turtle ships." Used very effectively during the Imjin War, these swift and impregnable ships ran circles around the larger and slower Japanese boats, causing havoc and sinking a majority of their floating fleet.

Hyeonchungsa was established in 1706 on the site of Yi's home. After being destroyed by royal decree in the late 1800s, it was reconstructed in 1932. In 1966, the property was designated a national shrine, and over the next three years was greatly expanded. In the '70s, additional landscaping was done. This monstrous shrine is indeed impressive! In the compound lie wide, well-manicured lawns, groves of trees, a pond, and an archery range flanked by huge ginkgo trees used for practice by the famous admiral. Here as well you'll find Admiral Yi's restored house and an exhibition hall containing his war diaries (N.T. #76), a two-meter-long broadsword, and other personal articles (T. #326). Admiral Yi's war diaries, written on mulberry paper, are still in excellent condition after nearly 400 years. These writings are still studied by military men; portions are required reading for all schoolchildren. To the rear, occupying the uppermost position, is the main shrine hall, housing his portrait. People from all over the nation come here to pay their respects and bow in reverence.

Every day incense and fresh flowers are offered at the main shrine hall, and every year on April 28 a memorial service is held. The shrine is open from 0900 to 1800 every day except Tuesday; ₩300 entrance. Neat and clean attire is expected, and no smoking is allowed. Use city bus no. 41 or 90, which carry on to Cheonan.

North of this shrine, 11 kilometers straight up the road from Asan, sits **Admiral Yi's tomb** (충무공묘지) (H.S. #112). Use the city bus to Ŭmbong. Killed by rifle fire during the last major sea battle of the Hideyoshi Invasions, Admiral Yi was originally buried on an island off the south coast but was moved to the present tomb site in 1614. The size of this grave and its accompanying stone figures befit the stature of the man.

Oeam-ni Folk Village 외암리

Eight kilometers south of Asan is Oeam-ni, a semi-traditional village that has been designated a folklore preservation area. Like Hahoe Village in Andong and Nagan-eup in Jeollanam-Do, this village largely escaped the modernization movement of the 1960s and 1970s. For some 500 years, members of the Yean Yi family have made this village their home and still predominate in this community of 300 people. A pair of wooden *jangseung* totem poles and a pavilion greet you on the outskirts of the village. Some five dozen tile- and thatch-roofed traditional houses are scattered here and there on the pine-covered hill. Perhaps the best preserved are Yeonam, Champan, and Seonghwa, all *yangban* houses built during the Joseon Dynasty. Farming equipment, storage containers, furniture, household utensils, and numerous other items of traditional daily life are seen in nearly every yard; a water-wheel grain mill and traditional graves are also a feature of the village. Handsome stone walls separate many of these compounds, making a spider web of narrow lanes. By all means visit, but as it's a lived-in community, respect the privacy of those who make this village their home. Ask before entering any front gate or taking pictures. A small information booth and restaurant sit at the village entrance. A city bus stops at this village on its way to Gangdang Valley, one of the nearby places city residents head to for a cool summer getaway.

Practicalities

Set between the train station and the Onyang Hot Spring Hotel is the town's market. The post office is nearby while the Telecom office sits along the main drag heading uphill from the train station.

With its reputation built on the hot spring and cultural sites, the hotel industry in Asan has boomed. The town's best accommodations are the first-class **Jeil Hotel** (tel. 041/544-6111), **Onyang Hot Spring Hotel** (tel. 041/545-2141), and **Onyang Grand Park Hotel** (tel. 041/543-9711), all with Korean- and Western-style rooms and restaurants, lounge, game room, nightclub and, of course, a hot spring bath. Rates start at about ₩85,000. Also good quality is second-class Hoseo Hotel. With basically the same amenities, minus the nightclub, rates here start at ₩40,000.

Many *yeogwan* cluster in the center of the city. You'll find the Ocheonjang Yeogwan (오천장여관) down toward the Onyang Hotel, and behind the post office in the market area are the Shinshinjang Yeogwan (신신장여관) and Suwon Yeoinsuk (수원여인숙).

From Asan, over a dozen daily trains run to Seoul and Janghang. The train station is in the center of the city; bus terminals have been moved to the periphery of downtown. Selected intercity bus destinations and fares are Seosan (₩5,200), Hongseong (₩3,200), Daejeon (₩4,300), Cheongju (₩3,700), Cheonan (₩1,200), and Suwon (₩4,900). City buses run frequently between Asan and Cheonan. Board them along the main east-west street. City buses to the folk museum and Hyeonchungsa run up the street away from the train station.

CHEONAN 천안

Cheonan [Ch'ŏnan] is the second-largest city (pop. 430,000) in Chungcheongnam-Do, and, after Daejeon, its most important transportation hub. It is conveniently located on the Gyeongbu rail line and the country's central expressway. The Janghang rail line branches off the Gyeongbu rail line in Cheonan and makes its way through the province to Janghang. Cheonan

is the principal market center in the northern portion of the province. Although Cheonan is industrializing, there is less spirited growth here than in Daejeon to the south or Suwon to the north. Hoseo University, and branch campuses of Dankook University and Sangmyeong Women's University are here. When Koreans think of Cheonan, one of the things that comes to mind is walnuts. This region also produces a sweet striped melon, pears, grapes, and apples.

The importance of this location is not all modern, however. Southeast of downtown is **Samgeori Park.** On this site the major historical transportation route to the southern provinces split, one road going to the Gyeongsang-Dos, the other to the Jeolla-Dos, and a resting place for travelers was built there. It was through this city that much travel and communication between the capital and the south passed.

Taejo-san Bronze Buddha
태조산좌불상

On the slope of Taejo-san, only a few kilometers from the center of Cheonan, is the temple **Gakwon-sa** [Kakwon-sa] the site of a huge seated bronze Buddha, one of the largest in Asia. Made with 60 tons of bronze, this 14.5-meter-tall figure (with ears 1.75 meters long!) was the largest cast-metal statue in the country until the late 1980s, when the Beopju-sa standing Buddha was erected—in 1994, the seated bronze Buddha of Songgok-sa also surpassed it in weight. From the cluster of shops at the end of the bus line, 203 steps lead up the mountainside to the temple precinct. In the middle of an open courtyard on the ridge to the side of the main compound rests this dominating image, sitting peacefully on a stylized lotus-bud base, benevolently looking out over the countryside. Its left arm lies on its lap, palm up, while the right hand is raised, imparting a benediction to all who approach. Its pursed lips, bold nose, and almond eyes also add a realistic touch to this well-proportioned figure. Started in 1976, this Amita Buddha was raised as a prayer for the reunification of the peninsula. It has a striking resemblance and a similar spiritual bearing to the Daibatsu of Kamakura, Japan. The Taejo-san Buddha, however, has its right

Taejo-san bronze Buddha

hand raised, its clothes draped in more classical Korean style, and the foot of its right crossed leg more visible. In this respect, then, it has greater similarity to the Daibatsu of Todaiji in Nara, Japan.

Since the early 1990s, much new construction has taken place at Gakwon-sa. Its once-insignificant buildings have been replaced with structures of grand proportion, seemingly proportionate in size to the seated Buddha figure. Of particular note is the massive main hall, one of the largest wooden buildings in the country. City bus no. 102 connects downtown Cheonan to Gakwon-sa.

Other City Temples

About 20 kilometers southwest of the city is **Gwangdeok-sa** (광덕사). Dating from the Silla Dynasty, and rebuilt after its burning in the 1590s, this temple used to be the largest in the province. Of its many buildings, the most visually unusual is the bell pavilion with its eight-sided roof. Originally from this temple but taken to Dongguk University for preservation is a six-

volume copy of a history of the Goryeo Dynasty (T. #390). Two other old books (T. #1246, #1247) are kept here as is a large painted mural (T. #1261). You can reach Gwangdeok-sa by city bus.

Beyond the Overseas Korean Cemetery is **Cheonheung-saji,** the site of a Goryeo Dynasty temple, the remains of which are a thick five-tier stone pagoda (T. #354) and banner pole support (T. #99).

Overseas Korean Cemetery

During the Japanese occupation of the Korean Peninsula, many Koreans were taken to Japan. Since those days, the number of Koreans in Japan has continued to grow, to nearly one million. Many of these people, and Koreans in other countries of the world, have expressed a desire to be buried in their ancestral homeland when they die. The Korean government has set aside land for overseas Koreans to be interred; the cemetery is six kilometers north of Cheonan. Every year the numbers of Koreans making their final journey home grows.

Independence Hall 독립기념관

Finished in 1987, the Independence Hall of Korea, called **Dongnip Ginyeomgwan**, is dedicated to all who struggled for the freedom and independence of the Korean nation during the Japanese colonial period. It's devoted to keeping alive the memory of these people, honoring their actions, and instilling in the youth of this country the spirit to pursue those same goals. In this way, its unstated goal is the spiritual guidance of all Korean people in the pursuit of liberating democracy and the fight against enslaving socialism. This is a chance for Korea to stand up and cheer for itself for persevering through adversity to self-determination, yet the hall also leaves open the painful wound of a still-divided peninsula. Set in a semicircle around the Grand Hall of the Nation, the centerpiece structure, there are seven other halls, each with a separate theme: National Heritage Hall, Nationalist Movement Hall, Japanese Aggression Hall, the March First Independence Movement Hall, Independence Hall, the Korean Provisional Government Hall, and the Republic of Korea Hall. Historical items, photographs, dioramas, and models all help bring to life this struggle. In addition, the grounds also hold several monuments, outdoor sculptures, fountains, and restaurants. To see everything could take half a day, but doing so might be overwhelming, anyway. Ten kilometers east of Cheonan, the Independence Hall is open 0930–1830 (1730 in winter) every day except Monday; ₩1,500 entrance fee. Take express city bus no. 500 from in front of the train station.

Another Cultural Shrine

Of related interest is a shrine to Ryu Gwan-sun (H.S. 230), eight kilometers farther down the road. Ryu was a 17-year-old student who rallied sentiment and instigated action against the oppressive Japanese occupation. Punished and killed for her participation in the 1919 March First Independence Movement, Ryu is held up as an example of selfless devotion to the cause of freedom from repression. Every October 12 a memorial ceremony is held here in her honor. Her birthplace is located nearby.

Practicalities

Cheonan has many accommodations and restaurants in front of the train station; fewer accommodations but more restaurants and drinking establishments are located in the newer section of town near the bus terminals. The train station sits in the center of the old part of town; a tourist information booth is located here. Through Cheonan run many dozen daily trains up the line to Seoul and down the line toward Busan. Additional trains run to Janghang, Mokpo, Gwangju, Yeosu, Suncheon, Jinju, Ulsan, and Pohang. Under the road leading up from the station you'll find an underground shopping arcade.

The city's two bus terminals stand next to each other about one kilometer north of the train station. The express bus terminal is on the left, the intercity bus terminal on the right; both are in the basement level of department stores. Express buses run to Seoul (₩3,600), Daejeon (₩3,100), Ulsan (₩13,300), and Gwangju (10,000). Intercity bus destinations and fares include Cheongju (₩2,500), Daejeon (₩3,100), Gongju (₩3,200), Hongseong (₩4,400), Seosan (₩6,400), Asan (₩1,200) and Suwon (₩4,100). From the train station, city bus nos. 26, 45, 70, 100, and others run to the bus terminals, and no. 102 goes to Gakwon-sa. From across the street, and going in the opposite direction, nos. 90 and 91 run a route to Hyeonchungsa and the Onyang Station, and nos. 42 and 500 go to the Independence Hall.

CHUNGCHEONGNAM-DO

Chungcheongbuk-Do

충청북도

Chungcheongbuk-Do [Ch'ungch'ŏngbuk-Do] is a crescent-shaped, landlocked province in the center of the country. With a population of just fewer than 1.5 million in an area of 7,436 square kilometers, it's only larger and more populous than the island province of Jeju-Do. Chungcheongbuk-Do is bounded on its east side by the formidable Sobaek Mountains, which separate it from Gyeongsangbuk-Do. The lower Charyeong Mountains form its northern boundary with Gyeonggi-Do and Gangwon-Do. Its western border with its sister province, Chungcheongnam-Do, doesn't follow any obvious physical boundaries. The two mountain ranges consist basically of gray granite much more ancient than the lighter rock of the Gyeongsangbuk-Do region. Between them lie the province's lowlands, an area widely underlaid by a schist formation that, at over 1 billion years old, is some of the oldest rock on the peninsula.

Dodam-sambong

Patches of this ancient rock are exposed in various places, the most well-known being Dodam-sambong of Danyang. Chungcheongbuk-Do's undulating lowlands are undistinguished, but a trip through them yields unadulterated, country-Korea scenes. Much is of cultural, historical, and scenic interest, however; look toward its eastern region for national parks, remote valleys and peaks, mountain fortresses, temples, and hot springs. This province is drained by two rivers; its northern half lies in the Han River drainage basin, while the Geum River flows through its southern half, providing the province with its widest alluvial plains.

Koreans regard the two Chungcheong provinces as one cultural entity. Its people are characterized by other Koreans as refreshingly forthright and frank, genuine and gentle: solid country folk. People here appear to live at a slower pace than those of other regions of the country. This is even reflected in the local dialect, which tends to draw out sounds and "round" its vowels, in comparison to the smooth and metered Seoul dialect, or the clipped Busan speech. This province has a long and honorable *yangban* tradition of scholarship and service to the state which, because of the class structure, rode for centuries on the backs of the peasants. Chungcheongbuk-Do is the repository of ten National Treasures (N.T.), 47 Treasures (T.), 17 Historical Sites (H.S.), and numerous other cultural properties, many found in the lofty heights of the Sobaek Mountains.

Of the dozen or so cultural festivals held yearly in the province, the most well-known and popular are the Nangye Korean Classical Music Festival held in Yeongdong County in September or October, the Ureuk Cultural Festival of Chungju in October, the Chungju World Martial Arts Festival in mid-autumn, the Sobaeksan Royal Azalia Festival of Danyang in May, the Cheongju Handicraft Biennale in autumn, and the Chungbuk Art Festival held in Cheongju in October.

For information online about the province, check out www.provin.chungbuk.kr or www.cbtour.net.

History

From tools and other archaeological evidence discovered in caves near Jecheon and Danyang, it's known that Paleolithic man dwelt in this area 40,000–50,000 years ago. Since recorded times, the earliest well-organized people here were the Mahan. By the 3rd century A.D., the Baekje Kingdom controlled the entire southwestern corner of the peninsula, including what is now Chungcheongbuk-Do. The province's northeastern corner lay at the junction of the old Three Kingdoms boundaries, and this pivotal area changed hands several times. By the 6th century it was under Goguryeo control, and in the 7th century it fell to the Silla Kingdom, then in the process of unifying the entire peninsula. In 1106, during the Goryeo Dynasty, modern Chungcheongbuk-Do and Chungcheongnam-Do became one administrative area, known as Chungcheong-Do. It remained unified until 1895, when the province was split into north and south units, although geographically the division is more eastern and western. While as affected as the rest of the peninsula by the Mongol invasions in the mid-1200s, this region suffered less from the Japanese invasions of the late 1500s than did the southern coastal provinces. In 1892, as part of the Donghak rebellion, Chungcheongbuk-Do witnessed many demonstrations by farmers distraught over their deteriorating living conditions at the hands of the usurious gentry. During the Japanese occupation, there were additional disturbances. Six of the 36 signers of South Korea's Declaration of Independence hailed from this province.

Industry and Agriculture

Cheongju, Chungju, and Jecheon—Chungcheongbuk-Do's major population centers—are also the province's largest and most established industrial sectors; two other burgeoning sites of industry are the towns of Okcheon, just east of Daejeon, and Danyang, in the north. Industries in the province produce ceramic tableware and earthenware pottery, cloth fiber, electronic parts, chemical fertilizers, and cement, among other things. To supply these industrial sites with elec-

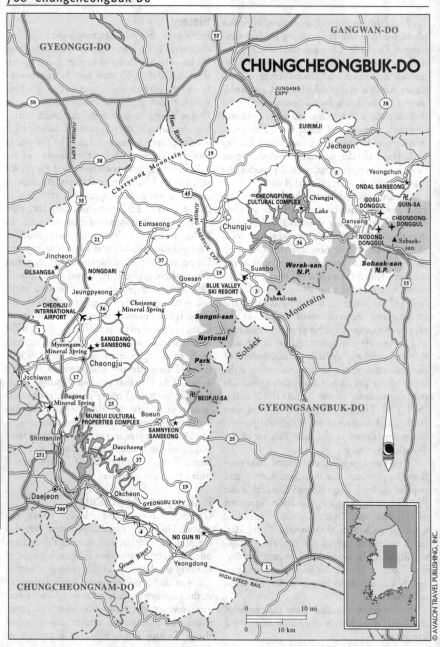

tricity, and the surrounding rural area with water control, two huge dams have been constructed. Completed in 1980, the Daecheong Dam, fifth-largest in the country, blocks the Geum River just outside Daejeon. The dam itself is in Chungcheongnam-Do, but most all of the reservoir backs up into Chungcheongbuk-Do. East of Chungju is the newer Chungju Dam. Completed in 1985, and second-largest in the country, its inundation has caused thousands of home and farm relocations, as far away as Danyang. Newer and much smaller, a lower and broader irrigation dam just west of Chungju has created a shallow lake on a stretch of the south branch of the Han River and one of its tributaries. A good deal of mining is also done in the province, including gold, tungsten, iron, graphite, and natural slate. Although manufacturing and mining are vital factors in the economy of the province, Chungcheongbuk-Do has always been predominantly agricultural. Rice is the principal cash crop, but the province is especially known for garlic, red pepper, *insam*, and high-quality tobacco, while apples, grapes, dried persimmons, and jujube are being produced in ever-increasing amounts.

Transportation

The only commercial airport in Chungcheongbuk-Do is outside Cheongju. Opened in 1997, the **Cheongju International Airport** has domestic connections to Jeju City and a few international flights to China. The Gyeongbu rail line cuts across the extreme southern tip of the province, with major stations only at Okcheon

and Yeongdong. Cutting across the northeastern corner is the Jungang rail line, which passes through Jecheon and Danyang. Connecting the province's cities is the Chungbuk rail line, from Jecheon to Jochiwon via Chungju and Cheongju, running through the flat plains between the Sobaek and Charyeong mountains. A fourth line's terminus is in Jecheon; it runs over the spiny backbone of the peninsula to the East Sea. Traffic up and down the Chungbuk line is frequent and convenient, but a continuation to the adjoining lines usually requires a change of trains in either Jecheon or Jochiwon, unless you're headed for Daejeon.

Cutting across the southern tip of the province and pretty much following the Gyeongbu rail line is the Gyeongbu Expressway (no. 1). Heading north from Cheongju to the eastern outskirts of Seoul is the Jungbu Expressway (no. 35). Cutting across the northern tier, running past Danyang and Jecheon, is the Jungang Expressway (no. 55). When work is completed, the Jungbu Naeryuk Expressway (no. 45), connecting Yeoju and Gumi, will split the province at a diagonal west of Chungju; and a yet-unnamed expressway (no. 40) will cut across the northern tier of the province through Eumseong, Chungju, and Jecheon. Express buses run to Cheongju, Chungju, and Jecheon. A widespread network of highways extends through the province like a spider's web, reaching nearly every little out-of-the-way village. This extensive system makes bus travel the most common and convenient means of transportation.

Cheongju 청주

Cheongju [Ch'ŏngju] (pop. 588,000) is the provincial capital. Lying on the Miho Plain, the largest basin along the upper reaches of the Geum River, it straddles the Mushim Stream and backs up against Uam-san. Reflecting its importance as an early population center and strategic site is the earthen fortress of Jeonbuk-dong (H.S. #415) north of the city center along the Miho Stream near the mouth of the Mushim Stream. Old Cheongju, then known as

Seowongyeong, functioned as a secondary capital during the United Silla period, and as a provincial army command center during the early Joseon Dynasty (15th-16th centuries). In 1908 the provincial government moved here from Chungju, and in 1949 Cheongju was elevated to city status. Cheongju is also the province's leading industrial and educational center, and is known throughout Korea for medicinal-quality mineral water. Expansion has taken

© ROBERT NILSEN

No Gun Ri (Nogeun-ni) incident site at railroad tunnel

place mainly on the west side, pushing the city limits nearly halfway to Jochiwon. Over 180 companies have factories in Cheongju. The largest and best known is the giant Daenong Fiber Co. However, chemicals, electronic goods, and semiconductors make up the greatest percentage of sales from these companies. Much ceramic ware and packaged foods are produced here as well. These factories attract many rural young people to the city, and the city is expanding in all directions trying to meet these needs with new housing complexes, markets, and bus lines. Cheongju also boasts a national museum, city arts center, five universities, dozens of lower-level schools, and the Korean Air Force Academy. Opened in 1997 and adjoining a military airfield north of the city, the Cheongju International Airport has become one of the country's newest international air-entry points. Information about the city can be found online at www.cheongju.chungbuk.kr.

SIGHTS

Central Park 중앙공원
Even though Cheongju has pushed way beyond its former boundaries, the city center is still vibrant and retains several historical and cultural sites. In the midst of the downtown area is the city's somewhat claustrophobic Central Park. Situated between the post office and Nambu market, it contains a traditional-style pavilion which was once part of a military headquarters for this region, several old monuments and memorials, and a 700-year-old ginkgo tree. Old gentlemen who come here to play *baduk* with their cronies are joined at noon by office workers out for fresh air and a stroll on their lunch breaks.

Iron Banner Pole
Surrounded by department stores and other shops is the city's most unusual historical artifact, an iron banner pole (N.T. #41) from the former temple Yongdu-sa. Erected in 962, this 13-meter-

NO GUN RI INCIDENT

Taking the highway or expressway from Daejeon to Gimcheon brings you through pastoral country scenes of rural Korea. Here are shaggy hills and low mountains that hem in narrow valleys sporting rice fields and vineyards, scattered villages, and small country roads. It's a tranquil farming area where nothing seems to happen too quickly. Yet, just east of the Chungcheongbuk-Do/Gyeongsangbuk-Do border is the site of one of the most infamous incidents in the Korean War that has only recently become widely known. No Gun Ri (노근리) (Nogeun-ni or Nogŭn-ni) is a tiny village where several hundred Koreans were killed in the very early days of the Korean War. These men, women, and children were fleeing south in front of North Korean troops. U.S. troops were in the area with orders to try to stop this push. While there is great confusion as to exactly what happened to whom and when, shots were fired by U.S. troops on a group of people in the No Gun Ri railroad tunnel resulting in several hundred being killed. Many Koreans hold that the U.S. troops fired on them with no apparent reason and the U.S. troops counter that they suspected North Korean troops hidden amongst the fleeing people and that they were returning fire from shots aimed at them by those troops. Survivors and relatives of this incident have been trying to get acknowledgment of and reparation for this incident from both the Korean and U.S. governments for years but with little success.

Yonghwa-sa 용화사

Large ancient iron artifacts are seldom seen, and wooden objects rarer yet, but stone remains are numerous. Some of these have been well-preserved, others defaced, and still others, like the Buddha images of Yonghwa-sa, lay buried in the earth to be discovered centuries after their making. Found in the muck of a streamside swamp in 1901, these seven statues (T. #985) were raised, cleaned, and enshrined at this temple. Each of the figures is a different representation of the Mireuk Buddha (Buddha of the Future), and all are well-proportioned and finely garbed, even though the skill of their carving leaves something to be desired. The largest has a feature rarely found on representations of the Buddha: a large swastika, an ancient symbol of the radiation in all directions of Buddha's embracing power, is carved in bold relief on its chest. Several of these figures were broken at the bottom, and each has a new base, some cut to fit the original stone. The difference in stone color and workmanship has been disguised and each now looks whole. These statues are now housed in a finely constructed wooden building with a two-tier roof, a much better home than the drab cement structure that served as their temporary quarters. Standing to its front is a five-tier stone pagoda. A stone arch gate with topping wooden pavilion and temple bell fronts the compound, very much like the entrance gate to an ancient mountain fortress. The compound sits over the levee from the stream, just north of the city's main bridge and is in easy walking distance from downtown.

Heungdeok-saji 흥덕사지

The newest of the old sites in Cheongju was discovered in 1985, when a housing subdivision was being developed just north of the athletic stadium complex and city arts center. This is the site of the Silla Dynasty temple Heungdeok-sa [Hŭngdŏk-sa] (H.S. #315). Although scholars previously knew of a temple by this name in the area, the exact location was a mystery until roof tile from this site with the date 849 and bronze gongs carrying inscriptions indicating that they belonged to a Heungdeok Temple were unearthed. From charred remains,

high, sectioned Buddhist flagpole was once adorned with banners, murals, or flags on special festive occasions or to announce special temple activities. Its granite supports are more artistically embellished than most such stone supports. This flagpole is very much like the one at Beopju-sa, in Songni-san National Park, from which a huge mural of the Buddha is hung every year on Buddha's birthday. Yet Beopju-sa's pole has recently been reconstructed. The only other original, intact iron flagpole standing where it was erected many centuries ago is at Gap-sa in Gyeryong-san National Park.

MYEONGAM
PARK HOTEL

To Sandang
Sanseong

Myeongam
Mineral Spring

0.5 mi

0.5 km

0

0

Uam-san

CHEONGJU NATIONAL
MUSEUM

Samil Park

SEE
DETAIL

25

To Cheongju
International Airport

CHEONGJU
UNIVERSITY

CITY HALL

36

17

CENTRAL
MARKET

17

CHEONGJU UNIVERSITY OF
EDUCATION

YONGHWA-SA

HEUNGDEOK-SAJI

CHEONGJU ART
CENTER

SEOWON
COLLEGE

JINYANG
HOTEL

EARLY PRINTING
MUSEUM

CHEONGJU
TOURIST HOTEL

CHUNGBUK
UNIVERSITY

CHEONGJU

INDUSTRIAL
AREA

NEWVERA HOTEL

LIHO
HOTEL

EXPRESS BUS
TERMINAL

INTERCITY BUS
TERMINAL

To Cheongju Train Station

JUNGBU EXPRESSWAY

35

DETAIL

CHEONGJU
HYANGGYO

Sangdang
Park

POLICE BOX

PROVINCIAL
GOVERNMENT
OFFICE

POST OFFICE

BANNER POLE

TELECOM

NAMBU MARKET

CHOHUNG
BANK

CHEIL BANK

GONGWONJANG
YEOGWAN

SUBUKJANG
YEOGWAN

HUBANGJANG
YEOGWANI

Central
Park

Mushim Stream

it is speculated that the temple burnt sometime in the mid- to late Goryeo Dynasty, never to be rebuilt. Although not an active temple today, the main hall and a stone pagoda have been re-created as they probably looked when in use. Archaeologists unearthed foundation stones for a lecture hall, dormitories, and corridors, and the outlines of these can be seen around the main hall. Many bronze religious artifacts, bowls and spoons, and clay and tile pieces were excavated and are on display at the small exhibition hall here and at the national museum across town. During the Goryeo period, this temple apparently functioned as one for the propagation of religious materials—a text preserved at the Seoul National Museum has a reference to being printed in 1377 at Heungdeok-sa near Cheongju. This is important not only for identifying the temple itself, but more significantly because it's the world's oldest known extant example of a text printed with movable metal type.

Cheongju Early Printing Museum
청주고인쇄박물관
Appropriately located next to Heungdeok-saji is the mushroom-top Cheongju Early Printing Museum. Hours are 0900–1800 (1700 in winter) daily except Monday and some holidays; ₩600 entrance fee. The museum is small but the material is well displayed, with explanations in Korean and English providing a capsule interpretation of the evolution of Korean printing. Shown is the woodblock printing process of the Silla period, with a replica of the oldest known printed text in the world (the original, *Jikjisimcheyojeol,* is stored at a museum in France). A well-executed model shows Buddhist monks in each stage of this process, from carving block plates to binding copies. The Goryeo Dynasty development of wood and metal movable type is shown, with examples of each. Further development of various font styles, for Korean and Chinese, in both wood and metal, was done during the Joseon Dynasty, and the process of making type pieces is also illustrated in detail. It's interesting to note that on the outside of this building, stone tiles molded into Chinese characters have been set into the wall; those on the right side of

the main door show these characters as if printed on the wall, while those on the left side are shown in the reverse, as on a type mold.

Also displayed here are articles dug up during the excavation of Heungdeok-saji. Important less for artistic merit than for historic value, these pieces still tweak the imagination into considering what the temple was like when it was a functioning entity.

Cheongju Hyanggyo 청주향교
The Cheongju Hyanggyo lies at the end of a long tree-lined boulevard behind the provincial government offices. Located on this site in 1683 for the education of sons of local aristocrats and government officials, this public Confucian academy no longer holds classes, but functions only as a shrine to 29 Chinese and Korean sages. Every year ritual ceremonies are held in their honor.

Of older vintage and located on the eastern periphery of the city is the Shinhang Seowon, a private school that taught local *yangban* children the basics of a classical education.

Samil Park 삼일공원
Directly north of the Confucian academy is Samil Park. This park has been set up to honor those who were instrumental in the March First Independence Movement, particularly the six signers of the Declaration of Independence who called this province home. Statues of these six stand in a semicircle as the centerpiece of the park. The leader of this group, Son Pyeong-hui, a member of the Cheondo-gyo church, was born in a thatched-roof house in a rural community north of Cheongju.

Cheongju National Museum
청주국립박물관
The small Myeongam Reservoir, on the eastern edge of the city, is popular with leisure fishermen and weekend boaters. Above the reservoir is the Cheongju National Museum, open 0900–1800 (1700 in winter) daily except Monday and January 1; ₩400 entrance fee. Finely displayed are items mainly from the Chungcheong provinces, with a concentration of articles from prehistoric times through the Goryeo Dynasty.

Some of the more notable items on display are bronze gongs and bells, a delicate Buddha statue, a well-cast temple bell, prehistoric stone and iron tools, and a huge decorative roof tile endpiece from Heungdeok-sa temple site in the city. This roof tile and numerous other pieces of religious import came from three excavated temple sites in the province. Some articles on display have been unearthed from the Baekje-era tombs (H.S. #319) on the hills north of Heungdeok-saji. A special exhibition hall and children's museum are located here as well.

Just up the road and on the opposite side is the city zoo. Open since 1997, it's a small but decent collection with a pair of Siberian tigers; entrance ₩800. Above it is the temple Hwajang-sa.

Mineral Springs
Cheongju reputedly has some of the best medicinal springs in the country. South of Cheongju, and one kilometer south of the Bugang train station, is the **Bugang mineral spring** [Pugang]. **Chojeong mineral spring** [Ch'ojŏng], 16 kilo-

meters northwest of the city, is the most famous in the area and known for its naturally carbonated water. It's now being developed for its hot spring potential with hotels, baths, and spas touting the medicinal effects of its water. The closest and easiest to reach is **Myeongam mineral spring** [Myŏngam], just beyond the national museum. You'll have no trouble locating this spring; people come here to fill jugs with the mineral-rich water. They swear by it! Have a refreshing sip before ascending the road or trail to the mountain beyond, or stop at one of the restaurants for lunch before returning to the city. The Myeongam Park Hotel is located here.

Sangdang Sanseong 상당산성
Three kilometers up the winding road from Myeongam mineral spring, over the pass and up a secondary road leading off to the left, sits the hilltop fortress (H.S. #212) Sangdang Sanseong, the west wall of which can be seen from the museum. This fortress commands a clear view of the surrounding countryside, a natural for such a

© ROBERT NILSEN

Sandang Sanseong south gate and wall

defensive fortification. Originally a Baekje fortress, it was refurbished and expanded by Silla forces when they conquered this area. After seeing battle during the Imjin War of the 1590s, it was rebuilt in the early 1700s. Recently reconstructed, its thick granite wall circles four kilometers around the hilltop, and is punctuated by three principal gates and two secret gates. Walk along the top of the partially rebuilt wall and survey the countryside as Baekje troops did some 1,500 years ago. Count on 1.5–2 hours to circumnavigate the wall, and from the west side you can see Cheongju at your feet. On the south gate, a "ferocious" tiger's head was painted, ostensibly to frighten the enemy, though its comical grin will put a smile on your face. This at one time was the principal garrison for the provincial army. All the military buildings, palace villas, and temples that once stood inside the wall have long since disappeared and been replaced by a small village that's located along the banks of the one remaining reservoir. Many of the villagers have cashed in on the notoriety of this fortress being a spot for a weekend outing, and have converted their traditional-style homes into fancy restaurants and drinking places. From the western section of the wall, a narrow path leads down to Myeongam mineral spring, a pleasant alternative to the twisting, roundabout road. One of the graves passed on the trail is the tomb of Kwak Ye, a Goryeo Dynasty scholar and civil servant who traveled to both Japan and China on government business. About every 30 minutes throughout the day, city bus no. 231 runs to the fortress village from Cheongju.

Muneui Cultural Properties Complex
문의문화재단지

Due to the rising waters of Daecheong Lake outside Daejeon, numerous old structures, shrines, prehistoric dolmen, and other stone remains had to be moved from their original locations for preservation. To accommodate and pull many of these into one place, the Muneui Cultural Properties Complex was constructed some 16 kilometers south of Cheongju on the banks of the lake, in a manner similar to the larger and more well-established Cheongpung Cultural Complex

near Danyang. Opened in 1999, this site sits on a hillside in part of what was a mountain fortress. A reconstructed fortress gate lets you into the complex, in which you find a *yangban*'s house and several commoner's houses filled with old-style items of everyday use, a *gaeksa*, two shrines to loyal citizens, several dolmen, and an exhibition hall that displays small artifacts from the area. This complex is open 0900–1800 (until 1700 in winter) and admission is free.

Sites North of Cheongju

To the north within easy distance of the city are several cultural and historic sights worth mentioning. Just beyond the airport and before you reach Cheungpyeong is the birthplace of Son Pyeong-hui (송병희선생허지), one of the authors and signers of the 1919 Declaration of Independence from Japan. Northwest of there and within a stone's throw of the expressway is **Nongdari** (농다리). Supposedly built in 1250, Nongdari is a low 24-span stone abutment bridge that, as it's said, has stood the test of time and never been washed away. It crosses the slow-moving upper reaches of the Miho Stream and is still used by locals to cross the stream by foot. On the outskirts of Jincheon [Chinch'ŏn] sits **Gilsangsa** [Kilsangsa] (길상사), a shrine dedicated to the Silla Dynasty general Kim Yu-shin. Set on a steep forested hillside, this shrine with portrait was reconstructed here in 1976, having been built elsewhere and later destroyed. A few kilometers to the west is the supposed birthplace (H.S. #414) of this famous and respected general. As he lived some 1,400 years ago, it's impossible to know with certainty what the living situation was like, yet a building has been built here that represents what a typical house of that era might have looked like. Still rather undeveloped, this site also holds a monument raised in 1983 to commemorate the man.

PRACTICALITIES
Accommodations and Food

There are six hotels in Cheongju. Most convenient to the center of the city is the second-class

Cheongju Royal Hotel (tel. 043/221-1300). Near the industrial area on the western edge of town are the second-class **Cheongju Tourist Hotel** (tel. 043/264-2181) and third-class **Jinyang Hotel** (tel. 043/267-1121). Newer are the **Liho Tourist Hotel** (tel. 043/233-8800) and **Newvera Hotel** (tel. 043/235-8181) near the bus terminals, and the old standby **Myeongam Park Hotel** (tel. 043/257-7451) is located at the mineral spring. Prices at these hotels range from about ₩50,000 and up.

More convenient and less expensive are the numerous *yeogwan* around the express and intercity bus terminals. Many of the better-quality and more expensive ones look like tall pseudo-Bavarian castles, but ordinary *yeogwan* are there as well. In the city center, try the Huibangjang Yeogwan (희방장여관) just south of Central Park, Subokjang Yeogwan (수복장여관) or Gongwonjang Yeogwan (공원장여관) just north of the park, or others near the Royal Hotel.

For a relaxed atmosphere and well-prepared food, try one of the dozens of restaurants on the pedestrian street or in the adjoining alleys.

Entertainment, Shopping, Services

Like many large Korean cities, Cheongju's pedestrian street is the center for upscale, high-quality mercantile shops, fine restaurants, and entertainment. Parallel to the main street, it runs from near the Nambu Market toward the city's main intersection at Sangdang Park and is closed to all but foot traffic in the evening. Here and in connecting alleys you'll find the best people-watching in town, and many good coffee shops and cinemas. Beer halls and other drinkeries are recognized by the throb of music filtering through their doors.

Numerous shops in this area specialize in clothes, sporting goods, handicrafts, and household items. Near city hall is the huge multi-level department store and Central Market, while close to Central Park are the Cheongju and Heungup department stores. South of Central Park is the traditional Nambu Market, selling everything from farm machinery to art objects, cabbage, and silks. Covering many city blocks, this tangle of individual shops is the central merchandising mart for the city and surrounding county. A few steps from the bus terminals is the newer Lotte Magnet Department Store.

In the heart of the city are the post office and Telecom office. Two blocks away, between the provincial government office complex and Sangdang Park, is a police box. Money can be exchanged at any of several banks located along the pedestrian street, or at the nearby Choheung Bank. Pick up brochures and maps at the **tourist information office** next to the intercity bus terminal at its location on the western edge of the city.

Transportation

The new **Cheongju International Airport** (청주 국제공항) is located about 10 kilometers north of the city center. It's a modernistic two-story structure that seems to have plenty of room to grow. When you face the building, domestic arrivals and departures are on the right, international on the left, with arrivals on the ground floor and departures on the upper floor. Ticket counters, shops, a foreign exchange bank, restrooms, telephones and the like are all close at hand. This airport is serviced by Korean Airlines, Asiana Airlines, and China Eastern Airlines. Domestic flights from Cheongju run only to Jeju-do and only four times a day, while international flights go to Shanghai and Shenyang in China. The international passenger service charge for foreigners is ₩9,000 per person, ₩4,000 for domestic use. Out front is a pay parking lot, and at curbside are city buses that run into Cheongju (₩1,000), Jochiwon (₩1,280), and Shintanjin (₩1,710). There are also frequent shuttle buses to Daejeon Dongbu Terminal (₩2,900) and occasional shuttles to Cheonan (₩2,900) and Chungju (₩4,200). A taxi into the city runs about ₩15,000. Just outside the airport parking lot and a 15-minute walk from the terminal is a small train stop on the Chungbuk line that's two stops north of Cheongju.

The Cheongju Station is inconveniently located 20 minutes west of the city on the Chungbuk line. Ten trains a day in both directions pass through Cheongju, with Daejeon and Jecheon as terminal points, except for one train that runs from Seoul to Andong. Going to Jecheon and beyond is convenient and pastoral, but for travel up or down the Gyeongbu rail line (except for the one train to Seoul), most people simply avoid a transfer by taking a frequent city bus to Jochiwon Station on the Gyeongbu rail line and boarding a train there direct to their destination.

With the Gyeongbu and Jungbu expressways meeting southwest of the city, there is steady traffic in and out of Cheongju, much of it along the beautiful Sycamore-lined Garosu Road that leads into town from the west. Express buses run to Seoul (₩5,200), Dong Seoul Station (₩5,600), Seoul Sangbong Station (₩5,500), Daegu (₩8,500), Busan (₩13,100), and Gwangju (₩8,800). The most frequent and convenient local transportation is via intercity buses. Selected destinations are Buyeo (₩5,600), Gongju

(₩3,000), Daejeon (₩2,600), Jeonju (₩6,600), Songni-san (₩5,100), Chungju (₩5,200), and Suwon (₩5,600).

Cheongju city buses crisscross and connect the city to the nearby tourist sights. The following list of buses from downtown Cheongju will be of most help:

nos. 210, 223: bus terminals

no. 231: national museum, Myeongam mineral spring, Sangdang Sanseong (also 233)

no. 642: Cheongju train station

nos. 500, 535: Jochiwon train station

no. 747: Cheongju International Airport

nos. 126, 131: Chojeong mineral spring

nos. 611, 612: Heungdeok-saji, Early Printing Museum

nos. 330, 331: Muneui Cultural Properties Complex

Songni-san Vicinity

BOEUN 보은

Known for its production of full-flavor jujubes, Boeun [Poŭn] is also the gateway to Songni-san National Park and the famous temple Beopju-sa. One of the nation's satellite communication earth stations is located east of town and on the mountain above it is a small astronomical observatory. Boeun's major historical claim involved *Donghak* religious members during the unstable end of the 1800s, when farmers became increasingly agitated over their deteriorating standard of living and growing exploitation by the gentry. Foreign ideas were filtering into the country, and the Korean royalty sought to legitimize its power based on diplomatic and economic relations with other countries, not on the will of its own citizens. While Japanese and Chinese merchants gained increasing control over the economy, to the detriment of Korean merchants, the religio-social *Donghak* movement aimed at ridding the country of all foreign influence. Socially, the movement believed in the equality of all Koreans, regardless of class, and an amicable working relationship among all men in order to raise everyone's standard of living. To dramatize

their beliefs, 20,000 vocal *Donghak* members assembled at Boeun in 1892. Violence was avoided, but in 1894 the *Donghak* peasant army actually instigated open rebellion in other regions of the country, creating great havoc for several weeks. This show of civil disobedience was defused by government troops, bringing to an end the militant action of this disenchanted group.

Of older historical interest are the partially reconstructed remains of **Samnyeon Sanseong.** This mountain fortress (H.S. #235) is located a few kilometers east of town, on the way to Songni-san National Park, and can be seen from town. Built by Silla troops to protect this area from Baekje incursion, this fortress is rather small in circumference but stoutly built.

On the eighth day of the fourth lunar month, the **Songni Festival** is held in Boeun. A lantern parade is held and fan dance performed in town, while the traditional Buddhist ceremony of circling a pagoda takes place at Beopju-sa temple.

Road to the Mountain

The road to Songni-san from Boeun leads past a sparkling reservoir, up a steep hill, and over a pass to a high valley from which Songni-san rises. The reservoir is new but the winding road, with its dozen hairpin turns over **Malchi-jae Pass** (800 meters), is not. When King Sejo visited Beopju-sa in 1464, he approached the temple by this route. Legend says that the king, thinking the strenuous climb up to Malchi-jae would be the end of his journey, was surprised when he reached the pass and discovered that a broad valley lay before him and the temple was nestled into the still-distant mountains. Songni-san, roughly meaning "Distanced from the Common," got its name from this incident.

A few kilometers farther, marking the edge of the park, is a lone red pine tree, majestically guarding the entrance to Beopju-sa and the inner mountain valleys. This 600-year-old, once-symmetrical tree (N.M. #103) has become the symbol of this mountain area. When King Sejo reached this spot, one of the tree's branches blocked the road. The king commanded that the branch be removed. At that moment, the tree—on its own accord—raised the limb, allowing king and company to pass. Surprised, yet pleased with the tree's courteous and gentlemanly manner, the king immediately bestowed upon it the rank of second minister, a rank it holds still. Having suffered a disease in recent years, the tree has lost a number of its branches, compromising its symmetric grace. Still majestic and noble, it's now a bit wizened. Today, the road must sweep around the tree, giving it wide berth.

SONGNI-SAN NATIONAL PARK
속리산국립공원

Situated in the geographical center of the country, Songni-san National Park takes its place as the central point in the Sobaek Mountains, lying over the Chungcheongbuk-Do/Gyeongsangbuk-Do border. Designated a scenic site of historic value in 1966, it was upgraded to a national park in 1970. With the incorporation of Hwayang-dong Valley, Seonyu-dong Valley, Ssanggok Valley, and adjacent northern sections into park lands in 1975, its size increased to 283 square kilometers; ₩3,200 entrance fee at the Beopju-sa entrance and ₩1,300 at all others. Tall and

rugged, this S-shaped mountain ridge is characterized by long, thickly wooded valleys that rise quickly to craggy peaks in the south, while lower peaks and serpentine valleys predominate in the north. Its forested valleys hide over a dozen temples, hermitages, and pavilions, and are home to some 300 kinds of small animals, birds, and insects. While spring brings cherry blossoms, summer a verdant green, and winter a stark white, perhaps the park is best appreciated in the autumn, when the hues and tints of fall are swathed across its hardwood canopy.

Songni-san draws great numbers of hikers to its many well-maintained trails—mostly in the southern section. Their lower portions are generally gradual and easy, becoming steeper up the trail; some sections necessitate metal stairways and railings. Nonetheless, on warm autumn days and public holidays, lines of people, including grandparents in billowy traditional clothes, trudge up the mountain for a view from the top. The ridge has half a dozen peaks over 1,000 meters, the highest being 1,057-meter Chonhwang-bong, "Celestial Emperor Peak," at its southern end. The most popular peak, however, is Munjang-dae (1,033 meters), from where there are superb views of the inner and outer valleys. Rippling off into the distance is a rugged jumble of hills that fight the valleys for space, and win. Munjang-dae means "Literary Competition Height," named when King Sejo and his courtiers climbed this peak and held some sort of scholarly contest.

Water running off this mountain flows into the country's three principal river drainage basins: the Nakdong River to the east, the Geum River to the southwest, and Han River to the north. Yet even with such fine natural attractions and good hiking trails, it is the temple Beopju-sa and its cultural inheritance that draws most people to this area.

Beopju-sa 법주사
Three kilometers above the minister pine, at the pivotal point of the mountain's fan-shaped inner valleys, sits Beopju-sa [Pŏpju-sa]. Largest in the province and one of the most important temples in the country, Beopju-sa is reached by a long, level walkway running through a colonnade of

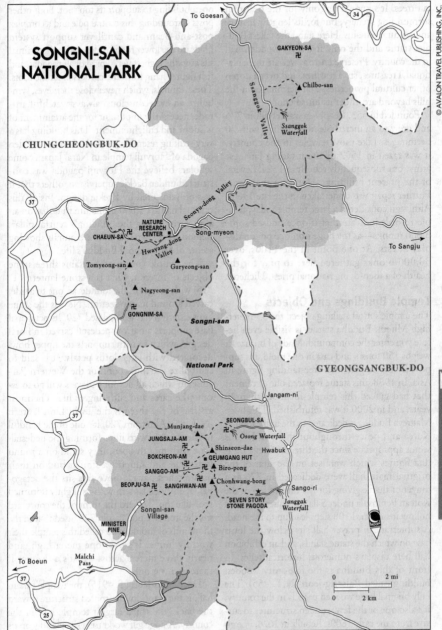

SONGNI-SAN
NATIONAL PARK

CHUNGCHEONGBUK-DO

To Goesan

GAKYEON-SA 卍

Chilbo-san ▲

Ssanggok Valley

Ssanggok
Waterfall

Seonyu-dong Valley

NATURE
RESEARCH
CENTER

Song-myeon

To Sangju

CHAEUN-SA 卍

Hwayang-dong
Valley

Tomyeong-san ▲

Garyeong-san ▲

Nagyeong-san ▲

GONGNIM-SA 卍

Songni-san

National Park

GYEONGSANGBUK-DO

Jangam-ni

SEONGBUL-SA 卍

Munjang-dae ▲

Osong Waterfall

JUNGSAJA-AM 卍

Shinseon-dae ▲

Hwabuk

BOKCHEON-AM 卍

GEUMGANG HUT ▲

Biro-pong ▲

SANGGO-AM 卍

Chonhwang-bong ▲

Sango-ri

BEOPJU-SA 卍   SANGHWAN-AM 卍

SEVEN STORY
STONE PAGODA ★

Janggak
Waterfall

Jangjak

Songni-san
Village

MOON

MINISTER
PINE ★

To Boeun

Malchi
Pass

0   2 mi

0   2 km

M CHUNGCHEONGBUK-DO

CHUNGCHEONGBUK-DO

tall trees. It's known not only for the beautiful surrounding scenery, but for its lengthy history and cultural remains. Here stand the tallest Buddha statue and the only five-story wooden hall in the country. Preserved here as well are three National Treasures, six Treasures, and over a dozen other cultural properties. Ten hermitages in the hills beyond are under its jurisdiction.

Founded in 553, Beopju-sa was rebuilt in 776 and grew to an incredible 60 buildings with 70 hermitages. Like most temples in the country, it was razed in 1592 by the invading Japanese army, but subsequently rebuilt in 1624. Several of the present buildings date from that time. Further repair was undertaken in the late 1960s. Although considered a large temple today, temple records indicate that it once housed some 3,000 monks—as the huge iron rice pot on display attests. At one point in the 1100s, over 30,000 monks gathered here to pray for the health of a then-dying national priest, Uicheon.

Temple Buildings and Objects

The temple's most striking object, the 33-meter-high Mireuk Buddha statue, is visible even before you enter the compound. Made of bronze (it weighs 150 tons!), and cast in one mold, it's supposedly the largest such freestanding figure in Asia. In 1988, this statue replaced one of cement that had graced this temple for more than 20 years, and in 2000 it was refurbished. This huge Maitreya Buddha is dedicated to the unification of Korea and peace throughout the world. This seems appropriate since the three Maitreya Buddha figures which were set on the altar of the original main hall were dedicated in 776 as a prayer of thanksgiving for the unification of the Korean Peninsula under Silla administration. It is hollow inside, and 108 steps lead up to the head. A subterranean prayer hall sits below the lotus base on which the statue stands, and an exhibition hall here displays numerous historical relics. In front of this Buddha is the five-story wooden building called **Palsang-jeon** (N.T. #55). The only original large wooden pagoda in the country, it's also one of the few wooden structures to survive from the early 1600s. Rebuilt in 1624, one gigantic pole runs up through the center of this open building to support its top roof. Four other posts surrounding this central pole and a complex post-and-beam and cantilever support system holds up the lower roofs. A decorative metal finial sits atop the highest tier, typical of all pagodas, and fish figures hang from the corners of all the roofs. These animals, which never close their eyes, symbolize an ever-conscious, always-watchful attitude, necessarily important for the attainment of wisdom and enlightenment. This building has a very striking resemblance to the famous wooden pagoda of Horyuji temple in Nara, Japan. Some scholars believe the Horyuji pagoda was constructed under Baekje supervision, others that it was only inspired by Baekje design. Inside this unusual hall are 1,000 miniature Buddhas on an altar surrounding the building's central pillar. Behind these, two to a side, are murals showing scenes of Seokgamoni Buddha's life.

The temple courtyard contains three stone objects of interest. First is a stone lantern (T. #15) with images of the four devas, one to a side, carved around its top section. Next is the stone lotus cistern (N.T. #64), dated 720. Its octagonal base supports a narrow pedestal carved in floral designs, which in turn supports the upper bowl decorated with large lotus petals. It is said to symbolize the lotus pond of the Western Paradise, to which all devout believers will go to escape the cares and suffering of life. The most artistic of the three is the Twin Lion lantern (N.T. #5). Also from 720, it's one of the handful in the country with lions forming the pedestal. One with mouth open, they stand on a round lotus bud and support a similar bud on their outstretched paws. Above this sits the octagonal, open-sided lantern with its slightly upturned roof-like top. Toward the front of the courtyard sits the iron rice pot, cast in 720, used to feed the thousands of monks who called this temple their worldly home. It's over one meter high, and nearly three meters across—that's a rice pot if there ever was one!

Daeungbo-jeon (T. #915), the temple's main hall, is the giant double-roofed structure toward the back, the third-largest temple hall in the country. A huge gilt wood triad sits placidly on its altar. Originally built in 553, it too was rebuilt

© ROBERT NILSEN

Beopju-sa courtyard

during the great reconstruction of 1624. In design and construction technique, this hall is similar to the slightly larger Mireuk-jeon at Geumsan-sa. On the inside, look for the cross-beams that support posts for the second-level roof. Its huge doors pivot in wooden holds. Other temple structures are Wontongbo-jeon (T. #916), with its seated, gilt wood statue of Gwaneum, the Goddess of Mercy; Neungin-jeon, the hall of the 16 Nahan; Samseong-gak, the Three Spirit shrine; a hall enshrining portraits of former monks and abbots of the temple; a two-posted front gate; an enclosed gate with four huge and colorful but not particularly ferocious devas; a bell pavilion; and offices and dormitories.

To the side of the compound is a Buddha image sculpted in bas-relief on the flat face of a fallen rock. This boulder, called Churaeam (T. #216), shows the Buddha seated on a lotus blossom, but unusually, with both feet flat on the ground. Much like the ancient banner pole in Cheongju, a 22-meter-tall iron pole is also seen at this temple. Originally built in 1007, it was pieced together again in 1972. On Buddha's

birthday, a huge mural depicting the Enlightened One is taken out of storage and hung from it. This once-a-year spectacle is a modern example of what must certainly have taken place at all major temples on special festival days. Finally, an old calligraphic inscription, originally presented to Saja-am, is now preserved in the main hall. The characters on this eight-panel folding screen were written by Joseon King Seonjo (1567–1608). Their age, and the fact that they were written by a king, give them immense historic and artistic value.

Seongbul-sa 성불사

Formerly called Munjang-sa, this temple has changed its name back to an even older appellation and is undergoing a complete revamping. In the early 1990s, the abbot of the temple had all the buildings pulled down and began building and landscaping anew. Sitting below Gwaneum Peak, this temple is dedicated to Gwanseeum Bosal, otherwise known as Gwaneum or the Goddess of Mercy. When all is completed, this temple

CHUNGCHEONGBUK-DO

will not only serve as a functioning temple but also as a Buddhist college to train novice monks.

Hiking in the Southern Section

The first and most often-used trail leads from Beopju-sa past Jungsaja-am to Munjang-dae. It's not particularly strenuous and offers great views from the top. Vary the return by going first to Shinseon-dae, then down past the Geumgang hut from there. The trail down is initially steep, but you get a wonderful view of the inner valley —round-trip from the village requires about seven hours. Or, from Munjang-dae, follow the ridge trail to Chonhwang-bong and return via Sanghwan-am and Sanggo-am. This long circular hike should take about 10 hours. Wear sturdy shoes and be prepared for a long day! Beyond this, two trails lead over the mountain ridge and down to Hwabuk. The more scenic goes via Munjang-dae, and down the far side past the stepped Osong Waterfall and Seongbul-sa to the village of Jangam-ni. The second goes up almost to Chonhwang-bong, before tracing its way down past a seven-story stone pagoda (T. #683) and Janggak Waterfall to the village of Sango-ri. Similar in style but in worse shape than the Central Pagoda outside Chungju, this stone structure was taken apart during the Japanese occupation but refitted in 1978. Believed to be from the Goryeo Dynasty, it probably marked the former temple Janggak-sa.

Trails are generally well-marked and maintained. Spring, because of Buddha's birthday, and autumn, because of the fall colors, bring the greatest number of tourists. Most young hikers and campers come during the summer, but even in winter people brave the slippery paths, though park officials occasionally close the trails due to heavy snowfalls. On occasion, other trails are closed due to overuse and the need for restoration. Check the status of trails with park officials before you climb.

Northern Sections

Fifteen kilometers straight north of Beopju-sa, but only reachable by more round-about roads, is the middle section of the park. Split into two areas, the largest is **Hwayang-dong Gugok**, a handsome, narrow valley where the white polished rock of its clear stream and luxuriant pine-covered hillsides blend in natural harmony. Along the bends in this stream are nine points of scenic beauty—odd-shaped boulders, thrusting promontories, and water pools. About six kilometers long, the valley can only be accessed on foot. At its western end is a monument to a Chinese Ming emperor who aided the Korean struggle against the invading Japanese in 1592. Across the river, perched on a streamside rock, is a pavilion. Above it, under a canopy of pines, is the temple Chaeun-sa. At the eastern end of this valley is the Nature Research Center. Hwayang-dong Gugok was the home of Song Shi-yeol during his retirement. This highly respected, Neo-Confucian scholar was probably the greatest statesman of the 1600s. Prime minister under King Injo, his policies were enlightened but were repudiated by later kings. Song was exiled and forced to commit suicide by drinking a poison potion. After his death, a *seowon* (private academy) dedicated to him was constructed along this stream; in 1756, his memorial tablet was enshrined in the National Confucian Academy on the grounds of Seonggyungwan University in Seoul—the highest possible honor for any Confucianist. Some four kilometers to the east and two kilometers above the village of Song-myeon is **Seonyu-dong Gugok.** A boulder-strewn stream runs through this quiet, secluded, and diminutive side valley. Although not outstanding, here, too, are rock outcrops and peculiar stone formations.

People come to this section of the park in the summer to swim, climb the rocks, picnic, and simply to get away from the stifling cities. A two-hour leisurely walk takes you from the Hwayang-dong entrance to the nature center. From the second bridge in the valley, a trail leads up to Tomyeong-san (643 meters). From the summit, a second trail returns to a point upriver, while another continues south over Nagyeong-san to the temple Gongnim-sa. A walk through the Seonyu-dong [Sŏnyu-dong] Valley along the stream should take no more than an hour up and back. Aside from the local population, these valleys are nearly abandoned in winter.

About 10 kilometers north of Seonyu-dong

Valley is the broad and plainer **Ssanggok Gugok Valley,** the upper portion of which has large rock sentinels, pools, and the Ssanggok Waterfall. At a bend in the river in the lower section, one riverside palisade of rocks is known as the Little Diamond Mountains. Set below Chilbo-san in the next valley to the north is the northernmost temple in the park, **Gakyeon-sa** [Kakyŏn-sa]. It houses a seated stone Buddha (T. #433).

Songini-san Village

One kilometer below Beopju-sa is the Songni-san village—a tourist village, pure and simple. It has look-alike souvenir shops, large restaurants, tearooms, drinking establishments, music halls, dozens of *yeogwan,* one first-class tourist hotel, several other hotels, a sculpture park, a campground, bus station, post office, police station, and the park office. All the usual tourist trinkets, Buddhist paraphernalia, and souvenir junk can be found in the shops. Also available for purchase are big bags of mushrooms and piles of *doraji* (bellflower), *gosari* (fern brake), and other wild mountain vegetables. Throughout the summer and into the autumn color season, crowds of people throng to the mountains, and the village is a hive of activity. For the remainder of the year, it's slower and more sedate, with a marked "after-season" atmosphere.

Accommodations and Food

At the north end of the village is the first-class **Lake Hills Hotel** (tel. 043/542-5281). Korean- and Western-style rooms run ₩129,500–278,000, with suites up to ₩507,000. The hotel also offers Korean and Japanese restaurants, a coffee shop, bar, game room, souvenir shop, tennis courts, and swimming pool. The regular hotels, of which there are half a dozen, like the

Aram Hotel (tel. 043/543-3791), have clean and comfortable rooms for ₩30,000–50,000. For less expensive rooms, many large and modern *yeogwan* and smaller *minbak* are spread throughout the village. *Minbak* generally run ₩20,000–25,000, while rates for *yeogwan* are ₩25,000–35,000, with some fancier places charging more than that. Across the road from Lake Hills Hotel is a public campground where a site runs ₩3,000–6000. Just outside the park, below the minister pine tree, is the **Songnisan Youth Hostel** (tel. 043/542-5799), where a bunk runs ₩10,000 with Y.H. membership. *Yeogwan* and a second campground are also available at Hwayang-dong while there are also a few *minbak* at Song-myeon.

Food prices are moderate to expensive, except for simple noodle dishes. While here, try the specialties of this mountain area: *pyogo deobbap* (mushroom-smothered rice), *peoseot cheongol cheongshik* (full rice meal with mushroom stew), or *sanchae cheongshik* (a full meal of rice, soup, and side dishes, prepared with various wild mountain vegetables). Although on the expensive side (₩10,000–15,000), they are hearty, savory, and nutritious meals; others run ₩5,000–8000.

Transportation

Express buses from the park run to Seoul Nambu bus station (₩10,300), Seoul Dongbu station (₩10,700), and Suwon (₩10,900). Frequent intercity buses connect Songni-san village to major provincial towns like Boeun (₩1,100), Cheongju (₩5,100), and Daejeon Dongbu Terminal (₩4,700). Buses also run to the park's back side, although less frequently, from Cheongju and Sangju to Song-myeon and Hwabuk; from Jeomchon to Hwabuk and Song-myeon; and from Goesan to Ssanggok, Hwayang-dong, and Seonyu-dong valleys.

CHUNGCHEONGBUK-DO

Northern Chungbuk

CHUNGJU 충주

Chungju [Ch'ungju], the province's second-largest city (pop. 220,000), is an overgrown farming community that exudes a country atmosphere. It lies at the confluence of the Han and Dalcheon rivers. Flanking the rivers are broad and rich alluvial farmlands, with rice, vegetables, and high-quality tobacco the principal crops. Apples are also produced here, mostly in the uplands. This low-lying city is in the throes of great expansion. Tall apartment complexes, new schools, recreational facilities, parks, and reservoirs have been constructed in all directions from the city center to keep up with population growth. In concert with its increasing size and modernity, a new administration center, with additional government and private offices, has been built on the north side of the city.

In 1956, Chungju was elevated to city status, and since the 1960s, there has been continual growth in industrialization, primarily in the light-industrial electronic and electrical goods sector and the fertilizer, chemical, and metal pipe sectors. More than 120 companies occupy the city's industrial estates—two on its northern edge near the Han River, and one south across the Dalcheon River from Chungyeolsa. In order to sustain the economic growth of this region, the Chungju hydroelectric dam was constructed a few kilometers outside the city. As a consequence of inundation, however, thousands of people and dozens of farms were relocated. Important cultural properties have also been moved and renovated. The 500-year-old residence of the writer Choe Ham-yeol, for example, now sits 12 kilometers outside Chungju on the road to Suanbo. Others have been gathered together at the **Cheongpung Folklore Preservation Site**, overlooking the lake halfway between Chungju and Danyang. In the late 1990s, a lower flood control dam was also constructed several kilometers north of the city creating a lake in this section of the Han River.

Every October, the **Ureuk Cultural Festival** is held in the city to honor the Silla Dynasty *gayageum* musician Ureuk. Events take place at various locations in the city and at Tan'geum-dae, and include *gayageum* music performances, a memorial ceremony honoring Ureuk, literary contests, a local shaman ritual, fireworks, and a parade re-creating a procession accompanying General Im Gyeong-eop to war. The general helped oppose the Manchu invasion of the peninsula in 1627.

Get information on the Web at www.chungju .chungbuk.kr.

Central Park 중앙공원

Set between the post office and the Telecom office, this diminutive green area graces the site of a Goryeo Dynasty fortress built in 1277. Below the towering trees are **Cheongnyeong-heon**, a city magistrate's office, and **Jegeom-dang**, part of the magistrate's residence, both rebuilt after a devastating fire in 1870. Both structures are of late Joseon Dynasty design, but Cheongnyeong-heon is perhaps the most appealing. Raised above the ground on short posts, it has a heated room on one end and a wood-floored open veranda on the other end. The **Chungju Cultural Center** flanks the park's eastern edge.

Historic Sites

North across the stream from Central Park is the **Chungju Hyanggyo** (충주향교). Built in 1398 and rebuilt in 1897, this Confucian academy educated local *yangban* children during the Joseon Dynasty. As at all such *hyanggyo* throughout the country, ceremonies are performed here twice a year in memory of Chinese and Korean Confucian sages.

Periodic memorial ceremonies are also performed at **Chungyeolsa shrine** [Ch'ungyŏlsa] (충열사), south of the city center along the Dalcheon River. First built in 1697 but greatly expanded in 1978, this shrine is dedicated to

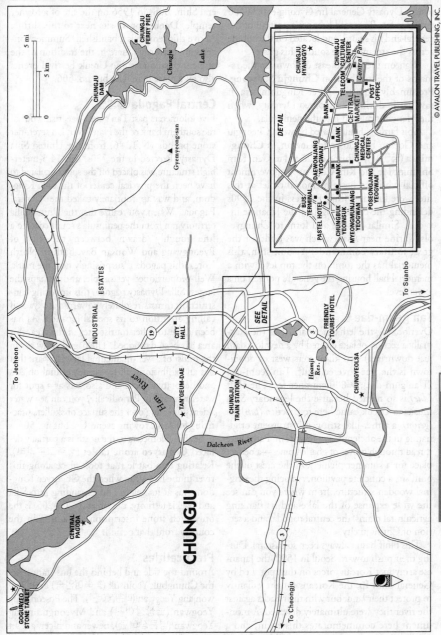

© AVALON TRAVEL PUBLISHING, INC.

DETAIL

CHUNGJU HYANGGYO

CHUNGJU TELECOM-CULTURAL CENTER

Central Park

BANK

CENTRAL MARKET

POST OFFICE

BANK

DAEWONJANG YEOGWAN

CHUNGJU MEDICAL CENTER

BANK

POSEONGJANG YEOGWAN

BUS TERMINAL

PASTEL HOTEL

CHUNGBUK YEOINSUK

MYEONGMUNJANG YEOGWAN

MYEONGMINJANG YEOGWAN

SEE DETAIL

CITY HALL

19

TAN'GEUM-DAE

CHUNGJU TRAIN STATION

Dalcheon River

Han River

INDUSTRIAL ESTATES

To Jecheon

CHUNGJU DAM

CHUNGJU FERRY PIER

Chungju Lake

Gyemyeong-san

CHUNGJU

To Suanbo

Hoamji Res.

FRIENDLY TOURIST HOTEL

3

CHUNGYEOLSA

CENTRAL PAGODA

GOGURYEO STONE TABLET

To Cheongju

3

5 mi

5 km

0

0

Joseon Dynasty General Im Gyeong-eop; ₩400 entrance fee. Preserved here are a portrait of the general and his sword, and located on the hillside across the stream to the south is his grave.

High on the hilltop east of town are the remains of the fortification **Chungju Sanseong.** Presumably from the Three Kingdoms era, it saw battle during the Goryeo Dynasty, when the Manchus pushed into the peninsula.

A bit farther afield, located between Cheongju and Goesan but closer to Goesan, is **Chungminsa** (충민사), a shrine dedicated to Gen. Kim Shi-min. He and Kim Chae-gap, a government official who also has a memorial tablet at this site, were killed at Jinju Fortress in the 1590s defending the country against the Japanese invaders. Similar in style and form to Chungyeolsa shrine near Asan which was built for the great military commander Yi Sun-shin, this memorial has the tomb on the top level with a memorial hall housing the general's portrait on a lower level.

Tan'geum-dae 탄금대

Overlooking the lethargic Han River (now actually a section of lake created by a new low dam just downriver) two kilometers west of downtown is the tree-covered bluff, Tan'geum-dae [T'an'gŭm-dae]; ₩800 entrance fee. The bluff *(dae)* is so named because the legendary Silla musician Ureuk came here to practice *(tan)* his *(geum)*, a zither-like stringed instrument originating in the ancient Gaya Kingdom. Paths here thread through groves of gnarled pines—a perfect place for a summer picnic. On the crest of the bluff sits a concrete pavilion, replacing the original wooden structure, from where you can see the wide expanse of the lake and its flanking agricultural plains, the central pagoda, and a section of Chungju city.

This bluff hasn't always been so pastoral. During their push toward Seoul in 1592, the Japanese army met Korean forces on this spot. Led by General Shin Ip, the Koreans fought valiantly to protect their land, but with their backs against the river they were ultimately defeated. A monument here commemorates this event, and a small shrine houses the memorial tablet of General Shin. Built in 1956 on the site of a former temple, **Daeheung-sa** sits next to this shrine. Above this temple is a bandshell. Summer concerts are performed here in the tradition of the ancient past, and some Ureuk Festival events also take place here. Use bus no. 506.

Central Pagoda 중앙탑

Five kilometers past Tan'geum-dae, rising out of the southern bank of the Han River, is a seven-tier stone pagoda (N.T. #6) from the United Silla Dynasty. Erected in the 780s, this 14.5-meter-high structure was placed on the spot calculated to have been the physical center of the Silla Kingdom, and was appropriately called the "Central Pagoda." When you realize that the United Silla territory ran from the peninsula's south coast to a line roughly drawn between the city of Pyeongyang and Wonsan Bay, both in North Korea, this pagoda is surprisingly near the mark. Well-proportioned yet simple, and perhaps the largest Silla Dynasty pagoda, this imposing construction thrusts resolutely toward the sky, as if calling attention to its special location. As has been done to other tourist sites in the area, this area has been developed. The pagoda now sits in the midst of a well-manicured lakeside park that has an exhibition hall for some cultural objects and decorative rocks and also acts as a spot for water recreation. Periodically, you can see water skiers skimming over the surface or skullers practicing for some rowing event. Use bus no. 506.

Several kilometers to the north is a partially defaced **Goguryeo stone tablet** (중주고구려비). Relating to a battle that took place along this river in the late 400s, when the Goguryeo Kingdom was at its height and expanding into Silla and Baekje territory, the tablet (N.T. #205) is the only such stone inscription remaining in the country from that period.

Practicalities

Around the side and behind the bus station are the Chungbuk Yeoinsuk (충북여인숙) and Daewonjang Yeogwan (대원장여관). The Poseongjang Yeogwan (보상장여관) and Myeongmunjang Yeogwan (명문장여관), newer and nicer, are set across from each other only a few steps away across the main street. Many other accommodations, as well as a multitude of restaurants, are dotted here and there between the bus station and the central downtown area which lies near Central Park. Conveniently located just down the street from the bus terminal is the second-class **Chungju Pastel Hotel** (tel. 043/848-1188), with rooms for ₩60,000–96,000. The finest place in town and just a bit pricier is the first-class **Friendly Tourist Hotel** (tel. 043/848-9900), situated south of downtown near the Hoamji Reservoir. For food, head for the areas along and near the pedestrian street and near the Central Park and post office.

Chungju has the same number, frequency, and destination of trains as Cheongju—only the times differ. Trains run to Jecheon—with one a day going farther, to Andong—and via Cheongju to Jochiwon and Daejeon—with one a day to Seoul. Bus travel is more convenient, and the terminal is more centrally located than the train station. However, due to increased traffic through its cramped inner-city quarters, the bus terminal may move to a newer part of town closer to the train station. Express buses run only to Seoul and Dong Seoul stations (₩5,700). Selected intercity bus destinations are Seoul (₩6,000), Wonju (₩4,200), Jecheon (₩3,300), Danyang (₩5,200), Cheongju (₩5,200), Suanbo (₩1,500), and Mun'gyeong (₩3,500).

City bus no. 506 runs to Tan'geum-dae and the Central Pagoda; no. 216, connects Chungju Station and the city center to Suanbo and Worak-san National Park; and no. 206, runs a back route to Songgye. A city bus also runs from in front of the bus station to the ferry terminal on the far side of the Chungju Dam. This bus doesn't always display a number but does have a sign indicating its destination. A taxi ride from town to the ferry terminal might run about ₩10,000.

CHUNGJU VICINITY

Chungju Lake 충주호

Completed in 1985, the concrete Chungju Dam is the second-largest dam in the country, but the largest concrete dam, providing electricity, irrigation, and flood control. This dam blocks the south branch of the Han River and forms a lake that winds almost 60 kilometers into the mountains, creating the largest inundated area in the country. Chungju Lake is one of two in the country with commercial ferry transportation. Ferries start from the **Chungju ferry pier** (충주나루) above the dam and run as far as Shin Danyang. A city bus with no number runs to the pier. Leaving approximately every hour from 0900 to 1600 from late spring to early fall, and four to five times a day starting at 1000 during winter, the 53 kilometers are covered in an hour and a half. All seats allow good views of the passing scenery. The trip is silky smooth over the broad lower half, but the lake narrows and squeezes between high rock cliffs and finely sculpted promontories as you approach Danyang. Other stops on the lake include the Worak pier, for access to Songgye Valley, Worak National Park, and the Mireuk-sa temple site; Cheongpung pier, near the folklore preservation village; Janghoe, closest stop to the cliffs Gudambong and Oksun-bong, two of the eight famous sites of Danyang; and Danyang pier, for Danyang town. When water is low, the ferry may not go all the way to Danyang. While more expensive than the bus between Chungju and Shin Danyang, the ferry is more scenic and a pleasant alternative. Fares from Chungju are Worak (₩6,000), Cheongpung (₩7,000), Janghoe (₩10,000), and Danyang (₩13,000).

A triple-decker excursion boat also runs round-trip from Chungju to Worak pier; the one-hour trip costs ₩6,000. Running on a regular schedule during the summer, it only goes sporadically the rest of the year. Motorboats can be hired from the Chungju, Janghoe, and Worak piers.

Cheongpung Cultural Complex
청풍문화재단지

Because of the inundation caused by the Chungju Dam, many historic and cultural properties had to be moved for preservation. A number of them were gathered together on a rise overlooking the lake, one kilometer from the town of Cheongpung, and named Cheongpung [Ch'ŏngp'ung] Folklore Preservation Site. This collection includes tile- and thatched-roof houses, Hanbyeong-nu Pavilion (T. #528), other pavilions, the Cheongpung Confucian school, Neolithic burial stones, the Cheongpung Standing Buddha image (T. #546), the stone remains of the small Mangwol Mountain Fortress wall, and an exhibition hall that displays articles of everyday use from decades past. Several restaurants, shops, and accommodations are located nearby. Open 0900–1800; ₩1,500 entrance fee. Bus from Jecheon (₩1,000) or Chungju. Ferries stop at the pier below this complex on their run between Chungju and Danyang.

Suanbo Hot Springs 수안보온천

Southeast of Chungju, on the western slope of the Sobaek Mountains, is the hot spring resort town Suanbo. While this area has been known for over 250 years, the first permanent bathhouse wasn't built until 1928. The waters here exit the earth at 53°C. Three natural springs and several drilled wells produce water for the numerous bathhouses in town—most are indoor facilities but a few have created more aesthetic outdoor pools. The valley supports farming, though Suanbo has mostly grown up around its liquid natural resource, with the attendant drinking and dancing establishments, restaurants, and brightly lit souvenir shops. Unlike Europeans, who "take the waters" or "visit the spa for a cure," Koreans generally enjoy the mineral-rich water more for the relaxation of a simple bath than for its medicinal nature. Yet those qualities are not overlooked. The water at Suanbo, as at similar hot springs on the peninsula, is credited with helping to cure skin disease, nervousness, and gastroenteric disorders.

In the vicinity are several sites of natural beauty. Five kilometers south of town is **Suok Waterfall**, where the stream tumbles over a ledge of horizontal layered rock, giving dynamic character to this wooded valley. To the southeast is **Mun'gyeong Saejae Provincial Park**, a deep and well-fortified mountain valley, once a principal route of travel between the old Gyeongsang and Chungcheong provinces. Nestled into the mountains to the east are remains of the former temple Mireuk-sa and Worak-san National Park. In the valley south of town is the small and mostly local **Suanbo Blue Valley Ski Resort**.

Suanbo is chockablock with hotels and *yeogwan*, nearly all with attached baths. The most upscale are the **Suanbo Park Hotel** (tel. 043/846-2331) and **Waikiki Suanbo Tourist Hotel** (tel. 043/846-3333), where room rates run generally ₩80,000–140,000. A notch lower are the **Suanbo Sangnok Hotel** (tel. 043/845-3500), **Royal Hotel** (tel. 043/846-0190), the **Suanbo Joseon Hotel** (tel. 043/848-8833), and others, where you can find a room from ₩35,000. Most large and modern buildings in town are *yeogwan*/bathhouses. While there are many, one is the **Shinheungjang Yeogwan** (신흥장여관) along the main street across from the post office, where rooms start at ₩28,000. With a Y.H. card, a bunk at the **Suanbo Sajomaul Youth Hostel** (tel. 043/846-0750), two kilometers west of town at the ski resort, will cost ₩9,000. The charge for a soak at any establishment is usually about ₩5,000, but may jump up to ₩10,000 for the finer hotel baths if you are not a guest there. Restaurants are as numerous as *yeogwan* in this compact community, and the bus station is conveniently located just off the highway at the north edge of town past the tourist information booth in Multang Park. Intercity bus fares from Chungju to Suanbo run ₩1,500, while buses also run to nearby provincial cities and other major cities in the country. Some city buses also run this route. Bus no. 216 from Chungju continues past Suanbo into Worak-san National Park, runs past Mireuk-saji to the trailhead for Deokju-sa, and continues on to the village of Songgye.

WORAK-SAN NATIONAL PARK
월악산국립공원

Worak-san [Wolak-san] was made a national park in 1984, and since has been expanded to the east to include several of the "Eight Sites of Danyang" and the former Geumsu-san Provincial Park, totaling 284 square kilometers. A few kilometers north of Mun'gyeong Saejae Provincial Park, Worak-san National Park straddles the spiny central mountain range of the country between Songni-san National Park and Sobaeksan National Park. Until a few years ago, this truly was a remote region, with only a few country

WORAK-SAN
NATIONAL PARK

© AVALON TRAVEL PUBLISHING, INC.

Shin
Danyang

Gu Danyang

Dodam-sambong

5

Soseonam

Haseonam

Sainam

Jungseonam

Dorak-san

Geumsu-san

Janghoe
Ferry Pier

Godam-bong

Oksun-bong

36

Sangseonam

Hwangjang-san

Daemi-san

CHEONGPUNG
CULTURAL COMPLEX

Chungju
Lake

Worak-san

Sillu-sa

Susan-ni

Bodeok-am

Worak-san

Songgye

Maitreya
Buddha Statue

Deokju-sa

East Gate

Waryong-dae

Munsu-bong

Yongha Valley

Worak-san
National
Park

GYEONGSANGBUK-DO

Deokju

South Gate

Camping

Camping

Pallangso

Pagoda

Mansu-bong

Camping

Mireuk-saji

Juheul-san

Songgye Valley

Worak
Ferry Pier

CHUNGCHEONGBUK-DO

CHUNGCHEONGBUK-DO

3

0   2 mi
0   2 km

CHUNGCHEONGBUK-DO

byways approaching its valleys. Apart from the local population, it's still relatively unknown and unfrequented even by Koreans. Here one finds an undisturbed harmony of stream, stone, and forest. The western section of this park, centered on Songgye Valley, is best reached from Chungju. The eastern section is closer to Danyang (see the Danyang and Vicinity section later in this chapter).

Regular city buses run from Chungju to Songgye (송계), passing Suanbo, Mireuk-saji, and Deokju, while intercity buses pass the Worak ferry pier on their way to Danyang. To the eastern-section sites, use city buses from Danyang. Perhaps the most unusual but not the most reliable way to the park is by ferry from Chungju to Worak pier, from where buses periodically run up to Songgye. The regular ferry runs several times a day to Shin Danyang (₩13,000), Janghoe (₩10,000), and Chungju (₩7,000), while excursion ferries depart when there are enough passengers. A handful of restaurants and accommodations are available in Deokju and Songgye villages. The park entrance fee is ₩1,300.

Mireuk-saji 미륵사지

A dozen kilometers east of Suanbo, at the upper end of Songgye Valley, is the temple site, Mireuk-saji [Mirŭk-saji]. Today, only stone objects remain to tell of its existence. Legend claims that during the first years of the Goryeo Dynasty, immediately after the dissolution of the Silla Kingdom, former Silla Prince Maui and Princess Deokju left Gyeongju for the Diamond Mountains, to embark upon a secluded religious life. On the way, they stopped in these mountains and had the temple Mireuk-sa constructed. It flourished for years, but eventually lapsed into decay. In 1977, the site was excavated and its terraced courtyard tidied up by an archaeological team from Chungju University. The most impressive object here, a 10-meter-tall Mireuk Buddha (T. #96), occupies an exposed sanctuary on the top terrace. Carved in the round from six blocks of stone, it's one of the few freestanding stone Buddha figures in the country. The figure's body is squarish and shallowly defined; though flat of feature, its head is obviously carved

with greater skill, possibly at a different time and/or by different craftsmen. A thin mortarboard hat balances on top. The figure's upper half is turned slightly to the left, as if nudged by ground movement over the centuries. Unlike the body stones, its head is spotless, yet villagers say it hasn't been purposefully cleaned. What mystery, then, keeps this head bright and incredibly unblemished? The surrounding stone walls have several alcoves, presumably for religious statuary. It's surmised that a wooden roof was once constructed over the figure, now only shadowed by a canopy of leaves. Foundation stones in front suggest that wooden walls enclosed the sacred spot. This building was undoubtedly the temple's main hall, the statue its central object of veneration; this would resemble the older and more revered Seokguram cave hermitage, which sits high on the mountain above Gyeongju, the ancient Silla capital. Uncharacteristically, and perhaps the only example of such in Korea, the overall directional lineup of this temple compound and the remains of its main hall are to the north rather than the south.

Also on this site is a six-meter-tall, five-tier stone pagoda (T. #95). Slightly thick in its support pieces and somewhat damaged, it's made in the same style as the Central Pagoda west of Chungju. Although thrusting skyward, it's much less graceful and lacks the finesse of its newer brother. Other objects on the site include a foundation stone for a memorial stela and two lanterns. The huge foundation stone is in typical tortoise shape, but the carving is done with little flair or decoration. Expressionless, the tortoise looks like it's springing directly out of the rock, half emerged, frozen. One of the lanterns is predominantly squarish, its squat pedestal supporting an airy light receptacle. The other, taller and more slender, is octagonal. Additional terraces, carved stone figures, and foundation stones remain to give one an idea of the size of this former temple compound. This pastoral historic site (H.S. #317) was 1,000 years ago an active, religiously significant temple of the early Goryeo Dynasty, and near a major travel route between the southern Honam region and the Goryeo capital at Gaeseong. In 1952, the small temple

Segye-sa was constructed to the side of these remains, and more recently shops and *minbak* have been constructed for visitors.

Park Sites and Hiking

From Mireuk-sa, the road leads down the Songgye Valley toward Chungju Lake. About four kilometers down, past Pallangso, Waryong-dae, and wide rock plates over which the river flows (pretty picnic spots), is the south gate of the old Worak Mountain Fortress. Only the stone arch of this gate remains, from which a section of the fortress wall trails up into the trees on the hillside. Down the valley in the village of Songgye are the remains of the north gate. A short distance from the south gate, up a secondary road to the west, a stone pagoda (T. #94) sprouts from a field indicating the site of a long-since-disappeared temple. Originally of nine tiers, its four remaining levels are supported by four lion figures. From the small village of Deokju, where there are a few shops and *minbak,* a trail leads off to the east going into Deokju Valley. This is the major trail into the mountain. About one kilometer up this valley stands the east gate of the old fortress. Constructed in 1256, the fortress walls once presented a formidable defense for Goryeo troops. One-half kilometer farther along the valley's clear stream is the small, heavily painted temple **Deokju-sa** [Tŏkju-sa] (덕주사). Originally from the Silla Dynasty, this temple is undergoing a complete change. A whole new compound is being cut into the hillside, with heavy stone retaining walls and steps, and all new buildings erected. A 20-minute walk above this temple, carved in bas-relief on a flat rock face, is a figure of the Maitreya Buddha (T. #406). Legend relates that this Buddha's facial features were sculpted to resemble those of Princess Deokju, namesake of this valley and the temple below. The path follows a steep incline to the main ridge, where there is a helipad, and from there on up to the top of the mountain (1,094 meters), where you can see Juheul-san in Mun'gyeong Saejae Provincial Park to the south and Chungju Lake to the north. Aside from the *minbak* at Deokju and Songgye, the **Woraksan Youth Hostel** (tel. 043/ 651-7004), just a five-

minute walk east of the Worak ferry pier, has beds for ₩10,000 a person. The two camping sites in the park (₩3,000) are located at Deokju and halfway between there and Mireuk-saji.

Trails go down three of the mountain valleys from here. The trail to the west leads to Songgye, the most convenient way out of the park. The trail to the east goes past Silleuk-sa to exit on a back road, and the northern path runs down the ridge first to Bodeok-am and then out to the village of Susan-ni by the lake. A walk to the top of the mountain and down any valley should take five to six hours. In the eastern section of the park, a two-hour trail leads up to Dorak-san from Sangseonam, and a moderate hike from a roadside trailhead leads to Oksun-bong from near the Janghoe ferry pier.

DANYANG AND VICINITY 단양

As a result of the inundation caused by the Chungju Dam, numerous changes have taken place in Danyang [Tanyang] since 1985: the creation of Shin ("New") Danyang, the near abandonment of Gu ("Old") Danyang, a new expressway, the rerouting of highway and rail routes, and construction of a new train station. Because of the rising water level, the old town has shrunk in size, yet a few remnants of this gray community still persist. Set in the middle of a large coal- and limestone-mining area, the cement and coal briquette factories contributed to the old town's industrial image, not to mention its dust problem. **Shin Danyang** (신단양) (now often simply referred to as Danyang), on the other hand, is a young and rapidly developing, if somewhat sterile, lakeside community several kilometers uplake. Graced with a new location that is somewhat confined by mountains at the bend in the river, new buildings, neatly laid-out streets, a handsome arch bridge, and fine scenery, it's in the process of developing a personality.

Set along the waterfront road is the Shin Danyang ferry pier. Up from the waterfront are several square blocks of businesses, government offices, accommodations, restaurants, shops, and a market. At the townside end of the bridge is the bus station; the pier is about 200 meters down

© ROBERT NILSEN

village near Danyang

the road. The town stretches to the west past the blufftop Sogeumjeong Park, and follows the curve of the lake toward the railroad line and a second highway bridge. Connected by city bus, the Danyang train station is on the far side of this bridge, several kilometers from the new town center toward the old town. The Jungang Expressway passes just to the west of Danyang as it cuts through the center of the country; it has opened this community to express-bus traffic.

Danyang is situated between Worak-san National Park and Sobaek-san National Park. The eastern section of Worak-san National Park reaches very close to Danyang, and within its boundary are five of the eight scenic sites of Danyang. Just outside of Sobaek-san National Park are well-known limestone caves, a Goguryeo Dynasty mountain fortress, and a temple that is the headquarters of one of the major sects of Korean Buddhism.

Practicalities

Many accommodations in Shin Danyang are located up from the lake between the ferry pier and the bus station. Start by checking the Cheoniljang Yeogwan (천일장여관) or Busan Yeogwan (부산여관). Restaurants, tearooms, and drinking halls are also found here and along the main street which is a few blocks uphill. For a bit better accommodation, head for the Danyang Tourist Hotel (단양관광호텔), which is located just outside of town near the new highway bridge.

Ten trains a day—in both directions—pass through Danyang, traveling to Seoul Cheongnyangni, Jecheon, Andong, Dong Daegu, and Busan. Selected intercity-bus destinations are Jecheon (₩2,100), Wonju (₩5,100), Chungju (₩5,200), Guin-sa (₩2,100), Huibang-sa (₩2,100), and Andong (₩6,900). City buses, which start near the bus terminal along the waterfront, run to all eight of the Danyang Palgyeong sites, the nearby caves, Guin-sa, and Huibang-sa. Several times a day, a ferry from the Shin Danyang ferry pier (신단양선착장) connects Danyang to Chungju (₩13,000), stopping at Cheongpung (₩7,000) and Janghoe (₩3,000) on the way. When the lake's water level is low, the ferry will not run as far up as

Danyang. Excursion ferries also ply the upper part of this lake from the Shin Danyang pier when water levels are sufficient and when there is enough demand. Contact the pier office for additional information.

Danyang Palgyeong

Clear streams, odd-shaped rock outcrops, and riverside cliffs are some of what the vicinity offers. Perhaps the most famous attractions to the area are the "Eight Sites." Called Danyang Palgyeong, these riverside rock formations are roughly grouped into three areas. South of town, up a serpentine valley, are **Haseonam**, **Jungseonam**, and **Sangseonam**, stretches of a swift stream where wide rock plates and huge boulders have been scoured white by pebbles on the riverbottom. Jungseonam is loveliest, a perfect place to picnic, sunbathe, or dip into the cool mountain water. Jungseonam, and Sangseonam are within Woraksan National Park so you will have to pay the entrance fee to see these two spots. Below Haseonam, and not considered part of these eight sights, is **Soseonam**, a pretty rock face at the turn of the river. Four kilometers down an adjoining road is Sainam, a tree-topped cliff rising from the stream.

In the second area, Oksun-bong and Gudambong, lakeside bluffs that rise precipitously from the water, stand in close proximity about 10 kilometers west of Shin Danyang and just through the gorge west of Janghoe ferry pier. Excursion ferries ply this picturesque narrow stretch of the river from the ferry pier.

Dodam-sambong [Todam-sambong] and Seong-mun make up the third section. The most famous and photographed of the eight sites is **Dodam-sambong** (도담삼봉), a group of three pointed "peaks" piercing the placid lake three kilometers around the bend from Shin Danyang. A traditional tile-roof pavilion nestles on the middle rise. Largest of the three, it's romantically referred to as the "husband peak"; the peak to the north is called "wife peak" while that to the south is the "concubine peak." When the lake is low, this stretch reverts to a lazy river as it was for eons before the building of the dam. Part of a rock stratum calculated to be over a billion years old, and one of the few examples of this exposed

ancient rock, these peaks can be seen from either the bus or train. A small group of restaurants with ample parking and a small pier have been constructed directly across from these peaks. Sightseeing boats cruise from a dock here during fine weather and there is a ferry to the village on the far side. On the hillside above this little community sits a small pavilion where you have a fine view down onto these peaks in the river and distant views of the Sobaek Mountains to the southeast. Around 300 meters farther upriver, on the cliff above the lake, is Seong-mun ("Stone Gate")—the last of the eight sites—a simple stone arch that forms an opening on the hillside. All the river sights can be reached by city bus from Danyang, but it follows a different route than the ferry to Chungju, which passes Gudambong and Oksun-bong.

Caves

Discovered in the early 1970s, **Gosu-donggul** [Kosu-donggul] (고수동굴) is the area's best-known cave. A series of vertical and horizontal caverns, serpentine corridors, curtained walls, fluted columns, canopies of stalactites, and upthrusting stalagmites, this 1,300-meter cave (N.M. #256) is well worth the entrance fee of ₩3,000; open 0900–1700. Overall, it's more pleasing than Seongnyu-gul, outside Uljin, and has a greater variety of formations than Gossidonggul, south of Yeongwol. Many tourist shops and restaurants have popped up here. This cave is about one kilometer east of Shin Danyang.

Four kilometers farther up this country road is **Cheondong-donggul** [Ch'ŏndong-donggul] (전동동굴); ₩2,600 entrance. Discovered in 1977, this 300-meter-long cave, basically a vertical drop into the ground, is a lighter gold than its big brother down the road. The village below marks the end of the city bus line and the start of a 12-kilometer trail to Biro-bong, highest peak in Sobaek-san National Park.

In the same vicinity, but up a different road, is **Nodong-donggul** (노동동굴); ₩3,000 entrance. This outstanding cave (N.M. #262), the most recently discovered, has a total length of over one kilometer, a 300-meter drop, and a 40- to 50-degree declivity. An extensive stairway and railing system makes the descent possible. Along with the usual limestone formations, this cave also has some novel variety: encrusted lines of rime, cave pearls, and bubbly formations that look like huge bunches of grapes. Its most spectacular sights are near the bottom.

City buses run from Shin Danyang to all three caves.

Guin-sa 구인사

Northeast of Shin Danyang, near the rural community of Yeongchun, is Guin-sa [Kuin-sa]. Located in a claustrophobic valley on the north slope of Sobaek-san, this temple is the headquarters of the Cheontae sect of Korean Buddhism. Meaning "Salvation Benevolence Temple," Guin-sa was founded in 1945 by the monk Sangwol Wongak, when the Cheontae order was reestablished—after centuries of non-existence in Korea—following the precepts of the Chinese monk Jijang Daesa's elucidation of the *Lotus Sutra*, with emphasis on the integration of both the meditative and doctrinal elements of Buddhism. This group of 34 buildings is set so close together that they are nearly stacked one on top of another up this steep and narrow valley. Because the temple was founded so recently, all the buildings here have been constructed since the 1960s and most are made of cement. Although the cement is not as pleasing as wood, traditional designs and decoration have been employed. While there are two front gates, numerous dormitories, an administration hall, and several halls dedicated to various bodhisattvas, the focus is the five-story main hall, the only such building in the country. The main worship hall is the top level, extremely elaborate inside and out. A huge gilt Buddha, flanked by two large bodhisattvas, sits on its broad altar. Notice the spike-like mandala behind each figure and the highly carved mural behind the main altar. Additional painted murals adorn the walls and ceiling.

High on the ridge above the temple compound is the mound tomb of the temple's founder. An object of reverence, this tomb is unusual as most Buddhist monks are cremated after death, and the *sarisa* of important and in-fluential monks are placed in a *sari budo* for preservation.

Although relatively new, the Cheontae sect is gaining in popularity among Korean Buddhists and the number of adherents is growing—there are more than 300 branch temples and teaching seminaries throughout the country. On a slow day, several hundred visitors go to Guin-sa; on days of celebration or teaching, several thousand may visit. The big celebration is Buddha's birthday, when the compound dazzles with paper lanterns. To cater to the crowds, a cluster of shops, restaurants, *minbak*, and a bus station has sprung up below the temple.

Guin-sa can be reached by bus directly from the nearby communities of Shin Danyang (₩2,100), Jecheon (₩3,480), Yeongwol (₩2,200), and Yeongchun (₩650), as well as from Seoul, Cheongju, and Busan.

Ondal Sanseong 온달산성

Capping a riverside hill between Yeongchun and Guin-sa are the stone remains of Ondal Sanseong, a tiny mountain fortress from the Three Kingdoms period (pre-A.D. 660). This fortification (H.S. #264) was built by General Ondal of the Goguryeo Dynasty, who was charged with blocking the advance of the invading Silla army during its march north to gain control of the Han River basin. Unfortunately, food and supplies ran out, and the Goguryeo soldiers were eventually overcome. There is little to be seen here now except for the walls of neatly piled, flat stones. A 20-minute walk or a short bus ride out of Yeongchun brings you to the Ondal National Tourist Resort village below the fortress. Follow the path through the village and up the hill to a modern pavilion, and continue up the improved path to the fortress walls; entrance ₩2,500. From this hilltop vantage, you have a wonderful view of the river turning, riverside agricultural plains, and Sobaek-san in the distance to the south. Near the village at riverside is the entrance to Ondal cave (N.M. #261), which can be entered for only a short ways.

Other points of historical interest in the immediate area are the Yeongchun Confucian Academy, in the town of Yeongchun, and the three-tiered, Silla-style Hyangsan stone pagoda (T. #405), some kilometers down river.

In 1897, the intrepid traveler Isabella Bird traveled through the Korean Peninsula. One of her jaunts was up the Han River, and she was able to get as far as Yeongchun before returning to Seoul. At that time there was commercial boat traffic on the river as far as Danyang, but smaller boats could even make it to this village.

Jecheon 제천

North of Danyang and much larger is Jecheon [Chech'ŏn], the third city in the province. A transportation hub and growing commercial center, Jecheon is known for few historic or culturally significant places except for Euirimji [Ŭirimji]. **Euirimji** (의림지) is the oldest known man-made reservoir in the country. From the Three Kingdoms period, this pond is shallow, about two kilometers around, and lined with weeping willows and other trees. It's been reworked several times throughout its history. The last major renovation took place in 1973 following extensive flooding and damage the year before. While not an extraordinary place, it is pleasant enough for a stroll around the perimeter on a warm summer evening. Two small pavilions capture spots along the bank, and the pond itself is set next to a natural stream that has a small waterfall just past the reservoir. To reach this ancient pond, take city bus no. 301 or 306 (₩600) about four kilometers north along the main street from downtown Jecheon toward Saemyeong University. There is a larger and modern reservoir farther up the valley.

One of the other significant sites nearby is the **Holy Site of Baeron**. This is where one of the early Korean Catholic Fathers, Choe Yang-eop, ran a seminary and where he was later killed.

Resources

Glossary

Note: Additional terms for Korean food and drink are listed in the Food section of the On the Road chapter.

aak—ritual Confucian ceremonial music
-am—Buddhist hermitage
Amita—Amithaba, the Buddha of Infinite Light
anju—a snack, finger food
Arhat—disciple of Buddha, one aspiring to become a bodhisattva
Arirang—most popular Korean folk song, with over 2,000 different lyrics and more than 50 melodic variations
aspara—mythical celestial figures, often painted inside Buddhist halls or molded into temple bells

baduk—(Japanese *Go*); board game using black and white stones
baegae—firm cylindrical pillow filled with rice or wheat hulls
baegil—100th day celebration for a baby
baeksam—ginseng in its root form with skin and tiny hairs removed
baksu—male shaman
banchan—side dishes
bap—boiled rice
-bawi—huge rock
biguni—female Buddhist monk
bodhisattva—in Buddhism, those who have attained enlightenment, but who have stayed in this world to help all sentient beings escape the cycles of suffering and death
bojagi—large square of cloth used to wrap and carry items
bomul—designated Treasure
-bong—mountain peak
boricha—roasted barley tea
bosal—bodhisattva; title of lay female attendant at a Buddhist temple
budo—stone reliquary for the cremated remains of a distinguished Buddhist monk (also called *sari budo*)
bulgogi—marinated, broiled beef strips
Bul-gyo—Buddhism
buncheong—casual, earth stoneware from the Joseon Dynasty
bunjae—bonsai
byo—milled rice

cha—tea
chaemyeon—"face," dignity, self-respect, honor, reputation
chajeon nori—a large-group game involving two massive pole and rope "tanks"
chapsang—roof-ridge animal figurines on Joseon Dynasty buildings. Of Chinese origin, they are guardians against evil and fire.
Cheondo-gyo—an indigenous religion, called the "Heavenly Way"; blend of shaman, Confucian, and Buddhist beliefs, formulated in 1860 by Ch'oe Je-u and originally known as *Donghak*
Chilseong—"Seven Star God," spirit of shamanistic origin, often enshrined at Buddhist temples with Sanshin and Dokseong
chorten—a stupa or stylized pagoda, particularly of Tibetan design, that is generally mounded in shape with a spire on top
Chuseok—autumn harvest festival. Along with lunar new year, the most important traditional holiday

dabang—tearoom; also *dashil* or *chatjip*
-dae—bluff or rock outcrop of size
daegeum—transverse bamboo flute
Daehan Minguk—official name of the Republic of Korea
Daejong-gyo—indigenous Korean religion that honors Dan'gun, the mythical founder of the Korean nation
dancheong—art of painting geometric and floral designs and human figures with natural pigments in bright colors on buildings and murals

-dang—small traditional-style structure

Dan'gun—mythical founder (2333 B.C.) of the Korean nation

Dano—traditional spring holiday held on the 5th day of the 5th lunar month to celebrate the end of planting

deva—a diety or god

-do—island

-Do—province

Do-gyo—Taoism, also called *Seondo-gyo*

dojagi—utilitarian earthenware pottery

dojang—seal (stamp) used in place of a signature; a gym or building for the practice of a martial art

Dokseong—"Lonely Arhat," a spirit of shamanistic origin now enshrined at many Buddhist temples, often in the company of Sanshin and Chilseong

dol—first birthday

dolharubang—volcanic "stone grandfather" figures of Jeju-do

dolmen—prehistoric grave indicated by a flat stone covering supported by upright stone pieces

-dong—city ward; rural sub-*myeon* area

Donghak—"Eastern learning," a combination of Confucian, Buddhist, and shaman beliefs

dubu—bean curd (Japanese: tofu)

eum/yang—negative/positive cosmological forces (Chinese: yin/yang)

-eup—town, with a population of 20,000-50,000 people

-ga—"block" of a street

gaeksa—guesthouse for official, traveling government employees during the Joseon Dynasty

gagok—long lyrical song with ensemble accompaniment, which in its entirety may last several hours

-gak—pavilion, small open-sided structure

gan—traditional structural measurement delineating area inside four posts, equal to about four square meters

gang—river

ganggangsullae—a gently swirling circle dance

performed by females

gasa—a slow narrative song

gat—wide-brim horsehair hat worn by males, usually black

gayageum—12-string zither

geobukseon—metal-clad warship created during the 1590s

geukjang—large theater or cinema

geun—dry measure of 600 grams

geune—long rope swing

gibun—one's mood or inner feeling

gimchi—a type of seasoned and fermented vegetable dish

gimjang—*gimchi*-making

gisaeng—female hostess/entertainer, similar to Japanese *geisha*

gomungo—six-string zither

gongwon—park; *gungnip gongwon*: national park

Goryeo cheongja—Goryeo Dynasty celadon; modern celadon made to approximate Goryeo Dynasty celadon

gosok bus—express bus

-gu—district of a large city

gujeolpan—sectioned, octagonal appetizer tray

gukbo—designated National Treasure

-gul (donggul)—grotto, cavern, (cave)

-gun—county

-gung—palace

gungdo—traditional Korean archery using a short double-curve bow and bamboo arrows

gusul—round red object (often with a tiny flame decoration) held in the hand of a Buddha statue or in the mouth of a dragon, representing the "flaming jewel" of Buddhist truth

gut—a shaman ceremony

Gwaneum (Gwanseeum Bosal)—Goddess of Mercy, Avaloketesvara (Chinese: Kwan Yin; Japanese: Kannon)

gyegok—mountain valley

-gyo—religion (e.g. Bul-gyo: Buddhism); bridge (e.g. Gumcheon-gyo)

hae—sea

haegeum—vertical two-string fiddle without a fingerboard

haenyeo—women divers of Jeju-do

haetae—mythical animal (resembling a lion) reputedly able to eat fire; set to the front of important government buildings, palace and temple halls, and tombs for protection

hanbok—traditional Korean clothing

haneuiwon—herbal (Oriental) medicine doctor's office

han'geul—Korean script

hanja—Chinese characters used in Korea

hanyak—herbal (Oriental) medicine

hanyakbang—herbal (Oriental) medicine pharmacy

hapgido—(aikido) martial art similar to taekwondo

hapseung—shared taxi ride

-ho—class of trains

hongsal-mun—"red arrow gate"; red wooden gate constructed of two posts and a lattice lintel set at the entrance to royal graves and Confucian shrines

hongsam—an unpeeled and steamed variety of *insam* (ginseng)

hun—globular clay flute

hwamunseok—mats, screens, and baskets woven of rush leaves, often using dyed leaves to make floral, animal, and Chinese character designs

hwangap—celebration marking ones 60th birthday, the end of one "cycle" of life based on the Eastern zodiac

hwarang—("flower youth") elite military, social, and religious group of young men of the Silla Dynasty

hwatu—card game using 48 small plastic cards—12 suits of four, each suit representing a month

hyanggyo—public-funded Confucian school and shrine of the Joseon and Goryeo dynasties set up to train the scion of the landed *yangban* class

ibul—sleeping quilt

Ijo baekja—Joseon Dynasty white porcelain

Ilju-mun—first gate along the entrance path to large Buddhist temples, characterized by a broad roof structure set on stout posts

insam—ginseng

inwang—mythological temple guards, either painted on a door or carved in the round and set at one of the temple gates

jaebol—family-run, industrial conglomerates

janggi—Korean board game similar to chess

janggo—hourglass-shaped drum

jangma—heavy summer rains

jangseok—handmade metal fittings for traditional-style Korean furniture

jangseung—totem poles, usually wood but sometimes stone, topped by stylized male and female heads and inscribed with Chinese characters, set at a villages entrance to protect the village from harm and evil spirits

-je (-che)—festival

-jeon—large Buddhist temple hall

jeonbul—payment in advance

jeongak—slow and ritualistic classical court music

jeongshik—full-course Korean meal of rice, soup, fish and/or meat, and side dishes, *table d'hôte*, (also called *hanjeongshik*)

jeosuji—reservoir

jesa—Confucian ancestor memorial ceremony, usually performed on the anniversary of the death, on *Chuseok,* and the first day of the lunar new year

jige—wooden A-frame carrying device with straps shouldered like a backpack, used principally by farmers and men who carry goods through narrow market streets

jikhaeng bus—intercity bus, limited stops

jing—metal gong

jultarigi—tug-of-war

jung—central, middle

Koreana Tripitaka—the Buddhist canon of literature, carved onto over 80,000 wood printing blocks and stored at Haein-sa; includes sutras, commentaries, and rules governing the lives of Buddhist monks

li (ni, ri)—distance equaling about 400 meters

ma—length of cloth equaling 91.4 centimeters

maedeup—tied decorative knots and tassels

maekju—beer

makkeolli—milky-white fermented rice wine

meolmiyak—seasickness medicine

minbak—private home that rents rooms

minyo—traditional folk songs of love, despair, and work

Mireuk—Maitreya; Buddha of the Future

mogyoktang—public bathhouse

moktak—hollow wooden gong used in Buddhist prayer recitations

mudang—shaman priestess

mugunghwa—rose of Sharon hibiscus; unofficial national flower of Korea

-mun—gate, door

-myo—shrine; commoners grave

-myeon—rural township with a population below 20,000

Nahan—disciples of Buddha, often shown as 16 or 500 figurines enshrined in a Buddhist hall

najeon chilgi—mother-of-pearl lacquerware

nam—male

neolddwigi—Korean seesaw

-neung—royal tomb

-no (-ro, -lo)—street

nogo—round drum

nongak—traditional farmers' music characterized by percussive instruments (drums and gongs) and a shrill flute, often accompanied by spirited dance movements

norigae—decorative pendent hung from the bow at the front of a woman's dress

nunchi—sense, intuition, ability to "read" a situation

oncheon—hotspring

ondol—floors in Korean homes heated by hot air (or water) running through flues beneath the floor

onggi—utilitarian brown earthenware pottery; also called *tojagi*

orakshil—amusement arcade

pansori—classical and lengthy, dramatic sung and spoken opera-like narrative, usually accompanied by a drummer

piri—small vertical bamboo flute

pojang macha—movable food cart/drinkery set up at streetside in the evening

pungsu jiriseol—geomantic theory of correct placement and location (Chinese: feng shui)

pyojunmal—the "standard" dialect of modern spoken Korean

pyeong—a measurement of area slightly less than four square meters

pyeon'gyeong—stone chimes

-ri (-ni, -li)—rural village, hamlet, or cluster of houses

-ru (-nu, -lu)—pavilion

-ryeong (-lyeong)—mountain pass

-sa—Buddhist temple

sadang—shaman shrine

saekdong—multicolored, striped cloth often incorporated into *hanbok*

Saemaul—"New Village," a countrywide community self-help economic program

saeng—gourd panpipe

saetakso—laundry

sajeokji—designated historical site

-saji—former temple site

samhan saon—winter weather pattern characterized by three cold days followed by four successive warmer days

samul nori—("the play of four instruments"), energetic percussion musicians that often includes gymnastic dance. Instruments include the hourglass drum, round drum, and large and small gongs.

-san—mountain

sanjang—mountain hut

sanjo—improvisational solo instrumental music, sometimes an accompaniment to lyrical or narrative song

sansam—wild variety of *insam* (ginseng)

sanseong—mountain fortress

Sanshin—"Mountain Spirit" of shamanistic origin, now enshrined at Buddhist temples, often in the company of the spirits Dokseong and Chilseong

sari (sarisa)—calcified remains of different sizes and colors found in the ashes after cremation of monks and holy men; preserved at temples, often in a reliquary container kept in a *sari budo*

sari budo—stone container of calcified human remains, sometimes called *sari tap*

Seohak—"Western learning"; refers to Western thought, particularly Catholicism, which filtered into the country during the 18th century

Seokgamoni—Siddhartha Gautama, Buddha of the Present Age

seon—Buddhist meditative practice (Japanese: Zen; Chinese: chan)

seowon—private Confucian schools of the Joseon Dynasty; village-level schools were called *seodang*

seowon seongchwitap—rock piles or conical towers erected as a prayer or supplication for good fortune, most often found on the way to a Buddhist temple

seunim—male Buddhist monk

-shi—city, with a population more than 50,000

shijang—market

shikdang—restaurant

shinseon—mythical Taoist beings of supernatural power

sijo—lyrical song from a three-line (or multiple) Korean poem, or that poem

Silhak—"practical learning" or "pragmatism," an intellectual movement, a reaction against the rigid Confucianism of the 18th century

soju—clear potato liquor

somokjang—traditional Korean furniture

ssal—unmilled rice

ssireum—traditional Korean wrestling

taegeuk—yin/yang symbol (as in the red/blue circle on the Korean flag) of two commas swirling in on themselves, symbolizing eternal duality, the union of opposites, balance and harmony

taegeukgi—Korean national flag

taekwondo—Korean martial art similar to karate

taekyeon—ancient martial art, predecessor of *taekwondo*

taepyeongso—conical wooden oboe

talchum—masked dance drama popular with

the lower classes during the Joseon Dynasty, often performed at cultural folk festivals today

tap—pagoda

usnisa—head protuberance on statues of the Buddha, symbolizing wisdom

wang—king

wanhaeng **bus**—rural bus that stops upon request

won—Korean monetary unit (₩)

Wonbul-gyo—indigenous Korean religion founded in 1924 that incorporates basic Buddhist beliefs and pragmatic social doctrines

wondumak—temporary shelters set up alongside agricultural fields

yakguk—(also yakbang) pharmacy

yaksu (teo)—mineral water (spring)

yangban—most often used to denote upper-class landed gentry of Joseon Dynasty; from Goryeo Dynasty denoting the two groups of civil servants: civilian and military. When used in modern speech, it means something akin to a respected male elder.

yeo (nyeo)—female

yeogwan—inn, traditional Korean accommodation

yeoinsuk—low-class inn

yeondae—Joseon-era beacon site for signaling emergencies

yeontan—pressed coal briquettes formerly used for home heating and cooking fuel

yo—sleeping mattress

yudo—martial art (Japanese: judo)

Yu-gyo—Confucianism

yujeokji—designated historical site

yut—traditional Korean games involving tossing four wooden sticks

yuwonji—recreation area

Korean Language Basics
국어어휘

Speaking Korean

The new government-instituted Romanization system not only changed the spelling of some Korean letters but also got rid of the apostrophe and diacritical marks above vowels. These marks are included in the following explanation because they are still often used and seen throughout the country, and words with these spellings still appear in this book.

The consonants g/k, d/t, b/p, and j/ch are, for all practical purposes, interchangeable; you will see the same word spelled with one or the other, depending on the system of transliteration. The same is true of the vowels and diphthongs eo/ŏ, yeo/ŏ, eu/ŭ, weo/wo, and eui/ŭi. The following examples will illustrate these differences: Gyeongju/Kyŏngju, Daegu/Taegu, Busan-Pusan, Jeonju/Chŏnju, Euiseong/Ŭisŏng, and Geumsan/Kŭmsan.

A few points to remember when speaking: With g/k, d/t, b/p, and j/ch sounds, the "hard" sounds, no matter the spelling, are the initial position sounds of a phoneme, while the "soft" sounds, no matter the spelling, are the medial position sounds. The s sound becomes sh before an ee sound, as in shin (new), but is written only as s in the new Romanization system. An "o" symbol has no sound when in the initial position and a ng sound in the final position. In the McCune-Reischauer (M-R) system, the apostrophe, as in the name Mokp'o, indicates an aspirated sound (sound made by quickly released breath, as the English "h," or as the English "p," "t," or "k" after a stopped consonant)—don't be self-conscious about really letting go of some air! It's also used to distinguish between an "ng" sound, and a final "n" sound in one phoneme followed by a "g" sound in the initial position of the next phoneme, as in the word han'gŭl. Although not part of the new government Romanization system, the apostrophe in this case has been kept in this book to make it more obvious for pronunciation purposes. Tense (double) consonants, as in ttaettaero, are all stressed (more so than in English stressed sounds), except in the final position, when they are unstressed and stopped. The r/l sound, as in Miryang, is made much like a non-initial Spanish r. An r sound followed by another r sound and an n sound followed or preceded by an r sound yield an l sound (Han rim becomes Hallim); the r and l sounds become an n sound when preceded by another consonant other than n (Dam ra becomes Damna). Before the nasal consonants n and m, and the r consonant, all non-nasal consonants in turn become nasal (hap nida becomes hamnida). In the final position, d, s, j, ch, and t sounds are pronounced as unreleased or stopped d (stopped consonans are formed by completely stopping the release of breath before the pronunciation of the following sound), the r sound becomes an l sound, the aspirate p becomes an unreleased p sound, and the tense s becomes a glottalized d sound (a glottal sound is made by a short closure of the glottis, as the "tt" in "bottle" in some English dialects). In the final position of the syllable, where two different consonants occur together, the sound of the "stronger" consonant will prevail and the weaker will be silent; nasal sounds are stronger than stopped sounds, and these in turn are stronger than the fricatives s, j, ch and h (a fricative is a sound made by forcing breath through a narrow opening formed by the mouth). Vowel sounds are constant and always pronounced the same. They tend to be run together when spoken rapidly.

Pronunciation Chart 발음

CONSONANTS 자음

Korean	New Romanization System	M-R Romanization	Pronunciation Guide
ㄱ	g (k)	k (g)	guide, kind
ㄴ	n	n	none
ㄷ	d (t)	t (d)	day, to
ㄹ	r (l), (n), [l]	r (l),(n) [l]	roll
ㅁ	m	m	meal
ㅂ	b (p)	p (b)	been, pen
ㅅ	s	s (sh) [t]	soup, dish
ㅇ	silent [ng]	silent [ng]	
ㅈ	j [t]	ch (j) [t]	jam, champ
ㅊ	ch [t]	ch' [t]	church
ㅋ	k	k'	kitchen
ㅌ	t	t' [t]	tag
ㅍ	p	p' [p]	plop
ㅎ	h	h	him
ㄲ	kk	kk (gg)	gum
ㄸ	tt	tt (dd)	duck
ㅃ	pp	pp (bb)	bin
ㅆ	ss	ss [t]	super
ㅉ	jj	jj	jolt

VOWELS 모음

Korean	New Romanization System	M-R Romanization	Pronunciation Guide
아	a	a	father
야	ya	ya	yacht
어	eo	ŏ (eo)	son
여	yeo	yŏ (yeo)	young
오	o	o	so
요	yo	yo	yoke
우	u	u	moon
유	yu	yu	you
으	eu	ŭ	put *
이	i	i	be
의	ui	ŭi (eui)	week *
애	ae	ae	hat
얘	yae	yae	yam
에	e	e	bait
예	ye	ye	yea
와	wa	wa	want
왜	wae	wae	wax
외	oe	oe	way
워	wo	wo (weo)	won
웨	we	we	went
위	wi	wi	we

( )—alternate pronunciation
[ ]—sound when in final position of syllable
'—indicates an aspirate sound

double consonants are stressed
*—lips slightly drawn apart, not rounded

Korean Numbers

Koreans use two systems for counting from one to 99, and one system from 100 onward. One system uses words of Korean origin while the other uses words of Chinese origin. It's all categorical and extremely confusing until you learn which system is used with which concepts. Simply speaking, for the traveler's use, Korean numbers are used with time (o'clock), hours, months, age, and counting things; numbers of Chinese origin are used with money, minutes, names of months, years, and floor numbers. The decimal system is used with Arabic numerals. Occasionally, Chinese characters are used for prices in Chinese restaurants. Ordinal numbers also use words of Korean and Chinese origin.

Number Chart 수자

Korean		Arabic	Chinese		
Korean	Romanized		Korean	Romanized	Hanja
하나	hana	1	일	il	一
둘	dul	2	이	i (ee)	二
셋	set	3	삼	sam	三
넷	net	4	사	sa	四
다섯	daseot	5	오	o	五
여섯	yeoseot	6	육	yuk	六
일곱	ilgop	7	칠	chil	七
여덟	yeodeol	8	팔	pal	八
아홉	ahop	9	구	gu	九
열	yeol	10	십	ship	十
열하나	yeol hana	11	십일	ship il	十一
열둘	yeol tul	12	십이	ship i	十二
스물	seumul	20	이십	i ship	二十
스물하나	seumul hana	21	이십일	i ship il	二十一
서른	seoreun	30	삼십	sam ship	三十
마흔	maheu	40	사십	sa ship	四十
쉰	shwin	50	오십	o ship	五十
예순	yeseun	60	육십	yuk ship	六十
일흔	irheun	70	칠십	chil ship	七十
여든	yeodeun	80	팔십	pal ship	八十
아흔	aheun	90	구십	gu ship	九十
		100	백	baek	一百
		1,000	천	cheon	千
		10,000	만	man	一萬
		100,000	십만	shimman	十萬
		1,000,000	백만	baengman	一百萬
		100,000,000	일억	il eok	一億

ORDINAL NUMBERS 서수

Korean		Arabic	Chinese	
Korean	Romanized		Korean	Romanized
첫째	cheot jjae	first	제일	je il
둘째	dul jjae	second	제이	je i
세째	set jjae	third	제삼	je sam
네째	net jjae	fourth	제사	je sa
다섯째	taseot jjae	fifth	제오	je o
여섯째	yeoseot jjae	sixth	제육	je yuk
일곱째	ilgop jjae	seventh	제칠	je chil
여덟째	yeodeol jjae	eighth	제팔	je pal
아홉째	ahop jjae	ninth	제구	je gu
열째	yeol jjae	tenth	제십	je ship

Vocabulary 용어

ENGLISH	ROMANIZED	HAN'GEUL

SENTENCE STRUCTURE

Statements, questions, requests, suggestions, and desire are all expressed with different verb endings.

statement:	*. . . imnida, . . . yo.*	. . . 입니다, . . . 요.
question:	*. . . imnikka?, . . . yo?*	. . . 입니까, . . . 요?
Please . . .	*. . . shipshiyo, . . . seyo.*	. . . 십시요, . . . 세요.
Let's . . .	*. . . eupshida.*	. . . 읍시다.
I want to . . .	*. . . goshipseumnida*	. . . 고싶습니다.

QUESTION WORDS

who	*nugu*	누구
what	*myeot*	몇
when	*eonje*	언제
where	*eodi*	어디
why	*wae*	왜
how	*eoddeoke*	어떻게
which (thing)	*eoneu (geot)*	어느(것)

INTRODUCTION AND PLEASANTRIES 인사말

ENGLISH	ROMANIZED	HAN'GEUL
Hello. (greeting used any time of day, meaning, "Are you at peace?")	*Annyeong hashimnikka, Annyeong haseyo?*	안녕하십니까? 안녕하세요?
Hello. (for answering a greeting)	*Ne, Annyeong hashimnikka?, Ne, Annyeong haseyo?*	네, 안녕하십니까?, 네, 안녕하세요?
Hello. (for answering the phone and getting someone's attention)	*Yeoboseyo.*	여보세요.
Good-bye. (when the other person leaves and you stay, or when both you and the other person leave)	*Annyeonghi gaseyo.*	안녕히가세요.
Good-bye. (when you leave and the other person stays)	*Annyeonghi gyeseyo.*	안녕히계세요.
Thank you.	*Gamsahamnida, Gomapseumnida.*	감사합니다., 고맙습니다.

ENGLISH	ROMANIZED	HAN'GEUL
Thank you. (when someone has helped you beyond what you might expect)	Sugo hashyeoseumnida.	수고하셨읍니다.
How do you do? (literally "I'm seeing you for the first time.")	Cheoeum boepgeseumnida.	처음뵙겠읍니다.
It's nice to meet you.	Mannaseo ban'gapseumnida.	만나서반갑습니다.
See you again.	Tto boepgeseumnida.	또뵙겠읍니다.
It's a long time since we've met.	Eoraegan manimnida.	어래간만입니다.
How have you been?	Eoddeoge jinaeseumnikka?	어떻게지내셨읍니까?
I'm fine.	Jal jinaeseumnida.	잘지냈읍니다.
What's your name?	Ireumi mueoshimnikka?	이름이무엇입나까?
Let me introduce myself.	Sogae hageseumnida.	소개하겠읍니다.
My name is . . .	Je ireumeun . . . imnida.	제이름은 . . . 입니다.
I understand.	Ihae hamnida.	이해합니다.
I don't understand.	Ihae mot hamnida.	이해못합니다.
Do you understand?	Ihae hashimnikka?	이해하십니까?
Do you know?	Ashimnikka?	아십니까?
Yes, I know.	Nae, amnida.	네, 압니다
I don't know.	Jal moreumnida.	잘모릅니다.
Please explain to me.	Jom seolmyeong haejuseyo.	좀설명해주세요.
I speak only a little Korean.	Han'gungmal jogeumman hamnida.	한국말조금만합니다.
Please speak slowly.	Mal cheoncheonhi hashipshiyo.	말천천히하십시요.
Please say that again.	Dashi malsseum haejusaeyo.	다시말슴해주세요.
How do you say that in Korean?	Han'gungmallo eoddeoke mal halsuisseumnikka?	한국말로어떻게말할수 있읍니까?
What do you call this in Korean?	Igeoseul han'gungmallo mworago hamnikka?	이것을한국말로뭐라고 합니까?
Do you speak English/Korean?	Yeongeo/Han'gungmal halsuisseumnikka?	영어/한국말할수있읍니 까?
Please speak in English/Korean.	Yeongeoro/Han'gungmallo malhaseyo.	영어로/한국말로말하세 요.
Is there someone here who speaks English?	Yeogi Yeongeo haneun saram isseumnikka?	여기영어하는사람있읍니 까?

ENGLISH	ROMANIZED	HAN'GEUL
Please write that down on paper for me.	Jongi ae jom jeogeojuseyo.	종이에좀적어주세요.
Is that right? (You don't say.)	Geureoseumnikka?	그렇습니까?
That's good.	Joseumnida.	좋습니다.
Of course.	Mullonijyo	물론이죠.
That's interesting.	Jaemi isseumnida.	제미있습니다.
Please help me.	Dowajuseyo.	도와주세요.
Please wait a moment.	Jamganman gidaryeojuseyo.	잠간만기다려주세요.
I'm sorry, excuse me. (following some "impolite" action)	Mian hamnida, Joesong hamnida.	미안합니다, (죄송합니다)
Pardon me. (used prior to an "impolite" action)	Shille hamnida.	실례합니다.
That's all right, never mind.	Sanggwan eopseumnida, gwaenchanseumnida.	상관없습니다, 괜찮습니다.
You're welcome; don't mention it.	Cheonmaneyo.	천만에요.
Please come in.	Deuleo oseyo.	들어오세요.
Congratulations.	Chukahamnida.	축하합니다.
Be careful.	Joshim haseyo.	조심하세요.
Hurry.	Ppalli.	빠리.

TRANSPORTATION 교통

airplane	bihaengi	비행기
airport	gonghang	공항
train	yeolcha, gicha	열차, 기차
electric (commuter) train	jeoncheol	전철
train station	yeok, gichayeok	역, 기차역
seat number	Jwaseok beonho	좌석번호
express/intercity/city bus	gosok/jikhaeng/shinae beoseu	고속/직행/시내버스
express-bus terminal	gosok beoseu teominal	고속버스터미날
bus terminal (stop)	beoseu teominal (jeongnyujang/jeongnyuso)	버스터미날 (정류장/정류소)
expressway/freeway	gosok doro	고속도로
national highway	ilban gukdo	일반국도
provincial highway	jibang doro	지방도로
subway	jihacheol	지하철

ENGLISH	ROMANIZED	HAN'GEUL
passenger ferry	*hwaeri, yeogaekseon*	훼리, 여객선
(. . .) ferry terminal	*(. . .) hang yeogaekseon teominal*	(. . .)항여객선터미날
first-class	*ildeung*	일등
second-class	*ideung*	이등
third-class	*samdeung*	삼등
auto, passenger car	*jadongcha, seungyongcha*	자동차, 승용차
taxi	*taekshi*	댁시
rental car agency	*Jadongcha daeyeojeom*	자동차대여점
parking (no parking)	*jucha (jucha geumchi)*	주차(주차금치)
ticket (window)	*pyo (paneun got)*	표(파는곳)
information window	*annae mun*	안내문
timetable	*shigan pyo*	시간표
one-way	*han banghyangeuro*	한방향으로
return (round-trip)	*wangbok*	왕복
I want to make a reservation.	*Yeyak hagoshipsumnida.*	예약하고싶습니다
I want to cancel my reservation.	*Yeyakul chuiso hagoshipsumnida.*	예약을취소하고 싶습니다
How much is the fare?	*Yogeumi eolmamnikka?*	요금이얼마입니까?
What time does it leave/arrive?	*Myeotshi ae chulbal/dochak hamnikka?*	몇시에출발/도착 합니까?
Which platform?	*Myeot beonhom aeseo tamnikka?*	몇번홈에서탑니까?
Is there a bus to . . . ?	*. . . ae ganeun beoseu isseumnikka?*	. . . 에가는버스 있읍니까?
How long does it take?	*Eolmana geolimnikka?*	얼마나걸립니까?
Where must I transfer?	*Eodi aeseo garataya doemnikka?*	어디에서가라 타야됩니까?
Please let me know when we get there.	*Dochak hamyeon alleojuseyo.*	도착하면알려주세요.
Please take me to . . .	*. . . ro gapshida.*	. . . 로갑시다.
I'm lost.	*Gileul ireoseumnida*	길을잃었읍니다.
Please help me.	*Jom dowajuseyo*	좀도와주세요.
Let's go.	*Gapshida.*	갑시다.
Please go slower/faster.	*Jomdeo cheoncheonhi / ppalli gaseyo.*	좀더천천히/빠리가세요.

M

Korean Language Basics

ENGLISH	ROMANIZED	HAN'GEUL
Please let me off here.	*Naeryeojuseyo.*	네려주세요.
Stop here.	*Sewojuseyo.*	세워주세요.

DIRECTIONS 방위

north	*buk (jjok)*	북(쪽)
south	*nam (jjok)*	남(쪽)
east	*dong (jjok)*	동(쪽)
west	*seo (jjok)*	서(쪽)
straight ahead	*ttok baro*	똑바로
right	*oreunjjok, ucheuk*	오른쪽, 우측
left	*woenjjok, jwacheuk*	왼쪽, 좌측
up	*wi (ae)*	위(에)
down	*mit (ae)*	밑(에)
this way	*ijjokeuro*	이쪽으로
that way	*keujjokeuro*	그쪽으로
here	*yeogi*	여기
there (referring to something distant from speaker, but near the listener)	*geogi*	거기
there (distant from both speaker and listener)	*jeogi*	저기
to	*ae, (euro)*	에, (으로)
from	*aeseo*	에서
Where is . . . ?	*. . . eodi issumnikka?*	. . . 어디있읍니까?
Is this the way to . . . ?	*Igeoseul . . . ae ganeun gil imnikka?*	이것을 . . . 에가는길입니까?
Is it near?	*Gakkapseumnikka?*	가깝습니까?
Please draw me a map.	*Jidoreul jom jeogeojuseyo.*	지도를좀적어주세요.
How can I get to . . . ?	*. . . eodiro gamnikka?*	. . . 어디로갑니까?

ACCOMMODATIONS AND FOOD 숙박와식사

(Refer to the Food section of the On the Road chapter for a list of specific foods.)

hotel	*hot'ael*	호텔
jang yeogwan	*jang yeogwan*	장여관
yeogwan	*yeogwan*	여관

ENGLISH	ROMANIZED	HAN'GEUL
yeoinsuk	*yeoinsuk*	여인숙
minbak	*minbak*	민박
youth hostel	*yuseu hoseutael*	유스호스텔
mountain hut	*sanjang*	산장
camping site	*yayeongjang*	야영장
parking lot	*juchajang*	주차장
proprietor	*juin*	주인
room	*bang*	방
reservation	*yeyak*	예약
heated floor (room)	*ondol (bang)*	온돌(방)
western-style bed (room)	*chimdae (bang)*	침대(방)
quilted sleeping mat	*yeo*	여
sleeping cover	*ibul*	이불
door	*mun*	문
window	*jangmun*	장문
air conditioning	*aeeokon*	에어꼰
fan	*seonpunggi*	선풍기
key	*yeolsoe*	열쇠
bathhouse	*mogyoktang*	목욕탕
tub	*tang*	탕
towel	*sugeon*	수건
soap	*binu*	비누
laundromat	*setakso*	세탁소
Can you recommend a good *yeogwan?*	*Joeun yeogwanul sogae haejugeseumnikka?*	좋은여관을소게해주겠읍니까?
Do you have a room?	*Bang isseumnikka?*	방있읍니까?
How much for one night?	*Haru eolmamnikka?*	하루얼마입니까?
Do you have a cheaper room?	*Deo ssanbang isseumnikka?*	더싼방있읍니까?
I'll be here one day (one week).	*Haru (iljuil dongan) meomureugesseumnida.*	하루(일주일동안) 머무르겠읍이다.
Where is the toilet?	*Hwajangshil eodi isseumnikka?*	화장실어디있읍니까?
Are you serving meals (can I eat)?	*Shiksa doemnikka?*	식사됩니까?
restaurant	*shikdang*	식당
bakery	*jegwajeom*	제과점

ENGLISH	ROMANIZED	HAN'GEUL
food	*eumshik*	음식
breakfast/lunch/dinner	*achim/jeomshim/jeonyeok shiksa*	아침/점심/저녁식사
Korean food	*Hanshik*	한식
Chinese food	*Junggukshik*	중국식
Japanese food	*Ilshik*	일식
Western food	*Yangshik*	양식
vegetarian food	*Chaeshik*	채식
chopsticks	*jeotgarak*	젓가락
spoon	*sutgarak*	숟가락
toothpicks	*issushigae*	이쑤시개
cup (glass)	*jan (keop)*	잔(컵)
barley tea	*boricha*	보리차
I'm hungry.	*Baega gopumnida.*	배가고픕니다.
I'm thirsty.	*Mogi mareumnida.*	목이마릅니다.
I'm full.	*Baega bureumnida.*	배가부릅니다.
I enjoyed the meal (I ate well).	*Jal meogeoseumnida.*	잘먹었습니다.
Please show me the menu.	*Menyu boyeojuseyo*	메뉴보여주세요
Please bring me a little of that over there.	*Jeogeotgwa gateun geoseuro juseyo.*	저것과같은것으로 주세요
Please bring me . . .	*. . . juseyo.*	. . . 주세요.
Please bring a little more of this.	*Igeoseul jogeumdeo juseyo.*	이것을조금더주세요.
Please bring more water.	*Mul jogeumdeo juseyo*	물조금더주세요
a portion for two/three/four people	*i/sam/sa inbun*	이/삼/사인분
One more bowl of rice please.	*Bap hangeureutdo juseyo.*	밥한그릇도주세요.
Please make it mild.	*Maepjiangae haejuseyo.*	맵지않게해주세요.
I cannot eat spicy food.	*Maeun geoseul mot mokseumnida.*	매운곳을못먹습니다.
Please leave out the meat.	*Gogireul jeonbu ppaeseyo.*	고기를전부빼세요
I only eat vegetables.	*Chaeshik man meokseumnida.*	채식만먹습니다.
I'm a vegetarian.	*Chaeshik juuija imnida.*	채식주의자입니다
How much is this?	*Igeoseul eolmamnikka?*	이것을얼마입니까?
It's tasty.	*Mashi isseumnida.*	맛이있습니다.

ENGLISH	ROMANIZED	HAN'GEUL
It's hot. (temperature)	*Tteugeopseumnida.*	뜨겁습니다.
It's spicy hot.	*Maepseumnida.*	맵습니다.
It's salty.	*Jjapseumnida.*	짭습니다.
It's sweet.	*Damnida.*	답니다.
It's bland.	*Shinggeopseumnida.*	싱겁습니다.
It's sour.	*Shipseumnida.*	십습니다.
It's bitter.	*Sseumnida.*	씁니다.
Please eat (help yourself).	*Mani japsuseyo.*	많이잡수세요.
Please bring me the bill.	*Gyaesanseoreul jom juseyo*	계산서를좀주세요.
I need a receipt.	*Yeongsujeung pilyeohamnida.*	영수증을필요합니다.
Do you take traveler's checks (credit cards)?	*Yeohaeng supyo (shinyong kadeu)gyesanhalsuisumnikka?*	여행수표(신용카드) 계산할수있읍니까?
payment in advance	*jeonbul*	전불
tea room	*dabang (dashil, chatjip)*	다방(다실,찻집)
tea	*cha*	차
coffee shop	*Keopi shyop.*	커피숖
coffee	*keopi*	커피
soft drink beverage	*eumnyo*	음료
alcoholic beverage	*sul*	술
drinking establishment	*suljip*	술집
beer hall	*hof*	호프

MARKET AND SHOPPING 시장

store, shop	*gage, sangjeom*	가게,상점
corner market	*supeo*	수퍼
market	*shijang*	시장
department store	*baekhwajeom*	백화점
souvenir shop	*ginyeompum sanghoe*	기념품상회
bookstore	*seojeom*	서점
What is this?	*Igeoseun mueoshimnikka?*	이것은무엇입니까?
Please show me another (a cheaper/larger/smaller) one.	*Dareun (ssan/keun/jageun) geoseul boyeojuseyo.*	다른(싼/큰/작은) 것을보여주세요.
Do you have (is there any . . .)?	*. . . isseumnikka?*	. . . 있읍니까?
Don't have (there is none).	*Eopseumnida.*	없읍니다.
I like it.	*Joahamnida.*	좋아합니다.

ENGLISH	ROMANIZED	HAN'GEUL
I don't like it.	Joahajianseumnida.	좋아하지않습니다.
How much is this?	Eolmamnikka?	얼마입니까?
It's cheap.	Ssamnida.	쌉니다.
It's too expensive.	Neomu pissamnida.	너무비쌉니다.
Please make it cheaper.	Ssage haejuseyo.	싸게해주세요.
Give me only one (two/three).	Hana man (duge/sege) juseyo.	하나만 (두게/세게) 주세요.
Fine, I'll take it.	Joseumnida, sageseumnida.	좋습니다, 사겠습니다.
May I use a credit card?	Shinyong kadeureul sayonghalsu issumnikka?	신용카드를사용할 수있읍니까?
Please wrap it for me.	Pojang haejuseyo.	포장해주세요

POST OFFICE, TELEPHONE 우체국, 전화

(central) post office	(jungang) uchaeguk	(중앙)우체국
poste restante	yuchi upyeonmulgwa	유치우편물과
stamp	upyo	우표
letter	pyeonji	편지
envelope	pyeongji bongtu	편지봉투
aerogram	hanggong seogan	항공서간
postcard	yeopseo	엽서
parcel, package	sopo	소포
airmail	hanggong upyeon	항공우편
sea mail	baepyeon	배편
postal rate (sheet)	upyeon yogeum (pyeo)	우편요금(표)
Telecom office	jeonshin jeonhwaguk	전신전화국
telephone	jeonhwa	전화
(long-distance/international) phone call	(janggeori/gukje) jeonhwa	(장거리/국제)잔화
I want to make a phone call.	Jeonhwareul hagoshipseumnida.	전화를하고싶습니다.
May I use the phone?	Jeonhwareul sseodo doemnikka?	전화를써도됩니까?
Let me speak to. . . .	. . . bakkwojuseyo.	. . . 바꿔주세요.
telegram	jeonbo	전보
Can I send a telegram?	Jeonbo chilsu isseumnikka?	전보칠수있읍니까?

ENGLISH	ROMANIZED	HAN'GEUL
TIME, WEATHER 시간, 날씨		
morning	*ojeon*	오전
afternoon	*ohu*	우후
evening	*jeonyeok*	저녁
night	*bam*	밤
minute	*bun*	분
hour	*shigan*	시간
o'clock (. . . thirty)	*shi (shiban)*	시(시반)
What time is it?	*Myeotshi imnikka?*	몇시입니까?
one (two/three) hour(s)	*han (du/sae) shigan*	한(두/세)시간
one day	*haru*	하루
yesterday	*oje*	오제
today	*oneul*	오늘
tomorrow	*naeil*	내일
now, currently	*jigeum*	지금
next	*daeum*	다음
day	*il, nal*	일, 날
month	*wol*	월
year	*nyeon*	년
weekday	*juil*	주일
weekend	*jumal*	주말
every day	*maeil*	매일
holiday	*gonghyuil*	공휴일
January	*ilwol*	일월
February	*iwol*	이월
March	*samwol*	삼월
April	*sawol*	사월
May	*owol*	오월
June	*yuwol*	유월
July	*chilwol*	칠월
August	*palwol*	팔월
September	*guwol*	구월
October	*shiwol*	시월
November	*shibilwol*	십일월

ENGLISH	ROMANIZED	HAN'GEUL
December	*shibiwol*	십이월
Sunday	*ilyoil*	일요일
Monday	*wolyoil*	월요일
Tuesday	*hwayoil*	화요일
Wednesday	*suyoil*	수요일
Thursday	*mogyoil*	목요일
Friday	*geumyoil*	금요일
Saturday	*toyoil*	토요일
spring	*bom*	봄
summer	*yeoreum*	여름
autumn	*gaeul*	가을
winter	*gyeoul*	겨울
climate	*gihu*	기후
weather	*nalsshi*	날씨
clear weather	*malgeun nalsshi*	맑은날씨
warm weather	*ttaddeuthan nalsshi*	따뜻한날씨
hot weather	*deoun nalsshi*	더운날씨
cool weather	*ssalssalhan nalsshi*	쌀쌀한날씨
cold weather	*chueun nalsshi*	추은날씨
wind	*baram*	바람
typhoon	*daepung*	대풍
rain	*bi*	비
heavy rains of summer	*jangma*	장마
autumn colors	*danpung*	단풍
snow	*nun*	눈
clouds	*gureum*	구름

TITLES 칭호

I	*jeo, na*	저, 나
you	*dangshin*	당신
he, she, that person	*geubun*	그분
we	*uri*	우리
they	*geubundeul*	그분들
Mr., Mrs., Ms., teacher, you (respectful), (respected elder)	*seonsaeng*	선생

ENGLISH	ROMANIZED	HAN'GEUL
mother	*eomeoni*	어머니
father	*abeoji*	아버지
grandmother (grandmother-age woman)	*halmeoni*	할머니
grandfather (grandfather-age man)	*harabeoji*	할아버지
aunt (middle-aged woman)	*ajumeoni*	아주머니
uncle (middle-aged man)	*ajeosshi*	아저씨
young woman (unmarried)	*agasshi*	아가씨
wife	*buin, samonim*	부인, 사모님
husband	*nampyeon*	남편
daughter	*dal*	딸
son	*adeul*	아들
student	*haksaeng*	학생
boyfriend, girlfriend, lover	*aein*	애인
person	*saram, bun*	사람, 분

BASIC VOCABULARY 기본단어

ENGLISH	ROMANIZED	HAN'GEUL
address	*juso*	주소
after	*hu*	후
again	*dashi*	다시
all	*modu*	모두
almost	*keoui*	거의
always	*hangsang*	항상
and	*hago, geurigo*	하고, 그리고
bank	*eunhaeng*	은행
bank card	*hyeongeum kadeu*	현금카드
bad	*nappeun*	나쁜
travel bag, suitcase	*gabang*	가방
beach	*haesuyokjang*	해수욕장
beautiful	*areumdaun*	아름다운
before, ago	*jeon, jeone*	전, 전에
big, large	*keun*	큰
boat	*bae*	배
book	*chaek*	책

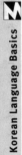

ENGLISH	ROMANIZED	HAN'GEUL
bridge	*dari*	다리
Buddhist monk	*seunim*	스님
Buddhist nun	*bigunni*	비구니
business card	*myeongham*	명함
business hours	*yeongeop shigan*	영업시간
but	*geurona, hajiman*	그로나, 하지만
child	*eorini*	어린이
cigarette	*dambae*	담배
city	*doshi*	도시
consulate	*yeongsagwan*	연사관
country	*nara*	나라
countryside	*shigol*	시골
credit card	*shinyong kadeu*	신용카드
date	*naljja*	날짜
date of birth	*saengil*	생일
danger	*wiheom*	위험
different	*dareun*	다른
difficult	*eoryeoun*	어려운
doctor	*uisa*	의사
driver	*unjeon gisa*	운전기사
driver's license	*unjeon myeonheojeung*	운전면허증
during, for (time length)	*dongan, gan*	동안, 간
early	*iljik*	일직
easy	*shwiun*	쉬운
embassy	*daesagwan*	대사관
enough	*chungbunhan*	충분한
entrance	*ipgu*	입구
exchange rate	*hwannyul*	환율
exit	*chulgu*	출구
family	*gajok*	가족
family name	*seong*	성
(hand) fan	*buchae*	부채
far	*meolli*	멀리
female	*yeoja*	여자

ENGLISH	ROMANIZED	HAN'GEUL
few, little	*jeogeum*	저금
first	*cheoeum*	처음
flower	*kkot*	꽃
foreigner	*oeguk saram*	외국사람
free (no cost)	*muryo*	무료
gas station	*juyuso*	주유소
gift	*seonmul*	선물
good	*joeun*	좋은
handsome	*minam*	미남
harbor	*hanggu*	항구
(mountain) hiking	*deungsan*	등산
hiking trail	*deungsangil*	등산길
hospital	*byeongwon*	병원
hot spring	*oncheon*	온천
house	*jip*	집
inside	*ane*	안에
Korean traditional clothing	*hanbok*	한복
lake	*hosu*	호수
last	*majimak*	마지막
later	*najunge*	나중에
length of stay (at an accommodation)	*sukbak gigan*	숙박시간
less	*deol*	덜
magazine	*japji*	잡지
male	*namja*	남자
many	*mani*	많이
married	*gyeolhonhan*	결혼한
married couple	*bubu*	부부
maybe, perhaps	*ama, hokshi*	아마, 혹씨
medicine	*yak*	약
money	*don*	돈
more	*deo*	더
motion sickness (medicine)	*meolmi (yak)*	멀미(약)
motion sickness bag	*wisaeng bongtu*	위생봉투
mountain	*san*	산

ENGLISH	ROMANIZED	HAN'GEUL
name	*ireum*	이름
nationality	*gukjeok*	국적
near	*gakkaun*	가까운
new	*saeroun*	새로운
newspaper	*shinmun*	신문
next	*daeum*	다음
no	*anyo, animnida*	아니오, 않입니다
no entrance	*chulip geumji*	출입금지
no smoking	*geumyeon*	금연
noisy	*shikkeureoun*	시끄러운
now	*jigeum*	지금
occupation	*jigeup*	직업
ocean	*bada, daeyang*	바다, 대양
office	*samushil*	사무실
often	*jaju*	자주
OK, good	*josseumnida*	좋습니다
or	*hogeun*	혹은
outside	*bakke*	밖에
park	*gongwon*	공원
passport (number)	*yeogwon (beonho)*	여권(번호)
pharmacy	*yakguk*	약국
photograph	*sajin*	사진
police station	*gyeongchalso*	경찰소
policeman	*gyeongchalgwan*	경찰관
pond	*yeonmot*	연못
pretty	*yeppeun*	예쁜
prohibited	*geumji*	금지
pull	*danggishiyo*	당기시요
push	*mishiyo*	미시요
quiet, silence!	*joyonghi, jeongsuk*	조용히, 정숙
receipt	*yeongsujeung*	영수증
river	*gang*	강
road, street	*doro, gil*	도로, 길
sea	*hae, bada*	해, 바다

M Korean Language Basics

ENGLISH	ROMANIZED	HAN'GEUL
same	*gateun*	같은
signature	*seomyeong*	서명
single, alone	*honja*	혼자
single, unmarried	*mihon*	미혼
small, little	*jageun*	작은
sometimes	*ttaettaero*	때때로
temple	*jeol*	절
temple (with proper name)	(. . . -sa)	(. . . 사)
ticket booth	*maepyoso*	매표소
toilet (restroom, bathroom)	*hwajangshil*	화장실
toilet paper	*hyuji*	휴지
tourist-information office	*gwan'gwang annaeso*	관광안내소
traveler's checks	*yeohaeng supyo*	여행수표
trees	*namu*	나무
umbrella	*usan*	우산
village	*maeul*	마을
visa	*bisa*	비사
walk (leisurely, for an appreciation of the natural surroundings)	*tambang*	탐방
waterfall	*pokpo*	폭포
yes	*ne*	네

Suggested Reading

Some books are followed by "OP," meaning out of print (or believed to be out of print). While these books are not generally or easily available for purchase, they are still good references, and are worth the trouble to locate for those serious about pursuing a subject.

General References

A Handbook of Korea. Seoul: Korean Overseas Information Service, 1998; 652 pages. An excellent, comprehensive, and easily readable general reference on all aspects of South Korean society and culture. The finest single-volume sourcebook available. Full of color photographs and charts.

Bartz, Patricia. *South Korea.* Oxford: Clarendon Press, 1972; 203 pages. While some sections are out of date, the material on physical features, geology, topography, weather, climate, and natural phenomena is still valid. One of the few concise sources for this information in English. OP.

Korea Annual. Seoul: Yonhap News Agency, 2002. Yearly publication providing historical and diplomatic highlights of the year, a who's who of Koreans, plenty of general information about the country, government, economy, business, society, and culture. Contains a short section on North Korea.

Savada, Andrea Matles, ed. *South Korea: A Country Study,* 4th ed. Washington: U.S. Government Printing Office, 1992; 408 pages. This study provides an overview of the historical, social, economic, political, and national-security concerns of South Korea. Contains a lengthy bibliography. *North Korea: A Country Study,* 4th ed. (1994) is a companion guide.

History

Alexander, Bevin. *Korea: The First War We Lost,* Rev. ed. New York: Hippocrene Books, Inc., 2000; 590 pages. An even-handed account of the causes of the Korean War, political strategies, and results of battle. Uses previously unavailable sources. Written by a military historian.

Cumings, Bruce. *Korea's Place in the Sun: A Modern History.* New York: W.W. Norton and Company, 1998; 528 pages. An insightful broad perspective on Korean history.

Eckert, Carter, et al. *Korea Old and New: A History* Cambridge, MA: Korea Institute, Harvard University, 1990; 454 pages. One of the best general histories, with good coverage of modern history to 1990.

Halliday, Jon, and Bruce Cumings. *Korea: The Unknown War.* New York: Pantheon Books, 1988; 224 pages. No traditionally accepted history of the Korean War, this book takes a fresh look at the conflict as an outgrowth of civil war with complications fraught by foreign intervention. Balances information, opinion, and analysis from all sides of the conflict. OP.

Hamel, Hendrik. *Hamel's Journal and a Description of the Kingdom of Korea, 1653–1666.* Translated by Jean-Paul Buys. Seoul: Royal Asiatic Society, Korea Branch, 1998; 107 pages. Translation of the record of the first Western group contact with Korea and their 13 years of captivity. First Western account of Korea.

Han, Woo-keun. *The History of Korea.* Translated by K.S. Lee and edited by Grafton Mintz. Seoul: Eul-yoo Publishing Company,

1970; 551 pages. One of the standard modern histories of Korea.

Joe, Wanne J. *A Cultural History of Modern Korea.* Edited by Hongkyu A. Choi. Elizabeth, NJ: Hollym International Corp., 2000; 876 pages. Insightful coverage from a Korean perspective.

Joe, Wanne J. *Traditional Korea: A Cultural History,* rev. ed. Edited by Hongkyu A. Choi. Elizabeth, NJ: Hollym International Corp., 1997; 446 pages. Basic scholarly work.

Kim, Yung-chung, trans. *Women of Korea: A History from Ancient Times to 1945.* Seoul: Ewha University Press, 1979; 327 pages. A classic work explaining the role and status of Korean women.

Ledyard, Gary. *The Dutch Come to Korea.* Seoul: Royal Asiatic Society, Korea Branch, 1971; 231 pages. Story of the shipwreck of the Dutch merchantman *Sparrow Hawk* and her crew's 13-year confinement and eventual escape from Korea. The only thorough analysis in English of the first Western group encounter with Korea.

Lee, Ki-baik. *A New History of Korea.* Translated by Edward W. Wagner and Edward J. Shultz. Cambridge, MA: Harvard-Yenching Institute Publications, Harvard University, 1985; 504 pages. Comprehensive, scholarly history to 1960, with extensive coverage of the ancient kingdoms. Best appreciated by the serious student of Korean history. Abundant bibliography and excellent index.

Merrill, John. *Korea: The Peninsular Origins of the War.* Newark, NJ: University of Delaware Press, 1989; 237 pages. Examination of the political, social, and military conditions in both South and North Korea that led to the hostilities known as the Korean War. OP.

Oberdorfer, Don. *Two Koreas: A Contemporary History,* rev. ed. New York: Basic Books, 2001;

544 pages. An examination of the historical relationship between South and North Korea and the impact other world powers have had on the unresolved situation of tension on the Korean peninsula.

Rutt, Richard. *James Scarth Gale and His History of the Korean People.* Seoul: Royal Asiatic Society, Korea Branch, 1972; 396 pages. New edition of the anecdotal history of Korea by one of Korea's earliest Western missionaries and foremost scholars.

Samguk Yusa: Legends and History of the Three Kingdoms of Ancient Korea. Translated by Ha Tae-Hung and Grafton Mintz. Seoul: Yonsei University Press, 1972; 456 pages. Intriguing tales, legends, and anecdotes of early Korea by a 13th-century Buddhist monk. One of the few extant classical Korean histories.

Business and Economy

Cho, Lee-Jay, and Yoon Hyung Kim, eds. *Economic Development in the Republic of Korea: A Policy Perspective.* Honolulu: East-West Center, 1991; 649 pages. Essays by leading Korean economists focusing on a handful of major policy initiatives since the 1960s that have dramatically and fundamentally changed Korean economic development.

Clifford, Mark. *Troubled Tiger: Businessmen, Bureaucrats, and Generals in South Korea,* rev. ed. Armonk, NY: M.E. Sharpe, Inc., 1997; 392 pages. Eminently readable telling of the interrelation of government, business, and the military in the formation of the modern South Korea state.

Eckert, Carter J. *Offspring of Empire: the Koch'ang Kims and the Colonial Origins of Korean Capitalism 1876–1945.* Seattle: University of Washington Press, 1991; 406 pages. This book skillfully portrays conditions that led to the rise of the Korean capitalist system during the Japanese colonial period, countering long-held prevalent beliefs and assertions that the Korean capitalist economy was able to blossom only after the end of the Japanese colonial domination.

Kwon, Jene K. ed. *Korean Economic Development*. Westport, CT: Greenwood Press, 1990; 446 pages. Collection of essays on a broad range of significant issues concerning the development of the Korean economy since 1961, focusing on policies, strategies, trends, strengths, and weaknesses.

McNamara, Dennis L. *The Colonial Origins of Korean Enterprise: 1910–1945*. Cambridge, England: Cambridge University Press, 1990; 208 pages. A study of Korean business culture during the Japanese colonial period, and characteristics that lead to the emergence of the large Korean conglomerates known as *chaebol*.

Ogle, George. *South Korea: Dissent within the Economic Miracle*. London: Zed Books, 1990; 189 pages. A no-holds-barred account of the history of labor unionism in Korea, exposing the unflattering underside of Korea's economic miracle by examining restrictive and repressive management policies, manipulative labor practices, the suppression of civil and democratic rights, and the collusion of successive authoritarian governments to de-emphasize the human side of industry.

Song, Byung-Nak. *The Rise of the Korean Economy*, 3rd ed. New York: Oxford University Press, 2002; 278 pages. Insightful examination by a prominent Korean economist of how and why the South Korean economy has become strong and vibrant, and its prospects for the future. Korean point of view. Draws mostly from Korean sources.

Culture and Sociology

Amnesty International. *Korea (the Republic of)*. Annual report of the status of human rights and other related issues in South Korea. *Korea (the Democratic People's Republic of)* is the companion report on North Korea. Amnesty International also issues periodic news releases and special reports pertaining to specific issues relating to human rights on these two countries.

Brandt, Vincent S.R. *A Korean Village: Between Farm and Sea*. Prospect Heights, IL: Waveland Press, Inc., 1990; 252 pages. Reissue of a classic ethnographic study of the social structure of a rural farming and fishing community in the mid-1960s. Valuable as an indicator of the times and a reference for change that followed. OP.

Breen, Michael. *The Koreans: Who They Are, What They Want, Where Their Future Lies*. London: Orion Publishing Group, 1998; 276 pages. Fairly objective look at the character of the Koreans, their history, and what shapes their collective personality.

Choe, Sang-su. *Annual Customs of Korea: Notes on Rites and Ceremonies of the Year*. Seoul: Seomun Dang, 1983; 168 pages. Thorough coverage of games and cultural practices of traditional lunar holidays and festivals.

Crane, Paul S. *Korean Patterns*, reprint of the 1967 edition. Seoul: Royal Asiatic Society, Korea Branch, 1999; 188 pages. This book attempts to explain to foreigners what makes Koreans tick, by concentrating on traditional ethics, etiquette, and cultural patterns. Still largely relevant, but somewhat superseded by current social changes.

Culin, Stewart. *Korean Games*. New York: Dover Publications, Inc., 1991; 177 pages. Republication of the 1895 edition of this work. Explains dozens of traditional Korean games—many still played today— that have corresponding games in China and Japan. Offers a theory linking some of these games to means of divination found in primitive societies.

Ha, Tae-hung. *Guide to Korean Culture.* Seoul: Yonsei University Press, 1978; 455 pages. Basic introduction to Korean cultural life.

Kendall, Laural. *The Life and Hard Times of a Korean Shaman: Of Tales and the Telling of Tales.* Honolulu: University of Hawaii Press, 1988; 168 pages. An anthropological "life history." A window into the little-known and much less understood world of a Korean shaman.

Kendall, Laural. *Shamans, Housewives, and Other Restless Spirits.* Honolulu: University of Hawaii Press, 1985; 248 pages. A "behind-the-scenes" look at the world of Korean shamans, their rituals, relationships, and practices. An insightful look at the human side of this spiritual element of Korean folk life. Contains a useful glossary and good reference to related works in Korean and English.

MacDonald, Donald S. *The Koreans: Contemporary Politics and Society,* 3rd edition. Edited by Donald N. Clark. Boulder: Westview Press, 1996; 352 pages. A general survey from the perspective of the mid-1990s. One of the best.

Mason, David. *Spirit of the Mountain.* Elizabeth, NJ: Hollym International Corp., 1999; 224 pages. Discussion of the Sanshin (Mountain Spirit) and its relation to Korean religious and social thought.

Pares, Susan, and James Hoare. *Simple Guide to Customs and Etiquette in Korea.* Kent, England: Paul Norbury Publications, 1996; 64 pages. Clear and concise, this brief pamphlet introduces newcomers to a few important points about Korean social customs, values, and traditions.

Pratt, Keith and Richard Rutt. *Korea: A Historical and Cultural Dictionary.* London: Curzon Press, 1999; 240 pages. A dictionary-style text presenting basic facts on a broad range of subjects relating to Korean history, historical

persons, and culture. A good reference for a quick understanding.

Rutt, Richard. *Korean Works and Days.* Seoul: Royal Asiatic Society, Korea Branch, 1978; 205 pages. One-year account (1957–58) of significant events in a rural village by one of the most astute observers of Korean life.

Ryu, Je-Hun. *Reading the Korean Cultural Landscape.* Elizabeth, NJ: Hollym International Corp., 2000; 340 pages. An examination of Korea and Koreans in terms of their cultural diversity and how this helps form an emerging national culture.

Steenson, Gary P. *Coping with Korea.* Oxford: Basil Blackwell Inc., 1987; 148 pages. Work on understanding Korean ways.

Yu, Chai-shin, and R. Guisso, eds. *Shamanism: The Spirit World of Korea.* Berkeley, CA: Asian Humanities Press, 1988; 190 pages. Essays by noted Korean academics on the social, cultural, medical, and psychological aspects of Korean shamanism. Valuable addition to standard works on Korean shamanistic beliefs, practices, and rituals.

Religion and Philosophy

Choi, Min-hong. *A Modern History of Korean Philosophy.* Seoul: Sung Moon Sa, 1980; 269 pages. Comprehensive coverage of current philosophical thought.

Clark, Charles Allen. *Religions of Old Korea.* New York: Garland Publishing, 1981; 295 pages. Reprint of a classic work. One of the earliest examinations of the religions and cults of Korea, plus comments on the introduction of Christianity to the peninsula. OP.

Clark, Donald N. *Christianity in Modern Korea.* Lanham, MD: University Press of America, 1986; 55 pages. Short study on the growth of Christianity in Korea.

Grayson, James H. *Korea: A Religious History.* London: Routledge Curzon, 2002; 320 pages. Survey of the major religions in Korean within a historical perspective.

International Cultural Foundation. *Main Currents of Korean Thought.* Korean Culture Series #10. Seoul: Si-sa-yong-o-sa, 1983. Overview of the foundation and basic threads of contemporary Korean intellectual orientation.

Keel, Hee-sung. *Chinul: The Founder of the Korean Son Tradition.* Berkeley, CA: Berkeley Buddhist Studies Series, 1984; 211 pages. Scholarly work on the life, philosophy, and legacy of the great monk Chinul, the force behind the resurgence of the Korean Zen tradition.

Keum, Jang-tae. *Confucianism and Korean Thought.* Korean Studies Series #10. Seoul: Jimoondang Publishing Co., 2000. Examination of the evolution of Confucian thought through the Joseon Dynasty with insights into how that has influenced modern Korean thought.

Korea Buddhist Chogye Order. *What is Korean Buddhism.* Seoul: Korea Buddhist Chogye Order, 2000; 233 pages. A non-philosophical collection of articles on main aspects of Korean Buddhism, temples, and monks' lives.

The Korean Buddhist Research Institute. *Buddhist Thought in Korea.* Seoul: Dongguk University Press, 1994; 385 pages. A study of Korean Buddhist sects. Also by Dongguk University Press: *The History and Culture of Buddhism in Korea* and *Chant'ae Thought in Korean Buddhism.*

Lancaster, Lewis R., and C.S. Yu., eds. *Introduction of Buddhism to Korea: New Cultural Patterns.* Berkeley, CA: Asian Humanities Press, 1989; 229 pages. Scholarly essays exploring various cultural aspects of the propagation and early growth of Buddhism in Korea. A welcome addition to standard works covering the philosophy and theology of Korea's predominant religion. Also from Asian Humanities Press: *Assimilation of Buddhism in Korea: Religious Maturity and Innovation in the Silla Dynasty.*

Lee, Jung Young. *Korean Shamanistic Rituals.* The Hague: Mounton Publishers, 1981; 249 pages. Somewhat repetitive, this is a well-researched, scholarly work on the most oft-performed Korean shamanistic rituals, with brief descriptions of other key rituals, ritual instruments, and photos of ceremonial garb and practices. While somewhat detailed for the casual reader, it's a good introduction for the serious student. Extensive booklist of English, Korean, and Japanese sources. OP.

Palmer, Spencer J. *Confucian Rituals in Korea.* Seoul: Kyobo Books, 1991; 270 pages. Brief explanation of traditional national Confucian ceremonies, with a short biography of each individual enshrined at the national Confucian shrine in Seoul.

Language

For dictionaries and other language texts, please see Language in the Introduction.

Choe, Miho, and William O'Grady. *Handbook of Korean Vocabulary.* Honolulu: University of Hawaii Press, 1996; 384 pages. A "root dictionary" useful for learning Korean words, related words, and their relationships. For the serious student of the Korean language.

Grant, Bruce K. *A Guide to Korean Characters: Reading and Writing Hangul and Hanja.* Elizabeth, NJ: Hollym International Corp., 1979; 367 pages. A list of the 1,800 basic Chinese characters used in Korea, their stroke order, basic definition in Korean and English, pronunciation in Korean, and sample usages. Very useful for the serious student.

Lukoff, Fred. *A First Reader in Korean Writing in Mixed Script.* Seoul: Yonsei University Press, 1982; 300 pages. Presents 1,800 basic Chinese characters used in Korean publications.

Literature

Chung, Chong-wha, ed. *Korean Classical Literature: An Anthology.* London: Kegan Paul International, Ltd., 1989; 221 pages. General introduction to Korean prose and *sijo* poetry.

Chung, Chong-wha, ed. *Modern Korean Literature: An Anthology, 1908–1965.* London: Routledge, 1995; 443 pages. Survey of the works of major modern Korean writers. Reveals the depth of the Korean soul and the indomitable spirit of a people under suppression and domination.

Fulton, Bruce, and Ju-Chan Fulton, trans. *Words of Farewell: Stories by Korean Women Writers.* Seattle: The Seal Press, 1989; 277 pages. These seven short stories by three well-known Korean writers focus on modern themes and carry a decidedly modern outlook.

Kim, Jaihiun, ed. *Classical Korean Poetry.* Berkeley, CA: Asian Humanities Press, 1994; 171 pages. An anthology of *sijo* poetry through the centuries. Also by Asian Humanities Press: *Modern Korean Poetry.* (1994).

Lee, Peter H., ed. *Anthology of Korean Literature from Early Times to the Nineteenth Century.* Honolulu: University of Hawaii Press, 1981; 342 pages. Encompassing collection covering 1,500 years of Korean prose and poetry of all genres.

Lee, Peter H., ed. *Pine River and Lone Peak: An Anthology of Three Choson Dynasty Poets.* Honolulu: An East West Center Book, University of Hawaii Press, 1991; 197 pages. Translation of poems by three 16th-century Korean poets, masters of the uniquely Korean forms of writing called *sijo* and *kasa.*

Rutt, Richard, trans. *The Bamboo Grove: An Introduction to Sijo.* Ann Arbor, MI: University of Michigan Press, 1998; 177 pages. Scholarly, annotated volume introducing this indigenous three-line Korean verse form to the West. Masterful work.

Seo Dae-eok. *Myths of Korea.* Comp. by Peter H. Lee. Korea Studies Series #4. Seoul: Jimoondang Publishing Co., 2000.

Zong, In-sob. *Folk Tales From Korea,* 3rd ed. Elizabeth, NJ: Hollym International Corp., 1995; 257 pages. Valuable collection of myths, legends, fairy tales, fables, and novellas of old Korea.

Art and Archaeology

Cho, Oh-Kon, trans. *Traditional Korean Theater.* Berkeley, CA: Asian Humanities Press, 1988; 364 pages. An annotated collection of masked-dance dramas and one puppet play. One of the few available translations of such work in English. Having been transferred from oral to written form only in the 20th century, these selections bring alive some of the more lively, pointed, and humorous folk plays of the Korean people.

The Folkcrafts of Korea. Seoul: Kemyongsa, 1980; 538 pages. Color plates and descriptions in English and Korean.

Kim, Won-Yong. *Art and Archaeology of Ancient Korea.* Seoul: Taekwang Publishing Co., 1986; 416 pages. Written by a leading archaeology professor and former curator of the National Museum of Korea, this richly illustrated and highly descriptive volume surveys the broad scope of Korean archaeology in an easy-to-read style.

Lee, Hye-gu. *An Introduction to Korean Music and Dance.* Seoul: Royal Asiatic Society, Korean Branch, 1977; 54 pages. Synopsis of types of Korean music and dance, with pictures and explanations of 49 traditional musical instruments. For the general reader.

Lee, Hye-gu. *Essays on Korean Traditional Music.* Translated by Robert C. Provine. Seoul: Royal Asiatic Society, Korea Branch, 1980; 278 pages. Considered the best single-volume text in English on the subject.

Nelson, Sarah Milledge. *The Archaeology of Korea.* Cambridge, England: Cambridge University Press, 1993; 323 pages. Examines the archaeological evidence of the Korean Peninsula through the end of the Three Kingdoms Period (668 A.D.), noting its unique features.

Park, Sam Y. *Korean Architecture.* Hawaii Book Distribution Co., 1992; 2 vols. Expansive compendium of traditional Korean architectural styles and motifs, with building and site plans.

Van Zile, Judy. *Perspectives on Korean Dance.* Wesleyan University Press; 328 pages. By all accounts, the first comprehensive text on all aspects of Korean dance.

Wright, Edward R., and Man Sil Pai. *Traditional Korean Furniture.* New York: Kodansha International, Ltd., 2000; 192 pages. This book is the first cohesive treatment of the wide spectrum of Korean furniture. Includes descriptions and illustrations, a short historical synopsis, and considers decorative metal fittings, finishing techniques, joinery, wood types, and tools. This book is the best place to start the study and appreciate the simple elegance of Korean furniture.

Geology

Lee, Dai-Sung, ed. *Geology of Korea.* Seoul: Kyohak Publishing Company, 1987; 514 pages. Comprehensive text by Korean geologists.

Flora and Fauna

Yoon, Moon-Boo. *Wild Birds of Korea.* Seoul: Kyohak Publishing Co., Ltd., 1995; 545 pages. Comprehensive coverage of the birds of Korea. This company also publishes a number of other related books: *Wild Flowers of Korea, Woody Plants of Korea, Wild Insects of Korea,* and *Wild Fungus of Korea.*

Food

Hyun, Judy. *The Korean Cookbook,* 2nd Edition. Elizabeth, NJ: Hollym International Corp., 1979; 294 pages. Well-used recipes with cultural anecdotes.

Lee, Chun Ja, Hye Won Park, and Kim Kwi Young. *The Book of Kimchi.* Seoul: Korea Information Service, 1998. Everything you always wanted to know about this most typical of Korean foods.

Noh, Chin-hwa. *Practical Korean Cooking.* Elizabeth, NJ: Hollym International Corp., 1985; 209 pages. Authentic recipes; easy-to-follow instructions. Combined volume of Noh's three other cookbooks: *Healthful Korean Cooking, Low-Fat Korean Cooking,* and *Traditional Korean Cooking.*

O'Brian, Betsy. *Let's Eat Korean Food.* Elizabeth, NJ: Hollym International Corp., 1997; 192 pages. An introduction to types of Korean food and specialties. Good for the cook and traveler.

Rutt, Joan, and Sandra Mattielli, ed. *Lee Wade's Korean Cookery.* Elizabeth, NJ: Hollym International Corp., 1985; 96 pages. Over 50 recipes; easy instructions.

Yoon, Sook-Ja. *Korean Traditional Desserts: Rice Cakes, Cookies and Beverages.* Seoul: Ji-Gu Publishing Co., 2001. All about tasty after-dinner treats.

Description and Travel

Adams, Edward B. *Korea Guide: A Glimpse of Korea's Cultural Legacy,* rev. ed. Seoul: Seoul International Tourist Publishing House, 1995; 399 pages. Basic introduction to Korea, with an expanded coverage of a select few tourist sites and important temples. Includes important cultural notes, but minimal practical details.

Adams, Edward B. *Korea's Golden Age: Cultural Spirit of Silla in Kyongju,* rev. ed. Seoul: Seoul International Tourist Publishing House, 1991; 421 pages. In-depth treatment of the historical sites of Gyeongju and the legacy of the Silla Dynasty.

Adams, Edward B. *Palaces of Seoul.* Seoul: Taewon Publishing Company, 1982; 216 pages. In-depth guide to the royal palaces of Seoul.

Adams, Edward B. *Through the Gates of Seoul: Trails and Tales of Yi Dynasty.* Vol. I. Seoul: Taewon Publishing Company, 1974; 393 pages. Complete account of palaces, shrines, temples, tombs, city gates, mountain fortresses, and hiking trails in and near Seoul, with in-

formative appendixes, useful maps, and several hundred photographs. OP.

Adams, Edward B. *Through the Gates of Seoul: Trails and Tales of Yi Dynasty.* Vol. II. Seoul: Seoul International Tourist Publishing House, 1977; 410 pages. Guide to major sites in the Seoul-surrounding province of Gyeonggi-Do. OP.

Bird, Isabella L. *Korea and Her Neighbors: A Narrative of Travel, with an Account of the Recent Vicissitudes and Present Position of the Country.* London: Kegan Paul, 2002; 488 pages. Reprint of two volumes written in the mid-1890s by this intrepid woman traveler. Curious for the impressions of the country and astute observations, a mere decade after the country's opening to the West.

Clark, Donald N. and James A. Grayson. *Discovering Seoul: An Historical Guide.* Seoul: Royal Asiatic Society, Korea Branch, 1986; 358 pages. An account of the history and points of interest of Seoul by two long-time residents of this ancient city.

Internet Resources

South Korea Tourism Information
www.visitkorea.or.kr or www.knto.or.kr
The official site of the Korean National Tourism Organization, the government tourism arm. The primary site for tourism-related information about the country of South Korea. Packed with useful information and links. See also www.tour2korea.com.

www.koreainfogate.com, www.lifein korea.com, www.1stopkorea.com
Commercial general information sites pertaining to South Korea.

Cities and Provinces
The following are the main websites for the provinces and metropolitan cities in South Korea, plus for the city of Gyeongju, with accompanying separate sites (if any) dedicated to their culture and tourism. While each is different, these sites generally cover overview facts and figures, city government, tourism opportunities, transportation, useful information, issues of daily life for visitors, and business and economic issues. They usually have multiple links to related websites. Aside from being presented in Korean, these sites are also available in Japanese, Chinese, and/or English.

Seoul
www.visitseoul.net, www.metro.seoul.kr

Gyeonggi-Do
www.provin.kyonggi.kr

Incheon
www.incheon.go.kr

Gangwon-Do
www.provin.gangwon.kr

Gyeongsangbuk-Do
www.provin.gyeongbuk.kr,
    www.gbtour.net.

Daegu
www.daegu.go.kr, http://tour.daegu.go.kr

Gyeongju
www.gyeongju.gyeongbuk.kr

Gyeongsangnam-Do
www.provin.gyeongnam.kr

Ulsan
www.metro.ulsan.kr

Busan
www.metro.busan.kr, www.visit.busan.kr

Jeju-do
www.jeju.go.kr

Jeollanam-Do
www.provin.jeonnam.kr,
    www.jeonnam.go.kr/tour

Gwangju
www.metro.gwangju.kr

Jeollabuk-Do
www.provin.jeonbuk.kr

Chungcheongnam-Do
http://chungnam.net

Daejeon
www.metro.daejeon.kr

Chungcheongbuk-Do
www.provin.chungbuk.kr, www.cbtour.net

Korean Government
www.korea.net
Maintained by the Korean Oversees Information Service, this site is the official Korean government homepage. Contains a wealth of information about government, business, and

tourism, news about the country, and many web links to other related sites.

www.cwd.go.kr
Homepage for the office of the president of the Republic of Korea.

Transportation
www.korail.go.kr
Official site of the Korean National Railroad, with information on tickets, schedules, and related links.

www.airport.co.kr
Site pertaining to domestic airports in South Korea.

www.airport.or.kr
Site for Incheon International Airport, South Korea's primary international entry point.

www.koreanair.com
Korean Air homepage.

www.asiana.co.kr or http://us.flyasiana.com
Asiana Airlines homepage.

www.seoulsubway.co.kr
Site of the Seoul subway system; provides links to other South Korean city subway websites. Includes information on ticketing, routes, timetables, and tourist sites.

Customs and Immigration
www.moj.go.kr
The official website of the Ministry of Justice; helpful for immigration issues.

www.customs.go.kr
The official website of the Korea Customs Service.

Accommodations
www.worldinn.com
Government-authorized site for information about all types of affordable accommodations in South Korea, with reservations capability. Contains a great amount of other information about transportation, eating, shopping, and events.

www.hotelguide.co.kr
Contact information and basic summary of services and amenities for about 250 of South Korea's best hotels.

Buddhism
www.buddhpia.com/english/index.html
http://www.human.toyogakuen-u.ac.jp/~acmuller/Buddhism-Korean.html
These sites provide general information on Korean Buddhism and links to Buddhist-related sites.

M

Climate Charts

Climate
Temperatures in degrees Celsius*

	SEOUL	GANGNEUNG	DAEJEON	DAEGU	BUSAN	GWANGJU	JEJU	AVERAGE COUNTRYWIDE HUMIDITY
JAN	-3	-1	-2	-1	2	0	7	59%
FEB	-3	1	0	1	4	1	6	58%
MAR	4	5	5	6	8	6	9	66%
APR	12	12	12	13	13	12	14	60%
MAY	18	16	17	18	17	18	18	63%
JUNE	22	20	22	22	20	22	22	75%
JULY	24	24	25	26	24	26	26	81%
AUG	25	25	25	26	26	26	25	76%
SEPT	21	20	20	21	22	21	23	73%
OCT	14	15	14	15	17	15	17	62%
NOV	7	9	6	8	11	9	12	59%
DEC	0	3	0	1	5	2	9	67%

* To compute Fahrenheit temperatures, multiply Celsius by 1.8 and add 32.

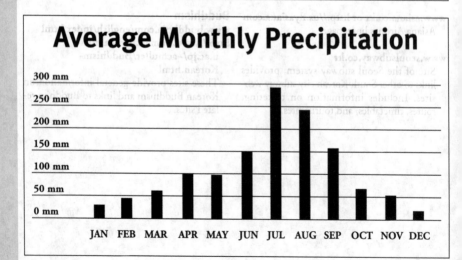

Average Monthly Precipitation

Index

Acknowledgments

The book that you hold in your hands represents great energy of the dedicated and talented Avalon Travel Publishing staff. Hearty thanks is also extended to Bill Dalton, traveler, writer, and friend, with whom a chance encounter at the Trowulan Museum on Java helped make this book a possibility and subsequent encouragement made it a reality; and to Joe Bisignani, my late friend and fellow travel writer, who always encouraged me to give my best.

Special thanks go to John Dennis, who graciously read and gave instructive suggestions on the Language section; Pak Yong-su, who shared knowledge about his country and would have given more had there been time; Park Yong, who offered constructive criticism on the Korean Language Basics appendix; Mr. Kwon of Gyeongju, who with insight and exuberance offered many suggestions, friendly surroundings, and homemade wine; Brian Zigmart and David Kendall for information I was unable to get elsewhere; Mr. Jooan Kang, Immanuel Park, Johann Choi, and Janice Tan for help in getting me to and from and around Korea; to Hans and Monique who taught me how to travel; and last but not least, to my wife Linda for her encouragement and support, and for spending time together on the road.

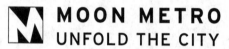

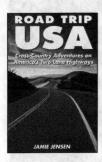

 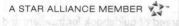

U.S.~Metric Conversion

1 inch	=	2.54 centimeters (cm)
1 foot	=	.304 meters (m)
1 yard	=	0.914 meters
1 mile	=	1.6093 kilometers (km)
1 km	=	.6214 miles
1 fathom	=	1.8288 m
1 chain	=	20.1168 m
1 furlong	=	201.168 m
1 acre	=	.4047 hectares
1 sq km	=	100 hectares
1 sq mile	=	2.59 square km
1 ounce	=	28.35 grams
1 pound	=	.4536 kilograms
1 short ton	=	.90718 metric ton
1 short ton	=	2000 pounds
1 long ton	=	1.016 metric tons
1 long ton	=	2240 pounds
1 metric ton	=	1000 kilograms
1 quart	=	.94635 liters
1 US gallon	=	3.7854 liters
1 Imperial gallon	=	4.5459 liters
1 nautical mile	=	1.852 km

To compute Celsius temperatures, subtract 32 from Fahrenheit and divide by 1.8. To go the other way, multiply Celsius by 1.8 and add 32.

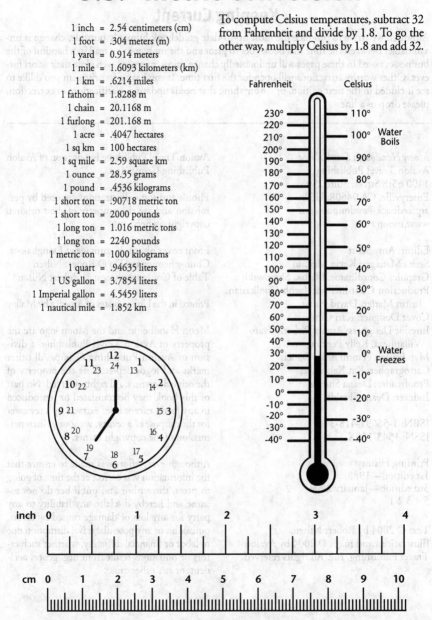

Keeping Current

Although we strive to produce the most up-to-date guidebook humanly possible, change is unavoidable. Between the time this book goes to print and the moment you read it, a handful of the businesses noted in these pages will undoubtedly change prices, move, or even close their doors forever. Other worthy attractions will open for the first time. If you have a favorite gem you'd like to see included in the next edition, or see anything that needs updating, clarification, or correction, please drop us a line.

Moon Handbooks South Korea
Avalon Travel Publishing
1400 65th Street, Suite 250
Emeryville, CA 94608, USA
atpfeedback@avalonpub.com
www.moon.com

Editor: Amy Scott
Series Manager: Kevin McLain
Graphics Coordinator: Melissa Sherowski
Production Coordinators: Jacob Goolkasian,
  Justin Marler, David Hurst
Cover Designer: Kari Gim
Interior Designers: Amber Pirker, Alvaro
  Villanueva, Kelly Pendragon
Map Editor: Naomi Adler Dancis
Cartographer: Kat Kalamaras
Proofreader: Deana Shields
Indexer: Deana Shields

ISBN: 1-56691-418-3
ISSN: 1543-155X

Printing History
1st edition—1988
3rd edition—January 2004
5 4 3 2 1

Text © 2004 by Robert Nilsen.
Illustrations and maps © 2004 by Avalon
Travel Publishing, Inc. All rights reserved.

Avalon Travel Publishing is a division of Avalon
Publishing Group, Inc.

Photos and some illustrations are used by permission and are the property of their original copyright owners.

Front cover photo: Hermitage at Donghak-sa,
Chungcheongnam-Do © Robert Nilsen
Table of Contents photos: © Robert Nilsen

Printed in the United States of America by Malloy